THE TIMES
Atlas of the Oceans

Atlas of

Edited by Alastair Couper

THE TIMES
the Oceans

VAN NOSTRAND REINHOLD COMPANY
NEW YORK   CINCINNATI   TORONTO   LONDON   MELBOURNE

Published by Van Nostrand Reinhold
Company Inc.
135 West 50th Street
New York, New York 10020

Cartography by
Hunting Surveys Ltd, Boreham Wood, Herts
Typesetting by
Nene Phototypesetters Ltd, Northampton
Index setting by
Stibo Sats, Åarhus, Denmark
Colour separations by
R & B Litho Reproductions Ltd, London
Excel Litho Plates Ltd, Slough
Printed and bound in Italy by
Mondadori, Verona

Editorial direction:	**Assistant editor:**
Alison Freegard	Julian Mannering
Cartographic direction:	**Cartographic assistant:**
Paul Middleton	Fiona Harvey
Art direction:	
Adrian Field	
Place names consultant:	
P. J. M. Geelan	
Index compilation:	
Geographical Research Associates, Maidenhead	

16 15 14 13 12 11 10 9 8 7 6 5 4 3 2 1
Library of Congress Cataloging in Publication Data
Main entry under title:
The Times atlas of the oceans
  Includes index
  1. Oceanography—Maps.   I. Couper, A. D.
  G2800.T5 1983   912′.155146   82–675461
  ISBN 0–442–21661–0

Contents

Contributors   *page* 6
Introduction   7
Description of main contents   8

THE OCEAN ENVIRONMENT

The geography of the oceans and seas   16
The ocean basins   26
The ocean–atmosphere system   44
The oceans and life   68

RESOURCES OF THE OCEAN

Living resources   80
The fisheries   90
Offshore hydrocarbons   102
Mineral and energy potentials   110

OCEAN TRADE

Ports of the world   122
Ships and cargoes   136
Shipping routes   146
The hazardous sea   160

THE WORLD OCEAN

The health of the oceans   170
The strategic use of the oceans   178
The study of the sea   192
The management task   208
The law of the sea   218

Appendices I–XI   225
Glossary   248
Sources and bibliography   255
Acknowledgements   257
Index   258

Contributors

EDITOR

Alastair D. Couper, MA, DIPEd, PhD, Master Mariner, FCIT, FNI, MRIN
Consultant to United Nations Agencies on Shipping
Professor and Head of Department of Maritime Studies, University of Wales Institute of Science and Technology (UWIST), Cardiff

CONTRIBUTORS

L. M. Alexander, AB, MA, PhD
Director, Office of the Geographer, Department of State, Washington DC

A. A. Archer, BSc, FIMM
Assistant Director, Head of Mineral Strategy and Museum Division, Institute of Geological Sciences, London

E. D. Brown, BL, LLM, PhD
Professor of Maritime Law and Director of Centre for Marine Law and Policy, UWIST, Cardiff

Captain W. Burger, MSc, Extra Master, CEng, FRIN, MRINA, MNI
Hon Lecturer, Department of Maritime Studies, UWIST, Cardiff

Captain A. G. Corbet, MSc, Extra Master Mariner, FRIN, MNI, Hon MAIN
Lecturer in Marine Traffic Control and Maritime Law, Department of Maritime Studies, UWIST, Cardiff

C. H. Cotter, BSc, MSc, PhD, Extra Master Mariner, FRIN
Late Senior Lecturer, Department of Maritime Studies, UWIST, Cardiff

C. M. Davies, BSc, PhD, MIGeol, FGS
Lecturer in Marine Geology, Department of Maritime Studies, UWIST

E. R. Jefferys, MA, PhD
Department of Mechanical Engineering, University College, London

J. King, BSc, MSc, Master Mariner, MRINA, FNI, MRIN
Professor of Maritime Technology, Department of Maritime Studies, UWIST, Cardiff

H. A. G. Lewis, OBE
Geographical Consultant to The Times

Captain A. M. Maclean, BA, MSc, Extra Master, MRIN, FR Met S
Hon Lecturer, Department of Maritime Studies, UWIST, Cardiff

D. J. McMillan, BSc, MSc, FGS
Demonstrator in Marine Geology, Department of Maritime Studies, UWIST, Cardiff

N. Merrett, MSc
Institute of Oceanographic Sciences, Wormley, Surrey

A. J. G. Notholt, BSc, MIMM, CEng, MAIME, FGS
Minerals Strategy and Economics Research Unit, Institute of Geological Sciences, London

E. S. Owen Jones, BSc, PhD
Assistant Keeper, Welsh Industrial and Maritime Museum, Cardiff

R. Reynolds, BA, MA, FR Met S
Scientific Officer, Department of Meteorology, University of Reading

A. L. Rice, DSc, PhD
Institute of Oceanographic Sciences, Wormley, Surrey

P. L. Richardson, PhD
Associate Scientist, Woods Hole Institute of Oceanography, Woods Hole, Mass.

A. H. Ryan, MA, FR Hist S
School of History, University of Liverpool

R. J. Schmidt, B Pharm, PhD, MPS
Lecturer in Pharmaceutical Chemistry, Welsh School of Pharmacy, UWIST, Cardiff

H. D. Smith, MA, PhD
Lecturer in Maritime Geography, Department of Maritime Studies, UWIST, Cardiff

M. W. Stubbs, BSc, FR Met S
Meteorological Office, Bracknell, Berkshire

B. J. Thomas, BSc, PhD, MCIT, MMS
Senior Lecturer in Port Administration and Planning, Department of Maritime Studies, UWIST, Cardiff
Principal Port Consultant to the United Nations (UNCTAD)

J. M. Walker, BSc, MSc, M Inst P, DIC, FR Met S
Senior Lecturer in Meteorology and Physical Oceanography, Department of Maritime Studies, UWIST, Cardiff

C. F. Wooldridge, BSc, PhD, FRGS
Lecturer in Maritime Geography, Department of Maritime Studies, UWIST, Cardiff

J. Zinn, AB, MA, PhD
Congressional Research Staff, Washington DC

CARTOGRAPHIC EDITOR

H. Dobson
Chief Cartographer, Department of Maritime Studies, UWIST, Cardiff

Introduction

THE world ocean covers 71 per cent of the surface of the globe. This distinguishes the planet earth from all other bodies in the solar system. Recent pictures from space emphasise the earth as the 'blue planet', with the ocean as the most dominant feature of its surface.

The ocean is regarded as the last major frontier on earth for the exploration and development of resources to sustain mankind in the future. The *Times Atlas of the Oceans* appears at a time when increased interest is focussed on the resource aspect of the ocean. It is designed, therefore, to be of value to the marine specialist, useful for the policy-maker and comprehensible to any intelligent person who wishes to know more about ocean research, resources, uses and policies.

Population growth, the near depletion of vital minerals and fossil energy sources on land, scarcity of additional good cultivable soils, crop failures, advances of the desert margins, food scarcity and protein deficiency in third world countries, pollution, the deployment of nuclear weapons, and the problems of the disposal of dangerous wastes have all led to intense interest in the oceans. They are perceived as future sources of food, energy, minerals, chemicals and space. We are already sustained by the oceans as the primary source of water, and no country, not even the USA or the USSR, can support its industries and populations without recourse to ocean transport. Throughout the world there is a move of populations and economic activities to coastal areas, and most great cities are ports. However, only a very small fraction of world food supply comes from the ocean, although most of the life of the planet exists within this vast volume. Similarly, apart from hydrocarbons, few of the minerals and chemicals within the oceans are at present utilised.

The ocean is a hazardous environment for man due to storms, ice, and its great depths. The possibility of more use of the ocean has emerged with advances in the sciences of marine geology and oceanography, research in fish finding, marine processing and breeding techniques, and the development of marine technology allowing the exploitation of hydrocarbons and minerals in deeper and more difficult regions of the ocean, and the construction of vessels of enormous size and complexity capable of voyaging even in ice covered regions. These advances have been accompanied by concern for the health of the ocean due to accidents, discharge of waste, over-fishing of a number of species, and conflicts between countries over access to and ownership of maritime areas.

The greater awareness of the value of the ocean has brought about some remarkable changes in jurisdiction over maritime zones in a very short time. During the past decade about 35 per cent of waters previously recognised as part of the high seas have been enclosed as national zones. At the same time the Third United Nations Conference on the Law of the Sea (UNCLOS III) has been meeting (1974–82) to bring about a Convention establishing a legal order for the ocean which would protect and preserve the marine environment, conserve the living resources, facilitate international communication, promote efficient and peaceful uses of the ocean, and advance the interests and needs of mankind as a whole. The Convention was opened for signature at the end of UNCLOS III in December 1982. It is of great historic significance. It was not, however, totally acceptable to several of the major states, and it may be many years before it enters into force for some of them. Consequently a very complicated era of ocean policy looms ahead.

In compiling the Atlas all of these important aspects have been considered. It is therefore more than an inventory of ocean resources and transport linkages—vital as these are. It goes a long way towards explaining physical and biological interactions, the trans-national character of living resources, the reasons behind the flow of merchant ships and deployment of naval vessels, management concepts, and the legal regime of the oceans. It provides an informed starting point for a sound understanding of the ocean-resource system involving man and the marine environment.

In exploring particular themes related to different aspects of the oceans the Atlas aims to be comprehensible to a wide range of specialists and non-specialists and there are many cross-references which emphasise relationships between diverse phenomena. Users of the Atlas involved in shipping, fishing, offshore hydrocarbons, minerals, renewable energy, naval strategy, law, history, conservation or recreation and research will recognise and make their own correlations of particular interest and importance in what is regionally and globally a highly mobile environment.

The oceanic world is a fitting subject for the latest in the deservedly renowned series of Atlases published by Times Books of London.

Alastair D. Couper
Cardiff, 1983

Contents: the ocean environment

THE GEOGRAPHY OF THE OCEANS AND SEAS

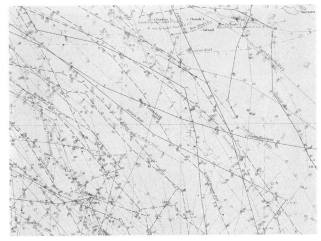

THE first systematic attempt to map the physical geography of the sea bottom was made by the US Naval Officer Matthew Fontaine Maury in his book *The Physical Geography of the Sea*, 1850. Maury showed a rudimentary generalised bathymetry of the North Atlantic. Increased submarine cable laying revealed more knowledge of this topography, and in recent decades advanced surveying and diving has produced a wider coverage. However, still only a relatively small amount of detail of many areas of undersea mountains, ridges, hills, shelves, slopes, plains and trenches has been revealed. Knowledge of these has become very important in matters as diverse as the deployment of nuclear submarines and understanding of fish locations.

THE OCEAN BASINS

OVER time-scales measured in millions of years, ocean basins are continually changing their shape and this affects the circulation of ocean currents, sea levels and climates. The changes are due to sea floor spreading and plate tectonics. On either side of the great ocean ridges the sea floor is spreading, pushing the plates apart as new material is extruded from Earth's interior. In other parts of the ocean basins some plates are moving against each other and part of the ocean crust is returned to the interior. Evidence for these movements is found in magnetic observations, geological sampling, deep drilling, deep diving and other visual and instrumental observations. The continental shelves and the deep sea bed are the subjects of many research programmes. These provide evidence as to the very origins of the ocean floor, seismic activities, new sources of hydrocarbons, deep sea minerals and marine life.

THE OCEAN–ATMOSPHERE SYSTEM

THE oceans and the atmosphere are constantly in motion, and without these motions life as we know it would be impossible. Atmospheric motions shape the globe's patterns of weather and climate and also arouse the surface of the sea. In return, the oceans provide the atmosphere with heat and moisture. The spectrums of atmospheric and oceanic motion range widely through time and space, from the tiny turbulent eddies which survive for but a few seconds to the variations in ice-cover and the global climatic fluctuations which extend over centuries. Monsoons, tropical cyclones, wind-waves, storm surges, tides, tsunamis, the great currents in the upper ocean; these and indeed all motion systems in the atmosphere and the sea affect maritime activities. They also spread pollution. Thus it is vital to advance understanding of these systems, and major research programmes of recent years have gone some way towards this.

THE OCEANS AND LIFE

LIFE in the oceans is closely interrelated, extending from the vegetable phytoplankton through complex food chains to the largest fish and mammals. Vegetable and animal life varies in distribution according to sea water composition, and interactions of sea water with nutrients, light, temperature, circulation, and predators, including man. There are zones of high primary production, which include areas of upwelling, and zones which appear to be virtually deserts. However, the latter, such as the abyssal plains, have, on closer inspection, been shown to contain many previously unknown species. Much biological research is centred on determining whether the oceans can yield more food for the world's growing population, and whether man's activities, including waste disposal, are in danger of causing irreversible damage to fragile marine ecosystems.

photos from top to bottom: part of map by M. F. Maury, showing depth soundings in the Pacific, off Mexico; White Island, a volcanic crater rising from the sea, off New Zealand; waterspout 900 metres high off the coast of Huntingdon Beach, southern California; the amphipod shrimp, *Cystisoma*, which apart from its eye pigment and stomach content is glass clear.

The North Atlantic Ocean   page   16   *Map* Sea floor and surface features of the North and Central Atlantic Ocean, the Caribbean, the Baltic, the Mediterranean and the Red Seas.

The South Atlantic and Indian Ocean   18   *Map* Sea floor and surface features of the Central and South Atlantic Ocean, the Indian Ocean, Arabian Sea and Bay of Bengal.

The North Pacific Ocean   20   *Map* Sea floor and surface features of the North Pacific Ocean, Gulf of Alaska, Bering Sea, Sea of Japan, Sea of Okhotsk, Yellow Sea and East China Sea.

The South Pacific Ocean   22   *Map* Sea floor and surface features of the South Pacific Ocean, the South China Sea, Philippine Sea, the Banda, Arafura, Timor and Coral Seas, the Tasman Sea.

The Arctic and the Antarctic   24   *Maps* Sea floor and surface features of the Arctic Ocean, the Chukchi, East Siberian, Laptev, Kara, Norwegian, Lincoln and Beaufort Seas, and Baffin Bay; Antarctica, and the Ross, Amundsen, Bellingshausen, Weddell, Lazarev, Riiser-Larsen, Cosmonaut, Cooperation, Davis and Dumont D'Urville Seas.

The limits of the sea   26   *Map* The major oceans and their areal extent. *Features* Cross-sectional perspective view up the Atlantic, Pacific and Indian Ocean basins; names and extents of ocean zones; comparison of land and ocean areas and depths; the main morphological features of ocean basins.

The shape of the ocean basins   28   *Map* The broad topography of ocean basins (continental margins, abyssal hills and plains, ocean ridges and rises). *Features* Cross section of active ridge profiles in the Atlantic, Pacific and Indian Oceans; types of continental margin; primary, secondary and relict abyssal plains.

Magnetism and sea floor dating   30   *Maps* Dating of the ocean floor by magnetic anomalies; the Earth's magnetic poles and fields; magnetic anomalies off California; the anomalies of the Reykjanes Ridge near Iceland. *Features* The magnetic time scale; the Earth as a magnet.

Sea floor spreading and plate tectonics   32   *Map* The Earth's crustal plates and their boundaries (ocean trenches, spreading ridges and hot spots). *Features* Poles of rotation of the crustal plates and fracture zones; how plates 'move': subduction.

The drifting continents   34   *Maps and features* The evolving theory of continental drift from Wegener to plate tectonics; geometrical and geological evidence for continental drift; the case of 'polar wandering'; convection currents within the Earth's mantle; beginnings of a new ocean: the Red Sea.

The topography of the deep ocean floor   36   *Maps* Seamounts and undersea volcanoes, volcanic islands and island arcs; the Hawaiian island chain; size of undersea mountains compared with Mt Etna.

Earth's unstable foundations   38   *Map* Earthquake belts and depth ranges. *Features* Seismic waves and how they tell us about Earth's interior; the internal structure of the Earth; ocean crustal layers and models for their likely composition; ophiolites.

Deep sea drilling   40   *Map* The age of ocean crust and the drill sites of the *Glomar Challenger* that helped confirm it. *Features* Drilling method of the *Glomar Challenger*; confirmation of continental drift from the expedition's sediment samples.

Sea floor sediments   42   *Map* The types, distribution and thickness of sea floor sediments. *Features* Land derived sediments, beaches, hydrocarbon deposits, sediment stacks on continental shelves, turbidity currents.

The water planet   44   *Maps and features* Earth's areas of high and low pressure; Atlantic winds and surface currents; Atlantic water movement and cross-section of the Gulf Stream; the Ekman Spiral.

Global winds and weather 1   46   *Maps* Wind and pressure systems for January and July; average annual rainfall; exceptional wind and gust speeds over the North Sea. *Feature* Formation of a depression.

Global winds and weather 2   48   *Maps* Occurrence of force 4 and force 8 winds for January and July; the monsoonal year. *Features* The Beaufort Scale and sea states; how monsoons occur over the Arabian Sea.

Oceanic circulation 1   50   *Maps* Surface currents for January and July; circulation of bottom water. *Features* Temperature profiles for longitudinal sections of the oceans; the thermocline.

Oceanic circulation 2   52   *Maps* Currents in the Mediterranean; the Gulf Stream; upwelling areas and seasonal upwelling in the East Pacific and Arabian Sea; coastal fog and fog in the North Pacific and North Atlantic oceans.

Cyclone and hurricane disasters   54   *Maps and features* The hurricane regions of Central America, Australasia, East and South Asia; the Philippines and Madagascar.

Tropical cyclones, thunderstorms and waterspouts   56   *Maps* Tropical cyclone storm tracks and sea surface temperatures; frequency of thunderstorms over the oceans globally; waterspout sightings from ships. *Features* Average monthly hurricanes and cyclones for different sea areas; a tropical cyclonic storm over the Irrawaddy Delta.

Waves, swell and tsunamis   58   *Maps* World wave environments and wave heights; exceptional waves in the North Sea; Pacific tsunamis and warning stations. *Features* Freak waves off south east Africa.

Tides and surges   60   *Maps* Global cotidal lines and amphidromic points; distribution of tidal range at spring tides; tidal types and their curves. *Feature* Storm surges in the North Sea.

The polar oceans   62   *Maps* Arctic surface currents, seasonal ice limits and ice flows; Antarctic surface currents and seasonal ice limits. *Features* Perspective views of the Arctic Ocean basin and Antarctica and the Southern Ocean showing ice limits, ice shelves, and topography.

The icy surface   64   *Maps* North Atlantic iceberg limits and exceptional sightings of icebergs; iceberg limits in the Southern Ocean; likelihood of icing on ships in the North Atlantic and Southern Ocean. *Features* The formation of icebergs, satellite views of ice cover of the polar regions; the travels of Trolltunga, a giant iceberg.

The salt sea   66   *Maps* Surface salinity and density for February and August. *Features* Salinity profiles for longitudinal sections of the oceans.

The biological environment   68   *Map* Biogeographic regions of the world. *Features* The water column and the biological zones; examples of marine life at different ocean depths.

The plankton   70   *Maps* Global distribution of phytoplankton and zooplankton. *Features* The start of the ocean food chains; examples of plankton species.

The benthos   72   *Map* Distribution of the benthic biomass. *Features* Examples of sea floor life at different levels – the continental margin, the abyssal floor, mid ocean vent communities.

The fishes   74   *Features* Types of fish at different ocean depths; colour and pigmentation, bioluminescence, fish structure at depth.

Ocean bird life   76   *Maps* Migrations and breeding grounds of the albatross, penguin, petrels, shearwaters and some tropical birds distributions. *Feature* Seabird feeding methods.

The Southern Ocean   78   *Map* The biological resource: example of distribution (krill, whales and some fish species). *Feature* Whales and the Southern Ocean food chain.

Contents: resources of the ocean

LIVING RESOURCES

Production of food, together with navigation, was perhaps the earliest use of the sea by man. Traditional, or artisanal, fisheries remain the foundation of fishing activities in many parts of the world. These small scale fisheries are principal sources of animal protein for coastal communities in Africa, Asia and the Pacific. The world commercial catch in the 1970s appeared to stabilise in the 60–75 million tonnes per annum range, some two-thirds being used for human consumption and the remainder reduced to meal and oil for the production of fertilisers and animal feeds. There is considerable technological change taking place in the world fishery and production could increase by around one-third by the beginning of the 21st century. As most usable stocks are already fully or nearly fully exploited, further expansion will have to rely increasingly upon unconventional species and the expansion of aquaculture.

THE FISHERIES

The focus of the commercial fisheries are the urban industrial areas of the world, which are in significant, albeit fortuitous, juxtaposition to the high-yielding biomass of the temperate and boreal waters of the North Atlantic and North Pacific, although much of the stock in these waters is over-fished. The migratory stocks of whales pursued by the long-range fleets from some of the industrial countries have also declined, as has the North Atlantic salmon. In tropical areas there is high species diversity, but the complex ecosystem is sensitive to biological disturbance, while the traditional fishery communities and methods are equally sensitive to the introduction of new vessels and gear. Worldwide problems are those of managing the various types of fisheries to ensure a maximum yield commensurate with the protection of the fishery and the fishermen; the fair division of sea fishery zones; and the allocation of allowable catches between States.

OIL AND GAS

The realisation that the continental shelves are rich in petroleum resources has dawned gradually in the 20th century, but large scale exploitation has had to await the combination of rising oil prices and the scarcity of land-derived supplies in some areas, coupled with the advanced technology required for the installation and operation of production facilities at sea. By the early 1980s over one-fifth of world petroleum production was derived from offshore sources, a proportion which will increase by the end of the century. This enormous advance has been accompanied by the development of new industrial and rig building sites, development of service bases, offshore communities, and disputes over extraction rights. The coastal villages and towns in areas not previously associated with the oil industry have often been faced with extensive environmental and social change.

MINERAL AND ENERGY POTENTIALS

The richest ocean mineral potential is to be found in the aggregates (sand and gravel) and placers (for example tin) which have to some extent been worked for decades, and in the chemical precipitates or authigenic minerals which occur in a diversity of forms ranging from the manganese nodules of the deep sea floor to the metalliferous muds of the Red Sea. However, technological and economic factors are such that most of the deposits are economically not worth exploiting at present. Despite this, the mineral question has presented a significant obstacle to the negotiating of the Law of the Sea treaty. The potential of seawater itself as a mineral resource, though much talked about, is probably limited. Considerable research is, however, being devoted to the use of the sea for the production of renewable energy, for example from both tidal and wave power stations. In the future it may even prove to be a virtually unlimited source of fuel for nuclear fusion power stations.

photos from top to bottom: bluefin tuna off the Spanish coast; hauling in a seine trawl off Iceland; an oil rig in the Brent Field withstanding a winter gale in the North Sea; source of minerals on the ocean bed: a 'smoker' releasing sulphurous substances on the East Pacific Rise.

The traditional fisheries   page **80**   *Map* Development from an artisanal fishery in the Shetland Isles, Great Britain. *Features* Artisanal fishing methods. Fishing in the Pacific islands of Kiribati.

Farming the sea   **82**   *Maps* The farming of finfish, crustaceans and molluscs around the world. Mussel and oyster farming in France. The distribution of milkfish at sea. Seaweed gathering.

The world fishing industry   **84**   *Map* Consumption of fish protein around the world. *Features* The vertical distribution of pelagic and demersal fish and shellfish. Fishing gears. The structure of the modern fishing industry.

The world fishing fleet   **86**   *Map* The worldwide distribution of fishing vessels over 100 grt. *Feature* Examples of modern fishing vessels.

The world catch   **88**   *Map* The tonnages of fish caught and an estimation of potential. *Feature* The major commercial species and the tonnages landed.

World fish production   **90**   *Map* The fish catches of the world's major fishing nations. *Features* The world catch and estimated catch until the year 2000.

The North Atlantic   **92**   *Maps and features* The tonnages of fish caught in the North Atlantic and the distribution of important commercial stocks; the extension of Iceland's fishing limits and principal fishing ports; eight year trends for the cod, herring and the industrial fisheries.

The Central and South Atlantic   **94**   *Maps and features* The tonnages of fish caught in the tropical and South Atlantic and the distribution of important commercial stocks; the fishing ports of the Moroccan coast; eight year trends for the hake and menhaden.

The North Pacific   **96**   *Maps and features* The tonnages of fish caught in the North Pacific and the distribution of the important commercial stocks; Japan's fishing ports, worldwide fishing activities, and world catch and its value.

The Indo-Pacific   **98**   *Maps and features* The tonnages of fish caught in the Indo-Pacific and the distribution of the important commercial stocks; fishing in Indonesia; eight year trends for the Californian sardine and Peruvian anchovy.

Ocean fisheries   **100**   *Maps and features* Distribution of the sperm whale between 1729 and 1919; distribution of baleen whales; the migration of humpback whales; distribution of tuna; the migration of the skipjack tuna; tuna catches around the world; the migration of the pink salmon in the North Pacific; the migration of the North Atlantic salmon; whale catches from 1670 to 1977.

Oil basins and production   **102**   *Map* The world's offshore oil basins and production fields. *Feature* Present oil production and estimated reserves.

Oil and gas 1   **104**   *Maps* Offshore oil and gas production by countries; offshore oil and gas production in the Los Angeles Basin, Gulf of Mexico, Venezuela and Trinidad. *Feature* Exploration and production platforms.

Oil and gas 2   **106**   *Maps* Offshore oil and gas production in the North Sea, Eastern Canada and North USA, Cook Inlet and the Canadian Arctic. *Feature* Undersea technology in the North Sea.

Oil and gas 3   **108**   *Maps* Offshore oil and gas production off the west coast of Africa, Indonesia and Malaysia, the Gulf, North-West Australia and Southern Australia.

Seabed minerals   **110**   *Map* The distribution of marine economic minerals. *Feature* Onshore production and the principal consumers of cobalt, copper, nickel and phosphate.

Marine minerals — continental margin   **112**   *Maps* The world distribution of offshore aggregates and placers; North Sea aggregates; aggregates off the Eastern USA coast; gold deposits in Alaska; offshore tin in Indonesia.

Marine minerals — shelf and trench   **114**   *Maps* The world distribution of offshore metalliferous deposits; metalliferous deposits in the Red Sea; the world distribution of offshore phosphorite deposits—insets of Chatham Rise, Agulhas Bank and Santa Monica Bay.

Marine minerals — ocean floor   **116**   *Maps* The world distribution of manganese nodules; metal concentrations in nodules in the Indian and Pacific Oceans. *Feature* Frequency distribution of grade of nodules.

Sea water   **118**   *Maps* Distribution of mineral extraction plants; distribution of seawater desalination plants. *Features* The elements which make up seawater; drugs from the sea.

Renewable energy from the oceans   **120**   *Maps* Sites suitable for tidal power—insets of the Bay of Fundy, White Sea, Severn Estuary, Northern France; potential areas for generating wave power; potential areas for generating thermal power. *Features* Devices for extracting wave energy and thermal energy.

Contents: ocean trade

PORTS OF THE WORLD

Pᴏʀᴛs are the meeting point of land and sea transport. Enormous quantities of cargo move through ports and the speed and efficiency of this transfer is vital for the economies of the countries concerned and for the profitability of marine transport. Technological changes have been towards reducing port storage, faster handling and larger consignments. This has involved highly specialised bulk handling equipment, container technology, and changes in the depth, layout and in the manning of ports. Many ports serve vast hinterlands, some others concentrate on importing for a port-located bulk-using industry, or on exporting a single commodity. Ports themselves have become locational factors for industries, and most of the worlds great cities are ports.

SHIPS AND CARGOES

Tʜᴇ modern world economy is bound together by sea transport. Over 70 per cent of world trade is carried by ships, and no country is independent of the fuels, raw materials, food stuffs or manufactured goods moved across the world's oceans. Modern ships are highly complex and specialised and many are of enormous size. They are owned primarily by companies in the industrial countries, although many such owners register their ships in Liberia and other 'flag of convenience' states. Increasingly, developing countries are entering into shipping. The world recession affects shipping very severely as demand for cargoes declines. This also affects shipbuilding. Consequently the shipping industry as a whole is undergoing great changes.

SHIPPING ROUTES

Sᴇᴀᴍᴇɴ normally attempt to follow the shortest routes commensurate with safety. As a result, high densities of marine traffic occur at specific places such as headlands, straits, port approaches and the entrances to canals. At several such places there are traffic separation zones. Canals have been constructed to reduce ocean distances, and like natural straits they are of strategic importance. Navigational aids have their greatest coverage in these zones of densest traffic, and more ships are being fitted with satellite receivers giving high positional accuracy. Ships are also weather-routed in high latitudes using both onboard and shore information for the determination of passages through the areas of lowest wave gradients.

THE HAZARDOUS SEA

Dᴇsᴘɪᴛᴇ improvements in navigational aids, accidents at sea still occur. Even quite large vessels disappear without trace due to structural failure or cargo shifting in bad weather. Collisions and strandings are also prevalent accounting for the total loss of about 300 ships each year, and many more are damaged. Often these casualties are due to human error. Some flags have a bad casualty record which can be ascribed to inadequate training and qualifications of staff, and poor quality vessels. There are areas of the sea which are particularly hazardous, notably where the density of traffic is high, many crossing situations exist, and where poor visibility, bad weather and draught constraints prevail.

photos from top to bottom: the new oil terminal at the Port d'Antifer, northern France; iron-ore, bound for Europe, loading at Vitória, Brazil; ships passing through the Suez Canal; storm-wave conditions in the North Atlantic.

Port development and location —Europe 1	page 122	*Maps and insets* European ports distribution, Golfe de Fos and Venice.
Europe 2	124	*Maps and features* Port of London past, present and future, Rotterdam, Göteborg and Port Talbot; river ports.
The Americas 1	126	*Maps* North America and South America ports distribution.
The Americas 2	128	*Maps and features* Ports of New York, San Francisco and Valparaiso.
Japan and the East	130	*Maps and features* Far East ports distribution; Singapore, Calcutta and Tokyo.
Australia, Africa and the Middle East	132	*Maps and features* Australasia, Africa and Middle East ports distribution; Sydney, Papeete and Dakar.
Commodity ports	134	*Maps* World commodity loading ports; comparison of North West Europe and South East USA major commodities export/import. *Features* The world's top twenty ports by tonnage and ship throughput; world bulk loading ports.
Commodity flows	136	*Maps* World trade flows of iron ore, grain, bauxite/alumina and phosphates, coal, crude oil and gas; container routes. *Features* Trends in world seaborne trade; movement of minor bulk commodities.
Modern merchant ships	138	*Features* Gas carrier, chemical tanker, products tanker, oil carrier, combination carrier, bulk carrier, ore carrier, general cargo ship, barge carrier, container ship and RoRo ships.
Ownership of merchant fleets	140	*Map* National and beneficial ownership of the world's fleets and flag of convenience (FOC) countries. *Features* The top ten flags; growth of merchant ship types.
Shipbuilding	142	*Maps* Shipbuilding countries: who orders and who builds; distribution of dry docks. *Features* Major shipbuilders 1970–80; ships laid up and tramp time charter index.
Dependence on seaborne trade	144	*Maps* World seaborne trade: exporting and importing countries. *Features* Index of national interest in seaborne trade; ratio of freight rates to prices of selected commodities.
The world pattern	146	*Maps* World shipping distances and cross-continental land bridges; inland maritime transports in Western Europe and South East USA.
Seasonal shipping routes	148	*Maps* Arctic Ocean seasonal trade routes and future submarine tanker routes; weather routeing across the North Atlantic and North Pacific. *Features* Icing up of the St Lawrence River and the Baltic Sea; the *Manhattan*.
World straits and canals	150	*Map* International straits and canals, and straits minimum widths and other data.
World straits and canals—four major canals	152	*Maps* The Suez Canal, Panama Canal, Kiel Canal and St Lawrence Seaway.
World straits and canals—strategic straits 1	154	*Maps* The straits of Hormuz, Bab-el-Mandeb, Dardanelles, Malacca and Singapore.
World straits and canals—strategic straits 2	156	*Maps and features* The straits of Dover and Gibraltar; world shipping density patterns.
Navigational aids and safety	158	*Maps* Loran, Decca and Omega world navigational coverage; radio warning areas. *Features* Buoyage systems; the navigational chart.
The weather	160	*Maps* World weather hazards and load line areas; weather forecast areas for North West Atlantic and North Sea.
High risk environments	162	*Maps* Types of ship loss in high risk casualty areas; oil rig mishaps; ships lost in ice casualties reported 1890–1980; loss of the *Titanic*.
Shipping casualties	164	*Map* Analysis of total world shipping casualties by type over a two-year period.
Collision at sea	166	*Features* Case studies of collisions between ships at sea: *Stockholm* v. *Andrea Doria*; *Crystal Jewel* v. *British Aviator*; *Niceto de Larrinaga* v. *Sitala*; *Statue of Liberty* v. *Andulo*; *Rattray Head* v. *Tillerman*; *Hagen* v. *Boulgaria*; *Sea Star* v. *Horta Barbosa*.
Stranding and loss: three tanker disasters	168	*Features* Case studies of three major tanker disasters: the *Torrey Canyon* (1967), the *Argo Merchant* (1976) and the *Amoco Cadiz* (1978).

Contents: the world ocean

THE HEALTH OF THE OCEANS

IN many coastal areas pollution has reached intolerable social, aesthetic and ecological levels. In the deep sea tar balls on the surface, mercury in fish, and the dumping of nuclear and other noxious waste present problems, although not as yet critical. Marine accidents bring concentrated oil pollution to coastal zones with consequent damage to marine life, sea birds, fragile habitats and the loss of amenities for recreation. By far the most serious sources of pollution are continuous discharges from the land. In particular, the enclosed and semi-enclosed seas, which are surrounded by high density populations, have run-off from many rivers which contain pesticides, fertilisers and industrial waste. They are receiving specific attention under UN regional seas programmes.

THE STRATEGIC USE OF THE OCEANS

ALL the oceans and seas are used for strategic purposes. Their great depth, vast expanse and the freedom which prevails over navigation on the high seas renders them of fundamental importance for the strategic mobility policies of many states. Naval forces operate widely in the world ocean. They monitor each other, protect their merchant and fishing fleets, and take action periodically in defence of high seas, territorial seas and other perceived rights. Nuclear submarines armed with long-range missiles operate in ocean areas and at great depths beyond detection. This invulnerability of the nuclear submarine renders it a powerful second strike force. Such a capability is highly valued by the USSR and USA as part of their strategic deterrent policy.

STUDY OF THE SEA

THE oceans are studied so as to understand their dynamic nature and characteristics. Because the world ocean is vast, much research can only be carried out satisfactorily through international cooperation. For instance, some programmes concern the relationship between the atmosphere and major ocean currents involving data collection over large areas of the oceans and need substantial funding, specialised vessels and equipment, skilled personnel and logistical support. In contrast, research into problems of pollution, mineral extraction or fish migration may take place at a more local scale, as will exploration of the coastal seas which hold some of the heritage from the world's maritime past in the form of submerged ancient ports or historic wrecks. Research in the field of marine archaeology has benefited greatly from the underwater technology developed in ocean research generally.

THE MANAGEMENT TASK

THE need to manage the resources and environment of the sea became evident in the second half of the 19th century and was reflected in the promotion of navigational safety regulations and attempts at prevention of overfishing. The requirements for management have intensified with increasing use of the oceans, including mineral extraction, waste disposal and tourism—the latter having greatly increased the awareness of many people of the need to conserve the integrity of the marine environment. The complex web of interactions involved in sea uses is most readily perceived regionally, especially in the coastal zones of developed countries which are subject to intense and often conflicting uses. There are also special areas of concern in the tropical and polar seas which possess fragile ecosystems. Legislation on the preservation of endangered species and protection of fragile habitats has become an essential part of management, as has the allocation of quotas and restricted areas in fishing, and control of whaling, marine mining and tourism.

THE LAW OF THE SEA

FOR centuries the vast expanse of the ocean has been free and open to all users. Coastal states exercised control over all activities in their 3-mile territorial sea, and fishing up to 12 miles, but the only law governing activities on the high seas was the law of the state whose flag a ship flew. The recent transformation of the biologically richest areas of the sea within 200 nm of the coast into national zones, the discovery of vast mineral resources on and under the seabed, the move by industry and population to coastal areas, and the great increase in diversity of uses of the sea surface, water column and seabed, has called for a more extensive and clearly defined legal regime in order to allocate and control space and resources and preserve the ocean environment. The United Nations Law of the Sea Convention which opened for signature on the 10th December 1982 is the most important comprehensive Treaty ever to be produced in relation to the sea.

photos from top to bottom: a major source of coastal pollution is untreated sewage; the nuclear aircraft carrier USS *Nimitz*; archaeologists surveying the wreck site of the *Rapid*, western Australia; merchant ships and sailing vessels vie for space to manoeuvre off Brest, France; sea floor nodules—these minerals have proved a major stumbling block in Law of the Sea Treaty negotiations.

Oil pollution — page 170 — *Map* Major oil spillages (over 50 000 barrels) from tankers. *Feature* Sources of oil entering the oceans.

Sources of marine pollution 1 — 172 — *Map* Coastal discharges and polluted river run-off: parts of the oceans badly affected by pollution.

Sources of marine pollution 2 — 174 — *Maps* Pollution in the North Sea: discharge and dumping; the industries and nations of the Baltic and the state of pollution of a closed sea.

Sources of marine pollution 3 — 176 — *Maps* Pollution in the Mediterranean: the impact of industry, tourism and oil routes.

Sea power of the major states — 178 — *Map* Strength of surface fleets. *Features* Types of modern naval craft; balance of power between NATO and allied forces, and the USSR and Soviet bloc.

Submarine strategy and defense — 180 — *Maps* The submarine nations; evolution of submarine deployment and missile range. *Features* Nations with intercontinental ballistic missiles; size comparison of nuclear and conventional submarine types.

Naval operations 1 — 182 — *Maps* Northern hemisphere deployment of sonar arrays and major naval bases; deployment of Soviet and US fleets; the strategic position of the Arctic Ocean and the Greenland–Iceland–UK gap.

Naval operations 2 — 184 — *Maps and features* The Atlantic Ocean and the Falklands crisis 1982; territorial claims in Antarctica; strategic importance of the Indian Ocean.

Maritime disputes and conflicts 1 — 186 — *Maps and insets* Areas of actual and potential dispute between nations; Svalbard; Rockall, the Beagle Channel; the Eastern Mediterranean.

Maritime disputes and conflicts 2 — 188 — *Maps and features* Continuing conflicts and claims on the East Asian continental shelf and peripheral seas; Arab/Israeli crisis 1973 and involvement of the major powers.

World naval operations and gunboat diplomacy — 190 — *Map* Naval involvement in power politics and gunboat diplomacy.

Historical routes and navigation — 192 — *Maps* The voyages of discovery from the 15th to 18th centuries; the view of the world in the 15th and 16th centuries according to Plotemaic geography, Martin Behaim, and Abraham Ortelius.

Undersea archaeology 1 — 194 — *Maps and insets* Major world archaeological sites reported between 1970 and 1980 and brief descriptions of each.

Undersea archaeology 2 — 196 — *Maps and features* The dispersal of a shipwreck over the centuries; location and scientific examination of a wreck site and retrieval of artefacts; the Kyrenia shipwreck; the Armada and its wrecks; the *Mary Rose*; submerged ports and cities.

The scientific discovery of the oceans — 198 — *Maps and features* The early voyages of scientific discovery.

Submarine cables — 200 — *Map and insets* The world network of submarine cable routes.

Ocean exploration since 1945 — 202 — *Maps and features* Scientific ocean exploration since 1945; the state of undersea topographical surveying; polar research; sonagraphs; new technology.

Space technology and the oceans — 204 — *Maps and features* The geoid and the accurate measurement of the Earth and Ocean distances; the Landsat and Seasat series of satellites; radar imagery.

International ocean research — 206 — *Maps* Types and size of research fleets and major projects. *Features* International cooperation in ocean research and the world data centre.

The problems of multiple sea use — 208 — *Features* Compatible and conflicting sea uses and concentrations of activities, from the coastal zones to the high seas.

Conservation of species and habitats — 210 — *Maps* Endangered species and habitats and projects to protect them, the UN environmental programmes; fisheries commissions and the management of stocks.

The conservation of special areas — 212 — *Maps* Special areas: protected zones of the Great Barrier Reef; reserves and reefs in the Caribbean; multiple sea use in Chesapeake Bay.

The European seas — 214 — *Maps and features* Activities and management in the North Sea; the Dutch sector.

Recreational sea use — 216 — *Maps and features* Ocean cruises, yacht races; impact of offshore recreation; sports fishing.

The territorial sea — 218 — *Maps* The state of territorial sea claims and landlocked countries.

Maritime jurisdictional zones — 220 — *Maps and features* The zones of national jurisdiction from inland waters to the high seas; methods for settling territorial claims between opposite or adjacent states; the recognition of archipelagic waters; the evolution of the economic zone (EEZ); claims to resources within and beyond the EEZ; freedom of navigation and research.

The continental shelf — 222 — *Maps and features* The geological continental shelf and margin and limits of the 200-mile EEZs; methods for determining a state's continental margin territory.

Control of marine pollution — 224 — *Maps and features* Pollution control globally and regionally.

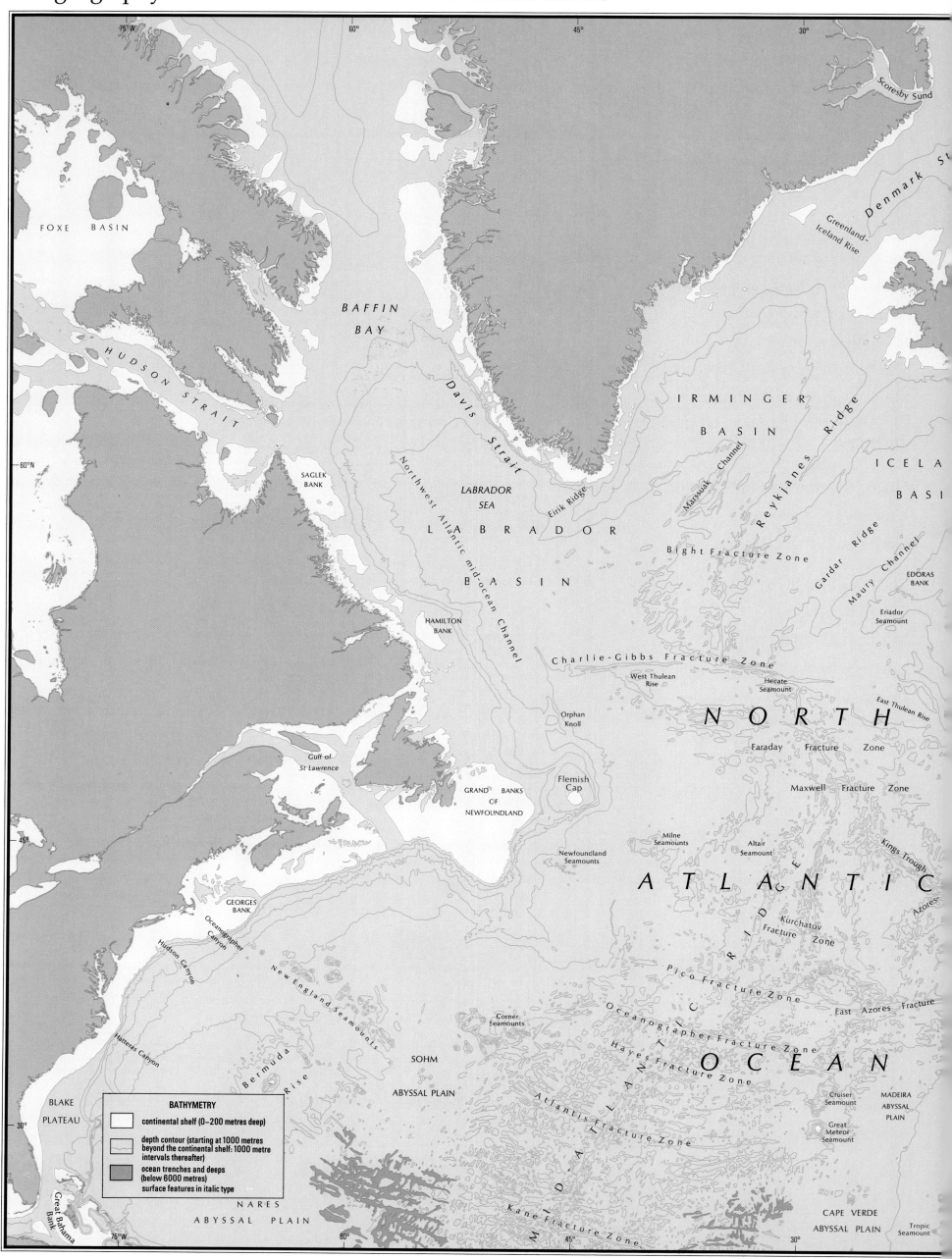

BATHYMETRY

☐ continental shelf (0–200 metres deep)

☐ depth contour (starting at 1000 metres
beyond the continental shelf: 1000 metre
intervals thereafter)

■ ocean trenches and deeps
(below 6000 metres)

surface features in italic type

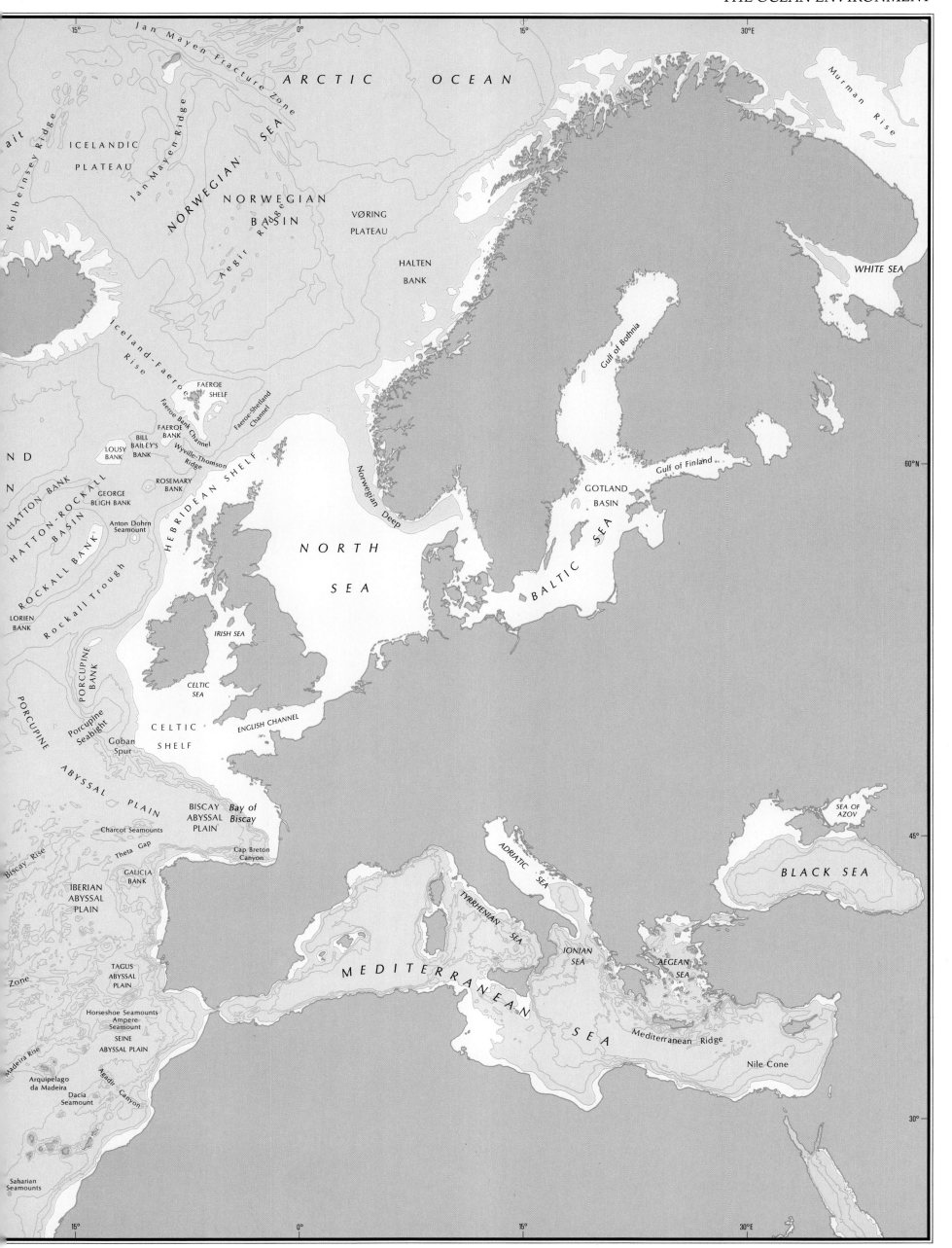

ARCTIC OCEAN

Jan Mayen Fracture Zone

Murman Rise

ICELANDIC PLATEAU

Kolbeinsey Ridge

Jan Mayen Ridge

NORWEGIAN SEA

WHITE SEA

NORWEGIAN BASIN

Aegir Ridge

VØRING PLATEAU

HALTEN BANK

Iceland-Faeroe Rise

Gulf of Bothnia

FAEROE SHELF

Faeroe Bank Channel

Faeroe-Shetland Channel

FAEROE BANK

BILL BAILEY'S BANK

LOUSY BANK

Wyville-Thomson Ridge

Gulf of Finland

60°N

ROSEMARY BANK

Norwegian Deep

GOTLAND BASIN

HATTON BANK

GEORGE BLIGH BANK

HEBRIDEAN SHELF

HATTON-ROCKALL BASIN

Anton Dohrn Seamount

NORTH SEA

BALTIC SEA

ROCKALL BANK

Rockall Trough

LORIEN BANK

IRISH SEA

PORCUPINE BANK

CELTIC SEA

CELTIC SHELF

PORCUPINE

Porcupine Seabight

Goban Spur

ENGLISH CHANNEL

ABYSSAL PLAIN

BISCAY ABYSSAL PLAIN

Bay of Biscay

SEA OF AZOV

Charcot Seamounts

Theta Gap

Cap Breton Canyon

45°

Biscay Rise

GALICIA BANK

ADRIATIC SEA

BLACK SEA

IBERIAN ABYSSAL PLAIN

TYRRHENIAN SEA

Zone

TAGUS ABYSSAL PLAIN

MEDITERRANEAN

IONIAN SEA

AEGEAN SEA

Horseshoe Seamounts

Ampere Seamount

SEINE ABYSSAL PLAIN

SEA

Mediterranean Ridge

Madeira Rise

Nile Cone

Arquipelago da Madeira

Dacia Seamount

Agadir Canyon

30°

Saharian Seamounts

15°   0°   15°   30°E

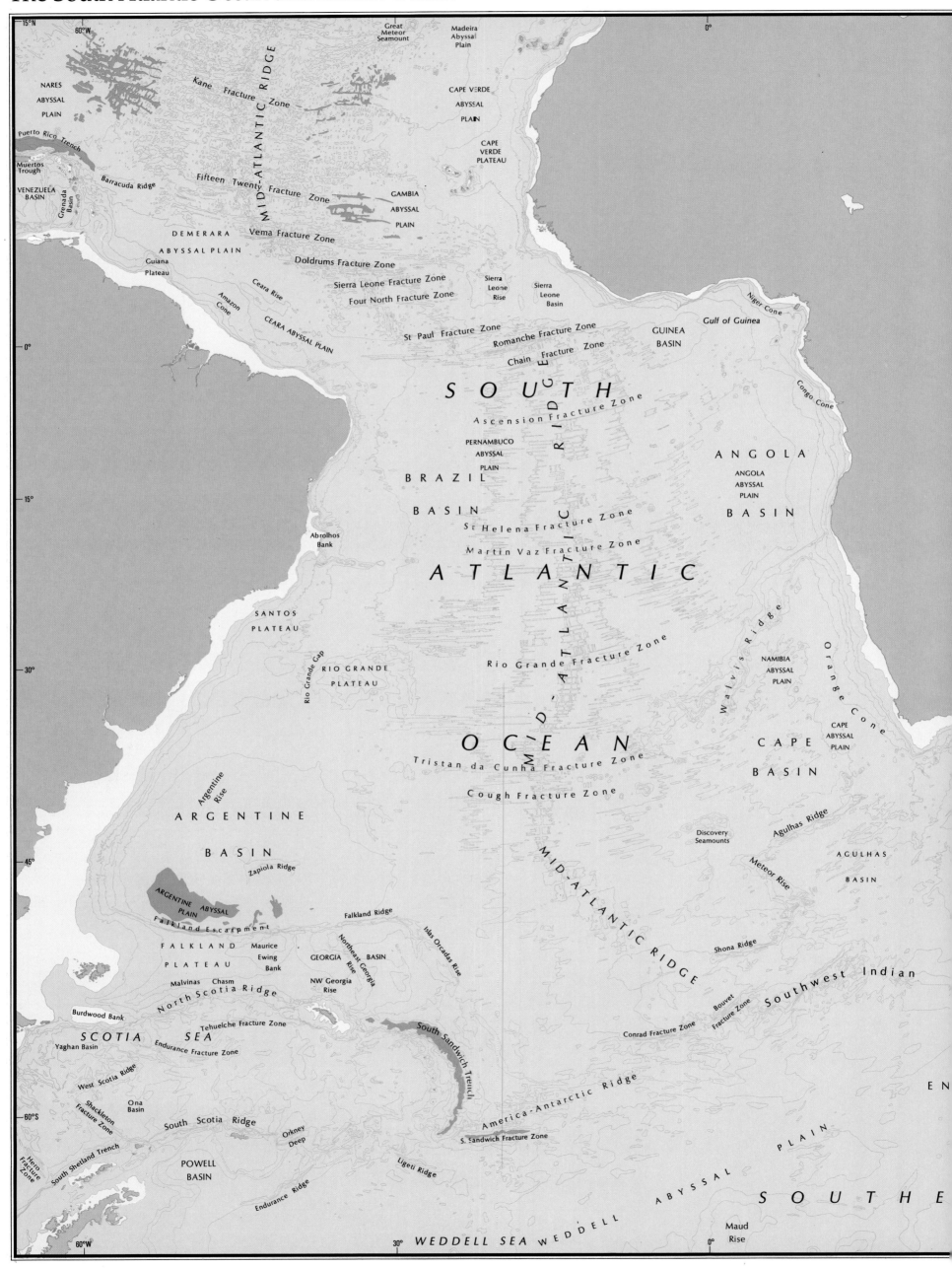

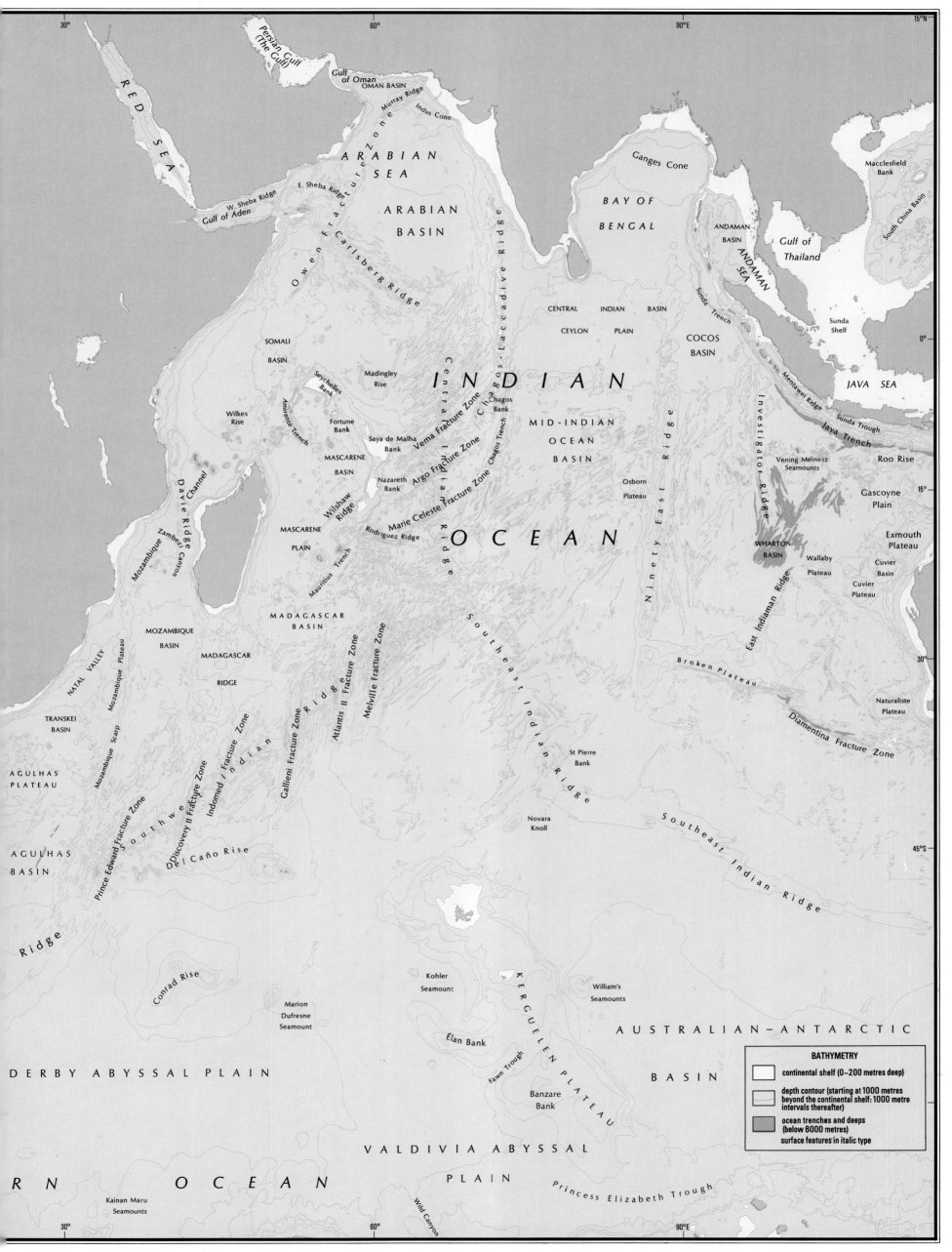

30°   60°   90°E   15°N

Persian Gulf
(The Gulf)
Gulf of Oman
OMAN BASIN
Gulf of Oman
Murray Ridge
Indus Cone

RED SEA

Ganges Cone

Macclesfield Bank

ARABIAN SEA

ARABIAN BASIN

BAY OF BENGAL

ANDAMAN BASIN

Gulf of Thailand

South China Basin

W. Sheba Ridge   *E. Sheba Ridge*
Gulf of Aden

Owen Fracture Zone

Carlsberg Ridge

Chagos-Laccadive Ridge

CENTRAL   INDIAN   BASIN

CEYLON   PLAIN

ANDAMAN SEA

Sunda Trench

Sunda Shelf

0°

SOMALI BASIN

Madingley Rise

Seychelles Bank

Wilkes Rise

Amirante Trench

Fortune Bank

Saya de Malha Bank

MASCARENE BASIN

Nazareth Bank

Argo Fracture Zone

Central Indian Fracture Zone

Vema Fracture Zone

Chagos Bank

Chagos Trench

MID-INDIAN OCEAN BASIN

COCOS BASIN

Mentawei Ridge

JAVA SEA

Sunda Trough

Java Trench

Roo Rise

I N D I A N

Osborn Plateau

Ninety East Ridge

Investigator Ridge

Vening Meinesz Seamounts

WHARTON BASIN

Gascoyne Plain

Exmouth Plateau

15°

Davie Channel

MASCARENE PLAIN

Wilshaw Ridge

Marie Celeste Fracture Zone

Rodriguez Ridge

Mauritius Trench

O C E A N

Wallaby Plateau

Cuvier Basin

Cuvier Plateau

Zambezi Canyon

Mozambique Plateau

MOZAMBIQUE BASIN

MADAGASCAR BASIN

MADAGASCAR RIDGE

Southeast Indian Ridge

Broken Plateau

30°

Naturaliste Plateau

Diamentina Fracture Zone

Natal Valley

Mozambique Scarp

TRANSKEI BASIN

Ridge II Fracture Zone

Gallieni Fracture Zone

Atlantis II Fracture Zone

Melville Fracture Zone

St Pierre Bank

AGULHAS PLATEAU

Prince Edward Fracture Zone

Southwest

Discovery II Fracture Zone

Indomed I Fracture Zone

Indian Ridge

Novara Knoll

Southeast Indian Ridge

45°S

AGULHAS BASIN

Del Caño Rise

Ridge

Conrad Rise

Kohler Seamount

KERGUELEN PLATEAU

William's Seamounts

A U S T R A L I A N – A N T A R C T I C

Marion Dufresne Seamount

Élan Bank

Fawn Trough

B A S I N

DERBY ABYSSAL PLAIN

Banzare Bank

BATHYMETRY

continental shelf (0–200 metres deep)

depth contour (starting at 1000 metres beyond the continental shelf: 1000 metre intervals thereafter)

ocean trenches and deeps (below 6000 metres)

surface features in italic type

VALDIVIA ABYSSAL

R N   O C E A N   P L A I N   *Princess Elizabeth Trough*

Kainan Maru Seamounts

Wild Canyon

30°   60°   90°E

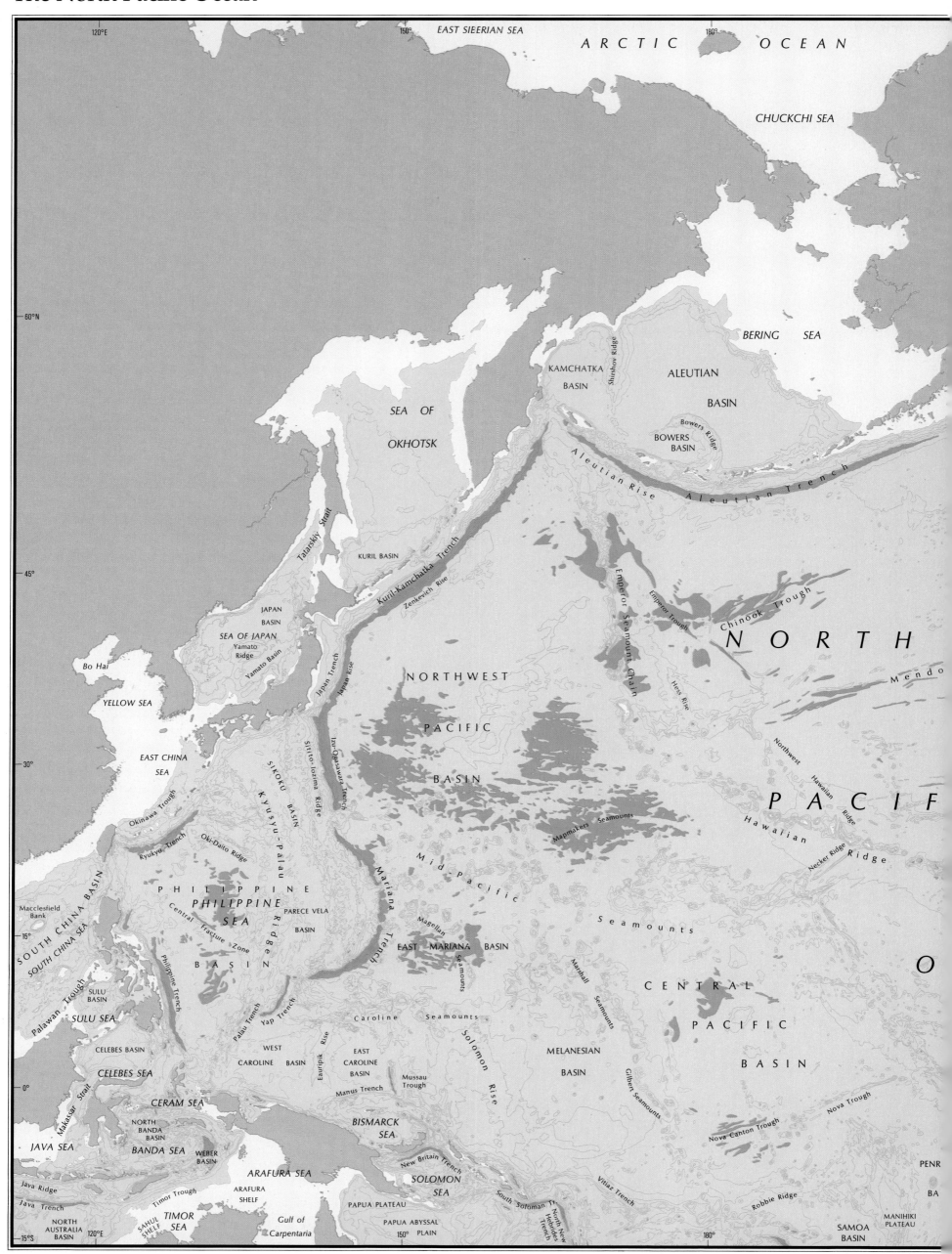

ARCTIC OCEAN

EAST SIBERIAN SEA

CHUCKCHI SEA

BERING SEA

KAMCHATKA BASIN

ALEUTIAN BASIN

Shirshov Ridge

BOWERS BASIN

Bowers Ridge

SEA OF OKHOTSK

Aleutian Rise

Aleutian Trench

KURIL BASIN

Kuril-Kamchatka Trench

Zenkevich Rise

Chinook Trough

Emperor Trough

N O R T H

Tatarskiy Strait

JAPAN BASIN

SEA OF JAPAN

Yamato Ridge

Yamato Basin

Emperor Seamount Chain

Hess Rise

Mendo

Bo Hai

Japan Trench

Japan Rise

NORTHWEST PACIFIC BASIN

Northwest Hawaiian Ridge

YELLOW SEA

EAST CHINA SEA

Okinawa Trough

Ryukyu Trench

SIKOKU BASIN

Sitito-Iozima Ridge

Izu-Ogasawara Trench

P A C I F I C

O

Oki-Daito Ridge

KYUSYU-PALAU RIDGE

Mapmakers Seamounts

Hawaiian Ridge

Necker Ridge

Mid-Pacific

PHILIPPINE

PHILIPPINE SEA

PARECE VELA BASIN

Seamounts

Macclesfield Bank

Central Fracture Zone

BASIN

Mariana Trench

Magellan

Seamounts

CENTRAL

SOUTH CHINA BASIN

Philippine Trench

EAST MARIANA BASIN

Seamounts

Marshall

SOUTH CHINA SEA

Palawan Trough

SULU BASIN

Palau Trench

Yap Trench

Caroline Seamounts

Seamounts

PACIFIC

SULU SEA

WEST CAROLINE BASIN

EAST CAROLINE BASIN

Eauripik Rise

Solomon Rise

MELANESIAN BASIN

Gilbert Seamounts

BASIN

CELEBES BASIN

Manus Trench

Mussau Trough

CELEBES SEA

Makassar Strait

CERAM SEA

BISMARCK SEA

Nova Canton Trough

Nova Trough

PENR

NORTH BANDA BASIN

WEBER BASIN

SOLOMON SEA

New Britain Trench

Vitiaz Trench

Robbie Ridge

JAVA SEA

BANDA SEA

ARAFURA SEA

South Solomon Tr

BA

Java Ridge

ARAFURA SHELF

PAPUA PLATEAU

North New Hebrides Trench

Java Trench

Timor Trough

SAHUL SHELF

TIMOR SEA

Gulf of Carpentaria

PAPUA ABYSSAL PLAIN

SAMOA BASIN

MANIHIKI PLATEAU

NORTH AUSTRALIA BASIN

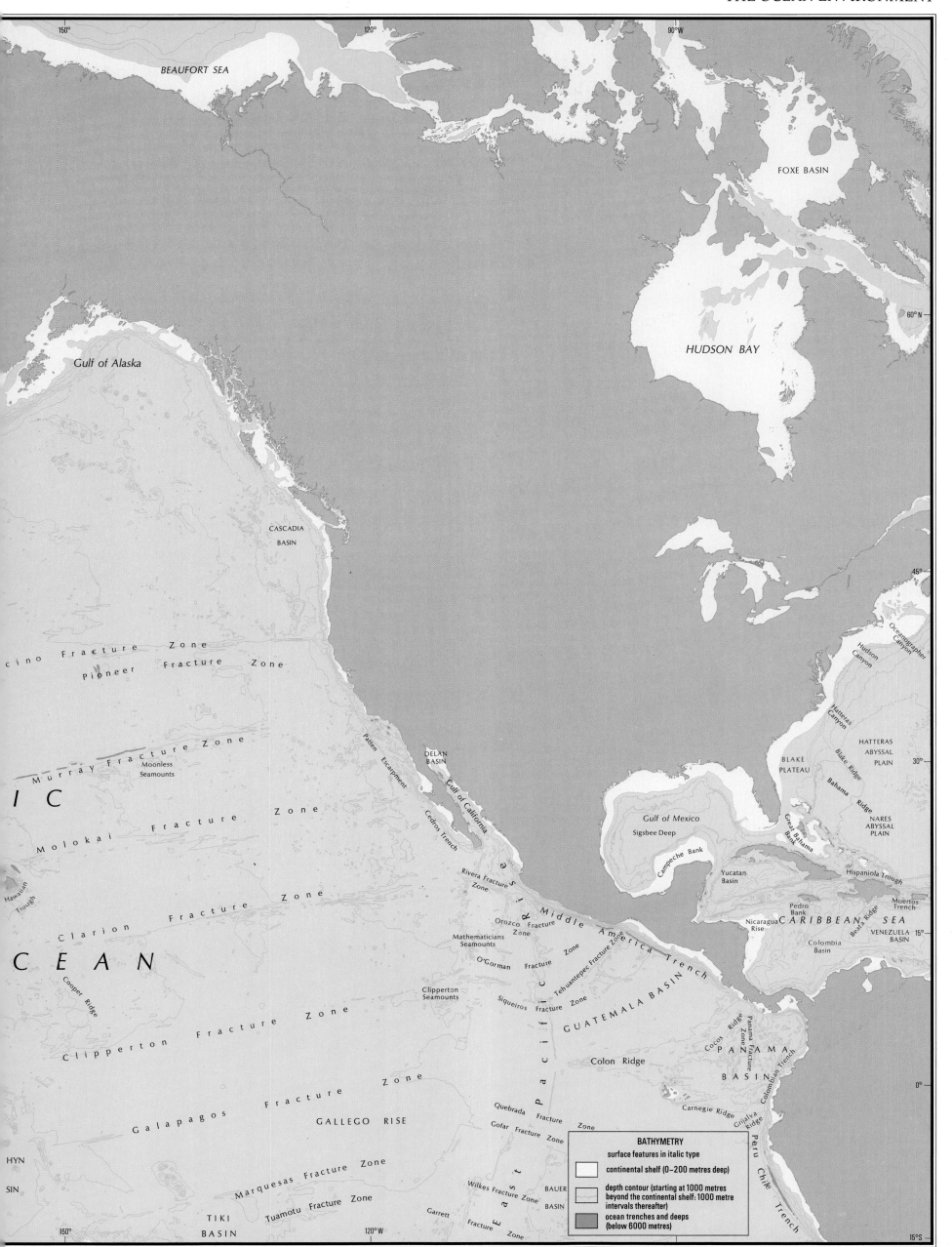

BATHYMETRY

surface features in italic type

continental shelf (0–200 metres deep)

depth contour (starting at 1000 metres beyond the continental shelf: 1000 metre intervals thereafter)

ocean trenches and deeps (below 6000 metres)

The South Pacific Ocean

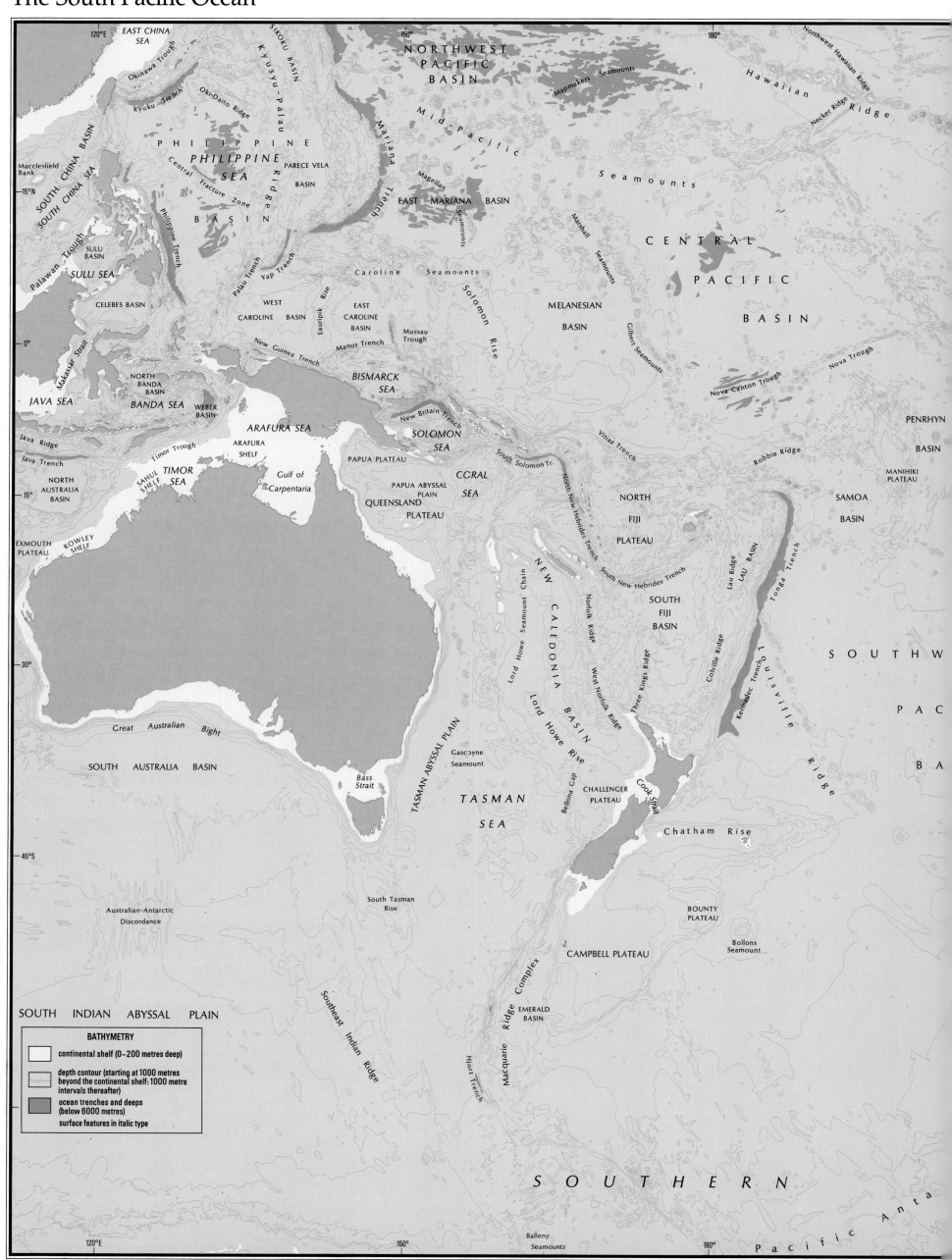

EAST CHINA SEA
120°E
NORTHWEST PACIFIC BASIN
150°
180°
Northwest Hawaiian Ridge

Okinawa Trough
Sikoku Basin
Kyusyu-Palau Ridge
Mid-Pacific
Mapmakers Seamounts
Hawaiian
Necker Ridge
Ridge

Ryuku Trench
Oki-Daito Ridge
Mariana Trench
Seamounts

Macclesfield Bank
15°N
PHILIPPINE
PHILIPPINE SEA
Central Fracture Zone
PARECE VELA BASIN
Magellan Seamounts
EAST MARIANA BASIN
Marshall Seamounts
CENTRAL PACIFIC BASIN

SOUTH CHINA BASIN
SOUTH CHINA SEA
Philippine Trench
BASIN

Palawan Trough
SULU BASIN
SULU SEA
Palau Trench
Yap Trench
Caroline Seamounts
Gilbert Seamounts
Nova Trough

CELEBES BASIN
0°
WEST CAROLINE BASIN
Eauripik Rise
EAST CAROLINE BASIN
Solomon Rise
MELANESIAN BASIN
Nova Canton Trough

New Guinea Trench
Mussau Trough
PENRHYN BASIN

JAVA SEA
NORTH BANDA BASIN
Manus Trench
BISMARCK SEA
MANIHIKI PLATEAU

BANDA SEA
WEBER BASIN
New Britain Trench
Vitiaz Trench
Robbie Ridge

ARAFURA SEA
SOLOMON SEA
South Solomon Tr.
SAMOA BASIN

Java Ridge
ARAFURA SHELF
PAPUA PLATEAU
NORTH FIJI PLATEAU

Java Trench
Timor Trough
PAPUA ABYSSAL PLAIN
North New Hebrides Trench
Lau Ridge
LAU BASIN

NORTH AUSTRALIA BASIN
15°
TIMOR SEA
SAHUL SHELF
Gulf of Carpentaria
CORAL SEA
QUEENSLAND PLATEAU
South New Hebrides Trench
SOUTH FIJI BASIN
Tonga Trench

EXMOUTH PLATEAU
ROWLEY SHELF
NEW CALEDONIA BASIN
Norfolk Ridge

Lord Howe Seamount Chain
West Norfolk Ridge
Colville Ridge
Kermadec Trench
Louisville Ridge
SOUTHW
PAC
BA

30°
Lord Howe Rise
Three Kings Ridge

Great Australian Bight
SOUTH AUSTRALIA BASIN
Gascoyne Seamount
TASMAN ABYSSAL PLAIN
Bellona Gap
CHALLENGER PLATEAU
Cook Strait

Bass Strait
TASMAN SEA
Chatham Rise

45°S
South Tasman Rise
BOUNTY PLATEAU

Australian-Antarctic Discordance
Southeast Indian Ridge
Macquarie Ridge Complex
EMERALD BASIN
CAMPBELL PLATEAU
Bollons Seamount

SOUTH INDIAN ABYSSAL PLAIN
Hjort Trench

SOUTHERN

Balleny Seamounts
150°
180°
Pacific Anta
Pacific

BATHYMETRY
- continental shelf (0–200 metres deep)
- depth contour (starting at 1000 metres beyond the continental shelf: 1000 metre intervals thereafter)
- ocean trenches and deeps (below 6000 metres)
- surface features in italic type

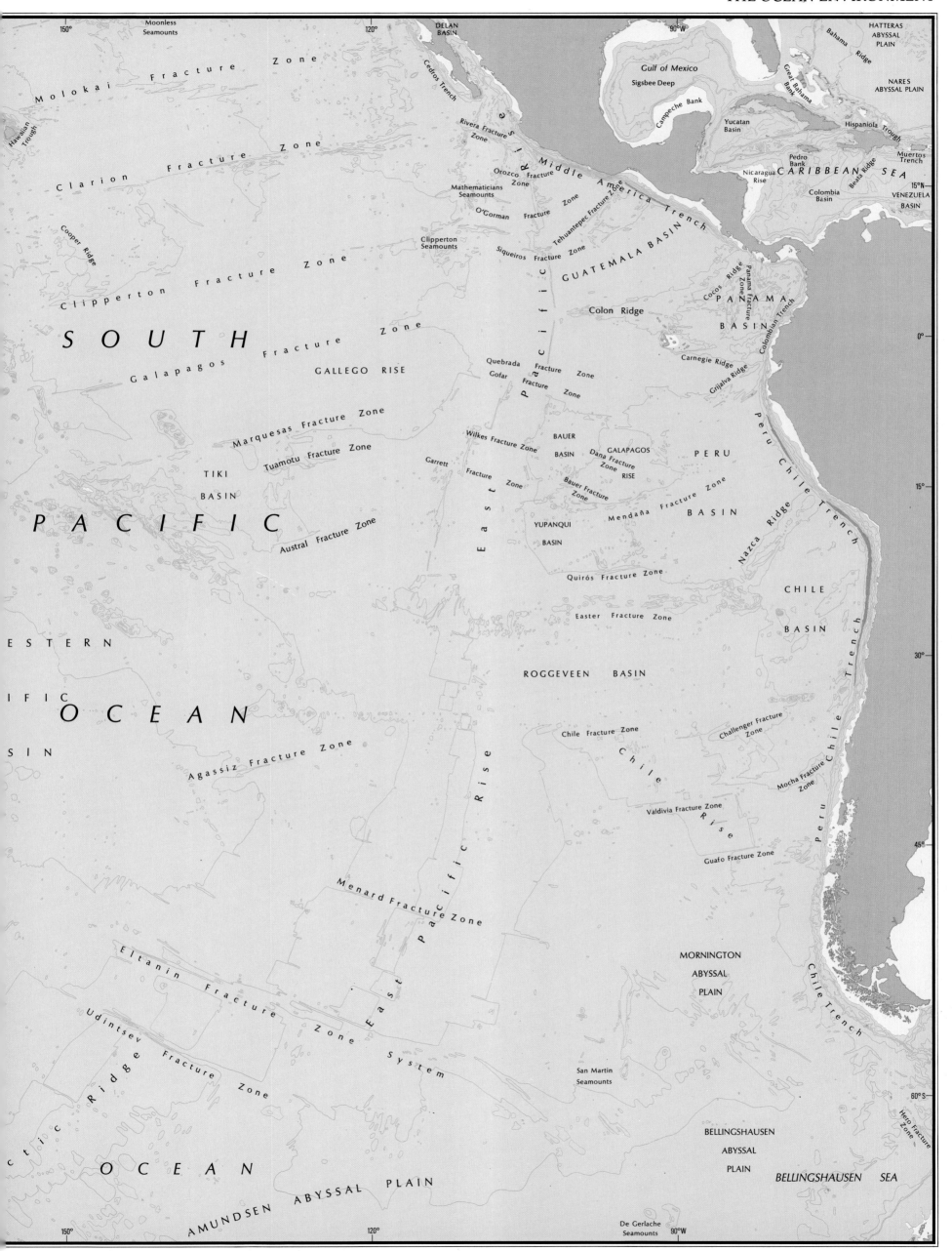

The Arctic and the Antarctic

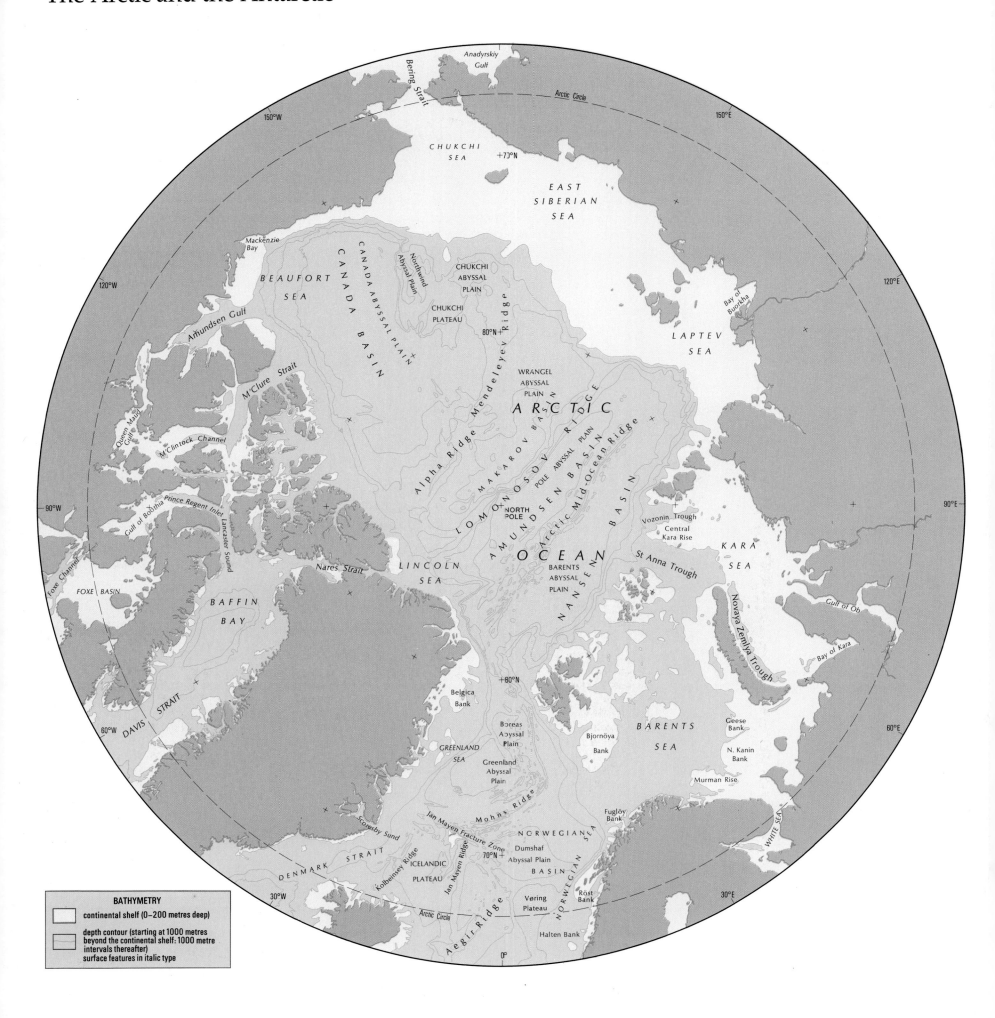

BATHYMETRY

continental shelf (0–200 metres deep)

depth contour (starting at 1000 metres beyond the continental shelf; 1000 metre intervals thereafter) surface features in italic type

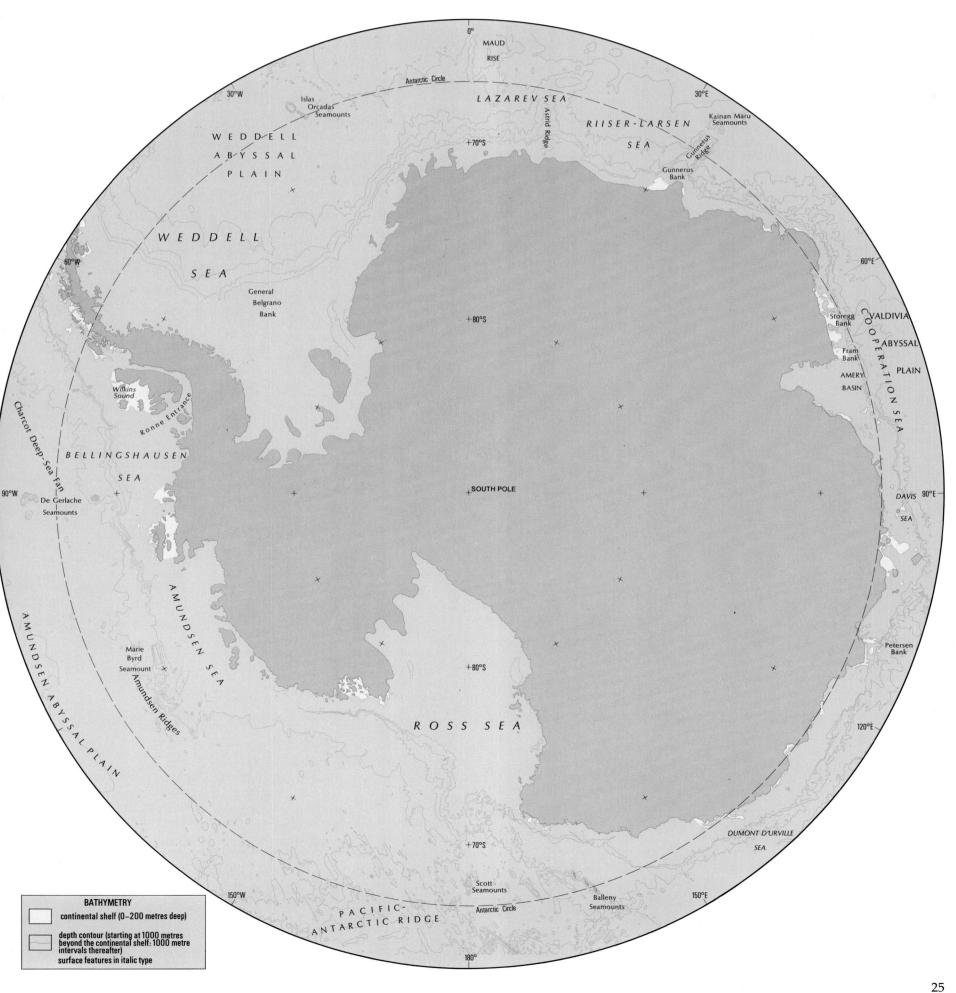

0°

MAUD
RISE

Antarctic Circle

30°W   LAZAREV SEA   30°E

Islas
Orcadas
Seamounts   RIISER-LARSEN   Kainan Maru
                                                                             Seamounts

W E D D E L L   Astrid Ridge   SEA
                                                    +70°S
A B Y S S A L   Gunnerus
                                                                      Ridge
P L A I N   Gunnerus
                                                             Bank

W E D D E L L

S E A   60°E

60°W
                                                                        Storegg   VALDIVIA
        General   Bank
        Belgrano   ABYSSAL
        Bank   +80°S   Fram   PLAIN
                                                                         Bank
                                                                        AMERY   Co
                                                                        BASIN   o
Wilkins   p
Sound   e
                                                                                   r
        Ronne Entrance   a
                                                                                   t
                                                                                   i
BELLINGSHAUSEN   o
                                                                                   n
SEA   S
                                                                                   E
Charcot Deep-Sea Fan   A

90°W   +   SOUTH POLE   +   DAVIS   90°E
De Gerlache   SEA
Seamounts

                                                                                  Petersen
                                                                                  Bank

AMUNDSEN   AMUNDSEN SEA

Marie
Byrd   +80°S
Seamount

Amundsen Ridges
                                                                                  120°E

AMUNDSEN ABYSSAL PLAIN

                        ROSS SEA

                                                                        DUMONT D'URVILLE
                                      +70°S   SEA

Scott
Seamounts   150°E

150°W   Balleny
                                Seamounts

PACIFIC-   Antarctic Circle
ANTARCTIC RIDGE

                        180°

The limits of the sea

EARTH'S surface has three primary components: the hydrosphere or surface waters, salt and fresh; the lithosphere, the surface outer shell of rock which consists of continental crust and sediment-covered oceanic crust; and the atmosphere, the surrounding layer of gases.

The total surface waters cover an area of about 361 million sq. km, compared with the total surface area of the Earth of 509 million sq. km. Ocean basins and associated seas thus cover 71 per cent of Earth's surface. The largest is the Pacific and its associated seas, followed by the Atlantic, including the Arctic Ocean basin, and the Indian Ocean. A fourth basin, the Southern Ocean, is sometimes recognised but is not well defined by surrounding land masses (its areal components have therefore been incorporated with the other three oceans). The largest sea (that is, definable area within the ocean expanse) is the South China Sea and, defined by shoreline length, the largest bay is Hudson Bay.

Mountain ranges dominate the Pacific coastline and effectively block the flow of major rivers so that little land-derived sediment enters the Pacific basin. In contrast, the Atlantic basin receives large quantities of terrigenous sediment from rivers such as the Amazon, Congo and Niger, and indirectly from rivers such as the Mississippi and St Lawrence, which discharge into the Atlantic's marginal seas.

The ocean floor can be divided into zones

1 *world map* The ocean basins are unevenly distributed over Earth's surface. Continental areas mainly occupy the northern hemisphere, while the Pacific, Atlantic and Indian Oceans extend northwards from the circumpolar basin of the Southern Ocean.

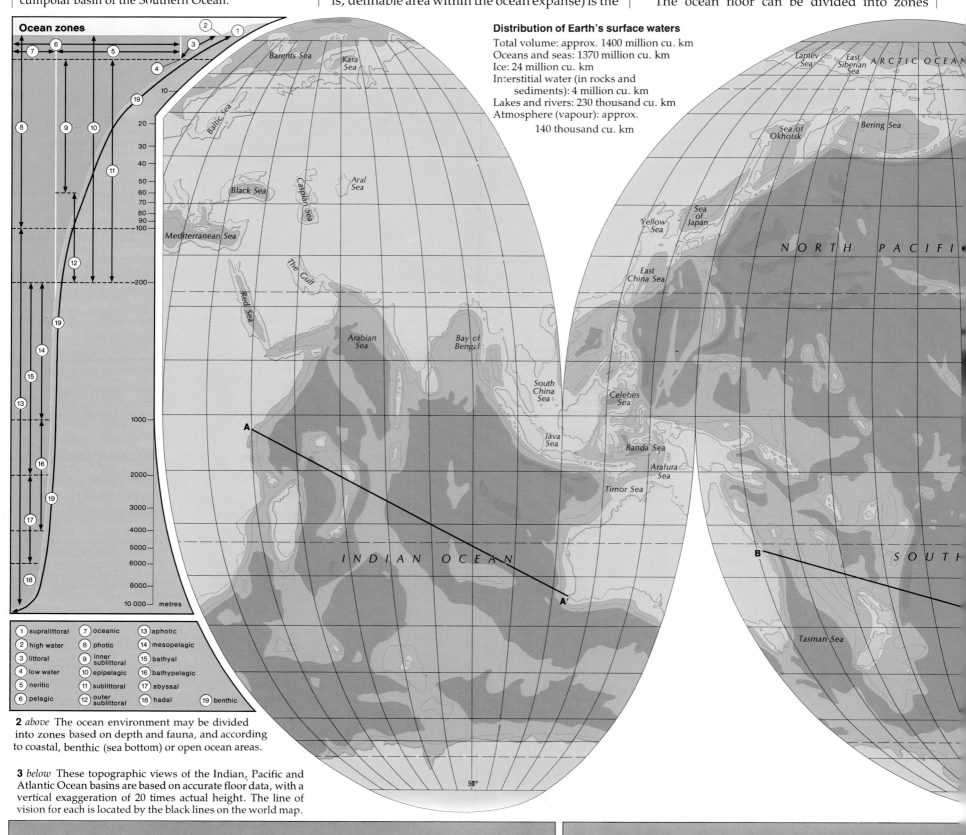

Distribution of Earth's surface waters
Total volume: approx. 1400 million cu. km
Oceans and seas: 1370 million cu. km
Ice: 24 million cu. km
Interstitial water (in rocks and sediments): 4 million cu. km
Lakes and rivers: 230 thousand cu. km
Atmosphere (vapour): approx. 140 thousand cu. km

Ocean zones

1	supralittoral
2	high water
3	littoral
4	low water
5	neritic
6	pelagic
7	oceanic
8	photic
9	inner sublittoral
10	epipelagic
11	sublittoral
12	outer sublittoral
13	aphotic
14	mesopelagic
15	bathyal
16	bathypelagic
17	abyssal
18	hadal
19	benthic

2 *above* The ocean environment may be divided into zones based on depth and fauna, and according to coastal, benthic (sea bottom) or open ocean areas.

3 *below* These topographic views of the Indian, Pacific and Atlantic Ocean basins are based on accurate floor data, with a vertical exaggeration of 20 times actual height. The line of vision for each is located by the black lines on the world map.

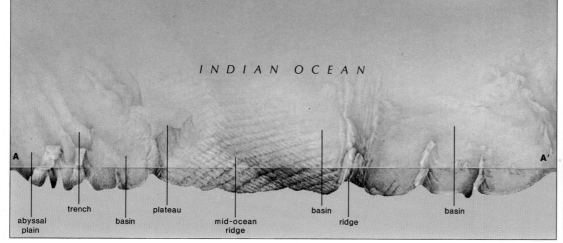

INDIAN OCEAN

abyssal plain — trench — basin — plateau — mid-ocean ridge — basin — ridge — basin

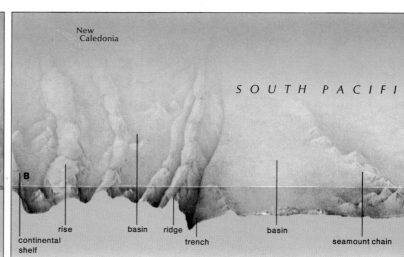

New Caledonia

SOUTH PACIFIC

continental shelf — rise — basin — ridge — trench — basin — seamount chain

based on water depth and incumbent fauna. Between high and low water is the littoral or intertidal zone. The sublittoral zone or continental shelf is a narrow coastal zone adjacent to the continents, sloping gently towards the shelf break and merging into the bathyal zone. The bathyal/abyssal zone boundary varies between 1000 and 3000 m; the hadal zone is confined to deep ocean trenches, below 6000 m.

4 *below* Two elevations stand out in the frequency distribution of levels on the Earth's surface: the continental platform at 0–1 km above sea level, and the abyssal floor at 4–5 km below sea level. From the highest elevation to the deepest ocean floor, the total vertical relief is a mere 0.31 per cent of Earth's equatorial radius.

5 *right* The hypsographic curve, the cumulative frequency of elevations of Earth's surface features, shows that ocean basins cover over twice the surface area of the continents. Indirectly, the curve indicates the ephemeral nature of coastlines, for during the course of an ice age, sea level can fall and rise by over 100 m.

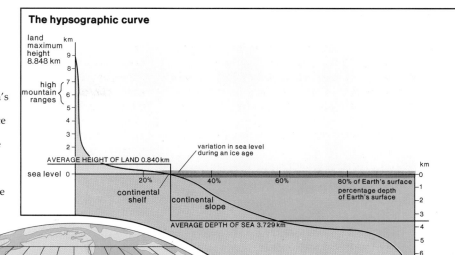

The hypsographic curve

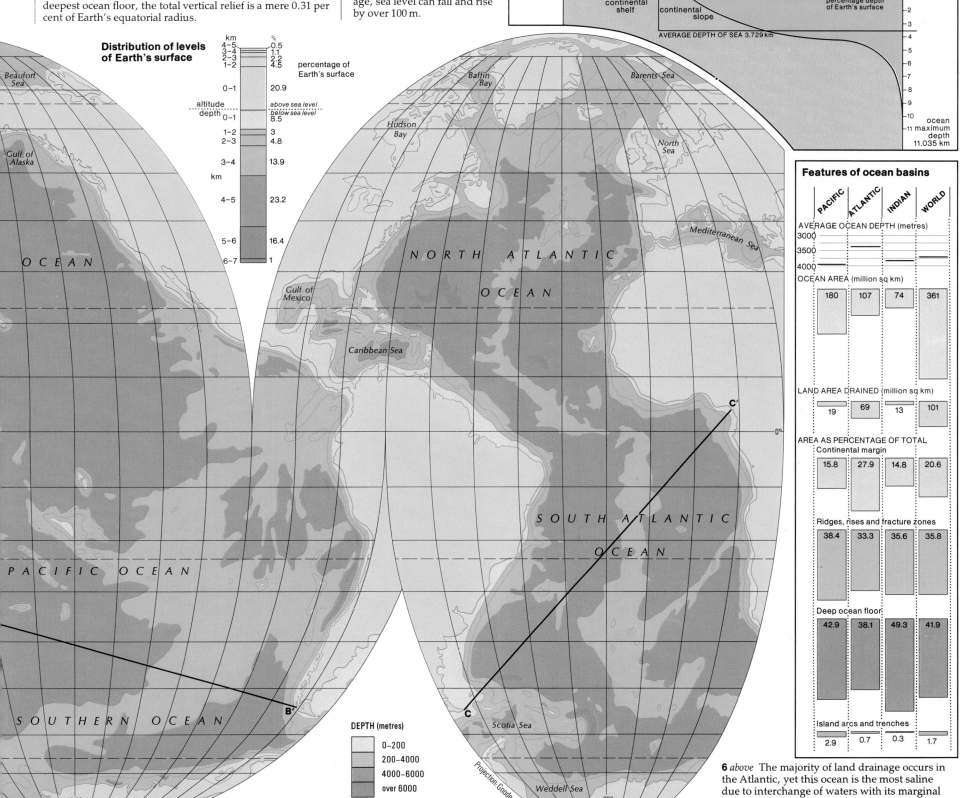

Distribution of levels of Earth's surface

km	%
4–5	0.5
3–4	1.1
2–3	2.2
1–2	4.5
0–1	20.9

percentage of Earth's surface

altitude depth	above sea level / below sea level
0–1	8.5
1–2	3
2–3	4.8
3–4	13.9
4–5	23.2
5–6	16.4
6–7	1

km

DEPTH (metres)
- 0–200
- 200–4000
- 4000–6000
- over 6000

Features of ocean basins

	PACIFIC	ATLANTIC	INDIAN	WORLD
AVERAGE OCEAN DEPTH (metres)				
OCEAN AREA (million sq km)	180	107	74	361
LAND AREA DRAINED (million sq km)	19	69	13	101
AREA AS PERCENTAGE OF TOTAL				
Continental margin	15.8	27.9	14.8	20.6
Ridges, rises and fracture zones	38.4	33.3	35.6	35.8
Deep ocean floor	42.9	38.1	49.3	41.9
Island arcs and trenches	2.9	0.7	0.3	1.7

6 *above* The majority of land drainage occurs in the Atlantic, yet this ocean is the most saline due to interchange of waters with its marginal seas. The continental margins are economically the most important provinces, but they constitute only about 21 per cent of the ocean floors.

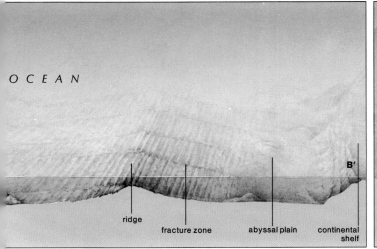

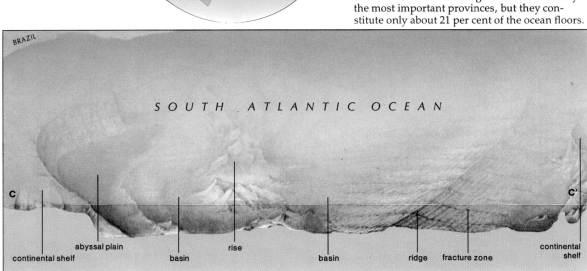

The shape of the ocean basins

THE ocean floor can be divided into physiographic provinces using criteria such as depth, relief, gradient and composition. Two groups of provinces are generally recognised: continental margin and (deep) ocean basin.

The continental margin comprises the continental shelf, slope and rise. Continental shelves are shallow platforms adjacent to land masses; many are characterised by an irregular topography comprising banks, basins and valleys, but some have relatively smooth floors. The seaward limit is usually defined by a shelf break, a distinct gradient change from the shelf to the steeper continental slope; here water depths range from 35 m to over 250 m. Continental slope gradients range from about 1:40 such as off major deltas, to over 1:3, such as off Blake Plateau and other submarine terraces. Often the slope is dissected by submarine canyons. These features have steep sides and V-shaped profiles, probably formed

from erosion during the lower sea levels of Pleistocene glaciation and subsequent widening and deepening by turbidity currents (see pages 42–3).

Seaward of the continental slope is the continental rise with gradients of between 1:50 and 1:800. It is composed of a long wedge of sediments usually several kilometres thick, which accumulate through sliding or slumping or transportation by turbidity currents down the slope. Atlantic and Indian Ocean rises are wide, whereas Pacific rises are narrow or even absent. Ocean basin provinces lie seaward of the continental margins. Ocean ridges cover about one-third of the ocean floor and form an almost continuous range through the ocean basins. Their crests are 2–3 km below sea level and 1–4 km above the surrounding floor. The ridges, such as the mid-Atlantic ridge, are sites of seismic activity, where new oceanic crust is formed from basaltic rocks being intruded and extruded at the ridge crest, and then spreading laterally away. Ocean rises,

such as the Bermuda rise, are aseismic and result from a gentle upwarping of oceanic crust. (The East Pacific Rise is therefore a misnomer, for it is a seismic ocean ridge.)

The physiographic character of the deep ocean floor is determined mainly by the extent to which sediment masks relief in oceanic crust and the extent of volcanic activity penetrating weakness in the crust. It consists mainly of plains and abyssal hills, the latter formed from volcanic material or sometimes from folded sediments. Abyssal hills can be several hundred metres high and up to 10 km in diameter; they occur mainly in clusters. Seamounts are hills over 1 km high, with steep sides and often a circular base, and guyots are a flat-topped variation: both features have a volcanic origin. Abyssal plains have a flatness unique on Earth's surface, with gradients not exceeding 1:1000. They consist of sediments dispersed via turbidity currents and augmented by pelagic deposits which mask the underlying,

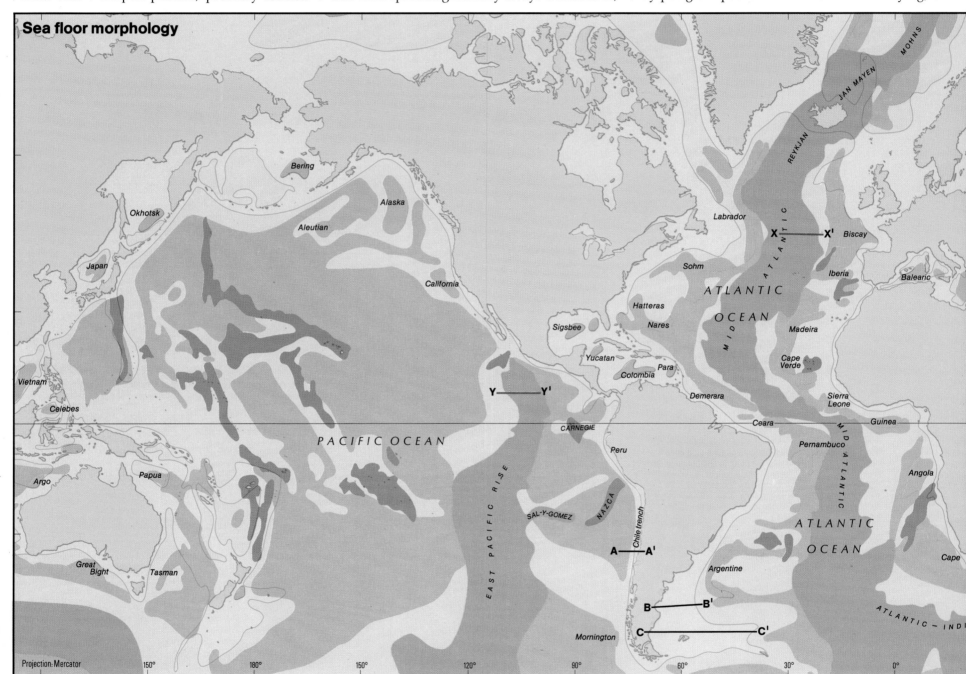

Sea floor morphology

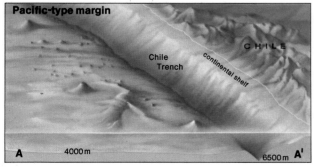

Pacific-type margin

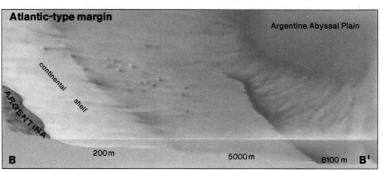

Atlantic-type margin

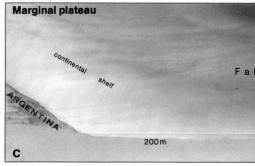

Marginal plateau

2 There are two main types of continental margins: 'Atlantic' and 'Pacific'. A third, the 'marginal plateau', is sometimes recognised but it is closely linked to the Atlantic type. Atlantic-type margins have a shelf width of up to 1500 km; a slope of from 20 to 100 km width, often dissected by submarine canyons; and a

well-developed rise. Pacific-type margins have a narrow shelf from 20 to 40 km, and a steep slope descending to a trench (over 6000 m), or trough (under 6000 m) parallel to the margin. These margins are neither restricted nor exclusive to the ocean basins after which they are named, but are the more dominant in each.

Marginal plateaus are platforms, with steep sides (1000–2000 m deep) falling to abyssal depths. An example is the Falklands Plateau.

Atlantic-type margins are known as 'passive' because they are seismically inactive. The connected continent and adjacent ocean belong to the same

jagged oceanic crust.

The deepest parts of the ocean are the long, often narrow trenches which occur either near some continental margins or are associated with some island arc systems. Trenches are formed by one lithospheric plate being subducted beneath another plate (see pages 32–3).

1 *world map* In the Atlantic Ocean, physiographic provinces follow a simple pattern: the ridge occurs in mid ocean and dominates much of its basin. Smooth-floored, elongate abyssal plains occur parallel to the ridge, and wide continental margins lie adjacent to the land. The Pacific and Indian Oceans show more complex morphology: the ocean ridges are offset to the sides of the basins and there are much greater areas of rough topography, due to sediment cover being thin or absent (for example, the abyssal hills west of North America). In the Pacific Ocean, clusters of abyssal hills occupy the greater area, but in the Atlantic and Indian Ocean basins, abyssal plains are more widespread due to the greater influx of terrigenous sediment from continental margins, mainly via turbidity currents.

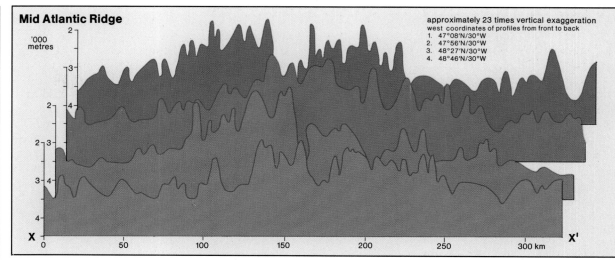

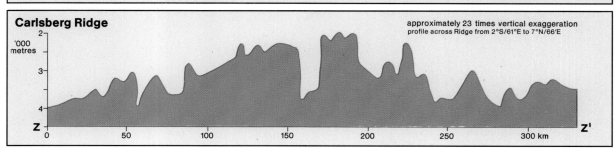

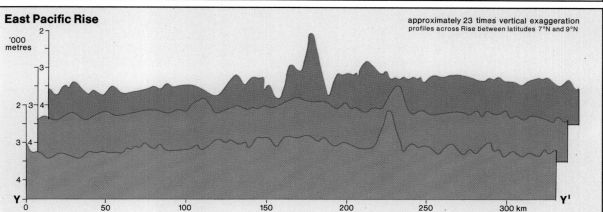

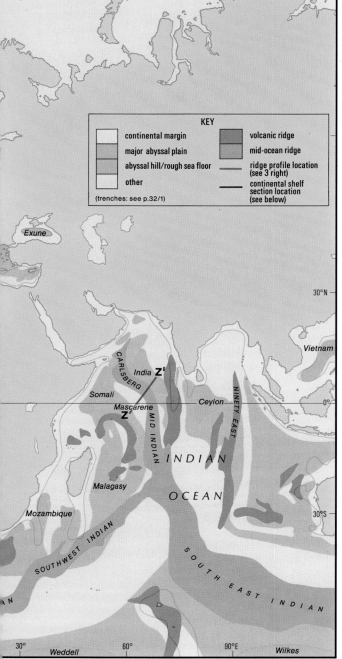

3 *above* Profiles of mid-ocean ridges in the Atlantic, Pacific and Indian Ocean basins. When new oceanic crust is formed, it spreads as parallel crests which together form a ridge. Spreading at either side is usually at an even rate. Some ridges have a slow spreading rate, as do, for example, the Mid Atlantic Ridge and the Carlsberg ridge in the Indian Ocean, where the crustal plates are moving apart at a rate of about 2 cm per year. Other ridges, such as the East Pacific Rise, have a fast spreading rate of 12–16 cm per year. Fast spreading ridges have a relatively subdued topography and deepen gradually away from the ridge axis. Slow spreading ridges are characterised by a high relief, as much as 2 km near the ridge axis, where a median rift valley about 20–40 km wide is formed by normal faults with usually a downward throw into the valley.

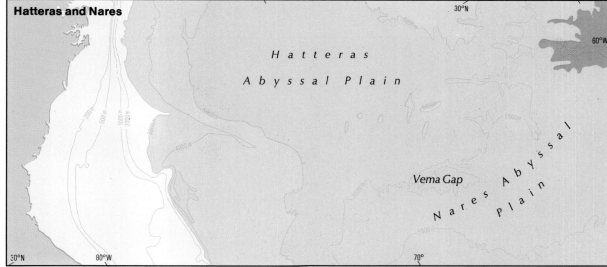

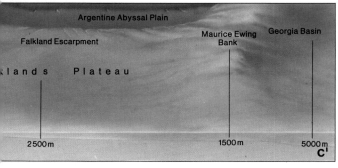

lithospheric plate (see *Sea floor spreading and plate tectonics* page 32). Pacific-type margins are active: the continent and adjacent floor are on different plates, with the oceanic plate being subducted (downwarped) beneath the continental plate because of seismic activity.

4 *above* Abyssal plains tend to lie parallel to the continental margin, and may be elongated (thousands of kilometres long and hundreds of kilometres wide), equilateral or irregular in shape. Abyssal plains are classified as primary, secondary or relict, according to the type of sediment influx. Primary abyssal plains have a direct influx. An example is the Sohm abyssal plain in the North Atlantic covering over 900 000 sq. km. The Gulf of Maine and the Laurentian Channel are the chief sediment sources and the presence of coarse sands some 1000 km south of the Laurentian Channel indicates the effectiveness of turbidity currents in transporting sediment. The Nares abyssal plain, one of the deepest in the North Atlantic, is an example of a secondary plain. There is an inflow of sediment from the Hatteras (primary) plain via the Vema Gap; the sediment is finer than in the primary plain. The Aleutian abyssal plain in the Pacific is relict, with the sediment source no longer evident.

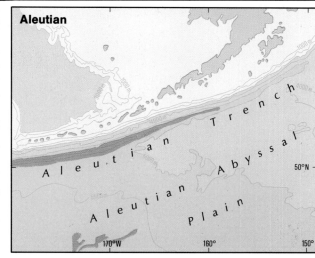

Magnetism and sea floor dating

STUDIES of Earth's magnetic field have been undertaken for over 400 years from the time when the magnetic compass was first recognised as being fundamentally important to navigation. In the past three decades, studies of the remnant magnetisation of rocks have provided valuable evidence to the history of lithospheric movements and the evolution of ocean basins.

Because Earth's core is believed to be composed largely of iron, it was once thought that the core behaves as a permanent magnet. However, heat destroys magnetism, and magnetic materials lose permanent magnetism at a temperature called the Curie point (usually 500–800°C), which is undoubtedly exceeded in the core. It is now widely considered that within the core there exists a self-exciting dynamo which generates the magnetic field.

The geomagnetic field is similar to that of a strong bar magnet with north and south magnetic poles located presently near 75°N 101°W and 67°S 143°E; this means that a line joining the two poles does not pass through Earth's centre but is displaced by about 1200 km towards Indonesia. The axis of the field is aligned at a small but varying angle (less than 12°) to Earth's axis of rotation.

When hot rocks which contain magnetisable material (such as new oceanic crust forming at ocean ridges) cool below the Curie point, they become magnetised in the direction of the existing field. This remnant magnetisation is retained by rocks long after the field has changed. Recent studies of remnant magnetism in rocks have led to three important discoveries: polar wandering, geomagnetic field reversals, and the significance of magnetic anomalies at ocean ridges.

By examining rock formations of various ages in different countries, positions of ancient magnetic poles can be determined for the times when rocks became magnetised. In reality, it is the lithosphere which has moved, and polar wandering curves are simply a convenient way to illustrate the feature (see *The drifting continents* pages 34–35).

Palaeomagnetic research has also shown that some rocks were magnetised in directions diametrically opposite to the present (or normal) field. Some 171 such reversals have occurred in the past 76 million years. The reason why the field reverses is unknown, but a simple, self-exciting dynamo can have either polarity, so it is possible that Earth's dynamo may be similarly changed. Within the past 45 million years, reversals have become more frequent. Periods of up to half a million years or so of constant polarity are called magnetic epochs, but superimposed are much shorter-term reversals called magnetic events. The time taken for the field to reverse is uncertain, but is possibly of the order of 1000–10 000 years.

1 *below* From the accurate dating of magnetic anomalies, it is possible to compile a magnetic isochron map and determine the age of many ocean floors. Newest oceanic crust is located at mid-ocean ridges and the age increases with distance away from the ridges.

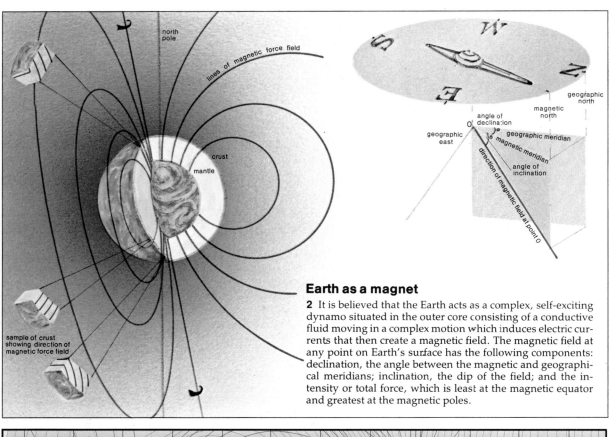

Earth as a magnet

2 It is believed that the Earth acts as a complex, self-exciting dynamo situated in the outer core consisting of a conductive fluid moving in a complex motion which induces electric currents that then create a magnetic field. The magnetic field at any point on Earth's surface has the following components: declination, the angle between the magnetic and geographical meridians; inclination, the dip of the field; and the intensity or total force, which is least at the magnetic equator and greatest at the magnetic poles.

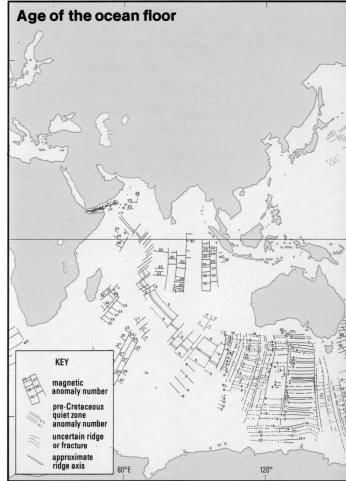

Age of the ocean floor

KEY

magnetic anomaly number

pre-Cretaceous quiet zone anomaly number

uncertain ridge or fracture

approximate ridge axis

Magnetic reversal time scale

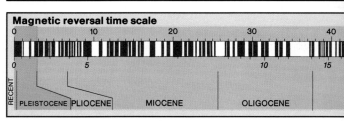

RECENT   PLEISTOCENE   PLIOCENE   MIOCENE   OLIGOCENE

3 *left* The map shows values of declination for 1977, together with the rate at which declination is changing over the Earth's surface. The declination, inclination and intensity of the geomagnetic field vary continuously over the globe. Because the direction of the field changes slowly with respect to geographical coordinates, navigators have to apply corrections, measured as declination, to compass bearings. Charts showing lines of equal declination are known as isogonic maps.

4 *above and* **5** *right* When it was recognised in the late 1960s that the magnetic anomalies (or stripes) at ocean ridges recorded the history of magnetic field reversals, earth scientists established a numbering system for key anomalies: numbers 1 to 32 from the present back to the upper Cretaceous period (c. 76 million years ago) and numbers M1 to M22 from the lower Cretaceous back to the Jurassic period. These sequences are separated by a long, stable period of normal polarity known as the Cretaceous Quiet Zone.

Magnetic poles

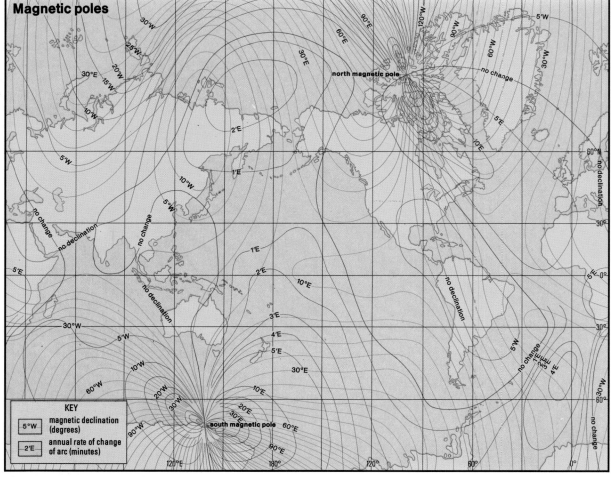

KEY

5°W   magnetic declination (degrees)

2°E   annual rate of change of arc (minutes)

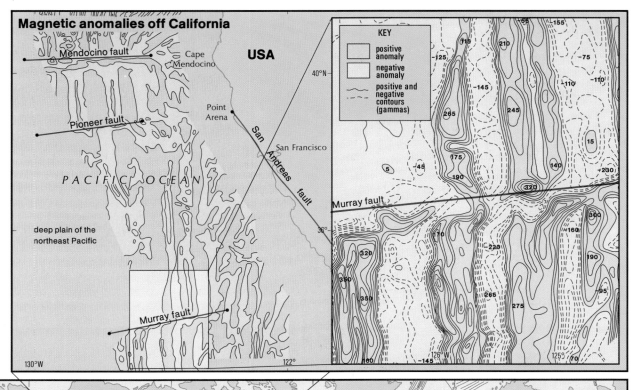

Magnetic anomalies off California

USA

KEY
- positive anomaly
- negative anomaly
- positive and negative contours (gammas)

Mendocino fault
Cape Mendocino
Point Arena
Pioneer fault
San Francisco
San Andreas fault
PACIFIC OCEAN
deep plain of the northeast Pacific
Murray fault

6 *left and* **7** *below* In places the ocean floor resembles a 'magnetic tape recorder'. A symmetrical pattern of magnetic anomalies occurs either side of the axes of ocean ridges. Positive anomalies result from rocks which were magnetised in a normal field, whereas negative anomalies result from magnetisation in a reversed field.

The map (left) shows linear magnetic anomalies off the west coast of California. Such anomalies occur widely over the ocean floor; these are parallel bands hundreds or thousands of kilometres in length, where the geomagnetic field intensity is higher (positive) or lower (negative) than the average value for an area. Such local variations arise from differences in the remnant magnetisation of rocks on the ocean floor; those magnetised in a normal field add to the average value giving a positive anomaly, whereas rocks magnetised in a reversed field produce a negative anomaly.

Many magnetic anomaly patterns have a pronounced symmetry in relation to the axes of ocean ridges. An example is the Reykjanes Ridge (below). In the early 1960s, earth scientists proposed the following explanation: material from within Earth's mantle rises to the surface at ocean ridges, forming new crust which moves slowly (a few centimetres a year) and laterally away from the ridge; as the crustal material cools, it becomes magnetised in the existing geomagnetic field, whether normal or reversed. This is the hypothesis of sea floor spreading.

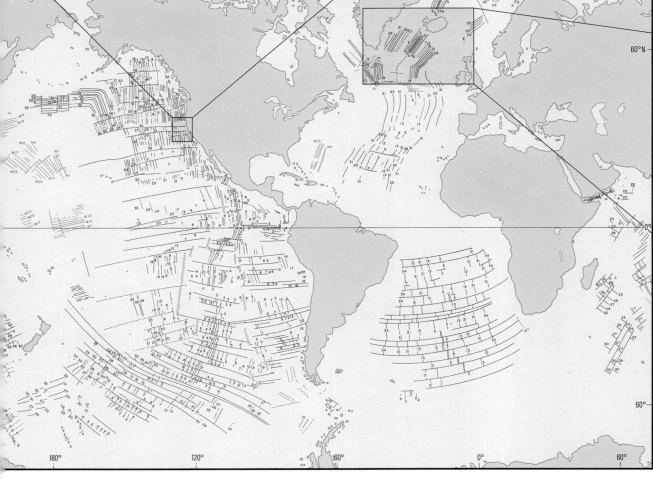

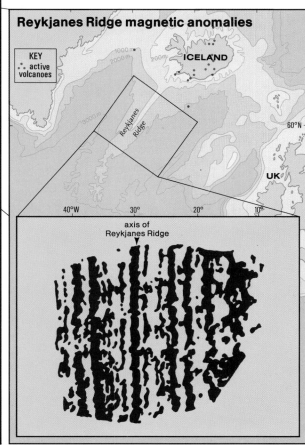

Reykjanes Ridge magnetic anomalies

KEY
- active volcanoes

ICELAND
Reykjanes Ridge
UK

axis of Reykjanes Ridge

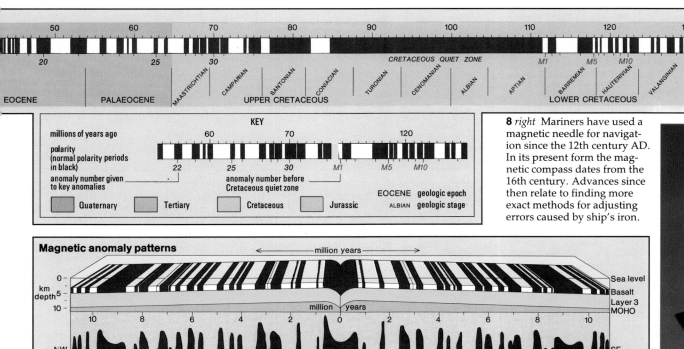

CRETACEOUS QUIET ZONE

| EOCENE | PALAEOCENE | MAASTRICHTIAN | CAMPANIAN | SANTONIAN | CONIACIAN | TURONIAN | CENOMANIAN | ALBIAN | APTIAN | BARREMIAN | HAUTERIVIAN | VALANGINIAN | BERRIASIAN | PURBECKIAN | PORTLANDIAN | KIMMERIDGIAN | OXFORDIAN | CALLOVIAN |

UPPER CRETACEOUS — LOWER CRETACEOUS — UPPER JURASSIC — MIDDLE JURASSIC

KEY

millions of years ago

polarity (normal polarity periods in black)

anomaly number given to key anomalies

anomaly number before Cretaceous quiet zone

EOCENE geologic epoch
ALBIAN geologic stage

- Quaternary
- Tertiary
- Cretaceous
- Jurassic

8 *right* Mariners have used a magnetic needle for navigation since the 12th century AD. In its present form the magnetic compass dates from the 16th century. Advances since then relate to finding more exact methods for adjusting errors caused by ship's iron.

Syeds & Davis Azimuth Compass 1837

Magnetic anomaly patterns

million years

Sea level
Basalt
Layer 3
MOHO

km depth

million years

NW
SE

km

Sea floor spreading and plate tectonics

THE theory of plate tectonics was formulated by earth scientists in the late 1960s. It unifies continental drift and sea floor spreading, and provides an explanation of the geodynamic mechanism of ocean basin and continent evolution over the past 200 million years.

The lithosphere, Earth's rigid outer layer, is divided into a number of blocks, or plates. The majority of plates consist of continental masses and adjacent ocean floor, whereas the remainder consist solely of oceanic areas. The rigid, relatively cool plates move over a hot, partially molten plastic layer known as the asthenosphere which lies at a depth of 60–70 km. There are three types of boundary between plates: divergent, convergent and conservative, consisting of transform faults and fracture zones.

Ocean ridges occur at divergent boundaries, where partially molten mantle material rises in irregular pulses along the ridge axes forming new lithosphere. As new oceanic crust is formed, the earlier crust spreads away from the ridge axis, which is a zone of high heat flow, extensive volcanism, and shallow-focus earthquakes.

Trenches are created at convergent boundaries. When two plates meet, one overrides the other, the latter being 'subducted' or forced into the mantle where the lithosphere is resorbed (reassimilated). Beneath ocean trenches, shallow (up to 70 km), intermediate (70–300 km) and deep-focus (300–700 km) earthquakes occur on a plane inclined at about 45°. When the oceanic portions of two plates collide, a volcanic island arc develops on the overridden plate; examples are the complex Japan arcs, or the simpler Tonga–Kermadec arc in the south-west Pacific. Collision of oceanic and continental areas results in a mountain range of volcanic material and folded sediments, such as the Andes.

A conservative boundary consists of a transform fault and occurs between offset ridge axes. Here, plates slide past each other without accretion or subduction processes, although some shallow-focus earthquakes occur. Where there is no related lateral motion outside the offset axes, the inactive line of the former transform fault is known as a fracture zone; this structure is particularly common on the East Pacific floor.

The main driving force of plate movement is thermal energy and involves processes in the deep mantle. The mechanism is probably a complex convective flow in the mantle, extending down to at least 700 km, a depth attained by some lithospheric slabs before being resorbed.

Hot spots result from plumes of magma rising to the surface from deep in the mantle, with irregularly pulsed extrusions forming volcanoes

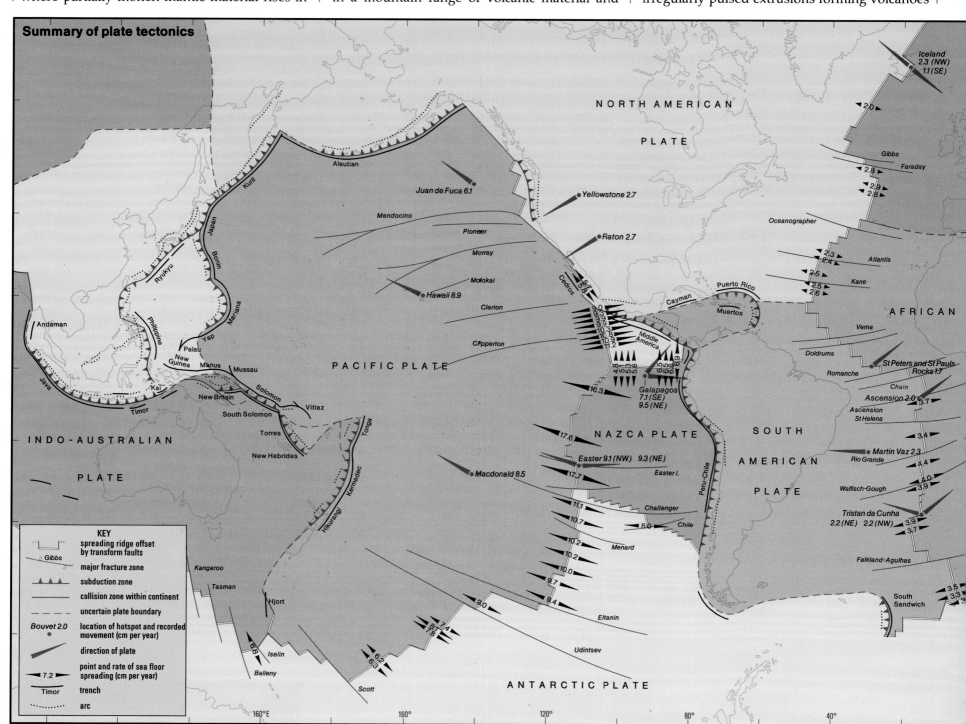

Summary of plate tectonics

KEY

- spreading ridge offset by transform faults
- *Gibbs* major fracture zone
- subduction zone
- collision zone within continent
- uncertain plate boundary
- *Bouvet 2.0* location of hotspot and recorded movement (cm per year)
- direction of plate
- *7.2* point and rate of sea floor spreading (cm per year)
- *Timor* trench
- arc

1 *above* Classifications of the global distribution of lithospheric plates have so far ranged from 6 to 26 plates covering Earth's surface. Several plate boundaries are conjectural, for example that around Scotia Arc in the South Atlantic, while some are uncertain, for example, that across China, within the Eurasian plate. Most classifications acknowledge 12 plates, although some of these have imprecise boundaries. Of the other possibilities, a Somalian plate, between the Carlsberg Ridge and the East African Rift system, is often recognised, but its southern boundary is very uncertain. A few small plates are vestiges of older plates which have been consumed in the continual process of plate evolution. For example, the Gorda plate, west of Seattle, USA, is possibly a remnant of the so-called Farallon plate which existed within the past 30 million years west of North America.

2 *right* A triple junction is a point where three plates come together. An example is the point where the Pacific, Cocos and Nazca plates meet, consisting of a spreading ridge, a subduction zone and transform faults. Fracture zones, found in all ocean basins, are typically 50–100 km wide and may be up to about 4000 km long. They mark the inactive extension of transform faults away from ridge axis offsets, where differential plate motions no longer exist.

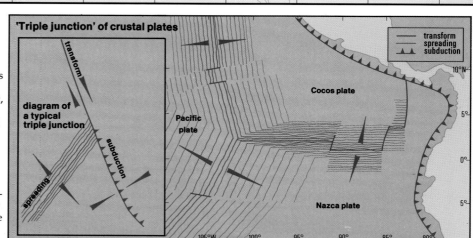

'Triple junction' of crustal plates

diagram of a typical triple junction

— transform
— spreading
▲▲ subduction

comprising a different type of basaltic lava to that generated at spreading ridges. Hot spots occur both on and away from plate boundaries, and as volcanoes often occur in chains decreasing in age away from the spot, they have been used to gauge plate motions. Sixteen hot spots are generally recognised. Although the concept is widely accepted, a particular problem is an explanation for how a spot can remain relatively fixed for millions of years in a convecting mantle.

The Pacific/Nazca plate boundary has the fastest total spreading rate (over 16 cm/yr), whereas the African/Arabian boundary has the slowest rate (just over 1 cm/yr); the Eurasian/North American spreading rate is about 2 cm/yr.

Plate tectonics provides an explanation for the relatively young ocean floor (no more than 200 million years old) in relation to the much older continents (possibly more than 4000 million years), in which the continental crust is too 'buoyant' to be subducted.

Poles of rotation of crustal plates

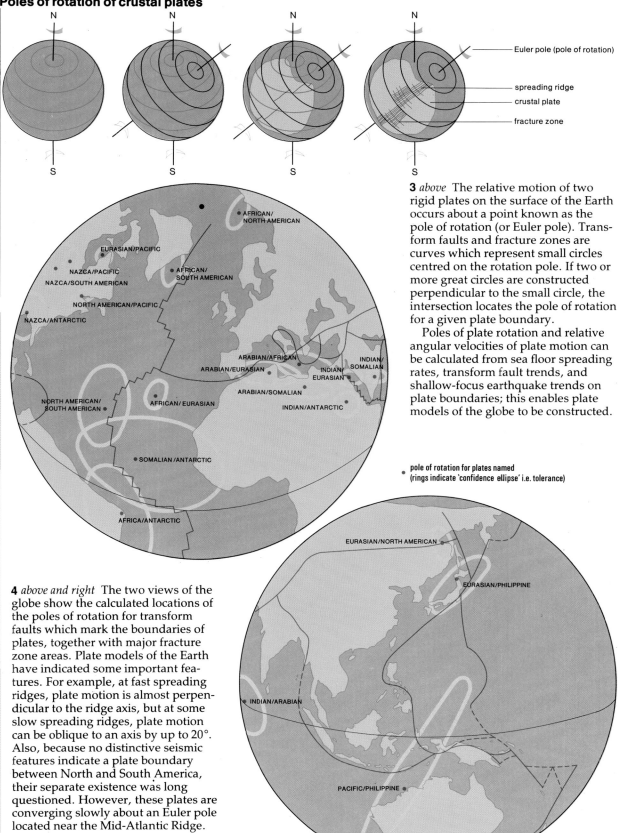

3 *above* The relative motion of two rigid plates on the surface of the Earth occurs about a point known as the pole of rotation (or Euler pole). Transform faults and fracture zones are curves which represent small circles centred on the rotation pole. If two or more great circles are constructed perpendicular to the small circle, the intersection locates the pole of rotation for a given plate boundary.

Poles of plate rotation and relative angular velocities of plate motion can be calculated from sea floor spreading rates, transform fault trends, and shallow-focus earthquake trends on plate boundaries; this enables plate models of the globe to be constructed.

• pole of rotation for plates named (rings indicate 'confidence ellipse' i.e. tolerance)

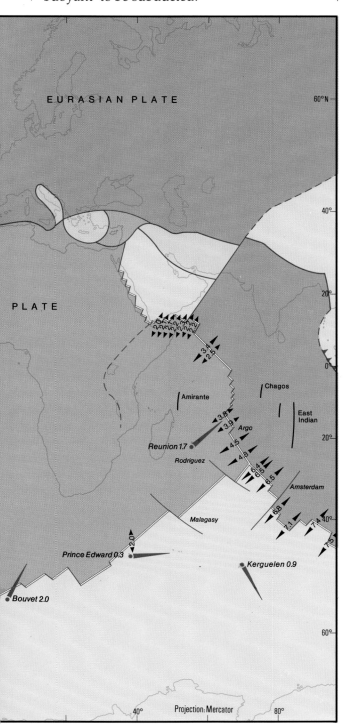

4 *above and right* The two views of the globe show the calculated locations of the poles of rotation for transform faults which mark the boundaries of plates, together with major fracture zone areas. Plate models of the Earth have indicated some important features. For example, at fast spreading ridges, plate motion is almost perpendicular to the ridge axis, but at some slow spreading ridges, plate motion can be oblique to an axis by up to 20°. Also, because no distinctive seismic features indicate a plate boundary between North and South America, their separate existence was long questioned. However, these plates are converging slowly about an Euler pole located near the Mid-Atlantic Ridge.

5 *below* At constructive margins, ocean or spreading ridges are underlain by a network of magma (molten rock) chambers located within the oceanic crust. Mantle material, on partial melting, rises into the magma chambers, where complex crystallisation processes occur accompanied by irregular ejection of magma to the surface. Although subduction zones are considered as destructive margins, not all of the lithosphere is resorbed into the mantle; some igneous material partially remelted from descending lithospheric slabs rises upwards, adding to the continental crust. This results in the creation of new crust at island arcs or a thickening of existing continental crust at a continental plate edge, by as much as 20 km over a 50–60 km width per 100 million years.

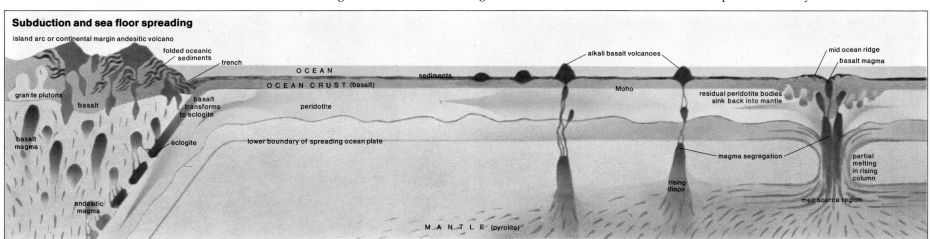

Subduction and sea floor spreading

The drifting continents

THE theory of plate tectonics, widely accepted today, embodies several aspects of an earlier concept known as continental drift. This proposed that the present distribution of continents on the surface of the Earth has resulted from the dissociation and migration of previous continental areas.

An examination of an atlas or globe shows that the Atlantic coasts of Africa and South America seem to have a jigsaw-puzzle fit. At the end of the 19th century, an Austrian, Suess, suggested that because of not only geomorphological similarities but also certain geological correlations, Africa, South America, India and Australia once formed a supercontinent. In 1912, a German scientist, Wegener, proposed that about 200 million years ago, a single supercontinent existed called *Pangaea*, comprising two principal land areas, *Laurasia* and *Gondwanaland*. These were partly separated by a large marginal sea, *Tethys*, and the remaining surface consisted of a vast ocean, *Panthalassa*, the precedent of the Pacific Ocean. He also suggested that since the early Mesozoic era, global history records the break-up of Pangaea.

There were many ambiguities in the geological evidence, and geophysicists at that time were doubtful that a mechanism could exist to drive large areas of continental crust across strong, resistant oceanic crust, let alone without major distortion of the continental blocks. Consequently the drift concept was largely abandoned in the 1920s. However, the theory of continental drift was revived in the 1960s with the concept of sea floor spreading, according to which oceanic crust is continuously formed at ocean ridges and spreads away laterally. In the late 1960s these ideas were incorporated into the theory of plate tectonics.

Pangaea was not a permanent, primordial land mass, but resulted from the merging of scattered blocks of continental crust over a long period of time up to the Permian period (280–225 million years ago). Geological evidence on land indicates that Gondwanaland (i.e. South America, Africa, India, Australia and Antarctica) existed as a single continent as early as 600 million years ago, at which time North America, Europe and much of Asia (later to become Laurasia) existed as separate masses.

During the Permian and Triassic periods, Pangaea remained relatively intact but began to dissociate about 200–180 million years ago with the gradual separation of Laurasia from Gondwanaland. Resulting from a clockwise rotation of Laurasia, the southern North Atlantic started to open and the Tethys Sea began to close through subduction, so that during the Jurassic period (180–135 million years ago), an almost continuous equatorial seaway existed. At the beginning of the Jurassic period, India became detached, to drift northward at a relatively fast rate, and Australia–Antarctica were separated from South America–Africa, beginning the formation of the Indian Ocean. During the Jurassic, the North Atlantic continued to widen, extending northward, but North America was still connected to Eurasia. At the end of the Jurassic, the South Atlantic started to open along a rift extending southward from the relative location of the Cameroons. About 65 million years ago, the South Atlantic was over 3000 km wide, Africa had drifted slowly northward with a gradual anticlockwise rotation and Eurasia had rotated clockwise, closing the Tethys Sea to form the Mediterranean. By the mid-Tertiary, Australia, separated from Antarctica, was drifting northward, and the Indian plate had collided with Asia forming the Himalayas. North America became connected to South America, and the North Atlantic rift extended into the Arctic basin, separating Europe from Greenland, so that the continents were almost in their present positions.

Extrapolating into the future, the Americas will continue drifting westward, Australia will drift northward, and the Red Sea and East African Rift system will begin to open as embryonic basins.

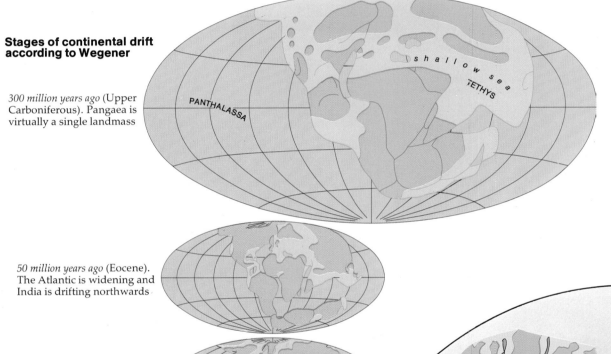

Stages of continental drift according to Wegener

300 million years ago (Upper Carboniferous). Pangaea is virtually a single landmass

50 million years ago (Eocene). The Atlantic is widening and India is drifting northwards

1.5 million years ago (Early Pleistocene). The continents are in their present-day positions, but South America is still connected to Antarctica

1 *above* In support of the theory of continental drift, in 1915 Alfred Wegener published *Die Entstehung der Kontinente und Ozeane* ('The Origin of Continents and Oceans') which not only contained detailed geodetic, geophysical, geological, palaeontological, and palaeoclimatological arguments but also showed reconstruction maps of continents and oceans at different periods in time to illustrate the break-up of Pangaea.

2 *right* Although the Atlantic coastlines of South America and Africa appear to have a jigsaw-puzzle fit, a coastline is not, as a feature, a suitable elevation for geometrical fitting because major coastline changes can arise from sea-level fluctuations. As continental margins are underlain primarily by continental crust, a more realistic contour for fit should be at some depth down the margin.

In the early 1960s, numerical methods using computers were used to examine the geometrical fit of continents. The best fit obtained for Africa and South America uses the 500 fathom (914 m) isobath with a rotation pole at 40°N, 30.6°W. A number of overlaps and gaps arise, the largest misfit being the Niger delta, but as each overlap comprises geological features younger than 200 million years, the geometric reconstruction shows good results. Similarly, closure of the North Atlantic continental masses on these computer models gives a reasonable fit provided that Iceland (composed of rocks younger than 65 million years) is excluded. The fit of the northern to the southern continents is comparatively poor, requiring the rotation of Spain to close the Bay of Biscay, and the omission of Central America, with large gaps in the Mediterranean and Caribbean seas.

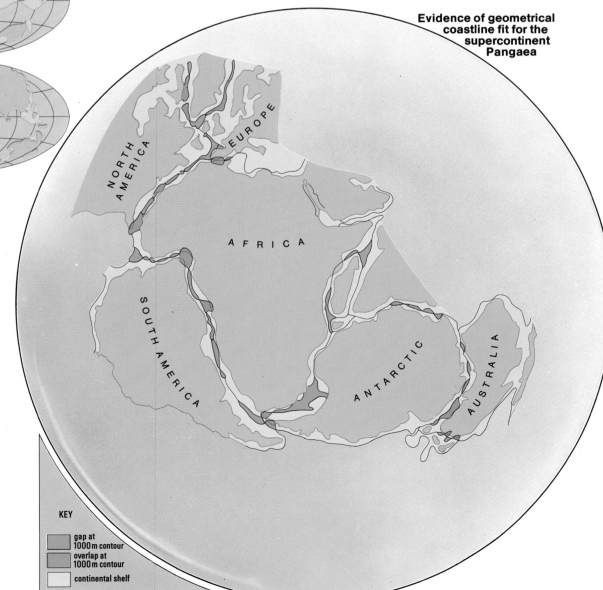

Evidence of geometrical coastline fit for the supercontinent Pangaea

KEY

gap at 1000 m contour

overlap at 1000 m contour

continental shelf

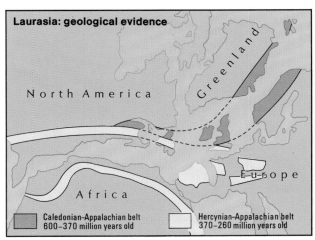

Laurasia: geological evidence

Caledonian–Appalachian belt
600–370 million years old

Hercynian–Appalachian belt
370–260 million years old

3 *left* and **4** *below* The correlation of geological features of separate continents also suggests that they were once joined. The most significant types of such evidence are stratigraphic and fossil similarities, and continuity of structural trends. A matching of Laurasia in the North Atlantic is more difficult than for Gondwanaland. However, the structural continuity of the Hercynian–Appalachian orogenic belt (260–370 million years ago) indicates that North America was probably linked with Europe at about 370 million years ago. For Gondwanaland, evidence of correlation includes the structural continuity of fold belts from South America across Antarctica to Australia; the close correlation across all continents of Permo-Carboniferous glacial tilts, Permian coal deposits, and Jurassic volcanic deposits; and the structural and age similarities of cratons (or shields) between Brazil and West Africa.

6 *above* Glossopteris, a fossil plant, has been found in rocks dating from the late Palaeozoic Era (225 million years ago), in South Africa, India, Australia and South America, further evidence that they were once joined.

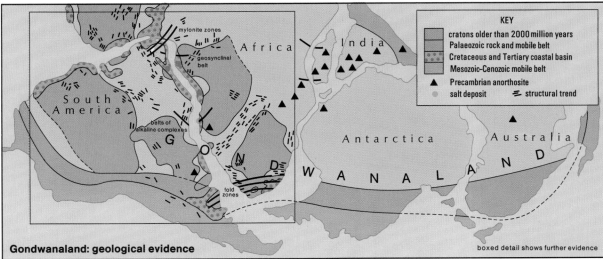

KEY

cratons older than 2000 million years

Palaeozoic rock and mobile belt

Cretaceous and Tertiary coastal basin

Mesozoic-Cenozoic mobile belt

▲ Precambrian anorthosite

• salt deposit   ⧫ structural trend

Gondwanaland: geological evidence   boxed detail shows further evidence

Two possible models of heat flow within the Earth

7.1 layered convection

7.2 convection throughout mantle

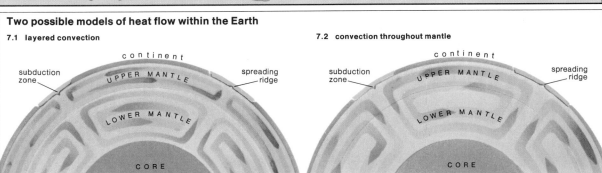

continent

subduction zone   UPPER MANTLE   spreading ridge

LOWER MANTLE

CORE

continent

subduction zone   UPPER MANTLE   spreading ridge

LOWER MANTLE

CORE

5 *below* Shoreline fit indicates that Arabia and Africa were once joined. Over the past 200 million years the Red Sea has spread, forming the beginning of a new ocean.

7 *above* Convective heat flow in the Earth's mantle was first proposed as a driving force for continental drift by the British geologist Holmes in the 1930s. However, the precise pattern of the flow remains unknown. It is unlikely to be a simple convection cell because of the variable nature and size of heat sources, phase changes, and also the movement of plates. For example plates will have edge forces such as ridge-push near the ocean ridges and the stronger slab-pull of a subducting plate due to density forces. These forces probably contribute to convective flow in the mantle.

8 *right* The movement of the British Isles demonstrates the degree of 'continental drift' over a period of 600 million years. It is important to note that the present-day coastline has, however, only been in existence since the late Tertiary; the present outline is used in the diagram to illustrate the process.

9 *below* Assuming that the overall configuration of Earth's magnetic field has remained almost constant and that rocks have not been magnetically agitated, it is possible to plot former pole positions from the remnant inclinations and declinations for rock formations of various ages. Apparent 'polar wandering' curves have been compiled from these data. (It is considered that the magnetic poles themselves did not actually wander, but that the continents have moved over the surface relative to the poles.) It is believed that the difference between the European and North American curves arises from the opening of the Atlantic Ocean in the past 200 million years.

'Polar wanderings'

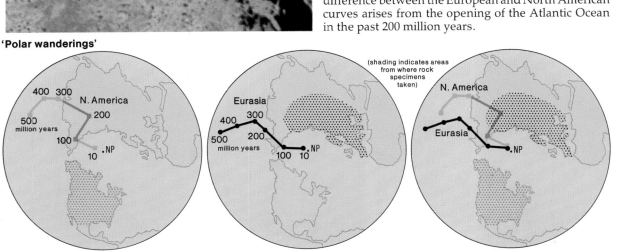

(shading indicates areas from where rock specimens taken)

Movement of Britain through 600 million years

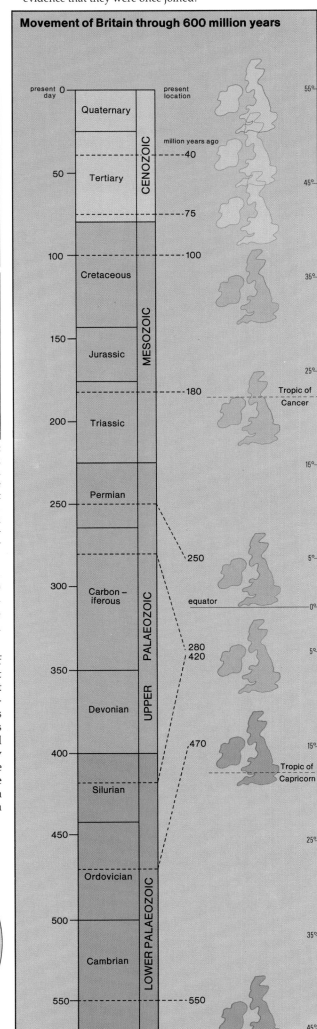

The topography of the deep ocean floor

THE deep ocean floor contains features of low relief, such as abyssal hills, and of high relief, such as oceanic islands, seamounts and guyots. Abyssal hills, which rise less than 1000 m above the surrounding ocean floor and are up to about 10 km in diameter, cover about 50 per cent of the Pacific floor but are much less abundant in the Atlantic and Indian basins. Most are of volcanic origin, though some might comprise folded sediments and some, possibly, are caused by upwarping due to igneous intrusions.

Oceanic islands are almost all of volcanic origin, created either at spreading ridges or at hot spots (see pages 32–33). On plate boundaries there are isolated islands, such as Ascension Island, and island arcs, such as the Marianas. Away from plate boundaries, islands are either aligned in chains or completely isolated. Between latitudes 30°N and 30°S, most oceanic islands are encircled by reefs, massive colonies of coral, coralline algae, and other shelly organisms. Some occur as fringing reefs extending up to 100 m from the shore, and others as barrier reefs detached and encircling the island at up to several kilometres distance. Some oceanic islands are closely grouped in chains and have extruded so much lava that they have become connected, forming submarine ridges. An example is the Hawaiian Islands.

Seamounts are submarine volcanoes similar in profile to oceanic islands but smaller, rising several kilometres above the ocean floor, with a circular or elliptical base and steep slopes (as much as 25°). Many are grouped in lines of between 10 and 100, for example the Emperor Seamounts, but some are isolated. Seamounts are particularly abundant in the Pacific and are less widespread in the Atlantic and Indian Oceans.

Guyots are seamounts with a flat-topped profile; they are not completely planar but have an extremely shallow slope from near the centre. They are seamounts which at some time were quite near sea level, became truncated by wave activity and later submerged due to ocean floor subsidence. Depth of submergence ranges from 200 m to about 2500 m, the majority being in the range 1000–2000 m, and some have tilted profiles, considered to be the result of subsidence. It has been estimated that the number of sea-

1 *main map* Seamounts and guyots are most common in the Pacific. Most have volcanic origins but are now totally extinct. Where they rise above the surface, they form islands or atolls. Most are broadly conical: the largest, Great Meteor seamount in the NE Atlantic, has a basal diameter over 100 km and a height of 4 km. Guyots are truncated seamounts, their tops eroded by wave action.

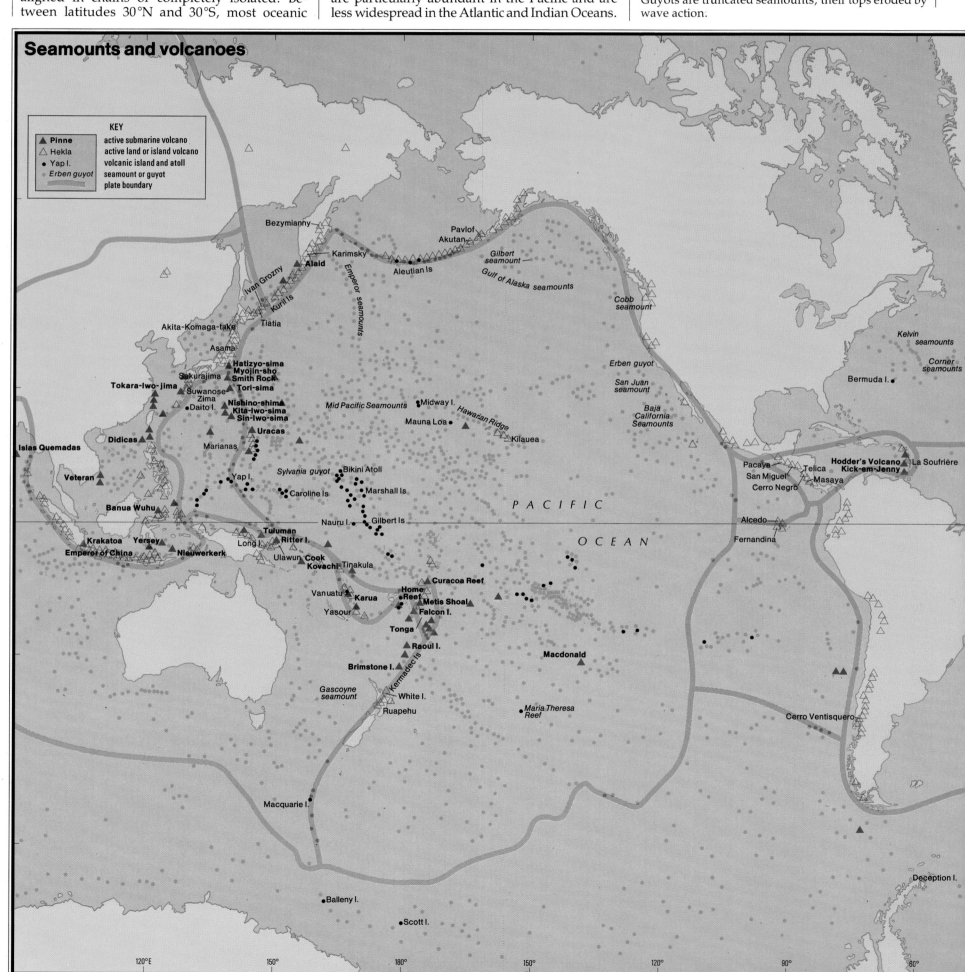

Seamounts and volcanoes

KEY
▲ Pinne — active submarine volcano
△ Hekla — active land or island volcano
● Yap I. — volcanic island and atoll
· *Erben guyot* — seamount or guyot
— plate boundary

mounts (including guyots) exceeds 10 000.

Atolls are annular reefs at or near sea level, encircling a lagoon, which have developed atop a volcanic island that has either subsided or been truncated by wave action. Atolls are particularly common in the Pacific Ocean.

Oceanic islands and seamounts can be dated from the age of the basaltic lava and reef sediments. No seamount older than the surrounding ocean floor has been found: some are the same age, suggesting that they formed on or near an ocean ridge; others are younger, formed more recently at a hot spot.

2 *right* The Hawaiian islands are part of an island chain formed by volcanoes moving with the crustal plate away from a hot spot. Radio-isotope dating of the lava confirms the increase in age along the chain, with the active crater of Kilauea at the eastern end, and Midway Island along the chain with lavas 25 Ma (Tertiary). The seamounts at the north-west end of the chain have lavas of 100 Ma (Cretaceous).

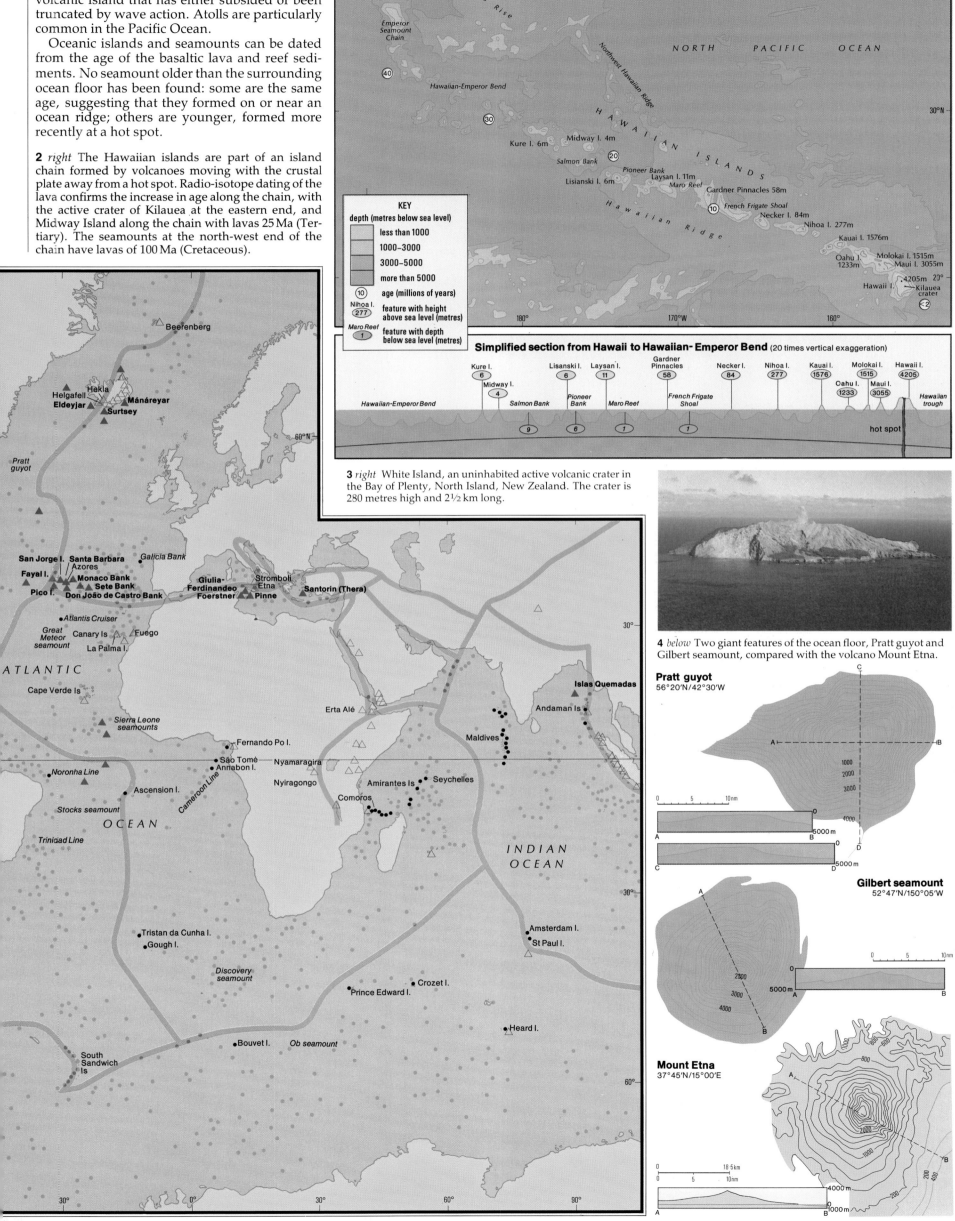

3 *right* White Island, an uninhabited active volcanic crater in the Bay of Plenty, North Island, New Zealand. The crater is 280 metres high and 2½ km long.

4 *below* Two giant features of the ocean floor, Pratt guyot and Gilbert seamount, compared with the volcano Mount Etna.

Pratt guyot
56°20′N/42°30′W

Gilbert seamount
52°47′N/150°05′W

Mount Etna
37°45′N/15°00′E

Earth's unstable foundations

SEISMOLOGY, the study of seismic waves generated by earthquakes, is the most important means of investigating Earth's interior. Seismic waves can be divided into body waves (P and S waves) which travel within the Earth, and surface waves. Only earthquakes and nuclear explosions contain sufficient energy to transmit seismic waves within the Earth, and from a global network of recording stations the precise location of each source can be determined. From recording stations, travel-time curves can be calculated for P and S waves, and from these the wave velocities can be calculated for different depths within Earth. A graph of these velocities versus depth show a number of discontinuities, which indicate that Earth's interior has a concentric structure consisting of a crust, mantle and core. The irregularities suggest subdivisions into an inner (solid) and outer (liquid) core, and into a lower, transitional and upper mantle. One important irregularity (a decrease in velocity), occurs at 100–200 km depth. It is known as the low-velocity zone (LVZ) and coincides roughly with the asthenosphere.

Earth's mean density is about 5520 kg/cu. m, but the density of surface rocks is no more than 2500–3000 kg/cu. m; material in the inner zones must therefore have a much higher density. The density distribution of the interior is not precisely known: a number of models have been based mainly on P and S wave velocity distributions, the total mass of Earth (deduced from the gravity field) and the moment of inertia about

Earth's rotational axis. From these models likely composition of the Earth can be deduced, but large variations in density of the upper mantle occur in all models, suggesting a heterogeneous composition.

A close relationship exists between the upper mantle and oceanic crust. The latter is produced from mantle material at spreading ridges, and up to several hundred million years later is resorbed into the mantle at subduction zones. The mantle's likely composition and the source of rocks contained in oceanic crust have been deduced from three types of study: firstly, ophiolite sequences, slices of oceanic crust found on continents, a result of upper mantle being thrust upward (or obducted) when continental masses collide at a convergent plate boundary; secondly, seismic velocity and calculated density distribution; and thirdly, high-temperature and pressure experiments on likely mantle materials.

The mantle is probably composed of various forms of peridotite, a rock which near the surface consists mainly of olivine and pyroxene minerals. At ocean ridges, partial melting occurs near the top of the mantle, supplying melt to a network of overlying magma chambers, in which rocks such as gabbro crystallise, and basalt lava is extruded in pulses, forming new oceanic crust. With increasing depth in the mantle, density increases through structural changes in minerals, but without their chemical composition altering. For example, olivine (orthorhombic crystalline form) is altered to spinel (octahedral) form.

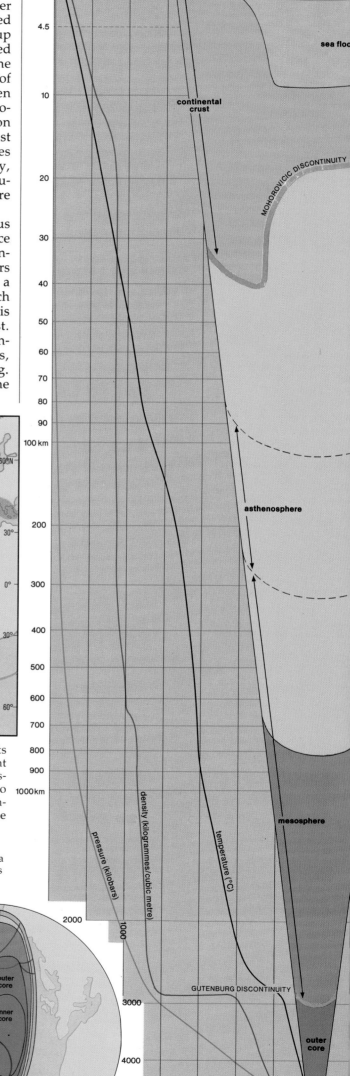

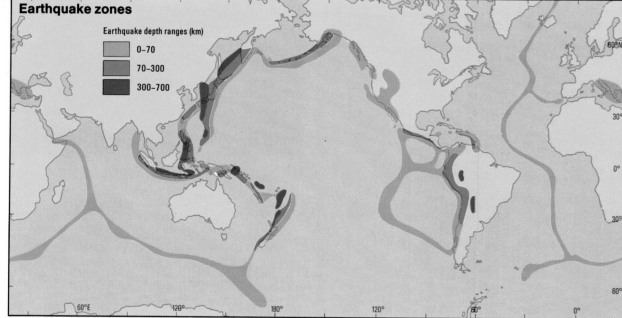

Earthquake zones

Earthquake depth ranges (km)
- 0–70
- 70–300
- 300–700

1 *above* Earthquakes are caused by displacement of crustal or upper mantle material and occur in belts along plate boundaries. They are classified as shallow-focus (less than 70 km), intermediate (70–300 km) and deep-focus (more than 300 km). They have a depth limit of about 700 km where, due to high temperatures, stress is relieved by melting and the faulting which constitutes an earthquake no longer occurs. Earthquake intensities are measured on the Richter magnitude scale; the largest ever had a magnitude of 8.50.

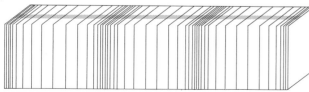

2 *above* P (or primary) waves oscillate backward and forward in the direction of propagation, like sound waves. They can travel through solids or liquids (e.g. molten rock or water).

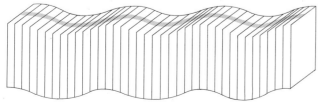

3 *above* S (or secondary) waves oscillate transverse to the direction of motion, shearing rock sideways. They can travel only through solids. Their speed is about half that of P waves.

4 *right* The diagram of the Earth's structure shows its division into various layers according to the present state of knowledge which is mainly deduced from seismic surveys. A logarithmic scale has been used to show Earth's layers more clearly, with estimated density, temperature and pressure values shown to the left of the diagram.

5 *right* In a similar manner to light waves passing through a water surface, seismic waves are bent or refracted at Earth's internal boundaries. The increase in velocity with depth eventually constrains the waves to bend back towards the surface. Some waves are reflected back to the surface.

At the mantle–core boundary, P waves are refracted towards the vertical due to the sudden decrease in velocity here; this causes a shadow zone through which P waves are not directly transmitted. S waves disappear at this boundary. Since S waves cannot travel through liquids, it is likely that the outer core is in a 'liquid' state. Recently S waves have been detected in the inner core, which is therefore probably solid.

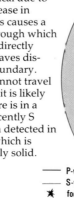

— P-wave
— S-wave
✳ focus

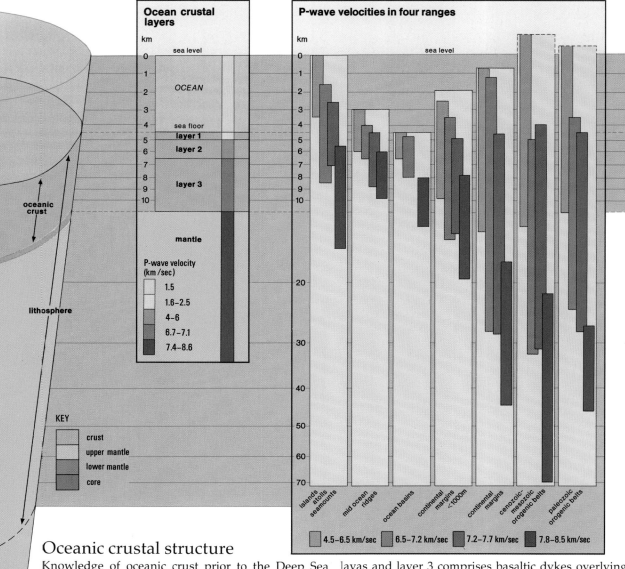

Ocean crustal layers

km — sea level
0
1
2 OCEAN
3
4 sea floor
5 layer 1
6 layer 2
7
8 layer 3
9
10

mantle

P-wave velocity (km/sec)
- 1.5
- 1.6–2.5
- 4–6
- 6.7–7.1
- 7.4–8.6

KEY
- crust
- upper mantle
- lower mantle
- core

oceanic crust

lithosphere

P-wave velocities in four ranges

islands stolls seamounts | mid ocean ridges | ocean basins | continental margins <1000m | continental margins | cenozoic-mesozoic orogenic belts | paleozoic orogenic belts

- 4.5–6.5 km/sec
- 6.5–7.2 km/sec
- 7.2–7.7 km/sec
- 7.8–8.5 km/sec

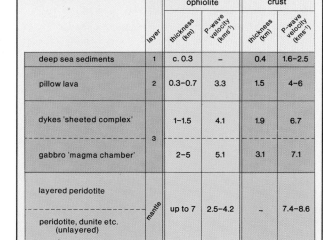

Models of ocean crust

km	SERPENTINE	STRUCTURAL	METAMORPHIC	IGNEOUS
0–3	OCEAN	OCEAN	OCEAN	OCEAN
4	sediment	sediment	sediment	sediment
5–6	basaltic igneous rocks	fractured and uncompacted basalt	greenschist facies basalts	basaltic lavas
7				basaltic dykes
8	partially serpentised peridotite	massive basalt and gabbro	amphibolite facies basalts and gabbro	gabbro
9–10	peridotite	peridotite	peridotite	peridotite

Ophiolite sequence

	layer	typical ophiolite thickness (km)	typical ophiolite P-wave velocity (kms⁻¹)	typical ocean crust thickness (km)	typical ocean crust P-wave velocity (kms⁻¹)
deep sea sediments	1	c. 0.3	–	0.4	1.6–2.5
pillow lava	2	0.3–0.7	3.3	1.5	4–6
dykes 'sheeted complex'	3	1–1.5	4.1	1.9	6.7
gabbro 'magma chamber'	3	2–5	5.1	3.1	7.1
layered peridotite	mantle	up to 7	2.5–4.2	–	7.4–8.6
peridotite, dunite etc. (unlayered)	mantle				

Oceanic crustal structure

Knowledge of oceanic crust prior to the Deep Sea Drilling Project was obtained primarily from dredged rock samples and geophysical measurements, particularly seismic refraction surveys. The latter showed that oceanic crust had three distinct seismic layers, that continental crust was much thicker (25–90 km) than oceanic crust (5–10 km), and that there were more widespread bands of seismic wave velocity beneath the structural provinces of the continents.

The seismic layers of oceanic crust are known as layers 1, 2 and 3. From coring evidence, the low P wave velocity and latterly drilling evidence, layer 1 has been found to consist of unconsolidated sediment. Drilling has confirmed the composition of layer 2 to be mainly the volcanic rock basalt, the top layers being pillow lavas formed by the more rapid cooling of lava by sea water. Seismic evidence indicates that layer 2 is 1000–2500 m thick (see **6** and **7** *above*).

Layer 3 lies below the deepest drill hole to date and four models of oceanic crust have been proposed from available evidence, differing mainly on the state and composition of layer 3 (see **8** *top right*). In the early 1960s, the American, Hess, proposed a serpentinite model, in which layer 3 was considered to be partially serpentinised peridotite, a rock formed by the reaction of peridotite with water; however, this model is not as widely accepted as the others. The other models have a similarity in that layer 2 comprises basaltic pillow lavas and layer 3 comprises basaltic dykes overlying gabbro. The igneous model is the fundamental type, its layers 2 and 3 boundary being simply a change in rock type.

Metamorphic rocks have also been encountered in drilling ocean crust. Metamorphic rocks occur in oceanic crust where there is interaction with sea water and the extent of metamorphism is related to the degree of sea water circulation within the crust. A varying intensity of metamorphism produces different assemblages of minerals, or facies, and layers 2 and 3 boundary in the metamorphic model represents a facies change. In the structural model, the boundary between layers 2 and 3 represents a change from fractured, pervious basalt to massive, compacted basalt and gabbro. It is likely that the structure of oceanic crust varies in different areas, and that the three latter models are all valid.

Ophiolites

Ophiolite 'suites' or sequences are one-time slices of oceanic crust found on shore. They consist particularly of iron- and manganese-rich muds and siliceous sediments which overly, in sequence, pillow lavas, basaltic dykes, gabbro and peridotite. They occur in many places, such as the Alps and the Himalayas, but perhaps the best known example is the Troodos Massif of Cyprus. They are believed to be sections of oceanic crust and upper mantle obducted in the last stages of ocean closure when two continental masses collide. However, some of their characteristics differ from present-day ocean crust: the ophiolite sequence is thinner, no magnetic anomalies are apparent, and their seismic velocities are lower.

A number of theories may explain the mechanism behind obduction: these include reverse-dipping subduction zones, detachment from the descending plate by process unknown, and plate uplift and ophiolite detachment either seaward or landward of the subduction zone.

9 *above* Comparison of an ophiolite sequence with normal ocean crust to show differences in thickness and seismic velocity.

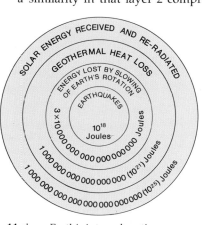

11 *above* Earth's internal motions are driven by radioactively generated heat and the conversion of gravitational to thermal energy. The radioactively generated heat that developed soon after the planet formed was sufficient to melt and restructure the interior into core, mantle and crust. Apart from the Sun, heat flow from the interior is the most important energy source on Earth.

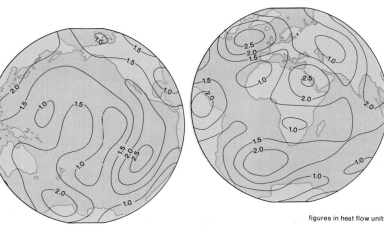

figures in heat flow units

12 *above* Heat flow measurements on land require deep boreholes to avoid the effects of diurnal and seasonal variations, but ocean waters mask the ocean floor from such effects and holes only several metres deep are sufficient for measurements. Heat flow is highest at ocean ridges due to rising magma.

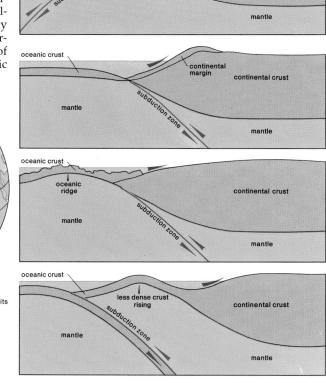

10 *above* Four examples of how oceanic crust might have been emplaced on continental crust.

Deep sea drilling

THE Deep Sea Drilling Project (DSDP) was started in 1968 with the objective of a major ocean floor reconnaissance of all basins except the Arctic. Early in the project it was decided to concentrate on investigation of problems relating to ocean crust evolution, continental margins and ocean palaeo-environments. Initially the project was developed and funded in the USA, but its scope expanded when five other nations, the UK, USSR, West Germany, France, and Japan, agreed to contribute. In 1975 DSDP evolved into an International Programme of Ocean Drilling (IPOD).

Both DSDP and IPOD have been accomplished using the 11 000-tonne drilling vessel *Glomar Challenger*. Although major results have been achieved, the drilling has been restricted to shallow penetration (100–1500 m) in non-hazardous areas. This means high latitudes as well as ocean floors with potential petroleum-bearing sediment have been avoided. Because *Glomar Challenger* could not be fitted with some of the standard features used in commercial offshore drilling (such as a riser system and blow-out preventors), future drilling phases such as the planned Advanced Ocean Drilling Programme (AODP) may use the 60 000-tonne *Glomar Explorer* (formerly owned by the millionaire-recluse, the late Howard Hughes). This ship will be capable of deploying up to 10 500 m of drill string and penetrating deeper than 1500 m.

Scientific ocean drilling has provided a better understanding of Earth's surface features and processes. It has also contributed, through sediment dating and analysis, strong evidence in support of plate tectonics. Considerable information has been gained on the nature of oceanic crust and the processes occurring at spreading ridges. It was also discovered that magma generation and emplacement is a pulsed, instead of continuous process; and that vertical magnetic reversals occur within the basalt crust, in addition to horizontal anomalies (see *Magnetism and sea floor dating* pages 30–31).

Drilling data from areas such as the Blake Plateau, Rockall Plateau, and Bay of Biscay have contributed important knowledge on the formation and evolution of passive (aseismic) continental margins. Cores sometimes contain organic-rich sediments and small amounts of petroleum hydrocarbons have been detected. Thus the outer areas of passive margins might contain important oil and gas regions and future drilling programmes will need to use riser systems and blow-out preventors for exploration in such areas.

Deep-sea drilling has also provided important data on physicochemical changes in the sedimentary column. These changes record the palaeo-oceanographic evolution of the world oceans from the warm, stagnant oceans at the time of the continental mass Pangaea and immediately after, to the cold, well-oxygenated waters of the present oceans.

1 *main map* Sediment cores from DSDP and IPOD drilling have provided considerable confirmation of the age of the ocean floor. Drilling is undertaken in 'legs' consisting of about five to fifteen drill sites within a localised geographical area, concentrating on one or more geological aspects. Deeper geophysical measurements have also been taken at many sites. By early 1982, 85 legs had been completed over 575 sites with one or more holes drilled; some holes are reentered at a later date. The map shows the location of each drill site; for clarity only the routes taken by the *Glomar Challenger* during the first (DSDP) phase between 1968 and 1975 are shown. Each leg takes about 45 to 50 days, about half that time being spent in transit.

2 *top right* Sediment cores sampled by DSDP/IPOD are used in determining ocean basin evolution and rate of continental drift, as well as climatic changes on Earth. The oldest sediments drilled are about 155 Ma (million years old). More widespread are deposits of the Cretaceous oceans (135–65 Ma) which follow the initial break-up of Pangaea. From 65 Ma, the closure of Tethys and the middle-America gap caused major

The Glomar Challenger

The ship relies on computer controlled dynamic positioning with two main propellers at the stern and side thrusters at bow and stern to maintain a fixed position.

A hydraulic piston corer is lowered through the drill string to take sediment samples.

Sonar scanners enable the drill string to enter a 5-metre diameter cone for relocation of a drill hole.

changes in water circulation and biological productivity. At about 38 Ma, a major temperature decrease showed bottom waters falling below 10°C, with a marked difference between polar and equatorial surface waters. The first sea-ice developed around this time although the Antarctic ice sheet did not develop until about 18 Ma.

The ocean waters as we know them began to develop about 10–5 Ma. This included the development of the Antarctic ice sheet, the overflow of salty Mediterranean waters into the Atlantic; and the complete closure of the middle-America seaway. The latter is important because it led to the development of longitudinal surface water circulation in the North Atlantic, producing colder water masses in the northernmost part, and eventually glaciation.

3 *left* The *Glomar Challenger* has been engaged in sea bed research since 1968. Maximum penetration drilled into the sea bed was 1741 metres. The greatest depth reached by the drill string was 7060 metres.

Age of ocean floor

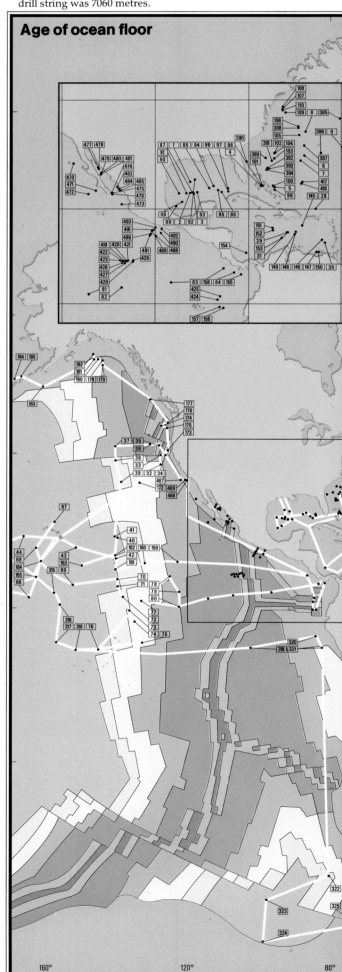

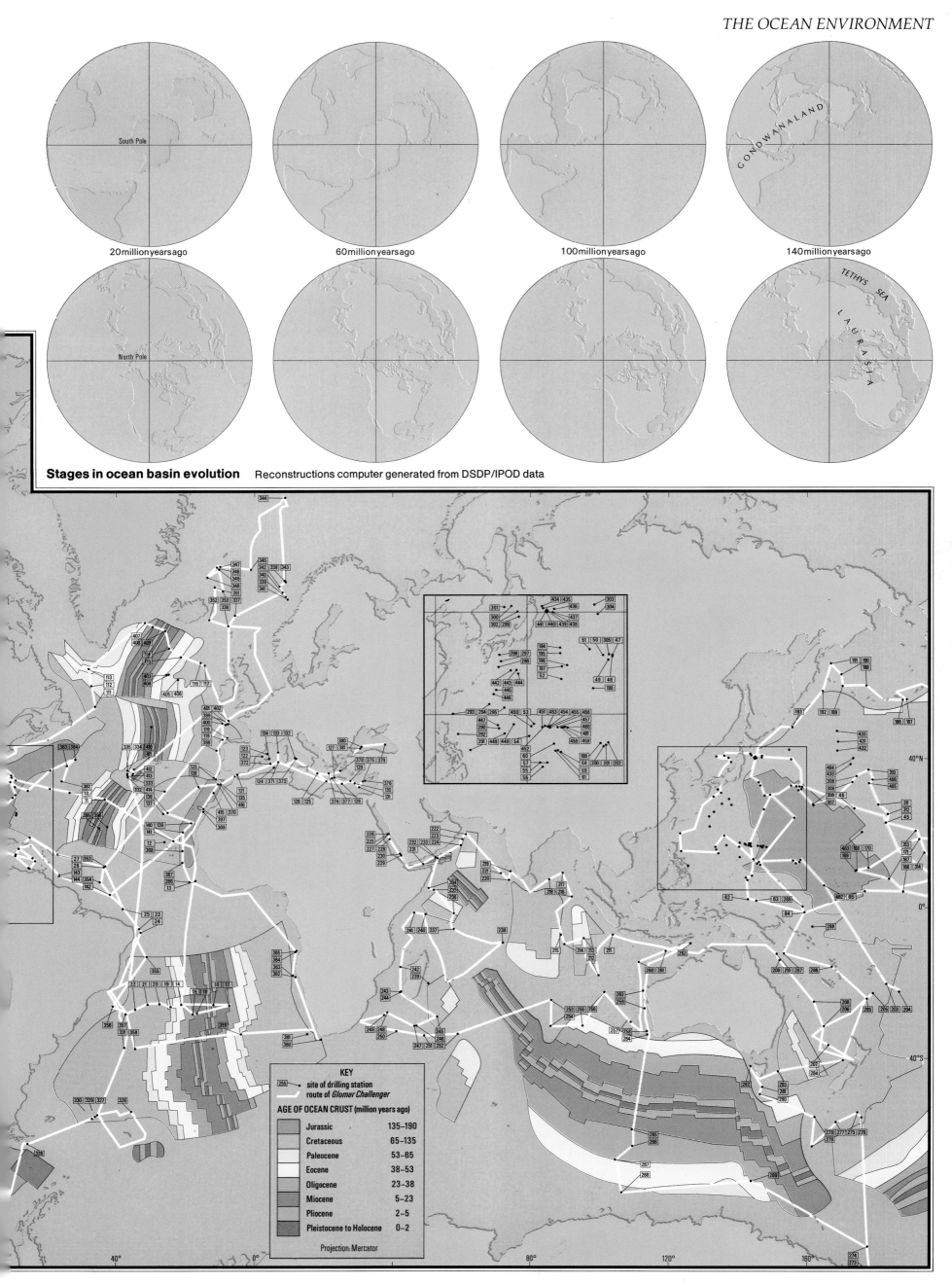

Stages in ocean basin evolution Reconstructions computer generated from DSDP/IPOD data

20 million years ago

60 million years ago

100 million years ago

140 million years ago

GONDWANALAND

TETHYS SEA

LAURASIA

South Pole

North Pole

KEY

255 site of drilling station

route of *Glomer Challenger*

AGE OF OCEAN CRUST (million years ago)

Jurassic	135–190
Cretaceous	65–135
Paleocene	53–65
Eocene	38–53
Oligocene	23–38
Miocene	5–23
Pliocene	2–5
Pleistocene to Holocene	0–2

Projection: Mercator

Sea floor sediments

DEEP-SEA sediments are classified as either pelagic or terrigenous. Pelagic sediments occur away from land in deep waters. In some deposits the remains of microscopic organisms fallen from surface waters are the main constituents, for example globigerina, pteropod, diatom, and radiolarian oozes, but in deeper areas only brown-red clays occur. Some pelagic deposits, such as manganese nodules, are authigenic: that is, they have formed in situ. Others include meteoric dust, or volcanic ash and dust. Pelagic sediment distribution is influenced by the calcite compensation depth (CCD) and the fertility of surface waters. The CCD is the depth where the supply of calcium carbonate towards the sea floor is balanced by the rate at which it dissolves; generally this is at a depth of 3.5–4.5 km. Above the CCD calcareous oozes are found, but below this depth only siliceous oozes and red clays occur.

Terrigenous sediments consist of land-derived material, occurring mainly on ocean basin margins. Sediments of glacial origin are common on continental shelves and also occur in deep water, as ice-rafted material which was deposited when the ice melted. Terrigenous muds occur mainly off the estuaries of large rivers. Slump deposits consist of large sediment blocks which have slid, or 'slumped' down the continental slope. Turbidites are formed by a turbidity current, or 'submarine avalanche', which causes coarse sediments, normally found only in shallow waters, to become interbedded with pelagic sediments.

Sediment thicknesses overlying oceanic crust have been measured by seismic surveys: in the Atlantic and Pacific, typical basin areas contain only about 500 m and 300 m of sediment, respectively; ocean ridges have much thinner cover, and it is only at some continental margins that thick sequences of 6–7 km occur.

Shallow-water, or shelf sediments are either siliciclastic (composed mainly of silicate minerals) or carbonate (composed of the minerals calcite and dolomite). Siliciclastic sediments are classified according to size as gravels, sands, silts and clays, and their distribution on continental shelves is controlled by a number of interdependent factors: the sediment supply from rivers, the extent of relict sediments (sediments deposited thousand of years ago), the intensity of wave and current activity, and fluctuations in sea level. Carbonate sediments occur on shelves devoid of large-scale siliciclastic deposition and having a high organic productivity, which generally increases towards the equator. Tropical areas where present-day carbonate sediments are forming include the Great Bahama Banks, the Great Barrier Reef and Pacific atolls. Carbonate sediments can form also in temperate waters.

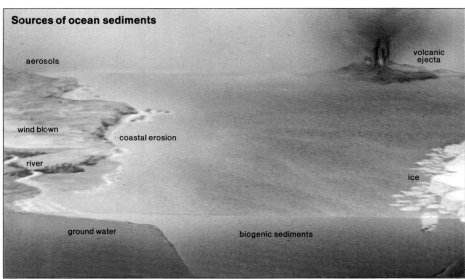

Sources of ocean sediments

1 *right* Illustration showing the various ways in which terrigenous sediments are deposited at sea.

aerosols

wind blown

river

ground water

coastal erosion

volcanic ejecta

ice

biogenic sediments

Sediment types across an ocean basin

3 *bottom* The diagram illustrates sedimentary sequences, structures and processes occurring along a section of ocean floor from a passive, or aseismic, continental margin to the deep abyssal floor. Illustrations **4** to **10** are examples of important sediment features occurring, their locations keyed by number along the profile. The greatest thickness of sediments is found on margins of the Atlantic Ocean, whereas the Pacific basin, overall, has the thinnest sediment cover.

4 *below* Beaches are accumulations of sediment, mainly sand, sometimes gravel or shingle, spread along the coastline. They are created by wave processes: small waves tend to stabilise beaches, but large or storm waves can drastically alter the beach profile. The backshore is inundated only during storms, the foreshore is the intertidal section, and the shoreface extends seawards to the depth at which passing waves no longer affect sediment movement, usually 12–20 m.

5 *above right* Much of the sediment on continental shelves is of relict origin (glacial sands and gravels); some is derived from rivers, and some from coastal erosion. The transport and deposition of shelf sediments are controlled by wave activity and the tidal current pattern. Some shelf seas, such as the east coast of the USA, are dominated primarily by storm waves. The seas around the British Isles exemplify a tide-dominated shelf; here bedform structures such as sand ridges, sand waves and sand ribbons are more common.

Sand waves and offshore sand banks

almost complete cover of sand waves

sand waves separated by gravel floor

sand banks

6 *below left* The same types of sedimentary formations, or traps, that produce oil and gas onshore occur offshore. These structures may be anticlinal traps (where the strata are uplifted in the form of an arch), structural traps (large dome forms with dimensions of several kilometres, such as those caused by salt plugs) and stratigraphic traps (where older rock formations are overlain by younger sequences of rocks). At present offshore oil is exploited on continental shelf areas, but in the near future exploration will begin on the continental slope and rise.

7 *below* Reef building corals are restricted to tropical regions where the water temperature never falls below about 18°C. Although the corals themselves are animals, related to the sea-anemones, they live in partnership with microscopic algae. Living reefs are consequently found only in shallow sunlit waters no more than 20–30 metres deep, where salinities are 30–40‰. Reef corals are colonial and each colony is made up of many hundreds or thousands of individual animals, or polyps. Each polyp secretes a chalkey, cup-like skeleton which, together with those of its neighbours, makes up the coral mass in a form which is characteristic of each species. Only the surface layer of a coral mass

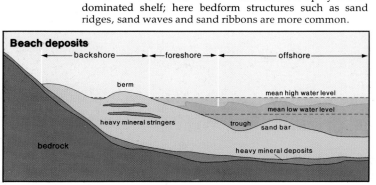

Beach deposits

backshore — foreshore — offshore

berm

mean high water level

mean low water level

heavy mineral stringers

trough

sand bar

bedrock

heavy mineral deposits

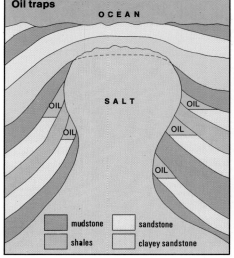

Oil traps

OCEAN

SALT

OIL

mudstone

shales

sandstone

clayey sandstone

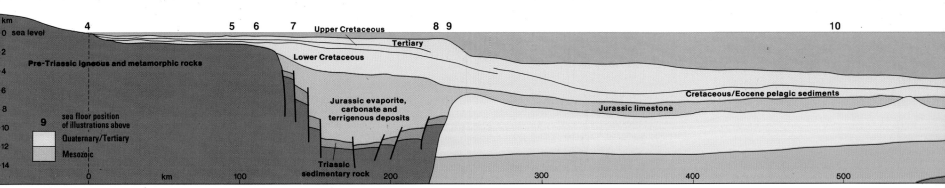

km

sea level

Upper Cretaceous

Tertiary

Lower Cretaceous

Pre-Triassic igneous and metamorphic rocks

Jurassic evaporite, carbonate and terrigenous deposits

Cretaceous/Eocene pelagic sediments

Jurassic limestone

9 sea floor position of illustrations above

Quaternary/Tertiary

Mesozoic

Triassic sedimentary rock

km

Distribution of deep sea sediments

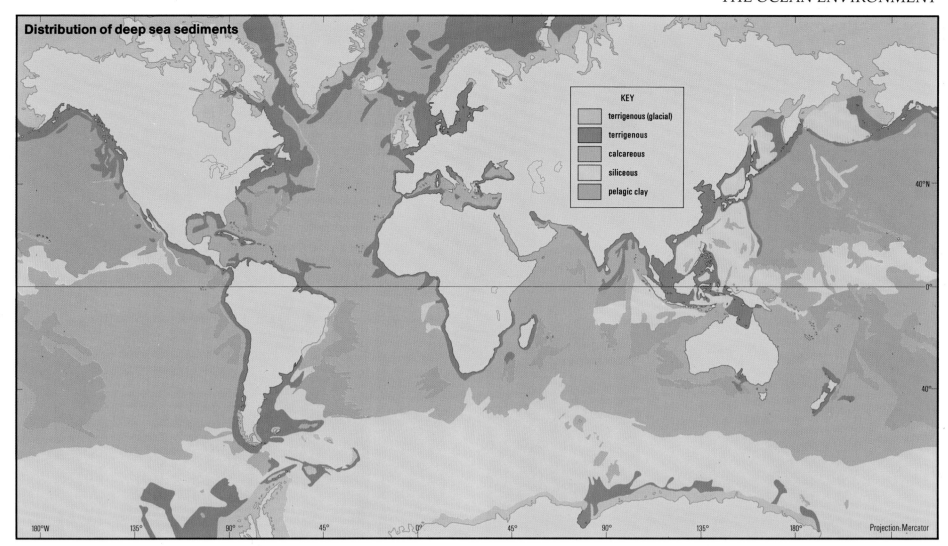

KEY
- terrigenous (glacial)
- terrigenous
- calcareous
- siliceous
- pelagic clay

40°N

0°

40°

180°W   135°   90°   45°   0°   45°   90°   135°   180°   Projection: Mercator

is living, the deeper layers being formed of the countless skeletons of previous generations of polyps. These skeletons are unpigmented, white calcium carbonate, for the brilliant coloration of coral reefs is truly 'skin deep' being produced entirely by pigments within the bodies of the living polyps.

Reefs can be classified into three main types: fringing reefs, which are linear structures adjacent to the shore; barrier reefs, linear structures separated from land by a lagoon; and atolls, near-circular structures enclosing a central lagoon.

8 *right* A turbidity current is a submarine avalanche in which sediment (of sizes ranging from mud to gravel) is carried down from the upper continental slope, mixed in suspension and travelling at up to 80–100 km per hour. These currents can erode and enlarge submarine canyons and are the main cause of large accretions of sediment on the continental rise. Material can be transported thousands of kilometres out onto the abyssal plains (see pages 28–29).

9 *below* The upper continental slope has a relatively steep gradient. This often means that sediment masses up to several kilometres in length and width and up to hundreds of metres thick, slip downslope, either by sliding, slumping, debris flow or turbidity currents. This seismic reflection profile illustrates the effect of slumping: a scar is evident upslope from which the sediment has slipped, and downslope there is an irregular hummocky topography where material has come to rest. The process is very similar to a landslip.

Turbidity current

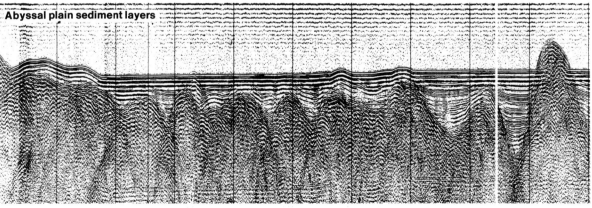

shelf
shelf
abyssal plain

2 *above* The distribution of sediments in the ocean basins can be related to other features, most notably bathymetry and the proportion of land drainage. For example, calcareous sediments define ridges, rises and platform areas, while red clay outlines the deeper basins. Terrigenous sediments are more widespread on passive continental margins than active margins and glacial deposits are abundant only in high latitudes and temperate regions.

The map of sediment distribution is mainly a refinement, from modern data, of maps produced from the *Challenger* expedition of the 1870s.

10 *below* As turbidity currents extend further down the ocean basin, they weaken and the sediment becomes finer as particles settle. As shown in this seismic profile, such deposits, together with the normal pelagic sediments, blanket the oceanic crust over large areas, producing abyssal plains, features of unparalleled smoothness on Earth's surface. Turbidity currents were more frequent when the sea level was lower, such as during the Pleistocene glaciations. Many of the turbidite deposits near the surface of abyssal plains were formed during this period.

Sediment masses on continental slope

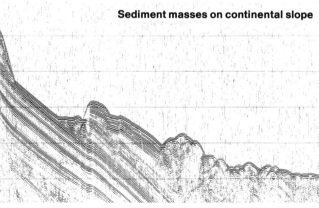

Abyssal plain sediment layers

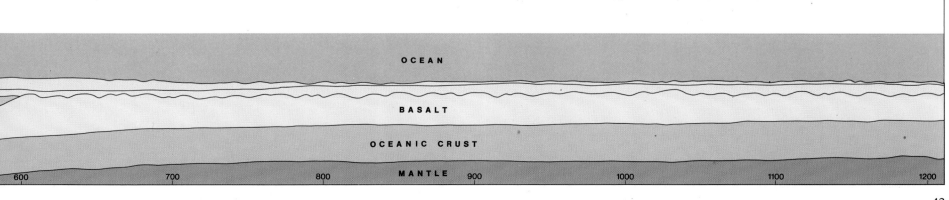

OCEAN

BASALT

OCEANIC CRUST

MANTLE

600   700   800   900   1000   1100   1200

The water planet

THE atmosphere is constantly in motion, shaping the complex patterns of weather and climate of the globe and arousing the surface of the sea. The great storms over sea and land are manifestations of air in motion; rain clouds result from ascent of air; fog forms when warm air flows across a cooler surface; currents in the uppermost layers of the oceans are largely wind-driven; and it is the wind which raises waves and storm surges. Even on an otherwise calm day the occasional light breeze ruffles the surface of the sea. Oceanic circulations depend upon atmospheric motions and also help maintain those motions. In a sense, the atmosphere and the oceans constitute a single system of two fluids interacting with each other.

Until recently meteorologists and oceanographers paid rather little heed to the mutual influences in what has come to be called the 'ocean–atmosphere system'. However, since the early 1960s there has been an upsurge of interest in the interdependence of atmospheric and oceanic circulations and a number of international research projects have placed considerable emphasis upon ocean–atmosphere interactions.

There is a whole spectrum of atmospheric motion ranging from tiny turbulent eddies, which survive as recognisable entities for just a few seconds, to global climatic fluctuations, which extend over decades or even centuries. All atmospheric systems affect maritime activities to some extent, and mariners, fishermen, drillers and divers all have to take into account the climate of the area where they work.

The Gulf Stream velocity field

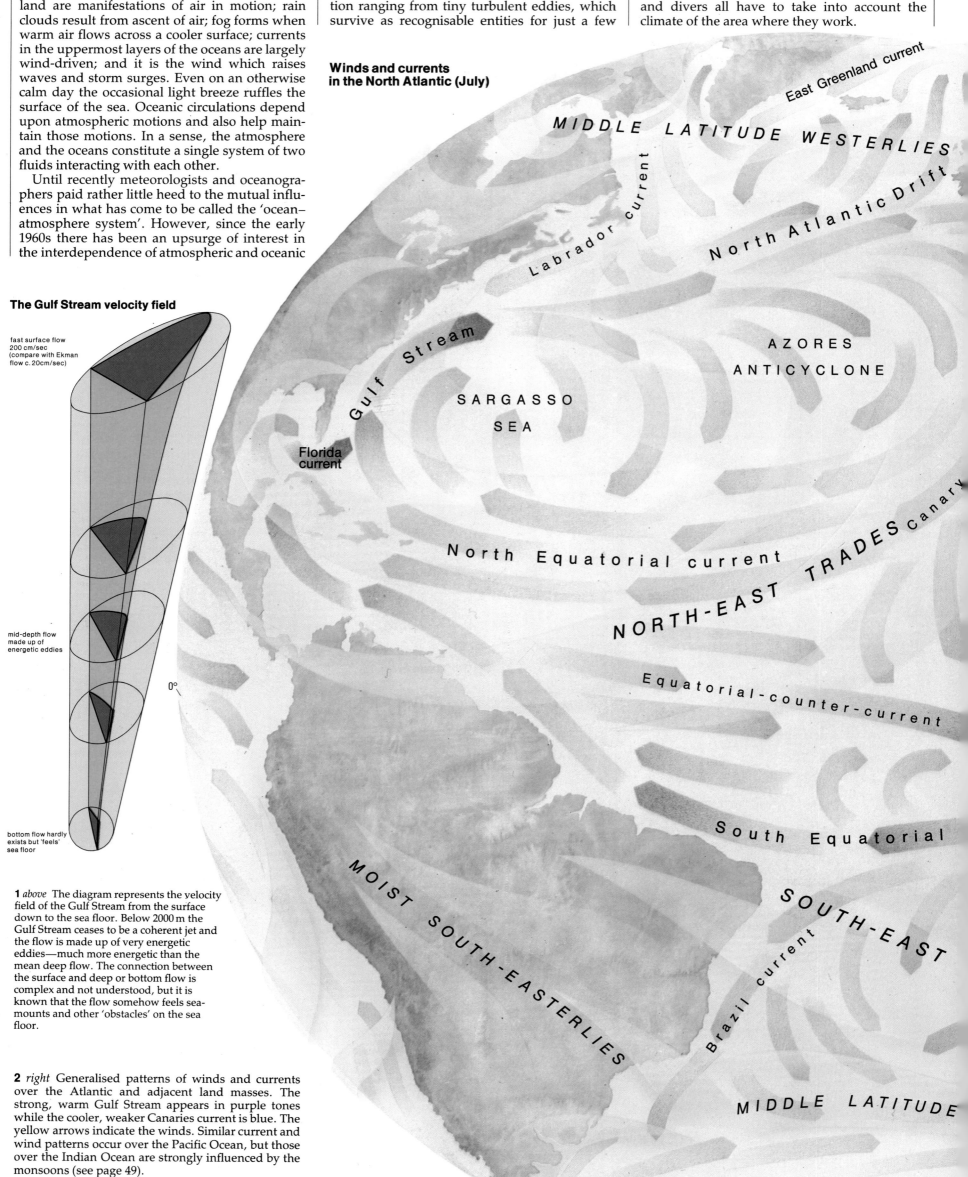

fast surface flow
200 cm/sec
(compare with Ekman
flow c. 20cm/sec)

mid-depth flow
made up of
energetic eddies

0°

bottom flow hardly
exists but 'feels'
sea floor

**Winds and currents
in the North Atlantic (July)**

East Greenland current

MIDDLE LATITUDE WESTERLIES

Labrador current

North Atlantic Drift

Gulf Stream

AZORES
ANTICYCLONE

SARGASSO
SEA

Florida
current

North Equatorial current

Canary

NORTH-EAST TRADES

Equatorial-counter-current

South Equatorial

MOIST SOUTH-EASTERLIES

SOUTH-EAST

Brazil current

MIDDLE LATITUDE

1 *above* The diagram represents the velocity field of the Gulf Stream from the surface down to the sea floor. Below 2000 m the Gulf Stream ceases to be a coherent jet and the flow is made up of very energetic eddies—much more energetic than the mean deep flow. The connection between the surface and deep or bottom flow is complex and not understood, but it is known that the flow somehow feels seamounts and other 'obstacles' on the sea floor.

2 *right* Generalised patterns of winds and currents over the Atlantic and adjacent land masses. The strong, warm Gulf Stream appears in purple tones while the cooler, weaker Canaries current is blue. The yellow arrows indicate the winds. Similar current and wind patterns occur over the Pacific Ocean, but those over the Indian Ocean are strongly influenced by the monsoons (see page 49).

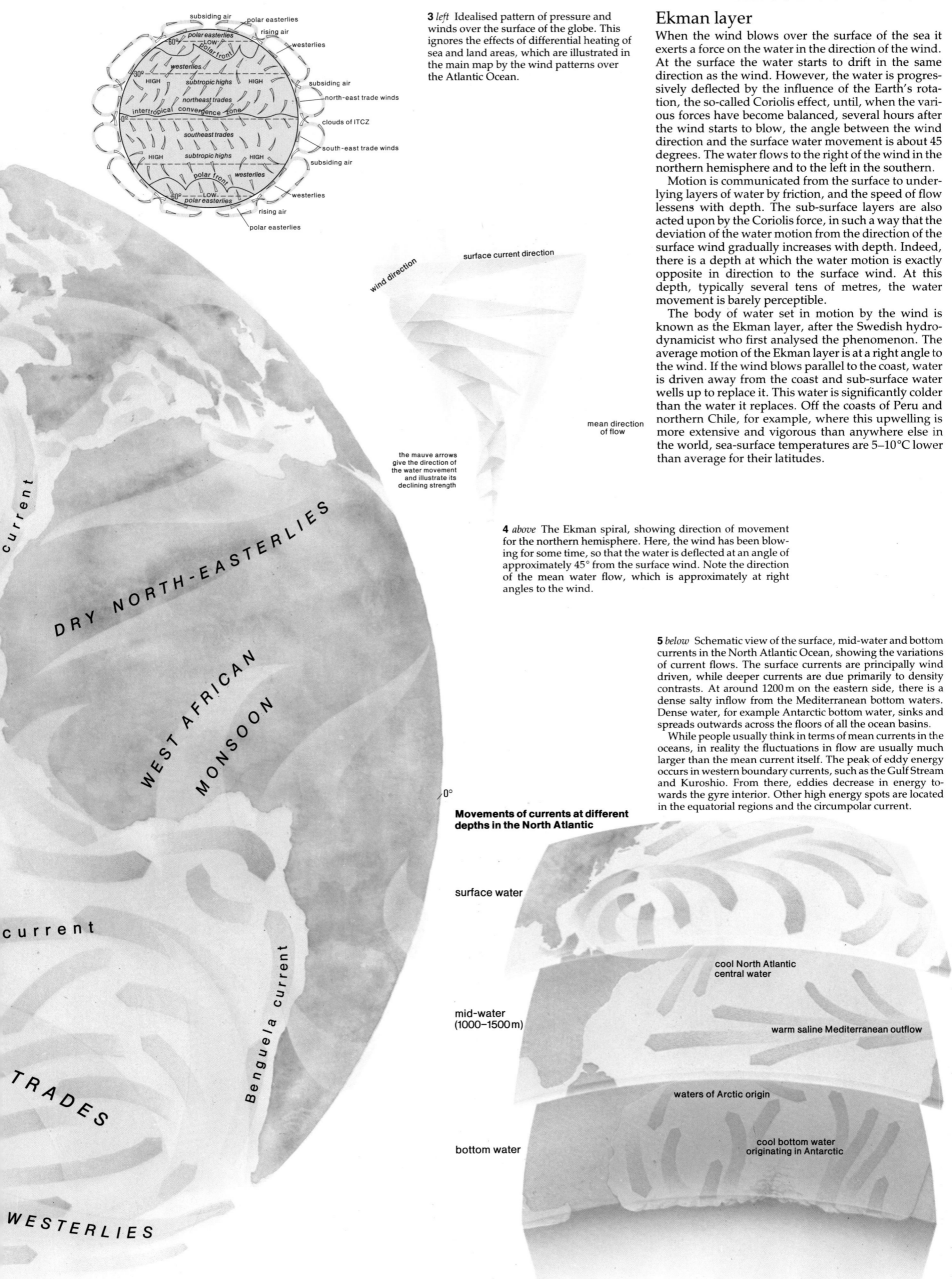

3 *left* Idealised pattern of pressure and winds over the surface of the globe. This ignores the effects of differential heating of sea and land areas, which are illustrated in the main map by the wind patterns over the Atlantic Ocean.

Ekman layer

When the wind blows over the surface of the sea it exerts a force on the water in the direction of the wind. At the surface the water starts to drift in the same direction as the wind. However, the water is progressively deflected by the influence of the Earth's rotation, the so-called Coriolis effect, until, when the various forces have become balanced, several hours after the wind starts to blow, the angle between the wind direction and the surface water movement is about 45 degrees. The water flows to the right of the wind in the northern hemisphere and to the left in the southern.

Motion is communicated from the surface to underlying layers of water by friction, and the speed of flow lessens with depth. The sub-surface layers are also acted upon by the Coriolis force, in such a way that the deviation of the water motion from the direction of the surface wind gradually increases with depth. Indeed, there is a depth at which the water motion is exactly opposite in direction to the surface wind. At this depth, typically several tens of metres, the water movement is barely perceptible.

The body of water set in motion by the wind is known as the Ekman layer, after the Swedish hydrodynamicist who first analysed the phenomenon. The average motion of the Ekman layer is at a right angle to the wind. If the wind blows parallel to the coast, water is driven away from the coast and sub-surface water wells up to replace it. This water is significantly colder than the water it replaces. Off the coasts of Peru and northern Chile, for example, where this upwelling is more extensive and vigorous than anywhere else in the world, sea-surface temperatures are 5–10°C lower than average for their latitudes.

4 *above* The Ekman spiral, showing direction of movement for the northern hemisphere. Here, the wind has been blowing for some time, so that the water is deflected at an angle of approximately 45° from the surface wind. Note the direction of the mean water flow, which is approximately at right angles to the wind.

5 *below* Schematic view of the surface, mid-water and bottom currents in the North Atlantic Ocean, showing the variations of current flows. The surface currents are principally wind driven, while deeper currents are due primarily to density contrasts. At around 1200 m on the eastern side, there is a dense salty inflow from the Mediterranean bottom waters. Dense water, for example Antarctic bottom water, sinks and spreads outwards across the floors of all the ocean basins.

While people usually think in terms of mean currents in the oceans, in reality the fluctuations in flow are usually much larger than the mean current itself. The peak of eddy energy occurs in western boundary currents, such as the Gulf Stream and Kuroshio. From there, eddies decrease in energy towards the gyre interior. Other high energy spots are located in the equatorial regions and the circumpolar current.

45

Global winds and weather

A<small>N</small> approximately meridional circulation prevails in low latitudes. Trade winds blow over the tropical oceans, from the northeast in the northern hemisphere and the southeast in the southern hemisphere, wind-speeds normally being in the range 4–7 m/sec. The trades of the two hemispheres converge in a zone near the equator, the so-called Intertropical Convergence Zone (ITCZ) where air rises to an altitude of 12 to 15 km in cumulonimbus systems and heavy rain falls. In this zone winds are light and rather variable, hence the popular designation, the 'doldrums'. Over the tropics and subtropics there is widespread descent of air, except in the lowest kilometre or two of the atmosphere, where air motions are predominantly convective and turbulent. On account of the descent, cloud and rainfall amounts are small.

Ascent of air is associated with low pressure at sea-level and descent with high pressure. Thus, a belt of low pressure coincides with the ITCZ and extensive areas of high pressure, the quasi-permanent subtropical anticyclones, dominate the tropics and subtropics.

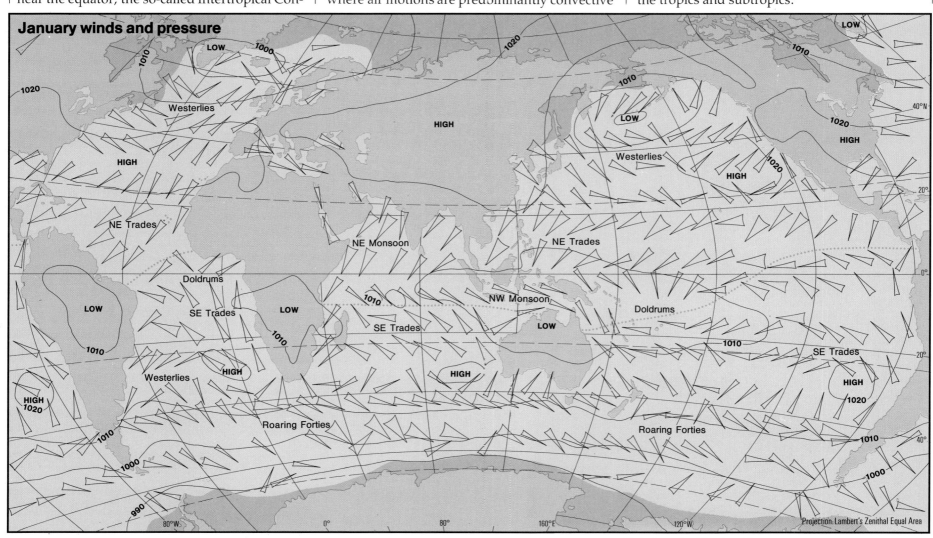

1 *above and* **2** *below* Prevailing surface winds and monthly mean values of sea-level pressure are shown. The patterns are broadly similar, except over the South China Sea, the northern half of the Indian Ocean and western parts of the Pacific, where monsoonal reversals occur. In general, winds tend to be light and variable near the equator, trade winds dominate in the tropics, and westerlies prevail in middle latitudes.

WIND VELOCITY (metres/second)

below 3 | 5–7 | ⋯⋯ intertropical convergence zone
3–5 | above 7 | ▨ mean extent of ice

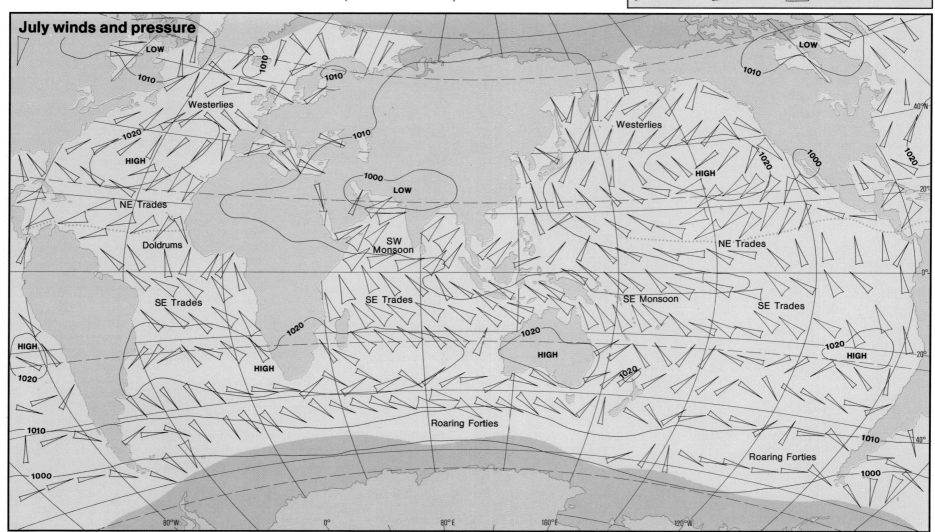

Polewards of these major anticyclones weather is controlled by transitory depressions and anticyclones. Depressions, which are low-pressure systems, are the principal sources of cloud, poor visibility, rain and strong winds outside the tropics. They are highly mobile systems several hundred to a few thousand kilometres in diameter and their general direction of movement is eastwards, although they may move in any direction. Anticyclones are high-pressure systems and are characteristically areas of light winds, good visibility and settled weather. They are rather slow-moving and as a rule are considerably more extensive than depressions.

Over the oceans depressions tend to be at their most intense when their centres of low pressure lie between latitudes 50° and 70°, whereas anticyclones tend to favour somewhat lower and higher latitudes. Accordingly, monthly-mean

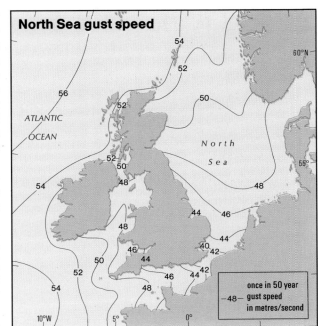

3 *above* Apollo 17 view taken in December 1972 showing the south polar ice regions, the ITCZ over the equatorial Indian Ocean, and an anticyclone over the Horn of Africa.

charts show minima of pressure near the polar circles. However, some depressions extend their influence well into polar regions and a few reach the poles themselves. Precipitation totals are small in high latitudes, partly because depressions are infrequent and partly because cold air is incapable of supporting large quantities of water vapour. The precipitation is mostly in the form of snow. Winds from an easterly point occur on the poleward flanks of depressions. Consequently, easterly winds prevail in polar regions.

The wind, pressure and precipitation regimes described above migrate towards the pole of the summer hemisphere and lie farthest from the equator about two months after the solstice. Thus, there are seasonal rhythms in global patterns of wind, pressure and precipitation. For example, as a result of the migration of the ITCZ and the associated trade-wind belts, winds are north-easterly off the mouths of the river Amazon in January and south-easterly in July.

In a given locality marked variations of wind direction may occur from day to day, in association with the ever-changing nature of the weather systems. The strongest winds occurring in depressions are generally the westerlies on their equatorward flanks, but it is possible for strong winds to blow from any direction. The stormiest waters in the world are those of the Southern Ocean and extra-tropical parts of the North Atlantic and North Pacific Oceans.

6 *above right* Three-second gust speeds and 7 *right* hourly mean values of wind-speed in the North Sea recurring on average once every fifty years at a height of 10 m above the surface of the sea.

These values are based on observations made at coastal stations, light vessels, Ocean Weather Ships, offshore platforms and the North Sea rescue ship *Famita* (57½°N 3°E). Such figures are important for the offshore industry. Knowledge of extremes is required particularly for estimating the wind forces that structures must withstand and for assessing the dangers faced by the crews of helicopters and supply vessels.

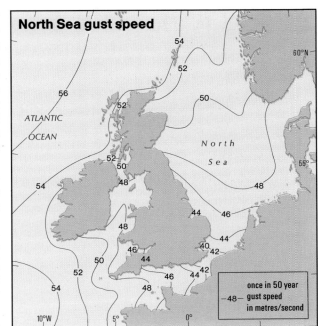

North Sea gust speed

—48— gust speed in metres/second — once in 50 year

North Sea Wind speed

—36— wind speed in metres/second — once in 50 year hourly mean

section illustrated 4 right

4 The diagrams show three stages of a depression or cyclone. Where cold and warm air masses meet, a kink of warm air sometimes penetrates the mass of cold (1). The circulating cold air increases this wedge (2), which is lower in pressure than the surrounding cold air and forms the depression. The depression dies when the cold front catches the warm front up and squeezes out the warm air (3).

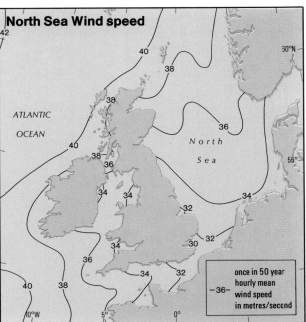

Three-dimensional section through a depression

jet stream

warm air mass

cirrus cloud (mare's tails)

cumulonimbus cloud

stratus clouds

nimbostratus (rain) clouds

dense , cold air mass

winds circulating the depression

warm front

cold front

5 *right* It is wettest near the equator (where the cumulonimbus systems of the ITCZ provide the rain), in middle latitudes (where extratropical depressions yield most of the precipitation), and in monsoonal regions (where it is wet for only a few months of the year). Tropical cyclones supply rain over the western parts of tropical oceans, but, again, only at certain times of year. The driest areas are those permanently under the influence of the subtropical anticyclones, and it is exceptionally dry where upwelling occurs. There the cold sea surface stabilises air masses, so that the formation of rain-bearing clouds is hindered.

It is difficult to measure rainfall accurately from aboard ships at sea, and techniques for estimating rainfall amounts from satellite observations of clouds are as yet in their infancy. Furthermore, the rainfall statistics of island and coastal stations are not necessarily representative of adjacent oceanic areas. Accordingly, charts showing rainfall amounts over the oceans are open to question.

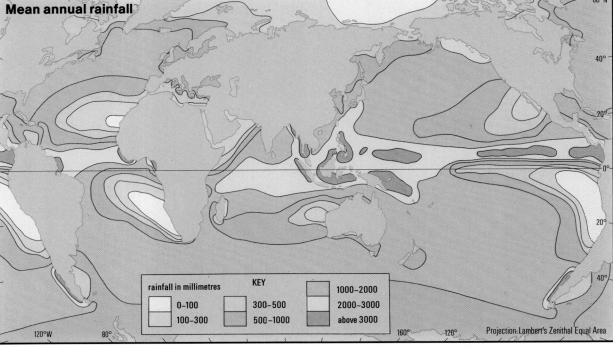

Mean annual rainfall

rainfall in millimetres KEY

0–100
100–300
300–500
500–1000
1000–2000
2000–3000
above 3000

Projection: Lambert's Zenithal Equal Area

Global winds and weather—The Beaufort Scale

The Beaufort scale was devised by Francis Beaufort, an admiral in the British Navy, in 1805 as a means of classifying wind conditions at sea. Later it came to include observations of sea state and land phenomena and later still wind speeds. For example, force 4 on the Beaufort scale corresponds to a wind speed of about 5 m/sec (18 km/hour), and force 8 to a wind speed of about 18 m/sec (65 km/hour). As it relies upon subjective visual interpretation it has been largely replaced during this century by more scientific methods. However, in remote areas and on board ships which do not have wind instruments it remains a useful means of determining wind speeds and sea conditions.

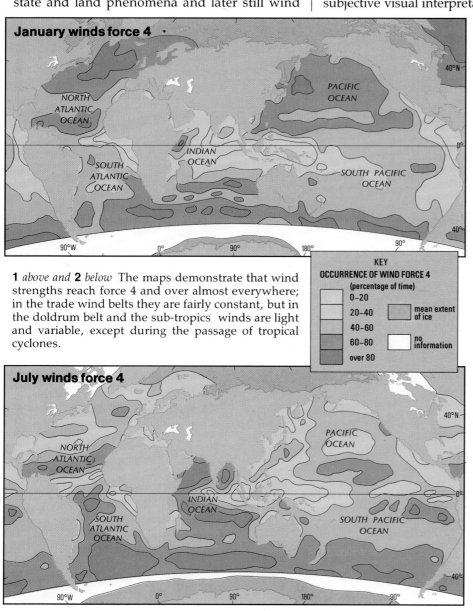

January winds force 4

July winds force 4

1 *above and* **2** *below* The maps demonstrate that wind strengths reach force 4 and over almost everywhere; in the trade wind belts they are fairly constant, but in the doldrum belt and the sub-tropics winds are light and variable, except during the passage of tropical cyclones.

KEY
OCCURRENCE OF WIND FORCE 4
(percentage of time)
- 0–20
- 20–40
- 40–60
- 60–80
- over 80
- mean extent of ice
- no information

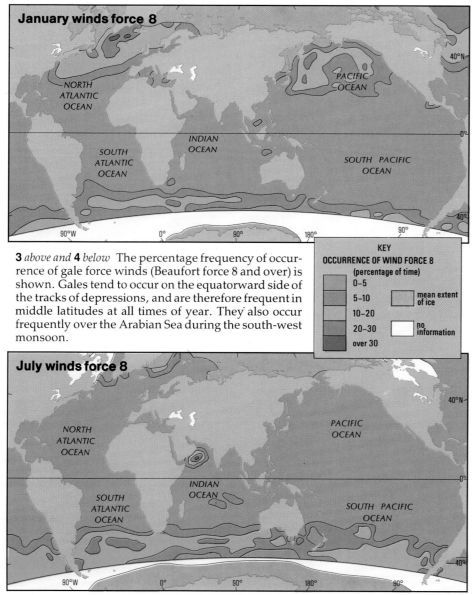

January winds force 8

3 *above and* **4** *below* The percentage frequency of occurrence of gale force winds (Beaufort force 8 and over) is shown. Gales tend to occur on the equatorward side of the tracks of depressions, and are therefore frequent in middle latitudes at all times of year. They also occur frequently over the Arabian Sea during the south-west monsoon.

KEY
OCCURRENCE OF WIND FORCE 8
(percentage of time)
- 0–5
- 5–10
- 10–20
- 20–30
- over 30
- mean extent of ice
- no information

July winds force 8

5   BEAUFORT SCALE OF WIND FORCE

Sea state force 3   Sea state force 4

Sea state force 6   Sea state force 7

Sea state force 8   Sea state force 10

Beaufort scale number	descriptive terms	sea criterion	probable height of waves (m)	probable max. height of waves (m)
0	calm	sea like a mirror	0	0
1	light air	ripples with the appearance of scales are formed but without foam crests	0.1	0.1
2	light breeze	small wavelets, still short but more pronounced; crests have a glassy appearance and do not break	0.2	0.3
3	gentle breeze	large wavelets; crests begin to break; foam of glassy appearance; perhaps scattered white horses	0.6	1.0
4	moderate breeze	small waves, becoming longer; fairly frequent white horses	1.0	1.5
5	fresh breeze	moderate waves, taking a more pronounced long form; many white horses are formed; chance of some spray	2.0	2.5
6	strong breeze	large waves begin to form; the white foam crests are more extensive everywhere; probably some spray	3.0	4.0
7	near gale	sea heaps up and white foam from breaking waves begins to be blown in streaks along the direction of the wind	4.0	5.5
8	gale	moderately high waves of greater length; edges of crests begin to break into spindrift; foam is blown in well-marked streaks along the direction of the wind	5.5	7.5
9	strong gale	high waves; dense streaks of foam along the direction of the wind; crests of waves begin to topple, tumble and roll over; spray may affect visibility	7.0	10.0
10	storm	very high waves with long overhanging crests; the resulting foam in great patches is blown in dense white streaks along the direction of the wind; the surface of the sea takes a white appearance; the tumbling of the sea becomes heavy and shock-like; visibility affected	9.0	12.5
11	violent storm	exceptionally high waves; small and medium-sized ships might be lost to view behind the waves; the sea is completely covered with long white patches of foam lying along the direction of the wind; everywhere the edges of the wave crests are blown into froth; visibility affected	11.5	16.0
12	hurricane	the air is filled with foam and spray; sea completely white with driving spray; visibility very seriously affected	14 or over	—

Monsoons

Monsoons are characterised by seasonal reversals of wind and weather systems which occur in tropical areas, mostly in the eastern hemisphere. South of the equator marked monsoonal changes occur only near northern Australia. Monsoons are associated with temperature contrasts between land and sea areas. In summer the land masses become hotter than the sea, so that winds blow from the oceans to the land. The process is reversed in winter. The most spectacular seasonal changes occur over southern Asia, the North Indian Ocean, the China Seas and the western North Pacific Ocean.

On the west coast of India, monsoon rains typically commence during the first ten days of June and end in mid-September. Active periods of monsoon intensity last from one to three weeks, with heavy rain and strong winds (17–20 m/sec) over the sea and coastal areas. Lulls usually last only a few days but may be as prolonged as two or three weeks.

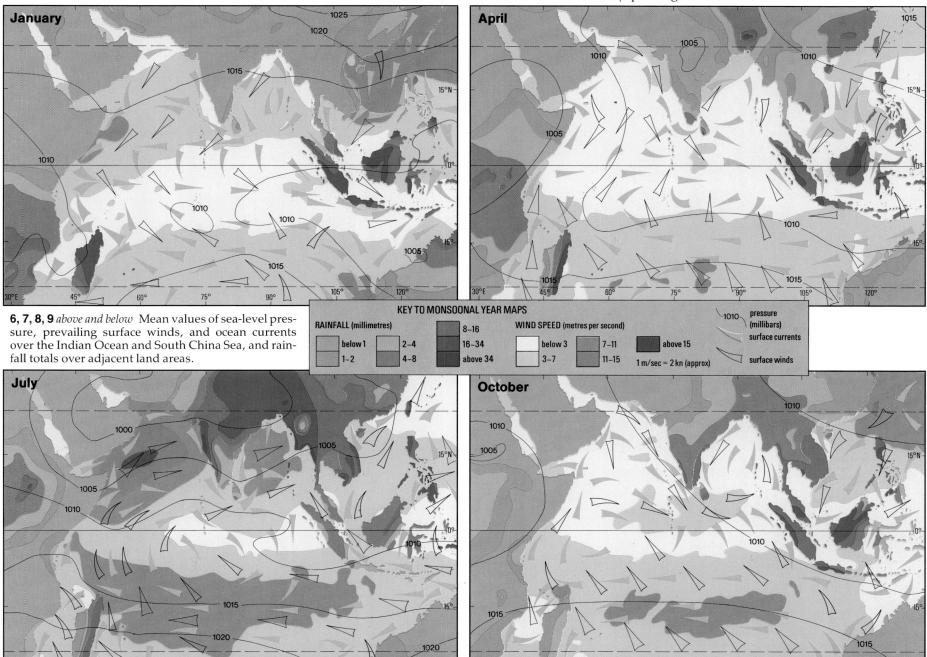

6, 7, 8, 9 *above and below* Mean values of sea-level pressure, prevailing surface winds, and ocean currents over the Indian Ocean and South China Sea, and rainfall totals over adjacent land areas.

KEY TO MONSOONAL YEAR MAPS

RAINFALL (millimetres)
below 1
1–2
2–4
4–8
8–16
16–34
above 34

WIND SPEED (metres per second)
below 3
3–7
7–11
11–15
above 15
1 m/sec = 2 kn (approx)

1010 pressure (millibars)
surface currents
surface winds

The monsoonal year

Mid-December to mid-March During January the north-east monsoon is fully developed. Characteristically, clear skies and north to north-east winds prevail over South and South East Asia and adjacent oceans; monsoon rain systems and north-west winds affect southern Indonesia and northern Australia; south-east trade winds blow over much of the tropical South Indian Ocean; and the Intertropical Convergence Zone (ITCZ) lies a little to the south of the equator.

Mid-March to early June Transition period: over the Indian subcontinent temperatures slowly rise and barometric pressure gradually falls, while over the Arabian Sea and Bay of Bengal winds become first variable and then light southwesterly, and ocean currents respond to these changes. Rain systems become increasingly frequent over the Bay of Bengal and south-eastern parts of the Arabian Sea, and in May a few reach tropical cyclone intensity (see page 56). Apart from a very occasional cyclone the rest of the Arabian Sea remains free of rain systems. The ITCZ migrates northwards, reaching Sri Lanka and southern India in late April. Throughout the period south-east trade winds and the associated South Equatorial Current occupy the whole of the tropical zone of the South Indian Ocean.

Early June to mid-September The south-west monsoon holds sway over the Arabian Sea, the Indian subcontinent, the Bay of Bengal, South East Asia and the China Seas; and its influence on winds and currents extends much farther afield, particularly to the South Indian Ocean and the western Pacific Ocean. For example, the trade winds over the South Indian Ocean are significantly stronger than at any other time of year. The wind speed in these trades, 9 m/sec, is the highest mean value experienced in any of the world's trade-wind belts.

Mid-September to mid-December Another transition period. Winds over the Arabian Sea and Bay of Bengal become first variable and then north-easterly. The trade winds over the South Indian Ocean diminish in strength immediately the south-west monsoon retreats from western India and the Arabian Sea and their strength is typically 4–6 m/sec throughout the period. The ITCZ continues to be active over southern India and Sri Lanka until November and then migrates southwards. Rain systems are frequent over the southern half of the Bay of Bengal throughout this period and some reach tropical cyclone intensity.

Monsoon over the Arabian Sea

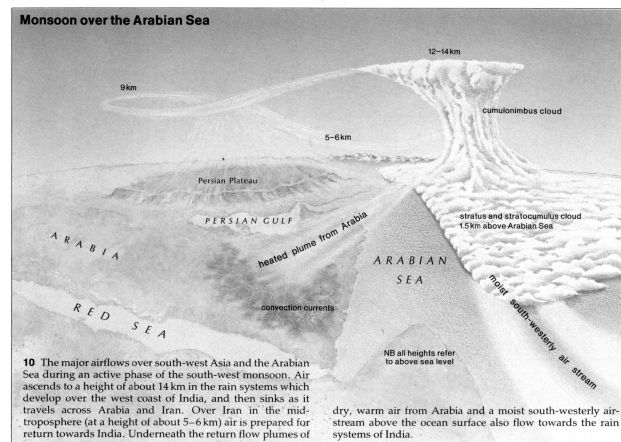

10 The major airflows over south-west Asia and the Arabian Sea during an active phase of the south-west monsoon. Air ascends to a height of about 14 km in the rain systems which develop over the west coast of India, and then sinks as it travels across Arabia and Iran. Over Iran in the mid-troposphere (at a height of about 5–6 km) air is prepared for return towards India. Underneath the return flow plumes of dry, warm air from Arabia and a moist south-westerly airstream above the ocean surface also flow towards the rain systems of India.

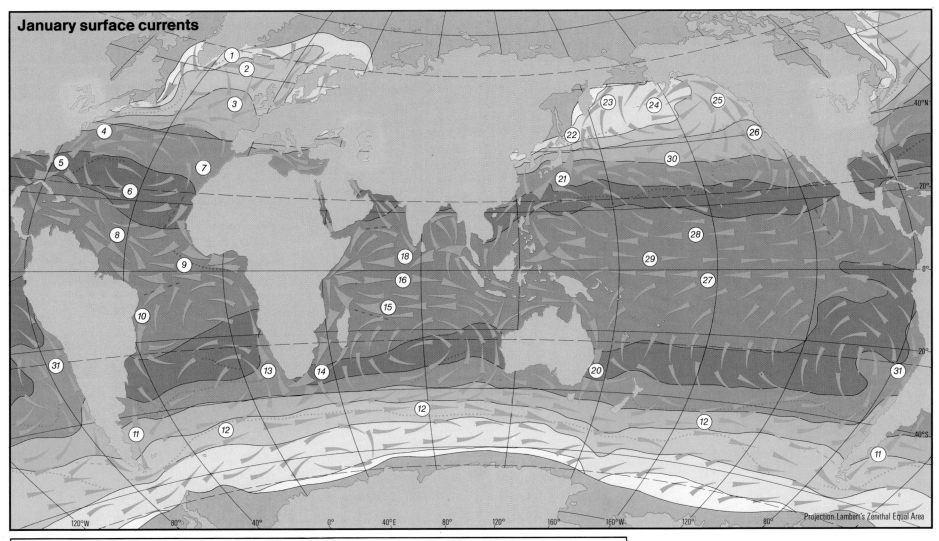

January surface currents

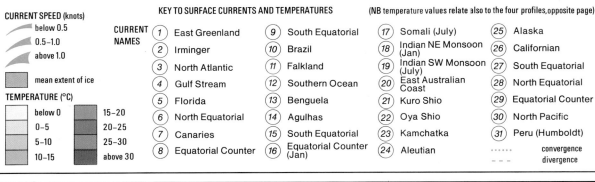

CURRENT SPEED (knots)		KEY TO SURFACE CURRENTS AND TEMPERATURES				(NB temperature values relate also to the four profiles, opposite page)	

CURRENT SPEED (knots)
- below 0.5
- 0.5–1.0
- above 1.0

mean extent of ice

TEMPERATURE (°C)
- below 0
- 0–5
- 5–10
- 10–15
- 15–20
- 20–25
- 25–30
- above 30

CURRENT NAMES

1. East Greenland
2. Irminger
3. North Atlantic
4. Gulf Stream
5. Florida
6. North Equatorial
7. Canaries
8. Equatorial Counter
9. South Equatorial
10. Brazil
11. Falkland
12. Southern Ocean
13. Benguela
14. Agulhas
15. South Equatorial
16. Equatorial Counter (Jan)
17. Somali (July)
18. Indian NE Monsoon (Jan)
19. Indian SW Monsoon (July)
20. East Australian Coast
21. Kuro Shio
22. Oya Shio
23. Kamchatka
24. Aleutian
25. Alaska
26. Californian
27. South Equatorial
28. North Equatorial
29. Equatorial Counter
30. North Pacific
31. Peru (Humboldt)

- ⋯⋯ convergence
- – – – divergence

1 *above and* **2** *below* The maps show prevailing surface currents and monthly-mean values of sea surface temperature for January and July. The patterns strikingly resemble those of prevailing winds in the atmosphere above, as is to be expected, since the winds provide the motive force for the major surface currents. However, equatorward flows are generally slow and broad, while poleward flows are rapid and concentrated near the western margins of ocean basins. Isotherms are oriented approximately east–west, except where they are distorted by warm and cold currents and the effects of persistent upwelling.

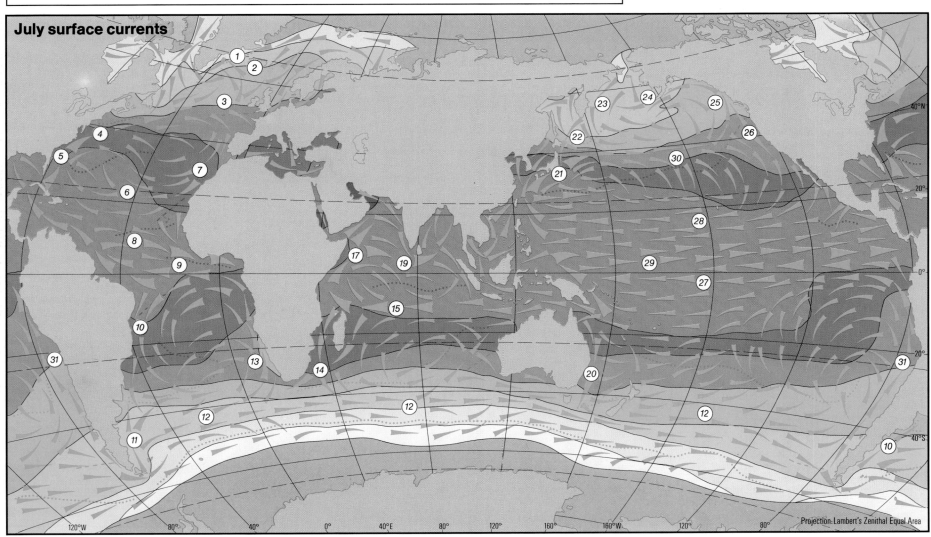

July surface currents

OCEANIC circulations derive partly from the action of wind on the surface of the sea and partly from convective processes. Surface currents are predominantly wind-driven, whereas deep-water motions stem largely from density contrasts between water masses. Intense surface flows, known as Western Boundary Currents, occur near the western sides of oceans. Examples are the Gulf Stream, the Kuro Shio and the Agulhas Current. These are permanent features of the global pattern of ocean currents. The Somali Current is also a Western Boundary Current but is present only when winds over the Arabian Sea are south-westerly, that is between May and October (see *Monsoons* page 49).

Surface water movements are such that well-marked zones of convergence and divergence occur. For example, there tends to be a convergence of water under subtropical anticyclones. The trade-winds on the equatorward flanks of these anticyclones transport water polewards and the westerlies on their poleward flanks drive water equatorwards. Water accumulates and is forced downwards. Conversely, upwelling of water takes place where divergence occurs. These vertical motions are of considerable importance to the biological economy of the sea. Ascending (cold) water is rich in nutrients which

are essential to marine life. Descending (warmer) water tends to be comparatively barren.

Perhaps the best-known example of such an oceanic feature is the Antarctic Convergence, which is found in the Southern Ocean between the latitudes of 50° and 60°S. This convergent zone separates the cold, ascending and extremely productive waters surrounding Antarctica from the warmer, biologically less significant waters of middle latitudes. Across it there is an abrupt change of temperature, occasionally as much as 5°C over a short distance.

Vertical motions associated with large-scale convergences and divergences are important elements of oceanic circulation systems. Indeed, some of these motions extend to depths of 1000 m or more.

As data-averaging processes are used in their production, charts of mean conditions tend to show ocean currents as steady, curvilinear flows. They provide no information about the ever-changing meanders, eddies and filaments which are now known to be characteristic elements of oceanic circulations in both surface and deep water. Many of the eddies and fragments of current are very extensive, not uncommonly covering areas of several thousand, or even tens of thousand square kilometres. They can also be

remarkably persistent as identifiable features. Durations of several months are usual, and some eddies first observed near Newfoundland have been tracked for many hundreds of kilometres across the North Atlantic Ocean towards Europe. Associated with them are complex fields of sea-surface temperature, which are of importance in the formation and intensification of extratropical depressions, through the agency of heat transfer from the ocean surface to the overlying atmosphere.

4 *below* Under sea ice, water becomes so dense by cooling and addition of salt drained from the ice above that it sinks to the bottom of the ocean. This occurs beneath the ice shelves of Antarctica, particularly in the Weddell Sea, the Ross Sea and the waters off Adélie Land. This Antarctic bottom water then spreads northwards and eastwards along the ocean floor.

Bottom water is also formed in the Arctic Ocean and in the sea between Greenland and Svalbard, where it is known as Arctic bottom water, and to the south and south-east of Greenland, where it is called North Atlantic deep water.

Bottom currents are strongest on the western margins of ocean basins, where they sometimes exceed 20 cm/sec (0.4 knots). Elsewhere bottom water moves very slowly, with flow rates typically of no more than a few millimetres a second.

3 *right* The graph provides a schematic representation of a typical oceanic temperature profile in tropical and subtropical areas. It generalises the actual temperature structures shown in the four profiles below, where it can be seen that there are differences only in the surface layer of water. The thermocline is a layer of abrupt temperature change which separates the mobile, well-stirred waters of the upper ocean from the cold, slow-moving waters beneath. It lies at a depth of a few hundred metres, the precise depth depending on latitude, season and prevailing meteorological conditions. It is absent in high latitudes where surface and deep-water temperatures are similar.

Vertical temperature structure of the ocean

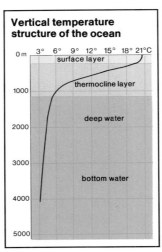

Movement of bottom water

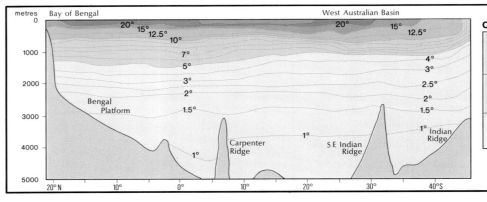

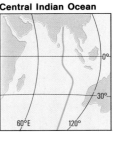

5–8 *right and below* The four meridian sections indicate vertical temperature structures; for temperature values refer to map key opposite. Locations of the ocean cross-sections are shown on the right of the profiles. It can be seen that the ocean basins are largely occupied by cold water with temperature less than 5°C. An almost isothermal layer of water extends from the surface to a depth of a few hundred metres. The temperature of the surface layer is determined by solar heating, large-scale horizontal movements of water, and mixing due to waves and currents.

Between the surface layer and the deep water there is a sharp gradient of temperature known as the thermocline. In parts of the Western Atlantic (see right of profile) the temperature of the surface water is comparable with that of the deep water, so there is no thermocline. To the east of Iceland the thermocline is seasonal; it is absent when surface water temperatures are less than 4–5°C.

The temperature profile of the Red Sea illustrates the effectiveness of the Bab-el-Mandeb sill as a barrier (see also *The salt sea* page 66). High temperatures (up to 56°C) at the bottom are caused by 'hot spots' or fissures which are associated with centres of sea floor spreading (see page 32).

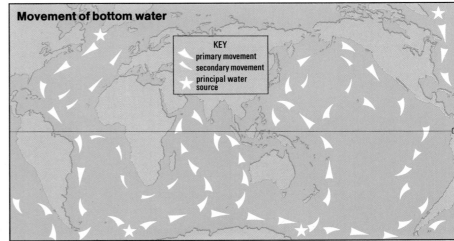

Eastern Pacific Ocean

Red Sea

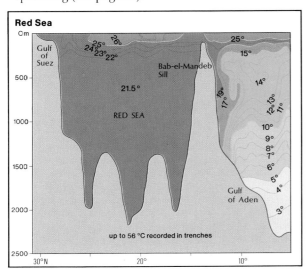

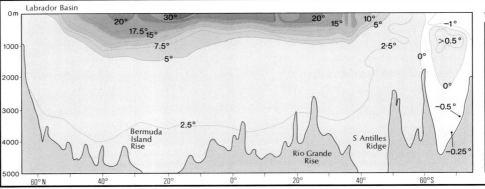

Western Atlantic Ocean

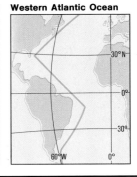

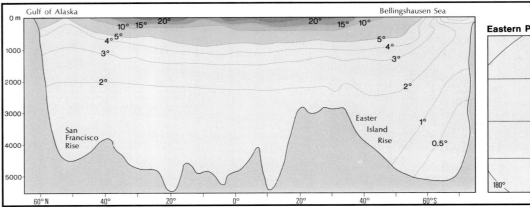

Central Indian Ocean

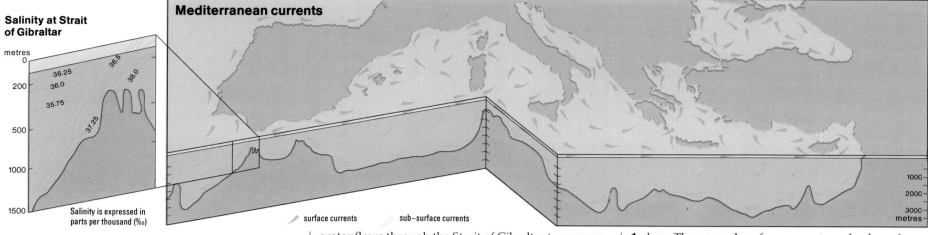

Salinity at Strait of Gibraltar

metres
0
200
500
1000
1500

36.25
36.5
36.0
35.75
38.0
37.25

Salinity is expressed in parts per thousand (‰)

Mediterranean currents

surface currents   sub-surface currents

1000
2000
3000
metres

Mediterranean circulation

The pattern of surface currents in the Mediterranean Sea is relatively simple. There is a general eastward movement of surface water, with anticlockwise circulations in each of the topographic subdivisions of the Mediterranean Sea.

In the eastern North Atlantic Ocean, south and west of Spain, there is a tongue of water of high salinity at a depth of about 1200 m (see *The salt sea* page 66). This phenomenon has its origins in convective processes in the Mediterranean Sea.

For much of the year skies over the Mediterranean Basin are largely cloud-free. Rainfall is scanty and evaporation rates are high. Thus, there is a net loss of fresh water from the Mediterranean because precipitation and inflow from rivers are insufficient to counterbalance evaporation. Atlantic Ocean surface

water flows through the Strait of Gibraltar to compensate for the deficiency. The evaporation causes the salinity, and hence the density, of the surface water in the Mediterranean Sea to increase, and this surface water sinks, to be replaced by less dense water; eventually a bottom current flows over the sill at the Strait of Gibraltar into the Atlantic Ocean. During the Second World War submarines made use of this strong outflow to be swept through the Strait of Gibraltar with their engines stopped, and so enter the North Atlantic undetected. This warm, highly saline outflow from the Mediterranean Basin reaches its equilibrium depth at about 1200 m and flows southward with North Atlantic deep water.

The surface layer of water from the Atlantic Ocean is relatively shallow, its depth ranging from 150 to 200 m along the north coast of Africa to only a few metres off southern Europe. Consistent with the tendency for

1 *above* The general surface currents and sub-surface circulation in the Mediterranean. The inset shows the vertical distribution of salinity at the Strait of Gibraltar.

aridity to increase eastwards across the Mediterranean region, surface salinity values also rise, from about 36.5‰ off Gibraltar to over 38.5‰ in the waters between Turkey and Egypt. The salinity of the Black Sea is only 18‰, but transport of water through the Dardanelles is unimportant and the effect on the Mediterranean negligible.

The Mediterranean is badly polluted in some areas. The renewal rate (or circulation period) of its waters as a whole is about 75 years. If the input of pollutants is too rapid there will be a net accumulation and the possibility that the Mediterranean could become a 'dead sea' (see pages 176–177).

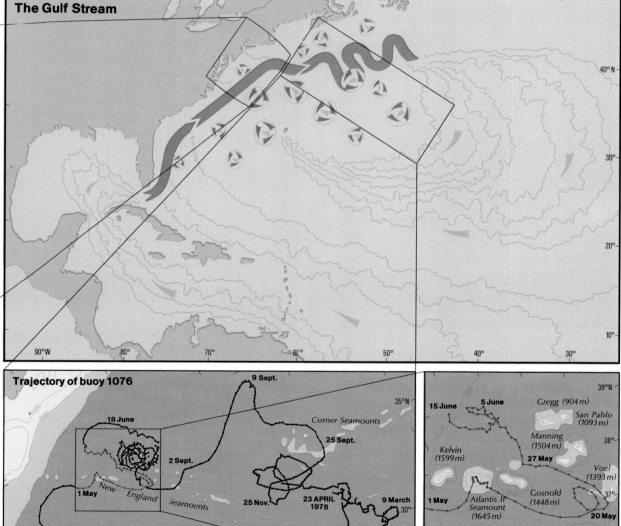

The Gulf Stream

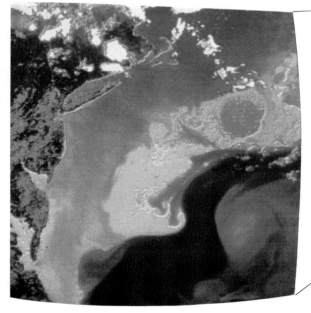

4 *above* This photograph of the Gulf Stream on 13 April 1977 is a colour-enhanced, infrared image from NOAA-5. A warm-core ring north of the dark red Gulf Stream and a cold-core ring (named 'Bob') to the south appear in orange. The colours correspond as follows to temperature (°C): white (cloud areas), less than 3; dark to light blue, 3–13; orange to red, 13–19; deep red-brown, 19–27.

The Gulf Stream

Of the surface currents that circulate in the North Atlantic gyre, the Gulf Stream is the fastest and most energetic, travelling off the north-east coast of North America at up to 220 km per day. But its strong northeast movement is characterised by complex meanders, eddies and also self-enclosed 'rings' which break off from the main current. Between 1975 and 1980, satellite tracking of free drifting buoys and infrared images provided new information on the flow of the Stream. The complex criss-crossing of the main flow, as shown by trajectories of these buoys, probably occurs in all major currents, but to date the Gulf Stream's movements have been best studied.

The Gulf Stream recognisably starts inside the Florida Straits and ceases to exist as a swift current around 45°N, 45°W, off the Grand Banks of Newfoundland. Off Cape Hatteras the average rate of flow is about 65 km per day and the jet of water carried extends to a depth over 1000 m. Some water flows north-east with the North Atlantic Current; some continues south-east around the subtropical gyre; and some (probably the greatest volume) recirculates within a narrow gyre north of Bermuda. This recirculation is thought to be driven by the energetic eddies and rings generated by the unstable Gulf Stream.

Trajectory of buoy 1076

9 Sept.
35°N
Corner Seamounts
18 June
25 Sept.
2 Sept.
New England
1 May
Seamounts
25 Nov.
23 APRIL 1978
9 March
30°
15 APRIL 1977
70°W   65°   60°   55°   50°

39°N
15 June   5 June   Gregg (904 m)
San Pablo (1093 m)
Kelvin (1599 m)
Manning (1504 m)
27 May   38°
Voel (1393 m)
1 May   Atlantis II Seamount (1645 m)
Gosnold (1448 m)   37°
20 May
65°W   64°   63°   62°   61°

2 *main map* The main flow of the Gulf Stream (*purple*) and some typical rings are shown in a synoptic view based on a variety of data. Outside the main current, the surface flow is shown schematically. Irregular curves are used to reflect the presence of mesoscale eddies. In general three rings at a time may occur to the north of the Gulf Stream. Here they will be circulating in a clockwise motion. South of the Gulf Stream and west of 50° will be as many as 8 to 14 rings; others may occur further east. These will be moving in anticlockwise circulation, but like the northerly rings will be travelling more or less against the main current and usually will become reabsorbed into it. The detailed behaviour of these currents remains largely unknown.

3 *above left and inset above right* The trajectory of one buoy (between 15 April 1977 and 23 April 1978) shows how near-surface currents of the Gulf Stream are affected by subsurface features. This buoy looped into ring 'Bob' (see photo) during April 1977 and later became locked into a series of eddies and loops around the New England seamounts between May and September (shown in red on map and inset). The diameter of the loops varied between 20 and 150 km. Thus the Gulf Stream somehow 'feels' the sea floor and is affected by it. The process of ring formation and duration is, through complex transfers of energy, similarly affected.

Upwelling

Upwelling is a climatic feature wherever winds persistently drive water away from a coast; as a result, cold sub-surface water rises to replace it (see *The water planet* page 44). Upwelling is a process of great biological importance. The ascending, cooler waters cause surface waters to become rich in nitrates and phosphates. These are nutrients for phytoplankton, on which zooplankton depend (see *The plankton* page 70). In turn, fish and birds thrive. This is especially so off the west coast of South America, where the birds are so numerous that their guano has proved a significant resource in the economies of Ecuador, Chile and Peru. Unfortunately, much of it is worked out now.

Wherever upwelling occurs there is some seasonal fluctuation of its intensity, associated with the annual rhythm of global wind patterns. In general the intensity is least in autumn and winter, but off Peru there is a summer minimum of intensity. Occasionally, however, upwelling unexpectedly ceases altogether, and the ecological and economic consequences can be disastrous. The effects are particularly severe along the Peruvian coast. The cessation is due to a replacement of the prevailing southerly winds by northerly winds which drive warm surface water shoreward and therefore downward. The warm waters cannot support the life cycle and vast numbers of fish and birds die.

The anomalous behaviour of the Peru Current is known as *El Niño* and in the years when it occurs (in this century in 1925, 1941, 1957–58, 1965, 1972–73, 1976) it develops soon after Christmas (whence *El Niño*, which is Spanish for 'The Child'). The anomaly typically lasts for several weeks, although it may persist for several months. The mechanism of *El Niño* remains largely unexplained but the phenomenon is known to be associated with anomalous behaviour of the atmosphere and oceans in other parts of the world. For example, connections have been found between *El Niño* and sea surface temperature anomalies in the western Pacific Ocean, deficiencies of monsoon rain in the Indian subcontinent, drought in the Sahelian zone of North Africa and cold winters in the USA.

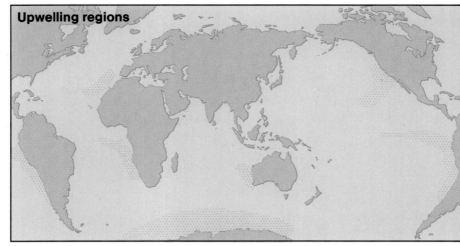

Upwelling regions

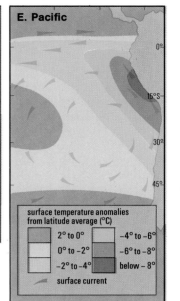

E. Pacific

surface temperature anomalies from latitude average (°C)

2° to 0°	-4° to -6°
0° to -2°	-6° to -8°
-2° to -4°	below -8°

surface current

5 *above and* **6** *above right* Upwelling occurs mainly in the trade-wind belts of the tropics and subtropics off the western coasts of continents, and around Antarctica. The surface waters of the South Pacific Ocean off the coasts of Peru and northern Chile are conspicuously cold for their latitudes, and this is due to upwelling. The motions of the Pacific Ocean spread the cooling, so that water temperatures are lower than average for the latitude, well to the west of South America. Indeed, immediately to the south of the equator a tongue of cold water extends almost halfway across the ocean.

In addition to the example of the Arabian Sea *right*, seasonal upwelling occurs in the California Current. Upwelling tends to be strongest in spring and autumn, and is weak or absent in late autumn and early winter.

7 *right* The map shows August sea surface temperatures in the Arabian Sea. Upwelling is seasonal off the coasts of Somalia and Arabia, occurring only between May and October, when winds are persistently southwesterly over the Arabian Sea. The upwelling causes the waters to be comparatively cool. Downwelling occurs during the north-east monsoon.

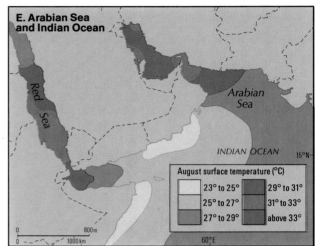

E. Arabian Sea and Indian Ocean

August surface temperature (°C)	
23° to 25°	29° to 31°
25° to 27°	31° to 33°
27° to 29°	above 33°

Fog

Fog and mist occur when visibility is reduced by water droplets suspended in the atmosphere. By definition, fog is present when visibility is less than 1000 m; mist when it is over 1000 m. Haze is caused by fine particles of smoke or dust. The three basic types of fog are sea smoke, advection fog and radiation fog.

Sea smoke is a patchy, shallow fog, rarely more than a few metres deep, which occurs where cold air passes over water at least 10°C warmer. Steam, or 'smoke', appears to rise off the surface of the water. Sea smoke is not normally a hindrance to navigation, as visibility at eye level and above is rarely impaired. However, there is a danger of very small boats being obscured. Sea smoke occurs chiefly in autumn and winter and is most common in the Arctic and Antarctic and off the eastern coasts of continents.

Advection fog (or sea fog) is the type most often encountered at sea, where it occurs mainly in spring and summer. It forms where warm, moist air meets a colder surface. It may form or disperse at any time of day or night, and may persist for many hours, or even a few days. Banks of advection fog can be several hundred metres deep and can present a serious hazard to shipping.

During summer, advection fog is very persistent over the pack ice and open waters of the Arctic and the Canadian Archipelago. On average, it occurs every other day between June and September. It is frequently widespread in several other regions: over the pack ice and open waters close to Antarctica; the Sea of Okhotsk and the Bering Sea; and the Oya Shio and Aleutian Currents of the North Pacific. Where advection fog is local there may be considerable daily variation of its density. This happens on the coast of California, near San Francisco, where fog forms when sea breezes cross the cool inshore waters of the California Current.

Radiation fog forms when air in contact with the ground is chilled to saturation point by nocturnal cooling of the ground. It is essentially a land fog but banks may drift over coastal and estuarine waters. It forms during the night and disperses by mid-morning.

8 *map and insets below* The map shows the number of mornings per year when visibility over coastal waters is less than 1 km. Fog is most frequent in middle and high latitudes and is uncommon in the tropics, but prevailing winds between October and March are such that visibility on the Guinea coast of Africa is frequently reduced by Saharan dust, particularly in December and January. The insets show the percentage frequency of fog for July in the North Atlantic and North Pacific, showing that greatest frequency occurs over the cool western waters.

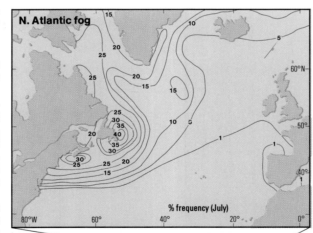

N. Atlantic fog

% frequency (July)

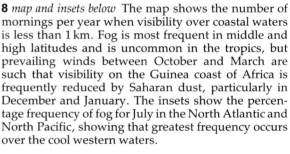

N. Pacific fog

% frequency (July)

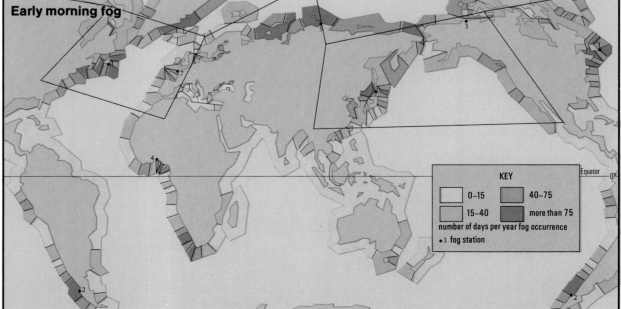

Early morning fog

KEY	
0–15	40–75
15–40	more than 75

number of days per year fog occurrence
• 3 fog station

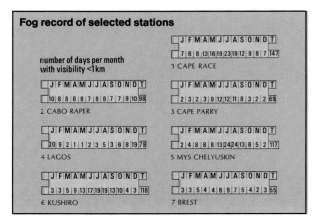

Fog record of selected stations

number of days per month with visibility <1km

	J	F	M	A	M	J	J	A	S	O	N	D	T
1 CAPE RACE	7	6	8	13	16	19	23	19	12	9	8	7	147
2 CABO RAPER	10	8	8	8	8	7	8	8	7	7	9	10	98
3 CAPE PARRY	2	3	2	3	9	12	12	11	8	3	2	2	69
4 LAGOS	20	9	2	1	1	2	3	5	3	6	8	19	79
5 MYS CHELYUSKIN	2	4	8	8	8	13	24	24	16	5	2	1	117
6 KUSHIRO	3	3	5	9	13	17	19	19	13	10	4	3	118
7 BREST	3	3	5	4	4	6	9	7	5	4	2	3	55

Cyclone and hurricane disasters

TROPICAL cyclones are violent storms accompanied by hurricane force winds and torrential rain. They occur most commonly between 5° and 30° latitude and roughly two-thirds are in the northern hemisphere. Tropical cyclones form in preferred oceanic areas of the tropics (see following pages). The majority follow a generally westward track across the ocean until curving poleward over the western ocean basin. The mature, violent systems thus tend to affect islands and continental regions on the western flanks of the subtropical oceans, for example, across South Asia and the Caribbean and southeastern United States in the northern hemisphere, and Madagascar and Australian tropical and subtropical coastal regions in the southern hemisphere. Hurricanes forming west of Central America may affect the Hawaiian Islands, but the absence of favourable generating conditions across the tropical South Atlantic and South East Pacific means that 'downstream' land areas (for example, eastern Brazil) do not suffer cyclones. The areas most vulnerable to damage are densely populated coastal zones and delta regions, and isolated groups of islands.

Of all natural disasters, tropical cyclones cause the greatest damage. At sea, wind and waves are a threat to shipping. But the effects are most severe when a storm reaches land, where heavy rain and storm surges cause flooding, damage to buildings, destruction of crops and livestock, and loss of human life. Death tolls are sometimes enormous, especially in heavily populated and ill-prepared underdeveloped countries. Thousands of people may die in a single storm: as many as 300 000 perished when the surge of water raised by a cyclone over the Bay of Bengal swept across the Ganges Delta on 12 November 1970. In contrast, in developed countries where storm warning systems are sophisticated and evacuation procedures clearly defined, comparatively few lives are lost but economic damage may be very great.

Paradoxically, tropical cyclones can bring benefits. Insurance compensation and grants-in-aid create short-term booms. Rain after drought can improve agriculture and help replenish reservoirs.

Harbingers of a tropical storm include vivid sunrise and sunset, rising swell, lines of cirrus cloud, a falling barometer and progressively muggy conditions. The US Weather Bureau broadcasts special hurricane bulletins covering the Atlantic and northern Pacific. In the Pacific port towns, such as Suva in the Fiji Islands, public buildings traditionally fly black flags when a hurricane is imminent. Many ports in hurricane-prone regions have specially designed or strengthened harbours and anchorages.

THE NAMING OF TROPICAL CYCLONES

Various regional names for tropical cyclonic storms are commonly used. Those which occur over the North Atlantic, West Indies and north-east Pacific Ocean are called *hurricanes*; those which occur over the south-west Pacific, the Arabian Sea, the Bay of Bengal and the south Indian Ocean are called *cyclones*; and those which occur over the China seas and the north-west Pacific are called *typhoons*. Of the many local names the best known are *baguio* (Philippines) and *cordonazo* (Mexico and the west coast of Central America). *Willy-willy* is sometimes used in north-west Australia. Many mariners use the term *tropical revolving storm* (TRS).

The practice of assigning names to individual storms was started by the US forces during the Second World War in the Pacific. From 1953 feminine names were allocated to Atlantic hurricanes. Since 1975 in Australia, and 1979 in the USA, alternate male and female names have been used. Names are allocated in advance in alphabetical order beginning with the letter 'A' each season. If a storm is severe its name is not repeated. Thus, hurricane Allen specifically identifies the North Atlantic hurricane of August 1980.

In India, cyclones are assigned numbers or letters instead of names.

1 *world map and insets* Locations of major cyclone disasters for 1974–82. It should be noted that in general only the point of landfall is plotted, as this is where most damage occurs. Individual cyclones travel considerable distances, change direction and increase and decrease in intensity over a period of several days. This complex behaviour is illustrated by the tracks of ten selected cyclones.

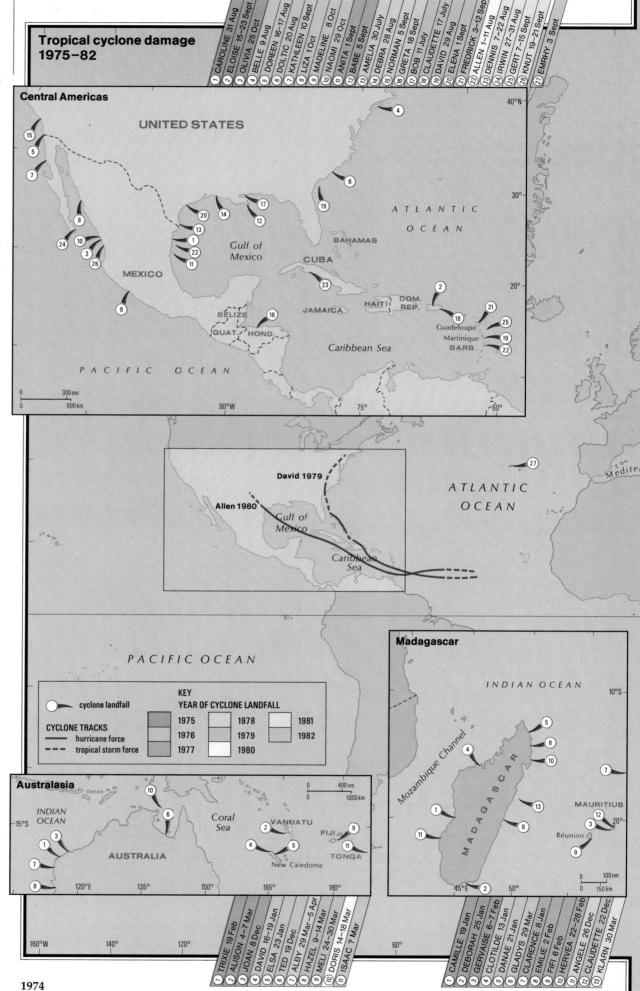

1974
Hurricane Fifi wreaked its damage on 18–19 September in Honduras and Guatemala. As many as 18 000 people died, 25 000 homes were destroyed and a total 100 000 people were affected. An area of 90 000 sq. km suffered damage.

On 25 December, hurricane Tracy devastated Darwin: 5000 houses were destroyed and 65 people died; about 35 000 of the city's population of 45 000 population were evacuated. The cost of damage was close to 1000 million Australian dollars.

1975
On 22 October, typhoon Flossie passed 250 miles south of Hong Kong, and two freighters, the *Ming Sing* and *Kinabalu Satii*, sunk. Forty-four lives were lost.

1976
Typhoon Olga struck Quezon Province, Luzon, on 21 May. In the ensuing flooding, 200 died, 15 000 homes were under water, dykes and bridges collapsed, and crops were damaged.

In Baja California State, Mexico, on 1 October, hurricane Liza left 600 dead, 200 000 injured and the city of La Paz devastated. The cost was estimated at $700 million. The damage was compounded by hurricane Madeline on 8 October and Naomi on 29 October.

1977
At the beginning of February, hurricane Emilie passed across Tamatave Province, Madagascar. The extensive storm surge caused severe flooding, 31 people died

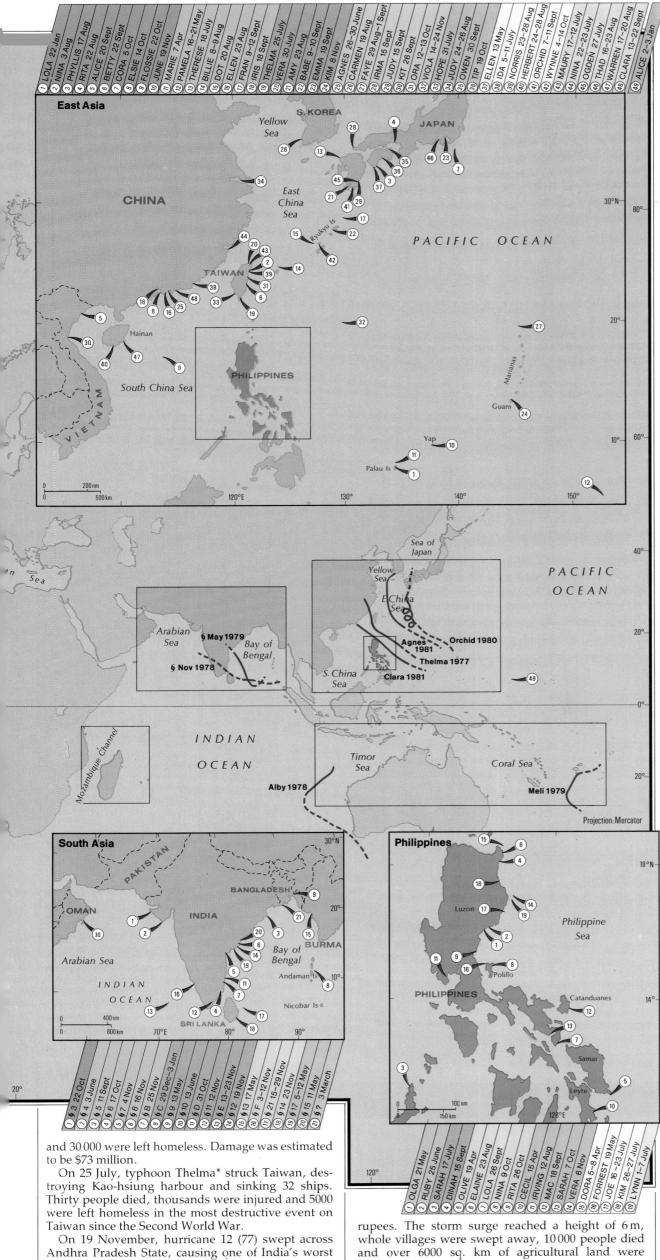

East Asia

South Asia

Philippines

2 above Hurricane David's storm waves overwhelming the coasts of Martinique, in the Caribbean, September 1979.

1978

In early April, hurricane Alby* approached Perth, Australia, where farmers were burning off pasture, and caused widespread blackouts, bushfires and severe damage to property and crops.

Late on 23 November, hurricane 21 (78)* swept west across Sri Lanka, having developed near the Nicobar Islands a few days earlier. $50 million damage was caused by high winds, flooding and landslides, with sea water inundating rice fields for up to 8 km inland. A total of 373 people perished and 80 000 homes were destroyed or damaged.

1979

Hurricane Meli* devastated the Fijian Islands during March, with a 12 to 15 m storm surge drowning 52 people and destroying 205 houses on Mbengga, 550 homes on Thithia and 3 villages on Ngau.

In early May, hurricane 17 (79)* brought extreme winds and 3 to 6 cm rain to Andhra Pradesh, India. Floods washed two bridges away and led to the loss of 700 people and 300 000 head of cattle. Water levels up to 3 m above normal inundated some coasts and with high winds produced serious erosion along parts of the Madras coast. Damage to houses, public utilities and crops was estimated to be 1700 million rupees.

Hurricane David* proved the worst disaster this century in many Caribbean islands. During late August and early September, over 1200 people perished and some 200 000 were made homeless in the Dominican Republic, while tiny Dominica witnessed 56 deaths and 60 000 homeless along with the virtually complete destruction of its staple banana crop. Damage in the region totalled $2000 million.

1980

In the Port Hedland area, Australia, there was a most exceptional occurrence of three major tropical cyclones within a space of six weeks (Amy and Dean in January, Enid in February).

Hurricane Allen* created widespread destruction in the Caribbean in early August, with 18 deaths and severe damage to the banana crop on St Lucia and 7 m waves washing several barges ashore on St Kitts. On 7 August flash floods in Haiti were responsible for 220 deaths and 835 000 homeless; damage was estimated at $400 million. The previous day saw the cargo vessel *Georgios* sink in heavy seas with the loss of 27 lives.

A helicopter crashed, killing 13, during the evacuation of an offshore oil rig near Louisiana. Almost 500 000 people were evacuated from Texas and Louisiana coastal districts where exceptionally high seas, strong winds and heavy rain caused $600 million damage.

In September, typhoon Orchid* created severe conditions in the seas around Japan where an ocean container broke its tow east of Shikoku and the *Derbyshire* sank with the loss of 44 lives as it neared Japan en route from Canada with a cargo of 158 000 tonnes of iron ore.

1981

During August, typhoon Agnes* wreaked havoc along the south and east coasts of South Korea where 5 to 10 cm rain produced floods and landslides, leading to 58 deaths and $24 million damage. Over 150 fishing vessels were sunk or damaged while in the Shanghai region of China about 300 fishing junks capsized and sea walls collapsed, leading to severe damage to extensive areas of rice and cotton fields.

September saw typhoon Clara* produce the Philippines' worst maritime disaster since the Second World War with the loss of the 1220 tonne destroyer *Datu Kalantiaw* and over 50 crew on a reef north of Manila. A little later it produced flooding in Fujian Province, China, where 200 sq. km of rice and 1200 sq. km of sugar cane were destroyed.

*indicates track of cyclone shown on the map.

and 30 000 were left homeless. Damage was estimated to be $73 million.

On 25 July, typhoon Thelma* struck Taiwan, destroying Kao-hsiung harbour and sinking 32 ships. Thirty people died, thousands were injured and 5000 were left homeless in the most destructive event on Taiwan since the Second World War.

On 19 November, hurricane 12 (77) swept across Andhra Pradesh State, causing one of India's worst disasters, with damage amounting to 3500 million rupees. The storm surge reached a height of 6 m, whole villages were swept away, 10 000 people died and over 6000 sq. km of agricultural land were damaged.

Tropical cyclones, thunderstorms and waterspouts

TROPICAL cyclones are the most energetic and destructive of all weather systems. Torrential rain falls from their towering cumulo nimbus clouds and wind speeds commonly exceed 50 m/sec. On land areas the heavy rain and violent winds cause serious flooding and widespread devastation, while at sea the severe wind, weather and sea conditions are a great danger to shipping. Low-lying coastal areas are prone to inundation by storm surges (see *Tides and surges* page 60).

The storms of tropical latitudes are classified according to their intensity. *Tropical cyclones* contain winds of Beaufort force 12 (33 m/sec) or more, *severe tropical storms* contain winds of forces 10 and 11 (24–32 m/sec) and *moderate tropical storms* contain winds of forces 8 and 9 (17–23 m/sec). If they are less intense they are called *tropical depressions*.

Satellite photographs have revealed that tropical cyclones develop from disturbances generated in the Intertropical Convergence Zone or ITCZ (see *Global winds and weather* page 46), but the precise physical circumstances which determine whether or not a disturbance will develop into a cyclone are still not adequately known.

The winds of tropical storms rotate anti-clockwise in the northern hemisphere and clockwise in the southern hemisphere. Tropical cyclones tend to travel in broadly curvilinear trajectories, following the general wind circulation trends, but their movement along these trajectories is erratic, in both speed and direction. Storms move very slowly in their early stage of development, when they are just diffuse areas of low pressure. As they intensify they accelerate and gradually become more compact until, when fully established, they are some 600–800 km in diameter and their speed of travel is 6–8 m/sec. The erratic movement may be a response to the complex fields of sea-surface temperature which are associated with ocean currents.

Of the storms which reach middle latitudes the majority do not survive for long because the surface of the sea is too cool to sustain them, but some develop fronts and become virtually indistinguishable from extratropical depressions. All storms dissipate rapidly over land, where they are starved of moisture.

The main energy source in a tropical cyclone is the heat released by the condensation of water vapour contained in air lifted from close to the ocean surface. The warmer the air, the more water vapour it can hold and, therefore, the greater the amount of energy released when condensation takes place. Thus, storm activity tends to be greatest over the western parts of oceans during late summer and early autumn, where sea-surface temperatures are highest, for example in the Caribbean.

Cyclones over the Arabian Sea and Bay of Bengal (North Indian Ocean) are atypical, however, for they are most frequent in the weeks preceding the onset of monsoon rains in western India and in the weeks following their retreat, that is in May, early June and November. This inconsistency appears to be unrelated to sea-surface temperature, because extensive areas of the North Indian Ocean are warm enough for the development of cyclonic storms throughout the rainy period in western India. Rather, it is believed that development of cyclones is inhibited by the persistently strong vertical windshear which exists over southern Asia and adjacent oceans while the summer monsoon is active.

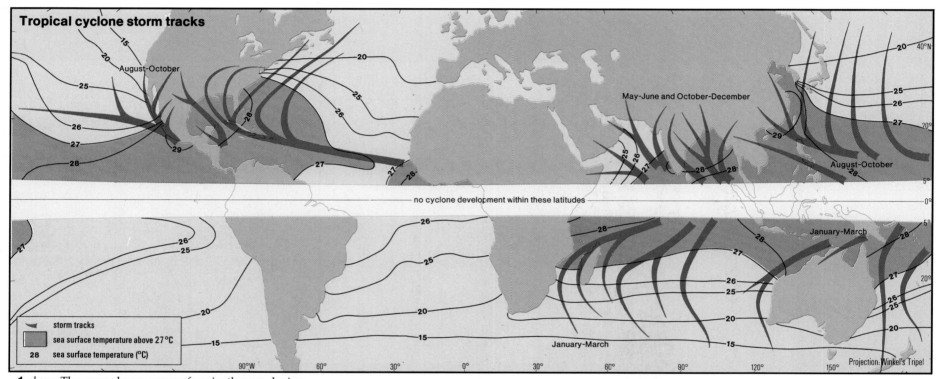

Tropical cyclone storm tracks

storm tracks
sea surface temperature above 27°C
28 sea surface temperature (°C)

no cyclone development within these latitudes

Projection: Winkel's Tripel

1 *above* The map shows sea surface isotherms during the warmest season and paths typically taken by tropical cyclones. Most storms curve around the subtropical anticyclones and enter middle latitudes, but some continue moving to the west. For a tropical cyclonic storm or hurricane to develop, sea surface temperature must be at least 26.5°C. The Earth's rotation is also instrumental, and such storms never develop within 5° from the equator. While it is not possible to predict where or when cyclones will strike, their probable tracks and thus areas of high vulnerability are well established. Especially at risk are coastlines and estuaries where tidal range exceeds 4 metres.

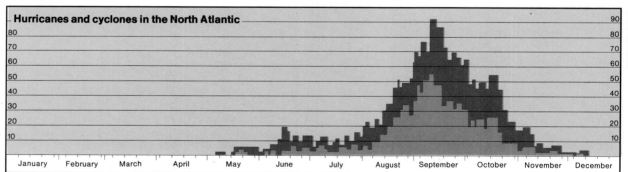

Hurricanes and cyclones in the North Atlantic

2 *above* The graph shows the total number of storms observed in the North Atlantic on each day throughout the period 1886–1977. The lighter colour represents those storms that developed into hurricanes. For example, during this period more than 90 storms, of which 55 were of hurricane intensity, were recorded on 10 September. In any one year a particular storm may persist over several days, and will have been recorded on each day for its duration. Also, more than one storm may be in progress on a single day. In the North Atlantic storms occur only from May to December and reach a peak in mid-September.

Average number of tropical storms and hurricanes per month

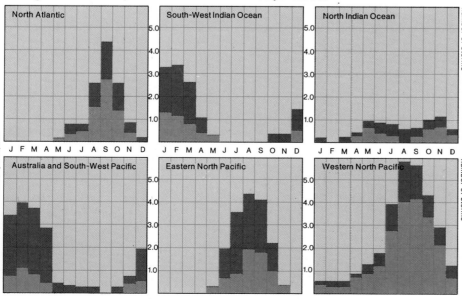

hurricanes, typhoons etc. (wind above force 12)
tropical storms (wind force 8–11)

Average storms per year

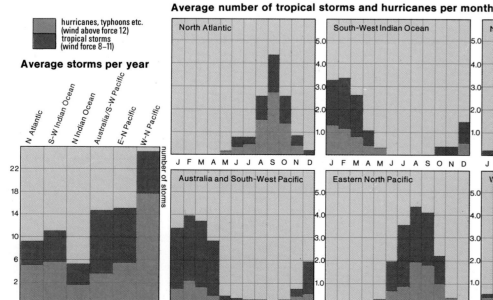

North Atlantic

South-West Indian Ocean

North Indian Ocean

Australia and South-West Pacific

Eastern North Pacific

Western North Pacific

3 *left* These monthly figures show the same trends as the more detailed record for the North Atlantic, with a peak occurring in late summer/early autumn, except for the North Indian Ocean where there are two peaks, just before and just after the monsoon.

4 *far left* The annual averages show that the western North Pacific has the most storms; in fact, the number of storms there that develop into cyclones is greater than the total of storms in each of the other areas.

Tropical cyclone over the Irrawaddy Delta

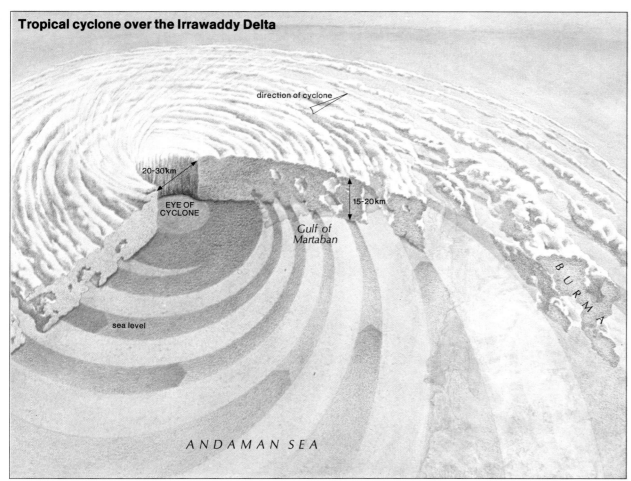

direction of cyclone

20-30km

EYE OF
CYCLONE

15-20 km

*Gulf of
Martaban*

B U R M A

sea level

A N D A M A N   S E A

5 *left* This illustration depicts a mature tropical cyclone in the northern hemisphere (in the southern hemisphere the rotations are in the opposite directions). On average, a tropical cyclone reaches maturity three days after forming as an incipient disturbance; it has then reached a stage of minimum central pressure and maximum wind strength and its diameter is characteristically 600–800 km. Warm, very moist air converges into the system at low levels, spiralling in more and more rapidly, and ascends quite abruptly in the 'throat' of the eye wallcloud some 30–40 km from the axis. This ascending air ultimately spirals out anticyclonically at upper levels, between 12 and 15 km, and appears as a vast cirrus shield which caps the cyclone. The eye is on average 20–30 km in diameter and is a region of subsiding air, clear or well-broken skies and calm conditions.

Hurricane-force winds occur typically within 250 km of the low centre, with the strongest winds (150–170 km/h) and heavy rain confined to a belt approximately 20 km wide near the eye wall. Gales are observed more widely, and winds tend to be strongest on the cyclone's right flank (left in the southern hemisphere) looking along its direction of motion, where the carrying current and the circulation reinforce each other. Bands of deep cumulus clouds with heavy showers spiral into the centre, embedded within an extensive region of clear skies where the air is sinking.

Surface wind waves can be up to 10 m high although most coastal inundation comes with the wind-generated storm surge, which is often 5 m above normal tidal levels. A sea-surface pressure fall of 1 mb is associated with an increase of roughly 1 cm in sea-surface elevation; in a typical cyclone this can add 0.5 m to water levels.

6 *right* The map shows the average number of days per year thunderstorms occur. Approximately 44 000 thunderstorms and almost one hundred million lightning discharges occur in the Earth's atmosphere every day. About 2000 storms are in progress at any given moment. The storms are invariably associated with cumulonimbus clouds and are typically accompanied by strong, gusty winds and outbreaks of rain or hail. Over the sea, storms tend to be most frequent at night, particularly in the tropics. The thunder is harmless, but the squally weather and lightning discharges present dangers and difficulties to the mariner. For example, the discharges cause sferics, which interfere with radio communications.

Thunderstorms are most frequent in low latitudes, and are particularly common in southern Mexico, Panama, Central Brazil, Madagascar and Indonesia. In all these areas storms occur on more than 100 days per year. On the island of Java the frequency exceeds 220 days per year. Storms are rare in subtropical anticyclones and over the cold waters off coasts affected by upwelling, and are almost unknown in polar regions. In middle latitudes storms are most common during summer.

Thunderstorms

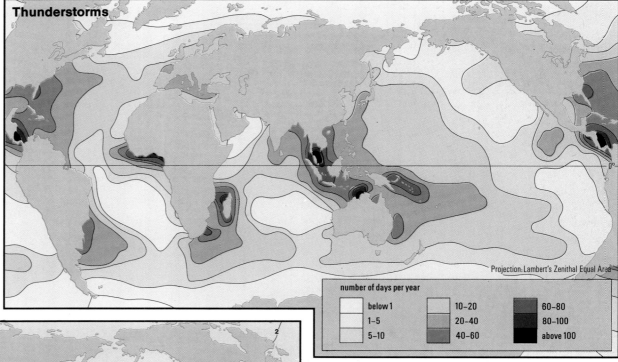

Projection: Lambert's Zenithal Equal Area

number of days per year

below 1	10–20	60–80
1–5	20–40	80–100
5–10	40–60	above 100

Waterspouts

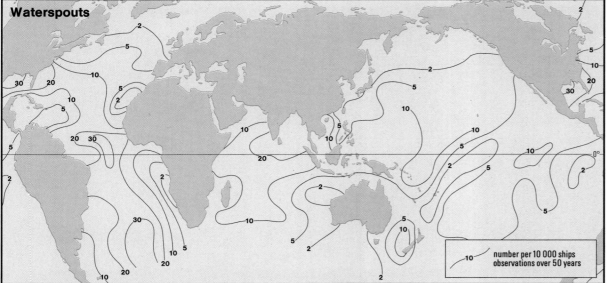

number per 10 000 ships
observations over 50 years

7 *above* The map shows the number of waterspouts recorded per 10 000 ship observations. Waterspouts are whirling vortices of air which descend from the base of a cumulus or cumulonimbus cloud to the sea below. They occur most frequently in the tropics and subtropics, particularly over the South Atlantic Ocean, the Gulf of Mexico, the Mediterranean Sea and the Bay of Bengal, and are rare over cold water. They are most likely to occur in summer and early autumn. The diameter may be as little as 1–2 m or as much as 300 m, and the height is usually a few hundreds of metres. They travel with their parent cloud at a speed of a few metres per second and typically exist for between ten

and thirty minutes. In and around their base the sea is agitated and a column, or cascade, of spray is thrown up. Even the most seaworthy of ships may be damaged if a spout passes directly over it. Damage is caused partly by the winds, which may exceed 60 m/s, partly by the sudden reduction of pressure, and partly by the release of water carried aloft by the vortex.

8 *right* A waterspout measuring 900 metres high off the coast of Huntington Beach, southern California, December 1969, which caused the deaths of 3 people and seriously injured 17 others. The pier-head and other beach property were totally destroyed; it cost the Santa Ana Fire Department $200 000 to clean up the damage.

Waves, swell and tsunamis

THE waters of the sea are disturbed by a number of natural forces. The gravitational influences of the Sun and Moon cause the tidal undulations which propagate around ocean basins (see *Tides and surges* page 60); seismic movements or other major underwater disturbances cause tsunamis (the so-called tidal waves which have nothing to do with tides); the action of wind on the surface of the sea causes wind-waves; and hydrodynamic forces excite internal waves within the oceans along layers of strong density contrast. Swell is the name given to residual wind-waves which are no longer under the influence of the forces which generated them.

Waves interact with each other, with currents and with the wind, as well as with swell from distant weather systems. At a given spot there is a synthesis of mutually interfering wave trains of different heights, periods and also directions. Superimposed is a wave disturbance consistent with the local wind at that particular spot.

Tides and wind-waves are potentially beneficial because energy can be extracted from them (see *Renewable energy* page 120). It is the destructive energy of waves, however, that is more familiar. Tsunamis can devastate low-lying coastal areas and the largest wind-waves can move objects weighing hundreds of tonnes as though they were mere pebbles; even a moderate swell can deliver 40 kW per metre of coastline. It is quite common for wind-waves to damage large ships, offshore structures and coastal defences. In-

ternal waves can make maintenance of trim difficult for submarines; they can also impede a surface vessel or affect its rudder control.

Quantitative knowledge of wave conditions is lacking because waves are observed or recorded systematically at very few locations far removed from coasts. Only at Ocean Weather Stations and offshore platforms are wave data obtained regularly. Accordingly, reliable wave climatologies exist only for coastal waters and the small number of offshore areas which have been the

subjects of special study, for example the waters around the British Isles. Mariners' legendary tales of monster waves, once treated with scepticism, have in the last three decades been confirmed by better understanding of the nature of waves by use of both measurement and theory to determine their size, speed and energy with reasonable accuracy.

There have been few detailed analyses of the circumstances of freak, or more precisely, episodic waves. However, it is probable that the

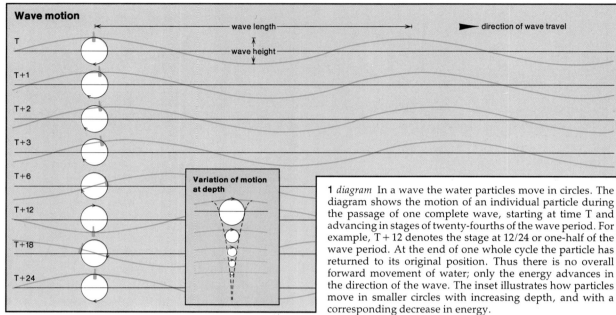

Wave motion

1 *diagram* In a wave the water particles move in circles. The diagram shows the motion of an individual particle during the passage of one complete wave, starting at time T and advancing in stages of twenty-fourths of the wave period. For example, T + 12 denotes the stage at 12/24 or one-half of the wave period. At the end of one whole cycle the particle has returned to its original position. Thus there is no overall forward movement of water; only the energy advances in the direction of the wave. The inset illustrates how particles move in smaller circles with increasing depth, and with a corresponding decrease in energy.

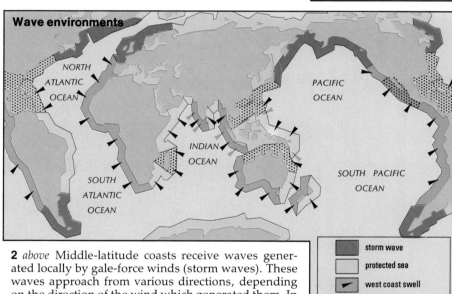

Wave environments

2 *above* Middle-latitude coasts receive waves generated locally by gale-force winds (storm waves). These waves approach from various directions, depending on the direction of the wind which generated them. In the tropics and subtropics, where gale-force winds are rare, coasts receive swell generated in the tradewind zones, monsoonal regions and the storm belts of temperate latitudes. The longest swells experience little attenuation and reach coasts thousands of kilometres from their source. Swells from the trade-wind zones predominate on east coasts, those from temperate-latitude storms on west coasts. Protected environments occur where swell fails to penetrate. This happens in

- storm wave
- protected sea
- west coast swell
- east coast swell
- monsoon influence
- tropical cyclone influence

Wave heights

greatest height with over 3% occurrence (metres)
- above 6
- 5–6
- 3.5–5
- 2.5–3.5
- less than 2.5

seas which are almost enclosed or where there is a cover of sea-ice. However, some protected environments are affected by waves and swell produced by tropical cyclones.

3 *above* Reliable wave climatologies exist only for coastal waters and a small number of offshore areas, where regular observations are made at ocean weather stations and offshore platforms. They confirm that wave conditions tend to be worst where winds are strongest, that is, off southern Africa, southern Australia, southern South America, western North America, Greenland, Iceland and North West Europe. In these waters the temporal frequency of waves at least 6 m high is more than 3 per cent while the occurrence of waves at least 2.5 m is more than 30 per cent. Large waves are also common on the Arabian Sea during the south-west monsoon.

Abnormal waves off southern Africa

SOUTH AFRICA

Agulhas Current

West Wind Drift

20-metre high wave

wave trains of wave length 260 m 150 m 55 m

Agulhas Current 4–5 kn

4 Off the east coast of South Africa, waves of different lengths become superimposed. This happens when waves generated far away in the Southern Ocean arrive as swell and combine with waves from other distant or local storms (see *above left*). These southern or south-westerly waves meet the Agulhas current head on and are steepened and shortened.

Some become so steep that their forward face is close to breaking (see *above right*). Here, an exceptionally high 'episodic', or freak, wave is about to crash on to the ship, the weight of water either crushing it or holing its bows. Such waves may be preceded by a correspondingly deep trough or 'hole in the sea', and ships have been known to founder and

disappear. The holes, though rare, are particularly dangerous as they can only be seen by a vessel on the brink of the wave. An exceptional wave crest, however, can often be seen from some distance away and avoiding action can be taken.

common denominator is a combination of large waves and swell opposing a strong tidal stream or a strong current near a continental edge. The Agulhas Current off southern Africa is a renowned area (see below) but the highest reliably measured wave in the open sea is still that encountered by USS *Ramapo* on the North Pacific in 1933. The ship, a tanker 146 m long, en route from Manila to San Diego, was overtaken by waves of period 14.8 seconds travelling at 55 knots. The greatest wave height observed was 34 m.

Measurement of waves

Waves are described by wave period (the time it takes for two successive wave crests to pass a point), by wave length (the distance between the two crests), and by wave height (the vertical distance between a trough and succeeding crest). The height of waves is a function of three wind factors: mean speed of the wind which raises the waves, the length of time the wind has been blowing (duration), and the distance over which the wind has blown (the fetch).

Because the surface of the sea typically possesses a disordered, even chaotic appearance, statistical methods have to be employed to measure the height, power and frequency of waves. When employing statistical methods, the term significant-wave height is often used. This is simply defined as the average height of the highest one-third of waves in a particular time interval (usually ten minutes). This concept is all the more useful because it approximates closely to wave height estimated visually by an experienced mariner. Similarly, the significant-wave period is the average period of the highest one-third of the waves. The significant-wave concept is useful for many engineering purposes, but where knowledge of distribution of wave energy in relation to wave period is required, for example the response of ships to complex motions of interacting waves, the wave spectrum concept is applied.

The energy of a wave is proportional to the square of the wave height; the wave spectrum is the distribution of wave energy with respect to wave period.

Tsunamis

Tsunami is a Japanese word which has been used to define a special type of ocean wave which is generated by seismic disturbances. The characteristics of these waves are very different from those of wind-waves. Whereas a wind-wave may have a length of, say, 100 m, the length of a tsunami can be measured in hundreds of kilometres. In addition, they travel at terrifying speeds, exceeding 650 km per hour. Thus, the time which elapses between their generation and their arrival on a distant coast is only a matter of hours. While travelling in deep water tsunamis are quite harmless as they attain only a metre or so in height. However, on reaching shallow, coastal water the velocity and wave length quickly diminish but as the period of the wave remains the same, it rears up, sometimes to heights of 16 m or more, and sweeps ashore, often causing widespread destruction and loss of life. It has been known for people on board ships at anchor to be unaware of a tsunami travelling beneath them but to see, only seconds later, a whole shoreline being devastated by monstrous waves. Tsunamis occur most frequently in the Pacific Ocean, which is ringed with a belt of earthquakes and volcanic activity; and no Pacific island or coastal settlement is safe from their onslaught. Honolulu is the centre of the system of warning stations and thus of tsunami research, since a great number of seismic waves strike the island as they cross the Pacific from their point of origin.

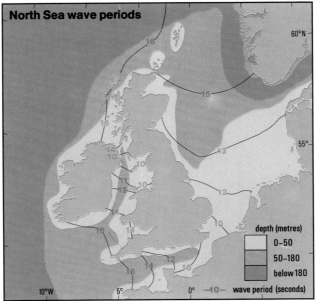
North Sea wave periods

depth (metres)
0–50
50–180
below 180
—10— wave period (seconds)

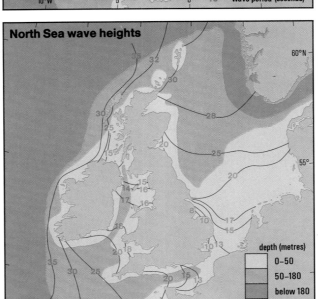
North Sea wave heights

depth (metres)
0–50
50–180
below 180
—16— wave height (metres)

5 *and* **6** *below* Graphs such as these are used by engineers to calculate wave periods and heights in relation to speed and fetch or duration of wind on the open ocean. For example, a surface wind of 40 knots with a fetch of 50 nm will give a wave period of 10 seconds and height of 22 feet (6.7 m). Where the wind speed is 40 knots and duration only 2 hours, the wave height will be 14 feet (4 m), regardless of fetch.

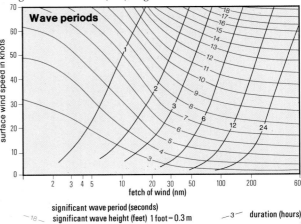
Wave periods

significant wave period (seconds)
significant wave height (feet) 1 foot = 0.3 m
duration (hours)

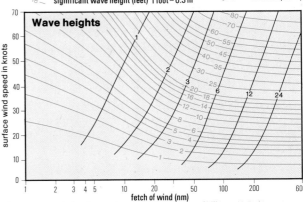
Wave heights

7 *above left* and **8** *left* Wave periods and heights that recur in the North Sea on average once every fifty years in a fully-developed twelve-hour storm. These values are derived from instrumental measurements and estimates based on wind data. Knowledge of such extreme conditions is important in the building of structures such as offshore platforms which are designed to withstand exceptional waves.

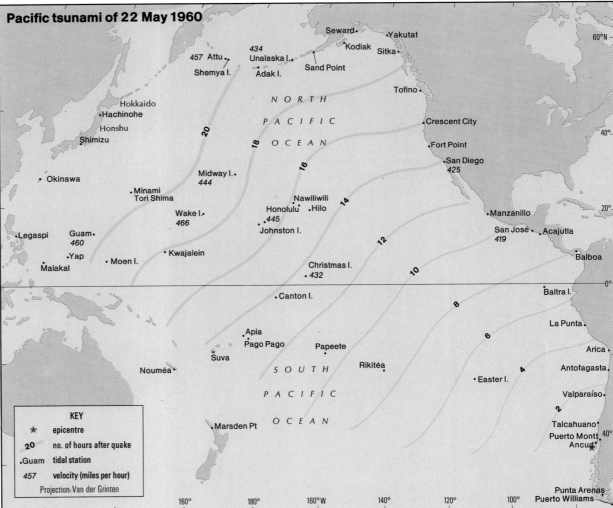
Pacific tsunami of 22 May 1960

KEY
★ epicentre
20 no. of hours after quake
.Guam tidal station
457 velocity (miles per hour)
Projection: Van der Grinten

9 *above* On 22 May 1960 an earthquake of exceptional intensity affected southern Chile, and though local damage was severe it was little compared to the trail of havoc that swept the Pacific during the following 24 hours. Minutes after the earthquake, massive

10 *left* The remains of wooden houses in the Philippines which were destroyed by a tsunami in August 1976.

waves broke along the Chilean coast and hundreds of people were killed at Ancud and Puerto Montt. About 15 hours later the tsunami hit the Hawaiian Islands. They suffered severe flooding and damage along waterfronts and hotels were badly affected along the famous Waikiki beach. The wave increased both in size and speed as it propagated and it was Japan, over 10 000 miles away from the original disturbance, which suffered the worst effects, many lives being lost along the coast of Hokkaido and Honshu.

Tides and surges

TIDES, the alternating rise and fall of sea level due to the gravitational pull of the Sun and the Moon, occur in all seas and oceans and the associated water movements can be observed on all coasts of the world. These movements take the form of currents and periodic oscillations of water level. The currents vary in strength and direction according to the state of the tide, and both currents and oscillations vary in magnitude from day to day and from place to place.

Tidal characteristics do not conform to any simple pattern. On a shelving beach the dominant pattern is one of ebb and flow while on a steep coast the most conspicuous tidal feature is a regular rise and fall of water level. Off some coasts tidal currents are imperceptible while in estuaries and straits they can be very strong.

The complex behaviour of the tides is still not fully understood. Though the relative motions of the Sun, the Moon and the Earth, and the gravitational forces exerted by the Sun and the Moon on the Earth, can be estimated with some precision, the exact prediction of oceanic responses to these forces presents a problem which has so far proved intractable. Nevertheless, tidal behaviour can be forecast sufficiently accurately to be

of practical value. The tide tables for a locality are constructed from astronomical data and from analyses of previous tidal times and heights in that locality.

The force exerted by the Moon upon the oceans is more than twice that exerted by the Sun so oceanic tidal responses owe more to the Moon's influence than the Sun's. It is because of the dominant lunar influence that tides occur fifty minutes later than on the previous day, for the interval between consecutive meridian passages of the Moon is 24 hours 50 minutes. Where the solar influence is dominant, as at Tahiti, tides occur at the same time each day.

The tide-generating force of the Sun and Moon is modified by the shape of the oceans. A body of water contained in an ocean basin possesses an inherent natural frequency of oscillation which is determined by the shape and dimensions of the basin and depth of water. If this frequency is the same as one of the principal harmonics of the tide-generating force, resonance occurs, amplifying further the rise and fall of the tides. The largest tidal ranges are found in the bays, gulfs and estuaries of the oceans where resonance occurs. In the Severn Estuary in Britain the range

exceeds 13 m and in the Bay of Fundy, Nova Scotia, it sometimes tops 16 m. Schemes already exist for harnessing the tidal energy in some waters, for example La Rance, Brittany (see *Renewable energy* page 120).

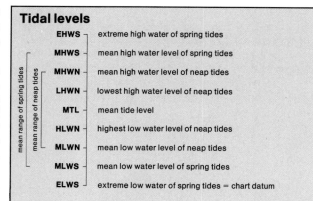

Tidal levels

EHWS	extreme high water of spring tides
MHWS	mean high water level of spring tides
MHWN	mean high water level of neap tides
LHWN	lowest high water level of neap tides
MTL	mean tide level
HLWN	highest low water level of neap tides
MLWN	mean low water level of neap tides
MLWS	mean low water level of spring tides
ELWS	extreme low water of spring tides = chart datum

mean range of spring tides
mean range of neap tides

1 There is a fortnightly cycle of tidal heights on all coasts. The tides of greatest range are called spring tides and those of smallest range neap tides. Tidal levels are defined in the diagram. Mean levels are calculated by taking the tides over a two-day period; average levels over a period of a fortnight or more.

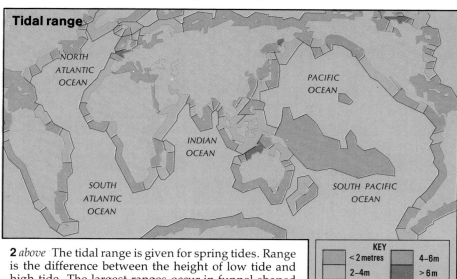

Tidal range

NORTH ATLANTIC OCEAN — PACIFIC OCEAN — INDIAN OCEAN — SOUTH ATLANTIC OCEAN — SOUTH PACIFIC OCEAN

KEY

< 2 metres		4–6m	
2–4m		>6m	

Tidal types

NORTH ATLANTIC OCEAN — Immingham — San Francisco — PACIFIC OCEAN — Do-son — Manila — INDIAN OCEAN — SOUTH ATLANTIC OCEAN — SOUTH PACIFIC OCEAN

KEY

diurnal		mixed
semi–diurnal		• tidal example

2 *above* The tidal range is given for spring tides. Range is the difference between the height of low tide and high tide. The largest ranges occur in funnel-shaped bays while on open ocean coasts the range is typically only 2–3 m. Spring tides are largest during spring and autumn; the smallest tides occur in summer and winter. Enclosed seas are almost tideless.

4 *below* Co-tidal lines are isolines which join places where high tide occurs simultaneously. The points where sea level remains constant are known as am-

phidromic points. Tidal ranges increase outwards from these points though precise values are largely unknown except on coasts.

3 *above right* Three types of tide can be distinguished on the world's coasts. Where there is a cycle of one high tide and one low tide every 24 hours 50 minutes,

as around Vietnam and in the Caribbean, the tide is said to be diurnal. Where there are two cycles in that period and the heights of high and low water vary little from one cycle to the next, as on most Atlantic Ocean coasts, the tide is said to be semi-diurnal. On some coasts tidal cycles are more complex and combine characteristics of both diurnal and semi-diurnal patterns. These tides are referred to as mixed and occur mainly on Pacific and Indian Ocean coasts. Examples of typical tidal curves are given in **5** *opposite page top* for the four locations shown on the map.

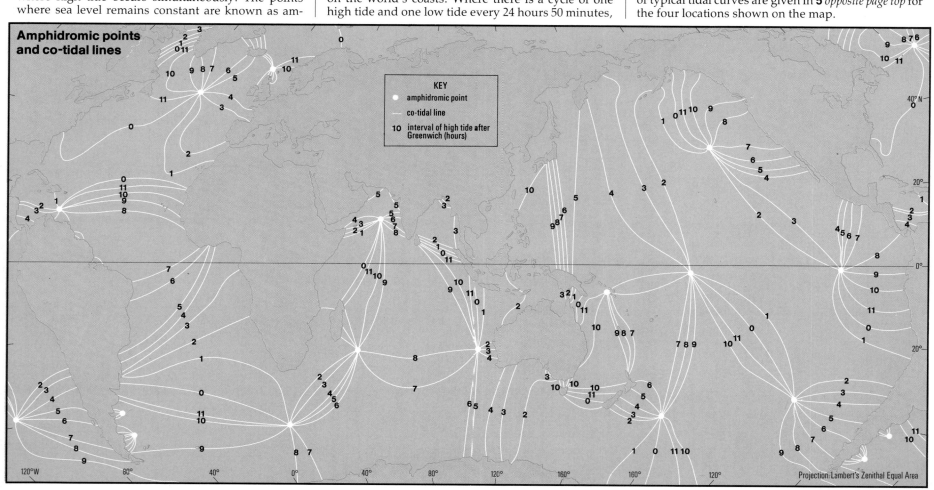

Amphidromic points and co-tidal lines

KEY

- ● amphidromic point
- — co-tidal line
- **10** interval of high tide after Greenwich (hours)

Projection: Lambert's Zenithal Equal Area

Tidal curves

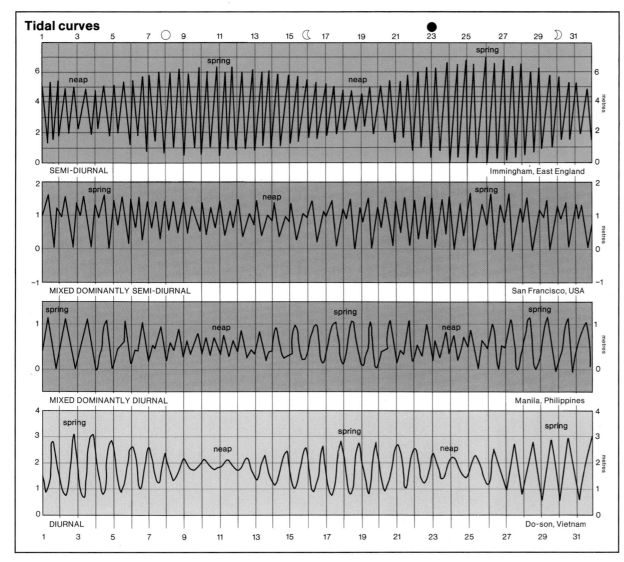

SEMI-DIURNAL — Immingham, East England

MIXED DOMINANTLY SEMI-DIURNAL — San Francisco, USA

MIXED DOMINANTLY DIURNAL — Manila, Philippines

DIURNAL — Do-son, Vietnam

North Sea tides

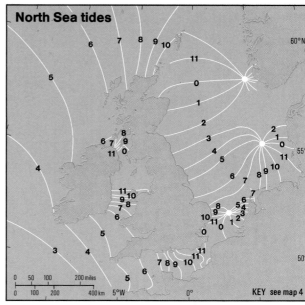

KEY see map 4

6 *above* The North and Irish Seas show a pattern as complex as the large oceans. The North Sea has three amphidromic systems. In the Irish Sea and English Channel, on the other hand, there are no amphidromic points. The co-tidal lines on the map are labelled in hours in relation to high water at Greenwich occurring at 0 hours.

5 *left* These tidal curves from four locations illustrate the typical tidal types. Tidal height varies with the phases of the Moon and with the changing declinations of the Sun and the Moon, so that fortnightly and semi-annual cycles of tidal height occur. Spring tides generally do not coincide with full moons and new moons. In some localities spring tides lag behind them, in others they precede them. This curious behaviour of the oceans remains unexplained.

Surges

Abnormal meteorological conditions cause the observed tide at a given place and time to differ from the computed astronomical tide. Strong winds can drive water towards or away from coasts, and variations of atmospheric pressure are accompanied by fluctuations of sea level. Of these two factors the first is the more significant, for severe gales are capable of raising or lowering coastal water levels by two or three metres, whereas atmospheric pressure variations alter sea level at the rate of only one centimetre per millibar. A raising of water level is known as a positive surge and a lowering as a negative surge.

Only on coasts and in shallow water are surges of any practical significance. Positive surges can give rise to flooding while negative surges can present navigational hazards to mariners, especially in the southern North Sea where traffic of deep-draught ships has grown in recent years.

Certain coastal areas are particularly susceptible to inundation. In the Netherlands and eastern England, for example, some stretches of coast have been flooded repeatedly, and on the Atlantic seaboard of the United States, the coasts of the Gulf of Mexico, at the head of the Bay of Bengal, and along the Pacific seaboard of Japan, surges raised by tropical cyclones constitute a recurrent danger (see *Cyclone and hurricane disasters* page 54).

Surge residual in the North Sea

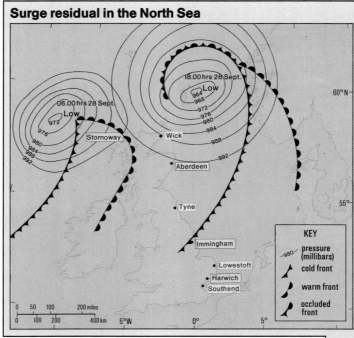

KEY
—980— pressure (millibars)
cold front
warm front
occluded front

7 *above and right* The storm surge of 28–29 September 1969 was initiated by a deep depression moving in a north-easterly direction. In Scotland, winds of 90 knots were recorded. The diagram shows the differences between actual and astronomically predicted water levels. It illustrates how a positive surge is preceded by a negative surge, and how the amplitude of a North Sea surge increases as it propagates.

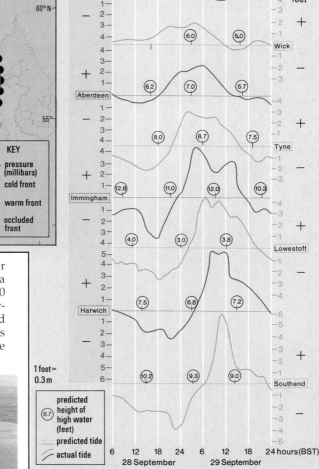

1 foot = 0.3 m

predicted height of high water (feet)

---- predicted tide
—— actual tide

8 *left* Aerial view of works in progress on the Eastern Scheldt storm surge barrier. In 1953, a devastating tidal surge caused extensive flooding and loss of life along the North Sea coasts of England and in the Netherlands. To protect the polders and other low lying areas of land in the south-west Netherlands, the Dutch Government started the Delta Project consisting of a series of ten dams and tidal barriers. The Eastern Scheldt storm surge barrier presently under construction is a part of the Delta Project. It will consist of three man-made islands and 63 concrete piers supporting steel sluice gates which may be closed to prevent flooding. The barrier will be 9 km in length. For ecological reasons a barrier with sluices which open and shut was preferred to a fixed dam.

The polar oceans

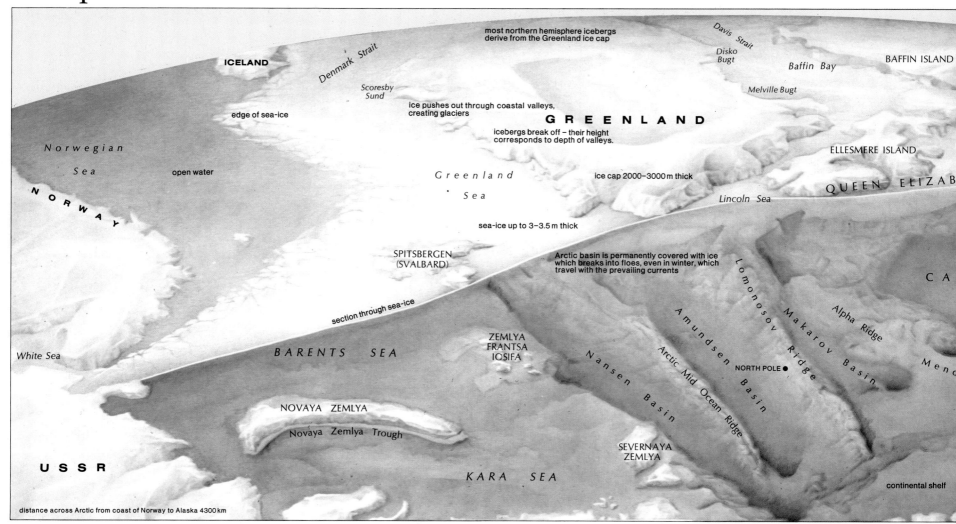

distance across Arctic from coast of Norway to Alaska 4300 km

THE Arctic and Antarctic regions are physically dissimilar. The Arctic Basin contains an ocean 12.2 million sq. km in area which is largely covered by a skin of ice some 3–3.5 m thick, and is almost encircled by land areas. Antarctica, in contrast, is a continent (or perhaps an archipelago) surrounded by oceans, and buried beneath an ice sheet, the surface area of which is about 13.5 million sq. km, average thickness approximately 2 km. More than 90 per cent of the Earth's permanent ice is contained in this ice sheet. The belt of sea ice surrounding the continent is broadly similar to that in the Arctic Ocean, although Arctic ice exists in more complex forms and can survive longer because of the ocean's relatively small size and landlocked situation.

The combination of cold air, high winds and snow make Antarctica's climate the severest in the world. The annual mean temperature along the coast is −30°C and only during summer (December to March) does the temperature ever rise above freezing point. In the Arctic, on the other hand, temperatures during summer (May to July) rise to well above freezing, especially in coastal areas of the bordering continents.

1 *above* The Greenland ice-cap, which covers an area of 1.8 million sq. km and is more than 3 km thick in places, contains about 90 per cent of all land-ice in the northern hemisphere and accounts for more than 90 per cent of all icebergs of the Arctic region, the only other noteworthy sources being the glaciers of Svalbard, Novaya Zemlya, Severnaya Zemlya and Zemlya Frantsa-Iosifa. While a number of bergs stem from Greenland's east coast glaciers, particularly those near Scoresby Sund, the majority are derived from glaciers terminating on the west coast, particularly those which discharge into Disko Bugt and Melville Bugt.

The belt of sea-ice distributed about the North Pole is markedly asymmetric, reflecting the influence of ocean currents. For example, coastal waters and fjords

The Antarctic and the Southern Ocean

Projection: Polar Zenithal

KEY
surface current
permanent ice
land above present sea level

mean minimum ice
mean maximum ice

Antarctica, showing view through the sea-ice to the continental shelves and deep ocean floor, and section through the ice cap revealing land contours

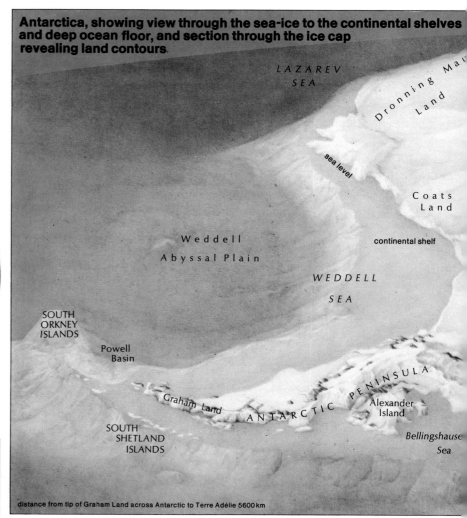

distance from tip of Graham Land across Antarctic to Terre Adélie 5600 km

View of the Arctic Ocean basin showing the sea floor beneath the polar ice and waters

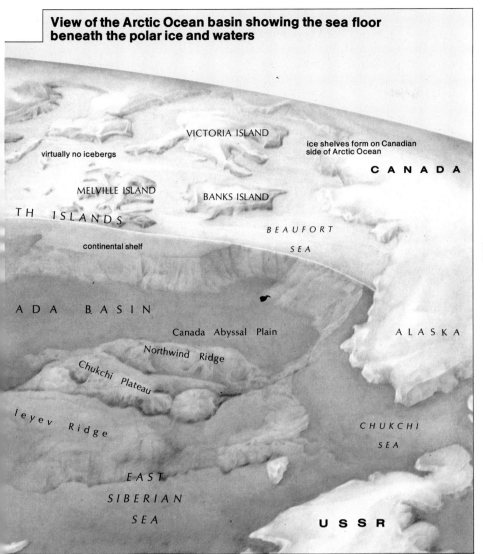

VICTORIA ISLAND

virtually no icebergs

ice shelves form on Canadian side of Arctic Ocean

C A N A D A

MELVILLE ISLAND   BANKS ISLAND

TH ISLANDS

B E A U F O R T
S E A

continental shelf

A D A   B A S I N

Canada Abyssal Plain

Northwind Ridge

Chukchi Plateau

A L A S K A

leyev Ridge

C H U K C H I
S E A

E A S T
S I B E R I A N
S E A

U S S R

Arctic Ocean

180°

Bering
Strait   Arctic Circle

Alaska   CHUKCHI
SEA   EAST
SIBERIAN
SEA

BEAUFORT
SEA

C A N A D A   Amundsen Gulf   A R C T I C   Novosibirskiye
Ostrova

Victoria I.   Prince Patrick I.   LAPTEV
SEA   U S S R

Prince of
Wales I.   Melville I.   O C E A N
Axel Helberg I.

90°W   Somerset I.   NORTH POLE   Severnaya
Zemlya   90°E

FOXE BASIN   Gulf of Boothia   Ellesmere I.   KARA SEA

Nares Strait   Lincoln Sea   Zemlya
Frantsa
Iosifa   Novaya
Zemlya

BAFFIN
BAY   Wandels Sea

Baffin I.

Svalbard   BARENTS
SEA
Beloye More

Greenland   GREENLAND
SEA

Davis Strait   Scoresby Sound

Denmark Strait   NORWEGIAN
SEA

0°

Projection: Polar Zenithal

KEY

- surface current
- ice drift
- permanent ice
- absolute maximum ice
- mean maximum ice
- mean minimum ice

of Norway remain open to shipping throughout the year, even well to the north of the Arctic Circle, whereas the coast of eastern Greenland is inaccessible to unassisted shipping for all but a brief period in summer. Moreover, the east coast of North America is normally ice-bound as far south as latitude 45°N in late winter; in a severe winter ice may stretch almost to Cape Hatteras (35°10′N).

An area of 6 million sq. km is permanently covered with multi-year pack ice (the Arctic pack) in which the ice concentration is everywhere greater than 70 per cent of the water surface; its average thickness is 2.5–4 m at the end of winter, and 1.5–3 m at the end of summer. Surrounding the Arctic pack is a field of loosely connected ice-floes; here the concentration is more than 40 per cent.

Drifting with the Arctic pack and floes are icebergs and ice-islands. The greatest average thickness of ice on the Arctic Ocean, approximately 3.5 m, occurs on the Beaufort Sea. Ice tends to converge on this area, resulting in the formation of a large number of ridges and hummocks. In contrast ice tends to be relatively thin along the Eurasian continental shelf line, a consequence of considerable water turbulence.

2 *below* The Antarctic coastline is in places formed by an ice shelf, the seaward extension of the ice sheet. This shelf, which attains a height of nearly 100 m above sea-level, is constantly being pushed seawards by the inland ice which, slowly, a metre or so per day, is forced outwards by pressure of weight of the ice above it from the central plateau towards the Southern Ocean. The Ross Ice Shelf (Ross Sea) and the Filchner–Ronne Ice Shelf (Weddell Sea) are especially noteworthy for their huge size.

Surrounding Antarctica and its ice shelves is pack ice. This covers 25.5 million sq. km at its maximum extent (September); its seasonal variation is about 75 per cent of this maximum. The action of wind and current carries the ice to the warmer waters of the Southern Ocean, so that pack ice is usually younger than its Arctic counterpart. Only in a few areas, such as the Weddell and Bellingshausen seas, where winds and currents drive ice on to coasts, is second- or multi-year pack ice commonly found.

Close to the continent, first-year ice is usually 2.75 m thick and multi-year ice more than 10 m thick. Pressure ridges and hummocks do occur but they are, in general, not as massive as those in the Arctic, largely because movements of sea-ice in the Southern Ocean are relatively unrestricted.

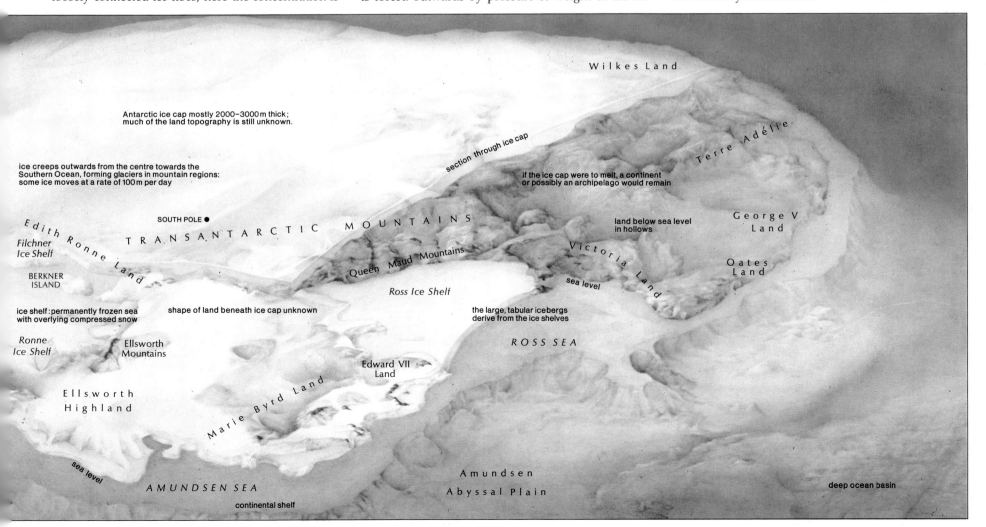

Antarctic ice cap mostly 2000–3000 m thick; much of the land topography is still unknown.

Wilkes Land

section through ice cap

Terre Adélie

ice creeps outwards from the centre towards the Southern Ocean, forming glaciers in mountain regions: some ice moves at a rate of 100 m per day

if the ice cap were to melt, a continent or possibly an archipelago would remain

SOUTH POLE ●

George V
Land

Edith Ronne Land

T R A N S A N T A R C T I C   M O U N T A I N S

land below sea level
in hollows

Filchner
Ice Shelf

Victoria Land

Oates
Land

BERKNER
ISLAND

Queen Maud Mountains

sea level

ice shelf: permanently frozen sea with overlying compressed snow

shape of land beneath ice cap unknown

Ross Ice Shelf

the large, tabular icebergs derive from the ice shelves

Ronne
Ice Shelf   Ellsworth
Mountains

Edward VII
Land

R O S S   S E A

Ellsworth
Highland

Marie Byrd Land

sea level

A M U N D S E N   S E A

Amundsen
Abyssal Plain

continental shelf

deep ocean basin

The icy surface

ICE in the polar regions exists as frozen sea-water (sea-ice) which in winter forms extensive pack ice, or as freshwater glaciers on or attached to land. Icebergs are fragments of these glaciers, calved in spring and summer melting seasons. The polar glaciers contain the major part of the world's fresh water. Although icebergs are a serious hazard to navigation, sea-ice constitutes the chief hindrance to shipping in high latitudes, particularly in river estuaries and harbours.

1 *below* Greenland's east coast bergs are carried south by the East Greenland Current and drift into the Davis Strait, where most of them melt. West coast bergs first travel in a counterclockwise direction around the head of Baffin Bay and then drift south to reach the shipping lanes and the warm waters of the Gulf Stream near Newfoundland during spring months. As the bergs drift, their numbers constantly decrease by grounding or melting and relatively few reach the Grand Banks.

Wind, waves, currents, tides and snow-cover all affect the formation of sea-ice. The first visible sign of freezing is minute crystals of pure ice or 'frazil'; these soon become hexagonal discs about 2.5 cm across and up to 1 mm thick. Wind and wave action cause the ice crystals to assume a variety of configurations which strengthens the ice. Waves and swell also cause the ice to fragment into angular pieces up to a few metres across which then collide, becoming rounded with raised rims. These 'pancakes' adhere to form a continuous sheet.

Constant atmospheric pressures and oceanic motions cause ice fields to fracture and floes to drive together into ridges and hummocks, which may extend 6 or 7 m above and 20–30 m below the water surface. In the Arctic more than 10 per cent of the ice cover is ridged or hummocked.

The melting of an ice cover can be rapid; a cover 2 m thick can melt completely in six weeks. Due to prevailing winds, even in winter about 10 per cent of the Arctic is open water, with leads or 'polynyas' running through the ice pack.

Arctic icebergs are mainly of the 'glacier' type and derive chiefly from Greenland—as many as 12 000–15 000 annually. These bergs can be as much as 70 m high at calving (170 m above sea level has been recorded) and over 1000 m long.

The colour of Arctic bergs ranges from white, with soft hues of green or blue, to browns and black. Many have veins of soil or debris. A different type of Arctic berg has blocky, precipitous sides with a flat top and, though much smaller, is most like the typical Antarctic 'tabular' berg. 'Ice islands', a special form of Arctic berg, originate from ice shelves at North Ellesmere Island and North Greenland. They stand about 5 m out of the water and are 200 m thick. Ice islands may

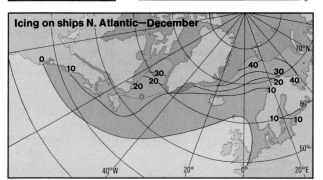

Iceberg movements North Atlantic

East Greenland Current

Labrador Current

Grand Banks

▲ Titanic 1912

▲ March 1921

▲ June 1926

Bermuda

Azores ▲ July 1921

KEY
annual iceberg southerly extent (estimated max.)
iceberg track
▲ unusual iceberg sighting

Iceberg sightings North Atlantic
approx. 200 icebergs sighted south of 48°N annually

Jan Feb Mar Apr May June July Aug Sept Oct Nov Dec

Icing on ships N. Atlantic—December

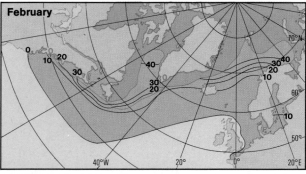

February

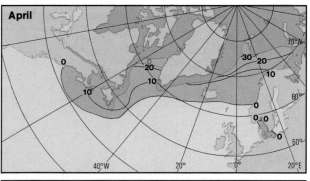

April

KEY
30 probable frequency moderate icing (per cent)
0 possibility of severe icing
average ice concentration more than 50 per cent

Projection: Conic

How icebergs are formed

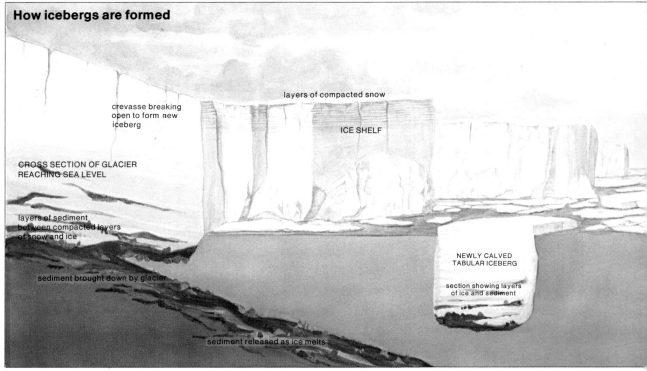

layers of compacted snow

crevasse breaking open to form new iceberg

ICE SHELF

CROSS SECTION OF GLACIER REACHING SEA LEVEL

layers of sediment between compacted layers of snow and ice

sediment brought down by glacier

sediment released as ice melts

NEWLY CALVED TABULAR ICEBERG

section showing layers of ice and sediment

Superstructure icing on ships

Superstructure icing jeopardises the safety of ships and probably constitutes the greatest danger to the lives of mariners navigating in extremely cold regions. Ice raises the centre of gravity of a vessel, reducing its stability; it increases the area exposed to wind and hence the heeling moment due to wind action; and it adversely affects steerability and alters trim. A vessel heavily coated with ice is, therefore, liable to become unstable and capsize.

The amount of icing depends upon air temperature, sea temperature, wind strength, sea state (a function of wind strength), the vessel's speed in relation to wind and sea, the duration of icing conditions and construction of the vessel affected. In extreme conditions ice can accumulate at more than 4 tonnes per hour on a 500-tonne trawler.

Ice accretion can occur on any vessel, but those with low freeboards and large top hampers are most at risk. Disasters have occurred mainly with trawlers, whalers and sailing ships, but ice may also form on offshore platforms such as drilling rigs. Although it is rare for the safety or stability of rigs to be seriously threatened, topside working conditions may become treacherous.

Shipboard icing from freezing rain, drizzle or fog can be dangerous, particularly underfoot. However, the largest accumulations of ice occur in heavy seas when sea-spray freezes on decks and superstructure. Snowfall aggravates the situation. The washing of hull plates clean by the sea adds to the problem, because the vessel is thereby made even more top-heavy.

3 *left and* **5** *opposite* The figures for potential icing on ships are based on the following air temperatures and wind speeds: N. Atlantic moderate icing, below −2°C, above 6.5 m/sec; severe icing, below −9°C, above 15.5 m/sec; Southern Ocean, below −2°C, above 8.5 m/sec. In the open ocean where the salinity of surface water is in the range of 30 to 35‰ (parts per thousand), ice forms only when the air temperature is below about −2°C (see *The salt sea* following pages). In the Baltic Sea, on the other hand, where salinities are much lower ice forms at a higher air temperature.

Thus, ice-growth relationships for the Baltic and the open ocean differ considerably.

On the fishing grounds of the Davis Strait, the Labrador Sea, the Denmark Strait, the Greenland Sea, the Barents Sea and northern parts of the Norwegian Sea, conditions suitable for the formation of moderate superstructure icing occur mainly between November and April, while severe icing normally occurs only in January and February. Icing is also a threat on the Sea of Okhotsk and northern parts of the Sea of Japan during winter months. Around Antarctica and close to the Arctic pack-ice, suitable conditions for at least moderate icing can occur at all times of year.

4 *below* Severe superstructure icing during winter in the Baltic Sea.

survive up to 30 years. They consist of old ice which is so tough that explosives are necessary if ships are to penetrate. Less formidable, but of great danger to shipping, are 'bergy bits' (floating pieces of ice up to 5 m above surface level and 10 m across) and their smaller relations, called 'growlers' (where the ice is almost awash).

The Antarctic ice shelves are remarkably free from undulations, so the icebergs calved from them are flat-topped and rectangular in vertical cross-section, unlike the more conical Arctic bergs. Production of Antarctic icebergs is probably tens of thousands per year. Most are no more than a few kilometres long when newly calved. They have a peculiar white colour and lustre due to a relatively high air content. The number of bergs freed varies in different years or periods of years. The calving of very large tabular bergs may result from disturbances caused by underwater movements of the Earth's crust or by tremors originating in Antarctica.

2 Icebergs are calved from glacier tongues or from ice shelves attached to land. The volume submerged is approximately 90 per cent while the depth under water compared with height above varies with type and shape of berg. Icebergs diminish by further calving, melting and erosion.

When a piece breaks off, the berg's equilibrium is disturbed and it may topple over. In cold water melting takes place mainly at the water line, and in warmer water mainly from below, causing the berg to calve frequently. Erosion is from wind and rain.

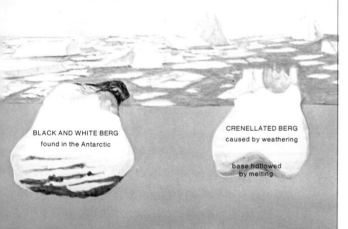

BLACK AND WHITE BERG
found in the Antarctic

CRENELLATED BERG
caused by weathering

base hollowed
by melting

Icing on ships S. Ocean—February

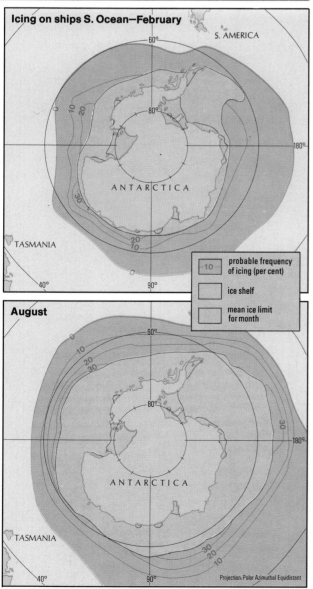

S. AMERICA

ANTARCTICA

TASMANIA

August

ANTARCTICA

TASMANIA

Projection: Polar Azimuthal Equidistant

probable frequency
of icing (per cent)

ice shelf

mean ice limit
for month

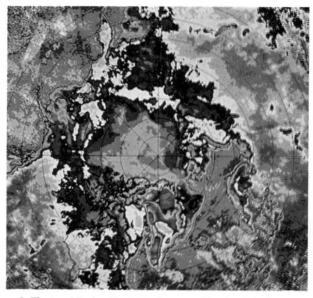

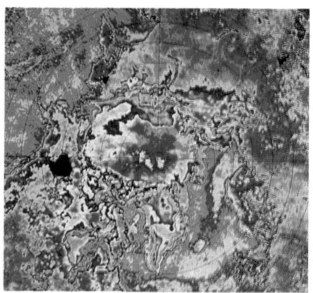

6 The two Nimbus 5 satellite images of the Arctic for January *above* and July *above right* (and similarly Antarctica and the Southern Ocean **7** *right*) record a characteristic called 'brightness temperature', that is a combination of the ice sheet's temperature and its reflectivity.
In January, the Arctic ice (light and dark browns) has extended south to cover northern Canada, Siberia and Greenland. In July the ocean remains largely frozen over, though the green areas round the north of Scandinavia and USSR coast show ice-free sea.
Note also the interior of Greenland which appears as water rather than yellow/pink land.

8 *below* Near their sources Antarctic icebergs typically drift in a west-north-west direction. Their tracks then become progressively more northerly; below about 63°S they come under the influence of the eastward-setting currents of the Southern Ocean. Bergs have been sighted off the Cape of Good Hope and the southern coasts of Tasmania and New Zealand; one has been seen as far north as latitude 26°S in the South Atlantic Ocean. Only near the tip of South America do icebergs present any significant threat on regular shipping routes.

Southern Ocean iceberg limits

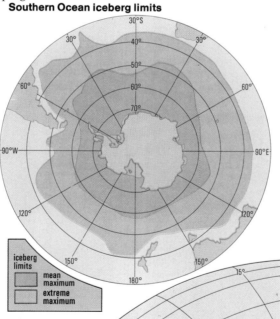

iceberg
limits

mean
maximum

extreme
maximum

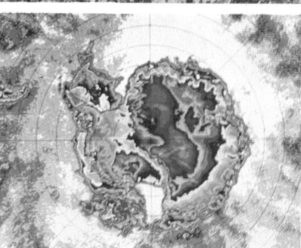

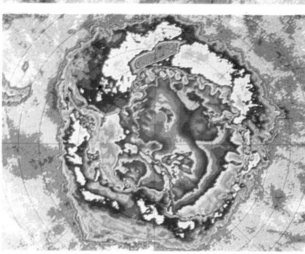

7 In the Southern Ocean in January *centre* the ice sheet is at its minimum extent, the great irregularities caused by the circumpolar current. In winter (August) *above* the pack ice stretches over a vast area.

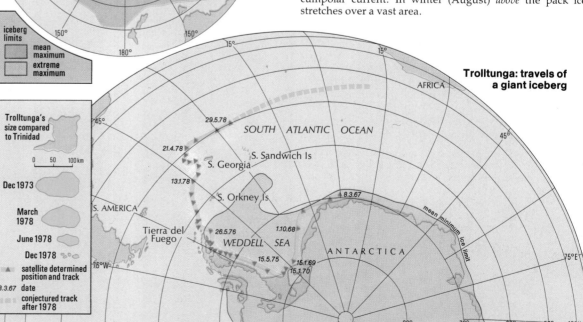

Trolltunga: travels of a giant iceberg

Trolltunga's
size compared
to Trinidad

Dec 1973

March
1978

June 1978

Dec 1978

satellite determined
position and track

conjectured track
after 1978

SOUTH ATLANTIC OCEAN
AFRICA
S. Sandwich Is
S. Georgia
S. Orkney Is
S. AMERICA
Tierra del
Fuego
WEDDELL SEA
ANTARCTICA

9 *above* The *Trolltunga* iceberg was discovered and intermittently tracked by satellite in 1967. It was then over 100 km in length and about 5000 sq. km in surface area. It appeared to have broken from an ice tongue at 69.5°S, 1°W some time in 1967. It became grounded just off the Filchner ice shelf in May 1969, and remained there until February 1975, when it started to drift again with the ice pack. Within two years it reached the north-east tip of the Antarctic peninsula,

and it then measured about 92 × 50 km. By March 1978 it was close to South Georgia. In May 1978 its dimensions were 56 × 23 km. However, *Trolltunga* soon began to disintegrate and by December 1978, when it was last sighted at 43°S, 11°E, it had become little more than a collection of small bergs.

The salt sea

SEA water is a complex solution in which approximately 80 naturally occurring elements have so far been detected. Over 99.5 per cent of the total dissolved matter in sea water is made up of chloride, sulphate, bromide, bicarbonate, sodium, potassium, calcium and magnesium, in the form of electrically charged ions. The remainder consists of very small amounts of nutrients, such as phosphate, silicate and nitrogen compounds, which are essential for marine animals and plant life. Dissolved atmospheric gases are also present. (See also *Sea water as a resource* page 118.)

Salts are washed into the sea by rivers, and they fall into the sea in precipitation. They are also introduced into the oceans from the Earth's crust at the ridges on the sea bed which are centres of sea floor spreading (see page 32).

Salinity may be regarded as the number of grams of salts dissolved in a kilogram of sea water. It is expressed in parts per thousand (‰) by weight. Although salinity varies considerably from place to place, the relative proportions of elements remain almost constant. This means the salinity of a sample of sea water can be calculated from the concentration of any one of the major constituents. Because electrically charged ions are present in sea water it is a good conductor of electricity, and its electrical resistance can be used to measure its salinity. In fact, this method is now used to define salinity.

Salinity is reduced by addition of fresh water: the melting of icebergs and glaciers, river runoff and rainfall. Some salts, such as calcium, are extracted by marine creatures for building shells and skeletons. Evaporation removes fresh water, thus increasing salinity. But the chemical balance of the oceans is not yet fully understood by scientists.

In the open ocean, where there is little influence from river runoff, salinity remains relatively constant. Such variations as there are reflect regional precipitation–evaporation patterns and the effects of ocean currents.

Density is a measure of the weight of a substance in a given volume. It is commonly expressed in kilograms per cubic metre (kg/m³). Together with temperature and pressure, salinity determines the density of sea water: density increases with increasing salinity. Thus, salinity has physical as well as chemical and biological significance, for large-scale circulations in the oceans result from density contrasts between water masses. It also has practical significance because the dependence of buoyancy upon water density relates to the loadline regulations which govern the limits of legal submersion of ships according to density distributions in the uppermost layer of the sea (see *Weather hazards for shipping* page 160).

February salinity

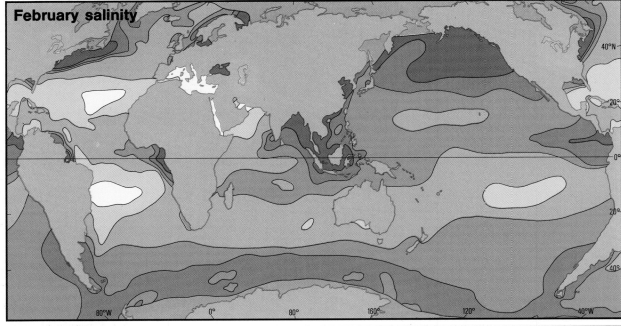

Elements dissolved in sea water

The total quantity of solids dissolved in the oceans is estimated to be about 5000 million million tonnes. The most abundant elements dissolved in sea water are sodium and chlorine, accounting between them for a little over 85 per cent of the weight of all solid substances dissolved in the sea. Sulphate, magnesium, calcium and potassium ions also occur in substantial quantities. Theoretically, all the naturally occurring elements should be contained in the sea, because they are brought from the land by rivers or from the Earth's crust by volcanic activity. Concentrations of the majority of the constituents of sea water are extremely small. Indeed, some are present only as traces and cannot be detected by direct chemical analysis of sea water. Their existence in the sea has been inferred from their presence in marine plants and animals, which possess the ability to extract the substances and concentrate them. Despite their minute concentrations, some trace elements are of great importance. For example, the oceans are our only source of iodine, an element vital to human metabolism.

3 *below* In these salterns in the San Francisco Bay area, salt is extracted from evaporating seawater. The salt precipitates on to the floors of the pools and is later gathered for distribution.

1 *left* and **2** *below* The maps show variations in surface salinity for February and August. The most saline water occurs in the largely landlocked seas adjacent to the arid regions of North Africa, where there is a considerable excess of evaporation over precipitation and river runoff. Salinity values exceed 40 parts per thousand by weight (40‰) in the northern half of the Red Sea and 38‰ in the Mediterranean Sea east of Sicily. High salinity also occurs in ocean areas dominated by subtropical anticyclones and trade winds where precipitation is scanty and evaporation is rapid.

Salinity values are lower where precipitation is plentiful, in regions affected by the Intertropical Convergence Zone and extratropical depressions. The least saline water is found in the areas which receive large discharges of river water. For example, off the west coast of Africa, salinities of less than 20‰ are recorded in the Bight of Biafra. Values are also comparatively low in high latitudes, where dilution is due not only to an excess of precipitation over evaporation but also to the availability of meltwater from ice. Salinity values are particularly low in the Black Sea and the Baltic Sea.

Away from coastal influences salinity varies comparatively little, both spatially and seasonally. In the surface waters of the open Atlantic Ocean values range from about 34‰ to a little over 37‰ and in the Pacific and Indian Oceans they range from about 32.5‰ to 36.5‰.

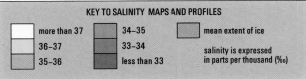

KEY TO SALINITY MAPS AND PROFILES		
more than 37	34–35	mean extent of ice
36–37	33–34	salinity is expressed in parts per thousand (‰)
35–36	less than 33	

August salinity

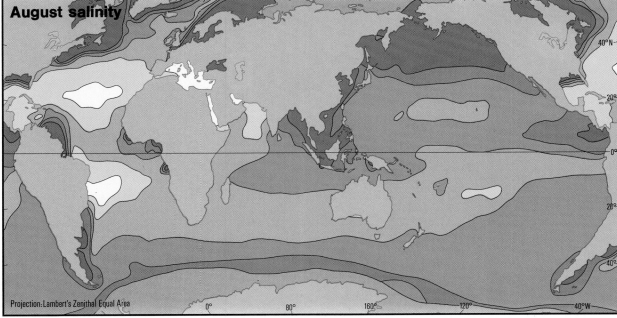

Projection: Lambert's Zenithal Equal Area

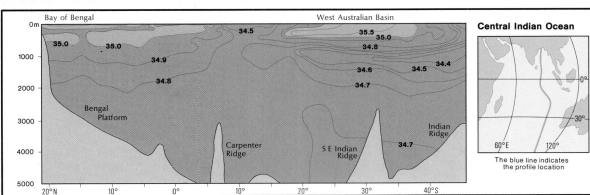

Central Indian Ocean

The blue line indicates the profile location

Density variations

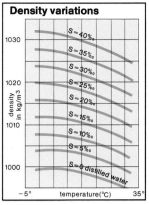

4 *right* For a given temperature and salinity, the density of sea water can be determined. For example, at a temperature of 10°C and salinity 35‰, the density is about 1027 kg/m³. Pure water (salinity = 0) has its maximum density at a temperature of 4°C. The temperature of maximum density decreases as salinity increases.

5 *right and* **6** *below* In the southern hemisphere there is a broadly zonal variation of density. The most dense water is found in the Antarctic, where values exceed 1027.8 kg/m³, and the least dense water off Indonesia (less than 1020 kg/m³). In the northern hemisphere density also tends to increase gradually from high to low latitudes, but there are exceptions.

In the Norwegian Sea during summer months density is maximum in the North Atlantic Drift Current

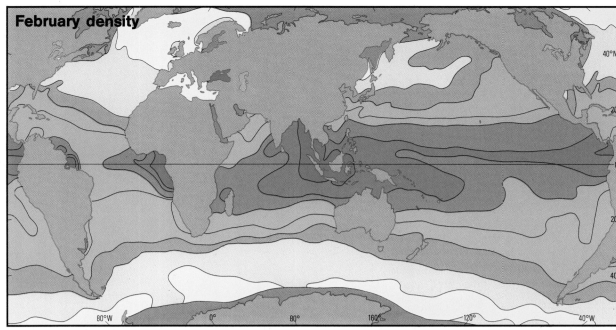

February density

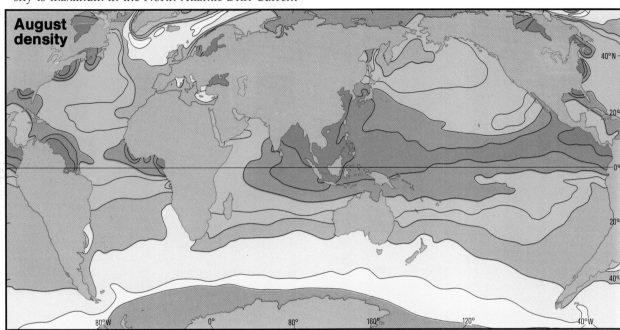

August density

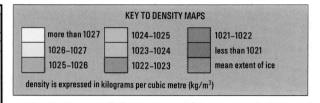

KEY TO DENSITY MAPS

more than 1027	1024–1025	1021–1022
1026–1027	1023–1024	less than 1021
1025–1026	1022–1023	mean extent of ice

density is expressed in kilograms per cubic metre (kg/m³)

and minimum off the coasts of Norway and Greenland. This is due to a plentiful supply of meltwater off these coasts during summer. The East Greenland Current contains melting sea ice and the glaciers of Norway and Greenland also provide meltwater.

The least dense sea water in the world is found in the Baltic Sea. In northern parts of the Gulf of Bothnia in summer the surface density falls to below 1003 kg/m³.

Water of low density also occurs in low latitudes off the deltas of the great rivers; for example, off the Irrawaddy Delta during the south-west monsoon values are less than 1015 kg/m³. In contrast, very dense surface water forms in the eastern half of the Mediterranean Sea during winter (more than 1029 kg/m³). The most dense water is found in deep ocean trenches, where it is compressed slightly, so raising its density to about 1070 kg/m³.

7–11 *bottom left, below and right* These salinity profiles show vertical variations of salinity. Locations of the ocean cross-sections are shown on the right of the profiles. Only in the surface waters of the sea is there much variation in salinity, and all the oceans follow this same general trend; the bulk of water is fairly homogeneous. Below a depth of 1000 m salinity values exceed 35.2‰ only in the tongue of water which flows from the Mediterranean Sea into the North Atlantic; below 4000 m salinity is almost constant. Surface salinities are more dependent upon atmospheric processes and proximity to rivers. In the tropics and subtropics surface salinities are high because there is little rain and a high rate of evaporation. In the Red Sea, salinities are far higher than in the open ocean. Rainfall is scanty and evaporation intense, salts are injected at the sea bed from the Earth's crust, and some are transported from the Bitter Lakes through the Suez Canal. In addition, the Red Sea is largely isolated from the Indian Ocean by the Bab el Mandeb Sill.

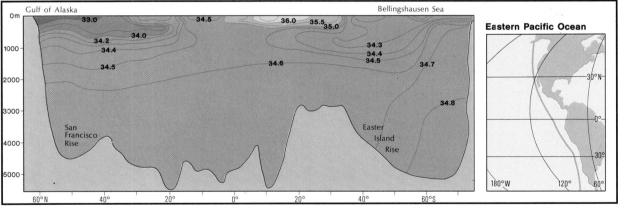

Eastern Pacific Ocean

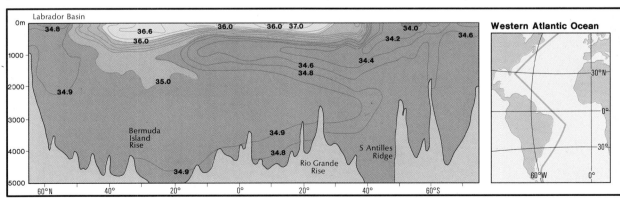

Western Atlantic Ocean

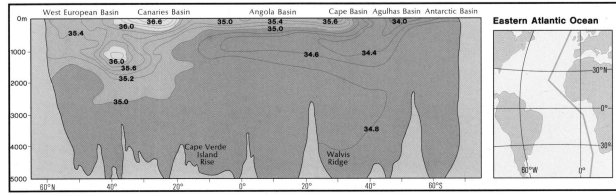

Eastern Atlantic Ocean

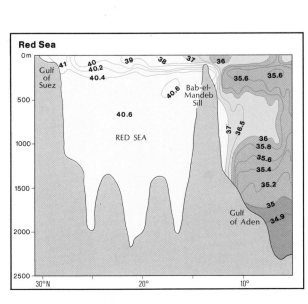

Red Sea

The ocean as a biological environment

THE world ocean is the largest biological environment on our planet. The ocean has a two-dimensional surface spread twice as extensive as that of all the land and freshwater areas combined; but the true vastness of the ocean becomes apparent only when its depth is also considered. Land animals and plants occupy a very narrow band, just a few tens of metres thick. Even if we include the highest flying birds, the occupied layer is extended to only a few hundreds of metres at most. In the oceans, overlying the sea floor where the animals and plants occupy an even thinner two-dimensional world, is the vast mid-water environment with an average thickness of almost 4 km, and the whole of its enormous volume, some 1370 million cu. km, is occupied by living organisms.

Despite their size, the oceans contain a disproportionately limited variety of species of animals and plants compared with the emergent land and fresh waters. Thus, of the well over a million described animal species, only about 160 000 live in the seas. Of these only 2 per cent or so live in mid-water, the remainder forming the benthic, or sea-floor community. But because of the enormous size of the mid-water realm, some of these species, for example the copepods, exist in truly astronomical numbers. This is not too surprising since the bulk of the plant life in the oceans, upon which all marine communities are ultimately dependent, is in the form of microscopic phytoplankton cells, unlike the large plants typical of land areas. The first link in almost all marine food chains is that between the phytoplankton and the tiny herbivorous zooplankton. Food chains in the sea also tend to be much longer than those on land, with as many as five or more links between the phytoplankton at one end and large predatory fish such as tuna at the other. Each link in such a chain involves an enormous loss of material which is used to provide energy for the animal at the higher end of the chain, no more than 10–15 per cent of the food surviving to form the tissues of the eater. These long marine food chains are inefficient from the fisherman's point of view; the unusually short chain from phytoplankton to krill to the blue whale is therefore very attractive (see *The Southern Ocean* page 78).

In the shallow, near-shore waters there is a

1 *below* Although the pattern of the world biogeographic regions is not as clear cut as that of the vegetation belts on land, it may be readily related to temperature. Cold water populations are found in the Arctic and Southern Ocean, south of the Antarctic Convergence, where surface temperatures lie between 5°C and a little below 0°C. Species diversity is low. Warm water populations are located where the surface temperatures remain above 18–20°C. There is high species diversity and rapid degeneration, although

2 *opposite* The water column indicates the depths at which the various oceanic creatures shown in the accompanying photographs dwell. Many oceanic animals, particularly within the upper 1000 m, make regular daily migrations from deep day-time depths to shallower night-time levels, sometimes covering several hundreds of metres. Since these migratory patterns vary from species to species, the population structure at any particular depth is changing continuously. Why so many animals should expend so much energy on such migrations is something of a mystery, but for many of them the reason must be related to the opposing requirements of feeding in the highly productive near-surface regions and at the same time avoiding predators in the sunlit zone.

good deal of environmental variation between, for instance, tropical lagoons, storm-beaten temperate shores and ice-covered polar waters. Much of the open ocean, on the other hand, provides remarkably stable and uniform environmental conditions. For example, while the total range of sea water temperatures extends from about −2°C to rather more than +30°C, temperatures in excess of +5°C are restricted to a narrow near-surface layer (see *Oceanic circulation* page 50). Similarly, although the salinity of sea water in near-shore regions may be reduced as a result of dilution by outflowing river water or melting ice, and increased by evaporation in shallow tropical seas, in the open ocean the salinity never varies by more than a few per cent, and the relative proportions of the constituent salts are remarkably constant (see *The salt sea* previous page).

There are consequently few clear-cut environments in the ocean compared with those on land, but it is possible to distinguish a number of general marine biological zones and provinces depending upon their distance from the nearest land and their depth beneath the surface.

The fertility of the sea determined by abundance of phytoplankton is generally high over continental shelves and in the great upwelling areas, which correspondingly are rich in animal life, such as the krill of the Southern Ocean and the pelagic fish populations of tropical upwelling areas. At a smaller scale, marine habitats are influenced by bottom conditions and local characteristics such as tides and currents.

the total biomass may be low. In a few areas, such as the Sargasso Sea, fertility is very low. In between are the temperate populations located between the 5°C and 18°C mean annual isotherms, commonly distinguished into a cool, or boreal, group and a warm temperate group. In these areas productivity is markedly seasonal, and, as in the tropical Indo-Pacific and the eastern Pacific, there is a broad distinction between Western and Eastern provinces separated by the deep ocean.

Creatures of light and darkness

2.1 *above* A number of animals are adapted for life in the specialised environment at the very surface of the sea. Like *Velella*, several of these surface-dwellers are supported by gas-filled floats and have sails which protrude through the air–water interface. They are centred on the warmer parts of the ocean, but from time to time winds and currents combine to bring vast numbers to the shores of temperate areas such as north-western Europe.

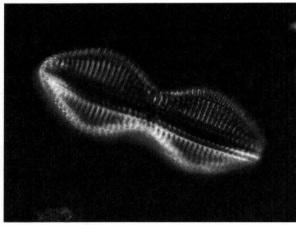

2.2 *above* Diatoms. The microscopic plants of the phytoplankton present a bewildering array of beautifully intricate shapes and colours. They are restricted to the sunlit euphotic or epipelagic zone. When they die the skeletal tissues generally dissolve rapidly before they reach the sea floor. But the siliceous remains of one group, the diatoms, are so resistant to solution that in many oceanic areas, particularly in high latitudes, the deep-sea sediments are composed almost entirely of diatomaceous oozes which have accumulated over millions of years.

MARINE BIOLOGICAL ZONES
The *epipelagic or euphotic zone* extends from the surface to a depth of about 100 m; a very thin layer in comparison with the total depth of the ocean. This is the most important layer in the sea for its lower boundary marks the limit of the penetration of sufficient sunlight to support photosynthesis, the process by which plants convert the Sun's energy into chemical energy. Almost all the world's fisheries resources live in this zone.

The *mesopelagic zone* extends down to the limit of the penetration of light from the surface, at about 1000 m. Many creatures living in this zone make daily vertical migrations. The food supply is either transported by the migrating animals or sinks in the form of dead bodies or fæcal material. In such a food-limited environment the dual requirements of obtaining sufficient food and not falling prey to other predators have resulted in many beautiful adaptations to camouflage, using reflective surfaces and light organs.

In the *bathypelagic zone* both the total amount of living material and the number of species is relatively small compared with the mesopelagic layer above. Luminous organs are less common, though many angler fishes use light organs to lure their prey. Black fishes, red shrimps and gelatinous squid seem to typify this zone. Few animals migrate, or do anything very active for at this depth conservation of energy is a cardinal principle.

The *abyssopelagic zone* extends from about 2000 m downwards. The already sparse mid-water fauna decreases still further until, within one hundred metres or so off the sea floor, there is an increase in the biomass. There is a pelagic community associated more or less closely with the sea bed which exists not only on the abyssal sea-floor, but also on the continental slope. Here live strange rat-tail fishes which have been the subject of exploratory fishing in recent years.

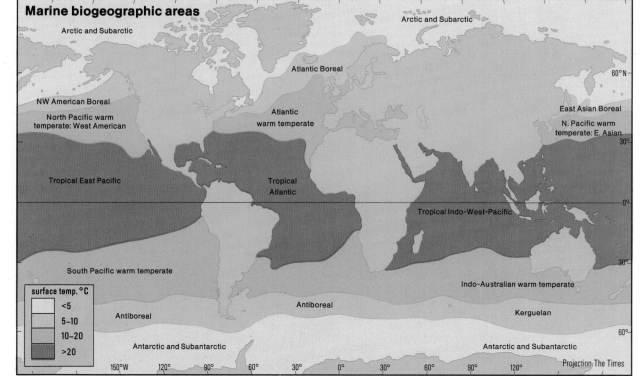

Marine biogeographic areas

Arctic and Subarctic
Arctic and Subarctic
Atlantic Boreal
NW American Boreal
North Pacific warm temperate: West American
Atlantic warm temperate
East Asian Boreal
N. Pacific warm temperate: E. Asian
60°N
Tropical East Pacific
Tropical Atlantic
Tropical Indo-West-Pacific
30°
0°
South Pacific warm temperate
Indo-Australian warm temperate
30°
Antiboreal
Antiboreal
Kerguelen
60°

surface temp. °C	
<5	
5–10	
10–20	
>20	

Antarctic and Subantarctic
Antarctic and Subantarctic
150°W 120° 90° 60° 30° 0° 30° 60° 90° 120°
Projection: The Times

metres

2.3 Foraminifera

2.1 Velella
(By-the-wind sailor)

2.2 Diatoms

2.5 Krill

2.4 Copepod

0

E P I P E L A G I C

100

2.6 Amphipod shrimp

2.8 Squid

200

2.7 Deep sea prawn

Lantern fish
(see page 74)

M E S O P E L A G I C

Rat tail fish
(see page 73)

500

Cyclothone
(see page 74)

1000

Ceratioid angler fish
(see page 74)

1500

B A T H Y P E L A G I C

2000

3000

A B Y S S O P E L A G I C

4000

5000
metres

2.3 *left* Foraminifera, *Orbulina universa*. Comparable in size to the phytoplankton, many of the foraminiferans and radiolarians have radiating spines and protoplasmic outgrowths reminiscent of snowflakes. The calcareous skeletons of the foraminiferans and the siliceous remains of the radiolarians both form important constituents of deep-sea oozes, the latter particularly in the very deep regions beneath the depth where calcareous remains disappear into solution.

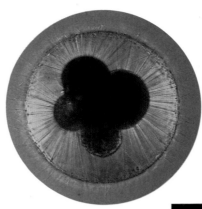

2.4 *right* Copepod, *Bradycalanus*. The shrimp-like copepods, ranging in length from about 0.5 to 17 mm, are found in almost every part of the ocean. *Bradycalanus*, for example, is a large deep-living form from depths of about 1000 m to 5000 m. A much more abundant shallow-living relative, *Calanus finmarchicus*, forms a major constituent of the diet of the large whale-bone whales and plankton-feeding fishes such as the herring.

2.5 *left* Krill, *Euphausia superba*. The euphausiacean shrimps are almost ubiquitous and, like the much smaller copepods, include herbivores, carnivores and omnivores. The largest epipelagic species, the krill, *Euphausia superba*, grows to about 60 mm and swarms in vast shoals in the Southern Ocean (see page 78).

2.6 *right* Amphipod shrimp, *Cystisoma*. Many of the planktonic animals of the epipelagic and upper mesopelagic zones camouflage themselves against predators by becoming transparent and therefore very difficult to see. The amphipod shrimp *Cystisoma*, apart from its eye pigment and its stomach contents, is glass clear. It is quite possible to read newsprint through the body of such a creature.

2.7 *left* Deep-sea prawn, *Notostomus*. Deep-sea prawns are widely distributed in the epipelagic and bathypelagic zones in temperate and tropical regions, but are much less abundant in high latitudes. Many of the mesopelagic species are deep-red or scarlet and undertake daily vertical migrations from a depth of 500 m or more during the day to within about 100 m of the surface at night.

2.8 *right* Squid, *Histioteuthis*. Squid are found at all depths from the epipelagic zone to more than 5000 m where finned octopods have been photographed in mid-water just above the sea-bed. Several of the mesopelagic forms, like *Histioteuthis*, possess cells which can change colour and emit light.

The plankton

THE biological economy of the ocean, like that of the land, is based almost entirely upon photosynthesis, the process by which plants use energy from sunlight to combine together carbon dioxide and water to produce carbohydrates. Being dependent upon sunlight, this primary productivity in the sea is restricted to the near surface layer, the epipelagic or euphotic zone. The depth level where light intensity is just sufficient to support photosynthesis varies with latitude, season, amount of suspended material in the water, including the plants themselves, and even with short-term weather conditions. In general, however, its greatest depth is about 100 metres in open oceanic conditions, such as in the Sargasso Sea, while in most inshore areas it will be at a depth of no more than 30 or 40 metres and may be reduced to only a few centimetres in some regions.

The large seaweeds which are anchored to the sea bed are therefore restricted to areas where the bottom is sufficiently shallow for light to penetrate. Since such regions represent only a fraction of one per cent of the total ocean area, the contribution of these large algae to the total economy of the seas is relatively insignificant.

In contrast to the large plants of the emergent land areas of the Earth, the main plant producers of the oceans are microscopic phytoplankton, and even the smaller terrestrial herbivores, such as rabbits, are enormous compared with their marine counterparts which are rarely more than a few millimetres long.

Many animal groups have representatives which graze directly on the phytoplankton, but the marine herbivores *par excellence* are the copepods, which row through the water feeding on phytoplankton cells and protozoans as they go. It has been estimated that copepods must outnumber all the other animals on Earth put together. With the other herbivores, the copepods form the basis of the animal communities of the ocean, for they are the first link in the food chain which leads from the phytoplankton to the larger organisms such as the fishes and whales.

Phytoplankton

Phytoplankton are microscopic algae which float free in mid-water, and live in the surface layers of the open ocean. They are the most important form of plant life in the oceans. The term 'plankton' is a rather loose one which means 'that which wanders or drifts'.

Apart from the overriding requirement of sufficient light for photosynthesis, the primary productivity of the oceans is affected by numerous other factors of which the two most important are the temperature and the supply of nutrient salts. As on land, biological processes in the ocean proceed at a much faster rate at high temperatures than at low ones. Consequently, although the number of phytoplankton cells present in a given volume of water may be much higher in temperate regions than in the tropics, particularly in spring and summer, the total number of cells produced over the whole year may be as great, or greater, in the warmer regions. The main importance of temperature, however, lies in its effect upon the stability of the water column; if there is no mixing between the cold deep water and the warm shallow water there will be no supply of nutrient salts to the surface layers. For this reason, the high surface temperatures in the tropics actually tend to reduce the primary production in such regions and make them less productive than the cooler temperate waters.

The supply of nutrients to the oceans, including the trace elements and vitamins necessary for plant growth, comes from two main sources. First, river waters entering the sea carry salts and other nutrients (see *The salt sea* page 66). This may result in high levels of phytoplankton productivity in the neighbourhood of major estuaries, but in the economy of the oceans as a whole it is relatively insignificant. For the total salt content of the oceans is so large that the river discharge increases the salinity by only about one part in three million per year. A much more important source of nutrients to the surface waters is the recycling of salts which have sunk into the deeper layers locked up in the bodies of animals and plants.

In the shallow waters overlying the continental shelves, nutrients cannot sink far beneath the euphotic zone since the water column is nowhere deeper than about 200 m. From these depths the nutrient-rich water is fairly readily brought back to the surface by currents and by the stirring effect of storms, particularly in mid and high latitudes where the temperature stability of the water column breaks down during winter (see *Oceanic circulation* page 50). Consequently, there is relatively high productivity in the coastal regions compared with that in the open ocean.

In very cold, near-polar latitudes the water column rarely develops a significant thermocline and therefore remains relatively unstable. Consequently currents and storms can bring nutrient-rich water to the surface even from considerable depths in these regions. In the Antarctic, the cooled waters which sink at the Convergence to form the Antarctic Intermediate Water are replaced by nutrient-rich water which rises to the surface from depths of 1000 m or more. Thus, there is high production in the polar and sub-polar regions, some parts of the Southern Ocean, for instance, being among the most productive of the world.

The sub-tropical and tropical regions have temperature and light regimes in the surface layers which would allow phytoplankton production to proceed throughout the year. However, because of the strong thermocline (a permanent feature of these regions, with a thin layer of warm water overlaying a much cooler sub-surface water mass), the water column tends to be very stable and the euphotic zone receives an adequate supply of nutrients in very specific and restricted areas. In the tropical regions of each of the oceans, such areas of relatively high productivity

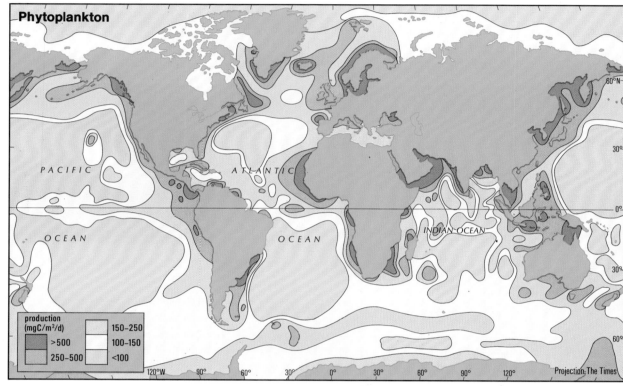

Phytoplankton

production (mgC/m²/d)
- >500
- 250–500
- 150–250
- 100–150
- <100

Projection: The Times

1 *above* The map shows phytoplankton production of the oceans measured in milligrams of carbon per square metre per day.

occur between the westward-flowing equatorial currents driven by the trade winds and the adjacent eastward flowing equatorial countercurrents (see *Upwelling* page 53).

Finally, there are restricted coastal regions of the tropics and sub-tropics where upwelling occurs, such as off north-west and south-west Africa in the Atlantic, off Somaliland and Arabia in the Indian Ocean, and off Peru and California in the Pacific. With the prevailing high surface temperature and light conditions, these regions support some of the highest phytoplankton productivity rates in the world.

Elsewhere in the tropics and sub-tropics the euphotic zone receives a very meagre supply of nutrients, and phytoplankton productivity is very low. The typical deep-blue sub-tropical oceanic waters, which look so lush and attractive, may therefore with some justification be referred to as the deserts of the ocean.

2 *below* Diatoms (Bacillariophyceae) are often the dominant component of the phytoplankton. They are particularly abundant in Arctic and Antarctic regions where their siliceous outer shells form sea floor sediment over enormous areas.
3 *bottom* Dinoflagellate, *Noctiluca miliaris*. The dinoflagellates have a cell wall made up of close-fitting plates of cellulose and can move through the water using their two whip-like flagella. Several of them, including *Noctiluca*, can produce a brilliant phosphorescence when disturbed.

4 *below* Different forms of radiolaria and dinoflagellate.

5 *below right* Several quite distinct algal groups are represented in the phytoplankton, all of them microscopic. The largest are no more than a millimetre or so across. Despite their small size, phytoplanktonic plants may be so abundant that they colour the surface layers of the sea green or brown, forming a 'red tide', as seen here.

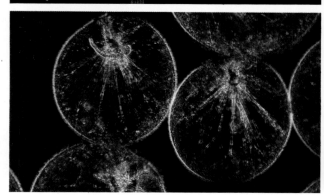

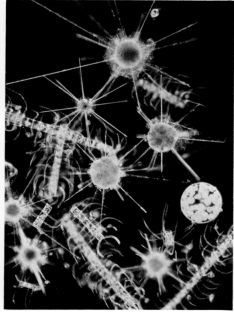

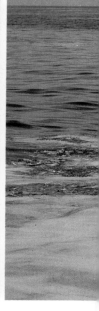

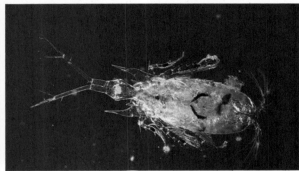

6 *above* and **9** *far right* Siphonophores, colonial relatives of the sea-anemones and jellyfish, in which different members of the colony are specialised for specific tasks such as swimming, flotation, food gathering and eating. Many siphonophores live in mid-water but some, such as the Portuguese man o'war, *Physalia far right* and *Porpita above* have gas-filled chambers which float at the very surface of the sea. While the float of *Physalia* may reach a length of 20 cm or more, the disc of *Porpita* rarely exceeds 3–4 cm across.

7 *centre above* Foraminiferan, *Globigerinoides*. Related to amoeba, most foraminiferans secrete a tiny calcareous shell pierced with many holes through which thin strands of protoplasm stream to capture floating food particles. Over wide areas of the deep ocean the dead shells of planktonic foraminiferans form a carpet of sediment many tens or even hundreds of metres thick.

8 *centre below* Copepod, *Coryeaeus speciosus*. The shrimp-like copepods are mostly very small, ranging from a fraction of a millimetre in length up to the size of a grain of rice. Many sur-

face-living copepods are at least partly herbivorous and form the first essential link in the food chain leading from the phytoplankton to the larger invertebrates and the fish.

Zooplankton

Although the herbivores are fed upon directly by some quite powerful swimmers such as the herring-like fishes and some mid-water shrimps, they are mainly eaten by other members of the planktonic community. The animal plankton, or zooplankton, therefore contains representatives of all the main animal groups, from the protozoans to larval fishes, and all sizes from microscopic forms to jellyfishes with discs a metre or more in diameter and with tentacles many metres long. Whether they feed directly upon the phytoplankton or upon other animals, the zooplanktonic creatures are ultimately dependent for their existence upon the primary productivity. The zooplankton therefore shows a similar distribution to that of the phytoplankton, being most abundant in moderately high latitudes and in upwelling regions.

Unlike the phytoplankton, the zooplankton is not restricted to the sunlit upper layers of the ocean and planktonic animals are accordingly found at all depths, though they are concentrated in the upper 1000 m or so. Many of them, including the herbivorous copepods, also undertake extensive diurnal vertical migrations, generally moving towards the surface during the night and descending, sometimes through hundreds of metres, during the day. Evidence of these migrations is often seen on ships' echo-sounder traces in the form of the 'deep scattering layer', though the organisms producing such traces must usually be shoals of fishes following their migrating prey rather than the zooplankton themselves.

As far as man is concerned, the zooplankton com-

11 *right* The distribution of zooplankton, measured in milligrams per cubic metre in the upper 100 m of the ocean, follows a similar pattern to that of the phytoplankton.

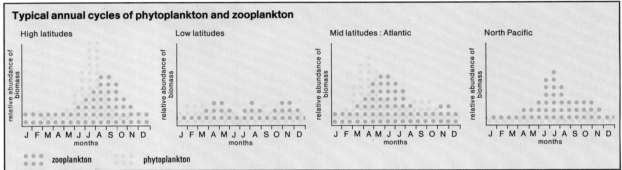

Typical annual cycles of phytoplankton and zooplankton

High latitudes | Low latitudes | Mid latitudes : Atlantic | North Pacific

relative abundance of biomass — J F M A M J J A S O N D months

zooplankton · · · · | phytoplankton · · ·

10 *above* Not only does the abundance of zooplankton correspond closely with the spatial variations in the primary productivity, but it also follows the seasonal changes in phytoplankton abundance. In tropical regions, where phytoplankton production proceeds at a fairly regular level throughout the year, the zooplankton also show rather minor changes. In high latitudes, on the other hand, where the phytoplankton productivity is restricted to a very short period in summer, the zooplankton similarly shows a single peak in abundance, lagging slightly behind the plants. In intermediate latitudes, where phytoplankton production can proceed at a high rate for some months, the zooplankton usually shows two peaks, the first following the spring phytoplankton bloom which is grazed by the animals to a low summer level and is succeeded by a smaller autumn bloom, and a corresponding smaller zooplankton peak.

munity is particularly important since it forms the link between the primary production of plant material and the commercially exploited animals. The total annual world production of phytoplankton has been estimated at between about 15 and 30 billion tonnes of carbon. The annual world fish production has been variously estimated at about 2.0 to 30.0 million tonnes of carbon, that is only about 0.01 per cent of the phytoplankton production. One important cause of this dramatic difference must be the nature of the trophic

relationships in the marine environment (that is, the number of links in a food chain, starting with phytoplankton). Four or five trophic levels are not uncommon between the phytoplankton and the higher carnivores. Moreover, the feeding relationships between these various levels are often complex, producing a food web rather than a simple chain. With transfer efficiencies of no more than 10–20 per cent in such a web the loss of material between the lower and upper levels is enormous.

Zooplankton

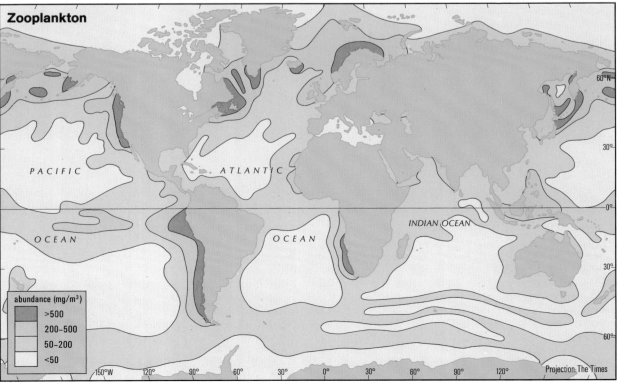

PACIFIC OCEAN | ATLANTIC OCEAN | INDIAN OCEAN

60°N | 30° | 0° | 30° | 60°

abundance (mg/m³)
>500
200–500
50–200
<50

150°W 120° 90° 60° 30° 0° 30° 60° 90° 120° Projection: The Times

The benthos

THE biological communities closely associated with the sea floor, from the intertidal zone to the bottom of the deepest ocean trenches, are collectively known as the benthos. In shallow seas, and particularly in regions of high phytoplankton productivity, the benthos is supplied with abundant food and is therefore correspondingly rich. Close to the continental coasts and along the mid-ocean ridges, the sea floor consists of rock outcrops where the benthic community is made up almost entirely of organisms anchored to the rock, filtering suspended matter from the overlying water or browsing over the rock surfaces. Such communities are extremely difficult to sample adequately except in shallow regions accessible to divers or submersibles, but they are relatively rare. More commonly the sea bed consists of sediments of various grades ranging from gravel and sands to the finest silts and muds. The coarse-grained sediments are largely restricted to the continental shelves, while the continental slope and abyss are almost everywhere carpeted with oozes made up of the calcareous or siliceous skeletal remains of microscopic mid-water organisms.

On the abyssal sea floor, 4–6 km beneath the surface, most of the benthic animals are no more than a millimetre or two long and live buried within the sediment. The larger animals which can be seen on deep-sea photographs are generally immobile suspension feeders or slow-moving detritus eaters which expend little energy in their search for food.

The form in which the food supply arrives at the sea bed largely determines the nature of the benthic community which it supports. In the shallow continental shelf regions there is a very close relationship between the benthos and the mid-water community of the euphotic zone. It takes a short time, hours or days, for material to sink to the bottom in these depths, and also many animals migrate daily or seasonally between the two environments and act as a very efficient transport mechanism between the two. But some 70 per cent of the sea floor lies under 4000 m or more of water and here the connection between the benthos and the euphotic zone is much more tenuous. Although mid-water animals are found at all depths, their numbers fall off dramatically beneath about 1000 m and there is little evidence of vertical migrations occurring below these levels. Consequently, there seems to be a gap of some 2000 m between the benthos and the main mid-water community across which food must pass almost entirely in the form of the dead bodies of mid-water organisms and their faecal material. Until recently it was assumed that this occurred solely as a fairly constant rain of very small particles. The corpses of the larger animals were thought to be mainly consumed in mid-water, so that those which reached the sea bed did not represent a significant source of food for the benthos. Also, deep sea samples contain few large or active forms. But it has been discovered that there is a small but important deep benthic community of highly mobile animals which are either active carnivores or feed on the carcasses of large animals which sink from the overlying water.

Benthic animals at different depths

2 Sea hares *Aplysia punctata* These marine gastropods (a pair is shown here mating) have the shell reduced to a flat plate and have prominent tentacles that suggest 'ears'. They dwell in the shallows of the continental shelf and feed on large seaweeds.

3 Gorgonian corals Gorgonians are related to the reef-building corals, but have a flexible horny skeleton rather than a rigid calcareous one. They are particularly abundant in shallow tropical seas where they often form thickets similar to plant thickets on land. This photograph was taken at a depth of 150 m on the summit of the Josephine seamount in the north-east Atlantic Ocean. The presence of the gorgonians, which are about 50 cm high, indicates the availability of abundant tiny suspended food particles on which they live.

4 Sea-pen, *Kophobelemnon stelliferum* (depth 1000 m) Like their gorgonian relatives, the sea-pens are suspension-feeding colonial animals with many individuals sharing a common horny skeleton, which in this case is unbranched. Sea-pens occur at all depths in the ocean but are particularly abundant on the continental shelf and upper continental slope. *Kophobelemnon* grows to only about 20 cm long, but some sea-pens reach a length of three or four metres. (Also shown is the feeding mark left by a starfish.)

5 Glass sponges, *Pheronema* (depth 1200 m) So-called because the skeleton is composed of spicules of pure silica, the glass sponges are mainly a deep-sea group. Food particles are collected from water which enters the sponge through thousands of tiny inhalant openings and leaves through the single large exhalant aperture. *Pheronema* reaches a diameter of about 15 cm and harbours a rich and varied community of small animals living on its surface and among the enlarged spicules which anchor the sponge to the sea-floor.

6 Deep-sea cod, *Lepidion eques* (30 cm long, depth 1400 m) *Lepidion*, which lives on the upper continental slope, looks very much like its shallow-water relatives except for the larger eyes and the enlarged dorsal fin ray which acts like a sensory antenna.

7 Raja raja (length more than 200 cm) The ray is a truly benthic species which cruises over the bottom hunting for its prey (fishes, crustaceans, molluscs, etc.) and only occasionally comes to rest. Some species are lighter coloured, from a pale bluish hue to pure white, while others can be quite dark-skinned, and range down to the continental rise depths and beyond.

150m deep
1000m

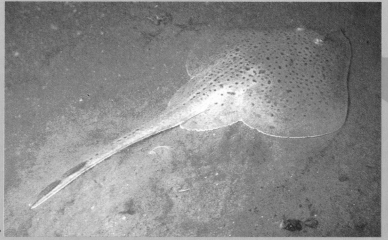

Zonation of the benthos

Individual benthic species have restricted vertical ranges, so that definite zones or layers can be recognised within the sea-bed communities. These zones are particularly narrow and obvious in the intertidal zone where an animal or plant has to withstand exposure and wave action. Consequently, clear bands of texture or colour are often visible, particularly on rocky coasts. Below low tide, benthic plants are usually found only close inshore. Many animals, including most of the commercially exploited fishes, are restricted to the continental shelf region where there is abundant food. Suspension feeders which filter small food particles from the water are particularly common.

On the upper part of the continental slope, down to a depth of about 1500 m, suspension feeding sponges, corals and sea pens are still quite abundant, but slow moving detritus eaters become more important. In this region, typical deep-sea groups such as the rat-tail fishes are also found.

On the lower part of the continental slope (1500–3500 m) and on the abyssal plain (3500–6000 m) detritivores become even more dominant. The most common species are detritivorous echinoderms, particularly the sea-cucumbers or holothurians.

With increasing depth the individual species become more widespread geographically. Many abyssal plain species are found in all the oceans of the world. In the very deepest parts of the ocean, however, the situation is reversed. The deep sea trenches (down to 11000 m) have their own special animal community and in many cases each species is found in one trench only.

1 *right* Benthic animals are found throughout the oceans, even in the deep-sea trenches at depths in excess of 10 000 m. This in itself is notable since little more than a century ago it was confidently believed that no life would be found below a depth of a few hundred metres. However, it is certainly true that as one moves away from the land masses towards the deep sea the benthic biomass decreases dramatically between the continental shelf and the continental slope, and there is a further decrease onto the abyssal plain. Towards the centres of the great oceanic gyre regions such as the central north Pacific, and also in the Mediterranean, the benthic biomass is reduced to an even lower level.

The abundance of the benthos follows very much the same pattern as that of the phytoplankton and the zooplankton. This is to be expected since wherever the sea bed is deeper than the euphotic zone the benthic communities are dependent for food upon the phytoplankton above them. Consequently, where the phytoplankton is rich the benthos should also be relatively abundant, but because of the attenuating effect of the water column the primary production pattern is less clearly reflected by the benthos.

Most estimates of benthic biomass are based on samples taken by grabs which tend to collect only the smaller organisms. The biomass figures are therefore considerable underestimates, but the map still gives a good indication of the general trends.

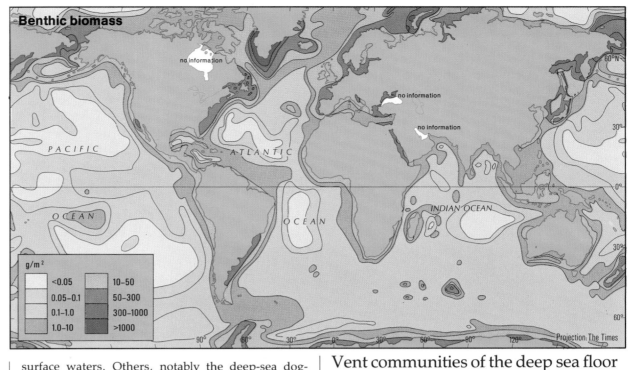

Benthic biomass

g/m²

<0.05	10–50
0.05–0.1	50–300
0.1–1.0	300–1000
1.0–10	>1000

no information

Projection: The Times

Benthic fishes

A relatively abundant and specialised fauna occupies the layer some tens of metres thick above the sea floor. It is recognisable from the top of the continental slope down to trench depths. This fish fauna is richest in both quantity and diversity around the oceanic rim, where the pelagic fauna impinges on the shoaling sea-bed to provide a valuable food source. Contact with the pelagic fauna diminishes with depth, so that by about 2500 m an impoverished abyssopelagic layer separates these two elements of deep-sea fish life. In contrast with their deep pelagic counterparts, benthopelagic fishes have undergone little loss of complexity. Indeed, many are robust and relatively large. Neutral buoyancy is commonplace, achieved in sharks and chimaeras by oily livers and in other groups by large gas-filled swim-bladders. There is a general trend to produce elongate forms with long-based dorsal and anal fins. The rat-tail fishes are adapted in this way. They are diverse and abundant over a wide range of depths. Males of many of these species utilise their swim-bladders for sound production, presumably for mate attraction. Like many bottom-living species, rat-tails produce buoyant eggs which develop in the rich

surface waters. Others, notably the deep-sea dog-fishes and ophidioid species, are live-bearers producing their offspring at depth.

Truly benthic fishes have no aides to buoyancy and spend much of their life in contact with the deep-sea floor. Among the elasmobranchs, deep-sea rays are typical benthic forms. They are probably rather more active than the 'sit-and-wait' predators that comprise the majority of benthic teleosts. On the upper slope the main such group is the scorpion fishes, lurking and well-camouflaged forms which feed largely on fish and crustaceans, but sometimes concentrate on the creeping brittlestar. Tripod fishes are well adapted to rest on the sea bed. They have anteriorly placed pelvic fins which bear elongate outer rays and together with prolonged rays in the lower lobe of the tail raise them up out of immediate bottom turbidity. Some, such as *Bathypterois* and *Benthosaurus*, have very long supporting rays while others, like *Ipnops*, are less pronounced. The tripod fishes are confined in their distribution to the deep-ocean, but sea-snails (Liparididae) and eel-pouts (Zoarcidae) are representatives of groups also found in shallow seas. The most numerous intertidal species of sea-snail have modified pelvic fins to enable them to cling to suitable surfaces, but this structure has become rudimentary in deep-sea forms.

Vent communities of the deep sea floor

In the late 1970s a startling discovery was made of some very localised benthic populations near active centres of sea floor spreading in the Galapagos Rift zone in the eastern Pacific. Water enters fissures in the sea bed and becomes heated and loaded with hydrogen sulphide, among other chemicals. There are bacteria which use this sulphide to produce organic matter from carbon dioxide, independently of the normal process of photosynthesis. These bacteria support an amazingly rich benthic community. Some of the animals in these vent communities are unknown elsewhere. These include a clam which grows up to 30 cm long, giant tube-worms several metres in length and 2–3 cm in diameter, and other organisms of unknown classification.

Despite the enormous productivity of these vent regions, they are very localised and are therefore insignificant in the oceans as a whole.

Deep sea scavengers

In the last twenty years experiments with baited traps and cameras have revealed the presence of a previously unsuspected community of highly mobile deep-sea scavengers. They range from amphipod crustaceans and shrimps through a variety of fishes to larger sharks many metres in length, and are rapidly attracted to any large food source, apparently over considerable distances. Within a few hours large numbers of these mobile scavengers arrive at the bait, and reduce it to a well-cleaned skeleton. The small food particles released by this activity in turn attract the much less active scavengers among the echinoderms and molluscs.

The active scavengers seem to be highly adapted opportunists which can survive for long periods without food and then rapidly home in on a suitable source when one arrives.

8 Sea cucumber, *Paelopatides gigantea* (30 cm long, depth 2000 m) The sea-cucumbers belong to the phylum Echinodermata which also includes the sea-urchins and starfishes. Some species live in mid-water, but most are detritus-eating bottom dwellers. They are the dominant echinoderm group in many parts of the lower continental slope and abyssal plain.

9 Tripod fish, *Bathypterois* The tripod fishes range in length from about 10 to 45 cm and range in depth from the upper continental slope at 200–300 m to more than 5000 m on the abyssal plain. Noteworthy are the greatly elongate outer rays of the pelvic fins and the lowest ray of the tail which are more than the overall length of the fish, and can hold the body above any turbidity close to the bottom. All tripod fishes are hermaphrodite and are capable of self-fertilisation; this may be an 'insurance' against the inability to find a mate in the low density deep-sea populations.

10 Rat-tail, *Odontomacrurus murrayi* (length 10 cm) Generally the rat-tails are one of the most successful benthopelagic families with more than 300 species, chiefly living around the continental slopes of the world ocean. Most rat-tails have a mixed diet derived from both pelagic and benthic habitats. Their eggs are buoyant and develop in the rich near-surface waters.

11 Giant pogonophora worms, *Riftia pachyptila* These giant tube worms were first seen by scientists exploring the sea bed north of the Galapagos Islands in 1977, where hot water rises from vents in the ocean crust. The vents contain hydrogen sulphide that supplies energy to bacteria which in turn is the food source of the giant worms and other life forms, such as the white crabs.

12 Suspension feeding cup sponge, *Hyalonema* (about 40 cm high, depth 4000 m) The stalk which raises the sponge clear of the bottom mud is made up of many strands of pure silica, each strand produced by a single specialised cell at the base of the 'cup'.

8

9

10

1500 m
2000–4000 m

11

12

The fishes

FISHES are but one of many groups of organisms which populate the deep ocean. A few species are exploited for food by man, but the vast majority are commercially unimportant. From an ecological viewpoint, the adaptations evolved by fishes to life in the deep-sea are fascinating and spectacular and many of these can be related to the global regime of vertical zonation which prevails despite horizontal physical discontinuities in the ocean, such as temperature and water movement, which affect geographic variability.

Fishes live at nearly all levels of the ocean, from the air–water interface down to the water–land boundary, to depths at least as great as 8300 m. Around 58 per cent of fish species are marine and of these only about 13 per cent occupy the deep ocean. Little more than 250 species are permanent residents in the epipelagic zone, yet there are approximately 1000 meso- and bathypelagic species and nearly 1300 benthic forms dwelling either on the continental slope or

5 *above and top* **Hatchetfish** *Argyropelecus* (length about 10 cm) Living at mid-twilight levels, hatchetfish are ideally suited to their surroundings. They are flattened from side to side, and so present a minimal silhouette from below; and in addition, they bear highly evolved photophores in half-silvered tubes which match the external twilight over a wide range of viewing angles. They have dark backs and highly silvered sides. Tubular eyes see vertically upward and yellow lenses in some species are special filters which may well enable these fish to detect animals above through their bioluminescent camouflage.

8 *below* *Opisthoproctus soleatus* (length less than 10 cm) This is a small, deep-bodied form living in the deep mesopelagic zone. Its upturned tubular eyes and small nibbling mouth indicate that small prey are hunted for by silhouetting them against the downwelling sunlight. Its own ventral camouflage is provided by luminescent bacteria located in an organ in the rectum and shining along a reflective tube running the length of the flattened underside. While the bacteria emit light continuously, pigment cells presumably regulate the output to the required intensity.

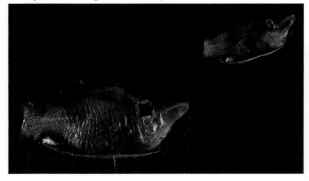

9 *right* *Cyclothone*. Most fishes of the bathypelagic zone belong to dark-coloured species of the genus *Cyclothone*. There are light-coloured species at depths of about 500 m while the deepest have been found at more than 2000 m. *Cyclothone* is very widely distributed and abundant and is probably the most numerous vertebrate genus on Earth.

the abyssal floor. When considered in terms of the theoretical volume 'available' for each species, those living along the shore and continental shelf to 200 m depth have about 290 cu. km per species. This compares with 500 000 cu. km for the inhabitants of the deep-sea: a 1700-fold difference. Such a discrepancy may be linked with the high plant production over the shelf.

The physical constraints of the environment are obviously reflected in evolutionary adaptations, from specialised species inhabiting the upper few centimetres of the ocean surface to those living on the ocean floor some 4000–11 000 metres below. Differences in form and function conspicuously relate to such survival pressures as concealment, feeding and reproduction. The examples here reflect not only these responses, but the variety of options evidently available. The headquarters of deep-sea fishes are in the tropical and sub-tropical regions where ocean clarity allows maximum penetration by sunlight.

Mesopelagic zone
This twilight zone often spans a temperature range of some 15 °C and is populated with a diverse fish fauna. Many are grazers and carnivores which make a nightly climb to feed in the epipelagic zone. Their migration may span several hundred metres, and these are typically small fishes of only around 10 cm in length. Others reside permanently at the lower levels, feeding on migrant prey entering or passing through their living depth. Exposure to predation is a major concern in such a habitat, which lacks shelter. The steady decline in the penetration of sunlight is a main feature of this zone and many adaptations to the decrease in light are found. Colour is important. Semi-transparent species occupy the shallower reaches and overlie dark-backed forms with silvery sides. Below 500 m, the predominant colour is black. Light organs are also important. Sunlight in the sea is largely unidirectional and descending light passing a fish in mid-water will render it conspicuous as a silhouette from below. By manufacturing their own light in organs ranged along the underside and matching it in intensity with the ambient sunlight, silhouetting may be reduced. The larger, more elaborate ventral light organs are generally found in upper mesopelagic species and they reduce in size and complexity in fishes living near bathypelagic levels. By the same token, many mesopelagic species, both grazers and carnivores, have upturned eyes to locate prey not so protected.

COLOURS AND PIGMENTS
The colours of mid-water animals are mainly related to concealment in the peculiar lighting conditions of the sea. Sunlight entering the ocean becomes more and more blue with increasing depth and its intensity is rapidly reduced so that little or none penetrates below about 1000 m. Close to the surface many animals adopt a vivid blue coloration while a little deeper many of the less active forms achieve camouflage by becoming transparent. An alternative and equally effective ploy is to 'pretend' to be transparent by acquiring highly reflective silvered flanks, as in many mesopelagic fishes. Deeper still, the animals become more and more heavily pigmented, crustaceans generally becoming vivid red while the fishes become brown or black. Both pigments are equally effective in that they do not reflect the predominantly blue ambient light.

Even then the percentage volumes of the euphotic, twilight (mesopelagic) and sunless zones (bathypelagic and deeper) are 2.5, 22.5 and 75.0 respectively. Hence most of the deep-sea living space occupied by fishes is not penetrated by sunlight. Yet it is not totally dark; in clear oceanic water biological background light becomes significant relative to daylight at depths greater than 500 m by day and 100 m on a moonlit night. In such a limitless environment as the deep ocean, light may be singled out as the main physical feature responded to in form and function by fishes, in ways not found in other living species. Body shape and colour, the capacity to produce light for, among other things, concealment purposes and the size and orientation of eyes are all influenced by living depth and hence ambient light. Lights built into elaborate lures attract prey, and therefore conserve energy, especially in bathypelagic species which live in a world lit only by other animals.
For benthic fishes, see pages 72–73.

6 *below* **Lanternfish** *Myctophum punctatum* (length, up to 10 cm) Lanternfishes are so called because of the pattern of small light organs on their flanks and undersides. The males of some species have light organs on the upper side of the tail stalk. Other species utilise light organs as 'headlights', pre-

BIOLUMINESCENCE
Many animals of the twilight and dark regions of the ocean can emit light produced by the oxidation of special chemicals called luciferins. Some creatures, including deep-sea angler fish, do not produce their own chemicals but instead maintain colonies of luminous bacteria in special organs with a shutter mechanism to control the light emission. Bioluminescence may be used to lure prey, as in several of the angler fish, or to deter predators, as in some crustaceans which either squirt a luminescent cloud or flash very brightly when attacked. Light organs may also be used for camouflage by lighting up the creature's underside which would otherwise be seen from below as a dark silhouette, while in other cases specific light organ patterns may enable animals to recognise other members of their own species or to distinguish between the sexes.

Epipelagic zone

The top of this well-lit zone is populated by a specialised group of fishes, which in the warm sea are typified by blue-backed forms such as flying fish, dorade or dolphin fish. There is also a wide variety of transparent, young stages of adult fish which live lower in the water column. This whole zone, its upper 150 m distributed with plant life, is the feeding ground for minute fish larvae hatching from buoyant eggs laid throughout the water column to the ocean floor. They mainly feed directly on planktonic plants. At night the epipelagic fish population is vastly swollen by migrants from the lower mesopelagic levels. Best known among these are the lantern fishes (family Myctophidae) that largely feed on crustacean grazers of the phytoplankton.

Large carnivores also dwell in the epipelagic zone. In tropical and temperate waters streamlined sharks (e.g. mako and blue sharks), tuna, marlin and swordfish spend much of their time at this uppermost level. Squid form a substantial part of the diet of these giants, but fish are their usual quarry. Indeed, smaller tuna may well fall prey to the other carnivorous forms.

1 *above* **Flying-fish** Cheilopogon sp. juvenile (length to about 30 cm) This species is typical of many in the sub-tropical and tropical ocean. Adults are cigar-shaped with a deep blue back and silvery underside, with wing-like pectoral fins emerging not far behind the large round eyes. Enlarged pelvic fins also assist in their gliding flight. A rapid burst of speed below the surface propels them into the air where they may glide for 10 seconds or so, over some hundreds of metres. Gliding may be prolonged by closing the pelvic fins to lower the elongate tip of the tail into the water and, with vigorous strokes, to gain speed and keep airborne.

2 *above right* **Blue shark** Prionace glauca (length up to 4 m) This abundant species has deep blue colouring with a pure white underside, with pointed snout and saw-edged teeth. It is a voracious predator and bears its young live, up to 100 offspring at one time. It lives on fish and squid in the upper zones.

3 *right* **Sailfish** Istiophorus platypterus (length up to 3.5 m) Like the shark, the sailfish dwells in warm and temperate waters. It differs from other billfish by its large dorsal fin. Often it will leap clear of the water surface. It is a popular sport fish in some areas.

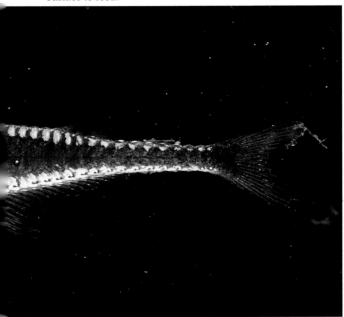

sumably to illuminate their prey. These small silvery-black fishes rarely exceed 20 cm in length, but the majority make nightly migrations of some hundreds of metres towards the surface to feed.

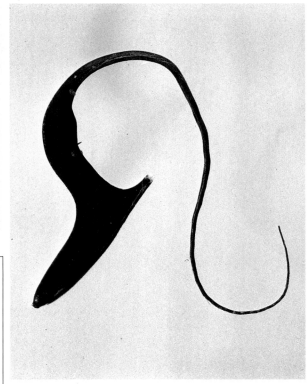

4 *above* **Bluefin tuna** Thunnus thynnus (length c. 3 m; weight around 370 kg) One of the swiftest and most mobile of predators, this tuna is blue-backed with silvery flanks. It has a finely streamlined body with crescentic second dorsal and anal fins, with grooves to accommodate the folded-back first dorsal and pectoral fins when swimming at speed. Tail finlets cut down drag, and lateral keels before the tail serve as horizontal stabilisers. One fish tagged off North America was recaptured off Norway some 50 days later, having averaged 80 miles per day.

7 *left* **Gulper eel** Eurypharynx pelecanoides (length up to 75 cm) This bathypelagic fish has gigantic pelican-like jaws relative to the small head. Its teeth are minute and, despite the size of the mouth, it feeds on small prey. It is silky-black in colour with a single light organ at the tip of its tail.

Bathypelagic and abyssopelagic zones

The bathypelagic zone contains a low density of animal life. It is possibly the largest biological environment on Earth and almost changeless in its physical surroundings. Few animals resident in other zones migrate to these depths. The resident fishes are largely carnivores with capacious stomachs to accommodate occasional meals of prey larger than themselves. Most are black and have much reduced ventral light organs. Many similar reductions in structural complexity occur in response to environmental conditions. Few fishes are equipped for sustained swimming. Many attract prey to voracious jaws with lighted lures, like the angler fishes, employing 'wait-and-dart' feeding tactics. Mate location in a poorly populated environment also necessitates specialisations. Female chemical signals appear to be common, for males of many species have elaborate nasal organs to follow scent gradients. Another specialisation is found, for example, in some angler fish where dwarf males have a short free-living existence before attaching themselves parasitically to a female many times their size, to form a self-contained breeding unit. Hermaphroditism is not uncommon, thus allowing two sets of viable eggs from one encounter.

The quantity of fish life decreases with depth to reach a minimum some 2.5 km below the sea surface. The impoverished abyssopelagic zone below can be considered an extension of the overlying zone for few physical differences are reflected in the fish fauna.

THE EFFECTS OF HYDROSTATIC PRESSURE

Life in the oceans is known to exist down to some 10 000 m, at which depth the pressure is about 1000 atmospheres. Since bone, muscle and fluids in fish are barely compressible, structural adaptations to avoid being crushed are only necessary for fishes which have a gas bladder, for gas is highly compressible. Such fishes have evolved means of regulating their density against pressure change. In the deepest known benthopelagic fish, from 7000 m or so, the swim-bladder gases still provide substantial buoyancy. On the other hand, activity and enzyme systems are considerably affected by the interplay of pressure and temperature, which limit the ranges of many deep-sea fishes. Some migratory mesopelagic fish accommodate wide ranges of conditions, often experiencing changes of 50 atmospheres pressure and 10°C temperature in an hour-long vertical migration.

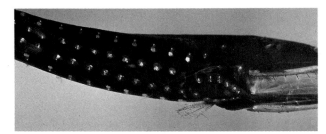

10 *above* Gonostoma bathyphilum. (length up to about 20 cm) This species lives deeper in the water column than other members of the genus and displays characteristic loss of complexity. In contrast with shallow-living relatives, it is black and not silvery, with reduced eyes and light organs. It undergoes no vertical migrations and has a regressed swim-bladder together with reduced musculature and robustness of skeleton.

11 *above* **Anglerfish** Melanocetus johnsoni (length up to 15 cm females; 3 cm males) This is a silky-black coloured bathypelagic predator with a huge, well armed mouth. The long fang-like teeth are hinged to allow large prey to be engulfed and not escape. Prey are attracted to the waiting jaws by the illuminated stalked lure between the eyes. In common with other deep sea anglerfishes, this species has dwarf males although unlike some others, these evidently do not form parasitic attachments with females.

Ocean bird life

OF the 8600 species of birds in the world fewer than 300 are truly marine in that the sea is their normal habitat and their principal source of food. Though divers, grebes, marine ducks and waders spend much of their lives on salt water they are excluded as they do not range widely over the oceans.

Seabirds are most numerous where turbulence and upwelling cause the upper layers of the sea to become rich in the nutrients which support an abundant supply of invertebrates and fish. Populations tend to be smallest over the tropical and subtropical oceans, where the biomass is relatively small, though large concentrations of birds can occur locally in these regions particularly around islands and over shallow water. The annual rhythm of atmospheric and oceanic circulations causes food supplies to vary and is reflected in the breeding cycles and migration habits of seabirds.

Three broad categories of seabirds can be distinguished according to habitat: those which feed near the coastline or forage inland (pelicans, cormorants, skimmers, most gulls and the coastal terns); those which dive for fish in offshore waters (penguins, diving petrels, gannets, boobies and frigate-birds); and those which frequent the open ocean and spend most of their lives on the wing (albatrosses, shearwaters and petrels).

All seabirds nest on land, though their choice of sites varies widely. These include cliff ledges or niches (tropic birds, cormorants, gulls and auks), grassy slopes (skuas, gannets, albatrosses and phalaropes), burrows (shearwaters, most petrels and some penguins), bushes and trees (cormorants, frigate-birds and noddies), coastal mangroves (pelicans), sandy shores or sand dunes (some terns) and bare rocky ground (some penguins). A few seabird species breed in small

colonies. An assembly of ten breeding pairs, for example, is about average for the flightless cormorant. The majority, however, breed in extremely congested colonies numbering many thousands or even hundreds of thousands of pairs. Some penguin rookeries contain a few million pairs of birds.

Some species remain comparatively close to their breeding quarters throughout the year, whereas many others disperse to feeding areas well away from their breeding localities. Some travel several thousand kilometres and these spectacular migratory journeys are possible because of superb aerodynamic design. By contrast, some species of birds are flightless, notably all members of the penguin family. However, this apparent disability does not restrict them greatly, for they accomplish migrations which take them considerable distances from their rookeries.

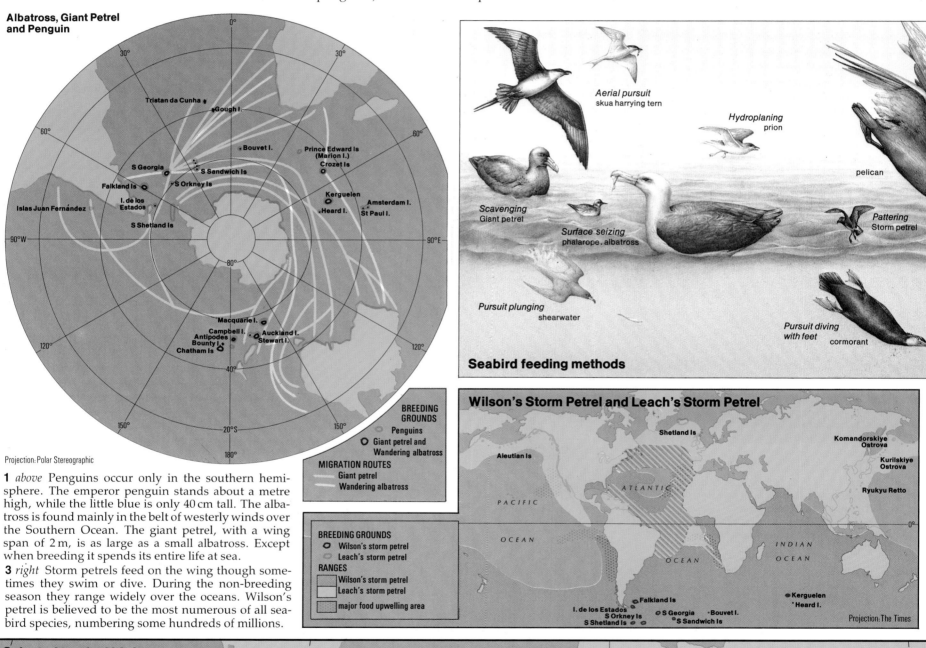

Albatross, Giant Petrel and Penguin

Projection: Polar Stereographic

BREEDING GROUNDS
○ Penguins
⊙ Giant petrel and Wandering albatross

MIGRATION ROUTES
Giant petrel
Wandering albatross

Seabird feeding methods

Wilson's Storm Petrel and Leach's Storm Petrel

BREEDING GROUNDS
◑ Wilson's storm petrel
○ Leach's storm petrel

RANGES
Wilson's storm petrel
Leach's storm petrel
major food upwelling area

Projection: The Times

1 *above* Penguins occur only in the southern hemisphere. The emperor penguin stands about a metre high, while the little blue is only 40 cm tall. The albatross is found mainly in the belt of westerly winds over the Southern Ocean. The giant petrel, with a wing span of 2 m, is as large as a small albatross. Except when breeding it spends its entire life at sea.

3 *right* Storm petrels feed on the wing though sometimes they swim or dive. During the non-breeding season they range widely over the oceans. Wilson's petrel is believed to be the most numerous of all seabird species, numbering some hundreds of millions.

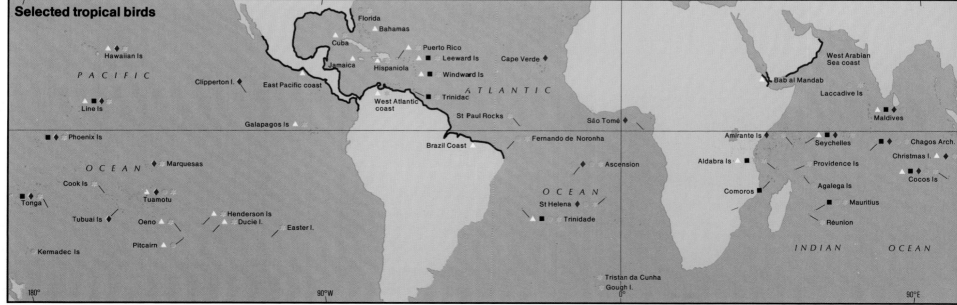

Selected tropical birds

Skuas

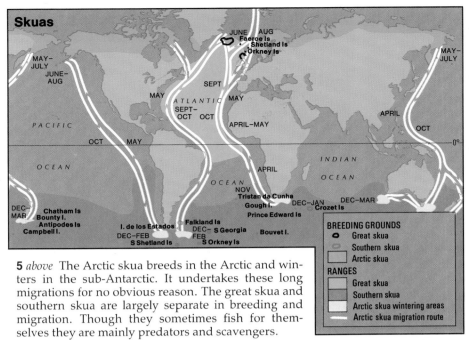

BREEDING GROUNDS
- ◐ Great skua
- ☐ Southern skua
- ☐ Arctic skua

RANGES
- Great skua
- Southern skua
- Arctic skua wintering areas
- — Arctic skua migration route

5 *above* The Arctic skua breeds in the Arctic and winters in the sub-Antarctic. It undertakes these long migrations for no obvious reason. The great skua and southern skua are largely separate in breeding and migration. Though they sometimes fish for themselves they are mainly predators and scavengers.

Shearwaters

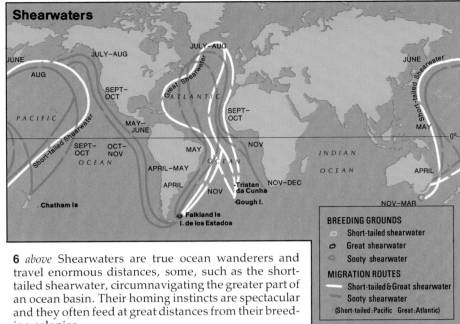

BREEDING GROUNDS
- ◐ Short-tailed shearwater
- ☐ Great shearwater
- ○ Sooty shearwater

MIGRATION ROUTES
- — Short-tailed & Great shearwater
- — Sooty shearwater

(Short-tailed:Pacific Great:Atlantic)

6 *above* Shearwaters are true ocean wanderers and travel enormous distances, some, such as the short-tailed shearwater, circumnavigating the greater part of an ocean basin. Their homing instincts are spectacular and they often feed at great distances from their breeding colonies.

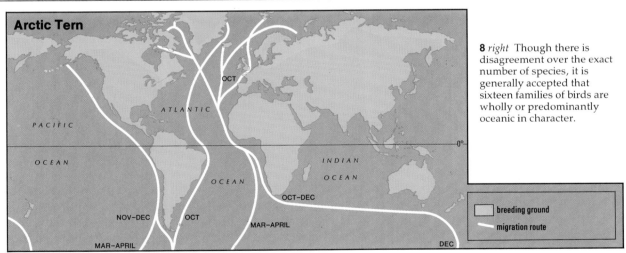

2 *left* Collectively, seabirds exploit all the resources of the upper ocean, taking small fish, large fish, flying fish, squid, krill, crustacea, and so on. They use various feeding techniques and most birds are capable of utilising more than one. Some feed while in flight, taking food from the surface of the sea or from just above or below it (petrels, albatrosses, shearwaters, terns and frigate-birds); the name 'petrel', after St Peter, is a reference to the birds' habit of walking or pattering across water. Some birds feed from the surface layer while swimming and also dive in pursuit of prey to a limited extent (shearwaters and albatrosses); some plunge-dive (gannets and boobies); some dive from the surface and engage in underwater pursuit to depths of ten metres or more (penguins and the small auks); some are skilled in piracy (skuas, frigate-birds and some terns); and many are adept at scavenging. The gulls are notorious scavengers, and in the last three or four decades some species, especially the lesser black-backed gull and the herring gull, have increasingly taken advantage of the untidy habits of humans. There are now colonies well inland and the birds are not only a nuisance in urban areas but also a possible danger to health as their droppings can spread diseases. Furthermore, the increased numbers of predatory gulls pose a threat to other seabirds because the large gulls take eggs and eat fledglings.

Arctic Tern

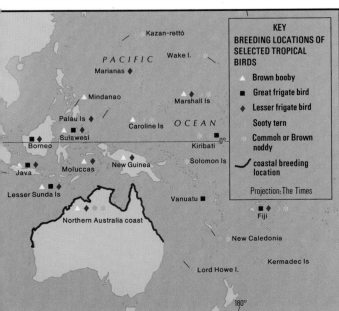

- ☐ breeding ground
- — migration route

8 *right* Though there is disagreement over the exact number of species, it is generally accepted that sixteen families of birds are wholly or predominantly oceanic in character.

THE SIXTEEN FAMILIES OF SEABIRDS

Sphenisidae	penguins
Diomedeidae	albatrosses and mollymawks
Procellariidae	true petrels and shearwaters
Hydrobatidae	storm petrels
Pelecanoididae	diving petrels
Phaethontidae	tropic birds
Pelecanidae	pelicans
Sulidae	gannets and boobies
Phalacrocoracidae	cormorants and shags
Fregatidae	frigate birds
Phalaropodidae	phalaropes
Stercorariidae	skuas and jaegers
Laridae	gulls
Sternidae	terns and noddies
Rynchopidae	skimmers
Alcidae	auks

KEY
BREEDING LOCATIONS OF SELECTED TROPICAL BIRDS
- △ Brown booby
- ■ Great frigate bird
- ◆ Lesser frigate bird
- ▲ Sooty tern
- ● Common or Brown noddy
- — coastal breeding location

Projection:The Times

7 *above* The Arctic tern makes migratory journeys thousands of kilometres in length, travelling to the Antarctic Ocean from its breeding grounds along the coasts of Alaska, Canada, Greenland, northern Europe and the Soviet Union, although its precise journeys are not known. The birds moult in the Antarctic during January and February before returning to the Arctic to breed.

4 *left* The dominant seabirds in the tropics are boobies, terns, frigate-birds, tropic birds, plus a few shearwaters, petrels and albatrosses. Their basic food consists of squid and flying fish. The tropics are relatively barren in comparison with some parts of the world, though upwelling areas are rich in bird life. Large communities also thrive in coastal waters enriched by minerals from inflowing rivers.

9 *right* The kittiwake is extremely abundant and ranges freely over the north Atlantic and north Pacific feeding on plankton. It breeds on cliff ledges in crowded colonies.

Common Kittiwake

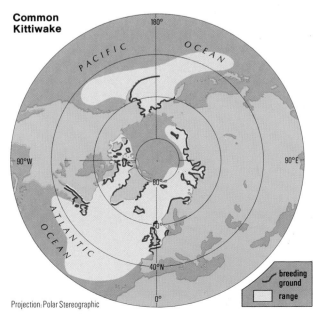

- — breeding ground
- ☐ range

Projection:Polar Stereographic

The Southern Ocean

THE Southern Ocean covers about 35 million sq. km, almost two-thirds of which freezes over each winter. It comprises all those oceanic areas to the south of the Antarctic convergence, where the cold northward-flowing Antarctic surface water dips sharply beneath the warmer water to the north. This sinking water, together with the even colder water which sinks close to the Antarctic continent to form the Antarctic bottom water, is replaced by upwelling, nutrient-rich water which is largely responsible for the enormous productivity of the Antarctic seas. Recent research has demonstrated that the biological communities of the Southern Ocean are not as universally rich as was once thought, for the really high productivity takes place only in the inshore waters, particularly in the Scotia Arc–Weddell Sea region and, at least as far as the phytoplankton are concerned, is restricted to a relatively short period of about 120 days each year. Nevertheless, at certain times and in certain seas, the Southern Ocean supports huge populations of phytoplankton, herbivorous zooplankton and predators, including seals, whales and seabirds.

The shortness of the food chain from the tiny planktonic plants, through krill to the baleen whales, in contrast with the length of most marine food chains, makes the exploitation of the whale populations by man very attractive since relatively little of the primary productivity of the ocean is 'lost' in intervening links (see *The plankton* pages 70–71). However, the well-documented collapse of the whale populations due to overfishing since the beginning of the Antarctic whaling industry in 1904 has led to the total prohibition of catching all but the small minke whale in recent years. To replace the lost whale harvest, there has been a growing interest during the last two decades in exploiting the krill populations directly, and thus getting even closer to the primary productivity.

It is estimated that before they were exploited, the Southern Ocean baleen whales were consuming around 190 million tonnes of krill each year, with further large amounts being eaten by the other predators. There must now be a huge potential for the exploitation of krill by man (see feature opposite).

Krill fishing is being seriously undertaken by several nations, particularly the USSR and Japan. The annual catch is now around 600 000 tonnes and is expected to rise rapidly. This relatively small amount will certainly have no significant effect on the Antarctic communities; but the lesson to be learned from the history of the whaling industry should act as a clear warning that much more knowledge of Antarctic biology is needed before the annual krill catch can be allowed to rise into the millions of tonnes. For krill are of prime importance, directly or indirectly, to many animals of the Southern Ocean other than the baleen whales. Reckless exploitation of krill could cause disastrous changes throughout the Southern Ocean ecosystem.

Whales

The whales (order Cetacea) are divided into two main groups. The baleen whales (Mysticeti) have enormous mouths and feed on small animals which they filter from the water through the baleen or whalebone plates suspended from their upper jaw. The toothed whales (Odonteceti), unlike the baleen whales, do not eat krill; they feed on larger prey ranging from fish to giant squid. Of the species illustrated here, only the sperm whale belongs to the Odonteceti. Almost all southern hemisphere baleen whales migrate into the Antarctic Ocean during the summer (November to April), consuming enormous quantities of the rich near-surface plankton, particularly krill and copepods. At the end of summer they migrate northwards towards the equatorial waters where mating takes place and the calves are born. During this warm-water sojourn the adults do not feed. The sperm whale more generally lives in warm and temperate waters.

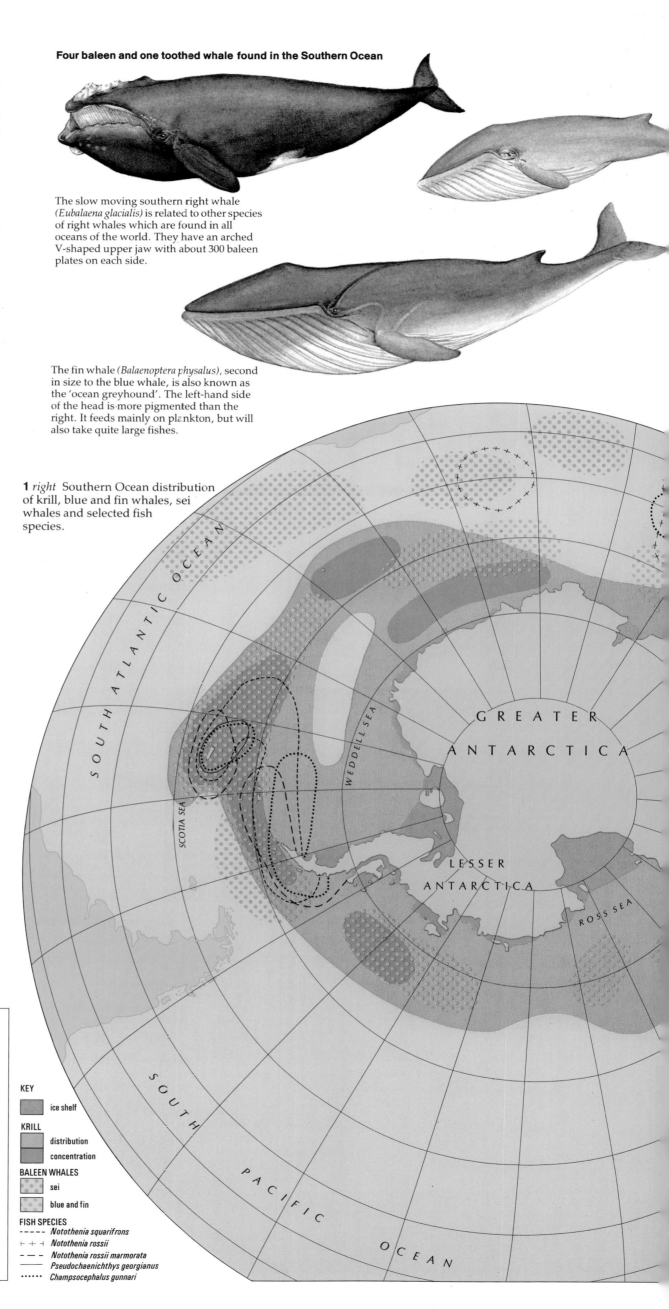

Four baleen and one toothed whale found in the Southern Ocean

The slow moving southern right whale (*Eubalaena glacialis*) is related to other species of right whales which are found in all oceans of the world. They have an arched V-shaped upper jaw with about 300 baleen plates on each side.

The fin whale (*Balaenoptera physalus*), second in size to the blue whale, is also known as the 'ocean greyhound'. The left-hand side of the head is more pigmented than the right. It feeds mainly on plankton, but will also take quite large fishes.

1 *right* Southern Ocean distribution of krill, blue and fin whales, sei whales and selected fish species.

KEY

▨ ice shelf

KRILL

▨ distribution
▨ concentration

BALEEN WHALES

▨ sei
▨ blue and fin

FISH SPECIES

- - - - - *Notothenia squarifrons*
+ + + *Notothenia rossii*
– – – *Notothenia rossii marmorata*
——— *Pseudochaenichthys georgianus*
········· *Champsocephalus gunnari*

The sei whale (*Balaenoptera borealis*) is very widely distributed. The sieves of its baleen plates are finer than those of most of its relatives and so it can eat smaller planktonic animals, particularly copepods.

Krill

The shrimp-like krill, *Euphausia superba*, measures a little over 5 cm in length when fully grown. With the present severely reduced whale stocks, some scientists believe that there is a krill surplus, which could be harvested by man, amounting to as much as 150 million tonnes annually, that is about twice as much as the current total world catch of all other marine species.

Despite the inhospitable regions in which they live, krill are rather easy to catch because they aggregate into extremely dense swarms 40–60 m across which can be spotted from the deck of a ship, from aeroplanes or even from satellites. In recent experimental fishing operations good catch rates of around 40 tonnes an hour have been achieved, with extreme rates of as much as 30 tonnes in eight minutes. Unfortunately, the small size of the animals and the rapidity with which they begin to spoil once landed make krill a difficult catch to process. Moreover, there is probably a rather limited potential for using krill directly for human consumption, the main use being in the form of a krill meal for feeding to animals.

The blue whale (*Balaenoptera musculus*) is the largest animal that has ever existed on Earth. During the feeding period a large adult may eat 3 tonnes of krill each day. Calves are over 7 metres long at birth. Blue whales live for about 50 years.

The sperm whale or cachalot (*Physeter catodon*) is the deepest diving species, descending regularly to depths of 1000 m, and can remain submerged for over an hour. The main food is squid, including giant species over 9 m long.

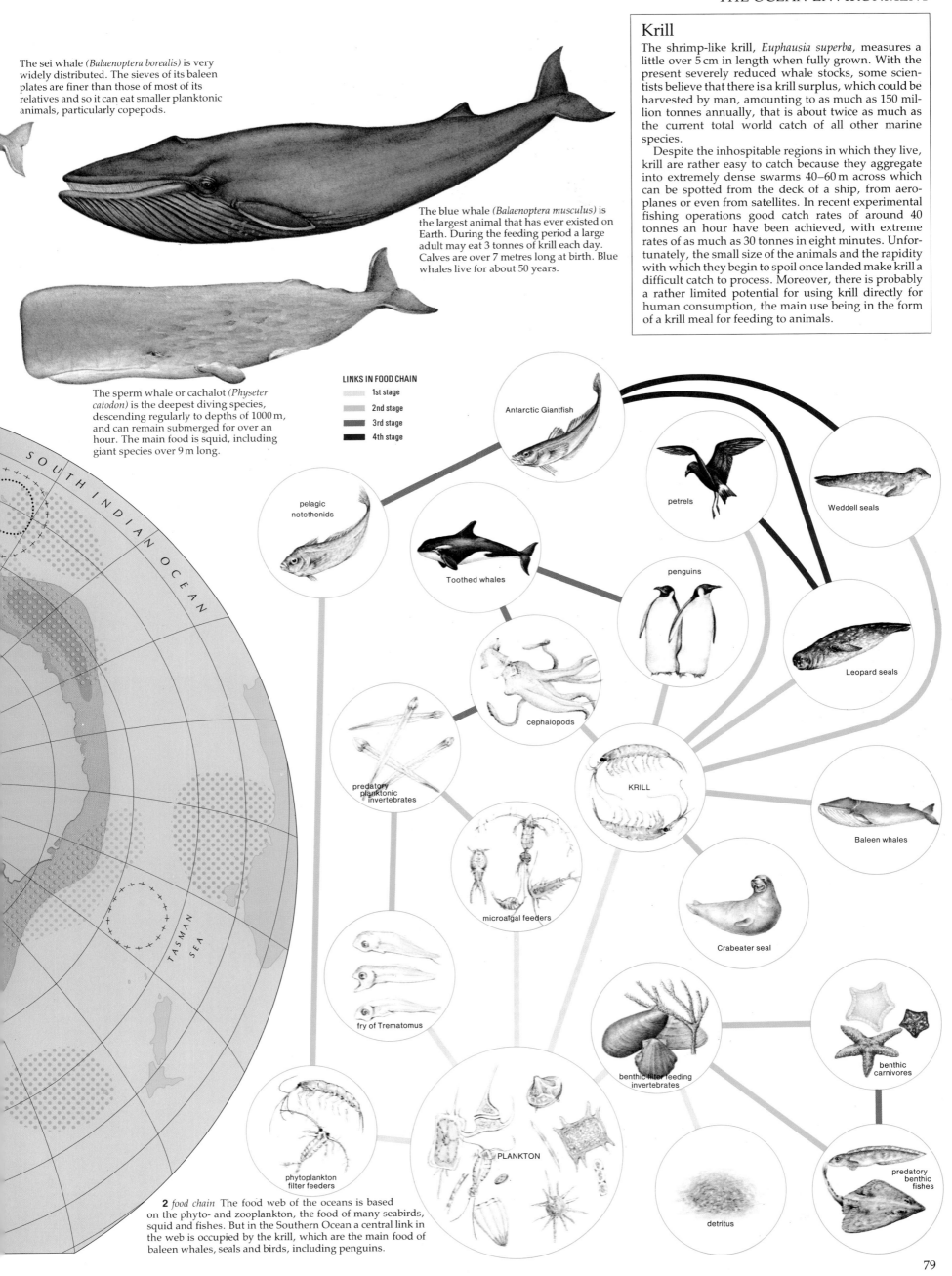

LINKS IN FOOD CHAIN
1st stage
2nd stage
3rd stage
4th stage

Antarctic Giantfish

pelagic notothenids

petrels

Weddell seals

Toothed whales

penguins

Leopard seals

cephalopods

predatory planktonic invertebrates

KRILL

Baleen whales

microalgal feeders

Crabeater seal

fry of Trematomus

benthic filter feeding invertebrates

benthic carnivores

phytoplankton filter feeders

PLANKTON

detritus

predatory benthic fishes

SOUTH INDIAN OCEAN

TASMAN SEA

2 *food chain* The food web of the oceans is based on the phyto- and zooplankton, the food of many seabirds, squid and fishes. But in the Southern Ocean a central link in the web is occupied by the krill, which are the main food of baleen whales, seals and birds, including penguins.

The traditional fisheries

THE sea, like the land, provides two main opportunities for the production of food; fishing (hunting) and aquaculture (cultivation). Unlike the land, for the sea the former is by far the more important of the two, both in terms of the number of people employed and economic returns.

The foundations of today's traditional or artisanal fisheries rest upon a vast range of regional gears which has evolved over a long period. The boats of the artisanal fishermen, for instance, are often simple dugouts, or planked craft locally built, or sailing vessels, sometimes with auxiliary engines. Though varied, much of the gear is also simple and includes numerous types of lines, lift and scoop nets, seines (beach and sea), gill nets, traps, rafts, spears and lures.

Fishing is frequently a dangerous occupation and demands skills as well as local knowledge; the risks are great, both physically and in terms of income, and many of the traditional fisheries are characterised by close-knit, sharing communities with distinct customs and rituals.

The traditional fisheries are mainly concentrated in the developing countries where fishing is usually combined as a part-time activity with agriculture. Though capital investment is minimal and incomes are low, these fisheries represent the largest single sector in world fishing and employ about 80 per cent of the world's fishermen. In addition, they directly support over 40

million people. In Asia and the Pacific in particular, artisanal fisheries predominate in manpower and number of vessels.

The trend in some countries, such as Thailand and Sri Lanka, has been towards rapid modernisation. In Thailand the new urban-based trawlers represent 15 per cent of the Thai fishing fleet yet produce 70 per cent of the landings. There are over 64 000 fishermen in Thailand located mainly in villages and they are feeling the impact of the efficient modern urban-based fishing on their stocks, and on their market opportunities. In this area, as in other parts of South East Asia, there is a conflict between the need to produce more fish, which can be done by the introduction of large modern vessels fishing out of

1 *left* In Japan, fishermen use cormorants to catch fish at night. A ring placed around the birds' necks prevents them from swallowing their capture.

2 *above* Near Weligman, Sri Lanka, small fish such as mullet and sea bass are caught with a rod by fishermen sitting on wooden stilts.

A lagoon atoll and its marine resources: Kiribati in the South Pacific

3 *below* The typical Kiribati village is made up of 20 to 60 houses built of coconut and pandanus materials of which the *Maneaba* (meeting house) is the largest. In ancient times it served as a navigation school. There may be a mission, cooperative, canoe sheds, fish traps, and always the lavatories extending outwards over the reef which are used as fishing platforms. Copra, dried shark fins or tuna are the only direct sources of cash incomes for most villagers. Many young men work away or serve as seamen on foreign ships. Population growth is a problem on all the atolls.

4 *right* The Kiribati atoll dweller lives close to the sea. The coral soils of the islands are poor but ecologically the coral reefs are rich with a great variety of habitats and marine life. Most of the fish are caught from canoes and by gathering from the reef flats. On heavily populated islands, lagoon and reef marine life has been seriously depleted. Some commercial deep sea fishing for tuna using powered vessels is being introduced to several of the atolls. The diagram and the accompanying captions indicate the marine resources and their locations.

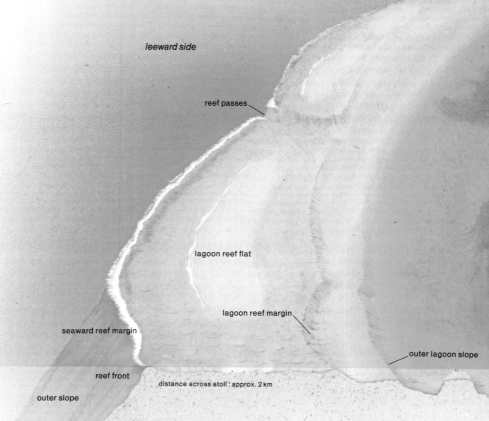

leeward side

reef passes

lagoon reef flat

lagoon reef margin

seaward reef margin

outer lagoon slope

reef front

distance across atoll: approx. 2 km

outer slope

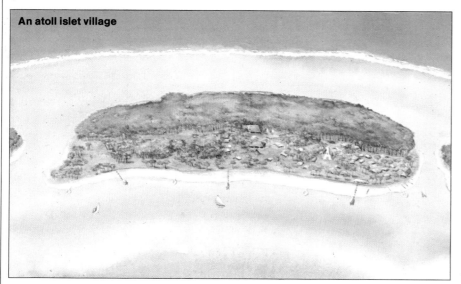

An atoll islet village

Marine resources of a coral atoll

Reef passes In the deep passages (boat passes) between the submerged reefs on the lagoon side there are shark, small tuna, surgeon fish, parrot fish, sardines and giant clams. Fishing is from canoes and by diving.

Reef margin, reef front and outer slope These areas have species similar to the corresponding areas on the windward side of the atoll, but fishing is more often possible on this sheltered leeward side.

Lagoon reef flat Line fishing and gathering at low water for small fish, clams, crabs, arc shells, and sea slugs.

Lagoon reef margin This area is fished for shrimps, eels, molluscs and shellfish using lines, spears and diving.

Outer lagoon slope Often good fishing for crabs, eels and shellfish, from canoes but also by diving.

Lagoon The vast expanse of the lagoon is less productive than the reef front and margins but around the hundreds of coral knolls there are many species of fish including whiting, mullet, sardines, false herring, urchins, oysters, shrimps, squid, clams, rays, and sometimes shark. Fishing is mainly from canoes.

Inner lagoon slope Mullet, sardines and sea slugs are caught from canoes with lines and nets, and by gathering.

Lagoon reef Small fish and some sea slugs, molluscs and bivalves are caught by

digging, gathering, line and net, and canoe fishing. Fish traps are built and fishing is also done from lavatory platforms extending from the beach.

Seaward beach and lagoon beach Snails and crabs are gathered here and used for bait. Now, however, small fish for bait are increasingly bred in beach hatcheries and sold to Japanese tuna fishermen. Milkfish are also reared in ponds behind the beach. Turtle eggs may be gathered, though no longer in populated islets.

The inner reef flat This area dries during low tide and women and children from the villages glean from the flat and the tide pools. At night, bright pressure lamps are used which blind the fish and make them easier to capture by hand. Seven days after full moon the reef flat may be covered by an edible jellyfish. Extending from the

beach are fish traps built of coral rubble into which fish swim during the ebb tide. The reef flats are often very overfished and depleted of much marine life. Species which may be obtained from outer and inner zones include bivalves, squid, lobster, crayfish, crabs, sea slugs, urchins, blennies, gobies, carrhitids, mullet, salmoneus, eels, octopus, sponges, shrimp, sea cucumbers, snails, and occasionally turtle.

Reef flat and tide pool zones The outer reef flat is normally covered by water at low tide. The village lavatories may sometimes reach here, perched at the end of long wooden causeways, and these also provide fishing platforms. Both men and women wade across the outer reef flat to water depths up to chest level, and form semicircles with nets; a beater herds the fish towards the entrance of the net. Here sea

the big ports, and the need to improve the standard of living of the artisanal fishermen. Modern fishing can result in the ruination of artisanal fishing villages, and attacks have been made on the crews of trawlers which have strayed near Indonesian artisanal fishing grounds. Many fishery experts now recognise the importance of the artisanal fishery to the majority of the population of island and coastal areas, and the need to introduce appropriate technology which will enable fishermen to extend their range from villages, and the need to reserve specific near-coastal zones of the sea for the artisanal fisheries.

Artisanal fishing around Kiribati

An example of the intimate and diverse relationships between people and the sea in an artisanal fishery can be seen in an atoll environment such as Kiribati.

The main region of Kiribati comprises a chain of low coral islands in the south-west Pacific extending over 400 miles from about lat. 3°30′N to 2°50′S and long. 173° to 177°E. The land surface areas, consisting of atolls and reef islands, total only 115 square miles and are inhabited by about 57 000 people. The islands are very isolated and many are subject to droughts. They have poor soils and a vegetational cover consisting primarily of coconut and pandanus trees. The resources of the sea and reef are, therefore, vital for the wellbeing of many communities.

The artisanal fishery on a typical atoll exploits a wide range of ecological conditions, and the fishermen have an intimate understanding of fish locations, habitats and behaviour. The coral reefs are extremely rich with hundreds of species of fish as well as other fauna.

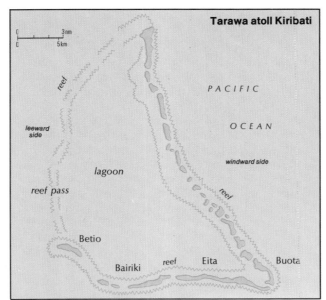

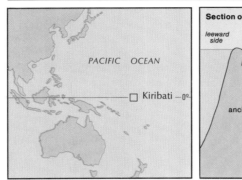

5 *above* Fishing boats in Lerwick harbour, Shetland, in the 1960s. The boats in the foreground, used mainly for recreation, are similar in design to the open boats of the past.

Development from an artisanal fishery

The process of specialisation in both gears and communities brought about by commercialisation and industrialisation over long periods is best seen in developed countries, even when traditional practices still persist. In the Shetland Islands, the basis was a long line, open boat fishery for ling and cod which was conducted by part-time fishermen and dated back to the medieval period. This was expanded for direct trade with Hanseatic merchant outlets in the 15th century. In the early 18th century the local landowners became the entrepreneurs, the lines became longer, the boats larger and the grounds more distant, the fisheries being conducted from outlying stations located as close as possible to the fishing grounds. In the 19th century this fishery was supplemented by a more specialised cod fishery using handlines and decked smacks, commencing in Shetland waters and ultimately ranging as far afield as Faeroe, Iceland and Rockall. After 1880, the fisheries became more specialised. The former fisheries disappeared, and winter fisheries for haddock and cod, with a great summer herring fishery using decked sailboats, took their place. Communities of full-time fishermen began to emerge, and out of these came the modern economically and technologically diversified industry.

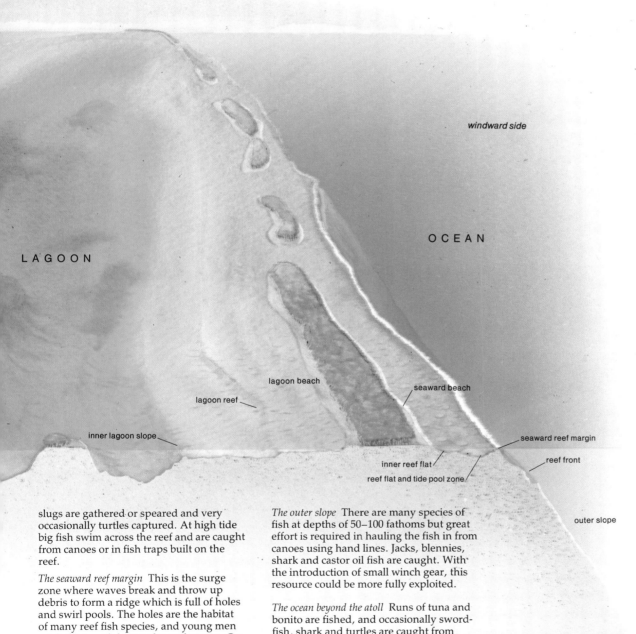

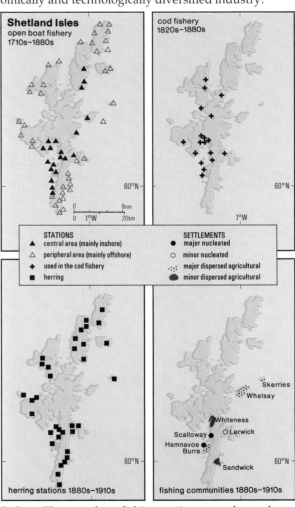

slugs are gathered or speared and very occasionally turtles captured. At high tide big fish swim across the reef and are caught from canoes or in fish traps built on the reef.

The seaward reef margin This is the surge zone where waves break and throw up debris to form a ridge which is full of holes and swirl pools. The holes are the habitat of many reef fish species, and young men catch them with long poles and spears. On the seaward side of the atoll lines are cast into the surf beyond the reef.

Reef front Here live many fish populations, including hundreds of reef species in the living coral, plus small tuna, shark and barracudas near the surface. The men use outrigger canoes and hand lines. Flying fish are caught at night using dip nets and lamps.

The outer slope There are many species of fish at depths of 50–100 fathoms but great effort is required in hauling the fish in from canoes using hand lines. Jacks, blennies, shark and castor oil fish are caught. With the introduction of small winch gear, this resource could be more fully exploited.

The ocean beyond the atoll Runs of tuna and bonito are fished, and occasionally swordfish, shark and turtles are caught from canoes at various distances from the islands. The islanders go out to sea in response to recognised signs. Birds flying high and scattered indicate poor fishing prospects. Birds concentrated near the surface, some diving, indicate dense shoals of sardines and other small fish, on which the tuna or bonito may be feeding. But the ocean is fished primarily by commercial vessels, mainly Japanese.

6 *above* The open boat fishing stations were located on beaches suitable for hauling up small boats and drying fish, as close as possible to the fishing grounds, so that there were many stations around the periphery of the islands. Cod fishing employed decked smacks and stations were located in the sheltered inlets (voes) in the central region of the archipelago. Herring sailboats also required sheltered harbours where stations could be constructed for salting and barrelling herring for export. Daily voyages favoured peripheral voes near the grounds. The fishing communities of the early 20th century emerged in locations most favourable to specialisation in all these types of fishing.

Farming the sea

THE origins of aquaculture can be traced back some four thousand years when it flourished in those areas which came under the influence of Chinese civilisation in southern and eastern Asia. It remains a widespread traditional practice. Most of this traditional aquaculture is based on rearing freshwater species and is closely related to agriculture. Brackish water culture in coastal locations appears to have developed around AD 1400 in the south-east Asian islands, now part of Indonesia.

Aquaculture statistics remain based upon estimates rather than accurate statistics due to the traditional nature of much of the activity, and the technical problems in obtaining data. However, indications show that production continues to increase. In 1980 finfish accounted for some two-thirds, while shellfish (largely molluscs) and seaweeds the remaining third of total world production. Unfortunately, in the finfish category it is not possible to distinguish accurately between freshwater and brackish and sea water production (mariculture), though it is thought likely that from one-quarter to one-third of finfish production is brackish and sea water based. There are also difficulties in estimating Chinese production, which may be considerably higher than the statistics suggest.

Aquaculture probably developed from simple holding and trapping of a single species. In fresh water the common carp was and remains important, although attention has been focused upon polyculture, whereby several compatible fish species and sometimes other aquatic organisms are raised together. Sometimes, this is further integrated with activities such as vegetable gardening, fruit growing or chicken or duck rearing. Most fish culture is carried out in ponds, though lakes, reservoirs, mangrove swamps, ricefields and rivers are also important.

Brackish water culture probably began with the milkfish which today is the most important marine species, being widely reared in Taiwan, the Philippines and Indonesia although it occurs naturally further afield throughout the Indo-Pacific region. As is commonly the case in traditional aquaculture, sustaining production is initially dependent upon the use of wild stocks. Milkfish fry are netted in coastal waters and raised in carefully prepared ponds in which food supply, pests and predators are controlled, and by using multiple stocking techniques two or three harvests can be made every year.

Greatest interest has always been in the cultivation of high value species which can best cover the considerable cost of provision and maintenance of specialised locations and equipment. In many industrial countries there is a strong interest in technological advancement with emphasis upon the securing of supplies of seed, breeding suitable strains, and using waste water and treated sewage as food supplies. In developing countries aquaculture is often seen as an important part of integrated rural development schemes which help promote, among other

things, employment and high quality food supplies. The FAO/UNDP ten-year aquaculture development programme which commenced in the mid 1970s aims to double output in Asia, Africa and Latin America.

In the developed countries in the late 1970s, over 800 companies in 26 countries were involved in farming the sea. The production of finfish tends to be restricted to high value species such as plaice and turbot, and salmonids, including salmon and trout, and there is a growing interest in the artificial propagation of juveniles which can then be released into the sea to be caught at a later stage. In these experiments in ocean ranching, salmon has been a prime candidate and over the past two decades the Japanese and others have been rewarded with some measure of success. The possibility of extending salmon ranges by introducing them to the southern hemisphere has long been recognised and still commands attention. Initial trials in Chile and South Island, New Zealand, in the early 1900s met with little success, as did Russian introduction of Pacific salmon into the North-east Atlantic. More recently, the Japanese have been

successful in a pilot operation in southern Chile, while other trials off Australia and New Zealand have also proved successful.

Of the shellfish, oysters and mussels are by far the most important. They are grown in numerous ways: on rafts, poles, hanging ropes and on the bottom. In the Netherlands, mussel seeds, garnered from natural beds, are planted in the shallower waters of the Wadden Zee and along the major channels of the Oosterschelde, and later transplanted into deeper water where they mature and are harvested by dredging. The gathering of natural seeds and the control of farming plots are strictly regulated by the government. The main markets for mussels are in France and Belgium and for oysters in Japan, North America and Western Europe.

1–4 *world map and insets* The nations of East Asia predominate in aquaculture production, much of which is traditional. European and North American production concentrates upon high value finfish such as salmon and trout, and shellfish—mainly oysters and mussels. France is the most important shellfish market in Europe and has important oyster and mussel rearing industries.

5 *below* By breeding oysters in artificial ponds, harvesting is made easier and the risk of contamination by pollution is avoided.

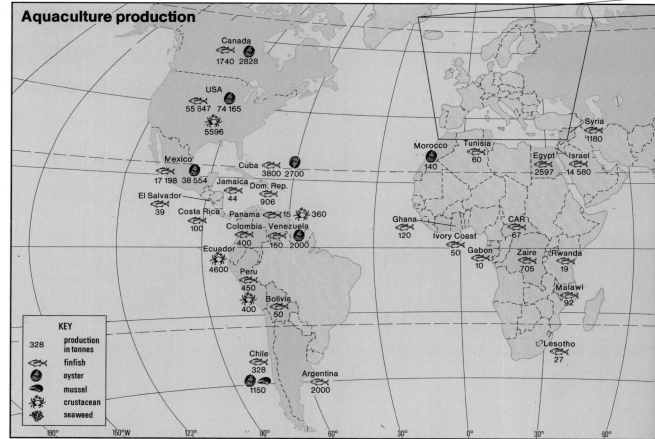

Aquaculture production

KEY
328   production in tonnes
finfish
oyster
mussel
crustacean
seaweed

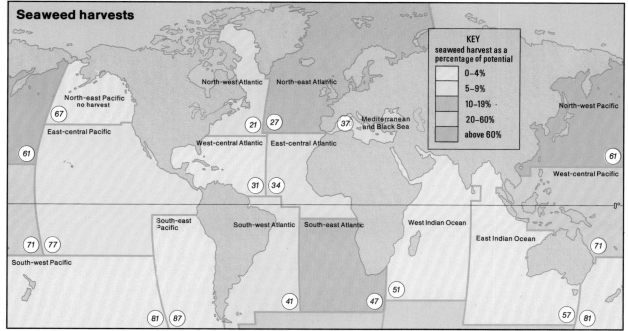

Seaweed harvests

KEY
seaweed harvest as a percentage of potential
0–4%
5–9%
10–19%
20–60%
above 60%

Red and brown algae production and potential harvest

red algae / brown algae
actual
potential
FAO area

all figures in '000 tons wet weight

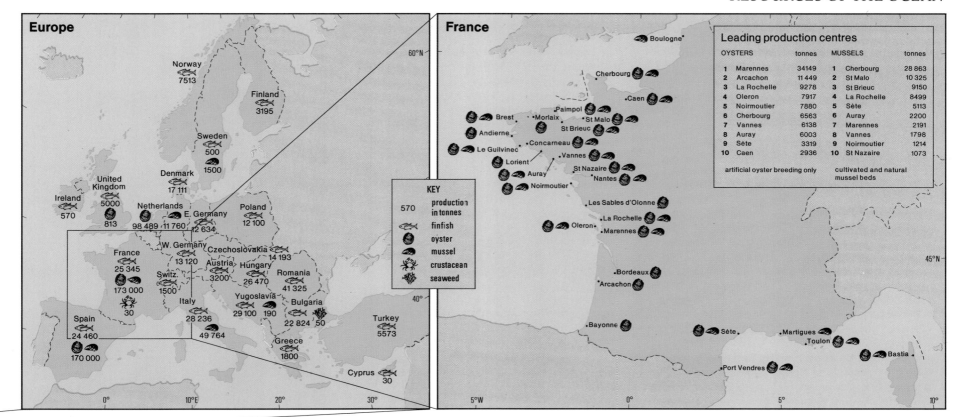

Europe

France

Leading production centres

	OYSTERS	tonnes		MUSSELS	tonnes
1	Marennes	34149	1	Cherbourg	28 863
2	Arcachon	11 449	2	St Malo	10 325
3	La Rochelle	9278	3	St Brieuc	9150
4	Oleron	7917	4	La Rochelle	8499
5	Noirmoutier	7880	5	Sète	5113
6	Cherbourg	6563	6	Auray	2200
7	Vannes	6138	7	Marennes	2191
8	Auray	6003	8	Vannes	1798
9	Sète	3319	9	Noirmoutier	1214
10	Caen	2936	10	St Nazaire	1073

artificial oyster breeding only — cultivated and natural mussel beds

KEY
570 production in tonnes · finfish · oyster · mussel · crustacean · seaweed

6 *below* The milkfish is distributed widely in the tropical Indo-Pacific. Although large mature specimens are sometimes caught at sea, they have never formed the basis for a large-scale sea fishery. They are, however, an important aquaculture resource. Their fry are collected in coastal waters by net and then transferred to ponds where they are reared for harvesting. Coastal industrialisation and pollution are, therefore, a hazard in the main farming area in the East Asian islands, which occupy the central location in the overall distribution of the milkfish.

East and South-east Asia

Milkfish

Milkfish distribution

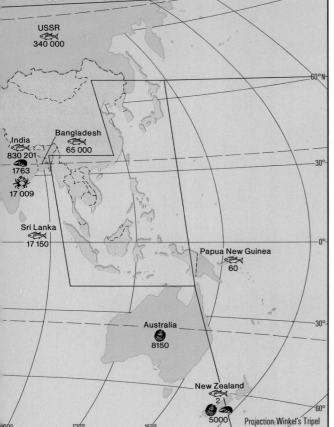

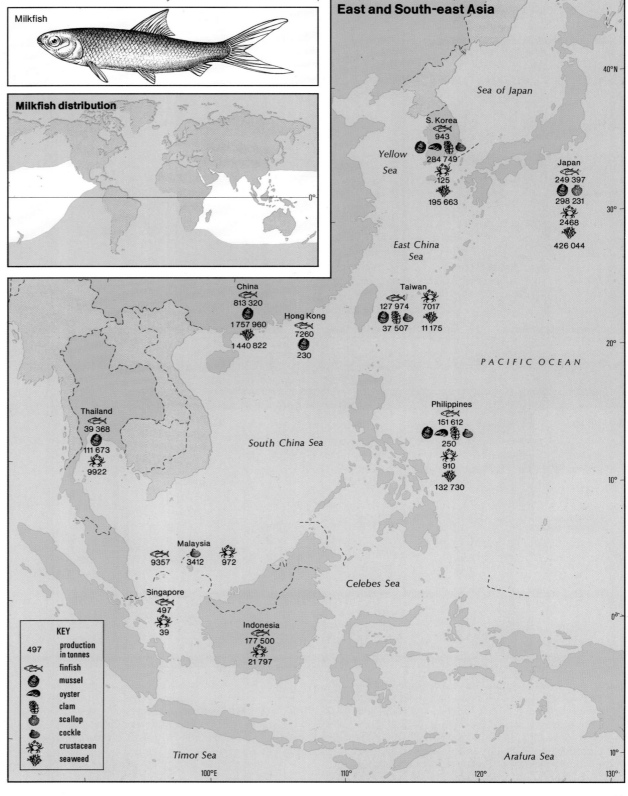

Seaweed

Seaweeds, or more precisely sea algae, are known to grow abundantly in many regions of the world's seas and oceans though the majority are located in the temperate and warm temperate waters. In regions where accessibility and transport are not problems, harvesting is often carried out. There is an increasing emphasis being placed upon cultivation though this is restricted to Japan, China and Taiwan where it is used primarily as a food resource. In Western Europe where seaweed was used originally as a fertiliser and for feeding animals, its uses are mainly industrial.

As a food seaweed offers a rich source of vitamins, iodides and calcium, which are synthesised from seawater. In industry, seaweeds are a source of vegetable gums (alginates from brown algae, carageenan and agar agar from red algae) and are used in a wide variety of manufacturing processes, particularly in the pharmaceutical, dairy, confectionary and textile industries.

7 *left* The concentration of production in the northwest Pacific reflects the cultivation of seaweed which is used primarily for human consumption. The smaller concentrations elsewhere are associated with industrial uses. The potential harvest of seaweeds remains very high in all the oceans between the polar ice and coral limits. However, the inaccessibility of much of the resource makes its harvesting prohibitively expensive so that cultivation is likely to increase.

KEY
497 production in tonnes · finfish · mussel · oyster · clam · scallop · cockle · crustacean · seaweed

The world fishing industry

THE great commercial fisheries of today are based upon the application and continuing development of technology for locating fish stocks and improving gear and vessel design. The rise of scientific methods of appraising resources as a tool in fisheries management has been a significant development. The methods apply principally to the epipelagic zone, though with the need to tap new resources, interest is being shown in deeper waters. Research relies on exploratory fishing, the use of acoustic soundings, egg and larvae surveys and fish tagging. Underwater observation may be used for deeper layers and aerial reconnaissance and remote sensing from space will undoubtedly play a greater role in the future. This research is supplemented by analysis of catch and landings data of the commercial fisheries by national fisheries administrations, regional fisheries management organisations and internationally by the FAO.

Ultimately more important than scientific resource appraisal, however, are the methods of locating fish stocks actually used by fishermen. In the traditional fisheries this is still based on local knowledge and visual observation of the sea surface, plankton, bird behaviour and other factors, together with the use of land bearings or dead reckoning for fixing positions on the fishing grounds. The focus of technological development has been upon the use of echo-sounders and sonar for fish detection, supplemented by radio-direction finding for location of grounds on the continental shelves of the major fishing regions.

The commercial fisheries are based on just a few gears which undergo a constant process of refinement and adaptation to a wide variety of fishery environments. The selection of suitable gears is influenced by tradition, the habits and value of the species sought, and such environmental conditions as the nature of the seabed.

1 *right* Pelagic fish live and feed close to the surface. Demersal and shellfish live for the most part on or near the bottom although some species such as cod and shrimp may adopt a pelagic habit at certain times. The pelagic fisheries are based mainly on shoaling species, such as sardine or anchovy, and are usually caught with purse-seines and pelagic trawls. Tuna are notable in being caught with a wide variety of gears. High value species such as whales and swordfish are caught individually with harpoons while salmon may be caught by gill nets or long lines at sea, or in traps as they enter the rivers. Important demersal gears include bottom beam and otter trawls, and seine nets, all of which may be operated for hours at a stretch in order to gain economic catches. Such fisheries normally catch several species simultaneously. Long line fishing is a selective way of catching large demersal species such as cod and ling. Among shellfish, the crustaceans, including lobsters and crabs, are highly mobile and are caught on the bottom using pots. Shrimps are caught using pelagic trawls. The molluscs, including mussels, oysters, clams and quahogs are relatively sedentary and may be dredged from the bottom.

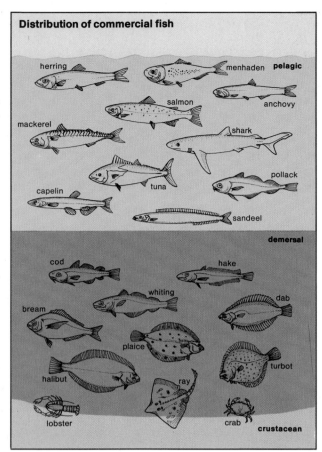

Distribution of commercial fish

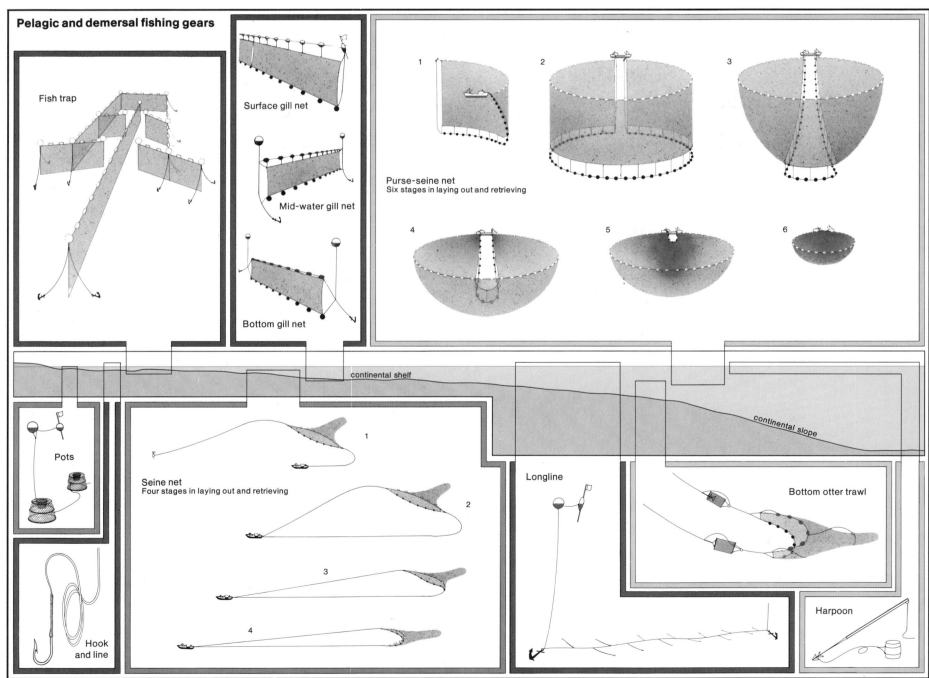

2 *above* Demersal gears may be classified into mobile and static categories. Chief among the former is the bottom otter trawl which appeared with the advent of steam trawling in the North Sea in the 1880s, and which is associated with overfishing of cod in the North Atlantic. Also important is the beam trawl, and the seine net, regionally adapted to a wide range of environmental conditions and fish stocks. Hand-lines are less important than formerly, while dredges are used for some shellfish. Static gears include long lines, gill nets, traps and pots. Pelagic gears are also mobile and static. The purse-seine, a mobile gear, is associated with the so-called 'industrial' fisheries in which the fish are reduced to meal and oil as distinct from being used for human consumption. It has undoubtedly contributed to overfishing of some stocks, such as the herring stocks in the North Sea. The mid-water or pelagic trawl is found in a wide variety of designs. Trolling, pole and line, and harpoon are used for high value species such as tuna and whales respectively. The static long line is important in the tuna fisheries. The famous drift net was the basis of the successive North Sea herring fisheries from medieval times until the 1950s.

The structure of the fishing industry

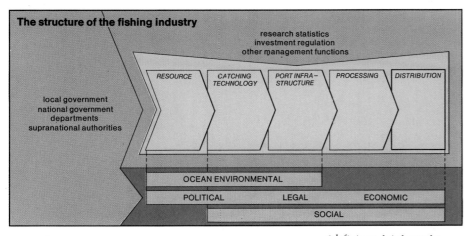

4 *left* A catch is brought alongside a purse-seiner.
6 *right* The Norwegian herring fleet in the port of Kristiansund in the 1960s. The fleet is now depleted because of the decline in the herring industry.

3 *above* The structure of the fishing industry consists of five major elements in which the resource—the subsistence and commercial fish stocks—are converted into food supplies. The degree of complexity of organisation is variable, and ranges from the simple subsistence fisheries, which probably produce around 10 per cent of the world catch and are not statistically recorded, to the highly organised commercial fishing industries which provide the bulk of the world supply of fish protein.

Each element in the structure is subject to a range of decision-making influences. Research investment is concentrated on resource evaluation and the development of technology and is supervised largely by national governments. In most regions investment in equipment is mainly by the fishermen, though some enterprises with large capital requirements, such as distant water fishing, rely more on private or state-owned companies. Regulations are exercised primarily by national governments and are concerned with such matters as mesh sizes, closed areas and seasons, quotas, vessel licensing, and with quality control of processed products. Because the industry involves so many decision-makers, including the individual fishermen, it is difficult to manage, and this has far-reaching implications for conservation.

Fisheries are also influenced by distinctive regional combinations of environmental, social, economic, legal and political factors. Environmental influences contribute to the pattern of grounds and catches. The continental shelves, upon which most of the currently exploited demersal stocks are located, and the upwelling areas associated with important tropical and subtropical fisheries, are the most important fishing grounds. All the seas, however, with their characteristic biomasses and fish fauna, offer some resource.

The cultural and economic patterns are dominated by the division between developed and less developed countries. In the industrial nations continuing technological advance combined with substantial investment have led to overcapacity in many fleets, which in turn leads to overfishing followed by social adjustment to a declining industry. Some developing countries with strong artisanal fisheries offer opportunities for building commercial fisheries in cooperation with the more developed fishing nations and the FAO.

5 *below* The countries which are particularly reliant upon seafood include the USSR, Poland and East Germany; the Scandinavian and Iberian countries; and Japan. There are also prominent groups of countries in South East Asia and West Africa where traditional fisheries are important. The fish products which are exported by developed countries are varied, with North American and Western European countries and Japan being active. The latter is, for example, a huge exporter of canned tuna. Exports from developing countries tend to consist of the more specialised high value products or bulk fishmeal and oil, as in the case of Peru.

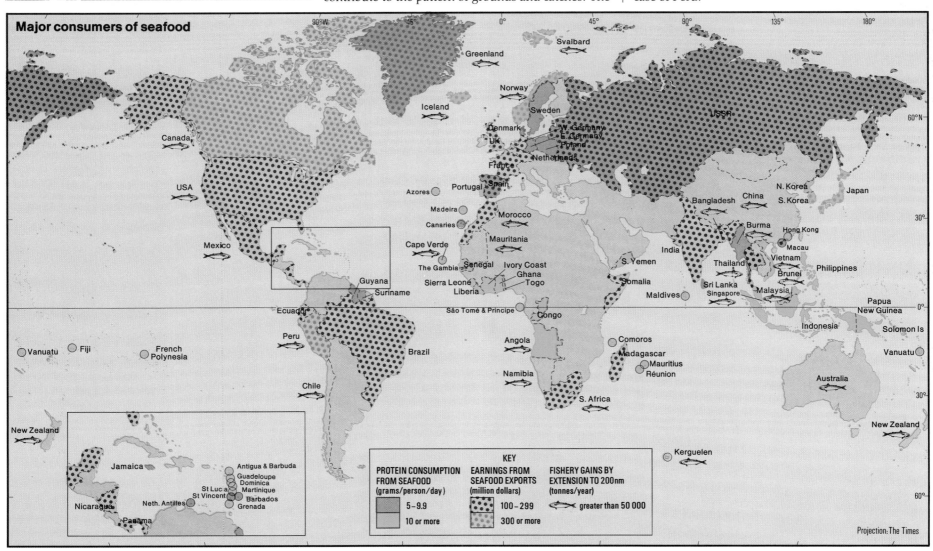

Major consumers of seafood

KEY		
PROTEIN CONSUMPTION FROM SEAFOOD (grams/person/day)	EARNINGS FROM SEAFOOD EXPORTS (million dollars)	FISHERY GAINS BY EXTENSION TO 200nm (tonnes/year)
5–9.9	100–299	greater than 50 000
10 or more	300 or more	

Projection: The Times

The world fishing fleet

THE world's fishing vessels may be numbered in millions, the vast majority being small craft employed in artisanal fisheries in developing countries, and those used for recreational fishing in the industrial nations. The true commercial fishing fleet is small by comparison, and only that part of it over 100 grt is mapped here, since only the larger vessels are influential in technological, economic and biological terms.

The commercial fleets are commonly classified either by the gear they carry, for example, seiners and trawlers; or by species caught such as tuna clippers and whale catchers; or geographically by operating range.

The nearshore fishing in a country's coastal zone is for shellfish, for diadromous species such as salmon, and for demersal stocks.

Further afield are the continental shelf fisheries within the Exclusive Economic Zone. Names for this fishery vary, for example the 'inshore' of Britain and the 'offshore' of Japan fall largely into this category. The maximum range of operation of the fleet is 200–300 miles from the home port. These continental shelf fisheries are often the most important sector of national fleets. The

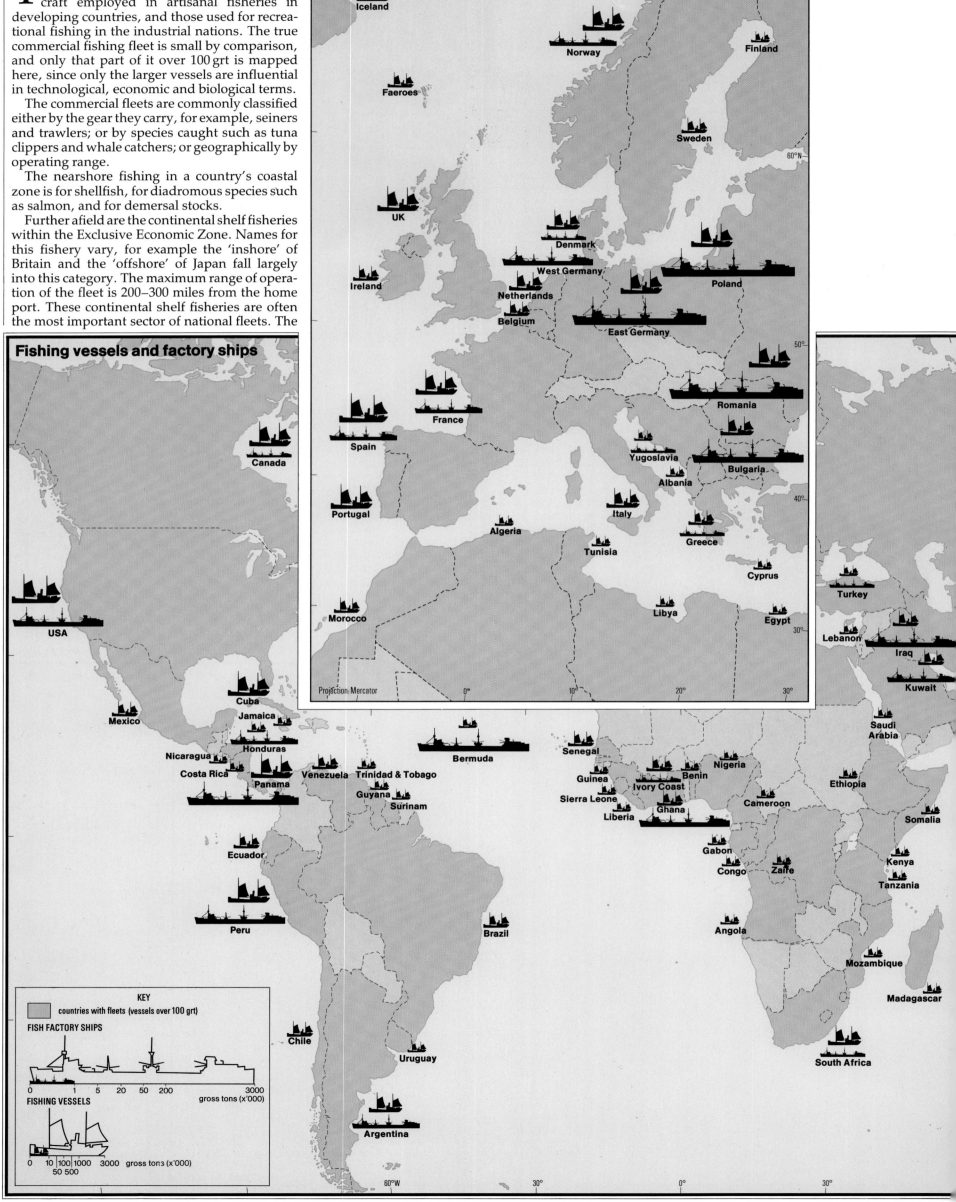

Fishing vessels and factory ships

Projection: Mercator

KEY

countries with fleets (vessels over 100 grt)

FISH FACTORY SHIPS

0   1   5   20   50   200   3000
gross tons (x'000)

FISHING VESSELS

0   10 100 1000 3000 gross tons (x'000)
        50 500

vessels are owned by the fishermen, and the fisheries have firm traditional roots, while at the same time they are innovative, notably in the development of multipurpose vessels able to use many types of gear. Such fisheries are attractive to developing nations aspiring to a substantial fishing industry based on their EEZ.

The terms 'middle' and 'distant' water fisheries originated in the north-east Atlantic trawling industries, and such fisheries are generally more specialised in gear and species sought than inshore/offshore fisheries. One type is based on distant water continental shelves—perhaps the best example is trawling for cod and other gadoids in the North Atlantic. These fisheries have in many cases been severely curtailed by extended fishing limits, leading to the rapid demise of some distant water fleets. Fleet operations are commonly concentrated in a small number of ports, vessels are company owned and the fishermen employees. The other type of distant water fishery is that in the deep ocean for species such as tuna, which are perhaps more responsive to direct economic pressures and overfishing.

Another category of fleet operates from remote shore or floating bases, historically a major element in the expansion of the greatest fishing nations of today, notably the USSR and other eastern European nations, especially Poland and East Germany, and Japan. It also opened up the Antarctic whaling industry. These fisheries have also been severely affected by the new EEZ regime, one response being the intensification of 'klondyking'—the buying of fish from coastal states' fleets by floating fish carriers belonging to nations formerly operating from remote bases as, for example, in the remaining herring and mackerel fisheries around Britain.

The design of vessels in the traditional fleets is a response to environmental conditions of operation and use of gears, and is the outcome of long periods of regional cultural evolution. In the case of the Shetland Isles (see page 81), for example, the open boat designs are now largely, though not entirely, used for recreational fishing. These 'Shetland models' are part of a large group of similar designs which originated at the time of medieval Viking influence and dominate traditional design throughout Scandinavia and the east coasts of Scotland and England.

1 *below* The major fishing fleets are concentrated in the industrial countries, while distant water factory ships are mainly from the communist bloc and flag of convenience states.

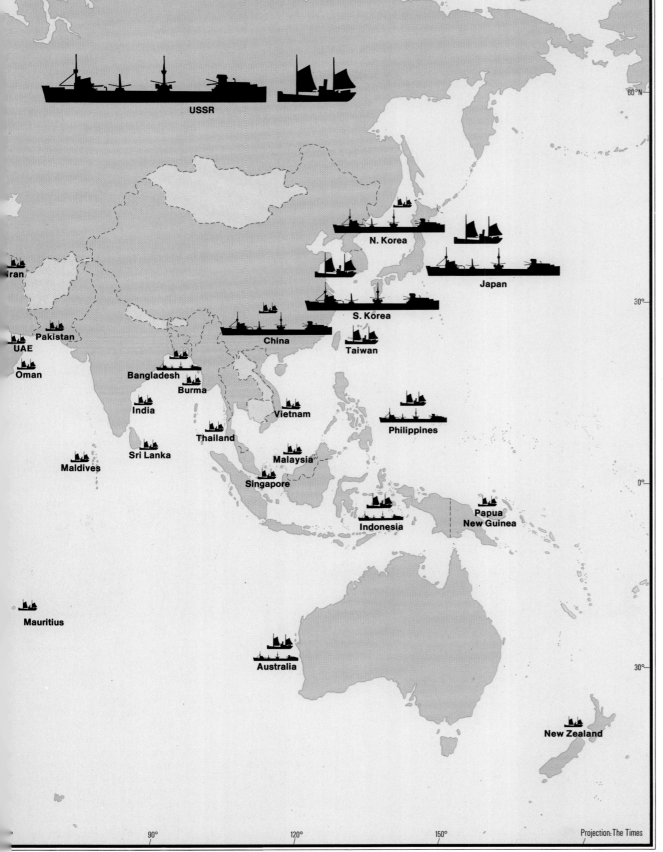

A seiner from Denmark. This vessel is also suitable for trawling, long-lining and purse-seining.

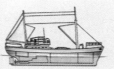

A trawler/drifter from the Netherlands. Drift netting for herring, once a major fishing activity in the North Sea, has practically ceased.

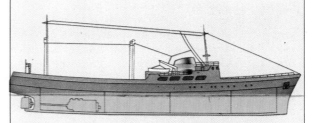

A stern trawler from the United Kingdom. This modern distant-water ship was designed to fish in the rich grounds of the North Atlantic.

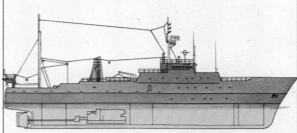

A small factory trawler from the United Kingdom equipped with the freezing and processing machinery which allows her to range far from her home base.

A small shrimp trawler from the Atlantic coast of the USA. These small vessels are used in the lucrative US shrimp fishery. A range of larger vessels is also used.

A tuna clipper from the USA. This is a combination vessel, rigged here as a tuna clipper. These boats may also be used as trawlers, tuna bait boats or purse seiners.

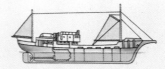

A pole and line tuna vessel from Japan which like the tuna long-liner is used in the oceanic tuna fisheries.

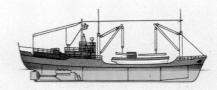

A tuna long-liner from Japan. These vessels range widely over the tropical and sub-tropical Indo-Pacific region in search of the high value tuna.

2 *above* These vessels represent some of the fishing craft used by the industrial fishing nations in the major fishing areas of the North Atlantic, American seaboard and the North Pacific. They have all evolved to meet the needs of particular fisheries and range from the small shrimp trawlers of about 16 metres (53 ft) to the factory trawler of over 100 metres (300 ft).

The world catch

LIVING resources, unlike the majority of mineral resources, are renewable and so there is a strong practical interest in assessing the state of fish stocks as well as the potential of the fisheries and of aquaculture. The impact upon living resources is greatest in the northern parts of the Atlantic and Pacific, adjacent to the major industrial cores of the world economy and declines with distance from these areas so that in the southern Atlantic and Indo-Pacific there still remain untapped resources. Pressure is particularly great upon shoaling pelagic species which are used for reduction into animal feed, and upon the high value pelagic species such as tuna, salmon and whale.

In the Atlantic, the foundations of the fisheries remain the gadoid stocks, notably the cod in the north and the hakes in the south. However, the most spectacular tonnages caught are those which make up the industrial pelagic fisheries such as the Atlantic and Gulf menhaden along the North American coast; the capelin, sandeel, blue whiting and Norway pout of the north east; and the sardinella species, anchovy, horse mackerels of the east and south east. The herring and mackerel of the north are now exploited mainly for human consumption. Also significant are the high value shell fisheries for oysters, ocean quahog and shrimps in North America, mussels in western Europe, and the oceanic tuna and cephalopod catches. There is limited development of fisheries for Antarctic fish species and krill.

The Pacific catches are dominated by the recent rise of industrial fisheries for pelagic species which began with the Peruvian anchovy. The two main concentrations are in the north-west Pacific, where Alaska pollack, chub mackerel and Japanese pilchard are predominant; and in the eastern and south-eastern Pacific, where thread herring, anchovy, pilchard, chub and jack mackerel have been landed in increasing quantities during the 1970s. The salmon of the north and tuna of the tropics are the main high value finfish, and the concentration of shellfish catches in the north east is also significant. The temperate demersal stocks are less in evidence than in the Atlantic, a reflection of the narrow continental shelves, although the hakes and yellowfin sole are caught in large quantities. Tropical demersal stocks are fished extensively but tonnages are low, reflecting in part the underdevelopment of the Indo-Pacific region.

The knowledge of all these resources bears a direct relationship to the pattern of fisheries effort which is greatest in the oceans of the northern hemisphere. Assessment of potential depends primarily upon scientific knowledge combined with fishing experience so, inevitably, due to the lack of data, the biological potential of the world ocean for increased yields is a controversial topic. Estimates vary widely, but it is generally thought that the present annual catch of between sixty and seventy million tonnes might be increased by twenty to thirty million tonnes by a judicious combination of more intensive fishing, better fisheries management, and improved utilisation of landings through more effective processing, storage and trade. In addition, the prospects for aquaculture appear to be improving, and the growth rate of production from this source may well outstrip that from con-

Examples of species caught and tonnages

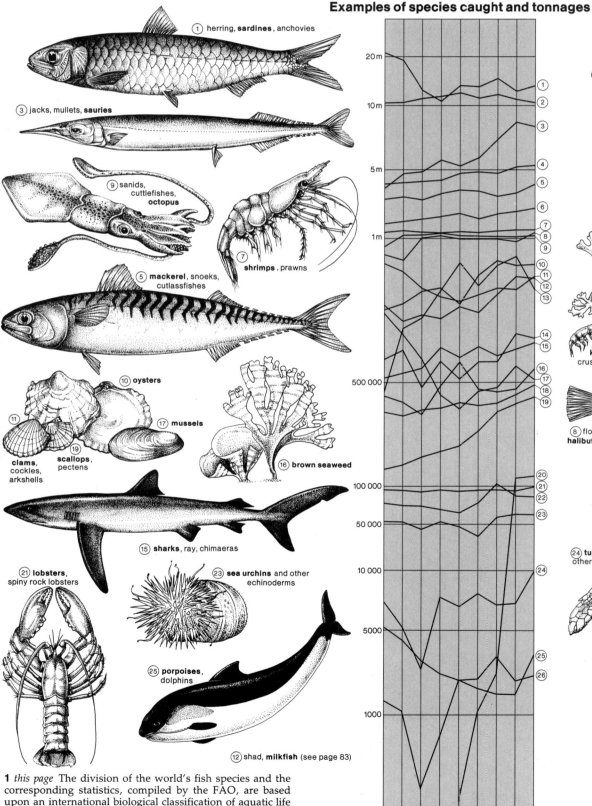

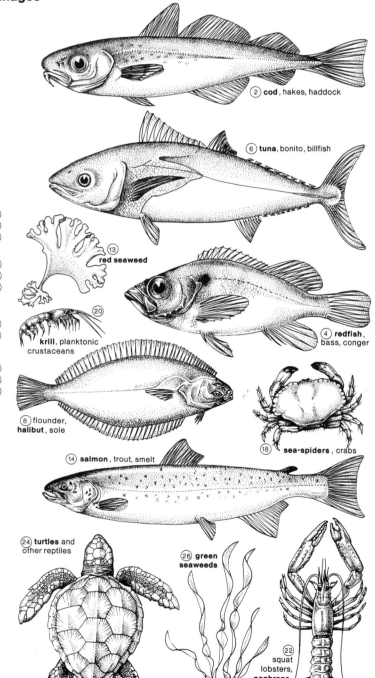

1 *this page* The division of the world's fish species and the corresponding statistics, compiled by the FAO, are based upon an international biological classification of aquatic life which, in the long run, permits detailed monitoring of the impact of fisheries and aquaculture upon marine life. Twenty-six species are illustrated and each represents one member of one classification. The graph shows recent trends of these classifications.

2 *opposite* The most intensively fished areas are in the North Atlantic and North Pacific which, together with southern temperate oceans, harbour mainly pelagic and demersal finfish resources. Both exploited and potential resources of crustaceans (shrimps, lobsters) and cephalopods (mainly species of squid) are greater in tropical seas. The degree of exploitation of resources and hence the potential for increased yields tends to vary with distance from the major industrial nations, potential being greatest in relatively remote areas in the tropics and southern latitudes, which, however, may not prove economic to exploit.

ventional fisheries in the foreseeable future.

The days of regarding the ocean as a vast, untapped reservoir of food are over as most major commercial stocks are now fully or near-fully exploited. The potential for greatly increased tonnages lies with the so-called 'unconventional' species such as krill (see *The Southern Ocean* page 78) and mesopelagic fish, notably lantern fishes

and lightfishes (see *The fishes* page 74). Cephalopods are already well in excess of one million tonnes per annum, most of which is caught by the Japanese.

Some of the most substantial changes in the environment tend to relate to the regional pattern of fisheries, rather than to any global pattern. One of the most pressing problems is to

assess the impact of the pelagic fisheries upon the ecosystem. Most of the major commercial stocks appear to be fully or over exploited and this may have contributed decisively to basic changes in the ecosystems in the North Sea where the herring stocks have collapsed and off southern Africa where the pilchard stocks have been devastated.

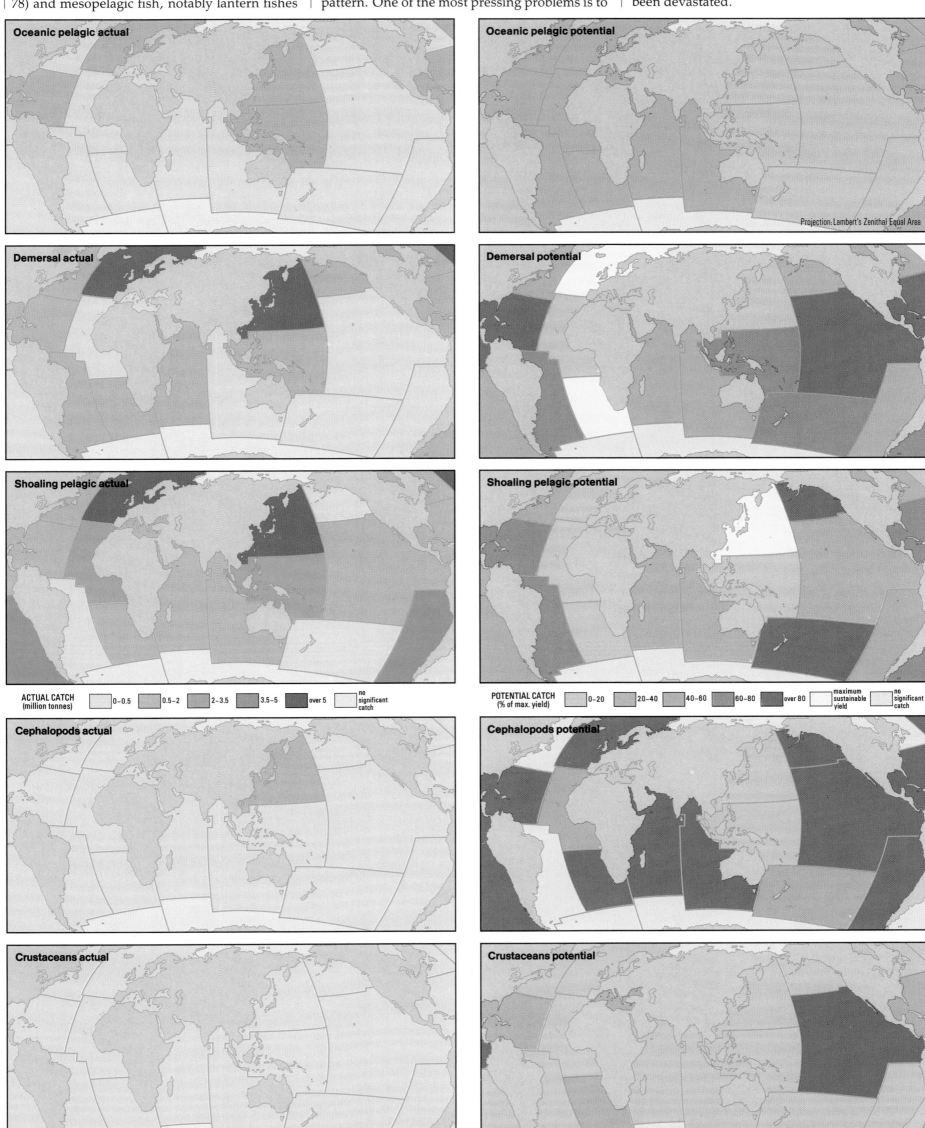

Oceanic pelagic actual

Oceanic pelagic potential

Projection: Lambert's Zenithal Equal Area

Demersal actual

Demersal potential

Shoaling pelagic actual

Shoaling pelagic potential

ACTUAL CATCH (million tonnes) 0–0.5 0.5–2 2–3.5 3.5–5 over 5 no significant catch

POTENTIAL CATCH (% of max. yield) 0–20 20–40 40–60 60–80 over 80 maximum sustainable yield no significant catch

Cephalopods actual

Cephalopods potential

Crustaceans actual

Crustaceans potential

World fish production

THE greatest catches come from the temperate and sub-polar continental shelves of the northern hemisphere, and from the upwelling areas of the great pelagic fisheries. Although there are some 20 000 species of fishes in the world ocean, only a small proportion is of real commercial significance. In temperate waters the biomass caught is relatively high and the species diversity low; in the tropics, outside of the upwelling areas, the reverse is the case. The greatest tonnages of individual species are caught by intensive purse-seining and trawling methods. With notable exceptions, such as the North Atlantic cod stocks and the South Atlantic hake stocks, individual hauls of demersal fish consist of a variety of species, often of smaller total weight than the average pelagic catch of a purse seine which is likely to consist of a single shoaling species.

The pattern of commercial fishing effort is dominated by the developed nations. Developing nations often possess an important subsistence element which is not statistically recorded, despite the fact that fish is frequently the principal source of animal protein in a diet otherwise deficient in this respect. The major commercial fishing nations may be grouped. First are the western European nations with their highly diversified fisheries and long history, concentrated in the north and mid-Atlantic and the Mediterranean and Black Seas. Developing from these through emigration and technological transfer are the commercial fisheries of North America, South America, Australia and New Zealand. The second major grouping are the centrally-planned, state-run fisheries of the Soviet Union and Eastern Europe, built upon distant water and remote-base operations. Third are the fisheries of Japan, the world's greatest and most diversified fishing nation, with a long history in the north-west Pacific and recent worldwide expansion. The fisheries of the developing countries remain primarily traditional, but significant developments are occurring locally, often with outside assistance, especially in South East Asia and parts of Latin America.

Landings are processed into a vast array of products but only a handful of basic techniques are used. These include fish sold fresh, freezing, dry salting, wet salting, smoking, canning, wind drying, marinating, and preparation of pastes. Markets are conservative and slow to change, which may prove to be the most important constraint upon the development of the unconventional species.

The world market has some striking regional variations. In the developed world there has been a marked shift over the past three decades

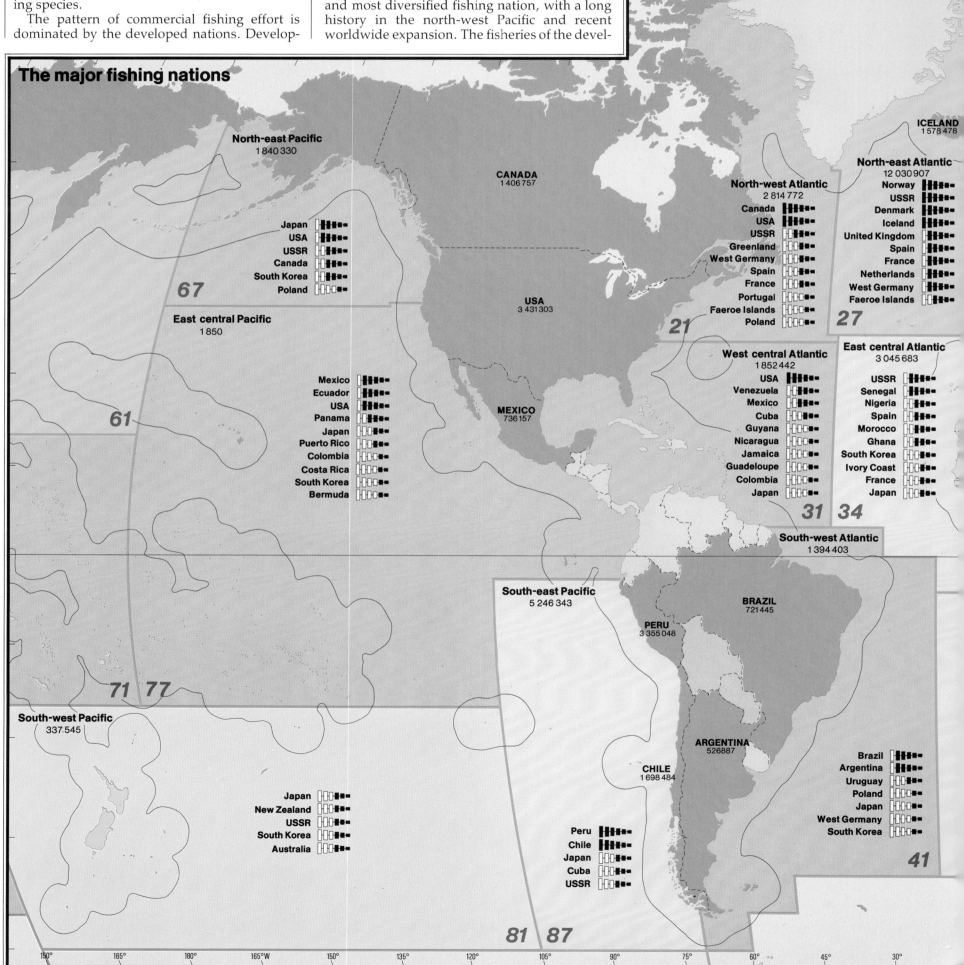

The major fishing nations

from fresh to frozen products, while the consumption of high value canned products such as salmon and tuna has also increased markedly. In many tropical markets, with their less well developed handling, marketing and storage facilities, traditional dried and salted products remain significant. Finally, approximately one-third of the world catch, mainly shoaling pelagic species, are reduced to meal and oil for animal feed and fertilisers.

A remarkably high proportion of fish products enter international trade—some 50 per cent in the early 1970s. The trade is dominated by the developed nations with the US market consuming some 50 per cent of world production of fish protein. Overall, current projected increases in production would do little more than keep pace with projected population increases, so that per capita consumption would be unlikely to alter significantly.

1 *below* Fishing fleets from all over the world converge on the well stocked seas of the North Atlantic and North Pacific and the areas of upwelling off the west coasts of Africa and South America, though protection has been afforded to local fleets through the introduction of EEZs. The largest landings are made by those countries in Western Europe, America and the Far East where fish has always been part of the staple diet. The increasing demand for animal feed has encouraged new fishing nations such as Peru, Poland and the USSR to become significant competitors.

2 *right* The table shows the trends in supply for the developed and developing countries. Conventional marine finfish offer relatively poor prospects for increased catches, though the situation is a little better for the developing countries where resources have been less exploited.

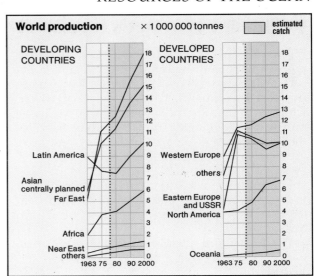

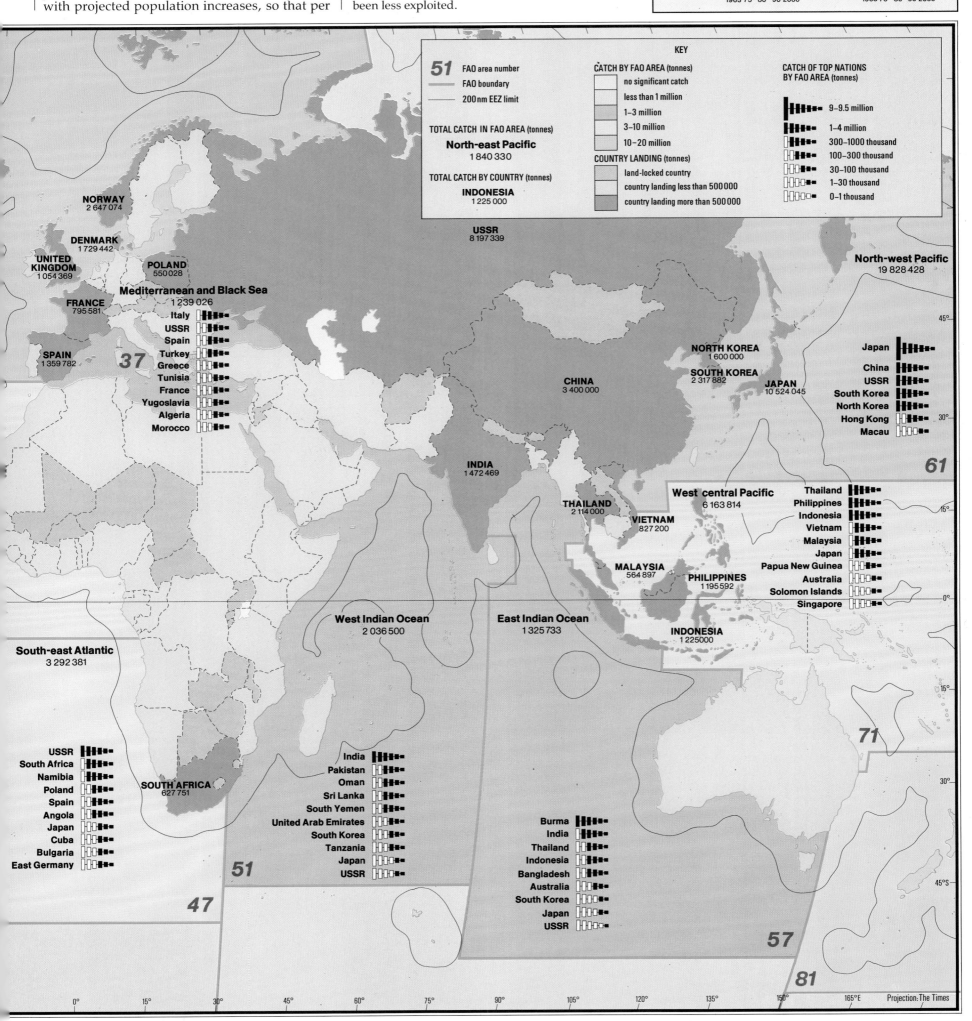

North Atlantic

THE North Atlantic is the cradle of the world's commercial fishing industry, pioneered by the nations of Western Europe. Today's industry has grown out of the thousands of coastal fishing communities of north-west and Mediterranean Europe, many of which date back to medieval times. However, it has become progressively more concentrated upon large inshore ports acting as centres of processing and marketing, while technological innovation has tended to lead towards specialisation and the ability to exploit a wide range of fisheries in both near and distant waters.

The fisheries of Canada and the United States were first concentrated in the Maritime Provinces (Newfoundland and Novia Scotia) and extend southwards from New England reflecting the pattern of settlement of immigrants from Western Europe. In contrast, the fisheries of the USSR and the Eastern European states are essentially a post-Second World War phenomenon. Organised on an enormous scale as state-run operations fishing in distant waters, they were severely curtailed in the 1970s when Canada, the Scandinavian states and the European Economic Community asserted the EEZ principle. Further important adjustments are in train within the EEC nations, and between them and the Scandinavian and North American states.

The artisanal element has now largely disappeared or has been converted into leisure activity, exceptions being the traditional Eskimo fisheries for whales and seals, and the pilot whale hunts around the Faeroe Islands (ironically, one of the most advanced of all the fishing regions).

The great fisheries with long historical roots are those based upon gadoid species and herring, augmented in the 1950s by an enormous industrial fishing effort. The chief object of exploitation among the gadoids were several of the 25 or so separate cod stocks. From the beginning these were caught by a number of promi-

Iceland

The degree of dependence of North Atlantic nations upon fisheries is considerable, though variable. The Scandinavian group is perhaps most dependent, notably the present or former Danish dependencies of Greenland, Faroe and Iceland. These countries rely almost entirely upon fishing. Iceland was a mecca as early as the 16th century for the English and Dutch who came to fish, and the Hanseatic merchants who came to buy fish. It was subsequently a centre for the smack fisheries and then trawlers.

Iceland's independence from Denmark came in 1943. Conflict between inshore fishing and trawling in the North Atlantic was widespread in some areas. For Iceland it was an international problem which culminated in the Cod Wars with Britain in the 1960s and 1970s (see *World naval operations and gunboat diplomacy* page 190) and the progressive extension of their fishing limits. Iceland's adoption of the Exclusive Economic Zone principle is of regional and global significance and appears already to be paying off in increased yields for local fleets.

1 *right* Icelandic fishing limits have been extended progressively seawards and now encompass the bulk of the fishing resources of the continental shelf, once intensively exploited by other nations. The crucial importance of fisheries is reflected by the wide distribution of fishing ports.

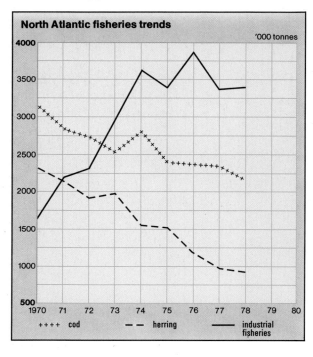

2 *above* The effects of overfishing and the decline of distant water fishing are reflected in the decline of the herring and cod catches. The rise of industrial catches reflects the switch in effort to the group of species, which principally includes Norway pout, capelin, blue whiting and sandeels. They are particularly important in the north east.

3 *main map* The cod, herring and industrial fisheries of the north-east Atlantic are largely exploited by the nations of Western and Eastern Europe. The main problem of reallocation of resources is within the waters of the European Economic community states. This was the reason deciding the Faroese to stay outside the EEC, and Greenland to withdraw from the EEC; it also influenced Norway's decision to stay out. In the north west, the once extensive activities of the European nations have been severely curtailed by the extension of the Canadian exclusive fishery zone to 200 miles.

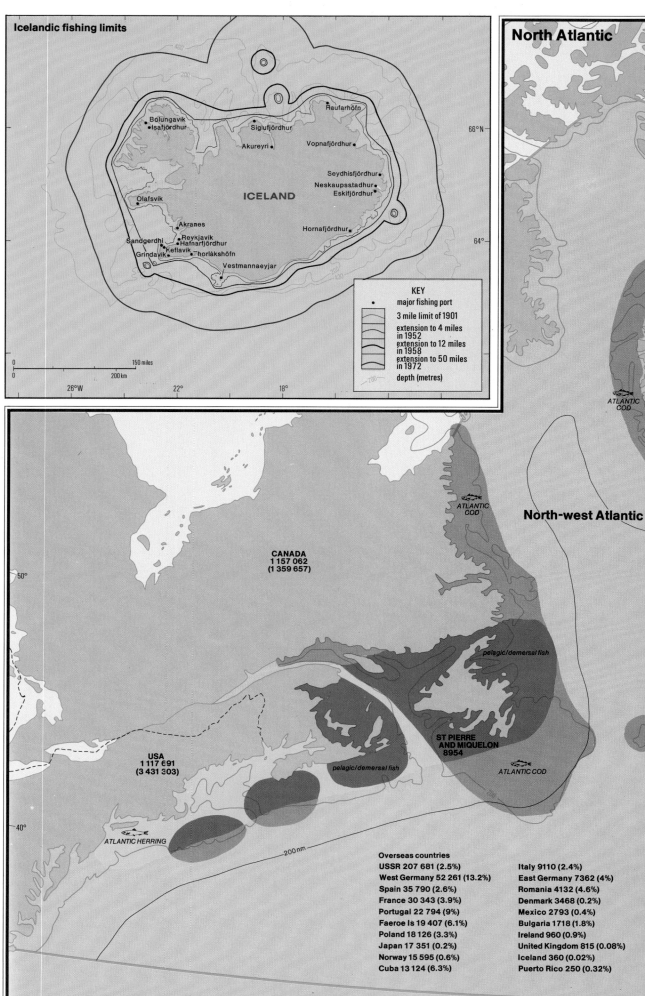

nent coastal fisheries, such as the Lofoten fishery of north Norway, and by distant water fisheries, such as the Portuguese on the Grand Banks. Fluctuations in the cod stocks may be related to long-run temperature changes, but the pressure of exploitation must be held primarily responsible for recent declines in catches, especially of those stocks which have been exploited by distant water trawlers.

The herring fisheries began with the Baltic herring catches in the Middle Ages. The great modern development, however, began with the Dutch North Sea fishery of the 16th and 17th centuries. In the 19th and early 20th centuries, the initiative passed to the Scots and English, followed by the Dutch, Norwegians, Icelanders and Germans; their catches aimed at the markets of the German and Russian Empires. Important regional fisheries developed based on the Atlanto-Scandian stocks and stocks west of Britain and Ireland. The drift net was replaced by the purse-seine in the 1960s, a development which resulted in overfishing, ultimately leading to a ban on fishing North Sea, Minch and Irish stocks at various times in the late 1970s.

The meteoric rise of industrial fisheries, led by the Scandinavian countries, took place in the 1960s and was linked to the enormous demand for animal feed in the countries of Western Europe, notably Denmark and the United Kingdom. Concentrations of these fisheries have been in the North Sea for sandeels, Norway pout and sprats; off the west of Britain for blue whiting, and further north for capelin.

4 *above* Vessels from Kristiansund pulling in a huge herring catch in the 1960s.

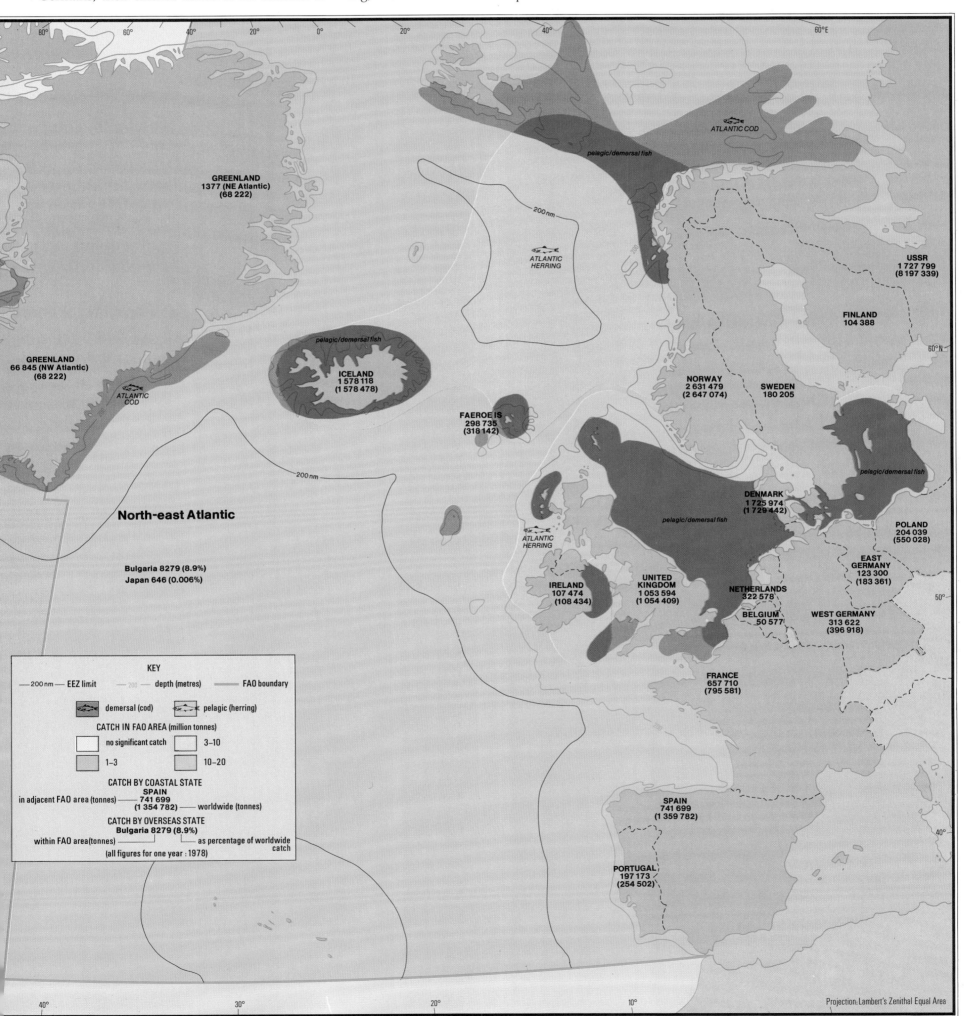

GREENLAND
1377 (NE Atlantic)
(68 222)

GREENLAND
66 845 (NW Atlantic)
(68 222)

ATLANTIC COD

pelagic/demersal fish

ICELAND
1 578 118
(1 578 478)

FAEROE IS
298 735
(318 142)

ATLANTIC COD

ATLANTIC HERRING

200 nm

ATLANTIC HERRING

North-east Atlantic

Bulgaria 8279 (8.9%)
Japan 646 (0.006%)

ATLANTIC HERRING

IRELAND
107 474
(108 434)

UNITED KINGDOM
1 053 594
(1 054 409)

NETHERLANDS
322 578

BELGIUM
50 577

FRANCE
657 710
(795 581)

pelagic/demersal fish

DENMARK
1 725 974
(1 729 442)

NORWAY
2 631 479
(2 647 074)

SWEDEN
180 205

USSR
1 727 799
(8 197 339)

FINLAND
104 388

POLAND
204 039
(550 028)

EAST GERMANY
123 300
(183 361)

WEST GERMANY
313 622
(396 918)

pelagic/demersal fish

SPAIN
741 699
(1 359 782)

PORTUGAL
197 173
(254 502)

KEY

—200 nm— EEZ limit   —200— depth (metres)   —— FAO boundary

demersal (cod)   pelagic (herring)

CATCH IN FAO AREA (million tonnes)

no significant catch   3–10
1–3   10–20

CATCH BY COASTAL STATE
SPAIN
in adjacent FAO area (tonnes) —— 741 699 ——
(1 354 782) —— worldwide (tonnes)

CATCH BY OVERSEAS STATE
Bulgaria 8279 (8.9%)
within FAO area(tonnes) —— —— as percentage of worldwide catch
(all figures for one year : 1978)

Projection: Lambert's Zenithal Equal Area

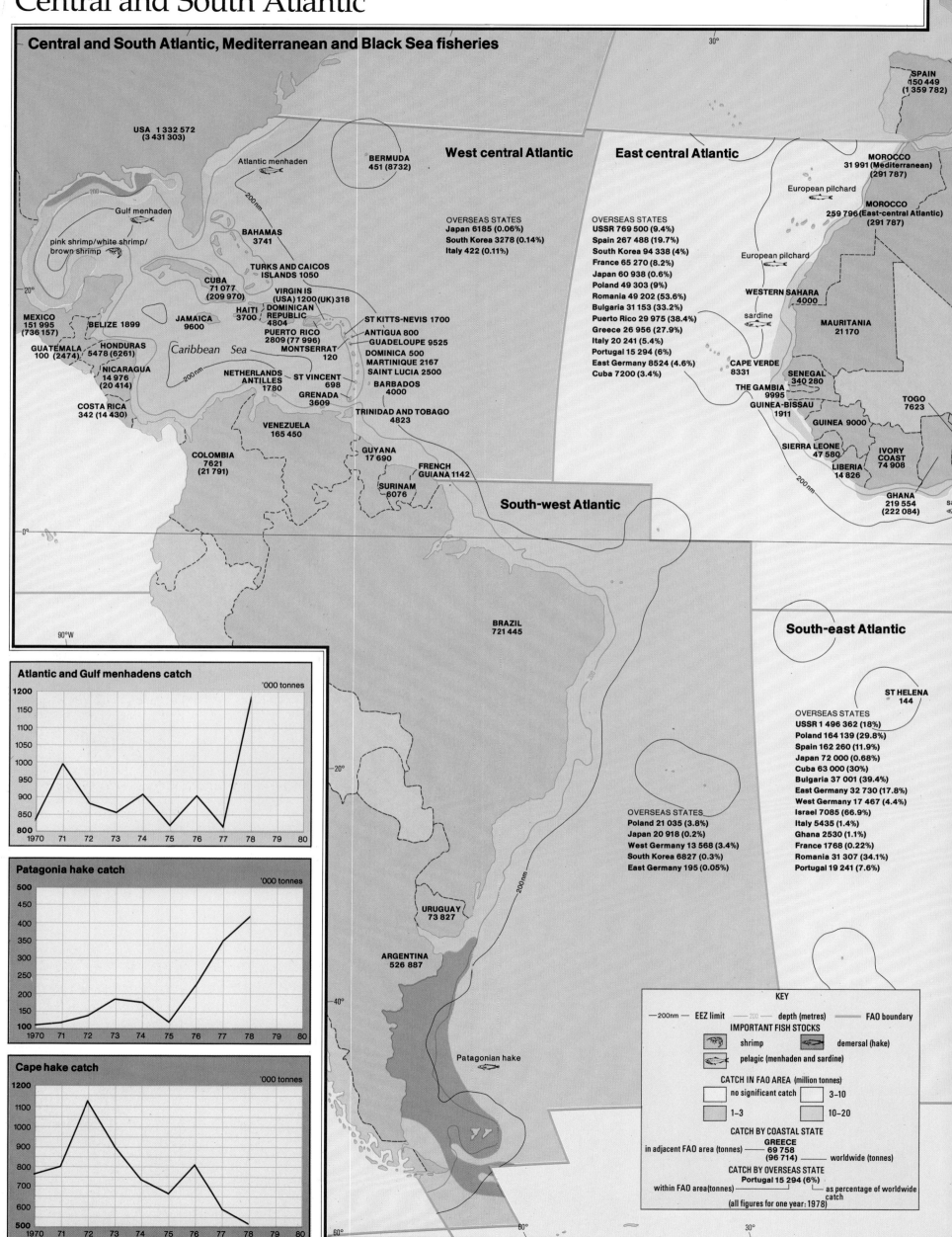

Central and South Atlantic, Mediterranean and Black Sea fisheries

30°

SPAIN
150 449
(1 359 782)

West central Atlantic

East central Atlantic

MOROCCO
31 991 (Mediterranean)
(291 787)

European pilchard

MOROCCO
259 796 (East-central Atlantic)
(291 787)

USA 1 332 572
(3 431 303)

Atlantic menhaden

Gulf menhaden

BERMUDA
451 (8732)

OVERSEAS STATES
Japan 6185 (0.06%)
South Korea 3278 (0.14%)
Italy 422 (0.11%)

OVERSEAS STATES
USSR 769 500 (9.4%)
Spain 267 488 (19.7%)
South Korea 94 338 (4%)
France 65 270 (8.2%)
Japan 60 938 (0.6%)
Poland 49 303 (9%)
Romania 49 202 (53.6%)
Bulgaria 31 153 (33.2%)
Puerto Rico 29 975 (38.4%)
Greece 26 956 (27.9%)
Italy 20 241 (5.4%)
Portugal 15 294 (6%)
East Germany 8524 (4.6%)
Cuba 7200 (3.4%)

European pilchard

WESTERN SAHARA
4000

sardine

pink shrimp/white shrimp/
brown shrimp

BAHAMAS
3741

MAURITANIA
21 170

TURKS AND CAICOS
ISLANDS 1050

CAPE VERDE
8331

CUBA
71 077
(209 970)

SENEGAL
340 280

VIRGIN IS
(USA) 1200 (UK) 318

THE GAMBIA
9995

MEXICO
151 995
(736 157)

HAITI
3700

DOMINICAN
REPUBLIC
4804

JAMAICA
9600

PUERTO RICO
2809 (77 996)

ST KITTS-NEVIS 1700
ANTIGUA 800
GUADELOUPE 9525
MONTSERRAT
120
DOMINICA 500
MARTINIQUE 2167
SAINT LUCIA 2500
BARBADOS
4000

TOGO
7623

GUINEA-BISSAU
1911

GUINEA 9000

BELIZE 1899

GUATEMALA
100 (2474)

HONDURAS
5478 (6261)

NICARAGUA
14 976
(20 414)

Caribbean Sea

NETHERLANDS
ANTILLES
1780

ST VINCENT
698

GRENADA
3609

SIERRA LEONE
47 580

IVORY
COAST
74 908

LIBERIA
14 826

COSTA RICA
342 (14 430)

VENEZUELA
165 450

TRINIDAD AND TOBAGO
4823

GHANA
219 554
(222 084)

COLOMBIA
7621
(21 791)

GUYANA
17 690

FRENCH
GUIANA 1142

SURINAM
6076

South-west Atlantic

0°

90°W

BRAZIL
721 445

South-east Atlantic

ST HELENA
144

OVERSEAS STATES
USSR 1 496 362 (18%)
Poland 164 139 (29.8%)
Spain 162 260 (11.9%)
Japan 72 000 (0.68%)
Cuba 63 000 (30%)
Bulgaria 37 001 (39.4%)
East Germany 32 730 (17.8%)
West Germany 17 467 (4.4%)
Israel 7085 (66.9%)
Italy 5435 (1.4%)
Ghana 2530 (1.1%)
France 1768 (0.22%)
Romania 31 307 (34.1%)
Portugal 19 241 (7.6%)

OVERSEAS STATES
Poland 21 035 (3.8%)
Japan 20 918 (0.2%)
West Germany 13 568 (3.4%)
South Korea 6827 (0.3%)
East Germany 195 (0.05%)

URUGUAY
73 827

20°

ARGENTINA
526 887

40°

Patagonian hake

60°W

30°

Atlantic and Gulf menhadens catch

'000 tonnes

1200, 1150, 1100, 1050, 1000, 950, 900, 850, 800

1970 71 72 73 74 75 76 77 78 79 80

Patagonia hake catch

'000 tonnes

500, 450, 400, 350, 300, 250, 200, 150, 100

1970 71 72 73 74 75 76 77 78 79 80

Cape hake catch

'000 tonnes

1200, 1100, 1000, 900, 800, 700, 600, 500

1970 71 72 73 74 75 76 77 78 79 80

KEY

—200nm— EEZ limit   — 200 — depth (metres)   ——— FAO boundary

IMPORTANT FISH STOCKS

shrimp   demersal (hake)

pelagic (menhaden and sardine)

CATCH IN FAO AREA (million tonnes)

no significant catch   3–10

1–3   10–20

CATCH BY COASTAL STATE

in adjacent FAO area (tonnes)
GREECE
69 758
(96 714) — worldwide (tonnes)

CATCH BY OVERSEAS STATE
Portugal 15 294 (6%)
within FAO area (tonnes) — as percentage of worldwide catch

(all figures for one year: 1978)

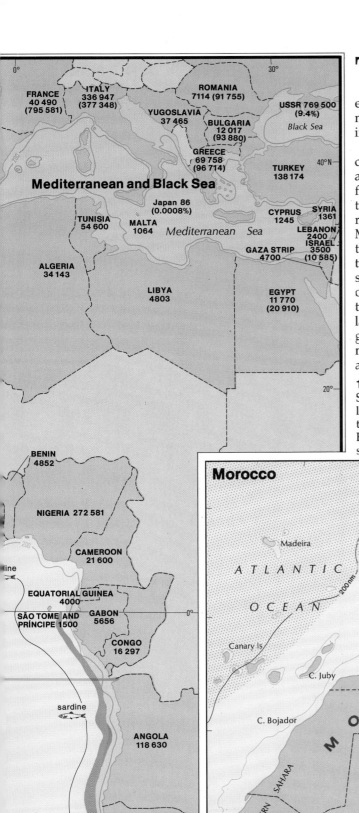

Mediterranean and Black Sea

FRANCE 40 490 (795 581)
ITALY 336 947 (377 348)
ROMANIA 7114 (91 755)
YUGOSLAVIA 37 465
USSR 769 500 (9.4%)
Black Sea
BULGARIA 12 017 (93 880)
GREECE 69 758 (96 714)
TURKEY 138 174
Japan 86 (0.0008%)
CYPRUS 1245
SYRIA 1361
TUNISIA 54 600
MALTA 1064
Mediterranean Sea
LEBANON 2400
ISRAEL 3500 (10 585)
GAZA STRIP 4700
ALGERIA 34 143
LIBYA 4803
EGYPT 11 770 (20 910)

BENIN 4852
NIGERIA 272 581
CAMEROON 21 600
EQUATORIAL GUINEA 4000
SÃO TOMÉ AND PRÍNCIPE 1500
GABON 5656
CONGO 16 297

sardine
ANGOLA 118 630
NAMIBIA 417 543 (417 543)
Cape hake
SOUTH AFRICA 624 607 (627 751)
pilchard/ Cape anchovy

Projection: Winkel's Tripel

Morocco

C. Spartel
Rabat
Casablanca
Safi
C. Sim
C. Rhir
Agadir
Madeira
ATLANTIC OCEAN
Canary Is.
C. Juby
C. Bojador
MOROCCO
ALGERIA
WESTERN SAHARA
MAURITANIA

KEY
• fishing port
200 nm EEZ limit
200 depth (metres)
upwelling area: source of nutrients

0   200 miles
0   300 km

TRADITIONAL fisheries are prominent along many coasts of the tropical and South Atlantic but the ocean expanses have been exploited mainly by the industrial nations of the north because these areas offer great potential for increasing their distant water fisheries.

The northern Mediterranean and Black Sea coasts lie on the southern fringes of European and Soviet industrialisation and, although the fisheries here are predominantly commercial, traditional methods have, on the whole, been retained. Along the southern shores of the Mediterranean and the western Sahara are the traditional fisheries of Islamic Africa; beyond these the artisanal fisheries of equatorial Africa stretch southwards to the desert coastal fringes of Angola and Namibia. In the New World, the traditions of the Indian populations have been largely obscured by European and Negro immigration. Of the three main areas of European migration – the eastern USA, southern Africa and eastern South America – only the first two

1 *main map* With the exceptions of the United States, South Africa and Morocco, the fisheries are relatively localised and small scale. There is intensive effort by the nations of eastern and to a lesser extent southern Europe in the eastern Atlantic aimed at the rich pelagic stocks off the desert coasts.

Morocco

Morocco is an example of a developing country which was affected early by European fishery expansion. Important fisheries in the area were the traditional tuna trap fishery, sardine fishing using purse-seines, and trawl fishing between Cape Sim and Cape Juby. The coast had been attractive to Iberian and French fishermen for centuries. The first sardine cannery was established in 1927, and the industry expanded rapidly on the basis of exports to European markets. Ground fisheries tend to be hampered by coral and the real potential was the offshore pelagic stocks in the upwelling areas, where Soviet bloc nations and Japan were attracted after the Second World War. Morocco's fishing industry now plays a key role in the economy of the country.

2 *above* The key to the fisheries of Morocco is the strong upwelling current which attracts the pelagic stocks, of which the sardine is the most important, and has encouraged intensive fishing efforts by a number of European nations. The Moroccan industry is located in a small number of ports along the open desert coast.

3 *far left* The menhaden industry has the longest history of any major pelagic fishery in the region and is based on separate stocks along the Atlantic and Gulf coasts of the United States. It is subject to wide annual fluctuations. Cape hake stocks have been intensively fished while the fishing effort for Patagonian hake has been increased.

have become major foci of large-scale advanced fisheries.

The two main areas of United States development are the Atlantic coast and the Gulf of Mexico. These fisheries grew up with the industrialisation of the country, fully exploiting the considerable range of sub-tropical and tropical groundfish and shellfish species. The leading sectors are now menhaden, shrimp, and recreational fishing.

There are records of using menhaden as fertiliser dating from 1812, but the modern industry got under way in the late 19th century when purse-seine fishing grew, backed up by processing plants along the Atlantic coast. The Gulf menhaden was intensively exploited only after the Second World War. In the early stages it was mainly used for fertiliser, but recently meal and oil have become the principal products.

The shrimp industry, based on the long-range fishing of several penaeid shrimp by trawlers, is the most valuable fishery resource in the United States. A notable problem of this fishery is the by-catch of other species which can sometimes account for three-quarters or more of the total catch but which are largely discarded at sea.

Both menhaden and shrimp spend the early part of their lives on the nursery grounds provided by the estuarine environments of the extensive coastal wetlands of the Atlantic and Gulf coasts. These areas are under enormous pressure from multiple use, including recreation (see *Regional management* page 213). It has been estimated that this major sports fishing industry contributes up to one-fifth of the total landings by weight in the FAO West central Atlantic statistical area.

The modern industry of South Africa was established at the turn of the century and based on Cape hake. It was modelled on British bottom otter-trawling. This was followed in the early 1940s by the pilchard and maasbanker fisheries off south-west Africa, mainly for fertiliser production, though significant quantities of pilchards were canned. The Namibian pilchard fishery has now virtually collapsed and the main pelagic fishery is a multi-species one off South Africa for anchovy, horse-mackerels and sardinellas.

The potential of the whole tropical and southern Atlantic for both pelagic and demersal stocks has attracted intensive exploitation by the Soviet bloc nations and Japan since 1945, especially off the Saharan coast, southern Africa, and briefly the Argentine hake grounds where the potential was amply demonstrated by Soviet fleets before the Latin American nations began to assert EEZ rights in the mid 1960s. Since then, continued assertion of coastal state rights by Latin American and African nations has caused distant water catches to drop steeply in many areas in the late 1970s, though the Japanese have continued to exploit the open ocean tuna and cephalopod resources.

4 *above* Inhabitants of Favignana, one of the Egadi Islands, near Sicily, engaged in tuna fishing, upon which most of the population depend for their livelihood. They employ small boats which are rarely more than 17 metres long.

The North Pacific

THE North Pacific is the second great centre of world fisheries development. Unlike the Atlantic, the continental shelves are more restricted (except in the East China Sea) and the fisheries are shared among a small number of large fishing nations. The pattern is dominated by the long-established fisheries of China and Japan, and by the relatively recent ones of Canada and the United States in the east and the Soviet Union in the west.

The eastern Asian realm of these fisheries is dominated by China which, together with Taiwan, Vietnam and the Korean States constitutes the greatest development of artisanal fisheries and aquaculture in the world. Modernisation of the fisheries in eastern China has proceeded apace recently. By 1978 the 860 000 or so fishermen of the People's Republic were producing some 4.7 million tonnes of aquatic products including 3.6 million tonnes of marine products (0.45 million tonnes farmed) and a further 1.05 million tonnes of freshwater products including 0.76 million tonnes produced by aquaculture. The strong traditional fisheries of China, based largely along the coast and on the adjacent continental shelf, contrast with the Japanese fisheries which have, over the past century, been built up into the largest commercial fishing industry in the world, and extend throughout the world ocean. South Korea and Taiwan have recently emulated the Japanese in developing distant water fisheries on an appreciable scale.

The Russian fisheries are a Soviet achievement based on Japanese foundations, later aided to some extent by Poland and East Germany. In 1913 the Far East fisheries constituted about one-tenth of the Russian catch; by the mid 1960s they contributed about a third, and produced around one-quarter of the gross value of the Soviet Far East economy.

On the west coast of North America, development of the fisheries has been relatively recent, parallelling the opening up of the West at the end of the 19th century. The principal focus was upon the coasts of British Columbia and Washington, centring on Vancouver and Seattle, and also to the north and west towards Alaska. The salmon has reigned supreme, though other fish (notably the herring and halibut) have been significant resources.

The North Pacific witnessed the birth of effective fisheries management. The first ever fisheries commission, for the North Pacific fur seal, was established in 1911 to control the fishing on the Pribilof Islands. The founding of the International Halibut Commission in 1924 marked the first successful attempt at regulating a fish species. The halibut was exploited to a limited extent by the Indians, and later by line fishermen of Scandinavian origin, but the fishery really expanded with the coming of the railways to the West Coast and the introduction of refrigeration to store and ship the fish to those east coast markets which could not be fully supplied from the north-west Atlantic grounds.

The herring fisheries, though less prominent than those of the North Atlantic, are nonetheless important, the major locations being northern Japan, Sakhalin, Korea, Siberia, Alaska and British Columbia. The British Columbian herring stock was probably one of the first to be depleted using the purse seine, though the most notable herring fishery was that of Hokkaido which grew with Japanese economic development in the latter half of the 19th century, and was the basis for the development of many fishing villages.

As in the North Atlantic, there has been considerable post-War growth of pelagic fisheries for industrial purposes.

1 *main map* The North Pacific continental shelf is generally narrow and oceanic fisheries are relatively important, for example, those for salmon and Alaska pollack. Groundfish stocks, such as the Pacific halibut, are exploited close to the coasts.

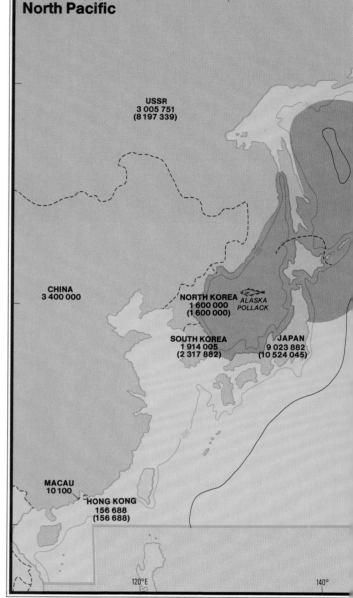

North Pacific

USSR
3 005 751
(8 197 339)

CHINA
3 400 000

NORTH KOREA
1 600 000
(1 600 000)
ALASKA POLLACK

SOUTH KOREA
1 914 005
(2 317 882)

JAPAN
9 023 882
(10 524 045)

MACAU
10 100

HONG KONG
156 688
(156 688)

120°E   140°

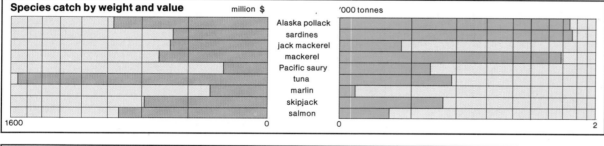

Species catch by weight and value

million $ '000 tonnes

Alaska pollack
sardines
jack mackerel
mackerel
Pacific saury
tuna
marlin
skipjack
salmon

1600   0   0   2

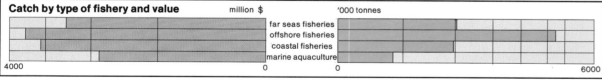

Catch by type of fishery and value

million $ '000 tonnes

far seas fisheries
offshore fisheries
coastal fisheries
marine aquaculture

4000   0   0   6000

2 *above* The fishing industry of Japan consists of three major divisions: the high (far) seas pelagic fisheries ranging throughout the world ocean, the offshore fisheries in the north-west Pacific much of which is within 200 nm of land; and the coastal fisheries close inshore. The pelagic fisheries include those for Alaska pollack, tuna, squid. The offshore fisheries total is swelled by shoaling pelagic catches. It is notable that all the species groups listed are pelagic, emphasising the relative unimportance of demersal stocks in the deep north-west Pacific. The relative values of species are also notable, with some one-and-a-half million tons of Alaska pollack (used for reduction and in preparation of surimi) worth little more than a mere 130 thousand tonnes of salmon. The growing importance of marine aquaculture is reflected in the high tonnage.

3 *left* In Japan yellow tail snapper fish are reared in massive 'net tanks' anchored to the bottom of the lagoon bed and kept afloat with buoys visible in the background. They subsist mainly on a daily diet of the small silver fish pictured in the foreground.

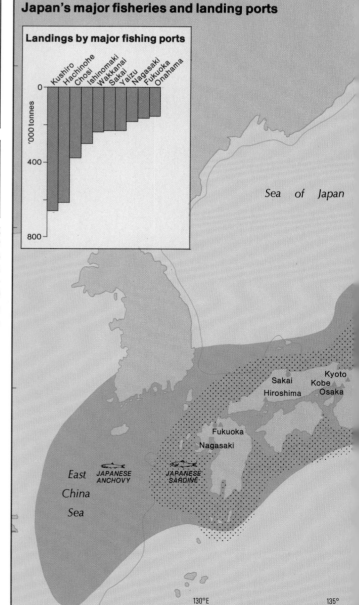

Japan's major fisheries and landing ports

Landings by major fishing ports

Kushiro
Hachinohe
Chosi
Ishinomaki
Wakkanai
Sakai
Yaizu
Nagasaki
Fukuoka
Onahama

'000 tonnes
0
400
800

Sea of Japan

Sakai
Hiroshima
Kyoto
Kobe
Osaka

Fukuoka
Nagasaki

East China Sea   JAPANESE ANCHOVY   JAPANESE SARDINE

130°E   135°

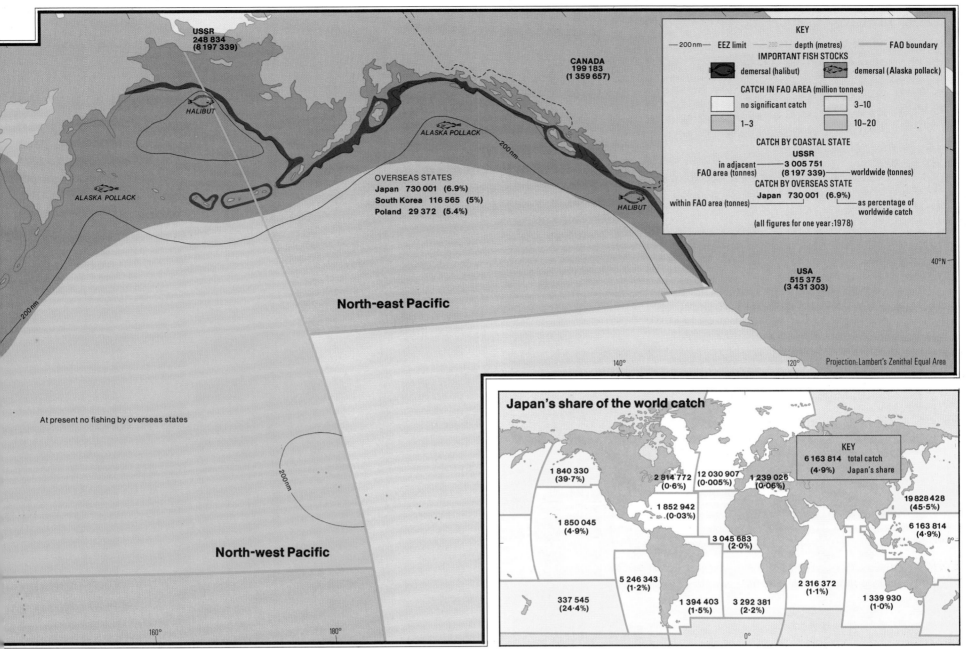

USSR
248 834
(8 197 339)

HALIBUT

ALASKA POLLACK

ALASKA POLLACK

CANADA
199 183
(1 359 657)

HALIBUT

OVERSEAS STATES
Japan 730 001 (6.9%)
South Korea 116 565 (5%)
Poland 29 372 (5.4%)

North-east Pacific

USA
515 375
(3 431 303)

40°N

At present no fishing by overseas states

200nm

North-west Pacific

KEY
— 200 nm — EEZ limit   200 — depth (metres)   —— FAO boundary
IMPORTANT FISH STOCKS
demersal (halibut)   demersal (Alaska pollack)
CATCH IN FAO AREA (million tonnes)
no significant catch   3–10
1–3   10–20
CATCH BY COASTAL STATE
USSR
in adjacent —— 3 005 751
FAO area (tonnes) (8 197 339) —— worldwide (tonnes)
CATCH BY OVERSEAS STATE
Japan 730 001 (6.9%)
within FAO area (tonnes) —— as percentage of
worldwide catch
(all figures for one year: 1978)

Projection: Lambert's Zenithal Equal Area

Japan's share of the world catch

KEY
6 163 814 total catch
(4.9%) Japan's share

1 840 330 (39.7%)
2 814 772 (0.6%)
12 030 907 (0.005%)
1 239 026 (0.06%)
19 828 428 (45.5%)
1 852 942 (0.03%)
1 850 045 (4.9%)
3 045 683 (2.0%)
6 163 814 (4.9%)
5 246 343 (1.2%)
2 316 372 (1.1%)
337 545 (24.4%)
1 394 403 (1.5%)
3 292 381 (2.2%)
1 339 930 (1.0%)

4 *left* The Japanese continental shelf is narrow and pelagic species have been of great importance in the development of the fisheries from the late nineteenth century onwards. Notable examples are the herring fishery of Hokkaido, and the sardine fisheries, both of which went into decline in the mid 20th century. There has been a subsequent resurgence in sardine landings which, together with several species of mackerel and also anchovy, constitute the principal shoaling pelagic stocks. The ports with the highest landings are concentrated in the northern part of the country.

Japan

The Japanese fishing industry emerged from the traditional village communities, and after 1900 began to develop very fast. Cooperative societies were a traditional feature of the communities though individual fishermen also fished independently, fishing being integrated with agriculture. The 'private right' fisheries grew rapidly relative to the community fisheries and became the basis of major coastal and offshore fishing. Further development occurred through the introduction of powered vessels in the inter-war and postwar periods and there was a steady reduction in the numbers of fishermen from some five million at the turn of the century to half a million in the 1970s.

There are now some 1500 fishing ports in Japan. The earlier ones began at locations where migrant fishermen made associations with wholesale fish dealers. A second type began as landing ports for boats from other ports. Later, and most numerous, were those which developed from the fishing villages and in which the shore industry was dominated by fishermen's cooperatives.

The coastal fisheries are important, contributing about one-fifth of the catch in the late 1970s. These are

5 *above* Japanese fishing activities, though concentrated in the North Pacific, extend to every ocean, and have been adversely affected in some areas (such as the north-east Pacific), by the extension of other countries' fishing limits. The Japanese industry is promoting joint ventures in fisheries development with many developing countries in order to boost production. The open ocean or 'far seas' fisheries in the Pacific, Atlantic and Indian Oceans concentrate on tuna, and squid, together with high seas salmon fishing and whaling in the Pacific.

mainly small scale, within the 12-mile limit, and include shell fisheries, seaweed gathering, and working set nets and beach seines. Offshore fisheries account for between two- and three-fifths of the catch and include important fisheries for major pelagic and demersal species. The distant water or 'far seas' fishing is dominated in tonnage by Alaska pollack, though of much longer standing are the tuna, squid and whale fisheries. Aquaculture contributes small but significant tonnages, and much research effort in Japan is directed at developing this side of the industry.

Fish contributes approximately one half of the animal protein intake in the Japanese diet, and demand is constantly increasing. Imports are substantial. The imposition of the EEZ, especially by the Soviet Union and Alaska, had serious implications for Japan's far seas fishery, especially for Alaska pollack. The challenge of meeting the demand is being met through negotiation with other countries, including the formation of joint ventures abroad, and continuing with a wide range of innovative ideas, such as krill fishing and salmon ranching.

Sea of Okhotsk

HERRING

Wakkanai

45°N

Sapporo Kushiro

Hachinohe

JAPANESE ANCHOVY

40°

Ishinomaki
Sendai

JAPANESE SARDINE

Onahama

JAPAN

Tokyo
Yokohama Chosi
Nagoya
Yaizu

35°

PACIFIC OCEAN

KEY
Japanese anchovy
Japanese sardine
herring
major fishing port
major wholesale fish markets

140°

6 *right* A modern Japanese deep sea fishing vessel which is typical of the boats in Japan's fishing fleet.

The Indo-Pacific

THE vast Indo-Pacific region, the oceanic half of the globe, remains the least developed apart from the tuna and whale fisheries. Generally speaking, the fisheries throughout the whole area can be classified as artisanal although they can be grouped by culture regions. Biogeographically, the area has a high degree of unity in its tropical and sub-tropical environment.

The traditional fisheries include those of eastern Africa, Madagascar (the Malagasy Republic); the Mascarenes and other Indian Ocean island groups, the desert coasts from the Horn of Africa to the mouth of the Indus, including the Red Sea and The Gulf, the Indian sub-continent including the west coast of India and the Bay of Bengal, the coasts and islands of South East Asia, northern Australia, and the Melanesian and Micronesian cultures of the tropical and South Pacific (see *The traditional fisheries* page 80). In most of these areas commercial development has been very limited, at least until recently, and then mainly in South East Asia. There is considerable potential in some areas, especially in the northern Indian Ocean and the shelf of Western Australia, and possibly round the oceanic islands of the western Indian Ocean.

The fisheries of the American west coast have artisanal foundations which were built up by the pre-Conquest civilisations. Industrialisation began after 1850 in California, based upon the Mediterranean techniques of fishing which were introduced by Italian, Spanish and Portuguese immigrants. Intensive commercial development commenced in the 1890s and 1900s in the sardine and tuna fisheries, the products being canned for the domestic and export markets. The sardine fishery collapsed in the 1950s.

The second major phase of industrialisation, in Peru during the 1950s and 1960s, was more spectacular and involved the anchovy. The rapid rise in the world demand for meal and oil was largely responsible for Peru's remarkable growth rate during that period. The collapse of the fishery in the 1970s appears to have been due to the combination of a change in the sea and overfishing, as in the case of the Californian sardine. Out of the decline of the anchovy has come diversification and expansion into other pelagic fisheries off the Central and South American coasts.

Industrialisation in the southern seas is relatively small-scale and isolated. In south-east and south-west Australia there are important shellfish and finfish sectors but, although Australia has the largest EEZ in the world, potential may be relatively limited. The small industry in New Zealand was, however, the fifth largest in the country and the fastest growing in 1978, with further expansion anticipated within the new EEZ. Likewise there is probably considerable potential in central and southern Chile for both the demersal trawl fisheries for hake and other species, and for pelagic fishing.

1 *below* Fish are a vital part of the Malaysian economy and diet. Pictured here are fish laid out to dry on wooden slats in Mersing, Malaysia.

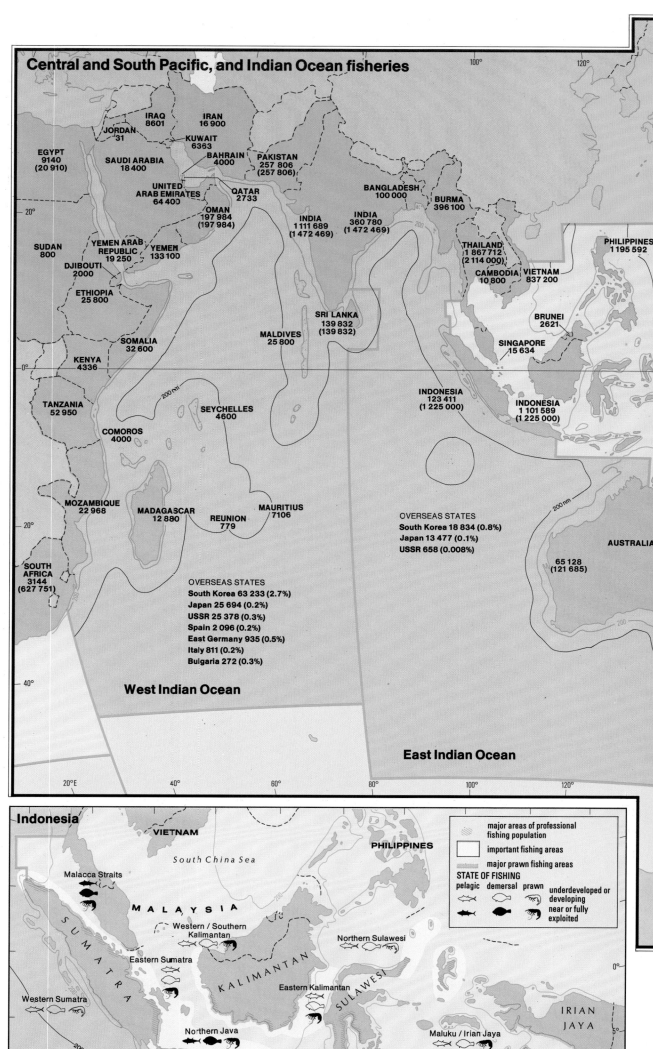

Central and South Pacific, and Indian Ocean fisheries

IRAQ 8601
JORDAN 31
IRAN 16 900
KUWAIT 6363
EGYPT 9140 (20 910)
SAUDI ARABIA 18 400
BAHRAIN 4000
PAKISTAN 257 806 (257 806)
BANGLADESH 100 000
BURMA 396 100
UNITED ARAB EMIRATES 64 400
QATAR 2733
OMAN 197 984 (197 984)
INDIA 1 111 689 (1 472 469)
INDIA 360 780 (1 472 469)
THAILAND 1 867 712 (2 114 000)
PHILIPPINES 1 195 592
SUDAN 800
YEMEN ARAB REPUBLIC 19 250
YEMEN 133 100
CAMBODIA 10 800
VIETNAM 837 200
DJIBOUTI 2000
SRI LANKA 139 832 (139 832)
BRUNEI 2621
ETHIOPIA 25 800
MALDIVES 25 800
SINGAPORE 15 634
SOMALIA 32 600
KENYA 4336
TANZANIA 52 950
SEYCHELLES 4600
INDONESIA 123 411 (1 225 000)
INDONESIA 1 101 589 (1 225 000)
COMOROS 4000
MOZAMBIQUE 22 968
MADAGASCAR 12 880
REUNION 779
MAURITIUS 7106
AUSTRALIA
65 128 (121 685)
SOUTH AFRICA 3144 (627 751)

OVERSEAS STATES
South Korea 18 834 (0.8%)
Japan 13 477 (0.1%)
USSR 658 (0.008%)

OVERSEAS STATES
South Korea 63 233 (2.7%)
Japan 25 694 (0.2%)
USSR 25 378 (0.3%)
Spain 2 096 (0.2%)
East Germany 935 (0.5%)
Italy 811 (0.2%)
Bulgaria 272 (0.3%)

West Indian Ocean

East Indian Ocean

Indonesia

VIETNAM
PHILIPPINES
South China Sea
Malacca Straits
MALAYSIA
Western / Southern Kalimantan
Northern Sulawesi
Eastern Sumatra
SUMATRA
KALIMANTAN
SULAWESI
Eastern Kalimantan
IRIAN JAYA
Western Sumatra
Maluku / Irian Jaya
Northern Java
JAVA
Southern Sulawesi
Southern Java
Arafura Sea
INDIAN OCEAN
Bali / Nusa Tenggara
AUSTRALIA

major areas of professional fishing population
important fishing areas
major prawn fishing areas
STATE OF FISHING
pelagic demersal prawn
underdeveloped or developing
near or fully exploited

Indonesia

Indonesia lies at the centre of the Indo-Pacific region and possesses richly varied artisanal fisheries, both shore and boat based, among its numerous islands. There are records of fishing expeditions further afield also, as far as the coast of northern Australia in colonial times. Post-war expansion has been largely based on the traditional fisheries and by the early 1970s the country was approaching self-sufficiency. The inter-regional trade is highly organised and as late as the 1960s it was still coordinated by a single firm in Djakarta.

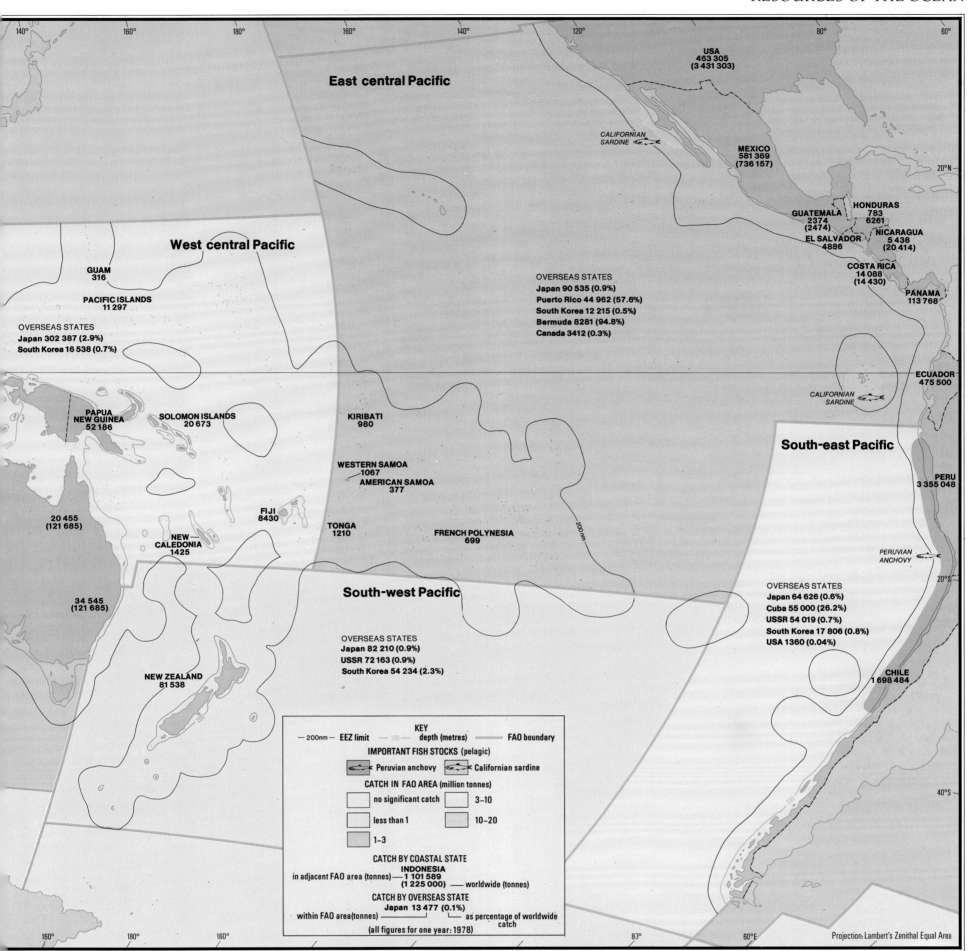

KEY

— 200nm — EEZ limit   200 depth (metres)   — FAO boundary

IMPORTANT FISH STOCKS (pelagic)

Peruvian anchovy   Californian sardine

CATCH IN FAO AREA (million tonnes)

no significant catch	3–10
less than 1	10–20
1–3	

CATCH BY COASTAL STATE

in adjacent FAO area (tonnes) **INDONESIA**
1 101 589
(1 225 000) — worldwide (tonnes)

CATCH BY OVERSEAS STATE

Japan 13 477 (0.1%)
within FAO area (tonnes) ——— as percentage of worldwide catch
(all figures for one year: 1978)

Projection: Lambert's Zenithal Equal Area

Although Indonesia probably has twice as many fishermen as Japan and perhaps the greatest potential stocks of any tropical country (six times the annual production in the early 1970s), productivity is low. Sea fisheries produce about one-tenth the catch of those of Japan, and only twice as much as Indonesia's own inland fisheries. Salt fish are the staple product and there is considerable spoilage. The country is thus attractive for joint fishing ventures to those hard-pressed major fishing nations such as Japan and Thailand and plans are afoot for modernisation. It is hoped that many of the small boats will be replaced by boats of 5 to 60 tonnes and trawlers of 100 to 400 tons. The new EEZ should lead to tighter control over foreign fishing vessels and a doubling of the present catch. In addition, a number of new fishing grounds have been discovered including areas stocked with giant prawns off Java, Sumatra and Kalimantan. Already the modernisation has, however, caused conflict between the artisanal and the mechanised fishermen. In Muncar, East Java, for instance, boats, nets and engines were destroyed by an angry mob who were demonstrating against the use of mechanised fishing boats by a few of the fishermen in the village.

2 *main map* With the exception of the tuna fisheries, and those of Chile, Peru, Mexico, the United States, Thailand and the Philippines, the Indo-Pacific is characterised by a predominance of small-scale artisanal fisheries operating from a large number of developing countries, many of which are small island states.

3 *right* The Californian sardine is an example of a major stock which collapsed after yielding a peak of over one million tons in the 1930s, and which is now showing some signs of recovery. The Peruvian anchovy stock is the most dramatic world example of a pelagic stock collapse in recent times. Both stocks have been partly replaced by other pelagic stocks in the course of fisheries development in the 1970s.

4 *left* The Indonesian archipelago is largely situated upon a shallow continental shelf with considerable potential resources in the large number of demersal and pelagic species. Though industrialisation is taking place, the fisheries are predominantly traditional with the greatest activity adjacent to the concentration of artisanal fishing populations along the central and western coasts.

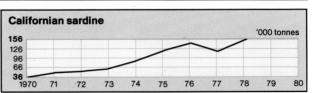

Californian sardine

'000 tonnes

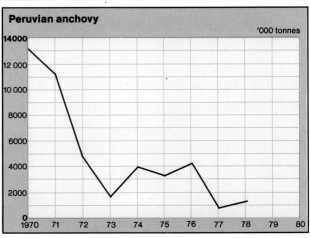

Peruvian anchovy

'000 tonnes

Ocean fisheries

BEYOND the shallow waters of the continental shelves are a group of fisheries which depend upon migratory pelagic stocks which spend varying proportions of their life cycles in oceanic waters. The main groups are the tuna, salmon and whales, and they have all been particularly vulnerable to over-exploitation on the high seas beyond the limits of national jurisdictions.

The most well publicised examples are those of whales. Depletion has in some cases become so severe that even aboriginal fisheries and related cultures are threatened. The bowhead whale which is fished by the Eskimoes is a sad example. Of all the fisheries, whaling is the only one subject to global management in the form of the International Whaling Commission. Even this has not yet been able to provide fully effective management because of conflicting interests.

In the case of salmon, severely affected both by overfishing at sea and by pollution and the industrialisation of native rivers, the enhancement of stocks through ranching techniques (see *Farming the sea* page 82) may redress the inroads of over-exploitation. To date, the management regime for tuna fisheries on a regional oceanic basis has perhaps been most effective, though they have also been the focus of serious conflicts and a factor in the seaward extension of jurisdiction by a number of Latin American states.

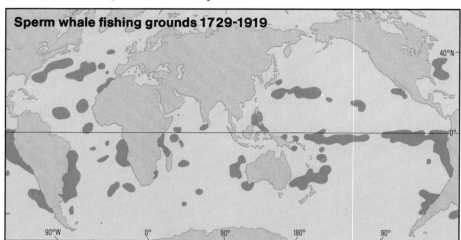
Sperm whale fishing grounds 1729–1919

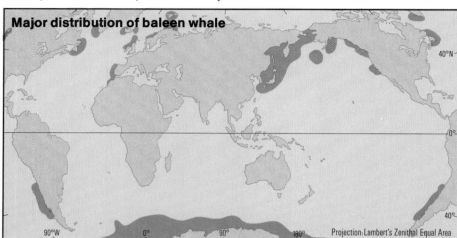
Major distribution of baleen whale

Projection: Lambert's Zenithal Equal Area

Whales

The whale fisheries represent striking examples of the destruction wrought by man upon wild populations, and the rise and fall of a great industry. Both leave enormous management problems in their wake.

The large-scale development of the whale fisheries began during the 17th century in the North Atlantic and was spearheaded by the Dutch at Spitsbergen (Svalbard), with competition from the English, French and Germans. Out of this came the great northern whale fishery of the 18th and 19th centuries led by Britain. The whales were harpooned from open boats which operated from a mother ship. In the 1860s steamships and explosive harpoons were introduced and the fishing expanded in effort to include seal populations, only to collapse in the 1880s. The revival of whaling in the North Atlantic by the Norwegians using ever remoter shore bases met with progressive decline and eventual extinction in the 1930s.

The establishment of whaling in New England also occurred during the 17th century. In the 18th century it was based on sperm whales, and expanded throughout the Atlantic, reaching the Pacific in 1789. The stocks and industry declined rapidly in the 1850s. Antarctic baleen whaling arose in the early 1900s and was pioneered by the British and Norwegians in the wake of the collapse of North Atlantic whaling. Shore bases were established on South Georgia, and factory ships introduced in 1925. This was the most spectacular fishery of all, reaching a peak in the 1930s, and finally dying out in the 1960s.

There are now three distinct fisheries: whaling from land stations; pelagic whaling in high latitudes mainly for baleen whales (the North Pacific industry dates from the 1950s) and pelagic whaling elsewhere. The only two ocean whaling nations now are the USSR and Japan, the former exporting much of its produce to the latter.

1 *and* **2** *above* The worldwide distribution of sperm whaling activity is graphically illustrated by the grounds of the New England whalers of the eighteenth and nineteenth centuries. The distribution of major baleen whale stocks is concentrated in boreal and polar waters in both hemispheres. The collapse of the great northern whale fishery in the North Atlantic provided a strong motive for the expansion of whaling in the Southern Ocean in the twentieth century.

The sequence of species depletion is striking, progressing from the more valuable or easily caught species to the less attractive. The right and bowhead stocks of the North Atlantic were depleted by the late 1700s, and southern hemisphere and North Pacific right stocks by the mid 1800s. Sperm whaling was all but finished by 1860 although there has been a resurgence in the North Pacific. The Antarctic blue whales were depleted by the 1950s, followed by the fin and humpback stocks in the early 1960s.

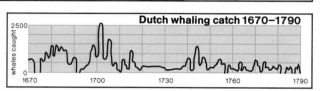
Dutch whaling catch 1670–1790

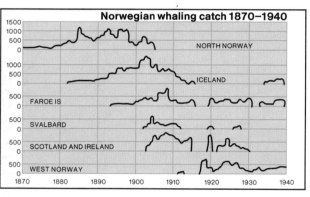
Norwegian whaling catch 1870–1940

NORTH NORWAY

ICELAND

FAROE IS

SVALBARD

SCOTLAND AND IRELAND

WEST NORWAY

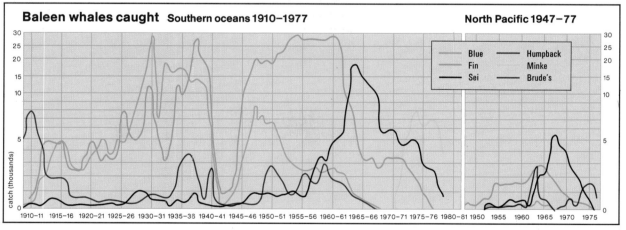
Baleen whales caught Southern oceans 1910–1977   **North Pacific 1947–77**

Blue	Humpback
Fin	Minke
Sei	Brude's

catch (thousands)

3–6 *above* The first graph provides a unique early statistical illustration of the activities of the Dutch in pioneering whaling in the Spitsbergen area, and the final extinction of the commercial industry in the North Atlantic is illustrated by the progressive collapse of Norwegian catches from bases ever more remote from Norway itself. The patterns of rise and decline in the Southern Ocean and North Pacific were relatively rapid due to the enormous effort and advanced technology employed.

7 *left and* **8** *below* The humpback whale and its now legendary migration routes.

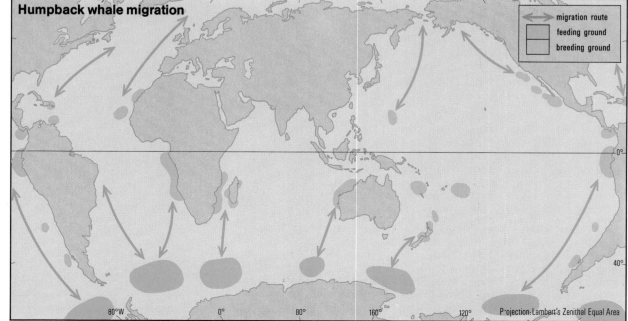
Humpback whale migration

migration route
feeding ground
breeding ground

Projection: Lambert's Zenithal Equal Area

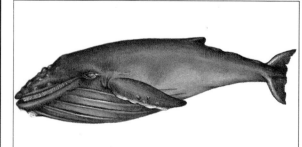

Tuna

Tuna have been an objective of traditional fisheries for centuries. The Mediterranean tuna traps, for example, were important in classical times and earlier. Today's major commercial industry has spread to all the world's oceans and the gears include long lines (the lines being set at depths of 80–140 m or more); pole and line, as used by the American bait boats; and purse-seining. Trolling is also employed.

There are six major market species which are widely distributed between 70°N and 35°S. In order of commercial importance these are skipjack, yellowfin, albacore, bigeye, southern bluefin and northern bluefin and, with the exception of skipjack, all are fully or almost fully exploited. In addition, there are a number of minor species, such as bonito.

The main centres of development are California and Japan. The Japanese have always had an important traditional bonito fishery in the Western Pacific but in the post-war period they have expanded into the Indian Ocean and Atlantic. The Californian fishery was founded on the pole and line baitboats and expanded southwards along the Mexican coast. Purse-seines, operated by tuna clippers, were introduced in the 1930s and the fishery subsequently expanded southwards and westwards. It became a starting point for conflict with the Latin American states over EEZs, and became the first tuna fishery to be regulated through the formation of the Inter-American Tropical Tuna Commission. Other significant tuna fishing nations are the Republic of Korea, Taiwan, Spain and France.

Tuna is a high value fish and is largely canned and consumed in the markets of the United States, Japan and Western Europe. Inevitably, it has become an export commodity for those less developed countries which possess substantial resources under the EEZ regime, such as the Philippines which is developing its own industry. Joint ventures between advanced fishing nations such as Japan and the countries of the Indo-Pacific are leading to the development of fresh tuna fisheries in those regions.

12 *right* These bluefin tuna were caught from purse-seiners operating in the Atlantic Ocean off the coast of south-west Spain. Unlike their American and Japanese counterparts, southern European fishermen tend to land relatively small catches of tuna using smaller boats.

Tuna distribution

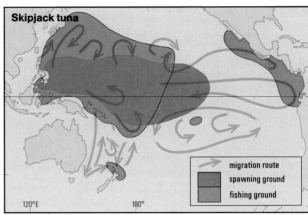

9 *above* The tunas are widely distributed in tropical and temperate waters though the exact limits of their ranges tend to be obscured at times, for example, in the case of the over-fished northern bluefin in the Atlantic, where it ranges northwards of the North Sea.

10 *right* The tuna's highly migratory habits are illustrated by the skipjack, the most important commercial species, which performs extensive migrations between breeding and feeding grounds in the Pacific.

11 *below* The world tuna catch statistics reflect the importance of the fisheries in the tropical and subtropical waters of the Pacific.

Skipjack tuna

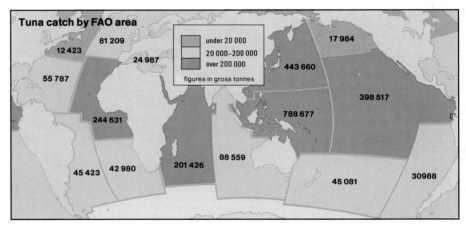

migration route
spawning ground
fishing ground

Tuna catch by FAO area

under 20 000
20 000–200 000
over 200 000
figures in gross tonnes

81 209
12 423
24 987
55 787
17 984
443 660
244 631
398 517
788 677
45 423
42 980
201 426
88 559
45 081
30 988

Salmon

The salmon spends part of its life in the oceans and the rest in the rivers where it migrates to spawn. Most fisheries are concentrated in the coastal areas and on the rivers.

The North Pacific, which is the most important area, contains five major commercial species of Pacific salmon: the pink, chum, sockeye, chinook and coho, distributed around the shores of the northern Pacific from Japan to California. Salmon of both Asian and North American origin appear to have overlapping oceanic distribution. Modern exploitation began in the second half of the 19th century in Japan, Russia (mainly by the Japanese) and North America. Large-scale canning commenced in the late 19th century. In coastal areas a wide variety of gears are used including set and floating traps, trolling and purse-seining. The Japanese high seas fishery which commenced in the 1930s and resumed after the war is based on gill netting and long lining using mother ships and fleets of catchers.

Although salmon fisheries are subject to natural production cycles, serious overfishing has occurred from time to time requiring strict regulation (for example, in British Columbia). In addition, there has been a serious decline in northern Japan and California due to pollution and modification of the rivers.

In the Californian case modification began with the Gold Rush in 1849. In the Soviet Union there has also been a substantial decline which is quite possibly related to the Japanese high seas fishery.

The story of the North Atlantic salmon is of its destruction brought about by industrialisation and overfishing. Pollution and river modification came about with the development of industry and salmon gradually disappeared from these rivers, notably in Germany, southern England, and New England. The threat of overfishing now comes from illegal drift netting in coastal waters, and drift netting and long lining in the relatively recently discovered oceanic feeding grounds off west Greenland, in the vicinity of the Faroe Islands, and in the northern Norwegian Sea. Salmon is an important recreational as well as commercial fishing resource, and this leads to conflict between river and sea fisheries interests. Fishing off Greenland was banned in 1976, and in January 1982 an international convention for the conservation of salmon in the North Atlantic was announced, the headquarters to be sited in Edinburgh.

Pink salmon

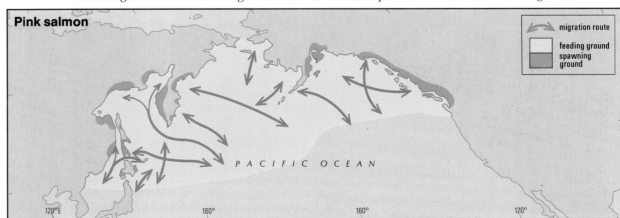

migration route
feeding ground
spawning ground

PACIFIC OCEAN

North Atlantic salmon

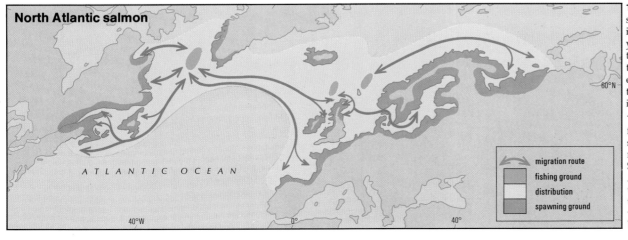

ATLANTIC OCEAN

migration route
fishing ground
distribution
spawning ground

13 *above and* **14** *left* The salmon distribution in the sea illustrates the extensive but as yet imperfectly known migrations. The effective range in the rivers has been restricted, especially in the North Atlantic, due to pollution and industrialisation of the rivers.

15 *right* Salmon migrating from the North Atlantic to spawn in their native river near Shin Falls, Lairg, Scotland. During adult life, Atlantic salmon may make two or three migrations to their home rivers to spawn while the Pacific salmon breeds only once.

Oil basins and production

THE modern petroleum industry originates from the 1850s, when wells were mechanically drilled in Pennsylvania. It was subsequently realised that some oilfield boundaries extended beneath the sea, and the world's first offshore well was sunk in 1896 off the coast of California, using wooden jetties from the land. The production of oil out of sight of land began in 1947 in the Gulf of Mexico.

Offshore oil production in 1980 was 14 million barrels per day (b/d), more than 20 per cent of total world production. The expenditure per year by the offshore oil industry is around $40 billion. It is estimated that by 1990 production will be about 24 million b/d and annual expenditure will be in excess of $100 billion.

1 map All potential hydrocarbon basins are shown. The oilfields in regular production are numbered and details as available given in the table.

basin name/ map ref. no.	field name	country	production, thousand barrels/ day*	estimated reserves, billion barrels	no. of wells
Cook Inlet Province					
1	MacArthur River	Alaska	70	0.105	66
2	Middle Ground Shoal	Alaska	15	0.039	42
Ventura					
3	Dos Cuadros	USA	26	0.063	146
Los Angeles					
4	Wilmington	USA	122	<0.001	2178
5	Huntington Beach	USA	29	0.085	968
Western Gulf					
6	Grand Isle 43	USA	25	0.141	216
7	Bay Marchand 2	USA	40	0.129	152
8	Timbalier Bay 21	USA	15	0.074	93
9	West Delta 30	USA	32	0.078	195
10	South Pass 24	USA	21	0.058	426
11	South Pass 61	USA	29	0.115	91
12	South Pass 62	USA	16	0.112	84
13	Ship Shoal 208	USA	12	0.100	104
14	Eugene Is 330	USA	61	0.156	203
Tabasco-Campeche					
15	Cantarell	Mexico	150	—	—

*averaged from first six months of 1979

basin name/ map ref. no.	field name	country	production, thousand barrels/ day*	estimated reserves, billion barrels	no. of wells
Magallanes					
36	Ostion	Chile	6	0.2	11
Talara					
37	Litoral	Peru	2	—	96
38	Humboldt	Peru	24	—	316
39	Providencia	Peru	1	—	49
Mid North Sea High					
40	Argyll	UK	18	<0.1	5
41	Auk	UK	21	<0.1	9

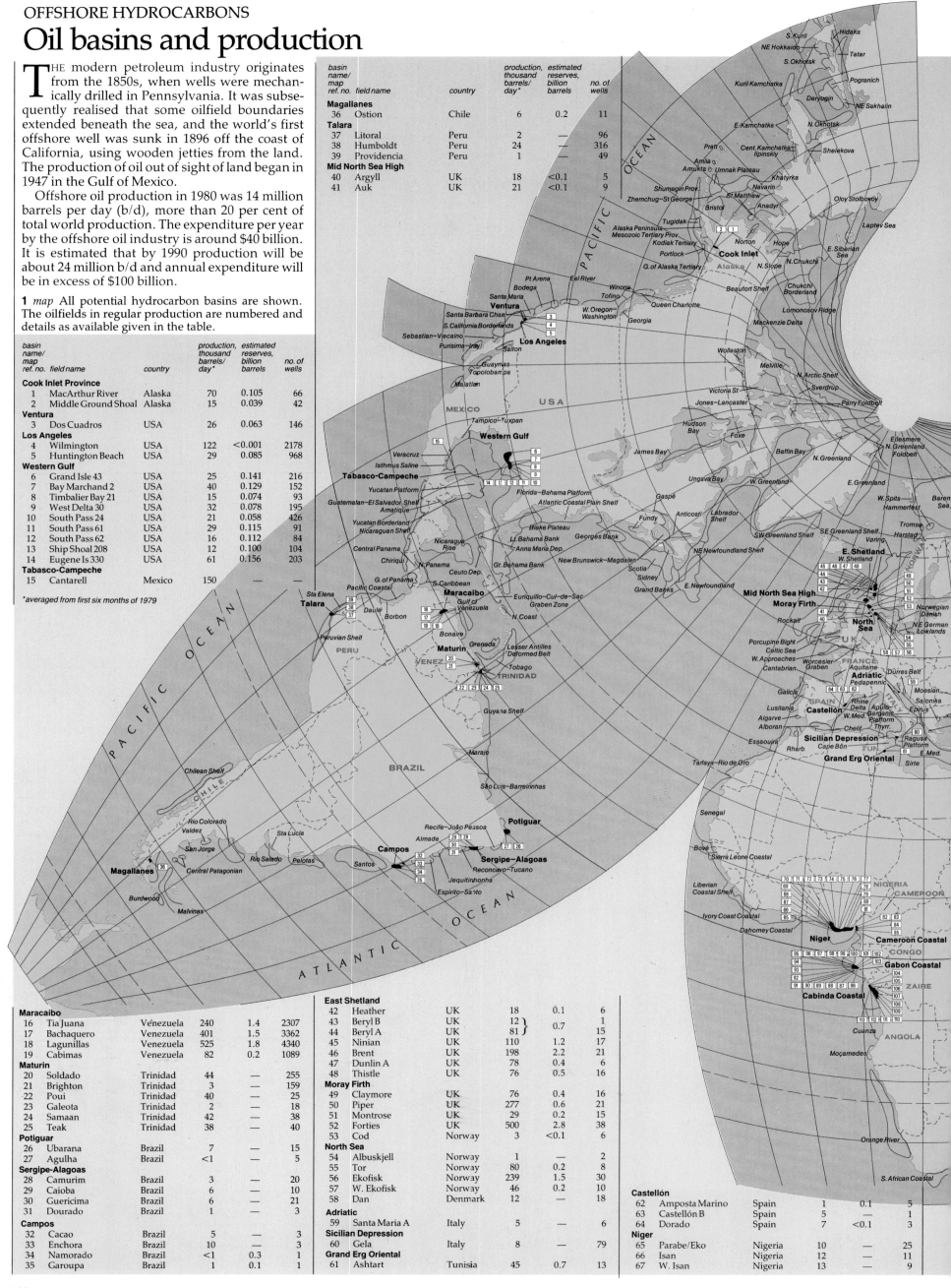

basin name/ map ref. no.	field name	country	production, thousand barrels/ day*	estimated reserves, billion barrels	no. of wells
Maracaibo					
16	Tia Juana	Venezuela	240	1.4	2307
17	Bachaquero	Venezuela	401	1.5	3362
18	Lagunillas	Venezuela	525	1.8	4340
19	Cabimas	Venezuela	82	0.2	1089
Maturin					
20	Soldado	Trinidad	44	—	255
21	Brighton	Trinidad	3	—	159
22	Poui	Trinidad	40	—	25
23	Galeota	Trinidad	2	—	18
24	Samaan	Trinidad	42	—	38
25	Teak	Trinidad	38	—	40
Potiguar					
26	Ubarana	Brazil	7	—	15
27	Agulha	Brazil	<1	—	5
Sergipe-Alagoas					
28	Camurim	Brazil	3	—	20
29	Caioba	Brazil	6	—	10
30	Guericima	Brazil	6	—	21
31	Dourado	Brazil	1	—	3
Campos					
32	Cacao	Brazil	5	—	3
33	Enchora	Brazil	10	—	3
34	Namorado	Brazil	<1	0.3	1
35	Garoupa	Brazil	1	0.1	1

basin name/ map ref. no.	field name	country	production, thousand barrels/ day*	estimated reserves, billion barrels	no. of wells
East Shetland					
42	Heather	UK	18	0.1	6
43	Beryl B	UK	12	0.7	1
44	Beryl A	UK	81		15
45	Ninian	UK	110	1.2	17
46	Brent	UK	198	2.2	21
47	Dunlin A	UK	78	0.4	6
48	Thistle	UK	76	0.5	16
Moray Firth					
49	Claymore	UK	76	0.4	16
50	Piper	UK	277	0.6	21
51	Montrose	UK	29	0.2	15
52	Forties	UK	500	2.8	38
53	Cod	Norway	3	<0.1	6
North Sea					
54	Albuskjell	Norway	1	—	2
55	Tor	Norway	80	0.2	8
56	Ekofisk	Norway	239	1.5	30
57	W. Ekofisk	Norway	46	0.2	10
58	Dan	Denmark	12	—	18
Adriatic					
59	Santa Maria A	Italy	5	—	6
Sicilian Depression					
60	Gela	Italy	8	—	79
Grand Erg Oriental					
61	Ashtart	Tunisia	45	0.7	13

basin name/ map ref. no.	field name	country	production, thousand barrels/ day*	estimated reserves, billion barrels	no. of wells
Castellón					
62	Amposta Marino	Spain	1	0.1	5
63	Castellón B	Spain	5	—	1
64	Dorado	Spain	7	<0.1	3
Niger					
65	Parabe/Eko	Nigeria	10	—	25
66	Isan	Nigeria	12	—	11
67	W. Isan	Nigeria	13	—	9

basin name/ map ref. no.	field name	country	production, thousand barrels/day*	estimated reserves, billion barrels	no. of wells
68	Malu	Nigeria	16	—	15
69	Meren	Nigeria	93	—	50
70	Delta	Nigeria	44	—	27
71	Delta S.	Nigeria	46	—	27
72	Meji	Nigeria	39	—	21
73	Okan	Nigeria	62	—	58
74	Mefa	Nigeria	8	—	5
75	Pennington	Nigeria	5	—	10
76	Middleton	Nigeria	4	—	6
77	N. Apoi	Nigeria	48	—	16
78	Ekpe	Nigeria	34	—	14
79	Asabo	Nigeria	24	—	11
80	Inin	Nigeria	29	—	8
81	Ubit	Nigeria	51	—	43

basin name/ map ref. no.	field name	country	production, thousand barrels/day*	estimated reserves, billion barrels	no. of wells
90	Torpille	Gabon	15	—	—
91	Dorée	Gabon	1	—	—
92	Grondin	Gabon	42	0.2	210
93	Breme	Gabon	18	—	—
94	Mandaros	Gabon	21	—	—
95	Barbier	Gabon	19	—	—
96	Girelle	Gabon	9	—	—
97	Anguille NE	Gabon	5	—	—
98	Anguille NNE	Gabon	1	—	—
99	Gonelle	Gabon	8	—	—
100	Lucina Marine	Gabon	3	—	8
101	PGS Marine	Gabon	3	—	—
102	Olendé	Gabon	1	—	—
103	Batanga	Gabon	<1	—	—

basin name/ map ref. no.	field name	country	production, thousand barrels/day*	estimated reserves, billion barrels	no. of wells
142	Marjan	Saudi Arabia	108	1.3	12
143	Zuluf	Saudi Arabia	557	5.2	37
144	Khafji	Divided Zone	405	1.4	128
145	Al Hout	Divided Zone	8	0.5	27
146	Bahregan Shahr	Iran	12	0.2	11
147	Hendijan	Iran	8	0.2	7
148	Nowruz	Iran	16	0.7	14
149	Ardeshir	Iran	35	1.6	50
150	Cyrus	Iran	2	0.5	8
151	Feridoon	Iran	53	1.5	39
152	Darius	Iran	19	1.0	16
153	Rostam	Iran	11	0.9	27
154	Rakhsh	Iran	21	0.8	14
155	Sassan	Iran	NA	1.0	28

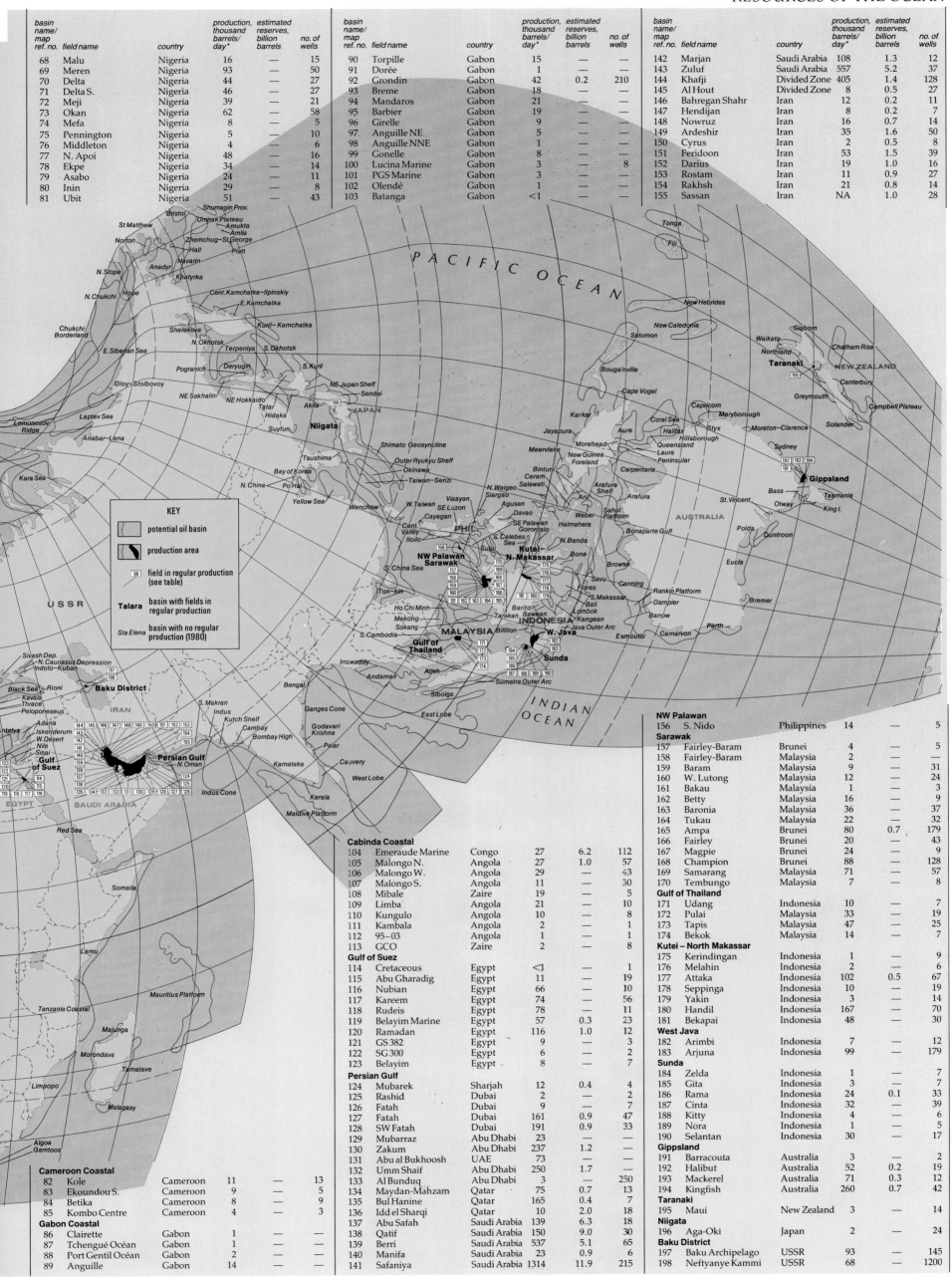

KEY
- potential oil basin
- production area
- 98 field in regular production (see table)
- **Talara** basin with fields in regular production
- Sta Elena basin with no regular production (1980)

Cameroon Coastal

	field name	country			
82	Kole	Cameroon	11	—	13
83	Ekoundou S.	Cameroon	9	—	5
84	Betika	Cameroon	8	—	9
85	Kombo Centre	Cameroon	4	—	3

Gabon Coastal

86	Clairette	Gabon	1	—	—
87	Tchengué Océan	Gabon	1	—	—
88	Port Gentil Océan	Gabon	2	—	—
89	Anguille	Gabon	14	—	—

Cabinda Coastal

104	Emeraude Marine	Congo	27	6.2	112
105	Malongo N.	Angola	27	1.0	57
106	Malongo W.	Angola	29	—	43
107	Malongo S.	Angola	11	—	30
108	Mibale	Zaire	19	—	5
109	Limba	Angola	21	—	10
110	Kungulo	Angola	10	—	8
111	Kambala	Angola	2	—	1
112	95–03	Angola	1	—	1
113	GCO	Zaire	2	—	8

Gulf of Suez

114	Cretaceous	Egypt	<1	—	1
115	Abu Gharadig	Egypt	11	—	19
116	Nubian	Egypt	66	—	10
117	Kareem	Egypt	74	—	56
118	Rudeis	Egypt	78	—	11
119	Belayim Marine	Egypt	57	0.3	23
120	Ramadan	Egypt	116	1.0	12
121	GS 382	Egypt	9	—	3
122	SG 300	Egypt	6	—	2
123	Belayim	Egypt	8	—	7

Persian Gulf

124	Mubarek	Sharjah	12	0.4	4
125	Rashid	Dubai	2	—	2
126	Fatah	Dubai	9	—	7
127	Fatah	Dubai	161	0.9	47
128	SW Fatah	Dubai	191	0.9	33
129	Mubarraz	Abu Dhabi	23	—	—
130	Zakum	Abu Dhabi	237	1.2	—
131	Abu al Bukhoosh	UAE	73	—	—
132	Umm Shaif	Abu Dhabi	250	1.7	—
133	Al Bunduq	Abu Dhabi	3	—	250
134	Maydan-Mahzam	Qatar	75	0.7	13
135	Bul Hanine	Qatar	165	0.4	7
136	Idd el Sharqi	Qatar	10	2.0	18
137	Abu Safah	Saudi Arabia	139	6.3	18
138	Qatif	Saudi Arabia	150	9.0	30
139	Berri	Saudi Arabia	537	5.1	65
140	Manifa	Saudi Arabia	23	0.9	6
141	Safaniya	Saudi Arabia	1314	11.9	215

NW Palawan

	field name	country	production, thousand barrels/day*	estimated reserves, billion barrels	no. of wells
156	S. Nido	Philippines	14	—	5

Sarawak

157	Fairley-Baram	Brunei	4	—	5
158	Fairley-Baram	Malaysia	2	—	—
159	Baram	Malaysia	9	—	31
160	W. Lutong	Malaysia	12	—	24
161	Bakau	Malaysia	1	—	3
162	Betty	Malaysia	16	—	9
163	Baronia	Malaysia	36	—	37
164	Tukau	Malaysia	22	—	32
165	Ampa	Brunei	80	0.7	179
166	Fairley	Brunei	20	—	43
167	Magpie	Brunei	24	—	9
168	Champion	Brunei	88	—	128
169	Samarang	Malaysia	71	—	57
170	Tembungo	Malaysia	7	—	8

Gulf of Thailand

171	Udang	Indonesia	10	—	7
172	Pulai	Malaysia	33	—	19
173	Tapis	Malaysia	47	—	25
174	Bekok	Malaysia	14	—	7

Kutei – North Makassar

175	Kerindingan	Indonesia	1	—	9
176	Melahin	Indonesia	2	—	6
177	Attaka	Indonesia	102	0.5	67
178	Seppinga	Indonesia	10	—	19
179	Yakin	Indonesia	3	—	14
180	Handil	Indonesia	167	—	70
181	Bekapai	Indonesia	48	—	30

West Java

182	Arimbi	Indonesia	7	—	12
183	Arjuna	Indonesia	99	—	179

Sunda

184	Zelda	Indonesia	1	—	7
185	Gita	Indonesia	3	—	7
186	Rama	Indonesia	24	0.1	33
187	Cinta	Indonesia	32	—	39
188	Kitty	Indonesia	4	—	6
189	Nora	Indonesia	1	—	5
190	Selantan	Indonesia	30	—	17

Gippsland

191	Barracouta	Australia	3	—	2
192	Halibut	Australia	52	0.2	19
193	Mackerel	Australia	71	0.3	12
194	Kingfish	Australia	260	0.7	42

Taranaki

195	Maui	New Zealand	3	—	14

Niigata

196	Aga-Oki	Japan	2	—	24

Baku District

197	Baku Archipelago	USSR	93	—	145
198	Neftyane Kammi	USSR	68	—	1200

Oil and gas 1

THE offshore oil industry is the impressive result of mineral exploitation in the marine environment, and it is at the forefront of technology for exploitation of marine minerals. Early developments in California and Lake Maracaibo were encouraged by the presence of natural seepages, and the industry originated in these areas and the Gulf of Mexico under the impetus of the continuing expansion of the world's leading petroleum consumer, the United States. The offshore industry is a very specialised part of the world oil industry, and remains centred along the northern coasts of the Gulf of Mexico.

The decisive expansion associated with the now familiar technological advances into deep water began in the 1960s and received a boost in the 1970s as the value of crude oil and natural gas spiralled upwards. Offshore locations, once too expensive to develop, became competitive with land sources, and as United States self-sufficiency in oil disappeared and imports rose rapidly throughout the 1960s and 1970s, the worldwide search by major oil interests in the United States and western Europe expanded rapidly. The North Sea became the main proving ground for deep water technology, and the development of technology for the North American Arctic is under way. The promise of wealth from offshore industries has been decisive in the emergence of the Exclusive Economic Zones (see *Maritime jurisdictional zones* page 220). Virtually all major industrial and developing nations with sea access are keen to develop their offshore oil and gas interests. In general, outside North America and the North Sea, the major centres of production are those which, like the United States, have developed from onshore provinces. This is particularly true in the Persian Gulf,

1 *below* The major offshore oil producers are Saudi Arabia, Abu Dhabi, the United States, the United Kingdom and Venezuela. In the Persian/Arabian Gulf, apart from Abu Dhabi and Qatar, there is very little unassociated gas production. Besides Nigeria and Indonesia, other developing countries including Ghana and the Philippines have started to develop their offshore oil resources, while others such as Brunei have initiated offshore gas production.

South East Asia, and the Gulf of Guinea.

Increasingly, however, the trend is to develop areas which have little or no land-based oil industry, and the distribution of prospective sites (see map, page 102) will ensure continuation of this pattern. The first stage in the development of a site is exploration and the build up of drilling rig activity and service bases in either existing or new port locations. Once full production is decided on, the massive operation of installing facilities begins. First, engineering yards to build production platforms are established, though wherever possible, existing shipbuilding and engineering yards are likely to be used. Then pipelines are laid at sea and on land and specialist oil and gas terminals are built at coastal locations. The production stage which follows requires the continued support of the service industry, while the demand for engineering equipment produced by the sequence of development tails off. This may be mitigated in a large oil province if there are several generations of production development involving groups of fields.

The major American and western European oil companies head a complex industrial structure consisting of four major divisions. In the offshore sector the oil companies co-ordinate complex development projects in which major tasks

2 *above* Oil rigs of an early type designed for the shallow waters of Lake Maracaibo, the largest of Venezuela's three main oil producing regions.

3 *above* Mobile jack-up rig off Texas, in contrast to the fixed seabed rigs of Lake Maracaibo, with service vessel in attendance.

are actually carried out by specialist high technology companies operating worldwide. The tasks include exploration drilling, well-logging, design and installation of production complexes offshore. Some large oil companies engage directly in these tasks through their exploration and production divisions. The related offshore engineering industry is dominated by a combination of specialist builders of exploration rigs, production platforms and modules, and a wide range of major civil engineering and shipbuilding companies which have expanded into the high technology area, notably in western Europe.

The firms involved in advanced technology tend to aim for a stake in world markets in order to lessen dependence on any one region. Regional and national stakes are maintained in the fields of servicing, finance, less specialised aspects of engineering and, of course, government participation and taxation arrangements which secure large national shares in the wealth produced regardless of the developers.

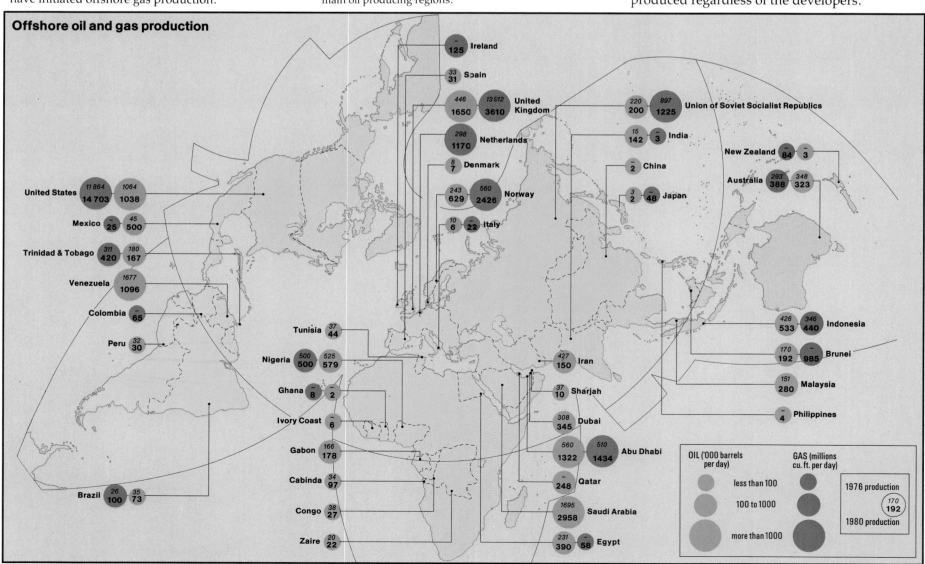

Offshore oil and gas production

Ireland — / 125

Spain 33 / 31

United Kingdom 446 / 1650, 13 512 / 3610

Union of Soviet Socialist Republics 220 / 200, 897 / 1225

Netherlands 298 / 1170

India 15 / 142, 3 / —

Denmark 8 / 7

China 2

New Zealand 84 / —, — / 3

Norway 243 / 629, 560 / 2426

Japan 3 / 2, — / 48

Australia 293 / 388, 348 / 323

United States 11 864 / 14 703, 1064 / 1038

Italy 10 / 6, 22 / —

Mexico 45 / 25, / 500

Trinidad & Tobago 311 / 420, 180 / 167

Venezuela 1677 / 1096

Colombia — / 65

Indonesia 426 / 533, 346 / 440

Peru 32 / 30

Tunisia 37 / 44

Iran 427 / 150

Brunei 170 / 192, — / 985

Nigeria 500 / 500, 525 / 579

Sharjah 37 / 10

Malaysia 151 / 280

Ghana 8 / —, 2 / —

Ivory Coast 6 / —

Dubai 308 / 345

Philippines — / 4

Gabon 166 / 178

Abu Dhabi 560 / 1322, 510 / 1434

Cabinda 34 / 97

Qatar 248 / —

Congo 38 / 27, 1695 / 2958 Saudi Arabia

Brazil 26 / 100, 35 / 73

Zaire 20 / 22

Egypt 231 / 390, 58 / —

OIL ('000 barrels per day) — less than 100, 100 to 1000, more than 1000

GAS (millions cu. ft. per day)

1976 production / 1980 production — 170 / 192

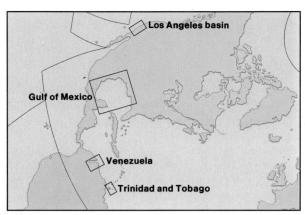

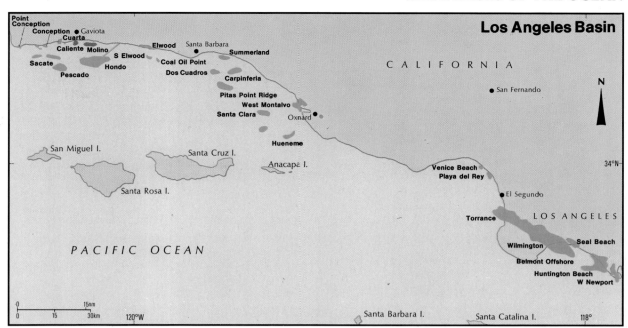

Los Angeles Basin

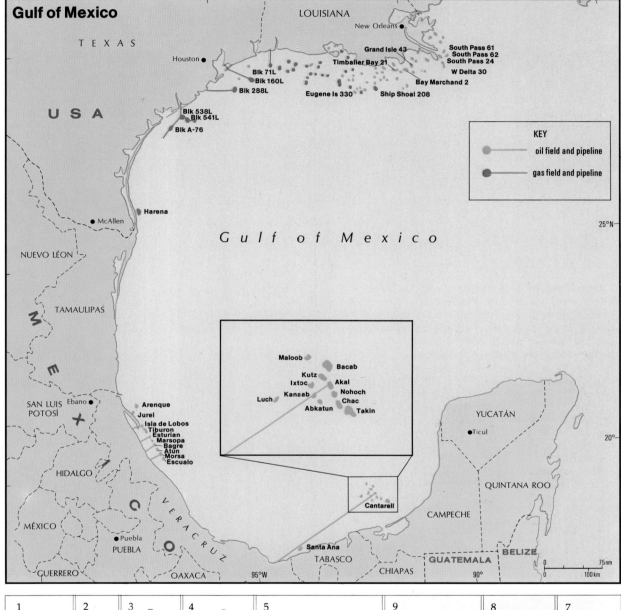

Gulf of Mexico

KEY
- oil field and pipeline
- gas field and pipeline

4 *top right* In the original heartland of offshore oil, activities developed from onshore sources. Drillers working from wooden piers exploited a seaward extension of the Summerland field in southern California in 1896—the first of over 400 such wells in the first United States venture into the offshore. **5** *below* In Lake Maracaibo, where Spanish Galleons were once caulked with bitumen collected from natural seepages, the first offshore wells began producing in the mid 1920s. **6** *right* The first offshore oil strike in the Gulf of Mexico occurred in 1938 on the Louisiana coast and this area now has the highest density of offshore production platforms in the world.

The shallow water and relatively favourable environmental conditions of the Gulf of Mexico and Lake Maracaibo have favoured great expansion of activity in these areas. By the end of 1978 some 16 000 wells had been completed on the United States Outer Continental Shelf since production commenced in 1947, with the number of active wells peaking at 5704 in 1971. The application of technology to deeper waters in offshore California, Gulf of Mexico, and perhaps the Gulf of Venezuela **7** *below*, is likely to sustain the leading position of these areas for the foreseeable future.

Venezuela

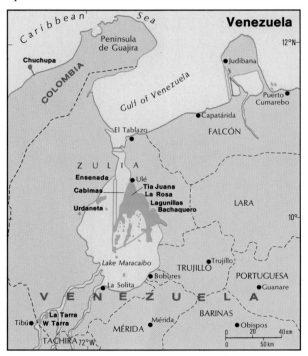

Trinidad

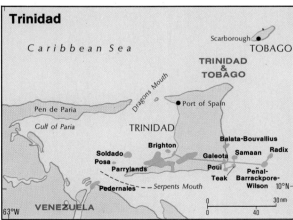

8 *right* Rigs can be divided into two categories: those used for exploration and those used for oil production. Submersibles and drill ships are mobile and can manoeuvre themselves over potentially promising oil-bearing ground. Production platforms are more permanent and are established once oil has been located. With advances in technology, offshore oil production has moved into ever deeper waters. The recent development of subsea completions, which can operate independently of the surface, means that production will be able to take place at depths hitherto inaccessible and thus open up new oil fields for exploitation.

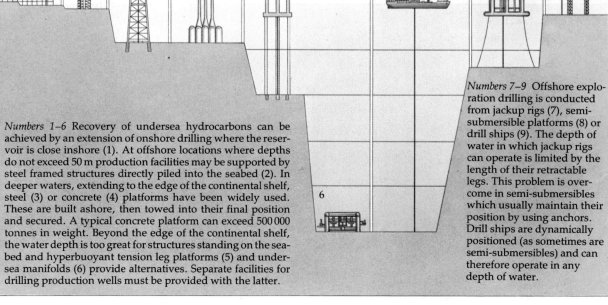

Numbers 1–6 Recovery of undersea hydrocarbons can be achieved by an extension of onshore drilling where the reservoir is close inshore (1). At offshore locations where depths do not exceed 50 m production facilities may be supported by steel framed structures directly piled into the seabed (2). In deeper waters, extending to the edge of the continental shelf, steel (3) or concrete (4) platforms have been widely used. These are built ashore, then towed into their final position and secured. A typical concrete platform can exceed 500 000 tonnes in weight. Beyond the edge of the continental shelf, the water depth is too great for structures standing on the seabed and hyperbuoyant tension leg platforms (5) and undersea manifolds (6) provide alternatives. Separate facilities for drilling production wells must be provided with the latter.

Numbers 7–9 Offshore exploration drilling is conducted from jackup rigs (7), semisubmersible platforms (8) or drill ships (9). The depth of water in which jackup rigs can operate is limited by the length of their retractable legs. This problem is overcome in semi-submersibles which usually maintain their position by using anchors. Drill ships are dynamically positioned (as sometimes are semi-submersibles) and can therefore operate in any depth of water.

Oil and gas 2: the technological frontier

The advance into deep water and increasingly severe environments is, in some respects, comparable to the simultaneous conquest of space. While advances in marine geology and exploration techniques have been almost revolutionary and have greatly aided the progressive exploration of the world's continental shelves, the main focus of interest has tended to be the development of high technology to cope with the inhospitable marine environment. There are three groups of environmental problems: increasing water depth; variable sea surface, sea bed and water column conditions; and the environmental impact of operations.

The pre-test drilling stages of offshore exploration are, if anything, more convenient at sea than on land and are carried out using aircraft and ships. The difficulties begin at the test-drilling stage when fixed or floating structures are required.

The centrepiece of production technology up to now has been the steel platform jacket, piled into the sea bed and topped by a steel deck on which are placed the production equipment and accommodation. Associated with this stage is the process of continuous pipe laying, which copes with depths in excess of 200 m. In deeper waters in the North Sea, reinforced concrete platforms containing storage space for up to 1 million barrels of crude oil are used. These platforms rest on the sea bed under their own considerable weight, which may be over 250 000 tonnes. Exploitation of oil beyond the edge of the continental shelf is likely to rely on subsea systems (called 'subsea completions') and floating platforms anchored to the sea bed. Most of these were still at the design stage in the early 1980s.

The great cost of production equipment is a major determinant of the viability of individual fields in deep water far from land. Grouped oil fields, which can then share transportation facilities, are favoured especially as pipelines to shore are a necessity for gas. For crude oil, large fields or groups of fields may be most economically exploited by pipeline, but small fields most frequently rely on tanker loading systems.

The installation and maintenance of offshore equipment necessitates a wider range of surface and sub-surface vessels. These include purpose-built supply vessels (and helicopters) for supplying rigs and platforms; pipe laying and trenching barges, crane barges and accommodation ships and rigs for installation; and fire-fighting and standby vessels for safety. Undersea technology is dependent on use of divers and submersibles.

Because the production installations are fixed, the industry has considerable environmental impact ranging from localised visual intrusion to pollution and interference with other uses of the sea, notably fishing and navigation.

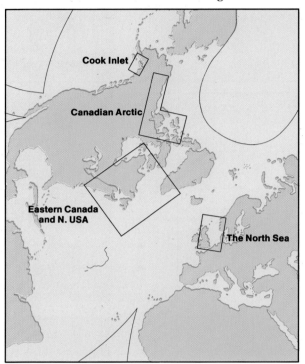

1 *right* The North Sea occupies a special place in the development of offshore hydrocarbon resources as it was the principal focus in the late 1960s and 1970s for the rapid evolution of offshore engineering technology brought about by the advance into deeper water and a more hostile environment.

Exploitation began with the discovery of the giant onshore Gronigen gas field in 1959. There then followed several generations of oilfield developments in the central and northern groups of basins. The strong incentive to extend exploration beyond the edge of the continental shelf west of Britain and Ireland and off northern Norway lies behind the continuing development of advanced technology.

The environmental, social and economic impact upon surrounding coastlands has been focused upon a series of ports including Great Yarmouth, Aberdeen (the main centre) and Stavanger where service bases are located. Specialist offshore engineering yards are situated partly in existing major shipbuilding centres and partly on scenically attractive greenfield sites in Scotland and Norway.

2, 3, *and* **4** *opposite page* Interest in the impact of the industry has been such that regions on the North American Atlantic and Arctic coasts have looked first at the North Sea to learn about developments in difficult and sensitive environmental, social and economic conditions. Such regions include the Canadian Maritime Provinces, off the coast of New England, and Cook Inlet in Alaska.

Further north, and in the Arctic Basin, ice is a major complicating factor. Strengthened rigs, platforms and ships are required, and scouring of the seafloor by icebergs may rupture pipelines. In shallow water artificial islands are feasible, and by 1979 no less than 15 had been constructed in the Beaufort Sea adjacent to the Mackenzie Delta. The Arctic environment is specially sensitive to pollution as the degradation of oil in cold conditions is very slow.

5 *opposite page centre and bottom* An aerial view of the centre of the Ekofisk complex which altogether measures 13 km long and 6 km wide. The complex supplies oil and gas to many parts of Western Europe and associated storage and processing facilities are located at Teesside, England, and Emden, West Germany. The illustration shows a below sea-level impression of the diverse equipment and servicing operations necessary for running an offshore oilfield complex.

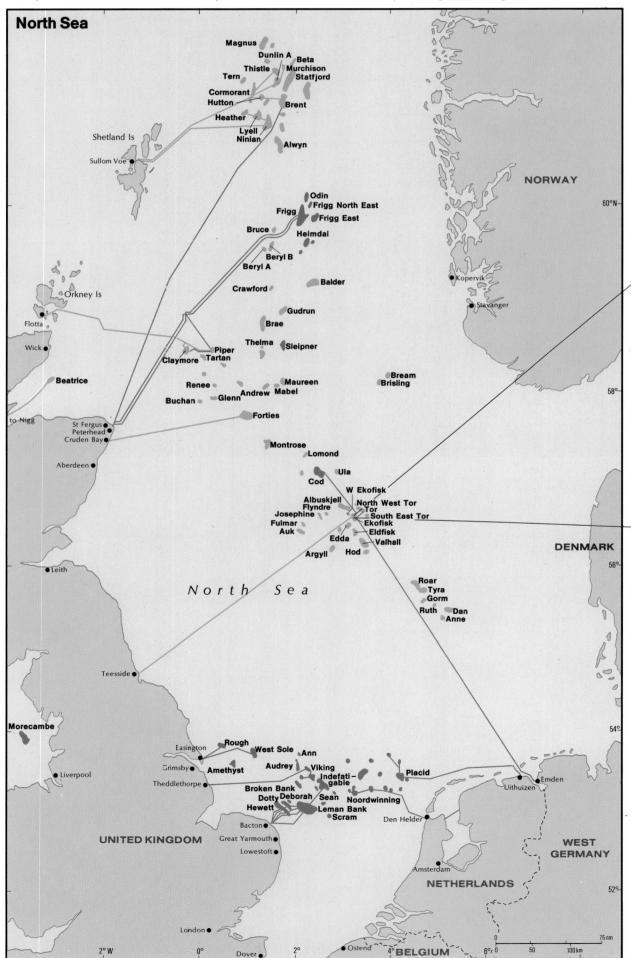

North Sea

Eastern Canada and N. USA

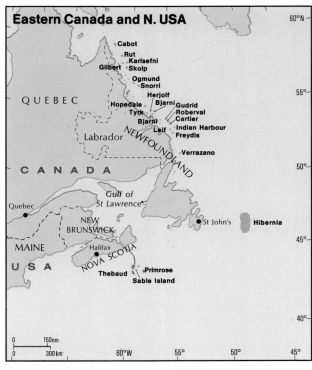

Canadian Arctic

6 *above* The *Discoverer Seven Seas*, a drill ship run by Texaco Canada heading towards St John's Harbour, Newfoundland.

Cook Inlet

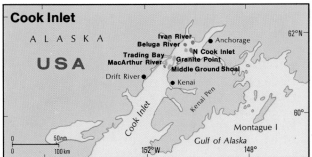

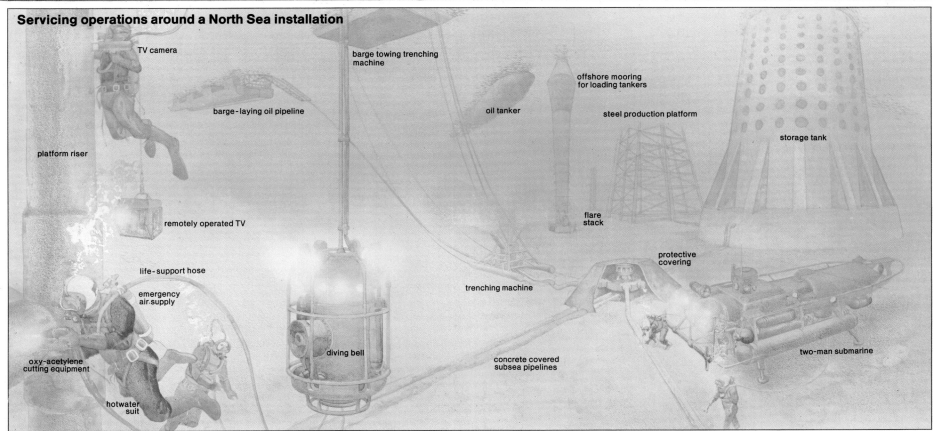

Servicing operations around a North Sea installation

TV camera

barge towing trenching machine

offshore mooring for loading tankers

barge-laying oil pipeline

oil tanker

steel production platform

storage tank

platform riser

flare stack

remotely operated TV

protective covering

life-support hose

emergency air-supply

trenching machine

oxy-acetylene cutting equipment

diving bell

concrete covered subsea pipelines

two-man submarine

hotwater suit

Oil and gas 3: the developing regions

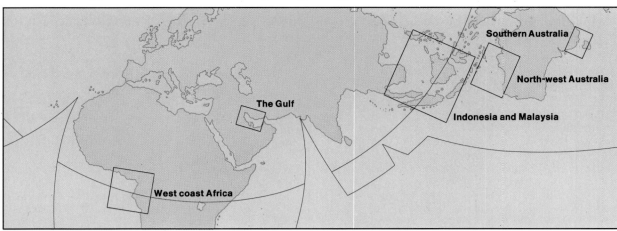

The Gulf

Southern Australia

North-west Australia

Indonesia and Malaysia

West coast Africa

In contrast to the pre-occupation with technology and environmental impact in North America and Western Europe, offshore developments in the rest of the world focus more clearly upon the resource potential of the continental shelf for developing countries, the political drive for coastal state participation, conflict among nations arising from the division of the connental shelf, and the development potential of both offshore and onshore oil wealth when channelled in other directions.

Development in the offshore oil industry outside the major producing areas is at present a function of their location in relation to the big world markets. As elsewhere, when onshore resources begin to deplete, offshore resources become more attractive. The need for offshore exploitation is greatest in the more developed countries which have witnessed industrialisation. Not all countries, however, are endowed with oil resources. In South Africa, for example, intensive exploration has yielded limited results. On the other hand the Australian offshore oil industry is developing rapidly and New Zealand, too, possesses an offshore gas field. The Mediterranean countries of Europe, principally Spain and Italy, but also Greece and Turkey, have offshore interests. Japan possesses very limited resources. Despite their production in the Caspian Sea, the Soviet Union's offshore resources are likely to lie mainly in the Arctic, Barents Sea, and Sea of Okhotsk.

The pattern in the developing world is characterised by the efforts of the countries of North Africa and the Middle East in the Mediterranean and Red Sea, notably Egypt, although overall production is very small. A second group consists of major industrialising states, principally Brazil, Argentina, Mexico, and India, all of which are achieving notable success. Sea areas of great potential in difficult environments far from

West Coast Africa

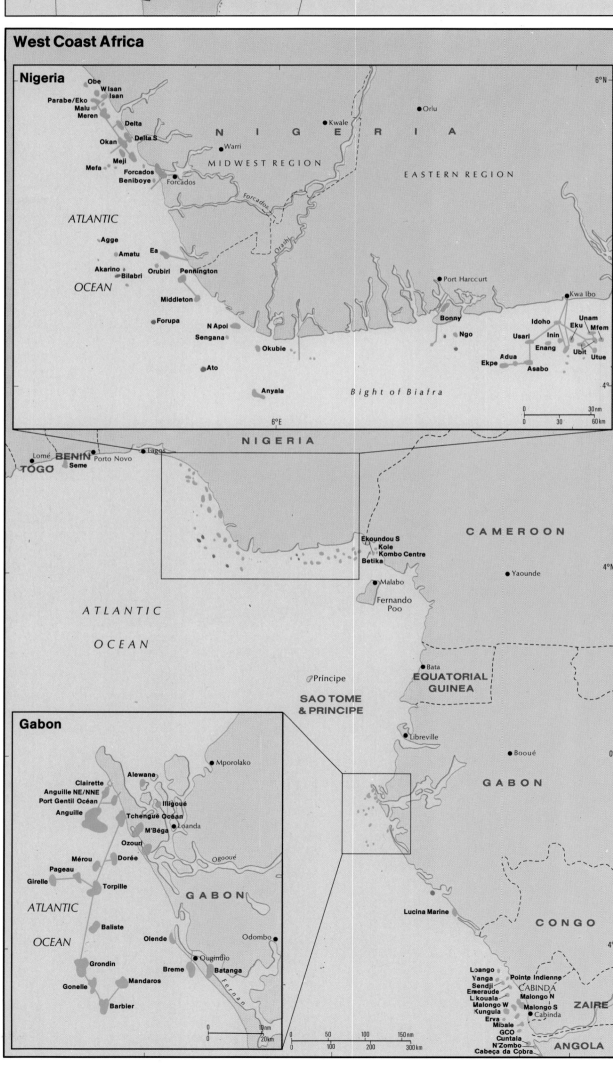

South East Asia

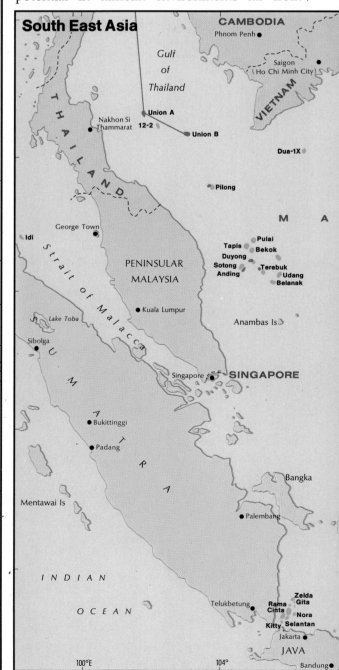

major markets may not be developed in the foreseeable future. This is particularly true of the polar regions. Political instability and competition from other energy sources are also deterrents.

The three major producing areas in the developing world, the Persian Gulf, the Gulf of Guinea and South East Asian waters, are the offshore extensions of major land provinces which have been in production for some time. Next in importance are a wide periphery of shelf seas off South America, the west coast of Africa, western India, north-west and south-east Australia, many of which are in tropical environments.

5 *below* Men working from an enormous floating barge on the assembly of an oil rig near Dubai.

1 *below* The Gulf is at the centre of the world's major concentration of land based oil resources and because of this offshore development has come relatively late. The potential is great, notably for the smaller states which have restricted land areas. The Gulf is sheltered from the open ocean, is shallow and relatively free of hazards. It is, of course, the most rapidly developing part of the industrialising world as its onshore and offshore wealth is re-invested in industry. Coastal installations associated with oil wealth are now being augmented by new ports. The Middle East is the leading region in growth of state participation, an idea now widely adopted, and influential in shaping the course of North Sea development.

2 *centre* In South East Asian waters and the China Seas offshore oil is becoming increasingly significant for a number of countries in this vast archipelagic area. As in the Gulf, these have grown from onshore interests, notably in Indonesia and Malaysia, where the main producing areas are off southern Sumatra and along the Indonesian and Malaysian shores of Borneo in the South China Sea. In Thailand reserves of gas are considerable, and it has now replaced oil as the principal energy source. One of the longest submarine

pipelines in the world joins the gas fields in the Gulf of Thailand to the mainland. Further north, in the East China Sea, considerable interest has attached to the prospects, especially by China, and this may have been a factor in the dispute over the Paracel Islands which resulted in forcible occupation by the People's Republic. As with the Gulf of Mexico and Caribbean, this is a tropical area subject to tropical storms, but it is a shallow water environment. South East Asian waters are regarded by the oil industry as one of the most promising for immediate expansion as the North Sea approaches full development.

3 *opposite page* Oil exploitation off the west African coast has resulted from the seawards move from the difficult mangrove swamps of the Niger Delta into the shallow seas. There are many small offshore fields in Nigeria producing less than 10 000 barrels per day. There is also an important producing area east of Gabon while, further south, the developments off Cabinda at the mouth of the Congo are in deeper water.

4 *bottom* Off both Western Australia and Victoria there are substantial reserves of oil and gas. Development of them was rapid in the 1970s.

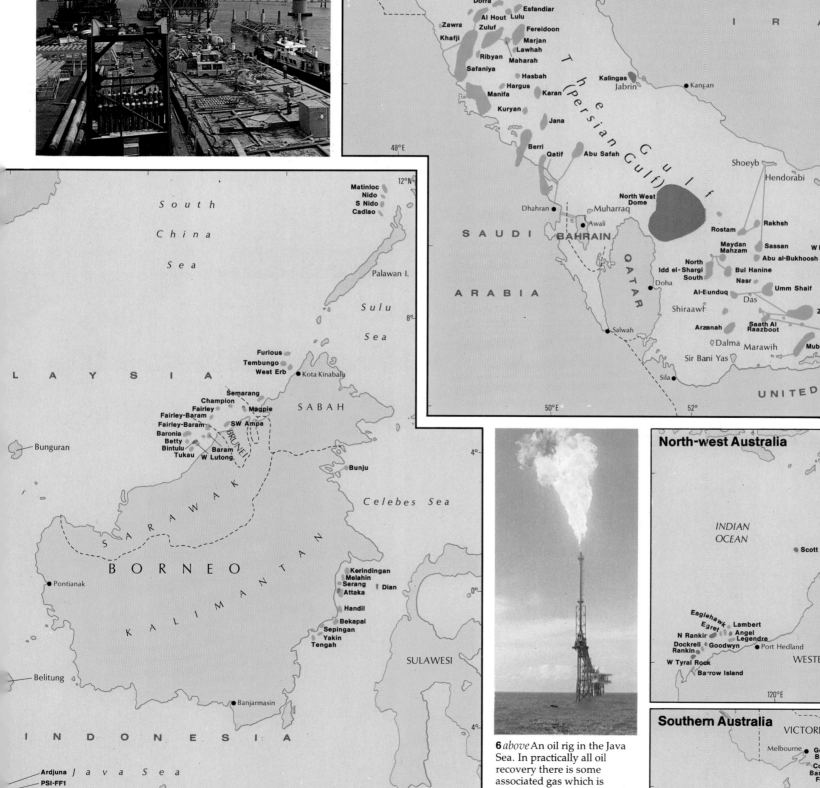

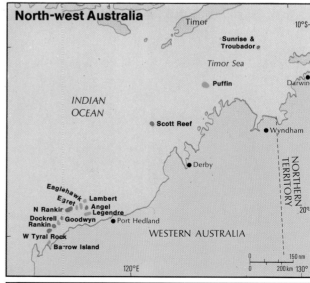

6 *above* An oil rig in the Java Sea. In practically all oil recovery there is some associated gas which is usually flared off, but now in some large oil fields it is collected and pumped ashore for use.

Seabed minerals

THE uneven world distribution of mineral resources on the land, the political sensitivity which this causes and a growing awareness of the importance of protecting and conserving the onshore environment have all been increasing the future significance of offshore minerals besides oil and gas. Knowledge of their distribution, genesis, grade and abundance is still imperfect but is increasing rapidly, particularly for those minerals likely to be economically significant in the near rather than the distant future.

At present (early 1980s) by far the most important of these commodities mined offshore, both quantitatively and by value, are aggregates (sand and gravel) for the construction industry, followed by tin from submerged placer deposits. Richly mineralised muds in the Red Sea seem likely to be exploited soon. Large quantities of manganese nodules are also likely to be mined, making a valuable contribution to the world supply of nickel, copper, cobalt and manganese. Some marine phosphatic deposits may also be exploited. Massive sulphide deposits discovered

recently in the east Pacific during marine scientific research may prove to be of interest in the future, but considerable technological developments will be required before they can be mined economically. The exploitation of marine mineral resources depends primarily on the cost competitiveness with other sources and in turn is related to the development of suitable low-cost technology as well as their relative grade and quantity.

Among the many factors that determine the distribution of marine mineral resources, the evolution of the oceans is one basic influence. Thus, the major locations of minerals were determined during different stages of ocean evolution. These stages are: the early stages of drifting of land masses when ocean spreading begins and the floor of the central rift is constructed of oceanic crust, for example, in the Red Sea; the stage when the rift has widened and a ridge is formed in the ocean, where more oceanic crust is formed spreading away from the ridge and cooling, as in the Atlantic Ocean; and a third stage

when oceanic crust collides with continental crust and is subducted below it, as for example, in the eastern Pacific (see *Sea floor spreading and plate tectonics* pages 32–33).

Polymetallic sulphides and metalliferous sediments can be deposited along these major fractures or plate boundaries on the crest of the ridges, during all these stages of ocean evolution and during periods of island arc volcanism. The deposits are formed by hydrothermal activity, particularly in tectonically active areas where the spreading rate is high.

The distribution of placers and aggregates is restricted to the continental shelf and is related to such factors as the proximity of source rocks on land and recent changes in sea level. Marine phosphatic deposits are restricted to the continental shelves.

High grade manganese nodules are most abundant in areas with very low sedimentation rates and stable oxidising conditions characteristic of large deep ocean basins, for example, in the north-east equatorial Pacific.

Marine economic minerals

COAL FROM BENEATH THE SEABED

Coal mining offshore has been carried out for many years. Usually it is by the extension of galleries from land into coal-bearing strata which dip under the sea. Enormous resources of coal lie at great depths under the continental shelf in many parts of the world, but their extent is unknown. Drilling in the North Sea gas provinces has confirmed the presence of large quantities of good quality coal in the carboniferous layers below the gas-bearing Permian rocks at depths of over 7000 metres beneath the sea bed. This is inaccessible with present day coal extraction technology. Very deep sources of coal may be exploited in the future by gasification techniques with plants located on artificial islands. In the Bay of Ariake, Japan, artificial islands have already been built but these are designed to facilitate the extension of coal mining from the land.

1 *main map* Seabed minerals can be found throughout nearly all the world's oceans, distributed across the continental shelf, along major fractures and on the deep ocean floor.

2 *right* The principal producers and consumers of cobalt, copper and nickel and, in the case of phosphates, the principal producers and importers.

Mined production and consumption of cobalt, copper, nickel and phosphate

PRODUCERS	cobalt	PRODUCERS	copper	PRODUCERS	nickel	PRODUCERS	phosphate
Zaire	14.7	USA	1168	Canada	195	USA	52.2
Zambia	3.3	USSR	1150	USSR	143	USSR	25.2
USSR	2.1	Canada	708	New Caledonia	86.3	Morocco	19.7
Canada	1.6	Zambia	596	Australia	69.8	China	11.5
Philippines	1.5	Zaire	460	Indonesia	40.5	Tunisia	4.6
Cuba	1.5	Peru	365	Cuba	38.2	Jordan	4.2
Morocco	1.0	Poland	343	Philippines	34.9	South Africa	3.0
Australia	1.0	Philippines	305	South Africa	25.7	Brazil	2.8
Finland	0.9	Australia	232	Dominican Rep.	15.5	Israel	2.4
New Caledonia	0.4	South Africa	212	Botswana	15.4	Togo	2.2

CONSUMERS	'000 tonnes	CONSUMERS	'000 tonnes	CONSUMERS	'000 tonnes	IMPORTS	'000 000 tonnes
France	7.0	USA	1866	USA	148	France	4.5
USA	6.9	Japan	1325	USSR	132	Canada	3.2
UK	3.1	USSR	1300	Japan	122	Poland	2.9
West Germany	1.9	West Germany	748	West Germany	68	Rumania	2.7
Japan	1.8	France	433	France	38.4	Spain	2.4
Sweden	0.5	UK	409	Italy	27	Belgium/Luxembourg	2.4
Italy	0.4	Italy	388	UK	22.8	Japan	2.3
Belgium	0.3	China	330	Sweden	20	Netherlands	2.1
Netherlands	0.3	Belgium/Luxembourg	304	China	18	West Germany	1.9
Finland	0.2	Brazil	246	Canada	12	Australia	1.9

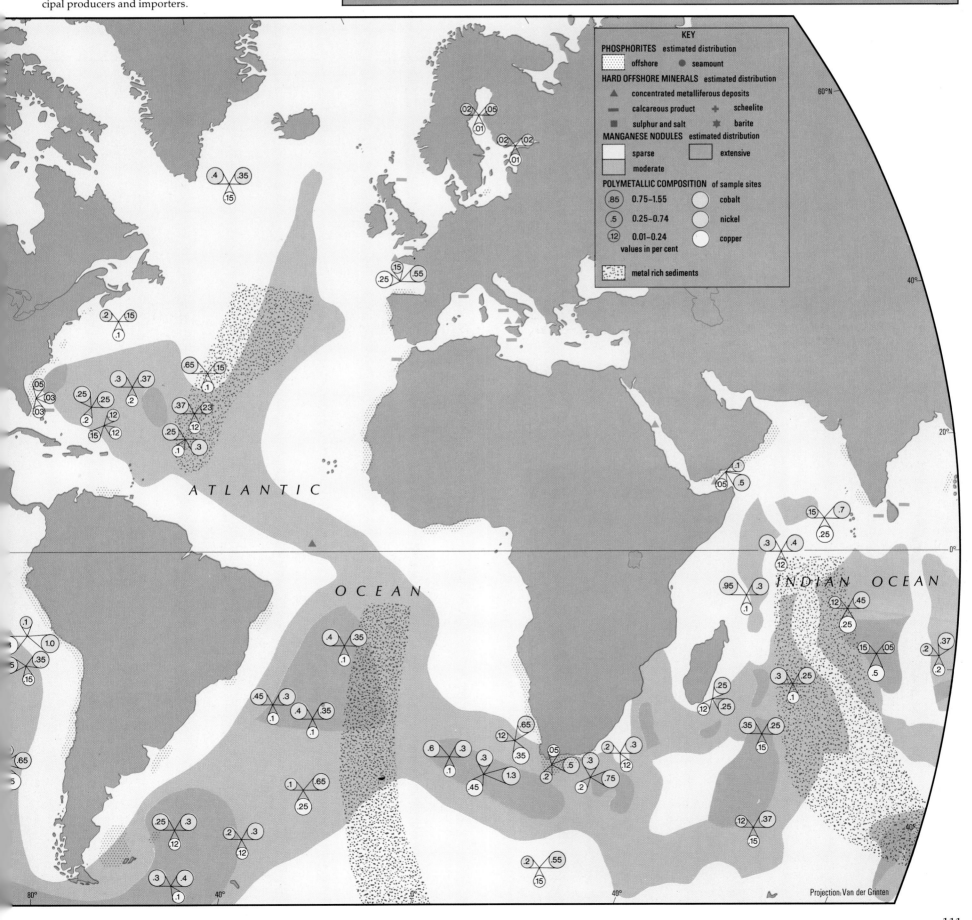

KEY

PHOSPHORITES estimated distribution
- offshore
- seamount

HARD OFFSHORE MINERALS estimated distribution
- concentrated metalliferous deposits
- calcareous product
- scheelite
- sulphur and salt
- barite

MANGANESE NODULES estimated distribution
- sparse
- moderate
- extensive

POLYMETALLIC COMPOSITION of sample sites
- .85 0.75–1.55
- .5 0.25–0.74
- .12 0.01–0.24
- values in per cent
- cobalt
- nickel
- copper
- metal rich sediments

ATLANTIC OCEAN

INDIAN OCEAN

Projection: Van der Grinten

Marine minerals—the continental margin

Aggregates

Marine aggregates comprise sand, gravel or shell deposits and are used primarily in the construction industry. They are, at present, quantitatively the most important hard marine mineral deposit mined.

Sand and gravel on modern beaches are derived from cliff erosion and from the redistribution of older sediments. Continental shelf deposits may also be derived from recent deposition of land materials, but most continental shelves are floored with relict sediments of Quaternary or earlier age. These include fluvial, fluvioglacial, glacial and beach sands and gravels deposited when the sea was lower relative to the adjacent coast, due mainly to variations in sea level during glacial periods and, to some extent, uplift of the land. Present day sediments of the tropics are often carbonate-rich. Quartz sands were brought on to some continental shelf areas in late Pleistocene and early Holocene times. This may occur where there is tectonic instability, such as off Taiwan. Some deposits owe their present position to such processes as wave action and tidal currents, long shore currents,

and ice pushing, while other deposits remain in their initial location of deposition.

Offshore calcareous deposits are formed by fragmentation of shells by waves and currents, or by precipitation from sea water. Segregation through density and shape of shell debris from detrital minerals, and their concentration into carbonate-rich deposits occurs in suitable hydrodynamic environments. One of the largest mining operations for shells for use in the manufacture of cement occurs off Iceland. The dredging of calcareous deposits, precipitated on the Bahamas Bank as aragonite, is also on a large scale.

There are several factors which influence the actual exploitation of offshore aggregates. The quality of the deposits is important for the construction industry and standards vary from country to country; only certain grain size distributions and compositions are suitable so that not all offshore deposits are in fact usable. Also, production and transport costs of offshore mining aggregates are normally high for such relatively low value products. The capital costs of equipment such as suction dredgers is also higher than for excavators on land. The 'economic mineral

depth' is about 35 metres. Offshore mining can be constrained due to adverse environmental effects. In some areas, in the absence of controls, dredging could affect coastal erosion by altering local wave and current environments or affect fishing by destroying the habitat of certain fish whose life cycle depends on gravel deposits. Aggregate dredging activities may conflict with shipping, oil and gas pipelines, and submarine cables. As a result, dredging may be prohibited over large areas. Only accessible and good quality deposits are consequently attractive and these can only be exploited after an acceptable environmental impact study has been made, and agreement has been reached with fishing authorities. Notwithstanding these problems for the offshore aggregate industry, the recovery of marine aggregates is likely to expand in the future due to shortages in many land areas.

1 *main map* Though there are considerable aggregate and placer resources deposited on the world's continental shelves, it is primarily the relatively easily dredged aggregates of sand and gravel which are exploited.

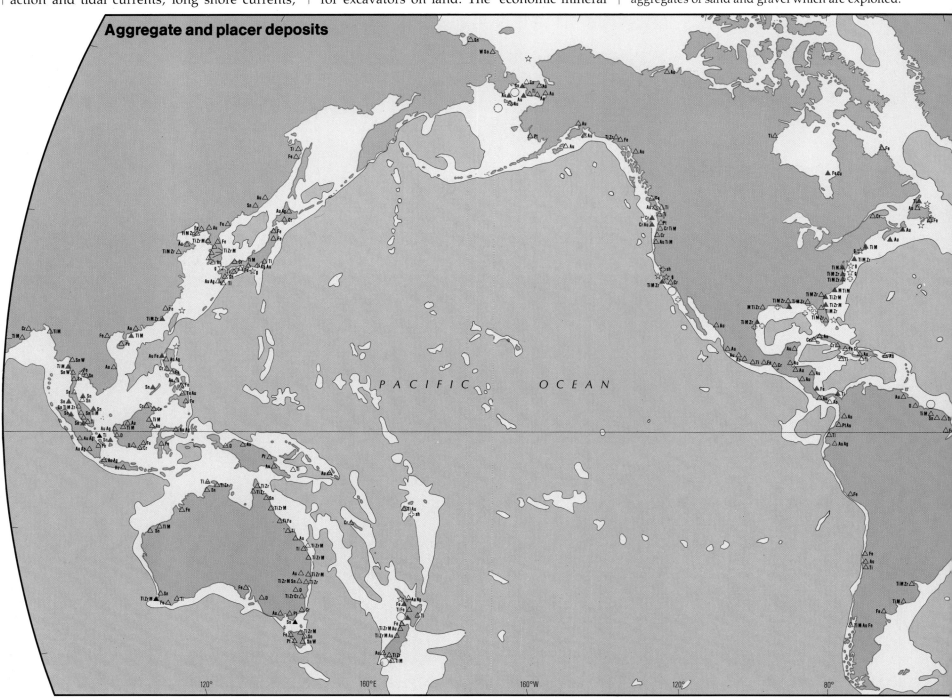

Aggregate and placer deposits

2 *left* A modern suction dredger heading out to sea and towards the aggregate banks. These vessels extract the sand and gravel by suction pipe. With modern navigational aids to provide accurate positions, detailed records can be kept of the dredged area and the quantities extracted.

5, 6 *right* Sand and gravel are the most important potential economic minerals by volume on the US continental margin. It has been estimated that nearly 500 billion tonnes occur on the Atlantic coast margin, of which 31.25 billion tonnes are gravel, and that the whole US continental margin may contain up to 1400 billion tonnes. These gravels were transported to the margin in the Pleistocene age by the action of glaciers.

7 *opposite far right* The North Sea, one of the world's richest areas of aggregates, has been divided into concession areas for the dredging of sand and gravel. Licences are issued by national agencies for the right to dredge but are subject to restrictions related to fish breeding areas and coastal protection.

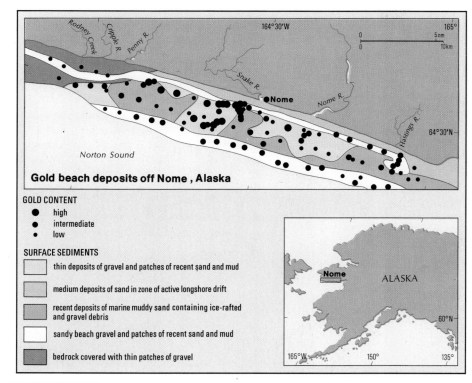

Gold beach deposits off Nome , Alaska

GOLD CONTENT
- high
- intermediate
- low

SURFACE SEDIMENTS
- thin deposits of gravel and patches of recent sand and mud
- medium deposits of sand in zone of active longshore drift
- recent deposits of marine muddy sand containing ice-rafted and gravel debris
- sandy beach gravel and patches of recent sand and mud
- bedrock covered with thin patches of gravel

Nome ALASKA

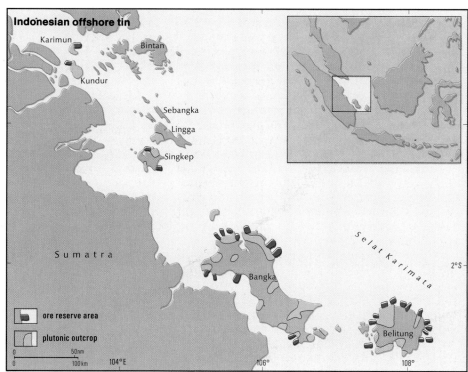

Indonesian offshore tin

- ore reserve area
- plutonic outcrop

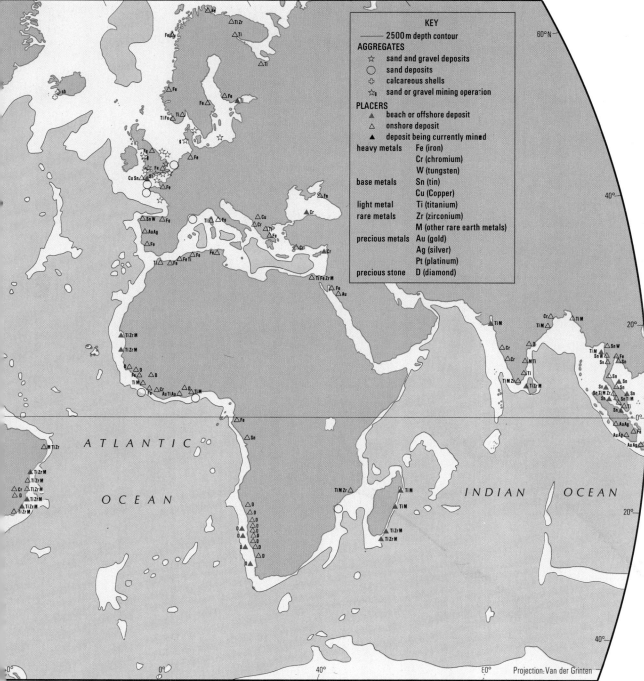

KEY
— 2500 m depth contour
AGGREGATES
- ☆ sand and gravel deposits
- ○ sand deposits
- ✛ calcareous shells
- ☆ sand or gravel mining operation

PLACERS
- ▲ beach or offshore deposit
- △ onshore deposit
- ▲ deposit being currently mined

heavy metals	Fe (iron)
	Cr (chromium)
	W (tungsten)
base metals	Sn (tin)
	Cu (Copper)
light metal	Ti (titanium)
rare metals	Zr (zirconium)
	M (other rare earth metals)
precious metals	Au (gold)
	Ag (silver)
	Pt (platinum)
precious stone	D (diamond)

Projection: Van der Grinten

Placers

Placer deposits are concentrations of heavy, resilient, and chemically-resistant minerals eroded from existing ore bodies by mechanical weathering. These minerals either remain *in situ* or become transported and concentrated in sands and gravels found in rivers and on beaches. Such deposits include the following minerals (metals in parentheses): native gold, native platinum, cassiterite (tin), rutile and ilmenite (titanium), magnetite (iron), zitcon (zirconium), wolframite (tungsten), chromite (chromium), monazite (cerium, thorium), and gemstones.

Although placer deposits have formed throughout geological time (e.g. the Rand gold deposits in South Africa, found in Precambrian rocks), most have been formed in the past 65 million years. Important deposits include gold on Alaskan beaches, titanium sands in Florida, Sri Lanka, India, Australia, and Brazil, tin in Malaysia and Indonesia, and magnetite on Japanese beaches.

3 *above left* The beaches at Nome have been known to contain gold since the late 19th century. Mining has been carried out on the beaches, later extending to onshore buried beaches. In the nearshore zone, the highest gold concentrations are found where thin relict gravel overlies glacial drift. The offshore deposits have been sampled by drilling from the ice that covers the sea for much of the year. The harshness and remoteness of Alaska adds considerably to the cost of mining, although with technological developments commercial interest in these deposits may increase.

4 *above* Indonesia is one of the main areas in the world where offshore placers are mined. Primary tin deposits occur in granitic rocks onshore and the heavy minerals (including cassiterite) have been concentrated and deposited in Quaternary and present river valleys and natural traps which extend offshore. Production costs are lower for these offshore deposits than for similar dredges inland, although capital and replacement costs are higher because of the more difficult marine environmental conditions. At present, exploitation is limited to 50 m depths but tin deposits known to occur at greater depths may be mined in the future. The Indonesian tin resource potential is estimated to be 1.6 million tonnes, about 40 per cent of which is offshore.

Gravel deposits
- more than 50%
- 25–50%

USA

Sand deposits
- more than 75%
- 50–75%

USA

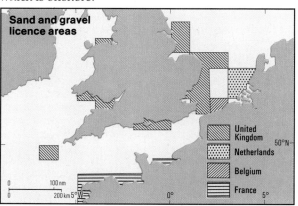

Sand and gravel licence areas

- United Kingdom
- Netherlands
- Belgium
- France

Marine minerals—the shelf and trench

Metalliferous deposits

As the theory of plate tectonics became generally accepted an economic factor came into play, for it was recognised that several different types of ore deposit are related to past or present plate boundaries. Chromite mineralisation, for example, occurs in ophiolites. This in turn provided an incentive to study active plate boundaries on the ocean floor and the active genetic processes.

Several investigators in the mid 1960s reported finding enrichments of manganese and iron in the sediments over wide areas of the ocean floor centred on the East Pacific Ride axis, and since then similar enrichments have been found elsewhere, associated with other mid-ocean ridges. Similar enrichments occur in some island arc areas, and examination of DSDP cores has shown that these metalliferous sediments overlie oceanic crust in many areas. In some cases they are buried beneath large thicknesses of sediment, as they have moved with the tectonic plates further from the mid-ocean ridges where they were formed.

In the late 1970s and early 1980s concentrations of zinc, copper and other metals were found in both metalliferous sediments and massive polymetallic sulphide deposits around the East Pacific Rise and associated similar structures, for example the Galapagos Ridge. The DSDP found copper sulphides in deep oceanic basalt. Some have been shown to be linked with very hot saline water issuing from fissures in the sea floor associated with spreading axes as in the Red Sea. This has led to suggestions that the leaching of base metals from the oceanic crust by convected saline water may be a widespread process, both now and in the past as on the Troodos Mountains in Cyprus.

2 *below* A black smoker, East Pacific Rise. The water ejected from these hydrothermal vents contains hydrogen sulphide.

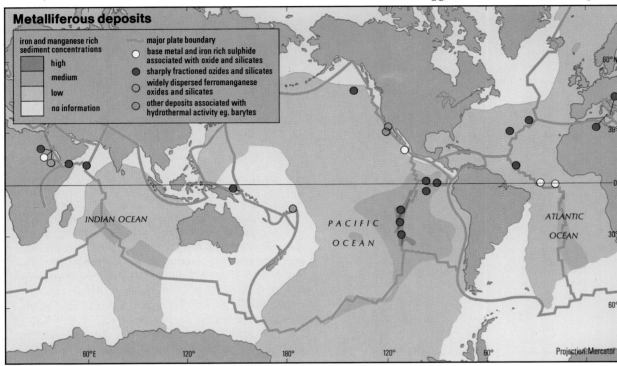

1 *world map* The first massive sulphide deposits were discovered by a manned submersible on the East Pacific Rise in 1978 in an area of volcanic hills with fissures and actively discharging hydrothermal vents close to the spreading axis. The deposits are roughly cylindrical and stand 3 to 10 m in height and approximately 5 m in diameter. Colours are variegated—ochre, white, grey, brown and red. Specimens collected contain iron, zinc and copper sulphides in substantial concentration. Further mineralised areas have since been discovered, including several zones between the Galapagos Islands and the mainland of Ecuador and on the Juan de Fuca Ridge off Oregon. More exploration will be necessary before the commercial importance of such deposits can be evaluated.

3 *right* The Red Sea metalliferous muds were first discovered in 1963. Although subsequent investigations have shown that there are several metalliferous deposits associated with hot brines, only the Atlantis II Deep is of current commercial interest. The deposits are all located in the northern and central parts of the Red Sea. They are very fine-grained, layered and multicoloured, and show considerable chemical variation. High concentrations of up to 6 per cent zinc, 1 per cent copper and 100 ppm silver, are found in sulphide, oxide and silicate.

The Atlantis II Deep covers an area of approximately 60 sq. km. The metalliferous mud is located some 2000 m below sea level and varies in thickness from 2 to 25 m, and is covered by 200 m of dense brine in which temperatures up to 62 °C have been recorded. This suggests that hydrothermal activity continues to deposit the metals. It is thought that cold saline water permeates through the hot, fractured, newly emplaced oceanic basalt. The heated brine then leaches the metals from the submarine rocks and transports them as chloride complexes until they reach the sea bed by convection, where they are precipitated when the hot brine is cooled by mixing with normal Red Sea water. The greater metal enrichment in the Atlantis II Deep sediments compared to other deposits is thought to be due to the proximity of a thick sedimentary sequence to the spreading centre. The Deep lies within the EEZs of both Sudan and Saudi Arabia and a joint Red Sea Commission has been set up to administer exploitation. It is hoped that they will be mined commercially before the end of the century.

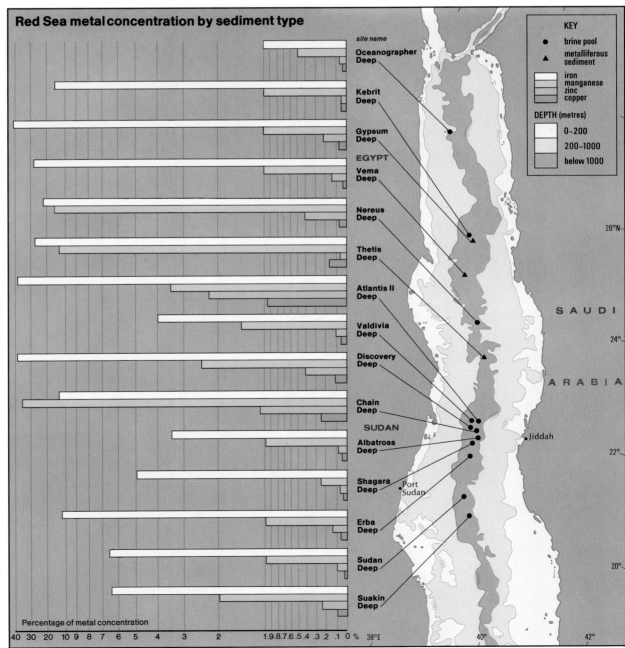

Red Sea metal concentration by sediment type

Percentage of metal concentration

Seafloor phosphorite

Phosphorite is a term normally used to describe rocks and unconsolidated sediments of marine origin in which the phosphate mineral (apatite) occurs in significant amounts. Phosphorite is valuable because it is the only suitable source of phosphorus for the manufacture of phosphate fertilisers and certain phosphorus-based chemicals. Most of the world's production of some 138 million tonnes of rock in 1981 was derived from marine sedimentary formations on land of Miocene-Pliocene, Cretaceous, Eocene Permian and Cambrian age. The USA and Morocco have dominated both world production and trade for many years.

The phosphate content or grade of phosphorite is invariably reported as phosphorus pentoxide (P_2O_5). In commercial deposits this may average as little as 6–8 per cent; most phosphate ores require processing to meet the requirements of the consumers, and the marketable material generally contains more than 30 per cent P_2O_5.

Attempts at commercial phosphate mining off southern California were made during the early 1960s, with unsuccessful results. None of the occurrences of seafloor phosphorite are of economic interest at present as large land-situated resources are readily available. The Chatham Rise deposits east of New Zealand are a possible exception and could conceivably replace New Zealand's traditional sources of supply.

Different opinions exist as to the precise mechanism of phosphate precipitation, but it is widely held that an influx of nutrient-rich oceanic waters, particularly where upwelling occurs (see *Upwelling* page 53), is an important source. Major phosphorite accumulations occur where there is a marked deficiency in terrigenous sediment and in oxygen-minimum zones. Vast numbers of organisms are supported by these nutrient-rich waters in which plankton bloom; organic discolouration and mass mortalities are characteristic phenomena. Further concentrations of phosphorus on the sea floor can occur where organic debris accumulates; the most widespread of organic sediments on the sea floor, diatom ooze, may contain the equivalent of up to 4 per cent P_2O_5 by dry weight.

Few sea floor phosphorites, however, are of modern origin but are dated between the Holocene and Cretaceous periods. The upper continental margin of Peru and Chile and the south-western African continental shelf are the only two areas where undoubted contemporaneous phosphorite formation has occurred.

Sea floor phosphorites most frequently occur as nodules which range in size from pebbles to boulders of several tonnes. They also appear as phosphatic muds, sands, loose pellets, slabs, relatively continuous pavements formed by cemented, coalescing nodules, as well as more or less phosphatised carbonate debris. Nodules vary in shape and often have a glazed polished surface, discoloured by the oxides of iron and manganese. Considerable fluctuations in phosphate content have also been recorded, some samples containing as much as 33 per cent P_2O_5. Non-phosphatic components comprise mainly clay minerals, quartz and feldspar and, to a lesser extent, minerals such as hornblende and pyroxene, and the secondary (diagenetic) minerals pyrite, goethite, calcite and dolomite. The iron-potash silicate, glauconite, is commonly present. Phosphorites on seamounts often contain volcanic fragments. They are composed predominantly of phosphatised limestone, although some are made up of crusts on and fillings in basalt blocks. In contrast with the occurrences on the continental margins, which are mainly Neogene, most of the seamount deposits are of Palaeogene and Cretaceous age.

4 *world map* Seafloor phosphorite was first discovered as nodules in dredge samples obtained from the Agulhas Bank off South Africa during the *Challenger* Expedition of 1872–76 and have since been found elsewhere, particularly off the western coasts of North and South America, the eastern coast of the USA, and off south-western Africa. They occur mostly on the continental margins and the upper parts of the continental slopes at depths of less than 500 m and, with few exceptions, between 40°N and 40°S. In addition, deposits have been found on some topographic highs such as flat-topped seamounts, rises, ridges and plateaux, notably in the western Pacific.

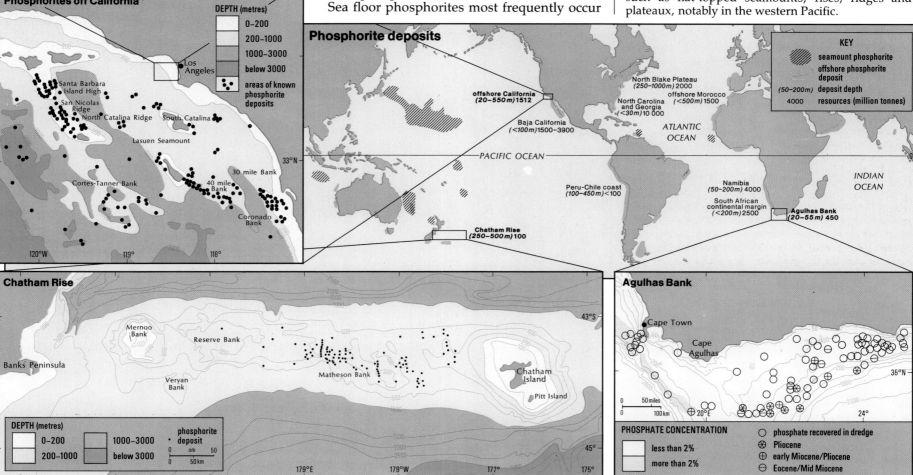

Phosphorites off California

Phosphorite deposits

Chatham Rise

Agulhas Bank

5 *top left* Phosphorite nodules were first recognised off California in 1937 during dredging by the Scripps Institution of Oceanography. They are now known to be of widespread occurrence, extending from Point Reyes, just north of San Francisco, to the Gulf of California, in water depths ranging from 60 m to 180 m and from a few kilometres offshore to the edge of the continental shelf. More than 30 individual deposits have been located in the southern California offshore area alone, ten of which were selected for detailed study in 1963–64. The deposits are estimated to contain about 50 Mt of nodules and 12.5 Mt of phosphatic sands, the P_2O_5 content of samples ranging from less than 1 per cent to 31.4 per cent. Of particular interest are the phosphorite sands in Santa Monica Bay because of their occurrence in relatively shallow water, averaging 55 m in depth.

6 *above left* Phosphorite nodules on Chatham Rise are widely distributed, occurrences having been traced over a distance of about 480 km along the crest of Chatham Rise. The largest accumulation occurs near the 180° meridian in water depths of between 350 m and 450 m. The nodules, which are predominantly 2–4 cm in diameter, represent phosphatised foraminiferal limestones that have been dated as Lower to Middle Miocene in age. They occur in greenish glauconitic sandy muds which overlie a white, soft, foraminiferal ooze of Oligocene age. Typically the nodules are olive grey to olive black in colour and have a smooth, glossy appearance. Samples show a range of 15–25 per cent P_2O_5.

7 *above right* Phosphorites are known to occur widely on Agulhas Bank and it has become one of the most intensely studied areas in the world. A variety of phosphorites have been identified, but the most important in terms of concentration and distribution are the phosphatised, organic limestones composed mainly of micro-fossils, chiefly planktonic foraminifera in an apatite cement, and phosphatic conglomerates which contain fragments of these limestones in a matrix of glauconite, micro-fossils and quartz sand, all cemented together by apatite. The two types of phosphorites can be correlated with limestones of Lower Miocene to Pliocene age which form extensive outcrops on the middle and outer continental shelf areas of southern and south-west South Africa. In addition, a third variety of comparable mineralogical composition, consists of phosphatised conglomerates characterised by a variable mixture of nodules with micro-fossils and bone debris, coinciding with the elongate outcrop of Palaeogene sediments on the inner Agulhas Bank parallel to the south Cape coast. Samples of phosphorites from Agulhas Bank show a range of between 10 and 25 per cent P_2O_5.

Marine minerals—the ocean floor

Manganese nodules were first discovered on the 1872–76 scientific voyage of HMS *Challenger*, but systematic exploration and detailed studies only started in the late 1950s when it was recognised that nodules might be a source of nickel, copper and cobalt.

Nodules occur in many different shapes, sizes and forms and are generally friable. They often have different upper and lower surface textures. Internally, they show concentric layering.

Areas of erosion or extremely low sedimentation rates such as red clay or siliceous ooze provinces, or areas with high currents at depths in excess of 4000 metres are particularly favourable for their occurrence. Globally, the composition of nodules varies considerably. The highest nickel and copper concentrations, for instance, occur in abyssal nodules, which grow at a rate of three to eight millimetres per million years.

Nodule genesis and metal enrichment processes are not fully understood. The major elements found in nodules may come from a variety of sources, but the areas of greatest enrichment are associated with high biological productivity in the overlying waters and depths greater than the calcium carbonate compensation depth (see *Sea floor sediments* page 42). High-grade nodules contain more todorokite, the manganese mineral capable of accommodating most nickel and copper into its structure.

Estimates of the reserves suggest that recoverable nickel and copper are of the same order as known land economic resources. At present, the only known economically attractive area lies between the Clarion and Clipperton fracture zones. Specialised mining systems have had to be developed to recover the nodules without lifting the underlying sediment, from depths in excess of 4000 m. Environmental conditions of potential mine sites have been ascertained, and the likely impact of mining on them has been assessed.

The technical problems, uncertainty over profitability, and the international debate over the rights and obligations of states in relation to the resources of the deep sea bed, has inhibited the exploitation of manganese nodules. However, several international consortiums have been formed for this purpose and have developed and tested systems for the recovery of nodules from great depths. The land mineral producers from the developing countries are particularly concerned that some controls are exercised over offshore production, while mining companies and several of the states in the developed world are wary of such controls.

1 *main map* The main element in a manganese nodule, or polymetallic nodule, is manganese, though the primary economic interest at present is in the copper, nickel and cobalt compositions of the nodules. Iron is also present. Although nodules occur over about 20 per cent of the ocean floor, only in relatively limited ocean areas are they found in sufficient abundance and of high enough grade to be of economic importance.

2 *below* Manganese nodules on the seabed in the Pacific Ocean. Nodules form gradually—over a period of several million years—around some foreign body such as a shark's tooth.

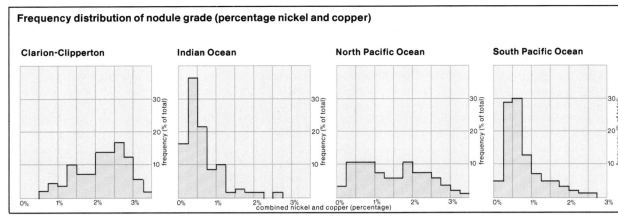

Frequency distribution of nodule grade (percentage nickel and copper)

Clarion-Clipperton | Indian Ocean | North Pacific Ocean | South Pacific Ocean

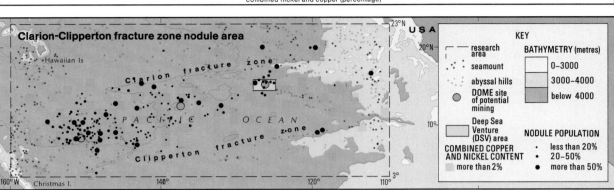

Clarion-Clipperton fracture zone nodule area

KEY

research area
seamount
abyssal hills
DOME site of potential mining
Deep Sea Venture (DSV) area
COMBINED COPPER AND NICKEL CONTENT
more than 2%

BATHYMETRY (metres)
0–3000
3000–4000
below 4000

NODULE POPULATION
less than 20%
20–50%
more than 50%

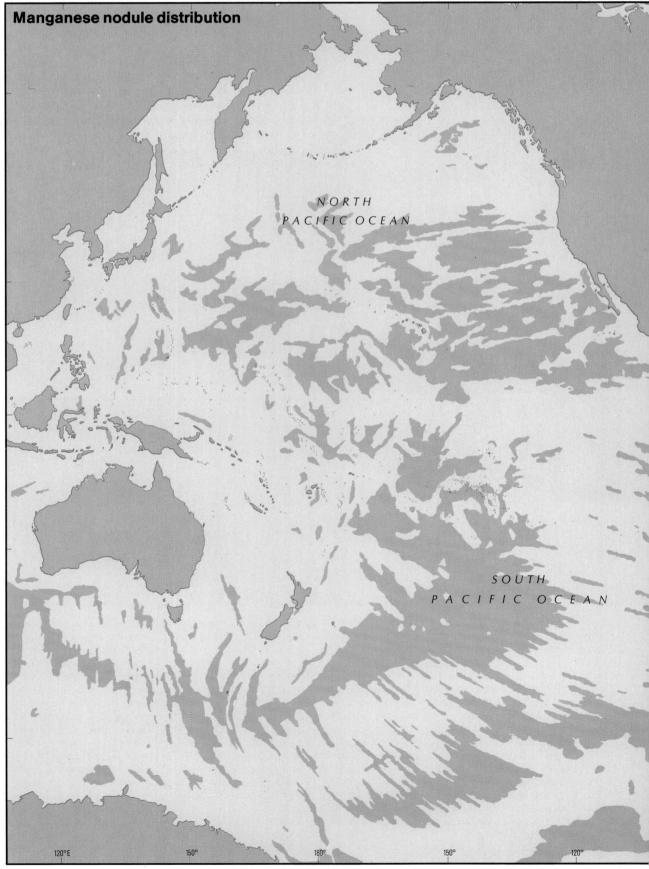

Manganese nodule distribution

NORTH PACIFIC OCEAN

SOUTH PACIFIC OCEAN

3 *left* Only if the combined nickel and copper content exceeds 1.75 per cent are nodules of any economic interest. In the Clarion Clipperton zone the majority of nodules are of this quality but in the other ocean areas the majority of nodules fall well below this grade.

4 *left below* The nodules in the Clarion Clipperton zone are generally rich in manganese, and it is estimated that the area contains 4–15 billion tonnes of them. Some 8–25 million tonnes of nickel, 6–23 million tonnes of copper, 0.9–3.5 million tonnes of cobalt, and 144–530 million tonnes of manganese could be recovered. Even within this province both nodule grade and abundance are irregular because of local variations in topography, currents, and the availability of suitable nuclei.

6 *right and* **7** *below right* The richest compositions of metals including cobalt and nickel can be found in the Pacific nodules. By contrast, metal values are significantly lower in the Indian Ocean and Atlantic nodules. At present, only in the north-east equatorial Pacific is mining thought to be economically viable.

5 *below* Part of a 200-tonne sample of manganese nodules dredged from the Pacific Ocean being emptied into the recovery ship.

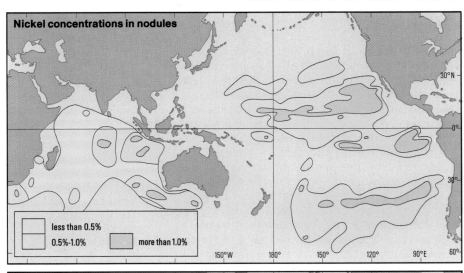

Nickel concentrations in nodules

less than 0.5%
0.5%-1.0%
more than 1.0%

Cobalt concentrations in nodules

less than 0.25%
0.25-0.5%
more than 0.5%

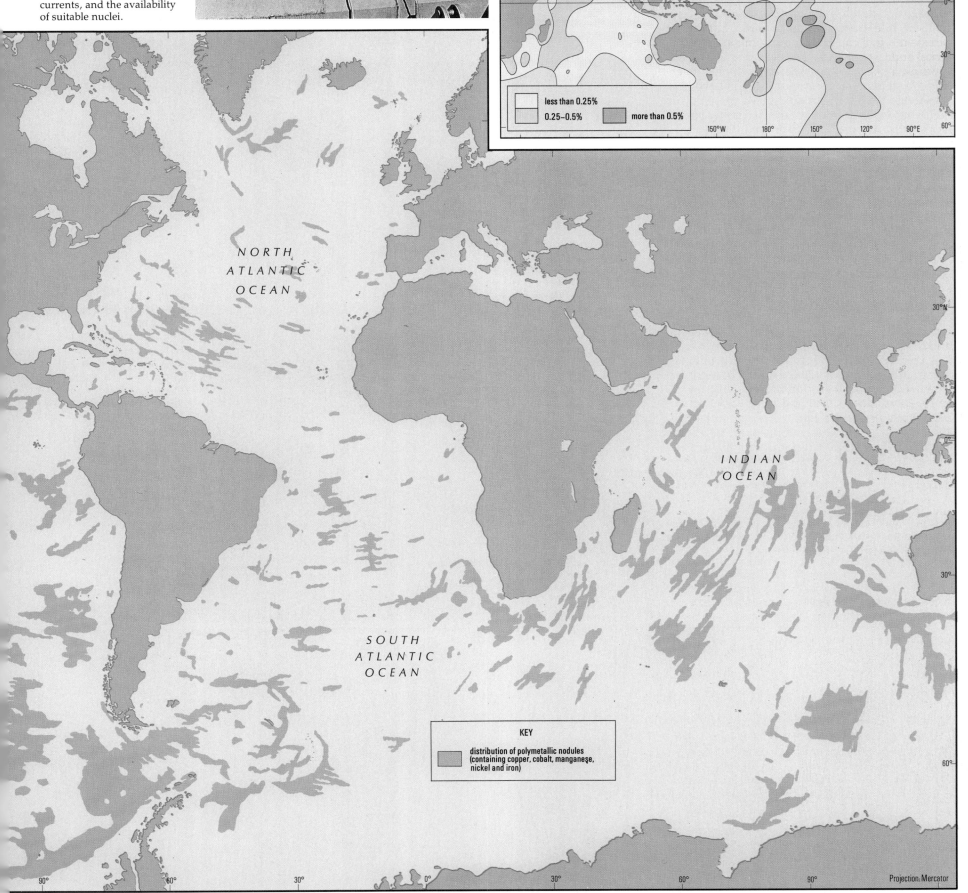

NORTH
ATLANTIC
OCEAN

SOUTH
ATLANTIC
OCEAN

INDIAN
OCEAN

KEY

distribution of polymetallic nodules (containing copper, cobalt, manganese, nickel and iron)

Projection: Mercator

Sea water

By far the most important use of sea water is for waste disposal of all kinds: its great volume, dynamism and distinctive chemistry allow it readily to break down and disperse many waste substances. Sea water is also used in vast quantities as cooling water, especially for coastal power stations in industrial countries.

The ocean waters probably originated at an early stage in the Earth's history, and their chemical composition reflects their relatively stable role in the geochemical cycles of the surface layers of the Earth. Chemical elements enter sea water from rivers, from submarine volcanic activity, from glacial debris and from the atmosphere. The proportions of the major elements and several of the minor elements (bromine, strontium and boron) are constant (termed conservative) in all but the most specialised environments, for example estuaries and the isolated bottoms of enclosed waters such as the Black Sea and deep fjords. The much larger range of non-conservative elements vary considerably in quantity, according to their reactivity. In particular, many important trace elements (such as lead, zinc, molybdenum, copper, nickel, vanadium, manganese, cobalt, phosphorus) are obtainable both from the authigenic minerals or from living resources such as seaweeds (for example potassium and iodine), which concentrate the elements from sea water much more effectively than man can do. Indeed, it is the very ability to concentrate elements that poses special dangers from certain types of pollution, such as organochlorines and heavy metals.

Not surprisingly, the sea has sometimes been regarded as an almost unlimited resource for new materials. It would appear to contain in solution all the naturally occurring elements, and over eighty have been detected. The concentrations of the great majority of these are very low, and indeed generally lower than in continental rocks, but the sheer volume of the oceans means that the quantities appear impressive.

Fundamental to exploitation of sea water are the technologies and economics of extraction enterprises, and also competition with land-based sources of supply which, in most cases, are easier and more economical to exploit. As technological and economic conditions for industry undergo continual change, sea water resources are subject to periodic reappraisal. Quantitatively, there exists a continuum from the most abundant, or major elements with a concentration greater than 100 parts per million (ppm), some of which are extracted; through the minor elements (between 100 and 1 ppm); to important trace elements (between 1 and .001 ppm): and many others beyond.

1 *below* Plants for producing freshwater from sea water range from basic distillation plants producing a few thousand cu. metres per day to industrial plants producing several million, for example that at Qatar for the aluminium industry. The trend is for very large units combined with electricity generation. In the 1880s steamships had distillation plants on board to feed their boilers.

Fresh water

The production of fresh water from the sea is an attractive proposition in settled coastal areas with an acute deficiency of natural freshwater supplies, for example, along desert coasts, or even in places with periodic shortfalls. The main demands are for drinking water (usually the first priority), and water for agriculture and industry. The first need may be met by relatively small scale production, as for example, on some of the Caribbean islands, while others require much larger scales of production.

The main means of freshwater production is by desalination plants. These use a variety of techniques, notably distillation and freezing processes. Most of the major plants are located on desert coasts in developing countries of the Mediterranean, Red Sea and the Gulf. Decisions to establish desalination plants must take account of the cost of the water obtained in relation to other sources, and the effects on coastal ecosystems of discharge of hot brine residues.

Considerable speculation has taken place regarding the possibilities of other techniques for economically obtaining very large quantities of fresh water from the sea. Of particular note is electrodialysis, but this is expensive for sea water for it requires abundant cheap electrical power. A second possibility which has been investigated is to tow large icebergs from the Antarctic ice shelves across the Southern Ocean to the desert coasts of South West Asia and south-west Africa, Western Australia and western South America. Although small icebergs were towed from southern Chile northwards along the coast for this purpose in the 1890s, further development depends upon competitiveness with desalination, long distance supply by pipeline from other land sources, and overcoming the problems of towing, docking and processing water from giant icebergs.

Minerals

The only two elements commercially extracted from sea water on a large scale are magnesium and bromine. Production is based primarily in the United States and, although the sea is the primary source of these elements, production from subsurface brines on

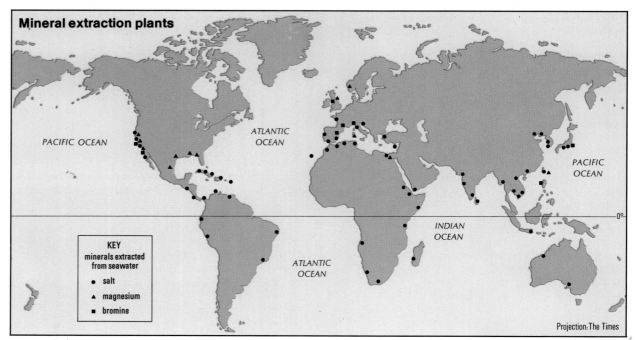

Mineral extraction plants

PACIFIC OCEAN

ATLANTIC OCEAN

PACIFIC OCEAN

INDIAN OCEAN

ATLANTIC OCEAN

KEY
minerals extracted from seawater
● salt
▲ magnesium
■ bromine

Projection: The Times

2 *above* The technology to extract more than a few of the elements dissolved in sea water is as yet not developed. The principle output is salt, magnesium metal, magnesium compounds and bromine, plus some gypsum and potassium.

3 *left* Use of salt pans for extracting salt from the sea still continues in many parts of the world, and salt making is an important source of income. The shallow pans on the Lebanon coast shown here have been carved out of a wave-cut platform. The windmills are used to pump up the sea water.

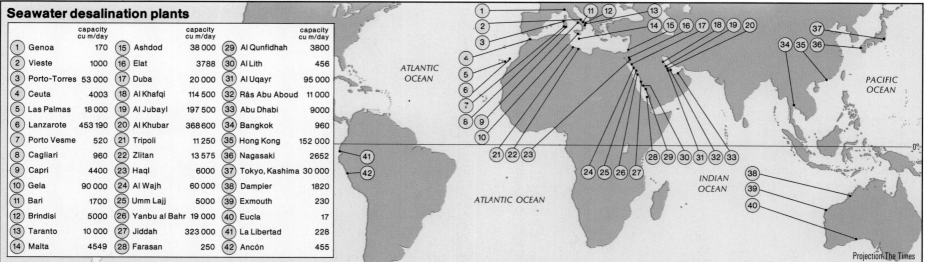

Seawater desalination plants

		capacity cu m/day			capacity cu m/day			capacity cu m/day
1	Genoa	170	15	Ashdod	38 000	29	Al Qunfidhah	3800
2	Vieste	1000	16	Elat	3788	30	Al Lith	456
3	Porto-Torres	53 000	17	Duba	20 000	31	Al Uqayr	95 000
4	Ceuta	4003	18	Al Khafqi	114 500	32	Râs Abu Aboud	11 000
5	Las Palmas	18 000	19	Al Jubayl	197 500	33	Abu Dhabi	9000
6	Lanzarote	453 190	20	Al Khubar	368 600	34	Bangkok	960
7	Porto Vesme	520	21	Tripoli	11 250	35	Hong Kong	152 000
8	Cagliari	960	22	Zlitan	13 575	36	Nagasaki	2652
9	Capri	4400	23	Haql	6000	37	Tokyo, Kashima	30 000
10	Gela	90 000	24	Al Wajh	60 000	38	Dampier	1820
11	Bari	1700	25	Umm Lajj	5000	39	Exmouth	230
12	Brindisi	5000	26	Yanbu al Bahr	19 000	40	Eucla	17
13	Taranto	10 000	27	Jiddah	323 000	41	La Libertad	228
14	Malta	4549	28	Farasan	250	42	Ancón	455

ATLANTIC OCEAN

PACIFIC OCEAN

INDIAN OCEAN

ATLANTIC OCEAN

Projection: The Times

land appear to be increasingly attractive economically. Large scale magnesium production dates from the Second World War. Magnesium is the lightest available structural metal and has a variety of uses in the chemical industry. It is produced by obtaining a solution of magnesium chloride which is then electrolysed to yield magnesium metal. Requirements include a source of pure calcium carbonate (such as sea shell beds), hydrochloric acid made from sodium chloride, sulphur and cheap electrical power. These requirements favour coastal sites along the Gulf of Mexico and in California.

Bromine, notably used in anti-knock compounds in petrol, is produced by initially reacting sea water with sulphuric acid and chlorine to release the elemental bromine which is then subjected to a series of processes culminating in the production of liquid bromine.

Two other elements which have been subject to special attention have been gold and uranium. Gold extraction from the sea was considered as a means of payment of Germany's First World War reparations until it was realised that concentrations were far below the economic level. A more serious possibility is the building of pilot plants to secure uranium from the sea for use in the nuclear industries. This is particularly attractive for countries such as Japan with no land-based source coupled with a desire to promote energy independence in the latest technology.

Again, in the event of nuclear fusion becoming a viable alternative to nuclear fission processes, using deuterium or hydrogen, the sea as the main source of these elements could indeed prove to be the ultimate source of energy.

Salt

The demand for salt, notably as a food preservative for meat and fish, dates from time immemorial, and sea salt has been produced for over 4000 years, the principal regions of production being the Mediterranean lands and East Asia. The most widespread method of production was, and remains, solar evaporation from large coastal pans. In Europe and elsewhere salt was also produced by heating sea water in pans fuelled by peat, timber and later coal. Such salt was generally considered inferior to solar sea salt. Early salt contained appreciable quantities of magnesium chloride, as well as sulphates of magnesium, calcium and potassium. Modern salt production uses a series of evaporating basins to separate the sodium chloride from the other salts, leaving a residue rich in magnesium and bromine which is presently largely unused. Sodium chloride is used directly for human consumption, as a de-icer on highways, and in the chemical industry. World production of sea salt is currently in the order of six million tonnes per annum.

Elements in sea water (milligrammes per litre)			
chlorine	19 000.0	bromine	65.0
sodium	10 500.0	carbon	28.0
magnesium	1 350.0	strontium	8.0
sulphur	885.0	boron	4.6
calcium	400.0	silicon	3.0
potassium	380.0	fluorine	1.3

argon	0.6	cerium	4×10^{-4}
nitrogen	0.5	yttrium	3×10^{-4}
lithium	(0.17) 17×10^{-2}	silver	3×10^{-4}
rubidium	12×10^{-2}	lanthanum	3×10^{-4}
phosphorus	7×10^{-2}	krypton	3×10^{-4}
iodine	6×10^{-2}	neon	1×10^{-4}
barium	3×10^{-2}	cadmium	1×10^{-4}
indium	2×10^{-2}	tungsten	1×10^{-4}
zinc	1×10^{-2}	xenon	1×10^{-4}
iron	1×10^{-2}	germanium	7×10^{-5}
aluminium	1×10^{-2}	chromium	5×10^{-5}
molybdenum	1×10^{-2}	thorium	5×10^{-5}
selenium	4×10^{-3}	scandium	4×10^{-5}
tin	3×10^{-3}	lead	3×10^{-5}
copper	3×10^{-3}	mercury	3×10^{-5}
arsenic	3×10^{-3}	gallium	3×10^{-5}
uranium	3×10^{-3}	bismuth	2×10^{-5}
nickel	2×10^{-3}	niobium	2×10^{-5}
vanadium	2×10^{-3}	thallium	1×10^{-5}
manganese	2×10^{-3}	helium	5×10^{-6}
titanium	1×10^{-3}	gold	4×10^{-6}
antimony	(0.0005) 5×10^{-4}	protactinium	2×10^{-9}
cobalt	5×10^{-4}	radium	1×10^{-10}
caesium	5×10^{-4}	radon	0.6×10^{-15}

Drugs from the sea

The toxic nature of certain fish was known to the Romans. As with all natural products used medicinally (at least since 2700 BC by the Chinese), their potential for medicinal use was first discovered as a toxic effect upon inadvertent ingestion. In modern times the study of marine organisms as sources of useful medicinal and pharmaceutical materials has become a rapidly expanding science. Several contemporary drugs are now produced from marine flora and fauna; however, there is little commercial exploitation of the sea for medicinally useful substances in relation to the total output of the pharmaceutical industry. A decreasing supply of crude oil as a starting material for the manufacture of drugs is expected to turn attention to the sea as an increasingly important source of raw material.

Thousands of marine organisms are known to be either toxic to eat, hazardous to touch, or venomous; only a small proportion has been studied in any detail. Research is hindered by the relative inaccessibility of the underwater world, and complicated by the transfer of certain chemical compounds down food chains. This makes it difficult to decide which particular organism should be picked, caught or cultivated to obtain the compound in large enough amounts. The transfer of chemicals up the food chain accounts for the variation in toxicity of fish from season to season as well as from location to location. It also accounts for sporadic outbreaks such as paralytic shellfish poisoning, caused for example by the ingestion of mussels that have filter-fed on toxic plankton.

The following marine organisms are potentially useful for their pharmaceutical, medicinal or toxicological properties.

Schizophyta (marine bacteria) are a potential source of antibiotics.

Certain cyanophyta (blue-green algae) contain amino acids which are toxic to the liver and nervous system. They can produce rapid death on administration to laboratory animals.

Rhodophyta (red algae). Some species are used as a source of agar, a gelling polysaccharide which is used in pharmaceuticals as an emulsion stabiliser, bulk laxative, and pastille base. Agar is also used in microbiology and plant tissue culture as a growth and support medium. Other species yield carrageenan, which is widely used in the food industry because it interacts with milk protein; in production of toothpaste because it forms rinsable gels; and as a research tool in the study of inflammation. Another variety is quite widely used as an anthelmintic, that is to destroy or expel round, whip or tape worms in infested intestines.

Phaeophyta (brown algae). Some yield commercially useful quantities of alginate used in the production of calcium alginate wool for use as a haemostatic, or in the food industry because of its ability to form non-thermoreversible gels. Another variety yields a choline derivative that can lower blood pressure. Other brown algae (kelps) are a useful source of iodine.

Chrysophyta (diatoms) are constituents of plankton and form diatomaceous earths which are used in cosmetics, as filtering aids and in chromatography.

Pyrrophyta (dinoflagellates or fire algae, also constitutents of plankton). Occasionally, individual species become unusually common and form 'blooms'

or 'red tides'. These species contain very important neurotoxins which render filter-feeding shellfish (and other organisms feeding on them) very poisonous to man.

Porifera (sponges). Developed from compounds found in a West Indian marine sponge are the antiviral compound idoxuridine, and the antitumour compound arabinosylcytidine, both of which are now widely used in Western medicine. Contact with sponges by bathers can lead to local skin inflammation, caused by fine sharp spicules.

Coelenterata, which include the jelly fish, sea anemones and corals, possess a stinging apparatus known as a nematocyst, which contains venom. Only a few species are capable of penetrating human skin, among them the Portuguese man of war (Physalia physalis). In some respects the toxins are similar to nettles on land. Heart stimulants may be extracted from certain sea anemones.

Echinodermata include the starfish, sea urchins and sea cucumbers. Some are toxic on ingestion; others have venomous defence organs, some of which contain holothurins, which are particularly potent neurotoxins in mammals.

Mollusca include the snails, octopus and squid; many are known to be poisonous or venomous. A wide range of compounds have been isolated from various species. Currently, an extract from the New

Zealand green-lipped mussel is being widely sold for its supposed beneficial effect on arthritic conditions.

Annelida include the marine worms; from one a marketable insecticide has been produced in Japan from an extract called nereistoxin.

Chordata, a vertebrate group comprising the fish, amphibians, sea-snakes, and mammals, includes a number of fish known to be poisonous, in particular the puffer fish (40 or so species). These, together with the porcupine fish (10 species) and the sunfish, contain tetrodotoxin, an exceedingly potent neurotoxin, which has found limited use as a local anaesthetic and muscle relaxant in terminal cancer patients. Other fish, such as the weever fish, stingrays and zebra fish, can inflict painful and even dangerous stings.

5 *left upper* Murex regius, a poisonous spiny shelled marine gastropod, or mollusca.
6 *left lower* Trichodesmium, a species of Cyanophyta (blue-green algae), contains a red photosynthetic pigment.
7 *centre* Laminaria saccharina, a species of Phaeophyta (brown algae), used in the food industry for its gel-making property.
8 *right top* Ceratium, a species of Pyrrophyta (dinoflagellates). Some cause shellfish poisoning in man.
9 *right centre* Puffer fish, Diodon, contains a substance which has anaesthetic properties.
10 *right bottom* Chondrus crispus (background), a red algae used in toothpaste and in the study of inflammation.

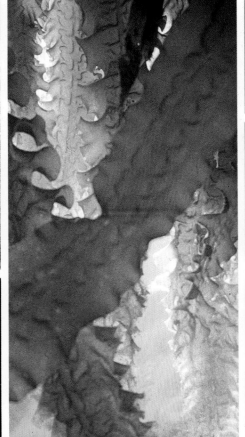

Renewable energy from the oceans

THE oceans absorb about three-quarters of solar energy received by the Earth. Derived from this energy are the winds, currents and waves, as well as the surface and near surface temperatures of the oceans; they in turn represent vast, potentially inexhaustible energy sources for the future. Other ocean energy sources include the tides; sea water itself, as raw material for nuclear fusion; salinity gradients; and the use of the marine biomass for energy generation by cultivating algae or kelp and converting them to methane or liquid fuels.

The limited life and rising prices of our non-renewable energy supplies mean that attention is being turned to the ocean with its renewable energy sources.

Tidal energy

The tides were used to drive mill wheels in Britain and Europe in ancient times; in the Bay of Fundy in Canada, tidal power was harnessed in the 17th century. A tidal range of over three metres, common in many areas, is needed to drive turbines and generate electricity. Tidal energy can be exploited at any site where the tidal range is adequate and coastal geography allows an economically short dam to impound a large area of water. The total estimated power available throughout the world is some 1100 gigawatts (GW, that is a unit of power equal to a thousand million watts). The tide carries out two rise-and-fall cycles in every lunar cycle of 24 hours, 50 minutes; high water advances by 50 minutes every day. Its range varies according to the position of the Earth,

Moon and Sun (see *Tides and surges* page 60). This variability complicates the extraction and use of tidal energy since the times of power production do not always coincide with electricity demand. Tidal electric systems must be integrated into a generating system with energy storage capability or flexible alternative power sources.

Tidal power schemes affect the environment in a number of ways. Coastal areas behind the barrage have higher mean water levels, but very high tides can be avoided. Sewage and industrial waste must be well treated before discharge into the basin since water is exchanged with the open sea less often and the change in salinity may alter the balance of aquatic life. Wide expanses of water with weaker tidal currents become available for recreational use and the smaller tidal range can improve the operation of harbours.

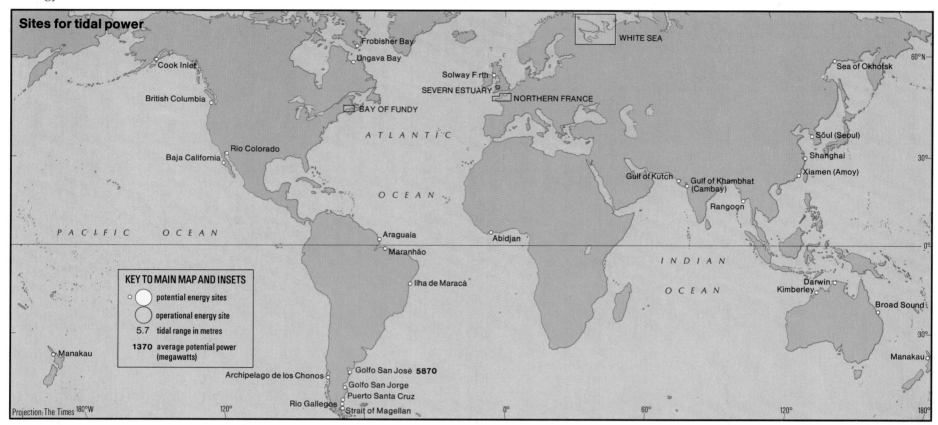

Sites for tidal power

KEY TO MAIN MAP AND INSETS
- ○ potential energy sites
- ◯ operational energy site
- 5.7 tidal range in metres
- 1370 average potential power (megawatts)

Projection: The Times

1 *map and insets* There are more than thirty sites in the world where conditions are suitable for the production of electricity from tidal energy. Three tidal power schemes are now operating, only one of which is commercial in scale. This is the concrete barrier across the mouth of the river Rance in Brittany, completed in 1967. It has been a technical and economic success; its operating costs are low and the equipment has suffered little corrosion.

Two small schemes were built at Kislaya Guba on the Barents Sea (20 MW) and in China (3 MW), but both are mainly experimental.

Two regions in the world have great undeveloped potential for tidal power production. Both the Bay of Fundy in Canada and the Severn Estuary in Britain have large tidal ranges and suitable sites for barrier

construction. Three sites in the Bay of Fundy have been chosen for development at Shepody Bay, Cumberland Basin and Cobequid Bay. In the UK the Severn Estuary Barrage Tidal Power Committee has investigated a variety of schemes and has selected the optimum site. The favoured single basin ebb generation scheme could supply about 6 per cent of Britain's electricity requirements at a cost of about £5600 million.

2 *below* The tidal power scheme at La Rance, Brittany. It has 24 turbines of 10 megawatts (MW; million watts) which generate a total of 540 GWh (gigawatt-hours) per year from the alternating tidal flows and can also pump water in or out of the basin; the energy so stored can later be released when demand for electricity is high. The barrier also has sluice gates which are opened near high and low tide to complete the filling and emptying of the basin.

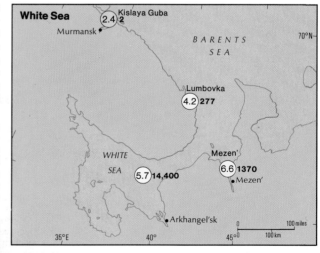

White Sea

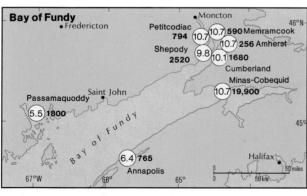

Bay of Fundy

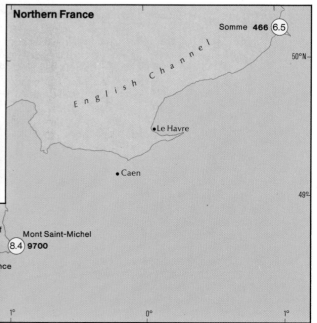

Northern France

Severn Estuary

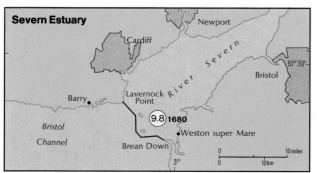

Wave energy

Waves are generated by the wind blowing for long periods over extensive 'fetches' of ocean (see *Waves, swell and tsunamis* page 58). The energy is transmitted very efficiently; typically, waves lose about half their energy in 1200 km.

At a small scale, wave energy already provides power for remote navigation buoys. This work, begun in Japan, is being extended to larger scale power production in the *Kaimei* ('Sea light') project run by Japan and the International Energy Agency. There are 24 openings in the base of a ship-like rectangular structure; waves move the water in them which forces air through a turbine, directed by valves. The air turbine absorbs the pneumatic energy and drives an electrical generator. An 80-metre long experimental device has been tested in the Sea of Japan and has yielded much valuable data.

Promising devices for exploiting wave energy include the OWC (oscillating water column), the Lanchester Clam (both illustrated), and the Lancaster flexible bag (similar to the Clam), the Salter Duck and the Evans cylinder. Many other concepts have been proposed. In Norway investigators are studying wave focusing and small cheap buoys which use sophisticated control to achieve high efficiency. In the USA the Scripps Institute has successfully demonstrated a power-absorbing buoy while Lockheed are investigating the 'Dam-Atoll', a saucer shaped structure which

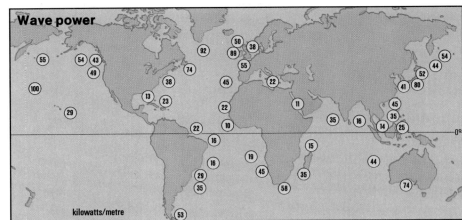

Wave power

kilowatts/metre

British Isles wave power

kilowatts/metre

focuses waves to drive a turbine at its centre. 'Passive' devices have been suggested for use in areas where the tidal range is small; waves simply run up a ramp and spill into a collecting pond behind. The water flows out through a low-head turbine. These systems are massive, relatively inefficient and may be environmentally unacceptable.

Wave power is a fluctuating resource, which conveniently is more plentiful in winter when electricity needs are highest. Studies indicate that up to 25 per cent of United Kingdom electricity demand might be met from variable supplies without extra energy storage or adverse effects on other power stations.

Before this target can be achieved, a great deal of research and development must be done to engineer cheap and reliable wave energy systems.

3 *above left* and **4** *above right* Some areas are subject to particularly powerful and regular waves. In the North Atlantic near the Hebrides, for instance, the average annual power has been measured to be 50 kW per metre of wave front. An experimental wave power station is likely to be built at Barvas, Lewis, in the Outer Hebrides. The total resource available from the coast of Britain and Eire is estimated to be about 120 GW, some five times Britain's electricity demand.

Energy absorption and transmission by waves

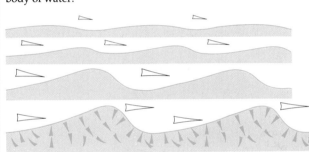

5 *above* Waves contain energy in two forms: kinetic energy due to motion and potential or stored energy. The potential energy is stored in the lower half of the wave pushed downwards and in the upper half raised above its mean level. As in a seesaw, there is a continual interchange between potential and kinetic energy as the water moves up and down. Energy is transmitted by pressure forces acting on the neighbouring body of water.

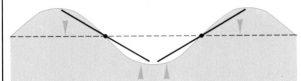

6 *above* The process by which waves are created when wind blows across the surface of the sea is not completely understood. Furrows begin to appear on the water surface as it absorbs energy from the wind. If the process is reinforced by continuing or stronger winds, the waves become progressively higher and longer. Energy is transmitted along the wave in the direction of the wind, although the mass of water remains in the same place. The wave will continue to travel

7 *right (above)* The Lanchester 'Clam' also uses air turbines but protects the power conversion system from sea water. Rubber bags, each connected to a separate Wells turbine, are supported on a floating hollow concrete beam. Air is squeezed from the bag, through the turbine and into the common chamber as wave pressure on the bag increases. When the wave retreats, the bag pressure drops and it is refilled with air from the common duct. At any one time, as many bags will be filling as are emptying, and the pressure inside the duct will only vary slightly. The Wells turbine can extract power from flows in either direction while rotating steadily.

8 *right (below)* Several devices convert the oscillatory wave motion to electricity by an air turbine and generator. The UK National Engineering Laboratory have developed floating and bottom standing designs which perform with high efficiency in model tests. Illustrated is a bottom standing system; here valves rectify the air flow so that it always passes through the turbine in the same direction. Alternatively a 'Wells' turbine could extract power from an alternating air flow, avoiding the mechanical complications of a valve system.

▷ energy derived from wind
▷ energy transferred to water

with little loss of energy until it reaches the sea shore or some other obstacle. If it meets an immovable barrier it will be reflected back, in a similar way to light reflected at a mirror. On the other hand, an object moving up and down in the water will create new waves. Wave power devices are designed to absorb the maximum amount of incoming energy, with very little loss from reflected or newly generated outgoing waves.

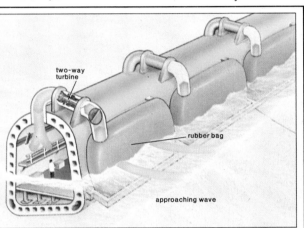

two-way turbine

rubber bag

approaching wave

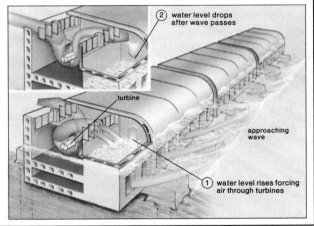

② water level drops after wave passes

turbine

approaching wave

① water level rises forcing air through turbines

Sea thermal power

The possibilities of utilising small temperature differences to produce energy have been known for some time. Limited success was achieved in the 19th century and now advances in heat transfer systems and new materials have made large scale projects feasible. A difference of at least 20°C between surface waters and waters at depths of between 1000 and 3000 m is required, conditions which are normally only found in tropical waters.

The energy produced may be transmitted to land by cable or used for ocean industry in situ: for example, the production of ammonia using hydrogen derived from seawater, the extraction of nitrogen from the air, desalination, the refining of ocean minerals such as manganese and aluminium, and for other energy-intensive processes.

Problems related to OTEC include mooring such a massive structure in deep water, and of corrosion

under operational conditions at sea, but the energy supply is continuous.

An experimental 'mini' OTEC installation is operating off Hawaii with private and state finance. Commercial plants may be operational by 1990.

The discovery of hot ocean springs at spreading ridges in the deep ocean has given rise to the possibility of locating an OTEC plant on or near the ocean floor, and using the hot water as an energy source. Since cold water would come from nearby, the lengthy cold water pipe would be eliminated.

9 *below* The Ocean Thermal Energy Conversion (OTEC) projects are based directly on the vast solar heat reservoir of the ocean and a temperature difference of around 20°C which exists between the surface water and ocean depths over 1000 m in tropical areas. The general and the most favourable zones for extracting thermal energy are mapped.

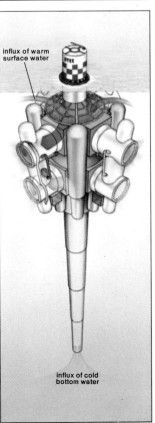

influx of warm surface water

10 *right* The OTEC device comprises a tube about 20 m in diameter and at least 500 m in length suspended from a platform moored in the ocean. The device contains liquid ammonia which has a low boiling point. The ammonia, vaporised by the warm surface water, is used to drive a turbine, and is then recondensed by cold water drawn from the depths of the ocean by the pipe.

influx of cold bottom water

Thermal energy

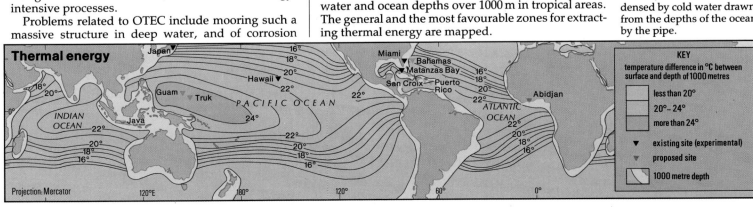

KEY

temperature difference in °C between surface and depth of 1000 metres

▢ less than 20°
▢ 20°– 24°
▢ more than 24°

▼ existing site (experimental)
▽ proposed site
▨ 1000 metre depth

Projection: Mercator

Port development and location

SEAPORTS are located in bays, creeks, lagoons, rivers, estuaries and, more recently, on entirely artificial man-made islands. Some ports developed where natural deep water and shelter existed, while others have been created by extensive harbour engineering works. Some have prospered on the handling of single commodities; others cater for a wide range of cargoes. Most ports are under public ownership (controlled by local, state or national governments); others are administered by railway corporations, customs authorities or by private companies.

A port's influence will often extend beyond the local environment or even national boundaries; many are growth centres stimulating industrial, manufacturing and commercial activities. Certain major ports, usually because of their strategic location, act as distribution centres for international regional trade while others have become the location for large maritime industrial areas.

Port development provides a valuable historical record of the commercial and military status and fortunes of metropolitan centres and individual nations.

The changing physical conditions in coastal regions influence the development of seaports.

This has assumed greater importance with the growth in size of vessels and the increased depth of water required in port approaches and in the vicinity of berths. However, there are two other equally important factors which affect the growth of ports: the first, those periods of expansion in seaborne trade which are clearly discernible; and the second, the impact of changing maritime technology and the move to greater specialisation in shipping.

The continuing success of a port depends also on the existence of efficient inland communications by road, rail or inland waterways to hinterlands of high production or consumption. If transportation inland is impeded, for example by physical barriers such as mountain ranges, the port's growth will be inhibited. A port's growth is also influenced by its proximity to a major shipping route. Ship-owners, in order to minimise their voyage costs, will try to conserve fuel or achieve economies in cargo handling by reducing the distance of sea passages or avoiding calls at too many ports. Thus savings can be made by concentrating on fewer ports of call, and by transhipping cargoes for other destinations in 'feeder' vessels.

THE DISTRIBUTION OF PORTS

The number, type and capacity of seaports required by a country are related to the volume of trade and dependence on maritime transport. The combination of these, and other special factors, has resulted in the present distribution of seaports in the world as illustrated in this section. Following the maps of Europe and north-west Europe on these pages, are North America (page 126), South America (page 127), Asia (page 130), Australasia (page 132) and Africa and the Middle East (page 133). A feature of these maps is the uneven distribution of ports throughout the world. However, this pattern disguises the relative importance of individual seaports in international maritime trade and their influence on the regions they serve. A hierarchical structure of seaports exists at the regional, national and international levels. At one end of the scale there are major international ports handling predominantly foreign seaborne trade while, at the other extreme, there are minor ports, many with primitive facilities, that concentrate on domestic coastal trade. Included here are all international seaports and ports with certain minimum facilities, comprising (1) all commercial seaports capable of accommodating vessels of 1000 grt; (2) seaports where reasonable anchorage facilities exist or where a minimum standard infrastructure allows the working of vessels; (3) single buoy moorings; (4) major dry docks; and (5) smaller ports which constitute the sole access to a state.

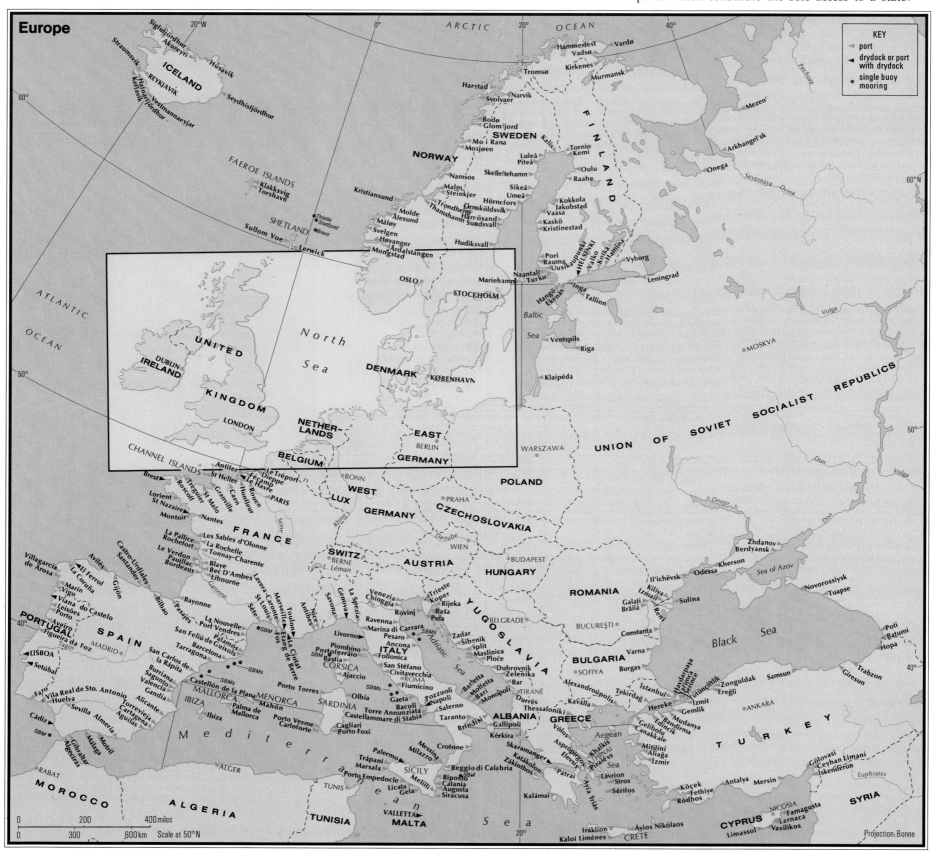

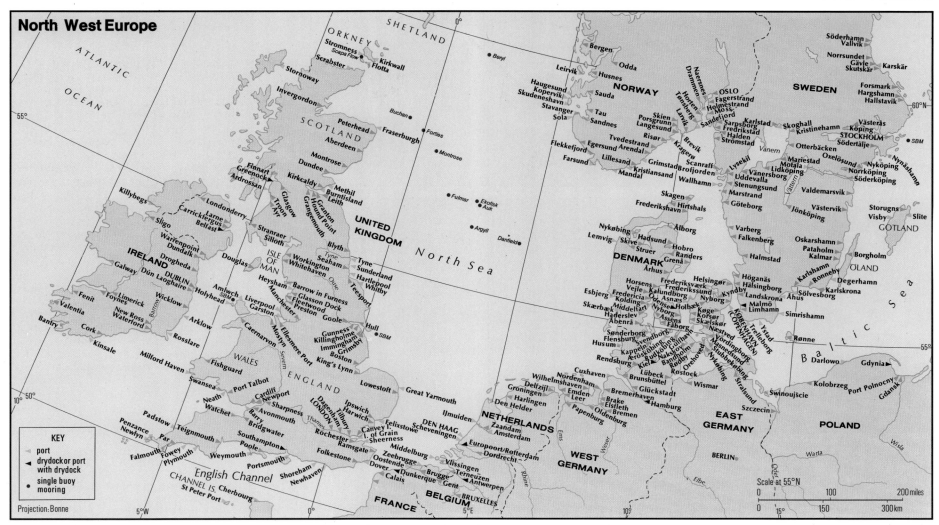

North West Europe

Ports of Europe

1 *main map opposite and* **2** *inset above* The heavy concentration of seaports along many coastlines reflects the importance that the industrial output of European nations, particularly that of member nations of the European Economic Community (EEC), has on international seaborne trade. However, seaports are not evenly distributed: there is no correlation between the length of a nation's coastline, its land area and the number of seaports. Major concentrations are found in north-west Europe and the western Mediterranean Sea, serving the region's most important hinterlands and industrial areas.

The physical geography of Europe provides a fascinating contrast, from the fjords of Norway through the peninsulas of north-west Europe to the bays and headlands of the Mediterranean. This, and the exist-

ence of so many independent sovereign states, explains the present distribution and also status of ports. Intense inter-port competition for the trade of the European hinterland with its large population, results from comprehensive and efficient inland transport networks. Not surprisingly, some traditional seaports have declined in importance. One example is the long-established west coast seaports of the UK which in the 1970s entered a period of decline largely because of a structural change in trading patterns. East coast ports, many of them relatively small in size, have assumed greater importance as the UK's trade with continental Europe, particularly the EEC member countries, has increased. Although west coast ports retain a major share of the traffic in bulk commodities because of their deep water locations, they have declined in the liner and unitised trades because of a shift to concentration on ports surrounding the English Channel and

North Sea.

The Mediterranean is effectively a closed sea, has relatively deep water and is virtually non-tidal. The topography of the region, particularly the proximity of mountain ranges on the northern shore, results in a narrow coastal strip with few navigable rivers. These features have restricted the inland penetration and hinterland development of seaports and encouraged the development of bay ports. Despite the physical limitations, considerable port development has taken place, particularly in the vicinity of the Rhone delta.

Many of the major Mediterranean ports that exist today have their origins in antiquity. Harbours, often involving considerable engineering works, were constructed by the Phoenicians in the 11th century BC, the Greeks in the 7th century BC, and later the Romans, to meet the maritime trading needs of countries bordering the Mediterranean. An example is the port of Fos.

Marseille

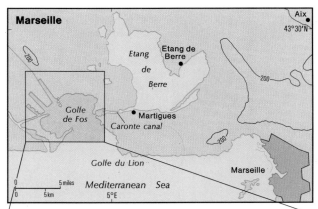

Golfe de Fos

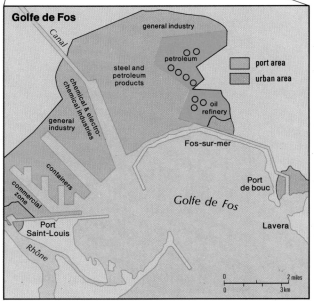

3 *left* The port of Fos in the Gulf of Fos is an extension of the port of Marseille, the largest seaport in the Mediterranean and the second largest port in Europe. The existing port facilities at Marseille were extended to the west to avoid the problems of siltation, with major new developments constructed at Etang de Berre and Lavera. However, these have been eclipsed by the construction of a vast modern industrial port at Fos. Like Rotterdam and Teesside, Fos is an excellent example of a maritime industrial development area (MIDAS). The existence of extensive flat land areas (120 000 ha) adjacent to deep water with nearby population areas and adequate communication, power and other services have encouraged the siting of large dependent industries in the dock estate. These include steel, petroleum, petrochemical, gas and heavy raw material industries and services to provide a major industrial complex dependent on the import and export of cargoes by sea.

The port of Fos consists of four huge dock basins, each of which extends from 2 to 4.5 km inland behind

which the industrial and commercial zones are located. The channel to the port is 9 km long and has a water depth of 23 metres allowing the berthing of 500 000 dwt tankers. Hinterland connections are also good and include pipeline distribution of crude oil and chemicals to Germany and Switzerland.

4 *below* Once the 'pearl of the Adriatic', Venice shared its enormous medieval trading prosperity with Genoa and Pisa. Venice is an example of a lagoon port protected by sand bars and one of its primary problems is the continual need for dredging. Passenger vessels and small cargo ships use the old port of Venice but tankers, container vessels, LNG and bulk carriers must berth at the industrial areas of Porto Marghera, 20 km along the canal (9.45 metres deep). Venice competes with Trieste at the head of the Adriatic and Genoa on the west coast of Italy, as well as with north-west European ports which, with Venice, share the hinterlands of Switzerland, southern Germany and northern Italy.

Golfo di Venezia

Venezia

Port development and location—Europe 2

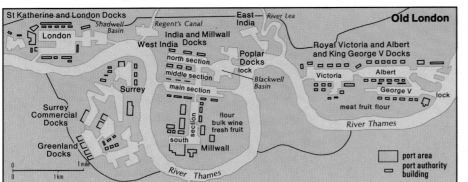

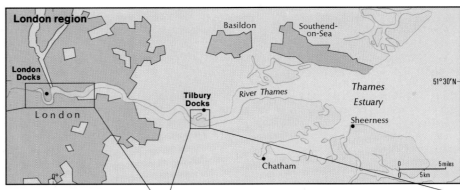

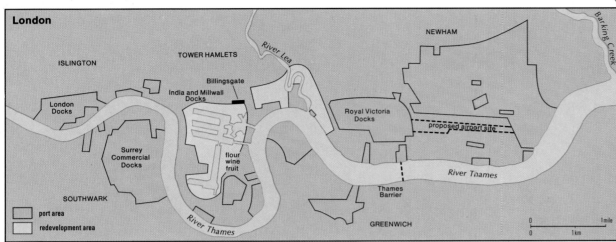

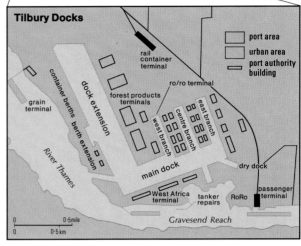

1 *above* The port of London developed at the Roman bridging point at the head of the Thames estuary, although there may have been some small port activities in the area before the Roman settlement around AD 30. The port had a major impact on the early development of the city and was a contributory factor in the subsequent emergence of London as a leading commercial centre. For over 200 years London was the largest city and the largest port in the world, the river berths and anchorages handling most of London's extensive traffic.

The old port of London comprises 152 km of the tidal river Thames. It provides a classic example of an enclosed dock system. Cargo handling facilities were initially provided at riverside quays and wharves but these were extended in the 19th century with the construction of enclosed dock basins. These basins, which were financed by private capital, often concentrated on a particular trade, or routes, or cargo types and provided the necessary specialised handling and storage facilities required by these trades.

The first major move downstream from the proximity of the City took place in 1886 when Tilbury Docks were constructed 37 km from London Bridge. The older enclosed docks continued to thrive until the late 1960s when because of changes in the dry cargo trades the facilities became obsolete. Restricted from expansion by urban development (which also caused great delays to road traffic travelling to and from the ports), and limited in the size of ship that could be handled by the dimensions of lock entrances, the trade of the upper docks began to decline rapidly. Some of this traffic transferred to Tilbury while other trades were attracted to other ports such as Felixstowe, Medway and Southampton which compete with London. The major enclosed dock systems in the upper reaches have now effectively closed and activities are concentrated at Tilbury, and the lower reaches of the Thames where oil, conventional and unitised general cargoes and grain are the principal trades.

RIVER AND ESTUARY PORTS

Many of the world's major seaports are located on the banks of rivers or estuaries. Several of today's larger ports were originally located up river at lowest bridging points or at the head of estuaries. Such locations offered safe anchorage and easy access to shallow draught vessels and reduced the distance between the port and its markets. In some cases the difficulties of maintaining adequate depths in rivers and the problems of large tidal variations in estuaries necessitated the construction of enclosed docks linked to the sea by lock entrances. Some ports still retain these inland locations, particularly those in major rivers such as the St Lawrence, the Amazon, and the Rhine. However, the survival of river and estuary ports, at least in their original locations, has been endangered by the increase in ship size and the consequent restrictions this imposes on the maximum permissible draught. Seasonal variations in the level of rivers, influenced by rainfall, ice melting and quantity of water extracted for domestic and industrial uses, are a further complication. Further restrictions on the survival of river ports have been imposed by urban expansion since this has reduced the availability of land for terminal development in the commercial centres of port cities. As a result, the older sections of river ports located at points where insufficient depth of water can be economically maintained by dredging have become obsolete and have had to be closed. These have been replaced by facilities built down river where deeper water is available, narrow navigable channels can be avoided and greater land areas are available.

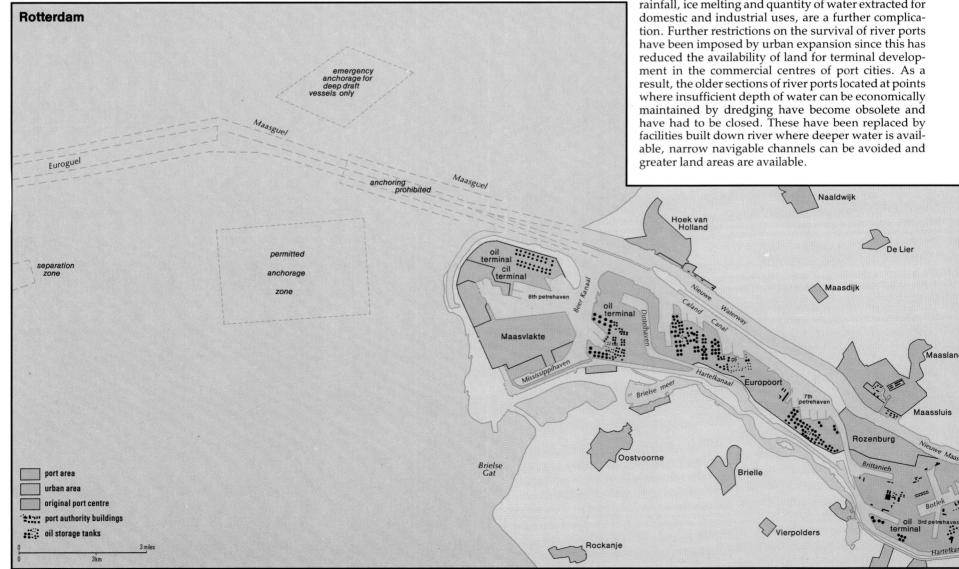

3 *below* Göteborg is Sweden's main trade outlet to the west and its major port. Located on the banks of the Gota river, it is a classic example of a river port, which over the past 350 years has seen the linear development of facilities on both banks of the river moving progressively downstream—a typical river port development process. The old river quays and harbours sited adjacent to the commercial centre of the city have gradually been closed or rebuilt and modernised to meet the needs of new traffic. As a result, the centre of gravity of the port has moved towards the deep water at the river entrance, and to major new developments at Skandia and Alvsborgs harbours. Here, large areas of land have been reclaimed and deep water berths constructed to accommodate large container vessels, roll-on roll-off (RoRo) and other specialised carriers. Göteborg acts as a pivot port for unitised traffic moving to and from Scandinavian countries. A major offshore terminal at Torshamenen is capable of handling crude oil tankers up to 250 000 dwt.

4 *right* Port Talbot tidal harbour illustrates the extent of harbour engineering works required to provide port facilities on exposed coastlines. The harbour, with a total water area of 188 ha, is a specialised bulk ore import port constructed to accommodate large dry bulk carriers. Two major breakwaters of 1950 and 1000 m respectively were constructed to provide protection from the sea and a deep water access channel is maintained. The jetty provides accommodation for two vessels. The southern side has been developed to receive fully laden vessels of 110 000 dwt in size and has a dredged basin of 22 m alongside to ensure that vessels remain afloat at all stages of the tide. The northern layby berth could be developed to accommodate vessels of 150 000 dwt. Iron ore and coal, destined for the adjacent steel works, are the principal commodities imported and they are handled by means of a continuous conveyor belt system feeding two separate stockpile areas on the shore. Iron ore destined for the steel works at Newport is now discharged at Port Talbot and transferred into specially constructed railway wagons (75 tonnes capacity) to enable economies to be made in the use of larger vessels.

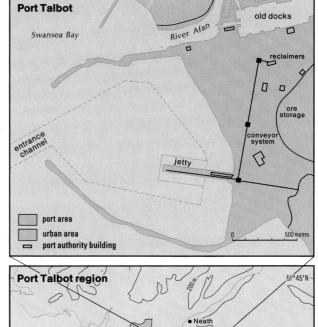

5 *bottom right* View of some of the oil terminals at the port of Rotterdam, looking east from the Oude Maas with the Nieuwe Maas to the left of the picture.

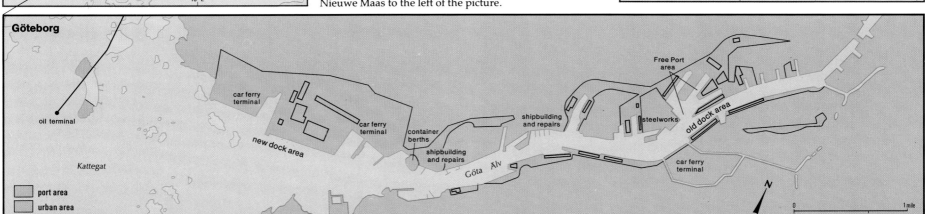

2 *below* Despite the generally accepted view that deltas provide poor locations for the siting of ports, Europe's—and the world's—largest seaport is located on the Rhine delta. Rotterdam, the 'gateway to Europe', forms the focal point of the transport communications network of north-west Europe and serves an extensive hinterland of 250 million people. It handles the seaborne trade of many countries.

Rotterdam's dominance has been maintained by continually responding to the technological requirements of shipping with improvements in approach channels and cargo handling systems. The Rhine, along with the Meuse and Shelde, has created an enormous delta extending into the North Sea. Vast quantities of silt are deposited and hundreds of islands, sand dunes and banks are formed. In the 1860s, a canal was built to cut through the sand dunes at the Hook of Holland and create the straight approach channel to the port. This channel was subsequently extended into the North Sea for a distance of 30 km and a depth of 24.5 metres and leads to Europoort, the enormous maritime industrial area of Rotterdam which was constructed between 1958 and 1970. The phenomenal growth of Rotterdam since the Second World War is largely based on the importation of oil. It is now the major oil refining centre in the world and also has large petrochemical complexes. Its other main trade is iron ore and grain although it handles all types of commodities. In 1973, Rotterdam handled a record 310 million tonnes of cargo and today approximately 100 million tonnes of cargo per annum passes through the port, to and from inland destinations along the Rhine and its related canal systems.

In the 1950s oil and petrochemical ports were constructed on reclaimed land at Pernis and Botlek. Noticeable is the extent to which industry, particularly oil refining and petrochemical complexes, occupy vast areas of the port. Rotterdam is also a major dry bulk and general cargo port and is the major container handling port in Europe. Most of the recent development of the port of Rotterdam is on the south bank of the Nieuwe Maas and Nieuwe Waterway where a succession of dock basins or oil harbours have been constructed. Subsequent developments have seen almost the entire south bank developed, mainly for the importation of bulk commodities.

Despite environmental concern, development continues with the reclamation and construction of an artificial island at Maasvlakte at the outer reaches of Europoort. This will have sufficient deep water to accommodate the world's biggest tankers and is suitable for industrial development, particularly that involving noxious and polluting industries. It will also be the site for future container terminal development.

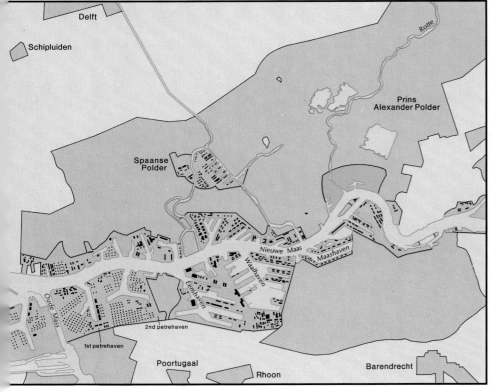

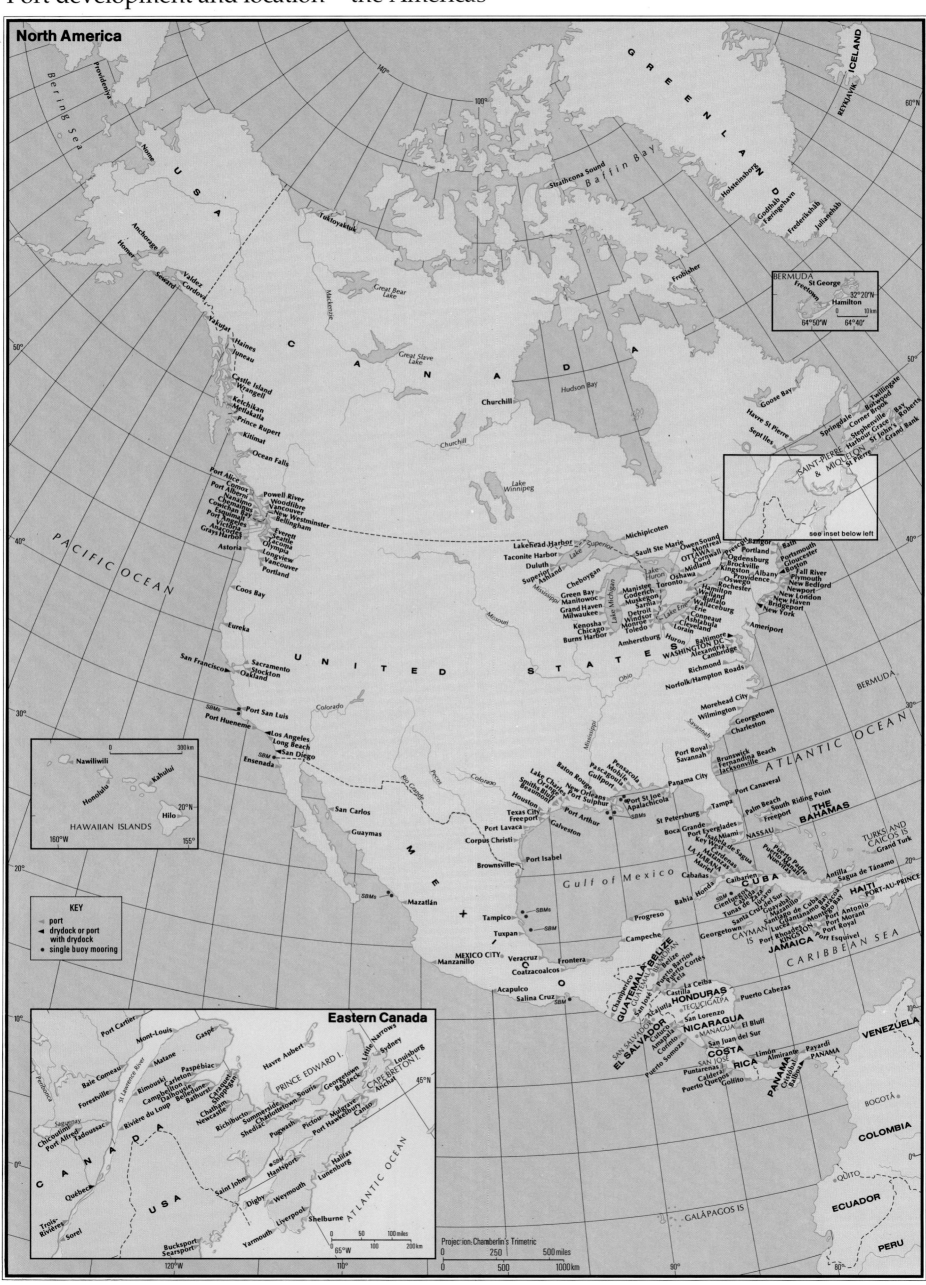

North America

Bering Sea

Providenya

USA

Nome

Anchorage
Homer

Seward
Valdez
Cordova

Yakutat

Haines
Juneau

Castle Island
Wrangell
Ketchikan
Metlakatla
Prince Rupert

Kitimat

Ocean Falls

Port Alice
Comox
Port Alberni
Nanaimo
Chemainus
Cowichan Bay
Esquimalt
Port Angeles
Victoria
Anacortes
Grays Harbor

Powell River
Woodfibre
Vancouver
New Westminster
Bellingham
Everett
Seattle
Tacoma
Olympia
Longview
Vancouver
Portland

Astoria

PACIFIC OCEAN

Coos Bay

Eureka

San Francisco
Sacramento
Stockton
Oakland

SBMs
Port San Luis
Port Hueneme
Los Angeles
Long Beach
San Diego
Ensenada

SBM

CANADA

Great Bear
Lake

Mackenzie

Great Slave
Lake

Churchill

Churchill

Lake
Winnipeg

UNITED STATES

Colorado

Colorado

Pecos

Rio Grande

San Carlos

Guaymas

MEXICO

SBMs
Mazatlán

Tampico
Tuxpan

MEXICO CITY
Manzanillo
Veracruz
Coatzacoalcos
Frontera

Acapulco
Salina Cruz

Tuktoyaktuk

Strathcona Sound

Baffin Bay

GREENLAND

ICELAND

REYKJAVIK

60°N

Godthåb
Færingehavn
Frederikshåb
Julianehåb

Holsteinsborg

Frobisher

Goose Bay

Havre St Pierre
Sept Iles

50°

Springdale
Corner Brook
Stephenville
Harbour Grace
St John's
Grand Bank

Twillingate
Botwood
Bay
Roberts

SAINT-PIERRE
& MIQUELON
St Pierre

see inset below left

Michipicoten

Lakehead Harbor
Taconite Harbor
Duluth
Superior
Ashland
Cheboygan

Green Bay
Manitowoc
Muskegon
Grand Haven
Milwaukee
Kenosha
Chicago
Burns Harbor

Lake Superior

Sault Ste Marie

Goderich
Sarnia
Detroit
Windsor
Monroe
Toledo

Lake Huron

Lake Michigan

Lake Erie

Owen Sound
Montreal
OTTAWA
Cornwall
Midland
Oshawa
Toronto
Hamilton
Welland
Buffalo
Wallaceburg
Erie
Conneaut
Ashtabula
Cleveland
Lorain

Amherstburg
Huron

Baltimore
WASHINGTON DC
Alexandria
Cambridge

Richmond

Norfolk/Hampton Roads

Morehead City
Wilmington
Georgetown
Charleston

Brunswick
Fernandina Beach
Jacksonville

Port Royal
Savannah

Prescott
Ogdensburg
Brockville
Kingston
Oswego
Rochester

Bangor
Bath
Portland
Portsmouth
Gloucester
Boston
Fall River
Plymouth
New Bedford
Newport
New London
New Haven
Bridgeport
New York

Albany
Providence

Ameriport

BERMUDA

ATLANTIC OCEAN

Ohio

Mississippi

Missouri

Houston
Texas City
Freeport

Port Lavaca

Corpus Christi

Brownsville
Port Isabel

Lake Charles
Orange
Smith Bluff
Beaumont

Baton Rouge
New Orleans
Port Sulphur
Port Arthur

Pensacola
Mobile
Pascagoula
Gulfport

Galveston

Port St Joe
Apalachicola

SBMs

Panama City
Tampa

St Petersburg

Boca Grande
Port Everglades
Port Miami
Key West

South Riding Point
Freeport

Palm Beach
Port Canaveral

THE
BAHAMAS

NASSAU

TURKS AND
CAICOS IS
Grand Turk

Gulf of Mexico

SBMs

Progreso

Campeche

Cabañas
Bahia Honda

Mariel
LA HABANA
Mariel
Cárdenas
Isabela de Sagua
Matanzas

SBM

Cienfuegos
Casilda
Tunas de Zaza

Caibarien

CUBA

Santa Cruz del Sur

Puerto Padre
Banes
Nuevitas

Antilla
Sagua de Tánamo

HAITI

PORT-AU-PRINCE

Guayabal
Nipe
Santiago de Cuba
Guantánamo Bay

Manzanillo

Lucea
CAYMAN
IS

Georgetown

Port Rhoades
KINGSTON
JAMAICA

Port Antonio
Montego Bay
Port Morant
Port Royal

Port Esquivel

CARIBBEAN SEA

Chambérico
GUATEMALA
GUATEMALA CITY
San José
Ocós
Acajutla
SAN SALVADOR
EL SALVADOR
Cutuco
Amapala
Corinto
San Juan del Sur

BELIZE
BELMOPAN
Belize
Puerto Barrios
Puerto Cortés
Tela

La Ceiba
Castilla
San Lorenzo
TEGUCIGALPA
HONDURAS
San José
NICARAGUA
MANAGUA
El Bluff
Corinto
Puerto Cabezas

Puerto Somoza

Limón
Almirante
COSTA
Puntarenas
Caldera
Puerto Quepos
RICA
Golfito

Payardi
PANAMA
Cristóbal
Balboa

VENEZUELA

BOGOTÁ

COLOMBIA

Quito
ECUADOR

PERU

GALÁPAGOS IS

BERMUDA

St George
Freetown
Hamilton

32°20'N

64°50'W   64°40'

0   10 km

HAWAIIAN ISLANDS

Nawiliwili
Honolulu
Kahului
Hilo

0   300 km

160°W   155°

20°N

KEY

▸ port
◂ drydock or port
  with drydock
• single buoy mooring

Eastern Canada

CANADA

Port Cartier
Mont-Louis
Gaspé

Baie Comeau
Matane
Forestville
Rimouski

Saguenay
Chicoutimi
Port Alfred
Tadoussac

Trois-Rivières
Sorel
Québec

St Lawrence River

Carleton
Campbellton
Dalhousie
Bathurst
Rivière du Loup
Belledune

Paspébiac
Caraquet
Shippagan

Chatham
Newcastle

Richibucto
Shediac
Buctouche

PRINCE EDWARD I.
Havre Aubert

Summerside
Charlottetown
Souris

Pictou
Mulgrave
Port Hawkesbury

Georgetown
Baddeck

CAPE BRETON I.

Little Narrows
Sydney
Louisbourg

Arichat
Canso

SBM

Hantsport
Halifax
Lunenburg

Saint John
Digby
Weymouth
Liverpool
Yarmouth
Shelburne

USA

Bucksport
Searsport

ATLANTIC OCEAN

0   50   100 miles
0   100   200 km

120°W   110°   65°W

Projection: Chamberlin's Trimetric

0   250   500 miles
0   500   1000 km

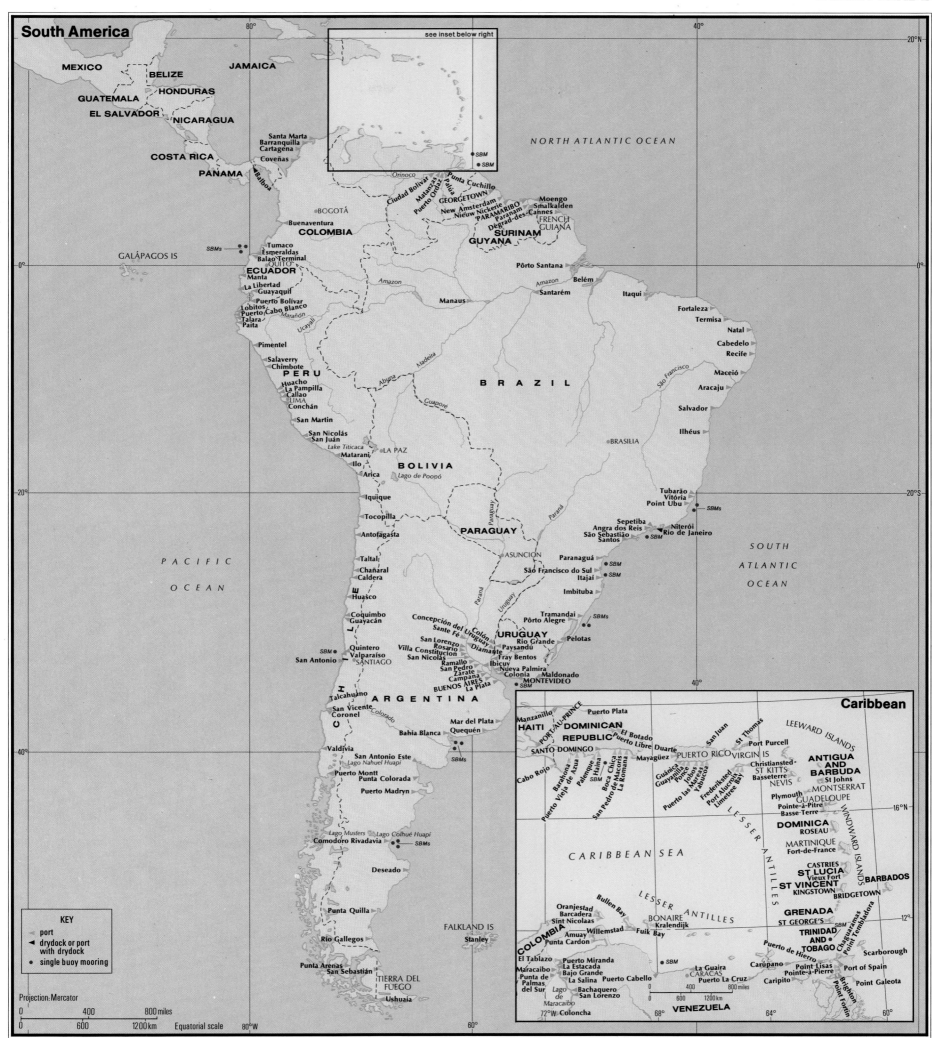

South America

KEY
➤ port
◄ drydock or port with drydock
• single buoy mooring

Projection: Mercator

Caribbean

1 *opposite* North America has four distinct and long coastal regions, the west coast, the east coast, Florida and the Mexican Gulf, and the Great Lakes. The prominent topographical feature of the west coast of the USA is the almost total absence, with the exception of the northern section, of bays, inlets or other natural indentations suitable for port location. Combined with the shortage of large suitable flat areas of land adjacent to the coast, this explains the sparse distribution of ports. Another relevant feature is the broad mountain range running parallel to the coast which restricts inland penetration.

On the east coast, the topography is dominated by the Appalachian mountain range. The coastline is indented, with the central section of the east coast consisting of a series of drowned river valleys (rias). These have provided sites for the major US ports serving the largest concentration of population in North America.

The least favourable coast for port development is the Florida peninsula and Mexican Gulf, but despite its physical and climatic disadvantages a number of large ports have flourished, largely as a result of the growth in the oil and related industries.

Finally, to the north, the Great Lakes, with such ports as Montreal, Toronto, Chicago, Detroit and Cleveland, serve the industrial regions and plains of the Mid West.

The trade of almost all US ports is dominated by bulk commodities, notably petroleum, iron ore, coal and grains. The USA's increased dependence on the importation of bulk commodities in the 1970s, notably oil, has directed greater attention to developing new ports with depths of water capable of accommodating the larger vessels employed in these trades. In the Gulf region these developments are often at offshore islands.

2 *above* Nowhere have the terrain conditions affected port location more obviously than in South America. On the west coast, the Andes run close to and parallel with the coast, restricting the coastal plain; the coast itself has few indentations or navigable rivers to provide natural protection for port development; and the region is affected by earthquakes. Artificial harbours are typical of most of west coast South America, and require the construction of moles or breakwaters to provide adequate protection from wind and waves, so that vessels may berth safely. On the east coast, by contrast, lie wide coastal plains and marsh areas; deltas and estuaries provide natural conditions for port development, although some of the great rivers present siltation problems. Rio de Janeiro is located in one of the finest natural harbours in the world and developed into a great metropolitan area and capital city like most major ports on the east coast.

1 *below* The port of New York is situated in the natural harbour of New York Bay at the mouth of the Hudson river. The location, formed by the drowned inlet of the ice-deepened river, provided good opportunities for adapting the site to meet the needs of technological change. Jointly administered (since 1921) by the states of New York and New Jersey, the port today is one of the largest ports in the world and the second major container handling port.

New York was founded in 1624 as New Amsterdam. At that time ships used to handle cargo at anchor in the East River. Later, private dock facilities were constructed along the East River to be followed by finger piers on the Manhattan shore of the Hudson river. The port's early growth in shipping was facilitated by the access to the interior through the Hudson–Mohawk Gap. The construction of the Erie Canal in 1825, linking New York with Buffalo and the industrial regions of the Great Lakes, improved access to the hinterland. By the end of the 19th century New York handled 60 per cent of all United States trade and 80 per cent of the overseas passenger traffic. Hinterland advantages declined with the arrival of the railways and the growth in inter-port competition, but New York has retained its role as America's premier port.

The most distinctive design feature of the port of New York is the large number of finger piers. By the end of the 19th century the port area was centred on developments on both sides of the Hudson river, with finger piers tightly pressed into the available land and

2 *above* The port of Savannah which began trading in 1744. The first steamboat to cross the Atlantic, the *Savannah*, sailed from here to Liverpool in 1819. The port now deals mainly in manufactured goods.

water areas. This presented cargo-handling difficulties since cargo discharged at Manhattan and destined for rail transport has to be placed in barges and ferried to the New Jersey shore for onward movement.

The construction of finger piers offered many economic operating advantages. They provide the maximum berthing area per length of shoreline, and are therefore advantageous where land is in short supply or very expensive. Finger piers enable ports to utilise deep water close offshore, thus reducing the cost of maintaining depths for deeper draught vessels. Before the advent of mechanical handling equipment, cargo was man-handled by dockworkers. The shorter the distance cargo was required to be moved, the less arduous the task for dockworkers; finger piers, with narrow quay aprons, provided an ideal solution. However, after the Second World War, cargo handling methods changed dramatically and greater emphasis was placed on mechanical means of handling which required larger areas of land. These changes presented a formidable challenge to the port of New York as finger piers became less suitable to meet the needs of modern shipping.

Restricted from expanding on the banks of the Hudson by urban developments, the port authority was forced to develop terminals in other areas of the bay. Initially, finger piers were adapted, largely by land reclamation, to provide larger terminal areas, particularly in the region to the south of the East River. Later, land was purchased at Newark Bay and major new container and bulk terminals were constructed with long marginal quays and extensive back-up areas.

Port Newark–Elizabeth port complex has the largest concentration of container terminals in the world with 26 berths extending over 7 km of quay along the Elizabeth Channel and Newark Bay and handling 1.86 million TEUs (twenty-foot equivalents) per annum.

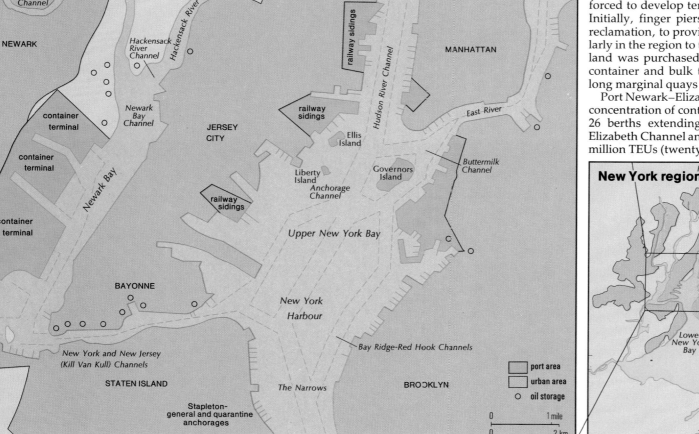

New York

Passaic River
Passaic River Channel
NEWARK
Hackensack River
Hackensack River Channel
container terminal
Newark Bay Channel
JERSEY CITY
container terminal
airport
Newark Bay
container terminal
BAYONNE
New York and New Jersey (Kill Van Kull) Channels
STATEN ISLAND
Stapleton-general and quarantine anchorages
The Narrows
New York Harbour
Upper New York Bay
Bay Ridge-Red Hook Channels
BROOKLYN
railway sidings
railway sidings
railway sidings
Liberty Island
Ellis Island
Anchorage Channel
Governors Island
Buttermilk Channel
East River
Hudson River Channel
MANHATTAN
passenger terminal
Hudson River
railway sidings

□ port area
□ urban area
○ oil storage

0 ___ 1 mile
0 ___ 2 km

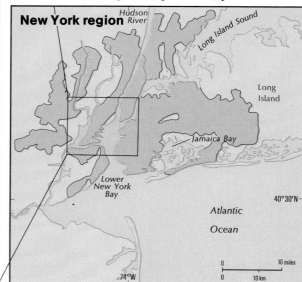

New York region

Hudson River
Long Island Sound
Long Island
Jamaica Bay
Lower New York Bay
Atlantic Ocean
40°30'N
74°W

0 ___ 10 miles
0 ___ 10 km

3 *below* The port of San Francisco is located on the west shore of San Francisco Bay. It is the main body of a series of connecting bays that form the largest natural harbour in the world with a shoreline of 320 km and depths up to 600 metres. With the ports of Oakland, Richmond, Stockton, Sacramento and San Pablo Bay, it forms the major series of port complexes on the US west coast.

The magnificent bay was discovered by Spanish missionaries travelling overland in 1775 although Sir Frances Drake landed on the shore to the north of San Francisco in 1579. Controversy still surrounds the claim that he entered the Bay. The approach to the Bay is through a strait some 20 km wide known throughout the world as the 'Golden Gate'.

The port of San Francisco dates primarily from the gold rush period of the 1850s. San Francisco became the main port and largest city on the west coast of the USA for sailing ships, Pacific whaling fleets and shipping to the Far East, Hawaii and Australasia. In its early years of development the port suffered from serious siltation problems. The building of a sea wall in the 1870s and the reclamation behind this stabilised the waterfront line and created the prime metropolitan land which remains the financial and commercial centre of the city today.

Like other major US ports, the port of San Francisco initially consisted of a series of narrow finger piers.

Technological changes in the shipping industry and competition from nearby ports have required drastic alterations to the layout of the port. This has been accomplished through land reclamation and the filling in of areas between the finger piers to provide the additional areas for modern cargo handling methods, particularly the handling of containers.

Despite these developments, other ports located in the Bay have taken over many of the activities from San Francisco. Timber is now concentrated at Stockton and Sacramento which are connected to the Bay by deep water channels. Oil terminals are located in San Pablo Bay, and the port of Oakland, located in the deeper water of the east shore, has one of the biggest container facilities in the USA, handling over half a million containers per annum.

In response to this competition the port of San Francisco is continuing to improve its facilities and services to attract more traffic. A modern grain terminal has been constructed at pier 90, container facilities are located at piers 94 and 96 and RoRo cargo is handled at piers 70 and 80. It remains, however, primarily a general cargo port. In an effort to expand the maritime industry within the city, a foreign trade zone, which was initially established in 1948, has been enlarged as part of the port's long term development plan. This area is considered outside the customs territory of the country, that is a 'free port'.

5 *above* View of San Francisco port with container terminals at piers 94 and 96 in the foreground.

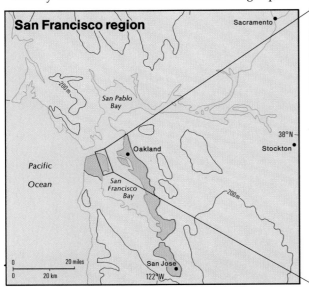

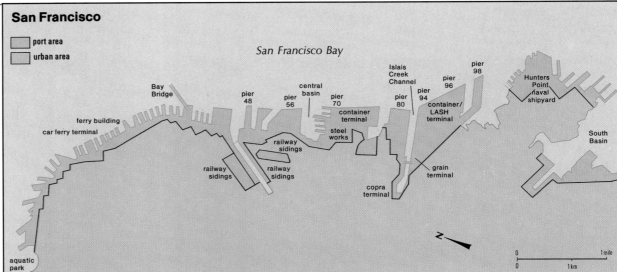

4 *right* Valparaiso, the major commercial centre on the west coast of South America, has been used as a port since the Spaniards conquered Chile in the 16th century. It played a prominent role in the formation of the fleet which carried Chilean and Argentinian troops to Peru which eventually brought an end to Spanish rule in South America. For the first 300 years of its existence the port remained small and concentrated largely on local trades, mainly providing a shipping connection to Callao in Peru. Since its completion as a modern international port in 1930, its main function has been to serve the population of the capital city of Santiago located 114 km inland. Its role is now diminishing, particularly in the handling of bulk cargoes, because of competition with the port of San Antonio located 64 km to the south and equipped with more modern handling facilities. Valparaiso remains the natural gateway for exported fruits from the Aconcagua valley and refined mining products which are exported by small companies from central Chile, and imports of general cargo largely destined for Santiago are still made mainly through this port.

Valparaiso is typical of port development on the west coast of South America. It is located in one of the few suitable sites in the area with some protection from the prevailing northerly winds in winter although an extensive breakwater has had to be constructed. The first section of the breakwater was built between 1912 and 1924 and stretches for 300 metres in an easterly direction. The second section was constructed between 1924 and 1930 in a south-east direction and provides a protected water area of approximately 50 hectares. This breakwater is constructed of concrete blocks and at the time of its completion was the deepest-based breakwater in the world, extending to water depths of 55 metres.

The original site of the port has been expanded by reclamation to provide a narrow linear strip of land on which a marginal quay has been constructed to provide eight major berths. Berths nine and ten are of the finger pier type and are located in the older section of the port to the north. The port is linked by road to Santiago where it connects with the Pan American Highway and by an electrified railway system with connections through to Argentina.

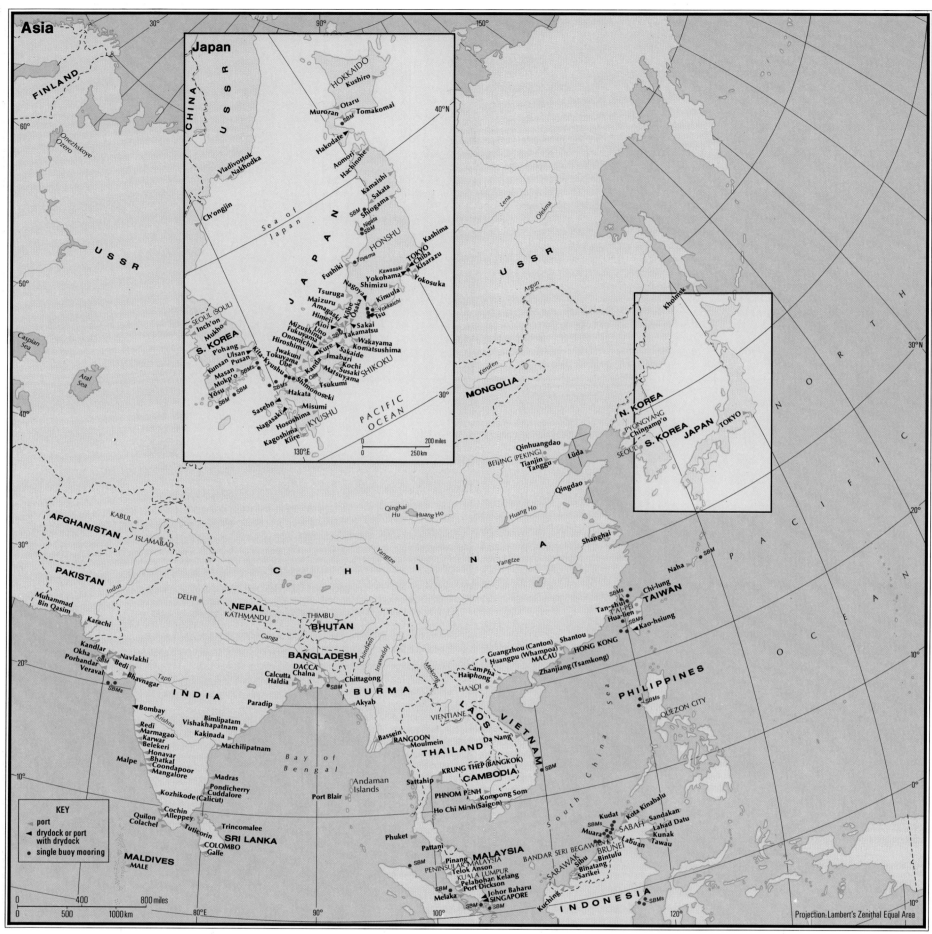

1 *main map above* The countries of Asia display a diverse geography. The dominant features are major peninsulas with long coastlines and extensive sea areas covered by island archipelagos. This is why sea transport is important in the area's domestic, regional and international trade and hence in the economic development of the countries bordering the sea.

Although the two countries are at vastly different stages of economic development, the concentration of ports in India and Japan is a striking feature. India, with its large population, boasts some of the biggest seaports in the region while Japan's rate of economic development has resulted in one of the heaviest concentrations of seaports in the world. The past two decades have seen an enormous growth in port construction and development largely funded by the World Bank and Asian Development Bank. Port facilities have been constructed in anticipation of newly discovered sources of raw materials, such as oil and gas in Indonesia. Technological changes in shipping have accelerated the need to adapt existing facilities and develop green field site expansion in other countries, notably Malaysia (Johore), Thailand (Sattahip) and Hong Kong (new territories). These developments are taking place against a backcloth of rapid economic development and industrialisation in countries such as South Korea, Taiwan and Singapore.

The location of seaports also provides a broad contrast, ranging from the enclosed dock systems of the major Indian ports, to the river sites of Chittagong, Rangoon and Bangkok and the natural bays of Hong Kong and Japan, notably Tokyo Bay and Osaka Bay. Japan, with its many islands and mountainous terrain, has a long history of dependence on sea transport, notably in domestic trades. As a result the long coastline is dotted with harbours of all sizes, many of which accommodate the major fishing fleets. The irregular coastline has produced large well-protected bays on the Pacific Ocean coast which, despite relatively shallow water, have been the sites for the development of the country's eight major ports.

The influence of the physical geography of a region on the number and location of ports is well illustrated in archipelagos such as the Philippines and Indonesia. Sea transport is extremely important to the commerce of these countries, consisting of thousands of islands stretching over very large sea areas. In many cases, the sea is the only means of commerce between islands and the main administrative and industrial centres of the country or region. Not surprisingly, they have large numbers of ports although many of them handle small quantities of cargo intermittently. In such cases a national network of major, secondary and minor ports is established with foreign seaborne trade being handled at comparatively few ports and then distributed to the smaller centres. Another contributory factor to the existence of so many ports, even on the larger islands like Java, is the poor inland transport infrastructure which restricts the movement of cargoes over long distances by road and rail.

Another feature of the region is the growth of and now intense competition between entrepot ports. Shipping economics play an important role in determining whether shipowners use a particular port. Shipowners often concentrate ships on a few ports of call and tranship cargoes for other destinations in feeder or coastal vessels. Good examples of these transhipment or 'pivot ports' are Singapore and Hong Kong. The latter owes its success to its links with mainland China and the large entrepot trade it handles.

There has been a rapid growth of unitisation in general cargo trades. The developing countries of Asia have some of the largest, most sophisticated and efficient operations in the world which handle the trade on the major European and transpacific routes.

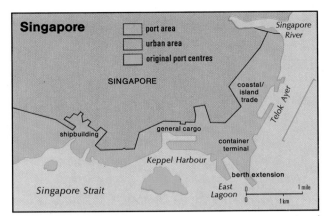

Singapore

port area
urban area
original port centres

SINGAPORE

Singapore River

coastal/island trade

Telok Ayer

shipbuilding

general cargo

container terminal

Keppel Harbour

berth extension

Singapore Strait

East Lagoon

0   1 mile
0   1 km

2 *above* Singapore's port facilities are sited on the southern coast of Singapore Island, and on islands close offshore. Founded by Sir Stanford Raffles in 1819 as a trading station for the East India Company, it was designated a free port by the British in 1824 and became the great entrepot port of South East Asia.

Singapore has few natural resources and no natural monopoly of transhipment cargo. Its success depends on its location as a focus of shipping, its reputation for efficiency, and the development of industries such as electronics and plastics together with ship repairing, food processing, banking and broking.

In addition to the original port on the Singapore river and the adjacent area of Telok Ayer, five other main port areas, or gateways, are administered or controlled by the Port of Singapore Authority.

Conventional general cargo handling facilities are centred on the 5 km of marginal quays at Keppel Wharves. Major reclamation in the vicinity of the East Lagoon provides the site of the container port of Singapore which began operation in 1972 and can accommodate the largest container vessels. The modern Pasir Panjang Wharves provide deep sea and coastal berths for general cargo trades, specialised LASH barge handling facilities and the major warehousing complex of the port. Sembawang Wharves, at the north of the island, specialise in handling low value, high volume cargoes such as timber and rubber. Jurong Port, at the south-western corner of Singapore, is the main bulk cargo handling port set up to serve the Jurong industrial estate. Facilities include 10 deep water berths and a quay length of 1792 metres. Oil tankers are berthed at terminals on adjacent islands where refineries are located. This has made Singapore a major bunkering place as well as an importer of crude oil and an exporter of refined products. Singapore also has shiprepair and shipbuilding facilities.

3 *below* Ohi container terminal, the main container and RoRo facility at the port of Tokyo. Ohi and Shinagawa terminal located close by are among the world's largest container terminals, and provide regular shipping ser-

4 *right* The port of Calcutta, situated 200 km up river from the mouth of the Hooghly, is the premier port of the eastern coast of India. This river is the western distributory of the combined delta of the Ganges and Brahmaputra. It forms the second largest delta in the world (after the Amazon) and has a high tidal range. The Hooghly river from its mouth to Calcutta is winding and has many sandbanks and changes in bottom contours. The maximum draught usually permitted is a little less than 8 metres.

Calcutta provides a good example of the problems confronted by ports in regions of sedimentary deposition. Although it has riverside jetties, enclosed dock systems had to be constructed to provide the necessary depth of water to accommodate general cargo vessels. To reach the docks, ships not only have to navigate a continually changing water area, but must negotiate sharp bends in the river and avoid sandbars which are subject to seasonal change. To enable the port to handle bulk carriers and oil tankers requiring deeper draughts, a deep water dock system has been constructed at Haldia, 90 km downstream from the existing facilities. Designed to accommodate ships up to 80 000 dwt, the long term objective of the project is to construct 6 bulk and 28 general cargo berths. The first phase of the project consists of 6 berths handling coal, iron ore, phosphate, containers and general cargo.

The site of this latest addition to the port avoids the sharp bends of the river in its upper reaches, which place restrictions on the length of ships that can enter the old port. The hinterland of the port of Calcutta has been reduced since Partition in 1947 but it is still the main port link with Delhi and the heavily populated regions of Bengal as well as the principal outlet for tea exports from Assam.

5 *below right* The primary ports of Japan have developed along the Pacific coast where there are many natural bays offering sheltered locations, and wide coastal plains. The maritime facilities of Tokyo Bay represent Japan's and the world's largest concentration of industrial ports, with the port of Yokohama as the major gateway.

The port of Yokohama handles a wide range of liquid and dry bulk cargoes, unitised and conventional cargo over a large number of private and publicly operated piers. Many industries own or lease and operate their own terminal facilities. Many of these are located in the coastal industrial zone reclaimed from the sea in huge artificial islands. Publicly operated berths are complemented by terminals leased to major shipping companies.

vices to ports worldwide. Adjacent to Ohi container wharf is the Ohi marine products wharf handling deep sea-fishing products from Africa, the North Sea and New Zealand.

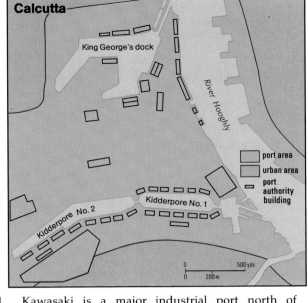

Calcutta

King George's dock

River Hooghly

Kidderpore No. 2

Kidderpore No. 1

port area
urban area
port authority building

0   500 yds
0   200 m

Kawasaki is a major industrial port north of Yokohama, where refineries, steel making, chemical and car assembly plants are located. It has terminals capable of accommodating 250 000 dwt tankers and 70 000 dwt dry bulk carriers and extensive tank storage and stockpile areas.

Expansion has also taken place at the existing port of Tokyo which primarily concentrates on domestic traffic. Although not an industrial port on the scale of Kawasaki, because of draught restrictions, it has several major industrial areas and associated bulk handling terminals and terminals for general cargo, cement, coal, timber, fish, oil and liquefied gas, and unitised trades. The main container and RoRo facility is the Ohi container terminal which comprises 8 berths with a quay length of 2300 m and an alongside water depth of 12 m. It is one of the major terminals of its type in the world, with 16 quayside gantry cranes and 362 000 square metres of storage.

Other major industrial ports in Tokyo Bay are located at Funabashi and Chiba. The latter is the newest industrial port and is located on an extensive reclaimed area stretching from the estuary of the Edo river to the Narawa region. Some 24 800 ha of this are allocated to port related industries and 690 000 square metres of waterfront area for cargo handling purposes. The port consists of 70 public and 290 private berths, mainly engaged in the bulk and semi-bulk trades, and can accommodate vessels of up to 250 000 dwt. The major industries are two large steel plants and four oil refineries. Major commodities handled are oil, liquefied gas and iron ore.

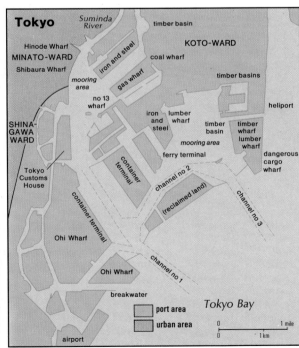

Tokyo

Suminda River

timber basin

Hinode Wharf

KOTO-WARD

MINATO-WARD

iron and steel

coal wharf

Shibaura Wharf

mooring area

gas wharf

timber basins

SHINA-GAWA WARD

no 13 wharf

iron and steel

lumber wharf

timber basin

timber wharf

lumber wharf

heliport

Tokyo Customs House

container terminal

mooring area

ferry terminal

channel no 2

dangerous cargo wharf

container terminal

(reclaimed land)

channel no 3

Ohi Wharf

Ohi Wharf

channel no 1

breakwater

Tokyo Bay

port area
urban area

0   1 mile
0   1 km

airport

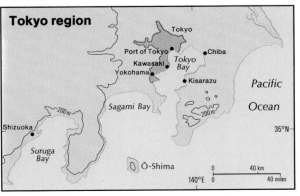

Tokyo region

Tokyo

Port of Tokyo

Chiba

Kawasaki

Tokyo Bay

Yokohama

Kisarazu

Pacific Ocean

Sagami Bay

200 m

35°N

Shizuoka

Suruga Bay

Ō-Shima

140°E

0   40 km
0   40 miles

Port development and location—Australia, Africa and the Middle East

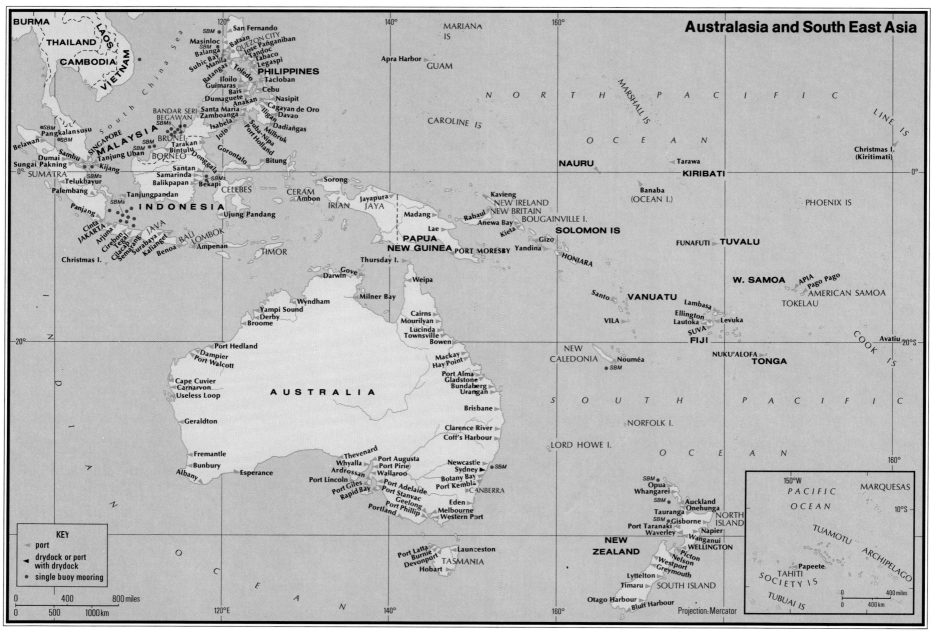

Australasia and South East Asia

Sydney (Port Jackson)

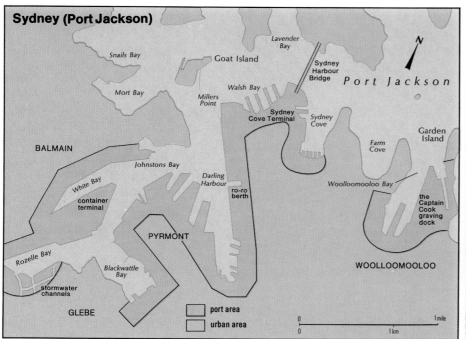

port area
urban area

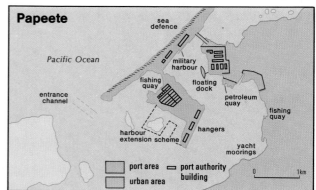

1 *main map top* The coastline features of Australasia and the Pacific range from fjords in New Zealand with their characteristically long lengths and steep sides, to the natural harbours of Australasia formed by the process of submergence and the thousands of coral islands of the Pacific.

There are some 55 ports on the Australian coast. Many of these developed as outlets for the export of wool and grain and for the arrival of immigrants and the import of goods from the United Kingdom.

Many Pacific islands are of volcanic origin and are fringed by coral reefs. Embayed volcanoes like Rabaul in Papua New Guinea and coral atolls, such as those found in the Marshall Islands, provide good harbour locations. The fringing reefs provide harbours with deep water lagoons inside. However, natural breaks in the coral reef restrict the size of entrance channels and require additional engineering works or dredging. Many of these ports are small but have provided suitable locations for naval bases.

2 *above* Situated in one of the finest natural harbours in the world, the port of Sydney is the largest port

3 *above right* Conventional berths at Darling Harbour, Sydney.

in Australia. It is a good example of port development in an area of subsidence comprising two large drowned river valleys separated by a headland. To the south the submerged entrance of Georges River forms Botany Bay and to the north the drowned valley of the Parramatta river forms the site of Port Jackson. The modern port is at Darling Harbour with extensions to White Bay, which has been developed as a container terminal. Timber is handled in Rozelle Bay, while a grain terminal and bulk soda ash berth are located at Glebe Island.

In 1971 work commenced to develop Botany Bay as a major new port location. The lack of adequate flat land at Port Jackson prompted this development to meet the needs of maritime related industries. The new port opened in 1979 to provide one of the largest container complexes in the southern hemisphere, a modern bulk liquids berth and a large area of reclaimed land for further expansion. A total of 260 hectares of land has been reclaimed and an entrance channel 1700 metres long and 19.2 metres deep constructed.

Papeete

port area
urban area
port authority building

4 *above* Papeete, the main centre of Tahiti, is a typical Pacific island port. Industry, services, population and trade have centred around the port town. The port has been built on the north-west of the island sheltered from the southeasterly winds and protected from seawards by a natural coral reef. The passage into the harbour requires dredging but vessels find a good anchorage and cruise passenger liners can lie alongside.

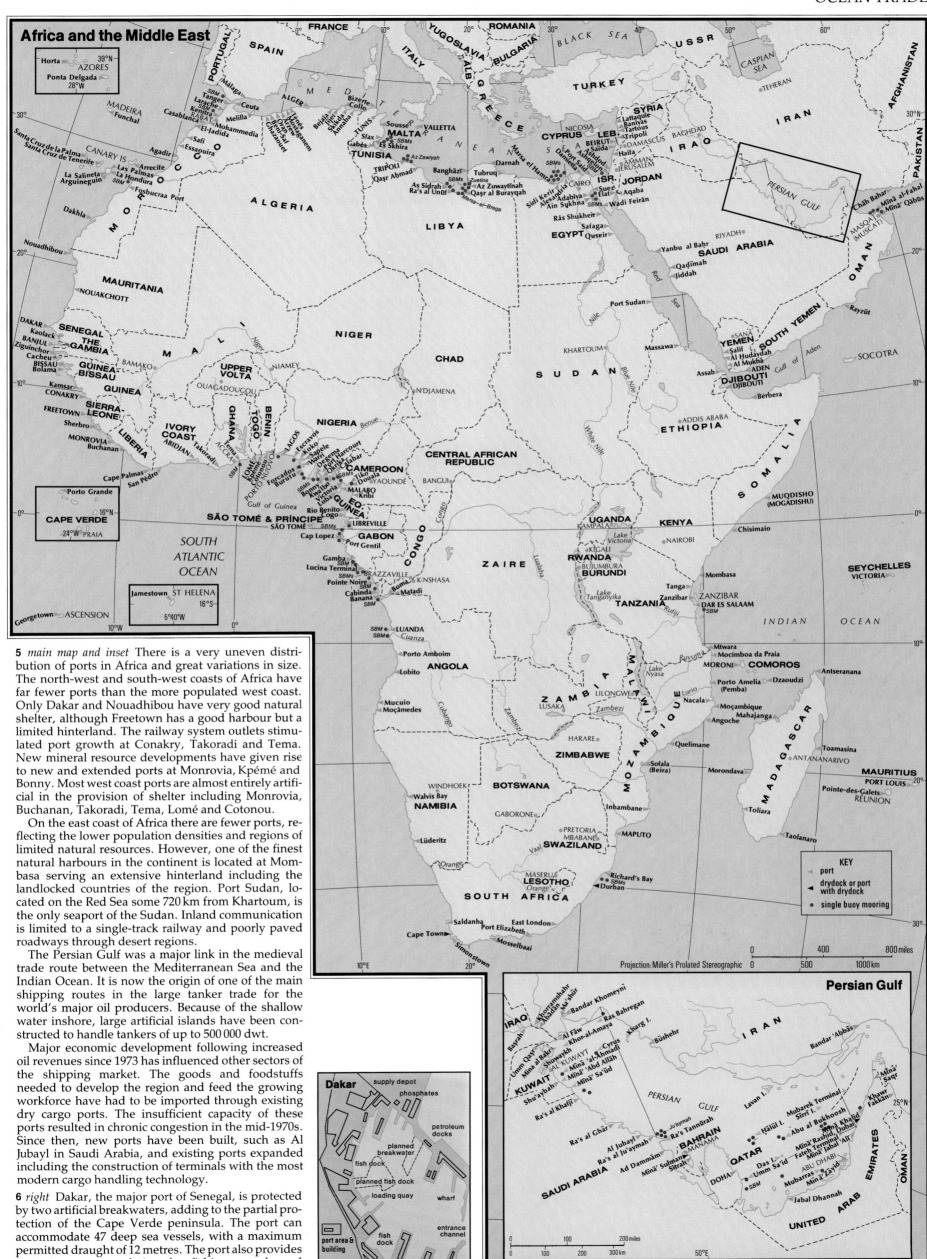

Africa and the Middle East

AZORES
Horta 39°N
Ponta Delgada 28°W

CAPE VERDE
16°N
24°W PRAIA
Porto Grande

ST HELENA
Jamestown 16°S
5°40'W

SOUTH ATLANTIC OCEAN

INDIAN OCEAN

KEY
port
drydock or port with drydock
single buoy mooring

Projection: Miller's Prolated Stereographic

0   400   800 miles
0   500   1000 km

5 *main map and inset* There is a very uneven distribution of ports in Africa and great variations in size. The north-west and south-west coasts of Africa have far fewer ports than the more populated west coast. Only Dakar and Nouadhibou have very good natural shelter, although Freetown has a good harbour but a limited hinterland. The railway system outlets stimulated port growth at Conakry, Takoradi and Tema. New mineral resource developments have given rise to new and extended ports at Monrovia, Kpémé and Bonny. Most west coast ports are almost entirely artificial in the provision of shelter including Monrovia, Buchanan, Takoradi, Tema, Lomé and Cotonou.

On the east coast of Africa there are fewer ports, reflecting the lower population densities and regions of limited natural resources. However, one of the finest natural harbours in the continent is located at Mombasa serving an extensive hinterland including the landlocked countries of the region. Port Sudan, located on the Red Sea some 720 km from Khartoum, is the only seaport of the Sudan. Inland communication is limited to a single-track railway and poorly paved roadways through desert regions.

The Persian Gulf was a major link in the medieval trade route between the Mediterranean Sea and the Indian Ocean. It is now the origin of one of the main shipping routes in the large tanker trade for the world's major oil producers. Because of the shallow water inshore, large artificial islands have been constructed to handle tankers of up to 500 000 dwt.

Major economic development following increased oil revenues since 1973 has influenced other sectors of the shipping market. The goods and foodstuffs needed to develop the region and feed the growing workforce have had to be imported through existing dry cargo ports. The insufficient capacity of these ports resulted in chronic congestion in the mid-1970s. Since then, new ports have been built, such as Al Jubayl in Saudi Arabia, and existing ports expanded including the construction of terminals with the most modern cargo handling technology.

6 *right* Dakar, the major port of Senegal, is protected by two artificial breakwaters, adding to the partial protection of the Cape Verde peninsula. The port can accommodate 47 deep sea vessels, with a maximum permitted draught of 12 metres. The port also provides extensive accommodation for fishing vessels and facilities for the handling of petroleum and fertilisers.

Dakar
supply depot
phosphates
petroleum docks
planned breakwater
planned fish dock
fish dock
loading quay
wharf
port area & building
fish dock
entrance channel
1 km

Persian Gulf
0   100   200 miles
0   100   200   300 km

133

Commodity ports

Most major ports still engage in diverse trades although there are a number of more specialised ports throughout the world. As the traffic in particular commodities has increased and the form in which it is handled has changed, so ports have had to adapt existing facilities or construct new purpose-built terminals. Until the early 1960s most ports consisted of the familiar all-purpose general cargo facilities with narrow quays and adjacent covered and open storage areas, handling all types of cargo from dry bulk to timber and break bulk. Since then there has been a move to greater specialisation in the design and equipment of port terminals.

General cargo ships have been succeeded by cellular lift-on lift-off (LoLo) container vessels carrying up to 3000 TEUs (twenty-foot equivalent units). These vessels need terminals with large land areas for storage and high capacity mechanical handling equipment to move and stack containers. Roll-on roll-off (RoRo) terminals, initially

1 *main map* Distribution of major bulk and container loading ports. Ports where large volumes of cargo originate in containers, or where enormous quantities of a single commodity are loaded for worldwide markets, tend to become highly specialised in their terminals. For example, the oil ports of the Arabian/Persian Gulf, North Africa and the Caribbean; the grain terminals of the United States, Canada, Australia and Argentina; coal ports in the USA, Australia and South Africa, or the exclusive phosphate loading gantry berths of Banaba (Ocean Island) which are gradually transferring much of the island's covering to ships for export!

2 *below* Loading iron-ore at the port of Vitória, Espírito Santo state, Brazil. The port also exports small amounts of coffee, monazite sands and lumber.

developed for ships engaged in short sea trades, have been constructed for larger vessels employed in deep sea trades. Movement of cargo between vessel and quay is by means of ship or shore mounted ramps; large areas are again needed for storage. Barge carrying ships increased in the early 1970s ('LASH' and 'SEABEE'). The barges are discharged from the mother ship and transferred alongside berths or towed directly to the consignor/consignee's premises, so avoiding the need for expensive infrastructure.

Dry bulk terminals are designed to handle large volumes of cargoes such as iron ore, coal, grain, phosphate, and cement, usually by continuous loading or discharging equipment such as conveyors. These terminals require extensive stockpiling facilities adjacent to the berths. Some bulk cargoes, such as copper, are handled as slurry (pulverised and mixed with water) and piped from inland areas to loading terminals.

Liquid bulk terminals handle petroleum and bulk chemicals as well as liquid natural gas (LNG) and liquid petroleum gas (LPG). Berthing facilities are normally at long jetties with pipeline connection to tank storage farms ashore.

The difficulties of finding deep water sites, particularly for the VLCCs engaged in the carriage of crude oil, initiated the development of offshore single buoy moorings (SBMs) which obviate the need for large-scale investment in port infrastructure but must still be constructed in protected coastal areas. The use of artificial islands, such as Das Island in the Arabian Gulf, has overcome problems of water depth and has also allowed infrastructure such as noxious gas processing plants to be located offshore. Artificial islands are being established in several areas for multi-purpose industrial port development.

Many ports have terminals for short sea ferry services or vessels engaged in regular oceanic services or cruising and these demand special facilities for large numbers of passengers and accompanying cars and also for freight vehicles which are a feature of short sea services.

3 *below* The original container terminal at the port of Singapore viewed from the control tower. Note the quayside gantry cranes and the yard stacking cranes.

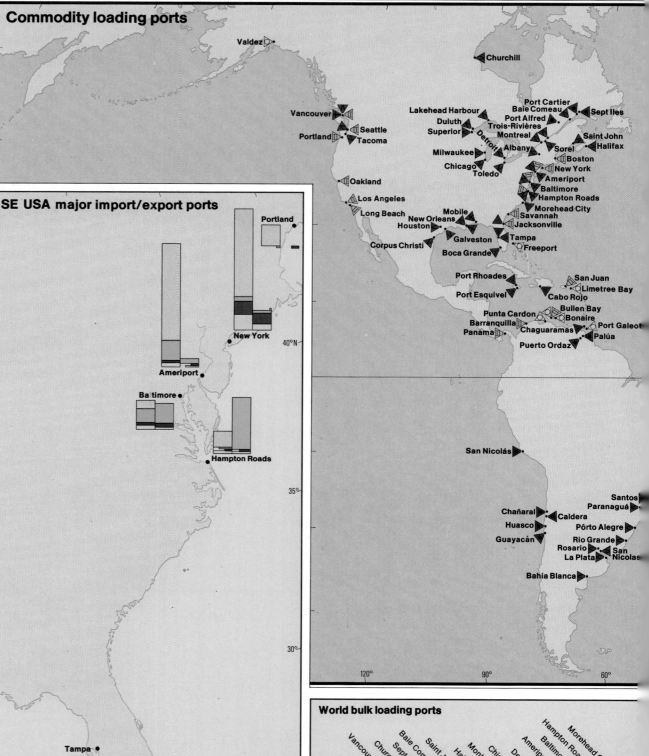

Commodity loading ports

(map with ports: Valdez, Churchill, Vancouver, Seattle, Tacoma, Portland, Lakehead Harbour, Duluth, Superior, Milwaukee, Chicago, Toledo, Detroit, Port Cartier, Baie Comeau, Port Alfred, Trois-Rivières, Montreal, Albany, Sorel, Sept Iles, Saint John, Halifax, Boston, New York, Ameriport, Baltimore, Hampton Roads, Morehead City, Oakland, Los Angeles, Long Beach, Mobile, New Orleans, Houston, Savannah, Jacksonville, Corpus Christi, Galveston, Tampa, Freeport, Boca Grande, Port Rhoades, Port Esquivel, San Juan, Limetree Bay, Cabo Rojo, Bullen Bay, Bonaire, Punta Cardon, Barranquilla, Panamá, Chaguaramas, Port Galeot, Palúa, Puerto Ordaz, San Nicolás, Santos, Paranaguá, Chañaral, Caldera, Huasco, Pôrto Alegre, Guayacán, Rio Grande, Rosario, San Nicolas, La Plata, Bahía Blanca)

SE USA major import/export ports

(chart map showing: Portland, New York, Ameriport, Baltimore, Hampton Roads — with bar charts; latitude markers 40°N, 35°, 30°)

(lower map showing: Mobile, Baton Rouge, Houston, Beaumont, New Orleans, Port Arthur, Freeport, Texas City, Corpus Christi, Tampa — with bar charts; 90°W, 85°)

only ports with import/export total over 10 million tonnes are shown (1978–82)

KEY

liquid bulk
dry bulk
containers
general cargo

import | export

(1sq.mm=approx. 400 000 tonnes)

World bulk loading ports

	Vancouver	Churchill	Sept Iles	Baie Comeau	Saint John	Halifax	Montreal	Chicago	Detroit	Ameriport	Baltimore	Hampton Roads	Morehead City
maximum quay length (m)			290	445	379		220				270		304
maximum vessel length					202								
maximum depth	15.2	9.5	11.3	8.2	10.9	13.7	10.7	8.2	8.2	12.2	10.5	10.7	12.2
maximum draft			8.2										
maximum dwt ('000 tonnes)		44									150		
loading rate per hour ('000 tonnes)	3.5	60*	8.1		1.7	2.0	1.5				6.0	9.0	

* '000 bushels

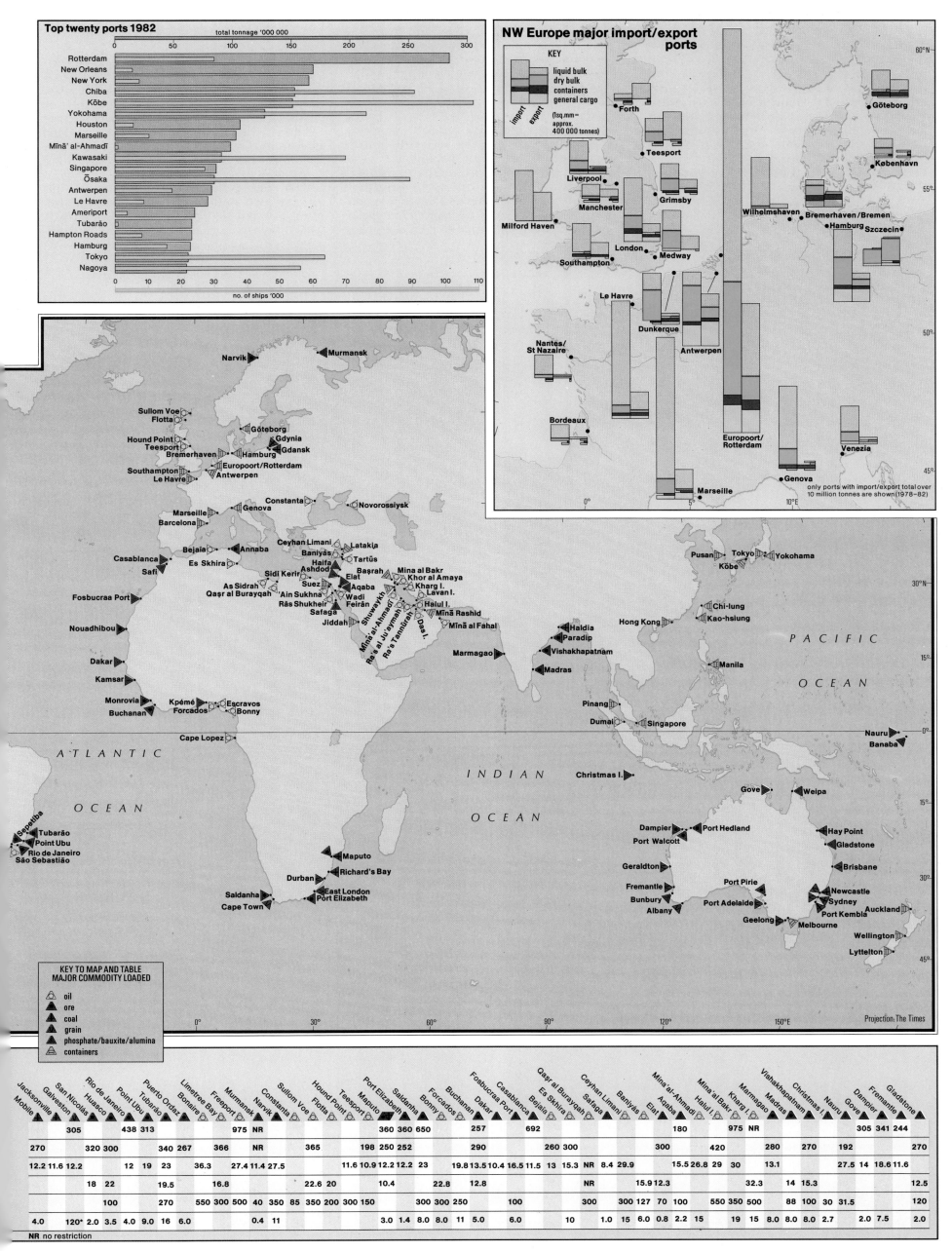

Top twenty ports 1982

total tonnage '000 000

	0	50	100	150	200	250	300

Rotterdam
New Orleans
New York
Chiba
Kōbe
Yokohama
Houston
Marseille
Mīnā' al-Ahmadī
Kawasaki
Singapore
Ōsaka
Antwerpen
Le Havre
Ameriport
Tubarão
Hampton Roads
Hamburg
Tokyo
Nagoya

no. of ships '000: 0 10 20 30 40 50 60 70 80 90 100 110

NW Europe major import/export ports

KEY
liquid bulk
dry bulk
containers
general cargo
import / export
(1sq.mm = approx. 400 000 tonnes)

only ports with import/export total over 10 million tonnes are shown (1978–82)

KEY TO MAP AND TABLE
MAJOR COMMODITY LOADED

- oil
- ore
- coal
- grain
- phosphate/bauxite/alumina
- containers

Projection: The Times

	Jacksonville	Mobile	Galveston	San Nicolás	Huasco	Rio de Janeiro	Point Ubu	Tubarão	Puerto Ordaz	Bonaire	Linetree Bay	Freeport	Murmansk	Narvik	Constanta	Sullom Voe	Flotta	Hound Point	Teesport	Maputo	Port Elizabeth	Saldanha	Bonny	Forcados	Buchanan	Dakar	Fosbucraa Port	Casablanca	Bejaia	Es Skhira	Qaṣr al Burayqah	Safaga	Ceyhan Limani	Baniyās	Elat	Aqaba	Mīnā al-Ahmadī	Ḥalul I.	Mīnā'al Bakr	Kharg I.	Marmagao	Madras	Vishakhapatnam	Christmas I.	Nauru	Gove	Dampier	Fremantle	Gladstone
		305			438	313				975	NR				360	360	650			257		692				180			975	NR					305	341	244												
	270		320	300			340	267		366		NR			365			198	250	252		290		260	300				300			420			280	270	192											270	
	12.2	11.6	12.2		12	19	23		36.3		27.4	11.4	27.5			11.6	10.9	12.2	12.2	23		19.8	13.5	10.4	16.5	11.5	13	15.3	NR	8.4	29.9			15.5	26.8	29	30		13.1				27.5	14	18.6	11.6			
				18	22			19.5		16.8				22.6	20			10.4		22.8		12.8						15.9	12.3					32.3		14	15.3										12.5	
			100			270			550	300	500	40	350	85		350	200	300	150			300	300	250		100			300			300	127	70	100		550	350	500		88	100	30	31.5				120
	4.0		120*	2.0	3.5	4.0	9.0	16	6.0			0.4	11			3.0	1.4	8.0	8.0	11	5.0		6.0		10		1.0	15	6.0	0.8	2.2	15		19	15	8.0	8.0	8.0	2.7		2.0	7.5			2.0				

NR no restriction

135

Commodity flows

THE volumes and patterns of seaborne trade reflect the world distribution of resources, population, location of industries, the characteristics of markets, economic growth rates, political and military factors, as well as short-term meteorological conditions. Seaborne trade accounts for over 80 per cent of international trade by volume. From the end of the Second World War until 1979 the growth in seaborne trade averaged 8 per cent per annum, but this rate declined with the world economic recession. (In 1980 about 3672 million tonnes of cargo was carried by sea, whereas the 1979 total was 3755 million tonnes.)

The major commodities transported are crude petroleum and petroleum products, iron ore, coal, grain, bauxite and alumina, and phosphate in bulk. Of dry cargoes, about 50 per cent are mixed products known as general cargo. This includes fruit, meat and other foodstuffs, manufactured goods, chemicals and raw materials. General cargo is carried by liner vessels, container ships, roll-on/roll-off ships, LASH ships and multi-decked tramps (see pages 142 and 148). It has a high value content and most is hauled between the developed countries; but rising incomes in a few of the developing countries, particularly the oil producers, are giving

rise to a higher demand for consumer goods.

Seaborne commodities are being transported over increasingly greater distances, e.g. iron ore from Australia to Europe, and coal from the east coast of the USA to Japan. The exception to this trend is a reduction in total distances in the crude oil trade with more use of pipelines, the re-opening of the Suez Canal, and the exploitation of oil sources closer to markets, namely the North Sea, Alaska and Mexico.

The basic patterns and quantities of commodity flows are likely to remain relatively stable for the immediate future. In the longer term (10 years) there may be a reduction in oil transport

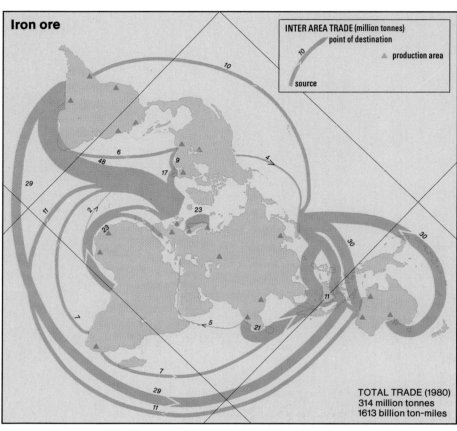

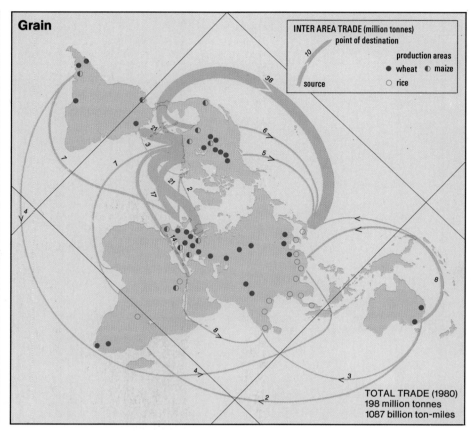

1 *above* Iron ore is the most important dry cargo in world seaborne trade. In 1980 about 314 million tonnes were transported, representing around 35 per cent of world production. This trade is determined by demand for steel. The countries with the highest ore imports are Japan, West Germany, the USA, the UK,

Belgium, France and Italy. Those with the highest exports are Australia, Brazil, Sweden, West Africa, India, Venezuela and Canada.
2 *above right* The world trade in grain changes irregularly with demand conditions, reflecting the harvest in various countries. In 1980 some 198 million tonnes

were shipped. Wheat is the principal cargo transported, followed by maize. The USA, Canada and Australia are the principal exporting countries. Grain is transported by bulk carrier and occasionally by tankers. It is a common cargo of tramp ships and has an important bearing on world tramp freight markets.

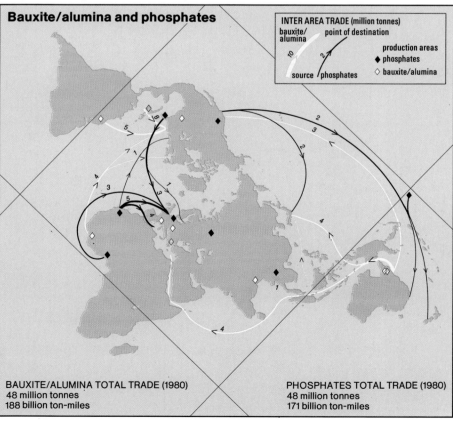

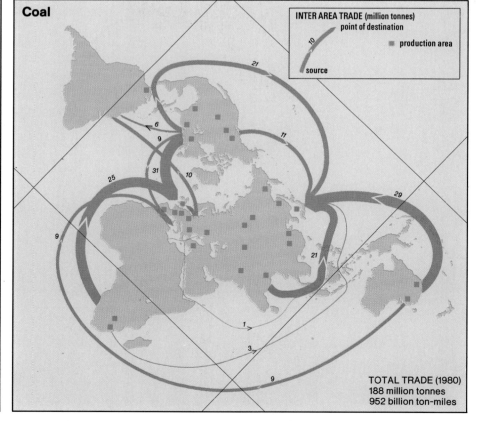

3 *above* Australia is the leading producer of bauxite (which is also exported as alumina). About 48 million tonnes of bauxite and alumina were hauled in 1980, mainly from Australia, Guinea and Jamaica to Europe and North America. Bulk phosphates amounting to about 48 million tonnes were carried during 1980 from

Morocco, USA and the Pacific islands to many parts of the world.
4 *above right* World production of hard coal is around 2800 million tonnes of which 188 million moved by ship in 1980: This is the second or third largest tonnage of dry bulk cargo carried by sea (vying with grain).

Most of the coal in international trade is coking coal used by the steel industry, and energy coal for power. The volume of the coal trade reflects the same factors governing the trade in iron ore; Japan (one-third of world imports) and Europe are the main importing areas.

flows due to opening of further sources in the Canadian Arctic and in Mexico closer to North American markets. The enlargement of the Suez Canal, new canals and greater use of pipelines will also alter patterns of trade and reduce demand for large ships. Gas carriage will certainly increase as a substitute for oil. Similarly, coal will be substituted for oil over the next decade.

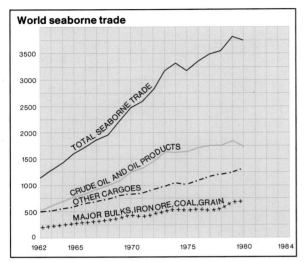

World seaborne trade

5 *above* Total seaborne trade 1962–80, with breakdowns for oil, the major bulk commodities, and other cargoes.

6 *right* Estimated trends for the major dry commodities and minor bulk cargoes, with projections to 1990.

7 *top right* There are about 22 major container routes in the world served by 463 specialised container ships with a total available capacity of 525 000 TEUs (1980). Some 180 shipping lines provide other container transport for general cargo and refrigerated commodities on various other routes. The focal points of the network are North America, Europe and the Far East.

8 *far right* The minor bulks comprise a range of industrial materials, fertilisers and agricultural products hauled by bulk carriers, conventional tramps and combined carriers.

9 *below* The pattern of movement of tankers carrying crude oil shown on the map will change with the future deepening and widening of the Suez Canal.

10 *below right* The trade in natural gas has increased greatly since 1965, with many discoveries of proven reserves. The map shows the major trade routes of liquid gas, and the graph indicates growth trends in LNG, with a projection to 1990.

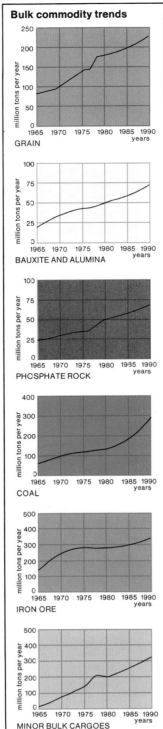

Bulk commodity trends

GRAIN

BAUXITE AND ALUMINA

PHOSPHATE ROCK

COAL

IRON ORE

MINOR BULK CARGOES

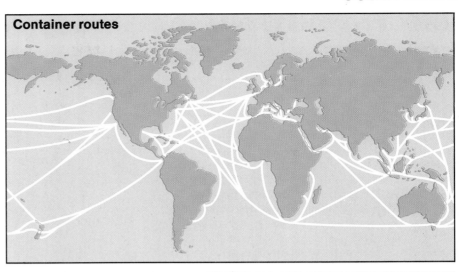

Container routes

Minor bulk commodities

MANGANESE ORE		
from	*to*	*000 tonnes*
Brazil	UK/Europe	252
Brazil	USA/Canada	73
Brazil	others	478
South Africa	UK/Europe	993
South Africa	Japan	1298
South Africa	others	746
other Africa	UK/Europe	693
other Africa	USA/Canada	189
other Africa	others	1183
India	Japan	519
Australia	Japan	613
other trades		947
total		7984

COPPER		
from	*to*	*000 tonnes*
Canada	Japan	705
Philippines	Japan	919
Papua N. Guinea	Japan	292
others	Japan	1187
total		3103

NICKEL		
from	*to*	*000 tonnes*
New Caledonia	Japan	2000
Indonesia	Japan	1310
Philippines	Japan	640
total		3950

ZINC		
from	*to*	*000 tonnes*
Canada	UK/Europe	512
Canada	Japan	259
Peru	Japan	197
Australia	Japan	272
total		1240

CHROME		
from	*to*	*000 tonnes*
South Africa	Japan	407
others	Japan	543
total		950

SULPHUR		
from	*to*	*000 tonnes*
USA/Canada	UK/Europe	1574
USA/Canada	Aus./N. Zealand	933
USA/Canada	Far East	1274
USA/Canada	Mediterranean	377
USA/Canada	Africa	1781
USA/Canada	South America	1051
Poland	North Africa	n.a.
Poland	others	n.a.
total		6990

PETROLEUM COKE		
from	*to*	*000 tonnes*
USA	UK/Europe	3550
USA	Mediterranean	1130
USA	Japan	1854
USA	others	2452
total		8986

RAW SUGAR		
from	*to*	*000 tonnes*
South America	USA/Canada	1347
W. Indies/Cent. America	USA/Canada	1517
W. Indies/Cent. America	UK/Europe	294
W. Indies/Cent. America	Japan	289
Africa	UK/Europe	929
Africa	USA/Canada	637
Africa	Japan	470
Australia/Pacific Is	UK/Europe	143
Australia/Pacific Is	USA/Canada	672
Australia/Pacific Is	Japan	793
Asia	USA/Canada	404
Asia	Japan	708
France	Africa	617
France	Asia	865
Cuba	USSR	2726
total		12411

SALT		
from	*to*	*000 tonnes*
Mexico	Japan	3759
Australia	Japan	3006
China	Japan	712
total		7477

n.a. = not available

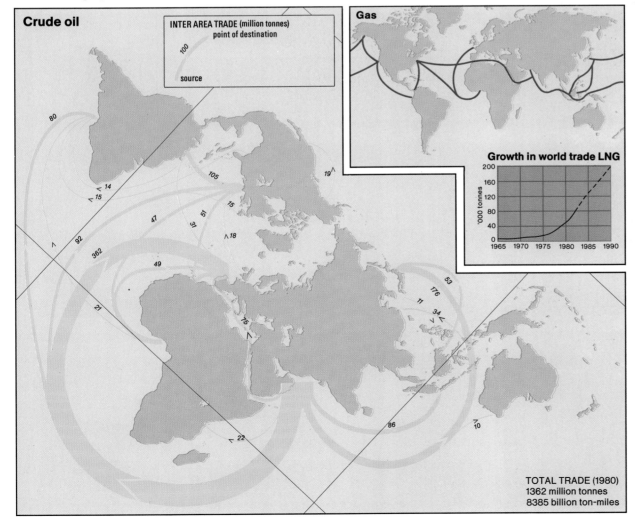

Crude oil

INTER AREA TRADE (million tonnes)
point of destination

source

Gas

Growth in world trade LNG

TOTAL TRADE (1980)
1362 million tonnes
8385 billion ton-miles

Liquid cargoes

Crude oil comes mainly from The (Arabian/Persian) Gulf to the markets of Europe, North America and Japan, and from West Africa and the Caribbean to North America and Europe. Crude oil from the North Sea is shipped to Europe and North America. In 1980 a world total of 1362 million tonnes was carried. Crude oil is hauled primarily by tankers in the size range 60 000 to above 500 000 dwt (with a predominance in the 200–300 000 dwt range), and to a lesser extent by combined carriers which can haul iron ore and other bulk cargoes on opposite legs of voyages.

Oil products include a wide range of types and grades of oil from gasoline and aviation fuel to heavy fuel oils. Cargoes are loaded mainly at refinery locations in Europe and the USA but increasingly in the oil-producing areas. In 1980 about 245 million tonnes of oil products were transported. Most of the trade is carried by some 1500 tankers in the size range 10–60 000 dwt, and by numerous coastal tankers.

The most practical way to transport natural gas over large distances is to liquefy it, which reduces its volume to 1/600 of its original. Liquefied natural gas (LNG) is transported from oil-producing areas and gas fields. Liquefied petroleum gas (LPG), like LNG, is carried by special gas tankers. It is a by-product of oil refineries and is often consumed close to areas of production. Japan is the main importer of LNG and LPG.

Many chemicals are transported in liquefied form by specialised tankers. Almost 1000 ships carry acids, alkalis, glycols, nitrates, phenols, ethylene, propylene, and raw materials in liquid form such as sulphur and phosphorus. Large chemical tankers ply routes from the Gulf of Mexico to Europe, Newfoundland to Europe and Japan; and smaller parcel tankers are used for the coasts of Japan and the USA and in European waters.

Modern merchant ships

THERE are fourteen main types of modern merchant ship, featured here. Other, more specialised vessels include carriers of wine, water, wood-chip, timber, livestock, refrigerated cargo (reefer ships), and cement, altogether totalling fifty types of merchant vessels. The world fleet of merchant ships (over 100 grt) totals about 40 500 vessels and equals 400 million grt. Over 59 per cent of the world fleet was under 10 years of age in 1980. Sweden and France had the most modern fleets (over 82 per cent less than 10 years old). Since the 1960s there has been a revolution in merchant shipping. Containerisation has reduced time in port from weeks to days and the vast increases in the size of bulk carriers and tankers have brought enor-

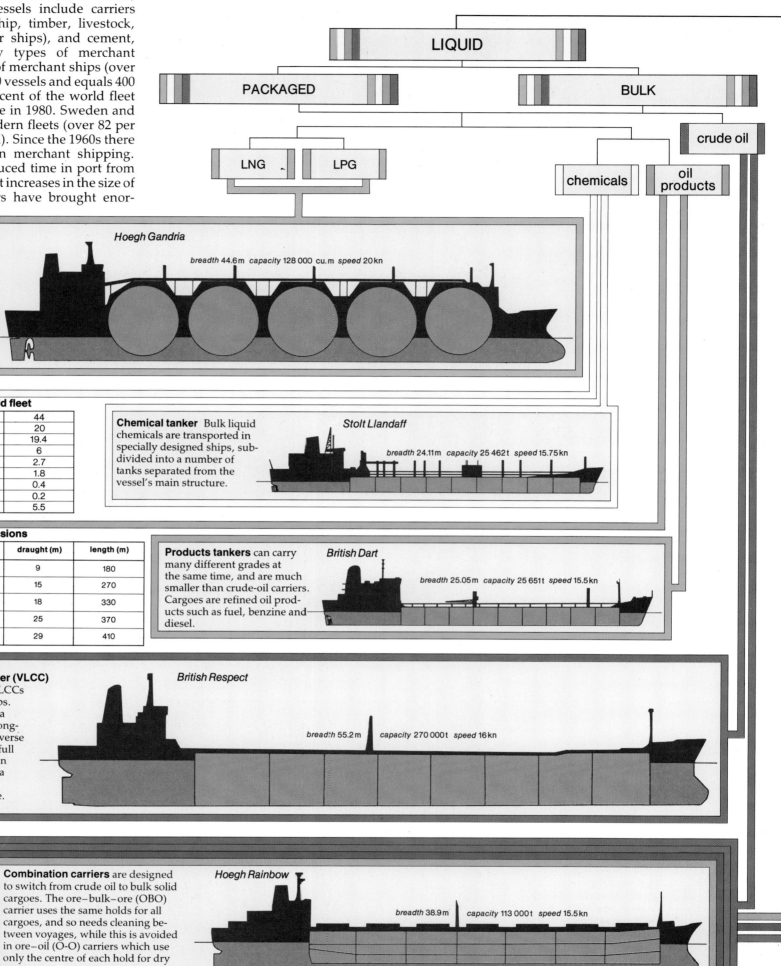

Gas carrier Liquefied natural gas (LNG) is contained in specially constructed insulated tanks at its boiling point (−161°C). LNG carriers are currently the most expensive ships in service. Liquefied petroleum gas (LPG) carriers are usually smaller than LNG carriers and their tanks can be pressurised.

Hoegh Gandria   breadth 44.6m   capacity 128 000 cu.m   speed 20kn

Percentage tonnage of world fleet

tankers	44
bulk carriers	20
general cargo	19.4
combined bulk/tankers	6
container ships	2.7
passenger/ferries	1.8
vehicle carriers	0.4
barge carriers	0.2
others	5.5

Chemical tanker Bulk liquid chemicals are transported in specially designed ships, subdivided into a number of tanks separated from the vessel's main structure.

Stolt Llandaff   breadth 24.11m   capacity 25 462t   speed 15.75kn

Approximate tanker dimensions

dwt	breadth (m)	draught (m)	length (m)
20 000	22	9	180
100 000	41	15	270
200 000	50	18	330
400 000	60	25	370
550 000	63	29	410

Products tankers can carry many different grades at the same time, and are much smaller than crude-oil carriers. Cargoes are refined oil products such as fuel, benzine and diesel.

British Dart   breadth 25.05m   capacity 25 651t   speed 15.5kn

Very large crude oil carrier (VLCC) Despite their great size VLCCs are essentially simple ships. They are subdivided into a number of tanks by two longitudinal and several transverse bulkheads extending the full depth of the hull. They can usually load or discharge a full cargo in less than 24 hours, whatever their size.

British Respect   breadth 55.2m   capacity 270 000t   speed 16kn

Combination carriers are designed to switch from crude oil to bulk solid cargoes. The ore–bulk–ore (OBO) carrier uses the same holds for all cargoes, and so needs cleaning between voyages, while this is avoided in ore–oil (O-O) carriers which use only the centre of each hold for dry cargo.

Hoegh Rainbow   breadth 38.9m   capacity 113 000t   speed 15.5kn

LIQUID

PACKAGED

BULK

LNG   **LPG**

crude oil

chemicals

oil products

mous economies of scale.

Future technological changes in shipping are likely to include developments in fuel consumption through changes from steam turbine to diesel; the return to coal burning; possibly wind-assisted vessels; more nuclear-powered craft (including perhaps submarine tankers or submarine tugs for oil dracoons in Arctic trade routes). Whatever developments occur, ships will certainly become more automated.

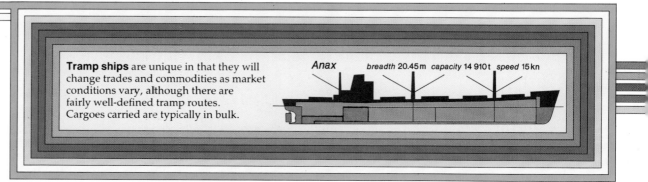

Tramp ships are unique in that they will change trades and commodities as market conditions vary, although there are fairly well-defined tramp routes. Cargoes carried are typically in bulk.

Anax   breadth 20.45m   capacity 14 910t   speed 15kn

CARGOES

The cargo types are colour coded and linked to one or more ship profiles so that the relation between cargo type and ship can easily be seen. All ships are to scale.

ship scale bar
0   50   100 m

SOLID

BULK   **PACKAGED**

timber   coal grain sugar bauxite phosphate   iron ore   breakbulk   unit loads

Bulk carrier Many of the world's raw materials are transported in bulk carriers. These are single-deck vessels with large hatchways and holds to facilitate the handling of cargo. They vary in size from 17 000 to 70 000 dwt corresponding to the largest ships that can enter the Panama Canal.

Irish Rowan   breadth 25 m capacity 26 900 t speed 15.5 kn

Ore carriers are usually strengthened to facilitate the carriage of ores and often have ballast tanks extending for the full length of the hold space along each side. They have no cargo-handling equipment.

Yachiyosan Maru   breadth 42 m capacity 122 000 t speed 16 kn

General cargo liner These multi-decked vessels have refrigeration and deep tanks. They usually carry breakbulk goods. Many such ships are in service, but they are gradually being replaced by container ships and small bulk carriers.

Ragna Bakke   breadth 21 m capacity 12 500 t speed 16 kn

Barge carrier A lighter-aboard ship (LASH) carries 70–90 rectangular barges of 370 dwt each, which are loaded over the stern and transferred forward for stowage. The larger SEABEEs carry 38 barges, each of 847 dwt.

Lash Italia   breadth 30.4 m capacity 29 820 t speed 21 kn

Container dimensions specified by the ISO are 2.43 × 2.43 m (8 × 8 ft) cross-section and 3.04 m, 6.09 m or 12.18 m (10, 20 or 40 ft) length. A 6.09 m container has a maximum payload of about 18.5 tonnes, so two cranes working 20 hours a day could handle 17 000 tonnes of cargo. Containers are also carried on road vehicles and trailers on board roll-on/roll-off (RoRo) ships.

Roll-on/roll-off (RoRo) container ship These ships transport unitised general cargoes on oceanic routes, and on a typical vessel one part is allocated to RoRo cargo while the deck and forward holds provide cellular space for containers.

Australian Emblem   breadth 30 m capacity 1450 × 7 m containers speed 24 kn

Container ship The holds of container ships are designed to take standard 20 ft containers. These ships can be loaded in 24 hours, usually at specially constructed berths. Cellular container ships have been in use since the late 1960s.

Dart Atlantic   breadth 30.6 m capacity 4500 × 7 m containers speed 23 kn

RoRo ferry Short-sea ferries are arranged so that cargo may be loaded and discharged rapidly. The cargo is mainly loaded commercial vehicles and private cars.

Duke of Yorkshire   breadth 17.5 m
capacity 90 passengers 52 trailers 60 cars
speed 18.5 kn

Car carrier Export vehicles are driven on and off this specialised ship via side ramps and 'hull doors'. There is parking space throughout the nine decks.

Toyota Maru No.10   breadth 23 m capacity 2 080 cars speed 20 kn

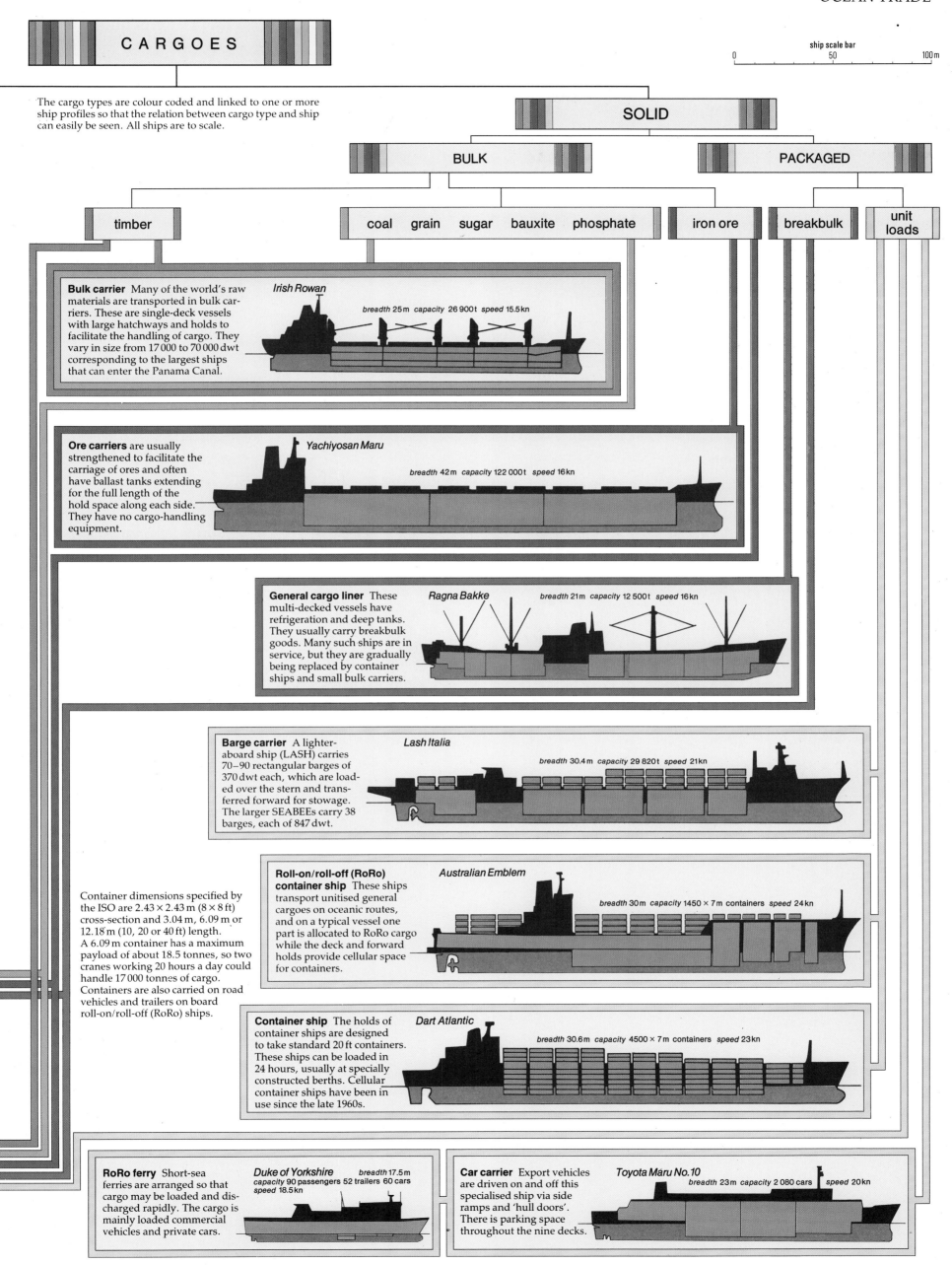

Ownership of merchant fleets

THE mid-nineteenth century saw the introduction of steam technology and with it the zenith of the British maritime trading empire. A brief challenge by fast sailing clippers was soon overwhelmed by improvements in steam propulsion and iron and steel shipbuilding, and by the opening of the Suez Canal in 1869. During this period the British were the world's major shipowners, and the most successful firms were the P & O Company, the Cunard Line, the White Star Line and the Inman Company. They received their impetus from government contracts to transport mail, increasing emigration and continuing export trade. The British maintained their position until the First World War, by which time German, Scandinavian, French, Japanese and American shipping were presenting a challenge. Three of the most notable new lines were the Dutch-owned Holland America Line, Germany's Hamburg America Line and the French Cie des Messageries Maritimes.

The pattern of world trade and shipping changed greatly during the period 1914–39. Oil imports to Europe increased and coal exports declined. As world oil trades expanded there

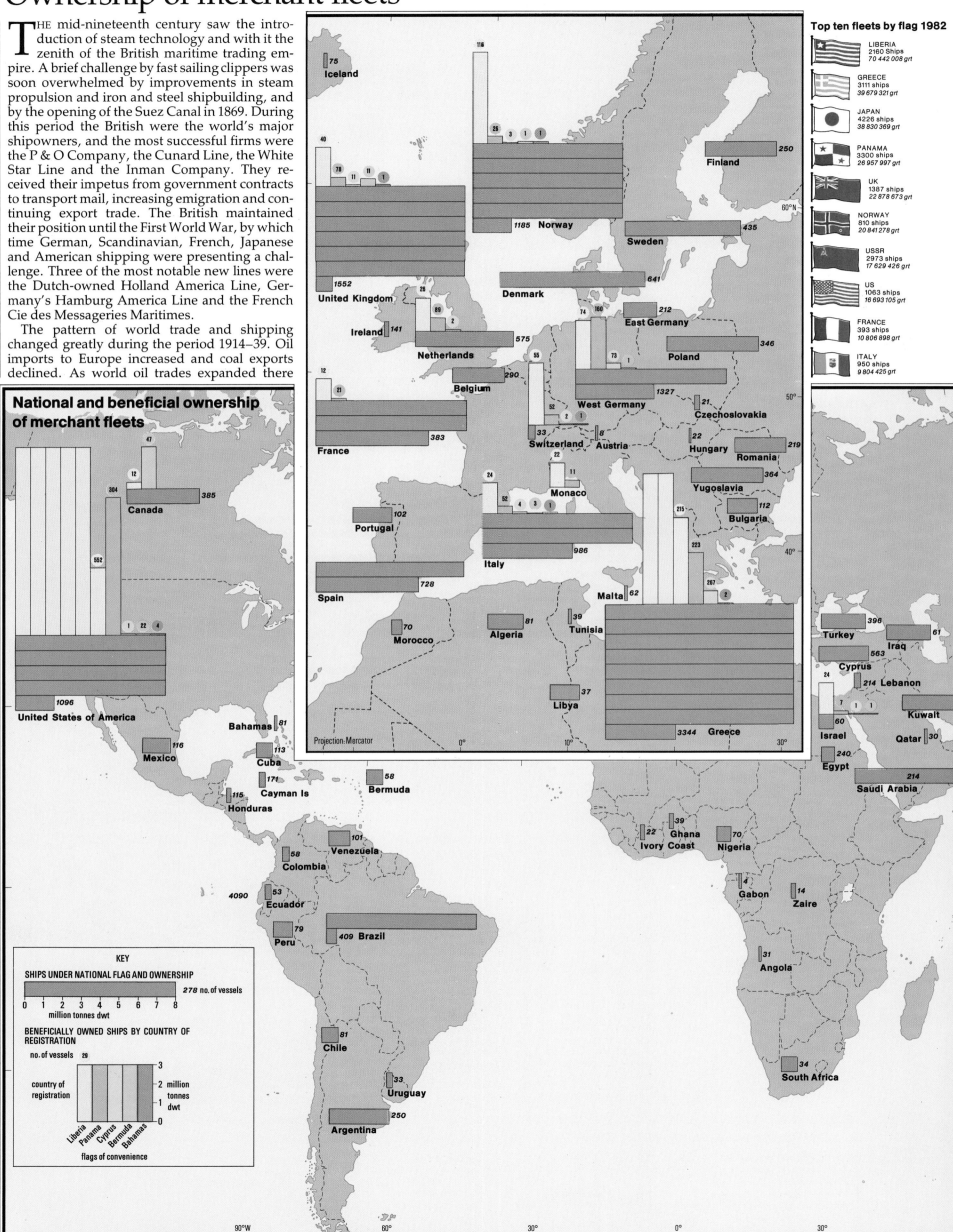

Top ten fleets by flag 1982

LIBERIA
2160 Ships
70 442 008 grt

GREECE
3111 ships
39 679 321 grt

JAPAN
4226 ships
38 830 369 grt

PANAMA
3300 ships
26 957 997 grt

UK
1387 ships
22 878 673 grt

NORWAY
810 ships
20 841 278 grt

USSR
2973 ships
17 629 426 grt

US
1063 ships
16 693 105 grt

FRANCE
393 ships
10 806 898 grt

ITALY
950 ships
9 804 425 grt

National and beneficial ownership of merchant fleets

KEY

SHIPS UNDER NATIONAL FLAG AND OWNERSHIP

278 no. of vessels

0 1 2 3 4 5 6 7 8
million tonnes dwt

BENEFICIALLY OWNED SHIPS BY COUNTRY OF REGISTRATION

no. of vessels   29

country of registration

3
2 million
1 tonnes
0 dwt

Liberia Panama Cyprus Bermuda Bahamas

flags of convenience

Projection: Mercator

was a growth in tanker fleets from 1.4 million tonnes in 1913 to 11.6 million tonnes in 1938. At this time, Western Europe, together with the USA and Japan, accounted for over 55 per cent of the world oil imports of 90 million tonnes, and the USA, Great Britain, Norway and other Western European countries owned nearly 90 per cent of the world tanker fleet.

During the Second World War the building of merchant ships accelerated. The United States was the main provider of many hundreds of standard series-built vessels. By the end of the war, the USA was the leading shipowner with nearly 30 million grt of shipping. Many of these ships were transferred to Panamanian flag of convenience (FOC) registry; others were bought by several countries to replace war losses.

Many Greeks were driven to FOC registers for vessels bought from the US government in order to take advantage of American loans which, due to the then political instability in Greece, were not available for ships to be registered in their home country. American owners were allowed to reap the benefits of lower crew costs and taxes by transferring tonnage to FOC registers, even in the case of ships of subsidised construction, provided that some were ordered in US shipyards for domestic registry.

Between 1945 and 1953, 11 million tonnes of US shipping were transferred to foreign registries (much of it to the Liberian flag). Surplus US tonnage which was not transferred or sold was withdrawn from service and placed in reserve as the 'mothball fleet'.

Of the world tonnage of 682.8 million dwt in 1980, the developed industrial countries owned just over 51 per cent, open registry countries accounted for 31 per cent, and socialist countries owned 7 per cent. The developing countries exceeded their target of 10 per cent ownership of world dwt. This group of countries will endeavour to increase their share to 20 per cent in the decade 1980–90. This may be achieved by allocating cargoes to national flag ships on the basis of 'cargo generation' (imports and exports), and by the phasing out of FOC.

2 *below* The *Bergen* (31 002 dwt) on sea trials off Bergen, Norway. The ship was built in 1977 and is registered in the fleet of Texaco, Norway.

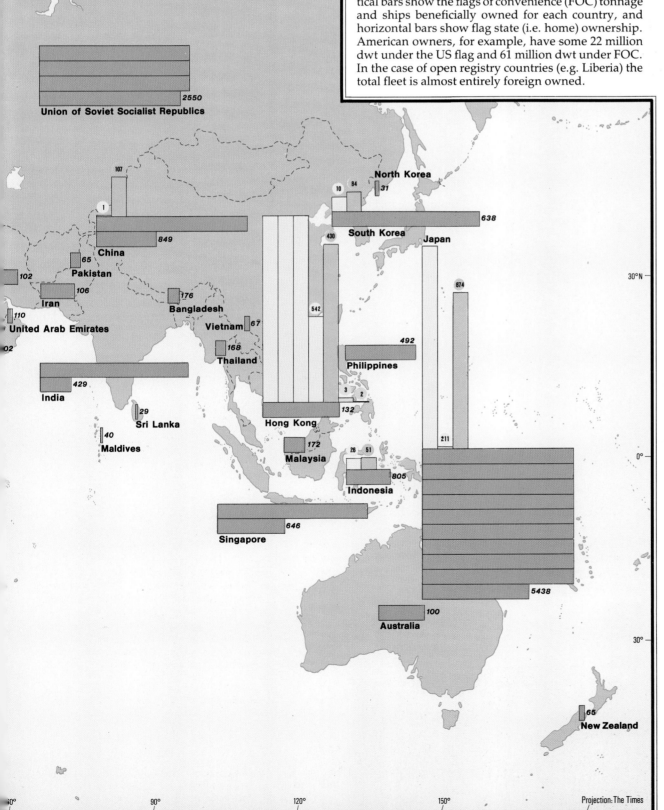

1 *map and inset* All fleets of over 100 000 dwt for 1981 (ships over 100 grt) are shown on the map by flag. Vertical bars show the flags of convenience (FOC) tonnage and ships beneficially owned for each country, and horizontal bars show flag state (i.e. home) ownership. American owners, for example, have some 22 million dwt under the US flag and 61 million dwt under FOC. In the case of open registry countries (e.g. Liberia) the total fleet is almost entirely foreign owned.

Flags of convenience

Flags of convenience are resorted to in order to employ lower-cost crew, to avoid corporation tax, and in some cases international regulations. The FOC fleets equal over 30 per cent of world tonnage. The open registry countries (those which provide FOC) include Liberia, Panama, Cyprus, Singapore, Somalia, Honduras, Bahamas and Lebanon; the Singapore government has declared that its flag will no longer be offered. The situation of Hong Kong highlights some of the many complications associated with FOC. Hong Kong owners have a substantial fleet under the Hong Kong flag; open registries are also provided under the Hong Kong flag; and some Hong Kong owners use the open registry facilities of Liberia. Similarly, there are a few Scandinavian owners who use the British flag for registration, while some British owners have their ships registered under Liberia and other FOC countries.

The main owners of FOC (the beneficial owners) are the USA, Greece, Hong Kong and countries in Western Europe. This is a situation which has met with criticism at the United Nations Conference on Trade and Development (UNCTAD), where it is argued that the developing countries whose flags are used do not receive sufficient economic benefits, and that the FOC is inhibiting the growth of developing countries' fleets. The system, it is argued, should be phased out. This is a view unacceptable to some developed countries which, because of the high costs of national crews, consider these as 'flags of necessity'.

3 *below* The graph shows the increase in tonnage (million grt) of merchant ships by type for the period 1970–81. 'Tankers' includes, from 1972, gas and chemical tankers. The world fleet increased from 33 000 ships, totalling 234 million grt (370 million dwt) in 1971, to 38 000 ships, totalling 399 million grt (683 million dwt) in 1981.

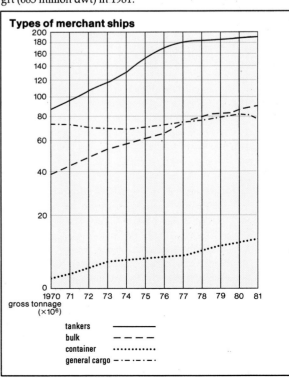

Shipbuilding

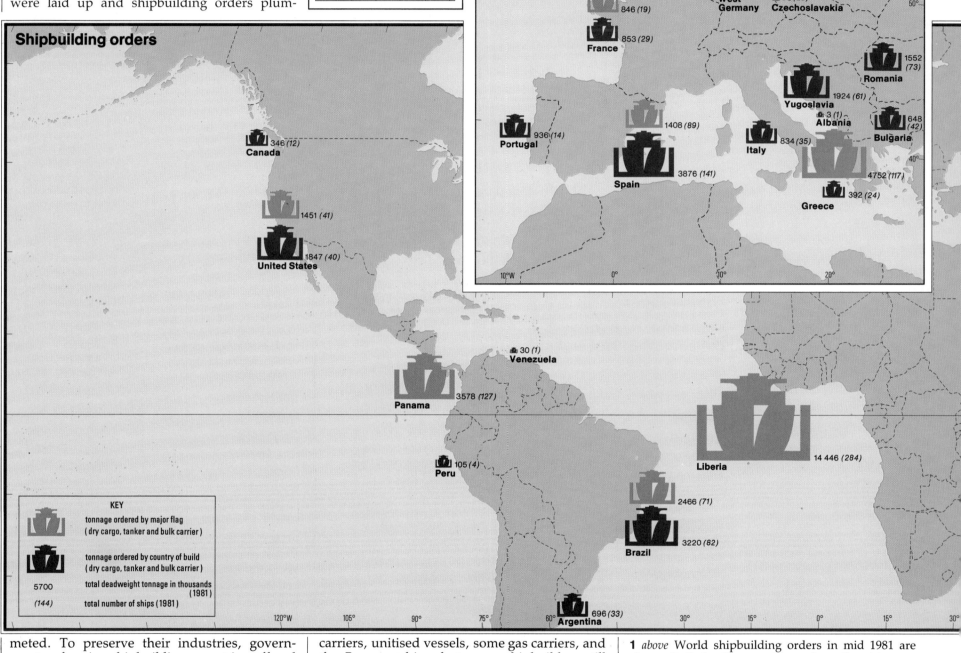

Tₕₑ post war boom in ship replacement and the demand for new types of vessels including giant tankers following the closure of the Suez Canal in 1956, led to massive expansion in the shipbuilding industry. New techniques and materials were introduced, old yards were modernised and many new ones established. The Japanese, in particular, established automated, mass-production shipyards and then offered low prices, good credit facilities and reliable delivery dates. Before the Second World War, European countries, especially the United Kingdom, were dominant; by the mid-1960s, however, Japan was attracting almost half the world's shipbuilding orders.

The oil price increases of 1973 and the recession which followed caused a decline in demand for shipping. However, vast numbers of ships were then on order and by 1977 the world fleet had excess tonnage of over 20 per cent. Ships were laid up and shipbuilding orders plum-

Shipbuilding trends

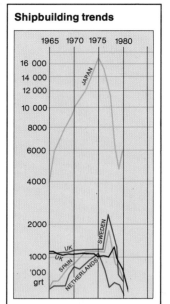

meted. To preserve their industries, governments of major shipbuilding countries offered subsidies and soft loans to induce further orders, but the crisis of demand was too formidable. Several shipyards were closed and others were adapted for rig construction. In some countries the industry was taken into public ownership in order to rationalise and preserve capacity.

The oversupply of ships remains an international problem and laid-up tonnage is again increasing. Many ships are being scrapped, and there is also disguised unemployment of tankers through the policy of slow steaming and use of vessels for oil storage. Attempts by the EEC and OECD to regulate shipbuilding and limit soft loans and subsidies have met with little success. Competition for orders remains fierce, particularly with the emergence of new shipbuilding countries such as South Korea, Taiwan and Romania.

Demand for shipping did improve in 1981, particularly for medium-sized tankers, bulk

carriers, unitised vessels, some gas carriers, and the *Panamax* ships, but many shipbuilders still depend on government support for survival. Prospects remain poor for future large tanker building and general cargo vessels.

1 *above* World shipbuilding orders in mid 1981 are shown both by the countries where the ships are being built and by the flag countries which have placed the orders. These ships, scheduled to appear on the market in 1983–84, show Japan clearly dominant with 634 vessels on order for building in Japanese yards. The orders for these ships came principally from flag of convenience owners (using, for example, the Liberian flag), and from Japan, Norway and the UK. In recent years South Korea has made the greatest relative increase in shipbuilding orders.

2 *top left* Shipbuilding trends for 1960–80 show that all countries have suffered a decline since the mid-1970s. Japan, however, is once more increasing her output.

3 *left* A ship undergoing repair in a Rotterdam floating dry dock.

5 *right* The chart represents the ships built (by grt) in each of the countries for the years 1970–80. Figures to the right of each bar are the totals built during the period, and numbers in brackets are the tonnages of vessels that were launched. Japanese yards produced 6 of the 13 million grt total in 1980.

Distribution of dry docks

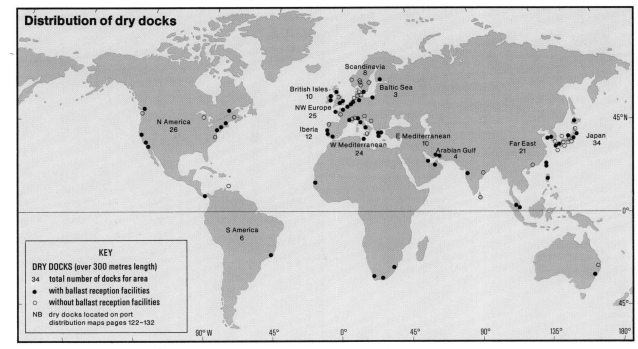

Scandinavia 8
British Isles 10
Baltic Sea 3
NW Europe 25
Iberia 12
W Mediterranean 24
E Mediterranean 10
Arabian Gulf 4
Far East 21
Japan 34
N America 26
S America 6

KEY
DRY DOCKS (over 300 metres length)
34 total number of docks for area
● with ballast reception facilities
○ without ballast reception facilities
NB dry docks located on port distribution maps pages 122–132

90° W   45°   0°   45°   90°   135°   180°
45°N   0°   45°

4 *left* The ship repair industry is distributed widely throughout the world as most major ports offer some repair facilities. Nevertheless, there are advantageous geographical locations which are close to busy shipping lanes and have good back-up links to marine supply industries. The evolution of the VLCCs and giant bulk carriers has called for the building of dry docks of enormous proportions and these have been established at focal points in regions of high density shipping such as Bahrain, Singapore and Lisbon. Others have been built at major shipbuilding centres as they can be used for construction as well as repair work. Because tankers must have their tanks clean and gas free before dry docking, and because they will be prohibited from discharging any tank washings in several parts of the sea in the future (see *Pollution conventions* page 224), many repair yards are providing reception facilities for oily ballast.

6 *above* A construction dock in South Korea. This country has had a remarkable record of shipbuilding growth in the last decade, compared with decline elsewhere.

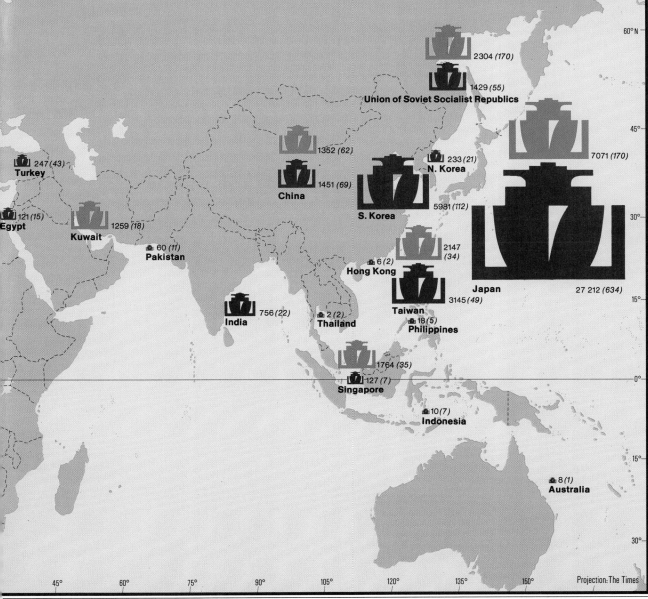

Turkey 247 (43)
Egypt 121 (15)
Kuwait 1259 (18)
Pakistan 60 (11)
India 756 (22)
Thailand 2 (2)
China 1451 (69)
1352 (62)
N. Korea 233 (21)
S. Korea 5981 (112)
Union of Soviet Socialist Republics 2304 (170)
1429 (55)
Japan 7071 (170)
27 212 (634)
3145 (49)
Hong Kong 6 (2)
2147 (34)
Taiwan 18 (5)
Philippines
Singapore 127 (7)
1764 (35)
Indonesia 10 (7)
Australia 8 (1)

60°N   45°   30°   15°   0°   15°   30°
45°   60°   75°   90°   105°   120°   135°   150°
Projection: The Times

World shipping orders

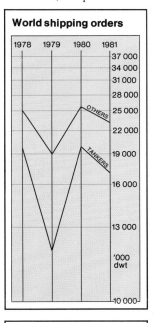

1978	1979	1980	1981

OTHERS
TANKERS

37 000
34 000
31 000
28 000
25 000
22 000
19 000
16 000
13 000
'000 dwt
10 000

7 *left* Reductions in world trade mean a decline in freight rates, ships laid up and reduced orders for new ships. For the major shipbuilding countries, the decline in demand after the 1973 oil crisis was alarming. At their lowest ebb in 1979, world shipping orders totalled some 31 million dwt.

8 *below left* Following the reduction in demand for trade there was a corresponding decline in the freight rates offered to shipping due to overtonnaging in the main trades.

9 *below* After a brief upturn, shipbuilding orders declined again and laid-up shipping has increased dramatically since 1981. At the end of July 1982, a world total of 64.5 million dwt was laid up.

Ships completed 1970–80

1 mm length represents 150 000 tonnes gross

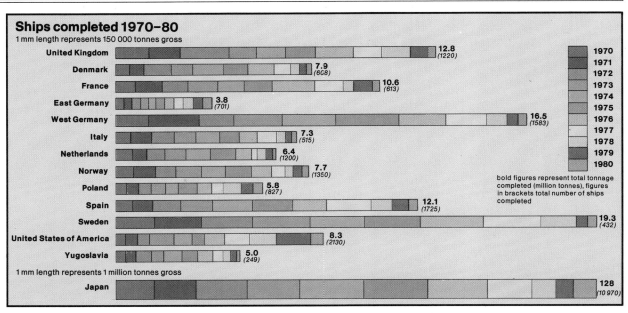

	1970
United Kingdom	12.8 (1220)	1971
Denmark	7.9 (608)	1972
France	10.6 (613)	1973
East Germany	3.8 (701)	1974
West Germany	16.5 (1583)	1975
Italy	7.3 (515)	1976
Netherlands	6.4 (1200)	1977
Norway	7.7 (1350)	1978
Poland	5.8 (827)	1979
Spain	12.1 (1725)	1980
Sweden	19.3 (432)	
United States of America	8.3 (2130)	
Yugoslavia	5.0 (249)	

bold figures represent total tonnage completed (million tonnes), figures in brackets total number of ships completed

1 mm length represents 1 million tonnes gross

| Japan | 128 (10 970) |

Tramp time charter index

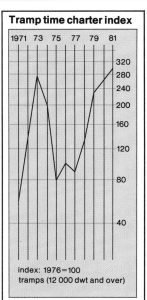

1971	73	75	77	79	81

320
280
240
200
160
120
80
40

index: 1976=100
tramps (12 000 dwt and over)

Ships laid up

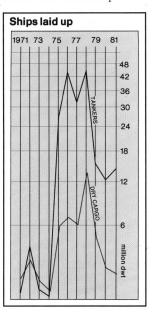

1971	73	75	77	79	81

TANKERS
DRY CARGO

48
42
36
30
24
18
12
6
million dwt

Dependence on seaborne trade

SEA transport is the cheapest means by far of moving large quantities of commodities over long distances. In 1980 a total of 3672 million tonnes of goods moved by sea, of which 1866 million were dry cargo and 1806 petroleum. A transport task of about 16710 billion ton-miles was performed by merchant ships at a freight cost of 0.6 cents per ton-mile. As a result of this economic method of transport, the world economy has been knit together by seaborne trade routes, and the trade flows (see pages 136–137) reveal the interdependencies between regions and reflect the economic relationships between the industrial countries and those with primary resources.

One of the most noticeable aspects of the world trade pattern is the imbalance that occurs between several regions and countries. The most pronounced imbalances are in relation to the producers of primary products. Saudi Arabia, for example, exports some 453 million tonnes of crude oil by tanker each year. By contrast she imports only 21 million tonnes of commodities which travel by cargo vessel. This means that tankers arrive empty and depart loaded while cargo vessels arrive loaded and depart practically empty. Similar imbalances occur in countries which produce ore and other minerals. The trade between many of the developed countries is somewhat better balanced and many ships carry various cargoes ensuring that they are full on both the outward and return legs of their voyages.

Empty haulage increases the cost of freight transport. There is little that can be done about this in relation to tankers, although the carriage of fresh water on voyages to Saudi Arabia and other Gulf countries has been contemplated.

Shipping organisations attempt to minimise this by careful route-planning to incorporate several ports in different countries, cross-trading, triangular voyages and the use of multi-purpose ships and combination carriers hauling oil in one direction and dry bulk in another. This sort of flexibility is crucial to the planning of shipping movements on an international scale.

1 *right and below right* Countries with a total seaborne trade (1980) of greater than 7 million tonnes are included in the upper map; those with total trade less than 7 million tonnes in the lower map. The USA economy generates the greatest tonnages of seaborne trade followed by Japan, Saudi Arabia, the Netherlands and France. However, some smaller nations such as Fiji which generate comparatively little trade, are almost totally dependent on sea transport (see also index *bottom*).

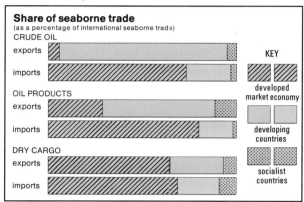

Share of seaborne trade
(as a percentage of international seaborne trade)

KEY
- developed market economy
- developing countries
- socialist countries

2 *above* The imbalances in world seaborne trade reflect the economic characteristics of groups of countries. The developed market economy group predominates in exports and imports of dry cargo and in imports of crude oil and oil products. The developing countries account for the greatest proportion of exports of oil and oil products, while the socialist countries of Eastern Europe and Asia (China) have a relatively low dependence on international seaborne trade.

Ratio of liner freight rates to prices of selected commodities

commodity	route	1970 1976 1977 1978 1979
sisal hemp	East Africa - Europe	
jute	Bangladesh - Europe	
rubber	Singapore/Malaysia - Europe	
tea	Sri Lanka - Europe	
coconut oil	Sri Lanka - Europe	
coffee	Brazil - Europe	
coffee	Colombia (Pacific ports) - Europe	
coffee	Colombia (Atlantic ports) - Europe	
cocoa beans	Brazil - Europe	
cocoa beans	Ghana - Europe	
tin	Singapore/Malaysia - Europe	

3 *above* If freight rates were allowed to rise through inefficiencies in sea transport, the movement of many commodities would no longer be viable. The graph shows freight rates as percentages of the prices of various commodities. Many exporters are greatly dependent upon the low level of these rates for the sale of their goods in distant markets.

4 *right* The two indexes (pink and yellow) show national interest in seaborne trade for selected countries. Both are derived from three factors. *Pink index:* 1. total seaborne trade (import and export); 2. seaborne trade as a percentage of gross national product; 3. size of merchant fleet by flag (home ownership and open registry). *Yellow index:* factors 1. and 2. as above; 3. total merchant fleet including the country's flag of convenience ships (i.e. its beneficial ownership). The numbers on the scale are simply to indicate the countries' relative positions.

In both indexes Japan is shown to have a very high dependence on maritime trade followed by Saudi Arabia, Kuwait, the Netherlands and the USA. Liberia has a low dependence on sea transport other than as an open registry country.

Index of national interest in seaborne trade

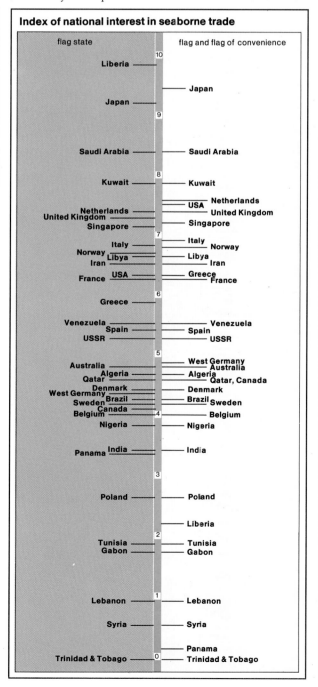

flag state | flag and flag of convenience

flag state		flag and flag of convenience
Liberia	10	Japan
Japan	9	Saudi Arabia
Saudi Arabia		Saudi Arabia
Kuwait	8	Kuwait
		Netherlands
Netherlands		USA
United Kingdom		United Kingdom
Singapore	7	Singapore
Italy		Italy
Norway Libya		Norway
Iran		Libya
France USA		Iran
		Greece France
Greece	6	
Venezuela		Venezuela
Spain		Spain
USSR	5	USSR
Australia		West Germany Australia
Algeria		Algeria
Qatar		Qatar, Canada
Denmark		Denmark
West Germany Brazil		Brazil
Sweden Canada		Sweden
Belgium	4	Belgium
Nigeria		Nigeria
Panama India		India
	3	
Poland		Poland
		Liberia
	2	
Tunisia		Tunisia
Gabon		Gabon
Lebanon	1	Lebanon
Syria		Syria
		Panama
Trinidad & Tobago	0	Trinidad & Tobago

World seaborne trade imports/exports

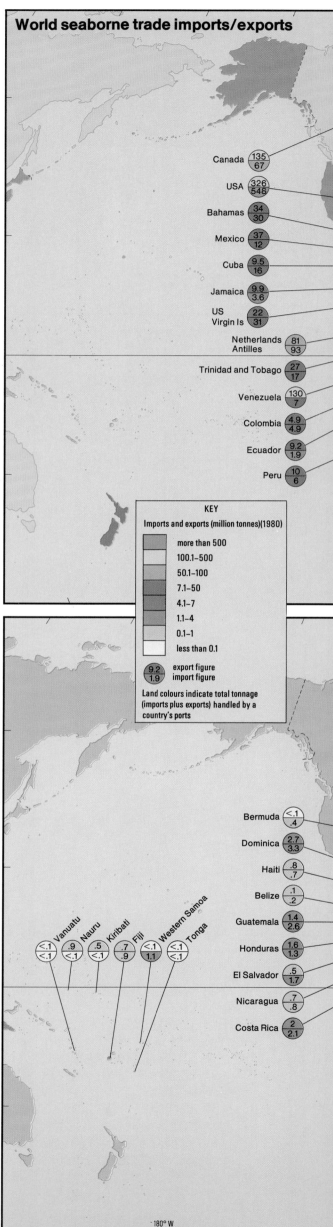

	export / import (million tonnes)
Canada	135 / 67
USA	326 / 546
Bahamas	34 / 30
Mexico	37 / 12
Cuba	9.5 / 16
Jamaica	9.9 / 3.6
US Virgin Is	22 / 31
Netherlands Antilles	81 / 93
Trinidad and Tobago	27 / 17
Venezuela	130 / 7
Colombia	4.9 / 4.9
Ecuador	9.2 / 1.9
Peru	10 / 6
Bermuda	<.1 / .4
Dominica	2.7 / 3.3
Haiti	.8 / .7
Belize	.1 / .2
Guatemala	1.4 / 2.6
Honduras	1.6 / 1.3
El Salvador	.5 / 1.7
Nicaragua	.7 / .8
Costa Rica	2 / 2.1
Vanuatu	<.1 / <.1
Nauru	.9 / <.1
Kiribati	.5 / <.1
Fiji	.7 / .9
Western Samoa	<.1 / 1.1
Tonga	<.1 / <.1

KEY
Imports and exports (million tonnes)(1980)
- more than 500
- 100.1–500
- 50.1–100
- 7.1–50
- 4.1–7
- 1.1–4
- 0.1–1
- less than 0.1

9.2 export figure
1.9 import figure

Land colours indicate total tonnage (imports plus exports) handled by a country's ports

180° W

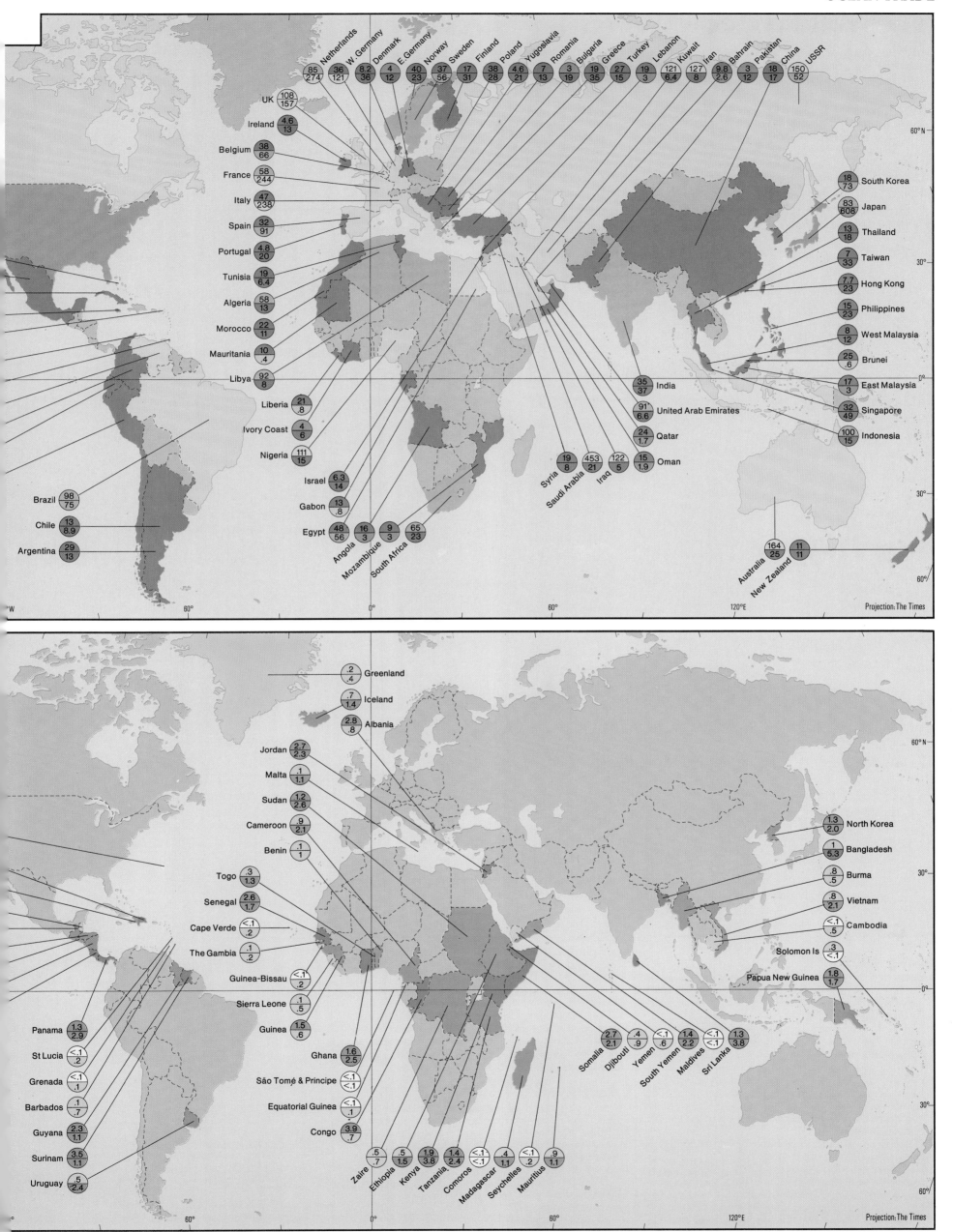

Netherlands 85/274
W. Germany 36/121
Denmark 8.2/36
E.Germany 4/12
Norway 40/23
Sweden 37/56
Finland 17/31
Poland 38/28
Yugoslavia 4.6/21
Romania 7/13
Bulgaria 3/19
Greece 19/35
Turkey 27/15
Lebanon 19/3
Kuwait 121/6.4
Iran 127/8
Bahrain 9.8/2.6
Pakistan 3/12
China 18/17
USSR 150/52

UK 108/157
Ireland 4.6/13
Belgium 38/66
France 58/244
Italy 47/238
Spain 32/91
Portugal 4.8/20
Tunisia 19/6.4
Algeria 58/13
Morocco 22/11
Mauritania 10/.4
Libya 92/8
Liberia 21/.8
Ivory Coast 4/6
Nigeria 111/15
Israel 6.3/14
Gabon 13/.8
Egypt 48/56

Angola 16/3
Mozambique 9/3
South Africa 65/23

Syria 19/8
Saudi Arabia 453/21
Iraq 122/5
Oman 15/1.9
Qatar 24/1.7
United Arab Emirates 91/6.6
India 35/37

South Korea 18/73
Japan 83/608
Thailand 13/18
Taiwan 7/33
Hong Kong 7.7/23
Philippines 15/23
West Malaysia 8/12
Brunei 25/.6
East Malaysia 17/3
Singapore 32/49
Indonesia 100/15

Brazil 98/75
Chile 13/8.9
Argentina 29/13

Australia 164/25
New Zealand 11/11

Greenland .2/.4
Iceland .7/1.4
Albania 2.8/.8

Jordan 2.7/2.3
Malta .1/1.1
Sudan 1.2/2.6
Cameroon .9/2.1
Benin .1/1
Togo .3/1.3
Senegal 2.6/1.7
Cape Verde <.1/2
The Gambia .1/2
Guinea-Bissau <.1/2
Sierra Leone .1/.5
Guinea 1.5/.6
Ghana 1.6/2.5
São Tomé & Principe <.1/<.1
Equatorial Guinea <.1/.1
Congo 3.9/.7

North Korea 1.3/2.0
Bangladesh 1/5.3
Burma .8/.5
Vietnam .8/2.1
Cambodia <.1/.5
Solomon Is .3/<.1
Papua New Guinea 1.8/1.7

Panama 1.3/2.9
St Lucia <.1/.2
Grenada <.1/.1
Barbados .1/.7
Guyana 2.3/1.1
Surinam 3.5/1.1
Uruguay .5/2.4

Zaire .5/.7
Ethiopia .5/1.5
Kenya 1.9/3.8
Tanzania 1.4/2.4
Comoros <.1/<.1
Madagascar .4/1.1
Seychelles <.1/.2
Mauritius .9/1.1

Somalia 2.7/2.1
Djibouti .4/.9
Yemen <.1/.6
South Yemen 1.4/2.2
Maldives <.1/<.1
Sri Lanka 1.3/3.8

Projection: The Times

145

The world pattern

THE main ocean routes of world shipping changed radically with the transition from sail to steam, and they have changed again over the past fifty years. Before the Second World War the North Atlantic was the busiest route regularly plied by large passenger vessels and cargo ships. Tramp ships transported coal outwards from Britain to the world's coaling stations, including Gibraltar, Port Said, Aden, Colombo, Panama, Suva, Singapore and Hong Kong, and liners called at these ports for bunkers. Grain cargoes from the Plate, timber from Canada and the Baltic, and raw materials from Africa, India and South East Asia were shipped to Europe, much of this through the canal routes.

The Panama and Suez Canals are still foci of world shipping but the Cape of Good Hope route now sees over 200 large ships per day passing en route from and to the Persian Gulf ports, Iran, East Africa, South East Asia and Australia. The deepening of the Suez Canal is redirecting more traffic back to the Mediterranean and Red Sea routes but the very large loaded tankers still continue around the Cape. Some passages have been made through the Straits of Magellan in recent years to avoid the congestion in the Panama Canal.

Recent increases in traffic have been on the short sea ferry services in north-west Europe and the Mediterranean, and in the shipping around South East Asia.

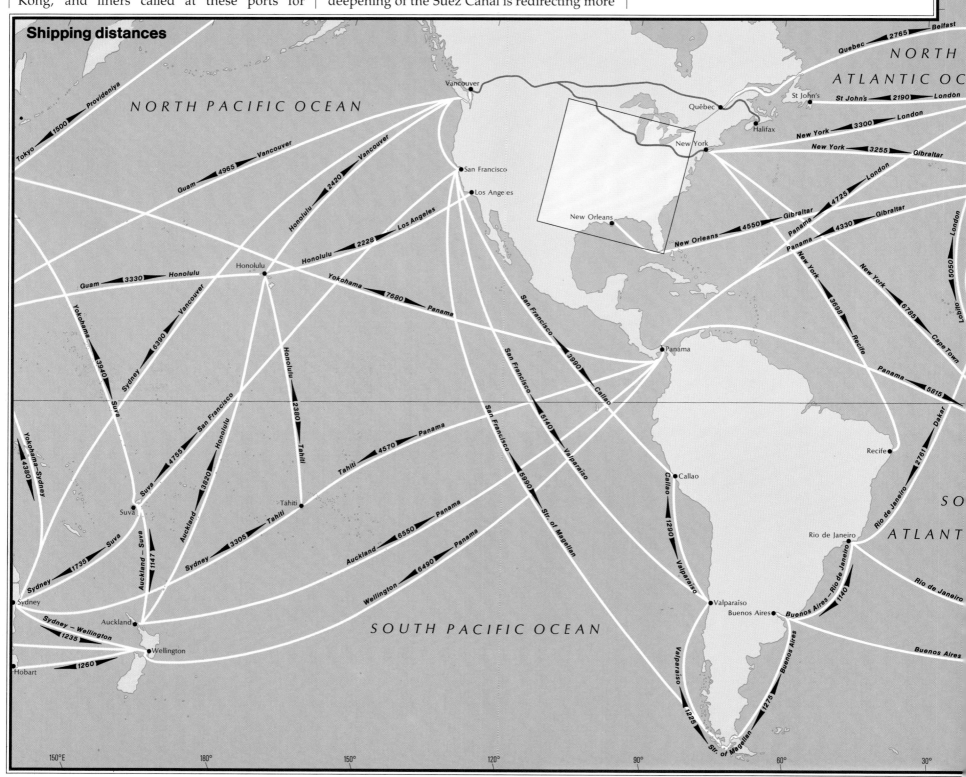

Shipping distances

Land bridges

Containerisation has encouraged the development of land bridges using high capacity railway links between ports at opposite sides of land masses for onward movement by sea. The most important railway land bridge links are the Trans-Siberian and the United States. The goods are generally transported on a 'through-rate' basis from origin to destination. There is also a land bridge across Canada from the port of Halifax to Vancouver; another is being developed across Mexico. Road land bridges link the port of Eilat on the Gulf of Aqaba with Ashdod and Haifa on the Mediterranean; and Syrian Mediterranean ports with Iran and Kuwait.

The Trans-Siberian land bridge conveys containers from Europe on the Trans-Siberian route via Nakhodka and Vladivostock to Hong Kong, Japan, and South East Asia. It grew in importance during the closures of the Suez Canal and continues to be used at a rate of about 2000 containers per month. This route is likely to increase for container traffic and provide formidable competition to container shipping for high value commodities between Western Europe and Japan. The Baikal–Amure–Magistrale branch of the Trans-Siberian railway should be completed by 1985, with a new port at Sovetskaya Gavan.

The United States land bridge links US east and west coast ports and is used mainly for containers moving between Europe and Japan. This route reduces the sea transit by seven days as compared with the Panama Canal route. It is also used for cargoes from Europe destined for the US west coast, and from Japan for the US east coast (the 'mini-bridge').

1 *main map* Shipping trunk routes between major ports or port representing a shipping area, such as London, are shown, with distances in nautical miles. Other sea distances are given in Appendix VII. Points of convergence for ocean shipping are still the principal straits and headlands and islands. Feeder routes (not shown) radiate from the major ports, and there is increasing use of barges from ports on the estuaries of some of the great rivers. Land bridges provide the overland transport links between legs of an ocean journey.

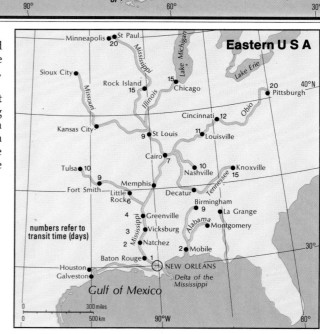

Eastern U S A

numbers refer to transit time (days)

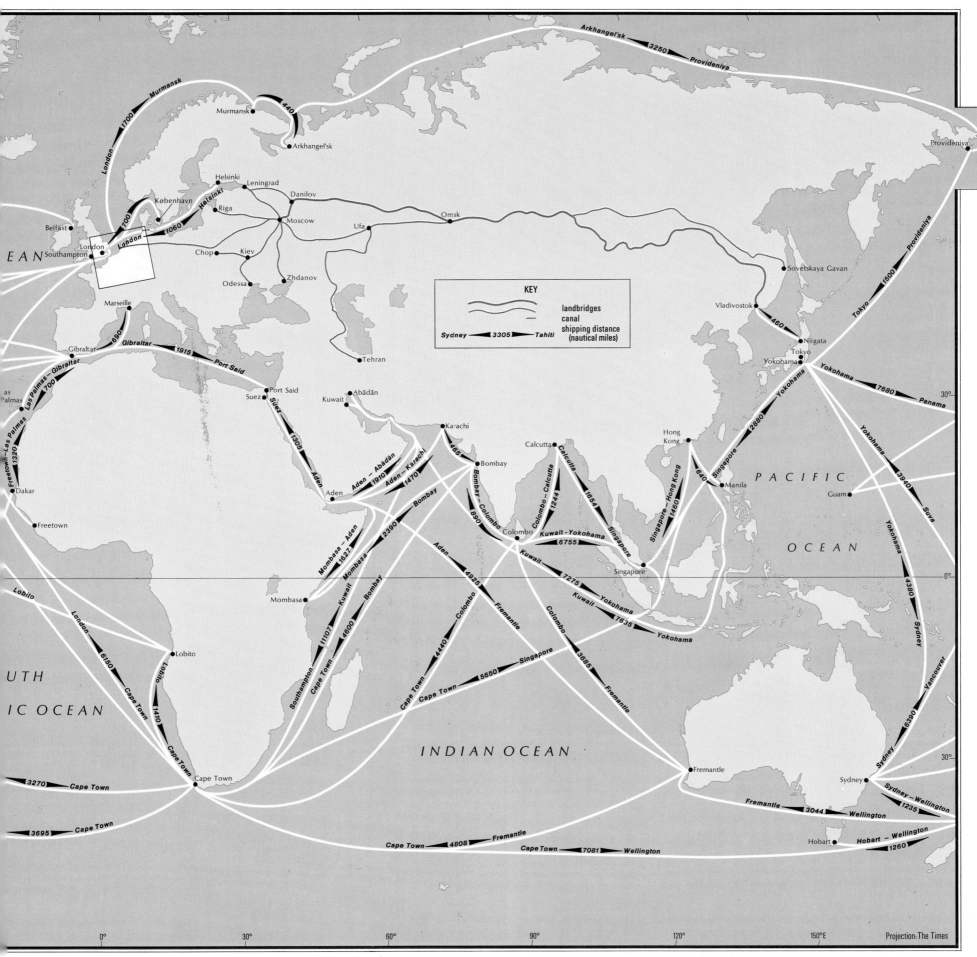

KEY

～～～ landbridges
──── canal

Sydney ◄──3305──► Tahiti   shipping distance (nautical miles)

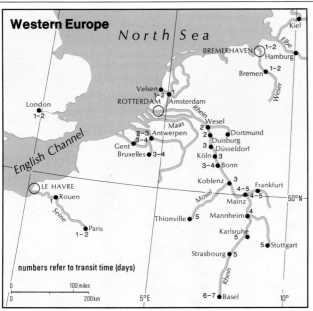

Western Europe

North Sea

BREMERHAVEN 1–2
Kiel
Elbe
Hamburg 1–2
Bremen 1–2
Weser

Velsen 1–2
ROTTERDAM Amsterdam
Maas Rhein Wesel
Antwerpen 2–3 Dortmund
Gent 3–4 Duisburg 2
Bruxelles 3–4 Düsseldorf 3
Köln 3
Bonn 3–4
Koblenz 3
London 1–2
Mosel 4–5 Frankfurt 4–5
English Channel
LE HAVRE
Rouen 1
Seine Mainz 4–5
Thionville 5 Mannheim 4
Paris 1–2 Karlsruhe 5
Strasbourg 5 Stuttgart 5
Rhein
6–7 Basel

numbers refer to transit time (days)

0 ─── 100 miles
0 ─── 200 km

2 *far left and* **3** *left* Inland extensions of maritime transport. In the past barges have been loaded at sea ports with transhipment cargoes from overseas ships. The barges then carry the cargoes to inland river ports. More recently barges have been carried aboard ships already loaded and the inland delivery made without intermediate loading and unloading. The three main systems are the LASH (lighter aboard ship), SEABEE and BACAT (barge aboard catamaran).

The USA has the most developed barge transport system, with trade to and from ports on the Mississippi and its tributaries. The map *(far left)* shows the inland origins and destinations of barge penetration of the USA and transit time in days to New Orleans, where the LASH vessels berth.

In Europe, LASH barge transport is still developing. The main activities are on the Rhine and its tributaries. The map *(left)* shows LASH origins and destinations on European waterway systems, and transit times in days to Rotterdam. When the Rhine–Main–Danube canal system is complete barges will travel as far as Romania.

4 *below* Barge carriers such as this Lykes Lines Seabee carry all forms of cargo such as containers, liquids, bulk refrigerated goods and vehicles but these are preloaded on to barges. An elevator platform fitted at the stern transports the barges on to one of the Seabee's three continuous decks which can hold up to 38 barges of 850 dwt each. This system reduces loading costs and time, and losses through damage and pilfering.

Seasonal shipping routes

THE Arctic Ocean has an area of about 12.2 million sq. km of which 11.7 million sq. km is ice covered in winter and 5.2 million sq. km in summer. The ocean has depths between 4000 m and 5000 m towards the Pole but is shallow in the Alaskan Coast and in Siberian coastal waters. Despite the appalling conditions of ice, storms, fog, low temperatures (−30°C to −45°C in winter) and overcast skies, navigation has always been possible in modern times during at least part of the year. The navigational season is continuously being extended with improvements in ice reconnaissance and ship design.

Since the voyage of the US nuclear-powered submarine *Nautilus* under the Arctic ice cap in 1958 there has been considerable use of submarine routes below the ice by military vessels. There has been consideration given to nuclear-powered submarine oil tankers or nuclear tugs towing oil barges below the surface.

The most immediate prospects for increased navigation in the Arctic in order to reduce distances, or to develop the hydrocarbons and mineral resources, lie in the use of large powerful surface vessels, some nuclear powered, and for sections of the routes accompanied by icebreakers.

A new trans-polar surface route was successfully explored in August 1977 when the Soviet vessel *Artica* made a voyage from Murmansk to the North Pole in eight days. This indicated the feasibility of very high latitude voyages following a direct route across the Arctic Ocean. This route is about 750 nm shorter than the Siberian Coastal Route between the east and west of the USSR and the ice is often thinner than that encountered on the margins of the land.

In the Canadian Arctic the exploitation of the natural gas of Melville Island, oil in the Beaufort Sea, and the mineral deposits of Baffin Island, and other areas, will require massively powerful vessels. Such a ship is the Canadian Oil/LNG ice-breaking tanker *Canmar Kigoriak* which made a passage to the Beaufort Sea in September 1979 having broken through severe multi year ice while traversing the North West Passage. In October she broke through the Polar Ice Packs. Special ice designed vessels will also include several 140 000 cubic m gas carriers for Arctic voyages. These are already designed and may be operational in the Arctic in the near future.

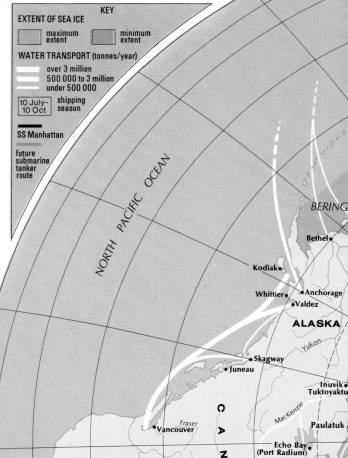

Arctic trade routes and future submarine routes

KEY

EXTENT OF SEA ICE

maximum extent / minimum extent

WATER TRANSPORT (tonnes/year)
over 3 million
500 000 to 3 million
under 500 000

10 July–10 Oct   shipping season

SS Manhattan

future submarine tanker route

North Pacific weather routeing

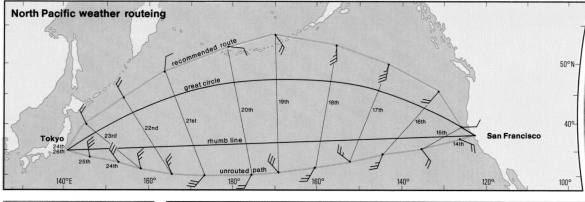

1 *above* In the case of the westerly voyage across the Pacific, weather routeing provided calm weather and the saving over an unrouted vessel of two days.

2 *right* In the case of the Atlantic example the non-routed ship ran into a deep depression which resulted in a loss of 14 days compared with the routed vessel.

KEY
BEAUFORT WIND SCALE

force 3   force 8

(half tooth=force 1 / one tooth=force 2)
direction of wind towards black dot at end of arm

15th   number of days from start of voyage

North Atlantic weather routeing

3 *below* The SS Manhattan crossing the North West Passage. She was the first commercial ship to test the Passage, having been converted in 1969 into an ice-breaking super-tanker to pioneer an Arctic sea route for oil transport between Alaska and the Atlantic Ocean. Despite a successful voyage, it was concluded that the Alaskan pipeline was the most economic vehicle for transporting oil from the North Slope to an ice-free tanker terminal on the west coast.

Weather routeing

Ships voyaging in both the North Atlantic and North Pacific experience notoriously bad weather conditions. Ice, fog and depressions are common in these regions and ships are often forced, especially during the winter months, to divert from the shortest routes.

Distance, time, and safety have to be balanced when a route is chosen. The master of a ship might, for example, wish to follow a great circle route across the Atlantic as it is the shortest distance on a sphere, but this is liable to carry him into regions of ice or bad weather, and he may therefore choose a composite great circle so as to avoid going too far north. For voyages over shorter distances than passages across the Atlantic or Pacific a rhumb line track is usually followed. Though this is a straight line on a mercator chart it is not the shortest distance. Unlike the great circle, however, it does not require continued alterations of course.

More recently seamen have sought the optimum route which takes account of weather conditions based on analysis and prediction. This is known as weather routeing and involves analysis of all available meteorological and oceanographic information to predict the most favourable passage for a vessel. The methods of weather routeing to give the optimum route are becoming well established in the Atlantic. It has the advantage of avoiding ship and cargo damage by routeing a vessel through regions of lowest wave gradients and results in shorter journeys and correspondingly lower costs.

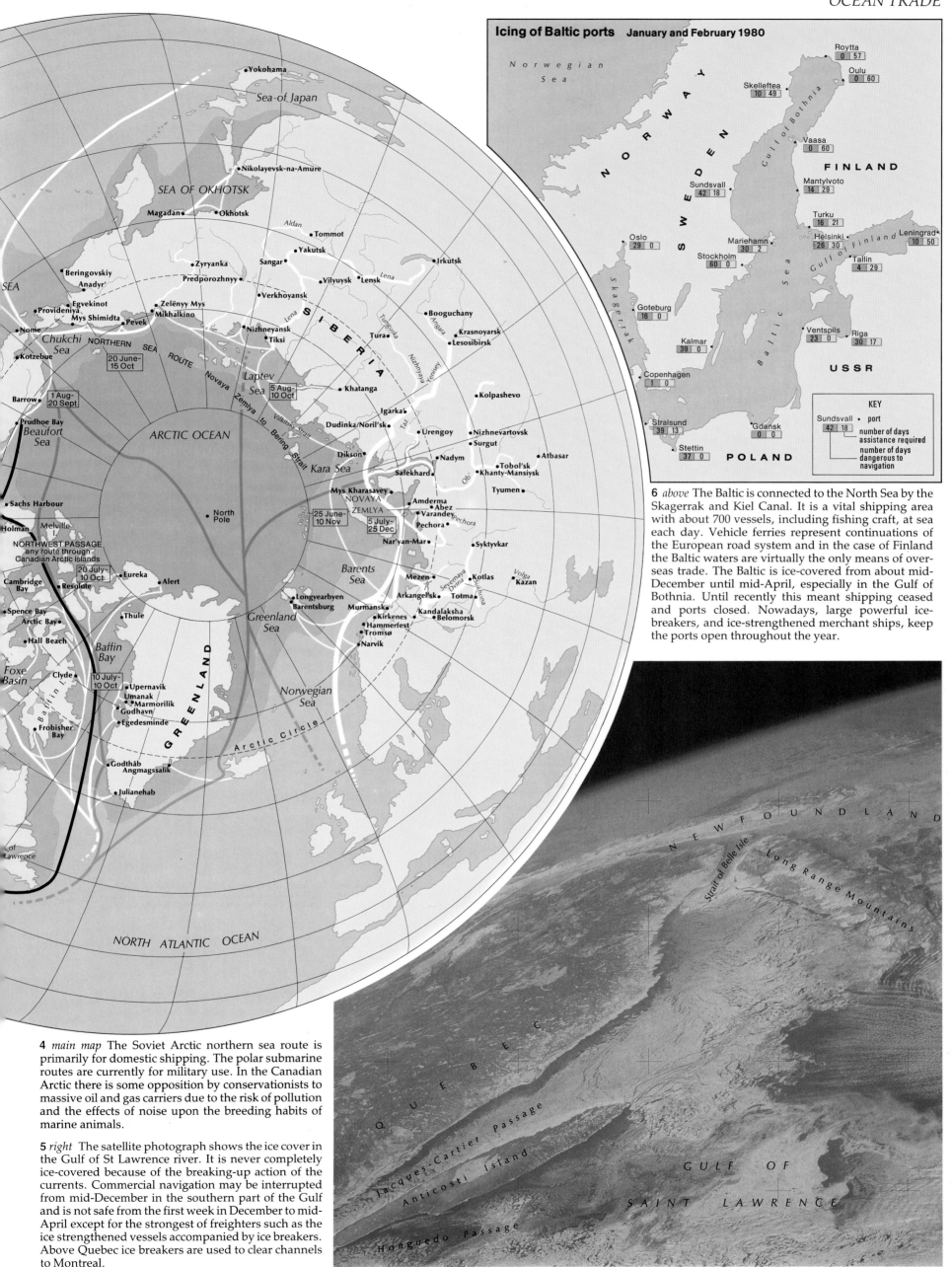

Icing of Baltic ports January and February 1980

6 *above* The Baltic is connected to the North Sea by the Skagerrak and Kiel Canal. It is a vital shipping area with about 700 vessels, including fishing craft, at sea each day. Vehicle ferries represent continuations of the European road system and in the case of Finland the Baltic waters are virtually the only means of overseas trade. The Baltic is ice-covered from about mid-December until mid-April, especially in the Gulf of Bothnia. Until recently this meant shipping ceased and ports closed. Nowadays, large powerful ice-breakers, and ice-strengthened merchant ships, keep the ports open throughout the year.

KEY

Sundsvall ● port
42 | 18 □ number of days assistance required
□ number of days dangerous to navigation

4 *main map* The Soviet Arctic northern sea route is primarily for domestic shipping. The polar submarine routes are currently for military use. In the Canadian Arctic there is some opposition by conservationists to massive oil and gas carriers due to the risk of pollution and the effects of noise upon the breeding habits of marine animals.

5 *right* The satellite photograph shows the ice cover in the Gulf of St Lawrence river. It is never completely ice-covered because of the breaking-up action of the currents. Commercial navigation may be interrupted from mid-December in the southern part of the Gulf and is not safe from the first week in December to mid-April except for the strongest of freighters such as the ice strengthened vessels accompanied by ice breakers. Above Quebec ice breakers are used to clear channels to Montreal.

Straits and canals

GEOGRAPHICALLY, a strait is a natural arm of the sea or a narrow sea channel which separates two land areas or connects two different water bodies. Legally, a strait is defined as any natural passage which connects two parts of the high seas, or one part of the high seas and the territorial sea of a foreign state (see *Maritime jurisdictional zones* page 220). In cases where the breadth of a strait is less than the combined territorial claims of the bordering states, conflicts of interest may arise between foreign states whose ships use the strait and the bordering coastal states (see *Maritime tensions and disputes* pages 186–8). Waterways are other natural passages which may or may not be included in the definition of a strait (for example, the North West Passage is not a strait).

Canals are artificial waterways. All of the main inter-oceanic canals were preceded by land transport transhipments, but as long ago as 2000 BC there was a canal across the isthmus of Suez. Places of transhipment and the inter-oceanic canals have played an important part in world seaborne commerce, and the main canals still exercise a great influence on the pattern and extent of world trade and on world politics. (See *Panama, Suez* and *Kiel Canals* and *St Lawrence Seaway* on following pages.)

The most important straits on which world shipping concentrates are *Bab el Mandeb, Dover, Dardanelles, Gibraltar, Hormuz, Malacca* and *Singapore* (see pages 154–5), as well as *Florida, Luzon, Lombok, Mona, Öresund* and *Windward*. Of historical interest, and with future potential, are the waterways of the North West Passage around North America and the North East Passage around Siberia (see *Seasonal routes and weather routeing* page 148). Of the major straits only Bab el Mandeb, Hormuz and Dardanelles have no alternative shipping routes and are therefore of great strategic importance, the first two as major oil routes. The only alternative to Malacca as a Far East route is via Lombok.

1 *below* The main world straits, waterways and canals and their minimum width in nautical miles. Straits and canals shown in heavier type are considered in greater detail on the following pages. The local term for 'strait' is always used. These include *estrecho* (Spanish), *haehyŏp* (Korean), *kaikyō* (Japanese), *proliv* (Russian), *selat* (Malay) and *stretto* (Italian).

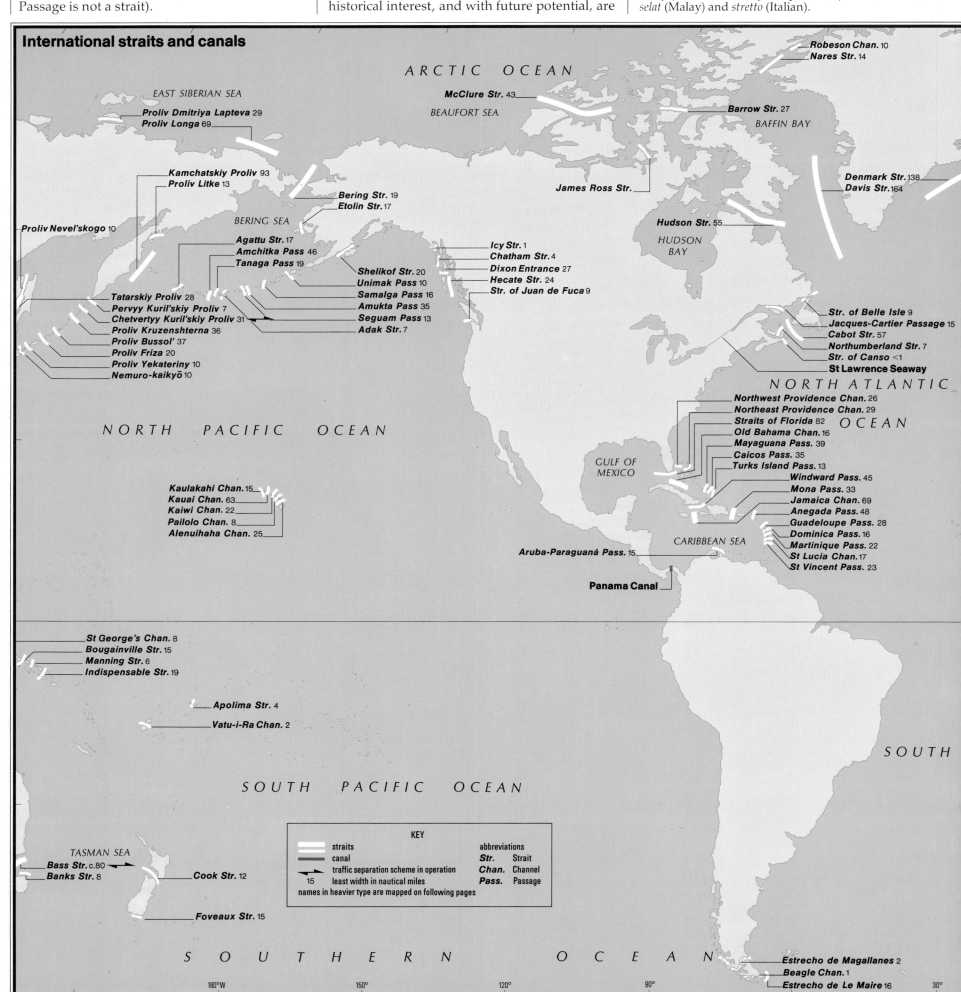

Main passages and straits used for international navigation

The table summarises the characteristics of the main world straits. Not all of those listed are considered by coastal states as legal straits. For example, the Danish government defines the Kattegat as a 'sea (fair water)'. For a complete list of passages and straits and their characteristics, see Appendices.

strait	sovereignty	depth (m)*	max. draft permitted or UKC†	length (nm)	average no. ships per day
Windward Passage	Cuba–Haiti	396	unlimited	40	—
Mona Passage	US–Dominican Rep.	61 274	unlimited	50	—
Florida	US–Bahamas–Cuba	1042	unlimited	330	—
Öresund	Denmark–Sweden	9	unlimited	58	—
Kattegat	Denmark–Sweden	17 124	(more than 40 000 dwt allow max. depth 15 m)	125	142
Dover	France–UK	20 37	UKC 5.2 m	30	350
Gibraltar	Spain–Morocco	82 1000	unlimited	36	140
Otranto	Albania–Italy	88 732	unlimited	40	—
Dardanelles	Turkey	45 90	unlimited	31	57
Bosporus	Turkey	70	unlimited	15	57
Tiran	Egypt–Saudi Arabia	73 183	unlimited	7	—
Bab el Mandeb	Djibouti–N. Yemen	42	unlimited (Large Strait W)	50	—
	S. Yemen–Ethiopia	305			
Hormuz	Iran–Oman	55 91	unlimited	100	80
Mozambique Channel	Madagascar–Mozambique	1830	unlimited	300	—
Malacca	Indonesia–Malaysia	21 97	UKC 3.5 m	500	150
Singapore	Indonesia–Malaysia–Singapore	21 55	UKC 3.5 m	75	150
Sunda	Indonesia	27 183	unlimited	70	—
Lombok	Indonesia	192 1280	unlimited	27	—
San Bernardino	Philippines	55 183	unlimited	35	—
Luzon	Philippines	55 183	unlimited	5	—
West Korea	S. Korea–Japan	62	unlimited	26	—

*Two figures indicate minimum and maximum depths.
†Quoted figures for maximum permissible draft do not allow for rise of tide. UKC—under keel clearance (m).

5 *right* Ships passing near Ismâ'ilîya during transit of the Suez Canal. Note waterway buoys (navigational width between buoys 180 m), and also mooring bollards which are spaced at 200 m intervals along the Canal so that ships can tie up in emergencies or during bad visibility. Maximum speed is 13 km per hour loaded and 14 km per hour in ballast. The Canal banks are protected against wash of passing ships. For much of the Canal's length there is only one traffic lane but there are four passing places.

6 *opposite right* A canal between the Nile and the Red Sea was built by the Egyptians around 4000 years ago. The construction of the present Suez Canal between the Mediterranean and the Red Sea, which was started by the French to de Lesseps' design in November 1854, was officially opened on 17 November 1869. The Canal was cut through a sandy isthmus of land, and through shallow lakes, for a distance of 86.4 nm (160 km). Originally it had a width of 21.9 m and a depth of 7.0 m. The Suez Canal is in its entirety a sea-level passage so that its construction and subsequent improvements have

1 *above* A Soviet freighter passes through the Miraflores locks in the Panama Canal. A treaty between the USA and Panama transferred ownership of land within the Canal Zone to Panama in 1980, and the Canal itself is to be ceded to Panama by the year 2000.

2 *right* The construction of a canal across the isthmus of Central America was considered by Spain as early as the sixteenth century. In 1880 an attempt was made by France, to the design of Ferdinand de Lesseps, to build a sea-level waterway over difficult country with dense equatorial forest and steep gradients. The French attempt was abandoned after a few years because of high costs, but in 1904 the enterprise was repursued by the United States to quite a different design involving lock systems. The canal was opened on 15 August 1914.

The Panama Canal has a length of 43.5 nm (80.5 km) and involves a series of locks which raise and lower vessels to and from a height of 25.9 m above sea level. Transit time is normally 8 to 10 hours. The permissible draught in the Canal varies from about 11.4 m to 12.2 m, according to water levels in the lakes; generally, however, about 12 m is the acceptable draught. Several vessels regularly trading between the Atlantic and the Pacific have been designed to Panama Canal maximum dimensions and are known as Panamax ships. Maximum ship dimensions are 274.3 m length and 32.3 m breadth.

The Panama Canal is vital to the strategic and commercial intercoastal shipping of the United States, and to the Europe–west coast North and South America trades, especially in bulk commodities. In the long-distance Pacific trades the Panama Canal reduces the passage between London and Auckland to 11 380 nm, compared with 12 670 nm by the Suez Canal and 12 480 nm via the Cape of Good Hope. The Canal is regularly used by reefer ships in the New Zealand trade.

The Panama Canal is in danger of becoming congested. Containerisation has alleviated this by reducing the number of liner vessels, but there is still a possibility of saturation of the canal in the future. Because of this a second 33 m deep sea-level canal route is expected to be established. Meanwhile, a widening programme has been undertaken since 1975 with special attention to the curves which have been a hazard to large ships.

Growth in canal trade

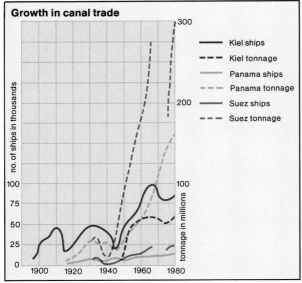

Legend:
- Kiel ships
- Kiel tonnage
- Panama ships
- Panama tonnage
- Suez ships
- Suez tonnage

3 *above* The graph shows the trends by tonnage and by numbers of ships transiting the Kiel, Panama and Suez Canals. The Suez Canal was closed between 1967 and 1975.

4 *right* A comparison of canal dimensions shows that Suez is the longest and deepest, while Panama has the greatest bottom width.

Panama Canal cross – section

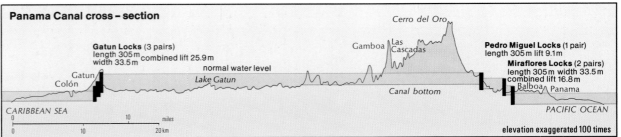

Gatun Locks (3 pairs) length 305 m combined lift 25.9 m width 33.5 m

Pedro Miguel Locks (1 pair) length 305 m lift 9.1 m

Miraflores Locks (2 pairs) length 305 m width 33.5 m combined lift 16.8 m

normal water level
Lake Gatun
Canal bottom
Cerro del Oro
Gamboa
Las Cascadas
Gatun
Colón
CARIBBEAN SEA
Balboa
Panama
PACIFIC OCEAN
elevation exaggerated 100 times

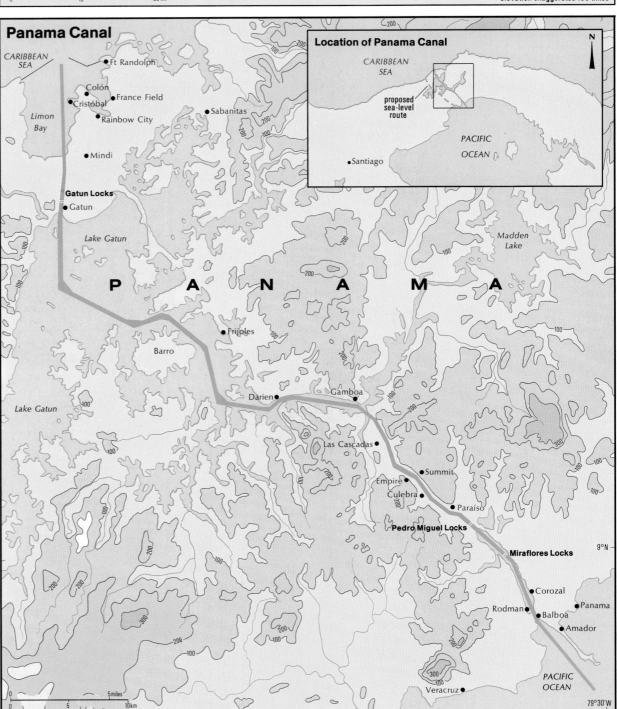

Panama Canal

Location of Panama Canal

Comparison of Panama, Suez, Kiel and Corinth canals

	bottom min. width metres	min. depth metres
Panama	91.4	12.5
Suez	90.0	19.5
Kiel	43.9	11.0
Corinth	21.0	7.9

vertical depth scale

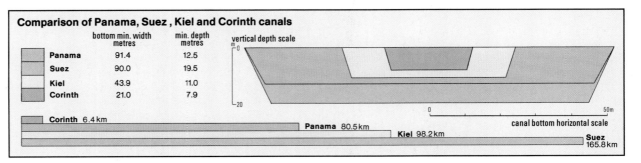

Corinth 6.4 km
Panama 80.5 km
Kiel 98.2 km
Suez 165.8 km
canal bottom horizontal scale

Suez Canal

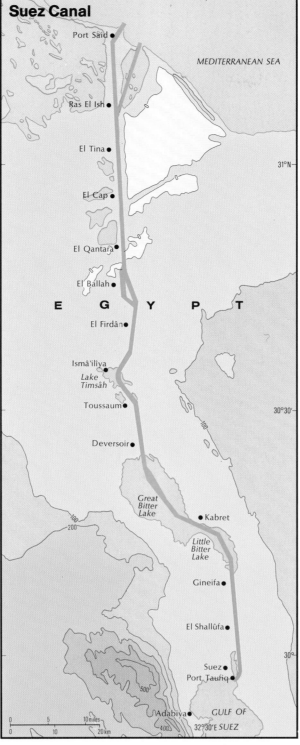

Port Said

MEDITERRANEAN SEA

Ras El Ish

El Tina

31°N

El Cap

El Qantara

El Ballah

E G Y P T

El Firdân

Ismâ'iliya
Lake Timsâh

Toussaum

30°30′

Deversoir

Great Bitter Lake

Kabret

Little Bitter Lake

Gineifa

30°

El Shallûfa

Suez
Port Taufiq

Adabiya

GULF OF
32°30′E SUEZ

Kiel Canal

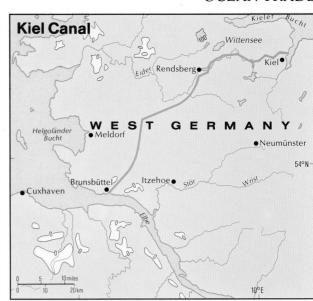

Kieler Bucht

Wittensee

Eider Rendsberg

Kiel

W E S T G E R M A N Y

Helgoländer Bucht

Meldorf

Neumünster

54°N

Brunsbüttel

Itzehoe Stör

Wrist

Cuxhaven

Elbe

10°E

been relatively easy; its construction cost less than half that of the Panama Canal.

The opening of the Suez Canal had an immediate effect on shipping and trade. It made dramatic reductions in voyages from Europe to Asia; for example, the distance between London and Bombay is 6260 nm via Suez, compared with 10 700 nm via the Cape, and London–Kuwait 6500 nm compared with 11 300 nm. As a result most of world shipping shifted from the Cape route to that of the Mediterranean and the Red Sea. By the 1960s some 15 per cent of world seaborne trade used the Canal.

Major changes came late in the history of the Suez Canal, because shipowners tended to tailor the dimensions of their vessels to canal requirements. It was not until the 1950s that the desire of shipowners for canal access for much larger ships influenced the canal authorities. Then a long-term programme for deepening the canal was started. By 1956 the maximum permissible draught had been increased to 10.7 m and in 1961 to 11.3 m.

The canal was closed between 1967 and 1975. The volume of shipping has been building again since 1976 and it remains one of the world's most important shipping routes. However, the majority of very large laden tankers continue to use the Cape route: about 570 million tonnes of oil were exported from the Middle East to destinations west of Suez in 1980 and only 28 million passed through the Canal. In March 1981, 45 tankers of over 250 000 dwt passed south, and one north. The first stage of the development project to widen and deepen the Canal was completed in October 1980. The draught was then 16.1 m. When development plans are complete fully loaded tankers of 250 000 dwt (draught 20 m) will be able to transit the Canal. Traffic will depend on the level of Canal charges compared with fuel costs and time by the Cape route.

The majority of the maritime nations use the Suez Canal. In 1980 the percentage distribution by flag (net registered tonnage) was: Greece 13.9; Liberia 12.1; USSR 7.0; UK 6.5; Norway 6.1; Panama 5.5; Japan 4.9; France 4.5; W. Germany 3.8; Singapore 2.7. Some 20 795 vessels made the transit. Of these, 2921 were tankers and 190 were warships.

It takes ships about 24 hours to make the passage (12 hours in transit). Some 80 ships per day can pass through, in two convoys southbound and one northbound.

7 *above* The Kiel Canal, opened in 1895, links the North Sea with the Baltic. It has a length of 53 nm (98.2 km). The permissible breadth is 40 m and draught 9.4 m. Although it is a sea-level canal it has a lock system in order to render it independent of the tidal fluctuations of the North Sea. The Canal is navigable for ships with draughts to 9 m, about 20 000 dwt.

This Canal provides a saving in distance of 190–290 nm (depending on the draught of the vessel and its route through the channels between Denmark and Sweden) on passages to the Baltic compared with sailing around the Skagen. The average transit time is 7 hours at the speed limit of 8 knots.

The Kiel Canal is particularly important for West German (16.6 per cent of tonnage) and for Polish (11 per cent) shipping, followed by Greek (10.4), Soviet (9.6), Swedish (6.9) and Finnish (5). It is especially important for short-sea and coastal vessels; more than three-quarters of the ships using the Kiel Canal are of about 1000 grt.

8 *below* Ships entering Kiel Canal from Kiel Harbour in the Baltic Sea. The Canal is an important route for Baltic shipping and some 90 000 ships pass through it each year. Originally built during 1887–97 to serve German military needs, it was widened to accommodate commercial ships.

The Suez Canal's two-stage expansion

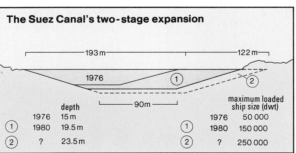

193 m

122 m

1976

① ②

90 m

	depth			maximum loaded ship size (dwt)
① 1976	15 m	①	1976	50 000
1980	19.5 m		1980	150 000
② ?	23.5 m	②	?	250 000

KEY TO ALL MAPS

heights in metres

below sea level	200–300
0–100	300–400
100–200	above 400

canals and locks

● major settlement

jetty

St Lawrence Seaway

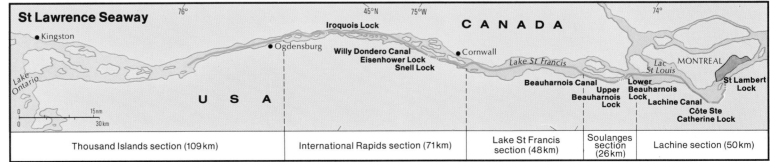

76° 45°N 75°W 74°

CANADA

Iroquois Lock

Kingston

Ogdensburg

Willy Dondero Canal
Eisenhower Lock
Snell Lock

Cornwall

Lake St Francis

Lac St Louis

MONTREAL

Lake Ontario

USA

Beauharnois Canal

Upper Beauharnois Lock

Lower Beauharnois Lock

Lachine Canal

Côte Ste Catherine Lock

St Lambert Lock

15 nm
30 km

| Thousand Islands section (109 km) | International Rapids section (71 km) | Lake St Francis section (48 km) | Soulanges section (26 km) | Lachine section (50 km) |

9 *right* As early as 1825 there was a canal by-passing the Lachine Rapids near Montreal. The St Lawrence Seaway was completed in 1959 jointly by Canada and the USA, at a cost of $470 million. It is of vital importance for the North American economy. The seaway allows deep-draughted vessels (7.92 m) to proceed from the Atlantic to the western end of Lake Superior, a distance of 2035 nm (3769 km). The navigation portion of the project completed this link and consists of five main sections between Montreal and Lake Ontario with a length of 164 nm (304 km). The Lachine and Soulange sections were completed by the Canadian government, and the International Rapids and

Location of St Lawrence Seaway

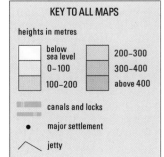

CANADA

Lake Superior

Québec

Lachine
Soulanges

Halifax

Ottawa

Lake Huron

Lake Michigan

Lake St Francis
International Rapids
Thousand Islands

Toronto

Lake Ontario

ATLANTIC OCEAN

Detroit

Buffalo

Boston

40°N

Lake Erie

Chicago

Cleveland

New York

90°W

Thousand Islands sections by the US government. The project also included the construction of plants to exploit the seaway's hydroelectric power.

The navigational season is normally from 1 April to 15 December; the period from mid-December until the end of March is subject to ice closure. Icebreakers maintain navigation up to Montreal throughout the winter.

The whole seaway system has 17 locks, including 8 locks in the Canadian Welland Canal built to provide a passage around Niagara Falls from Lake Ontario to Lake Erie. Ships travelling the length of the seaway are raised from sea level to an elevation of 183.5 m at Lake Superior.

1 *right* (Arabic for *Bāb el Mandeb* is 'Gate of Tears') The Strait's northern extremity is marked by Ras Bab al Mandeb and, about 14 nm away, by Ras Siyâne at its south-western limit. Perim I. (South Yemen) divides it in two: Large Strait and Small Strait. Large Strait is always used in preference to Small Strait because many casualties have occurred in the latter.

Currents and tidal streams mean that the surface set is variable; currents set in the direction of the wind, attaining a rate of 40 miles a day.

Large Strait is 9 nm wide and is deep at 322 m and free from dangers in the fairway, except for a bank at 11.9 m which lies about 30 m south-west of Pirie Point. A traffic separation scheme is in force.

Fog is rarely reported by ships in this area; generally visibility is good or very good. The mean monthly frequency of fog reported by ships never exceeds 2 per cent. However, poor visibility (less than 5 nm) can occur, especially in summer, but this is due mainly to dust particles.

Bab el Mandeb's strategic importance began with the opening of the Suez Canal, and this will increase with the widening and deepening of the Canal. The Strait takes in territorial waters of four coastal states: North Yemen, South Yemen, Djibouti and Ethiopia. The area is politically unstable with consequent risk of interference with shipping. About 50 ships a day pass through but only 10 per cent of Western Europe's oil supplies were transported via the Strait in 1980. The Strait is of great importance to Egypt in relation to the Suez Canal, to Israel for the port of Eilat, and to the Red Sea littoral states.

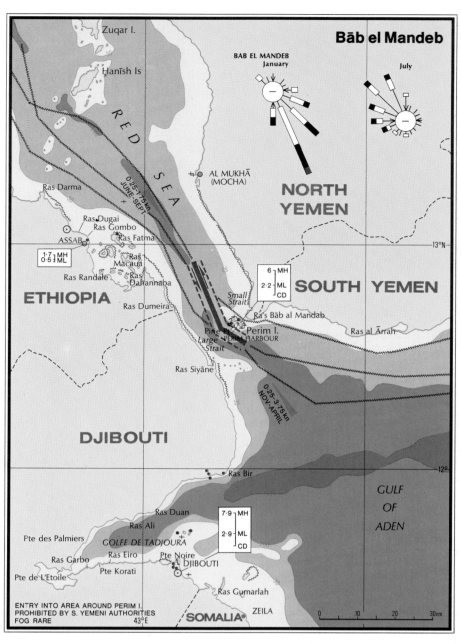

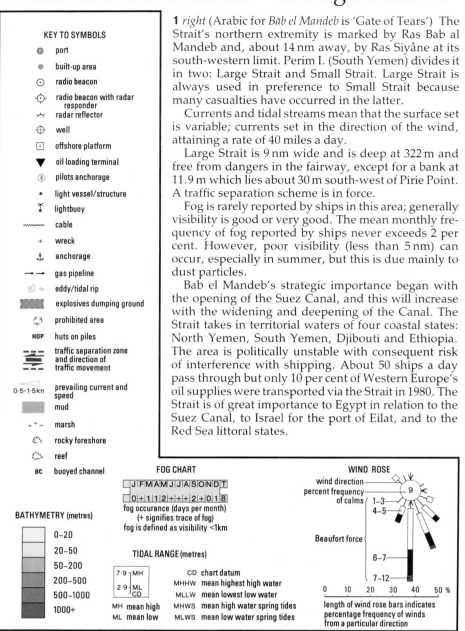

2 *left* Hormuz links the Persian Gulf with the Gulf of Oman and the Arabian Sea. Its width varies between 29 and 51 nm; length about 96 nm. It takes its name from the island Jazīreh-ye Hormoz on which stands a Portuguese fort dating from 1514. This testifies to the Strait's strategic and commercial significance for European powers. Anglo-Persian forces recaptured the islands in 1662.

Today Hormuz is one of the most vital channels of trade in the world since about two-thirds of seaborne trade in crude oil pass through it. It is also very vulnerable to mining and to rocket attacks. The world's largest tankers use the Strait and a total of about 80 ships per day make the transit. There is plenty of water for large tankers in the main channels. Traffic separation zones, which have to be used by deep draughted ships, are entirely in Oman territorial waters. The Strait's narrowest part measures 20.7 nm and is between the Iranian island of Jazīreh-ye Lārak and the Oman island of Great Quoin. Numerous islands and strong currents (0.4–0.8 knots in January and 0.6–1.7 knots in April), low swells, and bad visibility (often due to dust) may cause navigational difficulties. The northern peninsula of Oman is separated from the rest of the country by the United Arab Emirates. The peninsula is occupied primarily by fishermen. Oman is greatly concerned with pollution from tankers discharging ballast as it is already having adverse effects on local fish stocks.

Further west traffic routeing takes vessels through Iranian Territorial waters, since the seizure of the Tunb Islands by Iran in 1971 (see *Maritime tensions and disputes* page 187).

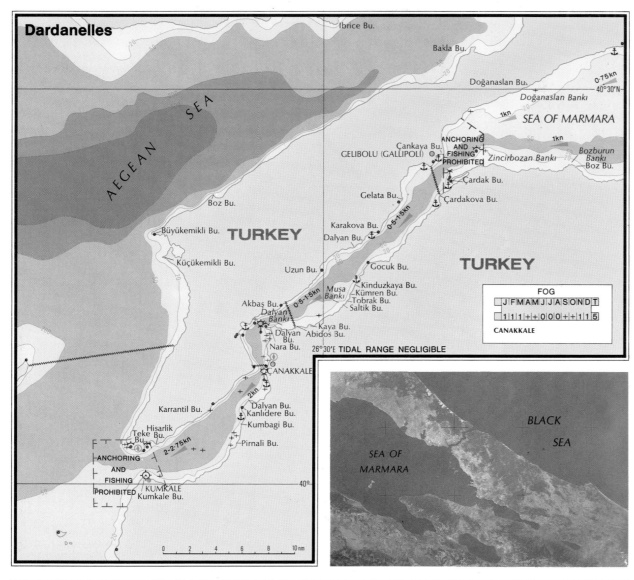

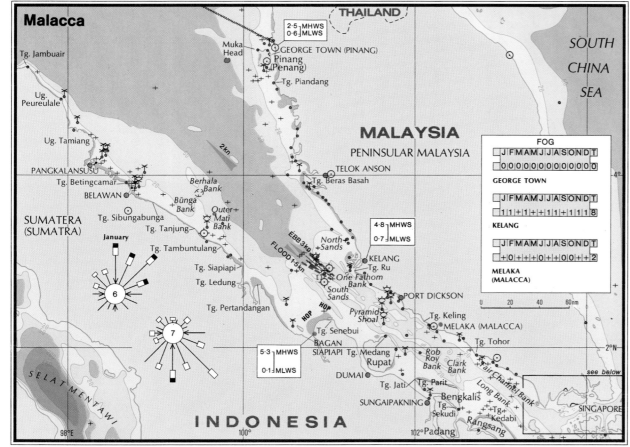

3 *left* (Dardanelles: Turkish *Çanakkale Bogazi*; ancient *Hellespont*) The Strait lies between the peninsula of Gallipoli in Europe (north-west) and Asia Minor (south-east) and connects the Aegean Sea with the Sea of Marmara. The latter is separated from the Black Sea by the Bosporus. The narrowest point is 1.2 km, the widest 6.4 km; its length is 33 nm; depth varies from 50 to 91 m in the main channel. The main current has an average rate of 1.5 knots (maximum 5 knots) and constitutes a surface flow of water from the Black Sea to the Aegean.

The Dardanelles is entirely within Turkish jurisdiction and vessels fly the Turkish courtesy flag and pay transit charges, but pilotage is not compulsory, except under certain conditions, despite several collisions and strandings.

Because the strait is of strategic importance (Turkey is a member of NATO), all warships must give 8 days' notice of transit along with details of their characteristics. About 262 warship passages were made in 1980 of which 229 were Soviet and 16 American.

Foreign aircraft carriers are prohibited from using the Strait under the Montreux Convention of 1936 but the Soviet carrier *Kiev* has made the transit as an anti-submarine cruiser. There are also restrictions on submarine passages, thus the Soviet Black Sea Fleet has few submarines.

The Dardanelles is of importance economically especially to the trade of Turkey, the USSR and the Black Sea States. Of the 20 755 merchant ships using the Strait in 1980 (including the Bosporus) 7656 were of Soviet flag, 2845 Greek, 1344 Rumanian, 789 Bulgarian and 544 Liberian.

The Dardanelles together with the Bosporus constitute the Turkish Straits. Since 1 May 1982 traffic schemes have been in accordance with IMO specifications throughout the Turkish Straits.

4 *left* This satellite view shows the Bosporus, a narrow strait connecting the Sea of Marmara and the Black Sea; it is only 0.5 nm at its narrowest point with a minimum depth of 30 m.

There is dense population on either bank and marine traffic accidents have caused concern. The crossing traffic has been alleviated by the 1074 m long Bosporus Bridge built in 1973. There are concentrations of small fishing boats in the Bosporus as it is the channel for fish migration between the Black Sea and the Mediterranean.

5 *left* Malacca Strait links the Indian Ocean (Andaman Sea) with the Pacific (South China Sea) and together with Singapore Strait (*below left*) has a length of 600 nm. Since ancient times it has had enormous economic and strategic significance and has in turn been controlled by Indians, Arabs, Portuguese, Dutch and British. In recent years Malaysia and Indonesia have shared jurisdiction over the Malacca Strait. It became of increased importance in 1869 with the opening of the Suez Canal, and since 1950 has been the main artery for transport of crude oil by tankers from the Gulf to Japan. About 140 vessels transit the Strait daily. The alternative passage to the Far East via the Lombok Strait adds 1200 nm to a voyage from the Gulf oil ports to Japan.

The width of the Malacca Strait varies between 8.4 nm in the south to about 140 nm in the north. Its waters are relatively shallow; in the south depth rarely exceeds 37 m, and averages about 27 m. Large vessels are funnelled through a channel 2 nm wide. The tidal range varies from 5.8 m in the south to 2.5 m in the north. Ships drawing more than 19.8 m should not use the Strait.

The climate is characterised by the north-east monsoon (northern winter) and the south-east monsoon (northern summer); from earliest times voyages were scheduled to take advantage of the prevailing winds. Throughout the year there is a residual, predominantly north-westerly current. Passage at the Strait's southern end is hindered by numerous small islands, some with reefs, and by sand ridges. Many shoals and migrating sand waves cause depths to vary. Depth is particularly critical near One Fathom Bank where the channel width for VLCCs is only 2 nm. There are also uncharted wrecks and unmarked shoals in the area.

The coastal areas contain some half million people dependent on the sea's living resources; there is great concern for the safety of navigation of ships with hazardous and pollutant cargoes.

6 *left* Singapore Strait (length 70 nm) has a width constantly less than 15 nm and its narrowest passage is 2.5 nm. Several shoals are less than 25 m and navigation is further complicated because ships bound to and from Japan have to turn almost 90° at this point. In 1981 several large vessels were boarded by pirates in the southerly traffic lanes passing through Indonesian waters.

7 *left* Shipping in Singapore Roads. About 150 large ships per day pass through the Strait.

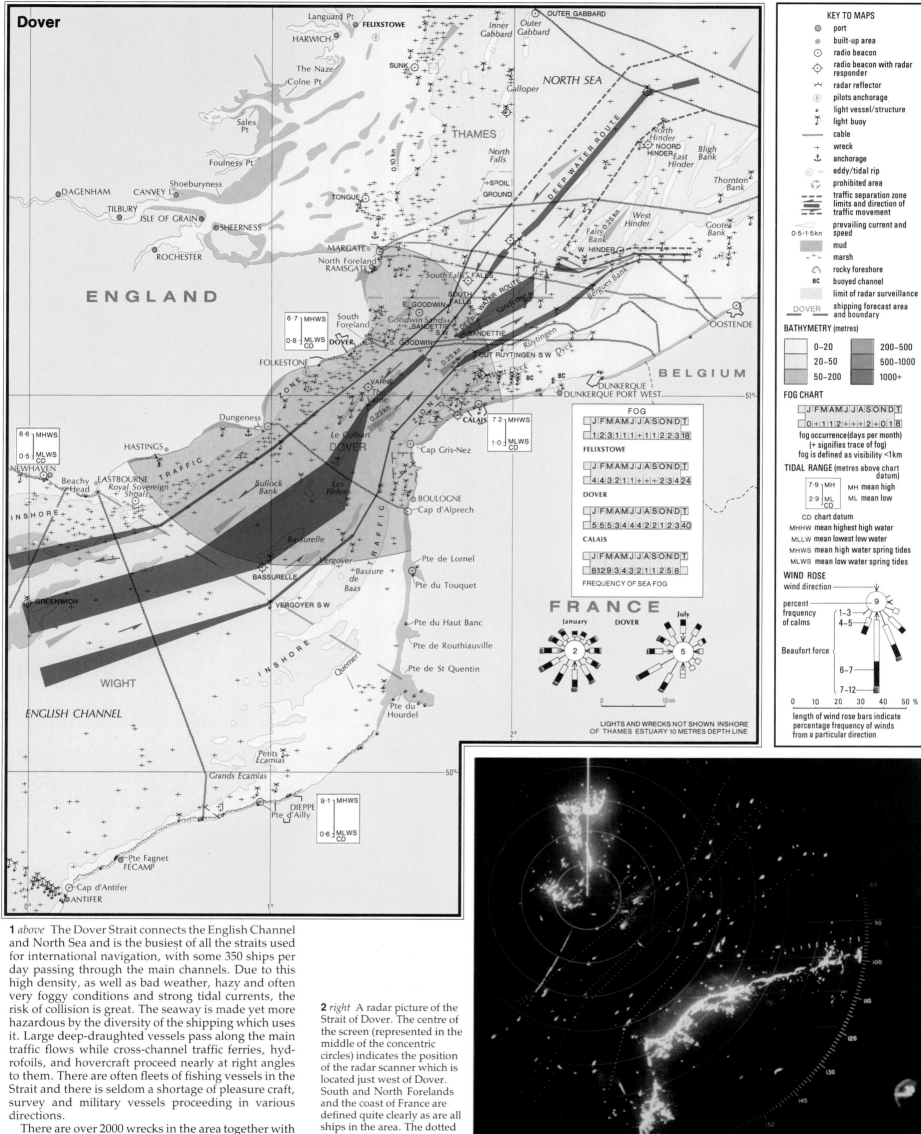

Dover

ENGLAND

NORTH SEA

THAMES

FRANCE

BELGIUM

ENGLISH CHANNEL

WIGHT

1 *above* The Dover Strait connects the English Channel and North Sea and is the busiest of all the straits used for international navigation, with some 350 ships per day passing through the main channels. Due to this high density, as well as bad weather, hazy and often very foggy conditions and strong tidal currents, the risk of collision is great. The seaway is made yet more hazardous by the diversity of the shipping which uses it. Large deep-draughted vessels pass along the main traffic flows while cross-channel traffic ferries, hydrofoils, and hovercraft proceed nearly at right angles to them. There are often fleets of fishing vessels in the Strait and there is seldom a shortage of pleasure craft, survey and military vessels proceeding in various directions.

There are over 2000 wrecks in the area together with numerous shoals. The tidal range varies considerably from place to place and the area is prone to negative storm surges (see *Tides and surges* page 60). Furthermore sand waves on the bottom tend to migrate. All these factors make navigation extremely difficult, and deep draughted ships cannot drastically alter course to avoid collision without running the risk of going aground. The Dover Strait is one of the blackspots for collisions but these have been reduced in number since 1973 (13 in 1970 and 11 in 1971, to 2 in 1978 and

2 *right* A radar picture of the Strait of Dover. The centre of the screen (represented in the middle of the concentric circles) indicates the position of the radar scanner which is located just west of Dover. South and North Forelands and the coast of France are defined quite clearly as are all ships in the area. The dotted lines on the screen indicate the traffic separation scheme.

8 in 1979). This is most likely due to the surveillance and broadcasting activities of the Channel Navigation Information Service (CNIS).

Collisions between ships proceeding in opposite directions have declined as a result of a mid-channel area which separates the traffic moving towards the North Sea along the French coast from the traffic moving on the English side towards the Atlantic. The number of ships contravening this separation scheme has been reduced steadily as a result of radar surveillance, aircraft monitoring and reporting, and naval presence.

3 *right* The Strait of Gibraltar separates Africa and Europe and lies between the Rock of Gibraltar and Mt Alyla in Morocco which formed the ancient Pillars of Hercules. The present name is derived from Jabel Tarik the Moorish invader of the area in 710 AD. The width of the Strait at the eastern end is 12 nm; to the westwards the Strait narrows to 8 nm and between Cape Trafalgar and Cape Spartel widens to 27 nm. The surface current is predominantly east going, reaching over three knots. This exceeds the deeper outflowing more saline west going current thus preventing the Mediterranean from becoming highly saline. The prevailing winds in the Strait are from the west but strong easterlies called *lavanters* also occur. There is deep water in the main channel of over 360 m but shoals lie within two to three nautical miles off the coast and need to be given a wide berth.

Traffic densities are high, about 200 vessels pass through the Strait each day, tankers predominate and carry over 200 million tonnes of oil through the Strait each year. In addition there are ferries and concentrations of fishing vessels. Navigation can be complex under reduced visibility and in 1979 a major collision incident cost 50 lives and spilled about 95 000 tonnes of crude oil. Separation zones are in force but there is no radar surveillance. Traffic is likely to grow as it is expected that with the continued deepening of the Suez Canal tanker volume will increase. There are plans for building a bridge across the Strait.

Strategically the Strait of Gibraltar is important, and there have been strong rivalries for control of the Rock of Gibraltar. The Strait is the only natural access by sea into the Mediterranean, and it also provides a corridor for planes who wish to pass through the area without overflying adjacent coastal states.

The rock and port of Gibraltar has been a British colony since 1713. Its role as a British naval base is less important than in the past but it contains Admiralty waters to which there is no entry without permission.

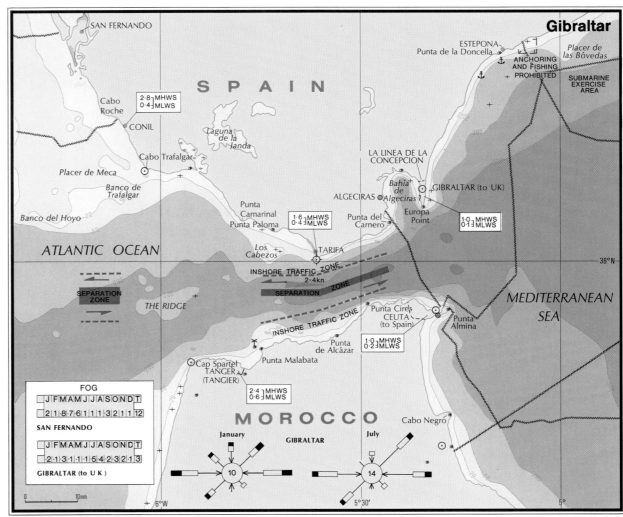

4 *right* A satellite view taken from Gemini X of the Strait of Gibraltar showing the northernmost tip of Morocco and south-west Spain, with storm cloud formations over the Atlantic Ocean.

Density of shipping at sea

The distribution of ships at sea is difficult to determine. Reasonably accurate figures for shipping density have been established at specific points such as the Straits of Dover, Gibraltar, and Singapore, where large numbers of ships concentrate. However, there is still only a crude estimate for most sea areas.

The density map (*right*) indicates the high concentration of merchant ships in north-west European waters, particularly the English Channel and southern North Sea, and in the seas around Japan. Concentration is also marked in straits and off headlands where ships tend to converge and along the major trade routes (see *Commodity flows* page 136 and *Shipping casualties* page 164). As there is a direct relationship between high density of shipping and incidence of collision, traffic separation schemes have been put into operation in many of these areas.

The fishing fleet density has been determined in relation to fish catch statistics but unfortunately there is not necessarily a close relationship between the fluctuating volume of fish catches and the number of fishing vessels so accurate plotting is not possible. However, since 1973 when the information for this map was plotted the fleets have, due to poor catches for several years, thinned out in the anchoveta and tuna industry off South America and there have been some fleet reductions in the North Atlantic, North Sea, and also in the Southern Ocean, the latter as a result of reduced whaling activities. There have been increases in fleets in the South Atlantic, Indian Ocean and south-west Pacific. The concentrations off the Galapagos Islands and to the south of Africa are made up primarily of tuna fishing fleets.

5 *right* The map is based on a projection, updated, which was made in 1973. The density patterns are for merchant ships and fishing vessels of over 100 grt. High densities in areas which are not on trade routes (see *The world pattern* page 146) indicate the presence of fishing fleets. Merchant vessels are plotted on the map in blue while fishing vessels are shown as red.

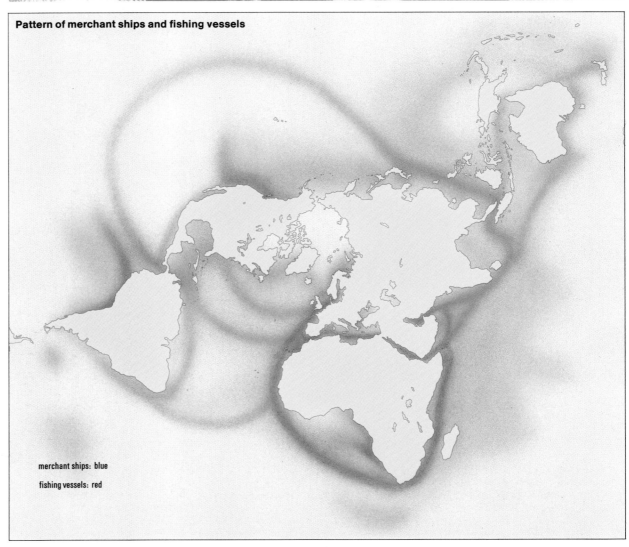

Pattern of merchant ships and fishing vessels

merchant ships: blue

fishing vessels: red

Navigational aids and safety

BEFORE the Second World War navigational equipment consisted of charts, sailing directions, tide tables, a list of lights, a compass, log, sounding equipment, sextant and chronometer. Lighthouses, lightships and buoys were, and are, fundamental external aids. In many confined waters pilotage authorities provide optional or compulsory services and coastguards frequently monitor ship movements

in coastal waters where there is congestion.

More modern aids include radar, sonar, Loran, Decca, Omega, satellite navigation, inertial navigation, and various hybrid and integrated systems. Not all ships possess these but the SOLAS Convention 1974 lays down minimum standards for navigational aids on ships. The development of VHF has been a further advance as it has permitted navigational information from shore

stations employing radar surveillance to be communicated to ships.

An important contribution to safety came when the International Maritime Satellite began to operate in 1982. It provides ships with very reliable contact for distress, safety communications, medical assistance, weather forecasts, navigational warnings, and management and social communications, in any part of the world.

Navigation systems

There are three types of assisted navigation systems; hyperbolic, satellite and inertial. Hyperbolic navigation is based on accurate measurements of differences in times taken by synchronised signals transmitted from each of two radio transmitters. They include Decca Navigator, Loran and Omega. The Decca Navigator employs chains of transmitters and the range of coverage is 250 nm day and 100 nm night. The positional accuracy obtained is ¼ to 2 nm.

The Loran System (Long Range Navigation) group of stations forms chains covering the North Atlantic and Pacific Oceans. The range is about 1200 nm and the accuracy of positions obtained is 15 to 500 metres.

The Omega System has spacing of stations at thousands of miles and gives an accuracy of about 1–2 nm anywhere at sea at any time. Radar (Radio Detection and Ranging) is a radio system in which the bearing and distance of an object can be detected if the object is within radar range which in turn depends on the heights of the radar aerial and the object as well as the re-radiation characteristics of the object. Radar is effective for ranges of 1–60 nm off land, and 3–15 nm from buoys and lightships. The detection of small objects can be increased if radar reflectors are attached to them. There are two other types of echo enhancers: Ramark, a transmitter which sends signals at regular intervals which can be detected by radars of ships in the vicinity, and Racon, comprising a receiver and transmitter. The transmitter responds to radar pulses detected by its receiver. The result is an echo flash on the radar screen.

Radar is also a valuable aid for collision avoidance. In order to improve this amenity, devices termed ARPA (Automatic Radar Plotting Aids) have been produced which automatically assess collison risks.

The satellite navigation system known as TRANSIT currently employs five satellites which trace out polar orbits having a period of 108 minutes. There are at least four opportunities each day when a vessel may be fixed from each satellite in the system. This gives the possibility of obtaining a position anywhere on the earth's surface at intervals of between 30 minutes and 3 hours to an accuracy of around 0.2 nm.

A more accurate satellite global positioning system (GPS) using high orbital satellites, known as NavStar, is planned for the mid 1980s. This system will provide continuous position fixing.

The system known as SINS (Ship's Inertial Navigation System), is a sophisticated self-contained dead reckoning navigation system. Using this system, the motion of a vessel is continually monitored so that its position, relative to its starting point, is known at all times. At present, its high cost confines its use to military vessels. Because it is self-contained and functions independently of weather conditions and radio signals it is particularly useful on board submarines which wish to avoid detection.

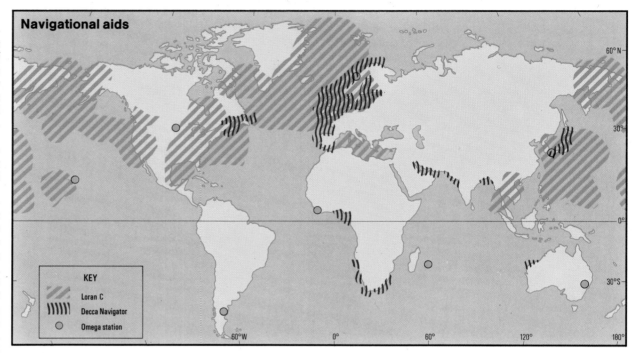

Navigational aids

KEY
Loran C
Decca Navigator
◯ Omega station

1 *above* This map shows the coverage areas of Loran and Decca Navigator systems, and the positions of the eight Omega transmitters which provide complete global coverage. The ground stations for the Transit Satellite Navigation system, which also gives global coverage, are all situated in the USA. Loran and Decca Navigator coverage areas depend on radio propagation conditions and so can vary considerably. The coverage areas depicted on the map represent only the minimum areas, having acceptable accuracy, which normally exist.

The radio propagation conditions depend on the ionisation of the atmosphere which depends on the

time of day and the season of the year at the observer's position.

2 *below* For the purposes of co-ordinating navigational warnings, the world has been divided into 16 geographical areas. For each area there is a co-ordinating country whose job it is to collate and issue warnings for that particular area. The warnings are all transmitted in English, but also in other languages as considered necessary. They relate to navigational aids, wrecks, mines, newly discovered hazards, offshore operations, malfunctioning of services and to special meteorological warnings (see *Weather hazards for shipping* page 160).

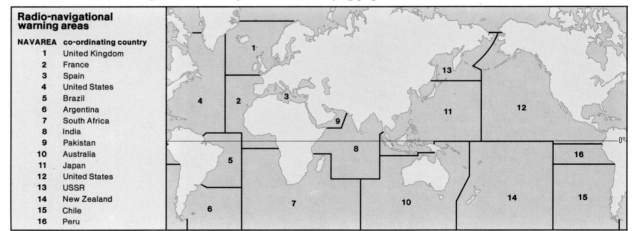

Radio-navigational warning areas

NAVAREA	co-ordinating country
1	United Kingdom
2	France
3	Spain
4	United States
5	Brazil
6	Argentina
7	South Africa
8	India
9	Pakistan
10	Australia
11	Japan
12	United States
13	USSR
14	New Zealand
15	Chile
16	Peru

The nautical chart

The chart is one of the most important navigational aids on which the safety of ships depends. The ordinary type is drawn on the mercator projection thus enabling compass bearings to be drawn as straight lines. The chart itself shows soundings, bathymetric contours, coastal detail, the particulars of navigation lights and buoys, navigational channels and undersea obstructions. Scales vary, and some charts cover whole oceans while others, at a scale as large as 1:7500, describe only a port or harbour.

Official charts in the United Kingdom are produced by the Hydrographic Department of the Ministry of Defence. Corresponding bodies in the United States and many other nations produce their own charts. There is widespread interchange of charts between nations which calls for a high degreee of standardisation in design and symbols. In this respect, the International Hydrographic Organisation in Monaco plays an important role as a co-ordinating body.

3 *left* The Eddystone Lighthouse stands on the Eddystone rocks, 14 nm off Plymouth, England. The present structure, the fourth to be built, stands 40.5 m (133 ft) above sea level. It is provided with a helicopter pad.

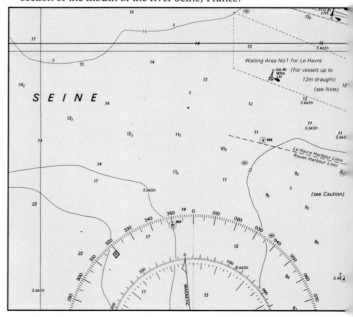

4 *below* A portion of a British Admiralty chart showing a section of the mouth of the river Seine, France.

SEINE

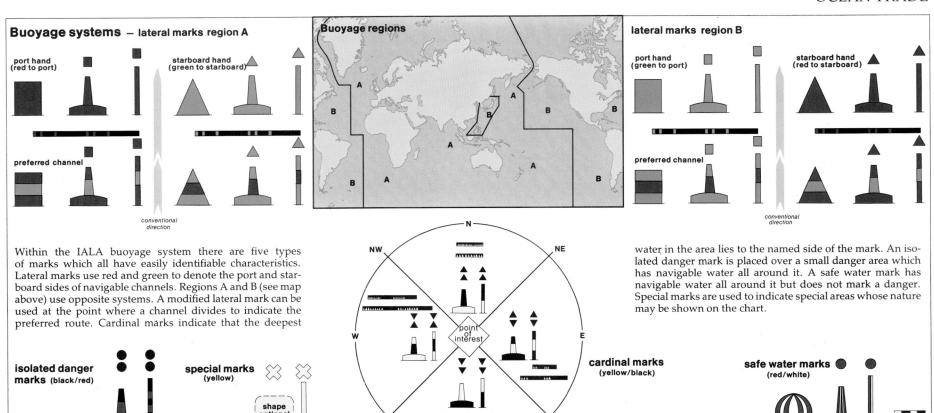

Buoyage systems – lateral marks region A

port hand
(red to port)

starboard hand
(green to starboard)

preferred channel

conventional direction

Buoyage regions

lateral marks region B

port hand
(green to port)

starboard hand
(red to starboard)

preferred channel

conventional direction

Within the IALA buoyage system there are five types of marks which all have easily identifiable characteristics. Lateral marks use red and green to denote the port and starboard sides of navigable channels. Regions A and B (see map above) use opposite systems. A modified lateral mark can be used at the point where a channel divides to indicate the preferred route. Cardinal marks indicate that the deepest

water in the area lies to the named side of the mark. An isolated danger mark is placed over a small danger area which has navigable water all around it. A safe water mark has navigable water all around it but does not mark a danger. Special marks are used to indicate special areas whose nature may be shown on the chart.

isolated danger marks (black/red)

special marks (yellow)

shape optional

N

NW

NE

W

point of interest

E

SW

SE

S

cardinal marks (yellow/black)

safe water marks (red/white)

Navigation buoys and marks (region A)

Navigation lights (region A)

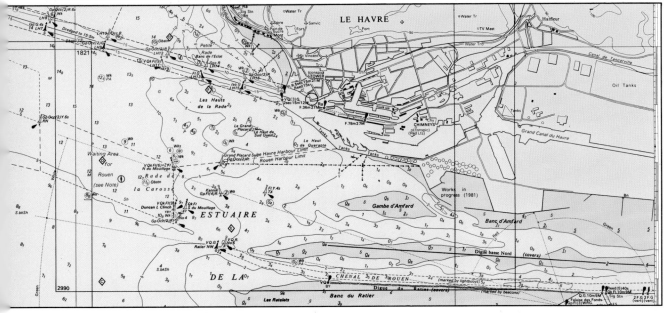

5 *above* Buoys for marking channels and dangers were introduced as long ago as the 16th century but only in piecemeal fashion in some estuaries and rivers. Since then, buoyage systems have spread to nearly all the world's coastlines but there is still no universal system. Indeed, as recently as 1976 there were more than 30 different buoyage systems, many of which were in complete conflict with each other. The International Association of Lighthouse Authorities (IALA) maritime buoyage system was agreed at a conference convened in Tokyo by IALA in November 1980. The world's oceans are now divided into two buoyage regions, A and B. The lateral marks differ in colour for the regions as shown in the diagram at the top of the page while the two drawings above illustrate the buoyage system, for both night and day, for region A only. When used with the conventional direction of buoyage, lateral marks indicate the port and starboard hands of the route to be followed. The conventional direction is either the direction taken by the mariner when approaching from seaward or a direction determined by the buoyage authorities and given in sailing instructions or indicated on a chart.

The weather

EACH region of the sea has its own characteristics of temperature, salinity, biology, currents and tides, and above all of sea state or character: the 'grey and stormy Bay of Biscay', the 'blue and placid Mediterranean', are typical popular perceptions. But any sea can change in a remarkably short time from calm to violent storm. Only in the tropical South Pacific outside the hurricane zones and in the tropical South Atlantic is the sea free from storms for any length of time. Elsewhere there are areas of constant or seasonal hazards which often coincide with shipping routes, fishing grounds, and areas of hydrocarbon extraction. The worst areas are the North Atlantic and adjacent seas, the high latitudes in the North Pacific and Southern Ocean, the regions of tropical storms, and the region of freak wave conditions off South Africa.

The force of the sea is such that it can expose the slightest structural weakness, bad cargo stowage, or lack of vigilance. Many ships have been lost in the North Atlantic by the sheer destructive force of the sea while many more have gone down when cargo has shifted due to excessive rolling. Even in short crossings such as the Irish Sea violent storms have taken their toll. There, on the night of 31 January 1953 a severe north-westerly gale drove a cargo liner ashore, sank five trawlers and overwhelmed the ferry *Princess Victoria* with the loss of 250 passengers.

Some container ships trading regularly in the North Atlantic have added foredeck protection against breaking seas, and many vessels are now 'weather routed' (see *Weather routeing* page 148). Rigs in the North Atlantic region are designed to withstand gales of 115 mph, and wave heights of 15 to 20 m (as high as a six-storey building).

Vessels trading regularly in ice-covered areas are specially strengthened and have extra engine power. In addition to the dangers of fog and collision with icebergs in high latitudes, severe gales combined with freezing conditions cause icing (see *The icy surface* page 64). The crews of the trawlers *Lorella* and *Rodrigo* described their plight to their families over the ship's radio as they lay head-on to gale force winds north of Iceland on 26 January 1955. Waves were breaking on board and spray froze on the superstructure. Nothing could be done to stop the accumulation of ice and the boats capsized with the loss of all hands.

On the Newfoundland Banks waves can become steep due to shoaling effects and refraction. On 15 February 1982 the semi-submersible rig *Ocean Ranger* sank in a storm while drilling on the Banks in winds recorded at 109 mph. All 84 people on board were drowned. In the same storm the next day a Soviet RoRo ship went down in the vicinity of the Banks.

Conditions can be even worse in regions of tropical cyclones (see *Cyclone and hurricane disasters* page 54). A ship caught near the centre experiences darkness, howling winds, swirling rain and enormously confused, high seas. This is the typical storm described by Joseph Conrad in *Typhoon*, a storm which attacks the mariner 'like a personal enemy, tries to grasp his limbs, fasten upon his mind, seeks to rout his very spirit'. It was under these conditions that the 166 374 dwt *Derbyshire* disappeared without trace in the South China Sea in September 1980. Heavy rain in the vicinity of a hurricane masked the radar pictures on the tankers *Atlantic Empress* (292 666 dwt) and the *Aegean Captain* (210 257 dwt) causing a disastrous collision near Tobago on 19 July 1979.

In spite of technological advances and our greater knowledge, shipbuilders, seamen, fishermen, yachtsmen, scientists, and rig operators all must remain wary of the hazardous sea areas.

1 *below* The world's oceans are divided into zones (load line areas) which correspond to the weather hazards threatening shipping. Load line marks for Tropical, Summer, Winter and Winter North Atlantic zones are drawn on a ship's sides and indicate the levels to which she is permitted to be loaded before sailing in any particular zone.

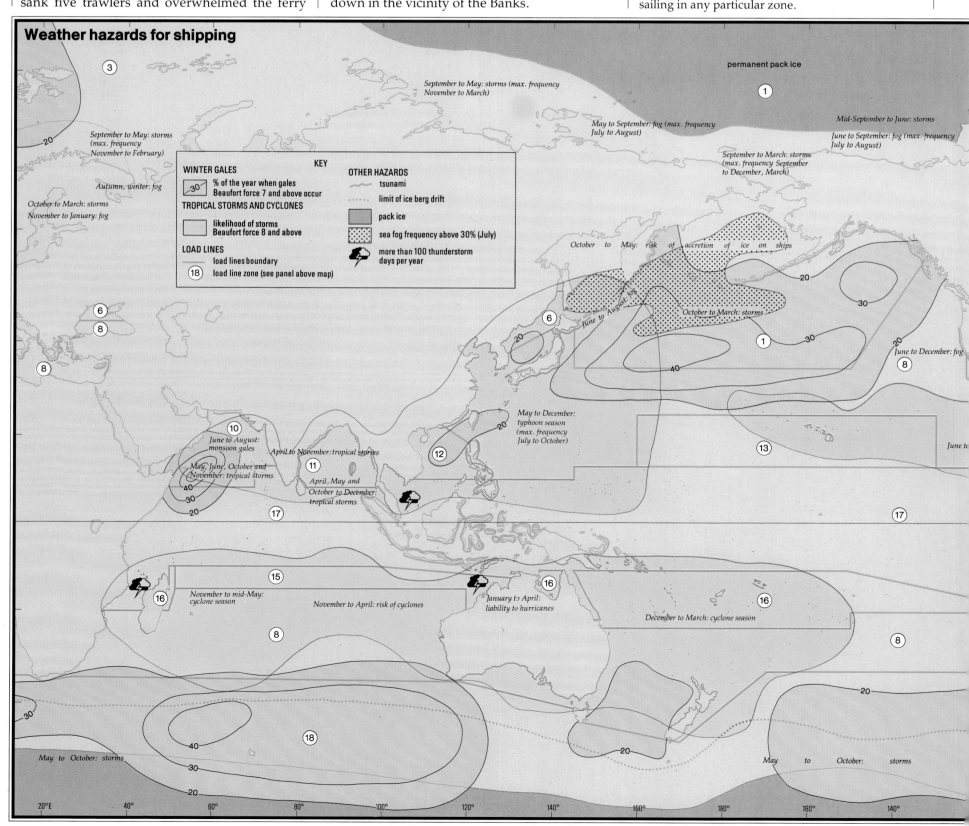

Weather hazards for shipping

permanent pack ice

September to May: storms (max. frequency November to March)

May to September: fog (max. frequency July to August)

Mid-September to June: storms

June to September: fog (max. frequency July to August)

September to March: storms (max. frequency September to December, March)

September to May: storms (max. frequency November to February)

Autumn, winter: fog

October to March: storms November to January: fog

October to May: risk of accretion of ice on ships

June to August: fog

October to March: storms

June to December: fog

KEY

WINTER GALES
- 30 — % of the year when gales Beaufort force 7 and above occur

TROPICAL STORMS AND CYCLONES
- likelihood of storms Beaufort force 8 and above

LOAD LINES
- load lines boundary
- 18 — load line zone (see panel above map)

OTHER HAZARDS
- tsunami
- limit of ice berg drift
- pack ice
- sea fog frequency above 30% (July)
- more than 100 thunderstorm days per year

May to December: typhoon season (max. frequency July to October)

June to August: monsoon gales

April to November: tropical storms

May, June, October and November: tropical storms

April, May and October to December: tropical storms

November to mid-May: cyclone season

November to April: risk of cyclones

January to April: liability to hurricanes

December to March: cyclone season

May to October: storms

May to October: storms

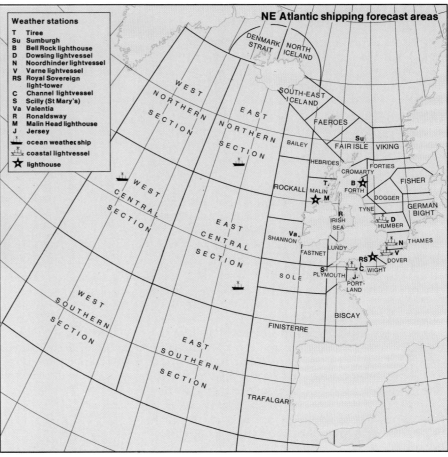

Weather stations

T	Tiree
Su	Sumburgh
B	Bell Rock lighthouse
D	Dowsing lightvessel
N	Noordhinder lightvessel
V	Varne lightvessel
RS	Royal Sovereign light-tower
C	Channel lightvessel
S	Scilly (St Mary's)
Va	Valentia
R	Ronaldsway
M	Malin Head lighthouse
J	Jersey

⊥ ocean weather ship
coastal lightvessel
★ lighthouse

NE Atlantic shipping forecast areas

2 *above* Running before high seas in the Bay of Biscay in winter.

3 *right* Broadcast weather reports originate from a variety of weather stations. The map shows the forecast areas for the north-east Atlantic region.

Load lines

The load line levels are Winter (**W**), Winter North Atlantic (**WNA**), Summer (**S**) and Tropical (**T**). '**W** 16 Oct–15 Apr; **S**' means that ships must load to the Winter depth between 16 October and 15 April but can load to the summer level during the rest of the year.

TF (tropical fresh)

F (fresh)

T

S

W

WNA

L R

LR = Lloyd's Register

1 **W** 16 Oct–15 Apr; **S**
2 **WNA** 16 Oct–15 Apr; **S**
3 **WNA** 1 Nov–31 Mar; **S**
4 Ships over 100 m LOA **W** 16 Dec–15 Feb; **S**
  Ships under 100 m LOA **W** 1 Nov–31 Mar; **S**
5 Ships over 100 m LOA **S** all year; ships under 100 m LOA **W**

6 Ships over 100 m LOA **S** all year; ships under 100 m LOA **W** 1 Dec–28/29 Feb; **S**
7 Ships over 100 m LOA **S** all year; ships under 100 m LOA **W** 16 Dec–15 Mar; **S**
8 **S** all year

9 **T** 1 Nov–15 July; **S**
10 **T** 1 Sept–31 May; **S**
11 **T** 1 Dec–30 Apr; **S**
12 **T** 21 Jan–30 Apr; **S**
13 **T** 1 Apr–31 Oct; **S**
14 **T** 1 Mar–30 Jun and Nov; **S**
15 **T** 1 May–30 Nov; **S**
16 **T** 1 Apr–30 Nov; **S**
17 **T** all year
18 **W** 16 Apr–15 Oct; **S**

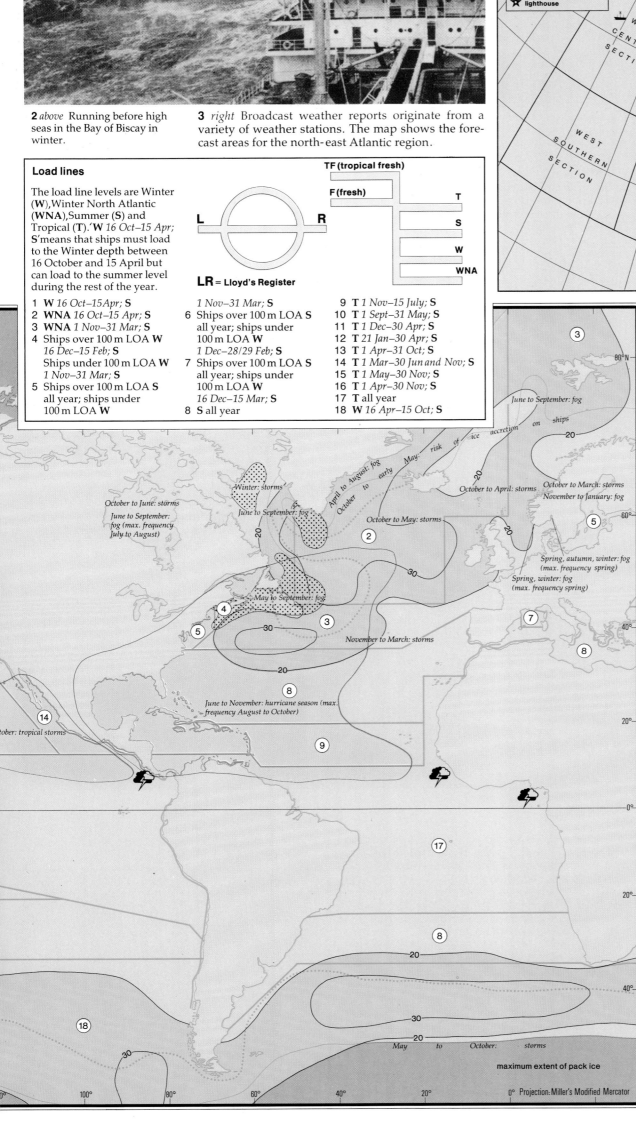

Weather forecasting

Weather forecasts provide the mariner with prognoses of hazardous conditions. Information is also provided for other aspects of seafaring, such as keeping costs down, taking advantage of favourable winds, or having a comfortable cruise.

The content of forecasts varies according to geographical location. In tropical areas, for example, the main features of note are the showers or thunderstorms which are accompanied by violent squalls. In certain regions such as the equatorial areas of the Indian Ocean and over the South China Sea, the monsoon winds are of greatest interest. These are often strong and blow for many days from the same direction causing heavy seas to build up. In many subtropical regions tropical storms are monitored. They often produce winds in excess of 100 knots as far as two hundred miles away from their centre and forecasters have to keep in mind that action must be taken by ships in order to avoid the storm or at least most of its force. Warnings of such features are required as far in advance as possible since a ship's relatively slow speed is of the same order as the speed of movement of tropical storms. Forecasts for sea areas in temperate latitudes are more concerned with the speed and direction of wind, visibility, and significant weather such as rain or snow. Thunderstorm activity would usually be mentioned in view of the squally winds that accompany such weather. In the colder areas towards the Arctic and Antarctic the possibility of ice forming on a ship has to be forecast.

Forecasts for short periods, usually from 24 to 48 hours ahead, are transmitted daily by radio. In return for this service, which is organised nationally by individual countries within the overall guidance of the World Meteorological Organisation, voluntary observations of the weather are made aboard many ships, sometimes as many as four a day. The reports are then inserted into the world-wide meteorological telecommunication system and within hours are available to forecasters all over the world.

Other information used by forecasters includes pictures taken by the various meteorological satellites. These pictures are useful in the identification of major weather features and have ensured, for instance, that no tropical storms go unnoticed.

Forecasts are usually issued as plain language statements of the expected weather for specific sea areas. However, many ships are now fitted with facsimile receivers which enable the mariner to receive charts depicting various forms of forecast information, for example, the forecast heights of waves over the North Atlantic Ocean.

There are also specialised forecast services which require the concentrated skills of experienced forecasters working in close co-operation with land-based master mariners. Such advice, usually tailored for a specific vessel and for which a charge is made, normally relates to a whole voyage and influences the actual route taken (see *Weather routeing* page 148).

High risk environments

THE sea is a dangerous environment for man, and it is not possible to go to sea without risk of accident. Casualty statistics for both ships and oil rigs reflect this, although, certainly in the case of ships, the figures also reflect a lack of proper vigilance towards hazards. Fire at sea is a case in point. Fires and explosions rate highest in casualty records for ships over 500 grt, and between 1979 and 1981 inclusive 188 ships were totally lost in this way. Fire at sea is particularly feared by mariners because no assistance can be offered from shore, and the situation becomes critical when passengers or explosive cargoes are carried, especially in bad weather conditions.

Storms are still a major cause of losses for large ships. The same period 1979–81 saw 160 ships of over 500 grt sink in bad weather. Human failure accounted for many of the 123 ship losses from stranding and 73 from collision in the same class and period. Failure to keep a proper lookout, poor passage planning, misinterpretation of information, and failure to update charts are the principal causes of these accidents.

Oil rig and platform losses are mainly due to bad weather and structural failure, but damage due to fire and explosion is also recorded. Many rigs are damaged while under tow.

It will never be possible entirely to eliminate accidents at sea, but they can be kept to a minimum by better officer training and qualifications, including the use of ship simulators, greater crew awareness of safety on board, lane separation schemes and traffic control, more and better use of instruments to prevent complex multi-ship encounters, as well as a monitoring of port conditions and the penalising of substandard vessels, crews and managers.

1 *right* The major shipping countries with the worst record for ship losses are shown. The figures are for the period 1976–80 for ships over 100 grt. The four different criteria provide a fair indication of the casualty records and contrary to popular opinion, it may be seen that Liberia, the chief flag of convenience country, by no means has the worst record. This is further emphasised by the total losses of the larger class of ships over 500 grt (not shown) for the years 1979–81: the ranking for numbers of ships lost is: Greece 172, Panama 149, Cyprus 53, Liberia 37, South Korea 33, and Japan 25.

2 *below* The cumulative total losses from foundering, collision or wrecking for 1975–80 are shown by sea region. The most hazardous areas are those with combinations of a high density and mix of traffic, particularly where there are deep draughted ships, crossing vessels, reduced visibility, complex tidal conditions, and variable sea floor contours. For example, the waters around Japan are made more hazardous by the dense concentrations of small craft. In 1979 some 2145 ships were involved in accidents in the sea around Japan. Many of them were under 100 grt, and therefore not recorded by Lloyds.

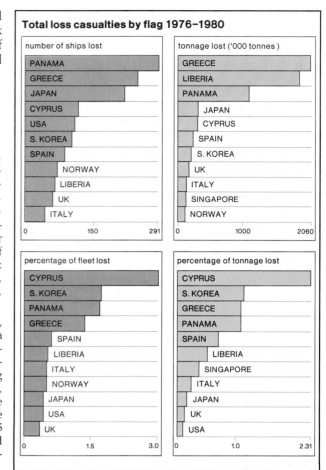

Total loss casualties by flag 1976–1980

number of ships lost

PANAMA	
GREECE	
JAPAN	
CYPRUS	
USA	
S. KOREA	
SPAIN	
NORWAY	
LIBERIA	
UK	
ITALY	

0   150   291

tonnage lost ('000 tonnes)

GREECE	
LIBERIA	
PANAMA	
JAPAN	
CYPRUS	
SPAIN	
S. KOREA	
UK	
ITALY	
SINGAPORE	
NORWAY	

0   1000   2060

percentage of fleet lost

CYPRUS	
S. KOREA	
PANAMA	
GREECE	
SPAIN	
LIBERIA	
ITALY	
NORWAY	
JAPAN	
USA	
UK	

0   1.5   3.0

percentage of tonnage lost

CYPRUS	
S. KOREA	
GREECE	
PANAMA	
SPAIN	
LIBERIA	
SINGAPORE	
ITALY	
JAPAN	
UK	
USA	

0   1.0   2.31

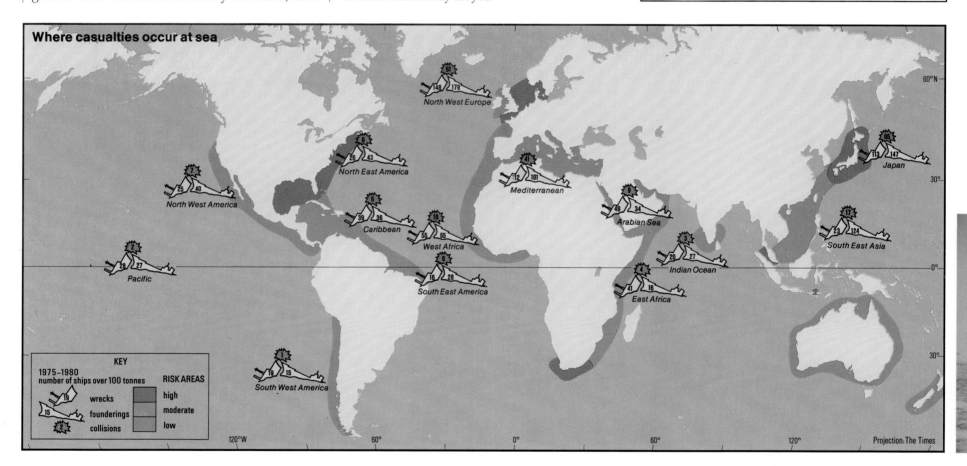

Where casualties occur at sea

North West Europe

North East America

North West America

Mediterranean

Caribbean

West Africa

Arabian Sea

Japan

South East Asia

Pacific

South East America

Indian Ocean

East Africa

South West America

KEY

1975–1980
number of ships over 100 tonnes

wrecks
founderings
collisions

RISK AREAS

high
moderate
low

Projection: The Times

60°N   30°   0°   30°

120°W   60°   0°   60°   120°

3 *below* An oil rig blowout in the Persian Gulf, 1978. If during drilling a large pocket of gas is penetrated, the explosive blast of gas may ignite destroying the rig.

Rig mishaps

Bad weather is a contributory cause in many rig mishaps. In the North Sea rigs are constructed to withstand waves of over 30 m, but hidden structural weaknesses and operational errors both when the rig is in position and when under tow during bad weather have led to severe damage and loss of life. The greatest disasters in recent years have been the capsizing of the semi-submersible accommodation platform *Alexander Kielland* in the North Sea Edda Field on 27 March 1980 with the loss of 123 lives, and the capsizing of the semi-submersible drilling ship *Ocean Ranger* in the Hibernean Field off Newfoundland on 15 February 1982 with the loss of 84 lives. The severest oil pollution from an oil rig occurred with the Ixtoc I blowout in the Bay of Campeche off the Yucatan Peninsula, Gulf of Mexico. The well released about 30 000 barrels per day into the sea from 3 June until September 1979. Some of the oil reached Corpus Christi Bay in Texas, a distance of some 800 km. During a blowout an immense amount of heat is generated which makes it difficult to control and may lead to the collapse of the structure. New fire fighting semi-submersibles have been designed and one is operational in the North Sea to deal with this type of emergency and specialised blowout teams are available for world wide action.

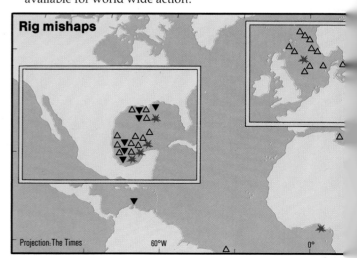

Rig mishaps

Projection: The Times

60°W   0°

Ice casualties

Ever since the loss of the *Titanic* shipping has been warned of the dangers of navigating in ice regions. But despite the presence of ice patrols, damage to ships and losses sometimes occur in the ice regions of North America and the Baltic, the North Pacific, and very occasionally in the Southern Ocean. Aircraft and now satellites are used in ice surveillance. The *Titanic*, while the most spectacular and tragic destruction of a vessel by ice, was not an isolated example.

Establishment of an ice reconnaissance and warning service, now known as the International Ice Patrol, was one outcome of the first International Convention for the Safety of Life at Sea, held in 1913 to consider the lessons of the *Titanic* disaster. The patrol observes sea-ice and icebergs, particularly in the shipping lanes; keeps shipping informed of ice conditions; issues warnings twice daily by radio; assists vessels in distress; and investigates the behaviour of sea-ice and icebergs, such as rate of melting, with particular reference to ocean currents.

5 *right* The black dots show locations of losses of ships over 100 grt in ice between 1890 and 1980. The hazardous nature of ice is revealed by the records which refer to ships being 'cut through', 'stove in', crushed or driven inshore.

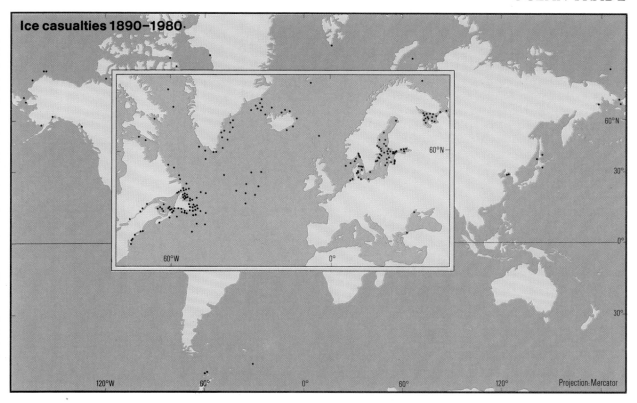

Ice casualties 1890–1980

Projection: Mercator

7 *below right* **Loss of the Titanic 14–15 April 1912**

Vessel description: British passenger liner, then the world's largest at 46 328 grt, length 260 m; propelled by triple screws at maximum speed 22 knots. Passenger capacity 2603 though at the time of her loss 1316 were on board together with 885 crew (2201 persons in total). Many thought the *Titanic* was unsinkable. She had 15 transverse watertight bulkheads and was designed to remain afloat with any two adjacent main compartments flooded. Her lifeboats could accommodate 1178 persons.
Voyage: Maiden voyage from Europe to New York. She sailed from Southampton, calling at Cherbourg and Queenstown, Ireland, departing from there on her Atlantic passage on Thursday, 11 April.
Time of collision with iceberg: 23.40 Titanic time; 21.38 New York time (Titanic time is used throughout the account below).
Date: Sunday, 14 April 1912.
Place: North Atlantic Ocean, probable position 41°33'N, 50°01'W, where survivors in lifeboats and wreckage were found, some 16 nm SE of the *Titanic*'s DR position of 41°46'N, 50°14'W which she broadcast by radio in her distress message.
Conditions: A dark moonless night, cloudless and perfectly clear, sea exceptionally calm.
At 17.50 the *Titanic*'s course was set to 266°; her speed was

21.6 knots despite radio warnings of ice from other ships. She relied solely on a sharp visual lookout. (Marine radar was not developed for some 30 years, and radio communication was still in its infancy.)

A lookout in the crow's-nest reported the dark silhouette of an iceberg right ahead at 23.40. The officer of the watch immediately ordered the helm to be put hardover to alter course to port and the engines full astern; he also closed the watertight doors. The iceberg, a small one, was almost black: when spotted it was only 500 m ahead. It was unavoidable.

A deceptively slight bump was felt as the iceberg scraped the starboard side, but five compartments in the forward section of the hull were seriously damaged and leaking beyond the capacity of the pumps. The extent of the damage was quickly realised. Radio distress signals were received by several ships. At 00.35 and 00.40 respectively, the *Carpathia* and the *Mount Temple* began heading towards the *Titanic*'s DR position, the *Carpathia* from 58 nm away and the *Mount Temple* from about 50 nm.

All *Titanic*'s lifeboats were lowered. As there were too few they were filled mainly with women and children. Some women could not be persuaded to leave, so men took spare spaces; many were left unfilled. A ship's lights were sighted, falsely claimed to be those of the *Californian*. Distress rockets and morse signals were used to attract her attention. Only about 5 nm distant, the mystery ship steamed slowly away.

The *Titanic* sank at 02.20.

The *Carpathia* arrived on the scene at 04.00 having proceeded in excess of her full speed of 14 knots, risking several close encounters with ice; she rescued 711 from the lifeboats. Many died floating in their lifejackets in the icy sea; 1490 lives were lost. The *Carpathia*'s track towards the *Titanic*'s (false?) DR position had fortunately intercepted the actual position of the disaster. (If the *Carpathia* had in fact reached the DR position her speed would have averaged 17 knots—most unlikely.)

6 *left* The International Ice Patrol operates off Newfoundland during the iceberg season between March and July. The Patrol is financed on a basis whereby each signatory nation pays in proportion to its total shipping tonnage.

The *Mount Temple* arrived at the ice barrier near the false position at 03.25 and found nothing.

The *Californian*, later alleged not to have offered assistance, had in fact stopped at 22.33 because of the ice conditions, some 33 nm north of the *Titanic*'s actual distress position, more than an hour before the *Titanic*'s collision. She remained there until just after dawn.

At about 06.00 the officer learned of the sinking, and immediately the *Californian* forced her way through the ice barrier and proceeded to *Titanic*'s DR position. After steaming about 20 nm at full speed she met the *Mount Temple* searching the area of the *Titanic*'s reported position but found nothing. She continued about ten miles south, skirting the ice barrier. She sighted the *Carpathia* at 08.00 and headed east towards her, again forcing her way through the ice. At 08.30 she joined *Carpathia* in the search but no more survivors were found.

Apart from the tragic loss of life on the *Titanic* caused by her reckless speed and inadequate lifeboat capacity, the disaster resulted also in the vilification of a remote and innocent bystander, the master of the *Californian*, by the ill-conducted Court of Inquiry.
Consequences: Various safety measures were introduced: 1. Regulations for life-saving appliances were amended. A vessel's lifeboat capacity had to be made adequate to accommodate all persons on board. Previously the Board of Trade regulations, to which the *Titanic* had complied, specified lifeboats merely in relation to a ship tonnage scale. 2. Specifications for lifeboats and their equipment were improved. 3. Regulations for emergency musters and drills were introduced. 4. Watchkeepers were required to pass eyesight tests. 5. The International Ice Patrol was formed to improve information and warnings about ice conditions in the North Atlantic. 6. Regulations for the improvement of radio installations and watchkeeping stated all vessels of any consequence must possess a radio and maintain a 24-hour radio watch for distress signals.

The foolhardy concept of a totally safe, unsinkable ship was no longer accepted. The memory of the *Titanic* stays firmly in the minds of those attending conferences for the Safety of Life at Sea.

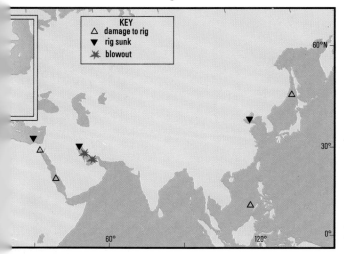

3 *below* Between 1978 and 1981 sixty accidents to rigs at sea were reported. Fourteen of these resulted in total losses. Ten were blowouts where serious pollution of the surrounding sea or coastal areas occurred.

KEY
△ damage to rig
▼ rig sunk
✳ blowout

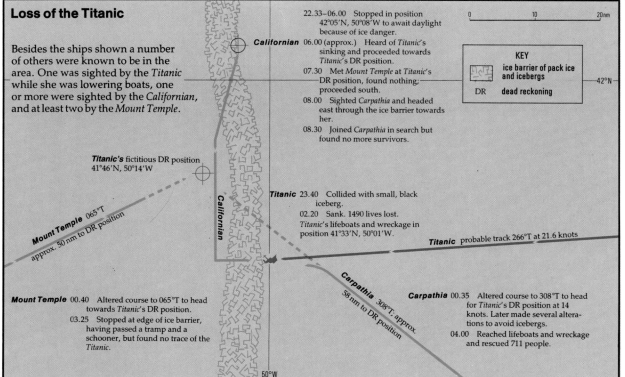

Loss of the Titanic

Besides the ships shown a number of others were known to be in the area. One was sighted by the *Titanic* while she was lowering boats, one or more were sighted by the *Californian*, and at least two by the *Mount Temple*.

Californian 22.33–06.00 Stopped in position 42°05'N, 50°08'W to await daylight because of ice danger.
06.00 (approx.) Heard of *Titanic*'s sinking and proceeded towards *Titanic*'s DR position.
07.30 Met *Mount Temple* at *Titanic*'s DR position, found nothing; proceeded south.
08.00 Sighted *Carpathia* and headed east through the ice barrier towards her.
08.30 Joined *Carpathia* in search but found no more survivors.

KEY
ice barrier of pack ice and icebergs
DR dead reckoning

Titanic's fictitious DR position 41°46'N, 50°14'W

Titanic 23.40 Collided with small, black iceberg.
02.20 Sank. 1490 lives lost. *Titanic*'s lifeboats and wreckage in position 41°33'N, 50°01'W.

Mount Temple 065°T approx. 50 nm to DR position

Titanic probable track 266°T at 21.6 knots

Carpathia 308°T; approx. 58 nm to DR position

Mount Temple 00.40 Altered course to 065°T to head towards *Titanic*'s DR position.
03.25 Stopped at edge of ice barrier, having passed a tramp and a schooner, but found no trace of the *Titanic*.

Carpathia 00.35 Altered course to 308°T to head for *Titanic*'s DR position at 14 knots. Later made several alterations to avoid icebergs.
04.00 Reached lifeboats and wreckage and rescued 711 people.

Shipping casualties

DESPITE the wider use and greater sophistication of navigational aids both on board ship and on shore, shipping accidents remain at a high level. The record of ships over 100 grt lost for 1976–80 is as follows:

year	no. of ships lost	million grt	ratio of losses to total grt (%)
1976	345	1.1	0.33
1977	336	1.0	0.31
1978	423	1.7	0.35
1979	465	2.2	0.56
1980	387	1.8	0.42

The total number of ships lost or seriously damaged in 1978 and 1979 was 2394. There are some clear black spots, particularly for collisions and strandings, which are located in narrow channels, around headlands and in areas where shipping density is high, especially in northwest European waters and the seas around Japan and South East Asia. The direct relationship between shipping densities and accidents is compounded by reduced visibility, strong tidal currents, deep-draughted vessels, the use of untrustworthy charts and equipment failure, and above all, human error. Since the advent of VLCCs in the 1960s the threat of disastrous pollution as a result of casualties has increased vastly (see *Oil spillages* page 170).

Weather conditions still account for most ship losses under 100 grt. Large ships are also at risk, hence the disappearance of the factory trawler *Gaul* in appalling conditions during a winter gale in 1974 in the northern North Sea.

The main causes of losses of the larger class of ships, over 500 grt, during 1981 were: fire and explosion, 69 ships (including two tankers struck by lightning after unloading); weather, 50 ships; stranding, 38 ships; and collisions, 30 ships. In addition to environmental damage and loss of property there is loss of life. In 1981 some 1094 people died in ship accidents, including 488 in two ferry disasters, and a volunteer lifeboat crew from a small village in Penlee, Cornwall, lost while on a rescue mission.

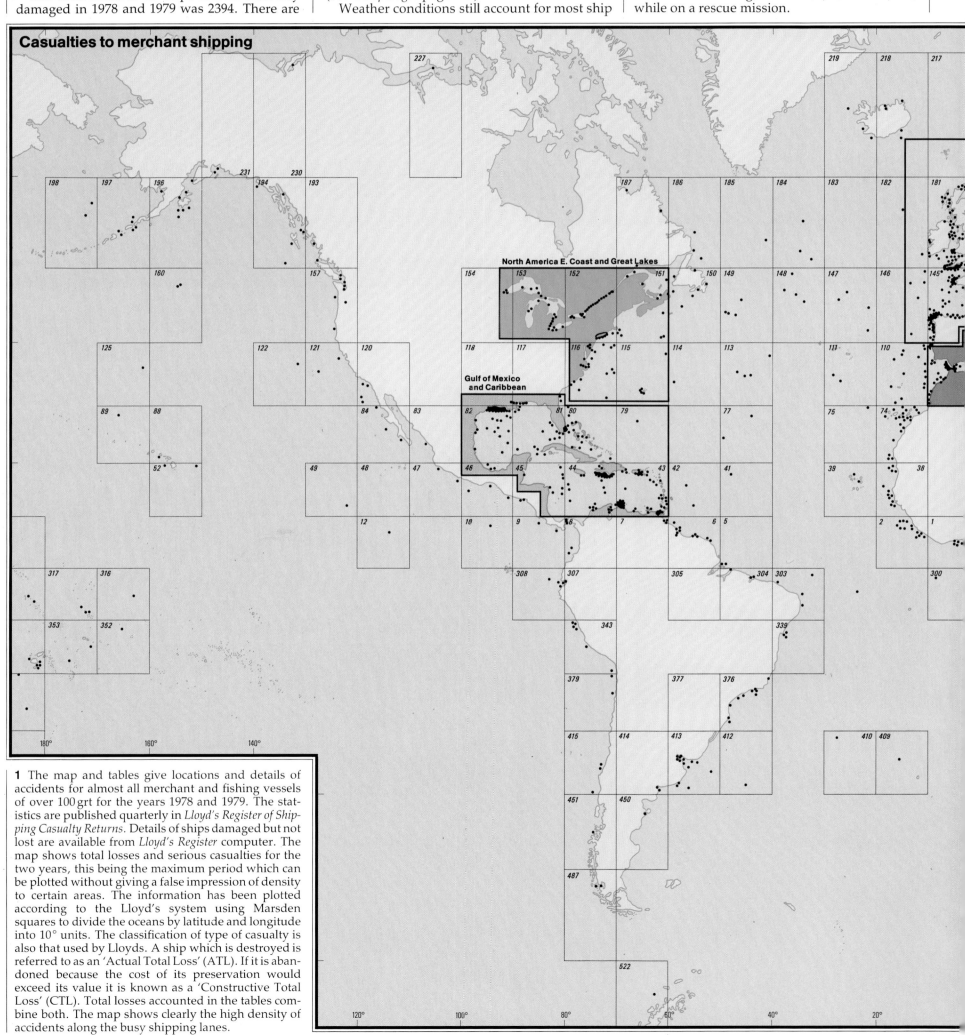

Casualties to merchant shipping

North America E. Coast and Great Lakes

Gulf of Mexico and Caribbean

1 The map and tables give locations and details of accidents for almost all merchant and fishing vessels of over 100 grt for the years 1978 and 1979. The statistics are published quarterly in *Lloyd's Register of Shipping Casualty Returns*. Details of ships damaged but not lost are available from *Lloyd's Register* computer. The map shows total losses and serious casualties for the two years, this being the maximum period which can be plotted without giving a false impression of density to certain areas. The information has been plotted according to the Lloyd's system using Marsden squares to divide the oceans by latitude and longitude into 10° units. The classification of type of casualty is also that used by Lloyds. A ship which is destroyed is referred to as an 'Actual Total Loss' (ATL). If it is abandoned because the cost of its preservation would exceed its value it is known as a 'Constructive Total Loss' (CTL). Total losses accounted in the tables combine both. The map shows clearly the high density of accidents along the busy shipping lanes.

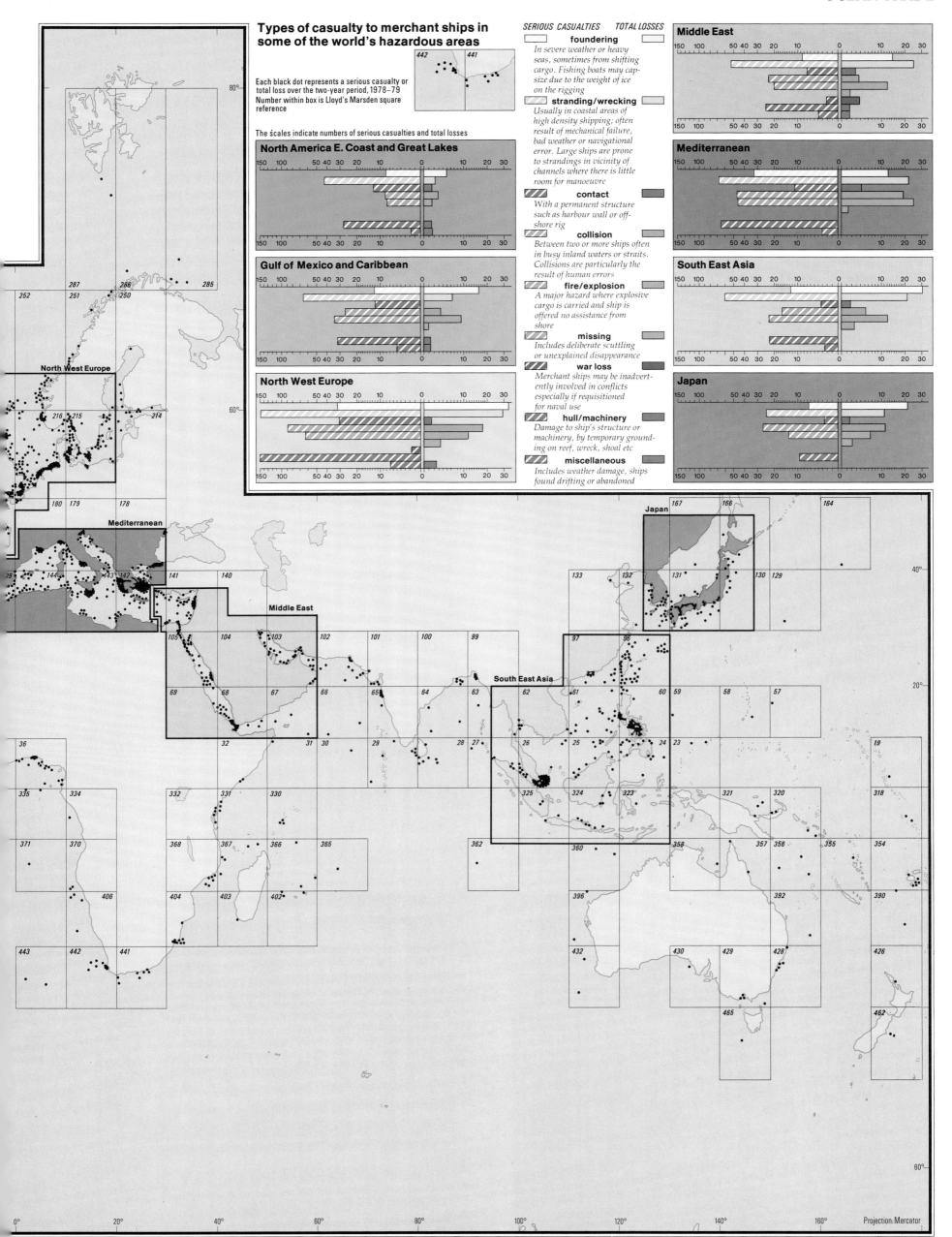

Types of casualty to merchant ships in some of the world's hazardous areas

Each black dot represents a serious casualty or total loss over the two-year period, 1978–79 Number within box is Lloyd's Marsden square reference

The scales indicate numbers of serious casualties and total losses

SERIOUS CASUALTIES   TOTAL LOSSES

foundering
In severe weather or heavy seas, sometimes from shifting cargo. Fishing boats may capsize due to the weight of ice on the rigging

stranding/wrecking
Usually in coastal areas of high density shipping; often result of mechanical failure, bad weather or navigational error. Large ships are prone to strandings in vicinity of channels where there is little room for manoeuvre

contact
With a permanent structure such as harbour wall or off-shore rig

collision
Between two or more ships often in busy inland waters or straits. Collisions are particularly the result of human errors

fire/explosion
A major hazard where explosive cargo is carried and ship is offered no assistance from shore

missing
Includes deliberate scuttling or unexplained disappearance

war loss
Merchant ships may be inadvertently involved in conflicts especially if requisitioned for naval use

hull/machinery
Damage to ship's structure or machinery, by temporary grounding on reef, wreck, shoal etc

miscellaneous
Includes weather damage, ships found drifting or abandoned

North America E. Coast and Great Lakes

Gulf of Mexico and Caribbean

North West Europe

Middle East

Mediterranean

South East Asia

Japan

Projection: Mercator

Collision at sea

INTERNATIONAL regulations for preventing collisions at sea have existed for a relatively short time. Before 1846 there were no statutory rules for avoiding collisions, but there were various rules of custom which formed part of the general maritime law. These rules were for sailing vessels and gave one vessel priority over another depending on relative wind directions.

In 1840 London Trinity House published rules for avoidance of collision between steamships. These required steamships approaching one another to alter course to starboard so that they passed on their port sides; and also required steamships to keep to their respective starboard sides of a narrow channel. The Steam Navigation Act of 1846 adopted London Trinity House rules.

Between 1846 and 1910 rules for ships' navigation lights, and penalties for proven failure to comply with regulations, were introduced. During these years there was some international agreement, and the International Regulations of

1910 proved to be very durable, remaining in force, with little change, until the 1948 Regulations came into force in 1954.

In 1933 the English system of helm orders was made illegal. Before then two systems of giving helm orders, the English and the French, had been used worldwide and had been the direct cause of accidents. In the English system, based on the use of the tiller, the call for 'starboard' meant that the tiller was moved to starboard in order to move the ship's head to port. The French call for starboard (tripord!) resulted in the ship's head turning to starboard. In an incident on the Thames in 1884, a local English pilot on a French vessel, the *Indus*, called 'tripord' and the ship, turning to starboard, struck the training vessel *Shaftesbury*.

The 1948 changes were mainly cosmetic (e.g. the term 'steam ship' was changed to 'power-driven vessel'). Radar was not mentioned as the danger of the so-called 'radar assisted' collision

had yet to be recognised. The *Stockholm* v. *Andrea Doria* collision (1956) highlighted the problem of using radar for collision avoidance, and the 1960 Regulations, which came into force in 1965, gave recommendations on the use of radar for avoiding collisions, and made clear that the basic rules for collision avoidance could be applied only by vessels in sight of each other. Despite notice of the 1960 radar recommendations, the *British Aviator* and *Crystal Jewel* collided in 1961. 'Radar-assisted' collisions of this type still occur.

The most common, 'end-on meeting' collisions are especially prevalent in straits and off main headlands. Traffic separation schemes in such areas, first introduced on a voluntary basis in the Straits of Dover in 1967, have significantly reduced collisions in North West European waters, from 156 in 1956–61 to 45 in 1976–81. (For straits having traffic separation schemes see pages 150–1.) The latest (1972) Collision Regulations came into force in 1977.

Stockholm
(Norwegian)
v.
Andrea Doria
(Italian)
Place: Open sea in the approaches to New York, about 20 nm west of Nantucket lightvessel
Date: 25 July 1956
Time: 23.10 local time
Conditions: Stockholm was approaching the fog bank from which *Andrea Doria* was emerging

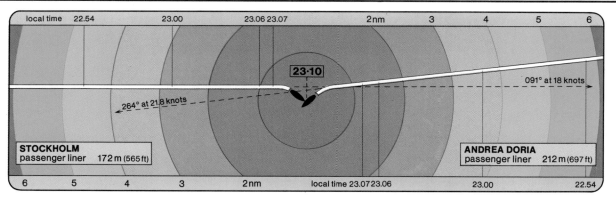

Cause: Lack of systematic radar observation together with immoderate speed. Possibility of some radar instrumental error.

Both vessels had observed each other on their respective radars for about 15–20 minutes before the collision. *Stockholm* was in clear weather but approaching a fog bank which was obscuring navigation lights. *Andrea Doria* emerged from the edge of the fog bank and the two vessels first sighted each other's navigation lights when they were about 1½–2 nm

apart. *Stockholm*'s speed was 18 knots and *Andrea Dorea*'s 21.8 knots, giving a relative approach speed of nearly 40 knots (i.e. 2 nm in 3 minutes).
Action: Stockholm, having the *Andrea Doria* fine on her port bow, went hard to starboard; *Andrea Doria*, having the *Stockholm* fine on her starboard bow, went hard to port.

Impact: Stem of *Stockholm* into starboard side amidships of the *Andrea Doria*. Angle of blow about 90°.
Consequences: Andrea Doria sank 11 hours after the collision, with the loss of 44 lives out of 1706. Most lives were lost by crushing in the initial impact. *Stockholm* had a severely damaged bow. The civil action was settled out of court.

Crystal Jewel
(British)
v.
British Aviator
(British)
Place: English Channel, 6 nm south-east of the Royal Sovereign lightvessel
Date: 23 September 1961
Time: 08.51 BST
Conditions: Both vessels in fog

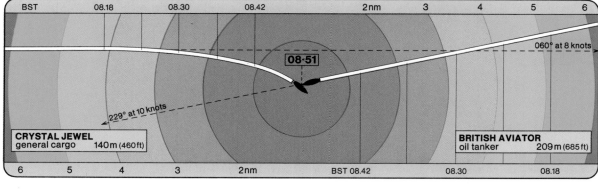

Cause: Lack of systematic radar observation. Succession of small alterations of course made by *Crystal Jewel* were confusing. The speeds of both vessels were immoderate in the later stages as they closed in on each other. Both vessels should have made substantial alterations of course at an early stage, or reduced speed considerably before coming into close quarters.

Both vessels were using radar and detected each other some 30 minutes before the collision. The *Crystal Jewel* was proceeding at a reduced speed of about 8 knots, and the *British Aviator* was also proceeding at a reduced speed of about 10 knots.
Action: The *Crystal Jewel*, believing that the vessels were going to pass close port to port, initially altered course 5° to starboard and then, as the *British Aviator* still appeared to be

coming too close, the *Crystal Jewel* made a series of small alterations of course to starboard. The *British Aviator* believed that the vessels were going to pass safely starboard to starboard and so maintained her course until a few moments before the collision when the *British Aviator* went hard to port, believing that the *Crystal Jewel* was still going to pass starboard to starboard, although much closer than previously anticipated.
Impact: Stem of *British Aviator* into port side amidships of the

Crystal Jewel. Angle of blow about 90°.
Consequences: Crystal Jewel had to be beached to avoid sinking. Both vessels later repaired. One life lost on the *Crystal Jewel.* The Court of Appeal found each vessel 50 per cent to blame.

It is notable that an almost carbon-copy collision occurred not far away in the English Channel a few hours later on the same day, the *Niceto de Larrinaga* v. *Sitala* collision (see below).

Niceto de Larrinaga
(British)
v.
Sitala
(French)
Place: English Channel
Date: 23 September 1961
Time: 18.32 local time
Conditions: Both vessels in fog

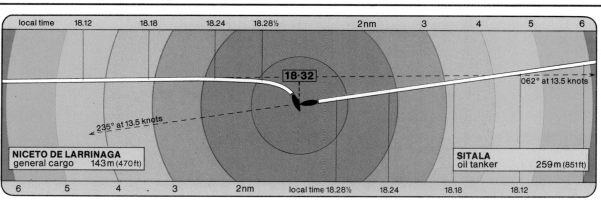

Cause: As for *Crystal Jewel* v. *British Aviator* collision (see above).

Like the *Crystal Jewel* v. *British Aviator* described above, this was a case of fine crossing in fog with both vessels using radar. The *Niceto de Larrinaga* (like the *Crystal Jewel*) believed it to be a close port to port passing whereas the *Sitala* considered it to be a safe starboard to starboard passing.
Action: The *Niceto de Larrinaga* made a series of small alter-

ations of course to starboard—keeping the radar echo of the *Sitala* on her port bow—and finally went hard to starboard at about a minute before the collision. The *Sitala* stopped her engines about a minute before the collision, which had by then become inevitable.
Impact: Stem of the *Sitala* into the port bow of the *Niceto de*

Larrinaga. Angle of blow was 65° leading aft on *Niceto de Larrinaga.*
Consequences: Both vessels were seriously damaged. Two lives lost on the *Niceto de Larrinaga.* Admiralty Division of the High Court found the *Niceto de Larrinaga* 60 per cent to blame, and the *Sitala* 40 per cent.

Statue of Liberty
(Liberian)
v.
Andulo
(Portuguese)
Place: About 3 nm SSW of
Cape St Vincent
Date: 8 June 1965
Time: 01.57 local time
Conditions: A fine, clear night

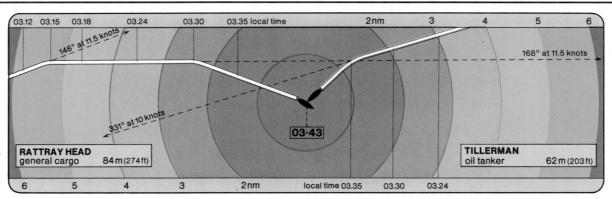

Cause: Defective look-out on
both ships, and very tardy
give-way action on behalf
of the *Statue of Liberty*.

The *Andulo* had sighted the *Statue of Liberty* on her port bow. The *Statue of Liberty* was the give-way vessel.
Action: The *Andulo*, believing that the *Statue of Liberty* was going to pass safely ahead of her, and that there was no further risk of collision, altered course to port to come onto the next leg of her track to her destination. Almost simultaneously with the *Andulo*'s alteration to port for navigational

reasons, the *Statue of Liberty* altered course to starboard to avoid collision. The vessels were less than a mile apart when their cancelling actions were taken and despite hard-over helm by both ships the collision had become inevitable. (The alteration of course made by the *Statue of Liberty* at 01.39 was for navigational reasons only; the *Andulo* was over 8 nm away at that time.)

Impact: Stem of *Statue of Liberty* into starboard side of *Andulo*. Angle of blow 85° leading forward on *Andulo*.
Consequences: Andulo sank the day after the collision; *Statue of Liberty* had severe damage to her bow and port side as she scraped past the *Andulo*. No lives were lost. House of Lords found *Statue of Liberty* 85 per cent to blame, and *Andulo* 15 per cent.

Rattray Head
(British)
v.
Tillerman
(British)
Place: North Sea, about 15 nm
off Blyth on the north-east
coast of Britain
Date: 24 June 1969
Time: 03.45 BST
Conditions: Both vessels in fog

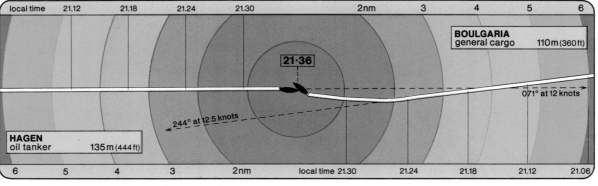

Cause: Poor look-out because
of discontinuous and
unsystematic radar
observation. Possibly poor
control design: in order to
alter course to starboard
(clockwise), the control verge
ring on the compass for the
autopilot had to be turned
anticlockwise, and vice versa.

Both vessels were using radar. The *Rattray Head* was following a course of 148° when she detected the echo of a vessel ahead.
Action: The *Rattray Head* altered course to starboard 20° to steer 168°. The echo passed clear on the port side but before resuming course the *Rattray Head* detected another echo ahead which was thought to be a vessel on an opposite course. The *Rattray Head* altered another 20° to starboard to

steer 188°. The officer of the watch left the radar in order to try to sight the oncoming vessel, which was to be the *Tillerman*. Meanwhile, the *Tillerman* had noticed the echo of the *Rattray Head* on her starboard bow, and that the echo was moving to pass ahead of the *Tillerman*. The officer of the watch of the *Tillerman* adjusted his automatic steering (autopilot), fully intending to alter course 25° to starboard but, in error, altered course 25° to port. The officer on watch did not realise his

mistake for some minutes, by which time it was too late. The vessels collided about 8 minutes later.
Impact: Stem of *Tillerman* struck the port side aft of the *Rattray Head.*
Consequences: Neither vessel incurred severe damage. The *Tillerman* stopped engines on sighting the *Rattray Head* about 0.2 nm ahead.

Hagen
(German)
v.
Boulgaria
(Greek)
Place: English Channel about
15 nm ENE of Casquets
Date: 4 July 1970
Time: 21.36 BST
Conditions: Both vessels in fog

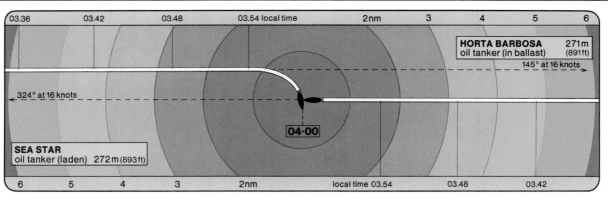

Cause: Hagen proceeding at
immoderate speed, and
Boulgaria proceeding at
immoderate speed and
failing to use radar properly.

This was another fine-crossing collision in fog where initially the vessels were going to pass close starboard to starboard. The *Boulgaria* was using radar; *Hagen*'s radar was not in use as it had broken down three days previously.
Action: It appears that in this case the *Boulgaria* crossed the

bow of the *Hagen* and then, in the belief that the vessels were in a more end-on situation, made a couple of small alterations of course to starboard, and then both vessels altered course hard to starboard, too late, as they came into sight, moments before the collision.

Impact: Stem of the *Hagen* into the port side aft of the *Boulgaria*. Angle of blow 75° leading aft on the *Boulgaria*.
Consequences: Boulgaria sank shortly after the collision, with the loss of 17 lives. Admiralty Court, Queen's Bench, found *Hagen* 40 per cent to blame and *Boulgaria* 60 per cent.

Sea Star
(South Korean)
v.
Horta Barbosa
(Brazilian)
Place: Gulf of Oman, in
approx. position 25°20′ N,
57°30′ E
Date: 19 December 1972
Time: 04.00 local time
Conditions: A fine, clear night
with a light breeze

Cause: Improper assessment
of the situation by the *Sea
Star*, which resulted in the *Sea
Star* altering course to
starboard too late. Defective
look-out by the *Horta Barbosa*
during the period in which it
was expected that the vessels
were about to pass close
starboard-to-starboard.

Both vessels had detected one another by radar when they were some 16 nm apart, and had seen each other's navigational lights at a substantial range, probably when they were more than 10 nm apart. The *Horta Barbosa* believed, by radar plotting confirmed by visual observation, that the vessels should pass each other starboard to starboard at a range of ¾–1 nm. The *Sea Star* decided that it was a nearly end-on meeting, a collision risk case which demanded that both vessels should alter course to starboard so each might pass on the port side of the other.
Action: The *Sea Star* altered course to starboard when the

vessels were 2–3 nm apart. This was not observed immediately by the *Horta Barbosa* because the officer of the watch was observing the land by radar to fix the position of his ship, and to complete his log book in readiness for handing over to his relief who was due on watch at 04.00. At the same time the cadet of the watch, and the look-out man, were engaged also in calling their reliefs. By the time the *Sea Star*'s alteration of course was observed, about a minute before collision, it was too late.
Impact: Stem of *Horta Barbosa* into port side of the *Sea Star*. Angle of blow about 90°.

Consequences: Sea Star exploded and caught fire, and later sank. *Horta Barbosa* was badly damaged. 11 lives were lost, all from the *Sea Star*, including four of the five who were on the bridge, namely the second officer, the chief officer who arrived on the bridge at 03.50 to relieve the second officer, the helmsman and the look-out man; of the bridge team only the cadet on watch survived. The Admiralty Court of the Queen's Bench found the *Sea Star* 75 per cent to blame, and the *Horta Barbosa* 25 per cent. This judgement was upheld by the Court of Appeal.

Stranding and loss: three tanker disasters

THE strandings of the *Torrey Canyon*, the *Argo Merchant*, and the *Amoco Cadiz* are notable for their effect on the formulation of various new international regulations. The impact of the *Torrey Canyon* loss (1967) was probably greater than that of the *Titanic*. Within two weeks, the Inter-governmental Maritime Consultative Organisation (see IMO, *appendices*) met in emergency session and adopted a comprehensive plan to obtain international agreements on routeing of ships; navigational aids; ship construction; training and certification of seafarers; watchkeeping standards; intervention on the high seas in the event of threat of pollution from a ship; liability of shipowners for pollution damage; and compensation for oil pollution damage.

The *Torrey Canyon* prompted half a dozen IMO conferences and conventions between 1969 and 1974, mainly concerned with oil pollution, such as the International Convention for the Prevention of Pollution from Ships (MARPOL 1973). (See *Pollution conventions*, page 224). This stranding also inspired the International Convention on the Safety of Life at Sea (SOLAS 1974), which came into force in 1980.

Similarly, the stranding of the *Argo Merchant* was one of a number of tanker accidents around the United States of America 1976–77 which inspired President Carter to make a request for further international action. This resulted in two Protocols which strengthen MARPOL 1973 and SOLAS 1974.

President Carter's initiative, together with the stranding of the *Amoco Cadiz* in March 1978, gave urgency to another international conference which was mainly concerned with the element of human error in accidents, and resulted in the 1978 International Convention on Standards of Training, Certification and Watchkeeping of Seafarers (probably in force in 1983).

It is also interesting to note that the *Amoco Cadiz* stranding was mainly caused by steering gear failure, and this accident added urgency to the requirements for dual steering gear systems in certain classes of ships, as well as to recommendations for improved steering gear specifications generally.

To help avoid stranding, IMO Routeing Instructions, besides designating Traffic Separation Schemes for collision avoidance, also specify a few well-surveyed Deep Water Routes for deep-drafted ships to pass along through relatively shallow seas of changing depths, and Areas to be Avoided because of inadequate survey.

1 *below* Argo Merchant

Vessel description: Liberian oil tanker, length 183.5 m. Normal service speed 16 knots; at time of her loss, owing to combination of weather conditions and boiler trouble, average speed was between 8 and 9 knots. Load carried 28 000 tonnes of dense fuel oil; draught about 10.7 m
Time of stranding: 06.00 local time
Date: Wednesday, 15 December 1976
Place: In position 41°02′N, 69°27′W, near Nantucket Shoals, off east coast of America
Voyage: From Puerto La Cruz, Venezuela, to Salem, Massachusetts

At 23.00 on Sunday, 12 December, the *Argo Merchant's* position was fixed off Cape Hatteras: Diamond Shoal lightvessel was bearing 310°T, at 9 nm; course was set directly towards Nantucket lightvessel, 415 nm ahead. The master's intention was to pass about 4 nm east of the lightvessel and east of Nantucket shoals.

On 13 and 14 December noon positions were calculated from celestial observations.

At 18.00 on 14 December the gyro compass system was noted to be erratic; thereafter the vessel was steered by reference to the magnetic compass.

At 22.00 one of the two radars onboard was switched on; during subsequent hours a number of vessels were detected but none was identified as Nantucket lightvessel.

At 01.00 on 15 December the master joined the second officer on the bridge. The depth sounder, switched on some time before 04.00, recorded a decrease to between 27 and 37 m, much less than expected.

At 04.00 the chief officer relieved the second officer; the latter remained on the bridge as did the master. All three were now concerned at not finding Nantucket lightvessel at the expected time of 03.30; the chief officer urged the master to 'do something' but the master decided not to change course or speed. Visibility was said to be about 7–8 nm; wind was strong southerly.

At 04.30 a radio bearing indicated that Nantucket lightvessel was right ahead but subsequent events prove that this must have been incorrect.

At 05.30 the chief officer desperately tried to obtain a celestial fix, though he knew conditions were unsuitable. In any case, in his haste he made a mistake in calculation: the position found was absurd and was discarded without further check. It was decided to wait until 06.00 when conditions for celestial observations might improve.

At 06.00 the *Argo Merchant* stranded; the master ordered the engines to be run astern but she was stuck firmly aground.
Cause: The probable track of the *Argo Merchant* was determined during the Liberian Marine Board Investigation, and is based on the magnetic courses steered as recorded in the ship's log. Comparison of gyro-compass and magnetic compass records indicate that the gyro was probably erratic some time before it was found to be so. Also, allowances being made for wind and current were declared not altogether appropriate.

The *Argo Merchant*, built in 1953 and so relatively old, was found to have some deficiencies which contributed towards her loss (e.g. faulty gyro and course recorder, and possibly a faulty radio direction finder). But the principal cause of her loss was navigational incompetence. The master had three clear warnings of impending danger: 1. Noon positions determined on 13 and 14 December indicated the probable track of the vessel towards the grounding position. 2. Nantucket lightvessel was neither sighted nor detected by radar, long after the expected time of 03.30, i.e. two and a half hours before grounding. 3. The depth soundings gave absolute proof that the vessel was off her proposed track and was running into shallow waters three hours before grounding.

Consequences: Some attempt was made at salvage but the weather worsened and the ship was abandoned two days after grounding. There was no loss of life. The vessel broke up but fortunately, with an offshore wind, most of the oil which leaked dispersed seawards. Nevertheless, costly precautions were taken to forestall possible pollution, and, as the disaster followed a number of other incidents in or near the USA, the American public was alerted to the dangers of pollution.

2 *right* Torrey Canyon

Vessel description: Liberian oil tanker, 297 m in length. At the time of loss she was fully loaded with over 119 000 tonnes of crude oil; her draught was about 16 m, full speed about 15¾ knots
Time of stranding: 08.50 GMT
Date: Saturday, 18 March 1967
Place: Seven Stones reef, about 7 nm north-east of the Scilly Isles, Great Britain
Voyage: From Mina al Ahmadi, Kuwait, to Milford Haven, Wales

On Tuesday, 14 March, after passing between Tenerife and the Grand Canary Island, the *Torrey Canyon's* course was set to 018°T, in order to pass 5 nm west of the Scilly Isles, which were then about 1400 nm away.

At about 02.30 on Saturday, 18 March, the master left night orders asking to be called either as soon as the Scilly Isles were detected by radar, or sighted, or in any case not later than 06.00. There was a moderate north-westerly wind with visibility about 10 nm.

The master was called at 06.00 and informed by the chief officer that the Scilly Isles had not yet been detected.

At about 06.30, the Scilly Isles were detected by radar on the port bow at a range said to be about 24 nm (about 26 nm is more likely to be correct). The vessel was several miles east of her intended track but there was still plenty of time to compensate for this displacement.

At 06.55 the chief officer altered course to port to 006°T, to head for what he initially thought was the radar echo of Bishop Rock; it was probably the echo of the eastern Scilly Isles. However, the vessel was only on 006°T for five minutes because when the master was informed of the course alteration by the chief officer, he asked if the original course of 018°T from their present position would take the vessel east of the Scilly Isles. The chief officer affirmed this so the master ordered him to alter course back to 018°T. This was at 07.00, when the master came to the bridge.

The vessel was now heading almost directly towards her graveyard, the Seven Stones reef. However, the master fully intended to alter course to port when the *Torrey Canyon* was east of the Scilly Isles in order to pass through the five-mile-wide passage between the Scilly Isles and the Seven Stones reef. He expected also to have the alternative of altering course to starboard to pass through the ten-mile-wide passage between the Seven Stones lightvessel and the Longships lighthouse.

4 *below* The US built *Torrey Canyon* lies impaled on Pollard Rock which opened a gash 200 m long in the 300 m hull.

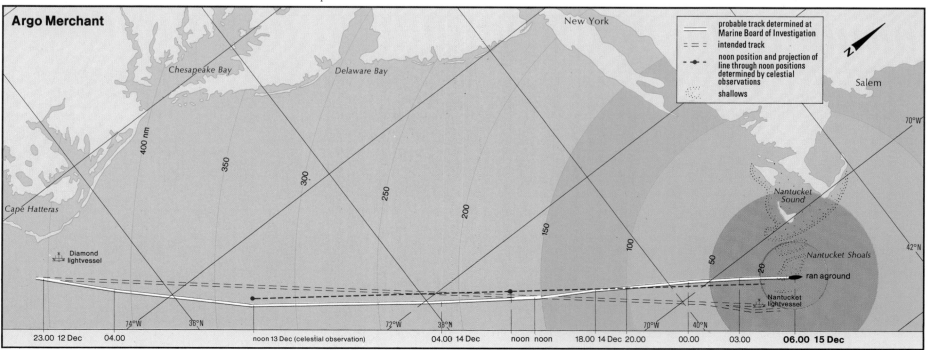

Argo Merchant

New York

Chesapeake Bay

Delaware Bay

Salem

		probable track determined at Marine Board of Investigation
		intended track
		noon position and projection of line through noon positions determined by celestial observations
		shallows

Cape Hatteras

400 nm

350

300

250

200

150

100

50

20

70°W

Diamond lightvessel

Nantucket Sound

Nantucket Shoals

ran aground

Nantucket lightvessel

42°N

74°W · 38°N · 72°W · 38°N · 70°W · 40°N

23.00 12 Dec · 04.00 · noon 13 Dec (celestial observation) · 04.00 14 Dec · noon noon · 18.00 14 Dec 20.00 · 00.00 · 03.00 · **06.00 15 Dec**

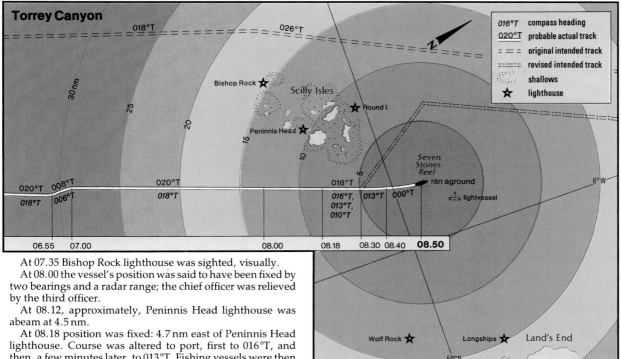

Torrey Canyon

016°T	compass heading
020°T	probable actual track
	original intended track
	revised intended track
	shallows
☆	lighthouse

At 07.35 Bishop Rock lighthouse was sighted, visually.

At 08.00 the vessel's position was said to have been fixed by two bearings and a radar range; the chief officer was relieved by the third officer.

At 08.12, approximately, Peninnis Head lighthouse was abeam at 4.5 nm.

At 08.18 position was fixed: 4.7 nm east of Peninnis Head lighthouse. Course was altered to port, first to 016°T, and then, a few minutes later, to 013°T. Fishing vessels were then sighted, at least two of them on the port bow.

At 08.25 the vessel's position was fixed again and the course altered to port by 3° to steer 010°T; however, because the tidal stream was setting easterly at a rate of probably between 0.5 and 1.0 knot, the course made good over the ground was about 018°T.

At 08.30 the course was altered to starboard by 3° to steer 013°T in order to keep clear of a fishing vessel on the port side. It was claimed that fishing nets were seen on both sides

at about this time.

At 08.38 the third officer plotted an incorrect position; however, the master realised that it was in error and new observations were made.

At 08.40 the position was fixed by observation of the Seven Stones lightvessel – it was bearing 033°T at a range of 4.8 nm. The *Torrey Canyon* was now only 2.8 nm from the rocks ahead.

At 08.42 the master switched from automatic steering to manual, and personally altered course to port to steer 000°T, and then switched back to automatic steering.

At 08.45, the third officer, now under stress, observed a bearing, forgot it, and observed it again. The position now indicated that the *Torrey Canyon* was less than 1 nm from the rocks ahead. The master ordered hard-to-port. The helmsman who had been standing by on the bridge, ran to the wheel and turned it. Nothing happened. He shouted to the master who quickly checked the fuse—it was all right. The master then tried to telephone the engineers to have them check the steering gear aft. A steward answered—wrong number. He tried dialling again, and then noticed that the steering selector was on automatic control instead of manual. He switched quickly to manual, and the vessel began to turn. Moments later, at 08.50, having only turned about 10°, and while still doing her full speed of 15¾ knots, the vessel grounded on Pollard Rock.

A number of cargo tanks were ruptured on impact, and crude oil began immediately to spread around the vessel. To make matters even worse, the moment of grounding was within minutes of the high-water neaps, and the vessel was soon to settle down further onto the rocks as she lost her reserve buoyancy and as the sea level fell.

Consequences: Despite almost immediate salvage operations, heavy seas pounding the vessel during the following days caused her to become a complete wreck. During these operations there was an explosion aboard which killed a member of the salvage team. No other lives were lost. The oil pollution was massive, the worst ever experienced; both British and French coasts suffered. After the vessel broke up in heavy seas it was bombed by the Royal Air Force in an attempt to burn up any remaining oil. However, although some fires were started, it is believed that only a small proportion of the oil burnt away before the *Torrey Canyon*'s remains sank out of sight on Thursday, 30 March 1967. Concern over the bombing by the RAF, which was of a Liberian vessel, outside British territorial waters, led to the 1969 Convention allowing for intervention on the high seas to prevent pollution.

3 *right* **Amoco Cadiz**

Vessel description: Liberian oil tanker, length 334 m, capacity 232 182 dwt, 109 700 grt. Single screw, and powered with a 30 400 bhp diesel engine. Maximum draught 19.8 m
Time of initial stranding: 21.04 GMT
Time of final stranding: About 21.30 GMT
Date: Thursday, 16 March 1978
Place: Near Portsal, north coast of France
Voyage: From Kharg Island, Iran, to Rotterdam via Lyme Bay, English Channel

The *Amoco Cadiz* was fully laden with crude oil, part of which was for discharge at Lyme Bay. On the morning of 16 March she passed through the traffic separation scheme off Ushant, though her exact path is uncertain. At 09.46 her steering gear system failed in a rough sea with a strong south-westerly wind, about 8 nm north of Ushant.

The ship, with rudder stuck initially in the hard-a-port position, started to veer north. The master, concerned about obstructing the approach to the west-going traffic lane, stopped the engine and transmitted radio warnings that the ship was not under command. He requested other vessels to keep clear of her but did not request outside assistance; the engineers were attempting to repair the steering gear.

By about 10.05 the vessel's original momentum was lost, and she began to drift under the influence of wind and tidal stream only. The latter, with rates up to 1 knot (neaps), was setting easterly from the time of breakdown until about noon; south-westerly until about 17.00; then north-easterly until grounding.

By 11.00 the vessel's heading had changed to 160°T, and she had drifted about 1½ nm in a south-easterly direction.

At 11.20 the engineers reported failure in repairing the steering gear; in the heavy seas the rudder swung about and could not be locked for them to carry out the work. The master, realising that he needed outside help, radioed for tugs.

The tug *Pacific*, then 15 nm away, responded promptly and arrived at the ship at 12.20. Making fast proved difficult in the heavy seas; a towing hawser was finally made fast on the starboard bow. Shortly after 14.00 the *Pacific* began towing off to starboard to try to turn the *Amoco Cadiz* onto a westerly heading. By then she had drifted about 6½ nm SSE from her 10.05 position and was less than 6 nm off Ushant Island. The tug stopped the *Amoco Cadiz* drifting south, but could not stop her drifting 2 nm further east. Her heading changed only 20° to starboard, from about 160°T to 180°T.

At 16.15 the towing hawser parted and the engine of the *Amoco Cadiz* was at once put to run astern with all possible power. As a result the heading changed to 130°T, i.e. the stern turned towards the wind, which was veering from SW to NW and continued to blow with gale force. For the next 2½ hours, with the engine running astern, the vessel's motion was towards the north-east.

By 19.00 the *Pacific* had prepared a new hawser and was ready to try again. This time the stern of the *Amoco Cadiz* was made fast. Her engine was stopped to enable the difficult operation to be carried out. But she swung round to head 260°T and drifted eastwards; at 20.04 the port anchor was dropped (1.3 nm west of Roche de Portsal buoy) but dragged, even though a large scope of cable was paid out. Seas were being shipped over the starboard bow and it was considered unsafe for the crew to try to drop the starboard anchor. (The French authorities later recovered the port anchor and found that both flukes had broken off.)

At 20.33 the crew got the towing hawser on board but it

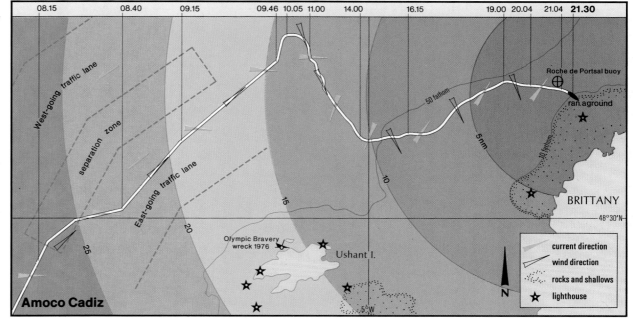

Amoco Cadiz

	current direction
	wind direction
	rocks and shallows
☆	lighthouse

5 *above* The *Amoco Cadiz* breaking up on the coast of Brittany, France, after a failure in the steering gear caused her to run aground.

was not made fast until 20.55. The *Pacific* moved off to begin towing but minutes later, at 21.04, the *Amoco Cadiz* struck the ground aft. The pump room was damaged and started to flood. Oil leaked and because of fire risk all power was switched off. At about 21.30 the vessel struck ground again and the engine-room flooded. The *Amoco Cadiz* was firmly aground. The *Pacific* continued to tow without effect until the towing hawser parted at 22.12. A second tug, the *Simson*, arrived about an hour later but could only stand by. The ship was doomed.

It was impossible to launch the lifeboats in the heavy seas. French naval helicopters were alerted and performed a daring rescue during darkness in the early hours of Friday, 17 March. No lives were lost.

Cause: The obvious cause of the disaster was the failure of the steering gear. However, the dangers of a lee-shore in the circumstances of breakdown are well known. The *Amoco Cadiz* on her passage to Lyme Bay could have passed much further offshore without increasing her passage distance or time significantly, but thus increasing her safety margin. Vessels are not compelled to enter the traffic separation zone off Ushant, but if they do they must comply with it.

After the breakdown, the hazardous position of the *Amoco Cadiz* was not fully appreciated by those on board. Even without steering, engine power could have been used more effectively; more urgent steps could have been taken to summon assistance from tugs and to prepare both anchors

Consequences: The entire oil cargo was lost and the resulting pollution was far in excess of the previous worst case (the *Torrey Canyon*). Following the *Amoco Cadiz* disaster the French Government introduced stricter regulations concerning laden tankers approaching the coasts of France. Radio reports have now to be made to the French marine authorities, and the areas in which laden tankers could operate are restricted. The French Government also insisted that IMO redesign and move further seaward some of the traffic separation schemes in the vicinity of the coast of France, to ensure that laden tankers pass further offshore.

Oil pollution

PETROLEUM oil is one of the most widespread pollutants in the sea. When it is spilt it spreads as a slick. One tonne of Iranian crude, for example, will cover an area of about 50 m diameter, to a thickness of 0.1 m within 10 minutes, before drifting with wind and current. In the case of the *Torrey Canyon* the initial 30 000 tonne spill covered 20 nm before drifting towards Brittany. Oil tends to be dispersed by waves and can be emulsified by absorption of water to change its texture to 'chocolate mousse'. Some oil will evaporate though this usually returns to the sea with rain; other attaches to sediment and sinks. Constituents of oil are also consumed by bacteria. The speed of disintegration depends on the type of oil and the ocean environment, particularly the temperature. Oil disintegrates in

warm water far faster than it does in cold. Hydrocarbons with the largest amounts of carbon atoms do not evaporate readily and are not biodegraded to any extent; they form tar balls which persist for many years in the sea. These can be found throughout the oceans, particularly along tanker routes.

Accurate comparisons of oil pollution between the 1970s and 1980s are difficult to make due to lack of comparable data, particularly for land sources. In the case of vessel-source pollution, however, there have been definite improvements. Despite the increased number of ships and the rising tonnage of oil carried, better operational procedures and new regulations have reduced the spills from 2.4 million in 1971 to 1.58 million in 1980.

Ship spills (barrels of oil)

1970

map ref. no.	barrels of oil spilled	name of tanker
1	232 500	Chryssi
2	153 000	Al Bacruz
3	139 500	Sofia P.
4	137 250	Silver Ocean
5	129 750	Ragny
6	123 000	Gezina Brovig
7	112 500	Polycommander
8	112 500	Warwick Trader
9	100 000	Marlena
10	82 500	Arrow
11	47 250	Pacific Glory
12	45 000	Oceanic Grandeur

1971

19	750 000	Texaco Denmark
20	480 000	Wafra
21	285 000	Towle
22	225 000	Texaco Oklahoma
23	139 500	Alkis
24	43 176	Juliana
25	37 500	Olympic Sun
26	24 750	Oregon Standard
27	12 000	Tasyca
28	10 500	Ampuria

1972

29	902 250	Sea Star
30	262 500	Trader
31	237 750	Golden Drake
32	150 000	Tien Chee

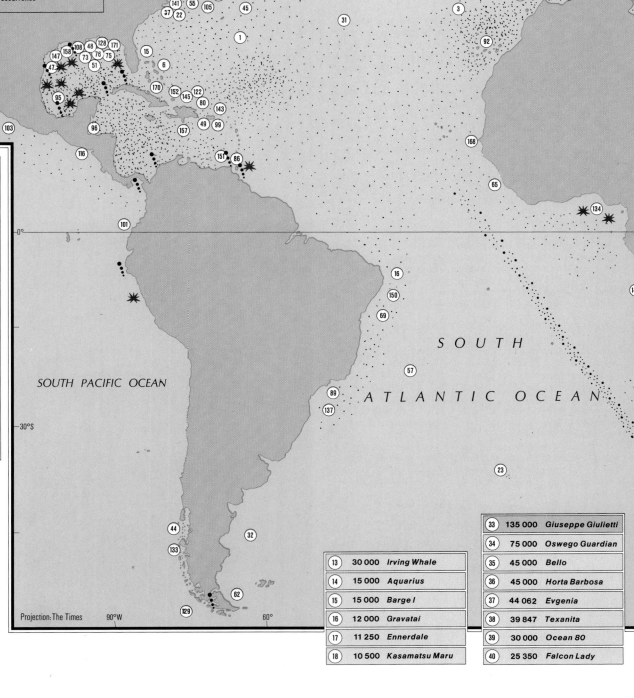

Major oil spillages

KEY

SHIP SPILLS (barrels of oil)
- less than 100 000
- 100 000–200 000
- over 200 000

✳ oil rig blowout

⋮ natural seep

map ref. no.	barrels of oil spilled	name of tanker
1	232 500	Chryssi

OIL SLICKS AND TAR BALLS
- high occurrence
- low occurrence

NORTH PACIFIC OCEAN

NORTH ATLANTIC OCEAN

SOUTH PACIFIC OCEAN

SOUTH ATLANTIC OCEAN

Projection: The Times

IMPACT OF OIL POLLUTION

The shoreline is most vulnerable. Damage to salt marshes, mangroves, sand and gravel beaches and living coral reefs, smothered by thick oil, can have a devastating effect. On exposed rocky coasts the effect is less severe. Around coastal areas the principal victims are diving birds which suffer from oil coating their feathers and from ingestion of oil (some 30 000 birds died when the Danish Waddensea area was covered by oil in March 1972). Fish and shellfish become inedible and therefore unsaleable from tainting, and there may be some damage to phytoplankton and to eggs and larvae in the upper layers of the sea, as well as to benthic communities from the oil which sinks. Furthermore, some oil dispersants used to remove oil have been more toxic to marine life than the oil itself. The extent of damage in the open sea is uncertain and it is frequently argued that the best course of action is to allow natural processes to deal with a spill. Once the oil approaches the coast, however, protection and dispersion procedures have to be initiated.

1 *main map* Most tanker accidents occur close to the coast and in congested sea routes. Tanker spillages for 1970–80 of over 50 000 barrels of oil are shown. Natural seeps are also shown, and the areas where tar balls occur. Rig blowouts have been few—only 28 accidents among 11 000 wells in the Gulf of Mexico, for instance—but they are potentially disastrous. The *Ixtoc I* exploration well in the Gulf of Mexico leaked three million barrels of oil before being brought under control in March 1980, nine months after the blowout.

13	30 000	Irving Whale
14	15 000	Aquarius
15	15 000	Barge I
16	12 000	Gravatai
17	11 250	Ennerdale
18	10 500	Kasamatsu Maru

33	135 000	Giuseppe Giulietti
34	75 000	Oswego Guardian
35	45 000	Bello
36	45 000	Horta Barbosa
37	44 062	Evgenia
38	39 847	Texanita
39	30 000	Ocean 80
40	25 350	Falcon Lady

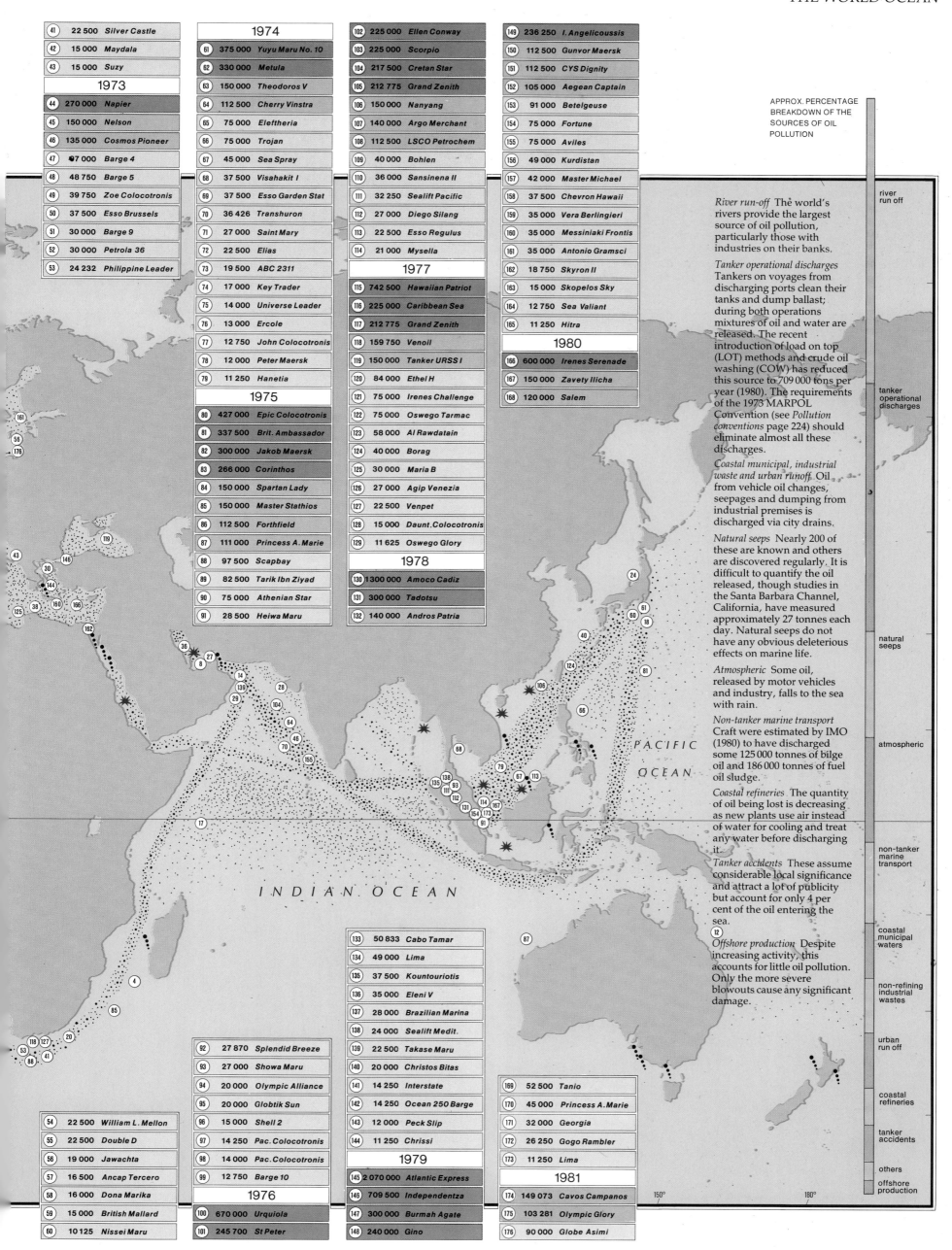

41	22 500	*Silver Castle*
42	15 000	*Maydala*
43	15 000	*Suzy*

1973

44	270 000	*Napier*
45	150 000	*Nelson*
46	135 000	*Cosmos Pioneer*
47	97 000	*Barge 4*
48	48 750	*Barge 5*
49	39 750	*Zoe Colocotronis*
50	37 500	*Esso Brussels*
51	30 000	*Barge 9*
52	30 000	*Petrola 36*
53	24 232	*Philippine Leader*

1974

61	375 000	*Yuyu Maru No. 10*
62	330 000	*Metula*
63	150 000	*Theodoros V*
64	112 500	*Cherry Vinstra*
65	75 000	*Eleftheria*
66	75 000	*Trojan*
67	45 000	*Sea Spray*
68	37 500	*Visahakit I*
69	37 500	*Esso Garden Stat*
70	36 426	*Transhuron*
71	27 000	*Saint Mary*
72	22 500	*Elias*
73	19 500	*ABC 2311*
74	17 000	*Key Trader*
75	14 000	*Universe Leader*
76	13 000	*Ercole*
77	12 750	*John Colocotronis*
78	12 000	*Peter Maersk*
79	11 250	*Hanetia*

1975

80	427 000	*Epic Colocotronis*
81	337 500	*Brit. Ambassador*
82	300 000	*Jakob Maersk*
83	266 000	*Corinthos*
84	150 000	*Spartan Lady*
85	150 000	*Master Stathios*
86	112 500	*Forthfield*
87	111 000	*Princess A. Marie*
88	97 500	*Scapbay*
89	82 500	*Tarik Ibn Ziyad*
90	75 000	*Athenian Star*
91	28 500	*Heiwa Maru*

102	225 000	*Ellen Conway*
103	225 000	*Scorpio*
104	217 500	*Cretan Star*
105	212 775	*Grand Zenith*
106	150 000	*Nanyang*
107	140 000	*Argo Merchant*
108	112 500	*LSCO Petrochem*
109	40 000	*Bohlen*
110	36 000	*Sansinena II*
111	32 250	*Sealift Pacific*
112	27 000	*Diego Silang*
113	22 500	*Esso Regulus*
114	21 000	*Mysella*

1977

115	742 500	*Hawaiian Patriot*
116	225 000	*Caribbean Sea*
117	212 775	*Grand Zenith*
118	159 750	*Venoil*
119	150 000	*Tanker URSS I*
120	84 000	*Ethel H*
121	75 000	*Irenes Challenge*
122	75 000	*Oswego Tarmac*
123	58 000	*Al Rawdatain*
124	40 000	*Borag*
125	30 000	*Maria B*
126	27 000	*Agip Venezia*
127	22 500	*Venpet*
128	15 000	*Daunt. Colocotronis*
129	11 625	*Oswego Glory*

1978

130	1 300 000	*Amoco Cadiz*
131	300 000	*Tadotsu*
132	140 000	*Andros Patria*

149	236 250	*I. Angelicoussis*
150	112 500	*Gunvor Maersk*
151	112 500	*CYS Dignity*
152	105 000	*Aegean Captain*
153	91 000	*Betelgeuse*
154	75 000	*Fortune*
155	75 000	*Aviles*
156	49 000	*Kurdistan*
157	42 000	*Master Michael*
158	37 500	*Chevron Hawaii*
159	35 000	*Vera Berlingieri*
160	35 000	*Messiniaki Frontis*
161	35 000	*Antonio Gramsci*
162	18 750	*Skyron II*
163	15 000	*Skopelos Sky*
164	12 750	*Sea Valiant*
165	11 250	*Hitra*

1980

166	600 000	*Irenes Serenade*
167	150 000	*Zavety Ilicha*
168	120 000	*Salem*

54	22 500	*William L. Mellon*
55	22 500	*Double D*
56	19 000	*Jawachta*
57	16 500	*Ancap Tercero*
58	16 000	*Dona Marika*
59	15 000	*British Mallard*
60	10 125	*Nissei Maru*

92	27 870	*Splendid Breeze*
93	27 000	*Showa Maru*
94	20 000	*Olympic Alliance*
95	20 000	*Globtik Sun*
96	15 000	*Shell 2*
97	14 250	*Pac. Colocotronis*
98	14 000	*Pac. Colocotronis*
99	12 750	*Barge 10*

1976

100	670 000	*Urquiola*
101	245 700	*St Peter*

133	50 833	*Cabo Tamar*
134	49 000	*Lima*
135	37 500	*Kountouriotis*
136	35 000	*Eleni V*
137	28 000	*Brazilian Marina*
138	24 000	*Sealift Medit.*
139	22 500	*Takase Maru*
140	20 000	*Christos Bitas*
141	14 250	*Interstate*
142	14 250	*Ocean 250 Barge*
143	12 000	*Peck Slip*
144	11 250	*Chrissi*

1979

145	2 070 000	*Atlantic Express*
146	709 500	*Independentza*
147	300 000	*Burmah Agate*
148	240 000	*Gino*

169	52 500	*Tanio*
170	45 000	*Princess A. Marie*
171	32 000	*Georgia*
172	26 250	*Gogo Rambler*
173	11 250	*Lima*

1981

174	149 073	*Cavos Campanos*
175	103 281	*Olympic Glory*
176	90 000	*Globe Asimi*

PACIFIC OCEAN

INDIAN OCEAN

APPROX. PERCENTAGE BREAKDOWN OF THE SOURCES OF OIL POLLUTION

River run-off The world's rivers provide the largest source of oil pollution, particularly those with industries on their banks.

Tanker operational discharges Tankers on voyages from discharging ports clean their tanks and dump ballast; during both operations mixtures of oil and water are released. The recent introduction of load on top (LOT) methods and crude oil washing (COW) has reduced this source to 709 000 tons per year (1980). The requirements of the 1973 MARPOL Convention (see *Pollution conventions* page 224) should eliminate almost all these discharges.

Coastal municipal, industrial waste and urban runoff Oil from vehicle oil changes, seepages and dumping from industrial premises is discharged via city drains.

Natural seeps Nearly 200 of these are known and others are discovered regularly. It is difficult to quantify the oil released, though studies in the Santa Barbara Channel, California, have measured approximately 27 tonnes each day. Natural seeps do not have any obvious deleterious effects on marine life.

Atmospheric Some oil, released by motor vehicles and industry, falls to the sea with rain.

Non-tanker marine transport Craft were estimated by IMO (1980) to have discharged some 125 000 tonnes of bilge oil and 186 000 tonnes of fuel oil sludge.

Coastal refineries The quantity of oil being lost is decreasing as new plants use air instead of water for cooling and treat any water before discharging it.

Tanker accidents These assume considerable local significance and attract a lot of publicity but account for only 4 per cent of the oil entering the sea.

Offshore production Despite increasing activity, this accounts for little oil pollution. Only the more severe blowouts cause any significant damage.

river run off
tanker operational discharges
natural seeps
atmospheric
non-tanker marine transport
coastal municipal waters
non-refining industrial wastes
urban run off
coastal refineries
tanker accidents
others
offshore production

Sources of marine pollution

POLLUTION of the marine environment has been defined by the United Nations as: 'The introduction by man, directly or indirectly, of substances or energy into the marine environment (including estuaries) resulting in such deleterious effects as harm to living resources, hazards to human health, hindrance to marine activities including fishing, impairment of quality for use of sea water, and reduction of amenities'.

Man has always used the sea to dispose of waste, but as natural sea water contains complex chemical substances it is often difficult, in the absence of accurate base levels, to measure the extent of pollution in the ocean. In some areas of the deep ocean, for instance, tar balls on the surface are prevalent but pollution may not be critical, as yet. However, in industrial estuaries and many areas of coastal waters, pollution is clearly evident. The migration of industries to the coast, development of new ports, the growth of massive urban centres and the use of insecticides, fertilisers and fungicide have led to highly polluted coastal zones often low in fish life and hazardous to man. Further out at sea, the dumping of waste material from military installations and shore industries has increased alarmingly since 1945. Military waste, including nerve gas, has been dumped for several years. In 1958, for example, the *William Ralston* was scuttled in the Atlantic carrying 8000 tonnes of mustard gas. Meanwhile, the increases in international seaborne trade, offshore mineral and oil extraction, and the many other uses of the sea and sea bed are continuously adding to ocean pollution, particularly in the coastal zones.

Pollutants

Chemicals entering the sea come direct from coastal industries and via rivers (including those receiving massive inputs of insecticides and fertilisers from agricultural runoff), and some are transported and deposited by the atmosphere, especially carbon monoxide and sulphur dioxide. Accidents to chemical tankers, loss of deck cargo at sea, and cleaning of tanks contribute still further. Massive quantities of cyanide compounds and other poisons have been dumped at sea from waste disposal ships. Toxic chemicals, particularly DDT and PCBs (polychlorinated biphenols), have been detected in marine animals ranging from Baltic herrings to Pacific whales and Antarctic penguins. They can cause thinning of bird egg shells and generally impair the reproductive ability of mammals. Chemicals such as chlorine, cyanides, and those contained in detergents all add to the pollution stress on marine life. Since the mid 1970s, special incinerator

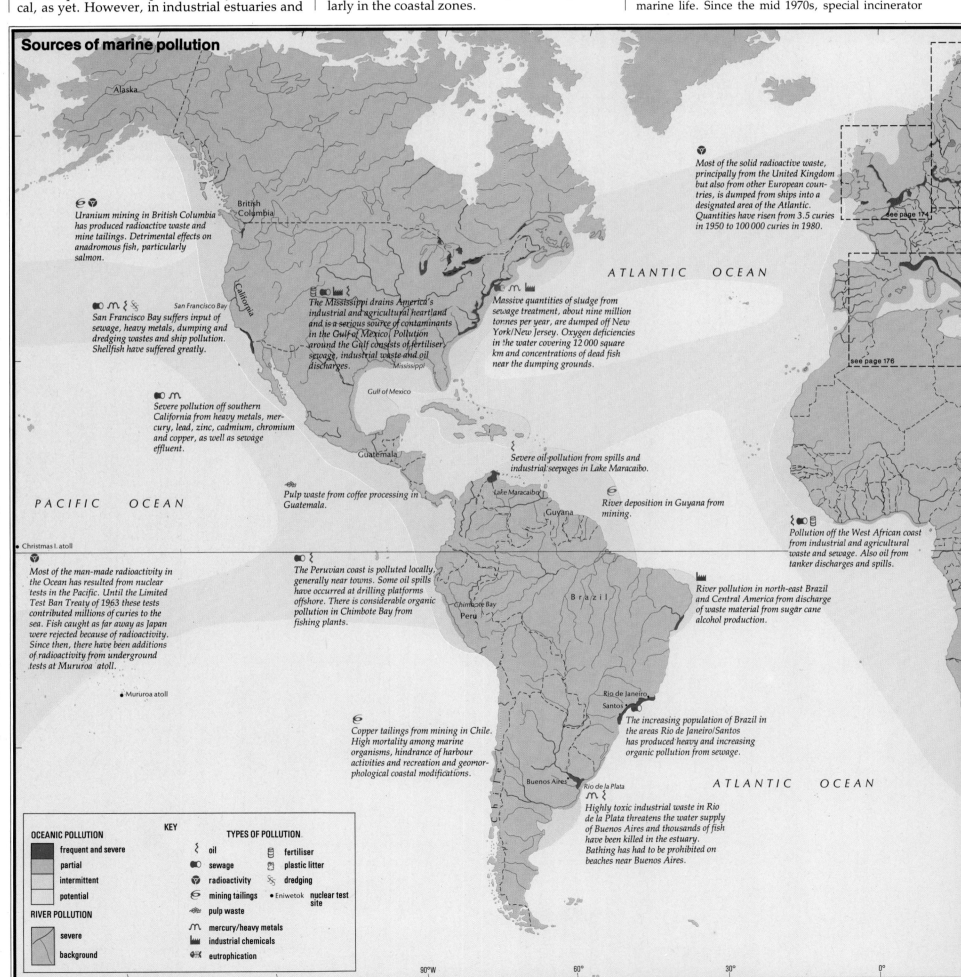

Sources of marine pollution

Uranium mining in British Columbia has produced radioactive waste and mine tailings. Detrimental effects on anadromous fish, particularly salmon.

San Francisco Bay suffers input of sewage, heavy metals, dumping and dredging wastes and ship pollution. Shellfish have suffered greatly.

Severe pollution off southern California from heavy metals, mercury, lead, zinc, cadmium, chromium and copper, as well as sewage effluent.

The Mississippi drains America's industrial and agricultural heartland and is a serious source of contaminants in the Gulf of Mexico. Pollution around the Gulf consists of fertiliser, sewage, industrial waste and oil discharges.

Massive quantities of sludge from sewage treatment, about nine million tonnes per year, are dumped off New York/New Jersey. Oxygen deficiencies in the water covering 12 000 square km and concentrations of dead fish near the dumping grounds.

Most of the solid radioactive waste, principally from the United Kingdom but also from other European countries, is dumped from ships into a designated area of the Atlantic. Quantities have risen from 3.5 curies in 1950 to 100 000 curies in 1980.

see page 174

see page 176

Pulp waste from coffee processing in Guatemala.

Severe oil pollution from spills and industrial seepages in Lake Maracaibo.

River deposition in Guyana from mining.

Pollution off the West African coast from industrial and agricultural waste and sewage. Also oil from tanker discharges and spills.

Most of the man-made radioactivity in the Ocean has resulted from nuclear tests in the Pacific. Until the Limited Test Ban Treaty of 1963 these tests contributed millions of curies to the sea. Fish caught as far away as Japan were rejected because of radioactivity. Since then, there have been additions of radioactivity from underground tests at Mururoa atoll.

The Peruvian coast is polluted locally, generally near towns. Some oil spills have occurred at drilling platforms offshore. There is considerable organic pollution in Chimbote Bay from fishing plants.

River pollution in north-east Brazil and Central America from discharge of waste material from sugar cane alcohol production.

Copper tailings from mining in Chile. High mortality among marine organisms, hindrance of harbour activities and recreation and geomorphological coastal modifications.

The increasing population of Brazil in the areas Rio de Janeiro/Santos has produced heavy and increasing organic pollution from sewage.

Highly toxic industrial waste in Rio de la Plata threatens the water supply of Buenos Aires and thousands of fish have been killed in the estuary. Bathing has had to be prohibited on beaches near Buenos Aires.

PACIFIC OCEAN

ATLANTIC OCEAN

ATLANTIC OCEAN

KEY

OCEANIC POLLUTION
- frequent and severe
- partial
- intermittent
- potential

RIVER POLLUTION
- severe
- background

TYPES OF POLLUTION
- oil
- sewage
- radioactivity
- mining tailings
- pulp waste
- mercury/heavy metals
- industrial chemicals
- eutrophication
- fertiliser
- plastic litter
- dredging
- nuclear test site

ships have been used by north-western European countries to burn toxic chemicals at sea and reduce dumping.

Heavy metals are carried down rivers from mining operations and industrial processes. They are persistent and cannot be broken down by bacterial action, though they do undergo chemical changes in the marine environment. Lead salts, for example, become the more poisonous methyl lead, and mercury is methylated into an even more highly toxic substance. Together with arsenic they represent the most dangerous pollutants. Zinc, cadmium and selinium also accumulate. Absorbed by marine organisms, these metals can affect animals, including man, further up the food chain. Traces have been found in fish as diverse as Pacific tuna and the Baltic herring. Persistent doses of heavy chemicals can cause brain damage, as at Minamata in Japan where, during the 1950s, members of a fishing community developed an illness characterised by numbness of their limbs, speech impairment and loss of coordination. The source of the illness was traced and proven to be effluents contain-

ing methylmercury which had infected fish in the bay. *Sewage* emanates either directly from cities' sewage systems or is dumped from barges within a few miles of the coast. It consists of phosphates, nitrates, ammonia, heavy metals and sometimes pathogenic bacteria and viruses. While phosphates and nitrates are vital nutrients, over supply of them causes an increase in growth of algae (entrophication) which in turn overwhelms other forms of life. Sewage puts demands on oxygen in the sea and in severe cases kills off marine life. The principle danger to humans from sewage is virus infection transmitted by shellfish consumption, while on beaches sewage presents a major aesthetic and social problem.

Radioactive pollution in the sea has resulted from nuclear tests. It comes now from industrial outfalls and the dumping of packaged industrial radioactive waste from ships. There are also continuous discharges of low level nuclear waste from coastal nuclear plants, such as Windscale in England, while small amounts are discharged from nuclear powered vessels. The vast increase in industrial nuclear wastes

which may accrue in the future could, if deposited in the sea, quickly cause ocean contamination beyond safe limits.

Dredging of channels and the dumping of spoil can cause turbidity, the reduction of light penetration, and the destruction of fish hatcheries. In some places holes may be left in the sea bed from aggregate dredging which contain water of low oxygen content and cause deleterious effects on marine life. In the case of manganese nodule mining from the deep sea bed there is likely to be destruction of benthic communities and their habitats. The near-surface species of the ocean may be affected by the dumping of dredged waste from ocean mining.

1 *main map* The great mass of the world's Oceans are not badly affected by pollution. However, in the coastal zones adjacent to industrial sites, large conurbations and river estuaries, pollution is sometimes severe. This is particularly true in Europe's peripheral seas (see following pages).

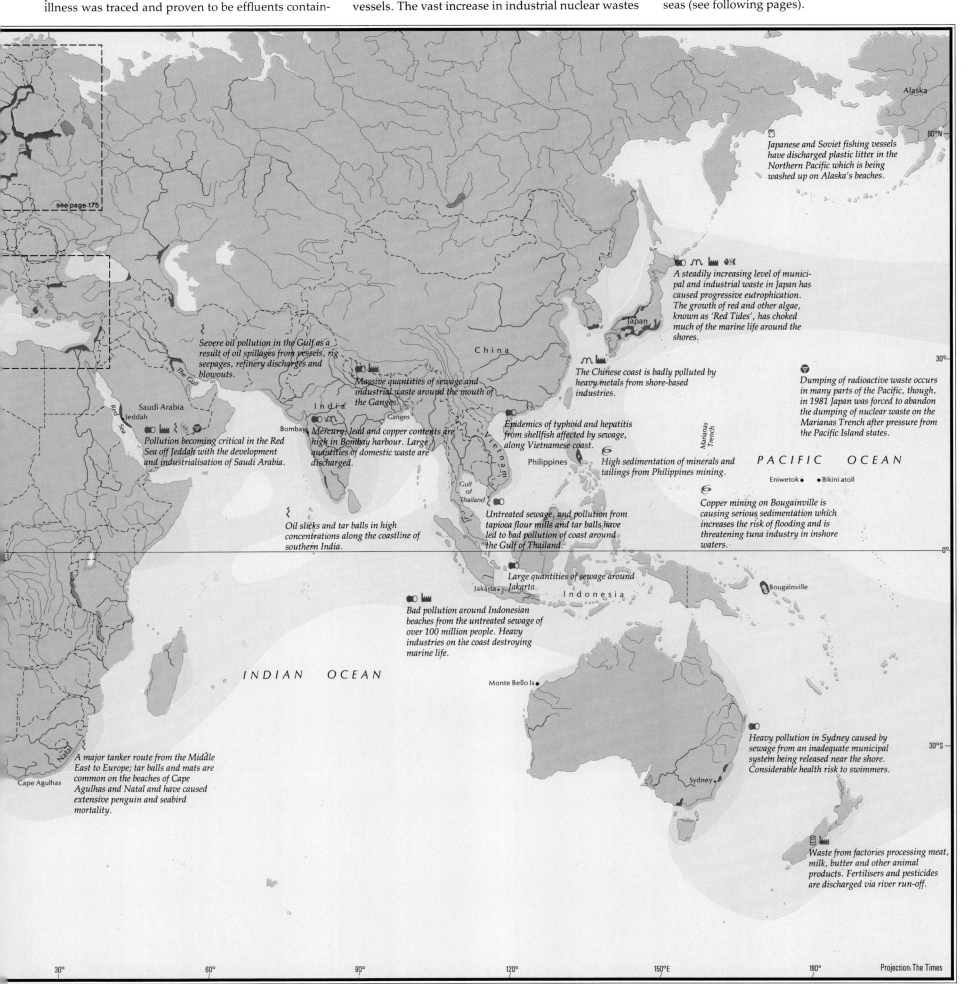

see page 175

Japanese and Soviet fishing vessels have discharged plastic litter in the Northern Pacific which is being washed up on Alaska's beaches.

A steadily increasing level of municipal and industrial waste in Japan has caused progressive eutrophication. The growth of red and other algae, known as 'Red Tides', has choked much of the marine life around the shores.

The Chinese coast is badly polluted by heavy metals from shore-based industries.

Dumping of radioactive waste occurs in many parts of the Pacific, though, in 1981 Japan was forced to abandon the dumping of nuclear waste on the Marianas Trench after pressure from the Pacific Island states.

Severe oil pollution in the Gulf as a result of oil spillages from vessels, rig seepages, refinery discharges and blowouts.

Massive quantities of sewage and industrial waste around the mouth of the Ganges.

Epidemics of typhoid and hepatitis from shellfish affected by sewage, along Vietnamese coast.

Mercury, lead and copper contents are high in Bombay harbour. Large quantities of domestic waste are discharged.

Pollution becoming critical in the Red Sea off Jeddah with the development and industrialisation of Saudi Arabia.

High sedimentation of minerals and tailings from Philippines mining.

Copper mining on Bougainville is causing serious sedimentation which increases the risk of flooding and is threatening tuna industry in inshore waters.

Oil slicks and tar balls in high concentrations along the coastline of southern India.

Untreated sewage, and pollution from tapioca flour mills and tar balls have led to bad pollution of coast around the Gulf of Thailand.

Large quantities of sewage around Jakarta.

Bad pollution around Indonesian beaches from the untreated sewage of over 100 million people. Heavy industries on the coast destroying marine life.

A major tanker route from the Middle East to Europe; tar balls and mats are common on the beaches of Cape Agulhas and Natal and have caused extensive penguin and seabird mortality.

Heavy pollution in Sydney caused by sewage from an inadequate municipal system being released near the shore. Considerable health risk to swimmers.

Waste from factories processing meat, milk, butter and other animal products. Fertilisers and pesticides are discharged via river run-off.

Alaska

60°N

30°

PACIFIC OCEAN

Eniwetok • Bikini atoll

Japan

China

India

Ganges

Saudi Arabia
Jeddah
Red Sea
The Gulf

Bombay

Vietnam

Philippines

Gulf of Thailand

Jakarta

Indonesia

Marianas Trench

0°

Bougainville

INDIAN OCEAN

Monte Bello Is.

30°S

Sydney

Cape Agulhas
Natal

Sources of marine pollution 2

The North Sea

The North Sea is one of the worst polluted sea areas in the world. However, the water mass is highly mobile and storms are frequent so that flushing and wave action mitigate some of the worst effects. Vast industrial complexes on its southern shores, a large coastal population, dense shipping, hydrocarbon extraction and dredging all contribute towards the problem.

It has been estimated that the sewage of some 31 million people enters the North Sea and amounts to some 7.3 million cubic metres per day, the bulk of which is untreated. The total flow of industrial effluent into the North Sea is estimated to be at about five million cubic metres per day and includes chemicals, heavy metals and oil.

The dumping at sea of sewage sludge and industrial waste is also prevalent and the latter includes waste from titanium dioxide, coal mines, mineral tailings, acids and alkalis. It is difficult to quantify the amount of oil being discharged from all the various sources, but it probably exceeds one million tonnes per year. In the case of the chemical tankers, a Norwegian study estimated that during the 1970s about 3600 tons of chemicals were discharged into the sea each year.

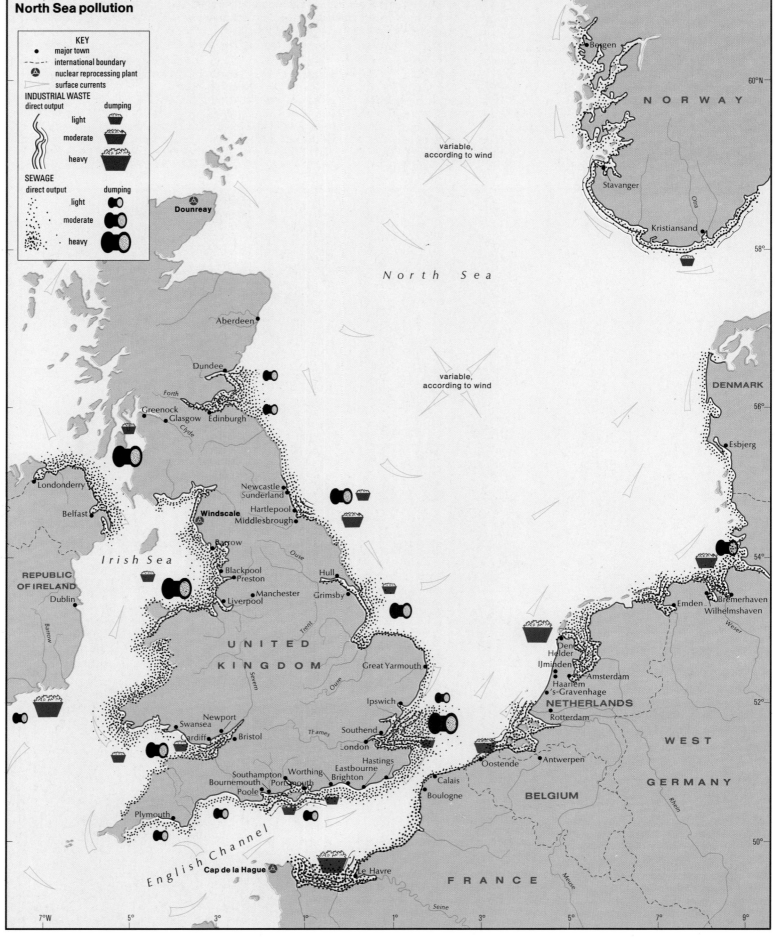

1 *right* The waste entering the North Sea can be divided into two basic categories: that which is dumped from barges or ships at sea, and that entering the sea from coastal and river sources and the atmosphere. In 1980, 153 million tonnes of waste were dumped into the North Sea from vessels alone. This included sewage sludge, dredged spoil, and rubble from building and demolition sites. The amount of pollution which enters the North Sea from dumping is exceeded by that entering from pipelines, rivers and the atmosphere. The input of radioactive material by pipeline spreads widely and comes from two types of sources: the nuclear reprocessing plants at Windscale, Cap de la Hague and Dounreay and the cooling water of nuclear power stations. The reprocessing plants are the most important sources since they contribute the greatest quantity of dangerous caesium, strontium and plutonium. Organic chemicals, particularly DDT and PCBs, enter the North Sea via dumping, pipelines and river run off. The Rhine contributes 10 500 tonnes per annum. Heavy metals are entering the North Sea at a considerable rate annually: 45 000 tonnes of zinc, 14 000 tonnes of lead, 10 000 tonnes of copper and 1000 tonnes of mercury, mainly through the river systems. Sewage is also a problem. It is dumped from barges from the UK, which causes the smothering of some marine life, and is discharged through pipelines from other states, causing zones of oxygen deficient waters in coastal areas.

Caesium

Zinc

Mercury

Phosphate

Nitrate

2–6 *left* The caesium originates principally from UK and French nuclear reprocessing plants. The highest levels of metals such as zinc and mercury are found along the coastal zones, adjacent to the major industrial areas. Phosphate and nitrate levels are highest in coastal areas where there are large sewage outlets.

The chemicals are measured in microgrammes per litre

Apart from specific incidents, such as the decline of inshore plaice stocks near estuaries, there is no conclusive proof that the living resources of the North Sea have, as yet, been seriously affected by pollution. Only in cases of mass mortality can pollution be clearly identified as a cause, as when many thousands of birds are lost, due usually to oil spillage. It is agreed, however, by the EEC that pollution must be reduced before more serious consequences become apparent.

The Baltic

The Baltic, like its neighbour the North Sea, is one of the world's most severely polluted seas. It is a cold sea and, being semi-enclosed, has a low rate of water exchange. The coastline around the Baltic is shared by seven countries and has many indentations and bays. About 250 river systems drain into it, and some 20 million people live on or near the coast.

Industries in the adjacent coastal states include copper smelting, aluminium, arsenic, lead, steel, textiles, petroleum, chemicals, zinc and chlorine plants, paper and pulp manufacturing, and food production. Fertilisers are used extensively in agriculture, and shipping is heavy. Inevitably, vast amounts of organic matter, nitrogen, phosphates, chemicals, heavy metals, and oil find their way into the Baltic via rivers, the atmosphere, and discharges from industry as well as marine accidents.

PCBs (polychlorinated biophenols), which affect the reproductive systems of birds and seals, are a serious problem. The whitetailed eagle is in real danger of extinction in the Baltic and the osprey, too, is threatened. The decrease in bird population has also been partly due to eggshell thinning as a result of feeding on polluted fish and mussels. The grey seal population has been decimated, due not to hunting but simply to the impairment of its reproductive capacity by PCBs accumulated in the Baltic herring, its main food.

Several industries discharge mercury into the sea, and it is also transported by the atmosphere. As yet there are few measurable effects on humans but in Sweden cod-liver oil from fish caught in the southern Baltic has been banned because of the high concentrations of mercury.

3 *below* Some 18 million people discharge sewage into the Baltic, and industries, ranging from pulp to metal production, unload waste. Quantities of pollutants are also carried into the Baltic by rivers and via the atmosphere, and there have been several oil spills from marine accidents. Pollutants persist a long time in this cold, semi-enclosed sea, where the average residence time for seawater is 35 years. Annual inputs of organic matter from sewage, industry and agriculture amount to 1 400 000 tonnes of BOD equivalent. This has led to areas of reduced oxygen which are avoided by cod and other fish. Inputs of metal include 60 tonnes of mercury, 14 000 tonnes of lead, 27 000 tonnes of copper and 68 000 tonnes of zinc per annum. Metal concentrations have been measured in fish, as have DDT and PCBs. Restrictions on waste disposal appear to be bringing improvements to the Baltic though lead levels continue to increase.

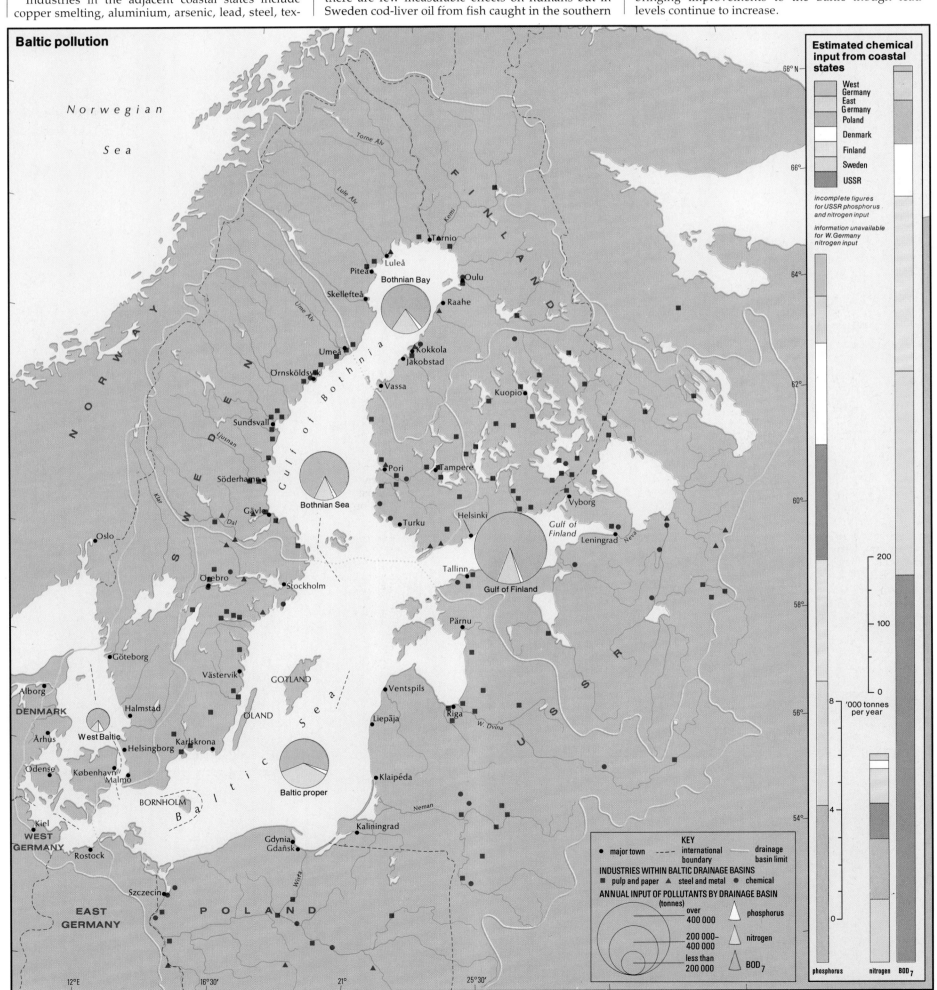

Baltic pollution

Estimated chemical input from coastal states

West Germany
East Germany
Poland
Denmark
Finland
Sweden
USSR

incomplete figures for USSR phosphorus and nitrogen input

information unavailable for W. Germany nitrogen input

'000 tonnes per year

KEY
• major town
--- international boundary
— drainage basin limit

INDUSTRIES WITHIN BALTIC DRAINAGE BASINS
■ pulp and paper ▲ steel and metal ● chemical

ANNUAL INPUT OF POLLUTANTS BY DRAINAGE BASIN (tonnes)
over 400 000
200 000–400 000
less than 200 000
△ phosphorus
△ nitrogen
△ BOD₇

phosphorus   nitrogen   BOD₇

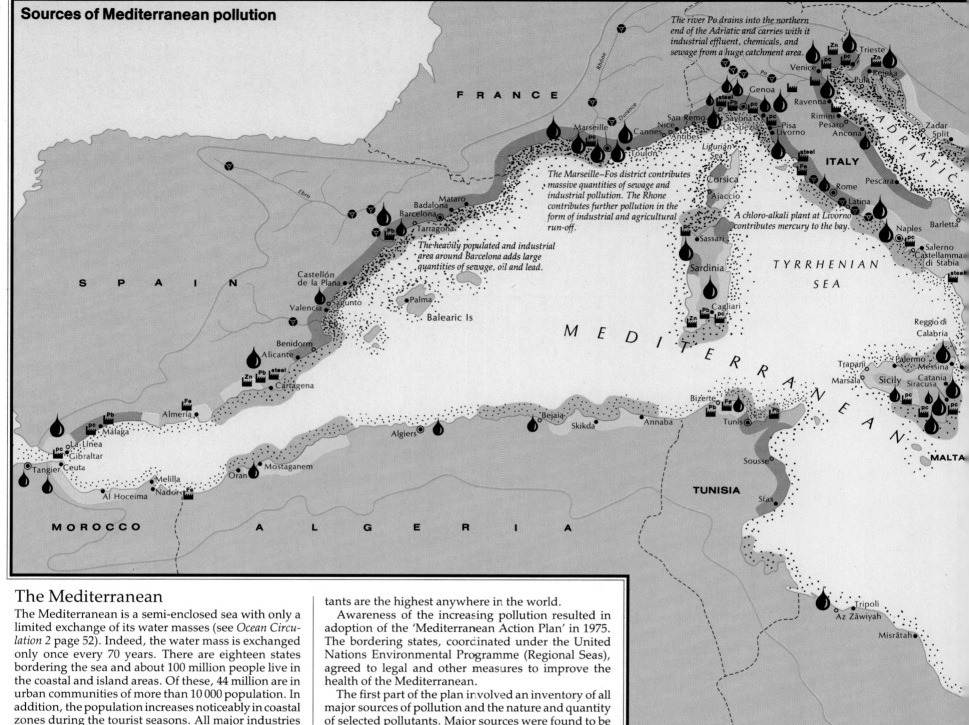

Sources of Mediterranean pollution

The river Po drains into the northern end of the Adriatic and carries with it industrial effluent, chemicals, and sewage from a huge catchment area.

The Marseille–Fos district contributes massive quantities of sewage and industrial pollution. The Rhone contributes further pollution in the form of industrial and agricultural run-off.

The heavily populated and industrial area around Barcelona adds large quantities of sewage, oil and lead.

A chloro-alkali plant at Livorno contributes mercury to the bay.

The Mediterranean

The Mediterranean is a semi-enclosed sea with only a limited exchange of its water masses (see *Ocean Circulation 2* page 52). Indeed, the water mass is exchanged only once every 70 years. There are eighteen states bordering the sea and about 100 million people live in the coastal and island areas. Of these, 44 million are in urban communities of more than 10 000 population. In addition, the population increases noticeably in coastal zones during the tourist seasons. All major industries and all sources of waste are represented. The density of every type of shipping is high, and is probably the highest in the world for both warships and pleasure craft. The Mediterranean is badly polluted by any standards and concentrations of some of the pollu-

tants are the highest anywhere in the world.

Awareness of the increasing pollution resulted in adoption of the 'Mediterranean Action Plan' in 1975. The bordering states, coordinated under the United Nations Environmental Programme (Regional Seas), agreed to legal and other measures to improve the health of the Mediterranean.

The first part of the plan involved an inventory of all major sources of pollution and the nature and quantity of selected pollutants. Major sources were found to be domestic sewage of urban areas and tourist concentrations; industrial plants; nuclear installations; river discharges; and agricultural run-off. Oil discharge from tankers is prohibited under the 1973 Marpol Convention (in force October 1984).

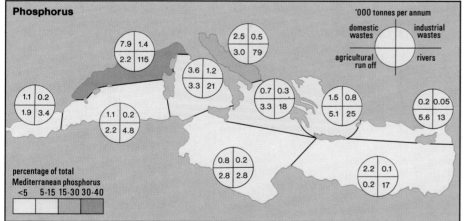

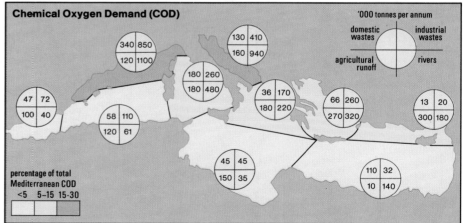

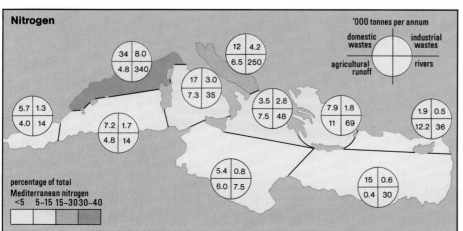

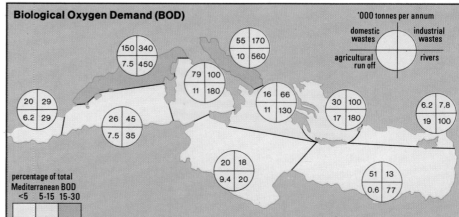

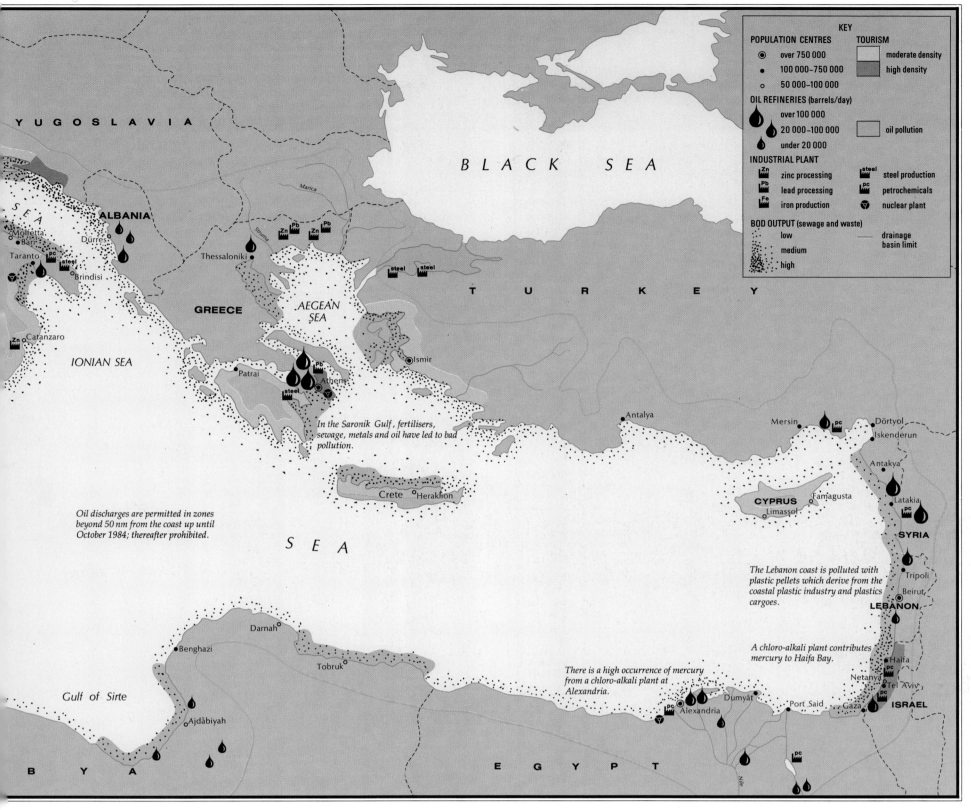

KEY

POPULATION CENTRES **TOURISM**
- over 750 000 — moderate density
- 100 000–750 000 — high density
- 50 000–100 000

OIL REFINERIES (barrels/day)
- over 100 000
- 20 000–100 000 — oil pollution
- under 20 000

INDUSTRIAL PLANT
- Zn zinc processing — steel steel production
- Pb lead processing — pc petrochemicals
- Fe iron production — nuclear plant

BOD OUTPUT (sewage and waste)
- low
- medium — drainage basin limit
- high

In the Saronik Gulf, fertilisers, sewage, metals and oil have led to bad pollution.

Oil discharges are permitted in zones beyond 50 nm from the coast up until October 1984; thereafter prohibited.

The Lebanon coast is polluted with plastic pellets which derive from the coastal plastic industry and plastics cargoes.

A chloro-alkali plant contributes mercury to Haifa Bay.

There is a high occurrence of mercury from a chloro-alkali plant at Alexandria.

1 *main map* The area between Spain, France and Italy receives about one-third of the total load of pollutants entering the Mediterranean. The northern end of the Adriatic receives about one quarter. The pollution comes from specific places with high densities of indigenous as well as tourist populations, concentrations of industry, rivers draining inland regions with industrial towns and intense agriculture which uses large quantities of fertiliser. The Marseille–Fos conurbation with its petroleum refining, steel, chemical, fertiliser and food processing plants, and power generation is particularly bad.

In Italy, Livorno is a centre of similar, although less extensive, industry. A chloro-alkali plant contributes mercury to the bay. Genoa has many polluting plants and the Bay of Naples has a major sewage problem. In Spain, the Barcelona region with its great concentra-

tions of coastal population, refineries and processing industries, adds sewage, oil and lead. In the Adriatic, industries near Venice and other northern Adriatic towns discharge oil and waste from tanneries and food processing plants. Eutrophication occurs in some localities due to the shallow sea and high loads of organic waste and nutrients.

The Gulf of Saronikos (in particular the harbour area of Piraeus) is badly polluted from sewage, fertilisers, zinc, iron, copper and oil. Between Cyprus and the Levant coast oil pollution is serious while Lebanon contributes waste from plastic and food processing, and Israel discharges chemicals and mercury from a chloro-alkali plant into Haifa Bay.

The North African coast suffers from oil pollution at loading terminals and refinery sites, while the Nile delta receives heavy sewage loads.

2–6 *opposite page and below* Pollutants entering the Mediterranean include organic matter (measured as BOD and COD, see *Glossary*), nutrients (phosphorus and nitrogen), specific organics (detergents, phenols, mineral oil), metals (mercury, lead, chromium, zinc), suspended matter (from natural erosion), pesticides, radioactive substances, and oil.

Phosphorus and nitrogen have high inputs from rivers in the northern parts of the basin and from domestic sources elsewhere. Over 60 per cent of BOD and COD comes from coastal sources and the rest is carried by rivers. Oil discharges are attributable to ships at sea, refinery sources and terminals. Of the heavy metal discharges mercury has caused most concern. Some of it comes from natural erosion, some from mercury mines, but the greatest part is from industry discharging into rivers.

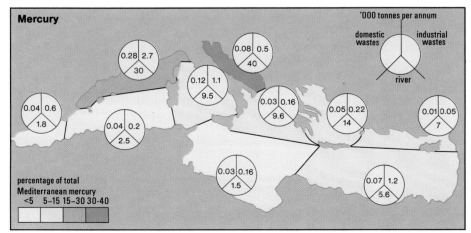

Mercury

'000 tonnes per annum

domestic wastes | industrial wastes

river

percentage of total Mediterranean mercury
<5   5–15   15–30   30–40

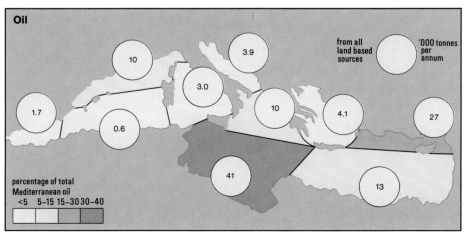

Oil

'000 tonnes per annum

from all land based sources

percentage of total Mediterranean oil
<5   5–15   15–30   30–40

Sea power of the major states

THE principal value of naval forces is their enormous capacity for geographical flexibility, and of increasing or reducing, in a relatively short time, the scale of military presence in distant regions. The major maritime powers have always demanded maximum freedom of the seas to allow their navies to be deployed at great distances from home waters.

Naval ships can be brought close to foreign coasts while on the high seas, posing a threat of intervention or punishment while remaining militarily uncommitted. Navies can thus exert a force on foreign governments much stronger than diplomacy but less dangerous than other forces. Conflict at sea can also be contained more readily, and there is less chance of escalation than is the case with armed conflict on land where territorial infringement and damage are more apparent and emotive.

These aspects of modern seapower, and the greater interests in acquiring sea territory and marine resources, are reasons why various forms of navies and naval activities have tended to multiply since the Second World War.

Accurate comparisons between the naval forces of the major powers are difficult to make. A simple comparison based on size of fleets, or numbers and types of craft, is useful, but not conclusive. In terms of ships the USSR fleet exceeds the combined strengths of NATO in relation to nuclear ballistic missile submarines (SSBNs), conventional submarines, cruisers and corvettes; the NATO naval forces exceed those of the USSR by numbers of aircraft and helicopter carriers, destroyers and ocean escorts.

But these general figures are inadequate as a basis for comparing the strengths of naval forces. Other factors such as weapon types and ranges, detection equipment, ship types, capabilities, cruising distances, endurance, speed, navigational and other technology, ship ages, and the manpower numbers and quality, are even more important. The Soviet numerical lead in submarines, for example, would appear less significant if the speed of response, accuracy, rate of missile delivery, numbers of missiles, target coverage, numbers of vessels at sea and variety of weaponry could be compared. In addition to surface craft and submarines, sea power involves the use of long-range aircraft from land bases, and ship-borne aircraft.

Even quite small Third World countries have navies and, with the increases in maritime jurisdictional areas and consequent regional disputes, their naval requirements are rising. The trend is towards small fast vessels, some equipped with powerful missiles, and with guns with very high rates of fire.

3 *right* A comparison of NATO and Warsaw Pact forces shows that NATO has superiority in surface ships and missile coverage capabilities, and in the strength of fleet air-arms, destroyers, nuclear powered aircraft carriers and nuclear powered cruisers (USA). The USA also has very large amphibious vessels capable of deploying over 300 helicopters, 100 landing barges and a division of marines. The European arm of NATO (including France) has more than half the NATO surface fleet. By contrast, the Eastern European members of the Warsaw Pact have very small naval capacities.

The USA has 14 aircraft carriers (totalling over one million tonnes displacement), with their anti-submarine warfare and strike aircraft, plus escorts and supply vessels. This represents a massive capability for deployment of sea power, which is also able to support land actions throughout the world. The USSR has five such craft (total 116 000 tonnes displacement): two Moskva-class helicopter carriers and three Kiev-class VTOL (vertical take-off and landing) carriers.

The Warsaw Pact countries have numerical superiority in submarine fleets, and perhaps in depth capabilities, but in terms of readiness, accuracy, and nuclear target coverage they are inferior. It should also be noted that the fleets of Australia, Japan, South Korea and Taiwan should be weighted in favour of the Western Alliance in the Far East area of operations.

1 *below* Since the 1950s the number of large surface warships has decreased, with the greater emphasis on submarines and the fitting of guided missiles to modern surface craft. In 1950 there were 1783 warships (over 1000 tonnes displacement); by 1978 there were 1065, and about half of these had missiles. The USA and USSR dominate in numbers of surface vessels.

2 *right* The trend in modern navies is to smaller ships and weapons (other than massive US aircraft carriers), and the use of submarine and air power. Helicopters are used in anti-submarine roles; long-range patrol and strike aircraft operating from ships can carry missiles. China and many Third World countries have adopted fast patrol boats, some armed with missiles, and there have been increases in the numbers of mine countermeasure vessels, both hunters and sweepers.

Selected fleet strengths (1982–83)	USSR	China	USA	Japan	UK	France	Italy	West Germany
ballistic missile submarines	70N+16	1	34N		4N	5N		
other submarines	123N+178	2N+102	94N+6	14	11N+16	20	10	24
rotary & fixed wing carriers	5		3N+11		3	3	1	
cruisers	43		9N+18		4	1	2	
amphibious ships	126	361	64	8	59	52	3	28
destroyers	66	16	89	33	13	19	6	7
frigates, escorts & corvettes	182	33	81	16	41	24	24	14
mine counter measure vessels	390	103	25	37	40	33	35	59
(fast) missile & patrol craft	475	925	35	19	19	13	12	42
naval aircraft	1350	850	4900	180	190	150	93	160

N = nuclear powered   figures do not include reserve fleets

Surface fleet strengths of principal navies

KEY
SURFACE FLEETS (1982–83)
NATO (including France)
Warsaw Pact
others
figures are load displacement tonnages

DENMARK 42 085
NORWAY 28 403
W. GERMANY 98 786
SWEDEN 35 470
NETHERLANDS 78 353
FINLAND 6 850
BELGIUM 19 172
UK 351 209
IRELAND 5 350
E. GERMANY 81 910
POLAND 52 586
FRANCE 270 531
ROMANIA 14 165
YUGOSLAVIA 22 261
SPAIN 190 372
ALB. 5452
BULGARIA 21 560
ITALY 130 959
TURKEY 119 666
SYRIA 5 573
PORTUGAL 35 952
GREECE 105 019
MOROCCO 8 821
TUNISIA 3 940
ISRAEL 16 292
IRAN 28 000
ALGERIA 12 747
LIBYA 24 863
IRAQ 10 369
PAKISTAN 44 883
EGYPT 46 214
SAUDI ARABIA 9 014
OMAN 3 922
S. YEMEN 10 482
CANADA 54 866
UNITED STATES OF AMERICA 3 930 321
MEXICO 38 337
CUBA 13 167
DOMINICAN REP. 9 529
VENEZUELA 28 630
COLOMBIA 12 766
ECUADOR 15 585
PERU 64 062
BRAZIL 107 355
NIGERIA 16 150
ETHIOPIA 5 306
ANGOLA 5107
URUGUAY 8 089
S. AFRICA 13 578
NEW ZEALAND 18 060
CHILE 75 710
ARGENTINA 79 089

Comparison of forces

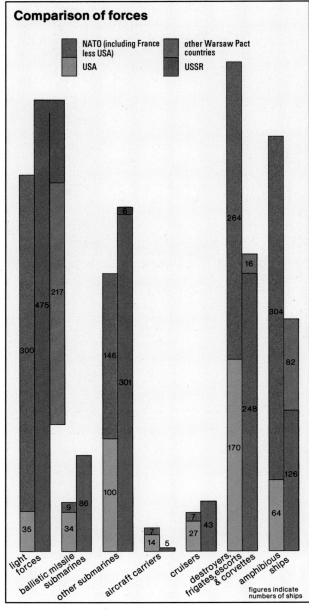

Legend:
- NATO (including France less USA)
- USA
- other Warsaw Pact countries
- USSR

Bar chart values:

light forces: 35, 300, 475, 217

ballistic missile submarines: 34, 9, 86

other submarines: 100, 146, 301

aircraft carriers: 14, 7, 5

cruisers: 27, 7, 43

destroyers, frigates escorts & corvettes: 170, 264, 248, 16, 6

amphibious ships: 64, 126, 304, 82

figures indicate numbers of ships

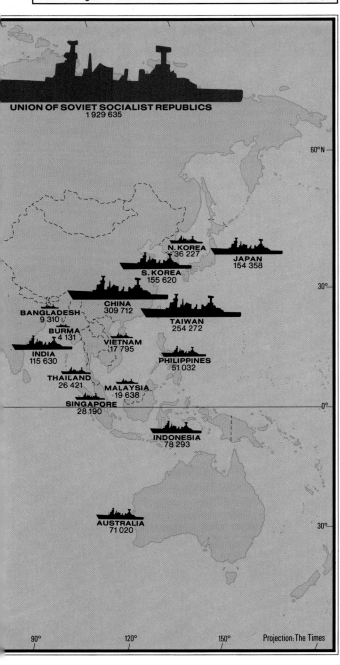

UNION OF SOVIET SOCIALIST REPUBLICS 1 929 635

N. KOREA 36 227
JAPAN 154 358
S. KOREA 155 620
CHINA 309 712
TAIWAN 254 272
BANGLADESH 9 310
BURMA 4 131
VIETNAM 17 795
PHILIPPINES 51 032
INDIA 115 630
THAILAND 26 421
MALAYSIA 19 638
SINGAPORE 28 190
INDONESIA 78 293
AUSTRALIA 71 020

60°N
30°
0°
30°
90°   120°   150°   Projection: The Times

Surface warship types

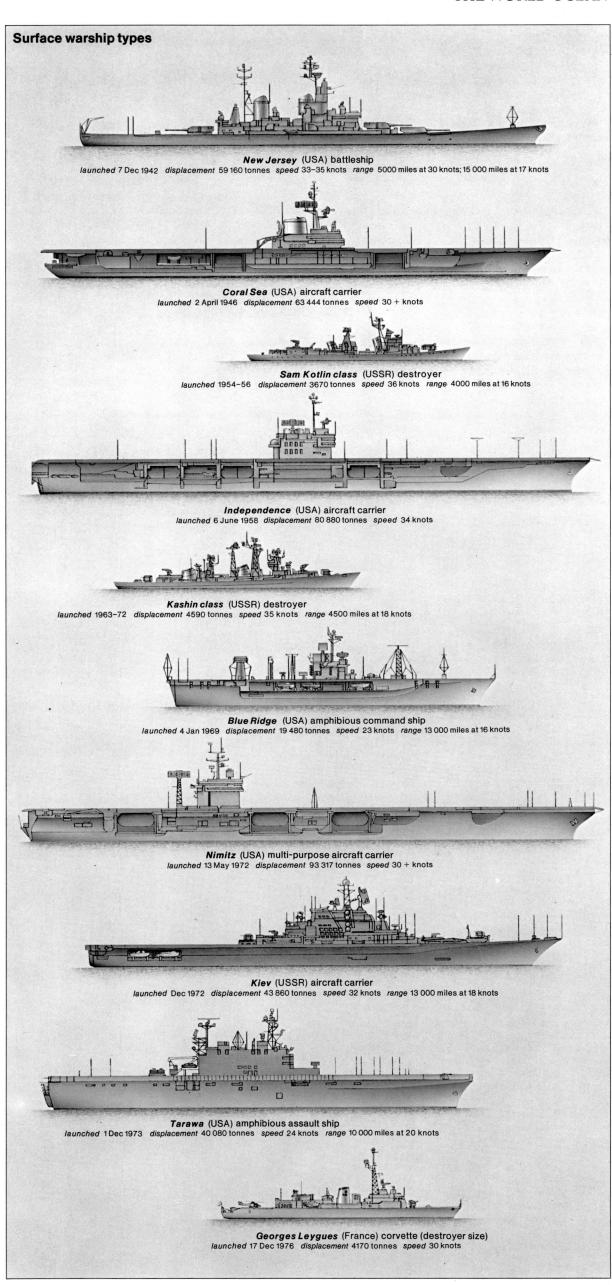

New Jersey (USA) battleship
launched 7 Dec 1942 *displacement* 59 160 tonnes *speed* 33–35 knots *range* 5000 miles at 30 knots; 15 000 miles at 17 knots

Coral Sea (USA) aircraft carrier
launched 2 April 1946 *displacement* 63 444 tonnes *speed* 30 + knots

Sam Kotlin class (USSR) destroyer
launched 1954–56 *displacement* 3670 tonnes *speed* 36 knots *range* 4000 miles at 16 knots

Independence (USA) aircraft carrier
launched 6 June 1958 *displacement* 80 880 tonnes *speed* 34 knots

Kashin class (USSR) destroyer
launched 1963–72 *displacement* 4590 tonnes *speed* 35 knots *range* 4500 miles at 18 knots

Blue Ridge (USA) amphibious command ship
launched 4 Jan 1969 *displacement* 19 480 tonnes *speed* 23 knots *range* 13 000 miles at 16 knots

Nimitz (USA) multi-purpose aircraft carrier
launched 13 May 1972 *displacement* 93 317 tonnes *speed* 30 + knots

Kiev (USSR) aircraft carrier
launched Dec 1972 *displacement* 43 860 tonnes *speed* 32 knots *range* 13 000 miles at 18 knots

Tarawa (USA) amphibious assault ship
launched 1 Dec 1973 *displacement* 40 080 tonnes *speed* 24 knots *range* 10 000 miles at 20 knots

Georges Leygues (France) corvette (destroyer size)
launched 17 Dec 1976 *displacement* 4170 tonnes *speed* 30 knots

Submarine strategy and defence

I N modern wars naval battles may be conducted between fleets entirely out of sight of one another. Much of the naval strategy of the major powers depends on hidden, highly mobile submarine forces; on the use of advanced technology to detect and monitor potential enemy forces from space; and on regular air and sea surveillance.

There are about 900 naval submarines in the world. They are divided into: diesel-electric with torpedoes, diesel powered with ballistic missiles, nuclear powered attack and nuclear powered ballistic missile submarines. The navies of 40 states employ submarines, including countries such as Chile, Ecuador and Libya.

Nuclear powered strategic ballistic submarines (SSBN) are very large vessels that can remain submerged for several months and have great navigational accuracy under sea and ice using inertial navigational systems. The Typhoon class of Soviet SSBN, for example, is of 30 000 tonnes displacement, has an underwater speed of 24 knots and carries 20 ballistic missiles. The great strategic value of SSBNs lies in their ability to range widely in the world below the sea surface, their capacity for long endurance and self-sustainment, their virtual undetectability once submerged in the deep ocean and their power to deliver nuclear missiles with great accuracy from almost any part of the surface or depth of

Abbreviations used in submarine strategy	
SS	strategic submarine
SSB	strategic submarine, ballistic missiles
SSG	strategic submarine, guided missiles
SSN	nuclear powered strategic submarine
SSBN	nuclear powered strategic submarine, ballistic missiles
SSGN	nuclear powered strategic submarine, guided (cruise) missiles
ULMS	undersea long range missile system

the seas. They have been conceived primarily as a defensive deterrent. Any country launching a first nuclear strike on military targets could expect massive 'second strike' retaliation from hidden nuclear missile submarines. Future developments in submarine detection methods and anti-submarine warfare to the extent of being able to pinpoint and attack submarines in the ocean depths would remove the invulnerability of the SSBN and with this the certainty of a retaliatory second-strike capability. This could increase the risk of an aggressor adopting a first-strike strategy, further endangering world peace by eroding the deterrent value of the SSBN.

In addition to the SSBN, the world powers rely on anti-submarine warfare (ASW) and detection forces, namely the hunter-killer submarines, helicopters, surveillance aircraft, and the sea surface, water column, seabed and satellite recording devices (see following pages).

1, 2, 3 *main map, table below and graph below right* The USSR has the greatest numbers of SSBNs and other nuclear missile submarines, followed by the USA with far less SSBNs but with multiple warhead capabilities covering twice the number of targets than the USSR. Only France, the United Kingdom and China have an additional, but limited, capability in SSBNs, nuclear powered attack (torpedo) submarines, and diesel powered ballistic missile submarines. The fleets of the other 35 submarine nations are entirely conventional diesel/electric vessels armed with torpedoes.

There has been a steady build-up of nuclear submarines by both NATO and the USSR since 1966, and in 1973 the Soviet nuclear submarine force overtook that of the Western Alliance numerically.

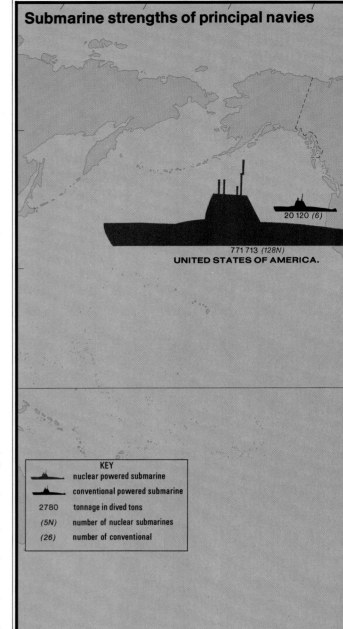

Submarine strengths of principal navies

20 120 (6)

771 713 *(128N)*
UNITED STATES OF AMERICA.

KEY	
	nuclear powered submarine
	conventional powered submarine
2780	tonnage in dived tons
(5N)	number of nuclear submarines
(26)	number of conventional

4 *above* The *Indomptable*, a French nuclear powered submarine, is armed with 18 self-guided torpedoes and travels at a speed of 20 knots. It measures 128 m long and 11 m wide and can accommodate a crew of 135 men.

5, 6, 7 *and* **8** *below left to right* The maps show the evolution of SSBN missile ranges and the operational areas from which SSBNs can strike their targets: by US submarines to strike anywhere in the USSR; by US submarines to strike 200 nm into the USSR; by Soviet submarines to strike anywhere in the USA; and by Soviet submarines to strike 200 nm into the USA.

The maps indicate the changes which have, and still are, coming about in nuclear missile developments and strategies. During the early 1960s Soviet submarines had to make long passages to their operational areas within about 700 nm of the American coast, thus rendering them vulnerable to detection en route and on station. By contrast, the Soviet Delta III's with missile ranges of 5200 nm are able to hide in the vastness of the Pacific (although they have to make long voyages through monitored areas to do so). They can also, more significantly, obtain geographic cover of Soviet sea and air space against detection in the contiguous waters of the Soviet Arctic and other home waters and still strike US targets. Similarly, the American Trident I and the Trident D5 could have operational areas in the Pacific (without being subject to close monitoring en route) and also within the geographic protection of US air and sea space against Soviet ASW forces.

The new generations of SSBNs under development also have improved delivery accuracy. Some of the new missiles utilise stellar inertial guidance and take star sights during flight. The Trident I has a strike accuracy of 225 m and the new Trident D5 possibly about 120 m. One of the implications of this is that these new missiles can destroy hard targets (i.e. highly protected land missile silos) from any azimuth. Sea based missiles could thereby become a possible first-strike threat against land missile launching sites. This adds another complicated dimension to the challenge and response strategies using the oceans.

The top submarine nations—number of submarines 1982–83

	ballistic		cruise		fleet	patrol	
	SSBN	SSB	SSGN	SSG	SSN	SS	reserves
USSR	70	16	49	18	66	155	108 SS
USA	34				94	6	2 SSBN 3 SSN
China		1			2	102	
UK	4				13	16	
France	5					20	
West Germany						24	
North Korea						17	
Turkey						15	
Norway						15	
Japan						14	
Peru						12	
Egypt						12	
Sweden						8	

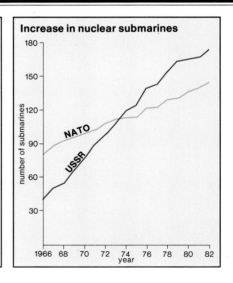

Increase in nuclear submarines

NATO

USSR

number of submarines — 30 60 90 120 150 180

1966 68 70 72 74 76 78 80 82
year

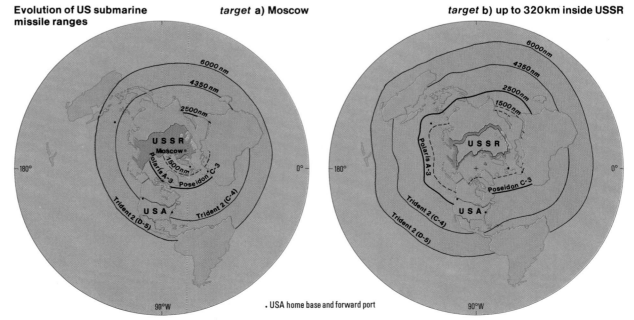

Evolution of US submarine missile ranges

target **a)** Moscow

target **b)** up to 320 km inside USSR

· USA home base and forward port

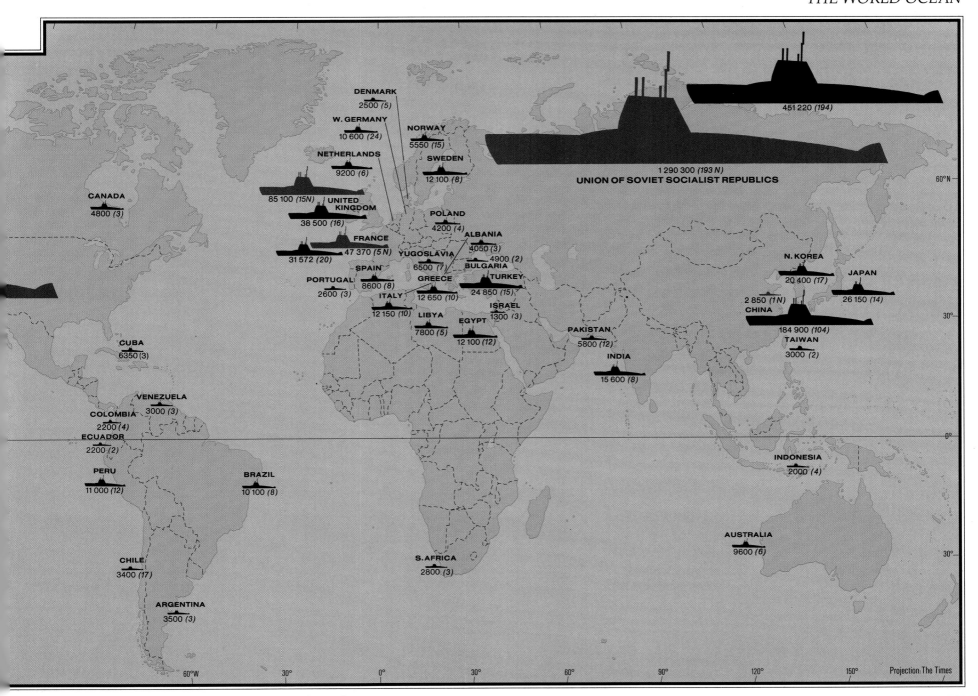

Map labels (country, tonnage, number of vessels):

DENMARK 2500 (5)
W. GERMANY 10 600 (24)
NORWAY 5550 (15)
NETHERLANDS 9200 (6)
SWEDEN 12 100 (8)
CANADA 4800 (3)
UNITED KINGDOM 85 100 (15N) / 38 500 (16)
POLAND 4200 (4)
FRANCE 47 370 (5 N) / 31 572 (20)
ALBANIA 4050 (3)
YUGOSLAVIA 6500 (7)
BULGARIA 4900 (2)
SPAIN 8600 (8)
GREECE 12 650 (10)
TURKEY 24 850 (15)
PORTUGAL 2600 (3)
ITALY 12 150 (10)
LIBYA 7800 (5)
ISRAEL 1300 (3)
EGYPT 12 100 (12)
PAKISTAN 5800 (12)
CUBA 6350 (3)
VENEZUELA 3000 (3)
COLOMBIA 2200 (4)
ECUADOR 2200 (2)
PERU 11 000 (12)
BRAZIL 10 100 (8)
CHILE 3400 (17)
ARGENTINA 3500 (3)
INDIA 15 600 (8)
S. AFRICA 2800 (3)
AUSTRALIA 9600 (6)
INDONESIA 2000 (4)
UNION OF SOVIET SOCIALIST REPUBLICS 1 290 300 (193 N) / 451 220 (194)
N. KOREA 20 400 (17)
JAPAN 26 150 (14)
CHINA 2 850 (1 N) / 184 900 (104)
TAIWAN 3000 (2)

Projection: The Times

Evolution of selected submarine launched ballistic missiles (SLBMs)

USA				USSR		
missile	range (nm)	submarine		missile	range (nm)	submarine
Regulus	—		1955	SS-N-4	300	Zulu V
Regulus	—	Growler	1958	SS-N-4	370	Golf I
—	—	—	1959	SS-N-4	370	Hotel
Polaris A-2	1500	Lafayette	1961	—	—	—
Polaris A-3	2500	Franklin, Washington	1963	SS-N-5	900	Golf/Hotel
			1967	SS-N-6	1300	Yankee
Poseidon C-3	2500	Lafayette	1970	—	—	—
—	—	—	1971	SS-N-6 II	1600	Yankee
—	—	—	1972	SS-N-8	4200	Delta I & II
—	—	—	1976	SS-N-8 I	5000	Delta II
—	—	—	1977	SS-N-17	2400	Yankee
				SS-N-18	5200	Delta III
Trident 1	4200	Lafayette	1979			
—	—	—	1980	SS-NX-20	4500+	Typhoon
Trident 2 C-4	4350	Ohio	1983	—	—	—
Long Trident 1	6000	Trident	1990s	—	6000	—
Trident 2 D-5.	6000	Trident				

9 The table compares the main developments of the USA and USSR in submarine nuclear missiles since the Second World War. The ranges of some are shown on the four maps **5, 6, 7** *and* **8** *below left and opposite. The submarines illustrated* below show the size difference between nuclear and conventional types.

Evolution of Soviet submarine missile ranges

target a) USA

SS-N-8 8000nm, 5000nm, 4200nm, 1300nm, 900nm, SS-N-6, SS-NX-20, USA, N. pole, USSR, SS-N-8 (1)

target b) up to 320km inside USA

SS-N-8 8000nm, 5000nm, 4200nm, 1300nm, 900nm, SS-NX-20, SS-N-5, SS-N-6, USA, N. pole, USSR, SS-N-8 (1)

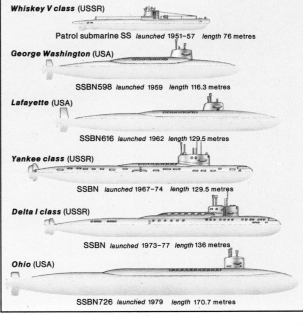

Whiskey V class (USSR)
Patrol submarine SS *launched* 1951-57 *length* 76 metres

George Washington (USA)
SSBN598 *launched* 1959 *length* 116.3 metres

Lafayette (USA)
SSBN616 *launched* 1962 *length* 129.5 metres

Yankee class (USSR)
SSBN *launched* 1967-74 *length* 129.5 metres

Delta I class (USSR)
SSBN *launched* 1973-77 *length* 136 metres

Ohio (USA)
SSBN726 *launched* 1979 *length* 170.7 metres

Naval operations 1

THE effectiveness of naval forces depends to a great extent on their deployment, as well as their speed and secrecy of movement. This in turn relates to their ease of access to operational areas and the availability of bases and other support facilities.

Several geographical constraints affect Russian oceanic strategic mobility. The northern seaboard is partially ice-bound. In winter, surface vessels and submarines from Murmansk reach the North Atlantic mainly through an area between Svalbard and Norway, the boundaries of which are in dispute (see page 187). The open ocean beyond is closely monitored by NATO countries. Nevertheless, it is the best ocean access available from the USSR. The Black Sea and Baltic Sea are far more confined and easily monitored. Access to the Pacific from the Soviet Far East through the Sea of Japan and the straits north and south is also well monitored.

This means that the Soviet Union has to divide its naval forces into four fleets: the Northern, Baltic, Black Sea and Pacific Ocean Fleets. Access from Soviet bases in these regions can be monitored at 'gateways' and, in any event, access is gained to areas distant from the main shipping lanes. The NATO forces by contrast have vast lengths of coastlines and more overseas bases available from which to deploy their vessels.

A vital element in naval strategy is judging the actions of potential adversaries and countering them by deployment of forces. For these purposes major powers use intelligence gathering ships (Soviet AGIs); gatekeepers at entrances to critical areas; vessels cruising within electronic earshot of bases; ship 'tattletales' shadowing other ships; submarines tracking other submarines; aircraft and helicopters using sonar, or magnetic anomaly detectors; sound surveillance systems (SOSUS), including the positioning of sonar buoy arrays on the sea bed or within the water column to detect submarine movement; fixed hydrophones moored to the sea bed; towed arrays of sonar sensors; and satellite monitoring. The USA has the greatest coverage of these systems but the USSR has similar acoustic devices although less widely distributed. It should be noted, however, that the Soviet Delta III class of submarine with missile ranges of 5200 nm can destroy targets in the USA and Europe from limited patrol areas within Soviet waters (sometimes with ice coverage) outside the SOSUS systems (see also maps on previous pages showing weapon ranges).

1 *main map* The locations of monitoring systems, bases and fleet strengths of NATO and Soviet navies.
2 *inset right* Surveillance of Soviet submarine activities in the Arctic.

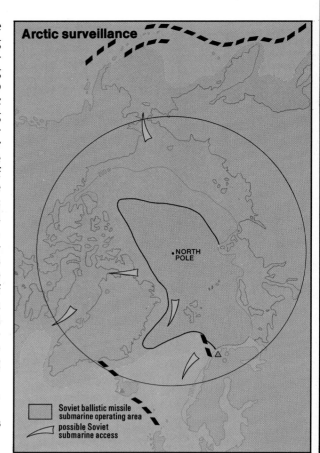

Arctic surveillance

■ Soviet ballistic missile submarine operating area
◣ possible Soviet submarine access

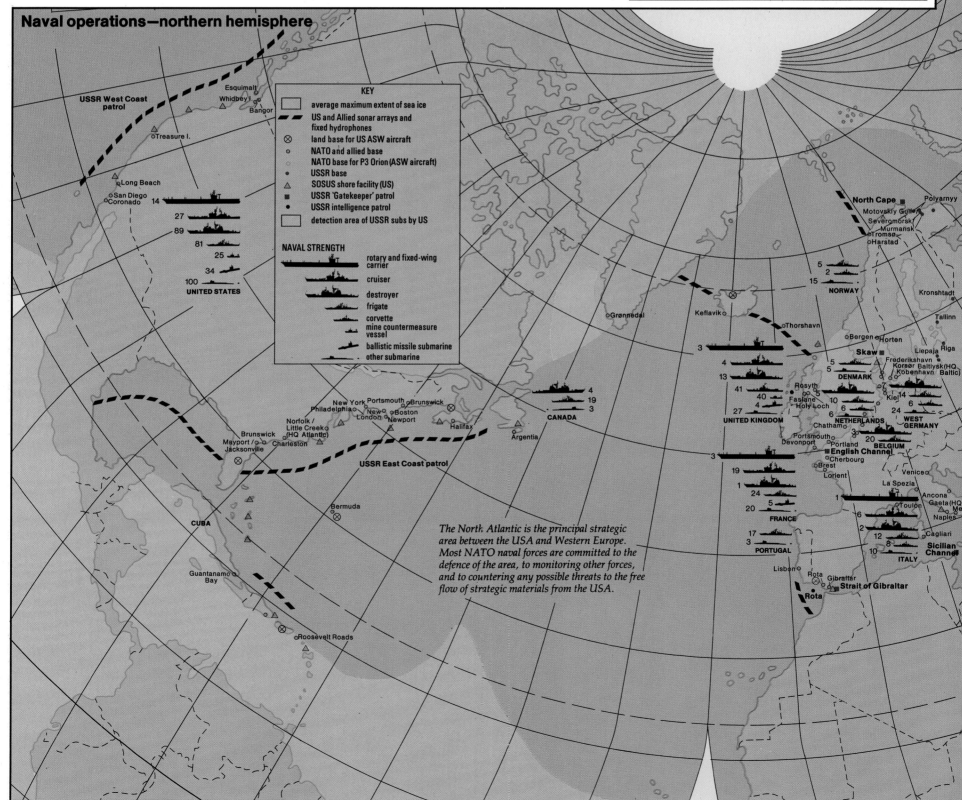

Naval operations—northern hemisphere

KEY
average maximum extent of sea ice
US and Allied sonar arrays and fixed hydrophones
⊗ land base for US ASW aircraft
○ NATO and allied base
◦ NATO base for P3 Orion (ASW aircraft)
• USSR base
△ SOSUS shore facility (US)
■ USSR 'Gatekeeper' patrol
● USSR intelligence patrol
detection area of USSR subs by US

NAVAL STRENGTH
rotary and fixed-wing carrier
cruiser
destroyer
frigate
corvette
mine countermeasure vessel
ballistic missile submarine
other submarine

UNITED STATES
14
27
89
81
25
34
100

CANADA
4
19
3

NORWAY
5
15

UNITED KINGDOM
3
4
13
41
40
27

DENMARK
5
10
6

NETHERLANDS
3
20
6

WEST GERMANY
14
24
6

BELGIUM
3

FRANCE
3
19
1
24
5
17
3

PORTUGAL

ITALY
1
2
12
8
6
10

The North Atlantic is the principal strategic area between the USA and Western Europe. Most NATO naval forces are committed to the defence of the area, to monitoring other forces, and to countering any possible threats to the free flow of strategic materials from the USA.

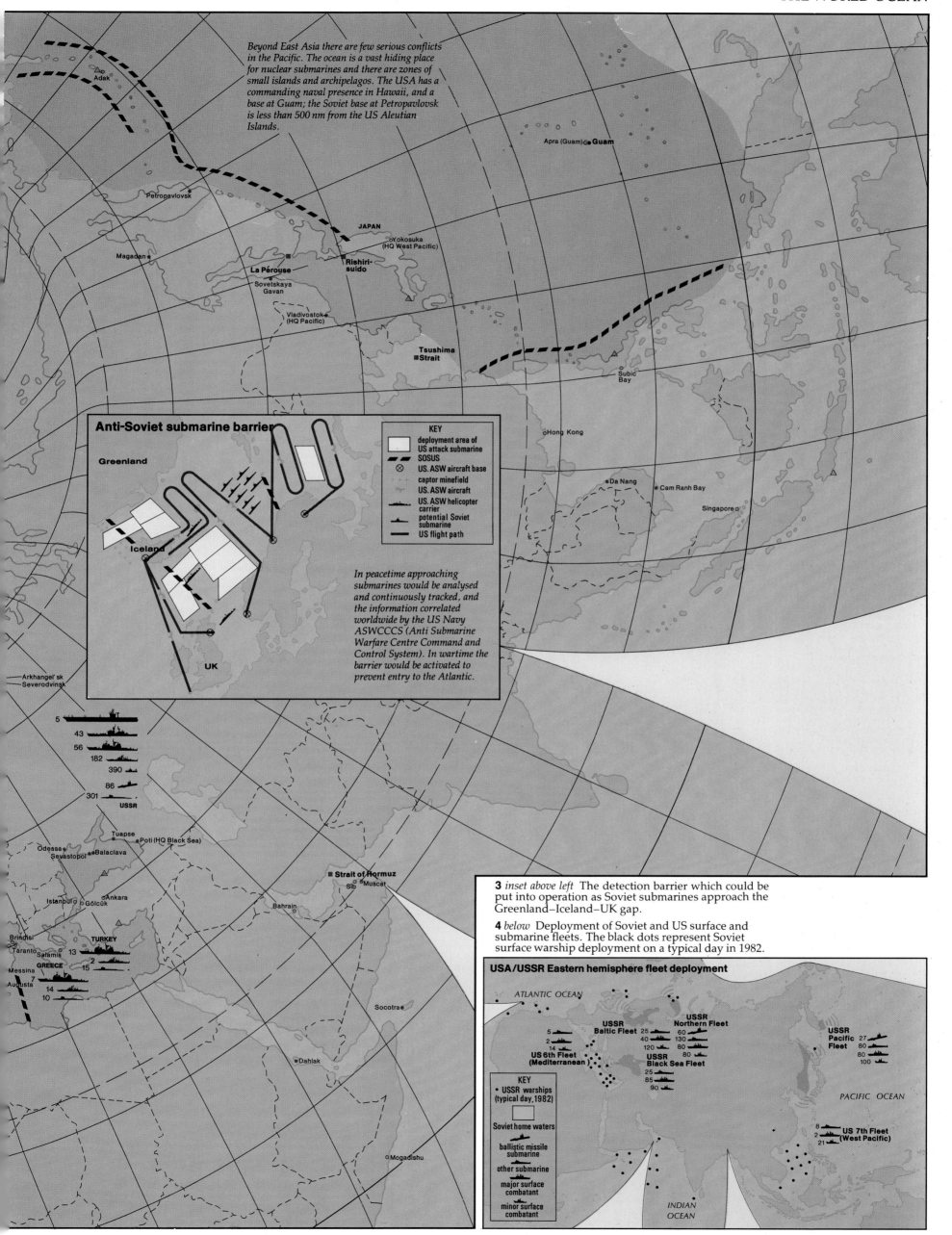

Beyond East Asia there are few serious conflicts in the Pacific. The ocean is a vast hiding place for nuclear submarines and there are zones of small islands and archipelagos. The USA has a commanding naval presence in Hawaii, and a base at Guam; the Soviet base at Petropavlovsk is less than 500 nm from the US Aleutian Islands.

Adak

Petropavlovsk

JAPAN

Magadan

Yokosuka
(HQ West Pacific)

La Pérouse

Rishiri-
suido

Sovetskaya
Gavan

Vladivostok
(HQ Pacific)

Tsushima
Strait

Apra (Guam) Guam

Subic
Bay

Hong Kong

Da Nang

Cam Ranh Bay

Singapore

Anti-Soviet submarine barrier

Greenland

Iceland

UK

Arkhangel'sk
Severodvinsk

KEY

deployment area of
US attack submarine

SOSUS

US. ASW aircraft base

captor minefield

US. ASW aircraft

US. ASW helicopter
carrier

potential Soviet
submarine

US flight path

In peacetime approaching submarines would be analysed and continuously tracked, and the information correlated worldwide by the US Navy ASWCCCS (Anti Submarine Warfare Centre Command and Control System). In wartime the barrier would be activated to prevent entry to the Atlantic.

5
43
56
182
390
86
301
USSR

Tuapse
Poti (HQ Black Sea)
Odessa
Sevastopol
Balaclava
Ankara
Istanbul Gölcük
TURKEY
Brindisi
Taranto
Salamis 13
GREECE 2
Messina 15
Augusta 7
14
10

Strait of Hormuz
Sib Muscat
Bahrain

Dahlak

Socotra

Mogadishu

3 *inset above left* The detection barrier which could be put into operation as Soviet submarines approach the Greenland–Iceland–UK gap.

4 *below* Deployment of Soviet and US surface and submarine fleets. The black dots represent Soviet surface warship deployment on a typical day in 1982.

USA/USSR Eastern hemisphere fleet deployment

ATLANTIC OCEAN

USSR
Baltic Fleet
5
2
14
US 6th Fleet
(Mediterranean)

USSR
Northern Fleet
25 60
40 130
120 80
80

USSR
Black Sea Fleet
25
85
90

USSR
Pacific
Fleet
27
80
100

PACIFIC OCEAN

8
2
21
US 7th Fleet
(West Pacific)

INDIAN
OCEAN

KEY

USSR warships
(typical day, 1982)

Soviet home waters

ballistic missile
submarine

other submarine

major surface
combatant

minor surface
combatant

Naval operations 2

The southern hemisphere, comprising the Antarctic ocean, the South Atlantic, the Indian Ocean and the South Pacific has been emerging as a zone of tension in maritime geopolitics for many years. The South Atlantic has seen the steady decline of North European territorial possessions, shifts in the balance of influence and power with the emergence of Soviet naval presence and bases, changes of governments within Africa and Latin America, armed conflicts in many countries, tension between South Africa and its neighbours, and the vulnerability of the tanker route via the Cape of Good Hope.

There is no equivalent in the South Atlantic of the North Atlantic Treaty Organisation (NATO), which provides a unified Western Allied defensive control of the sea region. Proposals for a South Atlantic Treaty Organisation (SATO) have not been successful due primarily to the lack of political unity and the many disputes in the region.

South Africa has the main naval force in Atlantic Africa but Nigeria is developing its forces rapidly. There are Soviet bases in Angola, Cape Verde, the Guineas and Benin. In Atlantic Latin American the most powerful states are Argentina, Brazil, Cuba, Mexico and Venezuela. The Latin American nuclear free zone now has little relevance for Brazil and Argentina, who are moving to nuclear capabilities, or for the main nuclear powers.

In the extreme south, Antarctica is politically unique. At present it is governed by the Antarctic Treaty of 1959, and none of the various territorial claims is entirely recognised internationally. In addition to its strategic value, and the many research projects in progress, its fisheries resources are becoming important and there is growing interest in the potential mineral resources. The dispute over possession of the Falkland Islands (and the dependencies of South Georgia, and the Sandwich Islands) between Britain and Argentina is also related to sectoral claims in the Antarctic. The seas surrounding the Falklands are rich in marine life and the continental shelf has a high potential for hydrocarbons.

The Indian Ocean has strategic value for the major maritime powers. The closures of the Suez Canal added to its importance as a routeway, especially for oil tankers, from the Straits of Hormuz to the Cape, and it is vital for the trade to Japan via the Malacca and Lombok Straits.

1 *below and* **2** *below left* The events of the Falklands crisis, March/June 1982, are shown on the maps and summarised in the table *below left*.

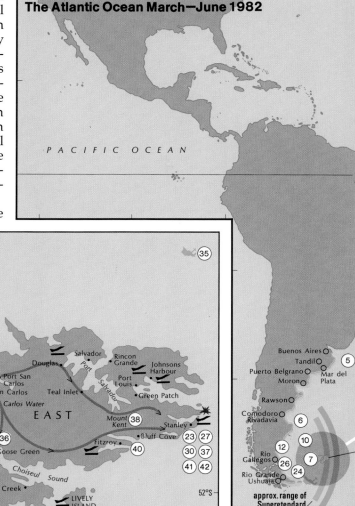

The Atlantic Ocean March–June 1982

PACIFIC OCEAN

Incidents numbered on maps

1. *18 March* Argentine party lands on South Georgia
2. *19 March* Argentine flag hoisted at Leith Harbour
3. *21 March* HMS *Endurance* ordered to stand by to remove Argentinians
4. *25 March* Additional supplies delivered by Argentine ship to South Georgia
5. *26 March* Argentine and Uruguayan fleets carry out manoeuvres in South Atlantic; Argentina announces its intention to protect party on South Georgia
6. *31 March* Argentine invasion fleet sails for the Falklands
7. *2 April* Argentine forces capture Falklands
8. *3 April* Argentine forces capture South Georgia
9. *5 April* First of UK Task Force sails from Portsmouth; includes carriers HMS *Hermes* and *Invincible*
10. *7 April* Britain declares 200 nm 'exclusion zone' around the Falklands
11. *7 April* 7 warships join task force off Gibraltar
12. *7 April* Argentina declares a 200 nm 'defence zone' from her coast and around Falklands and South Georgia
13. *9 April Canberra* sails from Southampton
14. *10 April* Warships arrive off Ascension I.
15. *16 April* Task force leaves Ascension, proceeds south; Ascension base expanded for operations for Vulcan (bombers), Nimrod (surveillance), Victor (refuelling), and Hercules (transport)
16. *17 April Canberra* calls at Freetown, Sierra Leone
17. *20 April* Second wave of UK fleet, including *Canberra*, arrives at Ascension I.
18. *20 April* Two Soviet Echo II class submarines reported in vicinity. Soviet Bear planes continue surveillance of task force and Primorye-class surveillance ship shadows *Canberra*
19. *21 April* Argentine Boeing 707 surveying task force chased off by Harriers
20. *23 April* Warships *Antrim* and HMS *Endurance* proceed to South Georgia
21. *25 April* Argentine merchant ship *Rio de la Plata* approaches task force and is warned off
22. *25 April* British forces recapture South Georgia; Argentine submarine *Santa Fe* crippled
23. *1 May* Harriers operating from HMS *Hermes* and *Invincible* and Vulcans from Ascension I. attack Port Stanley and other airfields
24. *2 May* Argentine cruiser *General Belgrano* sunk outside total exclusion zone by nuclear-powered hunter killer submarine HMS *Conqueror*
25. *4 May* HMS *Sheffield* destroyed by exocet missile from Argentine aircraft
26. *7 May* British military exclusion zone established 12 nm off Argentine coast
27. *9 May* Heavy air and sea bombardment of Argentine garrisons
28. *15 May* SAS marines land on Pebble I. and raid airstrip
29. *20 May* HMS *Fearless* and *Intrepid* lead invasion fleet into Falklands Sound
30. *20 May* HMS *Hermes* and *Invincible* steam south and attack Port Stanley installations by air and sea bombardment
31. *21 May* Invasion fleet including *Canberra* land troops and equipment at San Carlos Bay; naval bombardment covers landings
32. *21 May* HMS *Ardent* sunk during air attacks in San Carlos Bay
33. *23 May* HMS *Antelope* sunk during air attacks in San Carlos Bay
34. *25 May* HMS *Coventry* sunk on radar patrol
35. *25 May Atlantic Conveyor* sunk by exocet

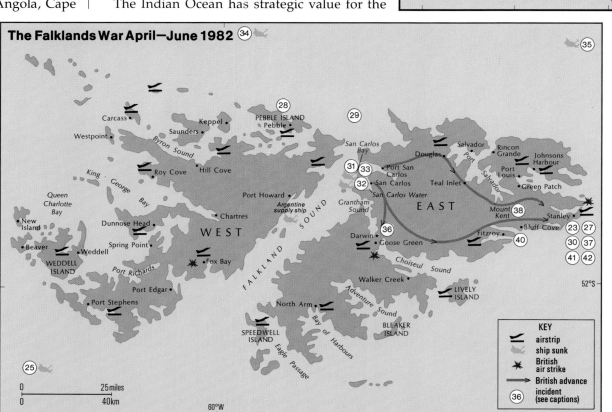

The Falklands War April–June 1982

Carcass
Westpoint
Saunders • Keppel
Byron Sound
PEBBLE ISLAND Pebble
San Carlos Bay
Salvador
Rincon Grande
Johnsons Harbour
King George Bay
Roy Cove • Hill Cove
Port San Carlos
Port Louis • Green Patch
Queen Charlotte Bay
Port Howard •
Argentine supply ship
San Carlos
Teal Inlet
San Carlos Water
Dunnose Head •
Grantham Sound
EAST
Mount Kent
Stanley •
New Island
WEST
Chartres
Darwin • Goose Green
Bluff Cove
Beaver • Weddell
Spring Point •
Fitzroy •
WEDDELL ISLAND
Fox Bay
Choiseul Sound
Port Richards •
Port Edgar •
Walker Creek •
Port Stephens •
North Arm •
Adventure Sound
LIVELY ISLAND
52°S
SPEEDWELL ISLAND
Bay of Harbours
BLEAKER ISLAND
Eagle Passage

0 __ 25 miles
0 __ 40 km
60°W

KEY
— airstrip
— ship sunk
✳ British air strike
→ British advance
㊱ incident (see captions)

Buenos Aires ○
Tandil ○
Puerto Belgrano ○ Mar del Plata
Moron ○
Rawson ○
Comodoro Rivadavia ○
Rio Gallegos ○
Rio Grande ○ Ushuaia ○

approx. range of Superetendard (with Exocet missile)
approx. range of A4 Skyhawk
60°W

Falkland crisis of 1982

The long history of disputes over the Falkland Islands commenced in the 18th century. Originally named the Falklands by the British in 1690, they were renamed the Malouines in 1722 by the French, who made the first official occupation and then sold East Falkland to Spain in 1767. There were conflicts between Britain and Spain over West Falkland, but eventually they both left the islands, unoccupied. Argentina claimed possession in 1820 after independence from Spain. Britain retook the islands in 1833. Argentina protested and has continued to claim sovereignty over the Falklands (Islas Malvinas). South Georgia was first claimed by Argentina in 1927, and the South Sandwich islands in 1948. These claims have been persistently rejected by Britain and by the Falklands population, who have affirmed that they wished to remain British. On several occasions the dispute came close to conflict, but a display of limited British sea power (as in 1966 and 1977) was sufficient to deter invasion.

The continuing dispute between Britain and Argentina resulted in open conflict in March 1982 when Argentine forces invaded the Falkland Islands and Dependencies. In response Britain despatched to the South Atlantic the biggest naval force assembled since the Second World War. The length of the voyage to the South Atlantic, the onset of winter, and the need to be self-sufficient in provisions, fuel and military supplies presented enormous logistical problems which had to be overcome in the short time before sailing. That Britain was able to charter and requisition a wide range of British merchant ships made the campaign preparations immediately possible.

The British task force was sent to the South Atlantic to take action on the grounds of self defence when Argentina failed to comply with the United Nations Security Council Resolution 502 of 3 April which called for the end of hostilities, the withdrawal of Argentine troops and a settlement by peaceful means.

The conflict led to considerable loss of life, particularly on the Argentine side. It also highlighted many positive and negative aspects of naval operations in an age of high technology. The successful deployment of the British force, over almost 8000 miles from home, showed the need for strong lines of supply provided by merchant ships and confirmed the value of a staging area and base such as Ascension Island.

The relative ease of detection of the surface ships was evident when an Argentine Boeing 707 approached the task force over 2000 miles from its destination. Possible sources of information may have been three Soviet surveillance satellites covering the region, Soviet submarines, planes and a 'tattletale' ship shadowing the troopship *Canberra*.

The Argentine fleet following the sinking of the cruiser *Belgrano* was kept in port due to the possible presence of British nuclear powered submarines which could not be detected. The Argentine diesel-electric submarines were less of a threat to the task force since they could be detected by ASW escort ships and Nimrod aircraft using Jezebel sonar buoys.

One of the most revealing aspects of the conflict was

36. *28 May* Darwin and Goose Green taken
37. *29 May* Heavy air and sea bombardment of Argentine positions at Port Stanley
38. *2 June* Mount Kent taken
39. *3 June* Harrier replacements proceed from UK; refuelled by Victors
40. *8 June* Logistic landing ships *Sir Galahad* and *Sir Tristram* and one landing craft bombed during Argentine air attacks on troops landing at Bluff Cove.
41. *12 June Glamorgan* damaged while supporting advance on Port Stanley
42. *15 June* British forces enter Port Stanley and fighting ceased
43. *20 June* British force retakes Sandwich Is

British fleet
aircraft/troop carrier
destroyer
assault ship
submarine

Argentine fleet
carrier
destroyer
fast attack craft

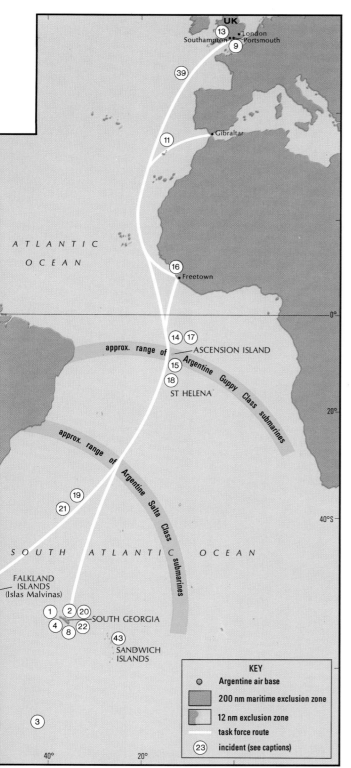

The Indian Ocean

The USA, USSR and the People's Republic of China have all shown strategic interest in the Indian Ocean. The vital Straits of Hormuz, Bal el Mandeb, Malacca and Lombok can all be commanded from it.

The USSR has a naval squadron permanently in the Indian Ocean and the US Seventh Fleet includes the Indian Ocean in its patrol area. During the initial period of the Soviet invasion of Afghanistan the warships of the USA, USSR, UK, France, West Germany and Australia took up positions in the region. The littoral states have only small navies with the Indian fleet predominating.

Attempts by the littoral states led by Sri Lanka to establish the Indian Ocean as a zone of peace have not progressed due to rivalries between India and Pakistan and strategic involvement of the major powers. However, the need to deploy missile submarines in the Indian Ocean by the USSR and USA has lessened with the development of longer range missiles.

Small islands such as the Maldives, Seychelles, Comoros and Diego Garcia are sought for bases. The UK Indian Ocean island of Diego Garcia has been made available to US air and naval forces; the USSR has no such facility. The former Soviet base of Berber in Somalia was lost in 1978 and since then only Aden, South Yemen, has provided a relatively stable base.

4 *below* The main naval bases controlled or used by the USSR, the USA and other powers in the Indian Ocean.

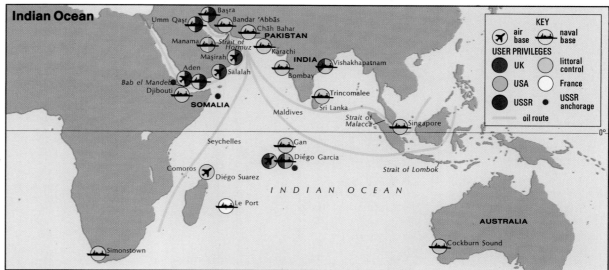

Antarctic claims

By 1943 the UK, New Zealand, France, Australia, Norway, Chile and Argentina had research bases established on Antarctica and had all made territorial claims. The claims of Britain, Argentina and Chile have a bearing on disputes outside the area. Argentina makes sectoral claims, based on demands of sovereignty over the islands of South Georgia and the Falklands and the Beagle Channel islands, which extend to the South Pole. Britain's claim in Antarctica dates from 1908. All claims, and especially overlapping claims have become more significant with the increased interest in krill and other fisheries, the hydrocarbon resources of the continental shelf and the rights of states to establish 200 nm exclusive economic zones.

In 1959 twelve states signed the Antarctic Treaty, which was ratified in 1961 for a period of 30 years. In addition to those countries which had made claims to sovereignty, the signatories were Belgium, Japan, South Africa, the USA and the USSR.

The Treaty is primarily related to research, with the aim that the Antarctic 'shall not become the scene or object of international discord'. It prohibits military activity and nuclear explosions in the Antarctic and ensures freedom of scientific investigation; it permits inspection of all bases. While no renunciation of existing territorial claims is implied, new claims of indefinite duration are not recognised; after 30 years (1991) any party can call a conference to review the Treaty.

Brazil, Poland, East Germany, Romania, Czechoslovakia, Denmark and the Netherlands have acceded to the Treaty, and have indicated claims and shown interests in both onshore and offshore resources. There could be many conflicts in the area in the future, particularly over mineral exploitation, which is not covered by the Treaty.

5 *below* At the time of the Antarctic Treaty, seven states had made claims to the territory. As the map shows, several of them overlap.

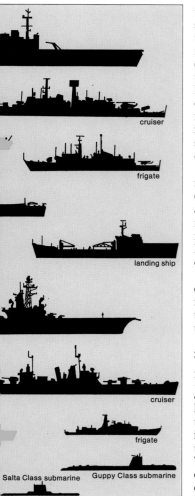

the ability of a single missile to destroy a very expensive and well equipped warship. Surface ships cannot take very certain or swift avoiding action against surface skimming computer-guided missiles, such as the exocet which can be launched from planes and relatively low cost platforms with high possibility of a first-hit. Clearly, even quite small countries in many parts of the world can now equip themselves with these missiles. The implications for naval forces are many, including the need to equip ships with even more sophisticated interceptor missiles, or to deploy less costly but a greater number of ships.

The close relationship required between air and naval action was well illustrated during the landing of British troops at San Carlos Bay. The bay provided a sheltered anchorage and surrounding high land masked the ships from low flying aircraft which therefore had only minimum time to pick their targets. However, ships were hit due to insufficient British air cover and airborne early warning craft.

The crisis also revealed design defects in some modern warships. These included the need to top up with fuel frequently on a long voyage to retain stability, and the vulnerability of the ships to spread of fire through use of inflammable materials.

3 *left* Examples of naval craft used by the British and Argentine fleets during the Falklands crisis. The British fleet amounted to 51 warships including two aircraft carriers, four nuclear powered and one hunter-killer submarine plus frigates, assault ships and logistic landing craft. There were 54 merchant vessels including tankers, passenger ships, cargo ships, ferries, tugs and trawlers along with 21 Royal Fleet auxiliaries. The Argentines had available 49 naval ships including one aircraft carrier, three conventional submarines, destroyers, frigates, patrol ships, amphibious craft and light forces; also transporters and fuel suppliers.

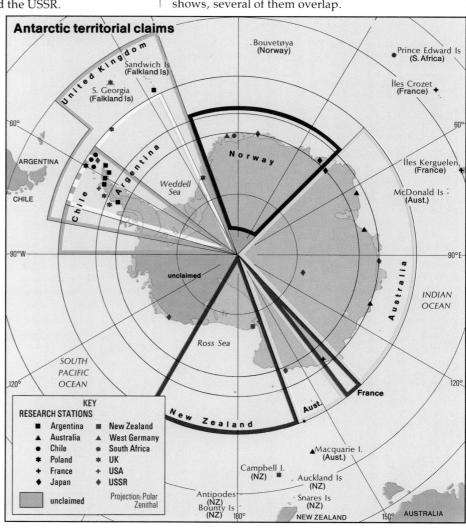

Maritime disputes and conflicts

SINCE 1946 disputes involving zones of the sea have regularly given rise to conflicts (on average about five per year). The number of disputes has continued to increase as more attention is focused on the sea as a source of food and scarce mineral resources, and coastal states have asserted jurisdiction over wider zones.

Questions giving rise to disputes include the validity of baselines, the methods of delimitation between opposite and adjacent states, ownership of rocks and islands, rights of fishing, rights of access; and now the incipient disputes over resources beyond the zones of national jurisdiction. (See *Maritime jurisdictional zones* pages 220–221.)

One of the main legal problems involved in dividing areas of the sea and sea bed is the principle of equidistance. This basically means that a median line is drawn at an equal distance from the coasts of opposite states, but it is complicated by the geographical characteristics of the coasts, especially where the presence of islands and bays may give one state an advantageous baseline. The International Court of Justice (in North Sea cases) has said there should be an application of 'equitable principles', but also that there is no legal limit to the considerations which states may take into account to ensure the application of these principles. It is clear that problems of dividing sea areas may easily lead to conflict.

As a result of greater determination to claim sea areas and ocean resources, more states have been developing modern, versatile and 'appropriate' levels of naval forces capable of defending their perceived rights and asserting claims in near and distant waters. Many of the types of disputes referred to in this section could give rise to more conflicts than in the immediate past, unless management measures and ocean laws are adopted and adhered to.

1 *main map and insets* The world map shows 'trouble spots' in principal sea regions and the insets cover those areas where more complex issues are involved; the inset for East Asia is on the following page.

3 *below* The three states involved in the dispute over the sea areas around Rockall are Britain, Denmark and Ireland. Geologically, the island is part of a 'micro-continent' which is separated from the continent on which the United Kingdom and Ireland lie. There is uncertainty about the geological conditions, and doubts about the applicable legal rules. If rocks such as Rockall are classifiable as islands they would be entitled to a legal continental shelf of their own (and an

Rockall map

exclusive economic zone or fishery zone). It also remains to be settled whether Rockall is situated on the natural prolongation of the continental margin of any of the three states.

The United Kingdom has annexed Rockall following physical occupation of the island, and is basing its extensive claim upon the capacity of this 'island' to generate a fishery zone and a continental shelf under present international law. Denmark and Ireland strongly oppose the United Kingdom's position and base their own claims upon natural prolongation arguments.

4 *right* In the dispute between Norway and the USSR over Svalbard (Spitsbergen), the Norwegians contend that the islands have no entitlement to a continental shelf apart from that under the territorial sea. Svalbard, it is argued by Norway, lies on the Norwegian continental shelf. However the Soviet Union, and some of the other signatories to the 1920 Treaty (which demilitarised Svalbard and stipulated sharing of the natural resources of the area), dispute this and claim that under the Treaty the islands have continental shelf entitlements.

The precise location of the boundary between Nor-

Areas of maritime tension and dispute

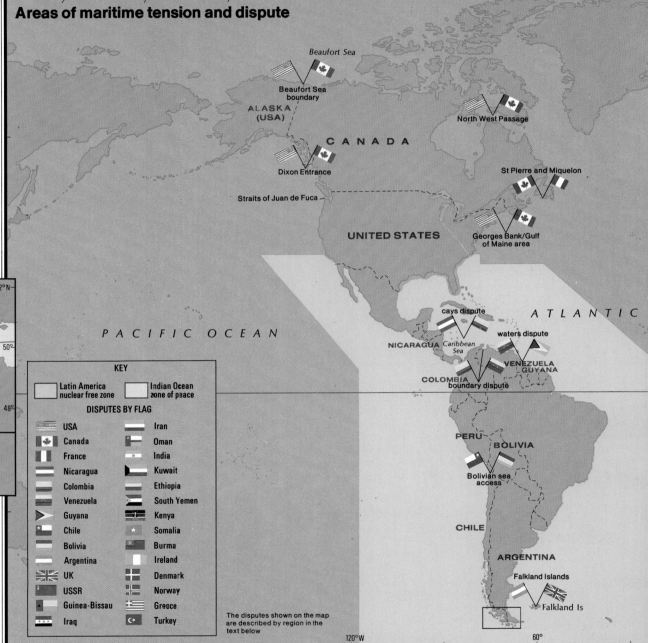

KEY

Latin America nuclear free zone	Indian Ocean zone of peace

DISPUTES BY FLAG

USA		Iran	
Canada		Oman	
France		India	
Nicaragua		Kuwait	
Colombia		Ethiopia	
Venezuela		South Yemen	
Guyana		Kenya	
Chile		Somalia	
Bolivia		Burma	
Argentina		Ireland	
UK		Denmark	
USSR		Norway	
Guinea-Bissau		Greece	
Iraq		Turkey	

The disputes shown on the map are described by region in the text below

Celtic Sea map

CONTINENTAL SHELF LINES
- continental shelf
- continental slope
- 200 nm from Lands End
- 200 nm from Isles of Scilly
- – – Irish formula (1st alternative draft convention)
- – ·· – Irish formula (2nd alternative draft convention)

ANGLO–IRISH LINE
equidistant using Irish base point (Cape Clear) and UK base point:
- – – Lands End
- ···· Isles of Scilly

2 *above* The delimitation of the continental shelf on the western approach to the English Channel is disputed between France, Ireland and the United Kingdom. If, as seems likely, the Anglo-French line meets the Anglo-Irish line landward of the outer limit of the continental shelf, the United Kingdom would be cut off from the more seaward part of the common continental margin. It would then be for France and Ireland to establish a bilateral boundary west of the tripoint formed by the intersection of the lines.

North America

Beaufort Sea boundary (Alaska–Yukon) Conscious of the area's oil potential, the Canadian and US Governments have claimed different continental shelf boundary lines.

Dixon Entrance (Alaska–British Columbia) and Straits of Juan de Fuca (Washington–Vancouver) The disputes between the Canadian and US Governments over these maritime boundaries have turned largely upon the equidistance principle.

Georges Bank/Gulf of Maine area Canada and the USA have been in dispute over the maritime boundary separating their fishery zones and continental shelves. The dispute, complicated by the introduction of 200-mile fishery zones and over-fishing, was submitted to the International Court of Justice for settlement in 1981.

North West Passage Canada claims internal water status for the Passage. The US regards these as international waters. Canada has unilaterally introduced the Arctic Waters Pollution Prevention Act 1970, enabling Canada to control shipping in an ecologically delicate region.

St Pierre and Miquelon There are problems of dividing the sea bed between France and Canada and also difficulties for Canada of fisheries management in a divided sea area.

South America

Falkland Islands See feature on pages 184–5.

Latin American Nuclear Free Zone The Latin American Nuclear Free Zone was created in 1967 by the Treaty of Tlatelolco. Not all Latin American states have ratified the Treaty, nor have all the nuclear weapon states outside the region.

Colombia–Nicaragua There is a dispute over a group of cays off Nicaragua which are claimed by Colombia.

Guyana–Venezuela Venezuela has a claim to sections of waters off Guyana.

Bolivian sea access Land-locked Bolivia wants a corridor to the sea through ex-Peruvian land in Chile. If Bolivia succeeds this may lead to coastal economic zone complications.

Venezuela–Colombia boundary in Gulf of Venezuela This dispute is complicated by differences over which legal principle is to be applied, the situation of a historic bay within the Gulf and the Monks Islands at the entrance to the Gulf.

Northern Europe

EEC–Iceland fisheries Following the Anglo-Icelandic 'cod wars' and the establishment of 200-mile fishery zones in North Atlantic and North Sea waters, the negotiation of fishery rights for EEC member states in Icelandic waters has not proved possible.

EEC–Norway fisheries Reciprocal fishing rights were provided for in an Agreement on Fisheries in 1980. The absence of effective EEC enforcement mechanisms and alleged overfishing contrary to agreed quotas have caused tensions.

British–Faroes boundary Both Britain and Denmark claim a 200-mile exclusive fishing zone. The determination of a fisheries boundary line is complicated by the existence of numerous small islands. The problem has to be seen in the

wegian and Soviet zones in the Barents Sea is of great significance strategically and in terms of resources. Norway favours a median line division while the Soviet Union wants a line of longitude to be adopted. The difference in delimitation involves an area of about 150 000 sq. km. The Norwegian claim could bring Norwegian fishing and oil activities closer to the approaches to Murmansk, and also makes the NATO monitoring of Soviet naval forces more effective, hence strong Soviet opposition to a median line.

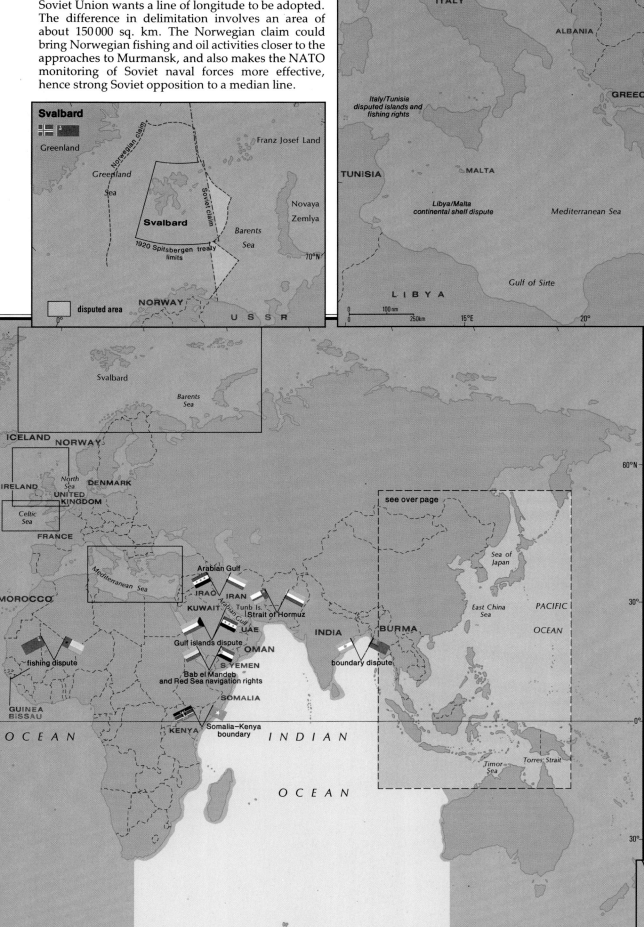

5 *above* The Mediterranean is a region of many disputes which have resulted in conflicts. They include Libya–Malta (median line), Italy–Tunisia (fishing), Spain–Morocco (fishing), Albania–Yugoslavia (fishing) and periodic conflict off the Lebanon–Syria–Israel coasts.

The dispute between Turkey and Greece relates primarily to continental shelf hydrocarbons. The feature which presents the greatest legal difficulty is the presence of a chain of Greek islands from Samothrace in the north to Rhodes in the south. The problem is aggravated by the fact that Greece is a party to the Geneva Convention on the Continental Shelf 1958, while Turkey is not.

Turkey maintains that the area in which the Greek islands are situated is part of the Turkish continental shelf and that the Greek islands do not possess a continential shelf of their own.

The Greek claim is that, in the absence of agreement between the two states and of any special circumstances justifying another boundary line, the delimitation should be based upon the median line between the Greek islands and the Turkish coast.

6 *below* The main cause of the dispute over the Beagle Channel between Argentina and Chile is ownership of the islands of Picton, Nueva and Lennox. These islands are under Chilean rule but are claimed by Argentina, while Barnvelt Island to the south has been 'occupied' by Argentina (by establishing a navigation light). Ownership of these islands ensures that Chile has command of the Straits of Magellan, and the related sea areas and shelves eastwards as EEZs. The dispute thus affects ownership of the potential resources of the South Atlantic, as well as territorial claims in the Antarctic (see page 185). Recommendations made by the Vatican in 1980 in an attempt to resolve the dispute were accepted by Chile, but not by Argentina.

context of the larger question of delimitation in the Rockall sector (see inset).

United Kingdom–Republic of Ireland boundary Maritime boundaries have still to be negotiated in the Rockall sector (see inset), the Irish Sea and the Celtic Sea. It has been agreed that the continental shelf problem will be referred to some form of judicial third-party settlement.

United Kingdom–France continental shelf boundary The boundary line was settled by a Court of Arbitration in 1977–78 but it will be necessary to reach agreement on the extension of this line seaward to the edge of the continental margin.

Indian Ocean
Indian Ocean Zone of Peace In 1971 the United Nations General Assembly adopted a resolution by the Indian Ocean community declaring the Indian Ocean a Zone of Peace. There is no absolute agreement on the application of this concept among all the littoral states, but it does represent an attempt by adjacent coastal countries to exercise more influ-

ence on the neighbouring high seas areas with respect to the military activities of distant maritime powers.

India–Burma boundary The dispute concerns the rights of Burma to draw a 222 nm baseline across the Gulf of Martaban and India's claim to measure the Indian maritime zone from the small uninhabited island of Narcondom.

Africa
Guinea Bissau Distant-water fishing by the USSR takes place in Guinea Bissau's waters. The problem includes the inability of local fishing to compete with large-scale, high technology operations.

Somalia–Kenya boundary There is a dispute over coastal territory.

Middle East
Strait of Hormuz The navigable waters of this vital access route to the Gulf are controlled by the State of Oman which provides facilities to United States forces in this oil-rich, politically explosive region (see also page 154).

Bab el Mandeb and Red Sea navigation rights This strait provides vital access to the Red Sea, the Israeli port of Elat and the Suez Canal. The navigable channel lies between Perim Island, controlled by South Yemen (People's Democratic Republic) and, to the west, Djibouti and southern Ethiopia (see also page 154).

Arabian Gulf There is a continued dispute and conflict between Iran and Iraq over the delimitation and sovereignty of the Shat el Arab River. The occupation by Iran of the Greater and Lesser Tunb Islands near the entrance to the Gulf continues to be a source of concern to other states in the region.

Islands Kuwait–Iraq There is a continuing dispute over ownership of islands in the Gulf.

Maritime disputes and conflicts 2

East Asia has been, and still is, a region of many disputes and conflicts. The area is rich in fish stocks and hydrocarbon deposits offshore, and it contains powerful states including China, Japan, Korea and Vietnam, with the USSR impinging to the north and large archipelagos, peninsular states and Australia to the south. There are many disputes over fishing rights, continental shelf boundaries, rocks and islands; and there is continuing tension over the command of marine space, often with the major powers backing one or other of the smaller contenders. The influence of Chinese policy in relation to maritime areas in East Asia is of fundamental importance to peace in the region and to the orderly development of offshore hydrocarbons in conjunction with international oil companies. The view of the Chinese Peoples' Republic is that the natural prolongation of the land should determine ownership of the continental shelf. Japan, on the other hand, bases its claims according to the median line principle. China claims most of the islands of the South China Sea, together with their continental shelves and exclusive economic zones.

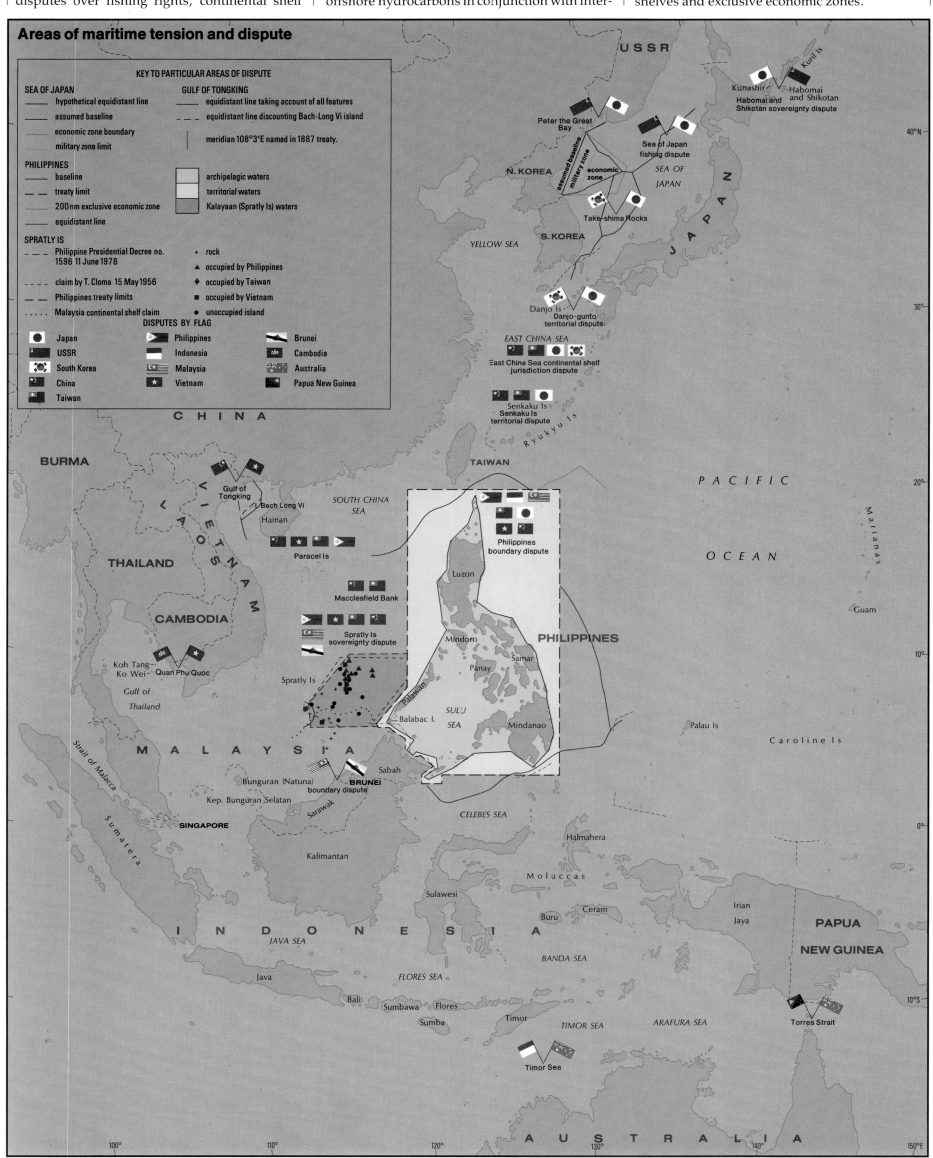

Areas of maritime tension and dispute

KEY TO PARTICULAR AREAS OF DISPUTE

SEA OF JAPAN
— hypothetical equidistant line
— assumed baseline
— economic zone boundary
— military zone limit

PHILIPPINES
— baseline
— treaty limit
— 200 nm exclusive economic zone
— equidistant line

SPRATLY IS
— Philippine Presidential Decree no. 1596 11 June 1978
— claim by T. Cloma 15 May 1956
— Philippines treaty limits
— Malaysia continental shelf claim

GULF OF TONGKING
— equidistant line taking account of all features
— equidistant line discounting Bach-Long Vi island
— meridian 108°3'E named in 1887 treaty.

archipelagic waters
territorial waters
Kalayaan (Spratly Is) waters

+ rock
▲ occupied by Philippines
♦ occupied by Taiwan
■ occupied by Vietnam
● unoccupied island

DISPUTES BY FLAG

Japan	Philippines	Brunei
USSR	Indonesia	Cambodia
South Korea	Malaysia	Australia
China	Vietnam	Papua New Guinea
Taiwan		

North East Asia

Claims in the Sea of Japan include the 1956 Soviet closing line across the mouth of Peter the Great Bay based on 'historic bay' rights and security arguments, but disputed by Japan; the Soviet occupation of the islands of Kunashir, Habomai and Shikotan north of Hokkaido; and the 200 nm fishery zones and continental shelf equidistant lines based on these. The Take-shima (Liancourt) Rocks were occupied by South Korea in 1954 but are claimed by Japan, and a military zone in that area has been declared by North Korea.

In the East China Sea the claim to the Danjo Islands by Japan and South Korea has similarities to the Greece–Turkey dispute in the Aegean Sea (i.e. South Korea's contention that the islands lie on its continental shelf). Japan, China and Taiwan, as well as South Korea, seek control of the Ryukyu Islands, again primarily for continental shelf resources.

The dispute between China and Japan in North East Asia stems from their baseline disagreements, the status of islands and sovereignty over the Senkaku (Tiao-Yu-Tai) Islands (claimed also by Taiwan). Both governments are seeking the orderly exploration of the rich and strategically located oil reserves in North East Asia seas and it is possible that agreement will be reached for joint ventures and close relationships with US oil companies.

1 *opposite page* Existing and potential conflicts resulting from disputed claims to islands and therefore to the continental shelves in the seas around East Asia are highlighted. Only those places actually disputed are shown; there are many other tensions throughout the region.

South East Asia

Prospects for the peaceful settlement of maritime disputes in South East Asia are more problematic. The South China Sea, containing some of the most sensitive areas, is virtually an enclosed sea bounded by China, Taiwan, the Philippines, Malaysia and Vietnam. The latter has offered foreign oil companies exploration contracts for many parts of the region which China will oppose. Similarly, Chinese contracts offered to foreign companies in the Gulf of Tonking have been opposed by Vietnam, and in 1979 two survey vessels working for US oil companies under Chinese contract were fired on by Vietnamese gunboats. The disagreement between China and Vietnam over the Gulf of Tongking relates partly to whether the Sino-French Treaty of 1887 prevails. If it does (China disputes this) there is a problem as to how the meridian was defined in relation to Tra Co. If the Treaty does not apply (the Chinese view) there is a problem of the use of the Vietnamese islands of Bach-Long Vi in drawing equidistant lines. If they are included they endow Vietnam with a considerable additional area of good fishing grounds and a potentially rich hydrocarbon basin.

Very few islands in the South China Sea are uncontested. China has claims over the Paracel (Xisha Qundao) Islands which also are claimed by Vietnam, Taiwan and the Philippines (see *left*); and the Macclesfield Bank is claimed by China and Taiwan. These islands are of little importance in themselves but they are rich in fish and offshore hydrocarbon resources; consequently Cambodia and Indonesia have also featured in some of the disputes. More significantly, the Vietnam claim to the Paracels has been supported by the USSR against China.

The strategic position of the Spratly (Nansha) Islands is significant as they lie on the shipping route from Singapore Strait to China and claims to them are numerous and complicated. The Philippines have occupied seven of the islands since 1968; Vietnam occupies five and Taiwan one; China claims ancient rights to them; Malaysia claims some of the southern islands; and Brunei also has claims. The claim by a Mr T. Cloma (a Philippine citizen engaged in a fishing business) in 1956 was reinforced in a decree signed by President Marcos in 1978 claiming islands in the group.

The Philippines comprise some 7100 islands. The delimitation of the maritime boundaries of the Philippines relate to Treaties of 1898 and 1930 and Acts of Decree from 1961 to 1978. The Treaty limits, the 200 nm EEZ, and the lines of equidistance with other states do not coincide. Disputes between the Philippines, Indonesia, Malaysia, Taiwan, Japan, Vietnam and China all occur in relation to these boundaries and islands in the South China Sea.

There are several disputes in the Gulf of Thailand between Thailand, Cambodia and Vietnam which relate mainly to sea bed boundaries. The dispute between Cambodia and Vietnam over the inclusion of Quan Phu Quoc Island and the Wei Islands within Vietnam has been the subject of recent negotiations.

Maritime boundaries in South East Asia are further complicated by the prevailing political conditions and the foreign policy interests of the USSR and USA, and particularly the Soviet involvement with Vietnam in joint exploration of the South China Sea continental shelf over which China has widespread claims.

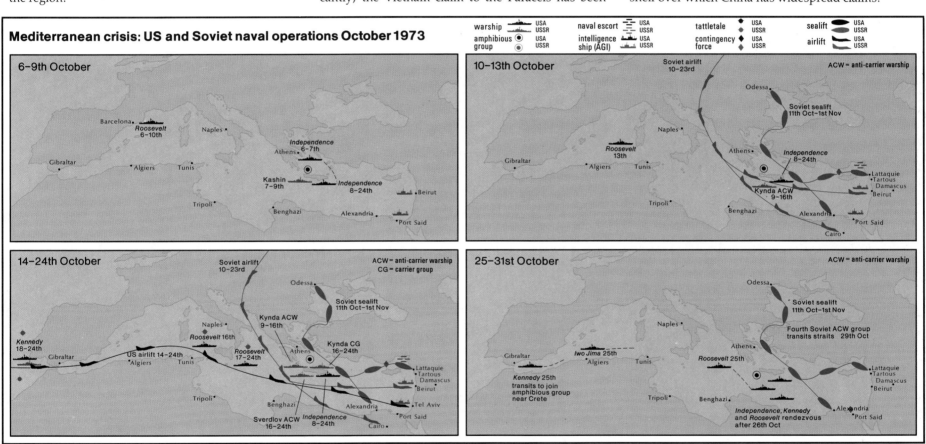

Mediterranean crisis 1973

In many conflicts between smaller nations the major powers deploy naval forces in the vicinity to indicate their support or hostility to the conflicting parties, to protect their merchant shipping, to evacuate nationals and to try to influence each other's attitudes and actions as the conflict develops. The role of the USA and USSR during the 1973 Mediterranean crisis illustrates these aspects of naval diplomacy.

On 6 October 1973 war broke out between Israel and Egypt and Syria. On 7 October ships of the US Sixth fleet were redeployed in the Mediterranean, including the aircraft carrier *Independence*, which sailed from Athens and took up a 'holding point' south of Crete. The Soviet Fifth Eskrada Mediterranean fleet was reinforced by units of the Black Sea fleet.

On 9 October *Independence* was joined by a Soviet Kynda-class anti-carrier missile vessel. This was to indicate to the USA that the Russians would resist any attempt to interfere with a Soviet air and sea lift of equipment and personnel to Egypt and Syria.

On 10 October the Russian air and sea lift began. Planes flew from Hungary across Yugoslavia and down the Adriatic to Syria and Egypt; many Soviet merchant ships sailed from Black Sea ports. The USA began flights through the Mediterranean with fighter–bomber reinforcements for Israel, and units of the

Sixth fleet moved to positions along the route.

During the first few days of the Soviet sea lift Israeli missile boats damaged a Russian merchant ship in the port of Latakia and sunk another in Tartus. The Russians responded by stationing SAM missile destroyers north of Cyprus to escort Russian ships and to provide missile cover for the airlift.

On 16 October the US carrier *Roosevelt* crossed the Strait of Sicily; the US helicopter carrier *Iwo Jima* sailed from the USA and was monitored in the Atlantic and Mediterranean by Soviet submarines and aircraft. The *Independence* and US amphibious forces in the Eastern Mediterranean were followed by Soviet submarines and surface warships. On 16 October the carrier *Kennedy* was met by a Soviet destroyer west of Gibraltar: they both entered the Mediterranean on 25 October.

A ceasefire agreed 22 October failed, and by 25 October the conflict had reached serious crisis level. The US fleet, which was strung out along the air route, began to consolidate and move to the Eastern Mediterranean where *Roosevelt* and *Kennedy* joined *Independence* and the amphibious group. The US fleet was put on defensive readiness. All the US carrier units were by then countered by heavy Soviet anti-carrier and other surface vessels and missile submarines, and the Russians had assembled sufficient men and supplies to intervene on land. Soviet patrols were active at various points off the coasts of Syria and Egypt. Vessels of

2 *above* A crisis during the Arab/Israeli war of 1973 illustrates use of gunboat-diplomacy tactics in the modern era. The USA and USSR used their naval forces to express their respective support for Israel and the Arab states.

the US Sixth fleet were in position off the Strait of Bab el Mandeb in the Indian Ocean, where Arab navies were attempting a blockade. US ships were also stationed at points along the Gulf–Cape of Good Hope oil tanker route. Soviet ships of the Far East fleet entered the Indian Ocean via the Strait of Malacca.

This explosive situation changed about 29 October, when a second ceasefire agreed on 24 October was considered effective. The US ships started to move back towards the Western Mediterranean on 30 October, and the Russians withdrew their Sverdlov anti-carrier cruisers, replacing them by lighter tattletales, which normally accompany US warships on exercises.

Two Soviet intelligence gathering ships, stationed off the coasts of Israel and Syria throughout the crisis, remained long after the end of the war.

The two major naval forces had been brought close to conflict; and their balance of sea power demonstrated, as well as their degree of speed and flexibility of response to a crisis which threatened their interests.

World naval operations and gunboat diplomacy

THE number of incidents at sea resulting from naval activities has continued to rise since 1946. The number of peacetime incidents for the period 1952–58 was 32, compared with 49 for 1973–79. The number of states involved rose from 51 to 86 during the same two six-year periods. All the activities illustrated, whether part of wartime action, or the purposeful patrol of a strait or territorial limit in peacetime, have had, or may still have, important strategic implications.

Most major naval incidents occurred during or in relation to regional wars, including: Korea 1950–53; Suez–Egypt–Israel 1956–57; China–Taiwan 1957–59; Cuba 1961–62; Indonesia–Malaya 1963–64; Cyprus 1964; Arab–Israel 1967; Vietnam 1964–74; Indo–Pakistan 1971–72; Arab–Israel 1973; China–Vietnam 1974–75; Syria–Lebanon 1976; Ethiopia 1978; Vietnam–Cambodia 1979; Iraq–Iran 1980–82; Britain–Argentina 1982; Israel–Lebanon (PLO) 1982.

An important function of the navies of the major maritime powers since 1946 has been that of 'standing by' on the high seas, just outside territorial waters of regional trouble spots, in order to render assistance to friendly governments if required, to evacuate nationals, or, more generally, to influence the course of events or activities of lesser powers by their presence. Many examples of this form of intervention or 'gunboat diplomacy' will be found.

Regional distribution of incidents located on the map includes: Mediterranean and Middle East 63; North East Asia 27; South East Asia 25; Caribbean 20.

The greatest number of involvements by flag, as victims or assailants, between 1946 and 1982 is: USA 73, UK 44, USSR 24, China 14, Israel 14, Egypt 12, France 12. The rest are less than ten incidents apiece, though in cases of war, such as between North and South Vietnam, many more naval actions than are recorded here have occurred.

Blockades

On many occasions naval forces have to be seen to threaten in order to be effective. This is particularly the case with the blockade. States have often justified the use of blockades on the grounds that alternative action, or lack of action, could lead to greater dangers. The Cuban Missile Crisis of 1962 is a case in point. The emplacement of Soviet missiles in Cuba was detected by US aerial reconnaissance. The US regarded this as a direct threat and a substantial change in the balance of power. A 'prohibited zone' was drawn around Cuba and the US Navy set up a blockade intercepting all ships in order to turn back any carrying 'prohibited material'. The objectives of the blockade were to force the Soviet Union to stop supplying missiles and to have those already in Cuba removed.

Naval blockades have mainly been conducted close to the ports blockaded, as with the Beira patrol during 1968, when the British Navy attempted to prevent oil reaching Rhodesia by intercepting vessels off the port of Beira. But long distance blockades have also been attempted, such as the patrolling of Bab el Mandeb by Arab navies in 1973 to prevent ships from reaching the Israeli port of Elat over 1200 miles away.

Warship visits to foreign ports

Port visits have been employed primarily to provide a visible presence of support, or coercion, which has often been successful in keeping the peace. The British Navy has been most active in this respect for over a century, and the US Navy particularly since the end of the Second World War. The Soviet Navy only began this type of naval diplomacy in 1967. From 1967 to 1976 Soviet ships made 170 such visits to Third World ports, compared with 37 visits from 1953 to 1966.

1 *right* The map summarises major naval incidents between 1946 and 1982; the activities are described in further detail in Appendix VIII. Only those incidents having important international strategic implications have been included; many actions which cannot be regarded as clear-cut events, such as routine manoeuvres or visits between states, are omitted.

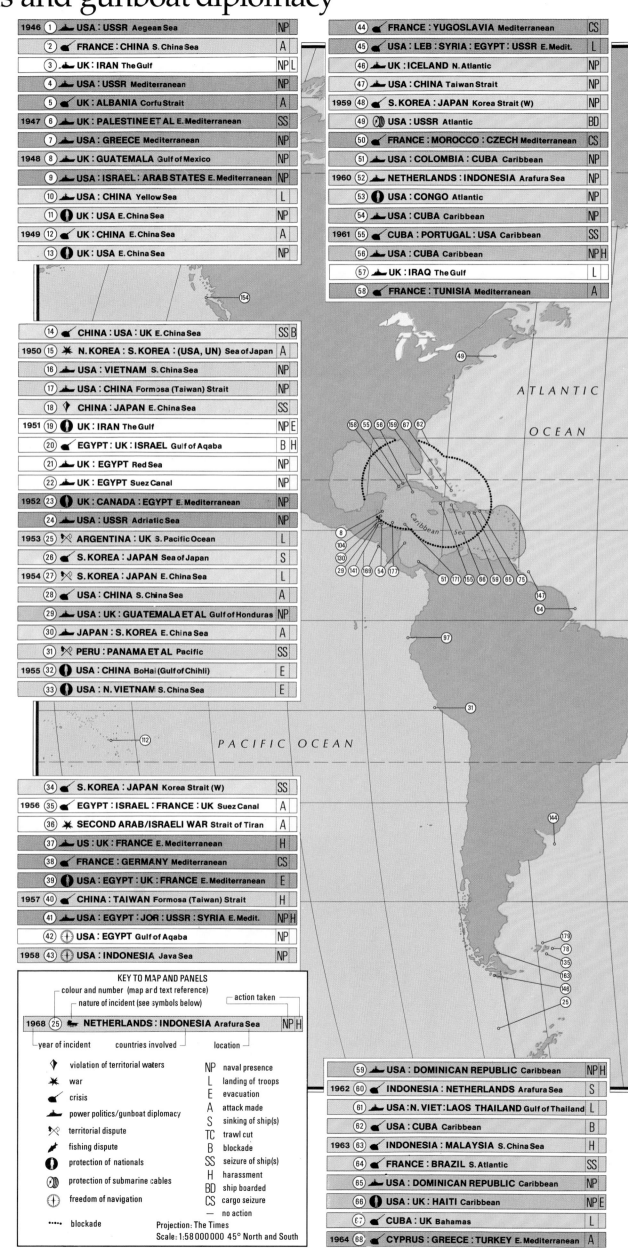

	Year	No.		Countries / Location	Action
	1946	1		USA : USSR Aegean Sea	NP
		2		FRANCE : CHINA S. China Sea	A
		3		UK : IRAN The Gulf	NP L
		4		USA : USSR Mediterranean	NP
		5		UK : ALBANIA Corfu Strait	A
	1947	6		UK : PALESTINE ET AL E. Mediterranean	SS
		7		USA : GREECE Mediterranean	NP
	1948	8		UK : GUATEMALA Gulf of Mexico	NP
		9		USA : ISRAEL : ARAB STATES E. Mediterranean	NP
		10		USA : CHINA Yellow Sea	L
		11		UK : USA E. China Sea	NP
	1949	12		UK : CHINA E. China Sea	A
		13		UK : USA E. China Sea	NP
		14		CHINA : USA : UK E. China Sea	SS B
	1950	15		N. KOREA : S. KOREA : (USA, UN) Sea of Japan	A
		16		USA : VIETNAM S. China Sea	NP
		17		USA : CHINA Formosa (Taiwan) Strait	NP
		18		CHINA : JAPAN E. China Sea	SS
	1951	19		UK : IRAN The Gulf	NP E
		20		EGYPT : UK : ISRAEL Gulf of Aqaba	B H
		21		UK : EGYPT Red Sea	NP
		22		UK : EGYPT Suez Canal	NP
	1952	23		UK : CANADA : EGYPT E. Mediterranean	NP
		24		USA : USSR Adriatic Sea	NP
	1953	25		ARGENTINA : UK S. Pacific Ocean	L
		26		S. KOREA : JAPAN Sea of Japan	S
	1954	27		S. KOREA : JAPAN E. China Sea	L
		28		USA : CHINA S. China Sea	A
		29		USA : UK : GUATEMALA ET AL Gulf of Honduras	NP
		30		JAPAN : S. KOREA E. China Sea	A
		31		PERU : PANAMA ET AL Pacific	SS
	1955	32		USA : CHINA BoHai (Gulf of Chihli)	E
		33		USA : N. VIETNAM S. China Sea	E
		34		S. KOREA : JAPAN Korea Strait (W)	SS
	1956	35		EGYPT : ISRAEL : FRANCE : UK Suez Canal	A
		36		SECOND ARAB/ISRAELI WAR Strait of Tiran	A
		37		US : UK : FRANCE E. Mediterranean	H
		38		FRANCE : GERMANY Mediterranean	CS
		39		USA : EGYPT : UK : FRANCE E. Mediterranean	E
	1957	40		CHINA : TAIWAN Formosa (Taiwan) Strait	H
		41		USA : EGYPT : JOR : USSR : SYRIA E. Medit.	NP H
		42		USA : EGYPT Gulf of Aqaba	NP
	1958	43		USA : INDONESIA Java Sea	NP

	Year	No.		Countries / Location	Action
		44		FRANCE : YUGOSLAVIA Mediterranean	CS
		45		USA : LEB : SYRIA : EGYPT : USSR E. Medit.	L
		46		UK : ICELAND N. Atlantic	NP
		47		USA : CHINA Taiwan Strait	NP
	1959	48		S. KOREA : JAPAN Korea Strait (W)	NP
		49		USA : USSR Atlantic	BD
		50		FRANCE : MOROCCO : CZECH Mediterranean	CS
		51		USA : COLOMBIA : CUBA Caribbean	NP
	1960	52		NETHERLANDS : INDONESIA Arafura Sea	NP
		53		USA : CONGO Atlantic	NP
		54		USA : CUBA Caribbean	NP
	1961	55		CUBA : PORTUGAL : USA Caribbean	SS
		56		USA : CUBA Caribbean	NP H
		57		UK : IRAQ The Gulf	L
		58		FRANCE : TUNISIA Mediterranean	A
		59		USA : DOMINICAN REPUBLIC Caribbean	NP H
	1962	60		INDONESIA : NETHERLANDS Arafura Sea	S
		61		USA : N. VIET : LAOS THAILAND Gulf of Thailand	L
		62		USA : CUBA Caribbean	B
	1963	63		INDONESIA : MALAYSIA S. China Sea	H
		64		FRANCE : BRAZIL S. Atlantic	SS
		65		USA : DOMINICAN REPUBLIC Caribbean	NP
		66		USA : UK : HAITI Caribbean	NP E
		67		CUBA : UK Bahamas	L
	1964	68		CYPRUS : GREECE : TURKEY E. Mediterranean	A

KEY TO MAP AND PANELS

- colour and number (map and text reference)
- nature of incident (see symbols below)
- action taken

| 1968 | 25 | | NETHERLANDS : INDONESIA Arafura Sea | NP H |

- year of incident
- countries involved
- location

	violation of territorial waters		NP	naval presence
	war		L	landing of troops
	crisis		E	evacuation
	power politics/gunboat diplomacy		A	attack made
	territorial dispute		S	sinking of ship(s)
	fishing dispute		TC	trawl cut
	protection of nationals		B	blockade
	protection of submarine cables		SS	seizure of ship(s)
	freedom of navigation		H	harassment
			BD	ship boarded
			CS	cargo seizure
	blockade		—	no action

Projection: The Times
Scale: 1:58 000 000 45° North and South

ATLANTIC OCEAN

PACIFIC OCEAN

Caribbean Sea

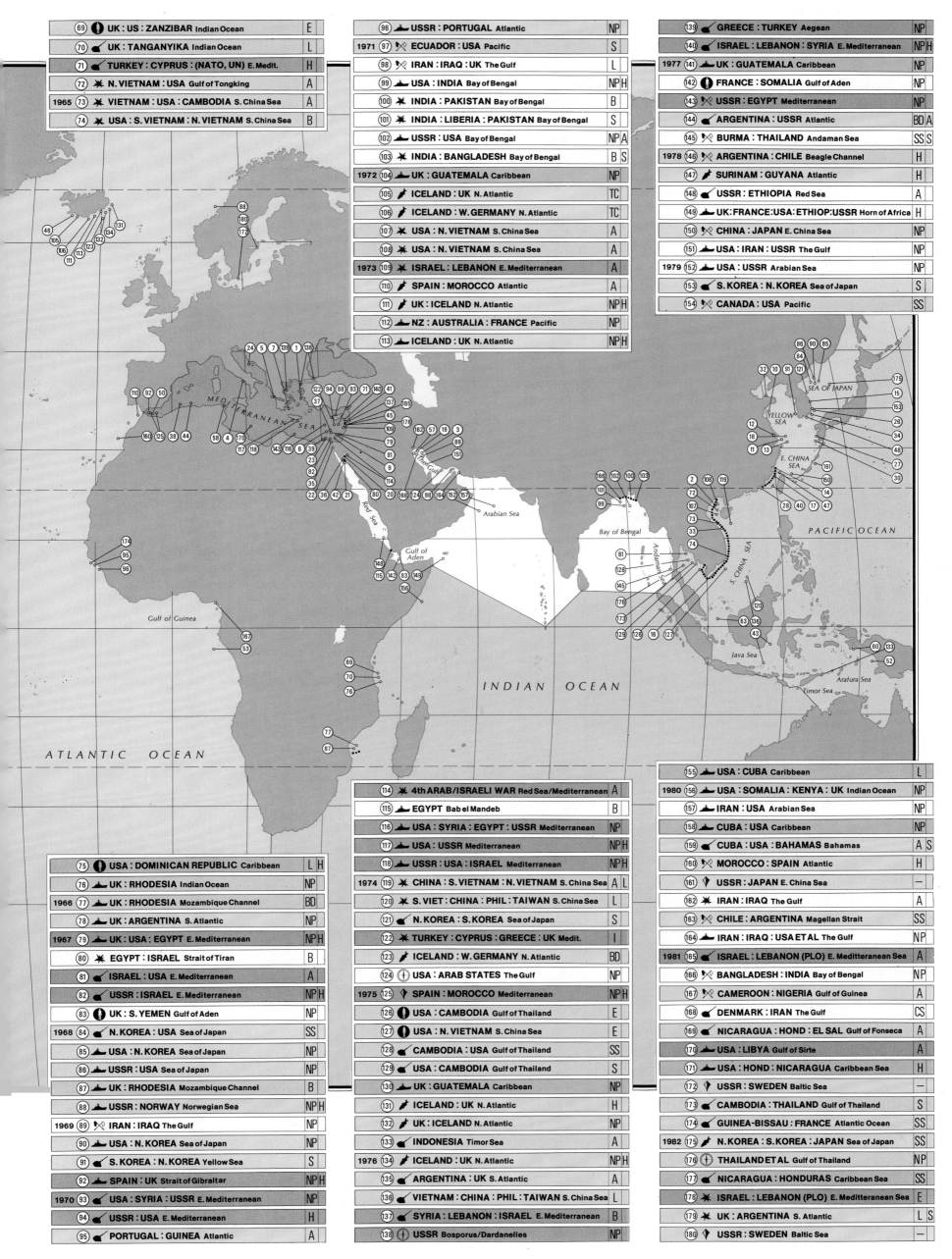

(69)	UK : US : ZANZIBAR Indian Ocean	E
(70)	UK : TANGANYIKA Indian Ocean	L
(71)	TURKEY : CYPRUS : (NATO, UN) E. Medit.	H
(72)	N. VIETNAM : USA Gulf of Tongking	A
1965 (73)	VIETNAM : USA : CAMBODIA S. China Sea	A
(74)	USA : S. VIETNAM : N. VIETNAM S. China Sea	B

(96)	USSR : PORTUGAL Atlantic	NP
1971 (97)	ECUADOR : USA Pacific	S
(98)	IRAN : IRAQ : UK The Gulf	L
(99)	USA : INDIA Bay of Bengal	NP H
(100)	INDIA : PAKISTAN Bay of Bengal	B
(101)	INDIA : LIBERIA : PAKISTAN Bay of Bengal	S
(102)	USSR : USA Bay of Bengal	NP A
(103)	INDIA : BANGLADESH Bay of Bengal	B S
1972 (104)	UK : GUATEMALA Caribbean	NP
(105)	ICELAND : UK N. Atlantic	TC
(106)	ICELAND : W. GERMANY N. Atlantic	TC
(107)	USA : N. VIETNAM S. China Sea	A
(108)	USA : N. VIETNAM S. China Sea	A
1973 (109)	ISRAEL : LEBANON E. Mediterranean	A
(110)	SPAIN : MOROCCO Atlantic	A
(111)	UK : ICELAND N. Atlantic	NP H
(112)	NZ : AUSTRALIA : FRANCE Pacific	NP
(113)	ICELAND : UK N. Atlantic	NP H

(139)	GREECE : TURKEY Aegean	NP
(140)	ISRAEL : LEBANON : SYRIA E. Mediterranean	NP H
1977 (141)	UK : GUATEMALA Caribbean	NP
(142)	FRANCE : SOMALIA Gulf of Aden	NP
(143)	USSR : EGYPT Mediterranean	NP
(144)	ARGENTINA : USSR Atlantic	BD A
(145)	BURMA : THAILAND Andaman Sea	SS S
1978 (146)	ARGENTINA : CHILE Beagle Channel	H
(147)	SURINAM : GUYANA Atlantic	H
(148)	USSR : ETHIOPIA Red Sea	A
(149)	UK : FRANCE : USA : ETHIOP : USSR Horn of Africa	H
(150)	CHINA : JAPAN E. China Sea	NP
(151)	USA : IRAN : USSR The Gulf	NP
1979 (152)	USA : USSR Arabian Sea	NP
(153)	S. KOREA : N. KOREA Sea of Japan	S
(154)	CANADA : USA Pacific	SS

(75)	USA : DOMINICAN REPUBLIC Caribbean	L H
(76)	UK : RHODESIA Indian Ocean	NP
1966 (77)	UK : RHODESIA Mozambique Channel	BD
(78)	UK : ARGENTINA S. Atlantic	NP
1967 (79)	UK : USA : EGYPT E. Mediterranean	NP H
(80)	EGYPT : ISRAEL Strait of Tiran	B
(81)	ISRAEL : USA E. Mediterranean	A
(82)	USSR : ISRAEL E. Mediterranean	NP H
(83)	UK : S. YEMEN Gulf of Aden	NP
1968 (84)	N. KOREA : USA Sea of Japan	SS
(85)	USA : N. KOREA Sea of Japan	NP
(86)	USSR : USA Sea of Japan	NP
(87)	UK : RHODESIA Mozambique Channel	B
(88)	USSR : NORWAY Norwegian Sea	NP H
1969 (89)	IRAN : IRAQ The Gulf	NP
(90)	USA : N. KOREA Sea of Japan	NP
(91)	S. KOREA : N. KOREA Yellow Sea	S
(92)	SPAIN : UK Strait of Gibraltar	NP H
1970 (93)	USA : SYRIA : USSR E. Mediterranean	NP
(94)	USSR : USA E. Mediterranean	H
(95)	PORTUGAL : GUINEA Atlantic	A

(114)	4th ARAB/ISRAELI WAR Red Sea/Mediterranean	A
(115)	EGYPT Bab el Mandeb	B
(116)	USA : SYRIA : EGYPT : USSR Mediterranean	NP
(117)	USA : USSR Mediterranean	NP H
(118)	USSR : USA : ISRAEL Mediterranean	NP H
1974 (119)	CHINA : S. VIETNAM : N. VIETNAM S. China Sea	A L
(120)	S. VIET : CHINA : PHIL : TAIWAN S. China Sea	L
(121)	N. KOREA : S. KOREA Sea of Japan	S
(122)	TURKEY : CYPRUS : GREECE : UK Medit.	I
(123)	ICELAND : W. GERMANY N. Atlantic	BD
(124)	USA : ARAB STATES The Gulf	NP
1975 (125)	SPAIN : MOROCCO Mediterranean	NP H
(126)	USA : CAMBODIA Gulf of Thailand	E
(127)	USA : N. VIETNAM S. China Sea	E
(128)	CAMBODIA : USA Gulf of Thailand	SS
(129)	USA : CAMBODIA Gulf of Thailand	S
(130)	UK : GUATEMALA Caribbean	NP
(131)	ICELAND : UK N. Atlantic	H
(132)	UK : ICELAND N. Atlantic	NP
(133)	INDONESIA Timor Sea	A
1976 (134)	ICELAND : UK N. Atlantic	NP H
(135)	ARGENTINA : UK S. Atlantic	A
(136)	VIETNAM : CHINA : PHIL : TAIWAN S. China Sea	L
(137)	SYRIA : LEBANON : ISRAEL E. Mediterranean	B
(138)	USSR Bosporus/Dardanelles	NP

(155)	USA : CUBA Caribbean	L
1980 (156)	USA : SOMALIA : KENYA : UK Indian Ocean	NP
(157)	IRAN : USA Arabian Sea	NP
(158)	CUBA : USA Caribbean	NP
(159)	CUBA : USA : BAHAMAS Bahamas	A S
(160)	MOROCCO : SPAIN Atlantic	H
(161)	USSR : JAPAN E. China Sea	—
(162)	IRAN : IRAQ The Gulf	A
(163)	CHILE : ARGENTINA Magellan Strait	SS
(164)	IRAN : IRAQ : USA ET AL The Gulf	NP
1981 (165)	ISRAEL : LEBANON (PLO) E. Mediterranean Sea	A
(166)	BANGLADESH : INDIA Bay of Bengal	NP
(167)	CAMEROON : NIGERIA Gulf of Guinea	A
(168)	DENMARK : IRAN The Gulf	CS
(169)	NICARAGUA : HOND : EL SAL Gulf of Fonseca	A
(170)	USA : LIBYA Gulf of Sirte	A
(171)	USA : HOND : NICARAGUA Caribbean Sea	H
(172)	USSR : SWEDEN Baltic Sea	—
(173)	CAMBODIA : THAILAND Gulf of Thailand	S
(174)	GUINEA-BISSAU : FRANCE Atlantic Ocean	SS
1982 (175)	N. KOREA : S. KOREA : JAPAN Sea of Japan	SS H
(176)	THAILAND ET AL Gulf of Thailand	NP
(177)	NICARAGUA : HONDURAS Caribbean Sea	SS
(178)	ISRAEL : LEBANON (PLO) E. Mediterranean Sea	E
(179)	UK : ARGENTINA S. Atlantic	L S
(180)	USSR : SWEDEN Baltic Sea	—

Historical routes and navigation

Before the 15th century transoceanic navigation was restricted. People lived in a number of small worlds, ignorant of what lay beyond the oceans which surrounded them. There are allusions in classical literature, among them Herodotus's account of a circumnavigation of Africa by Phoenician seamen in the 5th century BC, to oceanic voyages and to the possibility of the world being encompassed by the ship.

Well attested evidence of voyages in the Indian Ocean is in *The Periplus of the Erythraean Sea*, a navigational guidebook of the late 1st century AD. Based on the findings of Hippolus, a Greek seaman, it shows how traders sailed between the Red Sea and India by taking advantage of seasonal variations in the monsoon winds. When Chinese and Portuguese navigators entered these waters in the 15th century they found them still dominated by Arab and Indian seamen.

Norse literature and archaeological evidence tell of activity in the North Atlantic in the 9th and 10th centuries. This led, following Leif Eriksson's voyage from Greenland, to a short-lived Norse settlement in North America and created opportunities for trade and fishing in Icelandic waters.

The conquest of the Atlantic in the 15th century was pioneered by the Portuguese. Initially they were trying to alleviate social and economic difficulties though the acquisition of fertile Atlantic islands (Madeira and the Azores) and the opening of a sea-route to West Africa in opposition to the Moorish trans-Saharan caravan route. Their success bred new ambitions. They sailed the full length of Africa to the Cape of Good Hope; and in 1497–99 Vasco da Gama made a round voyage between Portugal and India, the object of which was to wrest the spice trade from Arab control. Through their discovery of the wind systems they established permanent sailing-ship routes between Europe and the Eastern Seas though the Dutch later added a useful alternative in the Indian Ocean.

In 1492 Christopher Columbus crossed the Atlantic. He and his Spanish backers hoped to forestall the Portuguese by finding a westward route to Asia. Instead they stumbled upon America and began the process of mapping and defining this continent. The English through the Bristol voyages (1480–1509) also made an important contribution, as did the French through those of Verrazzano (1524) and Cartier (1534–42). Fishermen of the western European seaboard were quick to enter the Newfoundland fishery. Regular transatlantic voyages had begun.

In 1494 by the treaty of Tordesillas the Iberian countries agreed to a demarcation on a meridian 370 leagues west of the Cape Verde Islands between their respective discoveries. The Spaniards hoped that the Asiatic Spice Islands might lie within their demarcation. They backed the voyage (1519–22), led by Magellan, which passed from the Atlantic into the Pacific by the straits of Magellan, crossed the Pacific and circumnavigated the world. By the 1560s the Spaniards knew enough about the North Pacific to begin the trade between the Philippines and Mexico carried by the annual Manila galleon. Dutch East Indiamen sighted Western Australia. A few, now of interest to nautical archaeologists, found their graveyards there. Much of the South Pacific, however, remained uncharted until the 18th century. Navigational problems were the chief obstacles. Seamen had compasses and a knowledge of celestial navigation, but lacked a practical means of fixing longitude at sea, a cause of serious errors in the vast oceanic spaces. A generation of 18th-century seamen, notably James Cook (1768–1779), equipped with the new clock method of fixing longitude and provided with better medical aids, created the modern map of the Pacific. The transoceanic routes thus created are associated with the voyages of the clipper ships between Europe, Asia and Australasia. The world was now truly encompassed by the sailing ship.

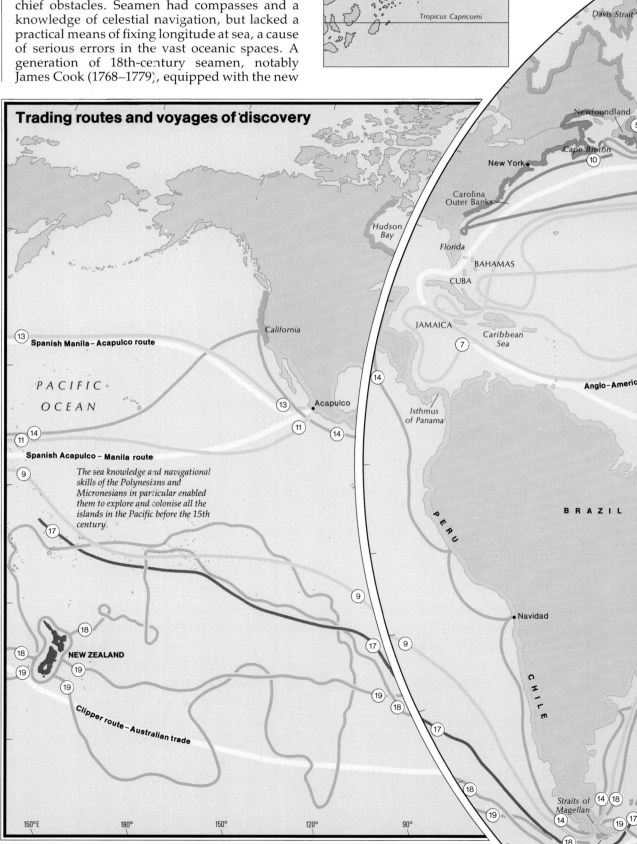

KEY TO NUMBERS ON MAP

1 Cheng-ho, Chinese admiral (1405–33), led voyages into the Indian Ocean extending as far as Indonesia, Ceylon and East Africa; a potential extension of Chinese power arrested by the adoption of a defensive policy by the Ming dynasty.
2 Dias (1487–8) extended Portuguese exploration of the west African coast to its southern extremity and revealed the way into the Indian Ocean.
3 Columbus (1492–3) made a landfall in the Bahamas which he identified as part of Asia; returned to Europe on a more northerly course thus picking up the westerlies.
4 Columbus (1493–4) established a colony on Hispaniola, explored south coast of Cuba and Jamaica.
5 John Cabot (1497) sailed from Bristol hoping to extend earlier Bristolean activity in the north Atlantic to a voyage to Asia; probably made a landfall at Cape Breton and returned, like Columbus, to make boastful claims; lost at sea (1498).
6 Vasco da Gama (1497–9) led the first Portuguese voyage to reach Calicut in India by circumnavigating Africa; his south-westerly sweep into the Atlantic from off Cape Verde shows that Portuguese seamen had mastered the Atlantic wind-systems.
7 Columbus (1502–4) coasted the Isthmus of Panama on his last transatlantic voyage.
8 The Portuguese (1511) reached and occupied Malacca and proceeded (1512–3) to the Moluccas and (1514) to Canton.
9 Magellan (1519–22) led the first expedition to pass from the Atlantic into the Pacific by the Straits of Magellan, an unsuitable route for regular commercial runs; crossed the Pacific on a north-westerly track to reach the Moluccas; Elcano took command after Magellan's death and completed the first circumnavigation.
10 Verrazzano (1524) sailed from Dieppe in hope of breaking the American barrier; revealed instead eastern seaboard of North America from Florida to Nova Scotia; misunderstood character of Carolina Outer Banks which he described as an isthmus.
11 Saavedra, a kinsman of Cortés, sailed (1527) from Mexico, picked up the east trade wind and revealed the outward passage across the Pacific to the Philippines.
12 Chancellor (1553) led first of English searches for a north-eastern sea route to Asia; rounded North Cape of Norway and reached Archangel; later searches blocked by ice.
13 Salcedo-Urdaneta (1565) pioneered the route of the Manila galleons from the Philippines to Acapulco (Mexico) in the northerly belt of west winds.
14 Drake (1577–80) became the first Englishman to circum-

1 *main map* The primary aim of oceanic pioneers was not discovery of unknown lands but discovery of new routes to lands already known however imperfectly: Africa, Asia and Atlantic islands. America emerged as an obstacle to a westward crossing from Europe to Asia and so took shape as navigators looked for passages through or around it. Tracks of exploring ships were plotted according to the world wind-systems and thus became the commercial routes of the sailing-ship era.

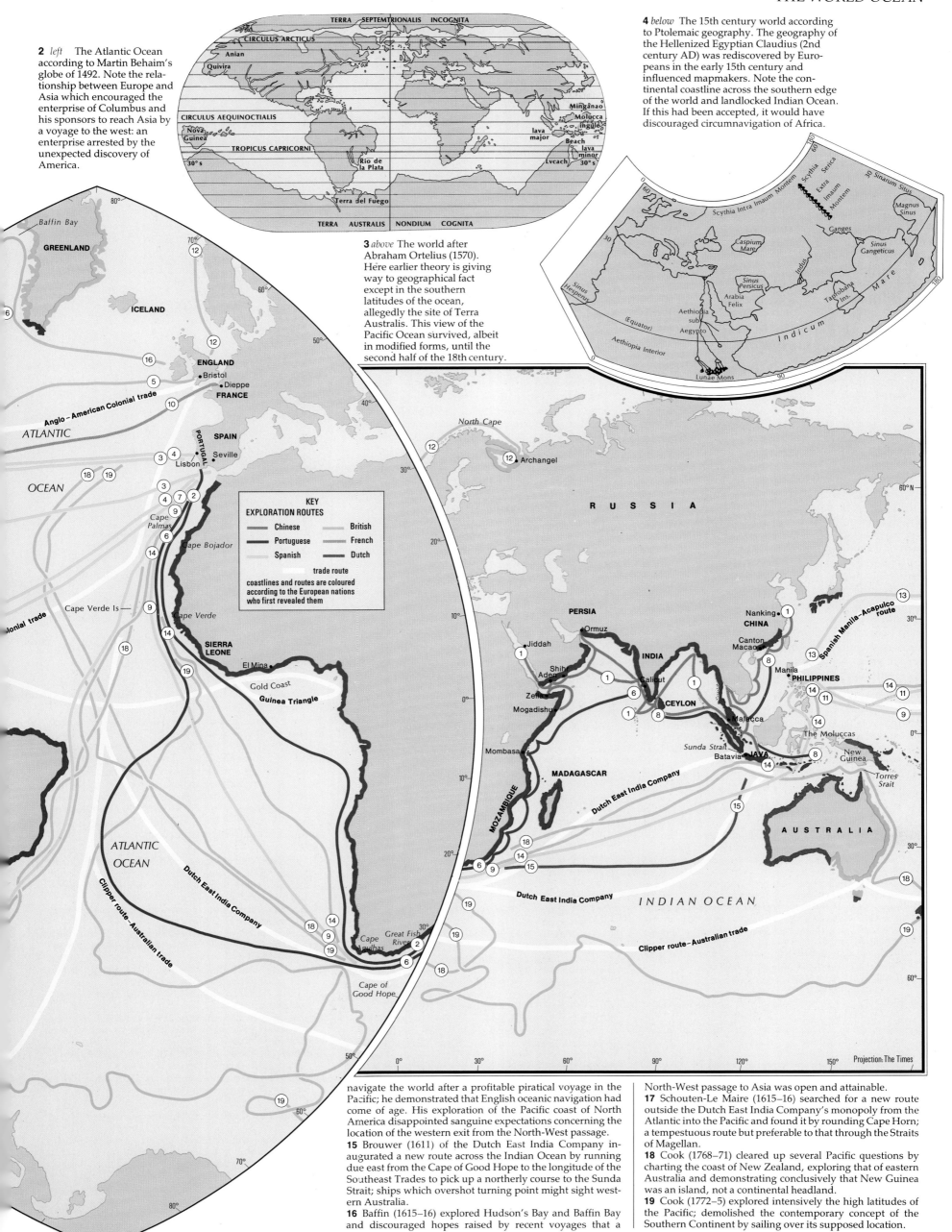

2 *left* The Atlantic Ocean according to Martin Behaim's globe of 1492. Note the relationship between Europe and Asia which encouraged the enterprise of Columbus and his sponsors to reach Asia by a voyage to the west: an enterprise arrested by the unexpected discovery of America.

4 *below* The 15th century world according to Ptolemaic geography. The geography of the Hellenized Egyptian Claudius (2nd century AD) was rediscovered by Europeans in the early 15th century and influenced mapmakers. Note the continental coastline across the southern edge of the world and landlocked Indian Ocean. If this had been accepted, it would have discouraged circumnavigation of Africa.

3 *above* The world after Abraham Ortelius (1570). Here earlier theory is giving way to geographical fact except in the southern latitudes of the ocean, allegedly the site of Terra Australis. This view of the Pacific Ocean survived, albeit in modified forms, until the second half of the 18th century.

KEY
EXPLORATION ROUTES

Chinese	British
Portuguese	French
Spanish	Dutch

trade route

coastlines and routes are coloured according to the European nations who first revealed them

navigate the world after a profitable piratical voyage in the Pacific; he demonstrated that English oceanic navigation had come of age. His exploration of the Pacific coast of North America disappointed sanguine expectations concerning the location of the western exit from the North-West passage.

15 Brouwer (1611) of the Dutch East India Company inaugurated a new route across the Indian Ocean by running due east from the Cape of Good Hope to the longitude of the Southeast Trades to pick up a northerly course to the Sunda Strait; ships which overshot turning point might sight western Australia.

16 Baffin (1615–16) explored Hudson's Bay and Baffin Bay and discouraged hopes raised by recent voyages that a

North-West passage to Asia was open and attainable.

17 Schouten-Le Maire (1615–16) searched for a new route outside the Dutch East India Company's monopoly from the Atlantic into the Pacific and found it by rounding Cape Horn; a tempestuous route but preferable to that through the Straits of Magellan.

18 Cook (1768–71) cleared up several Pacific questions by charting the coast of New Zealand, exploring that of eastern Australia and demonstrating conclusively that New Guinea was an island, not a continental headland.

19 Cook (1772–5) explored intensively the high latitudes of the Pacific; demolished the contemporary concept of the Southern Continent by sailing over its supposed location.

Undersea archaeology 1

THE increase in marine archaeological activity over the past two or three decades is directly related to the use of SCUBA (Self Contained Underwater Breathing Apparatus), which has facilitated undersea exploration, surveying, filming and recovery techniques of artifacts on the sea bed. The contribution of marine archaeologists to the knowledge of world maritime history is now widely regarded. From their evidence, details emerge of life on board ship, naval architecture and ship construction, ancient trade routes and cargoes, natural disasters, warfare at sea and the history of navigation, discovery and colonisation.

Two types of archaeological site represent the underwater cultural heritage. The first comprises fixed remains such as towns, villages or harbour works now submerged but once completely or partly above the surface. The Mediterranean is particularly significant and Apollonia on the north-east coast of Libya, Halieis in the western Peloponnesus, and Paulo Petri in the extreme south of Greece are researched examples. Shipwrecks, and the objects associated with them, make up the second type. The wrecks range from ancient classical sites consisting of a cargo mound and a few hull fragments, such as the vessel which sank carrying copper ingots off Cape Gelidonya, south-west Turkey (dated to around 1200 BC), to sites where the vessels have remained virtually intact. The *Wasa*, for example, was a Swedish warship which sank at the start of her maiden voyage from Stockholm harbour in 1628 and was salvaged between 1959 and 1961. Now reassembled, her good condition enabled archaeologists to retrieve some 25 000 listed artifacts from her remains.

Undersea archaeology is a discipline which involves much more than the discovery and retrieval of relics. Research often starts from documents and charts and proceeds through separate phases of underwater surveying and site excavation. Then follows the retrieval, conservation and restoration of timbers, cargo or other items brought to the surface. Finally, the presentation of the material to the public and the legal protection of the site are also considered to be part of a complete excavation project.

To carry out the excavation of a wreck or other site at sea is far more time-consuming and demanding than working on a land site. Problems caused by winds, waves and currents are common to all who work at sea but, in addition, a diver faces hazards related to the pressure, temperature and visibility of the water.

A major problem facing archaeologists at present is how to ensure proper protection for significant underwater sites. The main danger is modern piracy, where, as on land, unscrupulous people plunder sites and disperse archaeologically valuable items and therefore historical evidence. Some damage may also be caused by unintentional human interference in the form of dredging and fishing activities. Existing legislation is far from satisfactory and even where it exists, it is difficult to enforce effectively. However, support for suitable legislation to stop pilfering of wreck sites is developing at both national and international levels as the value of the underwater cultural heritage is at last being acknowledged and acted upon.

Many more sites lie awaiting chance discovery. Those selected here (and those detailed on the following pages) cover many aspects of man's involvement with the sea: the vessels in which he sailed, their cargoes and equipment, the ports and harbours on their routes. Also included are locations of some of the carvings or paintings found on land which give further valuable information to the archaeologist.

The present distribution of surveyed sites reflects to some extent the more popular places for SCUBA diving. The areas where diving is popular are the areas where wrecks are most likely to be discovered. Obviously the clear water of favoured diving areas presents a greater opportunity for sighting a wreck, or equally, a submerged city from aerial photographs. The actual distribution of wreck sites is of course related to the configuration of coastlines, the location of navigational hazards and their relation to trade routes and the severity of local sea conditions.

Eastern USA

(70) Conche
(57) Bay Bulls
(84) Isle-aux-Noir
(65) Yorktown
(37) Cape Hatteras
(13) Wilmington
(76) Black River
(77) Chinchorro Bank
(53) Quintana Roo
(87) Belize River
(3) Port Royal
90°W   80°   75°

1 *Map and insets* All the sites mapped were reported in the *International Journal of Nautical Archaeology* for the decade 1972 to 1982. While a vast number of actual and potential underwater sites of significance throughout the world are known, only a mere handful have been properly excavated. Recognising on one hand the vast numbers of sites known and on the other hand the paucity of sites so far reported in some areas, the map aims to illustrate a reasonable compendium of archaeological surveys.

1972

(1) *El Gran Grifon*, second-line, Spanish Armada vessel. Flagship of the squadron of supply ships. Wrecked 1588.

(2) *Amsterdam*, Dutch East Indiaman. Wrecked 1749. Huge collection of post-medieval antiquities

(3) Port Royal; excavation of 17th-century port destroyed by an earthquake in 1692.

1973

(4) Amphoras. Origins appear to be Mende, the Bosphorus area, and Motya.

(5) Amphoras of the 4th–3rd centuries BC; Potter's stamps indicate a cargo as having come from Heraclea Pontica.

(6) Punic vessel, possibly a warship from the mid-3rd century BC.

(7) Amphoras from ancient town of Callatis. Their ages range from 3rd century BC to the 6th century AD.

(8) *Mary*, Dutch yacht presented to Charles II of England upon his restoration and then wrecked in 1675.

(9) Harbour works; identification of sea level changes, 2000 BC–AD 200.

(10) King's Lynn; architectural and archaeological evidence of the town's waterfront during the middle ages.

(11) Amphoras of the Roman period found off Granada and Almeria indicate local trade only.

(12) Site of the Battle of Lepanto of 1571. Surface reconnaissance has located possible sites of wrecks.

(13) *Modern Greece*, British steamer, sunk 1862. Cargo discovered virtually intact.

(14) Anchors and amphoras of Greek and Roman origin, from the Hellenic, Roman and Byzantine periods.

(15) Roman cargo vessel of AD 600–650, transitional design of the era between the Roman period and the Middle Ages.

(16) *Vergulde Draeck*, Dutch East Indiaman, wrecked 1656. Its cargo included eight chests of silver.

(17) *Kennemerland*, Dutch East Indiaman, wrecked 1664. Bound for Batavia but was heading around Scotland to avoid interception by British in the English Channel.

(18) 17th- or early 18th-century Swedish merchantman. Cargo included stoneware, earthenware, glass and pewter.

(19) Ancient harbour of Phaselis. Findings indicate its development during the 1st and 2nd centuries AD.

(20) Roman port. A masonry embankment and other structural elements such as mooring stones remain.

1974

(21) Amphoras of the late 2nd century AD. Probably of Greek origin.

(22) *Santo Christo de Castello*, Spanish merchant ship, wrecked 1667. Cargo of lead ingots.

(23) *De Liefde*, Dutch East Indiaman, wrecked 1711. First to be found off the British Isles.

(24) Dutch galliot, wrecked 1677. Cargo of Dutch earthenware, delftware and clay pipes.

(25) *Lastdrager*, a flute (a fast narrow boat), wrecked in 1653 while engaged in trade with the Baltic.

(26) *Dartmouth*, British frigate, lost in an autumn gale in 1690 while at anchor.

(27) Sipontum, an ancient port founded by the Romans which flourished until the Middle Ages.

1975

(28) Wall paintings of ships; evidence of the hull shapes of bronze age craft.

(29) Engravings of ships. Evidence of the hull shapes of picene ships of 7th century BC.

(30) Anchors; indicate technical developments between 1st and 3rd centuries AD.

(31) *Wasa*, Swedish warship of 1628 which sank on her maiden voyage. Excavation of the sail locker; sails represent the oldest yet found. (The ship was raised in 1961.)

(32) *Batavia*, Dutch East Indiaman wrecked in 1629. Has survived despite the rigorous shallow-water conditions.

(33) *Nicholas*, Russian imperial frigate wrecked c.1790. Equipped with weaponry and navigation instruments purchased throughout Europe.

(34) Offshore structures of the harbour area. Evidence of the workings of the ancient port.

(35) Harbour and port of ancient Gythion. In AD 374 a large part disappeared under sea as a result of an earthquake.

(36) *Hollandia*, Dutch East Indiaman, wrecked 1743; 35 000 silver coins have been discovered.

(37) USS *Monitor*, a civil war ironclad sunk in bad weather in 1862. Her radical design make her a forerunner of the modern warship.

(38) *Adelaar*, Dutch East Indiaman wrecked 1728. (Explosives were used to separate concretions bonded to rock.)

(39) Anchorage of El Cabo de Higner. Roman wreck suggests that site was used as an anchorage even in antiquity.

1 *Map and insets* All the sites mapped were reported in the *International Journal of Nautical Archaeology* for the decade 1972 to 1982. While a vast number of actual and potential underwater sites of significance throughout the world are known, only a mere handful have been properly excavated. Recognising on one hand the vast numbers of sites known and on the other hand the paucity of sites so far reported in some areas, the map aims to illustrate a reasonable compendium of archaeological surveys.

1976

(40) Vessel from 2nd or 3rd century AD. Evidence of the traditions of Celtic shipbuilding.

(41) Hull of a wreck from 2nd or 1st century BC. Dated by amphoras and pottery discovered with it.

(42) Hull dated from the 4th century AD. Evidence of Byzantine shipbuilding trends.

(43) Harbour and town of Lapithos, kingdom of Cyprus which flourished between Archaic and Graeco-Roman times. Fish tanks discovered.

(44) *Meresteyn*, Dutch East Indiaman, wrecked 1702. Had on board a cargo of silver destined for Batavia.

(45) *Evstaffi*, transport ship of the Russian Imperial Navy wrecked in 1780.

(46) *James Matthews*, brig of British origin wrecked in 1841. She was a slave trade vessel and is the only one to have been discovered.

(47) Pottery dated around 1600 BC. The items would appear to have come from more than one wreck.

(48) Dutch East Indiaman wrecked in the 18th century. Cargo was removed when she broke up.

1977

(49) Vessel of 10–12 m loaded with amphoras containing pine resin.

(50) *Anne*, 70-gun British ship. Set on fire and sunk to prevent capture in 1690.

(51) *Curacao*, Dutch warship, lost while convoying a fleet of returning East Indiamen in 1729.

(52) Ancient harbour, anchorage and marine defenses. Flourished from 10th century BC to the middle ages.

(53) Fort excavations AD 300–AD 1000, Yucatan Peninsula held key position in trade between Mexico and central

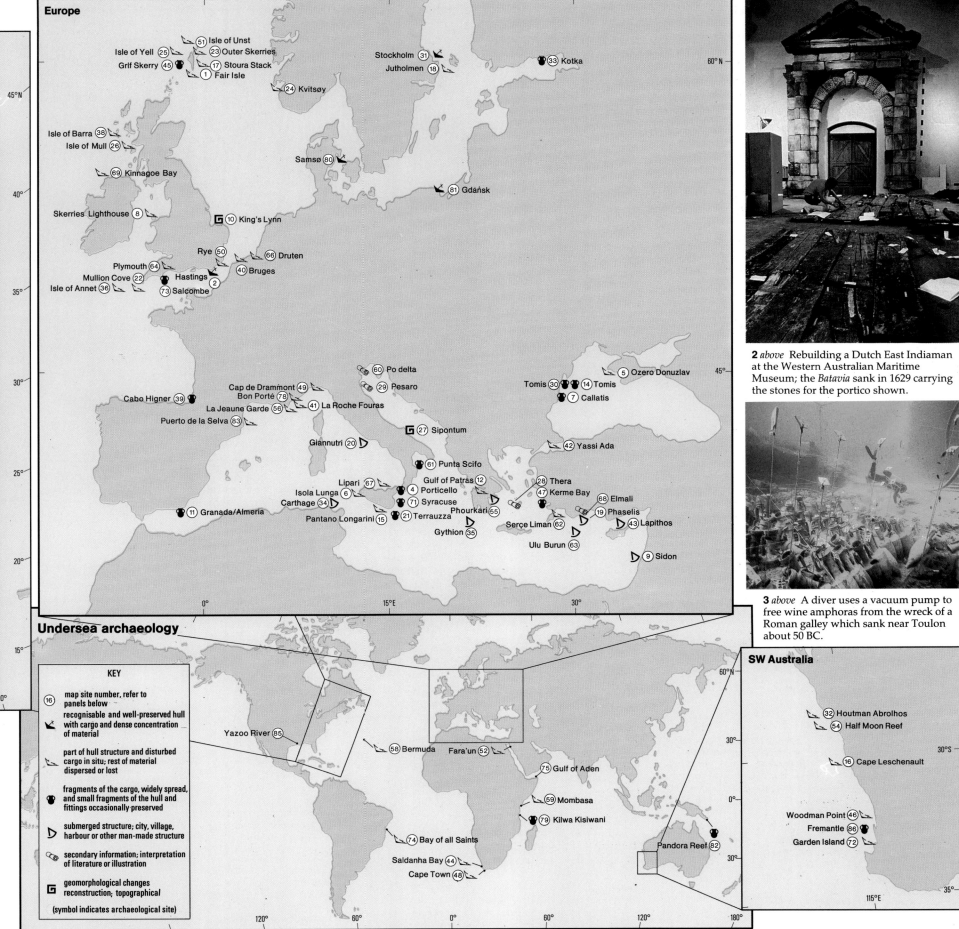

2 *above* Rebuilding a Dutch East Indiaman at the Western Australian Maritime Museum; the *Batavia* sank in 1629 carrying the stones for the portico shown.

3 *above* A diver uses a vacuum pump to free wine amphoras from the wreck of a Roman galley which sank near Toulon about 50 BC.

America during Maya period.

54 *Zeewijk*, Dutch East Indiaman wrecked in 1727; 82 survivors spent eight months as castaways before reaching Batavia Roads.

55 Villa complex of a Roman seaside resort which was used by the patrician class.

56 Amphoras, made in Calabria during early 2nd century BC, had held oil or other liquid.

57 *Sapphire*, British frigate, sunk whilst fighting the French off Newfoundland in 1669.

58 Spanish cargo vessel probably *en route* to Spain from Mexico when wrecked c.1650.

59 *Santo Antonio de Tanna*, Portuguese frigate, built in 1681. Remains of part of teak hull.

1978

60 Medieval lateen-rigged vessels. Evidence from floor mosaics, pictorial documents and wreck sites.

61 Cargo of marble dated c.AD 200. Reveals methods of Roman stone carving in quarry workshops.

62 Hull timbers and cargo consisting of Byzantine Greek coins, Arab glass weights, amphoras and Islamic glass. Dated c.1025.

63 Aperlae, submerged seaport. Thrived from 3rd century BC until devastation by Arabs in 7th century AD.

64 Keelson and fragments from gun assemblies of 16th-century ship.

65 Naval vessel, one of a number of ships scuttled by Earl Cornwallis during the siege of Yorktown in 1781. Eight more British naval wrecks were excavated in 1980.

66 Flat-bottomed Roman vessel of 2nd or 3rd century AD discovered in marsh silt.

67 Hull timbers, amphoras and pottery; little evidence of origins. Dated 3rd century BC.

1979

68 Tomb painting dated 525 BC, depicting small galley with ram bow. Vessel has many typical Greek features.

69 *La Trinidad Velencera*, Venetian merchantman requisitioned by Spain for Armada fleet and wrecked in 1588.

70 *Marguerite*, French vessel burnt by British warships in 1707.

71 Amphoras and domestic, possibly ceremonial, urn on a pedestal from a Corinthian vessel of the 4th century BC.

72 *Day Dawn*, ex-American whaler wrecked in 1886 in Careening Bay, an anchorage and haven for ship repair.

73 Bronze-age sword, blades and palstave indicate weapon depository.

74 *Sacramento*, Brazilian merchantman wrecked in 1668. Flagship of the general commercial company of Brazil.

75 Pre-Islamic ports of Heis, Daamo and Hafun. Traded with Mediterranean from 3rd century BC to 3rd century AD.

76 18th-century ferry. Good evidence of local shipbuilding

techniques in the south of North America.

1980

77 40-cannon frigate wrecked c.1790. Anchors and pottery also found. Nationality unknown.

78 Vessel of the 6th century BC; her remains (part of the keel and five ribs) are the oldest available for study.

79 Stone anchor shanks dated between the 8th and 11th centuries.

80 13th-century Viking ship, dated between 11th and 14th centuries.

81 Early 15th-century vessel, possibly single-masted; copper ingots found.

82 HMS *Pandora*, wrecked c.1791 en route from Tahiti to England. Vessel's gear and pieces of earthenware found.

83 Roman wreck of the 1st century BC. Amphoras found from north-eastern Spain. Some organic deposits including hair.

1981

84 Unidentified French flat-bottomed vessel sunk by British artillery c.1760. Frames and plankings have traces of soot.

85 USS *Cairo*, blown up and sunk in 1862 but found intact. First vessel to be sunk by electronically controlled mine.

86 Brig *James*, sunk c.1830; 6-pounder cannonade found. Gun carriage has been reconstructed.

87 Engravings on tombs and bones are evidence of type of canoes used by Mayas c.AD 100.

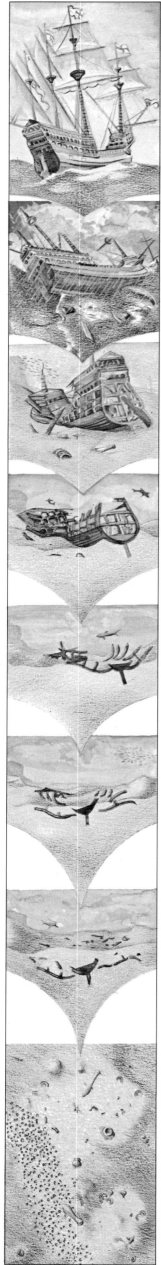

1 *left, top to bottom* The sinking and decay of a wreck.

Any ship, once at sea, whether a merchant-man, warship, or a ship bound on discovery, carries with her a record of contemporary ship-building and design, navigational techniques, cargoes, crews' belongings, and weaponry.

She can be wrecked by foundering in a storm, or by other hazards such as stranding, collision or fire, or be lost in a battle. She may capsize and sink or break up and sink in part. Some of her materials or contents are swept away by pounding waves, others are removed by currents during sinking.

The main structure of the ship together with the keel and ballast comes to rest on the seabed. The more buoyant objects float away. Unless the ship has been very badly broken up the cargo and other contents sink with her.

Contemporary or later attempts to salvage material such as canons, timber and cargo begins to deplete the wreck.

The chemical and biological agents in seawater degrade and destroy the hull and the scattered objects. Within a few decades much of the hull is broken up though the lower sections of the vessel will have sunk into the mud or silt.

The movement of unconsolidated seabed material (silt, sand, gravel, or shingle) by waves and currents further wears down and buries the remains.

The weight of the vessel, combined with the accumulation of sediment, cause the remains to sink deeper beneath the seabed.

Once all the remains and the artifacts have been buried the surrounding silt and mud protects them against further degradation so that they will last almost indefinitely. The remains will be hard to locate and the diver may have to rely upon contemporary source material and local knowledge as well as his own surveying. Once the site has been located, however, the removal of layers of silt will bring an increasing number of remains to light.

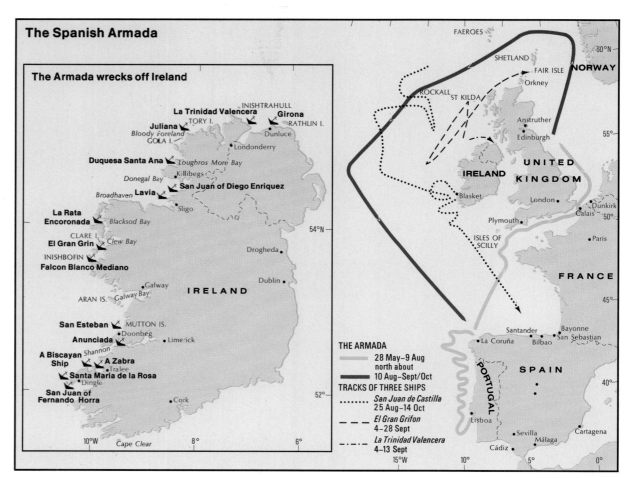

The Spanish Armada

The Armada wrecks off Ireland

2 *map and inset above* Around the Scottish and Irish coasts lies the physical evidence of the Armada. The bad seasonal weather which caused the catastrophe is still today referred to as 'Armada weather'.

The Spanish Armada

The Spanish Armada was launched against England by Philip II in May 1588 with the aims of defeating their Royal Navy and attempting a full scale invasion of southern England. With its show of strength of 130 ships, 2431 guns, 8000 seamen and 20 000 soldiers, the Armada might have inflicted heavy casualties on the English, or at least have achieved political concessions. However, delays at the start of the venture, an inadequate supply of guns and suitable ammunition, rotting food and dispirited men, were just precursors to a campaign that was to go badly wrong.

The Armada, on entering the English Channel to rendezvous with a Spanish army off Dunkirk and Nieuport, was met by Dutch and English resistance. The invasion barges intended for troop transportation were blockaded by a Dutch fleet of armed flyboats while the English set eight blazing fireships among the anchored Armada, causing it to scatter in confusion. Off Gravelines the English fleet attacked fiercely and inflicted considerable damage. With the English to the south the only return to Spain was a 3000 km route north and west around Scotland and western Ireland. On that return journey forty or more ships were wrecked. Only about one third of the total complement of men survived.

The wrecks of the Armada provide the opportunity to study a wide range of ship construction (this cosmopolitan fleet was requisitioned from across Europe and included ships from the Baltic and Mediterranean), as well as naval gunnery, field army accoutrements and social affairs, in late 16th-century Europe.

Analysis of artifacts from wreck sites has confirmed that many of the guns were of poor quality. Cannonballs show signs of hasty manufacture (some, made of poor-quality iron, are known to have shattered on impact against the heavy oak hulls of the English fleet). The siege guns incorporated into ships' armaments took up too much space and raised the centre of gravity, resulting in excessive recoil. Marine archaeology has therefore revealed some of the reasons why the Armada ended in disaster.

The *Santa Maria de la Rosa* wreck site is an interesting example of archival research and underwater survey. Built in 1587, she was requisitioned to become the vice flagship of the Armada's Guipuzcoan squadron of ten ships. With 27 guns and carrying 233 soldiers and 64 seamen, with a general cargo of munitions, stores and siege artillery, the *Santa Maria de la Rosa* was damaged by storm and battle and finally sank in Blasket Sound on 21 September 1588 with only one survivor.

A systematic swim-line search by divers in 1968, covering 10 sq km of seabed, eventually located a wreck site at a depth of 36 m just southeast of a submerged pinnacle of rock struck by the ship before she sank. In spite of the depth and difficult tide races the site was surveyed and artifacts recovered including a pewter plate bearing the name of 'Matute', a senior officer on board the *Santa Maria de la Rosa*.

Submerged cities and harbours

Changes in sea level and catastrophic events such as volcanic eruptions, earthquakes and associated tidal waves have sometimes led to the submergence of complete cities and harbours. Towns that once thrived and bustled with activity now lie as abandoned ruins on the seabed. The study of these submerged structures by archaeologists has added to our knowledge of ships and ports (from the dimensions of docks, slipways and boathouses), urban development and the life of

4 *right* An aerial photograph of Caesarea, Israel. The dark areas under the water are scattered rubble and constitute the remains of the harbour walls and quays which were built by Herod Agrippa in the 1st century AD.

the period during which the communities flourished.

Structures may have been submerged by a slow rise in sea level, sudden movements of the earth's crust, or a combination of the two. A city that sank slowly over hundreds of years would have undergone a gradual decline in its status as people, forewarned of the impending dangers, moved away. The buildings and harbour installations would have been allowed to fall into disrepair but the gradual inundation caused by adjustment of sea level would ensure that the buildings remained more or less intact and the stratigraphy of artifacts, building materials and rubbish from different periods, reasonably preserved. Well-surveyed examples are Apollonia and Paulo Petri.

In contrast, a city that was submerged violently and suddenly by an earthquake before the inhabitants could escape, would produce an archaeological site with all the facets of its activity preserved from a single moment. Such an event would smash and scatter many of the buildings and the smaller items such as pottery, jewellery and bones would be mixed with debris giving a poor stratigraphy. Examples are the several cities submerged along the northern shore of the Bay of Naples and Port Royal, a Jamaican pirate town in the Caribbean.

The Mary Rose

The Tudor warship *Mary Rose* was a carrack built in 1510 in Portsmouth for King Henry VIII and lost in action against the French in 1545. Her wreck is considered by many to be the most historically important yet discovered in European waters.

In 1536 the ship underwent a major reconstruction and refit and became one of the first purpose-built ocean-going warships capable of firing a broadside of guns. (Up to this time sea strategy had meant close contact, with ships locked together by grapnels, the fighting by archers and pikemen.) With an armament of 91 guns, made up of a balanced selection of bronze muzzle-loading and wrought-iron breach-loading guns, the *Mary Rose* is historically significant as the first true fighting ship that was not intended to perform trading tasks in time of peace.

The *Mary Rose* sank rapidly with a loss of up to 700 men. This was due to poor handling, a lack of discipline and overcrowding, as well as the gun ports being open ready for action. Lying under the murky waters of the Solent, the enveloping silts preserved her contents to create a time capsule of life at sea in the Tudor period. Apart from brief attempts at salvage in 1545–49 and 1836–40, she remained abandoned until rediscovery in 1967, since when a continuous programme of survey and study has been carried out with the aim of the recovery of the hull and the establishment of a Tudor ship museum in Portsmouth.

Although most of the clinker-built high castle structures and a large part of the port side of the hull have been eroded, the rest of the ship is well preserved. Just as significant as the hull timbers are the thousands of Tudor artefacts that have been recovered. These include sundials, arrows, long bows, sword scabbards, rigging blocks, ropes, the Barber-surgeon's chest (containing razors, syringes and ointment jars), clothing and footwear, guns and gun carriages. As well as helping to detail the ship's structure itself, these finds allow archaeologists to build a complete picture of life on board and of the people who crewed her. The wreck of the *Mary Rose* was raised successfully in October 1982 and moved to a dry dock in Portsmouth using a specially cushioned lifting frame.

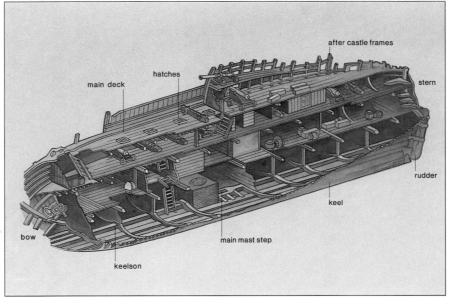

4 above right The only picture of the *Mary Rose* comes from the Anthony Roll, a list of the King's ships compiled by an officer of the Board of Ordnance at the Tower of London in 1546. It depicts her as she was after refitting in 1536.

5 right An artist's impression of the remains of the *Mary Rose* which were discovered on the seabed, taken from an isometric drawing. Even after reconstruction and preservation she will not, however, show the fine lines of this drawing.

6 below left Working from plans made during the excavation, a full-scale 2 m section was built. There are plans to build an exact replica and retrace the fateful voyage from the Aegean to Cyprus.

7 below The original Kyrenia ship is now on display in the Crusader Castle in Kyrenia, Cyprus.

8 right, bottom to top The stages in the recovery of a wreck from the predisturbance survey to the eventual exhibition for the public.

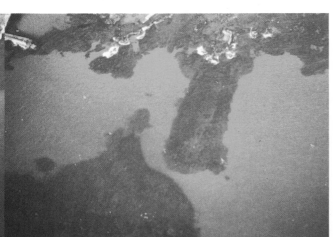

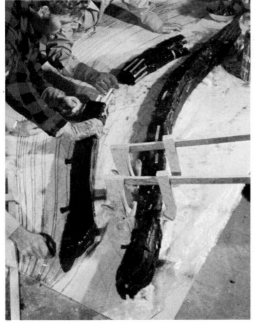

The Kyrenia shipwreck

This 4th-century BC Greek merchant vessel was found 2 km north-east of the ancient harbour of Kyrenia, Cyprus, in 30 m of water and it is an interesting example of how meticulous recording can reveal details of the tools and techniques used in ship construction, information on cargo and trading routes, facts about crew, and a vessel's eventual fate.

When first located, the site appeared as a cluster of ancient amphoras on a mud-sand seabed overgrown with Poseidon weed. Careful probing, mapping and removal of sediment by means of airlift revealed a major cargo of 400 amphoras. Their positioning showed that the ship had settled on her port side, her starboard side subsequently collapsing so that some of the pots spilled out. Most of the pots were from Rhodes (identified as dating to the last third of the 4th century BC) but a number were from Samos, further north. A secondary cargo of almost 10 000 almonds also came to light. Under the amphoras lay 29 grinding stones and because of their disparity in size, their odd number, and various states of finish, they are thought to be remnants of an earlier cargo serving as ballast. Crockery from the remains of the fore and aft cabins included four each of salt dishes, drinking cups, oil jars and wooden spoons, as well as pitches, ladles and copper vessels. The 'sets' of some of the items may indicate size of the crew. Information about the mariners' diet was gleaned from the recovery of garlic, olive stones, grape pips, fig seeds and lead weights used for fishing.

The wood of the hull was riddled with worm holes and extremely fragile. Nevertheless, after separation into manageable pieces, labelling, recovery, and extensive treatment to prevent cracking, warping and shrinking, 70 per cent of the ancient hull was found to have survived. Saw, adze and awl marks show that the ship was built by 'shell' construction. Using this method, the keel was laid first and the outer planking assembled and joined to it; frames were then laid down within the hull and fixed by copper nails driven in from outside. Lead sheathing encased both hull and keel to protect them from teredo worms.

The *Wasa*, Wasa Museum, Stockholm, raised 1961. The surviving structure, if suitably preserved, is exhibited.

Lifting the hull of the *Mary Rose*, 1982. It may be possible to recover a substantial part of the ship's hull.

The largest single piece of timber, found on the wreck site of the *Batavia*, Australia.

Bronze gun carriage on hull of *Mary Rose*. Individual items are cleared for lifting.

The wreck of a Spanish galleon near Portobelo, Panama. An air lift suction pump clears debris off excavated site.

The *Rapid* (China trader) wreck site, off Point Cloates, Australia. Timbers and artifacts are plotted in detail.

Orlop deck of *Mary Rose*. A predisturbance survey of the site is carried out before excavation using a specially erected grid system.

The scientific discovery of the oceans

THE first major scientific studies of the open ocean were carried out in the early 19th century. However, some attempts to obtain deep-sea soundings, to make sub-surface temperature and current measurements and to investigate other aspects of marine physics and chemistry had been made in the previous two centuries. In the late 17th century several Fellows of the Royal Society of London had been interested in the oceans: Robert Boyle studied the salinity of sea water; Robert Hooke devised instruments for measuring depth and temperature; Edmond Halley studied the trade winds; and the work of Isaac Newton on gravitation provided an explanation of the tides. In the early 18th century, Count Luigi Marsigli made systematic observations of currents, temperature and salinity in the Eastern Mediterranean. Later, Benjamin Franklin investigated the Gulf Stream; Benjamin Thomson (Count Rumford) studied ocean circulation; and Antoine Laurent de Lavoisier made the first full-scale chemical analysis of sea water.

In the period of relative peace at the end of the Napoleonic wars, Britain had a large and underemployed navy and therefore initiated a series of polar expeditions during which oceanographic observations were made. Moreover, the increasing importance of commercial shipping and the new technology of submarine telegraphy (see page 200) required improved knowledge of surface waves and currents, of the shape and nature of the deep sea floor, and of near-bottom water temperatures. Finally, the publication of Darwin's *Origin of Species* in 1859 stimulated interest in marine biology; deep sea dredgings brought up many hitherto unknown species including some which appeared to be 'living fossils' which confirmed Darwin's evolutionary theory.

As a result of these combined pressures, in 1868–70 the British government despatched the survey vessels *Lightning* and *Porcupine* on a series of short exploratory voyages in the North Atlantic and Mediterranean. The results were so encouraging that in 1872, HMS *Challenger* left England for a three and a half year scientific circumnavigation which is generally considered to mark the birth of modern oceanography.

Much of the information gathered previously was fragmentary or inaccurate. Even for the North Atlantic (the best known area because of the interest in the transatlantic telegraph cable) the available bathymetric charts were quite inadequate. For other regions, even the general shape of the ocean basins was unknown. Furthermore, virtually nothing was known about the mid-water life in the open ocean.

The important discoveries made by the *Lightning* and *Porcupine* were extended by the much more ambitious *Challenger* expedition to all the world oceans. The results in chemistry, physics, geology, and particularly biology amply justified the expenditure of £170 000 which the whole venture had cost. But perhaps the most important result of the expedition was the impetus it gave to other nations. By the end of the century, expeditions with a major interest in marine science had been despatched by the United States, Germany, Norway, Sweden, France, Italy, India, Monaco, Russia, Belgium, Denmark and the Netherlands.

Like the *Challenger*, several of these later expeditions visited all the major oceans, a tradition which continued during the first half of the present century until the Danish *Galathea* expedition of 1950–52 which was the last purely scientific circumnavigation. Other expeditions were directed to specific areas or particular problems. For instance, a German expedition in the Atlantic, on

the *Meteor* from 1925 to 1927, had as its main objective the study of currents and water masses in an entire ocean. Similarly, the British *Discovery* investigations, which began in 1925 and continued to the Second World War, were concerned with the physical, chemical and biological oceanography of the Southern Ocean, particularly in relation to the Antarctic whale fishery.

The history of oceanography has been closely linked with improvements in the technology of both ships and equipment. The ropes used up to the time of the *Challenger* to lower thermometers

and water bottles and to tow fishing nets were quickly replaced by stronger and less bulky wire, while the instruments themselves became much more accurate and sophisticated. Nevertheless, apart from the widespread use of echo-sounding after the First World War, much of the equipment on a research vessel in the 1930s was similar to that used on the *Challenger*. However, the growing use of electronics, acoustics and now satellites, together with purpose-built vessels including submersibles, has revolutionised oceanography since the Second World War.

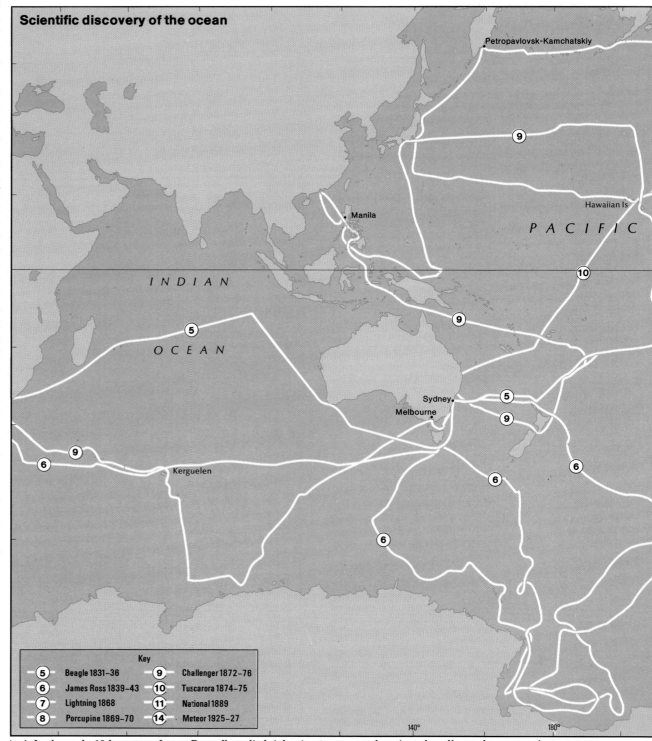

Scientific discovery of the ocean

Petropavlovsk-Kamchatskiy

Hawaiian Is

PACIFIC

Manila

INDIAN

OCEAN

Sydney

Melbourne

Kerguelen

140° 180°

Key

5	Beagle 1831–36	9	Challenger 1872–76
6	James Ross 1839–43	10	Tuscarora 1874–75
7	Lightning 1868	11	National 1889
8	Porcupine 1869–70	14	Meteor 1925–27

1 main maps (Indian and Pacific, and Atlantic Oceans) and inset *opposite top left* for the *Meteor*. Selected routes of some of the most significant international oceanographic explorations are plotted, the numbers corresponding to the numbers in bold type in the captions beneath the maps.

1 In the early 19th century James Rennell studied Atlantic currents, and William Scoresby investigated Arctic seas with special reference to the whale fisheries.

2 A circumnavigation by A. J. Krusenstern in 1803–06 on *Nadeshda* and *Neva*. This was the first cruise to use James Six's self-registering maximum–minimum thermometers, one of the most important instruments in physical oceanography until it was replaced by reversing thermometers in the late 19th century.

3 The voyage to the Antarctic under the Russian Bellingshausen in 1819–21 was important in terms of work carried out on plankton, rather than oceanography.

4 The Russians undertook a circumnavigation in 1823–26 under Kotzebue. On this voyage, the physicist Emil von Lenz was the first to demonstrate that the deep cold waters of the ocean basins originated in polar regions.

5 Charles Darwin was appointed naturalist on board HMS *Beagle* for her circumnavigation 1831–36. Though the cruise was not of great significance in the development of oceanography, Darwin's findings led directly to his theory of evolution.

6 On his first Antarctic expedition of 1839–43, James Clark Ross was accompanied by the scientist Hooker. Studies by Darwin and Hooker stimulated further interest in the scientific study of the ocean.

7, 8 The cruises of *Lightning* and *Porcupine* in 1868–70 dispelled two major misconceptions. First, using thermometers

protected against the effects of pressure, bottom temperatures well below the expected minimum of 4°C were recorded. Second, trawls used down to depths of 4450 m brought up a wide variety of animals, whereas previously it had been believed that no life existed below about 600 m.

9 The *Challenger* expedition of 1872–76 under Sir Charles Wyville Thompson covered 70 000 miles and made deep-sea investigations at 362 observation stations, including depth soundings, collection of sediment and water samples and specimens, and temperature measurements. The deepest sounding was obtained at over 8000 m, not far from the site of the present ocean record depth in the Marianas Trench in the Philippine Sea.

10 The USS *Tuscarora* in 1874–75 made many observations of sea temperature in the North Pacific, and made important deep sea soundings using piano wire incorporated in a device designed by William Thompson (later Lord Kelvin).

11 The German steamer *National*, under the leadership of Victor Hensen, cruised the Atlantic in 1889 in an investigation of plankton, and established the importance of quantitative methods in ocean biology.

12 The SS *Belgica* carried members of the Belgian Antarctic Expedition of 1897–99 and was the first ship to winter in the Antarctic. The crew and scientific staff were international and the results were worked out by more than 80 specialists from all parts of the world.

13 One important oceanographic voyage of the 20th century

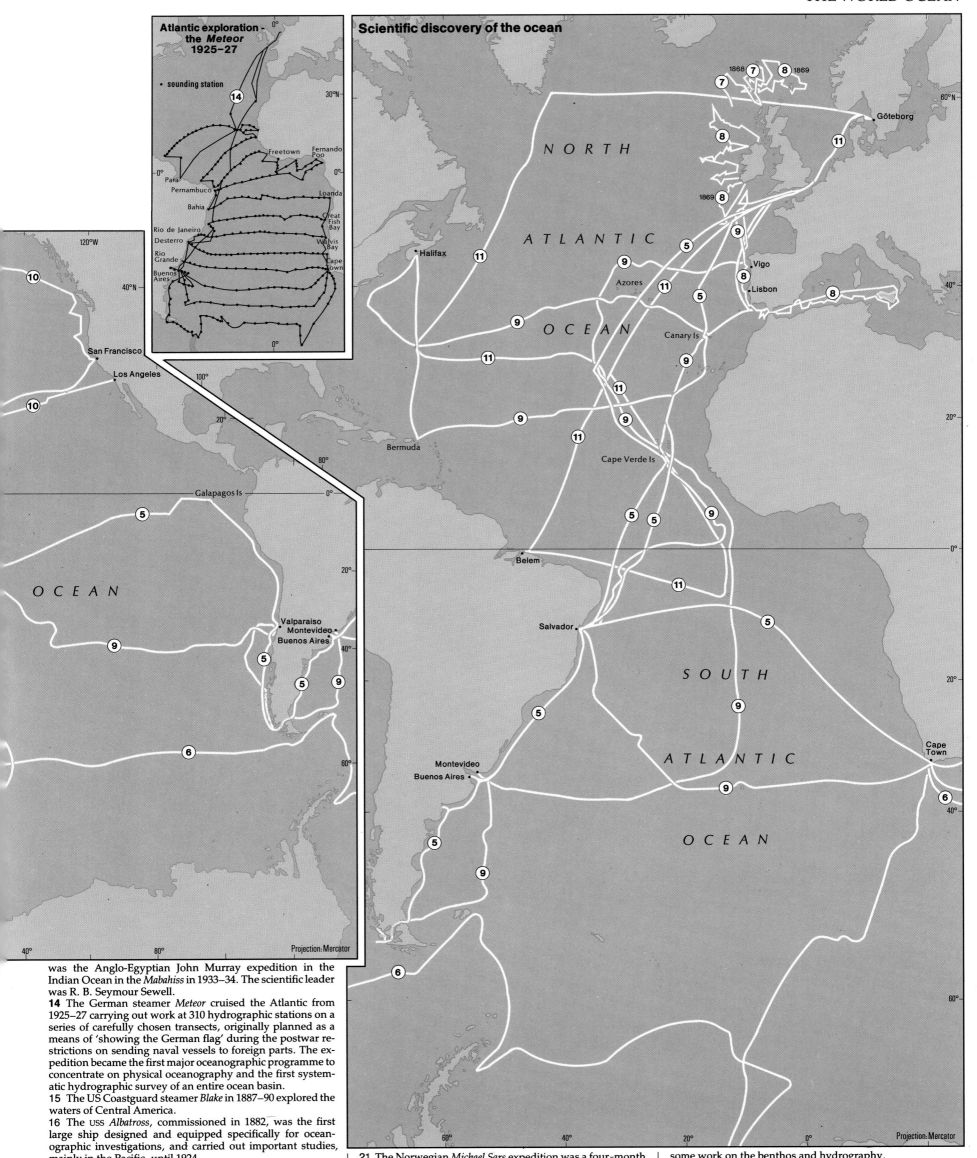

Atlantic exploration – the *Meteor* 1925–27

• sounding station

Scientific discovery of the ocean

Projection: Mercator

was the Anglo-Egyptian John Murray expedition in the Indian Ocean in the *Mabahiss* in 1933–34. The scientific leader was R. B. Seymour Sewell.

14 The German steamer *Meteor* cruised the Atlantic from 1925–27 carrying out work at 310 hydrographic stations on a series of carefully chosen transects, originally planned as a means of 'showing the German flag' during the postwar restrictions on sending naval vessels to foreign parts. The expedition became the first major oceanographic programme to concentrate on physical oceanography and the first systematic hydrographic survey of an entire ocean basin.

15 The US Coastguard steamer *Blake* in 1887–90 explored the waters of Central America.

16 The USS *Albatross*, commissioned in 1882, was the first large ship designed and equipped specifically for oceanographic investigations, and carried out important studies, mainly in the Pacific, until 1924.

17 The voyage of the *Fram* under Nansen in 1893–96 added greatly to knowledge of currents and ice in the Arctic.

18 The German Deep Sea Expedition in the *Valdivia* during 1898–99 made biological investigations in the Atlantic, Antarctic and Indian Oceans.

19 The Netherlands Deep Sea Expedition on board the *Siboga* in 1899–1900 studied the biology and physics of East Indian waters.

20 The German South Polar Expedition on board the *Gauss* in 1901–04.

21 The Norwegian *Michael Sars* expedition was a four-month cruise in the north Atlantic during the summer of 1910. The fisheries vessel *Michael Sars* and the scientific personnel were provided by the Norwegian government, while the other expenses were paid for by Sir John Murray, one of the scientists of the *Challenger* Expedition. The expedition carried out both hydrographic and biological work, but concentrated on mid-water life in the open ocean.

22 The Danish expedition of 1920–22 in the *Dana* covered the Atlantic and the Mediterranean. The expedition concentrated on the study of mid-water biology, but also included

some work on the benthos and hydrography.

23 The Royal Indian Marine Survey Ship *Investigator* in 1884–1914 carried out a great deal of work on deep sea biology, in the Laccadive Sea and Bay of Bengal, under a succession of surgeon-naturalists. It is difficult, if not impossible, to produce a track chart because the cruises were spread over such a long period.

For clarity, only those voyages numbered in bold type have been plotted on the map.

THE STUDY OF THE SEA
Submarine cables

THE expansion of British trade overseas in the mid-19th century demanded improved communications between London and the foreign markets. Once long distance overland telegraphy was established, newly available technology and materials made submarine cable laying a feasible proposition.

The first successful cable across the open sea was laid between England and France in 1851 and plans were soon made for larger ventures and particularly for a cable connecting Europe and North America. But before such ventures could be undertaken the prospective routes had to be surveyed to obtain closely spaced accurate soundings and samples of the bottom sediments to give some indication of the nature of the sea-bed. Moreover, it was important to know the range of water temperatures in which the cables would be laid. In the early days the surveys were carried out by the British and American navies, but later they were increasingly made by the cable companies, initially in chartered vessels and eventually in specially constructed ships.

The young science of oceanography benefitted enormously from this commercial interest, for it led to rapid improvements in the techniques of sounding, water-sampling and deep-sea thermometry, and the surveys also provided biologists and geologists with hitherto unobtainable specimens and information. The scientific results also helped to stimulate first Britain and later many other nations to mount major government-backed oceanographic expeditions.

The early cables were laid by conventional vessels fitted with enormous tanks below decks to hold the great lengths of coiled cable. Brunel's failed passenger liner the *Great Eastern*, for instance, which laid the first successful transatlantic cable in 1866, was able to carry some 2500 miles of cable. The first purpose-built cable vessel was launched in 1874; since then the vessels have become successively more sophisticated—and expensive—so that a modern cable ship with its distinctive clipper bows and large sheaves will cost upwards of $30 million.

A modern submarine cable is very different from its counterpart of the 1850s: the original copper, gutta-percha and iron have all been replaced by new materials and, to give greater flexibility, the cable's strength is now provided by a central core rather than an outer layer. The original cables could convey only a few simple electrical pulses each minute. By the time the first translatlantic telephone cable was laid in 1956 it could carry 36 simultaneous conversations, while a single cable could carry 1000 calls by the early 1970s and 5000 by 1980.

During their 130-year history submarine cables have had to face two major challenges from other communications systems. The first, the introduction of radio in the 1920s, was successfully beaten off mainly because cables were more reliable and could be more confidential. A second and more serious threat has been posed more recently by communication satellites, for submarine cables cannot compete in the transmission of television or other multi-destination traffic. Nevertheless, for point-to-point communication the cables are still cheaper and more reliable and they will continue to be heavily used over their more than 80 million circuit miles.

But increased capacity is no longer the key to the future of cables since few lines will require more than the existing capability. Instead, if the cables are to retain a role in competition with satellites it will be because of relative cheapness through the use of the new technology of fibre optics.

1 *main map and insets*
The cables forming the world submarine international network are shown, together with the nearest places to their landfall. Cable use and type are summarised in the table *top right*.

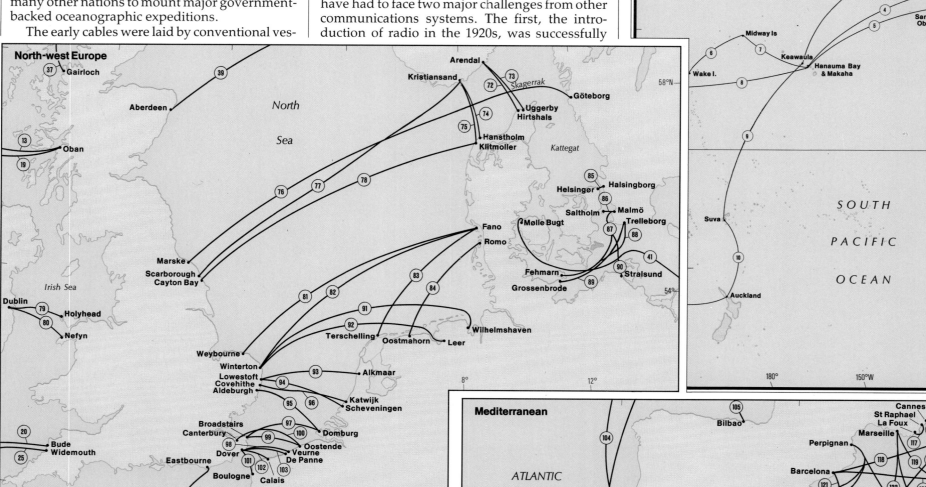

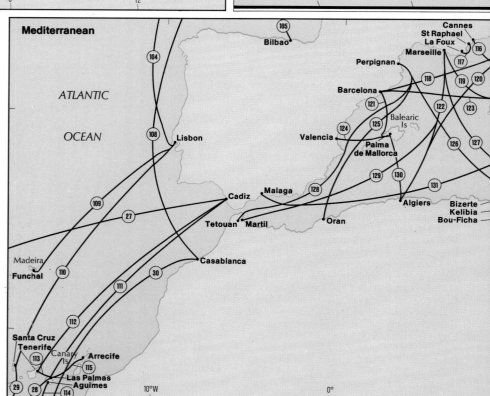

KEY TO CABLE NUMBERS

- **118** cable number
- **◄361** length of cable (kilometres)
- ○ voice–frequency telegraphy
- ■ telephony
- □ facsimile transmission
- ● sound programme transmission
- ☆ data transmission
- ★ direct-current telegraphy
- **1380** number of channels

No.	Length	Transmission	Channels
1	1370	○■ ☆	48
2	150	○■□○☆	80
3	4713	○■□●☆	80
4	4069	○■□ ☆	51
5	4413	○■□●☆	143
6	2052	■□	142
7	2295	○■	142
8	6760	○■□●☆	845
9	5691	○■□☆	80
10	2334	○■□○☆	85
11	1552	○■□	24
12	1576	○■	24
13	3723	○■□●☆	80
14	117	○■ ☆	24
	117	○■	80
15	505	○■	80
16	626	■	80
17	102	○■	80
18	4063	■	48
	4091	■	48
19	3597	○■□	48
20	5186	○■□●☆	1840
21	1389	○■ ☆	82
22	1482	○■□	640
23	1463	○■□☆	640
24	6660	■	138
25	6517	■	138
26	6258	○■□●☆	4000
27	6410	○■ ☆	845
28	5999	■	1840
29	1585	○■□●☆	360
30	2711	○■□●☆	640
31	4071	○■□●☆	640
32	5050	○■□●☆	160
33	3145	○■□●☆	360
34	2550	○■□●☆	480
35	746	○■□●☆	360
36	746	○■	30
37	530	○■□	26
38	569	○■□	36
39	569	○■□	36
40	63	■	
	48	■	60
41	128	○■ ☆	60
42	56	●	11
43	361	★	2
44	883	○■□☆	480
45	872	○■□☆	138
46	2656	○■□☆	138
47	1341	○■□☆	1600
48	880	○■□☆	1840
49	3819	○■□☆	480
50	2528	○■□☆	845
51	2041	○■□☆	85
52	2578	○■ ☆	128
53	1606	○■□●☆	85
54	2780	○■□☆	142
55	2576	○■□☆	170
56	900	○■□☆	480
57	2989	○■□☆	170
58	2204	○■□●☆	480
	2358	○■□●☆	85
59	220	○■ ☆	24
	196	○ ★	8
	185	○ ★	8
	181	○ ★	8
	239	○■	24
60	361	○■ ☆	1380
61	2184	○■ ☆	142
62	2446	■ ☆	720
63	1671	○■	80
	78	■ ●	12
64	2104	○■	50
65	1545	○■	144
66	693	○■	120
67	715	○■ ☆	128
68	1150	○■□●☆	144
69	1050	○■□●☆	160
70	235	○■ ☆	160
71	1009	○■□☆	83
72	124	○■	60
73	126 N.A.		2700
74	122	○■□	60
75	82	○■●☆	480
76	945	○■□●	60
77	726	○■□☆	480
78	683	○■ ☆	1260
79	119	○■	60
	117	○■	60
80	115	○■	24
	117	○■	24
81	574	○	192
82	541	○■	120
83	339	○■	120
84	257	○■●☆	120
	259	○■ ☆	120
85	6	○■	42
86	9	○■□☆	900
87	224	○■ ☆	480
88	200	○■ ☆	1200
89	202	○■ ☆	1200
90	119	■	12
	119	○■	42
91	519	○■ ☆	1260
92	465	○■	120
	461	○■□	120
93	222	■	N.A.
94	181	○■	60
	181	■	60
95	152	○■	180
	154	■	1260
96	202	○■	120
97	354	○■□☆	1380
98	107	○■ ☆	3900
99	119	○■□☆	1260
100	102	○■□☆	120
101	46	○■□	60
102	37	○■□	60
	39	○■□	60
	41	○■□	60
103	89	○■□●	420
104	1761	■	640
105	893	■	480
	861	■	1380
106	31	■	12
	33	■	12
107	191	○■●☆	2875
108	1926	○■□☆	640
109	1148	■	120
110	1363	○■□	360
111	1365	■	1840
112	1396	■	160
113	111	■	1840
114	5999	■	1840
115	346	■	480
116	196	○■●☆	96
117	35	○■□☆	2580
118	796	■	480
119	685	■	3440
120	1107	○■	480
121	339	■	1380
122	883	○■□●☆	80
123	950	■	1380
124	302	■	3900
125	1004	○■	60
126	943	○■□☆	640
127	3400	○■□☆	120
128	1404	○■□☆	96
129	1472	○■●☆	2580
130	339	■	480
131	1826	■	640
132	865	○■	128
133	156	☆	3
134	528	■	480
135	109	■	120
136	80	○■	60
137	98	○■	36
138	552	○■	120
139	320	■	1840
140	930	■	60
141	2713	○■□☆	1380
142	2495	■	640
143	1682	■	480
144	2006	○■□☆	480
145	3400	○■□☆	120
146	963	■	640
147	926	○■●☆	120
148	217	■	640

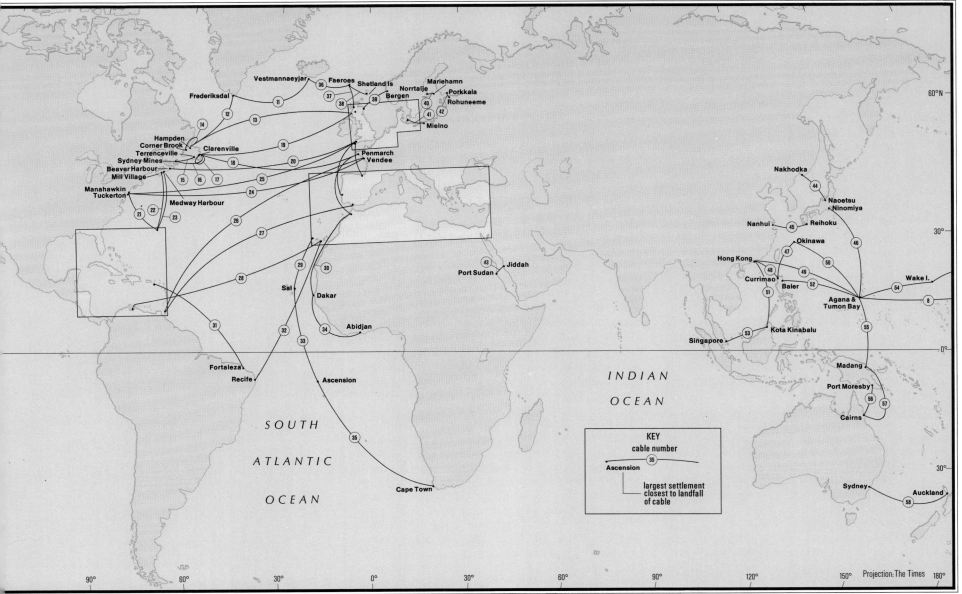

KEY

cable number — **35**

Ascension — largest settlement closest to landfall of cable

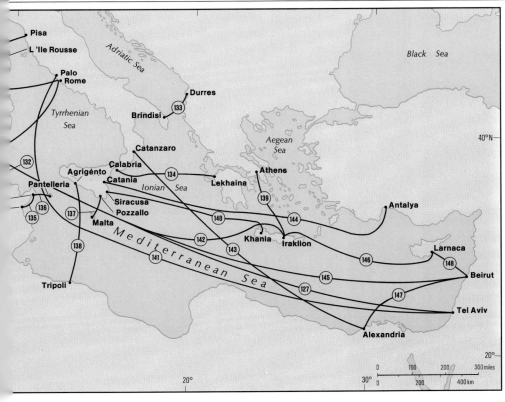

2 *above* Loading cable on to a cableship can take up to three weeks to complete. On board the cable is stowed in circular tanks. In order to keep the cable layers apart, thin pieces of wood are placed between them.

Ocean exploration since 1945

OCEANOGRAPHY has made enormous progress since the end of the Second World War. The era of the great scientific circumnavigations ended with the *Galathea* expedition. Since then, oceanographic cruises have tended to be much shorter, and have usually concentrated on relatively small sea areas which have been studied in much greater detail than was possible during the old expeditions. The numbers of scientists and ships involved in oceanic research has also increased enormously, so that it is much less easy to single out particular significant events.

Along with the more specialised approach there have been major technological advances in both ships and equipment. Although the first purpose-built oceanographic ship was launched as early as 1882, many research vessels before the Second World War had originally been built for fishing, cargo carrying or for military uses. Since the war, most ocean research ships have been designed for the purpose, with specialised winches, cranes, laboratories and navigational equipment. Many of these ships are used for all types of research, including biology, geology, chemistry and physics, but some even more specialised vessels have been constructed. The *Glomar Challenger*, for instance, is specifically designed for drilling into the deep ocean floor and has obtained thousands of deep cores from all parts of the world ocean for studies of submarine geology (see *Deep sea drilling* pages 40–41).

The equipment used on research vessels has also become much more sophisticated in the last few decades. Water sampling bottles, deep-sea thermometers and most biological samplers are basically similar to those used 50 or even 100 years ago, but the modern versions, made of new materials, tend to be more accurate and efficient. Some modern pieces of equipment, however, have no pre-war counterpart since they are based on developments in acoustics and electronics.

Sound is a particularly useful tool for the oceanographer. Since sound waves travel rapidly and efficiently through water they can be used to transmit information to and from a research vessel. The sidescan sonar system scans wide strips of the sea floor on either side of a ship to determine not only the shape of the sea-bed, but also the nature of the sediments and underlying rocks. Sound signals can also be used to monitor or control the behaviour of equipment lowered from or towed behind a ship. Plankton nets, for instance, can be opened and closed by sending a command sound signal, while a monitor on the net itself may transmit information back to the ship, such as its depth beneath the surface, the speed at which it is travelling and the temperature of the water through which it is passing. Since no wires are needed to transmit sound waves, acoustic communication is possible with

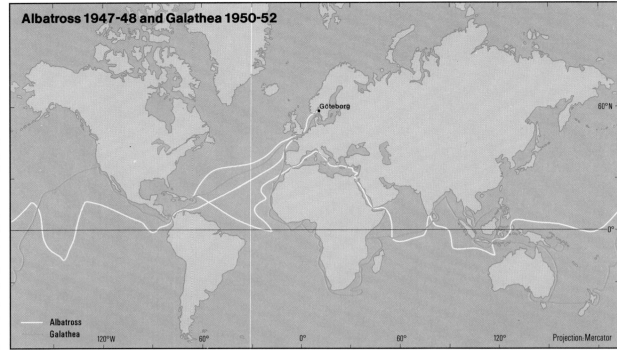

Albatross 1947-48 and Galathea 1950-52

Göteborg · 60°N · 0° · 120°W · 60° · 0° · 60° · 120° · Projection: Mercator

— Albatross
  Galathea

1 *above* The Swedish *Albatross* and the Danish *Galathea* expeditions were the last of the old-style oceanographic circumnavigating voyages. The main aim of the *Albatross* expedition was to study the deep ocean floor by both coring and seismic techniques. Biology was of secondary importance, but the deep-sea winch, which had been specially designed and built for use on the *Albatross*, was subsequently transferred to the *Galathea* and used most successfully to trawl animals from the bottom of the ocean trenches at depths of more than 10 000 metres.

pieces of equipment which are not attached to a ship. Gear can be moored to the sea floor using detachable weights which can be released after deployments lasting weeks or months, allowing the rest of the rig to float to the surface where it is picked up by the oceanographic ship. Deployed equipment may carry sensors which continuously monitor features such as current speed and direction, temperature, salinity and oxygen content, and record these data on magnetic tapes for subsequent analysis in the laboratory. In many cases it is no longer necessary for the research vessel and its scientists to be at sea throughout a sampling period, but only for the deployment and recovery of the recording equipment. These developments allow long term observations which were quite impracticable a few years ago.

With the rapid improvements in satellite technology, many oceanographic observations can now be made without going to sea at all. Moreover, satellites can rapidly cover vast areas which could not possibly be sampled by surface ships (see following pages).

At the other extreme, of course, it is sometimes necessary for the scientist to be as physically

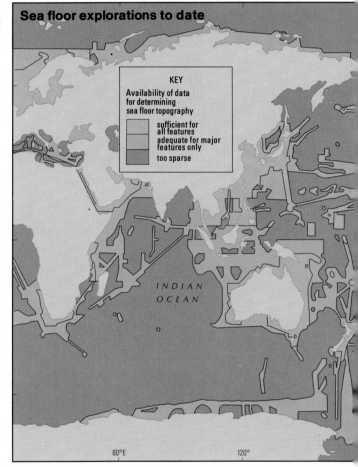

Sea floor explorations to date

KEY
Availability of data for determining sea floor topography
□ sufficient for all features
▨ adequate for major features only
■ too sparse

INDIAN OCEAN

60°E · 120°

close as possible to an area or phenomenon, either to make detailed observations or to carry out delicate manipulations. For these purposes numerous manned submersibles have been developed during the last 20 years, some capable of diving to abyssal depths. Submersibles have been used successfully in all the major oceanographic disciplines, but they have been particularly valuable for deep sea biology. Perhaps their most dramatic use has been in the study of the complex and fascinating communities living around hydrothermal vents, where American and French scientists have conducted detailed observations and experiments which would otherwise have been quite impossible.

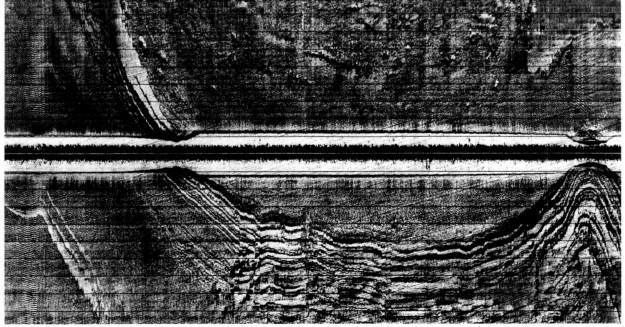

2 *left* The sidescan sonar evolved from the echo sounder principle, but instead of the echo sounder's cone-shaped ultrasonic beam directed vertically at the sea bed, the side scan beam is tilted and fan-shaped, with angles of about 1–2° in the horizontal plane and between 10° and 50° in the vertical plane. By emitting the ultrasonic beam as a series of pulses from a towed cylindrical body (the *towfish*), and scanning to both port and starboard, reflected signals are presented as closely-spaced lines on a graphic recorder, producing an acoustic map (sonograph) of the sea bed. This sonograph illustrates an area of sea bed scanning to 150 m either side of a vessel (the centreline) and showing folded sedimentary rocks outcropping on the sea bed (left and extreme right) surrounded by ripples of sand.

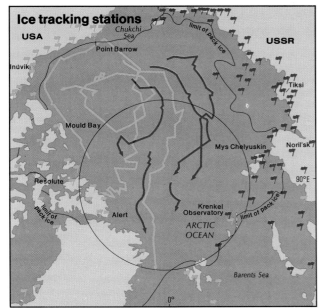

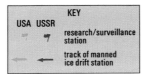

4 *left* From time to time scientists have maintained observations on ice islands (sections of ice-shelf up to 50 m thick and several hundred square km surface area), which drift with the Arctic ice pack. Shown on the map are the tracks of some of these between 1958 and 1975.

3 *below* Bathymetric information from GEBCO maps, supplemented by nautical charts and other maps, shows the present state of our knowledge of the topography of the sea floor to be adequate for 16 per cent of the oceans; sufficient for major features only for 22 per cent; and too sparse to determine for 62 per cent.

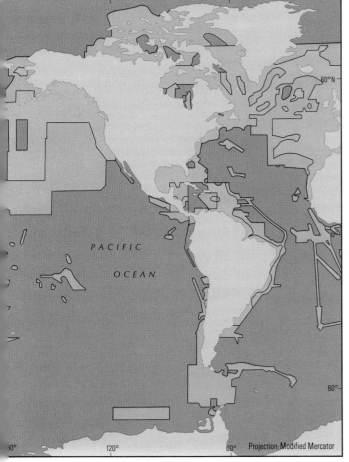

Mapping of the ocean floor

The systematic organisation of national hydrographic services began two centuries ago but in only a few countries. By the beginning of the 20th century, a need for common agreement was recognised on the (then) many methods of chart production. Following the world's first International Hydrographic Conference in 1919, an International Hydrographic Bureau (IHB) was established by 1921, based in Monaco. In 1967, the IHB was renamed the International Hydrographic Organisation (IHO), retaining the term IHB for the Monaco headquarters. At present, IHO comprises 46 member countries.

Production of the General Bathymetric Chart of the Oceans (GEBCO) was suggested first by Prince Albert of Monaco at the 7th International Geographical Congress, Berlin, 1899. In 1903 he assembled a small group of scientists who within seven months produced GEBCO first edition, consisting of 16 sheets on Mercator projection between 72°S and 72°N at a scale of 1:10 000 000, and 8 sheets on gnomonic projection covering the polar regions. The series was based on 18 400 depth measurements from lead-line surveys. A second edition appeared between 1912 and 1927. With the development of the echo sounder during the 1920s, the flood of depth data that became available motivated Prince Albert to ask the IHB to take over the GEBCO programme and a third edition began in 1932.

The science of marine geology expanded rapidly in the immediate post Second World War period, based largely on equipment and techniques researched and developed in wartime. New geological concepts evolved, such as seafloor spreading and plate tectonics. For the first time there was a need for detailed morphological maps of the ocean floor. Apart from detailed localised maps resulting from oceanographic cruises, only nautical charts and GEBCO were available.

The IHB recommended work on the third edition of GEBCO after the war, but still using plotting criteria established in the 1920s. The main item of criticism by geoscientists was the practice of transposing echo sounder profiles into discrete depth measurements, usually taking the shallowest point in the profile to plot the chart. However this method continued to the completion of the third edition in 1955 and when a fourth edition began the same erroneous method was still employed.

In 1970 a working group of the International Oceanographic Commission (IOC) of UNESCO recommended to the parent body that they should participate in the production of world bathymetric maps. In the early 1970s the methodology involved in producing world bathymetric maps was examined by a working group of the Scientific Committee on Oceanic Research (SCOR), and their findings were later endorsed by the GEBCO Guiding Committee. Therefore, it was decided that a 5th edition of GEBCO be developed, published jointly by the IHO and IOC. This latest series was published in 1982 and the maps on pages 16–24 derive from it.

6 *above* Retrieval of the submersible *Cyana* from a foray into the ocean depths. *Cyana* and *Archimede* were the two French submersibles which took part in the joint project FAMOUS (French-American Mid Ocean Undersea Study). *Alvin* was the US Navy's submersible. It was the first time manned submersibles were used in a scientific study of the ocean floor.

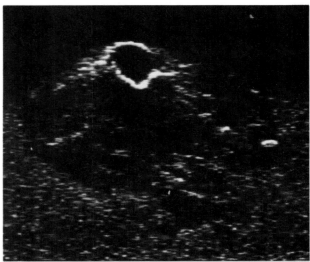

5 *above* Part of an early bathymetric chart showing depth soundings taken in an area of the Pacific Ocean off Mexico, with the island of Socorro (18°45′N, 111°W) top right. The soundings and charts were made under the supervision of the US naval officer Matthew Fontaine Maury between 1820 and 1845.

7 *right above* An undersea volcano observed by GLORIA (see **8**) in the Pacific Ocean. The volcano is 10 km across at its base and stands 1500 m above the sea floor at 4000 m depth.

8 *right centre* The long-range sidescan sonar GLORIA which produces images of areas of sea floor up to 60 km wide, seen here mounted on the stern of RRS *Discovery*, a research vessel of the Natural Environment Research Council's fleet (UK).

9 *right* Depth probe for measuring temperature and salinity.

Space technology and the oceans

SAFE passage in the oceans has always depended on weather, the state of the seas, hazards found in them and the ability to navigate far from land. Not surprisingly, communications, meteorology and navigation were amongst the first to benefit from satellites. Yet, surprisingly, it will be 1990 at the earliest before voice and telex by satellite have replaced morse code by radio, still used for 90 per cent of all ship-to-ship and shore-to-shore communications. Three maritime communications satellites in equatorial orbit can cover almost the whole world. At an altitude of 35 870 km (about 22 300 miles), they are in geo-synchronous orbit, remaining always over the same point on Earth.

Meteorological satellites in similar geo-synchronous orbits can view almost a whole hemisphere, whereas those in polar orbit image the Earth in swaths repetitively, monitoring weather patterns and tracking storms. Their optical and infrared scanners provide data for oceanography. The first needs daylight, the second does not; neither type of scanner can penetrate cloud.

Doppler navigation by satellite came about almost by accident when it was realised that the change in frequency of signals from satellites could give the position of an observer on the ground provided the orbit and the position of the satellite within it could be defined precisely by constant monitoring. Navigation satellites, in operation since 1964, and originally designed for use by Polaris submarines, now provide an accurate, world-wide, all-weather system. Great accuracy is obtained at fixed sites, for example, on shore or at an oil rig.

Almost as soon as satellites began to operate, special satellites in low orbit were employed on military reconnaissance. Their photographic capability steadily improved to the point where very small detail of 3 metres or less was identifiable. Those satellites produce real photographs, the film being returned from space.

Before 1990, it is hoped that Navstar, a greatly improved system, will be in use. At any one time four satellites will be within reception range to give continuous positions at sea to a few metres accuracy. From fixed sites accuracies down to 0.5 m will be possible.

Without question, Landsat has been the most widely used satellite imagery. Although Russian Salyut and Soyuz satellite photography can be of 20 m resolution, it has been little used in oceanography. Before Seasat, oceanography was a neglected science but the next decade promises to rectify the situation. The French 'SPOT' satellite, with resolutions down to 10 m, will be useful for coastal areas; other satellite systems will have special ocean functions. The European Space Agency's ERS1 will operate rather like an improved Seasat and Space Lab will also contribute to ocean studies. India's satellites, first launched in 1978, include ocean surveillance. Japan plans to launch satellites with similar capabilities. Canada, with UK cooperation, will operate a radar satellite designed for arctic and subarctic areas and study of ice.

Geodesy and geodetic satellites

Geodesy is the science of measuring the Earth and defining its shape. Before satellites were used almost all measurements of distance were confined to the land. There was no adequate means of measuring over the 70 per cent of the Earth's surface covered by the Oceans. Neither the amount by which the Earth is flattened at the poles nor the circumference at the equator were known to desired accuracy. However, there was also the need to discover the true shape of the Earth which does not conform exactly to the true geometric figure (a spheroid) to which it approximates.

If the Earth were at rest and the Ocean still, the water surface would not be, as one might expect, smooth and even. It would show hummocks and hollows attaining 100 m height or depth reflecting the uneven pull of gravity due to variation in density of the material of which the Earth is composed. Similar undulations (as they are called) are to be found in the motion of a satellite in orbit since it, too, moves under the influence of the Earth's gravity. But it is also affected by other forces, the attraction of the Moon and the Sun; the outward pressure of solar radiation and atmospheric drag. The resulting perturbations had to be identified and closely monitored, but that required knowledge of the precise locations of the monitoring stations. Hence the need to measure the Earth, and the inception of a geodetic satellite programme.

Geodetic satellites, active (transmitting a signal) or passive were used to determine the relative positions of a network of points covering almost the whole Earth. Active satellites gave the slant range from satellite to three or four ground stations, the position of at least one of which was known. The positions of the other stations were then calculated. The 'doppler principle' was applied to establish from active satellites the positions of further points. Passive satellites were either observed simultaneously from several places on

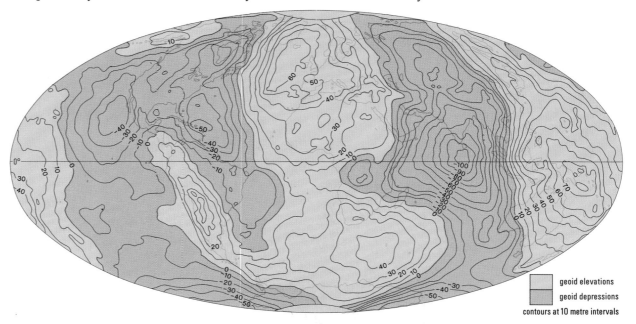

1 *above* The contours of the geoid at 10 m intervals based on the motion of satellites observed up to 1980. Where the geoid rises, gravity is less than its theoretical value, and greater where the geoid descends below the zero contour.

geoid elevations
geoid depressions
contours at 10 metre intervals

Earth or else photographed at night against the star background. By those means the Earth was found to be less flattened at the poles and almost 1.5 km smaller in equatorial circumference than had been assumed. In addition, the undulations of the geoid (the theoretical mean sea surface) were mapped over the continents and, less precisely, over the oceans. By monitoring satellite motions over a long period of time undulations over ocean areas were deduced more fully.

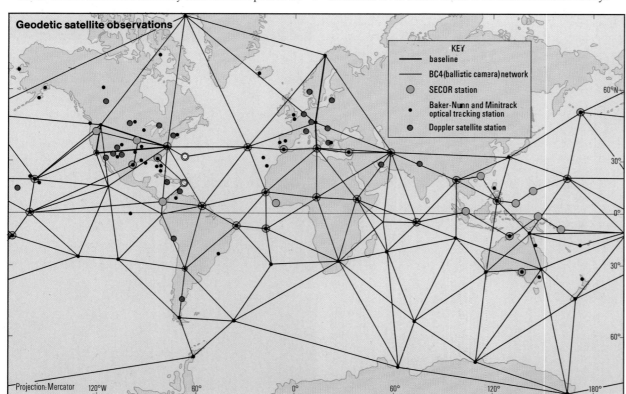

Geodetic satellite observations

KEY
— baseline
— BC4 (ballistic camera) network
○ SECOR station
· Baker-Nunn and Minitrack optical tracking station
● Doppler satellite station

Projection: Mercator

2 *left* Several kinds of satellite observation and other data were used in the measurement of the Earth. At various points ballistic cameras photographed satellites to create a world-wide geometric network of inter-related positions. Certain-accurately determined distances served as base-lines. A belt of SECOR (sequential observation of range) stations was established to girdle the Earth in the equatorial region. Various stellar cameras were used to photograph satellites against the stars of the night sky. Doppler observation of satellites added still further points. Finally all available measured gravity data was incorporated in the computations. The results showed the Earth to be of 6378.135 km radius at the equator and to be flattened at the poles in the ratio 1:298.25 of the equatorial radius. The accurate measurement of the Earth meant that exact distances across Oceans and locations of remote islands could be determined for the first time.

4 *right* Military reconnaissance satellites include photographic satellites operating in near-polar orbit to carry out area surveillance or 'close-look' photography of points of special interest. Capsules containing the high-resolution film are ejected to be recovered from the ocean after splash-down but more usually to be scooped out of the air at an altitude of about 15 km by a C-130 aircraft or a helicopter. Since the first launchings in 1959, the life of US satellites of this kind has increased from a few days to almost a year, a fact which is reflected in the reduced number of launchings each year. The orbit of the majority of Big Bird reconnaissance satellites is approximately 150 to 160 km perigee to 280 to 350 km apogee, but some operate in higher orbits.

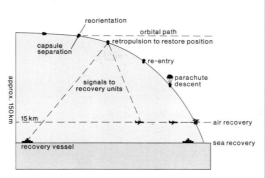

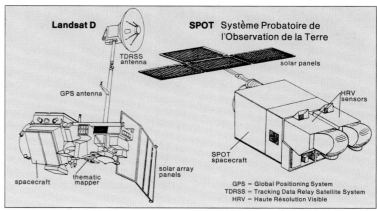

The Landsat series and Seasat

The US Landsat series of satellites designed to monitor Earth resources began to operate in 1972. Landsat 1, 2 and 3 transmitted images in digital form to obviate the need for collection and resupply of photographic materials. Operating from 930 km altitude, imagery was collected in different parts of the spectrum to help differentiate land–water boundaries, vegetation and thermal properties, for example. Of interest to oceanography were the disclosure of sandbanks, effluent from the land, ice formation and movement and concentrations of phytoplankton.

Landsat D, launched in July 1982 and operating at 730 km altitude, has a resolution of 30 m compared with the earlier Landsat 80 m resolution. As with its predecessors ocean data is rather limited; cloud is the major obstacle to the acquisition of such imagery.

Seasat, the first satellite dedicated to oceanography, was launched in 1978 but mechanical failure ended its operation after only 100 days. The need to observe the transient phenomena of the oceans repetitively requires a system not dependent on weather or daylight. Seasat was essentially a radar satellite. Its radar altimeter was capable of measuring mean wave height to about 50 cm, about the best possible from a vessel at

6 *above right* The latest satellite in the Landsat series, and the new French 'SPOT' satellite which will have particular application for coastal areas.

7.1 *right upper* Landsat colour composite of The Gulf near Abu Dhabi.

7.2 *right lower* The same scene after composite enhancement of the imagery revealing detail of the seabed quite invisible in the unenhanced imagery.

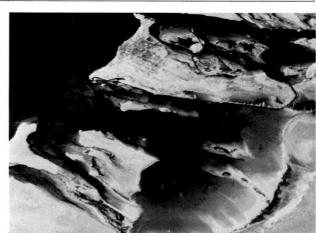

sea. Other devices permitted the measuring of surface roughness (the small waves produced by wind on the main waves) down to 2 cm, and an instrument for measuring surface temperature. A synthetic aperture radar supplied images much like an ordinary aerial photograph.

From Seasat wind speeds could be deduced to within 10 per cent of true speed, and direction to within 20°. It also gave surface temperature, atmospheric humidity, age and character of ice, pattern of waves and ocean currents; identification of oil and biological slicks and other ocean phenomena. It thereby set the pattern for its successors.

8 *below right* Satellite imagery is one of the tools for the monitoring of pollution. In this Landsat image of the Red Sea an oil slick shows up as a purplish area (bottom edge).

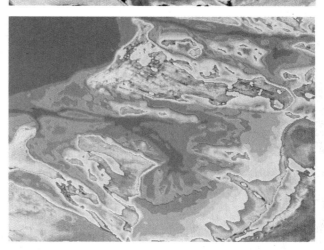

3 *opposite left* False colour composite of three bands (4, 5 and 6) of Landsat multispectral scanner (MSS) showing traces of blue-green algae in the Baltic Sea east of the Danish islands Mon and Falster. In July and August, blue-green algae (*Aphanizomenon flos acquae* and *Nodularia spumigena*) float to the surface when the sea is calm enough, to form chains up to 100 m long. Enhancement of the image to emphasise the algae appearance has resulted in the sandbanks appearing in blue.

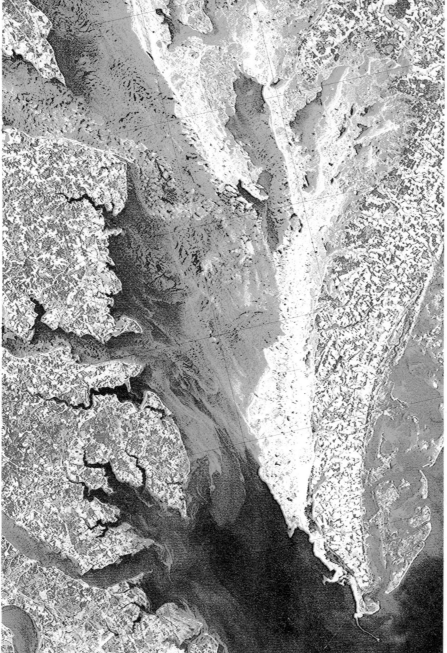

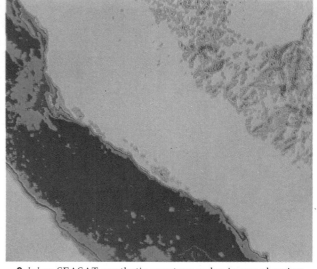

9 *below* SEASAT synthetic aperture radar image showing how sea patterns are affected by land (in this case an island). Radar images are not dependent on weather or cloud conditions. Images of this type can be acquired at night or through thick cloud.

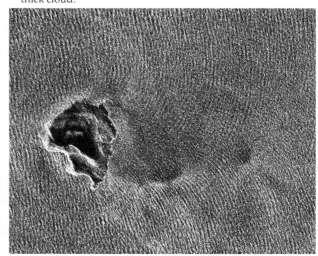

5 *right* A Landsat image of Chesapeake Bay just before the thaw in the coldest winter on record, February 1977. Ice has drifted up to 50 miles into the Atlantic. Thin ice has a greenish appearance. Older ice appears light blue to white, reflecting more light from its broken or snow-covered surface.

International ocean research

THE worldwide scale and breadth of ocean research has grown as the uses of the sea have multiplied and intensified, and it has now entered the league of 'big science' undertakings. The direction and purpose of this vast research effort have also changed in emphasis. Although the purely scientific investigations of the ocean sciences, exemplified by the famous research voyages, still occupy an important role, the emphasis is increasingly upon knowledge which can be applied to the management of ocean resources and the environment, including the promotion of safety at sea.

The principal organisational elements in the system of research are the national research laboratories and institutes, international agencies with regional and global responsibilities—especially those affiliated to the United Nations—and the marine industries. National organisations form the foundations of this panoply, and are particularly concerned with surveying for navigation and defence, with maintenance of capability in the ocean sciences, and with fisheries research and management. Much of the detailed mineral exploration is carried out by the oil and mining industries.

The nature of the marine environment and the massive scale of ocean research requires international and indeed often global approaches. The process of internationalisation began with the establishment of the International Council for the Exploration of the Sea (ICES) in 1902. Based in Copenhagen, it was the first body of its kind, and was concerned with biological and oceanographic research directed particularly to fisheries management. ICES has remained influential in this field. The scale of research now extends beyond specialist international organisations to planned global research programmes. Some, such as the International Decade of Ocean

Exploration (IDOE) are specifically focused upon the ocean environment. Others, such as the International Biological Programme (IBP), and the World Climate Research Programme (WCRP) have significant maritime components. The huge amount of data generated by these co-ordinated programmes has necessitated setting up extensive worldwide networks of data bases in order to monitor, control and disseminate information to scientists and policymakers.

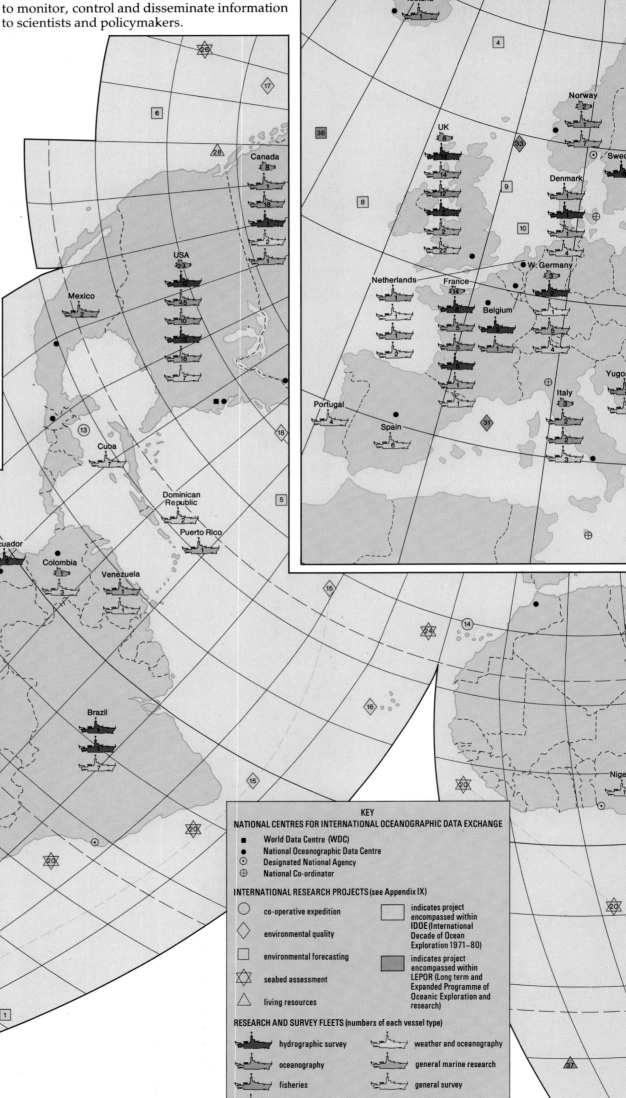

Research fleets and projects

KEY

NATIONAL CENTRES FOR INTERNATIONAL OCEANOGRAPHIC DATA EXCHANGE

- ■ World Data Centre (WDC)
- ● National Oceanographic Data Centre
- ⊙ Designated National Agency
- ⊕ National Co-ordinator

INTERNATIONAL RESEARCH PROJECTS (see Appendix IX)

- ◯ co-operative expedition
- ◇ environmental quality
- ▢ environmental forecasting
- ✡ seabed assessment
- △ living resources

- ▢ indicates project encompassed within IDOE (International Decade of Ocean Exploration 1971–80)
- ▨ indicates project encompassed within LEPOR (Long term and Expanded Programme of Oceanic Exploration and research)

RESEARCH AND SURVEY FLEETS (numbers of each vessel type)

- hydrographic survey
- oceanography
- fisheries
- geophysical
- weather and oceanography
- general marine research
- general survey
- submersible vessel

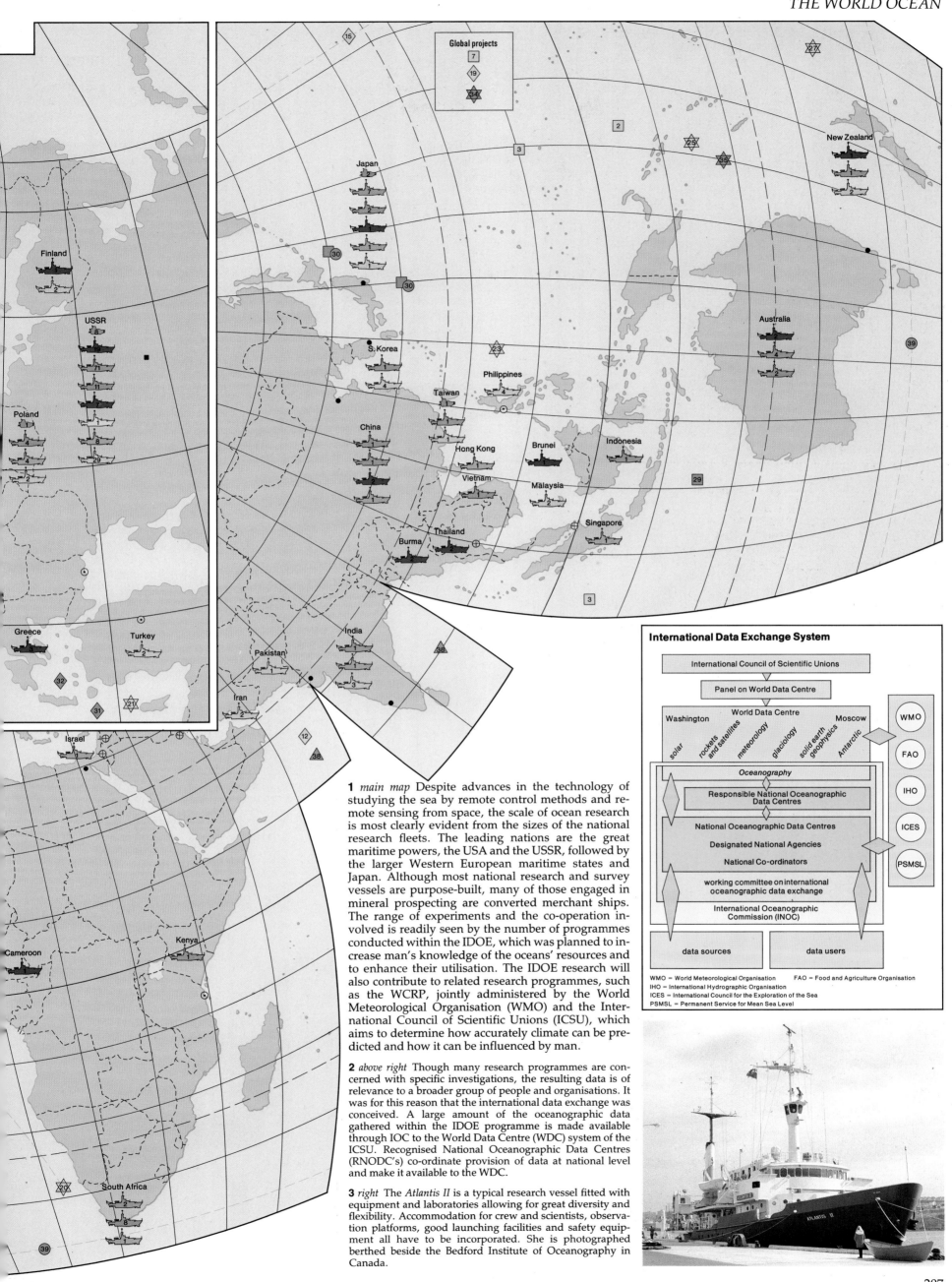

Global projects

New Zealand

Japan

Finland

USSR

Poland

S. Korea

Philippines

Taiwan

Australia

Greece

Turkey

China

Hong Kong

Brunei

Indonesia

Vietnam

Malaysia

India

Pakistan

Thailand

Singapore

Burma

Iran

Israel

Cameroon

Kenya

South Africa

International Data Exchange System

International Council of Scientific Unions

Panel on World Data Centre

Washington **World Data Centre** Moscow

solar | rockets and satellites | meteorology | glaciology | solid earth geophysics | Antarctic

Oceanography

Responsible National Oceanographic Data Centres

National Oceanographic Data Centres

Designated National Agencies

National Co-ordinators

working committee on international oceanographic data exchange

International Oceanographic Commission (INOC)

data sources | data users

WMO

FAO

IHO

ICES

PSMSL

WMO = World Meteorological Organisation FAO = Food and Agriculture Organisation
IHO = International Hydrographic Organisation
ICES = International Council for the Exploration of the Sea
PSMSL = Permanent Service for Mean Sea Level

1 *main map* Despite advances in the technology of studying the sea by remote control methods and remote sensing from space, the scale of ocean research is most clearly evident from the sizes of the national research fleets. The leading nations are the great maritime powers, the USA and the USSR, followed by the larger Western European maritime states and Japan. Although most national research and survey vessels are purpose-built, many of those engaged in mineral prospecting are converted merchant ships. The range of experiments and the co-operation involved is readily seen by the number of programmes conducted within the IDOE, which was planned to increase man's knowledge of the oceans' resources and to enhance their utilisation. The IDOE research will also contribute to related research programmes, such as the WCRP, jointly administered by the World Meteorological Organisation (WMO) and the International Council of Scientific Unions (ICSU), which aims to determine how accurately climate can be predicted and how it can be influenced by man.

2 *above right* Though many research programmes are concerned with specific investigations, the resulting data is of relevance to a broader group of people and organisations. It was for this reason that the international data exchange was conceived. A large amount of the oceanographic data gathered within the IDOE programme is made available through IOC to the World Data Centre (WDC) system of the ICSU. Recognised National Oceanographic Data Centres (RNODC's) co-ordinate provision of data at national level and make it available to the WDC.

3 *right* The *Atlantis II* is a typical research vessel fitted with equipment and laboratories allowing for great diversity and flexibility. Accommodation for crew and scientists, observation platforms, good launching facilities and safety equipment all have to be incorporated. She is photographed berthed beside the Bedford Institute of Oceanography in Canada.

The problems of multiple sea use

WITHIN any area of the ocean are habitats containing a mass of life forms. Many of them are highly mobile, and all of them have complex ecological relationships. Also, each sea area has its own identity in terms of its biology, its climatic conditions and its geographical and political situation. With the industrialisation of the world, man's activities have an ever growing impact upon the sea. Some of these activities seriously deplete ocean life; others threaten fragile habitats; many activities are in conflict with one another. The need to manage sea use in the interest of the ocean environment and to the best advantage for present and future generations has been recognised for many decades, but the concept of management belongs largely to the years since 1945. Earlier attempts at management consisted, for the most part, in formulation of laws to govern maritime activities such as navigation and coastal fisheries. In the days of sail and early steamships, the casualty rate and loss of life were very high. Navigational safety became a priority and from the 19th and early 20th centuries there were introduced collision avoidance rules, loadline rules, provision of lighthouse services, buoyage systems, improvements in pilotage, coastguard and lifeboat services, as well as safety regulations applied to ship design. After the Second World War came radio-position fixing networks and radar, then satellite navigation systems, improvement of hydrographic surveying, ship routeing schemes and legislation governing pollution from ships. Also, with the aid of an international legal framework and fishery commissions, some steps were taken to deal with the widespread problems of over-fishing, particularly in the North Atlantic and North Pacific.

More recently, the enclosure of areas of the sea by coastal states within 200-mile zones has been the principal means of establishing resource rights and controlling pollution from land and vessels, and providing a better basis for managing alternative uses of the national sea areas, including legislation to control the location and rate of exploration and exploitation of offshore hydrocarbon resources.

The priority aims of sea use management include: the reconciliation of conflicting uses, the maximising of yields from living resources commensurate with their conservation, the preservation of endangered marine species, and the protection of fragile ecosystems. Sea use management may also include the social dimensions of ensuring improvements in the livelihoods of those dependent on the sea in certain sea regions. The concept of sea use management is not, however, widely adopted due to the difficulties of coordinating activities between opposite and adjacent states. But even within national sea areas problems of cooperation between the various departments dealing with the sea may prove difficult. In many countries maritime administration is conducted within land departments; fisheries, for example, are often grouped with agriculture and forestry, marine hydrocarbons under energy, and shipping under transport.

Among the Western European states only France has completely reorganised its maritime administration to form a Ministry of the Sea (see *The European seas* page 214). In large federal states difficulty may arise in defining federal and state responsibilities for marine affairs. A particular problem for developing countries is finding sufficient administrative resources to cope with the continuing seaward extension of maritime jurisdiction.

The role of international bodies, notably agencies affiliated to the United Nations, such as the United Nations Environment Programme (UNEP), the International Maritime Organisation (IMO), and the Food and Agricultural Organisation (FAO), is complex and wide-ranging. Defence is arguably the most organised both nationally and internationally, primarily through NATO and the Warsaw Pact. Marine research is also extensively co-ordinated through international agencies.

Sea use management requires clear objectives, good research, multi-disciplinary approaches, and usually some structural changes in administration, or at least good methods of accessing diverse data under a strong coordinating team. The skills involved vary from biology to diplomacy.

The need to approach the use of the sea in a holistic way is particularly apparent in coastal waters where conflicting uses are most acute. The matrix shows the main conflicts which can arise. Too often, short term expediency for immediate gains overrides long term planning, to the detriment of many users and resources and the environment itself. The international and regional examples provided in this section highlight these problems and some of the solutions.

Global marine interactions

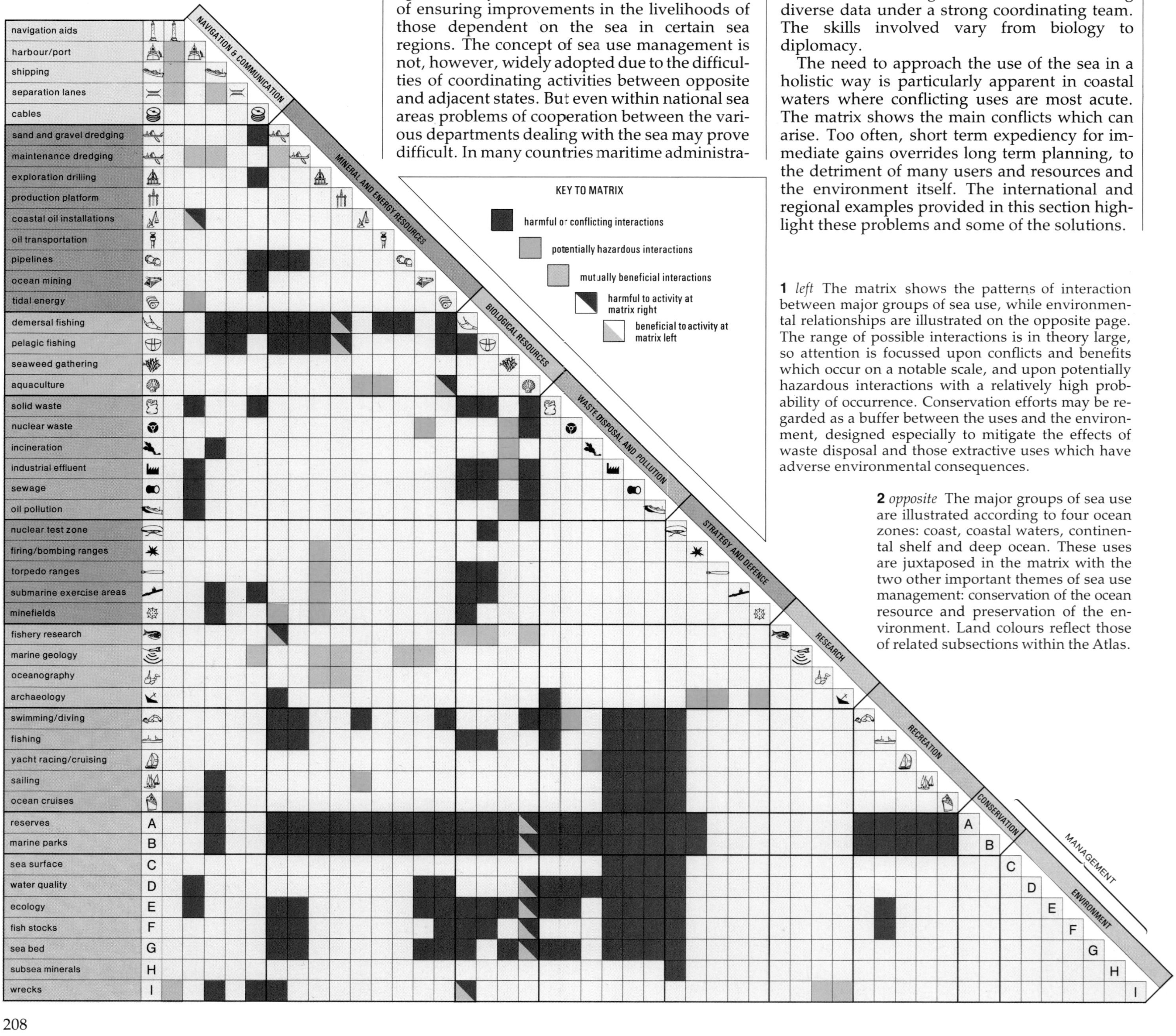

navigation aids
harbour/port
shipping
separation lanes
cables
sand and gravel dredging
maintenance dredging
exploration drilling
production platform
coastal oil installations
oil transportation
pipelines
ocean mining
tidal energy
demersal fishing
pelagic fishing
seaweed gathering
aquaculture
solid waste
nuclear waste
incineration
industrial effluent
sewage
oil pollution
nuclear test zone
firing/bombing ranges
torpedo ranges
submarine exercise areas
minefields
fishery research
marine geology
oceanography
archaeology
swimming/diving
fishing
yacht racing/cruising
sailing
ocean cruises
reserves A
marine parks B
sea surface C
water quality D
ecology E
fish stocks F
sea bed G
subsea minerals H
wrecks I
NAVIGATION & COMMUNICATION
MINERAL AND ENERGY RESOURCES
BIOLOGICAL RESOURCES
WASTE DISPOSAL AND POLLUTION
STRATEGY AND DEFENCE
RESEARCH
RECREATION
CONSERVATION
ENVIRONMENT
MANAGEMENT
KEY TO MATRIX
harmful or conflicting interactions
potentially hazardous interactions
mutually beneficial interactions
harmful to activity at matrix right
beneficial to activity at matrix left

1 *left* The matrix shows the patterns of interaction between major groups of sea use, while environmental relationships are illustrated on the opposite page. The range of possible interactions is in theory large, so attention is focussed upon conflicts and benefits which occur on a notable scale, and upon potentially hazardous interactions with a relatively high probability of occurrence. Conservation efforts may be regarded as a buffer between the uses and the environment, designed especially to mitigate the effects of waste disposal and those extractive uses which have adverse environmental consequences.

2 *opposite* The major groups of sea use are illustrated according to four ocean zones: coast, coastal waters, continental shelf and deep ocean. These uses are juxtaposed in the matrix with the two other important themes of sea use management: conservation of the ocean resource and preservation of the environment. Land colours reflect those of related subsections within the Atlas.

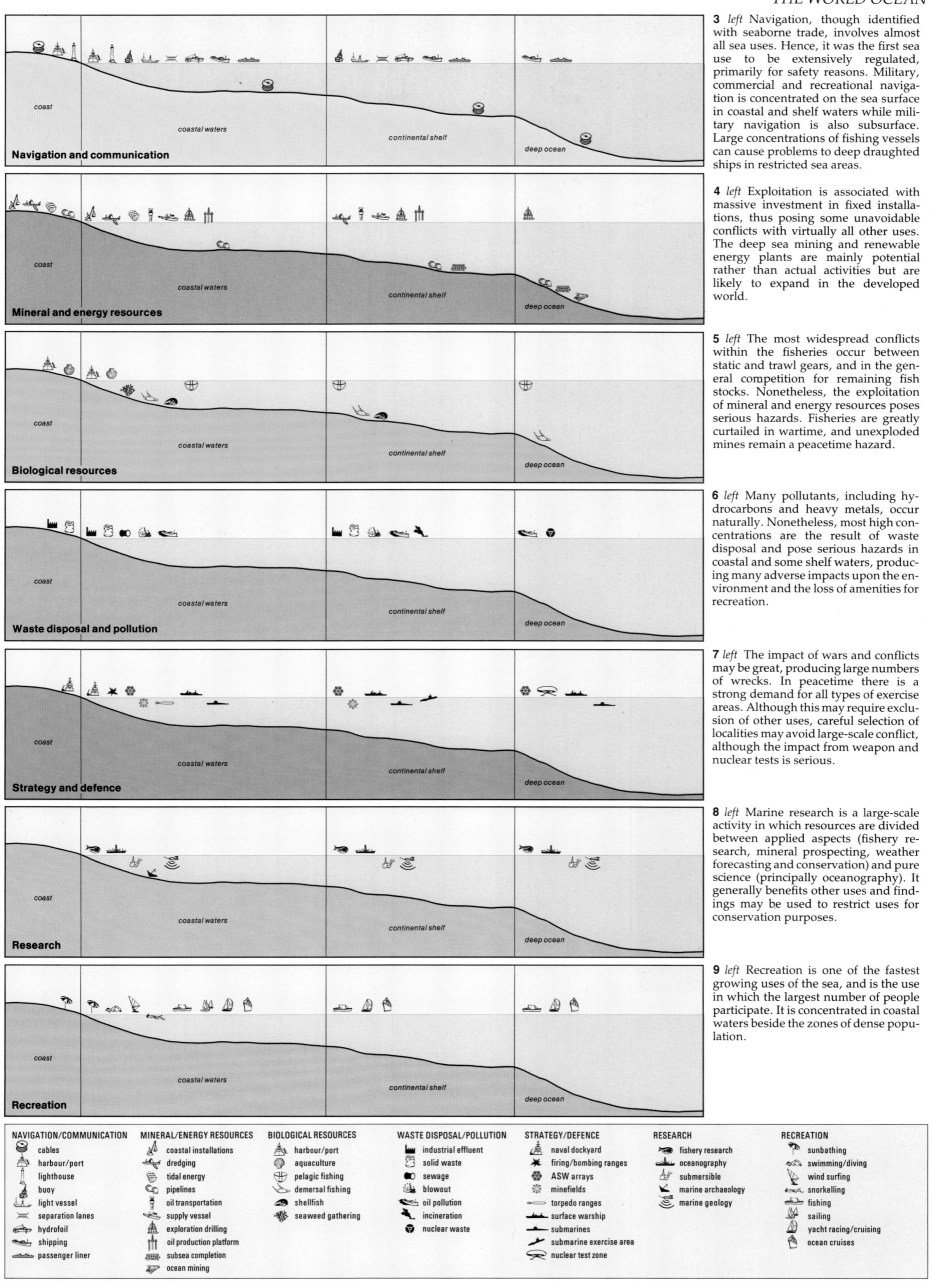

Navigation and communication

3 *left* Navigation, though identified with seaborne trade, involves almost all sea uses. Hence, it was the first sea use to be extensively regulated, primarily for safety reasons. Military, commercial and recreational navigation is concentrated on the sea surface in coastal and shelf waters while military navigation is also subsurface. Large concentrations of fishing vessels can cause problems to deep draughted ships in restricted sea areas.

Mineral and energy resources

4 *left* Exploitation is associated with massive investment in fixed installations, thus posing some unavoidable conflicts with virtually all other uses. The deep sea mining and renewable energy plants are mainly potential rather than actual activities but are likely to expand in the developed world.

Biological resources

5 *left* The most widespread conflicts within the fisheries occur between static and trawl gears, and in the general competition for remaining fish stocks. Nonetheless, the exploitation of mineral and energy resources poses serious hazards. Fisheries are greatly curtailed in wartime, and unexploded mines remain a peacetime hazard.

Waste disposal and pollution

6 *left* Many pollutants, including hydrocarbons and heavy metals, occur naturally. Nonetheless, most high concentrations are the result of waste disposal and pose serious hazards in coastal and some shelf waters, producing many adverse impacts upon the environment and the loss of amenities for recreation.

Strategy and defence

7 *left* The impact of wars and conflicts may be great, producing large numbers of wrecks. In peacetime there is a strong demand for all types of exercise areas. Although this may require exclusion of other uses, careful selection of localities may avoid large-scale conflict, although the impact from weapon and nuclear tests is serious.

Research

8 *left* Marine research is a large-scale activity in which resources are divided between applied aspects (fishery research, mineral prospecting, weather forecasting and conservation) and pure science (principally oceanography). It generally benefits other uses and findings may be used to restrict uses for conservation purposes.

Recreation

9 *left* Recreation is one of the fastest growing uses of the sea, and is the use in which the largest number of people participate. It is concentrated in coastal waters beside the zones of dense population.

NAVIGATION/COMMUNICATION	MINERAL/ENERGY RESOURCES	BIOLOGICAL RESOURCES	WASTE DISPOSAL/POLLUTION	STRATEGY/DEFENCE	RESEARCH	RECREATION
cables	coastal installations	harbour/port	industrial effluent	naval dockyard	fishery research	sunbathing
harbour/port	dredging	aquaculture	solid waste	firing/bombing ranges	oceanography	swimming/diving
lighthouse	tidal energy	pelagic fishing	sewage	ASW arrays	submersible	wind surfing
buoy	pipelines	demersal fishing	blowout	minefields	marine archaeology	snorkelling
light vessel	oil transportation	shellfish	oil pollution	torpedo ranges	marine geology	fishing
separation lanes	supply vessel	seaweed gathering	incineration	surface warship		sailing
hydrofoil	exploration drilling		nuclear waste	submarines		yacht racing/cruising
shipping	oil production platform			submarine exercise area		ocean cruises
passenger liner	subsea completion			nuclear test zone		
	ocean mining					

Conservation of ocean species and habitats

CONSERVING the biological structure of the oceans has become one of the leading issues in sea use management. Not only the living resources, which are such an important source of protein, but also the numerous endangered species and the fragile ecosystems in which the Ocean's populations live must now be encompassed within management schemes if they are to survive. Such schemes rely on good scientific data and research relating to the natural environment, and their analysis must take into account human requirements for food, minerals, employment, and recreation.

The most significant global developments include the FAO statistical system for fisheries and its related regional data base organisations, the inception of the EEZ of coastal states, and the UNEP for regional seas. Integrated multiple use management on a regional basis is still in its infancy. There is some application of it in the developed world though planning and management is also clearly visible in the warm temperate and tropical seas of the developing world under the direct influence of the FAO fisheries development programme and the UNEP regional seas programme.

The tropical and subtropical seas of the Indo-Pacific areas are prime targets for conservation management. Here is the world's largest archipelagic area and conservation management must take account of the fragile tropical island ecosystems as well as the open sea. In the East Asian archipelagos there is concern for the impact of offshore oil development and the dangers posed by tanker routes. The main ecosystems at risk include mangrove swamps, coral reefs, turtle nurseries, prawn fishing areas, and areas used in the production of algae. In Indonesia, protected areas have been designated for the conservation of marine turtles, seabirds and waders' habitats and dugongs.

Until recently, access to fishing areas was normally free with no restriction on catches. Under such a regime, the incentive was to maximise the individual catch. The resulting overfishing was reflected in the declining size and quality of catches, so that more effort and capital were expended to try and maintain the maximum levels. The need to reduce fishing effort to allow stocks to recover, and to establish a balanced level of effort, has long been recognised, if ignored. The

methods now used to regulate fisheries include closed areas and seasons, restrictions on gear (such as increased mesh sizes for nets to allow young fish to escape), quotas, and licensing a country to enter another country's EEZ. The last two have become popular as a means of barring competition from overseas fishing fleets. Some measures, particularly those that concern quotas, tend to lead to inefficiency and waste of capital as expensive boats and equipment may spend much time laid up in port.

Exploitation is not the only cause of decline in populations. In addition, many species have reached critical levels due to damage to or pollution of habitats, competition from other species (arising from exploitation), and the introduction of alien species. Some marine species have become extinct in modern times, notably the great auk and very likely the Caribbean monk seal; many others are on the endangered list.

1 *main map* The main classes of endangered species are the great whales, certain of the small whales, seals, sirenians, turtles, some fishes, and a range of seabirds including petrels, shearwaters, gulls and terns. The awareness that species are endangered has served to focus attention upon the wider issue of ecosystems. The destruction of these might arise through pollution, fishing, land reclamation, or industrial development. Conservation has been directed principally towards the more fragile areas, notably the Arctic and Antarctic, the coral reef habitats and the coastal wetlands.

2 *opposite* International fisheries commissions have been responsible for managing stocks in the high seas, particularly wide-ranging oceanic pelagic stocks such as tuna and whales. Other commissions are organised on a regional basis, but now with the advent of EEZs, the greater proportion of both demersal and pelagic stocks have been transferred from common property to coastal state resources, thus increasing the state's influence over their exploitation.

3 *above* A manatee (*Trichechus inungnis*) from the Amazon. This inoffensive mammal, related to the dugong in the Far East, is hunted only by man and faces possible extinction. It is now protected in many areas.

4 *below* The loggerhead turtle (*Caretta caretta*), like other sea turtles, digs a nest on land to bury eggs for incubation. In areas which have become overrun by tourists loggerhead populations have declined sharply.

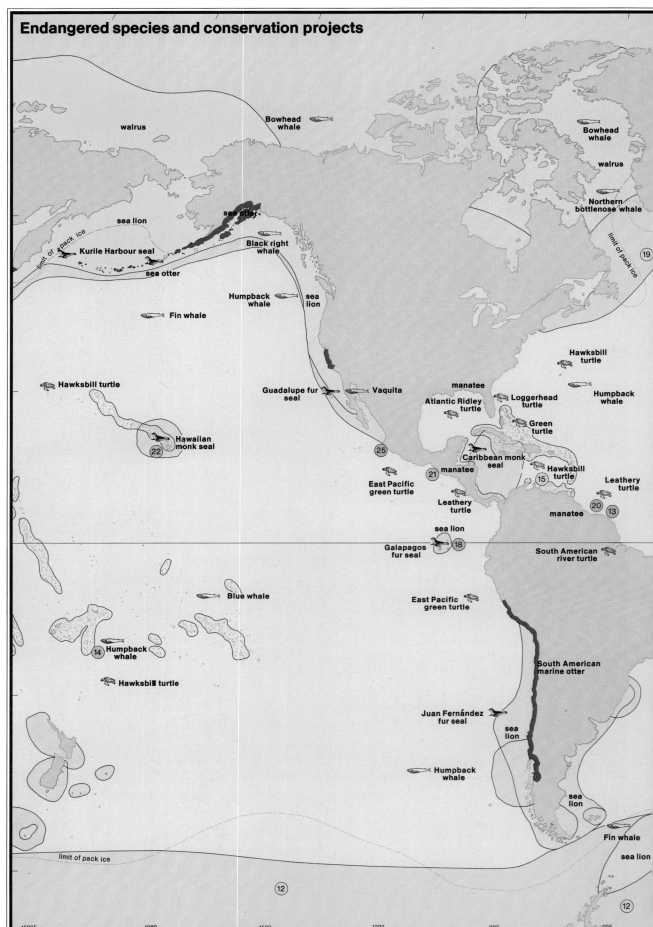

Endangered species and conservation projects

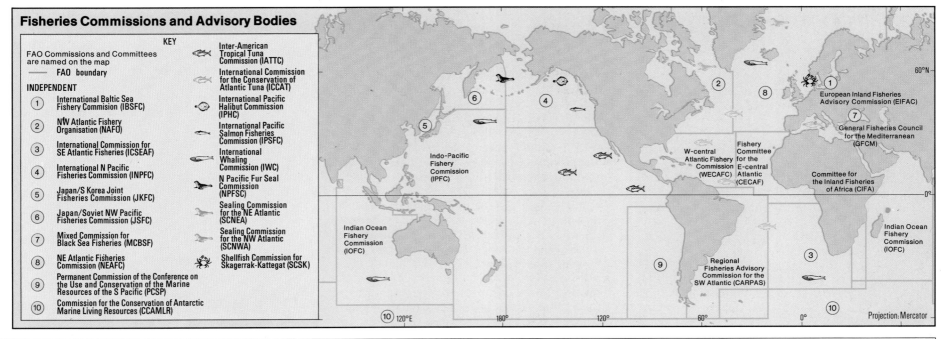

Fisheries Commissions and Advisory Bodies

KEY

FAO Commissions and Committees are named on the map

— FAO boundary

INDEPENDENT

1. International Baltic Sea Fishery Commission (IBSFC)
2. NW Atlantic Fishery Organisation (NAFO)
3. International Commission for SE Atlantic Fisheries (ICSEAF)
4. International N Pacific Fisheries Commission (INPFC)
5. Japan/S Korea Joint Fisheries Commission (JKFC)
6. Japan/Soviet NW Pacific Fisheries Commission (JSFC)
7. Mixed Commission for Black Sea Fisheries (MCBSF)
8. NE Atlantic Fisheries Commission (NEAFC)
9. Permanent Commission of the Conference on the Use and Conservation of the Marine Resources of the S Pacific (PCSP)
10. Commission for the Conservation of Antarctic Marine Living Resources (CCAMLR)

- Inter-American Tropical Tuna Commission (IATTC)
- International Commission for the Conservation of Atlantic Tuna (ICCAT)
- International Pacific Halibut Commission (IPHC)
- International Pacific Salmon Fisheries Commission (IPSFC)
- International Whaling Commission (IWC)
- N Pacific Fur Seal Commission (NPFSC)
- Sealing Commission for the NE Atlantic (SCNEA)
- Sealing Commission for the NW Atlantic (SCNWA)
- Shellfish Commission for Skagerrak-Kattegat (SCSK)

Projection: Mercator

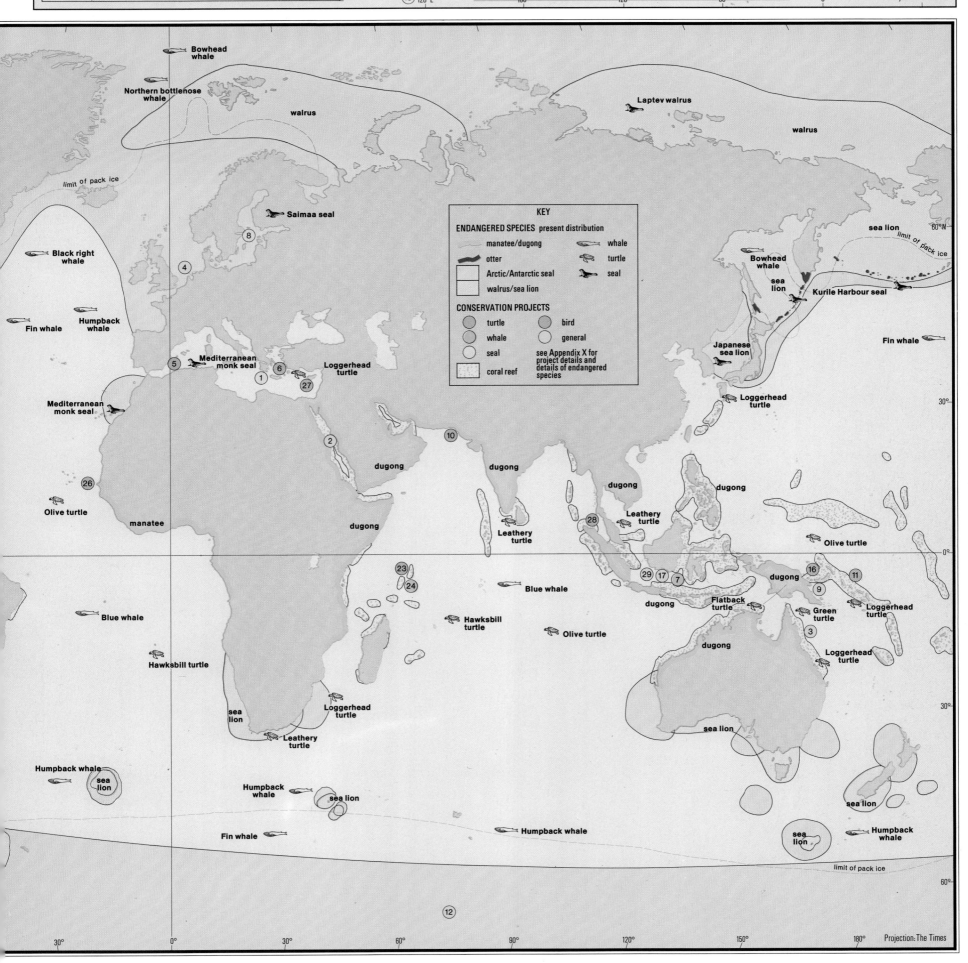

KEY

ENDANGERED SPECIES present distribution

- manatee/dugong
- otter
- Arctic/Antarctic seal
- walrus/sea lion
- whale
- turtle
- seal

CONSERVATION PROJECTS

- turtle
- whale
- seal
- coral reef
- bird
- general

see Appendix X for project details and details of endangered species

Projection: The Times

Conservation of special areas

Great Barrier Reef region

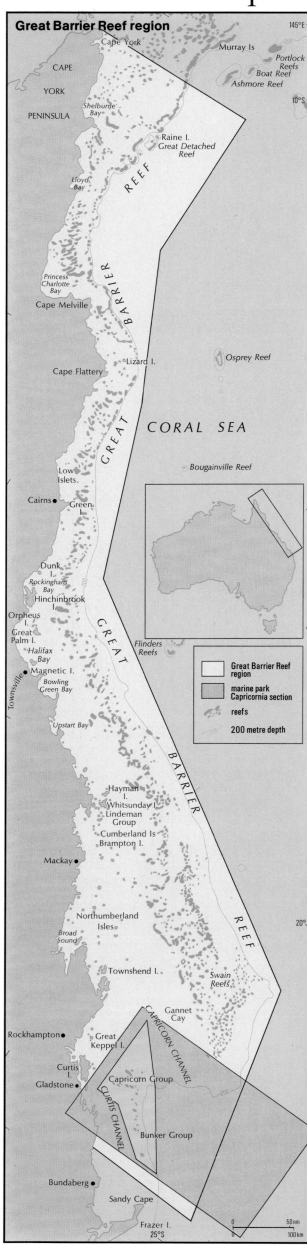

THE geographical scale of a special area depends on the nature of what is being conserved and may range from individual natural features, through large-scale national parks, to international regional seas.

The increasing use of the sea and the marked movements of populations and industries to coastal locations have placed marine environments under stress. In estuaries there is severe competition between human activities and the intricate web of marine life. On tropical coasts, delicate mangrove swamps are part of a complex ecosystem, while coral reefs are even more fragile and are rich habitats for myriad life forms.

Some of the strongest impacts of man's activities on marine life are to be found in the USA. Dense populations and advanced economic development on the eastern seaboard, the southern coasts and California have placed marine environments under considerable stress. The coastal wetlands, for example, offer ideal locations for recreation, settlement and industry, but nursery grounds for the important menhaden and shrimp stocks are situated here and need to be protected.

To ensure survival, these special areas require fewer people and less use, and reconciling these conflicts is a basic management task. Chesapeake Bay is a productive estuary in an industrial area with formidable management problems. The Caribbean, by contrast, is the home to populations of many developing island states and also a recreational zone for more distant areas; the Great Barrier Reef exemplifies planning to ensure preservation of a unique ecosystem while allowing a diversity of human activities.

The Great Barrier Reef

The Great Barrier Reef has been referred to as the largest living feature on Earth and was clearly visible from the Moon. It actually consists of some 2500 individual reefs and includes some 400 species of coral and 1500 species of fish, making it the world's largest and most complex expanse of living coral reefs to emerge in post glacial time. Before conservation measures were taken, the Reef was threatened by recreation, localised pollution and the possibility of large-scale oil prospecting and exploitation.

The Barrier Reef marine park is being developed in sections, beginning with Capricornia and Cairns. The Capricornia Section, for example, is divided into zones in order to control the impact of human activities. There are small preservation zones designed to conserve natural ecosystems and protect turtle and bird nesting sites. In scientific research zones, collecting and recreation are forbidden. In other zones only recreation is allowed. Further zones control commercial fishing.

1 and **2** *left and below* The Great Barrier marine park extends for over 2000 km. The Capricornia section, at the southern end, has been divided into zones to limit human interference.

3 *above* A SCUBA diver equipped with an underwater camera and flash unit examines part of the Great Barrier Reef around Heron Island. Many amateur divers enjoy their recreational diving more by contributing observations and assisting in programmed scientific projects, especially in biological and archaeological surveys.

Caribbean

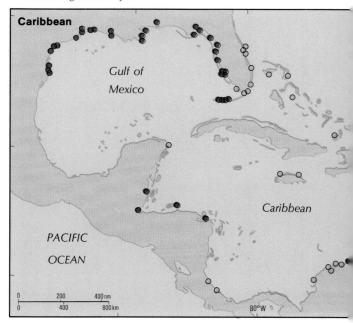

Capricornia section

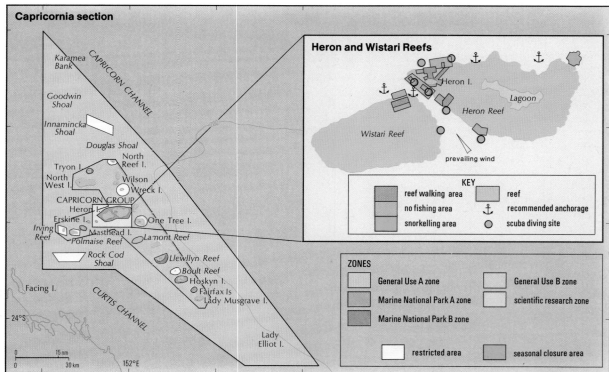

Heron and Wistari Reefs

KEY

reef walking area	reef
no fishing area	⚓ recommended anchorage
snorkelling area	○ scuba diving site

ZONES

General Use A zone	General Use B zone
Marine National Park A zone	scientific research zone
Marine National Park B zone	
restricted area	seasonal closure area

Chesapeake Bay

Chesapeake Bay, the largest estuary in the United States, covers an area of some 5250 sq. km. Bounded by the states of Maryland and Virginia, the bay measures approximately 304 km in length, and 5 to 36 km in width. It drains a region encompassing 105 037 sq. km and six states, and over 10 million people live within a radius of 80 km of the bay.

It contains one of the most productive marine ecosystems in the world. It is generally shallow, providing an environment in which large volumes of plant material are produced through photosynthesis. It has extensive beds of aquatic vegetation and is bounded by broad expanses of wetlands. The productive ecosystem supports a substantial commercial fishing industry and the bay is best known for its oysters and blue crabs. More than a quarter of the nation's oyster catch and half its blue crab catch come from the bay. In addition, more than 40 species of commercial finfish are harvested. The total commercial catch is valued at about $100 million annually.

Recreation is another major activity. On a typical summer weekend, an estimated 100 000 people fish the bay, and over 150 000 recreational craft, registered in Maryland and Virginia, utilise its waters. The presence of these vessels, together with more than 12 000 others engaged in commercial fishing, can create serious problems of congestion, particularly where they compete with the freighters, tankers, naval vessels and other ships which use the bay.

Industry and commerce add yet further stress. Baltimore is a major manufacturing centre, and, like the Hampton Roads complex at the mouth of the bay, is among the largest ports of the United States. The number of commercial vessel trips from Chesapeake Bay ports averages 50 000 a year, carrying over 90 million tonnes of cargo with a value of some $25 billion. A growing activity in the Hampton Roads complex is the export of coal from Appalachia.

Overall management of Chesapeake Bay and its resources is a complex process because of the conflicting demands and values of its various users, and of the multiplicity of local, state, and federal agencies associated with the bay. For example, local government has responsibility for zoning regulations along the shoreline; coordination of coastal zone management activities is carried out at the state level, while the federal government is concerned with managing federally-owned lands along the coast, the upkeep of navigable waters, maintaining certain environmental standards, establishing wildlife refuges, and other activities. Recently, the federal government has undertaken a five-year $25 million research programme to assess the changing conditions of the bay's natural ecosystem as a result of dredging, pollution, and similar processes. The states of Maryland and Virginia have also enacted legislation to encourage cooperative planning by both state legislatures in matters pertaining to the bay. Although talk of an overall Chesapeake Bay authority is frequently heard, there appears at present to be little prospect of such an organisation being established.

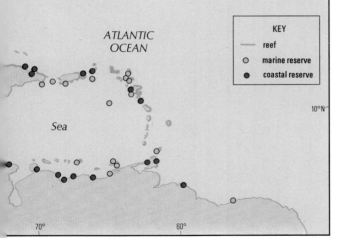

4 *above* Coastal and marine reserves have been developed, mainly during the 1970s, in order to maintain the fragile reef ecosystem of the Caribbean.

The Caribbean

The Gulf of Mexico and Caribbean are under pressure especially from the development of the world's largest economy to the north. The European image of the Spanish Main has been replaced by the immediately more attractive one of the Caribbean as one of the world's most glamorous tourist areas offering ocean cruising, yachting, sports fishing, and beach and reef activities to visitors from the US and to some extent Western Europe. Together with oil-related developments this has generated serious environmental risks in a region which consists of many small and very poor island nations with rising populations for which development is essential. The Caribbean is recognised as a priority area within the UNEP Regional Seas Programme and the IUCN Marine Programme and a network of marine reserves, has been established covering both the United States and the developing countries to the south.

5 *right* Chesapeake Bay, with its industry and commerce and natural resources and its huge population, will need careful management to retain environmental standards.

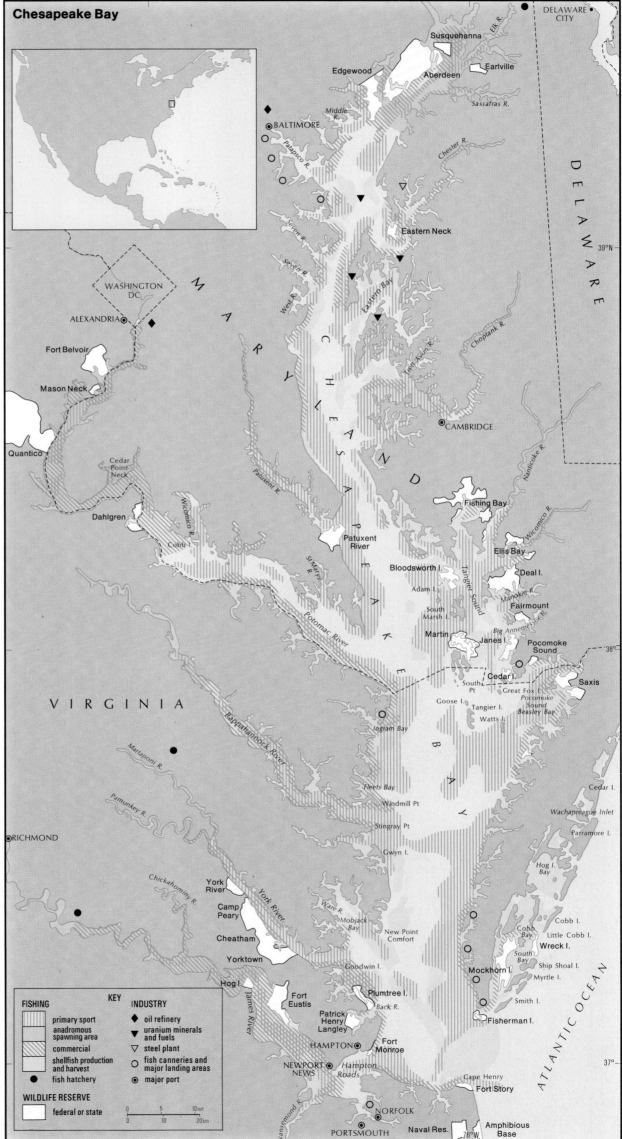

The European seas

T HE European seas, and in particular the North Sea, exemplify the tasks and problems of sea use management. Three major types of sea are represented: the enclosed Mediterranean, Baltic and Black Seas; the semi-enclosed Irish and White Seas and North Sea together with the Channel; and the open ocean areas like the Bay of Biscay, and the Norwegian and Barents Seas. Environmental conditions vary from arctic to warm temperate and from shallow shelf to deep ocean. In most areas there are several states directly or indirectly involved in management and control, and there are a number of uncertain or disputed boundaries such as between Greece and Turkey in the Aegean; the UK, Ireland and Denmark in the Rockall area; France and the UK in the Channel; and Norway and the USSR in the Barents Sea. Further, the North East Atlantic region and the Mediterranean are key strategic areas. The seas are rich in resources and make up the major maritime hub of the world trade system. The problems associated with multiple use are formidable, and the pollution of the enclosed seas (Baltic and Mediterranean) has become a major issue, as has coastal management, especially in the wetlands of the North Sea. Further, exploration and conservation of the maritime historical heritage of ancient ships and ports is important, especially in the North Sea and Mediterranean.

1 *above and* **2** *below* Fragile coastal environments such as the oyster farm in Cancale, Brittany, *above* are vulnerable to oil tanker disasters. When the *Amoco Cadiz (below)* ran aground off Brittany in 1978, 177 000 tonnes of oil were spilled.

The French seas

France is notable in Europe in having three major contrasting sea areas to administer: the Channel, the Bay of Biscay and the Mediterranean. Each of them requires a different approach. France has recognised the importance of developing coastal management to cope with the integration of conservation, recreation, aquaculture and industry, and the need for this was no more dramatically illustrated than by the impact of the oil spills of the two tankers *Torrey Canyon* and *Amoco Cadiz*. In both cases oil spread across Brittany's recreational beaches, oyster beds and bird sanctuaries. The *Amoco Cadiz* oil spill was instrumental in promoting reorganisation of the maritime administration of French national and local government authorities, leading in 1981 to France becoming the first country in the world to establish a Ministry of the Sea.

3 *main map* The areas of most intense marine activity are in the southern sector of the North Sea where coasts are densely populated and the seabed and water column rich in resources, notably aggregates, oil and gas, and fish. There are a number of busy ferry routes and congestion is caused by vessels making their way to and from the Dover Strait. In the north, most of the activity revolves around the oil and gas industry though fishing is also important.

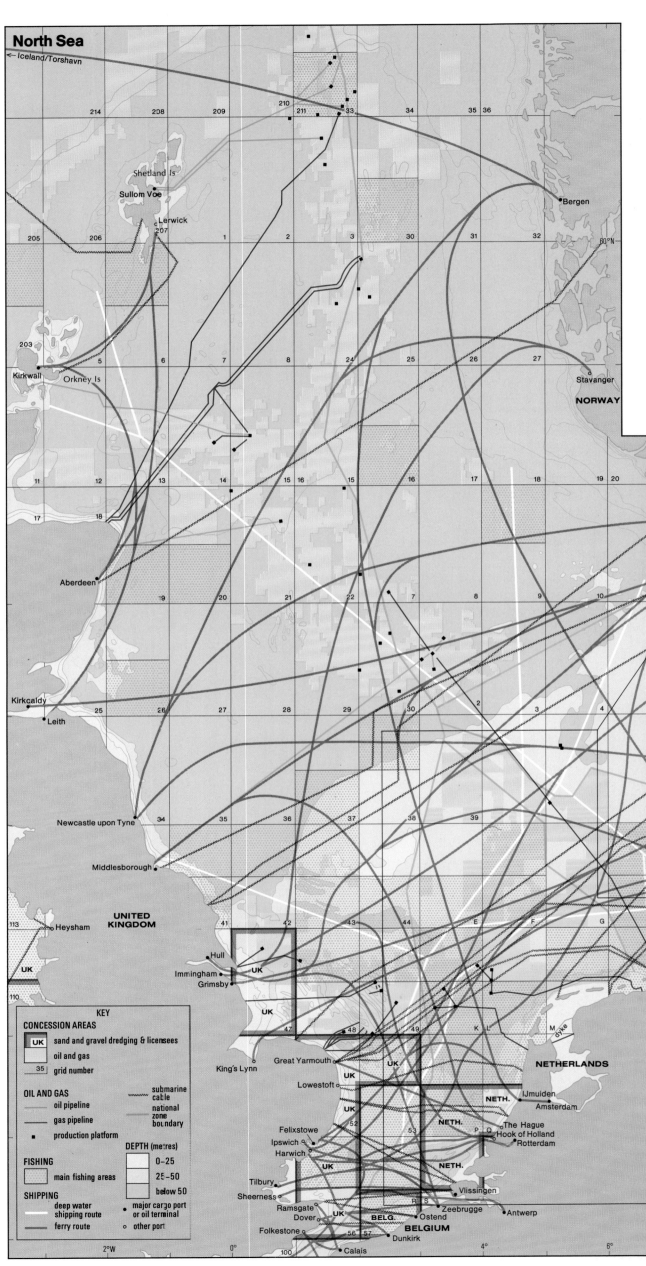

North Sea

KEY

CONCESSION AREAS

UK — sand and gravel dredging & licensees

— oil and gas

35 — grid number

OIL AND GAS

— oil pipeline

— gas pipeline

■ production platform

FISHING

main fishing areas

SHIPPING

— deep water shipping route

— ferry route

∿∿∿ submarine cable

— national zone boundary

DEPTH (metres)

0–25

25–50

below 50

● major cargo port or oil terminal

○ other port

The North Sea

The North Sea is the most intensively used of the European seas and is the richest in resources. Although management tends to operate at regional or national scales, the North Sea as a whole has given rise to a number of international management issues. These are fisheries conservation and allocation, the impact of offshore oil and gas activities, the use of coasts for recreation, settlement and industrial development, and use of the sea for waste disposal.

Management problems have been highlighted with the development of offshore oil and gas which has led to conflict with fisheries. It has led to the establishment of an emergency sector system to help cope with pollution and other safety hazards. The promise of oil and gas has meant a relatively rapid agreement on continental shelf divisions. The oil industry has also precipitated coastal planning problems in the rural areas of Scotland, and to some extent Norway, because of the environmental, social and economic impact of service bases, rig building yards and terminals.

The yield of North Sea fisheries has virtually doubled in the last twenty years to around 3 million tonnes per annum. There is a real possibility that serious overfishing of herring and mackerel stocks in the 1960s and early 1970s has led to a long-term restructuring of the ecosystem favouring species further down the food web. Also, the reallocation of the fisheries resources as a consequence of the entry of the UK, Ireland and Denmark into the European Community has led to intense fisheries competition, and has contributed to Norway, Faeroe and Greenland remaining outside the EEC in order to avoid its fishery regulations. The northern isles of Scotland have attempted to counteract the impending loss of resources by announcing local fishing plans. Negotiations over a common fisheries policy have proved to be a major stumbling block in the political progress of the Community, exacerbated by the virtual elimination of the UK's distant water trawling industry as a result of the implementation of 200-mile EEZs.

Marine traffic control to promote safety and reduce risks, particularly of oil pollution, is already established in the Channel and Dover Strait, as well as in port approaches in the southern North Sea, while the Sullom Voe Terminal, through which much of the North Sea offshore oil passes, has stringent controls on shipping bound for that port.

Pollution control is the subject of developing legal regimes such as the Oslo Convention regulating dumping at sea, and the Paris Convention regulating land-based pollution. The European Community is also developing roles in monitoring and controlling pollution. The greatest pressures from pollution are in the coastal zones, especially in the southern coasts and the Wadden Zee area where industrialisation, settlement and recreation are most intense.

Another aim is the conservation of maritime cultural remains including those from the Viking and Hansa periods, the era of exploration and trade development in the 16th–17th centuries, as well as the period of European industrialisation. Measures to protect maritime archaeological sites, conserve historic port areas and establish maritime museums are all part of this effort.

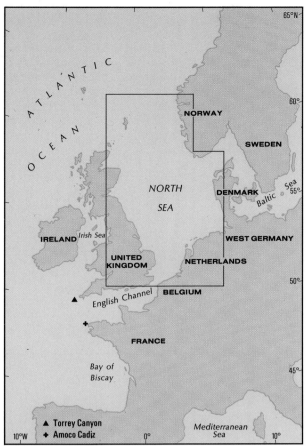

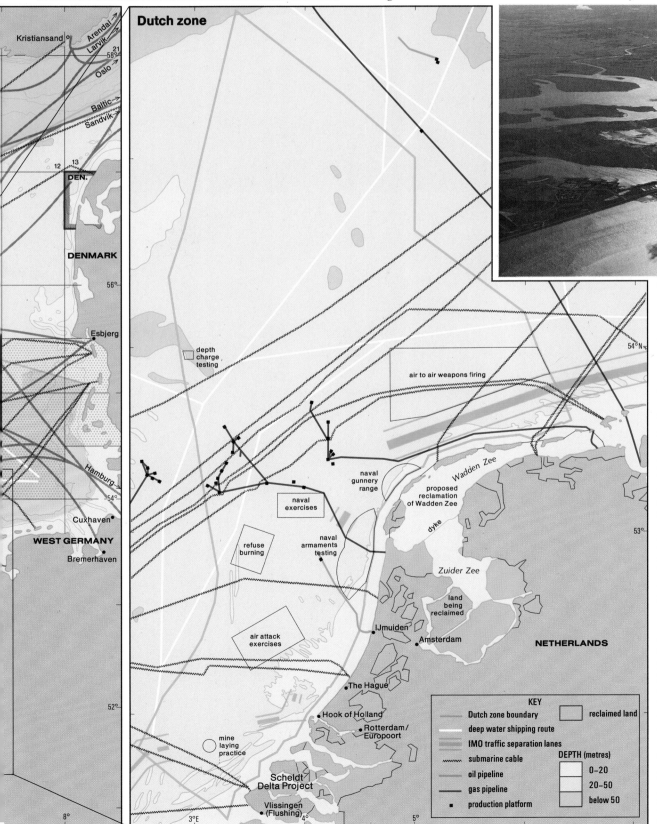

4 *above* Part of the Wadden Zee, a shallow sea, which is partly sheltered from the North Sea by low-lying islands. It is widely recognised as a sensitive area threatened by industrial and recreational uses.

5 *left* The traditional dependency of the Dutch on the sea has grown with the increasing extent of land reclamation, while the Dutch EEZ is one of the most intensively used in the world. Competing activities include fishing, dredging, gas extraction, shipping and naval exercises.

The Dutch Sea

The Dutch battle against the sea, and its people's history of dependence upon it are legendary. The great herring fishery of the 17th century, the East India trade, the dominance of northern European maritime trade in the early modern period, and the continuing process of land reclamation and coast protection, which has converted enormous shallow sea areas into land, are some of the central themes of Dutch history. In the present century the Zuider Zee has been reclaimed and the Delta Project is now nearing completion. The Wadden Zee could be reclaimed, but is valuable as a nursery ground for fish, for the culture of mussels and oysters, for bird life and for recreation.

Establishment of the North Sea boundaries has left the Netherlands with a continental shelf about twice as large as its land area. This is one of the most intensively used shelf seas in the world, with extensive fisheries, offshore gas installations, and Europe's major shipping lanes and port approaches. (Some 65 000 ships a year enter the approaches to Rotterdam, the Scheldt and Amsterdam, with further thousands of ships bound to and from the German North Sea ports, Scandinavia and the Baltic.) There are 17 restricted areas, either for the use of shipping or defence exercises. The need for conservation of the Wadden Zee coasts led to the establishment of the successful Wadden Zee Association. Dutch interests have been particularly active in regional management of the North Sea and in the co-ordination of national government maritime administrative interests.

Recreational sea use

RECREATIONAL enjoyment of the sea has made a huge impact upon coastal areas around the world in the last few decades, especially in the developed world where increased leisure time, easier mobility and larger disposable incomes, combined with the development of national tourist industries and the establishment of special areas for recreation, have given people new opportunities. The sea, which was once regarded simply as a hostile environment by those who worked on it, has now come to be regarded by many as an environment where they can relax and pursue interests far removed from those with which they are familiar on land. Swimming, surfing, fishing, snorkel diving, water skiing, sailing and ocean cruising are just some of the marine sports and pastimes and they are increasing rapidly in popularity. In the last twenty years, for example, sailing and sports fishing have become two of the fastest growing and most popular sports in Europe and around the American seaboard.

Holidays by the sea have led to the annual migration of hundreds of thousands of people to distant countries in the pursuit of better surfing conditions, more playful fish, clearer water for scuba diving, calmer seas for cruising or more challenging ones for ocean racing, or simply warmer weather for swimming and sunbathing. So although recreation on and beside the sea remains principally the privilege of the developed world, all the oceans and their coastlines have become an extended playground for those who can reach them and enjoy their facilities.

Seventy per cent of the world's population lives within 80 kilometres of a coast so that the potential demands by recreation upon the coastal zones is enormous and the steady growth of sea-based sports and activities has led inevitably to conflicts with other sea users as well as threats to the environment (see *Multiple sea use* page 208). In some areas traditional fishing industries have been displaced by tourism which offers better livings to local populations. Elsewhere, tourists have damaged or destroyed the very environments that they have chosen for their amenities. The most notable example can be found along the Mediterranean coasts of France and Italy (see *Mediterranean pollution* page 176).

1 *below* Ocean cruises vary enormously in their itineraries, and it is now possible to select a cruise in almost any part of the world. Cruises range from short, port-hopping voyages to round the world marathons. 'Cruise and fly' holidays, in which the traveller flies out to join the ship or flies home from the last port of call, are now offered widely as they provide greater flexibility. Shore excursions and land tours have become integral parts of many cruises. Some of them have a definite educational purpose, such as study of archaeology or wild life, others offer instruction in pursuits such as painting.

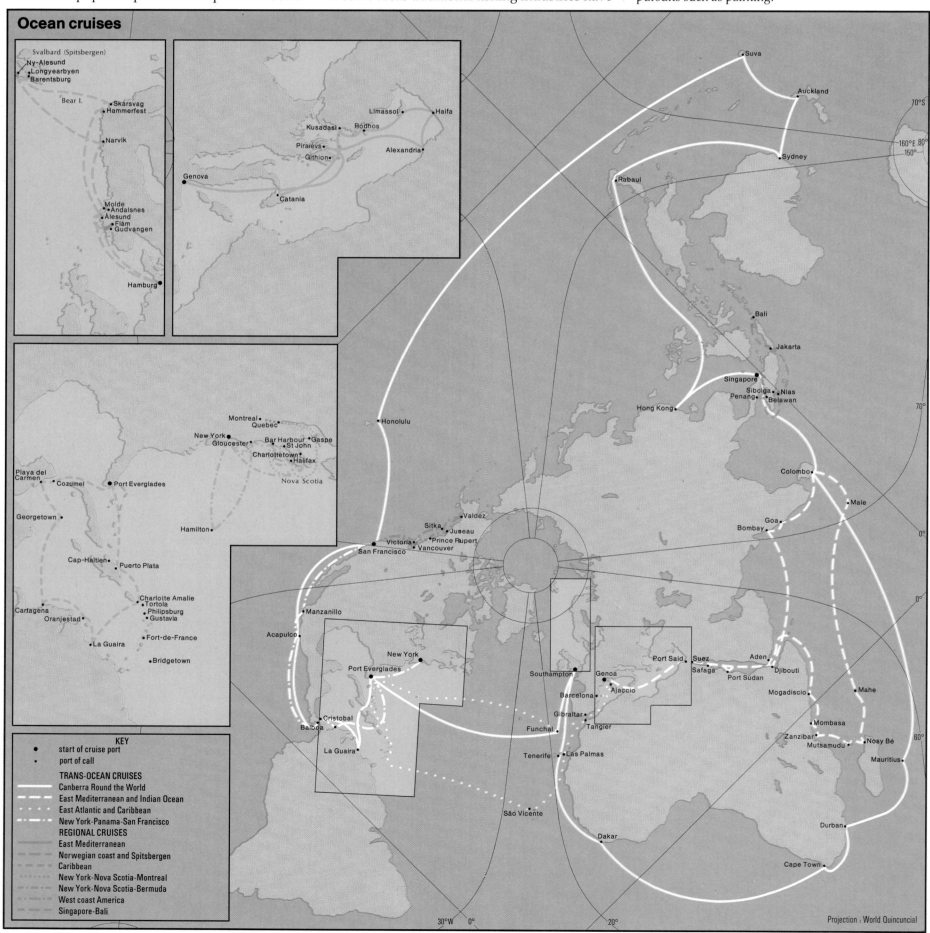

Ocean cruises

KEY
- • start of cruise port
- • port of call

TRANS-OCEAN CRUISES
- Canberra Round the World
- East Mediterranean and Indian Ocean
- East Atlantic and Caribbean
- New York-Panama-San Francisco

REGIONAL CRUISES
- East Mediterranean
- Norwegian coast and Spitsbergen
- Caribbean
- New York-Nova Scotia-Montreal
- New York-Nova Scotia-Bermuda
- West coast America
- Singapore-Bali

Projection : World Quincuncial

Ocean races

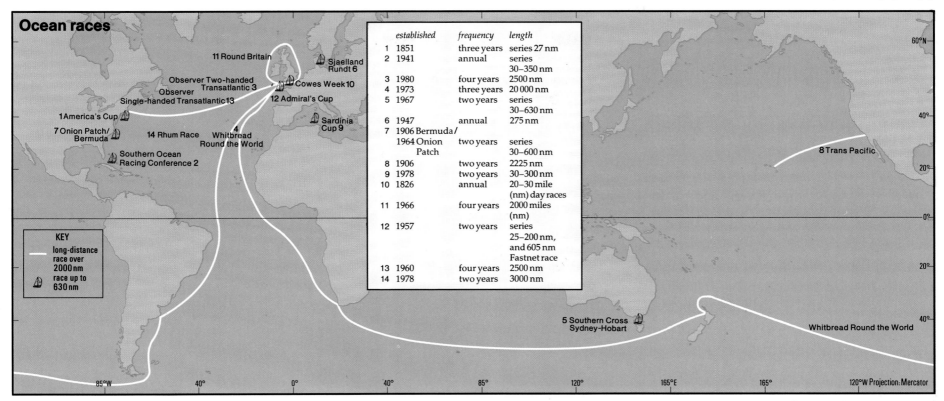

	established	frequency	length
1	1851	three years	series 27 nm
2	1941	annual	series 30–350 nm
3	1980	four years	2500 nm
4	1973	three years	20 000 nm
5	1967	two years	series 30–630 nm
6	1947	annual	275 nm
7	1906 Bermuda/ 1964 Onion Patch	two years	series 30–600 nm
8	1906	two years	2225 nm
9	1978	two years	30–300 nm
10	1826	annual	20–30 mile (nm) day races
11	1966	four years	2000 miles (nm)
12	1957	two years	series 25–200 nm, and 605 nm Fastnet race
13	1960	four years	2500 nm
14	1978	two years	3000 nm

11 Round Britain
Sjaelland Rundt 6
Observer Two-handed Transatlantic 3
Observer Single-handed Transatlantic 13
Cowes Week 10
12 Admiral's Cup
1 America's Cup
7 Onion Patch/ Bermuda
14 Rhum Race
4 Whitbread Round the World
Sardinia Cup 9
Southern Ocean Racing Conference 2
8 Trans Pacific
5 Southern Cross Sydney-Hobart
Whitbread Round the World

KEY
long-distance race over 2000 nm
race up to 630 nm

85°W 40° 0° 40° 85° 120° 165°E 165° 120°W Projection: Mercator
60°N 40° 20° 0° 20° 40°

2 *above* The major racing events cater for a wide variety of vessels and crews and range from the 27-mile races of the America's cup to the gruelling 20 000-mile Whitbread round the world race. By its very nature, however, it is an expensive and specialised pursuit and attracts comparatively few participants. Dinghy sailing, on the other hand, has brought the sport within the reach of millions.

3 *left* Participants in the Southern Ocean racing series off the Florida coast.

4 *right* Surfing has over three million participants. The major surf-sites are on those coasts which are exposed to great expanses of ocean where waves have room to propagate.

Surfsites

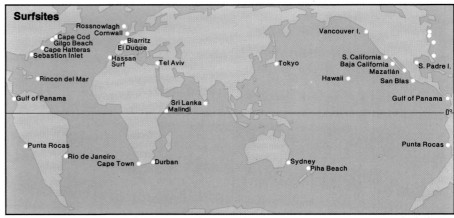

Rossnowlagh
Cornwall
Cape Cod
Gilgo Beach
Cape Hatteras
Sebastion Inlet
Biarritz
El Duque
Hassan Surf
Tel Aviv
Vancouver I.
S. California
Baja California
Mazatlán
S. Padre I.
Tokyo
Hawaii
San Blas
Rincon del Mar
Gulf of Panama
Sri Lanka
Malindi
Gulf of Panama
Punta Rocas
Rio de Janeiro
Cape Town
Durban
Sydney
Piha Beach
Punta Rocas

Brittany

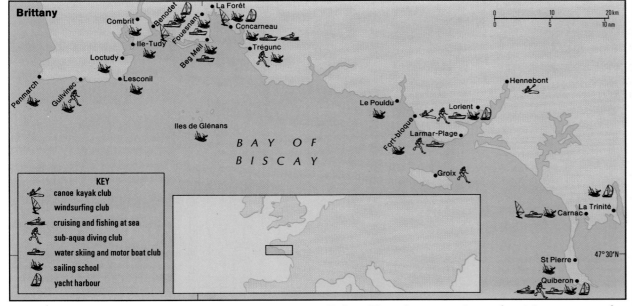

La Forêt
Combrit
Benodet
Fouesnant
Concarneau
Ile-Tudy
Beg Meil
Trégunc
Loctudy
Lesconil
Penmarch
Guilvinec
Iles de Glénans
Hennebont
Le Pouldu
Lorient
Fort-bloque
Larmar-Plage
BAY OF BISCAY
Groix
La Trinité
Carnac
St Pierre
47°30'N
Quiberon

KEY
canoe kayak club
windsurfing club
cruising and fishing at sea
sub-aqua diving club
water skiing and motor boat club
sailing school
yacht harbour

10 20 km
5 10 nm

6 *below* Windsurfers prepare for a regatta at Dinard, France. Windsurfing began only in the 1970s but is now one of the world's fastest growing water sports.

5 *above* Though ocean racing and cruising may extend across the widest expanses of water, most recreation takes place in the coastal zone and is heavily reliant on onshore amenities. Swimming, sand-yachting, dinghy sailing, canoeing, board sailing, water skiing and scuba diving all take place within the surf zone or just beyond. Much of the enormous growth of tourism has been directed towards the coasts and it is along these thin strips of land that most pressure has been placed upon the environment as well as on the life-styles of the local people. The Brittany coast of France around Lorient epitomises this situation. Sailing schools, diving clubs and marinas have sprung up in every convenient place while new roads and airports have been built to cope with the huge influx of holiday-makers. Careful management is required if many of the world's coastlines are not to suffer from this sort of impact.

7 *right* Saltwater sports fishing is now a worldwide recreation and in some areas the indications are that it has a greater impact on the economy than the commercial fisheries. In the USA, during 1975, for example, 22 million fishermen spent 4.5 million dollars on saltwater recreational fishing. The growing numbers of anglers have increased the demand on limited resources and in some cases the recreational stocks face the same problems as some commercial stocks. Catches of Californian barracuda, for example, have dropped from 14 lbs (30.8 kilos) per angler in 1935 to 2 lbs in 1970 and the fish has now been designated a 'depleted sports resource'.

In California, the wealth of the economy has generated a well-developed infrastructure of sporting facilities for a wide range of sports fishing and the statistics reflect a flourishing recreational industry.

San Diego county

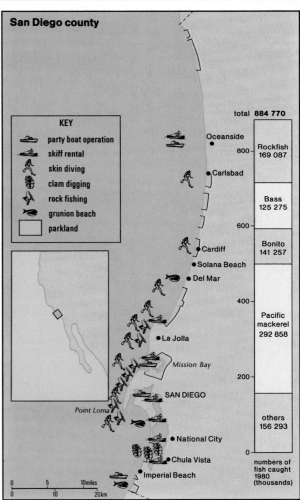

KEY
party boat operation
skiff rental
skin diving
clam digging
rock fishing
grunion beach
parkland

Oceanside
Carlsbad
Cardiff
Solana Beach
Del Mar
La Jolla
Mission Bay
SAN DIEGO
Point Loma
National City
Chula Vista
Imperial Beach

total 884 770
Rockfish 169 087
Bass 125 275
Bonito 141 257
Pacific mackerel 292 858
others 156 293

numbers of fish caught 1980 (thousands)

5 10 miles
10 20 km

The territorial sea

Iₙ 1982 the Third United Nations Conference on the Law of the Sea (UNCLOS III) adopted a new and comprehensive Convention on the Law of the Sea. This new Convention will, once in force, largely replace the present laws based upon international customary law and the four 1958 Geneva Conventions on the Law of the Sea. It will enter into force twelve months after ratification by sixty states. Many of the rules governing jurisdictional zones are uncertain under the present law and very complex under the new Convention; a summary and interpretation of the new rules is given in Appendix XI.

The new Convention will settle one particularly important question, that is the breadth of

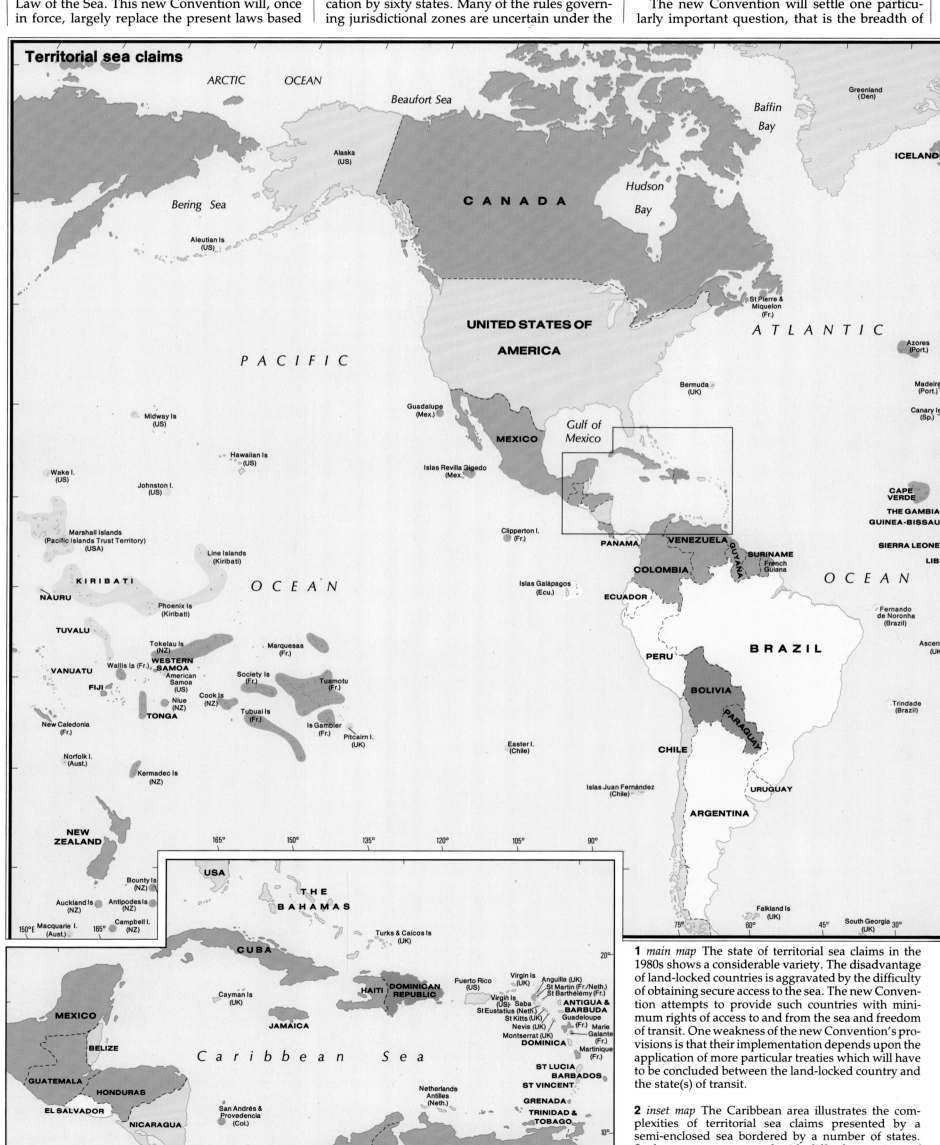

Territorial sea claims

1 *main map* The state of territorial sea claims in the 1980s shows a considerable variety. The disadvantage of land-locked countries is aggravated by the difficulty of obtaining secure access to the sea. The new Convention attempts to provide such countries with minimum rights of access to and from the sea and freedom of transit. One weakness of the new Convention's provisions is that their implementation depends upon the application of more particular treaties which will have to be concluded between the land-locked country and the state(s) of transit.

2 *inset map* The Caribbean area illustrates the complexities of territorial sea claims presented by a semi-enclosed sea bordered by a number of states. Such states are presented with difficult questions of delimitation due to the complex configuration of coastlines and the presence of a large number of islands.

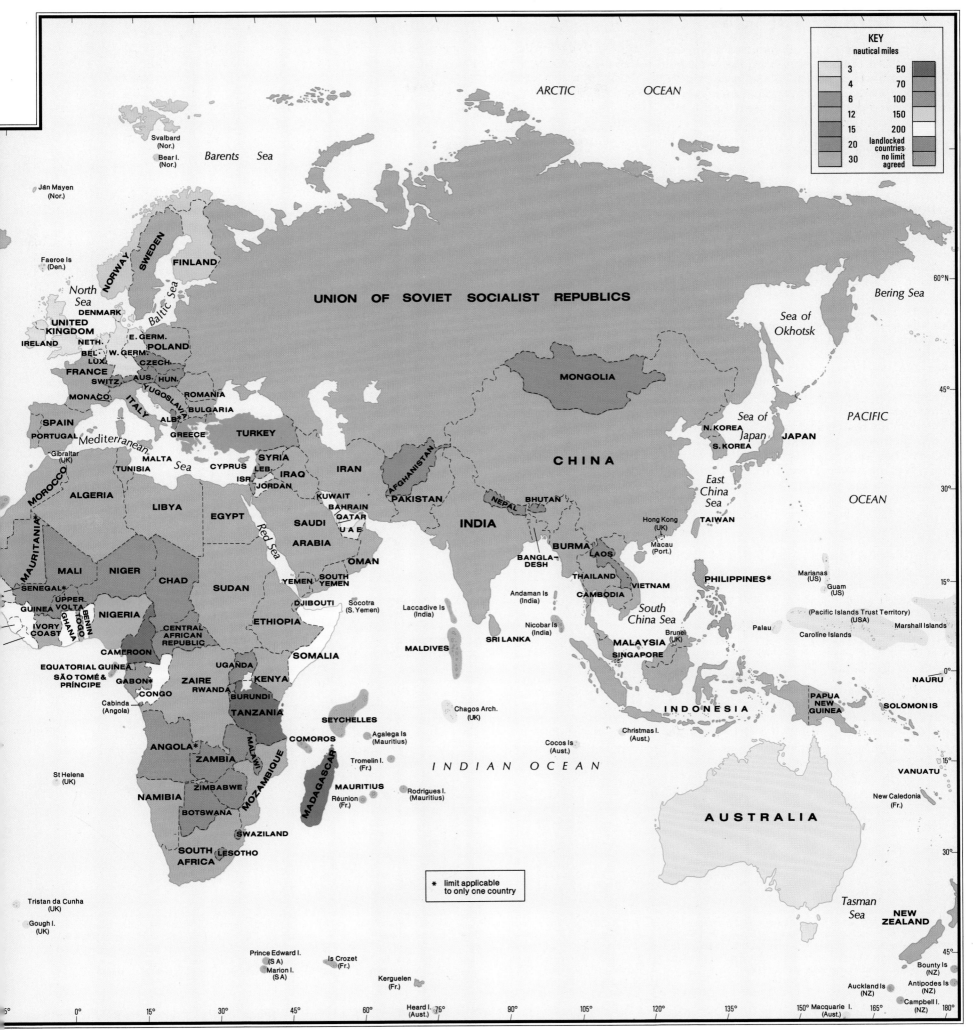

KEY
nautical miles

3	50
4	70
6	100
12	150
15	200
20	landlocked countries
30	no limit agreed

ARCTIC OCEAN

Svalbard (Nor.)

Bear I. (Nor.)

Barents Sea

Jan Mayen (Nor.)

Faeroe Is (Den.)

North Sea

NORWAY SWEDEN FINLAND

60°N

Bering Sea

UNION OF SOVIET SOCIALIST REPUBLICS

Sea of Okhotsk

DENMARK

UNITED KINGDOM

IRELAND NETH. E. GERM. POLAND

BEL. W. GERM. LUX. CZECH.

FRANCE AUS. HUN.

SWITZ. YUGOSLAV.

MONACO ITALY ALB. ROMANIA

BULGARIA

MONGOLIA

PACIFIC

45°

N. KOREA

Sea of Japan

S. KOREA JAPAN

SPAIN GREECE TURKEY

PORTUGAL Mediterranean

Gibraltar (UK) MALTA CYPRUS SYRIA LEB. IRAQ IRAN

MOROCCO TUNISIA Sea ISR. JORDAN

CHINA

East China Sea

OCEAN

30°

Hong Kong (UK)

TAIWAN

ALGERIA LIBYA EGYPT

KUWAIT BAHRAIN QATAR U A E

AFGHANISTAN NEPAL BHUTAN

PAKISTAN

Macau (Port.)

MAURITANIA SAUDI ARABIA

INDIA

MALI NIGER CHAD SUDAN YEMEN OMAN

SOUTH YEMEN

BANGLA-DESH BURMA LAOS

VIETNAM

PHILIPPINES *

Marianas (US) Guam (US)

15°

SENEGAL * UPPER VOLTA

GUINEA

DJIBOUTI Socotra (S. Yemen)

THAILAND

South China Sea

CAMBODIA

(Pacific Islands Trust Territory) (USA)

Marshall Islands

IVORY COAST GHANA BENIN TOGO NIGERIA ETHIOPIA

Laccadive Is (India)

Andaman Is (India)

Palau

Caroline Islands

CAMEROON CENTRAL AFRICAN REPUBLIC SOMALIA

Nicobar Is (India)

SRI LANKA

MALDIVES

MALAYSIA

Brunei (UK)

SINGAPORE

NAURU

0°

EQUATORIAL GUINEA GABON * CONGO ZAIRE UGANDA KENYA

SÃO TOMÉ & PRÍNCIPE RWANDA BURUNDI

Cabinda (Angola) TANZANIA

INDONESIA

PAPUA NEW GUINEA

SOLOMON IS

SEYCHELLES

Chagos Arch. (UK)

Christmas I. (Aust.)

St Helena (UK)

ANGOLA * ZAMBIA MALAWI MOZAMBIQUE

Agalega Is (Mauritius)

Cocos Is (Aust.)

INDIAN OCEAN

COMOROS

Tromelin I. (Fr.)

VANUATU

15°

NAMIBIA ZIMBABWE MADAGASCAR

BOTSWANA SWAZILAND

MAURITIUS

Réunion (Fr.)

Rodrigues I. (Mauritius)

New Caledonia (Fr.)

AUSTRALIA

SOUTH AFRICA LESOTHO

30°

Tristan da Cunha (UK)

* limit applicable to only one country

Tasman Sea

NEW ZEALAND

Gough I. (UK)

Prince Edward I. (S A)

Marion I. (S A)

Is Crozet (Fr.)

45°

Bounty Is (NZ)

Kerguelen (Fr.)

Heard I. (Aust.)

Auckland Is (NZ)

Antipodes Is (NZ)

Macquarie I. (Aust.)

Campbell I. (NZ)

5° 0° 15° 30° 45° 60° 75° 90° 105° 120° 135° 150° 165° 180°

---

the territorial sea. Traditionally, most states have claimed a territorial sea of 3 nm and the exercise of their sovereign jurisdiction over this zone was limited only by the obligation to allow innocent passage for foreign shipping. The outer limit of the territorial sea also marked the limit of the coastal state's exclusive fishing rights. In recent years, however, two trends have been noticeable. First, there has been a very marked increase in the breadth of territorial sea claimed and the majority of states now claim 12 nm or more; some states claim 200 nm. In contrast to this, the pressure to make excessively large, comprehensive territorial sea claims has to some extent been reduced by the appearance of new jurisdictional zones. The 'exclusive fishing zone' (EFZ) was

introduced in the 1960s. Although opposed initially by the distant-water fishing states, it has now been widely accepted, with states such as the members of the European Economic Community now claiming 200 nm EFZs. More recently, the 'exclusive economic zone' (EEZ) concept has been developed and is now incorporated in the new Convention. As a result of these developments, which provide for some protection of economic interests that had previously been sought in territorial sea claims, it has been possible to secure general agreement upon a 12 nm territorial sea. However, the settlement of this question raised a problem for the principal maritime powers which still recognised only a 3 nm territorial sea. Increasing the breadth of the

territorial sea from 3 nm to 12 nm means that some 116 straits, many of considerable strategic and economic importance, would lose their central belt of high seas and become entirely territorial sea straits. While foreign shipping would retain the traditional right of innocent passage through such straits, they would no longer enjoy the more liberal freedom of high seas navigation there. The Convention provides for a right of 'transit passage' through such straits, including a right to submerged passage for submarines and a right of overflight for aircraft. The straits in question include the straits of Dover, the Bering Straits, Bab el Mandeb and the Strait of Hormuz.

Maritime jurisdictional zones

THROUGHOUT history, the extent to which coastal states have encroached upon the area of the high seas by extending seawards their land-based jurisdictional claims has tended to reflect the interests of the predominant power or powers of the day. For example, in the 15th century, Spain and Portugal sought Papal support for their extensive claims to spheres of influence in the Atlantic. Similarly, competing sovereign claims between the Italian States virtually extinguished the high seas freedom of navigation in the Mediterranean between the 11th and 16th centuries. On the other hand, the Elizabethan and Dutch rejection of the Iberian claims helped to push back the frontiers of sovereign claims and preserve freedom of navigation and fishing.

In more recent times, maritime boundaries continued to reflect the interests of the leading powers. Thus, in the 19th century, Britain, as the leading maritime power, continued to defend freedom of the seas. For example, in 1821 she helped the United States against Russia's attempt to debar foreign shipping from all waters up to 100 miles from Alaska but opposed the United States in 1886 when that Power, too, attempted to extend its jurisdiction over the seal fishery in the Bering Sea. In the present century the United States, as the new leading maritime power, has carried on the traditional British policies of maintaining freedom of the high seas.

Any list of important formative factors in today's complex world of conflicting ocean territorial claims would include the growth of influence of the developing countries, and the emergence of new concepts such as the 'international economic order', the 'common heritage of mankind' and the 'exclusive economic zone'. It is the conflict between new power groupings and ideas such as these and the traditional interests of the advanced maritime states which has generated the new maritime jurisdictional zones.

1 *above* The zones over which coastal states claim jurisdiction today include the following: *internal waters*, that is all waters landward of the territorial sea baseline, including bays and estuaries, in which the sovereign jurisdiction of the coastal state is not even limited by the obligation to accord the right of innocent passage to foreign shipping; the *territorial sea*, the breadth of which has been set at 12 nm by the new 1982 Convention on the Law of the Sea; the *contiguous zone*, which presently extends to 12 nm from the territorial sea baseline under the 1958 Geneva Convention but will be increased to 24 nm by the new 1982 Convention; the *exclusive economic zone* (EEZ), which extends out to a distance of 200 nm from the territorial sea baseline. Many states at present do not claim a full EEZ but a more limited 200 nm *exclusive fishing zone* (EFZ). Lastly, the *continental shelf zone* (see pages 222–223) extends to at least 200 nm under the new Convention, but will be even more extensive in areas where the continental margin continues beyond that distance.

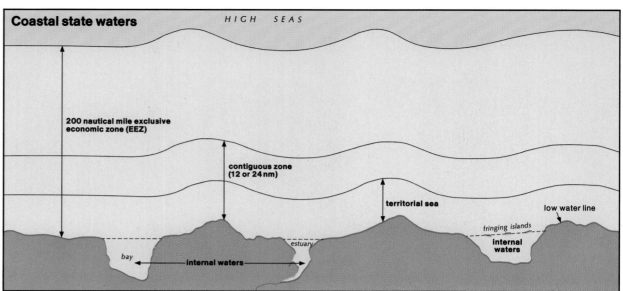
Coastal state waters
HIGH SEAS
200 nautical mile exclusive economic zone (EEZ)
contiguous zone (12 or 24 nm)
territorial sea
low water line
fringing islands
internal waters
bay
estuary
internal waters

Delimitation of the jurisdictional zones

The diagrams below illustrate some of the problems frequently encountered in determining territorial sea baselines or delimiting the territorial sea between neighbouring states.

In establishing the baseline from which the state's territorial sea is to be determined, it is important to distinguish between a bay and a mere curvature of the coast. The Convention provides that in the case of a curvature of the coast, the territorial sea baselines will simply follow the low-water along the curvature, whereas in the case of a legal bay, the coastal state is entitled to utilise as the territorial sea baseline a straight line enclosing the bay. It is first necessary to establish that the feature is a legal bay; it can then be determined where it is permissible to draw the closing line. Landward of this line will be internal waters over which the coastal states have practically unlimited sovereignty; the line itself will serve as the baseline from which the territorial sea is measured seawards.

Legal delimitation of the territorial sea between neighbouring (opposite or adjacent) states is another problem which the new Convention seeks to solve. Generally, delimitation is effected by application of the equidistance principle, that is, the 'equal' division of the sea area in relation to the coastlines. This principle may be altered or displaced either if the two states agree mutually to adopt another line, or if historic considerations or special circumstances decree that another line is adopted. One example of this might be if a headland or island protruded so far into the channel or sea area as to cause excessive distortion of the median line.

Rules on delimitation of the archipelagic waters of archipelagic states present different problems but here two points may be stressed: one, the right of archipelagic states to draw closing lines around the archipelago is generally recognised for the first time in the 1982 Convention; two, the new rule applies only to archipelagic *states*.

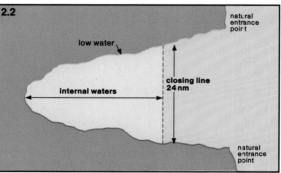
2.1 low water — natural entrance point — internal waters — closing line ≤24 nm — natural entrance point

2.2 low water — internal waters — natural entrance point — closing line 24 nm — natural entrance point

2.3 internal waters (a + b + c minus islands gives the diameter of the semi-circle) — internal waters — a — b — c

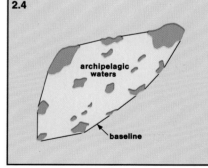
2.4 archipelagic waters — baseline

2.1 A juridical bay must have an area as large as, or larger than, that of a semi-circle whose diameter is a line drawn across the mouth. A closing line may be drawn across the mouth between low-water marks of the natural entrance points if that distance does not exceed 24 nm.

2.2 Where the width of entrance exceeds 24 nm a line of that length must be drawn so as to enclose the juridical bay.

2.3 Where islands form more than one entrance to a bay, the diameter of the semi-circle is the sum total of the lengths of line between the islands, i.e. **a + b + c**.

2.4 Archipelagic states may draw baselines between their outer islands enclosing archipelagic waters, recognised when the ratio of area of water to area of land is between 1:1 and 9:1. The length of any baseline may not exceed 100 nm, although 3 per cent of them may extend up to 125 nm.

3.1 Where the coast is deeply indented or fringed by islands straight baselines may be drawn which should follow the general direction of the coast. Local economic interests and the character of resultant internal waters may be taken into account in their delimitation, for example the islands off the coast of Yugoslavia (shown), Norway and Chile.

3.2 The median line between opposite states is equidistant from the nearest points on the baselines from which the breadth of the territorial sea of each state is measured. Departures from this principle are allowed either by agreement or to take into account historic title and special circumstances, for example, the continental shelf boundary between Saudi Arabia and Bahrain.

3.3 The lateral line between adjacent coasts is equidistant from successive nearest points on the coastline of either state. The line continues until some other part of the shoreline in one of the states is equidistant. At this point the line continues as a perpendicular bisector through successive turning points as new features on one or other shore become controlling points (Kenya–Tanzania).

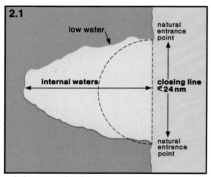
3.1 YUGOSLAVIA — Rijeka — Zadar — Split — Dubrovnik — baseline — Adriatic Sea

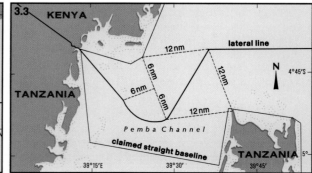
3.2 SAUDI ARABIA — Ra's al-Qurrayyah — Lubainah al-Saghirah — Kaskus — Lubainah al-Kabirah — Ra's al-Barr — Ra's al-Mazzala — BAHRAIN

3.3 KENYA — lateral line — 12 nm — 6 nm — 12 nm — TANZANIA — 6 nm — 6 nm — 12 nm — Pemba Channel — claimed straight baseline — TANZANIA

Exclusive economic zones and the area beyond

The exclusive economic zones (EEZs) extend 200 nm from the baseline of the territorial sea. Within the EEZ, the coastal state has sovereign rights for the purpose of exploring and exploiting, conserving and managing natural resources.

It must exercise these rights, however, with due regard to the rights of other states. For the extent of this limitation and information on the status and substantive regime of the EEZ, refer to Appendix XI. Coastal state jurisdiction over sea

areas has been extending since the 1950s in the form of EFZs and EEZs. As a result, some 35 per cent of what was previously high seas containing common property living resources now falls under the jurisdiction of the coastal states.

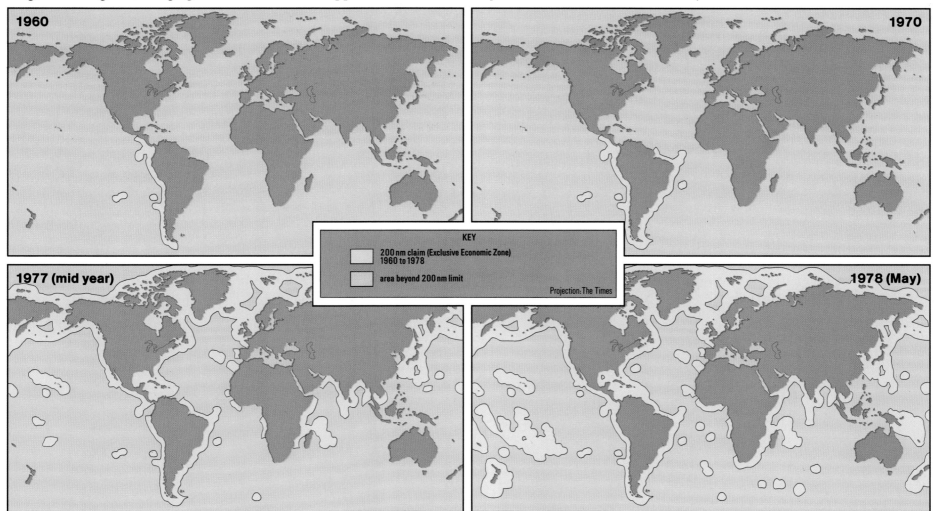

KEY

200 nm claim (Exclusive Economic Zone) 1960 to 1978

area beyond 200 nm limit

Projection: The Times

1960

1970

1977 (mid year)

1978 (May)

4–7 *above* Since 1950 vast areas of former high seas have come under national jurisdiction in the form of exclusive economic zones (EEZs), exclusive fishing zones (EFZs) or, in some cases, 200 nm territorial seas. The 1982 Convention on the law of the sea intends that all states will establish their 200 nm zones as EEZs.

Resources of the EEZ

The coastal state determines the allowable catch in the EEZ but is obliged to ensure that the maintenance of the living resources is not endangered by overexploitation. Conservation and management measures must be designed to maintain or restore populations of harvested species at levels which can produce the maximum sustainable yield (MSY), as qualified by relevant environmental and economic factors, including the economic needs of coastal fishing communities and the special requirements of developing states, and taking into account fishing patterns, the interdependence of stocks and any generally recommended subregional, regional or global minimum standards. The effects on associated species have also to be taken into consideration. It will be noted that the criteria to be applied by the coastal state are extremely vague, thus leaving it a considerable measure of discretion.

Having established, through its conservation measures, an allowable catch which will permit the maintenance of an MSY, as qualified by the factors mentioned above, the coastal state is next bound, without prejudice to these conservation measures, to

promote the objective of optimum utilisation. The procedure is as follows. The coastal state must determine the total allowable catch (TAC) and its own harvesting capacity (HC). If the total allowable catch exceeds the harvesting capacity, the surplus catch must be made available to other states, having particular regard to the interests of landlocked states and states with special geographical characteristics, especially the developing states among them. Here again, the scope of the coastal state's discretion is notable.

Resources beyond the EEZ

Beyond the EEZ there are the high seas. These contain stocks of migratory fish and marine mammals. All states have rights for their nationals to engage in fishing in the high seas but they have to observe certain obligations relating to conservation. Some marine species move from high seas to economic zones and between economic zones so that regional and international agreements are necessary. Of particular significance are the anadromous and catadromous species as well as the whales.

Lying on and beneath the sea bed, beyond the EEZ, are mineral resources. These are referred to in the 1982 Convention as resources of 'The Area'. The problems related to exploitation of these resources are referred to in detail in Appendix XI. They are the most formidable of all the problems concerned with the conduct of states in relation to ocean resource extraction at the present time.

Navigation and research in the EEZ and beyond

For states with large merchant fleets and naval forces the introduction of the EEZs appeared as a possible threat to freedom of navigation in what had once been high seas. However, the 1982 Convention provides all states with freedom of navigation within the EEZ, though subject to various provisions in the Convention. Beyond the EEZ the traditional high seas freedom of navigation continues as before.

In the case of navigation for purposes of scientific research there is no such freedom in the EEZ for foreign vessels. States tend to regard information derived from research as a resource. Consequently the Convention has a number of Articles which require consents from the coastal state to conduct research and lays down various conditions for carrying out research in the EEZ and sharing the results. There are also Articles governing research in the seabed 'Area' beyond the limits of national jurisdiction. However, on the high seas, and that includes the water column above the seabed area, scientific research is allowed to all states, and to competent international organisations, in conformity with the Convention.

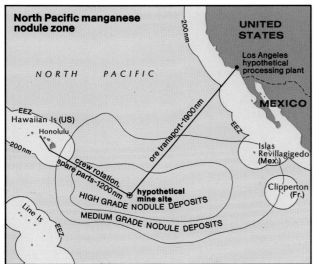

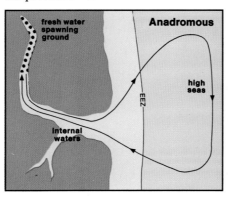

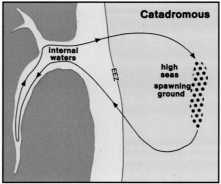

9 *centre* Organisms which spawn in fresh water, travel out to sea and then return to spawn are known as anadromous, an example being the salmon.

10 *left* Organisms which spawn at sea and travel to fresh water where they chiefly live before returning to sea to spawn are called catadromous, for example the mullet eel.

8 *left* An area in the North Pacific which is thought to be one of the more promising areas for polymetallic nodule mining both because of the grade of nodules found there and the location of the area from the point of view of transportation and supply. The map shows

the overlap of national zones and part of the international 'Area', which is the seabed beneath the high seas, as well as the advantages to states of island territories.

The continental shelf

Formulae for the determination of the outer limit of the continental shelf and for the delimitation of the continental shelf between opposite or adjacent states were first provided by the Geneva Convention on the Continental Shelf, 1958. Under this convention, the legal continental shelf was defined as the seabed and subsoil of the submarine areas adjacent to the coast but outside the territorial sea to a sea water depth of 200 metres, or, beyond that limit, to where the depth of the superjacent waters permitted the exploitation of the natural resources of the seabed and subsoil. There was thus an automatic entitlement to the shelf out to 200 metres depth but further extension of this entitlement was dependent upon technological capacity. The same formula applied to mainland and island coasts.

Since 1958 three important decisions on delimitation issues have been given. Two were by the International Court of Justice in the North Sea Continental Shelf case 1969 and the Continental Shelf (Tunisia–Libya) case 1982; the third by a Court of Arbitration in the Anglo-French Continental Shelf case 1977–78. The North Sea judgment (based on international customary law) has proved to be particularly influential in state practice and in the drafting of a new definition of the legal continental shelf in the 1982 Convention. Although, in the North Sea Continental Shelf case, the International Court of Justice was concerned not with the outer limit under the Geneva Convention but with a problem of delimitation between neighbouring States under international customary law, some of its most influential, if controversial, dicta did in fact *refer* to both the outer limit and the Geneva Convention. In particular the Court spoke of the coastal state as having inherent rights in the area of the shelf that constituted a 'natural prolongation' of its land territory into and under the sea.

The definition of the continental shelf in the 1982 Convention is complex and, like much of the Convention, is the product of compromise:

The continental shelf of a coastal State comprises the sea-bed and subsoil of the submarine areas that extend beyond its territorial sea throughout the natural prolongation of its land territory to the outer edge of the continental margin, or to a distance of 200 nautical miles from the baselines from which the breadth of the territorial sea is measured where the outer edge of the continental margin does not extend up to that distance *(Article 76, para. 1)*.

It is clear from this definition that the coastal state has an automatic right to a 'continental shelf' out to 200 nm, irrespective of the breadth of the 'continental margin'. It is in relation to the delimitation of the outer limit in situations where the continental margin extends beyond 200 nm that complex formulae are provided. It is not simply a question of determining the outer edge of the continental margin in geomorphological terms, but of identifying a legal outer edge. This may be established by reference to one of several methods, including the so-called 'Irish formula', which itself offers two options. The various formulae are illustrated and explained by the diagrams opposite.

In an effort to add an element of international objectivity to national determination of boundary lines in applying continental shelf formulae, the new Convention provides a role for a 'Commission on the Limits of the Continental Shelf'. The limits have to be established by the coastal state on the basis of recommendations made by the Commission, in accordance with Article 76.

In the matter of delimitation of the continental shelf between opposite or adjacent states, the 1958 Geneva Convention embodied a three-point formula under which such delimitations were to be effected (Article 6): (one) by agreement, which failing (two) by application of the equidistant principle, unless (three) another boundary was justified by special circumstances.

As with the question of the outer limit, the North Sea case has been particularly influential upon later developments. The Court empha-

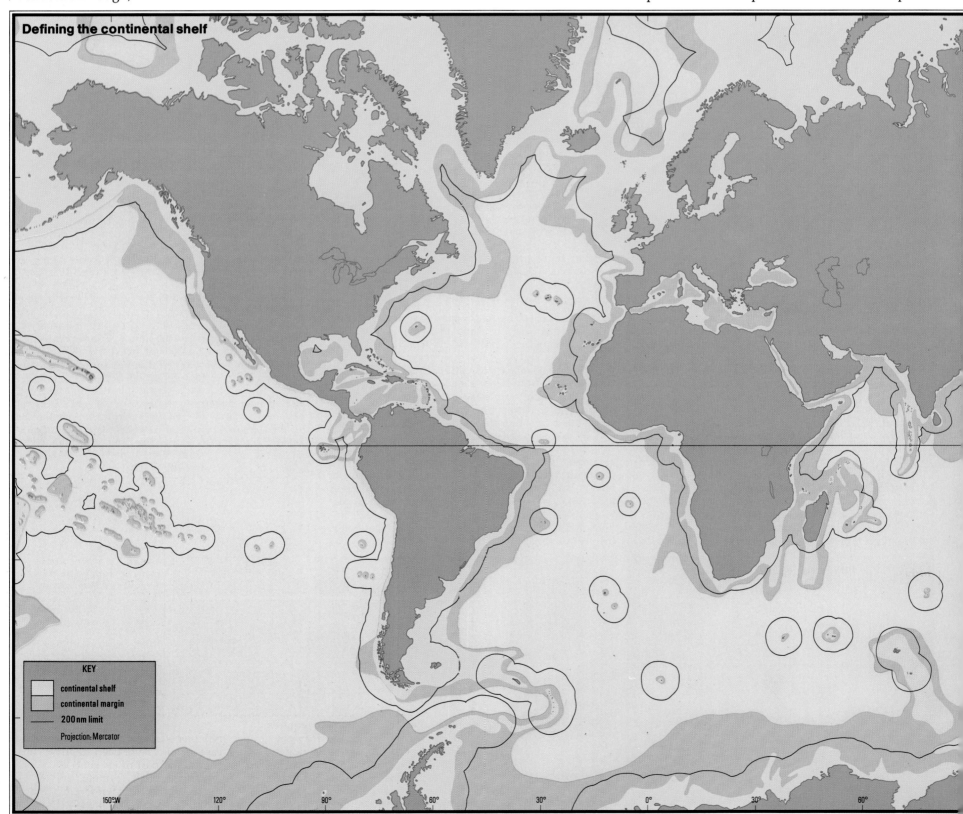

Defining the continental shelf

KEY
- continental shelf
- continental margin
- 200 nm limit

Projection: Mercator

150°W   120°   90°   60°   30°   0°   30°   60°

sised that, under international customary law, delimitation was to 'be effected in accordance with equitable principles, and taking account of all the relevant circumstances'. Although the Court gave an indication of the factors to be taken into account in the negotiations which were to follow its judgment, the fact remains that this decision provides little more than general guide-lines for the determination of boundary lines.

Unfortunately, the formula provided by the new 1982 Convention is even less precise. Under it delimitation would 'be effected by agreement on the basis of international law, as referred to in Article 38 of the Statute of the International Court of Justice, in order to achieve an equitable solution' (Article 83).

The unsatisfactory nature of this vague for-mula is only emphasised by the equally unsatis-factory provision made in the Convention for the settlement of such delimitational disputes. (For examples of the difficult problems to be solved concerning these rules see Maritime tensions and disputes pages 186–188.)

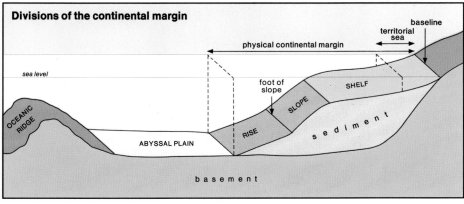

Divisions of the continental margin

2 *above* The principal physical divi-sions of a typical continental margin. In comparing this diagram with dia-grams **3–8** it will be seen that the legal terms do not necessarily bear the same meaning as their physical counterparts.

1 *main map* The extent of the physical continental shelf and margin and the 200 nm continental shelf limit.

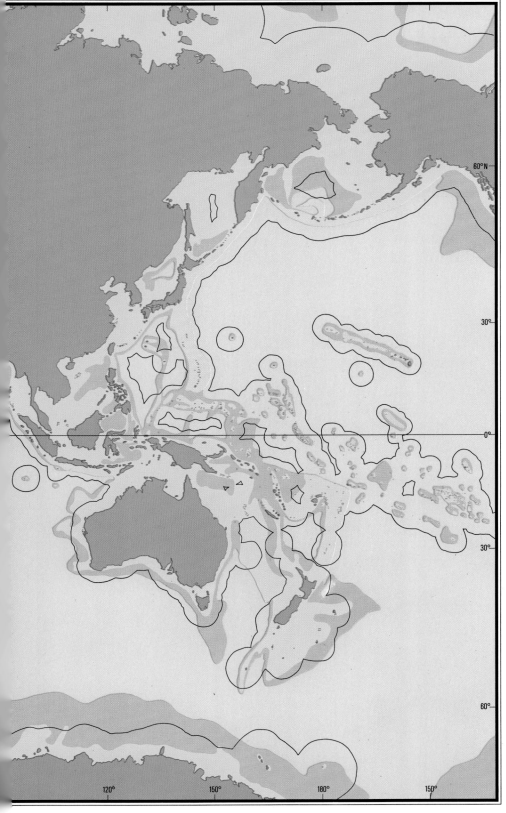

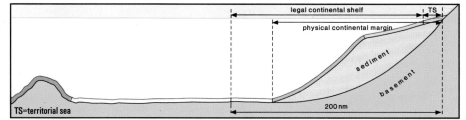

3 *above* Where the physical continental margin is less than 200 nm, the limit of its legal continental shelf may extend beyond the physical continental mar-gin to the abyssal plain. (This formula would apply to western USA, Chile and possibly to western Australia, for example.)

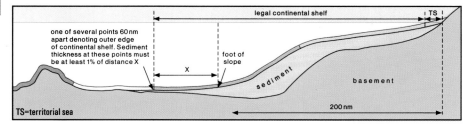

4 *above* This illustrates the first option of the 'Irish formula'. Wherever the continental margin extends beyond 200 nm from the baselines from which the breadth of the territorial sea is measured, the coastal state shall establish the outer edge of the margin by a line joining the outermost fixed points at each of which the thickness of sedimentary rocks is at least 1 per cent of the shortest distance from the point to the foot of the continental slope. The distance between any two fixed points must not exceed 60 nm.

5 *below* A variation of the Irish formula: the outer edge of the margin can be a line drawn by reference to fixed points 60 nm apart and not more than 60 nm from the foot of the physical continental slope.

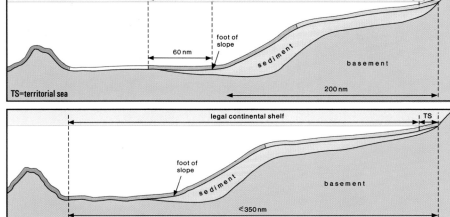

6 *above* A further limitation in the case of broad margin states requires that the fixed points employed in the delineation must not exceed 350 nm from territorial sea baselines. Thus it is possible for the line to terminate on the continental rise.

7 *below* An alternative for the broad margin state is that the fixed points must not exceed 100 nm beyond the 2500 m depth line. The limit could then extend on to the continental margin marine ridges.

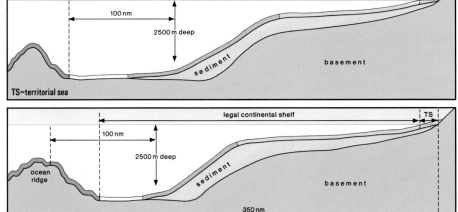

8 *above* A further provision requires that the continental shelf may not extend to encompass ocean ridges, such as the mid-Atlantic ridge. How-ever, this does not apply to submarine 'elevations' that are natural com-ponents of the continental margin, such as banks.

NB (*not shown*) Sri Lanka, a special case, would have been deprived of a substantial part of its continental rise under the Irish formula. It will be catered for in a 'Statement of Under-standing' to be published by the new Convention.

Control of marine pollution

DESPITE early attempts to introduce international pollution controls in 1926 and 1934, it was not until 1954 that the Oilpol Convention was adopted (enforced 1958). This Convention and its subsequent amendments were directed against operational pollution from ships at sea. The deliberate discharge of oil into the sea from tankers was common practice in the 1950s, either from tank cleaning en route to the loading port, or from discharge of ballast, or from ships bound for dry docks. Oilpol forbade discharge of oily mixtures into the sea within specified distances from the coast; required slop tanks on board for the retention of residue and encouraged the load on top (LOT) method. Tankers were also required to carry an oil record book.

The Safety of Life at Sea (SOLAS) Convention and the Collision Regulations have made an important contribution in reducing accidental oil spills. Added to these has been the IMO Convention on the Standards of Training Certification and Watchkeeping for Seafarers (1978). The *Torrey Canyon* stranding in 1967 initiated several changes. First, it led to the adoption at the Brussels Conference in 1969 of an International Convention relating to 'Intervention on the High Seas in case of Oil Pollution Casualties' (in force 1973). The conference also adopted the International Convention on Civil Liability for Oil Pollution Damage (in force 1975), to be followed in 1971 by a convention on an International Oil Pollution Compensation Fund (in force 1978). In addition, the *Torrey Canyon* incident resulted in the Tanker Owners' Voluntary Agreement concerning Liability for Oil Pollution (TOVALOP, 1969).

Attention was also focussed on marine pollution at the United Nations Conference on the Human Environment (Stockholm, June 1972), followed by a conference in London that November. The Convention on the Prevention of Marine Pollution by Dumping of Waste and other Matter was concluded as a result. An IMO Code was drawn up dividing chemicals into three types depending on their hazards and also laying down constructional requirements for chemical carriers. In this same year the Canadian Government unilaterally adopted the Arctic Waters Pollution Prevention Act in order to preserve the ecology of the Arctic against pollution.

Other Conventions in the 1970s included the Oslo Convention for Prevention of Marine Pollution by Dumping from Ships and Aircraft (1972) and the Paris Convention for Prevention of Marine Pollution from Land-based Sources (1974). As part of the United Nations Environmental Programme (UNEP), a Regional Seas Programme was adopted. The Barcelona Convention allowed a coordinated attack upon all sources of pollution in the Mediterranean region. Similar arrangements have been made for the Kuwait, the West and Central African and the Red Sea and Gulf regions.

In 1973 the International Convention for Prevention of Pollution from Ships (Marpol) was concluded to control all forms of pollution from ships. As a result of a protocol of 1978, only the provision on oil pollution will enter into force (October 1983), superseding OILPOL. One novel feature is the designation of special areas in the Mediterranean Sea, Baltic Sea, Black Sea and Arabian/Persian Gulf in which oil discharges are prohibited. It is hoped that MARPOL's provisions on chemicals will enter into force in 1986.

With respect to offshore activities, the Offshore Pollution Liability Agreement (OPOL), a contract concluded by a number of oil companies in 1974, came into force in 1975.

The 1982 United Nations Law of the Sea Convention provides a comprehensive framework of rules covering all sources of marine pollution (see Appendix XI).

1 *right* Marpol provides for special areas where no oil can be discharged from ships over 400 grt. It also requires that ports provide waste reception facilities for oily ballast.

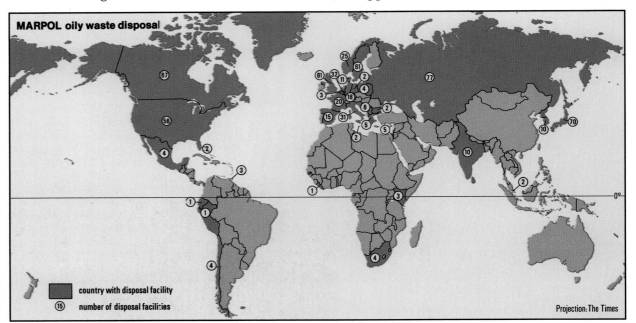

MARPOL oily waste disposal

■ country with disposal facility
⑮ number of disposal facilities

Projection: The Times

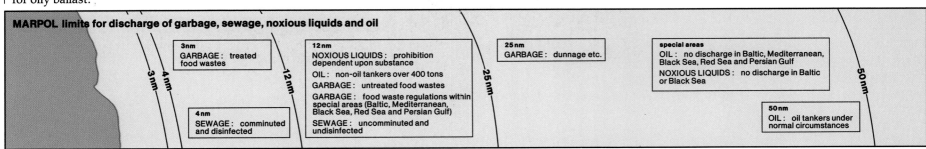

MARPOL limits for discharge of garbage, sewage, noxious liquids and oil

3nm
GARBAGE : treated food wastes

4nm
SEWAGE : comminuted and disinfected

12nm
NOXIOUS LIQUIDS : prohibition dependent upon substance
OIL : non-oil tankers over 400 tons
GARBAGE : untreated food wastes
GARBAGE : food waste regulations within special areas (Baltic, Mediterranean, Black Sea, Red Sea and Persian Gulf)
SEWAGE : uncomminuted and undisinfected

25nm
GARBAGE : dunnage etc.

special areas
OIL : no discharge in Baltic, Mediterranean, Black Sea, Red Sea and Persian Gulf
NOXIOUS LIQUIDS : no discharge in Baltic or Black Sea

50nm
OIL : oil tankers under normal circumstances

2 *above* Marpol was adopted to control all forms of pollution from ships and has limits within which dumping of oils, chemicals, packaged substances, sewage or garbage will eventually be forbidden.

3 *below and* **4** *right* Areas covered by the main regional Conventions which followed OILPOL in the 1970s. The Barrier Reef Amendment which makes this, too, a special area was adopted in October 1971, but is not yet in force.

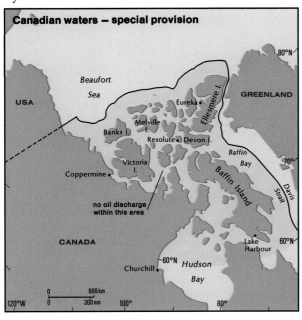

Canadian waters — special provision

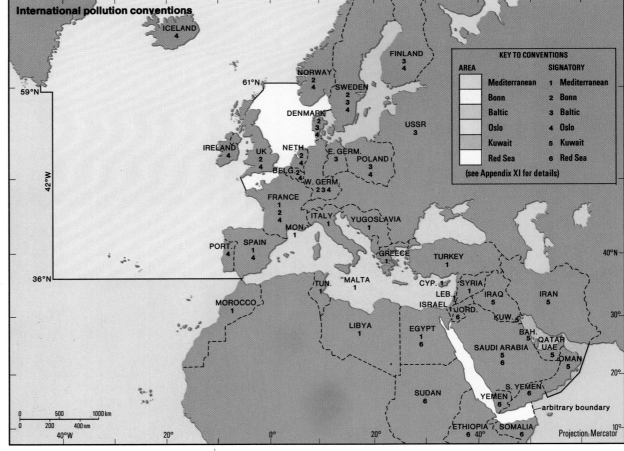

International pollution conventions

KEY TO CONVENTIONS

AREA	SIGNATORY
Mediterranean	1 Mediterranean
Bonn	2 Bonn
Baltic	3 Baltic
Oslo	4 Oslo
Kuwait	5 Kuwait
Red Sea	6 Red Sea

(see Appendix XI for details)

Projection: Mercator

End section contents

page

Appendix I Units of measurement   226

Appendix II Geography of oceans and seas   226

Appendix III The oceans and life   227

Appendix IV Living resources   228

Appendix V Oil and gas   228

Appendix VI Ships and cargoes   229

Appendix VII Shipping routes   230

Appendix VIII The strategic use of the sea   232

Appendix IX The study of the sea   234

Appendix X The management task   238

Appendix XI The law of the sea   241

Glossary   248

Sources   255

Bibliography   256

Acknowledgements   257

Index   258

Appendix I   Units of measurement

Conversion factors

DISTANCE
1 nautical mile = 1.852 kilometres = 1.15 statute miles
1 kilometre = 0.62 statute miles = 0.54 nautical miles
1 statute mile = 0.87 nautical miles = 1.6093 kilometres

DEPTH
1 fathom = 1.829 metres = 6 feet
1 metre = 3.281 feet = 0.547 fathoms
1 foot = 0.166 fathoms = 39.37 metres

1 shackle = 15 fathoms
1 cable = 608 feet (approx. 100 fathoms)
10 cables = 1 nautical mile

WEIGHT
1 tonne = 0.984 long tons = 1.102 short tons
1 long ton = 1.120 short tons = 1.016 tonnes
1 short ton = 0.907 tonnes = 0.893 long tons

CRUDE OIL (based on average gravity)
1 barrel = 0.136 tonnes = 35.6 gallons (Imp) = 42 gallons (US)
1 tonne = 256 gallons (Imp) = 308 gallons (US) = 7.33 barrels
1000 gallons (Imp) = 1201 gallons (US) = 28.6 barrels
1000 gallons (US) = 833 gallons (Imp) = 23.8 barrels

ENERGY

	heat units	million tonnes of oil
10 million million British thermal units	=	approx. 0.25
100 million therms	=	approx. 0.25
10 000 calorie/joules	=	approx. 1
1 million tonnes of coal	=	approx. 0.67

(1 million tonnes of oil produces about 4000 million kilowatt hours of electricity in a modern power station)

TIME
1 mean solar day = 24 mean solar hours
1 sideral day = 23 hours 56 minutes 04.1 seconds of mean solar time
(1 lunar day averages 24 hours 50 minutes of mean solar time)

TEMPERATURE

° centigrade (Celsius)		°Fahrenheit
100†	=	212†
75	=	167
50	=	122
40	=	104
35	=	95
30	=	86
25	=	77
20	=	68
15	=	59
10	=	50
5	=	41
0*	=	32*
−5	=	14
−10	=	14

*freezing point (fresh water)   †boiling point

To convert Fahrenheit to centigrade, deduct 32, multiply remainder by 5 and divide by 9.
To convert centigrade to Fahrenheit, multiply by 9, divide by 5 and add 32.

Tonnage definitions

Tonnage is a means of measuring a ship, and expressing its 'size' and earning capacity. It is used in assessing harbour and port dues and charges for the services rendered to a ship.

Frequently there is confusion over ship tonnages, arising from the use of *measurement* tons (at 100 ft to the ton) and *weight* tons (2240 lb), to express ship characteristics.

There are many forms of tonnage, as follows:

1 **Registered tonnage** The internal capacity of a ship, denoting the cubic capacity under the tonnage deck; a registered ton is 100 cu. ft of internal measurement.

2 **Gross registered tonnage (grt)** The registered tonnage (100 cu. ft), plus the measured tonnage 'over deck', such as the spaces for the bridge, accommodation, etc. GRT is a normal unit for passenger ships and cargo liners and is used as a basis for safety requirements and manning.

3 **Net registered tonnage (nrt)** A measure of the earning capacity of a vessel, expressed in units of 100 cu. ft. It is the grt less the volumes of certain spaces not used for the carriage of cargo (engine room, certain water tanks, etc). NRT is frequently the basis on which harbour dues and pilotage fees are levied. It is a normal unit for passenger ships and cargo liners.

4 **Displacement tonnage** The actual weight of a ship; it equals the weight of water displaced by a vessel when floating at the specific draught, the normal unit for warships.

5 **Light displacement** The weight of the ship when in a 'light' or unloaded state, but including the weight of water in boilers and any permanent ballast.

6 **Load displacement** The light displacement weight plus the weight of cargo fuel, stores, fresh water and water ballast.

7 **Deadweight tonnage (dwt)** The difference between light and load displacements. It is a measure of the carrying capacity of a vessel and is the weight of cargo, fuel, fresh water, and stores that it is able to carry at a specified draught. It is the normal unit for bulk carriers and tankers.

8 **Freight tonnage** Freight rates are assessed on weight or volume of cargo. If an item of cargo adds up to more than 40 cu. ft per ton (or 1 cu. ft per tonne) then the shipper pays on volume.

9 **New tonnage rules** In July 1982 a new convention for the tonnage measurement of ships came into force. Under the new convention the gross tonnage is based on the volume of all enclosed spaces, and net tonnage is the volume of cargo spaces plus the volume of passenger spaces, multiplied by a coefficient.

The gross and net tonnage under the new convention are no longer expressed in tons of 100 cu. ft but in cubic metres.

Among some of the results of the new rules will be large increases in the tonnages of RoRo ships, and reductions for many bulk carriers. However, existing ships need not change to the new system until 18 July 1994, so that the existing scheme will continue for most vessels. Full details of the new system are contained in the IMO Publication, *Tonnage Measurements of Ships* (1969).

Appendix II   Geography of oceans and seas

Digest of ocean facts and figures

The area of the Earth covered by sea is estimated to be 361 740 000 sq. km (139 670 000 sq. miles), or 70.92 per cent of the total surface. The mean depth is estimated to be 3554 m (11 660 ft), and the volume of the oceans to be 1 285 600 000 cu. km (308 400 000 cu. miles).

PACIFIC OCEAN
area 165 384 000 sq. km, covering nearly 40 per cent of the world's total sea area, the largest of the oceans. The greatest breadth (E/W) is 16 000 km and greatest length (N/S) 11 000 km.
depth an average of 4200 m, also the deepest ocean; generally the west is deeper than the east and the north deeper than the south. The greatest depths occur near island groups, including the Aldrich Deep (9400 m), the Marianas Trench (11 022 m) and the maximum depth, the Mindanao Trench (11 524 m).

ATLANTIC OCEAN
area total 82 217 000 sq. km, although commonly divided into North Atlantic (36 000 000 sq. km) and South Atlantic (26 000 000 sq. km). The greatest breadth of the North Atlantic is 7200 km (Morocco–Florida) and of the South Atlantic 9600 km (Guinea–Brazil).
depth an average of 3600 m, the greatest depth occurring in the Puerto Rico Trench (9560 m).

INDIAN OCEAN
area 73 600 000 sq. km, mainly confined to the southern hemisphere, and at its greatest breadth (Tasmania–Cape Agulhas) 9600 km.
depth an average of 4000 m; the greatest depth is the Amirante Trench (9000 m).

The table below shows comparative statistics of various seas, with approximate dimensions where applicable.

	sea area ('000 sq. km)	greatest distance N/S (km)	greatest distance E/W (km)	maximum depth (m)
Pacific Ocean	165 384	11 000	16 000	11 524
Atlantic Ocean	82 217	—	9 600	9 560
Indian Ocean	73 481	—	9 600	9 000
Arctic Ocean	14 056	—	—	5 450
Mediterranean Sea	2 505	960	3 700	4 846
South China Sea	2 318	2 100	1 750	5 514
Bering Sea	2 269	1 800	2 100	5 121
Caribbean Sea	1 943	1 600	2 000	7 100
Gulf of Mexico	1 544	1 200	1 700	4 377
Sea of Okhotsk	1 528	2 200	1 400	3 475
East China Sea	1 248	1 100	750	2 999
Yellow Sea	1 243	800	1 000	91
Hudson Bay	1 233	1 250	1 050	259
Sea of Japan	1 008	1 500	1 100	3 743
North Sea	575	1 200	550	661
Red Sea	438	1 932	360	2 246
Black Sea	461	600	1 100	2 245
Baltic Sea	422	1 500	650	460

Distance of objects at sea

The table shows the distance at which an object is visible at sea in clear weather and with natural refraction, and with the eye of the observer at sea level. In order to calculate the distance of visibility in practice, it is necessary to add to these the distance of visibility corresponding to the height of the observer's eye above sea level.

elevation of object above sea level (metres)	distance of visibility (nm)
1	2.1
3	3.6
5	4.6
10	6.5
25	10.3
50	14.6
100	20.7
200	29.3

River lengths

km	river	km	river
6 695	Nile *Africa*	2 780	São Francisco *South America*
6 570	Amazon *South America*	2 700	Ganges *Asia*
6 380	Yangtze *Asia*	2 655	Zambezi *Africa*
6 020	Mississippi-Missouri *North America*	2 570	Nelson-Saskatchewan *North America*
5 410	Ob-Irtysh *Asia*	2 430	Euphrates *Asia*
4 840	Huang He *Asia*	2 330	Arkansas *North America*
4 630	Zaïre *Africa*	2 330	Colorado *North America*
4 500	Paraná *South America*	2 200	Dnepr *Europe*
4 440	Irtysh *Asia*	2 090	Irrawaddy *Asia*
4 416	Amur *Asia*	2 060	Orinoco *South America*
4 400	Lena *Asia*	2 000	Negro *South America*
4 240	Mackenzie *North America*	1 870	Don *Europe*
4 180	Mekong *Asia*	1 859	Orange *Africa*
4 100	Niger *Africa*	1 799	Pechora *Europe*
4 090	Yenisey *Asia*	1 609	Marañón *South America*
3 969	Missouri *North America*	1 410	Dnestr *Europe*
3 779	Mississippi *North America*	1 320	Rhine *Europe*
3 750	Murray-Darling *Australia*	1 183	Donets *Europe*
3 688	Volga *Europe*	1 159	Elbe *Europe*
3 240	Madeira *South America*	1 094	Gambia *Africa*
3 180	Indus *Asia*	1 080	Yellowstone *North America*
3 058	St Lawrence *North America*	1 014	Vistula *Europe*
3 030	Rio Grande *North America*	1 006	Tagus *Europe*
3 020	Yukon *North America*	909	Oder *Europe*
2 960	Brahmaputra *Asia*	761	Seine *Europe*
2 850	Danube *Europe*	336	Thames *England*
2 820	Salween *Asia*	80	Liffey *Ireland*

Coastline lengths and areal extents of states

As the table shows, the jurisdictional area of some states (small island states in particular) would increase by a very large factor once a 200-mile Exclusive Economic Zone is established.

	length of coastline (nm)	sea area within EEZ limits ('000 sq. km)	total land area ('000 sq. km)		length of coastline (nm)	sea area within EEZ limits ('000 sq. km)	total land area ('000 sq. km)
Albania	155	12.3	28.7	Kuwait	115	12.0	17.8
Algeria	596	137.2	2 381.7	Lebanon	105	22.6	10.4
Angola	806	506.1	1 246.7	Liberia	290	229.7	111.4
Argentina	2 120	1 164.5	2 776.9	Libya	910	338.1	1 759.5
Australia	15 091	7 006.5	7 686.9	Madagascar	2 155	1 292.0	587.0
Bahamas (The)	—	759.2	13.9	Malaysia	1 853	475.6	329.7
Bahrain	68	5.1	0.6	Maldives	—	959.1	0.3
Bangladesh	—	76.8	144.0	Malta	50	66.2	0.3
Barbados	55	167.3	0.4	Mauritania	360	154.3	1 030.7
Belgium	34	2.7	30.5	Mauritius	87	1 183.0	1.9
Benin	—	27.1	112.6	Mexico	4 848	2 851.2	1 972.5
Brazil	3 692	3 168.4	8 512.0	Morocco	895	278.1	446.6
Bulgaria	134	32.9	110.9	Mozambique	1 352	562.0	783.0
Burma	1 230	509.5	678.0	Netherlands	198	84.7	40.8
Cambodia	—	55.6	181.0	New Zealand	2 770	4 833.2	268.7
Cameroon	187	15.4	475.4	Nicaragua	445	159.8	130.0
Canada	11 129	4 697.7	9 976.1	Nigeria	415	210.9	923.8
Cape Verde	—	789.4	4.0	North Yemen	244	33.9	195.0
Chile	2 882	2 288.2	756.9	Norway	1 650	2 024.8	386.6
China	3 962	1 355.8	9 597.0	Oman	—	561.7	212.5
Colombia	1 022	603.2	1 138.9	Pakistan	750	318.5	803.9
Comoros	211	228.4	2.2	Panama	993	306.5	75.6
Congo	106	24.7	342.0	Papua New Guinea	—	n.a.	461.7
Costa Rica	446	258.9	50.7	Peru	1 258	786.6	1 285.2
Cuba	1 747	362.8	114.5	Philippines	6 997	1 890.7	300.0
Cyprus	290	99.4	9.3	Poland	241	28.5	312.7
Denmark	686	68.6	43.1	Portugal	743	1 774.2	92.1
Djibouti	—	6.2	22.0	Qatar	204	24.0	11.0
Dominican Republic	325	268.8	48.7	Romania	113	31.9	237.5
East Germany	191	9.6	108.2	São Tomé and Principe	85	128.2	1.0
Ecuador	458	1 159.0	283.6	Saudi Arabia	1 316	186.2	2 149.7
Egypt	—	173.5	1 001.4	Senegal	241	205.7	196.2
El Salvador	164	91.9	21.0	Seychelles	—	729.7	0.4
Equatorial Guinea	184	283.2	28.1	Sierra Leone	219	155.7	71.7
Ethiopia	546	75.8	1 221.9	Singapore	28	0.3	0.6
Fiji	—	1 134.7	18.3	Somalia	1 596	782.8	637.7
Finland	735	98.1	337.0	South Africa	1 462	1 016.7	1 222.2
France	1 373	341.2	547.0	South Yemen	—	550.3	287.7
Gabon	399	213.6	267.7	Spain	2 038	1 219.4	770.8
Gambia (The)	38	19.5	11.3	Sri Lanka	—	517.4	65.6
Ghana	285	218.1	238.5	Sudan	387	91.6	2 505.8
Greece	1 645	505.1	131.9	Suriname	196	101.2	163.3
Grenada	—	n.a.	0.3	Sweden	1 359	155.3	450.0
Guatemala	178	99.1	108.9	Syria	82	10.3	185.3
Guinea	190	71.0	245.9	Tanzania	669	223.2	945.1
Guinea-Bissau	—	150.5	36.1	Thailand	1 299	324.7	514.0
Guyana	232	130.3	215.0	Togo	26	1.0	56.0
Haiti	584	160.5	27.8	Trinidad and Tobago	254	76.8	5.1
Honduras	374	200.9	112.1	Tunisia	555	85.7	163.6
Iceland	1 080	866.9	103.0	Turkey	1 921	236.6	780.6
India	2 759	2 014.9	3 280.5	USSR	23 098	4 490.3	22 402.2
Indonesia	19 784	5 408.6	1 904.3	United Arab Emirates	1 307	59.3	83.6
Iran	990	155.7	1 648.0	United Kingdom	2 790	2 336.5	286.7
Iraq	10	0.7	434.9	USA	11 650	7 825.0	9 372.0
Ireland	663	380.3	70.3	Uruguay	305	119.3	177.5
Israel	124	23.3	20.7	Venezuela	1 081	363.8	912.0
Italy	2 451	552.1	301.2	Vietnam	1 247	722.1	332.6
Ivory Coast	274	104.6	322.5	Western Samoa	—	96.0	2.8
Jamaica	280	297.6	11.0	West Germany	308	40.8	248.6
Japan	4 842	3 861.1	372.3	Yugoslavia	426	52.5	255.8
Jordan	15	0.7	97.7	Zaire	—	1.0	2 345.4
Kenya	247	118.0	582.6				

Landlocked countries

	outlet(s) to the sea
EUROPE	
Austria	Trieste, Hamburg Rotterdam
Czechoslovakia	Szczecin, Trieste
Hungary	Trieste, Constanța
Luxembourg	Rotterdam
Switzerland	Venice, Genoa, Marseille, Rotterdam
Andorra	Barcelona, Marseille
Leichtenstein	Venice, Trieste
San Marino	Ancona, Venice
Vatican City	Naples, Livorno
SOUTH AMERICA	
Bolivia	Matarani, Arica
Paraguay	Buenos Aires
ASIA	
Afghanistan	Karachi
Bhutan	Calcutta
Laos	Haiphong, Rangoon, Bangkok
Mongolia	Tanggu, Vladivostok
Nepal	Calcutta
AFRICA	
Botswana	Walvis Bay, Durban, Maputo
Burundi	Dar Es Salaam
Central African Republic	Douala
Chad	Lagos, Port Harcourt
Lesotho	Durban
Malawi	Sofala (Beira), Porto Amelia
Mali	Dakar, Conakry
Niger	Abidjan, Lagos
Rwanda	Mombasa, Dar Es Salaam
Swaziland	Maputo
Uganda	Mombasa
Upper Volta	Abidjan, Tema
Zambia	Sofala (Beira), Dar Es Salaam
Zimbabwe	Sofala (Beira), Maputo

Appendix III   The oceans and life

International Standard Statistical Classification of Aquatic Animals and Plants (ISSCAAP)

code	Division group of species
1	**Freshwater fishes**
11	Carps, barbels and other cyprinids
12	Tilapias and other cichlids
13	Miscellaneous freshwater fishes
2	**Diadromous fishes**
21	Sturgeons, paddlefishes, etc.
22	River eels
23	Salmons, trouts, smelt, etc.
24	Shads, milkfishes, etc.
25	Miscellaneous diadromous fishes
3	**Marine fishes**
31	Flounders, halibuts, soles, etc.
32	Cods, hakes, haddocks, etc.

code	Division group of species
33	Redfishes, basses, congers, etc.
34	Jacks, mullets, sauries, etc.
35	Herrings, sardines, anchovies, etc.
36	Tunas, bonitos, billfishes, etc.
37	Mackerel, snocks, cutlassfishes, etc.
38	Sharks, rays, chimaeras, etc.
39	Miscellaneous marine fishes
4	**Crustaceans**
41	Freshwater crustaceans
42	Sea-spiders, crabs, etc.
43	Lobsters, spiny-rock lobsters, etc.
44	Squat-lobsters, nephrops, etc.

code	Division group of species
45	Shrimps, prawns, etc.
46	Krill, planktonic crustaceans, etc.
47	Miscellaneous marine crustaceans
5	**Molluscs**
51	Freshwater molluscs
52	Abalones, winkles, conchs, etc.
53	Oysters
54	Mussels
55	Scallops, pectens, etc.
56	Clams, cockles, arkshells, etc.
57	Squids, cuttlefishes, octopuses, etc.
58	Miscellaneous marine molluscs

code	Division group of species
6	**Whales, seals and other aquatic mammals**
61	Blue-whales, fin-whales, etc.
62	Minke-whales, pilot-whales, etc.
63	Porpoises, dolphins, etc.
64	Eared seals, hair seals, walruses, etc.
65	Miscellaneous aquatic mammals
7	**Miscellaneous aquatic animals**
71	Frogs and other amphibians
72	Turtles and other reptiles
73	Sea-squirts and other tunicates
74	Horseshoe crabs and other arachnoids

code	Division group of species
75	Sea-urchins and other echinoderms
76	Miscellaneous aquatic invertebrates
8	**Miscellaneous aquatic animal products**
81	Pearls, mother-of-pearl, shells, etc.
82	Corals
83	Sponges
84	Aquatic bird guano, eggs, etc.
9	**Aquatic plants**
91	Brown seaweed
92	Red seaweed
93	Green seaweed and other algae
94	Miscellaneous aquatic plants

Appendix IV   Living resources

The International Convention for the Regulation of Whaling: amendment to quotas 1983

Numbers and notes in brackets ( ) are amendments to the schedule adopted at the 34th Annual Meeting of the International Whaling Commission, July 1982. They are not yet incorporated because during a period after adoption objections may be lodged, and 5 countries have lodged objections. Paragraph 13b(4) should be noted as covering a special case: 'The taking by aborigines of minke whales from the West Greenland stock and fin whales from the West Greenland stock is permitted and then only when the meat and products are to be used exclusively for local consumption. The number of whales taken in accordance with this sub-paragraph shall not exceed the limits shown in Table 1.'

SMS = sustained management stock
MSY = maximum sustainable yield
IMS = initial management stock
PS = protection stock

Toothed whale stock classifications and catch limits

	Sperm classification	Sperm catch limit	Bottlenose classification
SOUTHERN HEMISPHERE— 1982/83 season longitudes			
60°W–30°W	—	0	—
30°W–20°E	—	0	—
20°E–60°E	—	0	—
60°E–90°E	—	0	—
90°E–130°E	—	0	—
130°E–160°E	—	0	—
160°E–170°W	—	0	—
170°W–100°W	—	0	—
100°W–60°W	—	0	—
NORTHERN HEMISPHERE— 1982/83 season			
NORTH PACIFIC			
Western Division	—	l(4)	—
Eastern Division	—	0	—
NORTH ATLANTIC	—	0m	PSn
NORTHERN INDIAN OCEAN	—	0	—

Bryde's whale stock classification and catch limits

	classification	catch limit
SOUTHERN HEMISPHERE STOCK— 1982/83 season		
South Atlantic	—	0
Southern Indian Ocean	IMS	197 (0r)
South African Inshore	—	0
Solomon Islands	IMS	0 (r)
Western South Pacific	IMS	237 (0r)
Eastern South Pacific	IMS	188 (0r)
Peruvian Stock	SMS (—)	244P (165P) (76q)
NORTH PACIFIC STOCK—1982 season		
Eastern	IMS	0r
Western	IMS	507 (536)
East China Sea	SMSs (—)	19 (10)
NORTH ATLANTIC—1982/83 season	IMS	0r
NORTHERN INDIAN OCEAN— 1982/83 season	—	0

Baleen whale stock classifications and catch limits

	Sei classification	Sei catch limit	Minke classification	Minke catch limit	Fin classification	Fin catch limit	Blue classification	Hump-Back classification	Right, Bowhead, Pygmy Right classification	Gray classification	Gray catch limit
SOUTHERN HEMISPHERE —1982/83 longitudes											
120°W–60°W	PS	0	—	930 (852)	PS	0	PS	PS	PS	—	—
60°W–0°W	PS	0	—	1249 (656)	PS	0	PS	PS	PS	—	—
0°–70°E	PS	0	—	2198 (6116)	PS	0	PS	PS	PS	—	—
70°E–130°E	PS	0	—	1625 (1969)	PS	0	PS	PS	PS	—	—
130°E–170°W	PS	0	—	1187 (1896)	PS	0	PS	PS	PS	—	—
170°W–120°W	PS	0	—	1317 (937)	PS	0	PS	PS	PS	—	—
Total catch not to exceed	—	0	—	8102 (7072)	—	0	0	0	0	—	—
NORTHERN HEMISPHERE —1982/83											
ARCTIC STOCK	—	—	—	—	—	—	—	PS	—	—	—
NORTH PACIFIC STOCK											
Whole region	PS	0	—	—	PS	0	PS	PS	PS	—	—
Okhotsk Sea/West Pacific	—	—	SMS	421a	—	—	—	—	—	—	—
Sea of Japan—Yellow Sea— East China Sea	—	—	SMSb	940c	—	—	—	—	—	—	—
Remainder	—	—	IMS	0d	—	—	—	—	—	—	—
Eastern	—	—	—	—	—	—	—	—	—	SMS	179e
Western	—	—	—	—	—	—	—	—	—	PS	0
NORTH ATLANTIC STOCK											
Whole region	—	—	—	—	—	—	PS	PS	PS	—	—
West Greenland	—	—	SMS (—)	444f,i	SMSb (—)	6	—	—	—	—	—
Newfoundland/Labrador	—	—	—	—	IMS (—)	90 (0)	—	—	—	—	—
Canadian East Coast	—	—	—	0g	—	—	—	—	—	—	—
Nova Scotia	PS	0	—	—	PS	0	—	—	—	—	—
Central	—	—	SMS (—)	320 (300)	—	—	—	—	—	—	—
East Greenland/Iceland	—	—	—	—	SMS	194 (167)	—	—	—	—	—
Iceland–Denmark Strait	SMS	100f	—	—	—	—	—	—	—	—	—
Spain/Portugal/British Isles	—	—	—	—	SMS (—)	210 (120)j	—	—	—	—	—
Northeastern	—	—	SMS (—)	1790 (—)	—	—	—	—	—	—	—
West Norway/Faroe Islands	—	—	—	—	PS	0	—	—	—	—	—
North Norway	—	—	—	—	SMS (—)	61 (0)	—	—	—	—	—
Eastern	—	0	—	—	—	—	—	—	—	—	—
NORTHERN INDIAN OCEAN STOCK	—	—	IMS	0	—	—	PS	PS	PS	—	—

a The total catch of minke whales shall not exceed 1678 in the five years 1980 to 1984 inclusive.
b Provisionally listed as SMS for 1982 and 1983.
c The total catch of minke whales shall not exceed 3634 in the five years 1980 to 1984 inclusive.
d Pending a satisfactory estimate of stock size.
e Available to be taken by aborigines or a Contracting Government on behalf of aborigines pursuant to paragraph 13b(4).
f The total catch of minke whales shall not exceed 1778 in the five years 1981 to 1985 inclusive.
g Pending submission of data leading to an adequate assessment.
h The total catch of sei whales shall not exceed 504 in the six years 1980 to 1985 inclusive.
i The total catch of fin whales shall not exceed 270 in the three years 1983 to 1985 inclusive.
j Of the total numbers shown, a proportion corresponding to needs may be taken by aborigines pursuant to paragraph 13b(4).
k Available to be taken by aborigines pursuant to paragraph 13b(4).
l No whales may be taken from this stock until catch limits including any limitations on size and sex are established by the Commission. (The Government of Japan lodged an objection to footnote l within the prescribed period. This footnote came into force on 8th February 1982 but is not binding on Japan.)
m Provided that the remainder of 130 male sperm whales for the 1981 coastal season may be taken in the 1982 coastal season.
n Provisionally listed as PS for 1982 pending the accumulation of sufficient information for classification. Notwithstanding footnote l, catch limits for the 1982 and 1983 coastal seasons are 450 and 400 whales respectively, provided that included with each of these catch limits there may be a by-catch of females not to exceed 11.5 per cent and all whaling operations for this species shall cease for the rest of each season when the by-catch is reached.
p Available to be taken in a six months period starting in November 1982.
q Special remainder from 1981 coastal season that may be taken in a six months period starting in November 1981 making a total of 320 whales which may be taken during this period pursuant to this footnote and footnote P.
r Pending a satisfactory estimate of stock size.
s Provisionally listed as SMS for 1982.

Appendix V   Oil and gas

Total oil production (1981)

country	million tonnes	thousand barrels daily	percentage share of total	percentage change (annual average 1976–81)	country	million tonnes	thousand barrels daily	percentage share of total	percentage change (annual average 1976–81)
USA	481.6	10 150	16.6	+0.7	Oman	15.8	315	0.5	−2.9
Canada	73.7	1 565	2.5	−0.9	Qatar	19.5	405	0.7	−4.0
Argentina	25.8	495	0.9	+4.7	Saudi Arabia	491.6	9 990	17.0	+3.1
Brazil	10.6	220	0.4	+5.0	Sharjah	0.5	10	—	−23.1
Colombia	6.8	135	0.2	−1.7	other Middle East	11.0	210	0.4	−3.4
Ecuador	10.7	220	0.4	+3.3	Algeria	46.4	1 010	1.6	−1.5
Mexico	128.3	2 585	4.4	+24.1	Egypt	32.1	690	1.1	+14.4
Trinidad	12.0	240	0.4	+2.4	Libya	53.9	1 120	1.9	−10.4
Venezuela	112.1	2 170	3.9	−1.8	other North Africa	5.5	115	0.2	+9.2
other Latin America	12.6	265	0.4	+12.0	Gabon	7.6	150	0.3	−7.5
Austria	1.3	25	—	−6.9	Nigeria	71.3	1 445	2.5	−7.1
France	1.7	35	0.1	+9.6	other West Africa	16.5	330	0.6	+14.6
Italy	1.7	30	0.1	+9.2	South Asia	13.5	275	0.5	+6.2
Norway	24.9	505	0.9	+12.5	Brunei	8.2	165	0.3	−4.2
Turkey	2.4	45	0.1	−2.0	Indonesia	79.3	1 605	2.7	+1.2
United Kingdom	89.4	1 845	3.1	+50.0	other South East Asia	12.4	250	0.4	+10.1
West Germany	4.5	90	0.1	−4.0	Japan	0.4	10	—	−7.5
Yugoslavia	4.3	85	0.1	+2.0	Australasia	19.8	415	0.7	−0.8
other Western Europe	3.8	75	0.1	+1.4	USSR	609.0	12 370	21.1	+3.2
Abu Dhabi	54.8	1 140	1.9	−6.5	Eastern Europe	17.2	355	0.6	−2.9
Dubai	17.8	360	0.6	+2.7	China	101.0	2 035	3.5	+3.9
Iran	65.5	1 315	2.3	−26.0					
Iraq	44.2	900	1.5	−18.0	World total	2 890.3	59 100	100.0	−0.4
Kuwait	48.1	965	1.7	−13.3	OPEC members total	1 142.5	23 175	39.5	−5.8
Neutral Zone	19.2	370	0.7	−4.6					

World oil consumption (1981)

country/area	million tonnes	thousand barrels daily	percentage share of total	percentage change (annual average) 1976–81
USA	743.2	15 480	25.6	−2.0
Canada	81.6	1 745	2.8	−1.0
Latin America	227.8	4 745	7.8	+4.6
Austria	10.9	220	0.4	−1.3
Belgium & Luxembourg	25.6	520	0.9	−1.8
Cyprus/Gibraltar/Malta	1.4	30	—	+2.2
Denmark	11.7	240	0.4	−6.9
Finland	12.0	240	0.4	+1.4
France	99.3	2 070	3.4	−3.6
Greece	11.9	240	0.4	+2.4
Iceland	0.5	10	—	−1.8
Republic of Ireland	5.4	115	0.2	+0.4
Italy	95.5	1 935	3.3	−0.7
Netherlands	35.2	730	1.2	−2.1
Norway	7.5	155	0.3	−3.5
Portugal	8.9	180	0.3	+4.6
Spain	48.0	990	1.7	−0.1
Sweden	21.8	440	0.8	−6.0
Switzerland	11.9	250	0.4	−1.8
Turkey	15.4	315	0.5	−0.1
United Kingdom	74.6	1 555	2.6	−4.0
West Germany	117.6	2 465	4.1	−3.3
Yugoslavia	14.4	285	0.5	+1.6
Middle East	84.7	1 685	2.9	+2.6
Africa	75.9	1 565	2.6	+5.9
South Asia	43.4	890	1.5	+5.8
South East Asia	123.7	2 480	4.3	+6.9
Japan	224.3	4 700	7.7	−2.4
Australasia	36.3	770	1.3	−0.1
USSR	444.1	8 985	15.3	+2.9
Eastern Europe	102.4	2 110	3.5	+2.7
China	84.8	1 705	2.9	+2.0
World total	2 901.7	59 845	100.0	<−0.05

The production tables include onshore as well as offshore oil and gas statistics, for comparison with the tables on pages 102–104.

Total natural gas production (1981)

country	million tonnes (oil equiv.)	billion cu. ft daily	percentage share of total	percentage change (annual average) 1976–81
USA	499.2	19 565	36.2	+0.5
Canada	68.0	2 665	4.9	−0.4
Argentina	7.2	280	0.5	+1.7
Bolivia	2.4	95	0.2	+8.8
Chile	3.2	125	0.2	−2.7
Mexico	32.1	1 260	2.3	+16.8
Trinidad	2.2	85	0.2	+2.1
Venezuela	15.5	605	1.1	+4.8
other Latin America	3.7	145	0.3	+2.5
France	6.6	260	0.5	—
Italy	11.6	455	0.8	−5.8
Netherlands	65.0	2 550	4.7	−2.4
Norway	22.7	890	1.7	+138.2
United Kingdom	31.9	1 250	2.3	−1.1
West Germany	16.7	655	1.2	+3.5
other Western Europe	3.1	120	0.2	−3.4
Abu Dhabi	5.4	210	0.4	+34.3
Iran	5.7	225	0.4	−21.7
Kuwait	5.2	205	0.4	+0.7
Saudi Arabia	13.2	515	1.0	+16.6
other Middle East	8.5	330	0.6	+6.9
Algeria	19.6	770	1.4	+17.0
Libya	2.9	115	0.2	−3.3
Nigeria	0.7	25	0.1	+3.6
other Africa	1.8	70	0.1	+18.7
Pakistan	6.1	240	0.5	+5.6
other South Asia	7.0	275	0.5	+8.7
Indonesia	16.9	660	1.2	+51.5
other South East Asia	10.9	425	0.8	+2.0
Japan	1.8	70	0.1	−4.8
Australasia	12.0	470	0.9	+11.3
USSR	411.8	16 145	29.9	+7.3
Eastern Europe	46.3	1 815	3.4	−0.2
China	11.6	455	0.8	+3.0
World total	1 378.5	54 025	100.0	+3.2
OPEC members total	91.0	3 565	6.6	+7.6

Appendix VI Ships and cargoes

World fleets

GENERAL CARGO VESSELS

flag	1975	1980	1982
	million gross registered tons (grt)		
World	70.8	82.6	84.6
European Community	19.5	20.9	18.8
Denmark	1.2	1.0	0.7
France	1.4	1.3	1.2
West Germany	2.4	2.2	1.9
Greece	6.3	10.4	9.8
Italy	1.1	1.0	1.0
Netherlands	1.8	1.6	1.6
UK	4.9	3.0	2.3
Norway	1.9	1.3	1.4
Sweden	1.1	1.1	1.1
USA	3.9	3.5	4.0
Japan	5.2	4.3	5.0
Spain	1.0	1.1	1.1
USSR	7.3	7.6	7.7
Brazil	1.0	1.3	1.3
China	1.6	3.6	4.0
India	1.4	2.0	2.0
Liberia	3.6	3.4	3.6
Panama	4.8	8.9	10.0
Singapore	1.4	2.4	2.2

BULK CARRIERS AND COMBINATION CARRIERS

flag	1975	1980	1982
	million gross registered tons (grt)		
World	85.5	109.8	115.9
European Community	24.2	31.9	32.6
Denmark	0.6	0.6	0.7
France	1.4	1.5	1.6
West Germany	2.2	1.7	1.5
Greece	7.2	16.4	17.3
Italy	3.6	3.9	3.8
Netherlands	0.5	0.7	0.5
UK	8.1	6.2	6.0
Norway	9.2	6.0	6.3
Sweden	2.8	0.7	0.4
USA	1.9	2.0	1.9
Japan	12.4	13.0	13.2
Spain	1.1	1.2	1.2
USSR	0.6	2.1	2.3
Brazil	0.5	1.6	2.2
China	0.5	1.8	2.2
India	1.6	2.6	2.7
Liberia	19.7	23.9	22.9
Panama	2.6	6.1	9.3
Singapore	0.9	1.9	2.3

World merchant shipping laid up due to lack of employment

TANKERS/NON TANKERS

year	number	percentage of total tonnage (dwt)
1975	454/194	14/3
1980	77/325	2/1
1982	350/511	15/2

CONTAINER VESSELS

flag	1975	1980	1982
	million gross registered tons (grt)		
World	6.2	11.3	12.7
European Community	2.6	4.5	4.9
Denmark	0.2	0.5	0.8
France	0.1	0.4	0.5
West Germany	0.6	1.2	1.1
Greece	—	—	0.1
Italy	0.1	0.2	0.3
Netherlands	0.2	0.3	0.4
UK	1.3	1.7	1.5
Norway	0.1	0.1	0.1
Sweden	0.1	0.1	0.1
USA	1.8	1.9	2.1
Japan	1.1	1.6	1.7
Spain	—	—	0.1
USSR	0.1	0.3	0.3
Brazil	—	—	—
China	—	—	—
India	—	—	—
Liberia	0.2	0.5	0.4
Panama	—	0.3	0.6
Singapore	0.1	0.4	0.6

TANKERS

flag	1975	1980	1982
	million gross registered tons (grt)		
World	286.5	351.6	347.9
European Community	81.6	90.0	87.8
Denmark	4.2	5.5	5.0
France	13.5	15.7	14.0
West Germany	5.2	5.5	5.1
Greece	15.1	22.5	27.6
Italy	7.4	9.1	8.4
Netherlands	4.9	4.9	4.5
UK	30.8	26.1	22.4
Norway	26.6	25.6	25.6
Sweden	5.9	3.8	3.4
USA	9.4	16.3	17.3
Japan	33.4	34.7	34.4
Spain	4.7	9.2	9.6
USSR	5.5	7.4	7.5
Brazil	1.8	3.0	3.3
China	1.0	1.8	1.9
India	1.1	2.0	2.1
Liberia	84.1	107.1	96.0
Panama	10.6	13.6	16.8
Singapore	2.6	5.1	5.5

Appendix VII Shipping routes

Sea distance tables

Distances in nautical miles. Approximate time of voyage in days and hours at a speed of 15 knots

from **Ābādān** *to*

	nm	days	hours
Aden	1 939	5	9
Bombay	1 554	4	7
Cape Town	5 891	16	8
Colombo	2 500	6	22
Guayaquil	10 460	29	1
Karachi	1 157	3	5
København	7 027	19	12
Mombasa	2 850	7	22

from **Abidjan** *to*

	nm	days	hours
Bishop Rock (Scilly Is)	3 350	9	8
Bordeaux	3 376	9	12
Buenos Aires	3 933	10	22
Cape Town	2 679	7	11
Cristóbal (Panama)	4 592	12	18
Gibraltar	2 657	7	9
I. d'Ouessant (Ushant)	3 290	9	3
Lisboa	2 692	7	11
Montevideo	3 836	10	16
New Orleans	5 313	14	18
New York	4 429	12	7
Québec	4 550	12	15
St Nazaire	3 324	9	5

from **Aden** *to*

	nm	days	hours
Ābādān	1 939	5	9
Bombay	1 645	4	13
Cape Town (NE monsoon)	4 100	11	9
Cape Town (SW monsoon)	4 360	12	2
Colombo	2 094	5	12
Durban (NE monsoon)	3 350	9	7
Durban (SW monsoon)	3 600	10	0
Jakarta	3 885	10	19
Karachi	1 470	4	2
København	5 077	14	2
Madras	2 710	7	12
Mauritius (NE monsoon)	2 340	6	12
Mauritius (SW monsoon)	2 680	7	10
Melbourne	6 450	17	22
Mombasa	1 598	4	10
Port Adelaide	6 130	17	0
Seychelles Is	1 420	3	22
Singapore	3 640	10	2
Suez	1 310	3	15
Zanzibar	1 720	4	18

from **Antwerpen** *to*

	nm	days	hours
Aberdeen	458	1	6
Arkhangel'sk	2 064	5	17
Bergen	608	1	16
Bishop Rock (Scilly Is)	452	1	6
Buenos Aires	6 336	17	14
Dover	135	0	9
Dundee	454	1	6
Glasgow	806	2	5
Grimsby	254	0	16
Hull	265	0	17
I. d'Ouessant (Ushant)	441	1	5
Ijmuiden	132	0	8
Leith	418	1	3
Sunderland	347	0	23
Tyne	335	0	22

from **Auckland** *to*

	nm	days	hours
Balboa	6 510	18	2
Brisbane	1 358	3	18
Fremantle	3 202	8	21
Hobart	1 517	4	5
Honolulu	3 820	10	14
Port Adelaide	2 035	5	15
San Francisco	5 675	15	18
Singapore	4 990	14	3
Sydney	1 274	3	13
Thursday Island (Torres St)	2 560	7	2
Valparaíso	5 247	14	13
Wellington	543	1	12

from **Barcelona** *to*

	nm	days	hours
Algiers	279	0	19
Gibraltar	515	1	10
Marseille	185	0	12
Odessa	1 811	5	1
Port Said	1 588	4	10
Ródhos	1 309	3	15
Suez	1 675	4	16
Tanger	539	1	12
Trieste	1 300	3	15
Venezia	1 316	3	16

from **Bermuda** *to*

	nm	days	hours
Ascension	3 770	10	11
Barbados	1 220	3	9
Cape Town	6 180	17	4
Georgetown (Georgetown)	1 550	4	7
Gibraltar	2 925	8	3
Halifax (Nova Scotia)	752	2	2
Key West	1 088	3	0
La Habana	1 150	3	4
New York	695	1	22
Plymouth	2 810	7	19
St Thomas (Virgin Is)	870	2	10
Southampton	2 956	8	5

from **Bishop Rock (Scilly Is)** *to*

	nm	days	hours
Antwerpen	452	1	6
Boston (winter)	2 710	7	12
Boston (summer)	2 815	7	19
Cherbourg	191	0	12
Dover	310	0	20
Hamburg	765	2	3
I. d'Ouessant (Ushant)	100	0	6
Le Havre	258	0	17
Liverpool	283	0	18
New York (winter)	2 903	8	1
New York (summer)	2 991	8	7
Plymouth	97	0	6
Rotterdam/Europoort	453	1	6
Southampton	219	0	14

from **Bombay** *to*

	nm	days	hours
Ābādān	1 564	4	8
Aden	1 640	4	13
Calcutta	2 120	5	21
Cape Town	4 600	12	18
Galle (Sri Lanka)	960	2	16
Guayaquil	10 160	28	5
Karachi	465	1	7
København	6 732	18	16
London (docks)	6 260	17	9
Madras	1 450	4	0
Mauritius (NE monsoon)	2 540	7	1
Mauritius (SW monsoon)	2 960	8	5
Muscat	880	2	10
Rangoon	2 130	5	22
Seychelles Is (NE monsoon)	1 760	4	21
Seychelles Is (SW monsoon)	2 000	5	13
Singapore	2 460	6	20
Zanzibar	2 520	7	0

from **Booby Is (Torres Strait)** *to*

	nm	days	hours
Aden	6 002	16	16
Bahrain	6 051	16	19
Bombay	4 826	13	9
Calcutta	4 132	11	10
Cape Town	6 820	18	22
Chi-Lung	2 636	7	7
Colombo	3 960	11	0
Dumai (Sumatra)	2 712	7	12
Durban	6 841	19	0
Ho Chi Minh City	2 611	7	6
Hong Kong	2 711	7	12
Jakarta	2 131	5	22
Karachi	5 280	14	16
Kōbe	3 143	8	17
Manila	2 178	6	0
Miri (Sarawak)	2 259	6	6
Napier (via Gladstone)	2 845	7	21
Pelabahan Kelang	2 691	7	11
Shanghai	3 122	8	16
Singapore	2 508	6	23
Surabaya	1 796	5	0
Whangarei (via Gladstone)	2 487	6	22
Whangarei (via Basilisk)	2 568	7	3
Yokohama	3 228	8	23

(NB The route Sydney to Hong Kong is 224nm shorter via Torres Strait than via east of New Ireland. The route Sydney to Manila is 315nm shorter via Torres Strait than via east of New Ireland Is.)

from **Buenos Aires** *to*

	nm	days	hours
Antwerpen	6 335	17	14
Bahía Blanca	509	1	9
Brisbane (via Cape Town)	7 482	20	18
Cape Town	3 780	10	12
Cardiff	6 123	17	0
Cherbourg	6 073	16	20
Corunna	5 595	15	13
Fremantle	8 660	24	1
Glasgow	6 317	17	15
Guayaquil (via Magellan St)	4 443	12	8
Hobart (via Wellington, NZ)	7 095	19	17
København	6 761	18	18
Leixões/Oporto	5 460	15	4
Lisboa	5 300	14	17
Liverpool	6 258	17	9
Madeira	4 818	13	9
Melbourne (via Cape Horn)	7 384	20	12
Montevideo	115	0	7
New York	5 838	16	5
Plymouth	6 029	16	17
Port Adelaide (via Cape Horn)	7 775	21	14
Recife	2 170	6	0
Rio de Janeiro	1 140	3	4
Santos	998	2	18
Southampton	6 125	17	0
Sydney (via Cape Horn)	7 269	20	4
Tyne	6 495	18	1
Vigo	5 545	15	9

from **Cabo Finisterre** *to*

	nm	days	hours
Gibraltar	542	1	12
Istanbul	2 360	6	13
I. d'Ouessant (Ushant)	377	1	1
Pantelleria	1 368	3	19
Southampton	596	1	15

from **Calcutta** *to*

	nm	days	hours
Bombay	2 120	5	21
Cape Town (NE monsoon)	5 580	15	12
Cape Town (SW monsoon)	5 780	16	1
Colombo	1 230	3	10
Galle (Sri Lanka)	1 140	3	4
Guayaquil	12 015	33	9
Karachi	2 564	7	2
København	8 358	23	5
London (docks)	7 920	22	0
Madras	750	2	2
Mauritius (NE monsoon)	3 240	9	0
Mauritius (SW monsoon)	3 440	9	13
Singapore	1 530	4	12

from **Callao** *to*

	nm	days	hours
Antofagasta	725	2	0
Balboa	1 346	3	17
Coquimbo	1 100	3	1
Honolulu	5 130	14	6
London (docks)	6 135	17	1
Mazatlán	2 730	7	14
Papeete (Tahiti)	4 200	11	16
San Francisco	3 985	11	1
Valparaíso	1 290	3	4

from **Cape Town** *to*

	nm	days	hours
Ābādān	5 891	16	8
Aden	4 100	11	9
Ascension	2 380	6	14
Bermuda	6 180	17	4
Bombay	4 600	12	18
Brisbane	7 402	20	13
Buenos Aires	3 780	10	12
Calcutta	5 580	15	12
Colombo	4 350	12	2
Dakar	3 590	9	23
Durban	798	2	5
Freetown	3 120	8	16
Fremantle	4 951	13	18
Hobart	6 570	18	6
Karachi	4 665	12	23
København	6 585	18	7
Las Palmas	4 425	12	7
London (docks)	6 110	16	23
Madeira	4 675	12	23
Madras	4 960	13	18
Mauritius	2 280	6	8
Melbourne	6 445	17	21
Montevideo	3 660	10	4
New York	6 800	18	21
Port Adelaide	6 107	16	23
Rio de Janeiro	3 265	9	1
Singapore	5 630	15	15
Southampton	5 945	16	12
Sydney	6 904	19	4
Zanzibar	2 400	6	16

from **Casquets Lt** *to*

	nm	days	hours
Beachy Head	117	0	7
Cap Gris Nez	167	0	11
Dungeness	146	0	9
Eddystone Lt	79	0	5
I. d'Ouessant (Ushant)	128	0	8
Needles	64	0	4
Portland Bill	47	0	3
South Goodwin Lt	172	0	11

from **Colombo** *to*

	nm	days	hours
Ābādān	2 500	6	22
Aden	2 091	5	12
Brisbane	5 293	17	7
Calcutta	1 230	3	10
Cape Town (NE monsoon)	4 350	12	2
Cape Town (SW monsoon)	4 600	12	18
Fremantle	3 126	8	16
Hobart	4 827	13	9
Jakarta	1 830	5	2
Karachi	1 341	3	17
København	7 168	19	21
Madras	580	1	14
Mauritius (NE monsoon)	2 090	5	19
Mauritius (SW monsoon)	2 400	6	16
Melbourne	4 675	12	23
Pinang	1 284	3	13
Port Adelaide	4 364	12	2
Rangoon	1 257	3	11
Singapore	1 575	4	9
Suez (NE monsoon)	3 440	9	13
Suez (SW monsoon)	3 785	10	12
Sydney	5 161	16	14
Zanzibar	2 645	7	8

from **Dakar** *to*

	nm	days	hours
Bordeaux	2 228	6	4
Cape Town	3 590	9	23
Cardiff	2 360	6	13
Freetown	501	1	9
Gibraltar	1 495	4	3
La Pallice	2 174	6	7
Le Havre	2 460	6	20
Liverpool	2 475	6	21
Madeira	1 082	3	0
Marseille	2 188	6	2
Nice	2 265	6	7
St Nazaire	2 176	6	1
Tenerife	840	2	8

from **Dover** *to*

	nm	days	hours
Amsterdam	165	0	11
Antwerpen	135	0	9
Bishop Rock (Scilly Is)	314	0	20
Bordeaux	611	1	16
Calais	22	0	1
Dunkerque	38	0	2
Gibraltar	1 230	3	10
Hamburg	381	1	1
I. d'Ouessant (Ushant)	310	0	20
Le Havre	115	0	7
Liverpool	597	1	15
Plymouth	225	0	15
Rotterdam/Europoort	137	0	9
Southampton	119	0	8
Vigo	736	2	1

from **Durban** *to*

	nm	days	hours
Aden	3 350	9	7
Cape Town	798	2	5
Fremantle	4 240	11	18
Karachi	3 885	10	19
Maputo	298	0	19
Mauritius	1 553	4	7
Port Elizabeth	384	1	1
Sofala (Beira)	702	1	22
Toamasina (Madagascar)	1 360	3	18
Zanzibar	1 595	4	10

from **Fernando de Noronha Is** *to*

	nm	days	hours
Montevideo	2 364	6	13
Porto Grande (Cape Verde Is)	1 316	3	15
Recife	300	0	20
Rio de Janeiro	1 384	3	20

from **Gibraltar** *to*

	nm	days	hours
Azores	980	2	17
Barbados	3 250	9	0
Bermuda	2 930	8	3
Bombay	4 953	13	18
Brindisi	1 280	3	13
Cabo Finisterre	542	1	12
Cristóbal (Panama)	4 343	12	1
Dakar	1 500	4	4
Dover	1 230	3	10
Genova	860	2	9
Glasgow	1 373	3	19
Halifax (Nova Scotia)	2 675	7	10
I. d'Ouessant (Ushant)	920	2	13
Istanbul	1 820	5	1
Las Palmas	705	1	23
Liverpool	1 275	3	13
London (docks)	1 313	3	15
Madeira	610	1	16
Malta	990	2	18
Marseille	690	1	22
Napoli	975	2	17
New Orleans	4 550	12	15
New York	3 210	8	22
Plymouth	1 050	2	22
Porto Grande (Cape Verde Is)	1 560	4	8
Port Said	1 905	5	7
Southampton	1 142	3	4
Tenerife	720	2	0
Toulon	706	1	23

from **Guayaquil** *to*

	nm	days	hours
Ābādān	10 460	29	1
Amsterdam	5 695	15	19
Bergen	6 122	17	0
Bombay	10 160	28	5
Bremen	5 908	16	9
Brisbane	7 346	20	9
Buenos Aires (via Magellan St)	4 443	12	8
Calcutta	12 015	33	9
Fremantle (via Torres Strait)	8 922	24	18
Genova	6 067	16	20
Hamburg	5 926	16	11
København	6 085	16	21
Le Havre	5 480	15	5
Liverpool	5 511	15	7
London (docks)	5 596	15	13
Melbourne	7 410	20	14
Montreal	4 020	11	4
New Orleans	2 258	6	6
New York	2 849	7	21
Port Adelaide	8 130	22	14
Rotterdam/Europoort	5 670	15	18
Shanghai	8 882	24	16
Singapore	10 740	29	20
Wellington	6 020	16	17
Yokohama	7 996	22	5

from **Halifax (Nova Scotia)** *to*

	nm	days	hours
Bermuda	750	2	2
Gibraltar	2 670	7	10
La Habana	1 635	4	13
London (docks)	2 719	7	13
New York	590	1	15
Plymouth	2 400	6	16
Québec	250	2	2
St John's (Newfoundland)	540	1	12

from **Hong Kong** *to*

	nm	days	hours
Brisbane (via Torres Strait)	4 046	11	5
Fremantle	3 505	9	17
Honolulu	4 860	13	12
Manila	640	1	18
Melbourne (via Torres Strait)	5 014	16	4
Port Adelaide	4 789	13	7
Shanghai	850	2	8
Singapore	1 440	4	0
Sydney (via Torres Strait)	4 449	12	8
Vladivostok	1 640	4	13
Yokohama	1 585	4	9

from **Honolulu** *to*

	nm	days	hours
Auckland	3 815	10	14
Balboa	4 685	13	0
Callao	5 130	14	6
Esquimalt	2 360	6	13
Fiji Is (Kandavu)	2 780	7	17
Hong Kong	4 860	13	12
Papeete (Tahiti)	2 360	6	13
San Francisco	2 090	5	19
Seattle	2 405	6	16
Sydney	4 420	12	6
Valparaíso	5 911	16	10
Victoria (British Columbia)	2 349	6	12
Yokohama	3 385	9	9

from **Istanbul** *to*

	nm	days	hours
Batumi	586	1	15
Constanta	194	0	13
Gelibolu	132	0	8
Gibraltar	1 810	5	0
Malta	850	2	3
Novorossiysk	446	1	5
Odessa	344	0	23
Port Said	795	2	5

from **Jakarta** *to*

	nm	days	hours
Aden	3 885	10	19
Brisbane (via Torres Strait)	3 466	9	15
Colombo	1 842	5	2
Fremantle	1 761	4	21
Hobart	3 510	9	18
Melbourne	3 385	9	9
Padang	600	1	16
Port Adelaide	3 047	8	11
Shanghai	2 522	7	0
Sydney (via Torres Strait)	3 869	10	17
Thursday Island (Torres St)	2 165	6	0
Yokohama	3 220	8	22

from **Karachi** *to*

	nm	days	hours
Ābādān	1 157	3	5
Aden	1 470	4	2
Bombay	465	1	7
Calcutta	2 564	7	2
Cape Town	4 665	12	23
Colombo	1 341	3	17
Durban	3 885	10	19
Fremantle	4 438	12	7
Madras	1 910	5	7
Mombasa	2 359	6	13
Suez	2 772	7	16

from **La Habana** *to*

	nm	days	hours
Bermuda	1 145	3	4
Charleston	600	1	16
Cristóbal (Panama)	1 003	2	18
Halifax (Nova Scotia)	1 635	4	13
Key West	902	0	6
London (docks)	4 259	11	19
New Orleans	585	1	15
Norfolk	975	2	17
Plymouth	3 870	10	18
Savannah	610	1	16
Veracruz	860	2	9

from **Las Palmas** *to*

	nm	days	hours
Cape Town	4 425	12	7
Freetown	1 320	3	16
Gibraltar	705	1	23
I. d'Ouessant (Ushant)	1 306	3	15
Lisboa	712	1	23
Liverpool	1 650	4	14
Plymouth	1 432	3	23
Recife	2 445	6	19
Porto Grande (Cape Verde Is)	866	2	9
Tenerife	40	0	3

from **Le Havre** *to*

	nm	days	hours
Abidjan	2 460	6	20
Bordeaux	528	1	12
Dover	115	0	7
Guayaquil	5 480	15	5
I. d'Ouessant (Ushant)	235	0	15
La Pallice	463	1	7
Las Palmas	1 544	4	7
Lorient	342	0	23
Marseille	1 846	5	3
St Nazaire	398	1	2

from **Leningrad** *to*

	nm	days	hours
Aberdeen	1 261	3	12
Antwerpen	1 395	3	21
Arkhangel'sk	2 609	7	6
Calais	1 371	3	19

	nm	days/hours
Dover	1 374	3 19
Dunkerque	1 383	3 20
Gibraltar	2 179	6 2
Hamburg	868	2 10
Kiel Canal (Kiel)	832	2 8
København	699	1 22
Narvik	1 750	4 20
Oslo	965	2 6
Riga	457	1 6
Rotterdam/Europoort	1 299	3 14
Stavanger	1 073	2 23
Zeebrugge	1 342	3 17
from **Lisboa** *to*		
Buenos Aires	5 300	14 17
Cabo Finisterre	264	0 17
I. d'Ouessant (Ushant)	655	1 19
Las Palmas	712	1 23
Liverpool	995	2 18
Madeira	530	1 11
Plymouth	770	2 3
Southampton	865	2 9
from **Liverpool** *to*		
Bilbao	700	1 22
Bishop Rock (Scilly Is)	283	0 18
Bordeaux	670	1 20
Brisbane (via Torres Strait)	11 901	33 1
Buenos Aires	6 258	17 9
Dakar	2 475	6 21
Dublin	120	0 8
Fremantle	9 479	26 7
Gibraltar	1 275	3 13
Glasgow	212	0 14
Guayaquil	5 511	15 7
Hobart	11 140	30 22
København	1 035	2 21
Las Palmas	1 650	4 14
Lisboa	995	2 18
Melbourne	11 015	30 14
New Orleans	4 530	12 14
New York (winter)	3 073	8 12
New York (summer)	3 171	8 19
Oslo	958	2 15
Port Adelaide	10 677	29 15
Port Said	3 175	8 19
Santander	685	1 21
Sydney	11 474	31 20
from **London (docks)** *to*		
Antwerpen	180	0 12
Bishop Rock (Scilly Is)	405	1 3
Bombay	6 260	17 9
Brisbane (via Torres Strait)	11 936	33 3
Dover	90	0 6
Fremantle	9 514	26 10
Göteborg	581	1 14
Guayaquil	5 596	15 13
Hamburg	427	1 4
Hobart	11 175	31 1
København (via Kiel Canal)	587	1 15
Leith	404	1 2
Leningrad (via Kiel Canal)	1 212	3 8
Melbourne	11 090	30 19
New York	3 270	9 2
Port Adelaide	10 712	29 18
Rotterdam/Europoort	177	0 11
Sydney	11 509	31 23
from **Madeira (Funchal)** *to*		
Buenos Aires	4 818	13 9
Cape Town	4 675	12 23
Dakar	1 082	3 0
Gibraltar	610	1 16
I. d'Ouessant (Ushant)	1 090	3 0
Jamestown (St Helena)	3 059	8 11
Lisboa	530	1 11
New York	2 764	7 16
Plymouth	1 210	3 8
Porto Grande (Cape Verde Is)	1 040	2 21
Recife	2 650	7 8
Southampton	1 325	3 16
from **Madras** *to*		
Aden	2 710	7 12
Bombay	1 450	4 0
Calcutta	750	2 2
Cape Town	4 960	13 18
Colombo	580	1 14
Karachi	1 910	5 7
Rangoon	980	2 17
Singapore	1 590	4 10
from **Malta (Valletta)** *to*		
Alexandria	821	2 6
Algiers	582	1 14
Gibraltar	990	2 18
Istanbul	850	2 8
Marseille	650	1 19
Port Said	935	2 14
Singapore	5 970	16 14
from **Marseille** *to*		
Algiers	400	1 2
Brisbane (via Torres Strait)	10 235	28 10
Fremantle	7 813	21 16
Gibraltar	690	1 22
Hobart	9 474	26 7
London (docks)	2 005	5 13
Malta	650	1 19
Melbourne	9 349	25 23
Napoli	455	1 6
Port Adelaide	9 011	25 0
Port Said	1 510	4 4
Southampton	1 833	5 2
Sydney	9 808	27 5
from **Mauritius (Port Louis)** *to*		
Aden	2 340	6 12
Bombay	2 540	7 1
Calcutta	3 240	9 0
Cape Town	2 280	6 8
Colombo	2 090	5 19
Durban	1 553	4 7
Melbourne	4 595	12 18
Rangoon	3 208	8 21
Zanzibar	1 340	3 17
from **Mazatlán** *to*		
Acapulco	660	1 20
Balboa	2 006	5 13
Callao	2 730	7 14
Esquimalt	2 080	5 18
Guaymas	390	1 2
San Francisco	1 350	3 18
Valparaíso	4 100	11 9
Yokohama	5 782	16 1
from **Melbourne** *to*		
Aden	6 450	17 22
Balboa	7 928	22 0
Colombo	4 675	12 23
Guayaquil	7 410	20 14
London (docks)	11 090	30 19
Mauritius	4 595	12 18
Port Adelaide	495	1 9
Shanghai	5 235	14 13
Sydney	575	1 14
Wellington	1 480	4 2
from **Montevideo** *to*		
Brisbane (via Cape Horn)	7 388	20 12
Buenos Aires	115	0 7
Cape Horn	1 370	3 19
Cape Town	3 780	10 12
Fernando de Noronha	2 364	6 13
Fremantle	8 546	23 17
Hobart (via Cape Horn)	7 001	19 10
Magellan Strait (east entrance)	1 170	3 6
Melbourne (via Cape Horn)	7 290	20 6
New York	5 722	15 21
Plymouth	5 900	16 9
Port Adelaide (via Cape Horn)	7 681	21 8
Port Stanley (Falkland Is)	1 000	2 18
Rio de Janeiro	1 025	2 20
Sydney (via Cape Horn)	7 175	19 22
from **New Orleans** *to*		
Cristóbal (Panama)	1 403	3 21
Galveston	385	1 1
Gibraltar	4 550	12 15
Guayaquil	2 258	6 21
Kingston (Jamaica)	1 115	3 2
La Habana	585	1 15
Liverpool	4 530	12 14
London (docks)	4 782	13 6
New York	1 698	4 17
Plymouth	4 450	12 8
Veracruz	798	2 5
from **New York** *to*		
Bermuda	695	1 22
Bishop Rock	2 903	8 1
Brisbane (via Panama)	9 727	27 0
Buenos Aires	5 838	16 5
Cape Town	6 800	18 21
Cristóbal (Panama)	1 974	5 11
Fremantle (via E Aust and Panama)	11 829	32 20
Gibraltar	3 210	8 22
Guayaquil	2 849	7 21
Halifax (Nova Scotia)	590	1 15
Hobart (via Panama)	9 647	26 19
Kingston (Jamaica)	1 455	4 1
København	3 550	9 20
Liverpool	3 073	8 12
London (docks)	3 270	9 2
Melbourne (via Panama)	9 932	21 14
Montevideo	5 722	15 21
New Orleans	1 698	4 17
Port Adelaide (via Panama)	10 323	28 16
Rio de Janeiro	4 750	13 4
Southampton	3 090	8 14
Sydney (via Panama)	9 689	26 21
from **Piraévs** *to*		
Algiers	1 071	2 23
Barcelona	1 156	3 5
Beirut	643	1 19
Constanta	548	1 13
Gibraltar	1 481	4 3
Istanbul	352	0 23
Marseille	1 065	2 23
Nice	1 000	2 19
Odessa	694	1 22
Port Said	593	1 15
Suez	680	1 21
Tanger	1 505	4 4
Trieste	839	2 8
Venezia	855	2 9
from **Port Said** *to*		
Brisbane	8 811	24 11
Fremantle	6 301	17 12
Gibraltar	1 905	5 7
Hobart	7 962	22 2
Istanbul	795	2 5
Liverpool	3 175	8 19
London (docks)	3 213	8 22
Malta	935	2 14
Marseille	1 510	4 4
Melbourne	7 837	21 18
Port Adelaide	7 500	20 20
Suez	87	0 5
Sydney	8 296	23 1
from **Québec** *to*		
Belle Isle	734	2 0
Cape Race	826	2 7
Cape Ray	553	1 12
Fame Point	325	0 21
Father Point	157	0 10
Lizard (via Belle Isle)	2 610	7 6
Lizard (via Cape Race)	2 724	7 13
Montreal	139	0 9
New York	1 321	3 16
Plymouth	2 620	7 6
from **Rangoon** *to*		
Bassein	248	0 16
Bombay	2 130	5 22
Calcutta	735	2 1
Colombo	1 257	3 11
Madras	980	2 17
Moulmein	149	0 10
Mauritius	3 208	8 21
Singapore	1 080	3 0
from **Rio de Janeiro** *to*		
Ascension	1 900	5 6
Brisbane (via Cape Horn)	8 286	23 0
Buenos Aires	1 140	3 4
Cape Horn	2 350	6 12
Cape Town	3 265	9 1
Fernando de Noronha	1 384	3 20
Fremantle	8 177	22 17
Hobart (via Cape Horn)	7 899	21 22
Jamestown (St Helena)	2 110	5 20
London (docks)	5 205	14 11
Melbourne (via Cape Horn)	8 188	22 17
Montevideo	1 025	2 20
New York	4 750	13 4
Plymouth	4 900	13 14
Port Adelaide (via Cape Horn)	8 579	23 19
Porto Grande (Cape Verde Is)	2 688	7 11
Port Stanley (Falkland Is)	1 860	5 4
Recife	1 080	3 0
Salvador (Brazil)	710	1 23
Southampton	5 035	13 23
Sydney (via Cape Horn)	8 073	22 10
from **Rotterdam/Europoort** *to*		
Aden	4 660	12 22
Buenos Aires	6 345	17 15
Cape Town	6 170	17 3
Colombo	6 752	18 18
Fremantle	9 590	26 15
Genoa	2 215	6 3
Guayaquil	5 670	15 18
Hamburg	325	0 21
Hong Kong	9 745	27 1
København	485	1 8
Lagos	4 192	11 15
Lisboa	1 085	3 0
London (docks)	177	0 11
Mombasa	6 260	17 9
New Orleans	4 814	13 8
New York	3 320	9 5
Piraévs	2 825	7 20
Port Said	3 265	9 1
San Francisco	8 110	22 12
Singapore	8 310	23 2
Sydney	11 595	32 5
Yokohama	11 200	31 2
from **St Helena (Jamestown)** *to*		
Ascension	680	1 21
Cape Horn	3 550	9 20
Cape Town	1 700	4 17
Madeira	3 059	8 11
Plymouth	4 210	11 16
Porto Grande (Cape Verde Is)	2 270	6 7
Rio de Janeiro	2 110	5 20
from **Saint John (New Brunswick)** *to*		
Boston	290	0 19
New York	506	1 9
Philadelphia	675	1 21
from **St Thomas (Virgin Is)** *to*		
Barbados	440	1 5
Bermuda	870	2 10
Cristóbal (Panama)	1 020	2 20
London (docks)	3 773	10 11
Plymouth	3 500	9 17
Southampton	3 591	9 23
from **St Vincent (Cape Verde Is)** *to*		
Ascension	1 640	4 13
Buenos Aires	3 778	10 11
Cape Town	3 945	10 23
Fernando de Noronha	1 316	3 15
Freetown	875	2 10
Gibraltar	1 560	4 8
I. d'Ouessant (Ushant)	2 125	5 21
Jamestown (St Helena)	2 270	6 7
Las Palmas	866	2 9
London (docks)	2 526	7 0
Madeira	1 040	2 21
Plymouth	2 250	6 6
Rio de Janeiro	2 690	7 11
from **San Francisco** *to*		
Acapulco	1 880	5 5
Auckland	5 680	15 18
Balboa	3 245	9 0
Brisbane	6 193	17 4
Callao	3 990	11 2
Coquimbo	5 030	13 23
Esquimalt	700	1 22
Fiji Islands (Kandavu)	4 740	13 4
Fremantle	8 524	23 16
Hobart	6 923	19 5
Honolulu	2 098	5 19
Magellan Strait	6 300	17 12
Mazatlán	1 350	3 18
Melbourne	6 966	19 8
Port Adelaide	7 357	20 10
Seattle	800	2 5
Sydney	6 456	17 22
Valparaíso	5 135	14 6
Yokohama	4 535	12 14
from **Seattle** *to*		
Balboa	4 021	11 4
Honolulu	2 403	6 16
Manila	5 978	16 14
Nome (Alaska)	2 288	6 8
San Francisco	800	2 5
Victoria (British Columbia)	70	0 4
Yokohama	4 244	11 18
from **Shanghai** *to*		
Guayaquil	8 882	24 16
Jakarta	2 522	7 0
Kōbe	771	2 3
Manila	1 130	3 3
Melbourne	5 235	14 13
Singapore	2 183	6 1
Sydney	4 675	12 23
Yokohama	1 045	2 21
from **Sierra Leone (Freetown)** *to*		
Ascension	1 000	2 18
Cape Town	3 120	8 16
Dakar	470	1 7
Las Palmas	1 317	3 15
Malabo (Bioko, Fernando Póo)	1 500	4 4
Plymouth	2 700	7 12
Porto Grande (Cape Verde Is)	850	2 8
from **Singapore** *to*		
Aden	3 640	10 2
Bombay	2 460	6 20
Brisbane (via Torres Strait)	3 821	10 14
Calcutta	1 630	4 12
Cape Town	5 630	15 15
Colombo	1 575	4 9
Fremantle	2 220	6 4
Guayaquil	10 740	29 20
Hobart	3 967	11 2
Hong Kong	1 440	4 0
Jakarta	527	1 11
London (docks)	8 257	22 22
Madras	1 590	4 10
Melbourne	3 842	10 16
Port Adelaide	3 504	9 17
Rangoon	1 080	3 0
Shanghai	2 183	6 1
Sydney	4 306	11 23
Yokohama	2 888	8 0
from **Southampton** *to*		
Bermuda	2 956	8 5
Bishop Rock (Scilly Is)	219	0 14
Buenos Aires	6 125	17 0
Cabo Finisterre	596	1 15
Canary Islands	1 588	4 9
Cape Horn	7 258	20 3
Cape Town	5 945	16 12
Cherbourg	84	0 5
Dover	119	0 8
Gibraltar	1 142	3 4
I. d'Ouessant (Ushant)	215	0 14
Le Havre	105	0 7
Lisboa	865	2 9
Madeira	1 325	3 16
Marseille	1 833	5 2
New York	3 090	8 14
St Malo	149	0 10
Singapore	8 078	22 10
from **Suez** *to*		
Aden	1 310	3 15
Colombo	3 440	9 13
Jiddah	640	1 18
Karachi	2 772	7 16
Port Said	87	0 5
Port Sudan	708	1 23
Zanzibar	3 067	8 12
from **Sydney** *to*		
Antwerpen	11 569	32 3
Auckland	1 260	3 12
Brisbane	474	1 7
Cape Horn	5 750	15 23
Cape Town	6 278	17 10
Fiji Islands (Kandavu)	1 710	4 18
Glasgow	11 595	32 5
Hong Kong	4 470	12 10
Honolulu	4 415	12 6
Liverpool	11 464	31 20
London (docks)	11 558	32 2
Marseille	9 808	27 5
Melbourne	575	1 14
Shanghai	4 675	12 23
Singapore	4 306	11 23
Southampton	11 368	31 13
Valparaíso	6 257	17 9
Wellington	1 233	3 10
Yokohama	4 379	12 3
from **Tahiti** *to*		
Balboa	4 486	12 11
Callao	4 200	11 16
Honolulu	2 260	6 13
Sydney	3 050	8 11
Valparaíso	4 210	11 16
Wellington	2 340	6 12
from **I d'Ouessant (Ushant)** *to*		
Amsterdam	485	1 8
Antwerpen	441	1 5
Bishop Rock (Scilly Is)	100	0 6
Bordeaux	301	0 20
Bremerhaven	661	1 20
Cabo Finisterre	377	1 1
Cape Town	5 724	15 21
Dover	310	0 20
Gibraltar	920	2 13
Glasgow	1 005	2 19
Hamburg	703	1 22
Las Palmas	1 306	3 15
Le Havre	235	0 15
Lisboa	655	1 19
Lizard	90	0 6
London (docks)	399	1 2
Madeira	1 090	3 0
Plymouth	122	0 8
Porto Grande (Cape Verde Is)	2 125	5 21
Rotterdam/Europoort	440	1 5
Southampton	215	0 14
Tenerife	1 300	3 14
from **Valdez (Alaska)** *to*		
Cristóbal (Panama)	4 987	13 20
New Orleans	6 390	17 18
New York	6 959	19 8
San Francisco	1 715	4 18
from **Valparaíso** *to*		
Antofagasta	576	1 14
Arica (Chile)	879	2 10
Auckland	5 247	14 13
Balboa	2 616	7 6
Brisbane	6 487	18 0
Callao	1 290	3 4
Coquimbo	190	0 12
Fremantle	7 827	21 17
Hobart	6 100	16 22
Honolulu	5 911	16 10
Iquique	769	2 3
London (docks)	7 419	20 14
Magellan Strait	1 270	3 12
Matarani	960	2 16
Mazatlán	4 100	11 9
Melbourne	6 389	17 17
Papeete (Tahiti)	4 210	11 16
Port Adelaide	6 780	18 20
San Francisco	5 246	14 6
Southampton	7 218	20 1
Sydney	6 257	17 9
from **Venezia** *to*		
Algiers	1 256	3 11
Barcelona	1 316	3 16
Constanta	1 365	3 19
Gibraltar	1 364	3 19
Haifa	1 375	3 20
Marseille	1 220	3 9
Nice	1 155	3 5
Odessa	1 511	4 5
Port Said	1 311	3 15
Suez	1 398	3 21
Tanger	1 688	4 16
Trieste	66	0 5
Tunis	937	2 14
from **Victoria (British Columbia)** *to*		
Honolulu	2 349	6 12
Seattle	70	0 4
Tacoma	88	0 6
Yokohama	4 194	11 15
from **Wellington, NZ** *to*		
Auckland	543	1 12
Balboa	6 505	18 1
Brisbane	1 445	4 0
Cape Town	7 081	19 16
Fremantle	3 044	8 10
Guayaquil	6 020	16 17
Hobart	1 278	3 13
London (docks)	11 291	31 8
Melbourne	1 480	4 2
Papeete (Tahiti)	2 340	6 12
Port Adelaide	1 887	5 5
Southampton	11 091	30 19
Sydney	1 233	3 10
from **Yokohama** *to*		
Brisbane	3 980	11 1
Canton	1 668	4 15
Cebu	1 762	4 21
Esquimalt	4 220	11 17
Fremantle	4 460	12 9
Guayaquil	7 996	22 2
Hobart	5 014	16 4
Hong Kong	1 585	4 9
Honolulu	3 385	9 9
Inchón	1 033	2 20
Jakarta	3 220	8 25
Mazatlán	5 782	16 1
Melbourne	4 961	13 18
Port Adelaide	5 352	14 20
San Francisco	4 535	12 14
Seattle	4 244	11 18
Shanghai	1 045	2 21
Singapore	2 888	8 0
Suva	3 942	10 22
Sydney	4 379	12 3
Victoria (British Colombia)	4 194	11 15

Appendix VIII The strategic use of the oceans

World naval operations and gunboat diplomacy 1946–82

The incidents summarised here are located on the map on pages 190–191.

1946

1 **USA:USSR** To back Turkish resistance to Soviet territorial demands, USA sends body of deceased Turkish Ambassador to Washington home in battleship *Missouri*. US intention was to persuade the USSR to relax pressure on Turkey.

2 **FRANCE:CHINA** During a dispute over Chinese troop withdrawals in Vietnam, China withdraws after French cruiser *Emile Bertin* fires on Chinese troops at Haiphong.

3 **UK:IRAN** HMS *Norfolk* and HMS *Wild Goose* sent to Basra (Iraq) after rioting at the British oil refinery in Abadan (Iran) was fomented by the Soviet-backed Tudeh party. Troops landed. Intervention proved unnecessary but British interests were satisfied and Soviet influence in Iran suffered a setback.

4 **USA:USSR** The US Government announces that US Naval units will be permanently stationed in the Mediterranean to carry out American policy and diplomacy.

5 **UK:ALBANIA** Following shelling of HMS *Orion* and HMS *Superb* by Albania in Corfu Strait, and to assert right of innocent passage, British destroyers HMS *Saumorey* and HMS *Volage* entered the Straits but were severely damaged, and personnel killed, by mines. Most of the mines were later removed by British mine-sweepers.

1947

6 **UK:PALESTINE ET AL** For most of the year British naval patrols intercepted and seized ships carrying Jewish illegal immigrants to Palestine, thereby hoping to placate Arabs. However, a number of ships got through.

7 **USA:GREECE** On the day that Congressional authorisation was sought for President Truman's programme of aid to Greece against Communism, US Government announced the visit of a strong naval squadron (including carrier *Leyte*) to Greek ports.

1948

8 **UK:GUATEMALA** Cruisers HMS *Sheffield* and *Devonshire* sent to Belize to deter Guatemala from pursuing by force her claim to British Honduras.

9 **USA:ISRAEL:ARAB STATES** Three US destroyers assigned to Count Folke Bernadotte, UN Mediator for Palestine, to maintain peace between Arab and Jewish forces. While they had little hope of success, they did evacuate the UN team from Haifa in July 1948.

10 **USA:CHINA** 1500 marines landed to reinforce US naval base at Qingdao (abandoned February 1949).

11 **UK:USA** Two US cruisers and a British destroyer sent to Shanghai to protect nationals.

1949

12 **UK:CHINA** HMS *Amethyst* attempts to ascend Yangtze to continue mounting guard on HM Embassy at Nanking, but driven aground by Communist artillery fire. Attempts to rescue her by HMS *Consort*, and later HMS *London* and *Black Swan*, failed. HMS *Amethyst* finally escaped to rejoin the fleet. No further attempt to protect HM Embassy was made.

13 **UK:USA** Additional British and US cruisers sent to Shanghai for protection of Nationals.

14 **CHINA:UK:USA** Nationalist Chinese proclaim a blockade of the Chinese coast and, in spite of British and US protests, attack and occasionally seize British and US vessels.

1950

15 **N. KOREA:S. KOREA (USA, UN)** War began in June. The UN joined on the side of S. Korea with the US fleet deployed in Korean and Formosan waters. Naval incidents occurred throughout the war which ended in 1953.

16 **USA:VIETNAM** Two US destroyers sent to Saigon to demonstrate US support for Bao Dai's Government. Rioting against the visit broke out on 19 March.

17 **USA:CHINA** US Seventh Fleet ordered to patrol Formosa Strait to prevent Communists from invading Formosa or Nationalists from invading China.

18 **CHINA:JAPAN** Japanese fishing vessel *Dai-Ichi-Unzen Maru* seized by Communist Chinese warship—first of 158 vessels captured over the next four years until Japanese fishermen agreed to respect Chinese prohibited zones.

19 **UK:IRAN** Cruiser HMS *Mauritius* sent to Abadan to protect British subjects during dispute with Iran (no force employed). Destroyers helped the cruiser evacuate British subjects.

20 **EGYPT:UK:ISRAEL** Egyptian corvette stops, plunders and damages British merchant ship in Gulf of Aqaba as part of attempted Egyptian blockade of Israel.

21 **UK:EGYPT** British destroyer flotilla sent to Red Sea to prevent further incidents. Agreement on procedures for British ships using Gulf of Aqaba reached on 26 July.

22 **UK:EGYPT** British warships (27 in total, but usually two cruisers at a time) keep Suez Canal open to shipping when Egyptian labour withdrawn and clearance denied to British merchant ships; also provide protected labour force. Normal working resumed in February 1952.

1952

23 **UK:CANADA:EGYPT** After coup d'état in Egypt, a large British naval force (including two carriers, one Canadian) assembles off Egyptian coast in case British Nationals need protection.

24 **USA:USSR** President Tito goes to sea in USS *Coral Sea* to observe fire power demonstration during the carrier's visit to Split together with cruiser *Salem* and four destroyers. This indicated to Stalin that American help was available and acceptable to Yugoslavia.

1953

25 **ARGENTINA:UK** Argentine naval vessel lands party and erects buildings to signify occupation of disputed British territory of Deception I. On 16 February buildings demolished, intruders arrested and expelled by HMS *Snipe*.

26 **S. KOREA:N. KOREA** S. Korean navy seize Japanese fishing boats crossing the Rhee line (unrecognised by any other country). The practice continued for two years, the captive fishermen being exploited as hostages to secure concessions from Japan on other issues.

1954

27 **S. KOREA:JAPAN** S. Korean force lands on Take-shima Is, long disputed between S. Korea and Japan, and henceforth occupied by S. Korea.

28 **USA:CHINA** After six US Nationals killed on British airliner shot down by Chinese fighters, two US aircraft carriers (*Hornet* and *Philippine Sea*) sent to scene. Two Chinese aircraft shot down.

29 **USA:UK:GUATEMALA ET AL** To prevent Guatemalan Government importing arms to resist CIA-backed revolution, US Government threatens naval blockade; air-sea patrols established May–June. US induced British Government to discourage British ships from carrying arms.

30 **JAPAN:S. KOREA** Japanese patrol boat sent to investigate S. Korea seizure of Take-shima Is but withdrawn when fired on.

31 **PERU:PANAMA ET AL** Peruvian warships capture five whaling ships registered in Panama within 200 nm of Peruvian Coast, a limit not recognised by other countries. Similar incidents occurred with other S. American countries, but even major powers only voiced protests.

1955

32 **USA:CHINA** US Seventh Fleet (including five carriers) evacuate Chinese Nationalists from the Tachen Is, successfully deterring the Communists from interference.

33 **USA:N. VIETNAM** US Navy evacuates 300000 refugees from N. Vietnam which came under Communist control as result of the 1954 Geneva Agreement.

34 **S. KOREA:JAPAN** S. Korean warships capture 11 Japanese fishing vessels. Crews kept hostage.

1956

35 **EGYPT:ISRAEL:FRANCE:UK** In July President Nasser nationalised the Suez Canal Company. Israel, France and Britain launched a coordinated attack to secure the Canal but the exercise was unsuccessful due primarily to international diplomatic opposition. (Canal closed due to hostilities 1956–57, and from 1967 to June 1975.)

36 **SECOND ARAB/ISRAELI WAR** In February, actions in Red Sea, Gulf of Suez and Strait of Tiran.

37 **USA:UK:FRANCE** Harassing tactics employed by US Sixth Fleet against British and French warships to show disapproval of Anglo-French intervention at Suez.

38 **FRANCE:GERMANY** French warships arrest, in international waters, freighter *Helga Boge* carrying arms to Algerian rebels. First of many German ships intercepted.

39 **USA:UK:FRANCE:EGYPT** US Sixth Fleet lands marines at Alexandria and elsewhere to protect evacuation of 2000 Americans and other foreign Nationals during fighting between Egypt, Britain and France.

1957

40 **CHINA:TAIWAN** Periodic conflict from 1949, but 1957 saw much Chinese communist naval acitivity in Formosa Strait and islands in attempts to exert pressure on Nationalist Government in Taiwan.

41 **USA:EGYPT:JORDAN:USSR:SYRIA** US transports carrying 1800 marines anchor off Beirut in readiness to intervene in Jordan (when Egyptian subversion threatened independence) while the Sixth Fleet carried out manoeuvres. King Hussein reestablished authority.

42 **USA:EGYPT** US destroyers patrol Strait of Tiran and Gulf of Aqaba to prevent Egyptian interference with US merchant vessels bound for Israel.

1958

43 **USA:INDONESIA** US destroyer division 31 asserts right of innocent passage through Lombok and Makassar straits after territorial waters claimed by Indonesia.

44 **FRANCE:YUGOSLAVIA** Yugoslavian ship carrying arms to Algerian insurgents intercepted on high seas by French Navy; arms seized.

45 **USA : LEBANON : SYRIA : EGYPT : USSR** US Sixth Fleet lands 10000 marines in the Lebanon at request of Lebanese Government, from carriers stationed in the Mediterranean.

46 **UK:ICELAND** Royal Navy begins campaign to nullify ban on British fishing within 12 nm of Icelandic coast by protecting British trawlers from 1 Sept 1958 to 14 March 1959. RN foiled 65 Icelandic attempts to arrest British trawlers.

47 **USA:CHINA** US Seventh Fleet ordered to escort Chinese Nationalists to within three miles of Quemoy to prevent effective blockade by Chinese Communist Navy. This action successful; no fighting took place.

1959

48 **S. KOREA:JAPAN** S. Korean Government react to Japanese repatriation of certain Koreans to N. Korea by threatening to resume seizure of Japanese fishing vessels and extend detention of hostages they were going to release.

49 **USA:USSR** USS RO *Hale* sends party aboard Soviet trawler *Novorossisk* in international waters after series of breaks in Atlantic submarine cables. Trawler denied responsibility but no more breaks occurred.

50 **FRANCE:MOROCCO:CZECHOSLOVAKIA** French navy intercepts Czech freighter carrying arms to Morocco and confiscates arms destined for the Algerian rebels.

51 **USA:COLOMBIA:CUBA** US and Colombian warships patrol Caribbean coast off Panama to prevent further landing of Cuban guerrillas in that country.

1960

52 **NETHERLANDS:INDONESIA** To deter attacks by Indonesia on Dutch New Guinea (W. Irian) the Netherlands Government announce dispatch of aircraft carrier *Karel Doorman* and two destroyers to the colony.

53 **USA:CONGO** American carrier *Wasp* arrives off coast of Congo in readiness to evacuate Americans. She also delivers petrol to forces sent to the Congo by the UN.

54 **USA:CUBA** After armed uprisings (allegedly inspired by Castro) against the governments of Guatemala and Nicaragua, carrier USS *Shangri-La* and US destroyers patrolled the Caribbean coasts of both countries to prevent intervention on the part of Communist directed elements.

1961

55 **CUBA:PORTUGAL:USA** Insurgents seize Portuguese ship *Santa Maria*; USS *Western Union* seized by Cuba.

56 **USA:CUBA** Visible presence offshore of US Fleet encourages group of Cuban exiles organised by CIA to attempt overthrow of Castro régime by a landing at the Bay of Pigs. No actual naval support given and attempt fails.

57 **UK:IRAQ** Landing of troops together with naval concentration help deter Iraqi invasion of Kuwait.

58 **FRANCE:TUNISIA** After initial bombardment by aircraft from carrier *Arromanches*, cruisers *Colbert*, *Bouvet* and *Chevalier-Paul* force the entrance to Lake Bizerta and, with help from French troops, break Tunisian blockade of Bizerta naval base complex and reestablish French control.

59 **USA:DOMINICAN REPUBLIC** Presence offshore of US Fleet (including *Franklin D. Roosevelt* and *Valley Forge*) enables President Kennedy's representative to secure expulsion of the Trujillos; Government acceptable to US established.

1962

60 **INDONESIA:NETHERLANDS** Flotilla of Indonesian motor torpedo boats attempts to land infiltrators in Dutch New Guinea but is intercepted by Netherlands Navy which sinks one vessel. Irian later transferred to Indonesia.

61 **USA:N. VIETNAM:LAOS:THAILAND** Carrier covers disembarkation of US Marines in Thailand, an operation intended to demonstrate American readiness to intervene if Communists pushed their military successes too far.

62 **USA:CUBA** US establishes restricted zone around Cuba for vessels and aircraft carrying prohibited materials; also prescribes routes for those not carrying prohibited material.

1963

63 **INDONESIA:MALAYSIA** Confrontation period 1963–65; several incidents involving naval, merchant and fishing vessels. The basic cause was Indonesian opposition, under President Sukarno, to Malaysian federation.

64 **FRANCE:BRAZIL** French destroyer *Tartu* sent to fishing grounds off north-east coast of Brazil after three French lobster boats seized by Brazilian warships 60 nm off coast. Brazilians countered with a cruiser, five destroyers and two corvettes; *Tartu* withdrawn. Effect of these moves on compromise settlement reached in 1964 uncertain.

65 **USA:DOMINICAN REPUBLIC** US aircraft carrier *Boxer* anchors off Santo Domingo ready to send rescue helicopters in the event of trouble during Vice-President Johnson's visit to the Dominican Republic.

66 **USA:UK:HAITI** US naval task force (including carrier *Boxer* and 2000 marines) cruises off Haiti ready to protect US nationals in conflict between Haiti and Dominican Republic; also to intervene if Haiti Government overthrown. British destroyer and frigate stand by. No naval intervention; US nationals subsequently evacuated.

67 **CUBA:UK** Two Cuban warships land party on a British island in the Bahamas and seize 19 Cuban refugees and two fighting boats. HMS *Londonderry* investigated and found the normally uninhabited island used as base by Cuban exiles from US for attacks on Cuba. Steps taken by HM Government to discourage use of British territory for this purpose.

1964

68 **CYPRUS:GREECE:TURKEY** Following Civil War on Cyprus (1963), considerable tension between Greek and Turkish communities followed by attacks by Turkish sea and air forces on Greek Cypriot coastal towns. Many incidents.

69 **UK:USA:ZANZIBAR** USS *Manley*, HMS *Owen*, RFA *Hebe* evacuate US and British Nationals from Zanzibar following revolution there.

70 **UK:TANGANYIKA (TANZANIA)** Royal Marines landed from HMS *Centaur* to suppress mutiny in Tanganyikan army.

71 **TURKEY:CYPRUS (NATO, UN)** To reinforce threat of armed intervention, after failure to achieve satisfactory measures for protection of Turkish minority in Cyprus, Turkish fleet prepares for battle in show of force. This brought immediate concessions but no lasting solution.

72 **N. VIETNAM:USA** US destroyers patrolling Gulf of Tongking attacked by N. Vietnamese torpedo boats. If the objective was to discourage US naval activity it failed: US retaliation marked the moment when conflict with N. Vietnam first assumed the character of war.

1965

73 **VIETNAM:USA:CAMBODIA** Many US troops withdrawn from Europe and over 500000 committed to Vietnam; US Fleet active in the region. In 1970 focus shifted to Cambodia with many incidents at sea.

74 **USA:S. VIETNAM:N. VIETNAM** US and S. Vietnam blockade S. Vietnamese coast to prevent infiltration by vessels from north.

75 **USA:DOMINICAN REPUBLIC** 536 US marines landed from aircraft carrier to protect US citizens during civil war. Objective later extended to include prevention of communist influence in Dominican Republic government: US had 22000 men ashore and 9000 afloat. Four months later a provisional government acceptable to US established; US withdrew one year later.

76 **UK:RHODESIA (ZIMBABWE)** Pending arrival of British troops and aircraft in Zambia, aircraft carrier HMS *Eagle* cruises off Tanzanian coast to reassure Zambian Government that Rhodesian air attacks on Zambia would be prevented.

1966

77 **UK:RHODESIA (ZIMBABWE)** As authorised by UN Security Council's resolution in April, a party from HMS *Berwick* boards Greek tanker *Manuela* and persuades her not to continue her voyage to Beira. British naval patrol continues turning back tankers carrying oil to Rhodesia.

78 **UK:ARGENTINA** HMS *Puma* sent from Cape Town to Port Stanley (Falkland Is) following symbolic invasion of that colony by group of private Argentinian citizens; anti-British demonstrations in Argentina itself. Negotiations took place; naval force not employed.

1967

79 **UK:USA:EGYPT** After British Prime Minister stated that HM Government would join with other governments to assert right of passage by vessels of all nations through Strait of Tiran, the Admiralty announced that HMS *Victorious* and other warships were being held ready in the Mediterranean. Threat of purposeful force not pursued.

80 **EGYPT:ISRAEL** Egypt blockades Strait of Tiran near Sharm el Sheikh to prevent vessels entering or leaving Israeli port of Elat. This action and others leads to full scale Israeli strike (the Six Day War) and blockade and closure of the Suez Canal by the Egyptians until 1975.

81 **ISRAEL:USA** Israeli torpedo boats attack and drive off USS *Liberty*, a so-called 'technical research ship' apparently monitoring Israeli transmissions during war with Egypt. Several Americans killed and wounded. Israelis paid compensation.

82 **USSR:ISRAEL** Soviet naval squadron visits Port Said (eight ships) and Alexandria (four ships), declaring cooperation with Egyptian forces to repel any aggression. If the Israelis intended a further advance they did not make one. This gesture helped relieve Arab disappointment at the absence of earlier and more effective Soviet support.

83 **UK:SOUTH YEMEN** A naval concentration (originally planned for other purposes), assembles off Aden to cover withdrawal of British troops and is retained for protection or evacuation of British civilians from newly independent republic. No action; fleet dispersed.

1968

84 **N. KOREA:USA** N. Korean craft put stop to use of US vessels for close electronic surveillance of their coast by capturing and taking to port USS *Pueblo* before forces could intervene. US Government later made humiliating concessions to obtain release of crew.

85 **USA:N. KOREA** US naval task force including three carriers assembles in Sea of Japan as part of American reply to seizure of *Pueblo*. No action; force dispersed.

86 **USSR:USA** Soviet force of 16 ships manoeuvres between US warships and coast of N. Korea.

87 **UK:RHODESIA (ZIMBABWE)** Beira patrol continues although Rhodesia is obtaining oil by other routes.

88 **USSR:NORWAY** Major amphibious force supported by escort and missile-carrying destroyers, supply vessels, etc. sailed from Baltic Sea along entire Norwegian coast to Kola Peninsula. Explained by Soviet press as reply to NATO naval exercises of previous month, the action supported Soviet press campaign against Norway joining NATO.

1969

89 **IRAN:IRAQ** Iranian warships escort Iranian merchant ship from Khorramshahr to the Gulf in successful defiance of Iraqi threat to stop any ships with Iranian flag from sailing through waters claimed by Iraq. (Iran compelled to give way to similar claim in 1961 due to lack of warships, but naval action now secured her purpose.)

90 **USA:N. KOREA** Battleship USS *New Jersey* and a large task force including carriers sent to Sea of Japan following destruction of US surveillance aircraft by N. Korean aircraft a week before. No reaction from N. Korea and fleet eventually withdrawn without achieving anything.

91 **S. KOREA:N. KOREA** An armed N. Korean vessel sent to pick up a spy from S. Korean island of Huksando is intercepted at sea and sunk by S. Korean destroyer.

92 **SPAIN:UK** Spanish helicopter carrier *Dedalo* and 12 other Spanish warships sent to Algeciras Bay, apparently to demonstrate continued Spanish claims to Gibraltar.

1970

93 **USA:SYRIA:USSR** Sixth Fleet deployed in E. Mediterranean and subsequently reinforced in response to revolt in Jordan and invasion of that country by Syria.

94 **USSR:USA** Soviet Mediterranean Squadron reinforced to pose threat to Sixth Fleet including occasional training of guns etc. against US warships.

95 **PORTUGAL:GUINEA** In November, seaborne attacks made on Conakry, allegedly led by Portuguese officers. UN accused Portugal who denied involvement. Guinea responded by demanding immediate independence for Guinea-Bissau, Angola and Mozambique from Portugal.

96 **USSR:PORTUGAL** At request of Guinea, USSR institute naval patrol to deter any repetition of Portuguese threat. Successful, but patrol continues for years after threat has vanished.

1971

97 **ECUADOR:USA** Ecuadoran warships seize eight US fishing vessels in unrecognised 200-mile zone. Vessels subsequently released on payment of $500000.

98 **IRAN:RAS AL KHAIMAH (UAE):IRAQ** Iran forcibly occupies Abu Husa and Greater and Lesser Tunbs at entrance to the Gulf. Tunbs formerly held by Arab emirate Ras al-Khaimah. Occupation of islands resulted in fatalities.

99 **USA:INDIA** Alarmed by imminent defeat of Pakistan in India–Pakistan war, US assemble *Enterprise* task force which enters Bay of Bengal to protect American interests.

100 **INDIA:PAKISTAN** During Bangladesh War, Indian naval forces blockade Bay of Bengal. Aircraft from carrier *Vikrant* attack Chittagong and Cox's Bazar.

101 **INDIA:LIBERIA:PAKISTAN** Liberian Flag freighter MV *Venus Challenger* sunk by guided missiles from an Indian ship during India–Pakistan war: no survivors. Further three merchant ships and one tanker sunk in Karachi Roads, and Pakistani destroyer sunk by rockets from Indian MTB.

102 **USSR:USA** Soviet task force arrives to shadow *Enterprise*. If this encouraged India, there may have been some small success.

103 **INDIA:BANGLADESH:PAKISTAN** Indian naval forces continue blockade of Bay of Bengal; on 9 December Pakistani submarines sink Indian freighter in Arabian Sea. Pakistan capitulated due to Indian command of air and sea.

1972

104 **UK:GUATEMALA** HMS *Ark Royal* sent to Belize to deter apparent Guatemalan threat.

105 **ICELAND:UK** Icelandic gunboat cuts trawl wires of British boat *Peter Scott*. Further incidents follow.

106 **ICELAND:W. GERMANY** Icelandic gunboat *Aegir* cuts trawl wires of German fishing boat.

107 **USA:N. VIETNAM** For first time since 1968 hundreds of US Navy and Air Force planes strike military targets in N. Vietnam.

108 **USA:N. VIETNAM** In response to the massive N. Vietnamese offensive in S. Vietnam, President Nixon announces the mining by naval aircraft of Haiphong and other N. Vietnamese ports. Ships are given a 72-hour deadline to leave before the mines are activated.

1973

109 **ISRAEL:LEBANON** During 4th Arab/Israeli War (Yom Kippur), Israeli missile boats land commandos to attack Palestinian guerilla bases in the Lebanon.

110 **SPAIN:MOROCCO** Exchange of gunfire between Spanish and Moroccan warships over fishing rights; incidents continue.

111 **UK:ICELAND** After continued Icelandic harassment of British fishing vessels, British warships enter 50-mile zone claimed by Iceland; incidents and fishing continue.

112 **NEW ZEALAND:AUSTRALIA:FRANCE** NZ frigate *Otago* (relieved by *Canterbury*) supported by Australian naval auxiliary, enters French nuclear test danger zone off Mururoa to reinforce protests against nuclear tests. French agree to conduct future tests underground.

113 **ICELAND:UK** Icelandic gunboat chases British trawler for 150 miles but, owing to presence of British frigate, fails to make an arrest. One of many incidents between May and September.

114 **4th ARAB/ISRAELI WAR (YOM KIPPUR)** Many incidents both Red and Mediterranean Seas, particularly in straits.

115 **EGYPT** Egypt blockades Bab-el-Mandeb with the intention of preventing vessels reaching Strait of Tiran.

116 **USA:SYRIA:EGYPT:USSR** Sixth Fleet establishes a chain of communication and support across the Mediterranean to permit the airborne resupply of Israel.

117 **USA:USSR** Sixth Fleet reinforced and concentrated south of Crete as part of American response to threats of Soviet military intervention in Middle East.

118 **USSR:USA:ISRAEL** Soviet Mediterranean Squadron steadily reinforced. Undertakes aggressive surveillance of Sixth Fleet as well as escorting seaborne supplies to Arabs.

1974

119 **CHINA:S. VIETNAM:N. VIETNAM** Chinese warships engage in battle with N. Vietnamese; Chinese land troops to occupy Paracel Is.

120 **S. VIETNAM:CHINA:PHILIPPINES:TAIWAN** S. Vietnamese troops landed to occupy Spratley Is.

121 **N. KOREA:S. KOREA** Gunboats sink alleged S. Korean spy ship; four similar incidents during course of year.

122 **TURKEY:CYPRUS:GREECE:UK** Turkish sea-borne invasion of Cyprus.

123 **ICELAND:W. GERMANY** Gunboat *Aegir* arrests German trawler.

124 **USA:ARAB OIL PRODUCERS** US carrier *Constellation* enters Arabian Gulf to reinforce American objections to any interruption of oil supplies.

1975

125 **SPAIN:MOROCCO** Spanish naval task force sent to Ceuta and Melilla in response to Moroccan pressure; Morocco protests against violation of territorial waters.

126 **USA:CAMBODIA** After USA withdrawals from Indo-China war, US carriers *Okinawa* and *Hancock* send helicopters and marines to evacuate US citizens from Phnom Penh.

127 **USA:N. VIETNAM** US Seventh Fleet evacuate 15000 American and S. Vietnamese officials.

128 **CAMBODIA:USA** Cambodian patrol boats capture American merchant ship *Mayaguez*.

129 **USA:CAMBODIA** Successful rescue of *Mayaguez* undertaken by carrier *Coral Sea* assisted by destroyers and aircraft. Three Cambodian patrol boats sunk.

130 **UK:GUATEMALA** HMS *Zulu* sent to patrol off Belize (with air and ground reinforcements) in response to threatening Guatemalan concentration.

131 **ICELAND:UK** Following extension to 200 miles of Iceland's Exclusive Economic Zones, gunboats resume harassment of British trawlers. Numerous incidents follow.

132 **UK:ICELAND** HMS *Leopard* and two other frigates return to Icelandic Exclusive Economic Zone.

133 **INDONESIA** Naval bombardment and invasion of E. Timor, to counter insurgents from Timor independence organisation (Fretilin).

1976

134 **ICELAND:UK** After British warships withdrawn from Icelandic EEZ to permit negotiations, Icelandic gunboats resume harassment of British trawlers; British frigates return. Incidents continue but Iceland eventually successful.

135 **ARGENTINA:UK** Argentine destroyer fires on British research ship south of Falkland Is.

136 **VIETNAM:CHINA:PHILIPPINES:TAIWAN** Vietnamese Navy occupy Spratley Is; China protests.

137 **SYRIA:LEBANON:ISRAEL** Syrian naval blockade of Lebanese coast begun.

138 **USSR** Soviet aircraft carrier *Kiev* transits Bosporus and Dardanelles to assert Soviet interpretation of Montreux Convention.

139 **GREECE:TURKEY** Both countries threaten use of naval force over dispatch of Turkish seismic vessel to disputed waters of Aegean. Nothing happens, though Greece mobilises Aegean fleet on 1 September.

140 **ISRAEL:LEBANON:SYRIA** Israeli naval vessels patrolling in Lebanese waters intercept ships carrying arms to Palestine Liberation Organisation forces in the Lebanon.

1977

141 **UK:GUATEMALA** HMS *Achilles* sent to Belize in response to threatening attitude by Guatemala.

142 **FRANCE:SOMALIA** 18 French warships (including two aircraft carriers) deployed off Djibouti to cover referendum and for possible evacuation of French Nationals.

143 **USSR:EGYPT** According to President Sadat, helicopters from Soviet carrier *Moskva* are employed to jam Egyptian radio communications during frontier clashes between Egyptian and Libyan forces. An unusual but unauthenticated incident.

144 **ARGENTINA:USSR** After casualties inflicted by firing, Argentine Navy arrests seven Soviet and two Bulgarian trawlers inside 200-mile zone.

145 **BURMA:THAILAND** Burmese gunboat sinks Thailand fishing boat and captures another, allegedly in Thailand territorial waters.

1978

146 **ARGENTINA:CHILE** 25 Argentine warships carry out exercises in Beagle Channel (where ownership of three islands disputed with Chile). This threat of force gives an advantage in the subsequent negotiations.

147 **SURINAM:GUYANA** Surinam allegedly uses gunboats to harass Guyanese Nationals as part of a fisheries dispute eventually settled by negotiations.

148 **USSR:ETHIOPIA** Soviet warship opens fire to assist in defence of port of Massawa against Eritrean Liberation Front.

149 **UK:FRANCE:USA:ETHIOPIA:USSR** UK, France and US hold joint exercises off the Horn of Africa which are denounced by Ethiopia and the USSR as provocative.

150 **CHINA:JAPAN** After Japanese reiteration of their claim to the Senkaku Is, China sends flotilla of armed fishing boats in support of her claim. No Japanese naval reaction.

151 **USA:IRAN:USSR** US *Constellation* task force sails for Iranian waters with the intention of manifesting American concern at the chaotic situation in Iran. Move cancelled within few days after Soviet protests at 'gunboat diplomacy'.

1979

152 **USA:USSR** Carrier US *Constellation* and escorts sent to Arabian Sea as one of several moves intended to reassure Saudi Arabia and deter Soviet intervention.

153 **S. KOREA:N. KOREA** S. Korean authorities claim that on 28 April they sank N. Korean spy boat in S. Korean waters. N. Korea claimed this a fabrication.

154 **CANADA:USA** Canada seizes 19 American tuna boats in 200-mile zone off Pacific Coast. US retaliates by embargoing Canadian tuna; dispute continues.

155 **USA:CUBA** To manifest displeasure at presence of Soviet troops in Cuba, US carry out amphibious landing exercise in Guantanamo Bay.

156 **USA:SOMALIA:KENYA:UK** US continues requests for bases in Kenya and Somalia to build up Indian Ocean forces and is granted use of Mogadishu port and airfields by Somalia. US vessels sent to UK island base, Diego Garcia.

1980

157 **IRAN:USA** In response to the taking of US citizens as hostages (November 1979) by Iran, US warships *Nimitz*

(nuclear), *Midway* and *Kitty Hawk* deployed in the Arabian Sea area during January.
158 **CUBA:USA** Cuba closed port of Mariel ending exodus of boat traffic of refugees to USA. US coastguard patrols used to intercept boats during this period.
159 **CUBA:USA:BAHAMAS** In May, several Cuban MIG fighters attacked and sank the Bahaman Defence Force patrol boat *Flamingo* in Bahaman waters north of eastern Cuba after *Flamingo* had taken two Cuban fishing vessels in tow for poaching. Four members of *Flamingo* crew killed and several injured. Cuba apologised and paid compensation.
160 **MOROCCO:SPAIN** Armed Polisario (Popular Front for the Liberation of Sanguia el Hamra and Rio de Oro) guerrilla motor boats harass Spanish fishing vessels off coast of Western Sahara which Polisario claimed as territorial waters. 38 fishermen captured but released after negotiations in Algeria and recognition by Spain of Polisario.
161 **USSR:JAPAN** Soviet submarine on fire, 300 nm north-east of Okinawa, caused passage to be made through Japanese waters on voyage home ignoring Japanese conditions regarding carriage and leakage of nuclear materials. Japan described action as 'a very unfriendly act'.
162 **IRAN:IRAQ** At outbreak of war some small-scale clashes between opposing patrol boats. Iranian warships bombard Basra.
163 **CHILE:ARGENTINA** Chilean gunboat harrasses crew of newly constructed Argentine oil drilling platform at eastern end of Magellan Strait. Chilean fishing vessel seized by Argentine patrol off the Falklands. Cause was disputes over waters and islands in the Beagle Channel. Attempt to mediate by the Vatican suggesting a 'jointly patrolled zone of peace' was rejected by Argentina.
164 **IRAN:IRAQ:USA ET AL** Build-up of fleets of superpowers and allies in the Indian Ocean. In October there were over 60 American, French, British and Australian vessels in position (including 3 aircraft carriers and 8000 marines) to ensure freedom of navigation in the Persian/Arabian Gulf. Soviet strength in the area was increased to 29 naval vessels.

1981
165 **ISRAEL:LEBANON (PLO)** Naval actions taken by Israel against PLO bases and targets in Lebanon, including bombardment of PLO positions near Tyre and Sarafand, and seaborne commando force against Damour and Saksakieh.
166 **BANGLADESH:INDIA** Dispute involving deployment of naval vessels over an island in the river Hariabhanga estuary. The island (New Moore or South Talpatty I.), believed to have been formed by 1970 cyclone and tidal wave, was claimed by India in 1971 and Bangladesh in 1978.
167 **CAMEROON:NIGERIA** Five Nigerian soldiers killed and three wounded by gun fire from Cameroon patrol boat. Nigeria said the incident was within their territory, Cameroon said 20 miles within theirs.
168 **DENMARK:IRAN** Danish Merchant vessel *Elsa Cat* seized by Iranian navy on suspicion of carrying arms to Iraq. Cargo confiscated despite owners' protests that they were taking gelignite to Kuwait.
169 **NICARAGUA:HONDURAS:EL SALVADOR** Clashes between Nicaraguan and Honduran patrol boats in the Gulf of Fonseca. Nicaragua said El Salvador vessels were also involved.
170 **USA:LIBYA** US Sixth Fleet exercises in the Gulf of Sirte in international waters claimed by Libya as internal. Fighter planes from USS *Nimitz* engage in combat with Libyan aircraft. Both countries protest to the United Nations. President Reagan admits that the fleet was dispatched deliberately to challenge Libyan claims.
171 **USA:HONDURAS:NICARAGUA** Joint exercises held by US and Honduran navies off the Honduras/Nicaragua coast. Described by Nicaragua as 'a rehearsal of aggression against the Nicaraguan people'. Exercises in response to alleged build-up of Vietnamese/Cuban arms in Nicaragua.
172 **USSR:SWEDEN** Soviet Whiskey-class submarine runs aground in a restricted zone near Karlskrona naval base in Sweden. Sweden says submarine must have been involved in illegal reconnaissance or minelaying. Permission refused by Sweden for Soviet Flotilla to tow it off. Sweden protests at 'flagrant violation of territorial rights'.
173 **CAMBODIA:THAILAND** Cambodian patrol boat sunk by three Thai patrol boats as it was chasing a Thai fishing vessel. Cambodia claimed the incident took place in their own waters.

1982
174 **GUINEA-BISSAU:FRANCE** French trawler *Capitaine Cook* seized by Guinea-Bissau in area disputed between Guinea and Guinea-Bissau. A fine of Fr. 3 million was imposed. After the news was released the fine was halved and the vessel was released.
175 **N. KOREA:S. KOREA:JAPAN** Japan–N. Korean fishery agreement ended in June. S. Korean and Japanese fishing vessels seized by N. Korean navy 250 nm north of Iki island. S. Korean vessel seized 170 nm north-east of Ullung do. S. Korea claimed that since the end of the Korean war, 453 vessels and 3554 men had been captured, and 32 craft and 407 men were still held by N. Korea.
176 **THAILAND ET AL** Thai navy embark on a year-long, $36 m offensive against pirates, financed by 12 donor states through the UN High Commission for Refugees. There had been many attacks on fishing boats and Vietnamese refugees.
177 **NICARAGUA:HONDURAS** Honduras alleged that a Nicaraguan patrol boat seized a Honduran fishing vessel in Honduran waters, and many previous similar incursions. Nicaragua claimed Honduras was a refuge for anti-government right-wing guerrillas.
178 **ISRAEL:LEBANON (PLO)** Israel attacks on coastal cities of Lebanon. Bombardment from sea and landing of troops. Eventual forced evacuation of PLO by sea under UN supervison.
179 **UK:ARGENTINA** Invasion of Falkland Islands and South Georgia by Argentine forces (see page 184).
180 **SWEDEN:USSR** Swedish naval forces attempt to capture suspect Soviet submarine near Karlskrona naval base. Depth charges used but no submarine surfaced.

Appendix IX Study of the sea

Maritime museums

ANTIGUA, WEST INDIES
English Harbour The Nelson Museum, Nelson's Dockyard, English Harbour
ARGENTINA
Buenos Aires Museo Naval, Paseo Victórica 630, Tigre, Buenos Aires
AUSTRALIA
Echuca, Victoria Echuca Historical Society and paddle steamer *Adelaide*, Hopwood Gardens, Echuca
Fremantle, Western Australia Western Australian Museum, Fremantle
Mannum, South Australia Steamer *Marion*, Dry Dock, Mannum
Melbourne, Victoria Institute of Applied Science of Victoria, 204–328 Swanston Street, Melbourne
Port Adelaide, South Australia Port Adelaide Nautical Museum, St Vincent Street, Port Adelaide
Perth, Western Australia Western Australian Museum, Beaufort Street, Perth 6000
Swan Hill, Victoria Swan Hill Folk Museum, Box 524, Swan Hill
Sydney, New South Wales Port Jackson Marine Steam Museum—Steamer *Lady Hopetoun*, Sydney; Sydney Cove Waterfront Museum, Sydney
AUSTRIA
Fischamend Heimatmuseum, Fischamend
Linz Oberösterreichisches Landesmuseum, Tummelplatz 10 (Schloss), Linz/Donau
Petronell bei Wien Donau Museum, Schloss Petronell bei Wien
Spitz a.d. Donau Schiffahrtsmuseum, Schloss Erlahof, Ottenschläger Strasse, Spitz a.d. Donau (Wachau)
Stadl Paura Heimat-Haus Stadl Paura, Stadl Paura
Vienna Heeresgeschichtliches Museum, Arsenal, Wien III; Historisches Archiv der ersten Donaudampfschiffahrtsgesellschaft, Hinter Zollamistrasse, Wien; Technisches Museum, Mariahilfergasse 212, Wien
Wasserburg am Inn Heimatmuseum, Wasserburg am Inn
BELGIUM
Antwerp Nationaal Scheepvaartmuseum, Steenplein 1, 2000, Antwerpen
Brussels Gemeentelijk Museum van de Stad Brussel, Grote Markt, Brussel; Koninklijk Museum van het Leger en van Krijgsgeschiedenis, Halfeeuwfeestpark 3, Brussel
Oostduinkerke Nationaal Visserijmuseum, 8458, Oostduinkerke
Oostende Heemkundig Museum *De Plate*, Wapenplein, 8400, Oostende; *Mercator* (training ship), Opleidingsschip Mercator, Oostende
BERMUDA
Flatts Aquarium and Flatts, Bermuda Museum
Hamilton Bermuda Historical Society Museum, Hamilton, Bermuda
BRAZIL
Rio de Janeiro Museo da Marinha, Rio de Janeiro
BULGARIA
Varna Naval Museum, Cal. Tscherwenourmeiski 2, Varna
CANADA
Charlottetown, Prince Edward Island Seven Brothers Museum, Charlottetown
Collingwood, Ontario Huron Museum, Collingwood Institute, 128 St Paul Street, Collingwood
Dawson, Yukon Territory Steamer *Keno*, Yukon Dawson City
Halifax, Nova Scotia Nova Scotia Museum, PO Box 994, 1747 Summer Street, Halifax; Public Archives of Nova Scotia, Coburg Road, Halifax
Islet-sur-Mer, Quebec Bernier Maritime Museum, Islet-sur-Mer
Kaslo, British Columbia Kootenay Lake Historical Society, Steamer *Moyie*, Kaslo
Kingston, Ontario Kingston Marine Museum, Kingston
Montreal, Quebec Canada Steamship Lines Limited, PO Box 100, Montreal; Lake St Louis Historical Society, Marine Museum, Montreal; The Society of the Montreal Military and Maritime Museum, Ile Ste-Hélène, Casier Postal 1024, Montreal
Newfoundland Maritime History Group, Memorial University, Newfoundland
Penticton, British Columbia Penticton Museum and Archives Steamer *Sicamous*, Penticton
Pont Hill-Prince County, Prince Edward Island Green Park Provincial Historic Park, Pont Hill-Prince County
Quebec Cartier-Brébeuf National Historic Park, Quebec
Saint John, New Brunswick New Brunswick Museum (Marine Section), 277 Douglas Avenue, Saint John
St John's, Newfoundland Newfoundland Naval and Military Museum, St John's
Sarnia, Ontario Pilot House Museum, 2012 Wayne Street, Sarnia
Selkirk, Manitoba Lower Fort Garry National Historic Park, Box 7, Group 342, RR nr 3, Selkirk
Toronto, Ontario HMCS *Haida*, Ontario Place Corporation, 8 York Street, Toronto; HMS *Nancy* Museum, Queen's Park, Wasaga Beach, Toronto; Marine Museum for Upper Canada, Stanley Barrack, Toronto
Vancouver, British Columbia Maritime Museum, Cypress Street, Vancouver
Victoria, British Columbia Maritime Museum of British Columbia, Bastion Square, Victoria
Yarmouth, Nova Scotia Yarmouth County Historical Society, 22 Collins Street, Yarmouth
CUBA
Mariel, Pinar del Río Museo Histórico Naval *José Miguel Gómez*, Academia Naval del Mariel
CYPRUS
Kyrenia Kyrenia Ship Museum, Kyrenia
DENMARK
Aabenraa Aabenraa Museum, HP Hanssens Gade 33, Aabenraa
Aarhus Den Gamle By, Aarhus
Assens Willemoesgaardens Mindestuer, Østergade 36, Assens
Dragør Dragør Museum, Havnepladsen, Dragør
Ebeltoft Frigat *Jylland*, Ebeltoft
Esbjerg Fiskeri- og Søfartsmuseum, 6700 Esbjerg; Esbjerg Museum, Havnegade, Esbjerg
Frederikshavn Bangsbomuseet, Frederikshavn
Helsingør Handels- og Søfartsmuseum paa Kronborg, Kronborg Slot, Helsingør
Kerteminde Ladbyskibet, Ladby, Kerteminde
København B & W Museet, Trovegade 2, København 1449; Fiskerimuseum, Norregade 7, København; Nyboders Mindestuer, Sct Paulsgade 20, København; Oriogsmuseet, Sct Nicolai Kirkebygning, København
Kolding Museet paa Koldinghus, Koldinghus Slot, Kolding
Marstal Marstal og Omegns Museum, Prinsensgade 4, Marstal
Ribe Marinestuen, Weis' stue, Ribe
Ringkøbing Ringkøbing Museum, Ringkøbing (Jutland)
Rønne Rønne Museum, St Mortensgade 29, Rønne
Roskilde Vikingeskibshallen, Roskilde
Skagen Historiske Fyr, Skagen
Sønderborg Sønderborg Museum, Sønderborg Slott
Svendborg Svendborg Amts Museum, Fruestraede 3, Svendborg
Troense, Tåsinge I. Søfartssamlingerne ved Svendborgsund, Troense, Tåsinge
EGYPT
Alexandria Maritime Museum, Fort Kayyet Bay, Alexandria
FIJI
Suva The Fiji Museum, PO Box 2023, Government Buildings, Suva
FINLAND
Helsinki Suomenlinnan Museo, Suomenlinna (Sveaborg), Helsinki
Mariehamn Ålands Sjöfartsmuseum, Mariehamn (Åland)
Raahe Raahen Museo, Pekkahuonenkatu, Raahe
Rauma Rauman Museo, Kaupatori, Rauma
Turku (Åbo) Sjöhistoriska Museet vid Åbo Akademi, Åbo Akademi, Turku
FRANCE
Arromanches, Calvados Exposition permamente du débarquement, Arromanches 14117
Bandol, Var Musée de la Mer, Bandol, Ile de Bandol
Bordeaux, Gironde Musée Carrère, Bordeaux; Musée de Marine, Place de la Bourse 1, rue Fernand Philippart, Bordeaux
Brest, Finistère Salles Historiques du Château, Château de Brest, Brest
Camaret, Finistère Musée de la Marine, Tour Vauban, Camaret
Châteauneuf-sur-Loire, Loiret Musée de la Marine de Loire et du vieux Châteauneuf, au Château, Châteauneuf-sur-Loire
Compiègne, Oise Palais National De Compiègne, Compiègne
Concarneau, Morbihan Musée de la Pêche, Rue Vauban, Concarneau
Conflans-Sainte-Honorine, Seine-et-Oise Musée d'intérêt national de la Batellerie, Musée de la Batellerie, Conflans-Sainte-Honorine 78
Dieppe, Seine-Maritime Musée du Château, Château de Dieppe, Dieppe
Dunkerque, Nord Musée de Dunkerque, Rue Benjamin Morel, Dunkerque 59379

Fécamp, Seine-Maritime Musée Municipal, rue Alexandre-Legros 21, Fécamp
Granville, Manche Musée du Vieux Granville, Granville
Grasse, Alpes-Maritimes Mémorial Amiral de Grasse, rue Gazan 9, Grasse
Guidel, Morbihan Musée Sémaphore du Pouldu, Le Pouldu-en-Guidel
Honfleur Calvados Musée Maritime, Le Vieux Port, Honfleur
La Ciotat, Bouches-du-Rhône Musée Ciotaden, La Ciotat
Lanvéoc-Poulmic, Finistère Ecole Naval, Lanvéoc-Poulmic
La Seyne, Var Fort de Balaguier, La Seyne
Le Croisic, Loire-Inférieure Musée Naval du Croisic, Hôtel d'Aiguillon, Le Croisic
Le Havre, Seine-Maritime Musée de l'Ancien Havre, 1, rue Jérôme-Bellarmote, Le Havre; Musée-Exposition du Palais de la Bourse du Havre, Palais de la Bourse, Place Jules-Ferry 76, Le Havre
Lorient, Morbihan Musée Naval, Parc de la Compagnie des Indes, Lorient
Marseille, Bouches-du-Rhône Musée de la Marine de Marseille, Parc Chanot, Marseille 8e
Nantes, Loire-Inférieure Musée des Salorges, Château des Ducs, Nantes
Nice, Alpes-Maritimes Musée de la Marine, Tour Bellanda, Nice
Paris Musée de la Marine, Palais de Chaillot, Paris 16e; Musée du Conservatoire National des Arts et Métiers, 292, Rue St Martin, Paris IIle
Port-Louis, Morbihan Musée de la Citadelle de Port-Louis, Port-Louis
Quimper, Morbihan Musée departemental breton, Quimper
Rochefort, Charente-Maritime Musée Naval, Place de la Galissonnière, Rochefort
Saint-Malo, Ille-et-Vilaine Musée de Saint-Malo, Château de Saint-Malo, Saint-Malo
Saint-Martin-de-Ré, Ile-de-Ré Musée de Saint-Martin-de-Ré, Hôtel de Clerjotte, Saint-Martin-de-Ré
Saint-Servan, Ille-et-Vilaine Musée international du long-cours Cap Horniers, Tour Solidor, Saint-Servan
Saint-Tropez, Var Musée Naval de Saint-Tropez, Citadelle, St-Tropez
Toulon, Var Musée Naval de Toulon, Quai Stalingrad, Toulon; Tour Royale, Le Mowrillon, Toulon
Toulouse, Haute-Garonne Musée Languedocien des Transports, 5, Avenue du Lauragais, Toulouse

EAST GERMANY
Aken Kreis Heimatmuseum Aken, Parkstrasse 13, Aken (Elbe)
Dresden Armeemuseum der DDR, Kurt-Fischer-Platz, 806 Dresden; Verkehrsmuseum, Johanneum, Dresden
Havelberg Prignitzmuseum (Schiffahrt auf der Elbe und Havel), Havelberg
Oderberg Museum, Oderberg (Kreis Eberswalde Brandenburg)
Potsdam Museum der DDR Armee im Marmorpalast (Aussenstelle des Armeemuseum Dresden), Im Marmorpalast, Potsdam
Rostock Schiffahrtsmuseum, August-Bebel-Strasse 1, Rostock
Schönebeck/Elbe Museum Elbschiffahrt, Schönebeck (Elbe)
Stralsund Meeresmuseum, Katharinenberg 14a, 23 Stralsund
Warnemünde Heimatmuseum Warnemünde (part of the Schiffahrtsmuseum, Rostock), Theodor-Körner-Strasse, 31, Warnemünde

WEST GERMANY
Berlin Verkehrsmuseum Berlin, Hallesches Ufer 74/76, Berlin 61
Brake Schiffahrtsmuseum der Oldenburgischen Weserhäfen, Mitteldeichstrasse 36, 288 Brake (Unterweser)
Bremen Focke-Museum, Schwachhauser Heerstrasse 240, 28 Bremen; Übersee-Museum, Am Bahnhofplatz, Bremen
Bremerhaven Deutsches Schiffahrtsmuseum, 285 Bremerhaven-G; Nordseemuseum, Institut für Meeresforschung, Am Handelshafen, 285 Bremerhaven-G
Cuxhaven Buddelschiff-Museum, Kurmittelhaus, Cuxhaven-Duhnen
Duisburg Museum der Deutschen Binnenschiffahrt, Schifferbörse, Duisburg-Ruhrort
Düsseldorf Stadtgeschichtliches Museum, Bäckerstrasse 7-9, Düsseldorf
Emmerich Rheinmuseum, 424 Emmerich (Rhein)
Eutin Schloss Eutin, Schloss Eutin, Eutin (Holstein)
Flensburg Städtisches Museum Flensburg, Lutherplatz 1, Flensburg
Flensburg-Mürwik Marine Sammlung, Marine Schule, Flensburg-Mürwik
Glückstadt Detlefsen Museum, Glückstadt 43
Grömitz Kabinett der Seefahrt, Fischerstrasse 10, Ostseeheilbad, 2433 Grömitz
Hamburg Oevelgönner Seekiste, Oevelgönne 63, 2 Hamburg 52; Museum für Hamburgische Geschichte, Holstenwall 24, Hamburg; Museumshafen Oevelgönne, Oevelgönne 42, 2 Hamburg 52
Hamburg-Altona Altonaer Museum in Hamburg, Museumstrasse 23, 2000 Hamburg-Altona 1, PO Box 125
Juist Heimatmuseum, Juist (Friesische Insel)
Keitum, Sylt Sylter Heimatmuseum, Keitum (Sylt)
Kiel Kieler Stadt- und Schiffahrtsmuseum, Fischhalle am Wall, Kiel
Koblenz Rhein-Museum, Ehrenbreitstein, 54 Koblenz
Köln Städtisches Museum Köln, Zeughaus, Zeughausstrasse, Köln
Lauenburg Elbschiffahrtsmuseum, 59, Elbstrasse, Lauenburg (Elbe)
Leer Heimatmuseum Leer, Leer
Laboe Marine Ehrenmal, Laboe (Kiel)
Lübeck Museum im Holstentor, Holstentor, Lübeck; Museumchiff *Passat*, Senat der Hansestadt Lübeck; Sportamt, Kanzleigebäude, 2400 Lübeck
Minden Museum für Geschichte Landes -und Volkskunde, Minden
Mannheim Städtisches Reiss-Museum, Mannheim, Abteilung Rheinschiffahrtssammlung, Schloss, 6800 Manheim
München Deutsches Museum von Meisterwerken der Naturwissenschaft und Technik, Deutsches Museum, Museumsinsel Abholfach 8, München 26
Neustadt, Holstein Kreismuseum, Kremper Stadttor, Neustadt (Holstein)
Neuharlingersiel Buddelschiffsmuseum, Neuharlingersiel
Oldenburg Landesmuseum für Kunst und Kulturgeschichte, Oldenburg
Papenburg Heimatmuseum, Papernburg
Schleswig Schleswig-Holsteinisches Museum für Vor- und Frühgeschichte, Schloss Gottorp, Schleswig
Steinhudermeer Museum, Festung Wilhelmstein, Steinhuder Meer
Unterrodach Flössermuseum Unterrodach, Postfach 26, 8641 Unterrodach (Kronach-Bayern)
Vegesack Heimat Museum, Vegesack (Bremen)
Wasserburg am Inn Heimatmuseum, Wasserburg am Inn
Westrhauderfehn Fehn- und Schiffahrtsmuseum für Ostfriesland und Saterland, Westrhauderfehn 2953, Kreis Leer, Ostfriesland
Wiek auf Föhr Heimatmuseum, Wiek auf Föhr
Wilhelmshaven Kusten- und Schiffahrtsmuseum der Stadt Wilhelmshaven, Rheinstrasse 95, Wilhelmshaven
Worpswede-Schlussdorf Torfschiff-Museum, Heimatverein Schlussdorf, Worpswede-Schlussdorf
Wörth, Main Museum, Rathaud, Wörth (Main)
Zöns Kreismuseum, Zöns bei Köln

GREECE
Piraeus Nautical Museum, Freattys Marine Zeas, Piraeus

ICELAND
Reykjavik Pjoominjasafn Islands, Pjominjasafn Islands, Reykjavik

INDIA
Calcutta Birla Industrial and Technological Museum, Gurusaday Road 19a, Calcutta 19

INDONESIA
Djakarta Museum, Djakarta

IRISH REPUBLIC
Dublin Maritime Museum, St Michael's Wharf, Dun Laoghaire, Dublin

ISRAEL
Haifa Haifa Museum, Hanamal Street 2, Haifa
Tel Aviv Museum of Science and Technology, PO Box 17068, Tel Aviv

ITALY
Albenga Museo Navale Romano, Palazzo Peloso-Cepolla, Albenga
Bologna Museo delle Navi, Via Zamboni 33, Bologna
Camogli Museo Marinaro Municipale, Camogli
Genoa Civico Museo Navale, Piazza Bonavino 7, Genova (Pegli)
La Spezia Museo Tecnico Navale della Marina Militare, Arsenale Marine Militare, La Spezia
Marsala, Sicily The Punic ship *Mini-Museum*, Scuola Media 'V Pipitone', Via Sarzana 7, Marsala (Sicily)
Milan Civico Museo Navale Didattico, Via S Vittore 21, Milano
Naples Museo di San Martino, Soprintendenza alle Gallerie e alle opere d'arte della Campania, Pallazzo Real, Napoli
Nemi Museo delle Navi Romani di Nemi, Nemi
Trieste Museo del Mare, Via S Giorgio 3, Trieste
Venice Museo Storico Navale, Riva Degli Schiavoni campo S Biasio, 2148 Venezia

JAPAN
Kobe The International Ports and Harbours Museum, Naka-Tottei, Ikuta-ku, Kobe
Noo, Niigata-ken Maritime Museum, Noo-machi, Nishikubiki, Noo
Oarai, Ibarakari-ken Maritime Museum, 6890 Osohama, Oarai (Ibaraki-ken)
Tamano, Okayama-ken Maritime Museum, 250 Shibukawa, Tamano (Okayama-ken)
Toba Maritime Museum, Toba
Tokyo Transport Museum, 25, 1-Chrome, Kanda-Sudaco, Chiyodaku, Tokyo; Museum of Maritime Science, Landlot 13-1, Ariake-Chisaki, Koto-ku, Tokyo; The Japan Shipbuilding Industry Foundation, Senpaku Shinko Building, 35, Shiba-Kotohira-Cho, Minato-ku, Tokyo

MALTA
Valetta The National Museum, Auberge de Provence, Strada Mercanti, Valetta
Żabbar The Wickman Maritime Collection, *La Capitana*, Della Grazia Battery Road, Żabbar

MARTINIQUE
Fort-de-France Musée du Père Pinchon, Fort-de-France

NETHERLANDS
Amsterdam Rijksmuseum Nederlandsch Scheepvaart Museum, Kattenburgerplein 1, Amsterdam 1004; Rijksmuseum, Hobbemakade 19B, Amsterdam
Delfzijl Stichting Museum, Markstraat 39, Delfzijl
Den Helder Helders Marine Museum, *'t Torentje*, Hoofdgracht, Den Helder
De Rijp Oudheidkundig Genootschap *De Rijp*, Rechstraat 73a, De Rijp
Dordrecht Museum Meester Simon van Gijn, Nieuwe Haven 20, Dordrecht
Elburg Visserijmuseum, Vispoortstraat 24, Elburg
Enkhuizen Rijksmuseum Zuiderzeemuseum, Wierdijk 18, Enkhuizen
Gasselternijveen Kustvaarder *Gasselte*, De Hunze Recreatiepark Gasselternijveen (Drente)
Groningen Noordelijk Scheepvaartmuseum, St Walburgstraat 9, Groningen
Harlingen Hannema-Huis, Voorstraat 56, Harlingen
Hoorn West-Fries Museum, Rode Steen 1-8, Hoorn
Ketelhaven Zuiderzee Scheepvaartmuseum, Ketelhaven
Maassluis Gemeentelijk Museum, Hoogstraat 3, Maassluis; National Sleepvaart Museum, Hoogstraat, Maassluis
Rotterdam Maritiem Museum *Prins Hendrik*, Scheepmakershaven 48, 3011 VC Rotterdam; Nationaal Technisch Instituut voor Scheepvaart, Burg s'Jacobsplein 10, Rotterdam; Stichting Openlucht Binnenvaartmuseum, Calandstraat 34d, Rotterdam
Scheveningen Schevenings Visserijmuseum, Neptunusstraat, Scheveningen; Stichting Oud-Scheveningen, Ijmuidenstraat 120, Scheveningen
Schokland Museum voor de IJselpolders, Schokland, Noordoostpolder, Post Emmeloord
Sliedrecht Baggermuseum, Sliedrecht
Sneek Fries Scheepvaartmuseum en Oudheidkamer, Kleinzand 12, Sneek
Sommelsdijk Streekmuseum Goeree - Overflakkee, Kerkstraat, Sommelsdijk
Terschelling 't Behouden Huys, Terschelling, Isle of Terschelling
Veendam Veenkoloniaal Museum, Kerkstraat 18, Veendam
Veere De Schotse Huizen, Kade 25-27, Veere
Vlaardingen Museum voor Nederlandse Zeevisserij, Westhavenkade 45, Vlaardingen
Vlissingen Gemeentemuseum, Bellamypark 19, Vlissengen
Zaandijk Zaanlandse Oudheidkamer, Lagedijk 80, Zaandijk
Zierikzee Maritiem Museum, Noordhavenpoort, Zierikzee SS *Viera y Clavijo*, De Val Zierikzee

NEW ZEALAND
Auckland Auckland War Memorial Museum, Private Bag, Auckland

NORWAY
Aalesund Aalesunds Museum, R Rönnebergsgate 16, Ålesund; Sunnmøre Museum, Borgund-gavlen, Ålesund
Arendal Aust-Agder-Museet, Langsae Gård, Arendal
Bergen Bergens Fiskerimuseum, Bergen; Bergens Sjøfartsmuseum, Postboks 2636, Bergen; Hordaland Landsbrukmuseum, Stend Landsbrukskole, Bergen
Bodø Nordland Fylkesmuseum, Bodø
Drammen Drammens Museum, Konnerudgate 7, Drammen
Grimstad Grimstad Bymuseum og Ibsenhuset, Henrik Ibsens Gate, Grimstad
Haugesund Museet for Haugesund og Bybdens, Town Hall, Haugesund
Horten Marinemuseet, Horten
Kaupanger De Heibergske Samlinger - Sogn Folkmuseum, Kaupanger
Kristiansand Sjøfartsmuseum, Kristiansand Vest-Agder Fylkemuseum, Kongsgård, Kristiansand
Molde Fiskerimuseet paa Hjertøya, PO Box 70, Molde
Oslo Fram Museum, Bygdøy, Oslo; Kon Tiki Museum, Bygdøy, Oslo; Norsk Sjøfartsmuseum, Bygdøynesveien 37, Oslo 2; Norsk Veteranskibsklub SS *Børøysund*, Postboks 1287, Vika, Oslo 1; Vikingskiphuset, Bygdøy, Oslo
Sandane Nordfjord Folkemuseum, Sandane
Sandefjord Kommandør Chr. Christensens Hvalfangstmuseum, Sandefjord; Sandefjord Sjøfartsmuseum, Prinsengate 18, Sandefjord
Skien Fylkesmuseet for Telemark og Grenland, Skien
Stavanger Stavanger, Sjøfartsmuseum, Stavanger
Tönsberg Vestfold Fylkesmuseum, Farmannsveien 30, Tönsberg
Tromsø Tromsø Museum, Tromsø
Trondheim Trondheims Sjøfartsmuseum, Trondheim
Vardø Vardøhus Museum, Vardø

POLAND
Rozewie, near Gdańsk Muzeum Laternictwa, Województwo Gdanskie, Poczta Jastrzebia Góra
Gdynia Naval Museum, Bulwar Szwedzki, Gdynia
Gdańsk Maritime Museum, ul Szeroka 67/68, Gdańsk
Hel Fishery Museum, Bulivar Nadmorski 2, Hel
Szczecin Pomeraria Museum, Waly Chrobrego 1, Szczecin
Warsaw Museum Techniki, Palac Kultury, Warszawa

PORTUGAL
Faro Museu Maritimo de Almirante Ramalho Ortigao, Capitania do Porto, Faro
Figuéira da Foz Museu Municipal Dr Santos Rocha, Figueira da Foz
Ilhavo Museu Maritimo e Regional de Ilhavo, Ilhavo
Lisbon Museu da Sociedade de Geografia de Lisboa, Rua das Portas de Santo Antao 100, Lisboa; Museu de Marinha, Praça do Imperio, Lisboa 3
Provoa de Varzim Museu Etnografico Municipal, Rua de Vísconde, Povoa de Varzim

ROMANIA
Constanța Romanian Navy and Merchant Service Museum, Constanza

SENEGAL
Dakar, Ile de Gorée Museé de la Mer, Ile de Gorée

SINGAPORE
Singapore Maritime Museum, Singapore

SOUTH AFRICA
Cape Town South African Museum (Cultural History), Old Supreme Court Building, Adderley Street, Cape Town, PO Box 645

Port Elizabeth Port Elizabeth Museum, Humewood, Port Elizabeth

SPAIN

Aranjuez Casa de Marineros, Jardín del Príncipe Calle de la Reina, Aranjuez

Barcelona Museo Marítimo - Las Reales Atarazanas de Barcelona, Puerto de la Paz, 1, Barcelona; *Santa María*, Puerto de la Paz, Barcelona

Bueu, Pontevedra Museo Massó, Bueu

Cartagena Museo Arqueológico Municipal Navo *Santa María*, Cartagena

La Orotawa, Tenerife Museo Marítimo, La Oratawa

Luanco Museo Marítimo de Asturias, Calle Mariano Suárez-Pola, Luanco

Madrid Museo Naval, Ministerio de Marina, Montalban 2, Madrid

Palma de Mallorca Museo Marítimi, Palma de Mallorca

San Sebastian Museo Naval Provincial, San Sebastián

Seville Museo Marítimo, Torro del Oro, Sevilla

SWEDEN

Båstad Båstad Sjöfartssamlingar Vincent Andersson, Kyrkogatan 9, 260 90 Båstad

Falsterbo Falsterbo Museum, Sjövägen, 230 11 Falsterbo

Gävle Gävle Museum, S. Strandgatan 20, 802 22 Gävle

Göteborg Sjöfartsmuseet i Göteborg, Gamla Varvsparken, 414 59 Göteborg V; Fartygs Museum, Järntorget, Göteborg

Halmstad Hallands Museum, Tollsgatan, 302 31 Halmstad

Hälsingborg Hälsingborgs Museum, S. Storgatan 31, 252 23 Hälsingborg; Kalmar Läns Museum, Södra Storgatan 31, Hälsingborg

Härnösand Friluftmuseet Murberget, Murbergsgatan, 871 00 Härnösand; Kalmar Museum, Slottet, 381 00 Kalmar; Stiftelsen Kalmar Sjöfartsmuseum, Härnösand; Kulturhistoriska museet Murberget, Karlsham, Admiralitetsslätten

Hjö Steamer *Trafik*, Hjö

Karlshamn Karlshamn Museum, Drottninggatan 85, 292 00 Karlshamn

Karlskrona Marinmuseum och Modellkammaren, Amiralitetsslätten, 371 00 Karlskrona

Linköping Hantverks och Sjöfartsmuseum, Linköping; Linköpings Stads Museum, Vasavägen 16, 582 20 Linköping

Luleå Norrbottens Museum, Storgatan 2, 951 35 Luleå

Lysekil Bohuslänska Fornminnesällskapet Vikarvet, 453 00 Lysekil

Malmö Malmö Sjöfartsförening, Malmö; Tekniska Museet, Malmöhusvägen, 211 20 Malmö

Norrköping Norrköpings Museum, Kristinaplatsen, 602 34 Norrköping

Oskarshamn Oskarshamn, Sjöfartsmuseum, Varvsgatan 5, 572 00 Oskarshamn

Råå Råå museum för sjöfart och fiske, 255 90 Halsingborg

Roslagen Roslagen Sjöfartsminnesförenings Museum, Kaplansbacken Almstad, 101 10 Stockholm

Simrishamn Hembergska Huset, Simrishamn; Hoppets Lokal, Brantevik, 272 00 Simrishamn; Osterlens Museum, Storgatan 24, 272 00 Simrishamn

Skellefteå Skellefteå Museum, Nyborg, 931 00 Skellefteå

Stockholm Statens Sjöhistoriska Museum, Djurgårdsbrunnsvägen 24, 15 27 Stockholm No

Sundsvall Sundsvalls Museum, Storgatan 29, 852 30 Sundsvall

Torekov Föreningen Torekovs Sjöfarts och Hembygdsmuseum, 260 93 Torekov

Uddevalla Uddevalla Museum, Kungsgatan 30-32, 451 00 Uddevalla

Umeå Länsmuseet, Umeå; Västebottens Museum, Stiftelsen Gammlia, 902 44 Umeå

Väddö Roslagens Sjöfartsmuseum, Väddö

Västervik Tjustbygdens Kulturhistoriska Museum, Kullbacken, 593 00 Västervik

Växjö Smålands Museum, S Järnvägsgatan 2, 352 34 Växjö

SWITZERLAND

Basel Unser Weg zum Meer, Rheinhafen Kleinhüningen, 4000 Basel

Luzern Verkehrshaus der Schweiz, Lidostrasse 5, Luzern

TURKEY

Istanbul Bahruje Mûze ve Kütüphanesi, Besiktas, Istanbul

UNION OF SOVIET SOCIALIST REPUBLICS

Gor'kiy Technical Transport Museum, Gor'kiy

Leningrad Naval Museum, B-164 Ploshchad Pushkina 4, Leningrad

Odessa Maritime Museum of the USSR, Ul Lastochkina, Odessa

Riga Riga Museum of History and Navigation, Riga

Sevastopol Museum of the Black Sea Fleet, Sevastopol

Ventspils Fisheries Museum, Ventspils

UNITED KINGDOM

Aberdeen Aberdeen Art Gallery and Museum, Aberdeen

Annan Annan Museum, Annan, Dumfries and Galloway

Anstruther Scottish Fisheries Museum, Harbour Head, St Ayles, Anstruther, Fife

Bamburgh The Grace Darling Museum, Bamburgh, Northumberland

Barrow-in-Furness Barrow-in-Furness Museum, Barrow-in-Furness, Cumbria

Belfast, Ulster Belfast Transport Museum, 4 Withan Street, Belfast; Ulster Museum, Belfast

Bournemouth Rothesay Museum, Bournemouth, Hampshire

Bideford Public Library and Museum, Bideford, Devon

Bristol City Museum, Queens Road, Bristol; SS *Great Britain*, Great Western Dock, Gas Ferry Road, Bristol

Brixham Brixham Museum, Brixham, Devon

Buckler's Hard Buckler's Hard Maritime Museum, Beaulieu, Brockenhurst, Hampshire

Cardiff Welsh National Museum, Cathays Park, Cardiff

Castletown, Isle of Man Nautical Museum, Bridge Street, Castletown, Isle of Man

Chatham Dockyard Museum, Chatham, Kent

Cowes Steamer *Medway Queen*, Cowes, Isle of Wight

Devonport Devonport Museum, Devonport, Devon

Douglas, Isle of Man Manx Museum and Trust, Crellin's Hill, Douglas, Isle of Man

Dundee Dundee City Museum, Albert Square, Dundee; Shipping Museum, Barrack Street, Dundee

Edinburgh Royal Scottish Museum, Chambers Street, Edinburgh 1; Scottish United Services Museum, Crown Square, The Castle, Edinburgh

Exeter Exeter Maritime Museum, The Quay, Exeter

Falmouth Falmouth Maritime Museum, Falmouth, Cornwall

Glasgow Glasgow Museums and Art Galleries, Kelvingrove, Glasgow C3

Gosport Naval Ordnance Museum, RNAD, Priddy's Hard, Gosport, Hampshire; Submarine Museum HMS *Dolphin*, Gosport, Hampshire

Great Yarmouth Shipwrecked Sailor's Home, Great Yarmouth, Norfolk; Maritime Museum of East Anglia, Great Yarmouth

Greenwich National Maritime Museum, Romney Road, Greenwich, London SE10; The *Cutty Sark* Society, 2 Greenwich Church Street, Greenwich, London SE10

Grimsby Doughty Museum, Town Hall Square, Grimsby, Lincolnshire

Guernsey, Channel Islands Maritime Museum Castle Cornet, Guernsey

Hastings Fishermans Museums, Rock-a-Nor Road (Fishermans Church), Hastings, Sussex; Museum of Local History, Old Town Hall, High Street, Hastings, Sussex

Holywood, Ulster Ulster Folk and Transport Museum, Cultra, Holywood, Co Down

Hull Maritime Museum, Pickering Park, Kingston-upon-Hull

Ilfracombe The Museum, Ilfracombe, Devon

Isles of Scilly Valhalla Maritime Museum, Tresco Abay, Isles of Scilly, Cornwall

Lewes Anne of Cleves House, Southover, Lewes, Sussex

Liverpool City of Liverpool Museums, William Brown Street, Liverpool 3

London Museum of British Transport, Clapham, London SW7; HMS *Belfast*, Pool of London, near Tower Bridge; Science Museum, South Kensington, London SW7; The Imperial War Museum, Lambeth Road, London SE1

Maidstone Museum and Art Gallery, Maidstone, Kent

Middlesbrough Dorman Memorial Museum, Middlesbrough

Newcastle-upon-Tyne The Museum of Science and Engineering, Exhibition Road, Great North Road, Newcastle-upon-Tyne

Paisley Paisley Museum, Art Gallery and Observatory, High Street, Paisley, Strathclyde

Penzance Benbow Museum of Nautical Art, Penzance, Cornwall

Peterhead Public Library and Arbuthnot, St Peter Street, Peterhead, Grampian

Plymouth Buckland Abbey at Yelverton, Buckland Abbey, near Plymouth, Devon; Dockyard Museum, MOD Navy Devonport, Postal Code 1422, Plymouth PL1 4SG; Plymouth Museums and Arts Gallery, Tavistock Road, Plymouth, Devon

Portsmouth Royal Marines Museum, Eastney Barracks, Southsea, Portsmouth, Hampshire; HMS *Victory*, HM Dockyard, Portsmouth, Hampshire

Redcar Redcar Museum of Fishing & Shipping, Redcar, Cleveland

Rochester Eastgate House Museum, Rochester, Kent

St Peter Port, Guernsey, Channel Islands Lukis and Island Museum, St Barnabas Cornet Street, St Peter Port, Guernsey

Salcombe Overbecks Museum, Salcombe, Devon

Shoreham-by-Sea Marlipins Museums, High Street, Shoreham-by-Sea, Sussex

Sittingbourne Dolphin Yard, Crown Quay Lane, Sittingbourne, Kent

Southampton Southampton Maritime Museum, Southampton, Hampshire; Tudor House Museum, Bugle Street, Southampton, Hampshire

South Shields South Shields Public Library and Museum, Ocean Road, South Shields, Co Durham

Stromness, Orkney Stromness Museum, Alfred Street, Stromness, Orkney

Sunderland Sunderland Museum and Art Gallery, Borough Road, Sunderland, Co Durham

Swansea Royal Institution of South Wales, Swansea

Tilbury Tilbury Maritime Museum, Tilbury, Essex

West Hartlepool Gray Art Gallery and Museum, West Hartlepool, Cleveland

Whitby Museum of the Whitby Literary and Philosophical Society, Pannet Park, Whitby, Yorkshire

Whitehaven Public Museum, Whitehaven, Cumbria

Winchelsea Court Hall Museum, Winchelsea, Sussex

Worthing Worthing Museum and Art Gallery, Chapel Road, Worthing, Sussex

Yeovil Fleet Air Arm Museum, Yeovil, Somerset

UNITED STATES OF AMERICA

Annapolis, Maryland US Naval Academy Museum, Annapolis

Ann Arbor, Michigan University of Michigan Transport Library, Ann Arbor

Astoria, Oregon Columbia River Maritime Museum, 16th & Exchange Street, Astoria

Ausable Chasm, New York Lake Champlain Museum of Naval History, Ausable Chasm

Baker's Island, Lake Superior SS *Whaleback Meteor*, Baker's Island

Baltimore, Maryland Radcliffe Maritime Museum, Maryland Historical Society, Maritime Division, 201 West Monument Street, Baltimore 21201; The Peale Museum, 225 North Holliday Street, Baltimore; USS *Constellation*, Constellation Dock, Baltimore

Bath, Maine Bath Marine Museum, 963 Washington Street, Bath

Beach Haven, New Jersey Schooner *Lucy Evelyn*, Beach Haven

Beaufort, North Caroline Alphonso Whaling Museum, Beaufort

Blue Mountain Lake, New York Adirondack Museum, Blue Mountain Lake

Boothbay Harbor, Maine Grand Banks Schooner Museum, 100 Commercial Street, Boothbay Harbor

Boston, Massachusetts Boston Marine Society, 88 Broad Street, 9th Floor, Boston; Museum of Science, Science Park, Boston; USS *Constitution*, (IX-21), Boston Naval Yard, Boston

Bremerton, Washington Puget Sound Naval Shipyard Museum, Bremerton 98314

Bristol, Rhode Island Herreshoff Model Room, 125 Hope Street, Bristol

Brooklyn, New York The Long Island Historical Society, Pierrepont & Clinton Street, Brooklyn

Buffalo, New York Buffalo & Erie County Historical Society, 25 Nottingham Court, Buffalo

Cambridge, Massachusetts Frances Russell Hart Nautical Museum, Massachusetts Institute of Technology, Cambridge

Centerport, Long Island, New York Vanderbilt Museum, Commission of Suffolk County, PO Box F, Centerport, Long Island

Chatam, Massachusetts Whaling Museum, Chatham

Chicago, Illinois Chicago Historical Society, Clark Street and North Avenue, Chicago; Museum of Science and Industry, Jackson Park, 57th Street, and South Shore Drive, Chicago; The Adler Planetarium, 9090 East Achsah Bond Drive, Chicago

Clayton, New York Thousand Islands Museum, Riverside Drive, Clayton; Thousands Islands Shipyard Museum, Mary Street, Clayton

Cleveland, Ohio Cleveland Nautical Museum, Carnegie West Branch Library, Fulton Road and Bridge Avenue, Cleveland

Cleveland Heights, Ohio Great Lakes Historical Society, 320 Republic Building, Cleveland

Cohasset, Massachusetts Cohasset Maritime Museum, PO Box 205, Cohasset

Cold Spring Harbor, New York Whaling Museum, Main Street, Cold Spring Harbor, Long Island

Colombus, Georgia Confederate Naval Museum, Colombus

Detroit, Michigan Dossin Great Lakes Museum, Belle Isle, Detroit

Douglas, Michigan Saugatuck Marine Museum, PO Box 436, Douglas

Doylestown, Pennsylvania Bucks County Historical Society Marine Room, Doylestown; Mercer Museum, Doylestown

Duluth, Minnesota Maritime Museum, Duluth

East Greenwich, Rhode Island Varnum Military and Naval Museum, East Greenwich

East Hampton, New York East Hampton Town Marine Museum, Bluff Road, Amangasett, New York

Edgartown, Massachusetts Dukes County Historical Society, Edgartown

Erie, Pennsylvania Flagship *Niagara*, Erie

Essex, New York *Philadelphia*, Essex

Fairport Harbor, Ohio Fairport Harbor Marine Museum, 129 Second Street, Fairport Harbor

Fall River, Massachusetts Fall River Historical Society, 451 Rock Street, Fall River; Marine Museum, PO Box 1147, Fall River; USS *Massachusetts*, State Pier, Fall River

Fredericksburg, Texas Fleet Admiral Chester W. Nimitz Memorial Naval Museum, PO Box 777, Fredericksburg

Galveston, Texas Rosenberg Library, Galveston; USS *Cavalla*/USS *Stewart*, Submarine Seawolf Commission, PO Box 1595, Galveston

Glen Cove, New York Webb Institute of Naval Architecture, Crescent Beach Road, Glen Cove, Long Island

Gloucester, Massachusetts Cape Ann Scientific Literary & Historical Association, Gloucester

Groton, Connecticut The Submarine Library and Museum, US Naval Submarine Base, PO Box 157, Groton

Hackensack, New Jersey The Submarine Memorial Assoc (USS *Ling*), PO Box 395, Hackensack

Hannibal, Missouri Steamer *Mark Twain*, Hannibal

Hartford, Connecticut The Wadsworth Atheneum, 25 Atheneum Square North, Hartford

Hermann, Missouri Historic Hermann Museum, Hermann

Honolulu, Hawaii Falls of Clyde Maritime Museum, c/o Bernice P Bishop Museum, Honolulu

Hoodriver, Oregon USS *Banning*, Hoodriver

Houston, Texas Battleship *Texas*, The Battleship Texas Commission, San Jacinto Battlegrounds, Houston

Jeffersonville, Indiana Howard National Steamboat Museum, Jeffersonville

Kennebunk, Marine The Brick Store Museum, 117 Main Street, Kennebunk

Kings Point, New York United States Merchant Marine Academy, Kings Point, Long Island

Kingston, North Carolina CSS Neuse, Governor Richard Caswell Memorial, Kingston

Long Beach, California California Museum of the Sea Foun-

dation—*Queen Mary*, PO Box 20890, Long Beach
Los Angeles, California Cabrillo Beach Marine Museum, San Pedro 37200, Stephen White Drive; California Museum of Science and Industry, Museum of the Sea, 700 State Drive, Los Angeles
Louisville, Kentucky Steamer *Belle of Louisville*, Public Wharf, 4th and River Road, Louisville
Ludington, Michigan Mason County Museum, East Filer Street 305, Ludington
Mackinaw City, Michigan Mackinaw Maritime Park, Mackinaw City
Manitowoc, Wisconsin Manitowoc Marine Museum, North 8th Street, Manitowoc; Rahr Civic Center, 8th and Park Streets, Manitowoc
Marietta, Ohio Campus Martius Museum and Steamer *W P Snyder Jr*, 601 Second Street, Marietta; Ohio River Museum, Front Street, Marietta
Milton, Massachusetts Museum of the American China Trade and Captain Robert Bennet Forbes House, 215 Adams Street, Milton
Mobile, Alabama USS *Alabama* Battleship Memorial, PO Box 65, Location US, Highway 90 East, Mobile
Monterey, California Allen Knight Maritime Museum, PO Box 805, Monterey
Mystic, Connecticut Mystic Seaport, Mystic
Nantucket, Massachusetts Nantucket Whaling Museum of the Nantucket Historical Association, Broad Street, Nantucket
New Bedford, Massachusetts Old Dartmouth Historical Society and Whaling Museum, 18 Johnny Cake Hill, New Bedford
Newburyport, Massachusetts Historical Society of Old Newbury, 98 High Street, Newburyport
New London US Coast Guard Academy Museum, New London, Connecticut
New Orleans, Louisiana Louisiana State Museum, 757 Chartres Street, New Orleans
Newport, Rhode Island Newport Historical Society, 82 Touro Street, Newport; Revolutionary War Frigate *Rose*, Seaport '76, 60 Church Street, Newport
Newport News, Virginia The Mariners Museum, Newport News
New York Franklin D Roosevelt Library, Hyde Park, New York; India House, 1 Hanover Square, New York; Marine Museum of the City of New York, 1220 Fifth Avenue, New York; Marine Museum of the Seaman's Church Institute of New York, 25 South Street, New York 4; New York Yacht Club, 37 W 44 Street; Sailor's Snug Harbor, 914 Richmond Terrace, Staten Island, New York; The New York Historical Society, 170 Central Park West, New York 24; South Street Seaport Museum, 16 Fulton Street, New York
Pearl Harbor, Hawaii Pacific Submarine Museum, Pearl Harbor
Pemaquid Point, Maine Fisherman's Museum, Pemaquid Point
Pensacola, Florida Naval Aviation Museum, Naval Air Station, Pensacola
Philadelphia, Pennsylvania Atwater Kent Museum, 15 South 7th Street, Philadelphia; Commercial Museum, Philadelphia Civic Center, 34th and Convention Avenue, Philadelphia; Franklin Institute, Hall of Marine Transportation Parkway, Philadelphia; Heritage Ship Guild, North East Corner, 3rd and Chasmut Street; The Philadelphia Maritime Museum, 427 Chestnut Street, Philadelphia; USS *Olympia*/USS *Becuna*, Penn's Landing; USS *Olympic*, Delaware River, Pier 11 North, Philadelphia.
Plymouth, Massachusetts *Mayflower II*, PO Box 1620, Plymouth; Plymouth Plantation, Warren Avenue, Plymouth
Port Hueneme, California Seabee Museum, US Naval Station, Port Hueneme
Portland, Maine Maine Historical Society, 485 Congress Street, Portland
Portland, Oregon Oregon Historical Society, 1230 SW Park Avenue, Portland 97205
Portsmouth, Virginia Portsmouth Coast Guard Museum, Portsmouth; Portsmouth Naval Shipyard Museum, 2 High Street (PO Box 248), Portsmouth
Providence, Rhode Island Rhode Island Historical Society, 52 Power Street, Providence
Rockport, Massachusetts Sandy Bay Historical Society and Museum, Community House, Broadway, Rockport
Sag Harbor, New York Suffolk County Whaling Museum of Sag Harbor, Long Island, Main and Garden Street, Sag Harbor, Long Island (PO Box 327 A)
Saginaw, Michigan Trident Maritime Museum, 1202 Cass Street, Saginaw
St Louis, Missouri National Museum of Transport, Barrett Station Road, St Louis; The Missouri Historical Society, Jefferson Memorial Building, St Louis; The Waterways Journal, 666 Security Building, 319 North Fourth Street, St Louis
St Michaels, Maryland Chesapeake Bay Maritime Museum, PO Box 615, St Michaels
St Petersburg, Florida The Bounty Exhibit, 345 2nd Avenue North East, St Petersburg
Salem, Massachusetts Peabody Museum of Salem, 161 Essex Street, Salem; Salem Maritime National Historic Site, Custom House, Derby Street, Salem
San Diego, California Maritime Museum Association of San Diego, 1306 North Harbor Drive, San Diego. (Museum housed aboard the barque *Star of India*); Naval Training Center Museum, San Diego
San Francisco, California HM De Young Memorial Museum, Golden Gate Park, San Francisco; San Francisco Maritime Museum, Polk Street, San Francisco 9; Museum Ship *Balclutha*, Pier 43, San Francisco; San Francisco Maritime State Historical Park, Hyde Street Pier, San Francisco
San Pedro, California Ports O'Call Village and Whaler's Wharf, San Pedro
Sault Ste Marie, Michigan Museum Ship *Valley Camp*, PO Box 1668, Sault Ste Marie
Savannah, Georgia Ships of the Sea Museum, 503 East River Street, Savannah
Searsport, Maine Penobscot Marine Museum, Searsport
Seattle, Washington Museum of History and Industry, 2161 East Hamlin Street, Seattle
Sharon, Massachusetts Kendall Whaling Museum, Sharon
Staten Island, New York Library of the Steamship Historical Society of America, Inc. Mailing address: 414 Pelton Avenue, Staten Island (New York) 10310. Library address: 4 Broad Street, Staten Island; New York Public Library, St George Branch, 14 Bay Street, Staten Island
Treasure Harbor, Florida Keys McKee's Museum of Sunken Treasure, PO Box 165, Tavernier, Plantation Key
Vallejo, California Mare Island Naval Shipyard Museum, Vallejo
Vermilion, Ohio The Great Lakes Historical Society Museum, 480 Main Street, Vermilion
Vicksburg, Mississippi Sprague River Hall of Fame and Museum, Steamer *Sprague*, Vicksburg Waterfront, PO Box 484, Vicksburg
Washington, District of Columbia Lightship *Chesapeake*, 1200 Ohio Drive, SW Washington DC; Merchant Marine Exhibit, Maritime Adm Exhibit Hall, 441 G Street NW, Washington DC; Naval Gun Factory Museum, M Street at 8th SE, Washington DC; Smithsonian Institution, United States National Museum, Museum of History and Technology, Constitution Avenue, 12th–14th Streets NW, Washington DC; Truxtun-Decatur Naval Museum, 1610 H Street, NW, Lafayette Square, Washington DC; United States Coast Guard, Main Treasury Department Building, Room 2428, 15th and Pennsylvania Avenue, Washington DC; US Naval Historical Display Center, Washington Navy Yard, Washington DC; United States Navy Department, Constitution Avenue, Washington DC 25
Whitehall, New York Skenesborough Museum, Whitehall
Wilmington, North Caroline USS *North Carolina* Battleship Memorial, PO Box 417, Wilmington
Winona, Minnesota Transportation Museum on Board the *Julius C. Wilkie*, Winona
Yonkers, New York The Hudson River Museum, Yonkers
YUGOSLAVIA
Belgrade Museum of River Communication, Belgrade
Dubrovnik Maritime Museum of the Yugoslav Academy, Tvrgjava sv. Ivana
Kotor Maritime Museum, Trg Bokeljske mornarice br. 391, POB 58, Kotor
Oribic Maritime Museum, Oribic
Rijeka Maritime Museum, Rijeka
Split Maritime Museum of the Yugoslav Academy, Trg brade Radida 7, PO 100

Programmes conducted within the International Decade of Ocean Exploration (IDOE), 1971–80

1 **Sub-tropical convergence in SW Atlantic** Physical/chemical oceanography and upwelling *Argentina, Brazil, Uruguay*

2 **Equatorial undercurrent of W. Pacific** Origin and dynamics of the undercurrent *Australia, France*

3 **Sea surface current field in SW Pacific and E. Indian Ocean** Tracking of free drifting buoys by satellite *Australia, France, USA*

4 **Overflow studies** Fluctuations in water flow from Norwegian and Greenland seas into Atlantic *Canada, Denmark, France, W. Germany, Iceland, Norway, USSR, UK, USA*

5 **Mid-ocean dynamics experiment (MODE)** Medium scale eddies in general ocean circulation *France, W. Germany, Sweden, USSR, UK, USA*

6 **North Pacific experiment (NORPAX)** Large-scale fluctuations in ocean and atmosphere in mid-latitudes *Australia, Canada, France, W. Germany, Japan, UK, USA*

7 **Long-range investigation, mapping and prediction (CLIMAP)** Surface ocean climatic fluctuations associated with glacial and interglacial transitions *Denmark, W. Germany, Netherlands, Norway, Switzerland, UK, USA*

8 **Joint air-sea interaction project (JASIN)** Structure of oceanic and atmospheric boundary layers *Netherlands, UK, USA*

9 **Joint North Sea data acquisition project (JONSDAP)** Tide, current, chemical and pollution data for S. North Sea *Belgium, Netherlands, UK*

10 **Joint North Sea wave project (JONSWAP)** Dynamic processes at sea surface–German Bight *Canada, Denmark, France, W. Germany, Netherlands, UK, USA*

11 **El Niño** Oceanic circulation in SE Pacific *Chile, Colombia, Ecuador, Peru, USA*

12 **Monsoon circulation in the Arabian Sea (MONEX)** *India, USSR*

13 **Cooperative Investigations of the Caribbean and adjacent regions (CICAR)** Multidisciplinary programme *Brazil, Colombia, Cuba, France, W. Germany, Guatemala, Jamaica, Mexico, Netherlands, Panama, Trinidad and Tobago, USSR, UK, USA, Venezuela*

14 **Cooperative Investigations of the northern part of the E. Central Atlantic (CINECA)** Multidisciplinary study of oceanic area of Atlantic *France, W. Germany, S. Korea, Mauritania, Morocco, Norway, Poland, Portugal, Senegal, Spain, USSR, UK, USA*

15 **Geochemical ocean sections study (GEOSECS)** Application of geochemical and hydrographic measurements to the study of circulation and mixing processes of world oceans *Canada, France, W. Germany, India, Italy, Japan, UK, USA*

16 **Global atmospheric research programme (GARD) and Global Atlantic tropical experiment (GATE)** Convective and mesoscale systems and their relationship to larger scale tropical disturbances *Brazil, Canada, France, W. Germany, Mexico, Netherlands, Portugal, USSR, UK, USA, Venezuela*

17 **Controlled ecosystem pollution experiment (CEPEX)** Pollution ecology *Canada, UK, USA*

18 **Pollution and ecological investigations along the Halifax–Bermuda section** Marine pollution and chemical oceanography *Canada, W. Germany, UK, USA*

19 **Global investigation of pollution in the marine environment (GIPME)** Marine pollution research and monitoring *Most IOC (Intergovernmental Oceanographic Commission) member states*

20 **Continental margins of the S. Atlantic** Origin and evolution of present-day margins *Argentina, Brazil, Congo, France, Gabon, W. Germany, Ghana, Jamaica, Liberia, Nigeria, Portugal, Senegal, Sierra Leone, S. Africa, Spain, UK, Uruguay*

21 **Geochemical studies in the E. Mediterranean** Dispersion of ore elements *Greece, UK*

22 **Plate tectonics and metallogenesis (Nazca Plate)** Genesis of mineral deposits *Bolivia, Chile, Colombia, Ecuador, Peru, USA, Venezuela*

23 **Tectonic development of E. and SE Asia** Relationship between tectonics and natural mineral resources *Cambodia, Indonesia, Japan, S. Korea, Malaysia, Philippines, Singapore, Thailand, Vietnam*

24 **Mid-Atlantic ridge (FAMOUS)** Mechanism driving apart the plates of the earth and formation of a new ridge along the rift valley *Canada, France, Iceland, Portugal, UK, USA*

25 **Structure of the oceanic-island arc-continental margins of the SW Pacific** Interactions between coastal elements *Australia, Fiji, France, New Zealand, USSR, USA*

26 **Ocean minerals** Origin and distribution of nodules, environmental and technical problems of mining *France, W. Germany, New Zealand, UK, USA, Venezuela*

27 **Polymetallic nodule deposits, hot brines and metalliferous muds in the SW Pacific** Occurrence, formation and environmental factors *Australia, France, W. Germany, Japan, New Zealand, USSR, USA*

28 **Coastal upwelling ecosystems analysis (CUEA)** Studying the response of the system to change, predicted from monitoring a few biological, physical or meteorological variables *Canada, France, W. Germany, Japan, Mexico, Spain, USSR, UK, USA*

Long-term and expanded programme of oceanographic exploration and research (LEPOR) programmes

29 **Variability of sea surface temperature and salinity fields of SW Pacific and Indian Oceans** *Australia, France, Japan, New Zealand*

30 **Physical oceanography of the Kuroshio and adjacent regions** *China, France, Japan, S. Korea, Philippines, Thailand, USSR, UK (Hong Kong), Vietnam*

31 **Study of the physical oceanography of the Mediterranean** *Austria, Belgium, Egypt, France, W. Germany, Israel, Italy, Lebanon, Malta, Monaco, Morocco, Romania, Spain, Switzerland, Tunisia, UK, USSR*

32 **Saronikos system project** Existing and proposed Athens waste disposal *W. Germany, Greece, UK, USA*

33 **Study of North Sea pollution** Chlorinated aromatic hydrocarbons such as DDT, halogenated hydrocarbons, metals (mercury, lead, copper, zinc, cadmium, manganese), petroleum *Belgium, Denmark, France, W. Germany, Netherlands, Norway, Sweden, UK*

34 **General bathymetric chart of the oceans (GEBCO) with IHO** Morphological charting of the sea floor *All member states affiliated with IHO (International Hydrographic Organisation)*

35 **Studies of organic sedimentary processes on shelf slopes and deep ocean floor of SW Pacific** *New Zealand*

36 **Assessment of living resources in N. Atlantic** *Canada, UK, USA*

37 **Fish stock assessment in the S. Atlantic** *Argentina, Indonesia, Poland, Senegal*

38 **Indian Ocean fishery survey and development programmes** *Bahrain, Bangladesh, Burma, Ethiopia, India, Indonesia, Iran, Iraq, Jordan, Kenya, Kuwait, Madagascar, Malaysia, Maldives, Mauritius, Oman, Pakistan, Qatar, Singapore, Somalia, Sri Lanka, Tanzania, Thailand, N. Yemen, S. Yemen, UAE, UK*

39 **Southern Oceans** International coordination group for the southern oceans *Argentina, Australia, Belgium, Brazil, Chile, France, Japan, New Zealand, Norway, S. Africa, USSR, UK, USA*

Numbers 1–39 are indicated on the map pages 206–207.

Appendix X The management task

Some evolving regional commitments for the protection and conservation of the marine environment

Marine Pollution Prevention and Control

region	instrument	parties	type	status
ATLANTIC				
Mediterranean	UNEP Action Plan	multilateral	fully regional	approved in January 1975
West Africa (Gulf of Guinea and adjacent waters)	Draft UNEP Action Plan	multilateral	fully regional	submitted for approval in 1981
	Draft UNEP Regional Convention for the Protection of the Marine Environment of the West African Region	multilateral	fully regional	submitted for approval 1981
Caribbean (Caribbean Sea, Gulf of Mexico and adjacent waters)	Draft UNEP Action Plan	multilateral	fully regional	submitted for approval 1981
ARCTIC	—	—	—	—
INDO-PACIFIC				
Red Sea/Gulf of Aden	UNEP Action Plan	multilateral	fully sub-regional	approved January 1976
	Draft UNEP Regional Convention for the Environmental Protection of the Red Sea and Gulf of Aden	multilateral	fully sub-regional	subject to continuing consultations
Persian/Arabian Gulf	UNEP Action PLan ('Kuwait Action Plan Region')	multilateral	fully sub-regional	approved April 1978

Marine Pollution Prevention and Control

region	instrument	parties	type	status
East Asian Seas	Draft Action Plan for Asian sub-region (South China Sea and adjacent waters)	multilateral	fully sub-regional	subject to continuing consultations
South-east Pacific	Action Plan (short term)	multilateral	fully regional	adopted November 1978
	Draft UNEP Convention on the Protection of the Marine Environment against Pollution in the Southeast Pacific	multilateral	fully regional	subject to continuing consultations
	Draft UNEP Protocol on Regional Co-operation in cases of Pollution Emergencies	multilateral	fully regional	ditto
	Draft UNEP Action Plan	multilateral	fully regional	ditto
South-west Pacific	Draft Declaration of Principles on the Management and Improvement of the Environment in the Southwest	multilateral	fully regional	ditto
	Draft for a UNEP Regional Plan on Development and Environmental Protection	multilateral	fully regional	ditto

Regional organisations for the conservation of marine species

region	organisation	no. of members	type	established by
ATLANTIC				
General	International Commission for the Conservation of Atlantic Tunas (ICCAT)	12	quasi-regional	ICCAT Convention 1966
North-east Atlantic	Sealing Commission for the Northeast Atlantic (SCNEA)	2 (Norway, USSR)	fully regional	SCNEA Convention 1957
	North-East Atlantic Fisheries Commission (NEAFC)	14	fully regional	NEAFC Convention 1959
Baltic	Shellfish Commission for Skagerrak and Kattegat	3 (Denmark, Norway, Sweden)	fully regional	Agreement of 1952
	International Baltic Sea Fishery Commission (IBSFC)	7	fully regional	IBSFC Convention 1973
North-west Atlantic	Sealing Commission for the Northwest Atlantic (SCNWA)	?	quasi-regional	SCNWA Convention
	Northwest Atlantic Fisheries Organisation (NAFO)	?	quasi-regional	NAFO Convention 1978
	US–Canada East Fisheries Commission (apparently abortive)	2 (Canada, USA)	fully sub-regional	Fisheries Convention 1979
Atlantic	Fishery Committee for the Eastern Central Atlantic (CECAF)	27	quasi-regional	FAO Council Resolution 1967
West Central Atlantic	Western Central Atlantic Fishery Commission (WECAFC)	23	quasi-regional	FAO Conference
Mediterranean	General Fisheries Council for the Mediterranean (CFCM)	18	fully regional	GFCM Convention 1949
Black Sea	Mixed Commission for Black Sea Fisheries (MCBSF)	3 (Bulgaria, Romania, USSR)	fully regional	MCBSF Convention 1959
South-east Atlantic	International Commission for Southeast Atlantic Fisheries (ICSEAF)	—	quasi-regional	—
South-west Atlantic	Regional Fisheries Advisory Commission for the South-west Atlantic (CARPAS)	3 (Argentina, Brazil, Uruguay)	fully regional	FAO Conference Resolution 1962
Caribbean	—	—	—	—
ARCTIC	—	—	—	—
INDO-PACIFIC				
General	Indo-Pacific Fisheries Council (IPFC)	18	quasi-regional	IPFC Convention 1948
Indian	Indian Ocean Fishery Commission (IOFC)	29	quasi-regional	FAO Council Resolution 1948

region	organisation	no. of members	type	established by
North Pacific	International Pacific Halibut Commission (IPHC)	2 (Canada, US)	regional	IPHC Convention 1953 (replacing 1924 and other Conventions)
	North Pacific Fur Seal Commission (NPFSC)	4 (Canada, Japan, USSR, USA)	fully regional	NPFSC Convention 1957
North-east Pacific	International Pacific Salmon Fisheries Commission (IPSFC)	2 (Canada, USA)	sub-regional	IPSFC Convention 1930
	International North Pacific Fisheries Commission (INPFC)	3 (Canada, Japan, USA)	quasi-regional	INPFC Convention 1952 (amended 1978)
North-west Pacific	Japanese–Soviet Northwest Pacific Fisheries Commission (JSFC)	2 (Japan, USSR)	regional	JSFC Convention 1956
	Commission for Fisheries Research in the Western Pacific	4 (China, North Korea, USSR, Vietnam)	quasi-regional	Convention of 1956
	Japan–Republic of Korea Joint Fisheries Commission (JKFC)	2 (Japan, South Korea)	sub-regional	JKFC Convention 1965
	Japan–China Joint Fisheries Commission (JCFC)	2 (China, Japan)	sub-regional	JCFC Convention 1977
Eastern Pacific	Inter-American Tropical Tuna Commission (IATTC)	6	quasi-regional	LATTC Convention 1949
South Pacific	—	—	—	—
South-east Pacific	Permanent Commission of the Conference on the Use and Conservation of the Marine Resources of the South Pacific (PCSP)	3 (Chile, Ecuador, Peru)	fully regional	Agreement of 1952
	Fisheries Council of South Pacific Forum	?	regional	?
South-west Pacific	South East Asian Fisheries Development Centre (SEAFDEC)	4 (Japan, Philippines, Singapore, Thailand)	quasi-regional	Agreement of 1967
SOUTHERN				
	Commission for the Conservation of Antarctic Marine Living Resources	14	quasi-regional	Convention of 1981

Regional agreements for the conservation of marine species

region	agreement	parties
ATLANTIC General	International Convention for the Conservation of Atlantic Tunas, 1966	multilateral
	Agreement relating to Conservation of Atlantic Salmon, 1972	Denmark, USA
North-east	Agreement on Measures for Regulating the Catch and Conserving the Stocks of Seals in the Northeastern Part of the Atlantic Ocean, 1957	Norway, USSR
	Northeast Atlantic Fisheries Convention, 1959	multilateral
	Agreement Concerning the Regulation of Fishing of the Atlantic Scandinavian Herring, 1973	Iceland, Norway, USSR
Skagerrak, Kattegat and Sound	Convention Concerning the Preservation of Plaice and Dab, 1937	Denmark, Norway, Sweden
Baltic	Agreement Concerning Measures for Protection of the Stocks of Deep-Sea Prawns, European Lobsters, Lobsters and Crabs, 1952	Denmark, Norway, Sweden
	Agreement Concerning the Protection of the Salmon Population in the Baltic Sea, 1962 (with Protocol, 1972)	multilateral
	Agreement on Fishing and Sealing (in the Gulf of Finland), 1969	Finland, USSR
	Convention on Fishing and Conservation of the Living Resources in the Baltic Sea and Belts, 1973	multilateral
North-west	Agreement on Sealing and Conservation of Sea Stocks in the Northwest Atlantic	Canada, Norway
	Convention on Future Multilateral Co-operation in the Northwest Atlantic Fisheries, 1978	multilateral
	Agreement on East Coast Fishery Resources, 1979 [unperfected]	Canada, USA
Mediterranean	Agreement for the Establishment of a General Fisheries Council for the Mediterranean, 1949 (as amended 1963)	multilateral
Black Sea	Convention Concerning Fishing in the Black Sea, 1959	Bulgaria, Romania, USSR
South-east	Convention on the Conservation of the Living Resources of the Southeast Atlantic, 1969	multilateral
Caribbean	Agreement concerning Shrimp, 1972	Brazil, Trinidad and Tobago
South-west	Agreement on Fishing and Conservation of Living Resources, 1968	Brazil, Uruguay
	Agreement Concerning Shrimp, 1972	Brazil, Netherlands
ARCTIC General	Agreement on Conservation of Polar Bears, 1973	multilateral
North-east	Agreement on the Regulation of the Fishing of Northeast Arctic Cod, 1974	Norway, USSR, UK
INDO-PACIFIC General	Agreement for the Establishment of Indo-Pacific Fisheries Council, 1948	multilateral
North Pacific	Convention for the Preservation of the Halibut Fishery of the Northern Pacific Ocean and Bering Sea, 1953 (as amended 1979)	Canada, USA
	Interim Convention on the Conservation of North Pacific Fur Seals, 1957 (extended, 1969)	multilateral
	Agreement Relating to Fishing for King and Tanner Crab, 1974	Japan, USA
North-west Pacific	Agreement Regarding the King and Tanner Crab Fisheries in the Eastern Bering Sea	USSR, USA
	Agreement relating to the Crab Fisheries in the Northwest Pacific Ocean	Japan, USSR
	Convention in Concerning High Seas Fisheries of the Northwest Pacific Ocean, 1956	Japan, USSR
	Agreement on Fisheries, 1965	Japan, South Korea
	Agreement on Fisheries, 1975	China, Japan
North-east Pacific	Convention for the Protection, Preservation and Extension of the Sockeye Salmon Fishery of the Fraser River, 1939 (Protocol, 1956)	Canada, USA
	International Convention for the High Seas Fisheries of the North Pacific, 1952 (as amended 1978)	Canada, Japan, USA
	Agreement on Certain Fisheries Problems in Northeastern Part of the Pacific Ocean off the US Coast	USA, USSR
	Agreement Concerning Fishing off the West Coast of Canada, 1979	Canada, USA
Eastern Pacific	Convention of the Establishment of an Inter-American Tropical Tuna Commission, 1949	multilateral
South-east Pacific	Agreements on the Exploitation and Conservation of Marine Resources of the South Pacific, 1952 (as amended 1954)	Chile, Ecuador, Peru
SOUTHERN General	Convention on the Conservation of Antarctic Seals, 1972	multilateral
	Convention on the Conservation of Antarctic Marine Living Resources, 1980	multilateral

Regional instruments for the protection and conservation of the marine environment

region	instrument	parties
ATLANTIC North-east	Council of Europe Resolution 29 on the Protection of Coastal Areas, 1973	multilateral
	Convention for the Protection of the Environment (Nordic Convention), 1974	Denmark, Finland, Norway, Sweden
	Council of Europe Recommendation (847) on European Action to Prevent Oil Pollution of Waters and Coasts, 1978	multilateral
South-west	Treaty of the La Plata river and its Maritime Limits, 1973	Argentina, Uruguay
ARCTIC	—	—
INDO-PACIFIC Indian	Declaration of Indian Ocean as Zone of Peace, 1971	multilateral
South Pacific	Treaty on Sovereignty and Maritime Boundaries in the Area Between the Countries, 1978	Australia and Papua New Guinea
SOUTHERN	International Convention for the Regulation of Whaling, 1946	multilateral

Projects managed by the International Union for Conservation of Nature (IUCN) on behalf of the World Wildlife Fund (WWF)

The following projects (locations shown map pp 210–211) indicate the scope of the marine projects among the many undertaken by the World Wildlife Fund.

1 Mediterranean monk seal Conservation programme throughout Mediterranean.

2 Sudan, coral reefs The Sudanese Red Sea Reefs are being protected by the WWF as increasingly larger numbers of divers and tourists are attracted there.

3 Australia, Great Barrier Reef The WWF are supporting an information campaign to improve the prospects for conservation of the Reef from a renewed threat of oil drilling in the vicinity.

4 The Wadden Zee conservation programme Advisory committee for the Wadden Zee undertaking decisions on reclamation, pollution and tourism.

5 Mediterranean, Andouin's gull Protection of breeding places.

6 Turkey, marine turtles Investigation of sea turtles which visit the Aegean and Mediterranean coasts of Turkey for management of the resource.

7 Indonesia, sperm whales Considerable numbers of whales, both large and small, including a population of the critically endangered blue whale, were found at Lomblen Island during a survey by British, Australian and Indonesian experts.

8 Baltic sea, seals Decline in seals due probably to hunting, habitat destruction and effects of toxic chemicals on reproduction now monitored by Baltic countries.

9 Papua New Guinea, Dugong The Dugong Conservation, Management and Public Education Programme was started in 1978.

10 Pakistan, marine turtles Protection of nesting sites in recreational beaches.

11 Solomon Islands, marine turtles Study and management programme to maintain stocks of the five species of turtle known to inhabit the waters.

12 Krill and Southern Ocean management options The WWF is exploring management options for krill in the Southern Ocean.

13 French Guyana, turtle Protection of nesting beaches.

14 Tonga, humpback whale The King of Tonga, in discussion with WWF officials, has promised to establish a sanctuary for humpback whales.

15 Lesser Antilles, Bonaire underwater park Set up as part of IUCN's Eastern Caribbean natural areas management programme. The local reefs off Bonaire Island are encouraging increasing numbers of divers and tourists to the region.

16 Papua New Guinea, marine turtles Management, conservation and education programme to ensure the continued survival of the turtle resource.

17 Indonesia, marine conservation The project is designed by the IUCN to ensure full scientific and administrative co-ordination in establishing conservation areas in Indonesia and in advising on their management and administration.

18 Ecuador and Galapagos Island Sea- and lagoon-bird monitoring.

19 International workshop on biology and management of north-west Atlantic harpseals Newborn harpseals are slaughtered for their fur in the Gulf of St Lawrence and Newfoundland. The world conservation strategy does not recognise killing of species for 'fashion' as opposed to a compelling human need.

20 Surinam (Operation Headstart), Green Sea Turtle Study of tagged turtles to facilitate management for exploitation on a sustained yield basis.

21 Mexico, gray whale Becoming increasingly disrupted due to the presence of the offshore oil industry in the Gulf of Mexico.

22 Hawaii, humpback whale Project on these singing whales to establish communication with the species.

23 Seychelles, marine turtles Study of the hawksbill turtle in order to draw up conservation programme.

24 Seychelles Conference The protection of endangered birds by the Seychelles government was extended to that of marine turtles and whales. A publicity campaign was set up to support the conservation of all species on Aldabra Island.

25 Mexico, conservation of marine turtles Removal of eggs, otherwise taken for human consumption, to hatcheries in order to restore population.

26 Senegal, conservation of marine turtles Several coastal parks established to conserve, marine flora and fauna, including turtles and whales.

27 Cyprus, turtle Project initiated 1978 by Dept of Fisheries to deal particularly in conservation of green turtle, and investigate loggerhead.

28 Thailand, marine turtles (Tarutao National Park) Study of populations of turtles, depleted as result of poaching and illegal trawling.

29 Indonesia, conservation of marine resources
(Not shown)
Conservation of critical marine habitats
Monitoring of International Whaling Commission

Listed endangered marine species

Locations given map pages 210–211

Guadalupe fur seal Only known breeding colony in Guadalupe I., off north-west Baja, California; innate tameness makes it vulnerable to illegal hunting.

Japanese sea lion Almost certainly extinct on Japanese coastal islands; may exist on Dokto I., Japan and east coast of Korea

Juan Fernandez fur seal Existence vulnerable; located only on the Juan Fernandez archipelago off Chile.

Galapagos fur seal Thought extinct following sealing expeditions (1900s); two small colonies discovered (1932 and 1957). Hunting and capture prohibited.

Laptev walrus Protection from hunting since 1957, but numbers still low.

Kuril harbour seal Totally protected from commercial, sport or amateur hunting in the Far East but enforcement difficult.

Saimaa seal Totally protected by law since 1958; populations have increased to the extent that some control is necessary.

Mediterranean monk seal Population thought to be c.500–1000 and declining, due to human disturbance, persecution by fishermen and possibly marine pollution.

Caribbean monk seal Thought to be extinct following depletion of stocks in 18th century, and human persecution and disturbance since.

Hawaiian monk seal Protected throughout present and former range; regular breeding colonies restricted to five atolls of the leeward Hawaiian Chain.

Loggerhead turtle Found throughout tropical and temperate seas, but species is vulnerable; international agreements made for protection of nesting sites in Pacific and Atlantic sections of range.

Flatback turtle Restricted to tropical Australia; totally protected since 1968.

Green turtle Drastically reduced and totally eliminated in some areas (e.g. Bahamas, Florida) by over-exploitation; in other areas (e.g. Australia) population sound.

East Pacific green turtle Nesting grounds legally protected in the Hawaiian Is, elsewhere restrictions difficult to enforce (Mexico, Costa Rica).

Hawksbill turtle Thinly scattered throughout the Atlantic, Pacific and Indian Oceans (former range included the Mediterranean); USA has banned import of the species or any part of it (e.g. tortoiseshell); despite protected breeding/ nesting sites numbers still diminishing on account of continuing industrial and tourist markets.

Atlantic Ridley turtle Mexican Government has taken protection measures at its only known nesting site; efforts being made to establish breeding colony on Padre Island, Texas.

Olive turtle The species is totally protected in Sri Lanka and on islands off Borneo; reserves set up in Surinam and Guyana.

Leathery turtle (Leatherback or Luth) Laws have been enacted in several American countries, Sri Lanka and Australia to protect this species but it is still endangered in certain areas, particularly Costa Rica.

Northern bottlenose whale Confined to boreal and Arctic North Atlantic; population greatly depleted during last 100 years; full protection from exploitation recommended.

Vaquita (Cochito) Probably confined to northern half of Gulf of California. Mexico has banned all commercial and sport fishing of the species.

Fin whale Since late 1975 totally protected by IWC member nations except for small catches (sustained yields) in part of Antarctic and North Atlantic. Some exploitation almost certainly continuing.

Blue whale Totally protected by IWC member nations in the North Atlantic since 1960, in the Antarctic since 1965, in the North Pacific since 1966 and worldwide since 1967.

Humpback whale Totally protected by IWC member nations in the North Atlantic since 1955, in the southern hemisphere since 1964 and the North Pacific since 1966.

Bowhead or Greenland right whale Totally protected following an international convention for the regulation of whaling in 1935, but permitting aboriginal peoples to take small numbers for food.

Black right whale As for Bowhead whale.

Appendix XI Law of the Sea

1 General

This appendix mirrors the Atlas as a whole both in terms of subjects covered and sequence of treatment. However, understanding of the more specific legal questions considered below requires an introduction, in particular to (1) the sources of the international law of the sea and the significance of the Third United Nations Conference on the Law of the Sea (UNCLOS III); and (2) the maritime jurisdictional zones.

1 Sources of the international law of the sea and the significance of UNCLOS III

The two principal sources of international law in general and the law of the sea in particular are International Customary Law and Treaties.

Rules crystallise as rules of international customary law when two elements are present: (1) a particular usage is observed by the generality of states; and (2) they observe that usage out of a feeling of legal obligation. Thus, if the generality of states habitually permitted innocent passage for foreign merchantmen through their territorial sea and a point was reached when they believed themselves to be legally bound so to do, a rule of international customary law to that effect would then have come into existence. Treaties (or conventions, agreements, protocols, statutes, etc.) are agreements between states creating binding obligations under international law. Treaties create rules only for the parties to them, although a treaty may provide a model from which a rule of international customary law may grow. Treaties normally enter into force in accordance with a formula incorporated in the treaty itself.

Prior to the First United Nations Conference on the Law of the Sea (UNCLOS I) in 1958, most rules of the international law of the sea were rules of customary law, though even then there was a considerable network of treaty law on such matters as pollution, safety of life at sea and collisions. In 1958, however, most of the more fundamental rules of the law of the sea were incorporated in four Conventions, opened for signature at UNCLOS I, on: (1) the Territorial Sea and the Contiguous Zone; (2) the High Seas; (3) Fishing and Conservation of the Living Resources of the High Seas; and (4) the Continental Shelf. Collectively, they are known as the Geneva Conventions on the Law of the Sea, 1958. Frequent reference is made below to the new United Nations Convention on the Law of the Sea (hereafter 'UN Convention') adopted at UNCLOS III in 1982, but it is important to bear in mind that the Geneva Conventions are still in force for the parties to them and will remain so until superseded on entry into force of the new Convention. At the present time much of the law of the sea must be regarded as being in a transitional phase between the old regime, largely based on the 1958 Geneva Conventions and the new regime, based upon the 1982 UN Convention. The origins of the new regime can be traced back to 1967 when the Maltese delegation to the United Nations called for the delimitarisation of the seabed and the recognition of its resources as the 'common heritage of mankind'. After lengthy preparations, UNCLOS III met in 1973 and between then and December 1982, when the UN Convention was opened for signature, held 12 sessions extending in total over about 95 weeks. Over 150 states participated in the Conference which eventually produced a Convention running to 320 Articles and 9 annexes.

At present (1983), prospects for the early entry into force of the Convention are difficult to judge but there is little room for optimism following the signing ceremony held in Jamaica in December 1982. Although 117 states *signed* the Convention, some of the principal industrialised states were not among them: the Federal Republic of Germany, Italy, Japan, the United Kingdom and the United States. Altogether, 22 states decided against immediate signature, in many cases because they shared the dissatisfaction, first expressed by the United States, with the provisions of the Convention governing sea-bed mining. Even without this added complication, the early entry into force of the Convention on a global basis could not realistically have been expected. The Convention was negotiated as a 'package deal' and, accordingly, 'No reservations or exceptions may be made to this Convention unless expressly permitted by other articles of this Convention'. Such limited scope for reservations, when added to the complexity of the Convention and the need for sixty ratifications or accessions as a condition of entry into force, would in any event have thrown considerable doubt on the prospects for its widespread entry into force in the foreseeable future. It must be added, however, that regrettable though such delay or failure would be, it would not necessarily be fatal so far as concerns many of the rules in the Convention. As was noted above, unratified treaties very often form a humus in which rules of international customary law may take root. Some would see in this growth a desirable form of law creation responding to the realities of state practice. Others would deplore such a development as an unplanned and uncontrollable reaction to power, in which demands for equity and the establishment of a new international economic order could be too easily ignored.

2 Maritime jurisdictional zones

There are seven generally recognised jurisdictional zones stretching horizontally from internal waters out to the high seas. In some cases the status of the sea-bed and subsoil differs from that of the superjacent waters of the zone concerned. The more fundamental rules governing the status and delimitation of the zones will be outlined here; further comment on other aspects of these zones will be found in subsequent sections.

2.1 Internal Waters comprise all waters lying landward of the baselines from which the breadth of the territorial sea is measured. They include rivers, lakes, bays, ports and the waters landward of the low-tide line. The principal distinguishing feature of internal waters, as compared with the territorial sea, is that the sovereignty of the coastal state in these waters is not limited by a right of innocent passage in favour of foreign shipping. Though the question is not free from doubt, there is probably no *right* of entry into a foreign port except in distress, unless provided by treaty.

2.2 The Territorial Sea The breadth of the territorial sea has been a matter of controversy for over half a century, with claims varying all the way from 3 to 200 miles. Fortunately, it is now likely that a breadth of 12 miles will be generally recognised, following Article 3 of the UN Convention.

The coastal state's sovereignty over the territorial sea is limited by its obligation to accord a right of innocent passage to foreign shipping (see **3** *Shipping* below). The increase to 12 miles in the breadth of the territorial sea will mean that many straits through which there was previously a belt of high seas will become territorial sea straits. The 1958 Geneva regime of straits (a re-enforced form of innocent passage) has been replaced in the UN Convention by a regime of 'transit-passage', more favourable to foreign shipping.

The normal baseline from which the breadth of the territorial sea is measured is the low-water line as marked on large-scale charts officially recognised by the coastal state. The outer limit is the line every point of which is at a distance from the nearest point of the baseline equal to the breadth of the territorial sea.

Like the Geneva Convention on the Territorial Sea, 1958, the UN Convention makes special provision for baselines on highly indented coasts, at river mouths, in bays and around ports and roadsteads. Straight baselines joining appropriate points on the coastline may be employed where the coastline is deeply indented or there is a fringe of islands along the coast. The lines must not depart to any appreciable extent from the general direction of the coast, nor in general may they be drawn to or from a 'drying rock' unless a lighthouse or similar installation has been erected on it.

Bays, provided that they are more than mere curvatures of the coast, also have their baselines drawn in accordance with a special formula, first prescribed in the Geneva Convention of 1958 and retained in amended form in the UN Convention.

The delimitation of the territorial sea between opposite or adjacent states is effected by reference to a three-point formula: (1) by agreement, which failing (2) by a median or equidistance line, unless (3) another line is called for by reason of historic title or other special circumstances.

The coastal state is required to publicise baselines and lines of delimitation by publishing and depositing with the United Nations either adequate charts or lists of geographical coordinates of points, specifying the geodetic datum.

2.3 The Contiguous Zone Under the 1958 Geneva Convention on the Territorial Sea and the Contiguous Zone, the coastal state was entitled (but not obliged) to claim a contiguous zone extending out to 12 miles from territorial sea baselines. The residual status of this zone remained high seas and, accordingly, the various freedoms of the high seas continued to be enjoyed by other states. By way of exception (to be restrictively interpreted), however, the coastal state was entitled to exercise the control necessary to (1) prevent infringement of its customs, fiscal, immigration or sanitary regulations *within its territory or territorial sea*; and (2) punish infringement of those regulations *committed within its territory or territorial sea*. Under the UN Convention, the zone has been extended to 24 miles and the residual status is now that of the exclusive economic zone (see below) but otherwise the main features of the zone have been retained.

2.4 The Continental Shelf For a summary of the issues leading up to UNCLOS II, a definition of the outer limit and formulae for reaching agreement on this, see *The Continental Shelf* pages 222–223.

2.5 Exclusive Fishing Zones Prior to UNCLOS I and II in 1958 and 1960, no differentiation was generally recognised between the territorial sea and exclusive fishing zones. Following failure to agree upon a more extensive breadth for the territorial sea in 1958 and 1960, however, a new trend developed in state practice towards recognition of exclusive fishing zones beyond territorial sea limits. The trend can be traced through a series of bilateral fishery agreements, culminating in the multilateral European Fisheries Convention 1964 and the subsequent series of more extensive unilateral claims such as those made by Iceland. In the beginning, such extensive claims were strongly resisted but, by the 1970s, influenced by the growing support for the concept of a 200-mile exclusive economic zone, the major fishing states increasingly joined the ranks of states claiming 200-mile exclusive fishing zones. The trend in this direction was certainly helped by the decision of the International Court of Justice in the *Fishery Jurisdiction* case (1974, *United Kingdom* v. *Iceland*) to the effect that, although Iceland's 50-mile fishery limits were not 'opposable' to the United Kingdom, there was an obligation upon the parties to undertake negotiation and to take into account, *inter alia*, Iceland's entitlement to a preferential share of the fisheries within these limits.

It is likely that the more comprehensive exclusive economic zone provided for in the UN Convention will eventually be recognised generally. In the meantime there can be no doubt that the concept of the exclusive fishing zone is already well established.

2.6 The Exclusive Economic Zone (EEZ) Reference is made in a later section to the substance of the coastal state's rights in the EEZ. Here, it will suffice to note that the zone extends to 200 miles from territorial sea baselines; that the problem of delimitation between neighbouring states is similar to that considered above in relation to the continental shelf; and that the EEZ has a novel jurisdictional status as compared with other offshore zones.

Prior to the introduction of the new EEZ concept, a common pattern had been followed in relation to the status of specialised functional zones beyond the territorial sea. The outer limit of the territorial sea had been taken as marking the dividing line between a more landward area in which the fundamental principle of sovereignty had predominated and exceptions to it were restrictively interpreted, and the more seaward functional zones in which the fundamental principle of the freedom of the high seas predominated but the coastal state enjoyed limited rights by way of exception. For example, the continental shelf and the exclusive fishing zone were of this nature. Landward of the outer limit of the territorial sea there would always be, in case of doubt, a presumption in favour of the sovereignty of the coastal state. Seaward of this line, however, the presumption was in favour of the freedom of the high seas. The concept of the EEZ departs from this pattern. It is a zone *sui generis* in which there are no presumptions one way or the other, the rights of the coastal state and of other states being those actually specified in the UN Convention. This has of course been a matter of concern to the shipping community which feels that it has lost the pre-existing safeguards favouring freedom of navigation.

2.7 The High Seas The Geneva Convention on the High Seas 1958 defined the high seas as 'all parts of the sea that are not included in the territorial sea or in the internal waters of a state'. Given the introduction of the EEZ and of 'archipelagic waters' (see below), it was necessary to amend the definition in Article 86 of the UN Convention to

'all parts of the sea that are not included in the exclusive economic zone, in the territorial sea or in the internal waters of a state, or in the archipelagic waters of an archipelagic state'.

The principle jurisdictional feature of the high seas is the 'freedom of the high seas', which in reality comprises a bundle of freedoms. It includes the freedoms of navigation; fishing; the laying of submarine cables and pipelines; overflight; and 'others which are recognised by the general principles of international law' (Geneva Convention, Article 2). Under the UN Convention, two of these 'others' have been identified: freedom to construct artificial islands and other installations permitted under international law; and freedom of scientific research. Such freedoms have to be exercised with due consideration for the interests of other states in their exercise of the freedom of the high seas and also (a new element in the UN Convention) with due consideration for the rights under the Convention with respect to 'activities in the Area'.

The 'Area' in question is 'the sea-bed and ocean floor and subsoil thereof beyond the limits of national jurisdiction' for which a new and highly complex deep-sea mining regime is being established.

2.8 The regime of islands and archipelagos Under the 1958 Geneva Conventions on the Law of the Sea, islands were, in general, treated in the same way as mainland territories for the purposes of entitlement to maritime zones. Nor was there any difficulty over the definition of an island. It was understood to be 'a naturally-formed area of land, surrounded by water, which is above water at high tide'. As was noted above, the presence of 'a fringe of islands along the coast in its immediate vicinity' was one of the justifications for the adoption of a straight baseline system and it is also true that the position of an island or islands might be such as to constitute 'special circumstances' in relation to the delimitation of the continental shelf under the Continental Shelf Convention.

The UN Convention deals with islands rather differently, devoting a separate part to a 'regime of islands'. The general rule remains unchanged and the territorial sea, contiguous zone, exclusive economic zone and continental shelf of islands are to be determined in the same way as for 'other land territory'. There is one exception, relating to 'rocks which cannot sustain human habitation or economic life of their own'. Such rocks are not to have an EEZ or continental shelf of their own, though they may continue to have a 12-mile territorial sea.

The Geneva Conventions made no provision for special treatment for mid-ocean archipelagos, despite the fact that states like the Philippines and Indonesia had been pressing for recognition of their right to adopt a baseline system enclosing the archipelago within a series of straight lines joining the outermost islands and reefs of the archipelago.

In the UN Convention, however, there is a separate part on 'archipelagic states' which allows such enclosure within 'archipelagic baselines' and creates a new category of 'archipelagic waters' for the enclosed area (though there may also be internal waters within the archipelagic waters). The territorial sea, contiguous zone, EEZ and continental shelf of an archipelagic state are measured in the usual way—but from the archipelagic baselines.

The UN Convention recognises the right of ships of all states to enjoy a right of innocent passage through archipelagic waters similar to that enjoyed in the territorial sea. It also recognises, however, the right of the archipelagic state to designate sea lanes and prescribe traffic separation schemes within archipelagic waters. The right of 'archipelagic sea lanes passage' enjoyed by foreign shipping through such lanes is similar to the re-enforced right of innocent passage through territorial sea straits.

2 Fisheries: the international legal framework

1 Fishing as a freedom of the high seas

The starting point for any exposition of the rules of international law governing fisheries is the fundamental principle of the freedom of the high seas, long established in international customary law and codified in the Geneva Convention on the High Seas 1958, Article 2 of which includes freedom of fishing as one of the several freedoms comprised within the overall principle. Like other high seas freedoms, freedom of fishing is not an absolute freedom but one which has to be 'exercised by all states with reasonable regard to the interests of other states in their exercise of the freedom of the high seas'. Given the danger of overfishing certain stocks, this qualification implies the need for restraints to be accepted on fishing in the interests of conservation. This was indeed the purpose of another of the Geneva Conventions of 1958, that on Fishing and Conservation of Living Resources of the High Seas, which *inter alia* placed a duty on states 'to adopt, or to cooperate with other states in adopting, such measures for their respective nationals as may be necessary for the conservation of the living resources of the high seas'. However, this Conservation proved to be ineffective in practice and is now of little more than historical interest in view of the widespread extension of national fishery limits to 200 miles.

2 The role of fishery commissions

So long as national fishery limits extended no further than 12 miles, which was generally the case until the 1970s, the problem of conservation and allocation of fish stocks was very much an international problem and a network of treaties was set up to deal with the question, usually through regional fishery commissions, such as the North East Altantic Fisheries Commission (NEAFC) or the International Commission for the Conservation of Atlantic Tunas. Some of these Commissions have been more effective than others but many have been unsuccessful in preventing depletion of stocks through overfishing.

The International Commission for the Northwest Atlantic Fisheries (ICNAF), established in 1950, is a good example of such regional commissions. It had an excellent record in coordinating and publishing the results of national research programmes but was less successful as a regulatory agency, partly because of its limited powers prior to 1971 to deal with problems of overcapitalisation and allocation. However, under a Protocol which entered into force in 1971, it was empowered to adopt relatively more effective regulatory measures and introduced national quota arrangements.

One of the principal barriers to effective fishery regulation at international level has always been the reluctance of member states of these Commissions to depart from the traditional pattern of enforcement of international regulations by the flag state only.

3 The era of 200-mile limits

Given the recent trend towards 200-mile exclusive fishery limits and the provisions of the new UN Convention on the EEZ, the problems of fishery management have had to be tackled in quite a different context. In the North Atlantic area, for example, the adoption of 200-mile fishery limits by Canada, the United States and the member states of the European Economic Community (EEC) has necessitated the replacement of NEAFC and ICNAF. In the Northwest Atlantic, the North Atlantic Fisheries Organisation (NAFO) now has a regulatory role confined to the area beyond the 200-mile limit. In the North-East Atlantic, efforts to replace NEAFC have been frustrated so far by the refusal of the East European member states to accept the EEC as a party to the Convention.

For most coastal states, the extension of fishery limits to 200 miles means that what was largely an international problem of fishery conservation and allocation has now become predominantly a national problem. In the case of the EEC, however, the picture is much more complicated: Even before the adoption by EEC member states of 200-mile fishery limits in 1977, a common fisheries policy had been established, as required by the Treaty of Rome and the 1972 Treaty of Accession, in terms of which Denmark, Ireland and the United Kingdom joined the EEC. Following protracted negotiations, a regional fisheries policy was agreed upon in 1983.

4 The UN Convention and the EEZ

As was noted above, the UN Convention has introduced not a 200-mile exclusive fishery zone but the very much more complex 200-mile EEZ. While it is true that the coastal state is accorded 'sovereign' rights for the purpose of exploring, exploiting, conserving and managing the living resources of the EEZ (Article 56), it is also true that these sovereign rights have to be exercised subject to a number of constraints relating to, *inter alia*, conservation and utilisation of those resources; stocks in two or more EEZs or in the EEZ and adjacent areas; highly migratory species; marine mammals; anadromous stocks; and catadromous species. Brief notes are provided below on these aspects, as well as on the provision made for the enforcement of the laws and regulations of the coastal state.

4.1 Conservation (UN Convention, Article 61) Summarising the main points in Article 61:

1 The coastal state must determine the allowable catch.
2 The coastal state must ensure that the maintenance of the living resources is not endangered by over-exploitation.
3 The conservation and management measures adopted by the coastal state must be designed also to maintain or restore populations of harvested species at levels which can produce the maximum sustainable yield (MSY) as qualified by relevant environmental and economic factors, including the economic needs of coastal fishing communities and the special requirements of developing states, and taking into account fishing patterns, the interdependence of stocks and any generally recommended subregional, regional or global minimum standards.
4 Effects on associated species have to be taken into consideration.
5 There is an obligation to exchange scientific information.

It is left to the coastal state to determine in the first instance what measures are required to achieve such a highly qualified MSY, only 'taking into account' scientific evidence and, 'as appropriate', cooperating with international organisations. In the event of a dispute over such measures, the coastal state is not bound to accept anything more than 'compulsory conciliation,' which, despite its name, does not involve a binding recommendation or award.

4.2 Utilisation (UN Convention, Article 62)

1 The coastal state has an obligation to promote the objective of *optimum utilisation* of the total allowable catch which will permit maintenance of the qualified maximum sustainable yield referred to above.
2 The first step is for the coastal state to determine its own harvesting capacity. If it cannot harvest the whole total allowable catch, it must grant access to other states, having particular regard to the needs of land-locked states and states with special geographical characteristics in the same region.
3 In granting access to such surplus stocks, the coastal state may require nationals of other states to comply with conservation measures and other regulations on such matters as licences and fees; species to be taken and quotas; regulation of seasons, areas, gear and vessels; age and size of fish; landing of catches; and enforcement procedures. Although such regulations have to be consistent with the Convention, there is wide scope for coastal state discretion.

4.3 Stocks in two or more EEZs or in the EEZ and adjacent areas

Article 63 of the UN Convention provides for cooperation between the EEZ states concerned, or the EEZ states and the state or states fishing in the adjacent area, to seek agreement on measures necessary to coordinate and ensure conservation and development of such stocks. Also, Article XI(3) of the NAFO Convention establishes a Fisheries Commission to manage and conserve fishery resources in the regulatory area of the Northwest Atlantic beyond the 200-mile limit. The Commission may adopt proposals to achieve optimum utilisation of stocks and, in so doing, has to try to ensure consistency with measures applied to stocks within the EEZ.

4.4 Highly migratory species The species concerned are listed in Annex I to the Convention. Article 64 requires the coastal state and other states whose nationals fish in the region to cooperate directly or through appropriate international organisations to ensure conservation and promote the objective of optimum utilisation of such species throughout the region, both within and beyond the EEZ.

4.5 Marine mammals Article 65 requires states to cooperate to conserve marine mammals and in the case of cetaceans (whales, dolphins and porpoises) to work through the appropriate international organisations for their conservation management and study. Coastal states or international organisations may, however, prohibit, limit or regulate the exploitation of marine mammals more strictly than is provided for in the Convention. Under Article 120, these provisions apply also in the high seas beyond the EEZ. Note too that the cetaceans also appear in the list of highly migratory species.

4.6 Anadromous stocks Article 66, on the regulation of anadromous stocks such as salmon, does not lend itself to brief summary and it must suffice to say that:

1 The state of origin has the primary interest in and responsibility for the conservation of stocks.
2 It may establish a total allowable catch after consultation with other states allowed to fish the stocks beyond the EEZ and with states of migration.
3 There are reciprocal obligations of consultation and cooperation between the state of origin on the one hand and, on the other hand, states of migration and other states previously fishing the stock.

4.7 Catadromous species such as eels which breed in the high seas but spend the greater part of their life cycle in the waters of a coastal state, are governed by Article 67 of the UN Convention, as follows:

1 The coastal state (the 'management state') is responsible for their management and for ensuring their ingress and egress.
2 Harvesting may take place only landward of EEZ limits.
3 Where harvesting takes place in the EEZ, as opposed to the territorial sea or internal waters, it is subject to the other UN Convention provisions on EEZ fisheries.
4 Management (including harvesting) of fish in the EEZs of migrating states is to be regulated by agreement which must ensure 'rational management' and takes account of the management state's responsibility for the maintenance of the species.

4.8 Enforcement Under Article 73 of the UN Convention, the coastal state is accorded comprehensive powers of enforcement, including boarding, inspection, arrest and judicial proceedings. Foreign vessels must, however, be released upon the posting of a reasonable bond or other security and the punishments inflicted upon offenders must not include imprisonment or corporal punishment. There is also an obligation to notify the flag state of arrest and sentence.

5 High seas fisheries under the UN Convention

A framework for the management and conservation of the living resources of the high seas, beyond the 200-mile limits of the EEZ, is provided by Part VII, Section 2 of the UN Convention (Articles 116–120). It may be summarised as follows:

1 States have a duty to adopt for their nationals such measures as are necessary for conservation of the living resources of the high seas.
2 They also have an obligation to cooperate with one another in the management and conservation of these living resources. Where nationals of two or more states exploit the same resources or different resources in the same area, the states concerned must enter into negotiations to adopt the means necessary for conservation of these resources. They must, as appropriate, cooperate to establish subregional or regional fisheries organisations to this end.
3 In determining the allowable catch and establishing other conservation measures for high sea resources, states have to adopt measures designed to produce the maximum sustainable yield, as qualified by various specified factors. As in the similar provisions for EEZ fisheries, they must also take into consideration the effect of these measures on associated species and ensure that they are non-discriminatory between the fishermen of different states.

3 Shipping

The object of this section is to give an account of what might be called the legal framework of freedom of maritime navigation. This framework consists of a number of general rules of international law imposing restraints which vary in severity according to the maritime zone concerned and the type of vessel or the use to which it is being put. These rules are considered below in relation to the following zones: (1) internal waters, including ports and bays; (2) the territorial sea, straits used for international navigation and archipelagic waters; (3) the contiguous zone; (4) the continental shelf; (5) the EEZ; and (6) the high seas. Reference should be made to the 'General' section above as regards the geographical scope and jurisdictional status of these zones.

In relation to some of these zones there is no need to distinguish between the various categories of ships but in some cases it is necessary to note that the rules vary according to the class of ship concerned, including either warships, or merchant ships or private vessels.

In addition to the general rules considered below, there is an extensive network of more specialised rules which limit freedom of navigation in the interest of, for example, safety of navigation (e.g. the Collision Regulations), a pollution-free environment (see below) and safety of life (e.g. the Convention on Safety of Life at Sea). The special position of the warship is considered below in the section on legal aspects of the strategic use of the sea.

1 Internal waters, including ports and bays

As was seen in the General section above, internal waters comprise, *inter alia*, all waters landward of the baseline from which the breadth of the territorial sea is measured. They include, therefore, ports and the waters of certain bays landward of the 24-mile closing line. It is an established rule of customary law that foreign vessels are entitled to enter ports if in distress but, otherwise, they have no *right* of entry except by way of treaty. A number of states enjoy such rights as parties to the Geneva Convention and Statute of 1923 on the International Regime of Maritime Ports and, in addition, a right of entry is often provided for on a reciprocal basis by a bilateral treaty of commerce and navigation, or, less formally, entry is simply granted in recognition of the common interest in furthering trade relations.

2 The territorial sea, straits used for international navigation and archipelagic waters

The freedom of navigation on the high seas would be of little practical use if it were not complemented by rights of passage through the territorial sea, straits and the inter-island waters of mid-ocean archipelagos. The current state of the law can best be explained by examining first the relevant provisions of the Geneva Convention on the Territorial Sea and the Contiguous Zone, 1958, before turning, secondly, to the corresponding provisions of the UN Convention.

2.1 The Geneva regime

2.1.1 Innocent passage Under the Geneva Convention, foreign vessels enjoy a right of innocent passage through the territorial sea. Some indication of the conditions of innocence is provided in relation to fishing boats and submarines. Thus, fishing boats must observe the laws of the coastal state made to prevent them from fishing in the territorial sea and submarines must navigate on the surface and show their flag. For other vessels, however, it is provided simply that passage is innocent so long as it is not prejudicial to the peace, good order or security of the coastal state. This definition of innocence allows the coastal state to categorise the passage of a vessel as non-innocent by reference to the character or use of the vessel rather than by reference to an act committed by the vessel in the course of its passage. It is therefore more restrictive than the definition incorporated in the new UN Convention.

The Geneva Convention provides for the application of the coastal state's criminal and civil law to merchant vessels in innocent passage but only to a very limited extent (see Articles 18–20). In this context, government ships operated for commercial purposes are classified as merchant vessels. Government ships operated for non-commercial purposes (survey vessels, for example), on the other hand, retain their traditional immunity from the local jurisdiction.

The Geneva regime allows the coastal state, without discrimination among foreign ships, to suspend innocent passage temporarily in specified areas, if essential for the protection of its security.

As regards enforcement, Article 16 empowers the coastal state to take the necessary steps in its territorial sea to prevent passage which is not innocent. Moreover, where the ship is proceeding to internal waters, the coastal states may take the necessary steps to prevent any breach of the conditions to which the admission of the ship to internal waters is subject.

2.1.2 Passage through territorial sea straits Reflecting the vital importance of passage through certain strategically placed territorial sea straits, Article 16(4) of the Convention provides for what might be called a re-enforced right of innocent passage: the coastal state may *not* suspend innocent passage through territorial sea straits which are used for international navigation between one part of the high seas and another part of the high seas or the territorial sea of a foreign state.

2.1.3 Passage through archipelagic waters The Geneva Convention makes no special provision for such passage.

2.2 The UN Convention

2.2.1 Innocent passage After adopting the Geneva formula that passage is innocent so long as it is not prejudicial to the peace, good order or security of the coastal state, the UN Convention goes further by providing a list of activities in the territorial sea which would be considered to be prejudicial. It includes, in addition to such specific behaviour as weapons practice, fishing and research activities, the vague catch-all category of 'any other activity not having a direct bearing on passage'.

Two important novelties appear in the new Convention. The first relates to sea lanes and traffic separation scheme, while the second governs the passage of foreign, nuclear-powered ships and ships carrying nuclear or other inherently dangerous or noxious substances.

Sea lanes Where necessary, having regard to the safety of navigation, the coastal state may require ships in innocent passage to use designated sea lanes and traffic separation schemes. In particular, tankers, nuclear-powered ships and ships carrying nuclear or other inherently dangerous or noxious substances may be required to confine their passage to such sea lanes. The coastal state is obliged to indicate such sea lanes and traffic separation schemes on duly published charts. It is noteworthy that, in designating sea lanes and prescribing traffic separation schemes, the coastal state is obliged only to *take into account* the following factors: the recommendations of the competent international organisation; any channels customarily used for international navigation; the special characteristics of particular ships and channels; and the density of traffic.

Dangerous ships Foreign nuclear-powered ships and ships carrying nuclear or other inherently dangerous or noxious substances are required, when in innocent passage, to carry documents and observe special precautionary measure established for such ships by international agreements. Pending the conclusion and entry into force of such agreements, this is little more than a declaration of intent.

2.2.2 Passage through straits Given the trend towards more inflated territorial sea claims, the major maritime powers made it clear, from the start of UNCLOS III, that their recognition of a 12-mile territorial sea would be conditional upon the incorporation in a new convention of adequate safeguards for passage through territorial sea straits used for international navigation. It was pointed out that some 116 straits through which there had previously been a high seas corridor would become entirely territorial sea straits if a 12-mile breadth were to be generally accepted. The guarantee of non-suspension of innocent passage provided by Article 16(4) of the Geneva Convention was regarded as inadequate because (1) the applicability of the Convention's rules on innocent passage to warships was not beyond dispute; (2) under Article 14(6) of the Convention 'Submarines are required to navigate on the surface and to show their flag'; (3) the coastal state is free in the first instance to categorise a particular passage as non-innocent (for example, the passage of nuclear-powered vessels, or of mammoth oil tankers, or of vessels flying a particular flag, destined for a particular country, or carrying a particular cargo); and (4) there is no right of innocent passage for aircraft through the airspace above the territorial sea. Moreover, under international customary law, the position is, if anything, even less satisfactory, some states demanding prior notification and/or authorisation as a condition of passage.

As a result of the pressure brought to bear by the major powers to secure the incorporation of such safeguards in the treaty, the UN Convention devotes 12 Articles to 'Straits used for International Navigation' and makes provision for a new 'right of transit passage' in addition to innocent passage. It does not, however, seek to alter the legal regime of straits such as the Turkish Straits, regulated by long-standing international conventions. Nor does it apply if a high seas route or an EEZ route of similar convenience exists through the strait.

Transit passage. The principal characteristics may be summarised as follows:

1 It applies only when there is an area of high seas or EEZ at both ends of the strait. Where there is territorial sea at one end, only innocent passage applies.

2 Transit passage is the exercise of freedom of navigation and overflight solely for the purpose of continuous and expeditious transit of the strait.

3 Submarines in transit passage are not required to navigate on the surface and show their flag.

4 Where necessary to promote the safe passage of ships, the strait state may designate sea lanes and prescribe traffic separation schemes. The discretion of the strait state is more limited, however, as compared with the similar provisions for innocent passage through the territorial sea. Under the transit passage regime, it no longer suffices for the state simply to take into account various factors; it must now refer its proposals to the 'competent international organisation' and may actually designate and prescribe only following adoption by the international organisation.

5 There must be no suspension of transit passage.

'Re-enforced' innocent passage through straits Where there is only territorial sea at one end of a strait or where the strait runs between an island and the mainland and there is a high seas route or an EEZ route of similar convenience seaward of the island, the regime of transit passage does not apply. Instead, the re-enforced right of innocent passage (similar to that in Article 16(4) of the 1958 Geneva Convention) is provided for and thus such innocent passage is not subject to suspension by the coastal state.

2.2.3 Archipelagic sea-lanes passage Under Part IV of the UN Convention, a new status of 'archipelagic state' is recognised and this prescribes two regimes of passage through archipelagic waters: innocent passage and archipelagic sea lanes passage.

Innocent passage This is the normal regime of innocent passage as applying in the territorial sea generally and is therefore subject in appropriate circumstances to temporary suspension.

Archipelagic sea lanes passage The archipelagic state may designate sea lanes and air routes suitable for the continuous and expeditious passage of foreign ships and aircraft through or over its archipelagic waters and adjacent territorial sea. 'Archipelagic sea lanes passage' is enjoyed in such sea lanes and air routes and is similar to the right of transit passage through straits. The sea lanes and air routes must include all normal passage routes and their designation is subject to the same safeguard of prior adoption by the competent international organisation as in the case of transit passage. An additional safeguard is provided, however. If the archipelagic state does not designate sea lanes or air routes, the right of archipelagic sea lanes passage may be exercised through the routes normally used for international navigation.

3 The contiguous zone

The geographical scope and jurisdictional status of this have been considered above in the General section. Here, it will suffice to note that, subject to the exceptional jurisdictional powers of the coastal state (also dealt with above), foreign shipping enjoys the same right of passage in this zone as on the high seas or (under the UN Convention) in the EEZ.

4 The continental shelf

Pending its replacement by the new UN Convention, the Geneva Convention on the Continental Shelf 1958 will continue to govern the status of the continental shelf. Under the Convention, as was noted above, the coastal state enjoys certain sovereign rights over the shelf but, subject to these exceptions, the residual status of the waters above remains that of the high seas. In principle, therefore, freedom of navigation for foreign shipping continues to exist in those waters. Ships of all nationalities must, however, respect the 500-metre safety zones which the coastal state is entitled to establish around continental shelf installations and neither the installations nor their safety zones may be established where interference may be caused to the use of recognised sea lanes essential to international navigation. Moreover, due notice must be given of the construction of any such installations and permanent means for giving warning of their presence must be maintained.

If and when the new Convention enters into force, the waters of the continental shelf out to 200 miles will overlap with those of the EEZ. So far as the continental shelf is concerned, Article 78 of the UN Convention simply provides that the rights of the coastal state over the continental shelf do not affect the legal status of the superjacent waters (which will be that of the EEZ out to 200 miles and that of the continental shelf beyond 200 miles, if the legal continental shelf extends that far). Article 78 goes on to say that the exercise of the coastal state's rights in the continental shelf must not infringe or result in any unjustifiable interference with navigation. As regards installations on the continental shelf, Article 80 of the UN Convention applies the corresponding EEZ provision by cross-reference (see below).

5 The exclusive economic zone

In the EEZ the coastal state enjoys sovereign rights for the purpose of exploring, exploiting, conserving and managing the natural resources of the sea-bed, subsoil and superjacent waters and jurisdiction, as specified in the UN Convention, with regard to, *inter alia*, (1) artificial islands, installations and structures; (2) marine scientific research; and (3) the protection and preservation of the marine environment. Given also the exceptional juridical status of this new zone (see General section above), it is clear that the introduction of the EEZ poses much more of a threat to freedom of navigation than have any of the other offshore zones. Nevertheless, Article 58 of the UN Convention does provide that all states are to enjoy the freedom of navigation in the EEZ, though subject to the relevant provisions of the Convention.

As regards artificial islands, installations and structures, Article 60 is in similar terms to Article 5 of the Geneva Convention on the Continental Shelf. Safety zones must not exceed 500 metres from each point on their outer edge except as authorised by generally accepted international standards or recommended by the competent international organisation. All ships must respect these zones and comply with generally accepted international standards regarding navigation in their vicinity.

6 The high seas

The geographical scope and jurisdictional character of the high seas have been considered above in the General section. In this context, it will suffice to recall that all states, coastal and non-coastal, are entitled to exercise freedom of navigation on the high seas, subject to their having reasonable regard to the interests of other states. For the detailed rules governing such matters as nationality of ships, immunity of warships and other public vessels, safety measures to be taken by states, the duty of the Master to render assistance, piracy, hot pursuit, and pollution, reference should be made to the Geneva Convention on the High Seas 1958 and Part VII of the new UN Convention.

4 Exploitation of sea-bed hydrocarbons and minerals: the international legal framework

So far as international law is concerned, the rules governing the exploitation of sea-bed natural resources depend not upon the type of resource (be it gravel, placer deposits, coal, oil, natural gas or manganese nodules) but upon the maritime zone in which they are situated. In this context it is necessary to distinguish only three zones: (1) internal waters and the territorial seas; (2) the continental shelf; and (3) the area beyond the limits of national jurisdiction.

1 Internal waters and the territorial sea

In the zone landward of the outer limit of the territorial sea, the coastal state has sovereignty over all of the natural resources of the sea-bed and subsoil, and foreign states or their nationals may participate in the exploitation of these resources only with the consent of the coastal state.

2 The continental shelf

The geographical scope of the continental shelf and problems of delimitation have been considered in the 'General' section above. Here attention is focussed on the rules governing the exploitation of the continental shelf's natural resources.

Subject to a few exceptions, the most important of which is noted below, the exploitation regime established by the Geneva Convention on the Continental Shelf 1958 has been reincorporated in Part VI of the UN Convention on the Law of the Sea. Indeed, the most important Article in the present context, Article 2 of the Geneva Convention, has been taken over virtually unchanged as Article 77 of the UN Convention. It provides that the coastal state exercises over the continental shelf sovereign rights for the purpose of exploring it and exploiting its natural resources, the latter being defined as:

> '. . . the mineral and other non-living resources of the sea-bed and subsoil together with living organisms belonging to sedentary species, that is to say, organisms which, at the harvestable stage, either are immobile on or under the sea-bed or are unable to move except in constant physical contact with the sea-bed or the subsoil'.

As has been seen, the coastal state is empowered to construct on the continental shelf installations necessary for its exploration and the exploitation of its natural resources and to establish 500-metre safety zones around them.

Of the additions to this regime introduced in the UN Convention, one in particular deserves to be noted here. Article 82 requires that the coastal state must make payments or contributions in kind in respect of the exploitation of the non-living resources of the continental shelf beyond the 200-mile line. Such payments and contributions are to be made annually with respect to all production at a site after the first five years of production at that site. The rate rises from one per cent in the sixth year to seven per cent for the twelfth and subsequent years. Exemption is, however, granted to a developing state if it is a net importer of a mineral produced from its continental shelf. The payments or contributions have to be made through the International Sea-Bed Authority, a new institution set up under the UN Convention, and are to be distributed to states parties to the Convention 'on the basis of equitable sharing criteria, taking into account the interests and needs of developing states, particularly the least-developed and the land-locked amongst them'.

3 The Area beyond the limits of national jurisdiction

At the time of writing (January 1983), the law governing the deep-sea mining of manganese nodules and other natural resources of the sea-bed and subsoil beyond the outer limit of the continental shelf is in a state of flux. Several of the principal industrialised states, led by the United States, have declined to sign the UN Convention because of their dissatisfaction with the sea-bed mining regime contained in Part XI. This stance was taken despite the fact that a scheme for Preparatory Investment Protection (PIP) was grafted on to the Convention during the final session of UNCLOS III in an attempt to accommodate their concern. There must now be considerable uncertainty about the viability of the UN regime and at least a possibility that first-generation sea bed mining will take place under a Reciprocating States Regime based on national legislation. The Regime, embodied in Part XI and in a related PIP Conference Resolution, is exceedingly detailed, technical and complex. A broad outline is given here, together with a note on the alternative Reciprocating States Regime.

3.1 Background to the UN Convention regime The legal status of the natural resources of the sea-bed of the high seas under international customary law is uncertain. In recent years, it has been argued by the technologically advanced states, particularly the United States, that deep-sea mining is a high seas freedom and that, in its exercise, states may acquire exclusive rights in particular mine sites by discovery and public assertion of an exclusive claim, supported by due diligence in exploring, evaluating and working the deposit. Since 1967, however, there has been a powerful drive by the Group of 77 developing states to have the 'Area' and its resources recognised as the common heritage of mankind, in which no state or other entity may acquire exclusive rights. A major landmark in this campaign was the Declaration of Principles governing the Area adopted by the General Assembly of the United Nations on 17 December 1970, whereby the Area and its resources were 'solemnly declared' to be the common heritage of mankind. The object of the subsequent proceedings in UNCLOS III was to transform this non-binding resolution into binding, detailed treaty rules.

3.2 The UN regime for the Area is contained in Part XI of the UN Convention. The principal features of Part XI may be summarised as follows:

1 The Area and its resources are the common heritage of mankind and no state or other entity may acquire rights in the minerals of the Area except under the system established in

the Convention.

2 A parallel system is established under which all deep-sea mining would be under the control of an International-Sea-Bed Authority ('the Authority'), which would be empowered both to undertake mining operations through an organ called 'the Enterprise' and to enter into contracts enabling private and state ventures to acquire mining rights. The parallel system would work as follows: in applying for a contract, the applicant would identify two areas of equal estimated value and, in granting the contract, the Authority would allocate one of them to the applicant while reserving the other for exploitation by either the Enterprise or by developing countries.

3 The general policies of the Authority would be determined by the plenary Assembly, while their application in individual cases would be the responsibility of a 36-member Council. Because of the importance of its powers, the question of membership of the Council and its system of voting caused great difficulty in the negotiations. One of the Council's powers is that of approval of plans of work authorising miners to develop a mine-site.

4 The UN Convention contains a number of provisions designed to help the Enterprise to compete with private enterprise. They include a system of financing which places a considerable onus on states parties to the Convention, especially in the early years of operation, and a burdensome obligation upon contractors to transfer mining know-how to the Enterprise.

5 In order to avoid causing hardship to producers of land-based minerals, an elaborate production control system is incorporated in the Convention, under which mineral production by sea-bed miners is restricted in accordance with a formula based on 60 per cent of the projected annual increase in the world's demand for nickel.

6 Provision is made for a review of the system at the end of a 15-year period.

The PIP scheme was designed to provide acceptable safeguards for the heavy investments already made by Western mining consortia, while at the same time preserving the main features of the Convention regime as outlined above.

Under the PIP scheme it will be open to consortia to secure a preferential status (within the integrated PIP Convention regime) by registering as a 'pioneer investor', provided it meets specified conditions relating to signature of the Convention by parent states and the level of pioneer investment. The registered pioneer investor may then have a 'pioneer area' allocated to it, with the exclusive right to conduct 'pioneer activities' therein. Pioneers may not proceed beyond the preliminary 'pioneer activity' stage until the Authority has granted them a contract approving their plan of work. This is practically guaranteed, however, provided the parent states of the consortia members have all ratified the Convention. The Authority is bound also to grant one further permit—a production authorisation—provided the provisions of the regime are followed.

While it is true that the integrated PIP Convention regime offers a degree of protection for earlier investment in sea-bed mining and international security of tenure in the allocated mining site, it still imposes upon the principal industrialised mining states heavier burdens and limitations than some of them are prepared to accept. For this reason it is now likely that further exploratory work will continue under the unilateral legislation already adopted by the United States, the Federal Republic of Germany, the United Kingdom and France. Of these states, only France has so far signed the UN Convention. All four made arrangements to coordinate their legislation in September 1982. It remains to be seen whether in the years ahead the Convention can be further amended to accommodate the demands of the Western industrialised nations or whether, following changes of government, they may still be persuaded to accept the UN regime.

5 Prevention and control of marine pollution and liability for pollution damage

The conventions summarised here create rules of international law binding upon the states parties to them. It is left to governments to implement their terms through national legislation. An important role is, however, played by a variety of international institutions. Foremost among them is the *International Maritime Organisation* (IMO) which, in relation to vessel-source pollution, usually convenes conferences to draft or revise conventions and acts as the depository for their ratification. Other institutions which perform similar functions include the Assembly, Secretariat and Executive Committee of the Fund Convention (see *1.5* below); the Commissions established under the Oslo Dumping Convention (see *3.1* below), the Paris Land-Based Sources Convention (see *4.1* below) and the Helsinki Convention on the Baltic Sea Area (see *5.3* below). Mention should also be made of the work of the United Nations Environment Programme (UNEP) and, in particular, of its Regional Seas Programme under which marine pollution is being attacked through a series of regional conventions and Action Plans. Even in these cases where no specialised organs are established (and where, therefore, co-ordination and implementation are left to governments) the conventions frequently embody a pledge by the states parties to promote measures to protect the marine environment within the competent specialised agencies or other international bodies.

1 Conventions on vessel-source pollution

1.1 The International Convention for the Prevention of Pollution of the Sea by Oil, 1954–69 (OILPOL) The Convention was amended in 1962, 1969 and, in minor respects, in 1971. The 1969 amendments entered into force on 20 January 1978.

Subject to certain exceptions, tankers are prohibited from discharging oil or an oily mixture anywhere except where (1) the tanker is proceeding en route; (2) it is more than 50 miles from the nearest land; (3) the rate of discharge from cargo carrying space does not exceed 60 litres per mile; and (4) the total discharge on a ballast voyage does not exceed 1/15 000 part of total cargo-carrying capacity. Similar restraints are placed on non-tankers.

States parties are required to 'take all appropriate steps to promote the provision of' facilities for disposal of oil residues. It is envisaged that OILPOL will be superseded by MARPOL in 1983 (see *1.2* below) when the latter enters into force.

1.2 International Convention for the Prevention of Pollution from Ships, 1973 (MARPOL) The original MARPOL had five annexes, each dealing with a different type of pollutant. Parties were required to be bound by Annexes I (oil) and II (noxious liquid substances in bulk). By 1978 it was clear that technical problems over Annex II were delaying the ratification and entry into force of the Convention and a Protocol was therefore adopted to facilitate the early entry into force of oil pollution regulations in Annex I. MARPOL and the 1978 Protocol are now to be read as a single instrument which requires implementation of Annex I but defers the application of Annex II. The combined instrument has now been ratified by 15 states, accounting for 50 per cent of the world's merchant shipping (entry into force: 2 October 1983). The provisions of the five Annexes are summarised:

Annex I: Oil The main innovations as compared with OILPOL are as follows. The total discharge on a ballast voyage is reduced by half to 1/30 000 of cargo capacity. Five special areas (see page 224) have been designated in the Mediterranean, the Black Sea, the Baltic, the Red Sea and the Arabian/Persian Gulf area. Only 'clean ballast' discharges are permitted in such areas. The 'load-on-top' procedure is made compulsory for all oil tankers of 150 tonnes and over. A major innovation requires new oil tankers of 70 000 tonnes and over to be fitted with segregated ballast tanks. All ships of over 400 tonnes must have tanks for the retention of oil residues and, correspondingly, the Convention requires the provision of oil reception facilities at oil loading terminals, repair ports and other ports in which ships have oil residues to discharge.

The 1978 Protocol introduced further amendments: segregated ballast tanks would now be required on all new tankers of 20 000 tonnes and over (previously 70 000), and protective locations are specified for them. Under a sister Protocol of 1978 relating to the International Convention for the Safety of Life at Sea, 1974, provision is made for inert gas systems in all existing and new tankers of 20 000 tonnes and over and for improved steering gear and radar and collision avoidance aids.

Annex II: noxious liquid substances in bulk Four categories of noxious liquid substances are established, according to the degree of their threat to marine resources, human health, amenities and other legitimate uses of the sea. Over 400 substances have been evaluated and are included in the list appended to the Convention. The discharge of residues containing such substances is permitted only either to reception facilities or into the sea subject to specified conditions which vary with the categories of substances concerned. The Baltic and the Black Sea are designated as special areas in which the discharge of noxious liquid substances is prohibited.

Annex III: Harmful substances carried by sea in packaged form or in freight containers, portable tanks or road and rail tank wagons General requirements are laid down relating to the prevention of pollution from this source but detailed requirements on packaging, marking and labelling, stowage, quantity limitations, and other aspects are left to be developed within the framework of the International Maritime Dangerous Goods Code or in other appropriate form.

Annexes IV and V: Sewage and garbage Annex IV forbids discharge of sewage within 4 miles of the nearest land unless the ship has in operation an approved treatment plant. Between 4 and 12 miles, sewage must be comminuted and disinfected before discharge. As regards garbage, specific minimum distances from land have been set in Annex V for the disposal of all the principal kinds of garbage. The disposal of all plastics is prohibited.

1.3 International Convention relating to Intervention on the High Seas in Cases of Oil Pollution Casualties, 1969 and *Protocol relating to Intervention on the High Seas in Cases of Maritime Pollution by Substances other than Oil, 1973.* The scope of the Convention and Protocol comprises the area of the high seas, that is, the area beyond the outer limit of the territorial sea or, if and when the EEZ is generally recognised, the area beyond it. The Convention entered into force on 6 May 1975; the Protocol has not yet entered into force.

Parties 'may take such measures on the high seas as may be necessary to prevent, mitigate or eliminate grave and imminent danger to their coastline or related interests from pollution or threat of pollution of the sea by oil, following upon a maritime casualty or acts related to such a casualty which may reasonably be expected to result in major harmful consequences'. The related interests include commercial fishing and tourist interests, the health of the coastal population and the conservation of living marine resources and of wild life. The measures taken must be 'proportionate to the damage actual or threatened' and 'reasonably necessary'. The Protocol of 1973, once it enters into force, will extend the Convention to cases of pollution by substances other than oil which are liable to cause serious damage.

1.4 International Convention on Civil Liability for Oil Pollution Damage, 1969 (CLC) and Protocol 1976. As regards geographical scope, CLC applies 'exclusively to pollution damage caused on the territory including the territorial sea of a contracting state and to preventive measures taken to prevent and minimise such damage'. It should be noted, however, that the Convention also covers damage caused in the area outside the territorial sea by preventive measures designed to prevent or minimise pollution damage inside the territorial sea.

CLC entered into force on 19 June 1975. The Protocol has not yet entered into force.

The purpose of CLC is to provide uniform international rules and procedures for determining questions of liability and providing adequate compensation to persons who suffer damage caused by the escape or discharge of oil from ships. Liability is placed upon the owner of the ship. Liability is strict (no need to prove fault or negligence). The owner may limit his liability per incident to approximately $160 per ship's ton, with a ceiling of $16.8 million and the ship must be covered by insurance in such an amount. The Protocol is concerned with the unit of account used in CLC.

1.5 International Convention on the Establishment of an International Fund for Compensation for Oil Pollution Damage, 1971 and Protocol 1976. The Fund Convention entered into force on 16 October 1978. The Protocol has not yet entered into force.

The Fund Convention is supplementary to the Civil Liability Convention 1969 and its main purpose is to ensure the availability of additional compensation in cases where the protection afforded by the 1969 Convention is inadequate. Compensation is paid from a Fund financed by levies on importers of oil. The present aggregate ceiling of compensation available from the CLC and the Fund is $54 million. The Protocol is concerned with the unit of account used in the Convention.

2 Conventions on Pollution from the Continental Shelf

2.1 Geneva Convention on the High Seas, 1958 and **2.1.1 Geneva Convention on the Continental Shelf, 1958** The High Seas Convention entered into force on 30 September 1962 and the Continental Shelf Convention on 10 June 1964.

Article 24 of the High Seas Convention requires every state to draw up regulations to prevent pollution of the seas by the discharge of oil from pipelines or resulting from the exploration and exploitation of the seabed and its subsoil. In addition, the Continental Shelf Convention embodies a number of rules designed to ensure safety of offshore operations and prevention of pollution. For example, Article 5(7) requires the coastal state to undertake in the safety zones around shelf installations all appropriate measures for the protection of the living resources of the sea from all harmful agents.

2.2 Convention on Civil Liability for Oil Pollution Damage Resulting from Exploration for and Exploitation of Seabed Mineral Resources, 1976 The Convention applies to pollution damage: (1) resulting from an incident which occurred beyond the coastal low-water line at an installation under the jurisdiction of a controlling state, and (2) suffered in the territory, including the internal waters and territorial sea, of a state party or in the areas in which, in accordance with international law, it has sovereign rights over natural resources. It also applies to preventive measures, wherever taken, to prevent or minimise such pollution damage. On its entry into force, the area of operation of the Convention will thus be mainly the territory of states parties and their offshore waters out to the outer limit of the continental shelf. Pending the entry into force of the Convention, it is not practicable to illustrate the Convention area on a chart.

The Convention was prepared by the following nine states: Belgium, Denmark, France, Germany, Ireland, the Netherlands, Norway, Sweden, and the United Kingdom. Under Article 18, the parties may unanimously agree to invite other states bordering the North Sea, the Baltic Sea or the Atlantic north of 36 °N to accede to the Convention. It will enter into force 90 days after ratification by 4 states.

The operator of an installation is made liable for any pollution damage arising from an incident involving his installation. Liability is strict (no need to prove fault or negligence). Liability could have been limited to approximately $35 million until 1 May 1982 and after that date may be limited to approximately $47 million. States also have the option of providing for unlimited liability or a higher limit of liability. To cover his liability, the operator is required to carry insurance up to specified limits.

3 Conventions on Dumping

3.1 Oslo Convention for the Prevention of Marine Pollution by Dumping from Ships and Aircraft, 1972 See map page 224 for the area to which the Convention applies. Entered into force on 7 April 1974.

The pattern of control established by the Convention has four basic elements:

1 A requirement that no substance or material may be dumped without the approval of the national authorities.

2 No such approval may be given for specified highly hazardous substances (black list substances), the dumping of which is prohibited.

3 As regards other specified substances and materials requiring special care (grey list substances), there is a requirement that 'significant' quantities may be dumped only if the national authorities have issued a permit, having regard to specified precautionary requirements.

4 Finally, provision is made for limited exceptions in Articles 8 and 9.

3.2 London Convention on the Prevention of Marine Pollution by Dumping of Wastes and other Matter, 1972 The London Convention is of global effect, though, of course, only in relation to states parties. Entered into force August 1975.

The pattern of control is similar to that established in the Oslo Convention for the North East Atlantic (see *3.1* above).

4 Conventions on Pollution from Land-Based Sources

4.1 Paris Convention for the Prevention of Marine Pollution from Land-Based Sources, 1974 Adopted by 10 Western European states, the Convention requires ratification by 7 states to bring it into force and has not yet reached this number.

Through this regional instrument, states parties undertake to combat marine pollution from land-based sources by adopting individually and jointly the measures prescribed in the Convention. In particular, the parties undertake to *eliminate* pollution by substances listed in an annexed 'black list' and to *limit strictly* pollution by substances in a 'grey list'.

5 Regional Conventions on Marine Pollution

5.1 Bonn Agreement for Co-operation in Dealing with Pollution of the North Sea by Oil, 1969 The 'North Sea area' to which the Agreement applies is shown in the map on page 224. The Agreement entered into force on 9 August 1969.

The basic objective of the agreement is protection against oil pollution which presents a grave and imminent danger to the coast or related interests of one or more of the parties and 'active co-operation' is the chosen means. Such co-operation is of two kinds: preparatory and organisational co-operation, and co-operation following a casualty. Under the first, provision is made for exchange of information on competent authorities and means to deal with pollution and eight zones of responsibility are established. Prescribed co-operation following a casualty is of three kinds: provision is made for the speedy gathering of information; for monitoring and distribution of information by the zonal authority; and for assistance in dealing with the spill.

Under Article 5(2), masters of ships flying the flag of a state party are to be requested to report on casualties causing or likely to cause oil pollution.

5.2 Agreement between Denmark, Finland, Norway and Sweden concerning Co-operation in Taking Measures against Pollution of the Sea by Oil, 1971 No area is specified in the Agreement, which entered into force for all four states on 16 October 1971.

This Agreement provided for a system of cooperation similar to that established in the North Sea Agreement (**5.1** above).

5.3 Helsinki Convention on the Protection of the Marine Environment of the Baltic Sea Area, 1974 The Convention area, shown on page 224, is the 'Baltic Sea Area', defined as 'The Baltic Sea proper with the Gulf of Bothnia, the Gulf of Finland and the entrance to the Baltic Sea bounded by the parallel of the Skaw in the Skagerrak at 57°44'8"N. It does not include internal waters of the Contracting Parties'.

The Convention entered into force on 3 May 1980 after ratification by the seven signatory states. The Baltic Marine Environment Protection Commission held its first meeting in May 1980.

The fundamental obligation accepted by states parties is to take, individually and jointly, all appropriate legislative, administrative or other relevant measures in order to prevent and abate pollution and to protect and enhance the marine environment of the Baltic Sea area. More specifically, states accept particular obligations to (1) counteract the introduction into the area of hazardous substances; (2) control and minimise land-based pollution; (3) take measures to prevent pollution from ships and pleasure craft; (4) prevent, or in some cases control, dumping; (5) take measures to prevent pollution resulting from the exploration and exploitation of the seabed and subsoil; and (6) co-operate with the other parties in the framework of the Commission established by the Convention.

5.4 Barcelona Convention for the Protection of the Mediterranean against Pollution, 1976 Protocol 1 for the Prevention of Pollution of the Mediterranean Sea by Dumping from Ships and Aircraft, 1976; Protocol 2 concerning Co-operating in Combatting Pollution of the Mediterranean Sea by Oil and Other Harmful Substances in Cases of Emergency, 1976; Protocol 3 for the Protection of the Mediterranean against Pollution from Land-based Sources, 1980; Protocol 4 concerning Mediterranean Specially-Protected Areas, 1982.

The Mediterranean Sea Area, to which the Convention and Protocols apply, is defined as 'the maritime waters of the Mediterranean Sea proper, including its gulfs and seas bounded to the west by the meridian passing through Cape Spartel lighthouse, at the entrance of the Straits of Gibraltar, and to the East by the southern limits of the Straits of the Dardanelles between Mehmetcik and Kumkak lighthouses' (see page 224).

The Convention and Protocols 1 and 2 entered into force on 13 February 1978.

The Convention embodies general undertakings in relation to the prevention and abatement of pollution and the adoption of appropriate measures to combat pollution caused by dumping; discharges from ships; exploration and exploitation of the continental shelf and of the seabed and its subsoil; and discharges from land-based sources. It also provided for co-operation in dealing with pollution emergencies, monitoring and scientific and technological matters and binds the parties to adopt procedures for the determination of liability and compensation for pollution damage. However, the detailed rules on these matters are left to the four Protocols already signed and others in the course of development.

5.5 Kuwait Regional Convention for Co-operation on the Protection of the Marine Environment from Pollution, 1978 Protocol concerning Regional Co-operation in Combatting Pollution by Oil and Other Harmful Substances in Cases of Emergency, 1978.

For the Sea Area covered by the Convention and Protocol see page 224. It does not include the internal waters of the contracting states (i.e. waters landward of the baseline of the territorial sea) unless otherwise stated in the Convention or Protocol.

The Convention and Protocol entered into force on 30 June 1979.

The Convention is broadly similar to the Barcelona Convention (**5.4** above) but so far only the original Protocol has been developed.

5.6 Abidjan Convention for Co-operation in the Protection and Development of the Marine and Coastal Environment of the West and Central African Region, 1981 Protocol 1 concerning Cooperation in Combatting Pollution in Cases of Emergency, 1981.

The 'geographical coverage' of the Convention is defined as 'the marine environment, coastal zones and related inland waters falling within the jurisdiction of the states of the West and Central African Region, from Mauritania to Namibia inclusive, which have become Contracting Parties to this Convention . . .' (see page 224).

The Convention and Protocol 1 were signed on 23 March 1981 and will enter into force on the sixtieth day following the date of deposit of the sixth instrument of ratification or accession.

The Convention and Protocol 1 are broadly similar to those adopted for the Mediterranean (**5.4** above) and Kuwait Region (**5.5** above).

5.7 Other 'Regional Seas' Conventions Ten regions are covered by UNEPs Regional Seas Programme: (1) the Mediterranean, (2) the Kuwait Action Plan Region, (3) West and Central Africa. The Barcelona, Kuwait and Abidjan Conventions and Protocols reviewed in **5.4**, **5.5** and **5.6** above relate respectively to these three regions. More recently two more regions have been covered, namely: (4) the South-East Pacific and (5) the Red Sea and Gulf of Aden. The South-East Pacific is dealt with in two instruments adopted in November 1981: the Lima Convention for the Protection of the Marine Environment and Coastal Areas of the South Pacific and the Agreement on Regional Co-operation in Combatting Pollution of the South-East Pacific by Hydrocarbons and Other Harmful Substances in Cases of Emergency. The Red Sea and Gulf of Aden are covered by two instruments adopted in February 1982: the Jeddah Convention for the Conservation of the Red Sea and Gulf of Aden Environment and the Protocol concerning Regional Co-operation in Combatting Marine Pollution by Oil and Other Harmful Substances in Cases of Emergency. Similar instruments are expected to be adopted for (6) the Wider Caribbean region (1983). It is possible that similar provision will be made in due course for: (7) East Africa, (8) the East Asian Seas, (9) the South-West Pacific and (10) the South-West Atlantic.

6 The United Nations Convention on the Law of the Sea, 1982
Part XII of the new Convention, consisting of 46 articles, is the first attempt to provide a comprehensive framework of conventional rules covering all sources of marine pollution. It is possible here to give only a brief account of its principal provisions.

6.1 General obligation Article 192 embodies a 'general obligation', whereby 'States have the obligation to protect and preserve the marine environment'.

6.2 Best practicable means In honouring this obligation, states have a duty to use the 'best practicable means at their disposal and in accordance with their capabilities' (Article 194).

6.3 Legislating to prevent, reduce and control marine pollution Marine pollution may originate and cause damage in any geographical zone from land to mid-ocean and one of the functions of the UN Convention is to allocate responsibility to states for standard setting and for the enforcement of these standards in relation to the various maritime zones and sources of pollution. As regards standard setting, Section 5 of Part XII deals in turn with six sources of marine pollution:

First, states are placed under an obligation to tackle *pollution from land-based sources* through the adoption of national legislation and the establishment of global and regional rules, taking into account, however, the economic capacity of developing states and their need for economic development.

A similar obligation is next prescribed for *pollution from seabed activities*.

Thirdly, provision is made for the establishment of international rules, standards and recommended practices and procedures to prevent *marine pollution from activities in the Area*. States have a complementary obligation to adopt national legislation in relation to the activities in the Area of vessels, installations, structures and devices flying their flag, or of their registry, or operating under their authority.

A combination of national legislation and international norms is again envisaged to deal with *marine pollution caused by dumping*. National legislation must ensure that dumping is not carried out without the permission of the competent national authority. Moreover, dumping within the territorial sea or the EEZ, or onto the continental shelf, may not be carried out without the express prior approval of the coastal state.

A mixture of national and international law-making is also provided for in order to prevent, reduce and control *marine pollution from or through the atmosphere*.

Finally, Article 211 deals with *pollution from vessels*. Under this Article, states have an obligation to establish international rules and standards and national laws and regulations of at least the same effect. They have also to promote the adoption of routeing systems, wherever appropriate. Article 211 goes on to provide for standard-setting in ports and national waters; the territorial sea; and the EEZ.

Where states have established particular anti-pollution requirements as a condition for the entry of foreign vessels into their ports or national waters, or for calling at their off-shore terminals, they have an obligation to publicise them. In cases where co-operative arrangements have been made by two or more states to impose such requirements in identical form, foreign masters are to be placed under a duty to provide information about their destination and capacity to comply with these requirements when navigating in the territorial sea of one of these states.

As regards the territorial sea, coastal states have a sovereign right to adopt laws and regulations, provided they do not hamper the innocent passage of foreign vessels. Nor must such laws apply to the design, construction, manning or equipment of foreign ships, unless they are giving effect to generally accepted international rules or standards (*Articles 21 and 211*).

Article 211 includes two provisions on the EEZ. First, the coastal state may adopt laws and regulations giving effect to generally accepted international rules, thus making these rules enforcible in the EEZ. Secondly, provision is made for especially vulnerable areas of the EEZ where the normal international rules are inadequate to meet the special oceanographical and ecological circumstances. Subject to stringent safeguards to be applied by the 'competent international organisation', the coastal state may adopt special mandatory measures implementing international norms applicable to such special areas. Subject to the agreement of the competent international organisation, the coastal state may also adopt additional national laws and regulations on discharges or navigational practices. It is also entitled to adopt special rules for areas of the EEZ covered by ice for most of the year (*Article 234*).

Finally, provision is made to ensure that incidents involving or threatening discharges will be promptly notified to states which may be affected.

6.4 Enforcement The provisions of Part XII on standard setting, summarised above, are complemented by equally complex rules on the enforcement of these standards (*Articles 213–222*). Traditionally, anti-pollution laws could be enforced under two kinds of jurisdiction. By virtue of its *territorial jurisdiction*, the *coastal state* was entitled to enforce its anti-pollution laws on its land territory, and in its maritime 'territory': ports, internal waters and the territorial sea. Part XII employs this type of jurisdiction in relation to, for example, land-based sources of pollution, dumping and discharges landward of the 200-mile EEZ limit. Secondly, by virtue of its *quasi-territorial jurisdiction*, the *flag state* has traditionally enforced the law on ships flying its flag or registered in its territory, and Part XII again incorporates this type of enforcement. Hitherto, however, there has been no way of exercising jurisdiction over a foreign vessel which has caused pollution beyond the limits of any state's territorial jurisdiction. Subject to certain safeguards, this gap will be closed by Article 218 which embodies a third type of jurisdiction: port-State jurisdiction. Under this Article, when a vessel flying the flag of State A is voluntarily within a port or at an off-shore terminal of State B, State B may institute proceedings in respect of a discharge seaward of State B's EEZ in violation of applicable international rules.

6.5 Sovereign immunity Warships and other public vessels used only on government, non-commercial service, are not subject to the above rules as such, but states have a duty to apply the substance of these rules to such vessels 'so far as is reasonable and practicable' (*Article 236*).

6.6 Other pollution conventions The provisions of Part XII are without prejudice to earlier or later pollution treaties provided that the specific obligations assumed under such special treaties are carried out in a manner consistent with the general principles and objectives of the UN Convention (*Article 237*).

6 Legal aspects of the strategic use of the sea
The warship is the most obvious instrument of the state's strategic use of the seas and this section opens with a brief account of some of the more general rules of international law governing the warship's operations in time of peace. One of the warship's principal functions is to carry the maritime component of the nuclear deterrent and the second part of this section embodies a survey of the rules governing the testing and deployment of nuclear weapons. This is followed by three further outlines of the rules of international law relating to other important functions of the warship: the establishment and maintenance of blockades; naval surveillance activities; and the protection of sea-bed exploitation operations.

1 Warships (surface vessels and submarines)
If the warship is to operate effectively as part of the state's armed forces, it is imperative that it should enjoy a large degree of freedom of navigation and an unhindered right of passage through important straits and archipelagic waters. On the other hand, other states will wish to safeguard their security by placing certain restraints on these freedoms. It is one of the functions of international law to maintain a balance between these potentially conflicting interests. As will be seen below, the formula differs from one maritime jurisdictional zone to another.

High seas On the high seas, the warship's right to freedom of navigation is restricted only by the obligation not to interfere with the exercise by others of the freedom of the high seas and by rules imposed by its own government (though often having their origins in international agreements) on such matters as the avoidance of collisions, pollution and safety of life at sea. The warship is immune from the jurisdiction of other states except in very exceptional circumstances —on the basis of consent, for example, or following the conversion of the warship to piratical use.

The continental shelf and the exclusive economic zone The waters above the continental shelf are 'high seas' and, in general, the warship enjoys the same freedoms there as in the waters beyond the limits of national jurisdiction. There is, however, an obligation to respect the 500-metre safety zones around installations and structures on the continental shelf.

Under the United Nations Convention on the Law of the Sea, the coastal state enjoys a 200-mile exclusive economic zone (EEZ), the area of which will largely coincide with that of the legal continental shelf. Although the waters of the EEZ do not retain the same 'high seas' status as those of the continental shelf, there is nonetheless a right of freedom of navigation for warships in these waters provided it is exercised compatibly with the rights of the coastal state in its EEZ.

The territorial sea As noted above, foreign shipping enjoys a right of 'innocent passage' through the territorial sea. There is, however, some doubt about the extent to which warships share in this right. For states bound by the Geneva Convention on the Territorial Sea and the Contiguous Zone (1958), there is no doubt: warships enjoy a right of innocent passage, subject only to the obligation upon submarines to navigate on the surface and to show their flag. This right may, however, be temporarily suspended if essential for the protection of the coastal state's security. In substance, the rules are the same under the UN Convention. The position of coastal states which are not parties to the Geneva Convention is governed by the less certain rules of international customary law which, according to some states, allow them to make innocent passage of warships conditional upon prior authorisation or notification.

The foreign warship is obliged to observe the laws and regulations of the coastal state while exercising its right of innocent passage. On the other hand, it enjoys immunity from the local jurisdiction. If the warship disregards any request for compliance with the local laws which is made to it by the coastal state, it may be required to leave the territorial sea immediately.

Under the UN Convention, warships in general, and nuclear-powered ships or ships carrying nuclear weapons in particular, may be required to confine their passage to designated sea lanes.

Internal waters (including ports) For obvious reasons, foreign warships have no right of access to internal waters, including ports. Both the timing and the number of ships to be included in a foreign port visit are matters within the discretion of the port state. Elaborate security safeguards are usually negotiated before a nuclear-powered warship is permitted to enter port. Once granted access, however, the foreign warship enjoys immunity from the local jurisdiction and the local authorities may not board her without the master's consent.

Straits and archipelagic waters Where the dimensions of a strait are such that there is a belt of high seas or EEZ running through it, there is no problem. Where, however, the strait lies entirely within the territorial sea of the riparian state(s), it is of vital strategic importance to the maritime powers that the passage of their warships through the strait should have a specially protected status. Under the 1958 Geneva Convention on the Territorial Sea and the Contiguous Zone such protection was afforded by a provision banning suspension of innocent passage through straits used for international navigation.

Under the UN Convention, warships would enjoy a right of 'transit passage' through such straits. This right is more favourable to the foreign vessel than innocent passage and is more akin to the freedom of navigation enjoyed on the high seas. For example, submarines in transit passage would not be required to navigate on the surface and fly their flags. Warships, like other foreign ships, may, however, be obliged to use designated sea lanes and observe designated traffic separation schemes.

Prior to UNCLOS III, the waters between and around the islands of an archipelago had no special status. Under the UN Convention, however, the new status of archipelagic waters is similar to that of straits used for international navigation.

2 Nuclear weapons and arms control

Until recently, the seas provided the principal sites for nuclear-weapon testing and they still offer the most advantageous arena for the deployment of nuclear deterrent forces. However, in recent years the efforts of the world-wide anti-nuclear and environmental lobbies have resulted in changes in the law which have placed restraints on these uses of the oceans. This section provides a brief survey of these developments.

2.1 The Nuclear Test Ban Treaty Article 1 of the Nuclear Test Ban Treaty, which entered into force on 10 October 1963, provides that:

> Each of the parties to this Treaty undertakes to prohibit, to prevent, and not to carry out any nuclear weapons test explosion, or any other nuclear explosion, at any place under its jurisdiction or control: (a) in the atmosphere; beyond its limits, including outer space; or under water, including territorial waters or high seas; or (b) in any other environment if such explosion causes radioactive debris to be present outside the territorial limits of the State under whose jurisdiction or control such explosion is conducted. . . .

A party to the Treaty thus agrees not to test nuclear weapons 'under water, including territorial waters or high seas', but only 'at any place under its jurisdiction or control'. Though this provision is ambiguous, the intention seems to have been to regard a party conducting a test in the high seas as having temporary control there. Such a test would thus be within the scope of the ban.

As regards the subsoil, the Treaty is somewhat ambiguous, but the position seems to be that nuclear tests are forbidden if they cause radioactive debris to be present outside the territorial limits of the state under whose jurisdiction or control such tests are conducted. Accordingly, whereas an explosion in the subsoil of the territorial sea would be quite legal so long as it did not cause radioactive debris beyond the limit of the territorial sea, a test conducted in the subsoil beyond the outer limit of the territorial sea would be illegal even though no radioactive debris escaped to the superjacent waters or atmosphere, because the subsoil of the high seas is a place 'outside the territorial limits of the state' concerned.

Of the major powers, only China and France have failed to become parties to the Test Ban Treaty, although France made a unilateral statement in 1974 that it did not intend to conduct any further atmospheric tests.

Further and somewhat clearer restrictions on maritime nuclear tests have been introduced by two later treaties.

Article I of the Treaty on the Prohibition of the Emplacement of Nuclear Weapons and Other Weapons of Mass Destruction on the Seabed and the Ocean Floor and in the Subsoil Thereof, of 11 February 1971, forbids the emplacement in the subsoil of facilities specifically designed for testing nuclear weapons. It is, however, geographically less extensive than the corresponding ban in the Nuclear Test Ban Treaty since, unlike the latter, it does not extend without qualification to waters landward of the outer limit of the 12-mile coastal belt.

For parties to the Treaty for the Prohibition of Nuclear Weapons in Latin America, of 14 February 1967 (the Treaty of Tlatelolco), the position is also much clearer in relation to the subsoil of the maritime area covered by that Treaty, that is, the territorial waters of the states parties. The testing of nuclear weapons is absolutely banned.

2.2 Nuclear weapon-free zones A nuclear weapon-free zone has been established in Latin America. In addition, declarations have been adopted in the UN General Assembly and elsewhere, designed to create 'zones of peace' in the Indian Ocean, South-East Asia and Africa. It is unlikely, however, that they will lead in the foreseeable future to the establishment of further nuclear weapon-free zones on a treaty basis.

The Latin American nuclear-free zone was established by the Treaty for the Prohibition of Nuclear Weapons in Latin America of 14 February 1967. Under Article 1, parties are obliged to prohibit and prevent in their territories the testing, use, manufacture, production or acquisition by any means, as well as the receipt, storage, installation, deployment and any form of possession of any nuclear weapon. The Treaty does not, however, prohibit the transit of nuclear weapons in the treaty area.

Under Articles 1, 3 and 4(1), the nuclear-weapons ban extends to the territorial sea, air space and any other space over which the state exercises sovereignty in accordance with its own legislation. The ban accordingly already extends to a distance of 200 miles from the coasts of such states as Ecuador and El Salvador, which claim territorial seas of 200 miles breadth, and Peru, which claims sovereignty not only over the continental shelf but also over the superjacent waters out to 200 miles from the coast. In all, the zone of application already includes an area of 7 million sq. km. In addition, Article 4(2) provides for the extension of the zone of operation of the Treaty to vast areas of the Pacific and Atlantic Oceans but the conditions to which such extension is subject have not yet been fulfilled.

As at 31 December 1980, the Treaty was in force for 22 states but they did not include Argentina, Brazil, Chile or Cuba.

Under Additional Protocol I to the Treaty, it is open to 'all extra-continental and continental states having *de jure* or *de facto* international responsibility for territories situated in the zone of application of the Treaty' (France, the Netherlands, the United Kingdom and the United States) to undertake to apply 'the status of denuclearisation in respect of warlike purposes', as defined in the Treaty, to such territories. As at 31 December 1980, only the Netherlands and the United Kingdom had ratified Protocol I.

Under Additional Protocol II to the Treaty, it is open to the nuclear-weapon states to undertake to respect 'the status of denuclearisation of Latin America in respect of war-like purposes', as defined in the Treaty; not to contribute to acts involving a violation of the Treaty; and not to use or threaten to use nuclear weapons against the Parties to the Treaty. All five of the nuclear powers are now bound by these undertakings.

2.3 The Seabed Delimitarisation Treaty, 1971 The Treaty on the Prohibition of the Emplacement of Nuclear Weapons on the Seabed and the Ocean Floor and in the Subsoil Thereof of 11 February 1971 entered into force on 18 May 1972. Brief comment will be made on the scope of the Treaty both in terms of weapon systems covered and geographically, and also on the gaps in the Treaty.

Weapon systems covered Though the text is far from clear, it would appear that the prohibition contained in Article I of the Treaty extends to chemical and biological weapons and nuclear mines anchored to, or emplaced on, the seabed; that it probably includes vehicles, carrying or designed to carry weapons of mass destruction, that can navigate only when in contact with the sea-bed; that it would include certain other weapon systems if in fact they became weapons of mass destruction (for example, weather modifiers, lasers, anti-satellite weapons); and that it does not include conventional mines. Much more important, however, is the fact that vehicles which can navigate in the water above the sea-bed and submarines have to be viewed in the same way as any other ships; submarines would therefore not be violating the treaty if they were either anchored to, or resting on, the sea-bed. It is the failure of the Treaty to disturb in any way the deployment of nuclear missile-firing submarines which has lead to criticism of the Treaty as an agreement not to do what no one intended to do in any case.

Geographical scope A distinction must be made between (1) the area seaward of a 12-mile coastal zone and (2) the 12-mile coastal zone. Where a coastal state claims a territorial sea of a breadth of less than 12 miles, a further distinction is necessary between the territorial sea and the area between the seaward limit of the territorial sea and the seaward limit of the 12-mile coastal zone.

1 In the area seaward of a 12-mile coastal zone, the prohibition applies to all states parties to the Treaty. Under Article I(1) of the Treaty, the prohibition applies to the seabed and ocean floor, and the subsoil thereof, beyond the outer limit of the seabed zone as defined in Article II. Article II indicates that the outer limit is to be 'coterminous with the 12-mile outer limit' of the contiguous zone provided for in Article 24 of the Geneva Convention on the Territorial Sea and the Contiguous Zone and that it is to be measured 'in accordance with the provisions of part I, section II, of that Convention [which *inter alia* specifies the baseline from which the territorial sea and the contiguous zone are to be measured] and in accordance with international law' in those cases which the Convention does not regulate, for example 'historic waters' and bays the coasts of which belong to more than one state.

2 In the 12-mile coastal zone, the general rule is that the Treaty prohibitions apply to all states other than the coastal state. However, no limitation is placed on the right of the coastal state to invite other allied states to emplace weapons of mass destruction on the seabed of its territorial sea.

For coastal states claiming a territorial sea of less than 12 miles the position is slightly different. So far as the coastal state is concerned, the ban would not apply in any part of the 12-mile zone, even though it has no sovereignty over that part lying outside its territorial sea. Because of this lack of sovereignty, however, it has no right to invite allied states to install weapons of mass destruction in this intermediate area.

Gaps in the Treaty The main criticisms to which the Treaty has been subjected can be summed up as follows: the Treaty does not affect: (1) the stationing of submarines on the seabed; (2) the installation there of Anti-Submarine Warfare (ASW) devices; and (3) the installation of conventional weapons on the seabed. Moreover, it does not provide for the establishment of a satisfactory system of verification.

2.4 SALT Agreements

At the close of the first phase of the Strategic Arms Limitation Talks (SALT) between the Soviet Union and the United States on 26 May 1972, two agreements were signed: the Treaty on the Limitation of Anti-Ballistic Missile System (the 'ABM Treaty') and the Interim Agreement on Certain Measures with Respect to the Limitation of Strategic Offensive Arms (the 'Interim Agreement'). The two Agreements entered into force on 3 October 1972. There can be little doubt that the SALT Agreements have made a much more substantial contribution to the demilitarisation of hydrospace than the Seabed Demilitarisation Agreement, though, as will be seen, they leave intact the considerable nuclear submarine forces of the two super-powers.

In the present context, the Interim Agreement is the more important of the two but the ABM Treaty does refer to the marine environment to a limited extent.

The ABM Agreement The basic provision is contained in Article I(1), under which, 'Each Party undertakes to limit anti-ballistic missile (ABM) systems and to adopt other measures in accordance with the provisions of this Treaty'. One way in which this limitation is to be effected is specified in Article V(1), under which: 'Each Party undertakes not to develop, test, or deploy ABM systems or components which are *sea-based*, air-based, or mobile land-based' *(emphasis added)*.

The Interim Agreement The basic provisions of the Interim Agreement (so far as the marine arena is concerned) are contained in Articles III and IV and are spelled out in more detail in the Protocol to the Agreement:

> The Parties undertake to limit submarine-launched ballistic missile (SLBM) launchers and modern ballistic missile submarines to the numbers operational and under construction on the date of signature of this Interim Agreement, and in addition launchers and submarines constructed under procedures established by the Parties as replacements for an equal number of ICBM launchers on older submarines. *(Article III)*
>
> Subject to the provisions of this Interim Agreement, modernisation and replacement of strategic offensive ballistic missiles and launchers covered by this interim agreement may be undertaken. *(Article IV)*

Reading Articles II and IV and the Protocol together, the position is as follows. Quite unconditionally, the United States may have 656 SLBMs *on nuclear powered submarines* and the Soviet Union may have 740. In addition, the United States may have a further 54 SLBMs (making a total ceiling figure of 710) and the Soviet Union a further 110 SLBMs (making a total ceiling figure of 950), provided they satisfy the conditions laid down in the Protocol. These are that, if the additional SLBMs are to be deployed on nuclear-powered submarines, they may only become operational as replacements for equal numbers of the older type of ICBM launcher used prior to 1964 or of launchers on older submarines. If, however, the additional SLBMs are deployed on submarines other than nuclear-powered submarines, they are not required to be replacements but they do count in calculating the total SLBM arsenal of the state concerned and this total must not exceed the ceiling of 710 (United States) or 950 (USSR).

Finally, a ceiling is also placed upon the numbers of modern ballistic missile submarines which the two powers may have. The figures are 44 for the United States and 62 for the Soviet Union.

The Interim Agreement was intended to remain in force for a maximum of five years (until 3 October 1977) but the two Parties formally stated in September 1977 that they intended to refrain from any actions incompatible with its provisions or with the objectives sought in the SALT II talks. SALT II (Treaty on the Limitation of Strategic Offensive Arms) and a Protocol Thereof were signed on 18 June 1979 but have not entered into force. In 1982 SALT was succeeded by START (Strategic Arms Reduction Talks).

3 Blockades

The term 'blockade' covers a number of different types of naval operation undertaken on the basis of a number of different rules of international law. They may be classified as

(1) Wartime blockades; (2) Pacific blockades based on reprisal; (3) Blockades by way of self defence; and (4) Blockades authorised by the United Nations.

3.1 Wartime blockades Under the laws of war, a belligerent is entitled to establish a blockade of the enemy coast thus isolating the blockaded area from maritime communications. Paper blockades are forbidden; they must be effective and maintained by a force strong enough to prevent access to and egress from the ports concerned. Wartime blockades must be limited to enemy ports, applied impartially against ships of all states and declared and notified in advance to neutral states.

3.2 Pacific blockades based on reprisals A clear distinction must be made between the position under international customary law and that under the Charter of the United Nations.

Under international customary law, a state was entitled to resort to a pacific blockade by way of reprisal. If, for example, State A declined to make reparation for its unlawful detention of State B nationals, State B might bring pressure to bear by establishing a blockade of State A's ports. Such a retaliatory act, normally illegal, was regarded as an act of reprisal, justified by the prior tortious (wrongful) act of State A. Such acts of reprisal had to be more or less proportionate to the original offence. Such a blockade differed from the wartime blockade in that it must not disturb the ingress and egress of ships of third states.

The right to employ forcible reprisals for the recovery of debts owed by states to foreign nationals was limited by Hague Convention II of 1907 (the Porter Convention) but a much more far-reaching restriction is now embodied in Article 2(4) of the United Nations Charter. Under this Paragraph, the threat or use of any type of forcible reprisal is prohibited.

3.3 Blockades by way of self-defence Circumstances can be envisaged in which it would be lawful for State A to establish a blockade of State B's coast on the basis of the rules of international customary law on self-defence. It would be necessary to show, however, that as the result of the illegal act or omission of State B, the need for self-defence of State A was compelling and instant. Similarly, it might be possible to take such self-defensive action under Article 51 of the United Nations Charter. This notoriously ambiguous Article provides that 'Nothing in the present Charter shall impair the inherent right of individual or collective self-defence if an armed attack occurs against a Member of the United Nations. . . .'

The question of the legality of the Cuba Blockade established by the United States during the Cuban Missile Crisis in 1962 has been fully argued in the literature but it is difficult to square the action taken with either international customary law or the Charter.

3.4 Blockades authorised by the United Nations Under Chapter VII of the United Nations Charter, the Security Council may determine the existence of a threat to the peace, breach of the peace or act of aggression and may then decide what measures are to be taken to maintain or restore international peace and security. Such measures may include the complete or partial interruption of sea communications by means not involving the use of armed forces (Article 41) or such action as may be necessary by air, sea or land forces. Blockade is specifically included among these forceful measures (Article 42). A good example is provided by the Security Council's Resolution 221 of 9 April 1966, whereby it called upon the United Kingdom Government to prevent by the use of force if necessary the arrival at Beira of vessels reasonably believed to be carrying oil destined for Rhodesia.

4 Naval surveillance activities

Provided that the various forms of naval surveillance are practised on the high seas, they are in principle legitimate exercises of the freedom of the high seas. Equally clearly, such activities in the territorial sea of another state would be inconsistent with the conditions of innocent passage.

Doubts are sometimes raised about the legality of the emplacement on the seabed of another state's continental shelf of sonabuoys, hydrophones and other detection equipment. The better view probably is that such installations are not illegal provided they do not interfere with the sovereign rights of the coastal state for the exploration of the continental shelf and the exploitation of its natural resources.

The anxiety of naval commanders to derive maximum intelligence information from tattletale shadowing of other ships has in the past led to a dangerous deterioration in seamanship with increased risks of collision and consequent diplomatic conflict. In an attempt to reduce the dangers inherent in this practice of 'shadowing', 'buzzing' or otherwise harassing each other's vessels, the Soviet Union and the United States signed in 1972 an Agreement on Prevention of Incidents at Sea.

5 Protection of sea-bed exploitation

The protection from both terrorist attacks and inter-state hostilities of continental shelf installations and, in future, deep-sea mining sites is obviously an important strategic objective of naval forces. In such cases the principle of self-defence would usually provide the necessary legal basis for action. It will be recalled that under the Geneva Convention on the Continental Shelf, 1958 (Article 5), coastal states are entitled to establish 500-metre safety zones around continental shelf installations and to take in these zones measures necessary for their protection. Correspondingly, ships of all nationalities must respect such safety zones. Similar provisions are incorporated in Articles 60 (exclusive economic zone) and 80 (continental shelf) of the UN Convention.

7 The legal regime of scientific research

Ideally, the scientific researcher would be as oblivious of the existence of national maritime frontiers as are the fish and other objects of his research. Unfortunately, he does not enjoy such freedom but is subject to far-reaching restraints which vary from one jurisdictional zone to another.

Prior to 1945, which may be taken as the starting point for the development of rules on the continental shelf, there was little need for complex rules to govern the relatively small amount of marine scientific research which then existed. The only rules were implied in the two fundamental principles which operated in the marine arena. Thus, landward of the outer limit of the territorial sea, the principle of sovereignty implied that the consent of the coastal state was required for research in internal waters and the territorial sea. Beyond the territorial sea, the principle of the freedom of the high seas implied that scientific research was open to all.

However, by 1958 the coastal state had become concerned to protect its sovereign rights in the resources of the continental shelf and certain restraints on scientific research were incorporated in Article 5 of the Geneva Convention on the Continental Shelf. Since 1958, scientists have expressed growing concern over the obstacles placed in the way of their work by the ever-expanding claims of coastal states to jurisdiction over a variety of offshore zones and, partly as a result of their protests, expressed by bodies such as the Intergovernmental Oceanographic Commission and the International Council for the Exploration of the Sea, extensive provision is made to facilitate marine scientific research in Part XIII of the UN Convention on the Law of the Sea.

1 Research in internal waters

No scientific research may be conducted in the internal waters of a foreign state without that state's consent. Ports are an important part of internal waters and in the past, difficulties in connection with foreign port calls have created impediments to research in the offshore zones of the port states concerned. Sometimes extensive advance notice has been required, or visas have been delayed or customs difficulties encountered. Some attempt to improve the position has been made in the UN Convention but it is doubtful if it will be effective in changing the attitude of states which have applied a restrictive policy in the past.

Article 248 imposes a duty on states and competent international organisations intending to conduct research in the EEZ or on the continental shelf to provided specified details of their plans to the coastal state not less than six months ahead of the project. Article 255 complements this provision by requiring that:

> States shall endeavour to adopt reasonable rules, regulations and procedures to promote and facilitate marine scientific research conducted in accordance with this Convention beyond their territorial sea and, as appropriate, to facilitate, subject to the provisions of their laws and regulations, access to their harbours and promote assistance for marine scientific research vessels which comply with the relevant provisions of this Part.

2 Research in the territorial sea

Although the Geneva Convention on the Territorial Sea and the Contiguous Zone, 1958, made no express reference to scientific research, it is clear that the position as stated in Article 245 of the UN Convention is simply a codification of the existing rules. Article 245 provides that:

> Coastal states, in the exercise of their sovereignty, have the exclusive right to regulate, authorise and conduct marine scientific research in their territorial sea. Marine scientific research therein shall be conducted only with the express consent of and under the conditions set forth by the coastal state.

It is sometimes argued that certain kinds of scientific research could properly be conducted incidentally, in the course of innocent passage through the territorial sea. However, there is no question but that the coastal state has the right to prohibit all kinds of scientific research. While it seems that in practice meteorological research is not usually interfered with, there is abundant evidence that most coastal states will not tolerate the use of other kinds of electronic gear, with the exception of that required for navigational purposes. Given the information-gathering activities of Soviet 'trawlers' and American 'environmental research' vessels, not to mention the notorious involvement of the CIA in the operation of the *Glomar Challenger*, such an attitude is understandable, if highly regrettable, from the standpoint of genuine marine research.

Article 245 is complemented by Articles 19, 40 and 54, which make it quite clear that foreign ships, including marine scientific research and hydrographic survey ships, may not carry out any research or survey activities when engaged in innocent passage, transit passage or archipelagic sea lanes passage through the territorial sea, straits or archipelagic waters.

3 Research in the EEZ and on the continental shelf

Under Article 5(1) of the Geneva Convention on the Continental Shelf, 1958, it was provided that the coastal state, in exercising its sovereign rights for the exploration of the continental shelf and the exploitation of its natural resources, must not cause 'any interference with fundamental oceanographic or other scientific research carried out with the intention of open publication'. The significance of this safeguard was, however, considerably weakened by the provision in Article 5(8) that the consent of the coastal state had to be obtained 'for any research concerning the continental shelf and undertaken there'. The further requirement that consent should not be withheld if the request was submitted by a qualified institution, with a view to purely scientific research into the physical or biological characteristics of the continental shelf, was subject to the qualification that this should 'normally' be so, thus providing the coastal state with a virtually uncontrollable escape clause.

The corresponding provision in the UN Convention, Article 246, which applies not only to the continental shelf but also to the EEZ, embodies a very much more complex 'consent regime'. At first sight, this regime is much more favourable to the researcher than the Geneva regime, though there are loopholes here, too, for the coastal state which wishes to deny or delay the grant of consent. The principal features of the new regime may be summarised as follows:

1 The consent of the coastal state is required.

2 Coastal states must *in normal circumstances* grant their consent for projects by other states or competent international organisations, provided they are to be *(a)* carried out in accordance with the Convention, *(b)* exclusively for peaceful purposes and *(c)* in order to increase scientific knowledge of the marine environment for the benefit of all mankind. Compliance with the condition in *(a)* above, would require that the research was conducted 'with appropriate scientific methods and means compatible with' the Convention; that it did not 'unjustifiably interfere with other legitimate uses of the sea'; and that it complied with regulations for the protection and preservation of the marine environment' (Article 240). The inclusion of the phrase 'in normal circumstances' does of course offer the same escape clause as in the Geneva Convention.

3 Coastal states may withhold consent if the project *(a)* is 'of direct significance for' the exploration and exploitation of natural resources; *(b)* involves drilling, the use of explosives or the introduction of harmful substances into the marine environment; *(c)* involves the construction, operation or use of artificial islands, installations and structures; or *(d)* contains inaccurate information on its nature and objectives.

4 Consent may not be withheld under 3*(a)* above for projects concerning the natural resources of the continental shelf beyond the 200-mile line, provided the site of the research lies outside areas publicly designated by the coastal state as areas in which exploitation or detailed exploratory operations are occurring or will occur within a reasonable period.

5 Consent may be implied upon expiry of six months from the date of submission of the required information unless within four months of that date the coastal state has *(a)* withheld its consent under Article 246; *(b)* challenged the authenticity of the stated nature of objectives of the project; *(c)* required further information; or *(d)* drawn attention to outstanding obligations arising from an earlier project.

6 Article 264, read with Part XV(2) and Article 297, provides a major loophole for any coastal state wishing to avoid its obligations to consent to scientific research on its continental shelf or EEZ. Although disputes regarding the Convention's provisions on marine scientific research are in general subject to the compulsory settlement procedures laid down in Part XV(2), an exception is made for any dispute arising out of the exercise by the coastal state of a right or discretion in accordance with Article 246 or a decision by the coastal state to order suspension or cessation of a research project under Article 253. The coastal state is not obliged to subject such disputes to a binding settlement procedure and is bound only to accept resort to 'compulsory conciliation'. Unfortunately, the conciliation commission may not call in question the exercise of the coastal state's discretion to designate areas of the continental shelf beyond the 200-mile line as areas in which consent to research may be refused (see (4) above); nor its discretion to withhold consent under Article 246(5). More fundamentally, however, the conciliation commission is not in any event empowered to give a binding ruling on the dispute.

4 Research in the 'Area'

The provision made for scientific research in the sea-bed 'Area' beyond the limits of national jurisdiction (see *1 General* above) reflects the new status of the Area and its resources as the common heritage of mankind. Under Articles 143 and 256 of the UN Convention, the basic principle is that such research is to be carried out exclusively for peaceful purposes and for the benefit of mankind as a whole. The International Sea-bed Authority is empowered to carry out research and to promote and encourage such research by states parties and competent international organisations. It has also to coordinate and disseminate the results of such research. States parties, too, are authorised to conduct research and are under an obligation to promote international cooperation of such research by various specified means.

5 Research in the high seas

Prior to UNCLOS III, marine scientific research was simply one of the freedoms of the high seas to be exercised with reasonable regard to the interests of other states in their exercise of the freedom of the high seas. Under the UN Convention, however, the legal framework has been radically altered. As has been seen, a large part of what was formerly high seas is now incorporated in 200-mile EEZs and separate research regimes have been provided both for the EEZ and the 'Area', that is, the zone which used to be simply the seabed and subsoil of the high seas. Accordingly, to avoid confusion, Article 257 refers to research in 'the water column beyond the exclusive economic zone' and provides that all states and competent international organisations have the right, in conformity with the Convention, to conduct research in this zone.

Glossary

A

Abandonment (of shipping) When a constructive total loss (CTL) *q.v.* is claimed, the assured may either treat the loss as a partial loss or abandon the vessel to the underwriters and claim for total loss.

Abyssal Referring to that part of the ocean between a depth of about 2000 to 6000 m.

Abyssal hills Small irregular hills, rising to a height of 30 to 1000 m, that cover large areas of the ocean floor. They are especially common in the Pacific Ocean.

Abyssal plain A very flat portion of the ocean floor underlain by sediments. The slope of this feature is less than 1:1000.

Abyssopelagic zone The marine biological zone extending from about 2000 m downwards. Although life at such depths is sparse compared with more shallow ocean zones, a wide variety of organisms are found here, including sponges, worms, echinoderms, crustaceans and molluscs.

Advection fog Sea fog which forms where warm, moist air flows over a colder surface. It occurs mainly in spring and summer and can be a serious hazard to shipping.

Agar agar A jelly prepared from seaweeds and used in bacteria-culture, medicine, glue-making, silk-dressing and cooking.

Aggregates Gravel, crushed stone, sand and other materials which are mixed with cement and water to make concrete.

AGI Soviet intelligence gathering ship.

Algae Chlorophyll-containing plants of the division Thallophyta. Most marine plants are classed as algae.

Alginate A salt of alginic acid which is extracted from certain seaweeds and used in plastics, medicine, etc.

Amphidromic points The nodal points where sea level remains constant and around which tides rotate.

Amphipod One of the Amphipoda, an order of small sessile (flat) eyed crustaceans with both swimming feet and jumping feet.

Amphora A two-handled jar used by the Greeks and Romans for holding liquids.

Anadromous Animals that migrate from the sea to freshwater (usually a river) to spawn.

Anaerobic Refers to those organisms which are not dependent on the presence of oxygen in the sea or air.

Annelida A class comprising the red-blooded worms including marine worms, which have long bodies made up of jointed segments.

Antarctic convergence A narrow, meandering zone between latitudes 50° and 60° separating the cold water which surrounds Antarctica from the warmer water of middle latitudes; across the zone there is an abrupt change of temperature, occasionally as much as 5°C over a few hundred metres.

Antarctic intermediate water Cold Antarctic water which sinks beneath warmer water north of the Antarctic convergence.

Anthelmintic A drug extracted from red algae (Rhodophyta) used to destroy worms in infested intestines.

Anticyclones Weather systems in which air flows outwards from centres of high pressure. Light winds, good visibility and settled weather are characteristics of anticyclones.

Apatite A mineral consisting of calcium phosphate and fluoride found in all types of rock. As a result of weathering on the Earth's surface, much of it is dissolved and eventually reaches the sea where some is deposited on the sea floor and some taken up by plankton.

Aphotic zone That part of the ocean where not enough light is present for photosynthesis by plants.

Aquaculture The cultivation or farming of the ocean for food, usually by traditional methods.

Arabinsylcytidine An anti-tumour compound extracted from sponges.

Aragonite A calcium carbonate mineral found in near-surface deposits. It is the principal material in corals and pearls.

Archipelagic State Under the 1982 UN Convention on the Law of the Sea an archipelagic state (constituted by one or more archipelagos *q.v.*) may adopt a system of straight baselines *q.v.* enclosing the archipelago.

Archipelago A group of islands, interconnecting waters and other natural features so closely interrelated as to form an intrinsic geographical, economic and political entity.

Area, The The area beyond the limits of national jurisdiction (i.e. beyond the outer limit of the continental shelf) for which UNCLOS III has attempted to establish a new legal regime. Under the UN Convention on the Law of the Sea, the mineral resources of the Area, especially manganese nodules, would be the 'common heritage of mankind'.

ARPA (Automatic Radar Plotting Aids) Devices attached to ships which automatically assess collision risks.

Artificial harbour A harbour where the necessary protection from wind, sea and waves is provided by man-made jetties or breakwaters.

Artificial islands In some parts of the world the need for land to grow food, space for housing or industrial sites, or port extensions has led to the building of man-made islands, normally by filling in and reclaiming areas of sea near the coast. These islands are also used as offshore harbours for tankers and as deepwater ports. Many are located off the west coast of North America, and the coasts of Japan, the Netherlands and the Middle East.

Artificial propagation The captive breeding of sea fishes in controlled environments.

Artisanal fisheries Traditional fisheries which use simple fishing vessels and equipment; such fisheries employ most of the world's fishermen.

Asthenosphere A shell or layer within the Earth (also known as the upper mantle) beginning approximately 100 km below the Earth's surface and extending to a depth of 250 km.

ASW Anti-submarine warfare.

ASWC Anti-submarine warfare carrier.

ASWCCCS Anti-submarine warfare centre command and control system.

ATL Actual total loss; casualty classification of ship in Lloyds Register.

Atoll A circular or oval-shaped coral reef (which may have islands or islets in it) enclosing a body of water called a lagoon *q.v.*

Authigenic Applied to minerals, including manganese and phosphorite nodules, zealites, glauconite and other clay minerals, that are direct inorganic sediments from sea water.

Autotroph An organism which produces its own food from inorganic material using light or chemical energy.

Autotrophic bacteria Bacteria that produce their own food from inorganic compounds.

Azimuth The arc of the horizon between the meridian of a place and a vertical circle passing through any celestial body.

B

BACAT (barge aboard catamaran) System for carrying maritime cargoes on barges to inland river ports after unloading from a catamaran-type 'mother' ship.

Baguio Name for tropical cyclone in the Philippines.

Baleen Horny plates (whalebones) growing from palates of certain whales and used instead of teeth for sieving plankton.

Ballistic missile A guided missile or rocket, launched at a surface target, which follows a ballistic trajectory (i.e. moving under its own momentum and through force of gravity) through the outer atmosphere to reach its target.

Barratry In criminal law, includes any fraudulent practice committed by the master or crew to the prejudice of the owner or charterer of a vessel.

Barrier reef A reef mainly composed of coral that runs parallel to land but is separated from it by a deep lagoon.

Basalt Fine-grained, dark coloured igneous rock; the most abundant volcanic rock covering or underlying the sediments of ocean floors.

Baseline Line along the coast separating the state's internal waters *q.v.* from the territorial sea *q.v.* The breadth of the various maritime zones is measured from the baseline. Usually follows low water line but may consist of straight baselines off highly indented coasts or around archipelagos *q.v.*

Bathyal zone Zone between edge of continental shelf and ocean floor from about 200 m to 2000 m in depth, or to where temperatures do not exceed 4°C.

Bathymetry The measurement of the depth of an ocean, sea or other larger body of water.

Bathypelagic zone Marine biological zone at bathyal *q.v.* depths; amount of living material and number of species is relatively small, but includes black fishes, red shrimps and gelatinous squid.

Bathythermograph An instrument used to measure temperature in the ocean.

Bauxite Clay compound containing aluminium.

Bay Coastal indentation constituting more than a mere curvature of the coast. Legal bays may be closed by a straight baseline *q.v.* with enclosed waters being internal waters *q.v.*

Beaches Unconsolidated sediments (generally sand or gravel) that cover parts or all of the shore.

Beam trawl A bag-shaped net in which the top of the net is fastened to a heavy beam held above the sea bed by shoes so that the mouth of the net is kept open as it is dragged along the sea bed.

Beaufort scale Measure of wind speed which varies from 0 for calm to 12 for hurricane, devised in 1805 by Sir Francis Beaufort.

Beneficial ownership National ownership of ships registered under flags of convenience. The world's main beneficial owners are the USA, Greece, Hong Kong and Western European countries.

Benthic Relating to the bottom of the sea.

Benthopelagic zone Marine biological zone at the bottom of the sea characterised by a wide diversity of life, including slowing moving and sedentary organisms.

Benthos The sea floor.

Bergy bits Floating pieces of glacier ice rising up to 5 m above the surface level of the water they are floating in and usually about 10 m across.

Bicarbonate Acid salt of carbonic acid.

Bioluminescence Also called phosphorescence; emission of light by living marine organisms which appears as a shimmering glow on the ocean surface. It is most frequently found in warm, tropical seas.

Biomass Extent and variation of marine life in any given ocean zone, dependent on depth of water, availability of light, food, temperature and pressure.

Bivalves Aquatic animals having a shell in two valves or parts, e.g. oysters, mussels and clams.

Blockade Prevention by force or threat of force of ingress or egress of shipping to or from a port or coastal waters.

Blow-out preventers (BOP) In off-shore drilling, a series of valves, cutters and rams, controlled hydraulically from the surface and used to cut off pressure leaks of gas or oil.

BOD (biological oxygen demand) The amount of oxygen required to degrade the organic material and oxidise reduced substances in a water sample; used as a measure of the oxygen requirement of bacterial populations in serving as an index of water pollution.

Boreal Of or relating to the North.

Boron Non-metallic element existing as brown amorphous powder or dark crystals; occurs in borax or boric acid.

Bottom water Cold, dense water found at the bottom of an ocean basin.

Bottom water currents Usually slow-moving except on western margins of ocean basins where they can exceed 20 cm/sec.

Brackish water Water in which salinity ranges from approximately 0.50 to 17.00 parts per 1000 (‰).

Breakbulk cargo Unconsolidated loads of commodities in bales, boxes or loose. The term is to distinguish these from bulk homogeneous loads and unitised loads in containers.

Brightness temperature A measure of an ice sheet's temperature and its reflectivity.

Bromide A salt of hydrobromic acid.

Bromine A non-metallic element chemical which occurs in salts found in sea water.

Bulk cargoes Large consignments of loose cargo (grain, iron ore, coal) usually travelling in full ship loads between two named ports and normally arranged under the terms of a charter party.

Bulk terminal Purpose-built terminal facilities, often equipped with automatic handling equipment such as conveyor belts, pipelines, etc., at which bulk cargoes are loaded/discharged, stacked and stored ready for onward movement.

Bunkering facilities Points within a port at which ships can take on, either from shore side tanks or from tanker vessels moored alongside, heavy fuel oil and diesel oil for the propulsion of main and auxilliary engines.

C

Cadmium A bluish white metal, obtained mainly as a by-product in the processing of zinc ores.

Caesium Soft metallic element which ignites in air and combines vigorously with water to form powerful alkali. Used in photoelectric cells.

Calcareous Composed of calcium carbonate.

Calcite The main mineral of calcium carbonate ($CaCO_3$).

Calcite compensation depth (CCD) Depth where the supply of calcium carbonate towards the sea floor is balanced by the rate at which it dissolves; generally at depths of 3.5–4.5 km.

Calcium A metal which does not occur in the free state in nature, although its compounds are extremely abundant; an essential constituent of living organisms.

Calving Of icebergs; the breaking away of a mass of ice from a glacier or ice shelf.

Cannon shot rule A reference to the historical basis of the traditional (but now largely superseded) 3 nm breadth of the territorial sea; alleged to be based on the range of cannon from coast.

Carbonate Salt of carbonic acid.

Cargo sharing Allocating cargoes to national flag ships on basis of imports and exports.

Carnivores Flesh eaters. Seals, walruses, whales, etc., are marine carnivores.

Carrack Large cargo ship, also fitted for fighting, which sailed the Mediterranean in the 15th and 16th centuries.

Carrageen Reddish brown edible seaweed of N. Europe and N. America, the extract of which is used in jellies, lotions and surgical dressings.

Cassiterite Hard, dense oxide of tin; chief source of the metal.

Catadromous Of fishes, descending periodically for spawning to the lower parts of a river or to the sea (e.g. some eels).

Catastrophic waves Large waves which may result from intense storms or from slumping of submarine rocks or sediments, and which can cause immense damage and loss of life.

CCOP/SOPAC *See Committee for Coordination of Joint Prospecting for mineral resources in South Pacific offshore areas.*

Cellular container vessel A vessel in which the cargo holds are fitted with a cellular guide system to receive and stack containers. They are normally referred to as first generation (approximately 800 TEU capacity), second generation (approximately 1500 TEU capacity), and third generation (up to 3000 TEU capacity).

Centrifugal force A force due to rotation that causes motion away or out from the rotating object.

Cephalopod Class of molluscs including squid, octopus, cuttlefish with prehensile tentacles around the mouth and usually with no shell.

Chimaeras Cartilaginous fishes with long, thread-like tail and large pectoral fins, often ranked with rays and sharks.

Chloride A compound of chlorine with another element.

Chlorophyll A group of green pigments found in plants that are essential for photosynthesis.

Chordata Highest phylum of animal kingdom including the vertebrates.

Chrysophyta Constituents of plankton; form diatomaceous *q.v.* earths which are used in cosmetics, as filtering aids and in chromatography.

Clean Ballast Tanks (CBT) The reserving of certain cargo tanks solely for ballast water.

Climate: long-range investigation, mapping and prediction study (CLIMAP) To determine surface ocean climatic fluctuations associated with glacial and inter-glacial transitions over the past 700 000 years.

Closing line The line closing the mouth of a legal bay *q.v.* or a river and forming part of the baseline *q.v.*

CMG Commission for Marine Geology (of International Union of Geological Sciences). Established March 1961. It aims to contribute to the advancement of investigations relating to the study of the Earth, considered from theoretical and practical points of view.

CNES Centre National d'Etudes Spatiales de France.

CNEXO Centre National pour l'Exploitation des Océans (France).

Coelenterata Phylum of aquatic, mainly marine, animals; includes corals, sea anemones and also jellyfish.

Coking coal Contains c.80 per cent carbon and used as smokeless fuel and in preparation of metals from their ores in blast furnaces.

Combined carrier A general purpose merchant vessel designed to carry bulk homogenous and non-homogenous type of cargo (e.g. iron ore and oil). The ship may be volume or deadweight limited for tonnage, according to the type of cargo it carries. *See also Appendix I.*

Committee for Coordination of Joint Prospecting for mineral resources in South Pacific offshore areas (CCOP/SOPAC) Established 1966 under UN Economic Commission for Asia and the Far East. It aims to promote and coordinate exploration by geophysical surveys and other means for new sources of mineral wealth under the shallow marine shelves adjoining land areas of member countries.

Common adventure Where a number of persons have a common interest in a marine venture, e.g. shipowner, cargo owner and underwriter.

Community (marine) An integrated group of organisms inhabiting a common area. These organisms may be dependent on each other or possibly on the environment. The community may be defined by their habitat or by the composition of the organisms.

Compensation depth The depth at which the oxygen produced by a plant during photosynthesis equals the amount the plant needs for respiration (during a 24-hour period).

Conference A collection of shipowners formed together in mutual interest on a particular trade in order to guarantee service rates and times. Essentially they form a cartel on that particular trade.

Conservative elements Elements in seawater whose ratio to other conservative elements remains constant. Examples are chlorine, sodium and magnesium.

Container ship One designed to take large standardised metal boxes containing different types of cargo.

Container terminal Purpose-built berth designed to accommodate container vessels and to handle the import and export of containers. Normally equipped with quay-side gantry cranes, large mobile equipment for in-terminal movements of containers, and container freight stations for the packing and unpacking of cargo.

Contiguous zone Maritime zone lying seaward of territorial sea *q.v.* and extending to a maximum of 24 nm from the baseline *q.v.* Coastal state has limited jurisdiction in the zone in relation to customs, immigration, fiscal and sanitary matters.

Continental crust Thick, discontinuous layer of the outer zone of the Earth which forms the continental landmasses.

Continental Drift theory Theory proposed by Alfred Wegener in 1912 that continents are not static masses but are part of the Earth's crust which is in motion over the Earth's surface.

Continental margin Zone (consisting of shelf, slope and rise) separating the continent from the deep ocean floor.

Continental rise Most seaward zone of the continental margin, characterised by a gentle slope (1:100) descending to the oceanic depths.

Continental shelf Shallow, gently sloping zone extending from shoreline to a depth where there is a marked increase in slope towards oceanic depths; this usually occurs at about 128 m but may be between 35 m to 250 m.

Continental slope Zone extending from shelf edge to the beginning of the continental rise.

Continuous seismic profile A record produced by using a high energy acoustic device that shows thickness and structure of the upper layers of the ocean crust.

Convection currents Motion within a fluid due to differences in density or temperature.

Conventional weapon Any weapon, e.g. a missile, bomb or shell, fitted with a non-nuclear warhead.

Convergence zone (of surface water) Region where two converging currents meet, resulting in water of higher density sinking and then spreading out below the surface.

Cooperative Investigations in the Northern Part of the East Central Atlantic (CINECA) Comprehensive study comprising the monitoring of environmental and biological parameters over several years; surveys including exploratory fishing and acoustic surveys providing synoptic pictures of the area.

Cooperative Investigations of the Caribbean and Adjacent Regions (CICAR) A multidisciplinary programme studying upwelling, fisheries resources, marine pollution and coastal aquaculture in view of the possible construction of a sea-level canal.

Copepoda Class of minute crustaceans with single eye, no shell and oarlike swimming feet.

Coral Small marine organisms living in colonies in warm seas. Individuals (polyps) have calcareous skeletons which, after their death, accumulate to form coral reefs.

Coral reef Reef, often extending over large areas, composed chiefly of coral and coralline algae.

Cordonazo Name for tropical cyclone in Mexico and west coast of Central America.

Coriolis force An apparent force due to the Earth's rotation. This force causes moving objects to turn to the right in the northern hemisphere, and to the left in the southern hemisphere.

COW (crude oil washing) The cleaning or washing of crude oil tanks by dislodging residues of waxy and asphaltic substances using high pressure jets of crude oil.

Cratons Also known as shields; portions of continental crust composed of Precambrian rocks (600 million years or older), generally reduced by erosion to flat, low-lying areas.

Cruise missile A medium speed, tactical guided missile launched at a ship or other surface target. It uses a low trajectory or flight path to home on its target.

Cruiser Large surface gun- or missile-armed warship. Its original concept was a long-range vessel, independent of shore support for protracted periods while on trade protection.

Crustacean Large class of arthropods, mainly aquatic, including crabs, lobsters, barnacles, shrimps and water fleas.

CTL Constructive total loss; ship classification in Lloyds Register. Term applied when a ship is reasonably abandoned on account of its actual total loss being unavoidable or because it could not be preserved from actual total loss (ATL) without an expenditure which would exceed its value at the time when the expenditure occurred.

Cumulonimbus Towering mass of cloud usually topped by spreading anvil or plume, which brings heavy rain or snow and sometimes hail. It is frequently accompanied by lightning.

Curie Quantity of radioactive substance that undergoes 3.70×10^{10} radioactive transformations per second.

Curie point Temperature reached in cooling process of molten material at which any magnetic minerals present will begin to produce a magnetic field. Above this temperature magnetic properties are lost.

Cyanides Salts of hydrocyanic acid, used in extracting gold from low-grade metals, electroplating and steel hardening.

Cyanophyta Blue-green algae growing in water and on damp earth, rocks or bark.

Cyclone Weather system containing an approximately circular movement of air around a centre of low pressure. Strong winds, cloud formation and rain are typical of cyclones. *See also Tropical cyclones.*

D

Dam-atoll Saucer-shaped structure for exploiting wave energy which focuses waves to drive a turbine at its centre.

Dead reckoning Position determined in navigation based purely on direction and distance from a known point.

Decca navigation system Hyperbolic system giving position by measurement of phase differences between continuous-wave radio signals from land-based stations.

Decibar A measure of pressure equal to one tenth normal atmospheric pressure and approximately equal to the pressure change of 1 m depth in seawater.

Deep-focus earthquakes Originating from 300 km down to a depth of 700 km and generally confined to belts in western parts of Central and South America, Aleutian Islands and western margin of the Pacific Ocean.

Deep scattering layer A sound-reflecting layer caused by the presence of certain organisms in the water. The layer (or layers) rises toward the surface at night and descends when the sun rises.

Deep sea trenches Long, very deep depressions of the sea floor with relatively steep sides; usually found at depths over 6000 m.

Delta Roughly triangular area of alluvial deposits formed at the mouth of a river; also consists of distributory channels, lagoons and marshes.

Delta project (in the Netherlands) The coastal protection and water management scheme involving building of dams, sluices and storm-surge barriers in the Rhine–Scheldt delta region of Zeeland and south Holland.

Demersal Bottom-dwelling.

Density (of sea water) Mass of water per unit volume, which varies with pressure, temperature and salinity. Rises in temperature reduce density while increases in pressure and salinity increase it.

Depressions Weather systems in which air flows inwards towards centres of low pressure. They are characterised by strong winds and unsettled, cloudy, wet weather.

Desalination A variety of processes whereby the salts are removed from sea water resulting in water that may be used for human consumption.

Destroyer Medium-sized, high-speed warship with primary mission of supporting strike and amphibious forces.

Detrital deposits Sedimentary deposits resulting from the erosion and weathering of rocks.

Detritivores Detritus eaters, usually found on or near the sea floor, of which the most common are echinoderms.

Deuterium (H_3) Isotype of hydrogen, sometimes referred to as heavy water.

Diagenesis Chemical and physical changes to sediments after their deposition on the sea floor.

Diatom Microscopic aquatic plant with silica-containing shell which forms thick deposits of diatomaceous ooze on the sea floor.

Distant water fishery Conducted at ranges of hundreds or thousands of miles from home ports of vessels, in many of the oceanic tuna fisheries, sea fishing of salmon, and pelagic whaling.

Diurnal Occurring daily; referring to tides, one low and one high tide within one lunar day (about 24 hours 50 minutes).

Dived tons The difference between the fully submerged displacement and the displacement of the submarine when running on the surface.

Divergence zones Of surface water; region where ocean currents diverge, causing upwelling *q.v.* of cold, nutrient-rich water to the surface.

Doldrums Equatorial trough of low pressure between approx. 5°S and 5°N latitudes where the weather is unsettled and winds tend to be light and variable.

Dolomite Greyish-white mineral, carbonate of calcium and magnesium.

Domestic registry Of merchant ships, under same national flag and ownership.

Doppler principle The change in frequency of a signal received from a moving object. Frequency increases as the object approaches and decreases as it moves farther away.

Dracones Watertight rubber barges up to 90 m in length used to carry oil or other liquids in bulk.

Draught The depth of a loaded vessel in the water, from the level of the lowest point of the hull to the waterline.

Dredging Removal of sediment by mechanical or hydraulic techniques to provide required water depths.

Drift net A static gill net suspended from the surface of the sea by floats; drift nets may be joined end to end in fleets *q.v.* and hauled by a buss rope fixed below the line of nets, as developed by the Dutch for fishing herring in the North Sea.

DSDP (Deep Sea Drilling Project) Begun by US in 1968, later joined by UK, USSR, West Germany and France, with the objective of a major ocean floor reconnaisance of all basins except the Arctic.

Dugout Boat made by hollowing out the trunk of a tree.

DWT (Deadweight tonnage) *See Appendix I.*

Dysphotic zone The dimly illuminated zone in the sea between the euphotic and aphotic zones.

E

Earthquake A sudden motion of the earth caused by faulting or volcanic activity. Earthquakes can occur in the near surface rocks or down to a depth of up to 700 km. The actual area of the earthquake is called the focus; the point on the Earth's surface above the focus is called the epicentre.

Echinoderms Phylum of marine invertebrates, including starfish, brittle star, sea urchin, sea lily and sea cucumber.

Echo-sounder Device used to detect underwater objects and measure depths by projecting sound waves through water and registering the vibrations reflected back.

Ecology The study of the interactions of organisms with their physical, chemical, and biological environments.

Ecosystem A unit consisting of organisms and their effective environment.

Eddies (or ocean currents) Oceanic circulations ranging from a few metres to a few hundred kilometres in diameter. Typically they survive as recognisable entities for several days or a few weeks while moving within the surrounding ocean.

EEZ The 200-mile Exclusive Economic Zone in which the coastal state has extensive resource and management rights.

EFZ Exclusive Fishing Zones out to a distance of up to 200 miles from the coast have been widely claimed since the 1960s. Will probably now be gradually superseded by more comprehensive EEZs *q.v.*

Elasmobranchs Class of fishes, including sharks and skates, having a cartilaginous skeleton and plate-like gills.

Electrodialysis Use of electrical power to achieve separation or dissolution of materials, notably for the production of freshwater from sea water.

Enclosed dock Impounded area of water linked to port approaches by a lock entrance.

Energy coal Used in power plants, etc., and distinct from coking coal used in the steel industry.

Enforcement Enforcement of laws governing the use of the seas usually rests with the flag state unless, under a treaty (e.g. Fisheries Treaty), powers of enforcement have been granted to another state.

Epicentre *See Earthquake.*

Epipelagic zone Sunlit zone, extending from ocean surface to depth of about 100 m, where photosynthesis occurs;

biologically, the most important layer in the sea.

Episodic waves Also known as freak waves; generally produced by a combination of large waves and swell opposing a strong tidal stream or current near a continental edge.

Equidistance principle In maritime jurisdiction, the median line drawn at an equal distance from the coasts of opposite states.

Erosion The physical and chemical breakdown of a rock and the movement of its broken or dissolved particles from one place to another.

Estrecho Strait *(Spanish).*

Estuary Arm of the sea at the mouth of a tidal river where tidal effect is influenced by the river current.

Euler pole In plate tectonics, the pole of rotation for two plates migrating from each other.

Euphausiacea Shrimp-like crustaceans in which the gills are visible externally and the eight pairs of thoracic limbs are similar, with none modified as mouthparts. Includes the krill, principal food of the southern whalebone whales.

Euphotic zone The uppermost zone of the sea where there is sufficient light penetration for photosynthesis. In clear water the zone is typically 40 to 50 m deep in middle latitudes during summer and about 100 m deep in low latitudes.

Eutrophication Over-enrichment of a water body with nutrients, resulting in excessive growth of organisms and depletion of oxygen concentration.

Evaporation In meteorology, conversion of water into vapour; the rate of evaporation depends on the temperature, wind speed, turbulence and relative humidity of the air in the atmosphere.

Export processing zone Serving a similar purpose to free ports or free zones, it is normally located near a port or airport; it is equipped with the appropriate infrastructure facilities and provided with the regulations and incentives to encourage the importation and processing of raw materials.

F

FAMOUS *See French/American Mid-Ocean Underwater Study.*

FAO *See Food and Agricultural Organisation.*

Fathom A common unit measure of depth equal to 6 ft, or 1.83 m.

Fault In geology, a break or zone of fracture within the Earth's crust, along which movement of adjacent bodies of rock has occurred.

Feldspars Group of rock-forming aluminium silicate minerals which comprise about 50 per cent of the Earth's crust.

Fetch The distance over the sea surface that the wind blows in the area where waves are generated.

FGGE First GARP *q.v.* Global Experiment.

Fibre optics Branch of optics dealing with the transmission of light along very narrow, flexible glass cables.

Filaments The sinuous or meandering branches of the eastern edge of ocean currents, e.g. the Gulf Stream.

Finger piers Long, finger-shaped piers, typical of port of New York, designed to provide maximum berthing area per length of shoreline and to enable ports to utilise deeper water close inshore.

Fjord Narrow, elongated deep-water arm of the sea found along mountainous, glaciated coasts in high latitudes.

Flag discrimination Used to express policies adopted by governments to ensure a preferential treatment of the national fleet to the exclusion of other fleets and the carriage of a large percentage of nationally generated trade on national flag vessels. Also known as 'cargo preference'.

Flag of convenience *See FOC.*

Floating bases Also called factory ships; large vessels, often remaining at sea for months and which may be serviced periodically from home port, where daily catches from smaller ships are processed (salting, canning, freezing).

Floating policy One which describes ship insurance in general terms and leaves the name of ship or ships and other particulars to be defined by subsequent definition.

Flotsam Denotes goods which have been cast or lost overboard from a ship but can be recovered as floating objects.

Fluviatile Belonging to or formed from rivers.

Fluvioglacial Pertaining to glacial rivers.

FOC (Flag of convenience) A foreign flag under which a shipping company registers its tonnage to avoid taxation or other burdens at home.

Fold In geology, a structure formed by the bending or buckling of the Earth's crust.

Food and Agriculture Organisation (FAO) Established in Quebec in 1945. UN international agency based in Rome and promoting, among other activities, global exchange of information on fisheries, fish distribution and marketing.

Food chain Series of organisms connected by the fact that each forms food for the next higher organism in the series; in the sea, the chain goes from algae to sharks.

Foraminifera Class of microscopic animals with shells commonly made of calcium carbonate; skeletons of some species have accumulated to form thick deposits on ocean floor.

Fracture zone Major fault zone in Earth's surface forming extensive zone of irregular topography of the sea floor, with steep-sided ridges, troughs and escarpments.

Frazil The minute crystals of ice which form first when water begins to freeze.

Freeboard The distance between a vessel's deck and the water line.

Free port Port designated as a free trade zone where goods exported are exempted from customs duty and subjected to the minimum of customs regulations.

Freezing point The temperature at which a liquid freezes or solidifies at normal pressure. For freshwater this temperature is 0 °C (or 32 °F), for normal seawater (salinity about 35‰) the freezing temperature is −1.9 °C (28 °F).

French/American Mid-Ocean Underwater Study (FAMOUS) Study of the Mid-Atlantic Ridge plate tectonics, the formation of new crust and the possible formation of hydrothermal rocks and metalliferous sediments.

Frigate Medium sized warship of moderate to high speed, with primary mission of escort and independent deployment.

Fry Swarm of young fishes just spawned.

G

Gabbro A coarse-grained, dark coloured igneous rock consisting of olivine, pyroxene and plagioclase.

Gadoid Fishes of the cod family.

Gantry crane A rail-mounted or rubber-tyred metal structure supporting a travelling crane with a horizontal boom under which loads can be lifted and moved in both horizontal and vertical directions.

GARP Global Atmospheric Research Programme.

GATE GARP *q.v.* Atlantic Tropical Experiment.

Gears In fisheries, the equipment used to catch fish, e.g. nets, lines, pots and traps.

General Bathymetric Chart of the Oceans (GEBCO) Detailed map of the ocean floor; first edition published 1903, 5th and latest 1982.

Geodesy Science of measuring the Earth and determining its shape.

Geoid The geoid, the shape of the ocean at rest, approximates to a spheroid (a regular geometric figure) but it departs from the spheroid because the pull of gravity is not uniform, causing the mean ocean surface to form hummocks and hollows. At the zero contour, geoid and spheroid are in contact, and gravity agrees with its theoretical value. Where the geoid rises, gravity is less than the theoretical value (negative gravity) and greater where the geoid descends below the zero contour (positive gravity).

Geomorphology The study of the shape of the Earth's surface and the processes that control and modify these features.

GEOSECS Geochemical Ocean Sections Study. (Study of the oceanic circulation and mixing processes.)

Geostrophic current A current in which the horizontal pressure gradient is balanced by the Coriolis force *q.v.* These currents can be calculated by careful measurement of temperature and salinity at closely-spaced localities.

Gill nets Trap swimming fish by the gills; and may be set below the surface, mid-water or on the bottom.

GIPME *See Global Investigation of Pollution in the Marine Environment.*

Glaciation Covering and modification of the Earth's surface by glaciers; mountain glaciation generally increases sharpness and steepness of landscape, continental glaciation produces a flatter topography.

Glacier River of ice formed in high mountains and polar regions.

Glauconite Mineral formed in the sea; a hydrated potassium iron and aluminium silicate.

Global Investigation of Pollution in the Marine Environment (GIPME) Study of pollutants entering the sea from land by routes other than rivers; domestic and industrial outfalls, direct run off, ocean dumping.

Globigerina Species of foraminifera, shells of which form soft, fine-grained, limy material on ocean floor.

Gnomonic projection Used to produce a chart or map on which great circles appear as straight lines.

Goethite Hydrated iron oxide.

Gondwanaland A major landmass of the Mesozoic era that included most of the present landmasses of the southern hemisphere.

GPS (Global positioning system) A satellite navigation system using high orbital satellites.

Grazing The feeding by zooplankton upon phytoplankton.

Great circle The shortest distance between two places on the surface of the globe. The great circle track of a ship crosses the meridians at different angles.

Group of 77 Term used for the group of developing countries at many of the United Nations conferences as distinct from the socialist countries (Group C) and the developed countries (Group B).

Growlers Small icebergs which lie so low in the water that they are almost awash.

GRT (gross registered tonnage) *See Appendix I.*

Guano Accumulated excrement of sea birds, rich in phosphate and nitrogen, found especially in the islands off Peru.

Guyot Also called tablemount; submarine volcanic mountain having a comparatively smooth, flat top.

Gyre In ocean currents, a circulation several hundred kilometres in diameter.

H

Hadal zone Oceanic zone confined to deep ocean trenches below 6000 m.

Haehyop Strait *(Korean).*

Hanseatic (League) Medieval trading organisation of North German towns with companies at most seaports on Baltic and North Sea.

Harbour A stretch of water, protected from sea and swell and either natural or artificial, where ships can shelter.

Heeling Of a ship, inclining or leaning to one side, caused purely by the action of wind and waves.

Herbivores Organisms that eat plants.

Hermaphroditism Union of both male and female reproduction systems in one individual or body, e.g. limpets.

High seas The interlinking seas and oceans lying seaward of the 200-mile EEZ *q.v.*

Hinterland The region or area from which ports receive or dispatch their cargoes.

Holothurians Class of echinoderms comprising sea cucumbers which have elongated cylindrical bodies and move horizontally by means of tube feet.

Hornblende Dark green or black mineral of amphibole group; found widely among igneous and metamorphic rocks.

Hot spots Localised areas of the lithosphere beneath which plumes of magma rise to the surface from deep in Earth's crust with different basaltic lava from that at spreading ridge.

Hurricane Name for tropical cyclone *q.v.* in north Atlantic, West Indies, north-east Pacific and south-west Pacific Ocean.

Hydrocarbon Compound of hydrogen and carbon with nothing else, e.g. petroleum, coal, asphalt and natural waxes.

Hydrodynamics Science of forces acted on, or exerted by, liquids.

Hydrological cycle The system whereby the water is removed from the ocean by evaporation into the atmosphere and eventually returns to the ocean either directly as precipitation or indirectly by rivers.

Hydrosphere Earth's water found in the oceans, on land and underground, as well as water vapour in the atmosphere.

Hydrostatic pressure Pressure exerted by a homogenous fluid acting on an object.

Hydrothermal Pertaining to or produced by action of heated or super-heated water, especially in dissolving, transporting and re-depositing mineral material.

Hyperbolic navigation system Radio navigation system in which position lines, which are hyperbolae, are determined by measurement of phase differences between land-based transmitters.

Hypsographic curve Curve representing the relative heights of the Earth's features in proportion to their areas on the Earth's surface.

I

IAHS *See International Association of Hydrological Sciences.*

IALA *See International Association of Lighthouse Authorities.*

IAPH *See International Association of Ports and Harbours.*

IAPSO *See International Association for the Physical Sciences of the Ocean.*

IATTC *See Inter-American Tropical Tuna Commission.*

Icebergs Large masses of floating ice, more than 5 m in height, derived from floating glacier tongues or from ice shelves.

Ice-floes Relatively flat pieces of sea ice that can vary in size from 10 km across to less than 20 m.

Ice islands Large pieces of ice that have broken away from an Arctic ice shelf.

ICES International Council for the Exploration of the Sea.

Ice shelf Rather flat, floating ice sheet of considerable thickness, extending from 2 m to 50 m above sea level and usually of great horizontal length, attached to the coast.

ICNAF *See International Commission for Northwest Atlantic Fisheries.*

Idoxuridine An antiviral compound derived from a West Indian marine sponge.

Igneous rock Rock formed by solidification from a molten silicate material.

IGY International Geophysical Year.

IHB International Hydrographic Bureau.

IHO *See International Hydrographic Organisation.*

IMO *See International Maritime Organisation.*

Inchmaree clause This extends the insurance underwriters' liability to cover losses which may be caused by risks which do not come within the ordinary definition or maritime perils. (This clause takes its name from the well-known case dealing with damage to auxiliary engine room equipment in the steamer *Inchmaree.*)

Indemnity Security against loss or damage.

Industrial fisheries Large-scale fisheries in which the catch is used for purposes other than human consumption, e.g. animal feed. These account for approximately one-third of the world commercial catch, and consist mainly of shoaling pelagic fish.

Inert gas systems Replacement of flammable gas content in cargo tanks by inert gas from the ship's own boiler flue gas.

This method greatly reduces the chances of cargo tank explosion.

Inertial navigation system A self-contained independent navigational instrument, consisting of accelorometers mounted on a stabilised platform, and a computer which continuously determines directions and distances travelled from a known initial position, thereby constantly determining present position. Used mainly in civil and military aircraft and in warships.

Innocent passage Foreign shipping has a right of innocent passage through the territorial sea. Such passage must not prejudice the peace, good order or security of the coastal state.

Inter-American Tropical Tuna Commission (IATTC) Established by an international agreement of 1949 to be responsible for research, conservation and regulation relating to the tuna fisheries of the eastern Pacific.

Intergovernmental Oceanographic Commission (IOC) Established 1960 within UNESCO. Aims to promote the scientific investigation of the oceans, with a view to learning more about their nature and resources, through the concerted action of the 88 member states.

Intermediate earthquakes Occurring between 70 and 300 km depth.

Internal waters All waters lying landward of the baseline *q.v.* Include bays, rivers, harbours and inland waterways. No right of innocent passage *q.v.* for foreign shipping.

International Association for the Physical Sciences of the Ocean (IAPSO) Established 1919, it aims to promote study of scientific problems relating to the ocean and interactions taking place at its boundaries chiefly in so far as such study may be carried out by the aid of mathematics, physics and chemistry; initiate, facilitate and coordinate research into and investigation of, those problems of physical oceanography which require international cooperation; provide for discussion, comparison and publication.

International Association of Hydrological Sciences (IAHS) Founded in 1922, it aims to promote and develop the study of hydrology, initiate, facilitate and coordinate research or such hydrological problems as necessitate international cooperation; ensure discussion, comparison and publication of the result of research.

International Association of Lighthouse Authorities (IALA) Founded 1st July 1957. Aims to assemble lighthouse authorities around the world for discussion of technical interests such as leading lights, microwave aids to navigation, radionavigation systems, unification of buoyage systems, buoy moorings, etc., and has set up a working group to prepare a lighthouse dictionary.

International Association of Ports and Harbours (IAPH).

International Commission for North-west Atlantic Fisheries (ICNAF) Established 1950 in Washington. Aims are the investigation, protection and conservation of the fisheries of the north-west Atlantic Ocean, in order to make possible the maintenance of a maximum sustained catch from these fisheries.

International Hydrographic Bureau (IHB) Established 1921 in Monaco, with 19 member countries, for purpose of reaching common agreement on methods of navigation and charts used; now administrative headquarters of IHO.

International Hydrographic Organisation (IHO) Established 1921 in Monte Carlo. Aims to establish permanent association between hydrographic services of the various maritime countries; their work with a view towards rendering navigation easier and safer in all seas; endeavour to obtain uniformity in hydrographic documents and advance the science of hydrography.

International Ice Patrol Formed in 1913 to improve information and warnings about ice conditions in the North Atlantic.

International Maritime Organisation (IMO) UN agency originally established 1958 as IMCO (Intergovernmental Maritime Consultative Organisation), to promote co-operation and exchange of information among governments on technical matters related to international shipping, especially safety at sea and marine pollution.

International Maritime Satellite Operational 1982 and providing ships with contact for distress, safety communications, medical assistance, weather forecasts, navigational warnings, etc.

International Pacific Halibut Commission (IPHC) Established originally by a Convention of 1923 between the USA and Canada for the regulation of the halibut fishery in the North Pacific; it was the first of its kind, for a fish species, and one of the most successful.

International Programme of Ocean Drilling (IPOD) Evolved from DSDP *q.v.* in 1975 with object of ocean floor reconnaissance.

International Whaling Commission (IWC) Established by Convention of 1946 for the prevention of overfishing of whales through promotion of research and regulation.

Intertropical Convergence Zone (ITCZ) Zone of low pressure and wet weather near equator where trade winds of the two hemispheres converge.

Interstitial water Water in rocks and sediments.

Intertidal zone *See Littoral zone.*

Invertebrates Animals without backbones.

IOC *See Intergovernmental Oceanographic Commission.*

IODE Intergovernmental Oceanographic Data Exchange (IOC working committee).

Iodide A salt of hydriodic acid.

Iodine Non-metallic element of halogen family; compound found in seaweed and used in medicine, photography and organic synthesis.

Ions Electrically charged atoms or groups of atoms; can be created by collisions with charged particles, high energy radiation or by dissolving suitable compounds in water.

IOS Institute of Oceanographic Sciences (UK).

IPHC *See International Pacific Halibut Commission.*

IPOD *See International Programme of Ocean Drilling.*

Island A naturally formed area of land, surrounded by water, which is above water at high tide.

Island arc Curved chain of volcanic islands commonly associated with deep-sea trenches.

Isobar Line connecting places of equal pressure; commonly used on weather maps and on oceanic subsurface analyses.

Isobath Contour lines of equal depths.

Isotherm Line connecting points of equal temperature.

Isthmus Narrow neck of land connecting two larger land areas.

IUCN International Union for Conservation of Nature and Natural Resources.

IWC *See International Whaling Commission.*

J

JASIN *See Joint Air-Sea Interaction Experiment.*

Jetsam Denotes goods which are washed ashore from a ship after having been cast or lost overboard.

Jettison The throwing overboard of cargo or equipment in order to lighten a vessel in time of peril.

Joint Air-Sea Interaction Experiment (JASIN) Study of the structure of the oceanic and atmospheric boundary layers to establish fluxes of heat, momentum and water vapour, on time scales of up to one month, and over distances of up to 200 km.

Joint North Sea Data Acquisition Project (JONSDAP) Gathers data on tidal levels, current velocity, marine chemistry and pollution in the southern North Sea.

Joint North Sea Information Systems (JONSIS) Standing committee on ocean data systems for NERC. A project for the development of a network of moored ocean data stations for the mathematical modelling of the North Sea circulation.

Joint North Sea Wave Project (JONSWAP) Established 1968. A research project, involving personnel from West Germany, UK, USA and the Netherlands, concerning dynamic processes at sea surface at Sylt I., in the German Bight.

Joint Oceanographic Institution for Deep Earth Sampling (JOIDES) A large-scale scientific project which collects data by drilling numerous deep holes into the sediments on the ocean floor.

K

Kaikyo Strait *(Japanese).*

Kaimei 'sea light' project Eighty metre-long experimental device, developed in Japan, for harnessing wave energy; waves move water in ship-like structure driving air through a turbine which drives an electrical generator.

Kelp Large seaweeds of the brown algae, used as a source of alginates.

Kilometre A metric measure of distance equal to 1000 m, 0.62 statute mile or 0.54 nautical mile.

Klondyking Buying of fresh fish from local fisheries for immediate and direct transfer to distant markets.

Knot A unit of velocity equal to 1 nautical mile per hour. It is approximately equal to 50 cm per second.

Krill Shrimp-like plankton dweller, rich in protein, that constitutes basic food of baleen whales; now being exploited for human consumption.

L

Lagan Denotes goods cast overboard which can be recovered because they have been buoyed.

Lagoon Enclosed area of water separated from open sea by, usually, an elongated sand bank or barrier reef.

Lagoon beach Also called barrier beach; a long broken ridge of sediment separated from the coast by a lagoon.

Landsat satellites Series of US satellites, operation of which began in 1971, designed to monitor Earth's resources.

Larvae Free-living forms of animals emerging from egg, usually distinct from adults and incapable of sexual reproduction.

LASH (Lighter-aboard ship) Cargo-carrying system using specially built ships designed to carry 70–90 barges of 370 dwt which, at destination, are disembarked and towed to unloading berths.

Lateen-rigged Triangular sail still common on boats in the Mediterranean.

Laurasia Name given by German scientist Wegener to hypothetical landmass of Mesozoic era that included most of continents of Northern Hemisphere.

Leeward The direction towards which the wind is blowing.

LEPOR *See Long-term and Expanded Programme of Oceanic Exploration and Research.*

Levanters Strong easterly winds occurring in Strait of Gibraltar.

Lift and scoop nets Operated by hand from the shore or a vessel in traditional fisheries, catching the fish by an encircling movement.

Light displacement Weight of a ship when in 'light' or unloaded state but including weight of water in boilers and any permanent ballast. *See also Appendix I.*

Lithosphere Outermost portion of the Earth, consisting of the crust and upper mantle.

Littoral zone Narrow area along a coast that extends from the low-tide mark to the high-tide mark and is characterised by special flora and fauna.

Lloyds Register of Shipping A non-profit making society which surveys and classifies merchant ships. Ships which meet Lloyds requirements are classed '100 A1 at Lloyds' and this term has entered into the English language to denote the highest standards which can be achieved. Other similar classification societies are Bureau Veritas, Det Norske Veritas, and the American Bureau of Shipping.

LNG Liquefied natural gas.

LOA Length overall, a measurement of a ship's length to its extremities fore and aft.

Load displacement Weight of water displaced by a vessel when floating at her loaded draught and equal to the combined weight of the vessel and her contents; normal unit of measure for warships. *See also Appendix I.*

Load lines Lines on ship's side to mark limits to which ships may be loaded to provide safe freeboard *q.v.* in different areas of the sea during various seasons.

Load line zones The oceans of the world are divided into seasonal zones and seasonal periods, for example, the tropical zone and the North Atlantic winter seasonal zone. Ships when entering these zones must have the appropriate minimum freeboard.

Long lines Fishing gear, used especially for pelagic and demersal fish not swimming in close packed shoals.

Longshore currents Currents in the near-shore region that run essentially parallel to the coast.

Long-term and Expanded Programme of Oceanic Exploration and Research (LEPOR) Established 1968 by UN General Assembly. Aims are to increase knowledge of the ocean; its contents, subsoil, interfaces with the land, the atmosphere and ocean floor with a view to enhancing its utilisation and exploitation.

LORAN (Long Range Navigation) Hyperbolic navigation system with radio stations forming chains in North Atlantic and Pacific Oceans; range about 1200 nm.

LOT (load on top) Method of washing out oil tankers; oil washings from all cargo tanks are pumped into a single slop tank where oil and water separates; the water is drained into sea, oil remains on board and new oil loaded 'on top' of it.

LPG Liquefied petroleum gas.

Luciferins Protein-like substance in the luminous organs of certain animals.

M

Maasbanker A small, shoaling pelagic fish caught off the coast of southern Africa.

Magma Molten silicate material and dissolved gases generated within the mantle and extruded and intruded to higher elevations, solidifying to form igneous rocks.

Magnesium Light silver-white metallic element that occurs in magnesite, dolomite and sea water.

Magnetic anomalies Deviations from the uniform or idealised magnetic field of the Earth produced by forces within the Earth's crust and deep interior.

Magnetic declination Angle in degrees between true north and magnetic north.

Magnetic field Field of influence surrounding the Earth in which magnetic forces operate.

Magnetic reversal Periodic shift in which magnetic polarity of the Earth reverses itself so that north and south poles are interchanged.

Manganese nodules Potato-sized lumps distributed irregularly on the sea floor, rich in manganese and valuable for their copper, nickel and cobalt content; the largest recorded quantities are found in eastern central areas of the Pacific Ocean.

Mangrove swamps Feature of tropical waters; flat, low-lying areas of mud and silt lying between high and low water, covered by stilt-like roots of mangrove and associated vegetation.

Mantle Zone within the Earth that extends below the crust to the Earth's core; upper limit about 40 km below land surface (10 km below ocean floor), lower limit about 2900 km below Earth's surface.

Marginal plateau Platform on seaward side of continental margin with steep sides (1000–2000 m) falling to abyssal depths.

Marginal quay Straight length of quay running parallel to the shore at which ships berth to load and discharge their cargoes.

Marginal seas Seas between island arc and continent; seas located along margins of continents and having wide connections with open sea, e.g. Bering Sea, Caribbean Sea.

Mariculture Cultivation of marine or salt-water fishes.

Maritime industrial development areas (MIDAS) Large industrial zone located close to port facilities at which primary and secondary industries dependent on maritime transport for their raw materials or manufactured goods are concentrated.

MARPOL International Convention for Prevention of Pollution of the Sea from Ships. An IMO Convention, 1973, received sufficient signatures October 1982 to partially enter into force October 1983. *See also Appendix XI.*

MCM Mine countermeasure vessel.

Meanders Of ocean currents, twists and curves of water; can be as much as 100 km wide with distances of several hundred kilometres from curve to curve.

Median line division *See Equidistance.*

Menhaden A shoaling pelagic fish found off east coast of US, in the Atlantic and Gulf of Mexico, and the basis of a long established industrial fishery.

Merchant ship Ship that carries merchant cargo.

Mesopelagic zone Marine biological zone between depths of 200 and 1000 m, within which little light penetrates and temperature variations are small.

Metamorphic rocks Rocks formed by recrystallisation of pre-existing rocks in the solid state under extreme conditions of heat and/or pressure.

MGB (motor gunboat) Fast patrol boat with guns only as armament.

MIDAS *See Maritime industrial development areas.*

Mid-Ocean Dynamics Experiment (MODE) Studies fluctuations in mid-ocean flow currents by establishing the dynamics and statistics of medium scale eddies.

Milkfish A widely distributed species in the Indo Pacific which forms the basis of much industrial aquaculture in the East Asian islands.

MODE *See Mid-Ocean Dynamics Experiment.*

Molluscs Phylum of soft-bodied unsegmented animals often with hard shell; includes clams, oysters, mussels, octopus and squid.

Monsoon Wind system involving seasonal reversal of prevailing wind direction, found most often in tropics; summer monsoon brings warm, wet weather, winter monsoon cold, dry air.

Monsoon Experiment (MONEX) Studies the summer monsoon in the northern hemisphere; that is, the transport of air from the southern to the northern hemisphere. Of particular importance is the assessing of monsoon rainfall in the Indian sub-continent and East Africa.

MTB (motor torpedo boat) Fast patrol boat whose armaments include torpedoes.

N

NASA National Aeronautics and Space Administration (USA).

National ownership *See Domestic registry.*

NATO (North Atlantic Treaty Organisation) Member nations: Belgium, Canada, Denmark, Greece, Iceland, Italy, Luxemburg, Netherlands, Norway, Portugal, Turkey, UK, US, W. Germany.

NavStar High orbital navigation satellite providing continuous position fixing.

NEAFC *See North-east Atlantic Fisheries Commission.*

Neap tide Weak tides that occur about every two weeks when the Moon is in its quarter positions.

Nekton Animals that are able to swim independently of current action.

Nematocyst A stinging organ in jellyfishes.

Neritic zone Marine zone of shallow water near land.

Nitrogen Colourless, gaseous element that forms about four-fifths of atmosphere; essential constituent of living organisms.

NOAA National Oceanic and Atmospheric Administration (USA).

NORPAX North Pacific Experiment.

North-east Atlantic Fisheries Commission (NEAFC) An intergovernmental organisation established by conventions in 1959 for the regulation of fisheries in the North-east Atlantic.

NRT (net registered tonnage) *See Appendix I.*

O

OBO (ore-bulk-oil) carriers A variation of a bulk carrier which can carry ore, other bulk cargoes and oil.

Ocean basin That portion of the ocean seaward of the continental margin that includes the deep-sea floor.

Oceanic circulations Sum total of ocean currents including surface or wind-driven currents and deep water currents.

Oceanic crust Thin, continuous portion of the outer zone of the Earth comprising entire crust under the oceans where it is less than 8 km thick.

Ocean ridges Largest single feature on Earth's surface extending as submarine volcanic mountain range around the world for more than 50 000 km and characterised by much earthquake activity.

Ocean rises Large areas of the ocean basin elevated above the surrounding abyssal hills and thought to have originated as gentle upliftings of the ocean floor.

Octopods Genus of eight-armed cephalopods.

OECD Organisation for Economic Co-operation and Development.

Offshore fishery A Japanese term for fisheries beyond the immediate coastal zone but distinct from their distant water (far seas) fishery.

OILPOL International Convention for Prevention of Pollution of the Sea by Oil.

Olivine Green, usually transparent, mineral consisting of silicate of iron and magnesium.

Omega navigation system Very low frequency (VLF) radio navigation systems using phase comparison of continuous-wave transmissions to obtain hyperbolic lines of position.

Omnivores Organisms feeding on both animal and vegetable food.

O-O (oil-oil) carrier Combination carrier in which only the centre of each hold is used for cargo.

Ooze Marine sediment that contains more than 30 per cent of various microorganism shells.

OPEC (Organisation of Petroleum Exporting Countries) Formed in 1961 to administer a common policy for sale of petroleum. Member nations are: Algeria, Ecuador, Gabon, Indonesia, Iran, Iraq, Kuwait, Libya, Nigeria, Qatar, Saudi Arabia, United Arab Emirates and Venezuela.

Open registry *See FOC.*

Ophiolites A sequence of former deep-sea sediments found onshore, overlaying pillow lavas, basaltic dykes, gabbro and peridotite.

Optimum route For shipping, route decided upon by taking account of weather conditions based on analysis and prediction.

Organochlorines A class of organic chemicals containing chlorine.

OTEC (ocean thermal energy conversion) Device used for generation of energy from temperature differences in the water column.

Otter trawl Demersal fishing gear; cone-shaped net, held open by ropes, weights and floats in conjunction with angled otter boards which draw apart as trawl is pulled along the sea bed.

P

Pack ice Any area of sea ice no matter what form it takes or how it is disposed.

Panamax ships Ships so constructed that the dimensions of the Panama Canal are taken into account in their width and draught.

Pandanus trees Screw-pines, fruit is edible and leaves used for mat making.

Pangaea The supercontinent existing at the beginning of the Mesozoic era from which all our present continents originated.

Panthalassa The superocean which surrounded Pangaea *q.v.*

Parcel tankers Tankers which are capable of carrying more than one type of oil. Usually used for carrying oil products, e.g. kerosene, aviation spirit, lubricating oil, etc.

Pathogenic Producing disease.

Patrimonial sea A term used, chiefly by Caribbean spokesman, to refer to what is now generally known as the EEZ *q.v.*

PCBs (polychlorinated biphenols) Toxic chemicals affecting marine animals.

Pelagic Of, inhabiting, or carried out in the deep or open sea.

Pelagic sediments Sediments deposited in the deep sea that have little or no coarse-grained terrigenous material.

Penaeid Shrimps of the genus panaeus, adults of which live and spawn on the continental shelf and spend their juvenile periods in coastal regions.

Peridotite Rock composed essentially of olivine (85 per cent) and pyroxene (15 per cent).

Phaeophyta Brown algae, one of the main divisions of seaweeds.

Phosphate Salt of phosphoric acid.

Phosphorite A sedimentary deposit consisting largely of calcium phosphate.

Photic zone Uppermost layer of the sea where light penetrates.

Photophores Luminiferous organs.

Photosynthesis The production of organic matter by plants using water and carbon dioxide in the presence of chlorophyll and light; oxygen is released in the action.

Phytoplankton Vegetable plankton; microscopic floating plant life of oceans and basic food source for most marine life.

Pier Structure, often of iron, steel or timber, which extends out to sea as a promenade or landing stage. Term used in North America to describe finger-like quays where cargoes are loaded or discharged.

Pillow lavas Basaltic or andestic pillow-shaped lava formed in oceans, lakes and rivers that either erupted beneath water or flowed into it.

Pivot port Port selected by the shipowner as a point for the receipt and distribution of containers being transhipped by feeder services to other ports in the country or region. *See also Transhipment.*

Placer deposit Metalliferous mineral particles concentrated in some sand and gravel layers which occur in rivers and beaches.

Plankton Microscopic floating and drifting plant and animal life found throughout the world's oceans.

Plankton bloom A large concentration of plankton within an area, due to a rapid growth of the organisms. The large numbers of plankton can discolour the water, sometimes causing a red tide *q.v.*

Plate tectonics The concept that the lithosphere *q.v.* is divided into a number of large and small areas (plates) which are in motion at rates which can be measured in cm per year.

Pleistocene A geological epoch that ended about 10 000 years ago and lasted about 1 to 2 million years. This epoch has been subdivided into four glacial stages and three interglacial stages. The last of the pleistocene glacial stages is called the Wisconsin stage. The period we are now in, the Holocene epoch, is not part of the pleistocene and may be an interglacial stage.

Plimsoll mark The load line *q.v.* on ships which bears the name of Samuel Plimsoll who campaigned for safety measures against the overloading of ships.

Plutonium Transuranic element; used as fuel in nuclear reactors and nuclear weapons.

Polar wandering Changes in position of the magnetic pole at various periods of geologic time.

Polder Land reclaimed from the sea or fresh water. It is normally flat and lies below sea level. (Dutch.)

Polyculture In aquaculture, cultivation of several compatible fish species and sometimes other aquatic organisms simultaneously in the same environment.

Polynya Any area of open water enclosed in ice.

Porifera Phylum of sessile aquatic animals consisting of sponges.

Port Place where two-way exchanges between land and sea transport regularly take place. It is usually comprised of terminals and berths at the waterfront together with adequate back-up land for storage of goods used in the cargo transfer operation between ship and shore.

Potassium Soft metallic element occurring in a wide variety of silicate rocks and mineral deposits; essential to life processes.

Precipitation Water particles, either liquid or solid, that fall from the atmosphere and reach the ground.

Preparatory investment protection (PIP) Proposed scheme controlling exploitation of mineral resources of the deep sea Area, where investors may be allocated exclusive rights subject to certain conditions.

Proliv Strait (Russian).

Protective location A design concept in which segregated ballast tanks are placed in selected areas of the ship where they will minimise the possibility of oil outflow from the cargo tanks after collision or grounding.

Protoplasmic Of living water.

Protozoa Phylum of unicellular animals, consisting of naked mass of protoplasm surrounded by membrane.

Pteropod Any member of group of gasteropods that swim by wing-like expansion of the foot.

Purse-seines Fishing gear most suitable for catching large quantities of shoaling pelagic fish; circles of net that can be closed around the fish like a bag, and now hauled in through a powered pulley.

Pycnocline A zone where water density rapidly increases. The increase is greater than that in the water above or below it. The density change, or pycnocline, is due to changes in temperature and salinity.

Pyrite An abundant sulphide, known as 'fool's gold' because of its brassy colour.

Pyroxenes Group of rock-forming minerals composed mainly of silicates of calcium, iron and magnesium.

Pyrrophyta Dinoflagellates or fire algae which contain massive neurotoxins that can poison everything including fishes and sea birds.

Q

Quartz Mineral, oxide of silicon and important constituent in many igneous, sedimentary and metamorphic rocks; principal mineral in sandstones and unconsolidated sand and gravel.

Quay (jetty) Artificial structure of wood, concrete or steel lying alongside or projecting into water on which cargo is landed after discharge from a vessel or prepared for loading.

R

Racon Radar responder beacon (or transponder) emitting particular signal when triggered by emissions of ships' radar sets.

Radar (radio detection and ranging) Device employing transmitted and reflected radio waves to detect presence of objects and to determine their bearings and ranges.

Radiation fog Night and early morning fog sometimes found over coastal and estuarine waters and usually formed by nocturnal chilling of the ground.

Radioactive elements Those elements that are capable of changing into other elements by the emission of changed particles from their nuclei.

Radiolaria Minute protozoans which secrete shell of silica.

Radiolarian oozes Siliceous deep-sea oozes formed by skeletons of radiolaria and found in the Indian and Pacific Oceans.

Ramark (echo enhancer) Radar beacon which transmits independently without having to be triggered by emissions of ships' radar sets.

Ramp Concrete or metal structure, either of a rigged or adjustable design, at which Ro-Ro *q.v.* vessels berth.

Red Sea Commission Body set up to administer exploitation of metalliferous mud in Atlantis II Deep (north and central Red Sea).

Red tides Pollution hazard; appears when natural population explosion or 'bloom' of certain species of floating dinoflagellates (plankton) containing dangerous toxins occurs, imparting red tinge to water.

Reef Area of rocks or coral which, if just below sea level, may constitute a danger to surface navigation.

Reefer ships Ships designed for carrying refrigerated cargo.

Relict sediments Sediments occupying a location in which the environment has changed since the time they were deposited; usually refers to sediments on bottom of outer continental shelf.

Remote sensing Detection of an object or phenomenon by information gathering device (sensor) without direct contact.

Resonance of tides Occurs when the natural period of a water basin compares with that of a harmonic of the oscillatory force responsible for generating tides in the basins. As a result, tidal ranges in the basin are amplified.

Rhodophyta Red algae.

Rhumb line A curve on the Earth's surface which cuts all the meridians at the same angle. When a ship is maintaining the same true course she is sailing on a rhumb line track.

Ria Drowned river valley, or area where several rivers flow into broad indented bay; a configuration favoured for port building.

Rift Elongated trough created by sinking of Earth's crust and, during its formation, characterised by earthquake activity.

Right of access Foreign shipping has, arguably, no right of access to foreign ports except when in distress. In practice access usually permitted, often on basis of bilateral treaty of commerce and navigation.

Riser system In off-shore drilling for hydrocarbons, the pipes which connect well-heads on the sea floor to production platforms.

Roaring forties The stormy regions of the Southern Ocean between the parallels of 40° and 50°S, where westerly winds prevail.

Ro-Ro (roll-on/roll-off) ships Ships designed to carry cargo-loaded road vehicles and trailers which drive on and off when embarking and disembarking.

S

Salinity The total amount of dissolved material in seawater. It is measured in parts per thousand (‰) by weight in 1 kg of seawater.

Salt dome A large cylindrical mass of salt that has risen through the surrounding sediment. It can form a trap for oil or gas.

Salvage The rescue of ships, lives or cargo from danger is a salvage service. The reward paid to the salvor in respect of the successful performance of a salvage service is also called salvage.

SAM missile Surface to air missile.

Sand waves Wave-like sediment formations on the sea floor, mainly composed of sand and found in shallow seas where wave activity is pronounced.

Satellite navigation system Position determination by means of artificial Earth satellites, which are monitored by tracking stations on Earth and which transmit their orbital data (injected into their memories at regular intervals by Earth stations). Any vessel fitted with an appropriate receiver and computer can determine its position from the orbital data and doppler effect on the satellite transmissions.

Scientific Committee on Oceanic Research (SCOR) Established 1957 by ICSU Executive Board. Works jointly with Advisory Committee or Marine Resources Research; Committee on Marine Geology, International Council for Exploration of the Sea; and Advisory Committee on Oceanic Meteorological Research.

Scuba (self-contained underwater breathing apparatus; popularly called aqualung). A small portable gas cylinder which permits divers to move with relative ease underwater with no direct connection to surface.

SEABEE Type of barge carrier. First developed by US navy in the Second World War. Comprises a mother ship containing many independent barges, which are used to reach locations on a waterway/canal system that the mother ship cannot reach.

Seabirds Birds which are truly marine in that the sea is their normal habitat and their principal source of food. Sixteen avian families fulfil these two criteria.

Sea floor spreading Theory that sea floor grows outwards from a central ridge system located on floors of the oceans.

Seamount Isolated elevation, usually higher than 1000 m from the sea floor, usually conical in shape.

Seasat Radar satellite launched to observe transient phenomena of the oceans.

Sea smoke Patchy, shallow fog caused by cold air passing over considerably warmer waters; occurs in Arctic and Antarctic and off the east coasts of Asia and North America in autumn and winter.

Seaweed Sea algae, of which there are over 1000 species.

Secondary shoreline Shoreline where the coastal region has been formed mainly by marine or biological agents. Examples are coral reefs, barrier beaches and marshes.

SECOR (Sequential observation of range) Satellite stations girdling the Earth at determined distances over a specific area of latitude.

Sediment Solid material of organic or inorganic origin deposited by water, wind or ice; usually described in terms of origin or mode of transportation.

Sedimentary rocks Rocks that have formed from the accumulation of particles (sediment) in water or from the air.

Segregated ballast tanks (SBT) Special tanks on an oil tanker reserved for the carriage of sea water ballast. Required by 1973 MARPOL Convention (in force 1984).

Seine net A large class of fishing net which operates by an encircling movement.

Seismic wave Form taken by energy released when rocks within the Earth break apart or slip rapidly along fault lines during an earthquake.

Seismology Study of earthquakes and related phenomena.

Selat Strait *(Malay).*

Selenium Non-metallic element of sulphur group obtained from flue dust produced by burning sulphide ores; used in glass and ceramic industry.

Serpentine Greenish mineral consisting of hydrous magnesium silicate; the fibrous variety is a major source of asbestos. The term is also applied to rock which is a mixture of serpentine and other minerals.

Serpentinite Rock composed almost entirely of serpentine.

Sextant An instrument for measuring either horizontal or vertical angles in order to obtain a position line in navigation. Horizontal angles are used in coastal navigation and vertical angles are used in astro-navigation.

Sferics (contraction of the word *atmospherics*) The electrical impulses originating in lightning discharges; heard as crackling noises in a radio receiver.

Shallow-focus earthquakes Occurring at depths of less than 70 km, they are found in all seismic belts and produce the largest percentage of earthquakes.

Significant-wave concept For measurement of waves, average height of highest one-third of waves in a particular time interval (usually 10 minutes); significant wave period is the average period of the highest one-third of the waves.

Silicate One of group of minerals containing silica and oxygen; approx. 95 per cent of Earth's crust is composed of silicate materials.

Siliceous Of or containing silica.

Siliciclastic Sediments composed mainly of silicate mineral particles.

Sill A ridge separating a partially closed ocean basin from the ocean or another basin.

Siltation Deposition of mainly muddy sediments in estuaries, port approaches and harbour areas.

Single buoy mooring (SBM) Large mooring buoy in open water to which a vessel, such as a tanker, moors to load or unload.

SINS (Ship's inertial navigation system) Complex, self-contained dead reckoning system which continuously determines the ship's movement from an initial known position of the ship, and thereby continuously deduces the ship's existing position.

SIO Scripps Institution of Oceanography (USA).

SLBM Submarine-launched ballistic missile.

Smacks Fore and aft rigged vessels which, in Britain particularly, preceded stern trawlers in the development of demersal fishing in the 19th century and were used for trading.

Sodium Soft, silvery-white metallic element; reacts violently with water to form strong alkali sodium hydroxide.

Sonar (another name for an echo sounder) Used for sound navigation and ranging. A sonar uses high frequency sound in water to detect underwater objects, e.g. submarines.

SOSUS Sound surveillance systems.

Sounding The determination of the depth of the ocean either by lowering a line to the bottom, or electronically by noting how long sound takes to travel to the bottom and return.

Spinel A mineral found in crystalline limestones and gneisses; gem varieties accumulate sometimes in placer deposits *q.v.*

SPOT satellite French satellite with resolutions down to 10 m; useful for monitoring coastal areas.

Spreading ridges Of ocean ridges, occur when rock cools as it wells up through central rift zone and spreads outward forming new sea floor.

Spring tides Strong tides with greatest range that occur about every two weeks, when the Moon is full or new.

SS Strategic submarine.

SSB Strategic submarine, ballistic missiles.

SSBN Nuclear powered submarine, ballistic missiles.

SSG Strategic submarine, guided missiles.

SSGN Nuclear powered submarine, guided (cruise) missiles.

SSN Nuclear powered strategic submarine.

Stationary waves A type of wave in which the waveform does not move forward; however the surface moves up and down. At certain fixed points called nodes, the water surface remains stationary.

Storm surges Abnormally high water levels due to strong winds blowing on the water surface.

Storm waves Waves generated by gale to storm or hurricane force winds.

Straddle carrier A large and mobile piece of mechanical handling equipment, mainly deployed in container terminals, which is designed to lift, transport and stack containers up to three high.

Strait Narrow passage connecting two sections of the sea. Rights of passage through straits depend in part on status of waters at either end (i.e. whether they are territorial sea, EEZ *q.v.* or high seas *q.v.*). Usually at least a right of innocent passage *q.v.* but sometimes transit passage *q.v.* exists.

Strategic nuclear weapon A long range weapon, usually a ballistic missile armed with a nuclear warhead, which can be launched at targets deep in the enemy's homeland.

Strategic route (shipping) Route based on analysis of prevailing weather, without prediction to any significant degree.

Stratocumulus Low cloud in large globular or rolled masses, not rain-bringing.

Stretto Strait *(Italian).*

Strontium Metallic element resembling calcium in its chemical properties; radioactive strontium 90 occurs in fall-out.

Subduction zone Zone where one plate is deflected beneath another plate, the downwarped plate being resorbed in the upper mantle.

Subsea completions System for exploitation of oil beyond continental shelf. All items of equipment are mounted on the sea floor in an atmospherically controlled chamber and serviced by technicians lowered in a diving bell.

Sulphates Salts of sulphuric acid, e.g. calcium sulphate (gypsum).

Surf Breaking waves in a coastal area.

Surface current Current which occurs in the uppermost 100 m or more of the ocean.

Surge Difference in height between predicted and observed tide, due mainly to wind driving water towards or away from a coast.

Swell Waves which were originally generated by wind but have propagated out of the generation area.

Swim-bladders Gas-filled thin-walled sac, the means by which many bony fishes achieve buoyancy.

Symbiosis A relationship existing between two organisms in which neither is harmed but one or both benefit.

Synoptic measurements Numerous measurements taken simultaneously over a large area.

T

Tactical nuclear weapon A medium- or short-range nuclear-tipped weapon.

Telemetry A method, usually electronic, of measuring and then transmitting the measurement to a receiving station.

Teleosts Bony fishes with well-developed bones.

Teredo worms Ship-worm genus of molluscs.

Terrigenous sediments Sediments composed of material derived from the land. Usually these deposits are found close to land.

Territorial seas Traditionally, the width is 3 nm. Under the 1982 Conventions every state has the right to establish the width of its territorial sea up to a limit not exceeding 12 nm measured from baselines *q.v.* determined in accordance with the Convention. *See also Canon shot rule.*

Tethys In plate tectonics, a hypothetical large marginal sea in the Mesozoic era separating the principal landmasses of Laurasia and Gondwanaland.

Tetrodotoxin Potent neurotoxin found in some species of Chordata, e.g. puffer fish and porcupine fish.

TEUs (Twenty-foot equivalent units) Measure often used to describe carrying capacity of container ships, each unit being 20′ × 8′ × 8′ or 20′ × 8′ × 4′, etc.

Thermocline Narrow layer about 100–200 m below ocean surface where there is a sharp gradient of temperature beween the cold, deep water and warmer water above.

Through transport system An integrated door-to-door system for moving cargo from producer to receiver, such as by the use of container.

Thunderstorm Local storm always associated with cumulonimbus cloud and accompanied by lightning and thunder, gusty winds and heavy rain.

Tidal bore A large wave of tidal origin that travels up some rivers and estuaries.

Tidal currents Currents due to tide.

Tide Periodic rise and fall of sea-level; due to the gravitational influences of the Sun and Moon on ocean waters.

Todorokite Manganese mineral capable of accommodating nickel and copper.

Tonnage *See Appendix I.*

Tonne-mile A unit of measure of seaborne trade equal to one tonne of cargo carried for one mile.

Top hamper The equipment and accommodation, etc., above the deck of a ship.

Trace element Chemical element essential in plant and animal nutrition but only in minute quantities, e.g. iron, zinc, copper.

Trade winds Winds blowing constantly over the tropical and sub-tropical oceans, from the north-east in the northern hemisphere and the south-east in the southern hemisphere.

Tramp A dry cargo ship which is not normally being used for the provision of a regular service and usually finds employment in the carriage of homogenous dry cargoes in bulk.

Transform faults Sharp angular faults caused by spreading of sea floor away from oceanic ridges.

Transhipment (entrepôt) port A commercial centre where cargoes are assembled or consolidated before onward movement to other regions or states.

TRANSIT Satellite navigation system produced by US Navy in 1964 consisting of four satellites in 108-minute polar orbits 1100 km above Earth, four tracking stations, a computing centre and two injection stations.

Transit passage The right of passage enjoyed by foreign shipping through straits *q.v.* used for navigation between one part of the high sea *q.v.* or an EEZ *q.v.* and another part of the high seas or an EEZ. Similar to high seas freedom of navigation and includes right of submerged passage for submarines. More liberal regime than innocent passage *q.v.*

Transit shed A building, normally constructed on the quayside, the purpose of which is to store cargo temporarily while customs and other administrative formalities are completed.

Traps Geological structures which confine and contain hydrocarbons.

Trawl fishing Means of catching fish whereby a net is towed on wires in mid-water or along the bottom of the sea floor.

Trim (of a ship) The difference between the forward and after draughts. A ship may be trimmed 'by the head' (forward draught more than after draught) or 'by the stern' (forward draught less than after draught).

Trolling Fishing with towed lines.

Trophic Relating to nutrition.

Tropical cyclones Severe weather systems in which sustained winds exceed 32 m/sec; they originate over tropical oceans where the water temperature exceeds 26.5°C and they range in diameter from 500 to 1500 km.

Tropical depression Weather system in tropical latitudes containing wind speeds of less than 17 m/sec (below force 8 on Beaufort scale).

TRS (tropical revolving storm) Mariners' term for tropical cyclone, i.e. hurricanes, typhoons, etc.

Truman proclamation Issued by the US President in 1945, claimed exclusive rights in natural resources of the continental shelf. Usually taken as originating the new legal concept of the continental shelf.

Tsunami Japanese word for ocean waves of great length and high speed caused by submarine earthquake; often travel thousands of miles and cause widespread destruction on coastline. Commonly mis-called 'tidal wave'.

Turbidite Generally a mixture of coarse-grained and fine-grained sediment deposited from turbidity currents.

Turbidity current Submarine avalanche, caused by earth tremors or gravitational instability of sediment masses, that cut deep canyons in continental slope and sweep great quantities of sediment far out into ocean.

Turbulence A flow of water in which the motion of individual particles appears irregular and confused.

Typhoon Name for tropical cyclone over the China Seas and the NW Pacific.

U

ULMS Undersea long-range missile system.

UNCLOS UN Conference on the Law of the Sea: UNCLOS I in 1958; UNCLOS II in 1960; and UNCLOS III from 1974 to 1982.

UNCTAD United Nations Conference on Trade and Development.

UNEP (United Nations Environment Programme) Regional Seas Programme A conservation and environment programme with the governments of countries bordering certain seas.

UNESCO (United Nations Educational, Scientific and Cultural Organisation) Established 1946 with 152 member nations. Founded to promote international educational, scientific and cultural cooperation and assistance.

Unitised cargoes Loose cargoes which are packaged into units conforming to a uniform size (e.g. container, pallet, timber standard) to facilitate handling during transport.

Unit loading The practice of standardising the package of cargo to be handled between ship and shore, e.g. pallets, containers, barges.

Upwelling Upward movement of cold, nutrient-rich water to the surface of an ocean; occurs near coasts where winds persistently drive water seawards and in the open ocean where surface currents are divergent.

Uranium Hard radioactive metallic element, occurring in minute quantities in sea water.

V

Velella Floating marine organisms with stinging tentacles.

Velocity The rate of change of position (distance) in a given time such as 50 km per hour.

Vent communities Marine life found in localised fissures of deep sea floor near active centres of sub-floor spreading.

Ventral On side normally towards the ground.

VHF Very high frequency.

VLCC A very large crude oil carrier which is subdivided into a number of tanks. Oil may be discharged by use of under deck cargo pipelines, or by a 'free flow' system where the vessel is trimmed by the stern and oil flows through valves in the tank bulkheads into one big tank before being pumped ashore.

Voe A term for a type of sea inlet in the Orkney and Shetland Islands.

VTOL (of aircraft) Vertical take-off and landing.

W

Warsaw Pact Military alliance between Bulgaria, Czechoslavakia, East Germany, Hungary, Poland, Romania and USSR.

Water column Vertical cylindrical mass of water, usually in oceanography, from the surface to the sea floor; often represented schematically in the literature to show variations of temperature, salinity, currents, etc.

Waterspout Whirling column of water and spray about 200 m in diameter and up to 1500 m in height; occurs when the atmosphere is unstable.

Wave attenuation The decrease in the waveform or height with distance from a wave's origin.

Wave crest The highest part of a wave.

Wave height Vertical distance between trough and succeeding wave crest.

Wave length Distance between two wave crests.

Wave period Time it takes two successive wave crests to pass a point.

Wave refraction The change in direction of waves that occurs when one portion of the wave reaches shallow water and is slowed down while the other portion is in deep water and is moving relatively fast.

Wave spectrum Distribution of wave energy with respect to wave period.

Wave trough The lowest part of a wave between two successive crests.

Wave velocity The speed with which the wave proceeds. It is equal to the wave length divided by the wave period.

WCRP World Climate Research Programme.

Weather routeing A new science in which weather forecasting is specifically directed at optimising a ship's passage in terms of time and prevention of damage. The distance steamed may be somewhat longer than by direct route but storms and high wave fields are avoided as far as possible.

Well-logging in offshore drilling. The recording of the characteristics of the rock strata encountered in the drilling programme of a well.

Westerlies Prevailing winds of mid-latitudes in northern and southern hemispheres. Normally blow from the south-west in northern hemisphere and from the north-west in southern hemisphere.

Wharf Structure alongside which a ship is moored to load or discharge cargo.

WHOI Woods Hole Oceanographic Institution (USA).

Willy-willy Name for tropical cyclone in NW Australia.

Windshear Variation of wind-speed or direction or both together in either the vertical or the horizontal plane.

Wind-wave Water wave raised by the action of wind on the sea; size and velocity are determined by wind-speed, duration *q.v.* and fetch *q.v.*

World Meteorological Organisation (WMO) A specialised agency of the United Nations; responsible for fostering international collaboration, organising research and training programmes, and monitoring standards in theoretical and applied meteorology.

Wreck This term includes jetsam, flotsam, lagan and derelict, found in or on the shores of the sea or any tidal waters.

Z

Zooplankton Microscopic, drifting animal life of oceans containing larvae of larger swimming animals and fish.

Sources

The maps on pages 16–25 are all based on the General Bathymetric Chart of the Oceans (GEBCO), published by the Canadian Hydrographic Service, Ottawa, Canada, under the authority of the IHO and IOC (UNESCO).

Scientific coordinators G. L. Johnson, Dept of the Navy, Office of Naval Research, Arlington, Virginia, USA; D. Monahan, Canadian Hydrographic Service; G. Udintsev, Institute of Physics of the Earth, Moscow, USSR; J. Ulrich, Insitut für Meereskunde an Der Universität Kiel, West Germany; R. L. Fisher, Marie Z. Jantsch, R. L. Comer, Scripps Institution of Oceanography, La Jolla, California, USA; R. C. Searle, Institute of Oceanographic Sciences, Surrey, UK; J. Mammerickx, S. M. Smith, Geological Research Division, Scripps Institution of Oceanography, California, USA; Y. Iwabuchi, Hydrographic Dept, MSA no. 3–1, 5-Chome, Tsukiji, Chuo-ku, Tokyo, Japan; A. S. Laughton, Institute of Oceanographic Sciences, Surrey, UK; D. E. Hayes and M. Vogel, Lamont-Doherty Geological Observatory, Columbia University, New York, USA; J. La Brecque, P. D. Rabinowitz, C. Denner, Lamont-Doherty Geological Observatory, Columbia University, New York, USA; B. C. Heezen, M. Tharp, R. Bodnar, M. Bond, H. Jicha, M. McClellan, Lamont-Doherty Geological Observatory, Columbia University, New York, USA; R. H. K. Falconer, New Zealand Oceanographic Institute, Wellington, New Zealand; G. Grönlie, Universitetet i Oslo, Institutt for Geologi, Oslo, Norway; L. Sobczak, Earth Physics Branch, Dept of Energy Mines and Resources, Ottawa, Canada; S. Cande, Lamont-Doherty Geological Observatory, Columbia University, New York, USA.

Special coordinators (on topographic detail) D. J. Drewry and G. de Q. Robin, Scott Polar Research Institute, University of Cambridge, Cambridge, UK.

The sources for maps, diagrams, etc., listed below are in addition to the private research and correspondence conducted by the Department of Maritime Studies, UWIST, Cardiff, between 1978 and 1983.

pp 26–27 **2** modified from R. A. Davis, *Principles of Oceanography*, Addison-Wesley Publishing Co, Reading, Massachusetts, 1972. **5** *Oceanography: Introduction to the Oceans Course S334 Unit 1*, Open University Press, Milton Keynes, 1972. **6** M. Grant Gross, *Oceanography: a view of the Earth*, Prentice Hall Inc, New Jersey, 1977.

pp 28–29 **1** B. C. Heezen and C. D. Hollister, *The Face of the Deep*, Oxford University Press, 1971; M. N. Hill (Ed.) *The Sea vol. 3: The Earth Beneath the Sea*, John Wiley and Sons Inc, New York, 1963; *The Times Concise Atlas*. **2** GEBCO, Canadian Hydrographic Service. **3** G. L. Johnson and P. R. Vogt, 'Mid-Atlantic Ridge, 47–51°N', *Bulletin Geol. Soc. America* vol. 84, 1973; H. W. Menard, *Marine Geology of the Pacific*, McGraw-Hill, New York, 1964; D. H. Mathews, F. J. Vine and J. R. Cann, 'Geology of an Area of the Carlsberg Ridge, Indian Ocean', *Bulletin Geol. Soc. America* vol. 76, 1965. **4** B. C. Heezen and A. S. Laughten: M. N. Hill (Ed.) see **1** *op. cit*.

pp 30–31 **1,4** W. C. Pitman III, R. L. Larson and E. M. Herron, Lamont-Doherty Geological Observatory, drawn by M. M. Alvarez and H. Cason, Geological Society of America, 1974. **5** F. J. Vine, 'Seafloor spreading': I. G. Gass, P. J. Smith and R. C. L. Wilson (Eds), *Understanding the Earth*, Open University Press, 1972. **6** R. G. Mason and A. D. Raff 'A magnetic survey off the west coast of North America 32°N to 42°N': *Bulletin Geological Society America* vol. 72, 1961; F. J. Vine see *op. cit*. **7** J. R. Heirtzler, X. Le Pichon and J. G. Baron, 'Magnetic anomalies over the Reykjanes ridge': *Deep-Sea Research* vol. 13, 1966.

pp 32–33 **1** F. Press and R. Siever, *Earth*, Freeman & Co, San Francisco, 1974; X. Le Pichon, 'Sea-floor spreading and continental drift': *Journal of Geophysical Research* vol. 73, 1968; C. G. Chase, 'Plate kinematics: The Americas, East Africa, and the Rest of the World': *Earth and Planetary Science Letters* vol. 37, 1978; A. E. Ringwood, 'The petrological evolution of island arc systems': *Journal Geol. Soc. London* vol. 130, 1974. **2** F. Press and R. Siever, see **1** *op. cit.*; R. N. Hey, K. S. Deffeyes, G. L. Johnson and A. Lowrie, 'The galapagos triple junction': *Nature* vol. 237, 1974. **3** After: W. J. Morgan, 'Rises, trenches, great faults, and crustal blocks': *Journal Geophysical Research* vol. 73, 1968. **4** C. G. Chase, 'Plate kinematics: the Americas, East Africa, and the rest of the world': *Earth and Planetary Science Letters* vol. 37, 1978.

pp 34–35 **1** A. Wegener, *The origin of continents and oceans*, English trans. Dover Publications, New York, 1966. **2** E. C. Bullard, J. E. Everet and A. G. Smith, 'Fit of continents around Atlantic': P. M. S. Blackett, E. C. Bullard and S. K. Runcorn (Eds), *A Symposium on Continental Drift*, Royal Soc. London, 1965. **3** P. M. Hurley, 'The confirmation of continental drift': *Scientific American*, 1968. **4** A. G. Smith and A. Hallam, 'The fit of the southern continents': *Nature* vol. 225, 1970; Hurley see **3** *op. cit*. **8** A. G. Smith, J. C. Briden and G. E. Drewry, 'Phanerozoic world maps': *Palaeontology* vol. 12, 1973. **9** P. Wyllie, *The Way the Earth Works*, Wiley and Sons Inc, New York, 1975.

pp 36–37 **1** *The Times Comprehensive Atlas*; G. A. McDonald, *Volcanoes*, Prentice Hall, 1972; F. M. Bullard, *Volcanoes of the Earth*, University of Texas Press, 1977; B. C. Heezen and C. D. Hollister, *The Face of the Deep*, Oxford University Press, 1971. **2** GEBCO, Canadian Hydrographic Survey. **4** H. W. Menard and H. S. Ladd, 'Oceanic islands, seamounts, guyots and atolls': M. N. Hill (Ed.), *The Sea vol. 3: The Earth Beneath the Sea*, Interscience, New York, 1963.

pp 38–39 **1** T. Hatherton, 'Active continental margins and island arcs': C. A. Burk and C. L. Drake (Eds), *The Geology of Continental Margins*, Springer-Verlag, New York, 1974; F. J. Vine, 'Sea-floor spreading': I. G. Gass, P. J. Smith and R. C. L. Wilson (Eds), *Understanding the Earth*, Open University Press, 1971. **2,3** O. M. Phillips, *The Heart of the Earth*, Freeman, Cooper & Co n.d. **4** M. H. P. Bott, *The interior of the Earth*, Edward Arnold, London. **6,8** *Oceanography: Introduction to the oceans Course S334 Unit 2*, Open University Press, 1977. **7** P. J. Wyllie, *The Dynamic Earth: Textbook in Geosciences*, John Wiley & Sons Inc, New York, 1971. **9** G. C. Brown and A. E. Mussett, *The Inaccessible Earth*, George Allen & Unwin, London, 1981. **10** I. G. Gass, A. G. Smith and F. J. Vine, 'Origin and emplacement of ophiolites': *Geodynamics Today*, Royal Soc. of London, 1975.

pp 40–41 **1** *Initial Reports of the Deep Sea Drilling Project*, National Science Foundation, Washington DC. **2** *Palaeoceanic reconstructions*, National Science Foundation. **3** *Scripps Institution of Oceanography*.

pp 42–43 **2** After R. E. Sheridan, 'Atlantic continental margin of North America': C. A. Burk and C. L. Drake (Eds), *The Geology of Continental Margins*, Springer-Verlag, New York, 1974. **4** M. D. Rawson, W. B. F. Ryan, 'Ocean floor sediment and polymetallic nodules', Lamont-Doherty Geological Observatory, Columbia University, New York, 1978; C. A. Burk and C. L. Drake, see **2** *op. cit*.

pp 46–47 **1,2** *Russian World Ocean Atlas* vols 1 and 2, Pergamon Press Ltd, Oxford 1974, 1978; *Meteorology for Mariners*, 3rd ed, HMSO 1978. **3,4** *Guidance notes for offshore industry*, Meteorological Office/UK Department of Energy, 1977. **6** M. N. Hill (Ed.) 'The sea' vol. 1, *Physical Oceanography*, Wiley-Interscience, New York, 1962.

pp 48–49 **1,2,3,4** J. L. Davies, *Geographical variations in coastal development*, 1980. **6,7,8,9** *Russian World Ocean Atlas* vol. 2 Atlantic and Indian Oceans, Pergamon Press Ltd, Oxford, 1978; *India Climatic Atlas*, 1943; *Meteorology for Mariners*, HMSO.

pp 50–51 **1,2** *Russian World Ocean Atlas* vols 1 and 2, Pergamon Press Ltd, Oxford, 1974, 1978; *Meteorology for Mariners*, HMSO. **3,4** A. H. Perry and J. M. Walker, *The Ocean–Atmosphere System*, Longman, 1977. **4** H. Stommel, 'The circulation of the abyss', 1958, repr. in *Ocean Science*, Scientific American; P. Tchernia, *Descriptive Regional Oceanography*, Pergamon Press Ltd, Oxford, 1980. **5–8** P. Tchernia, *op. cit*.

pp 52–53 **1** P. Groen, *The Waters of the Sea*, 1967; A. H. Perry and J. M. Walker, *The Ocean–Atmosphere System*, Longman, 1977. **2** Dr P. L. Richardson, 'Gulf Stream Rings'. **3** Dr P. L. Richardson et al, 'North Atlantic subtropical gyre: SOFAR floats tracked by moored listening stations': *Science*, repr. ed. vol. 213, 1981. **5** R. V. Tait, *Elements of Marine Ecology*, 1981. **6** A. H. Perry and J. M. Walker *op. cit*. **7** *CIA Indian Ocean Atlas*; *Russian World Ocean Atlas* vol. 2, Pergamon Press Ltd, Oxford, 1978. **8** Admiralty pilots; *The Times Concise Atlas*; *Russian World Ocean Atlas*, vols 1 and 2, Pergamon Press Ltd, Oxford, 1974, 1978.

pp 54–55 **1** *Mariners' Weather Logs; World Meteorological Organisation Bulletin; Annual Reports of League of Red Cross Societies*; P. J. Herbert and G. Taylor, 'Everything you always wanted to know about hurricanes': *Weatherwise* vol. 32 no. 2, 1979.

pp 56–57 **1,3,4** A. H. Perry and J. M. Walker *op. cit.*; D. de Angelis, *The World of Tropical Cyclones*; *Mariners' Weather Log* vol. 19 no. 6, 1975. **2** *Tropical cyclones of the N. Atlantic Ocean*, US Dept. of Commerce, 1978. **6** *The Times Concise Atlas*; 'World distribution of thunderstorm days'; Tables of Marine Data; WMO *World Maps*. **7** A. H. Gordon, 'Waterspouts': *The Marine Observer* vol. 21, 1951.

pp 58–59 **2** J. L. Davies, *Geographical variations in coastal development*, 1980. **3** E. S. Meisburger, *Frequency of occurrence of ocean surface waves in various height categories for coastal areas*, US Army Engineer Research and Development Laboratories, 1962. **4** J. K. Mallory, 'Abnormal waves on the south-east coast of South Africa': *International Hydrographic Review* vol. 51, 1974. **5,6** M. Darbyshire and L. Draper, 'Forecasting wind-generated sea waves', *Engineering* no. 195, 1963. **7,8** 'Guidance notes for offshore industry', Meteorological Office/UK Dept of Energy, 1977. **9** M. G. Spaeth, 'The New Tsunami Warning System': *Mariners Weather Log* vol. 18 no. 2, 1974; A. H. W. Robinson, 'The Pacific Tsunami of May 22nd, 1960': *Geography* vol. 46, 1961.

pp 60–61 **1,3** J. L. Davies *op. cit.* **4** D. E. Cartwright, 'Deep sea tides': R. G. Pine (Ed.), *Oceanography: contemporary readings in ocean sciences*, Oxford University Press, 1973. **5** C. A. M. King, *Introduction to physical and biological oceanography*, E. Arnold, 1975. **6** P. Groen, *The Waters of the Sea*, Van Nostrand, 1967. **7** R. D. Hunt, *The Marine Observer* vol. 42, 1972.

pp 62–63 **1,2** *CIA Polar Regions Atlas; The Times Comprehensive Atlas; Philips University Atlas*.

pp 64–65 **1** *CIA Polar Regions Atlas*; Walker and Scott, article in *Weather* vol. 27, 1972. **3** Dick De Angelis *Mariners Weather Log* vol. 18 part 1, 1974. **8** *CIA Polar Regions Atlas; Meteorology for Mariners*, HMSO. **9** E. Paul McClain, 'Eleven year chronicle of one of the world's most gigantic icebergs': *Mariners Weather Log* vol. 22 no. 5, 1978.

pp 66–67 **1,2,5,6** *Russian World Ocean Atlas* vols 1 and 2, Pergamon Press Ltd, Oxford, 1974, 1978. **4** A. H. Perry and J. M. Walker *op. cit.* **7–11** P. Tchernia, *Descriptive regional oceanography*, Pergamon Press Ltd, Oxford, 1980.

pp 68–69 **1** R. B. Tait, *Introduction to Marine Ecology*, 3rd ed., 1981.

pp 70–71 **1,11** *Atlas of the Living Resources of the Seas*, FAO, 1982. **10** *Biological Environments* Course 5334 Unit 10, The Open University, Milton Keynes.

pp 72–73 **1** A. L. Rice, *Oceanologica Acta* vol. 1, 1978.

pp 76–77 **1,7** R. M. Lockley, *Ocean Wanderers*, 1974. **2** B. Nelson, *Seabirds: their biology and ecology*, 1981. **3,5,6,9** G. Tuck and H. Heinzel, *A Field Guide to Seabirds of Britain and the World*, 1978.

pp 78–79 **1** *Atlas of the Living Resources of the Seas*, FAO, 1982; I. Everson, *The Living Resources of the Southern Ocean*, 1977. **2** Modified from S. Z. El-Sayed, 'On the productivity of the Southern Ocean', 1970, in M. W. Holdgate (Ed.), *Antarctic Ecology* vol. 1. Academic Press, London and New York.

pp 80–81 **3** and **4** H. J. Wiens, *Atoll Environment Ecology*, Yale University Press, 1962; 'Mariana to Marakei': British admiralty chart; R. La Catala, *Report on the Gilbert Islands*, Report to the South Pacific Commission, 1952; **6** H. D. Smith, 'The development of Shetland fisheries and fishing communities': P. H. Fricke (Ed.), *Seafarer and Community*, Croom Helm, London, 1973.

pp 82–83 **1–4** T. Pillay, *FAO Statistics*, Rome, 1982; Centre Nationale pour l'Exploitation des Océans, Paris, 1980. **6** E. S. Iversen, *Farming the Sea*, Fishing News Books, Farnham, 1976; Shao-Wen, *Aquaculture in South East Asia: an Historical Overview*, University of Washington Press, Seattle/London, 1978. **7** FAO, *Seaweed resources of the oceans*, FAO, Rome, 1978.

pp 84–85 **1** J. C. Sainsbury, *Commercial fishing methods; an introduction to vessels and gear*, Fishing News Books, Farnham, 1976. **2** J. C. Sainsbury, *op. cit.*; **5** IUCN, *World conservation strategy; living resource conservation for sustainable development*, IUCN/UNEP/WWF, Gland, Switzerland, 1980.

pp 86–87 **1** Lloyd's of London, *Lloyd's statistical tables*, London, 1980. **2** J. O. Traung (Ed.), *Fishing boats of the world* (3 vols), Fishing News Books, Farnham, 1955–1975; P. Hjul, *The stern trawler*, Fishing News Books, Farnham, 1972.

pp 88–89 **1** *FAO statistics*, Rome 1980. **2** FAO, *op. cit.*; M. A. Robinson, 'World fisheries to 2000: supply, demand and management': *Marine Policy* vol. 4 no. 1, 1980.

pp 90–91 **1** FAO, *op. cit.* **2** M. A. Robinson, *op. cit.*

pp 92–93 **1** J. R. Coull, 'The background to the Icelandic fisheries dispute': *Aberdeen University Review* vol. 45 no. 4, 1974; *Astand nytjastofna á Islandsmidum og aflahofnar*, Hafrannstoknastofrunin, Reykjavik, 1982. **2** FAO, Yearbooks of fishery statistics: catches and landings, Rome, 1978. **3** FAO, *op. cit.*; FAO *Atlas of the living resources of the seas*, Rome, 1981.

pp 94–95 **1** FAO statistics, *op. cit.* **2** A. von Brandt, 'Fisheries off North-West Africa': Rapp P-V Réun. Cons. Perm. Explor. Mer 159, 231–239; FAO Atlas, *op. cit.* **3** FAO statistics, *op. cit.*; FAO Atlas, *op. cit.*

pp 96–97 **1** FAO statistics, *op. cit.*; FAO Atlas, *op. cit.* **2** Fisheries statistics of Japan, statistics and information department, Ministry of Agriculture, Forestry and Fisheries Government of Japan, 1980. **4** FAO Atlas, *op. cit.*; Fisheries statistics of Japan, *op. cit.* **5** FAO, *op. cit.*

pp 98–99 **2** FAO statistics, *op. cit.* **3** FAO statistics, *op. cit.*; FAO Atlas, *op. cit.* **4** F. Bartz, *Die grassen Fischereiraume der Welt, Versuch einer regionalen Darstellung der Fischereiwirtschaft der Erde*, Wiesbaden, Franz Steiner Verlag. Bibliothek geographischer Handbucher, 1964; M. J. Valencia. '*Shipping, energy and environment: southeast Asian perspectives for the 1980s*': Workshop report, East–West Centre, Honolulu, Hawaii, 1980.

pp 100–101 **1** D. H. Cushing, *Fisheries Biology* 2nd ed., University of Wisconsin Press, 1981. **2** N. A. Mackintosh, *The stocks of Whales*, Fishing News Books, London, 1965. **3** A. Beaujon, *The history of the Dutch sea fisheries*, International Fisheries Exhibition Literature, London, 1883. **4** N. A. Mackintosh, *op. cit.* **5–6** K. R. Allen, Conservation and management of whales, University of Washington Press, London/Seattle, 1980. **7** FAO Atlas, *op. cit.* **9** H. Nakamura, *Tuna: distribution and migration*, Fishing News Books, London, 1969. **10** FAO Atlas, *op. cit.* **11** FAO statistics, *op. cit.* **13** FAO Atlas, *op. cit.* **14** FAO, *op. cit.*; *Report of meeting of North Atlantic salmon working group* ICES, Copenhagen, 1981; A. Netboy, *Salmon: The World's Most Harassed Fish*, Collins, 1960.

pp 102–103 **1** *Oil and gas* 1979, 1980, 1981; *BP Statistical Review*, British Petroleum Co. Ltd; *International Petroleum Times* vol. 84, 1980; *American Association of Petroleum Geologists Bulletin* vol. 63 no. 10, 1979.

pp 104–109 *International Petroleum Encyclopaedia* 1980, Pennwell Publishing Co., 1980; *OPEC Annual Statistical Bulletins* 1979, 1980; *Pipeline Industries; International Petroleum Times; Offshore Services* 1979, 1980; *Petroleum 2000*.

pp 110–111 **1** V. E. McKelvey and F. H. H. Wang et al, 'World Subsea Mineral resources', US Geological Survey preliminary map 1970; Frazer and Wilson 'Manganese nodule resources in the Indian Ocean': *Marine Mining* vol. 2 no. 3, 1980; G. P. Glasby (Ed.) 'Deep sea nodules: distribution and geochemistry': *Marine Manganese Deposits* n.d. **2** 'World Mineral Statistics 1976–80', Institute of Geological Sciences, London, 1982; 'Metal statistics 1970–80': Metallgesellschaft Aktiengesellschaft 68th ed, 1980; 'Phosphate rock statistics 1981': Comité des matières premières groupe de travail, phosphate brut et acide phosphorique.

pp 112–113 **1** V. E. McKelvey and F. H. H. Wang *op. cit.*; F. C. F. Earney, Petroleum and Hard Minerals from the Sea, n.d.; E. Oele 'Sand and gravel from shallow seas': *Geologie en Mijnbouw* vol. 57 no. 1, n.d. **3** C. H. Nelson and D. M. Hopkins, 'Sedimentary processes and distribution of particulate gold in the Northern Bering Sea': US Geological Survey Professional Paper no. 689. **4** M. Simaptupang and P. T. Tambang, 'Indonesian offshore tin development': A. Prijorio (Ed.) et al, *Indonesian mining industry: its present and future*, Indonesian Mining Association, 1977. **5,6** 'Distribution of sand and gravel deposits on the continental margin': *Oceanus*, Fall, 1975. **7** *Atlas of the Seas around the British Isles*, Ministry of Agriculture, Fisheries and Food, 1981.

pp 114–115 **1** R. C. Coleman et al, *Ophiolites*, 1969. **3** Marine Mining vol. 1 no. 3 and vol. 4 no. 3, n.d. **4** V. E. McKelvey and F. H. H. Wang, *op. cit.* **5** 'The submarine phosphate deposits off Southern California' vol. 2: Offshore Technology Conference, Houston, Texas 1970; K. O. Emery, *The Sea off California*, n.d. **7** *Marine Geology* vols 28 and 29, 1978 and 1979; *Nature* vol. 277, 1979; 'Transactions of Geology Society of South Africa', 1973.

pp 116–117 **1** V. E. McKelvey and F. H. Wang, *op. cit.*; Rawson and W. B. F. Ryan, 'Ocean floor sediment and polymetallic nodules': Martine Dreyfuss, Office of the Geographer, US Dept of State, 1978. **2** H. Bastion Thiry et al, 'French exploration seeks to define mineable nodule tonnages on Pacific floor': *Energy and Mining Journal* vol. 178, 1977. **3** J. Z. Frazer, 'Manganese nodule reserves: an up-dated estimate': *Marine Mining* vol. 1 nos. 1–2, 1977. **4,5,6** D. S. Cronan and S. A. Moorby, 'Manganese nodules and other ferromanganese oxide deposits from the Indian Ocean': *Journal of the Geological Society* vol. 138, 1981.

pp 118–119 **1** Sir Peter Kent, Minerals from the Marine Environment, 1978. **3** 'Proceedings of the first Desalination Congress of American Continent', 1980.

pp 120–121 **1** P. R. Ryan, 'Harnessing power from tides—a state of the art': *Oceanus* vol. 22 no. 4, 1979/80. **3** D. Crabbe and R. McBride, 'Annual wave energy in specific sea areas': *The world energy book*, 1978; B. M. Count, *Wave power, progress and projects*, UK Central Electricity Generating Board, 1979. **4** J. N. Newman, 'Power from ocean waves': *Oceanus* vol. 22 no. 4, 1979/80. **7,8** Energy Technology Support Unit, AERE, Harwell, Oxfordshire; **9** 'Ocean thermal energy': *Ocean Industry*, Nov. 1978; 'Ocean thermal energy conversion programme summary': Energy, Research and Development Administration, Washington DC. **10** Lockheed Missiles and Space Company, Inc.

pp 122–133 *Ports of the world*, Lloyd's of London Press, 1982; *Lloyd's Maritime Atlas* 11th ed., Lloyd's of London Press, 1977; *The Times Comprehensive Atlas*; Port Authorities of: Marseille, London, Rotterdam, Götteborg, Port Talbot, New York, San Francisco; Tokyo, Singapore, Sydney; Calcutta Port Trust; p 134 N. Beard, 'London Docklands: an example of inner city renewal': *Geography* vol. 64 no. 3.

pp 134–135 **1** Containerisation International Yearbook; *UN Statistical Yearbook*; Galbraith's shipping map; Flexi-Van Corporation, *The State of Containerisation*, 1979; Statesman's Yearbook. **2** US Ports Foreign trade report 1977, US Dept of Commerce; individual port authorities. **3** C. Van Schirach-Szmigie, 'Foreign Trade in European Ports': Stockholm School of Economics; individual port authorities.

pp 136–137 **1,2,4,5,8** Fearnley and Egers Chartering Co. Ltd. **3** British Sulphur Co. Ltd. **6** 'Balance in maritime sectors': B & W Diesel, Copenhagen, 1980. **7** Containerisation International Yearbook. **9** Fearnley and Egers; *BP Statistical review of the world oil industry*, 1980/1981; *BP Statistical review of world energy*, 1981. **10** J. W. Kerr, 'Report on 14th World Gas Conference, Toronto, Canada 1979'.

pp 138–139 *Kawasaki Ship Review*, Kawasaki Heavy Industries Ltd, 1980; *Shipping World and Shipbuilder; Lloyd's Statistical Abstract*, 1982.

pp 140–141 **1** Based on data supplied to UNCTAD Secretariat by A. and P. Appledore Ltd, North Devon; *Open Registry Fleets*, UNCTAD, 1980 and 1981. **3** *Lloyd's Register of Shipping 1982* and *Lloyd's Register of Shipping Statistical Tables 1970–80*, Lloyd's Press, London, 1980.

pp 142–143 **1,5** 'Survey—world ships on order': Fairplay International 1981; Lloyd's register of shipping, Annual summary of completed ships throughout the world in 1977, Lloyd's Press, London. **2** General Council of British Shipping Annual Reviews, 1976–81. **4** *The Growth of Shiprepair*, Dock and Harbour Authority, 1978. **7** *Lloyd's register of shipping statistical tables, 1971–79*, Lloyd's Press, London, 1980. **8** General Council of British Shipping; *British Shipping Review 1982*. **9** H. P. Drewry, *Shipping Statistics and Economics*.

pp 144–145 **1** 'International seaborne trade 1980': UNCTAD. **2** Updated from J. K. Gamble, 'Law of the Sea Institute 8th Annual Conference 1973', using UN statistics and formula. **3** 'Review of Maritime Transport 1981': UNCTAD. **4** M. McGuire and W. Broeren, *Marine transportation index of national interest*, Dalhousie, Halifax, Nova Scotia, 1975.

pp 146–147 **1** *Lloyd's Maritime Atlas*, Lloyd's Press, London; D. Hilling, *Barge carrier systems*, Benn, London, 1978; wall chart by Mobil Oil Co. Ltd.

pp 148–149 **1,2** *Ships Routeing* 4th ed., IMO, 1978 (1981 amendments); *Weather Routeing North Atlantic* Ocean Routes (Europe) Ltd, Gravesend. **4** *CIA Polar Regions Atlas*, 1978; J. A. Cestone and E. St George Jar, 'Underwater Arctic Navigation': *Journal of Navigation* vol. 27 no. 3, July 1974. **5** *Meteorology for Mariners*, UK Dept of Energy/Met. Office.

pp 150–151 **1** 'World straits affected by a 12 mile territorial sea': (map) Office of the Geographer, US Dept of State; *Ships Routeing* 4th ed., IMO, 1978 (1981 amendments). **2** R. W. Smith, 'An analysis of the strategic attributes of international straits: a geographical perspective': *Maritime studies and management* no. 2, Admiralty sailing directions, 1974; 'Limits of oceans and seas': special pub. no. 28, International hydrographic bureau, 1953.

pp 152–153 **2** Panama Canal Company; Admiralty Charts; 'Panama Canal': *Lloyd's Shipping Economist*, 1980. **6** Suez Canal Company; Admiralty Charts. **7** 'Nord-Ostee Kanal Statistische Dokumentation', 1970–82.

pp 154–155 **1–6** *Admiralty Sailing Directions and Charts; Admiralty Tide Tables* vol. 2; *Russian World Ocean Atlas* vols 1 and 2, Pergamon Press Ltd, 1974, 1978; *Lloyd's Maritime Atlas; Meteorological Atlas of the Indian Ocean*, Meteorological Office; *Ship Routeing* 4th ed., IMO, 1978; *The Times Comprehensive Atlas*; M. Leifer, *Malacca, Singapore, Indonesia* vol. 2, Sijthoff and Noordhoff, 1978; G. Blake, 'Turkish guard on Russian waters': *Geographical Magazine*, Dec 1981

pp 156–157 **1,3** *Admiralty Sailing Directions and Charts; Admiralty Tide Tables; Lloyds Maritime Atlas*; **5** C. C. Bates and P. Yost (US Coastguard), 'Where trends the flow of merchant ships': 8th Annual Conference on Law of the Sea, Washington.

pp 158–159 **1** *Admiralty List of Radio Signals* vols 2 and 5, Hydrographer of the Navy; *Admiralty Manual of Navigation* vol. 1, HMSO. **4** International Assoc. of Lighthouse Authorities, *Maritime Buoyage Systems A and B* 2nd ed., Hydrographer of the Navy, 1980. **5** Admiralty Notices to Mariners, Hydrographer of the Navy.

pp 160–161 **1** Münchenen Ruchversicherungs Gesellschaft, West Germany. **1,3** Hydrographer to the Navy.

pp 162–163 **1** 'Serious Casualties to Merchant Ships 1978–79': Shipping Information Services of Lloyd's Register of Shipping, Lloyd's Press, London. **2** 'Lloyd's Register of Shipping Casualty Statistics 1980': Lloyd's Press, London. **4** *Offshore*, March 1981. **5** 'Lloyd's Register of Shipping Casualty Returns—Polar Record' vol. 19 no. 121, 1979. **7** P. Padfield, *The Titanic and the Californian*, Hodder and Stoughton Ltd, 1965.

pp 164–165 **1** *British Shipping Statistics*, General Council for British Shipping, May 1982; *Lloyd's Casualty Returns Annual Summary*, Lloyd's Press, London, 1980; J. F. Read, 'Shipping casualties around the British Isles 1970–79': NMI, 1981; Liverpool Underwriters Association, 'Hull casualty statistics (ships of 500 gross tons and over)': IUMI Conference, Corfu, 1981.

pp 166–167 **1** J. C. Carruthers, 'The *Andrea Doria/Stockholm* Disaster—Was there a conspiracy?': *Safety at Sea International*, Dec. 1972. **2** A. N. Cockroft, 'Sailor beware, full ahead in fog can spell disaster': *Safety at Sea International*, May 1969; The *Sitala* (1963) 1, Lloyd's Report 205. **3** A. N. Cockroft, 'Collision off Cape St Vincent': *Safety at Sea International*, Oct. 1972; The Statue of Liberty (1971) 2, Lloyd's Report 77. **4** P. M. Alderton, 'Two ships ignored the rules and a collision was the penalty': *Safety at Sea International*, July 1970; *The Rattray Head* and the *Tillerman* (1970), Lloyd's Report. **5** A. N. Cockroft, 'A radar-assisted collision': *Safety at Sea International*, September 1973; The *Hagen* (1973), Lloyd's Report 257. **6** HMSO Formal Investigation Report of Court no. 8021, '*Crystal Jewel* and the *British Aviator*', Feb 1962; The *British Aviator* (1965) 1, Lloyd's Report 271 (CA). **7** *The Sea Star* (1976) 2, Lloyd's Report 477 (CA).

pp 168–169 **1** 'Report of the Republic of Liberia Marine Board of Investigation on the loss of the Torrey Canyon': Monrovia/Liberia 1967; P. M. Alderton, 'Disaster stirred world action against a peril of the sea': *Safety at Sea International*, April 1970. **2** 'Final Report of the Republic of Liberia Marine Board of Investigation on the loss of the Argo Merchant': Bureau of Liberian Maritime Affairs, Oct 1977. **4** 'Final and Interim Reports of the Republic of Liberia Marine Board of Investigation on the loss of the Amoco Cadiz': Bureau of Liberian Maritime Affairs, Dec 1980.

pp 170–171 **1** Information from: IMO Reports, 1980–81; Centre for Short-lived Phenomena, 1979–80; 'Oil spills in 1978/1979: An International Summary and Review': *Oilspill Intelligence Reports* vol. 2 no. 12, Mar 1979, vol. 3 no. 21, May 1980; Ocean Affairs, 'Workshop on inputs, fates and effects of petroleum in the marine environment': Virginia, USA, May 1973; 'Petroleum in the Marine Environment': National Academy of Sciences, Washington DC, 1975; 'Higher Risk Sea Areas—A Risk Analysis': OCIMF, Aug 1979; R. D. Wilson, P. H. Monaghan, A. Osanik, L. C. Price and M. A. Rogers, 'Estimate of Annual Input of Petroleum to the Marine Environment from Natural Marine Seepage': Transactions Gulf Coast Association of Geological Societies vol. 23, 1973.

pp 172–173 **1** G. J. Hunt, 'Radioactivity in surface and coastal waters of the British Isles 1979': Ministry of Agriculture, Fisheries and Food Directorate of Fisheries Research, 1981; K. K. Landes, 'Mother Nature as an oil polluter': American Assoc. of Petroleum Geologists, Bulletin no. 4, Apr 1973; 'Assessment of the effects of pollution on fisheries and aquaculture in Japan': FAO Fisheries Technical Paper no. 163, Oct 1973; 'The Health of the Oceans': UNEP Regional Seas Reports and Studies, nos 1, 2, 4, 6, 13, 14, 16; 'Marine Environmental Impact due to Mining Activities of El Salvador Copper Mines' and 'Bottom sediment contamination in the Bay of Naples, Italy': *Marine Pollution Bulletin* vol. 9, 1978; D. W. Abecassis, 'Marine oil pollution': *The International Nature of Marine Pollution*, Dept of Land Economy, Cambridge, 1976; T. Vabiyana, 'Policies in pollution aquaculture and coastal management in Japan': *Marine Policy* vol. 3 no. 1, 1979; 'Economic Aspects of the Effects of pollution on the marine and anadromous fisheries of the western USA': FAO 1 paper 162, 1976.

pp 174–175 **1** A. J. Lee and J. W. Ramster (Eds), *Atlas of the Seas around the British Isles*, Fisheries Research Technical Report no. 20, 1979. **2–6** 'European Parliament Working Document on the Pollution of the North Sea' no. 298/81, 1981; 'International Council for the Exploration of the Sea Report of working group for the International study of the pollution of the North Sea and its effects on living resources and their exploitation': Cooperative Research Report no. 39, May 1974; 'Nuclear waste spreads across the North Sea': *Maritime Policy Bulletin*, 1979. **3** 'The Baltic': *AMBIO* (special issue) vol. 9 nos 3–4, vol. 6 no. 6, 1980; 'Prevention of Oil Pollution in the Baltic Sea area': Merchant Shipping Notice no. 966, Dept of Trade, 1981.

pp 176–177 **1–6** 'Pollutants from land-based sources in the Mediterranean': UNEP/WG/8/INF4, June 1979; 'Le Bassin Méditerranean, Cadre Geographique et Socio-Economique Du Plan Bleu': UN, Jan 1977; 'The Mediterranean': *AMBIO* (special issue) vol. 6 no. 6, 1977; 'Preliminary report on the state of the Mediterranean Sea': UNEP, Jan 1978.

pp 178–179 **1–3** Capt. J. Moore RN (Ed.), *Jane's Fighting Ships*, 1982–83, Jane's Publishing Co. Ltd, London, 1983.

pp 180–181 **1–3** *Jane's Fighting Ships op. cit.*; **5–8** H. Scoville Jnr, 'Missile Submarines and National Security': *Scientific American* vol. 226 no. 6, 1972; J. S. Wit, 'Advances in Anti-Submarine Warfare': *Scientific American* vol. 244 no. 2, Feb 1981.

pp 182–183 **1** B. Dismukes and J. McConnel, *Soviet Naval Diplomacy*, 1979; *Armaments and Disarmaments*, SIPRI Yearbook, 1979. **2** R. Humble, *Undersea Warfare*, 1981. **3** Pergamon Policy Studies no. 37, Pergamon Press Ltd. **4** British Maritime League, 1983.

pp 184–185 **5** *CIA Polar Regions Atlas*, Washington 1978.

pp 186–187 **1–6** B. Buzan, 'The Sea of Troubles: Sources of Dispute in the New Ocean Regime': Adelphi Papers no. 143, Institute of Strategic Studies, London, 1973; W. Epstein, 'Nuclear Free Zones': *Scientific American* vol. 233 no. 5, Nov 1975; US State Department, Washington

pp 188–189 **1** J. R. V. Prescott, *Maritime Jurisdiction in South East Asia*, East–West Centre, Honolulu, Hawaii, 1981; US State Dept, Washington DC; Keesings Contemporary Archives; M. S. Samuels, *Contest for the South China Sea*, Methuen, London, 1982; Belchman and Kaplan, *Force without War: US Armed Forces as a Political Instrument*, 1979. **2** B. Dismukes and J. McConnel, *Soviet Naval Diplomacy*, 1979.

pp 192–193 **2** Behaims's terrestial globe is at the National Museum, Nurnberg. **3** The 'Typus Orbis Terrarum' of Abraham Ortelius from *Theatnum Orbis Terrarum*, Antwerp, 1570 (facsimile ed. pub. N. Israel, Amsterdam, 1964). **4** from Ptolemaic 'Geography', ed. Nicolaus Germanus, in A. Bettex, *The Discovery of the World*, Thames and Hudson, 1960.

pp 194–198 Keith Muckelroy (Ed.), 'Archaeology under Water': *An Atlas of the World's Submerged Sites*, McGraw-Hill Book Company, 1980; The Mary Rose Trust, Portsmouth; 'The Underwater Cultural Heritage': Report of the Committee on Culture and Education, Doc. 4200, Council of Europe, 1978; D. J. Blackman (Ed.), *Marine Archaeology*, 23rd Symposium of Colston Research Society, University of Bristol, 1971; *The International Journal of Nautical Archaeology and Underwater Exploration*, Published for the Council for Nautical Archaeology, Academic Press, London; National Maritime Museum, London, UK; *Underwater World* vol. 4 no. 9, September 1981; 'Progress in Underwater Science': Annual Report of the Underwater Association, Pentech Press, London.

pp 198–199 **1** World Ocean Atlases, Atlantic, Pacific and Indian Oceans.

pp 200–201 **1** *List of cables forming the world submarine network*, 19th ed. International Telecommunication Union, Geneva, 1977.

pp 202–203 *CIA Polar Regions Atlas.*

pp 206–207 The International Decade of Ocean Exploration (IDOE), 1971–1980, Intergovernmental Oceanographic Commission Technical Services 13, Unesco 1974; Marine Information and Advisory Service, Institute of Oceanographic Sciences, Brook Road, Wormley, Godalming, Surrey GU8 5UB, UK; Marine Information and Advisory Service, News Bulletin Number 2, Natural Environmental Research Council; Research Vessels and Exploration of Marine Resources, Institute of Shipping Economics Bremen, Lecture and Contributions No. 25, Bremen, 1979; National Science Foundation, Division of Ocean Sciences, Washington DC; A. Varley (Ed.), Ocean Research Index, Frances Hodgson, Cambridge, England; W. S. Wooster, 'International Cooperation in Marine Science': Ocean Yearbook 2, edited by E. M. Borgese and Norton Ginsburg, University of Chicago Press, Chicago and London; 'Research Vessel Fleets by Country', 'Surface Research and Survey Vessels by Country', 'Submersible Research and Survey Vessels by Country': Ocean Yearbook 2, University Chicago Press, Chicago and London.

pp 208–209 **1** A. D. Couper, 'Marine Resources and Environment': *Progress in Human Geography* vol. 2 no. 2, 1978; *World conservation strategy: living resource conservation for sustainable development* IUCN/UNEP/WWF, Gland, Switzerland, 1980; G. Hardin, 'The tragedy of the commons': *Science* no. 162, 1968; S. A. Patin, *Pollution and the biological resources of the oceans*, Butterworths, London, 1982; D. M. Johnston, 'The Environmental Law of the Sea': International Union for Conservation of Nature and Natural Resources, Gland, Switzerland, 1981.

pp 210–211 **1** Red Data Books, vol. 1 *Mammalia*, vol. 4 *Pisces*, IUCN, Switzerland, 1980.

pp 212–213 **1,2** Great Barrier Reef Marine Park Authority: Bulletin no. 3, Nov 1981; Zoning Plan, Aug 1980; Annual Report 1980/81; *Great Barrier Reef Travellers' Companion*, Australian Tourist Commission, 1980; 'Reeflections' *(sic)* Great Barrier Reef Marine Park Authority, 1978. **4** IUCN 'A Strategy for the Conservation of Living Resources and Processes in the Caribbean Region': *Caribbean Data Atlas*, Gland/IUCN, Switzerland.

pp 214–215 **1** Hydrographer of the Netherlands; A. J. Lee and J. W. Ramster (Eds), *Atlas of the Seas around the British Isles*, Fisheries Directorate, MAFF, Lowestoft, 1981; A. D. Couper and H. D. Smith, 'Multi-use and multi-state management in the North Sea': Law of the Sea Institute 16th Annual Conference, Halifax, June 1982. **2** Rijkswaterstorat, Directie Noordzee, The Netherlands.

pp 216–217 **1** *ABC Shipping Guide*, Dunstable, UK. **2** *Yachting World*, London. **4** G. Fairmont, *The Surfer's Almanac; an International Surfing Guide*, New York, 1976. **5** *Bretagne Nautisme*, Regional Brittany Tourist Authority, 1980. **7** Department of Fish and Game, Resources Agency, Sacramento.

pp 218–219 *The Annual Summary of Notices to Mariners*, Hydrographic Dept, UK.

pp 220–221 'A map illustrating the various formulae for the definition of the continental shelf', a preliminary study prepared by the Secretariat at the request of the 2nd Committee of the 3rd UN Conference on the Law of the Sea; 'Limits in the Seas', US Dept of State, Bureau of Intelligence and Research, Office of the The Geographer, Washington

pp 222–223 P. B. Beazley, *Maritime limits and baselines: a guide to their delineation*, special pub. no. 2, The Hydrographic Society, London 1978.

Appendix II International Boundary Studies, Series A, Limits of the Seas, The Geographer, Dept of State, Washington, DC; UN Statistics, UNCLOS III; *Marine Policy*, July 1981; The Times Comprehensive Atlas; *Norie's Nautical Tables*, Imray Lowrie Norie & Wilson Ltd, 1973. *Appendix III* FAO Statistics, Rome. *Appendix IV* International Convention for the Regulation of Whaling 1946, with subsequent amendments up to and including the 34th annual meeting, Brighton, UK, July 1982. *Appendix V BP Statistical Review of the World*. *Appendix VI* General Council of British Shipping; John L. Jacobs & Co. Ltd, *World Tanker Fleet Review*; Fearnley and Egers Chartering Co. Ltd, Oslo. *Appendix VII Lloyd's Nautical Yearbook*, Lloyd's of London Press, 1982. *Appendix IX* J. van Beylan, *List of Maritime Museums and Collections*, Marine Academie, Antwerp, 1976. *Appendix X* Douglas M. Johnston (Ed.), *The Environmental Law of the Sea*, IUCN, Gland, Switzerland, 1981; Red Data Books, IUCN, Gland, Switzerland ; IOC, Technical Series 13, UNESCO.

Bibliography

The ocean environment

M. Grant Gross, *Oceanography: a view of the Earth*, Prentice Hall Inc, New Jersey, 1977; B. C. Heezen and C. D. Hollister, *The face of the Deep*, Oxford University Press, 1971; P. Weyl, *Oceanography: An introduction to the Marine Environment*, John Wiley, New York, 1970; B. C. Heezen and A. S. Laughton, 'The Earth Beneath the Sea': M. N. Hill (Ed.), *The Sea* vol. 3, Wiley-Interscience, New York, 1963; A. Cox (Ed.), *Plate Tectonics and Geomagnetic Reversals*, Freeman & Co, San Francisco, 1973; P. J. Wyllie, *The Dynamic Earth: Textbook in Geosciences*, John Wiley and Sons Inc, New York, 1971; A. Cox, G. B. Dalrymple and R. R. Doell, 'Reversals of the Earth's Magnetic Field': *Scientific American*, 1967; F. Press and R. Siever, *Earth*, Freeman & Co, San Francisco, 1974; F. J. Vine and D. H. Matthews, 'Magnetic Anomalies over Oceanic Ridges': *Nature*, nos 199, 974–949, 1963; F. J. Vine and H. H. Hess, 'Sea Floor Spreading': A. E. Maxwell (Ed.), *The Sea* vol. 4, Wiley-Interscience, New York, 1970; S. Vyeda, *The New View of the Earth*, Freeman & Co, San Francisco, 1978; G. C. Brown and A. E. Mussett, *The Inaccessible Earth*, George Allen and Unwin, London, 1981; A. G. Smith, 'Continental Drift': I. G. Gass, P. J. Smith and R. C. L. Wilson (Eds), *Understanding the Earth*, Open University Press, 1971; D. G. Smith, *The Cambridge Encyclopedia of Earth Sciences*, Cambridge University Press, 1981; P. J. Wyllie, *The way the Earth works*, Wiley, New York, 1976; B. F. Windley, *The evolving continents*, Wiley, Chichester, 1977; D. H. Tarling, *Evolution of the Earth's crust*, Academic Press, London, 1978; Open University, *Oceanography: Introduction to the Oceans*, Course S 334 Units 1–3, Open University Press, 1977; H. G. Reading, *Sedimentary Environments and Facies*, B. H. Blackwell and Sons Ltd, Oxford, 1978; W. H. Bergen, 'Deep-Sea Sedimentation': C. A. Burke and C. L. Drake (Eds), *The Geology of Continental Margins*, Springer-Verlag, New York, 1974; M. N. Hill (Ed.), *The Sea* vol. 1 'Physical Oceanography'; A. H. Perry and J. M. Walker, *The Ocean–Atmosphere System*, Longman, London and New York, 1977; P. Tchernia, *Descriptive Regional Oceanography*, Pergamon, 1980; *Meteorology for Mariners*, 3rd ed., Her Majesty's Stationery Office, London, 1978; *Encyclopaedia of Birds* part 3, Orbis, 1977; N. B. Marshall, *Developments in deep-sea biology*, Blandford Press, Poole, Dorset, 1979; F. S. Russell and M. Y. Yonge, *The Seas: an introduction to the study of life in the sea*, Frederick Warne, London and New York, 1975; A. C. Hardy, *The open sea—Its natural history: the world of plankton*, Collins, New Naturalist Series, London, 1956; A. C. Hardy, *The open sea—Its natural history: fish and fisheries*, Collins, New Naturalist Series, 1956; A. C. Hardy, *Great Waters*, Collins, London, 1967.

Living resources

F. Bartz, *Die grossen Fischereiraume der Welt. Versuch einer regionalen Darstellung der Fischereiwirtschaft der Erde. Bd 1: Atlantisches Europa und Mittelmeer, Bd 2: Asien mit Einschluss der Sowjetunion*, Wiesbaden, Franz Steiner Verlag, Bibliothek geographischer Handbucher, 1964; A. Von Brandt, *Fish catching methods of the world* 2nd ed., Fishing News Books, Farnham, 1981; C. A. Goodlad, *Shetland Fishing Saga*, The Shetland Times, Lerwick, 1971; H. D. Smith, 'The development of Shetland Fisheries and Fishing Communities': P. H. Fricke (Ed.), *Seafarer and Community*, Croom Helm, London, 1973; *Seaweed resources of the oceans*, FAO, Rome, 1978; J. A. Hanson, *Open sea mariculture: perspectives, problems and prospects*, Dowden, Hutchison & Ross, 1974; T. V. R. Pillay (Ed.), *Coastal aquaculture in the Indo-Pacific region*, Fishing News Books, Farnham, 1970; T. V. R. Pillay and W. A. Dill (Eds), *Advances in aquaculture*, Fishing News Books, Farnham, 1979; Shao-wen Ling, *Aquaculture in South East Asia: an historical overview*, University of Washington Press, Seattle/London, 1977; J. Thorpe (Ed.), *Salmon ranching*, Academic Press, London/New York, 1980; *Modern Fishing Gears of the World* (3 vols), Fishing News Books, Farnham; R. Morgan, *World Sea Fisheries*, Methuen, London, 1956; J. Sainsbury, *Commercial Fishing Methods: an introduction to vessels and gear*, Fishing News Books, Farnham, 1971; P. Hjul, *The Stern Trawler*, Fishing News Books, Farnham, 1972; J. A. Gulland, *The Fish Resources of the Ocean*, Fishing News Books, Farnham, 1971; *Atlas of the living resources of the seas* 4th ed., FAO, Rome, 1982.

The fisheries

G. O. Barney, *The Global 2000 Report to the President of the US* (fisheries section), Pergamon Press Ltd, 1981; G. Borgstrom, *Fish as Food*, Academic Press, 1961; N. G. Benson, *A century of Fisheries in North America*, 1970; J. R. Coull, *The Fisheries of Europe*, Bell, London, 1972; D. H. Cushing, *The Arctic cod*, Pergamon Press Ltd, 1966; A. J. Heighway and G. Borgstrom, *Atlantic Ocean Fisheries*, Fishing News Books, 1961; A. Underdal, *The politics of fisheries management: the case of the North-east Atlantic*, Oslo University Press, 1980; F. H. Bell, *The Pacific halibut: the resource and the fishery*, Alaska North-west Publishing, 1981; G. Borgstrom, *Japan's world success in fisheries*, Fishing News Books, London, 1964; O. Young, *Resource management at the international level: the case of the North Pacific*, Frances Pinter, London, 1977; A. Davidson, *Seafood of South East Asia*, Macmillan, London, 1978; M. H. Glantz and J. D. Thompson, *Resource management and environmental uncertainty: lessons from coastal upwelling fisheries*, Wiley, New York, 1980; P. Pownall, *Fisheries of Australia*, Fishing News Books, Farnham, 1978; R. S. Shomura et al, *The present state of fisheries and assessment of potential resources of the Indian Ocean and adjacent seas*, FAO, Fish Rep. 54, Rome, 1967; K. R. Allen, *Conservation and managament of whales*, University of Washington Press, Seattle/London, 1980; G. Jackson, *The British whaling trade*, London, 1978; N. A. Mackintosh, *The stocks of whales*, Fishing News Books, London, 1965; I. H. Matthews, *The natural history of the whale*, Weidenfeld and Nicolson, London, 1980; E. Mitchell, *Porpoise, dolphin and small whale fisheries of the world: status and problems*, Gland IUCN, 1975; E. Slipjer, *Whaling* 3rd ed , 1979; J. N. Tønnessen and A. O. Johnsen, *The history of modern whaling*, Hurst/ANU Press, London/Canberra, 1982; J. Joseph and J. W. Greenough, *International management of tuna, porpoise and billfish: biological, legal and political aspects*, University of Washington Press, Seattle/London, 1979; N. Nakamura, *Tuna distribution and migration*, Fishing News Books, London, 1969; W. J. McNeil and D. C. Himsworth, *Salmonid ecosystems of the North Pacific*, Oregon State University Press, 1980; A. E. J. Went, *The Atlantic salmon: its future*, Fishing News Books, Farnham, 1980.

Offshore hydrocarbons, minerals and energy potentials

Our Industry Petroleum 2nd ed., British Petroleum, London, 1977; F. C. F. Earney, *Petroleum and hard minerals from the sea*, Edward Arnold, London, 1980; A. Wildavesky and E. Tenenbaum, *The Politics of Mistrust Estimating American Oil and Gas Resources*, Sage Publications, 1981; M. S. Baram, D. Rice and W. Lee, *Marine Mining of the Continental Shelf*, Ballinger Publishing Co., 1978; *BP Statistical Reviews*, British Petroleum Co., London, 1979, 1980; J. G. N. Nelson and S. Jessine, *The Scottish and Alaskan Offshore Oil and Gas Experience and the Canadian Beaufort Sea*, University of Waterloo, 1981; K. Chapman, *North Sea Oil and Gas: A Geographical Perspective*, David and Charles, Newton Abbot, 1976; A. M. Hutcheson and A. Hogg, *Scotland and Oil* 2nd ed., Oliver and Boyd, Edinburgh, 1975; Oo Jin Bee, *The Petroleum Resources of Indonesia*, Oxford University Press, Oxford, 1981; C. M. Siddayao, *The Offshore Petroleum Resources of South East Asia: Potential Conflict Situations and Related Economic Considerations*, Oxford University Press, Oxford, 1981; D. J. Faulkner, 'The Search for Drugs from the Sea': *Oceanus* vol. 22 no. 2, summer 1979.

Ports of the world

A. Vigarie, *Ports de Commerce et vie Littorale*, Hachette Universelle, Paris, 1979; Y. Karmon, *Ports Around the World*, Crown Publishers, 1980; J. Bird, *Seaports and Seaport Terminals*, Hutchinson, 1971; R. S. Thomas, *Freeports and Foreign Trade Zones*, Cornell Maritime Press, 1980; B. Nagorski, *Port Problems in Developing Countries*, IAPH, 1979; R. Takel, *Industrial Port Development*, Scientechnica, 1974.

Ships and cargoes

Review of Maritime Transport 1981 (TD/B/64/251), UNCTAD, 1982; *Shipping Statistics Yearbooks*, Institute of Shipping Economics, Bremen; Richard G. Wooler, *Marine transportation of LNG and related products*, Cornell Maritime Press, 1975; R. Ffooks, *Natural Gas by Sea*, Gentry Books, London, 1979; E. Gold, *Maritime Transport: the Evolution of International Marine Policy and Shipping Laws*, Lexington Books, 1981; P. M. Alderton, *Sea Transport*, Thomas Reed, 1980; A. Branch, *Elements of Shipping*, Chapman and Hall, 1981; R. O. Goss, *Studies in Maritime Economics*, University of Cardiff Press, 1982; *The Growth of World Shiprepair*, UK Dock and Harbour Authority, 1978; A. D. Couper, *The Geography of Sea Transport*, Hutchinson, 1972.

Shipping routes

W. E. Butler, *Northeast Arctic Passage* vol. 1, Sijthoff and Noordhof, 1978; M. Leifer, *Malacca, Singapore and Indonesia* vol. 2, Sijthoff and Noordhoff, 1978; K. Shaw and G. Thomson, 'The Straits of Malacca': *Journal of Navigation* no. 55, 1972; R. P. Thomson, 'Establishing Global Traffic Flows': *Journal of Navigation* vol. 25 no. 4, Oct 1972; K. L. Koh, *Straits in International Navigation*, Oceana Publications, 1982.

The hazardous sea

D. K. Fleming, 'Seascapes': *Maritime Policy and Management* vol. 9, Jan 1982; 'Higher Risk Sea Areas—A Risk Analysis': Oil Companies International Marine Forum, Aug 1979; 'Mobile Rig Mishaps': *Ocean Industry*, Mar 1977; 'Ocean Ranger Sinks at Hibernia during storm': *Ocean Industry*, Mar 1982; Capt. P. Alderton, 'Loss of a Famous Liner': *Safety at Sea International*, Jan 1972; Anon, 'The Californian Incident': Mercantile Marine Service Assoc., Liverpool, 1965.

The health of the oceans

Finn et al, *Oil Pollution from Tankers in the Straits of Malacca: Policy and Legal Analysis*, East–West Centre, Hawaii, 1979; J. E. Kelly and C. E. Shea, 'The Sub-seabed Disposal for High Level Radioactive Waste—Public Response': *Oceanus*, 1978; R. Sengupta and T. Kureishy, 'Present State of Oil Pollution in the Northern Indian Ocean': *Marine Pollution Bulletin* vol. 12 no. 9, 1981; E. Miles, K. N. Lee and E. Carlin, *Sub-seabed Disposal of High Level Nuclear Waste: an Assessment of Policy Issues for the United States*, Institute for Marine Studies, Seattle; R. Johnston, *Marine Pollution*, Academic Press, 1976; S. A. Gertach, *Marine Pollution*, Springer-Verlag, New York, 1981; A. J. Lee and J. W. Ramster (Eds), 'Fisheries Research Technical Report' no. 20, *Atlas of the Seas around the British Isles*, MAFF, 1979; E. Porter, *Pollution in four industrialised estuaries*, Royal Commission on Environmental Pollution in the United Kingdom, 1973; G. J. Mangone, *Marine Policy for America*, 1977; C. Osterborg and S. Keckes, 'The State of Pollution in the Mediterranean': *AMBIO* vol. 6 no. 6, 1977.

The strategic use of the sea

S. Kaplan, *The Diplomacy of Power*, Brookings, 1981; Belchman and Kaplan, *Force without war: US armed forces as a political instrument*, 1979; H. W. Bagley, 'Seapower and western security: the next decade': Adelphi Papers no. 139, International Institute for Strategic Studies, London, 1977; D. L. Larsen, 'Security, Disarmament and the Law of the Sea': *Marine Policy* vol. 3 no. 1, Jan 1979; J. S. Wit, 'American SLBN Counter force options and strategic implications': *Survival* vol. 14 no. 4, 1982; 'Armaments and Disarmaments': *SIPRI Yearbook*, 1979; P. Polomka, *Ocean Politics in South East Asia*, Institute of South East Asian Studies, Singapore, 1978; M. Leifer, 'Conflict and regional order in South East Asia': Adelphi Papers no. 162, Institute of Strategic Studies, London; L. Joo-Dock, *Geo-strategy in the South China Sea Basin*, Singapore University Press, 1979; *To Use the Sea: Readings in Seapower and Maritime Affairs*, Naval Institute Press, Maryland, 1977; S. G. Gorshkov, *The Sea Power of the State*, Pergamon Press, Oxford, 1976; D. P. O'Connell, *The Influence of Law on Seapower*, Manchester University Press, 1975; V. R. Prescott, *The Political Geography of the Oceans*, David and Charles, 1975; Larsen and Tarpgard, 'Law of the Sea and ASW: National Security versus Arms Control': *Marine Policy* vol. 6 no. 2, 1982.

The study of the sea

K. Muckelroy (Ed.), *Archaeology under Water: an Atlas of the World's Submerged Sites*, McGraw-Hill Book Company, 1980; N. C. Flemming (Ed.), *The Undersea*, Cassell, 1977; D. J. Blackman (Ed.), *Marine Archaeology*, Butterworths, London, 1973 and Shoe String Press Inc, Connecticut, 1973; N. C. Flemming, *Cities in the Sea*, Doubleday, New York and New English Library, London, 1972; C. Martin, *Full Fathom Five*, Chatto and Windus, London, 1975; G. F. Bass, *Archaeology under water*, Praeger, New York and Thames and Hudson, London, 1966; K. Muckleroy, *Maritime Archaeology*, Cambridge University Press, Cambridge, 1978 and Macmillan, New York, 1979; G. F. Bass, 'Marine Archaeology: A Misunderstood Science': *Ocean Year Book 2*, University of Chicago Press, Chicago and London; *Jane's Ocean Technology 1979–80*, London, 1980; W. S. Wooster, 'International Cooperation in Ocean Science': *Ocean Yearbook 2*, University of Chicago Press, Chicago and London; A. E. J. Went, *Seventy years agrowing: a history of the International Council for the Exploration of the Sea, 1902–72*, 1972; M. Deacon, *Scientists and the sea, 1650–1900, a study of marine science*, Academic Press, London, 1971; S. Schlee, *A history of oceanography*, Robert Hale and Co., London, 1973; E. Linklater, *The voyage of the Challenger*, John Murray, London, 1972; A. McConnell, *No sea too deep. The history of oceanographic instruments*, Adam Hilger Ltd, Bristol, 1982.

The management task

A. D. Couper, 'Marine resources and environment': *Progress in Human Geography* vol. 2 no. 2, 1978; G. Hardin, 'The tragedy of the commons': *Science* no. 162, 1968; S. A. Patin, *Pollution and the biological resources of the oceans*, Butterworths, London, 1982; D. M. Johnston, 'The Environmental Law of the Sea': International Union for Conservation of Nature and Natural Resources, Gland, Switzerland, 1981; 'The biology, distribution and state of exploitation of shared stocks in the North Sea area': ICES, Copenhagen, 1978; C. M. Mason (Ed.), *The effective management of resources: the international politics of the North Sea*, Frances Pinter, London, 1979; D. Watt (Ed.), *The North Sea: a new international regime*, Westbury Press, Guildford, 1981; H. Van Hoorn et al (Eds), *The North Sea: environment and problems*, Werkgroop Nordzee, Amsterdam, 1980; A. D. Couper and H. D. Smith, 'Multi-use and multi-state management in the North Sea': Law of the Sea Institute 16th Annual Conference, Halifax, June 1982; 'Promotion of the Establishment of Marine Parks and Reserves in the Northern Indian Ocean including the Red Sea and Persian Gulf': IUCN, Gland, Switzerland, 1976; M. Falicon, *La protection de l'environnement marin par les Nations-Unies: programme d'activités pour les Mers Régionales*, CNEXO, Rapports économiques et juridiques, Brest, 1982; A. W. Koers, *International regulation of marine fisheries*, Fishing News Books, London, 1973; M. M. Sibthorp, *The North Sea Challenge and Opportunity*, 1975; L. Friedheim, *Managing Ocean Resources*, Westview Press, 1979; H. Knight, *Managing the Seas Living Resources*, Lexington Books, 1977; Lin Sien, Chia and MacAndrews, *South East Asian Seas: Frontiers for Development*, MacGraw-Hill, 1981; *Ocean Yearbook I*, Borghese and Ginsburg, 1978; *Ocean Yearbook II*, Borghese and Ginsburg, 1980; D. M. Johnston, *Marine Policy and the Coastal Community*, Croom Helm, 1976; K. A. Beriasher, V. V. Serebriakov, *International Marine Organisations: essays on structure and activities*, Martinus Nijhoff, 1981.

The Law of the Sea

C. J. Colombos, *The International Law of the Sea*, Longman, 1967; M. S. McDougal and W. T. Burke, *The Public Order of the Oceans*, Yale University Press, repr. 1976; D. P. O'Connell, *International Law of the Sea* (2 vols), Oxford University Press, Oxford, 1983; UN, *Third United Nations Conference of the Law of the Sea* (official records) vols I–XIV (further volumes in preparation); R. Platzoder (Ed.), *Third United Nations Conference on the Law of the Sea: documents*, Oceana vol. 1, 1982 (10 volumes projected); R. Churchill et al (Eds), *New directions in the Law of the Sea*, Oceana vols I–X; N. Papadakis, *International Law of the Sea: a Bibliography*, Sijthoff and Noordhoff, 1980.

Acknowledgements

Photographs and illustrations

Jacket: Popperfoto.
pp 8–9 Courtesy Trustees of the British Museum, London; Dick Roberts/Vision International; Peter Holthosen/Seaphot Planet Earth Pictures; Institute of Oceanographic Sciences, Wormley, Surrey.
pp 10–11 J. N. Perez/Seaphot Planet Earth Pictures; Peter Holthusen/Seaphot Planet Earth Pictures; A Shell Photograph; Woods Hole Oceanographic Institution, USA.
pp 12–13 C. Sappa/CEDRI, Paris; Marcus Brooke/Colorific; Zefa; The National Institute South Wales Branch.
pp 14–15 Warren Williams/Seaphot Planet Earth Pictures; Popperfoto; Western Australian Museum; Encyclopaedia Universalis, Paris; Robert Hessler/Seaphot Planet Earth Pictures.
p 26–27 **3** Oxford Illustrators Limited, Oxford.
p 28 **2** Swanston Graphics, Derby.
p 30 **2** Felicity Clark.
p 31 **8** Admiralty Compass Observatory 'Crown Copyright'.
p 33 **5** Felicity Clark.
pp 34–35 **5** NASA/Science Photo Library; **6** Institute of Geological Sciences; **7** Felicity Clark.
p 37 **3** Dick Roberts/Vision International.
p 40 **3** Oxford Illustrators Limited, Oxford.
pp 42–43 **1, 8** Felicity Clark; **7** Warren Williams/Seaphot Planet Earth Pictures.
pp 44–45 **2,4,5** Oxford Illustrators Limited, Oxford.
p 46 **3** NASA/Science Photo Library; **4** Oxford Illustrators Limited, Oxford.
pp 48–49 **5** Ambrose Greenaway/Topham (sea states 3,4,6,7,8), Peter Scoones/Seaphot Planet Earth Pictures (sea state 10); **10** Oxford Illustrators Limited, Oxford.
p 52 **4** Richard Legeckis/Science Photo Library.
p 55 **2** Sygma/Paris/John Hillelson.
p 57 **5** Oxford Illustrators Limited, Oxford; **8** Peter Holthosen/Seaphot Planet Earth Pictures.
pp 58–59 **4** Oxford Illustrators Limited, Oxford; **10** Dr George Pararas-Carayannis/International Tsunami Information Centre.
p 61 **8** Dept of Information & Documentation/Netherlands.
pp 62–63 **1,2** Oxford Illustrators Limited, Oxford.
pp 64–65 **2** Felicity Clark; **4** T. R. Hughes; **6,7** Dr Per Gooersen/Polar Record/Science Photo Library.
pp 66 **3** George Gerster/John Hillelson.
pp 68–69 **2** Oxford Illustrators Limited, Oxford; **2.1,2.2** Peter Parks/Oxford Scientific Films; **2.3** Claude Carre/Jacana Paris; **2.4,2.7,2.8** Institute of Oceanographic Sciences, Wormley, Surrey; **2.5** Kenneth Lucas/Seaphot Planet Earth Pictures; **2.6** Peter Holthosen/Seaphot Planet Earth Pictures.
pp 70–71 **2,4,6,7,8** Peter Parks/Oxford Scientific Films; **3** Claude Carre/Jacana Paris; **5** Dr R. Pingree/Oxford Scientific Films; **9** Flip Schulke/Seaphot Planet Earth Pictures.
pp 72–73 **2** David George/Seaphot Planet Earth Pictures; **3,4,5,6,8,12** Institute of Oceanographic Sciences; **7** Roy Manston/Seaphot Planet Earth Pictures; **9,10** Peter David/Seaphot Planet Earth Pictures; **11** Robert Hesslee/Seaphot Planet Earth Pictures.
pp 74–75 **1,5b,6,7,8,10** Peter David/Seaphot Planet Earth Pictures; **2** Steve Earley/Oxford Scientific Films; **3** Rod Salm/Seaphot Planet Earth Pictures; **4** Jesus Perez/Seaphot Planet Earth Pictures; **5a,9,11** Institute of Oceanographic Sciences.
pp 76–77 **2**, pp 78–79 **2** Oxford Illustrators Limited, Oxford.
pp 80–81 **1** Orion Press/Photri; **2** Jenny Pate/Alan Hutchison Library; **3,4** Oxford Illustrators Limited, Oxford; **5** Marcus Brooke/Colorific.
pp 82–83 **5** Zefa.
pp 84–85 **1** Oxford Illustrators Limited, Oxford; **2** Felicity Clark; **4** Reg Weir, Cornwall; **6** Fjellanger Widerøe A/S, Oslo, Norway.
pp 86–87 **2**, pp 88–89 **1** Oxford Illustrators Limited, Oxford.
p 93 **3** Fjellanger Widerøe A/S, Oslo, Norway.
p 95 **4** Leonard Freed-Magnum/John Hillelson.
pp 96–97 **3** Flip Schulke/Seaphot Planet Earth Pictures; **6** Paolo Koch/Vision International.
pp 98–99 **1** R. Ian Lloyd/Alan Hutchison Library.
pp 100–101 **8** Oxford Illustrators Limited, Oxford; **11** Jesus N. Perez/Seaphot Planet Earth Pictures; **15** Topham.
pp 104–105 **2** Alain Keler/Sygma/John Hillelson; **3** Michael Freeman/Bruce Coleman. **8** Oxford Illustrators Limited, Oxford;
pp 106–107 **5** *Photograph* courtesy of Phillips Petroleum Company, *illustration* Oxford Illustrators Limited, Oxford; **6** Texaco Canada Inc.
pp 108–109 **5** Hugh Jones/Seaphot Planet Earth Pictures; **6** David Nance/Seaphot Planet Earth Pictures.
pp 112–113 **2** Popperfoto.
pp 114–115 **2** Woods Hole Oceanographic Institution.
pp 116–117 **1** Robert Hessler/Seaphot Planet Earth Pictures; **2** Courtesy of Consolidated Goldfields PLC.
pp 118–119 **3** Paolo Koch/Vision International; **5** Christian Petron/Seaphot Planet Earth Pictures; **6,8** Peter Parks/Oxford Scientific Films; **7,9** Warren Williams/Seaphot Planet Earth Pictures; **10** Gillian & John Lythgoe/Seaphot Planet Earth Pictures.
pp 120–121 **2** M. Brigaud/Sodel-Edf, Paris; **7,8,10** Oxford Illustrators Limited, Oxford.
p 125 **5** Zefa.
pp 128–129 **1** Maurice & Sally Landre/Colorific; **5** Port of San Francisco.
p 131 **3** Port of Tokyo.
p 132 **3** Zefa.
p 134 **2** Marcus Brooke/Colorific; **3** Claus Meyer/Colorific.
p 141 **2** Courtesy of Texaco Inc.
pp 142–143 **3** Paolo Koch/Vision International; **6** David Burnett/Contact/Colorific.
p 147 **4** Ambrose Greenaway/Topham.
pp 148–149 **3** Charles Swithinbank; **5** NASA.
pp 152–153 **1** Koene/Explorer/Vision International; **5** Zefa; **8** Anderson/Fournier Explorer/Vision International.
pp 154–155 **4** NASA/Camera Press; **7** Popperfoto.
pp 156–157 **2** National Maritime Institute; **4** NASA/Science Photo Library; **5** Oxford Illustrators Limited, Oxford.
pp 158–159 **3** Alastair Black; **4** Produced from a portion of BA Chart No. 2146 with the sanction of the Controller, HM Stationery Office and of the Hydrographer of the Navy; **5** Oxford Illustrators Limited, Oxford.
p.161 **2** Mariners' Weather Log.
pp 162–163 **3** Submex Limited; **6** Charles Swithinbank.
p 168–169 **4** Bill Eppridge/Life Magazine 1967 Time Inc/Colorific; **5** Alain Dejeau/Sygma/John Hillelson.
p 180 **4** Etablissement cinématographique et photographique des armées, Paris.
p 195 **2** Western Australian Museum; **3** Chéné/CNRS, Paris.
pp 196–197 **1** Oxford Illustrators Limited, Oxford; **3** Avner Raban (2 photos); **4** By permission of the Master of Fellows, Magdalene College, Cambridge; **5** Courtesy of The News, Portsmouth; **6,7** Susan Womer Katzev; **8** Mary Rose Trust (3 photos), N. Goran Algard, P. E. Baker/Western Australian Museum (2 photos), Sydney Wignall.
p 201 **2** Standard Telephone and Cables Limited.
pp 202–203 **2** Waverley Electronics Limited; **5** Courtesy Trustees of the British Museum, London; **6** Besacier/CNEXO, Paris; **7,8** Institute of Oceanographic Sciences, Wormley, Surrey; **9** Peter David/Seaphot Planet Earth Pictures.
pp 204–205 **3** Dr Klaus A. Ulbricht, German Aerospace Research Establishment (DFVLR); **5** NASA/US Geological Survey; **7,8** Hunting Surveys Ltd; **9** SEASAT image by Rae Farnborough.
p.207 **3** David George/Seaphot Planet Earth Pictures.
pp 210–211 **1** Flip Schulke/Seaphot Planet Earth Pictures; **2** Kenneth Lucas/Seaphot Planet Earth Pictures.
p 212 **2** Bay Picture Library.
pp 214–215 **2** B. Regent/Alan Hutchison Library; **3** Leonard Freed-Magnum/John Hillelson; **5** Aerophoto Eelde.
p 217 **3** Alastair Black; **6** Fred Mayer/Magnum.

Editor's acknowledgements

The following people, companies or organisations have given assistance in the compilation of the Atlas:

Cartographers J. H. Mills-Hicks, Mrs S. Surman

Cartographic assistants Miss D. Gunning, Miss J. S. Harper, A. P. Rogers

Research assistants S. J. Davies, C. G. Fitzgerald, Miss A. M. Gay, Mrs A. Huntley, Miss C. Issac, M. Lyon, Mrs J. McCallum, C. Reynolds, A. Scott-Dickens, Miss D. R. Sell, Mrs R. Sherwood, G. Taylor, J. Weston

Dr Alistair J. Gilmour, Great Barrier Reef Marine Park Authority; International Maritime Organisation (IMO) UN, London; Food and Agriculture Organisation, United Nations, Rome; Eurocean, Monaco; Dept of the Interior, USGS, Washington DC, USA; Woods Hole Oceanographic Institution, Massachusetts, USA; Springer-Verlag Publishing Co. Ltd, New York; Institute of Geological Sciences, London; Offshore, Houston, USA; British Petroleum, London; Ocean Routes, Gravesend, UK; The Royal Swedish Academy of Sciences, Stockholm; Dept of State, Washington DC, USA; The Geographical Magazine, London; Containerisation International, London; The Maritime Councellor, French Embassy, London; Journal of the Geological Society, Oxford; Marine Mining, New York; Marine Geology, Amsterdam; Elsevier Scientific Publishing Co., Geo-Sciences Dept, Amsterdam; 'Science' American Association for the Advancement of Science, Washington DC; Lamont-Doherty Geological Observatory, Columbia University, New York; Dept of Oceanography, Florida State Univ., Tallahassie, USA; Offshore Technology Conference, Dallas, Texas; Edward Arnold (Publishers) Ltd, London; Geo-Journal, Wiesbaden, W. Germany; Royal Geological and Mining Society of the Netherlands, The Hague; Transactions of the Geological Society of South Africa, Transvaal, S. Africa; Blackwell Scientific Publications Ltd, Oxford; MacMillan Journals Ltd, London; Von Nostrand Reinhold (UK) Ltd, Wokingham; Meteorological Office, Bracknell, Berkshire; Dept of the Army, Equipment Research and Development Command, Fort Belvoir, Virginia, USA; Institute of Oceanographic Sciences, Godalming, Surrey; Ian Trelawney, Felixstowe Port Consultancy Service, Felixstowe; James Cable, British Embassy, Helsinki; The Port Authority of NY and NJ, New York; Marine Dept, Hong Kong; Dept of Trade, Maritime Rescue Co-ordination Centre, Dover; R-ADM D. C. Kapoor, International Hydrographic Bureau, Monaco; International Labour Office, Geneva; The International Institute for Strategic Studies, London; Lloyds Register Printing House, Crawley, UK; H. Tambs-Lyche, Gen. Sec., ICES, Copenhagen; W. H. Freeman & Co. Publishers, San Francisco, California; Penwell Publishing Co., Tulsa, USA; The East–West Centre, Honolulu, Hawaii, USA; Capt. R. Hill RN, Ministry of Defence, London; Capt. W. Burger, MSc, Dept of Maritime Studies, UWIST, Cardiff; E. S. Owen Jones, Welsh Industrial and Maritime Museum, Cardiff; Dr D. H. Maling.

Section contributors

THE OCEAN ENVIRONMENT
The ocean basins Dr C. M. Davies; *The ocean atmosphere system* J. M. Walker; *The oceans and life* Dr A. L. Rice, J. M. Walker

RESOURCES OF THE OCEAN
Living resources Prof. A. D. Couper, Dr H. D. Smith; *The fisheries* Dr H. D. Smith; *Oil and gas* Dr H. D. Smith, Prof. A. D. Couper, Prof. J. King; *Mineral and energy potentials* D. J. McMillan, Dr C. M. Davies, A. A. Archer, Dr R. J. Schmidt, Prof. A. D. Couper

OCEAN TRADE
Ports of the world Dr B. J. Thomas; *Ships and cargoes* Prof. A. D. Couper, Prof. J. King; *Shipping routes* Prof. A. D. Couper, Capt. A. G. Corbet, Capt. A. M. Maclean; *The hazardous sea* Prof. A. D. Couper, Capt. A. G. Corbet, J. M. Walker

THE WORLD OCEAN
The health of the oceans Prof. A. D. Couper; *The strategic use of the oceans* Prof. A. D. Couper, Prof. E. D. Brown; *The study of the sea* Dr C. F. Wooldridge, Dr A. L. Rice, Dr C. H. Cotter, Prof. A. D. Couper, H. A. G. Lewis; *The management task* Dr H. D. Smith, Prof. A. D. Couper, L. M. Alexander, Dr C. F. Wooldridge, Dr J. Zinn; *The law of the sea* Prof. E. D. Brown

Publishers' acknowledgement

The Times and John Bartholomew projections courtesy of John Bartholomew and Sons Ltd, Edinburgh

Index

Appearing in italic type are: 1. Gazetteer entries: sea features, ports, etc., accompanied by a grid reference; 2. Ship names; 3. Latin names (e.g. species of plants and animals); 4. Cross-references to another part of the index.

Often names will appear in both italic and roman type, the former because the name is given an accurate map location and the latter because it is treated as a subject in its own right.

The word '(map)' preceding a page number indicates a major reference to the entry.

A

Ābādān 30.20N 48.16E 133
Åbenrå 55.03N 9.26E 123
Aberdeen 57.09N 2.03W 106, 123
Abidjan 5.15N 3.58W 120, 133
Abrolhos Bank 18.30S 38.45W 18
Abu al Bu'Khoosh 25.26N 53.08E 133
Abu Dhabi: offshore oil & gas 104
Abū Mūsá 154
Abyss 72
Abyssal
  floor 27
  hills 28, 29, 36
  nodules 115, 116–117, 173, 221
  plains 28, 29, 43, 73
  plain, sediment layers 43
  species 72
  zone 26
Abyssopelagic zone 68, 75
Acajutla 13.35N 89.50W 126
Acapulco 16.51N 99.56W 126
Accidents at sea 162–171
Accra 5.35N 0.15W 133
Accra, port 133
Acids 174
Actual total loss (ATL) 164
Adabiya 29.52N 32.28E 133
Adak Strait 51.52N 176.40W 150
Ad Dammān 26.20N 50.11E 133
Ad Dawḥah, (Doha) 25.19N 51.35E 133
Adelaar, wreck 194
Aden 12.47N 44.58E 133
Aden 185
Aden, Gulf of 154
Aden, Gulf of 13.00N 47.00E 18
Admiral's Cup, racing event 217
Admiralty charts *see Charts*
Adriatic oil basin 102
Adriatic: pollution 177
Adriatic Sea 44.00N 15.00E 17
Advanced Ocean Drilling Programme (AODP) 40
Aegean Captain (tanker) 160
Aegean Sea 154, 155, 214
Aegean Sea 37.00N 27.00E 17
Aegir Ridge 66.00N 4.00W 17, 24
Africa, West
  offshore oilfields 108, 109
  pollution 172–173
Agadir 30.26N 9.38W 133
Agadir Canyon 32.30N 12.50W 17
Agar (agar agar) 83, 119
Agassiz Fracture Zone 38.15S 127.15W 23
Agattu Strait 52.50N 173.00E 150, 151
Aggregates & extraction of (map) 110, 112–113
Agnes, typhoon 55
Agueneiqin 27.45N 15.40W 133
Aguilas 37.24N 1.34W 122
Agulhas Bank: phosphorites (map) 115
Agulhas Basin 47.00S 27.00E 18–19
Agulhas current 51, 58, 59
Agulhas Plateau 40.00S 26.00E 19
Agulhas Ridge 40.00S 13.00E 18
Åhus 55.56N 14.19E 123
'Ain Sukhna 29.35N 32.21E 133, 135
Aioi 34.49N 134.26E 130
Aircraft carriers 178, 179
Ajaccio 41.56N 8.43E 122
Akita-Komaga-take 36
Akureyri 65.42N 18.03W 92, 122
Akutan 36
Akyab 20.08N 92.55E 130
Alaid 36
Ålands Hav. 60.00N 19.30E 151
Alaska 96, 136, 220
  gold, beach deposits (map) 113
  pipeline 148
Alaska, Gulf of 58.00N 145.00W 21
Alaska pollack 88, 96, 97
Albany, Australia 34.58S 117.53E 132, 135
Albany, USA 42.39N 73.49W 126, 134
Albatross, ship 199
Albatross expedition (map) 202
Albatross, seabird (map) 76, 77
Albert, Prince of Monaco 203
Ålborg 57.03N 9.56E 123
Albuskjell oilfield 102, 106
Alby, hurricane 55
Alcedo 36
Alenuihaha Chan. 20.30N 156.00W 150
Ålesund 62.29N 6.19E 122
Aleutian abyssal plain (map) 29
Aleutian Basin 57.00N 177.00E 20
Aleutian currents 53
Aleutian Is 36
Aleutian Rise 51.00N 173.00E 20
Aleutian Trench 51.00N 170.00W 20
Alexander Kielland, oil rig 162
Alexandria, Egypt 31.12N 29.54E 133
Alexandria, Egypt: pollution 177
Alexandria, USA 38.48N 77.06W 126
Alexandroúpolis 40.50N 25.53E 122
Al Fāw 29.58N 48.28E 133
Algae 83, 88, 205, 210
Algeciras 36.07N 5.28W 122
Algeciras 157
Alger 36.48N 3.02E 133
Algeria: naval fleet 178
Alginates 83
Al Ḥudaydah 14.50N 42.58E 133
Aliağa 38.51N 27.00E 122
Alicante 38.20N 0.30W 122
Al Jubayl, port 133
Alkalis 174
Allen, hurricane 54, 55
Alleppey 9.29N 76.23E 130
Almería 36.49N 2.27W 122
Almirante 9.17N 82.23W 126
Al Mukhā 13.20N 43.18E 133
Alpena 45.05N 83.25W 126
Alpha Ridge 85.30N 125.00W 24, 62
Altair Seamount 44.40N 34.00W 16
Ålvsborg 125
Alwyn oilfield 106
Alyla, Mt 157
Amagaski 34.40N 135.25E 130
Amapala 13.15N 87.43W 126
Amazon Cone 2.30N 48.00W 18
Amazon, R. 26, 124
Ambon 3.40S 128.11E 132
Amchitka Pass 51.40N 180.00W 150
America–Antarctic Ridge 60.00S 20.00W 18
America's Cup, racing event 217
Ameriport 40.00N 75.10W 126, 134
Amery Basin 68.00S 75.00E 25
Amery Ice Shelf 63
Amethyst oilfield 106
Amherstburg 42.06N 83.07W 126
Amirantes Is 37
Amirante Trench 8.00S 52.30E 19
Amoco Cadiz, tanker 168, (map) 169, 171, 214
Ampenan 8.34S 116.04E 132
Ampere Seamount 36.05N 13.00W 17
Amphibious ships 178, 179
Amphidromic points 60, 61
Amphipod crustaceans 72, 73
Amphipod shrimp 69
Amphoras 194, 195, 196
Amsterdam, 52.22N 4.53E 123
Amsterdam 215
Amsterdam wreck 194
Amsterdam I. 37
Amuay 11.44N 70.15W 127
Amukta Pass. 52.30N 172.00W 150
Amundsen Abyssal Plain 64.00S 120.00W 23, 25, 63
Amundsen Basin 88.00N 80.00E 24
Amundsen Gulf 70.00N 120.00W 24
Amundsen Ridges 69.00S 120.00W 25
Amundsen Sea 72.00S 115.00W 25, 63
Anacortes 48.30N 122.40W 126
Anadromous organisms 221
Anadyrskiy Gulf 65.00N 177.00W 20, 24
Anakan 8.51N 125.09E 132
Anchorage 61.10N 150.00W 126
Anchovy 84, 88, 95, 97
  collapse of fishery in Peru 98, 99
Ancona 43.36N 13.31E 122, 182
Ancud 59
Andaman Basin 10.00N 94.00E 19
Andaman Is 37
Andaman Sea 5.00N 96.00E 19
Andaman Sea 155
  cyclones 57
Andrea Doria, liner 166
Andrew, oilfield 106
Andulo, ship 167
Anegada Pass. 18.30N 64.00W 150
Anewa Bay 6.12S 155.33E 132
Angling 216
Anglo-French Continental Shelf case 1977–78 222
Anglo-Icelandic 'Cod Wars' 186
Angoche 16.10S 39.58E 133
Angola 104
  naval fleet 178
  offshore oilfields 108
Angola Abyssal Plain 13.00S 2.00E 18
Angola Basin 15.00S 3.00E 18
Angra dos Reis 23.01S 44.18W 127
'Annaba 36.52N 7.46E 133, 135
Annabon I. 37
Annapolis Royal 44.45N 65.31W 126
Anne, wreck 194
Annelida 119
Annual cycles of phytoplankton & zooplankton 70
Antalya 36.52N 30.46E 122
Antarctica (maps) 62–63
  bottom water 45, 51, 78
  expeditions 198
  fishery resources 78–79, 184
  icebergs, ice sheet & ice shelves 63, 65
  mineral resources 184
  territorial claims 184, 185
  whaling fishery and industry 78, 100
Antarctic Convergence 51, 78
Antarctic giantfish 79
Antarctic Peninsula 62
Antarctic Treaty 184
Antelope, frigate 184
Anthony Roll 197
Antibes 43.33N 7.08W 122
Anti-carrier cruiser 189
Anticosti I. 149
Anticyclones 46–47, 51, 56, 57
Antifer 49.40 0.08E 122
Antifer, Port d' 125, 156
Antigua: fishing catch 94
Antilla 20.50N 75.44W 126
Anti-submarine barrier (map) 183
Anti-submarine warfare (ASW) 178, 180, 182–183
Antofagasta 23.39S 70.25W 127
Anton Dohrn Seamount 57.30N 11.00W 17
Antrim, destroyer 184
Antseranana 12.16S 49.17E 133
Antwerpen 51.13N 4.23E 123, 135
AODP (Advanced Ocean Drilling Programme) 40
Aomori 40.49N 140.45E 130
Apalachicola 29.44N 85.01W 126
Apapa 6.28N 3.15E 133
Aperlae, submerged port 195
Apia 13.50S 171.55W 132
Apolima Str. 14.00S 172.00W 150
Apollonia 194, 196
Apra Harbour 13.27N 144.37E 132
'Aqaba 29.31N 35.00E 133, 135
Aqaba, G. of 146, 181
Aquaculture 80, 82–83, 96, 97
  origin 82
  production, world (map) 82, 83
  statistics 82
Arabian Basin 11.30N 65.00E 19
Arabian Gulf see Gulf, The
Arabian Sea 20.00N 65.00E 19
Arabian Sea 49, 53, 56, 58
Aracaju 10.55S 37.04W 127
Arachon: oyster production 83
Arafura Sea 7.00S 140.00E 20, 22
Arafura Shelf 10.00S 135.00E 22
Aragonite 112
Araguaia 120
Archaeology, undersea 194–195
Archangel 192
Archipelagic states: delimitation 220
Archipelagic waters: definition 220
Arctic mid-ocean Ridge 86.00N 90.00E 24, 62
Arctic
  bottom water 51
  Circle 63
  ice 62, 63, 148, 203
  icebergs 64, 104, 106
  navigation 148–149
  Ocean (map & view) 62–63
  routes (map) 148–149
Arctic skua 77
Arctic tern 77
Arctic Waters Pollution Prevention Act 186, 224
Årdalstangen 61.14N 7.42E 122
Ardent, frigate 184
Ardrossan, Australia 34.26S 137.55E 132
Ardrossan, Scotland 55.38N 4.49W 123
Arendal 58.27N 8.47E 123
Argentia 182
Argentina 108
  aquaculture 82
  Falkland war, 1982 184–185
  fishing catch 94
  fishing fleet 86
  naval submarine strength 181, 184–185
  naval surface fleet 178, 184–185
  pollution, marine 172
  territorial claims 184, 185
Argentine Abyssal Plain 47.30S 50.00W 18, 28
Argentine Basin 45.00S 45.00W 18
Argentine–Chile dispute 187
Argentine Rise 41.00S 48.00W 18
Argo Fracture Zone 13.45S 66.10E 19
Argo Merchant, tanker 168
Argyll, oilfield 102, 106
Argyropelecus (hatchetfish) 74
Århus 56.09N 10.13E 123
Ariaka, Bay of 111
Arica 18.29S 70.20W 127
Arichat 45.31N 61.02W 126
Arjuna 5.54S 107.17E 132
Arkhangel'sk 64.32N 40.31E 122
Arklow 52.48N 6.08W 123
Ark region 74
Arkshells 88
Armada and wrecks 196, 197
'Armada weather' 196
Ærøskøbing 54.51N 10.23E 123
ARPA (Automatic Radar Plotting Aids) 158
Arrecife 29.00N 13.30W 133
Artica, Soviet vessel 148
Artisanal fisheries 80–81, 95, 98–99
Aruba–Paraguaná Pass 12.20N 71.00W 150
Arzanha 24.45N 52.35E 133
Arzew 35.53N 0.19W 133
Asama 36
Ascension 7.55S 14.25W 133
Ascension Fracture Zone 7.20S 14.00W 18
Ascension I. 36, 184
Ashdod 31.50N 34.38E 133
Ashdod 135, 146
Ashland 46.35N 90.52W 126
Ashqelon 31.40N 34.33E 133
Ashtabula 41.55N 80.49W 126
Asian Development Bank 130
Asnæs, see Kalundborg
Asprópirgos 38.02N 23.35E 122
Assab 154
Assab 13.01N 42.44E 133
Assens 55.17N 9.53E 123
As Sidrah 30.38N 18.22E 133, 135
Asthenosphere 32, 38
Astoria 46.12N 123.48W 126
Astrid Ridge 68.00S 11.00E 25
Astronomical data, in predicting tides 60
ASW aircraft bases (US) 182–183
ASW (anti-submarine warfare) 178, 180, 182–183
ATL (actual total loss) 164
Atlantic Conveyor, container ship 184
Atlantic Empress, ship 160
Atlantic Express, ship 171
Atlantic menhaden 88
Atlantic Ocean 16–18
  currents 44–45
  exploration of sea floor (map) 203
  fishing industry & trends 92, 94
  fishing, total catch by FAO areas 90
  fog (maps) 53
  icing on ships (maps) 64
  mid-ocean ridge (profiles) 29
  North 182
  physiographic provinces 29
  rises 28
  saline current 53
  salinity 27, 53
  salinity profiles 67
  sounding 198, (map) 199
  storms, hurricanes & cyclones 56
  surface waters 53
  topographic view 26, 27
  voyages & exploration 192, 198
  waterspouts 57
  wave power 121
  weather hazards 160
  whaling industry 100
  winds 44–45
Atlantic Ridley turtle 210
Atlantis Cruiser 37
Atlantis Fracture Zone 30.00N 42.00W 16, 18
Atlantis II Deep 114
Atlantis II Fracture Zone 33.00S 57.00E 19
Atlantis II Seamount 52
Atmosphere 26, 44, 46, 53, 57, 60, 158
Atmospheric pressures affecting ice fields 64
Atolls 36, 37, 42, 80–81
Auckland 36.51N 174.49E 132, 135
Audrey, oilfield 106
Augusta, Italy 37.14N 15.13E 122, 183
Auk 76, 210
Auk, oilfield 102, 106
Australasia, hurricanes 54–55
Austral Fracture Zone 20.00S 127.00W 23
Australia 136
  aquaculture 83
  fisheries 96
  fishing fleet 87
  naval submarine strength 181
  naval surface fleet 178, 179
  offshore oil & gas 104, 108, (map) 109
  pollution 173
  ports 132
  storms per year 56
Australian–Antarctic Basin 60.00S 120.00E 19
Australian–Antarctic Discordance 50.00S 125.00E 22
Austria: aquaculture production 83
Authigenic minerals 118
Automatic Radar Plotting Aids (ARPA) 158
Avatiu 21.12S 159.47W 132
Aveiro 40.38N 8.40W 122
Avilés 43.35N 5.56W 122
Avonmouth 51.30N 2.43W 123
Ayia Triás 37.58N 23.24E 122
Áyios Nikólaos 35.12N 25.43E 122
Ayr 55.28N 4.39W 123
Azores 37, 192
Azores anticyclone 44
Azores–Biscay Rise 42.40N 19.00W 17
Az Zuwaytīnah 30.51N 20.03E 133
Azov, Sea of 46.00N 37.00E 17

B

Bab el Mandeb 51, 67, 154, 185, 187, 189, 190, 219
Bab el Mandeb 12.30N 43.20E 150, 151
Babuyan Chan. 18.50N 121.30E 151
BACAT (barge aboard catamaran) 147
Bachaquero 9.56N 71.08W 127
Bach Long Vi 188, 189
Bacillariophyceae 70
Bacton 106
Baddeck 46.06N 60.44W 126
Baffin Bay 62, 64
Baffin Bay 73.00N 65.00W 16, 24
Baffin I. 62, 148
Bagnoli 40.47N 14.05E 122
Bagotville 48.21N 70.53W 126
Baguio (hurricane) 54
Bahama Ridge 29.00N 75.00E 16
Bahamas 141
Bahia Blanca 38.49S 62.17W 127, 134
Bahrain 109, 143, 183, 185, 220
  fisheries 98
  fishing catch 94
Baie Comeau 49.15N 68.07W 126, 134
Baie Verte 49.56N 56.10W 126

Abbreviations

approx.	= approximately
cm	= centimetre
Chan.	= channel
cu.	= cubic
ft	= foot/feet
G.	= gulf
I.	= island
Is	= islands
km	= kilometre
kW	= kilowatt
m	= metre
mm	= millimetre
Ma	= million years
nm	= nautical mile
Pass.	= passage
Pen.	= peninsular
R.	= river
Str.	= strait
t	= tonne
%	= per cent
‰	= parts per thousand
°C	= degrees centigrade
°F	= degrees Fahrenheit

Baikal–Amure–Magistrale railway 146
Bailey, shipping forecast area 161
Bainbridge 30.54N 84.33W 126
Bais 9.32N 123.08E 132
Baja California 120
Baja California Seamounts 36
Bajo Grande 10.30N 71.36W 127
Baker–Nunn 204
Baku District, oil basin 103
Balabac Strait 7.40N 117.00E 151
Balaenoptera borealis (sei whale) 79
Balaenoptera musculus (blue whale) 79
Balaenoptera physalus (fin whale) 78
Balanga 14.40N 120.32E 132
Balao Terminal 1.02N 79.20W 127
Balboa 152
Balboa 8.58N 79.34W 126
Balder oilfield 106
Baleen whale 78, 100
  Antarctic fishery 100
  catch 1910–1977 (graph) 100
  distribution 1729–1919 (map) 100
Balikpapan 1.15S 116.48E 132
Balintang Chan 20.00N 122.00E 151
Ballast reception facilities 142
Balleny I. 36
Balleny Seamounts 66.00S 162.00E 22, 25
Ballistic cameras 204
Ballistic missiles 180
Ballistic missile submarines *see SSB's*
Baltic Sea 55.00N 18.00E 17
Baltic Sea 64, 67, 93, 149, 214, 215, 153
  Landsat image 204, 205
  pollution (map) 175
  ports: (map) icing 149
Baltimore 39.17N 76.35W 126
Baltimore 134, 213
Banaba (Ocean I.) 0.53S 169.32E 132, 135
Banana 6.00S 12.25E 133
Bandar 'Abbās 154
Bandar 'Abbās 27.12N 56.15E 133
Bandar 'Abbās new port 154
Bandar Khomeynī 30.25N 49.05E 133
Banda Sea 8.00S 125.00E 20
Bandholm 54.50N 11.30E 123
Bandırma 40.21N 27.57E 122
Banghazī 32.07N 20.03E 133
Bangkok see Krung Thep
Bangladesh
  aquaculture 83
  fisheries 98
  fishing fleet 87
Bangor 44.49N 68.47W 126, 182
Baniyās 35.15N 35.57E 133, 135
Banjul 13.27N 16.44W 133
Banks I. 63
Banks Str. 40.40S 148.00E 150, 151
Bantry 51.41N 9.27W 123
Banua Wuhu 36
Banzare Bank 58.50S 77.44E 19
Bar 42.05N 19.05E 122
Baracoa 20.21N 74.30W 126
Barahona 18.12N 71.10W 127
Barbados: fishing catch 94
Barcadera 12.29N 70.00W 127
Barcelona 41.23N 2.11E 122, 135
Barcelona Convention 224
Barcelona region: pollution 177
Barents Abyssal Plain 85.00N 35.00E 24
Barents Sea 62, 128, 120, 214
Barge aboard catamaran (BACAT) 147
Barge carriers 138, 139
Barges 134, 146, 147
Barge transport systems 147
Bari 41.08N 16.55E 122
Barking Creek 124
Barletta 41.19N 16.17E 122
Barnvelt I. 187
Barracuda 217
Barracuda Ridge 16.10N 57.00W 18
Barranquilla 10.58N 74.45W 127, 134
Barrier Reef marine park 212
Barriers, river 120
Barrow in Furness 54.06N 3.13W 123
Barrow Strait 74.40N 95.00W 150
Barry 51.23N 3.16W 123
Barvas 121
Basalt 32, 43
Baselines 186, 204, 220
Bases 182–183
  Ascension I. 184
  Indian Ocean 185
  NATO 182–183
  naval 185
  SSBN 182–183
  US, ASW aircraft 182–183
  USSR 182–183, 184, 185
Bashi Channel 21.20N 121.00E 151
Basins, ocean, *see Ocean: basins*
Başrah 30.30N 47.50E 133, 135
Bass 88, 217
Bassein 16.45N 94.43E 130
Basseterre 17.18N 62.42W 127
Basse Terre 16.02N 61.45W 127
Bass Strait 40.00S 147.00E 150, 151
Bastia 42.41N 9.26E 122
Bataan 14.32N 120.15E 132
Batangas 13.45N 121.03E 132
Batavia, wreck 194, 197
Bath 43.56N 69.50W 126
Bathurst 47.37N 65.39W 126
Bathyal zone 26
Bathymetric charts *see Charts*
Bathypelagic species 74
Bathypelagic zone 68, 74, 75
Bathypterois (tripod fish) 73
Baton Rouge 30.27N 91.11W 126, 134
Battleships 179
Batumi 41.39N 41.38E 122
Bauer Basin 10.00S 101.45W 23
Bauer Fracture Zone 15.00S 100.00W 23
Bauer Fracture Zone 23
Bauxite/alumina, trade 136, 137
Bay: legal definition 220
Bayonne 43.30N 1.28W 122
Bay Roberts 47.35N 53.15W 126
Baytown 29.43N 95.01W 126
BC 4 (ballistic camera 4) 204
Beach deposits (profile) 42
Beaches 42
Beachy Head 156
Beagle, ship 198, (map) 199
Beagle Channel 185, 187
Beagle Channel 55.00S 68.00W 150
Beam trawl 84
Beata Ridge 16.00N 72.30W 18
Beatrice oilfield 106
Beaufort, Francis 48
Beaufort scale of wind force 48, 56, 148, 160
Beaufort Sea 73.00N 140.00W 24
Beaufort Sea 63, 106, 107, 148
Beaufort Sea boundary 186
Beaumont 30.05N 94.05W 126, 134
Bec d'Ambès 45.02N 0.30W 122
Bedi 22.33N 70.02E 130
Beerenberg 37
Behaim, Martin 193
Beira Patrol 1968 190
Beira, see Sofala
Beirūt 33.54N 35.30E 133
Bejaïa 36.46N 5.04E 133, 135
Bekapi 1.00S 117.30E 132
Belawan 155
Belawan 3.48N 98.42E 132
Belekeri 14.42N 74.16E 130
Belém 1.25S 48.35W 127
Belfast 54.36N 5.56W 123
Belgian Antarctic Expedition 1897 199
Belgica, ship 198
Belgica Bank 78.28N 15.00W 24
Belgium 136, 156
  fishing catch 93
  naval fleet 178, 182
Belize 17.30N 88.12W 126
Belize: fishing catch 94
Belledune 47.55N 65.51W 126
Belle I, Str. of 51.30N 56.30W 149, 150
Bellingham 48.45N 122.31W 126
Bellingshausen Abyssal Plain 64.00S 90.00W 23
Bellingshausen Sea 75.00S 85.00W 25
Bellingshausen sea 62, 63
Bellingshausen, T. 198
Bellona Gap 36.45S 166.30E 22
Bell Rock lighthouse, weather station 161
Beneficial ownership 140, 141
Bengal, Bay of 12.00N 86.00E 19
Bengal, Bay of 54, 56, 57, 60, 199
Benguela current 45
Benin: offshore oilfields 108
Beni-Saf 35.19N 1.24W 133
Benito 88
Benoa 8.45S 115.14E 132
Benthic
  animals 72–73
  areas: zones 26
  biomass (map) 73
  communities 68, 72–73, 173
  fish 73
  species 72–74
  zone 72–73
Benthopelagic zone 73
Benthos 72, 73
Benthosaurus 73
Berber 184
Berbera 10.27N 45.01E 133
Berdyansk 46.45N 36.48E 122
Bergen 60.24N 5.18E 123, 182
Bergen, ship 141
Bering Sea 58.00N 175.00E 20
Bering Sea 53, 220
Bering Strait 150, 219
Bering Strait 66.00N 169.00W 20, 24
Berkner I. 63
Bermuda 36, 182
  fishing catch 94
  fishing fleet 86
Bermuda Rise 28
Bermuda Rise 32.30N 65.00W 16
Beryl A & B, oilfields 102, 106
Beta oilfield 106
Beypore 11.11N 75.48E 130
Bezymianny 36
Bhatkal 13.58N 74.35E 130
Bhavnagar 21.46N 72.09E 130
Big Bird reconnaissance satellites 205
Biafra, Bight of 66
Bight Fracture Zone 57.00N 35.00W 16
  offshore oilfields 108
Bikini Atoll 36
Bilbao 43.15N 2.55W 122
Bill Bailey's Bank 60.35N 10.15W 17
Billfish 74, 88
Billingsgate 124
Bimlipatam 17.55N 83.31E 130
Binatang 2.10N 111.38E 130
Bintula 3.03N 113.08E 130
Biological background light 74
Biological environment, ocean 68
Bioluminescence 74
Biomass 73, 76, 85, 90
Birds, sea 76–77, 210
Biscay Abyssal Plain 45.00N 7.15W 17
Biscay, B. of 45.00N 4.00W 17
Biscay, Bay of 40, 161, 214
Biscay, shipping forecast area 161
Bishop Rock 168
Bismarck Sea 5.00S 145.00E 20, 22
Bissau 11.52N 15.35W 133
Bitter Lakes 67
Bitumen 105
Bitung 1.26N 125.12E 132
Bizerte 37.15N 9.52E 133
Bjornöya Bank 76.00N 23.00E 24
Black right whale 210, 211
Black Sea 43.00N 35.00E 17
Black Sea 53, 66, 118, 154, 155, 214
Blake, steamer 199
Blake Plateau 28, 40
Blake Plateau 31.00N 79.00W 16
Blake Ridge 29.00N 73.30W 16, 18
Blarket Sound 196
Blaye 45.09N 0.42W 122
Bligh Bank 156
Blockades 181, (map) 190
Blow-outs, oil rig 162, 170, 171
Bluefin tuna 75, 177
Bluefin whale 101
Blue Ridge 179
Blue shark 75
Blue whale 68, 79, 210, 211
Blue whiting 88, 93
Bluff Cove 184
Bluff Harbour 46.36S 168.20E 132
Blyth 55.07N 1.30W 123
Board of Ordnance 197
Boca Chica 18.27N 69.36W 127
Boca Grande 26.43N 82.15W 126
BOD (Biological Oxygen Demand) 175, 176, 177, *see also Glossary*
Bodø 67.17N 14.25E 122
Bohai (Haixia) 151
Bolama 11.30N 15.30W 133
Bolivia: aquaculture 82
Bolivian sea access 186
Bollons Seamount 49.40S 176.10W 22
Boltek 125
Boma 5.51S 13.03E 133
Bombay 18.54N 72.49E 130
Bonifacio, Strait of 41.20N 9.00E 150
Bonito 88
Bonny 4.27N 7.10E 133
Bonny, port 108, 133, 135
Booby, (map) 76, 77
Boothia, Gulf of 70.00N 90.00W 24
Bordeaux 44.50N 0.35W 122, 135
Boreas Abyssal Plain 77.00N 1.00E 24
Boreholes 39
Borgholm 56.50N 16.40E 123
Borneo: offshore oilfields 109
Bornholmsgattet 56.00N 15.00E 151
Boron 118
Bosporus 155
Bosporus 41.05N 29.00E 151
Bosporus Bridge 155
Boston, England 52.58N 0.02W 123
Boston, USA 42.21N 71.05W 126, 134, 182
Botany Bay 34.00S 151.14E 132
Botany Bay, port 132
Bothania, G. of 65.00N 22.00E 17
Bothnia, Gulf of 67, 149
Bottom water (map) 45, 51, 78
Botwood 49.09N 55.20W 126
Bougainville Strait 7.00S 156.00W 150, 151
Boulgaria, ship 167
Boulogne 50.43N 1.35E 123, 156
Boundary disputes *see Territorial claims & disputes*
Bounty Plateau 49.00S 179.00E 22
Bouvet Fracture Zone 55.00S 2.00E 18
Bouvet I. 37
Bowen 20.01S 148.15E 132
Bowers Ridge 54.00N 180.00 20
Bowhead whale 100, 210, 211
Boyle, Robert 198
Bradycalanus (capepod) 69
Brae oilfield 106
Brăila 45.15N 27.59E 122
Brake 53.20N 8.27E 123
Brass 4.20N 6.18E 133
Brazil
  fishing catch 94
  naval submarine strength 181
  naval surface fleet 178
  offshore oil & gas 104, 108, 136, 184
  pollution, marine 172
Brazil Basin 15.00S 25.00W 18
Brazil current 44
Breakwaters 125, 129
Bream oilfield 106
Breeze, in Beaufort scale 48
Bremen 53.05N 8.47E 123
Bremerhaven 53.33N 8.35E 123, 135
Brent oilfield 102, 106
Brest 48.23N 4.30W 122, 182
Brevik 59.04N 9.43E 123
Bridgeport 41.10N 73.10W 126
Bridgetown 13.05N 59.36W 127
Bridgewater 44.23N 64.31W 126
Bridgwater 51.07N 3.00W 123
Brighton 10.16N 61.38W 127
Brimstone I. 36
Brindisi 40.39N 17.58E 122
Brisbane 27.28S 153.00E 132, 135
Brisling oilfield 106
Bristol Bay 57.00N 160.00W 20
Bristol, see Avonmouth
Bristol voyages 192
Britain, Great *see UK and British Isles*
British Admiralty charts *see Charts*
British Ambassador, ship 171
British Aviator, ship 166
British Columbia 96, 101, 120
British/Faroes Boundary 186
British Isles *see also UK*
  movement in 600 My 35
  offshore oil & gas 104, (map) 106
  pollution, marine 174
  wave power resources 121
British Task Force 184, 185
Brittany
  coastal recreation (map) 217
  tidal energy 60
  tidal power scheme 120
Brittlestar 73
Broadcast weather reports 161
Broad Sound 120
Brockville 44.35N 75.41W 126
Brofjorden 58.20N 11.24E 123
Broken Bank oilfield 106
Broken Plateau 31.30S 95.00E 19
Bromine 119
Brooklyn 128
Broome 17.59S 122.14E 132
Brouwer 193
Brown booby 77
Brown seaweed 88
Brownsville 25.54N 97.28W 126
Bruce oilfield 106
Brugge 51.13N 3.13E 123
Brunei
  boundary dispute 188
  fisheries 98
  offshore oil & gas 104, 109
Brunel, I.K. 200
Brunsbüttel 53.53N 9.08E 123
Brunswick 31.08N 81.29W 126, 182
Bruxelles 50.51N 4.20E 123
Bryde's whale 100
Buchanan 5.52N 10.02W 133
Buchanan, port 133, 135
Bucksport 44.35N 68.49W 126
Buenaventura 3.50N 77.01W 127
Buenos Aires 34.41S 58.25W 127
Buffalo 42.53N 78.55W 126
Bulgaria
  aquaculture 83
  fishing fleet 86
  naval submarine strength 181
  naval surface fleet 178
Bulk carriers 136, 138, 139, 141, 142, 143
Bulk commodity trends 137
Bullen Bay 12.11N 69.01W 127, 134
Bullock Bank 156
Bunbury 33.19S 115.38E 132, 135
Bundaberg 24.52S 152.21E 132
Bunkering: Singapore 131
Buorkha, Bay of 72.00N 130.00E 24
Buoyage systems, regions & marks 159
Buoys 158, 159
  Jezebel sonar 184
  mooring (SBMs) 122–133, 134
  navigation 121, 208
  trajectories 52
Burgas 42.30N 27.29E 122
Burma
  fisheries 98
  naval fleet 178
Burmah Agate, tanker 171
Burnie 41.03S 145.55E 132
Burns Harbour 41.38N 87.11W 126
Burntisland 56.03N 3.14W 123
Burriana 39.51N 0.04W 122
Burutu 5.21N 5.31E 133
Būshehr 28.59N 50.50E 133
By-the-wind-sailor 68, 69

C

Cabañas 23.00N 82.59W 126
Cabedelo 6.58S 34.50W 127
Cabinda 5.33S 12.11E 133
Cabinda Coastal, oil basin 102, 103, 104, 108, 109
Cableship 200, 201
Cables, submarine (maps) 200–201
Cabo Rojo 17.56N 71.40W 127, 134
Cabot, John 192
Cabot Str. 47.30N 60.00W 150
Cachalot *see Sperm whale*
Cacheu 12.18N 16.10W 133
Cádiz 36.32N 6.17W 122
Cadmium 173
Caen-Ouistreham 49.11N 0.22W 122
Caernarvon 53.08N 4.16W 123
Caesarea, submerged harbour 196, 197
Caesium 174
Cagayan de Oro 8.30N 124.39E 132
Cagliari 39.10N 9.07E 122
Caibarién 22.32N 79.28W 126
Caicos Pass. 22.00N 72.20W 150
Cairns 212
Cairns 16.55S 145.47E 132
Cairo, wreck 194
Calabar 4.58N 8.19E 133
Calais 50.58N 1.51E 123, 156
Calanus finmarchicus 69
Calcareous deposits 42, 43, 112
Calcareous ooze 72
Calcite compensation depth (CCD) 42
Calcium
  in sea water 66, 119
  in seaweeds 83
Calcutta 22.32N 88.19E 130
Calcutta, port of (map) 131
Caldera 27.03S 70.51W 127
Calicut 192
Calicut see also Kozhikode
California 30, 32, 102
  fog 53
  magnetic anomalies 31
  offshore oil & gas 104, 105
  phosphate mining 115

phosphorite nodules offshore 115
pollution, marine 172
recreation industry 217
sardine fishery collapse 98, 99, 100
tuna fishery 101
California current 53
Californian 163
Callao 12.02S 77.10W 127
Callatis 194
Cambodia 98
Cambridge 38.34N 76.05W 126
Camden, see Ameriport
Cameroon Coastal, oil basin 102, 103, 108
Cameroon Line 37
Camouflage 68, 73
Campana 34.15S 58.58W 127
Campbell Plateau 51.00S 170.00E 22
Campbellton 48.00N 66.40W 126
Campeche 19.51N 90.32W 126
Cam Pha 21.01N 107.21E 130
Campos, oil basin 102
Canada 153
aquaculture production 82
Arctic: gas, oil & mineral exploiation 106, 107, 148, 149
fisheries & exclusive fishery zone 92, 96
fishing catch total 90
fishing fleet 86
naval submarine strength 181, 182
naval surface fleet 178, 182
oilfields (maps) 106–107
Canada Abyssal Plain 80.00N 150.00W 24, 63
Canada Basin 80.00N 145.00W 24, 62–63
Canakkale 40.09N 26.24E 122
Canakkale 155
Canals 125, 137, 146, 147, 150, 152, 153
Kiel 153
Panama 152
Rhine–Main–Danube 147
St Lawrence Seaway 153
Suez 153
Canal trade 152
Canal Zone 152
Canary current 44
Canary Is 37
Canberra, liner 184, 216
Canmar Kigoriak, tanker 148
Canoe fishing 80
Canoeing 217
Canso 45.20N 61.00W 126
Canso, Str. of 45.20N 61.00W 150
Canton 192
Canton see also Guangzhou
Canvey I. 51.30N 0.39E 123
Canvey I., port 156
Canyons, submarine 28, 29, 43
Cap Breton Canyon 43.40N 1.50W 17
Cape Abyssal Plain 34.45S 12.00E 18
Cape Basin 37.00S 7.00E 18
Cape Breton 192
Cape Cuvier 24.12S 113.23E 132
Cape Flattery 212
Cape hake 95
Cape Hatteras 63
Cape Horn 193
Capė Juby 95
Capelin 84, 88, 93
Cape of Good Hope 152, 192, 193
Cape Palmas 4.22N 7.44W 133
Cape route 146, 153, 184
Cape Sim 95
Cape Spartel 157
Cape Town 34.00S 18.28E 133, 135
Cape Trafalgar 157
Cape Verde 192
Cape Verde Abyssal Plain 23.00N 26.00W 16, 18
Cape Verde Is 37
Cape Verde Plateau 18.00N 20.00W 18
Cape York 212
Cap Lopez 0.38S 8.42E 133, 135
Capricornia section, Gt Barrier Reef 212
Caracas Convention *see Unclos III*
Caraquet 47.48N 64.56W 126
Carbonate-rich deposits 112
Carbon monoxide 172
Car carriers 139
Cardenas 23.03N 81.12W 126
Cardiff 51.27N 3.09W 123
Careening Bay 195
Caretta caretta (loggerhead turtle) 210
Cargo
seaborne trade 144
ships 139, 141, 142, 144, 146
tonnes carried by sea 136
types 134, 138, 139
Caribbean Sea 15.00N 75.00W 21
Caribbean Sea, tanker 171
Caribbean 109
cables, submarine (map) 200
hurricanes (map) 54–55
recreation & tourism 212, 213
territorial sea claims: complexities 218
Caribbean monk seal 210
Caripito 10.09N 63.08W 127
Carleton 48.06N 66.08W 126
Carloforte 39.08N 8.18E 122
Carlsberg Ridge (profile) 29
Carlsberg Ridge 6.00N 61.00E 19
Carnarvon 24.53S 113.45E 132
Carnegie Ridge 1.00S 85.00W 23
Caroline Is 36
Caroline Seamounts 7.00N 145.00E 22
Carp 82
CARPAS (Regional Fisheries Advisory Commission for the SW Atlantic) 211
Carpathia, ship 163
Carpentaria, G. of 15.00S 140.00E 22
Carrageenan 83, 119
Carrickfergus 54.44N 5.47W 123
Cartagena, Colombia 10.19N 75.35W 127
Cartagena, Spain 37.37N 0.59W 122
Carúpano 10.40N 63.14W 127
Casablanca 33.36N 7.37W 133, 135
Cascadia Basin 47.00N 127.30 21
Casilda 21.51N 79.59W 126
Caspian Sea 108
Cassiterite 112, 113
Castellammare di Stabia 40.42N 14.29E 122
Castellón de la Plana 39.59N 0.01W 122
Castellón oil basin 102
Castilla, Pto. 16.01N 86.01W 126
Castries 14.02N 61.01W 127
Castro-Urdiales 43.23N 3.12W 122
Casualties at sea
ice 163
rigs, oil 162
shipping, merchant 164–171
tankers, oil 168–171
Catadromous organisms 221
Catania 37.28N 15.05E 122
Cayenne (Degrad-des-Cannes) 4.56N 52.20W 127
CCAMLR (Commission for the Conservation of Antarctic Marine Living Resources) 211
CCD (calcite compensation depth) 42
Ceara Abyssal Plain 0.00 36.30W 18
Ceara Rise 3.00N 42.00W 18
Cebu 10.18N 123.53E 132
CECAF (Fishery Committee for the E-Central Atlantic) 211
Cedros Trench 27.45N 115.45W 23
Celebes Basin 4.00 122.00E 22
Celebes Sea 0.00 120.00E 20
Celtic Sea 50.00N 8.00W 17
Celtic Sea 186
Celtic Shelf 49.15N 7.00W 17
Central African Rep: aquaculture production 82
Central America: cyclones (map) 54
Central Fracture Zone 17.00N 128.00E 22
Central Indian Basin 1.00N 82.00E 19
Central Indian Ridge 12.00S 66.00E 19
Central Kara Rise 81.00N 80.00E 24
Central Pacific Basin 11.00N 180.00 22
Cephalopod catches 88
Cephalopods 79
Ceram Sea 3.00S 130.00E 20
Ceratioid angler fish 69
Ceratium 119
Cerium 113
Cerro Negro 36
Cerro Ventisquero 36
Cetacea 78
Ceuta 35.54N 5.18W 133
Ceuta 157
Ceyhan Limani 37.00N 35.46E 122, 135
Ceylon Plain 4.00S 82.00E 19
Chagos Bank 7.00S 72.00E 19
Chagos–Laccadive Ridge 8.00S 71.00E 19
Chāh Bahar 25.17N 60.37E 133
Chain Fracture Zone 2.00S 16.00W 18
Challenger, ship 42, 115, 116, 198, 199
Challenger Fracture Zone 36.00S 85.00W 23
Challenger Plateau 40.00S 169.30E 22
Chalna 22.34N 89.35E 130
Champerico 14.18N 91.56W 126
Chañaral 26.20S 70.38W 127, 134
Chancellor 192
Chandler 48.22N 64.40W 126
Channel lighthouse, weather station 161
Channel Navigation Information Service (CNIS) 156
Charcot Deep-Sea Fan 66.00S 85.00W 25
Charcot Seamounts 45.00N 12.00W 17
Charleston 32.46N 79.55W 126, 182
Charlestown 17.09N 62.34W 127
Charlie-Gibbs Fracture Zone 52.45N 35.30W 16
Charlottetown 46.14N 63.07W 126
Charts 158–159, 194, 198, 203
Chatham 47.02N 65.28W 126
Chatham 124, 182
Chatham Rise 43.30S 180.00 22
Chatham Rise: phosphorites (map) 115
Chatham, Str. of 57.20N 134.40W 150
Cheboygan 45.40N 84.28W 126
Cheju Haehyŏp 34.00N 126.30E 151
Chemainus 48.55N 123.42W 126
Chemicals 177
Chemical tankers 137, 138, 141
Chemical waste disposal 206
Cheng-ho 192
Cherbourg 49.39N 1.38W 123, 182
Cherbourg: mussel production 83
Chesapeake Bay
Landsat image 205
Sea use management 212, (map) 213
Chesapeake, see Hampton Roads
Chester, Canada 44.32N 64.16W 126
Chester, USA see Ameriport
Chetvertyy Kuril'skiy Proliv 50.00N 155.00E 150, 151
Chiba 35.36N 140.07E 130
Chiba, port 131
Chicago 41.53N 87.45W 126, 134
Chicoutimi 48.25N 71.06W 126
Chile
aquaculture production 83
earthquake 59
fisheries 99
guano 53
naval submarine strength 181
naval surface fleet 178
phosphorites offshore 115
pollution, marine 172
territorial claims Antarctica 185
Valparaiso region 129
Chile/Argentine dispute 187
Chile Basin 25.00S 78.00W 23
Chile Fracture Zone 36.00S 100.00W 23
Chile Trench 53.00S 76.00W 23, 28
Chi-lung 25.09N 121.44E 130, 135
Chimaeras 73, 88
Chimbote 9.05S 78.35W 127
China, People's Rep. of 188
fisheries 96
fishing catch total 91
fishing fleet 87
naval fleet 178
naval submarine strength 181
offshore oil & gas 104, 109
pollution, marine 173
strategic interest in Indian Ocean 185
territorial claims 188–189
typhoon damage (map) 55
China Seas 109
Chinnamp'o 38.45N 125.28E 130
Chioggia 45.13N 12.17E 122
Chittagong 22.18N 91.50E 130
Chlorine in sea water 66, 119
Chondrus crispus 119
Ch'ŏngjin 41.43N 129.58E 130
Chonos, Arch. de los 120
Chordata 119
Chosi 96
Christiansted 17.45N 64.41W 127
Christmas I, Ind. Oc. 10.30S 105.40E 132, 135
Christmas I, Pac. Oc., see Kiritimati
Chrome, trade in 137
Chromite 112, 114
Chromium 113
Chrysophyta 119
Chryssi, tanker 170
Chub mackerel 88
Chukchi Abyssal Plain 77.00N 172.00W 24
Chukchi Plateau 78.00N 165.00W 24, 63
Chukchi Sea 69.00N 170.00W 20, 24, 63
Churchill 58.47N 94.12W 126
Cie des Messageries Maritimes 140
Cienfuegos 22.09N 80.27W 126
CIFA (Committee for the Inland Fisheries of Africa) 211
Cilacap 7.41S 109.05E 132
Cinta 5.25S 105.50E 132
Ciotat, la 43.10N 5.36W 122
Circulation, oceanic, *see Oceans: circulation*
Cirebon 6.43S 108.33E 132
Cirrus cloud 54, 57
Cities, submerged 196, 197
Ciudad Bolívar 8.08N 63.35W 127
Ciudad del Carmen 18.39N 91.51W 126
Civitavecchia 42.05N 11.48E 122
Claims
territorial *see Territorial claims & disputes*
territorial sea 218, 219
Clams 73, 83, 84, 88
Clara, typhoon 55
Clarence River 29.25S 153.23E 132
Clarion–Clipperton nodule area (map) 116, 117
Clarion Fracture Zone 116–117
Clarion Fracture Zone 18.00N 122.00W 23
Claymore, oilfield 102, 106
Cleveland 41.32N 81.40W 126
Clipper routes 192–193
Clippers 140, 192
Clipperton Fracture Zone 116–117
Clipperton Fracture Zone 10.00N 115.00W 23
Clipperton Seamounts 8.00N 111.00W 23
Cloma, T. 188, 189
Clydeport see Glasgow, Greenock
CNIS (Channel Navigation Information Service) 156
Coal
exports via Hampton Roads 213
mining offshore 111
trade 134, (map) 136, 137, 140
world production 136, 137
Coaling stations 146
Coastal fisheries 96, 97
Coastal zones, recreation in 216
Coats Land 62
Coatzacoalcos 18.10N 94.25W 126
Cobalt 110, 111, 116–117, 118
Cobb Seamount 36
Cobequid Bay 120
Cochin 9.58N 76.14E 130
Cockles 83, 88
Cocos Basin 2.00S 92.00E 19
Cocos plate 32
Cocos Ridge 5.30N 86.00W 23
Cod 72, 81, 84, 87, 88, 92, 93, 175
COD (Chemical Oxygen Demand) 176, 177 *see glossary*
Cod, oilfield 102, 106
'Cod wars' 92, 186
Coelenterata 119
Coffs Harbour 30.18S 153.10E 132
Cogo 1.00N 9.40E 133
Colachel 8.18N 77.12E 130
Collisions at sea 156, 157, 162, 164–167
aids for avoiding 158
avoidance rules 208
examples 166–167
regulations 166, 221
Collo 37.00N 6.34E 133
Colombia
aquaculture producton 82
fishing catch 94
naval submarine strength 181
naval surface fleet 178
offshore oil & gas 104
Colombia–Nicaragua dispute 186
Colombian Trench 4.45N 78.15W 23
Colombo 6.57N 79.51E 130
Colón 32.13S 58.15W 127
Coloncha 9.13N 71.42W 127
Colonia 34.28S 57.55W 127
Colon Ridge 2.00N 96.00W 23
Colours of ocean animals 74
Columbus 32.28N 84.59W 126
Columbus, Christopher 192
Colville Ridge 34.30S 177.30E 22
Combination carriers 138
Commercial fisheries 84, 85
Commission for the Conservation of Antarctic Marine Living Resources (CCAMLR) 211
Commissions, fisheries 211
Committee for the Inland Fisheries of Africa (CIFA) 211
Commodities/liner freight rates, ratios 144
Commodity flows 136–137
Commodity ports 134–135
Common noddy, (map) 77
Communications 204
Communication satellites 200, 204
Comodoro Rivadavia 45.51S 67.26W 127
Comóros 36, 185
fisheries 98
Comox 49.40N 124.56W 126
Compass 31, 158
Conakry 9.31N 13.43W 133
Conakry, port 133
Concepción del Uruguay 32.30S 58.15W 127
Conchán 12.20S 76.56W 127
Conger 88
Congo Cone 6.00S 9.00E 18
Congo: offshore oil & gas 104, 108
Congo, R 26, 109
Conneaut 41.57N 80.31W 126
Conqueror, submarine 184
Conrad Fracture Zone 56.00S 5.00W 18
Conrad Rise 54.00S 40.00E 19
Conservation management 208, 210–214, 221 *see also Appendix X*
Conservation projects: endangered species (map) 210–211, *see also Appendix X*
Conservation of salmon: convention 101
Constanța 44.10N 28.40E 122, 135
Constructive total loss (CTL) 164
Consumers of seafood (map) 85
Containerisation 152
Container ports 128, 129, 131–132, 134–135
Container routes 137
Containers 138, 139, 146
Container ships 136, 138, 139, 141, 160
Contiguous zones: definition 220
Continental
crust (diags) 38–39
drift 32, (maps) 34–35, 40
margin 27, 28–29, 40, 115, 222
rise 28, 43, 223
slope 27, 28, 43, 72, 73, 84, 223
Continental shelf 26, 27, 28, 42, 72, 73, 106, 109, 115, (maps) 222–223
Celtic Sea (map) 186
deposits 112
divisions & legal definitions (maps) 222–223
fisheries 84, 85, 90, 92, 96, 97, 100
Continental Shelf (Tunisia–Libya) case 1982 222
Convective heat flow 32, 35
Conventions
law of the sea *see UNCLOS III, see also Appendix XI*
pollution 168, 224
safety of life at sea *see SOLAS*
salmon conservation 101
standards of training etc. of seafarers 168
trade and development *see UNCTAD*
Cook I. 36
Cook Inlet 106, (map) 107, 120
Cook Inlet Prov. oil basin 102
Cook, James 192, 193
Cook Strait 41.00S 174.30E 150
Coondapoor 13.37N 74.40E 130
Cooperation Sea 65.00S 75.00E 19, 25
Cooper Ridge 10.15N 150.30W 23
Coos Bay 43.22N 124.13W 126
Copepod 68, 69, 70, 71, 79
Copper 110, 111, 113, 114, 116–117, 118, 174, 175
Copper: inter area trade 137
Coquimbo 29.57S 71.21W 127
Coral 42–43, 72
Coral reef 42, 80–81, 132, 155, 210–212
Coral Sea aircraft carrier 179
Coral Sea 17.00S 158.00E 22
Cordonazo, hurricane 54
Cordova 60.30N 145.52W 126
Corfu Channel 39.30N 20.00E 151
Corinth Canal 152
Corinthos, tanker 171
Corinto 12.28N 87.11W 126
Coriolis force 45
Cork 51.53N 8.28W 123
Cormorant oilfield 106

Cormorant 76
Corner Brook 48.57N 57.57W 126
Corner Seamounts 37, 52
Corner Seamounts 35.30N 51.30W 16
Cornwall 45.00N 74.43W 126
Coronado 182
Coronel 37.02S 73.05W 127
Corpus Christi 27.48N 97.23W 126, 134
Corvettes 179
Coryaeeus speciosus 71
Coryphaenoides 73
Cosmonaut Sea 63.00S 40.00E 19,
Costa Rica
   aquaculture production 82
   fisheries 99
   fishing catch 94
Cotonou 6.20N 2.27E 133
Cotonou, port 133
Coveñas 9.25N 75.42W 127
Coventry, destroyer 184
COW (crude oil washing) 171
Cowes Week, racing event 217
Cowichan Bay 48.46N 124.00W 126
Crab 84, 88, 213
Crabeater seal 79
Crawford oilfield 106
Cretaceous Quiet Zone 30
Cretan Star, tanker 171
Crisis
   Cuban 1962 190
   Falklands 1982 184
   Mediterranean 1973 189
Cristóbal 9.21N 79.54W 126
Cromarty, shipping forecast area 161
Crotone 39.05N 17.08E 122
Crozet I. 37
Cruden Bay 106
Crude oil washing (COW) 171
Cruise missiles 180
Cruisers 178, 179
Cruiser Seamount 32.00N 28.00W 16
Cruises, ocean (map) 216
Crustaceans 83, 89
Crustal plates 29, 32, 33
Crust, oceanic (diags) 38–39, 40–41, 43
Crystal Jewel, ship 166
CTL (constructive total loss) 164
Cuba
   aquaculture production 82
   fishing catch 94
   fishing fleet 86
   naval fleet 178
Cuban Missile Crisis 1962 190
Cuddalore 11.42N 79.43E 130
Cumberland Basin 120
Cumulo-nimbus clouds 47, 56, 57
Cumulus clouds 57
Cunard Line 140
Curacao, wreck 194
Curaçao Reef 36
Curie point 30
Currents (maps) 50–51
   Atlantic, N. 44–45
   Gulf Stream 44–45, (maps) 52
   Mediterranean (diags) 52
   straits 154–157
   surface 44–45, (maps) 50–51, 198
   tidal 60, 112
   upwelling 45, 53, 57, 71, 76, 78, 85, 95, 110, 114
Cutlassfish 88
Cuttlefish 88
Cutuco 13.19N 87.49W 126
Cuvier Basin 22.00S 111.00E 19
Cuvier Plateau 24.00S 108.00E 19
Cuxhaven 53.52N 8.42E 123
Cyanophyta 119
Cyclones 47, 48, 49, (maps & graphs) 54–57, 60, 160
Cyclothone 69, 74
Cyprus 141
   aquaculture 82
Cyrus 29.01N 49.28E 133
Cystisoma (amphipod shrimp) 69
Czechoslovakia: aquaculture 82

D

Daamo, pre-Islamic port 195
Dab 84
Dacca 23.43N 90.21E 130
Dacia Seamount 31.10N 13.42W 17
Dadiangas 6.05N 125.15E 132
Dagenham, port 156
Dagenham 51.30N 0.15E 123
Daito I. 36
Dakar 14.40N 17.26W 133
Dakar, port (map) 133, 135
Dakhla 23.43N 15.57W 133
Dalhousie 48.04N 66.22W 126
Dam-Atoll' 121
Damietta (Dumyât) 31.23N 31.48E 133
Dampier 20.45S 116.51E 132, 135
Dampier Strait 5.40S 147.00E 151
Dana, ship 198
Dana Fracture Zone 12.00S 96.00W 23
Da Nang 16.07N 108.12E 130
Danjo Islands 189
Dan, oilfield 102, 106
Dardanelles 40.20N 26.30E 150, 151, 155
Dar-es-Salaam 6.50S 39.17E 133
Darling Harbour, Sydney 132
Darlowo 54.27N 16.23E 123
Darnah 32.46N 22.39E 133
Darwin, Australia 12.28S 130.50E 132
Darwin, Australia 54, 120

Darwin, Charles 198
Darwin, Falkland Is 184
Das I. 134, 135
Das Island 25.09N 52.52E 133
Dating: radio isotope 37
Davao 7.05N 125.37E 132
David, hurricane 54
Davie Ridge 17.00S 41.30E 19
Davis Sea 65.00S 92.00E 19, 25
Davis Strait 62, 64
Davis Strait 66.00N 58.00W 16, 24, 150
Day Dawn, wreck 195
DDT 172, 174, 175
Deborah oilfield 106
Decca Navigator System 158
Deception I. 36
Deep scattering layer 71
Deep sea cod 72
Deep Sea Drilling Project (DSDP) 39, 40, 114
Deep sea expeditions 198
Deep sea prawn 69
Deep water technology 104, 106
Degema 4.44N 6.46E 133
Degerhamn 56.21N 16.03E 123
De Gerlache Seamounts 65.00S 90.00W 23, 25
Degrad-des-Cannes 4.56N 52.20W 127
Delan Basin 31.00N 114.00W 21, 23
Del Caño Rise 45.00S 41.00E 19
Delfzijl 53.20N 6.56E 123
Delimitation of the territorial sea 186, 220
Delta III submarine 180, 181, 182
Delta Project (Neths.) 60, 215
Deltas, as port sites 125
Demerara Abyssal Plain 10.00N 48.00W 18
Demersal
   fish 84, 85, 88, 90, 96, 210
   gears 84
   species 87
   stocks (map) 94–95
Den Haag 52.05N 4.15E 123
Den Helder 106
Den Helder 52.58N 4.45E 123
Denmark
   aquaculture production 83
   fishing catch total 93
   fishing fleet 86
   fishing zone claims 186
   naval submarine strength 181, 182
   naval surface fleet 178, 182
   offshore oil & gas 104
Denmark Strait 62, 64
Denmark Strait 65.00N 30.00W 16, 24, 150
Density of sea water (maps & graph) 38, 66–67
Deployment of fleets 182–185
Deposits (fluviatile, glacial etc.) 112–113
Depressions (low pressure systems) (diags) 47, 48, 51, 56
Derby 17.17S 123.36E 132
Derbyshire, ship 160
Derince 40.44N 29.50E 122
Desalination plants (map) 118, 119
Deseado 47.45S 65.55W 127
Destroyers 178, 179
Detritivores *see Detritus eaters*
Detritus 72
Detritus eaters 72
Detroit 42.20N 83.02W 126, 134
Deuterium 119
Devonport 41.11S 146.22E 132, 182
Dhiavios Karpáthou 151
Dhiékplous Kithiron 151
Diadromous species 87
Diamante 32.08S 60.35W 127
Diamentina Fracture Zone 36.00S 105.00E 19
Diamond 113
Dias, Bartholomew 192
Diatomaceous ooze 42, 68, 115
Diatoms 68, 69–70
Didicas 36
Diego Garcia 185
Dieppe 49.55N 1.05E 122
Digby 44.38N 65.45W 126
Dinoflagellate 72
Discoverer Seven Seas 107
Discovery, ship 198
Discovery, scientific, of oceans 198–199
Discovery Seamount 37
Discovery Seamounts 42.00S 0.10E 18
Disko Bugt 62
Disputes, *see* Territorial claims & disputes
Distances, shipping route 146–147, *see also Appendix VII*
Diurnal tide 61
Diving, SCUBA 194
Dixon Entrance 186
Dixon Entrance 54.30N 132.00W 150
Djakarta 98
Djibouti 11.36N 43.08E 133
Djibouti 154, 187
Dogger, shipping forecast area 161
Doha (Ad Dawþah) 25.19N 51.35E 133
Doldrums 46, 48
Doldrums Fracture Zone 8.00N 40.00W 18
Dolphin 75, 88
Dominica: hurricane damage 55
Dominican Republic
   aquaculture production 82
   hurricane damage 55
   naval fleet 178
Dominica Pass 15.50N 61.30W 150
Donggala 0.37S 119.44E 132
Don João de Castro Bank 37

Doppler navigation 204
Doppler principle 204
Dorade 75
Dotty, oilfield 106
Douala 4.03N 9.42E 133
Douglas, Falkland Is 184
Douglas, UK 54.09N 4.28W 123
Dounreay 174
Dover 51.07N 1.20E 123
Dover 156
Dover, shipping forecast area 161
Dover Strait 156, 157, 215, 219
Dover Strait 51.00N 1.30E 150, 151
Dowsing lightvessel, weather station 161
Drake, Sir Francis 129, 193
Drammen 59.45N 10.13E 123
Dredging 112, 123, 173
Drift net 84, 87, 93
Drill holes 39
Drilling 40–41, 202
Drill ships 105, 107
Drill slots 107
Drogheda 53.43N 6.20W 123
Dronning Maud Land 62
Drugs from the sea 119
Dry docks 122–133, 143
DSDP (Deep Sea Drilling Project) 39, (map) 40–41, 114
Dubai: offshore oil & gas 104, 109, 154
Dublin 53.21N 6.16W 123
Dubrovnik 42.38N 18.06E 122
Dugong 210, 211
Dumaguete 9.18N 123.18E 132
Dumai 1.45N 101.28E 132, 135
Dumont d'Urville Sea 65.00S 140.00E 25
Dumping 171, 174–175
Dumping conventions 224
Dumshaf Abyssal Plain 68.00N 5.00E 24
Dundalk 54.01N 6.25W 123
Dundee 56.28N 2.58W 123
Dungeness 156
Dunkerque 51.03N 2.23E 123, 135
Dunkirk 196
Dún Laoghaire 53.18N 6.08W 123
Dunlin A, oilfield 102, 106
Durban 29.52S 31.03E 133, 135
Durrës 41.19N 19.28E 122
Dutch East India Company 193
Dynamic positioning (ships) 40, 105
Dzaoudzi·12.50S 45.16E 133

E

Earthquakes 32, 33, 38, 59
Earth
   circumference 204
   core 30, 38, 39
   magnetic field 30, 35
   mantle 35, 38–39
   ridges 38
   shape & measurements 204
   structure & composition (diags) 38–39
   surface 26, 27, 40
   surface waters 26
Earth resources satellites 205
Easington 106
East Azores Fracture Zone 37.00N 25.00W 16–17
East Caroline Basin 4.00N 146.45E 22
East China Sea 28.00N 124.00E 20
Easter Fracture Zone 26.00S 95.00W 23
Eastern Scheldt storm surge barrier 60
East Germany 96
   aquaculture 83
   fishing fleet 86
   naval fleet 178
East Greenland current 44, 64, 67
East Greenland Current 131
East India Company 193
East India Docks 124
East Indiaman Ridge 25.00S 100.00E 19
East Korea Strait 34.20N 129.00E 151
East London 33.02S 27.58E 133
East Mariana Basin 14.00N 153.00E 22
East Pacific green turtle 210
East Pacific Rise 29, 114
East Pacific Rise 20.00S 115.00W 23
East Sheba Ridge 14.30N 56.15E 19
East Siberian Sea 73.00N 170.00E 24, 63
Eauripik Rise 3.00N 142.00E 22
Echinodermata 72, 73, 88, 119
Echo sounders 84, 202, 203
Ecosystems 78, 89, 208, 210, 212, 213
Ecuador
   aquaculture production 82
   fisheries 99
   guano 53
   naval submarine strength 181
   naval surface fleet 178
Edda oilfield 106, 162
Eddystone Lighthouse 158
Eden 37.04S 149.55E 132
Edincik 40.22N 27.52E 122
Edith Ronne Land 63
Edoras Bank 56.00N 22.00W 16
Edward VII Land 63
EEC 92, 123, 142, 175, 215, 219
EEC–Icelandic Fisheries 186
EEC–Norway Fisheries 186
Eel-pout 73
EEZ (Exclusive Economic Zone) 87, 91, 92, 94, 95, 97–99, 101, 185, 187, 210, 219, 221
EEZ limit 92 *see also Appendix II*
EFZ (Exclusive Fishing Zone) 219

Egadi Is 95
Egersund 58.27N 6.00E 123
Egypt 153
   aquaculture production 82
   fisheries 98
   naval submarine strength 181
   naval surface fleet 178
   offshore oil & gas 104, 108, 154
EIFAC (European Inland Fisheries Advisory Commission) 211
Eilat, *see Elat*
Eirik Ridge 58.40N 44.00W 16
Ekenäs 59.58N 23.26E 122
Ekman layer 45
Ekofisk & W., oilfield 102, 106, 107
Élan Bank 57.00S 70.00E 19
Elat 29.32N 34.56E 133
Elat 135, 146, 154, 181, 187, 190
Elbe, R. 158
El Bluff 12.00N 83.45W 126
El Botado 19.20N 69.30W 127
Elcano 192
Eldeyjar 37
Electricity power schemes, tidal energy 120, 121
Electrodialysis 119
Elefsis Bay 177
Elements, in nodules 116
Elements in sea water 66, (table) 119
Elevsis (Elefsis) 38.02N 23.32E 122
El Ferrol 43.30N 8.14W 122
El Gran Grifon, wreck 194
El-Jadida 33.16N 8.36W 133
Ellesmere I. 62
Ellesmere Port 53.18N 2.54W 123
Ellington 17.20S 178.14E 132
Ellsworth Land 63
Ellsworth Mts 63
El Niño 53
El Salvador
   aquaculture production 82
   fisheries 99
Elsfleth 53.14N 8.27E 123
El Tablazo 10.45N 71.32W 127
Eltanin Fracture Zone System 54.00S 130.00W 23
Emden 53.22N 7.13E 106, 123
Emerald Basin 55.00S 162.00E 22
Emily, hurricane 54
Emperor of China 36
Emperor penguin 76
Emperor Seamount Chain 42.00N 170.00E 20
Emperor Seamounts 36
Emperor Trough 43.00N 175.30E 20
Enderby Abyssal Plain 61.00S 40.00E 19
Endurance, patrol ship 184
Endurance Fracture Zone 56.50S 50.00W 18
Endurance Ridge 63.00S 40.00W 18
Energy
   sources 120–121
   thermal 32, 39, (map) 121
   tidal (maps) 60, 120, 121
   wave power (map) 121
English Channel 50.00N 2.00W 17
English Channel: collisions 156, 166–167
Ensenada 31.52N 116.38W 126
Entrepot ports 130, 131
Epic Colocotronis, tanker 171
Epipelagic Zone 68, 70, 74, 75, 84
Equatorial countercurrent 44, 70
Equatorial current 70
Equidistance, principle of 186
Equitable principles 186
Erben Guyot 36
Eregli 41.18N 31.27E 122
Eriador Seamount 55.00N 25.00W 16
Erie 42.07N 80.05W 126
Erie Canal 128
Eriksson, Leif 192
ERS 1 (Earth resources satellite) 204
Erta Alé 37
Esbjerg 55.28N 8.26E 123
Escort ships 178
Escravos 5.36N 5.11E 135
Esmeraldas 0.55N 79.38W 127
Esperance 33.52S 121.53E 132
Esquimalt 48.26N 123.27W 126, 182
Essaouira 31.31N 9.46W 133
Es Skhira 34.18N 10.09E 133, 135
Estrecho de Le Maire 55.00S 65.00W 150
Estrecho de Magallanes 53.30S 71.00W 150
Estuary ports 124
Etang de Berre 43.23N 5.00E 122
Ethiopia 154, 178
Etna, Mt 37
Etolin Strait 60.20N 165.30W 150
Eubalaena glacialis (southern right whale) 78
Euler pole 33
Euphausiacea 69
Euphausia superba (krill) 69
Euphotic zone 68, 70, 71, 72, 73, 74
Eurasia 35
Eureka 40.48N 124.10W 126
European Community 215
European Inland Fisheries Advisory Commission (EIFAC) 211
European Space Agency 204
Europe: distribution of ports 122, 123
Europoort/Rotterdam 51.55N 4.30E 123
Europoort/Rotterdam (map) 124–125, 135
Eurypharynx pelecanoides (gulper eel) 75
Evans cylinder, wave energy device 121
Evaporation, affecting salinity 52, 66, 67

Everett 47.59N 122.12W 126
Evstaffi, wreck 194
Exclusion zones, maritime 184, 185
Exclusive Economic Zone, *see EEZ*
Exclusive Fishing Zone *see EFZ*
Exmouth Plateau 19.00S 114.00E 19, 22
Exocet missile 184
Expeditions, ocean 192–193, 198–199, 202
Expenditure, offshore oil 102
Exploration, ocean 198–199, 202
Explosions (in casualty records) 162

F

Fåborg 55.05N 10.16E 123
Factory ships 86, 87, 100
Færingehavn 63.50N 51.20W 126
Faeroe Bank 60.55N 8.40W 17
Faeroe Bank Channel 61.00N 8.00W 17
Faeroe Is 81, 92, 93, 215
  exclusive fishing zone 186
  Salmon feeding grounds near 101
Faeroe Shelf 62.00N 8.00W 17
Faeroe–Shetland Channel 62.00N 2.00W 17
Faeroes, shipping forecast area 161
Fagerstrand 59.44N 10.36E 123
Fair Isle, shipping forecast area 161
Fairy Bank 156
Falcon I. 36
Falkenberg 56.53N 12.30E 123
Falkland War of 1982 184, 185
Falkland Escarpment 49.00S 45.00W 18
Falkland Islands 184
Falkland Plateau 51.00S 50.00W 18
Falkland Ridge 49.00S 33.00W 18
Fall River 41.42N 71.08W 126
Falmouth 50.09N 5.04W 123
Famagusta 35.08N 33.58E 122
Families of birds 77
Famita, ship 47
FAMOUS (French–American Mid Ocean Undersea Study) 203
FAO (Food & Agricultural Organisation) 208
  areas 84, 85, 210
  fisheries development programme 210
  fishery commissions & advisory bodies 211
  fishing catch totals by FAO area 90, 91, 94, 95
  tuna catch by FAO area 101
FAO/UN, ten year aquaculture development programme 82
Faraday Fracture Zone 49.50N 30.00W 16
Farallon plate 33
Farming the sea 82
Faro 37.01N 7.52W 122
Faroe Is *see Faeroe Is*
Farsund 58.05N 6.49E 123
Faslane 182
Fateh Terminal 25.36N 54.31E 133
Faults 29, 32, 33
Favignana 95
Fawn Trough 57.00S 75.00E 19
Fayal I. 37
Fearless, ship 184
Fécamp 49.45N 0.22E 122, 156
Felixstowe 124, 156
Felixstowe 51.57N 1.19E 123
Fenit 52.17N 9.50W 123
Fernandina 37
Fernandina Beach 30.35N 81.28W 126
Fernando Po 37
Ferries 149, 156, 157
Ferry services 134, 146
Fertilisers 83, 91, 95, 115, 134, 172, 175
Fethiye 36.39N 29.09E 122
Fifi, hurricane 54
Fifteen Twenty Fracture Zone 15.00N 45.00W 18
Figueira da Foz 40.09N 8.52W 122
Fiji 144
  fisheries 99
  hurricane devastation 55
Filchner–Ronne Ice Shelf 63, 65
Finfish 82, 83, 213
Finger piers 128, 129
Finland
  aquaculture products 83
  fishing catch 93
  naval fleet 178
Finland, G. of 60.00N 25.00E 17, 151
Finnart 56.07N 4.50W 123
Fin whale 78, 100, 210, 211
Fire at sea 162
Fish
  factories 86, 87
  locating methods 84
  products 90, 91
  species caught 88–89, *see also Appendix IV*
  species, vertical ocean zones 74–75
  stocks (map) 94–95, 206
  world production 91
Fisheries (maps) 92–101, 99, 209
  artisanal 80–81, 95, 98–99
  catch, world: species 88–89 *see also Appendix IV*
  commissions & advisory bodies 211
  control 84, 96, 100
  inshore 87
  lagoon & atoll 80–81
  offshore 87
  traditional 80–81, 84, 95, 96, 97
Fisher, shipping forecast area 161
Fishery Committee for E. Central Atlantic (CECAF) 211
Fishguard 52.00N 4.58W 123
Fishing 80
  boats 87
  commercial 84
  fleets, world (map) 86–87, 91, 157, 210
  gears 84
  industry: structure 84–85
  limits 87, 92, 186
  management 84
  nations (map) 90–91
  recreational 95, 216
  rights 186, 210, 219
  statistics, world 88
  zones 186, 215
Fishmeal 85
Fitzroy 184
Fiumicino 41.47N 12.15E 122
Flags
  casualties, loss distribution by 162
  of convenience (FOC) 141, 144
  ships 142
  warning, for hurricanes 54
Flatback turtle 211
Fleets, fishing
  distant & middle water 87
  world (map) 86–87, 91, 157, 210
Fleets, merchant
  national & beneficial ownership 140–141
  world 138–139, 141
Fleets, naval 178–183
  Argentine 184
  British 178, 182–185
  deployment 182–185
  Indian 185
  NATO 178–179, 182–183
  strengths, selected countries (table) 178
  Uruguayan 184
  USA 182–183, 189
  USSR 178–179, 182–183, 185, 189
  world (map) 178–179, (map) 181
Fleets, survey & research (maps) 206–207
Fleetwood 53.56N 3.01W 123
Flekkefjord 58.18N 6.39E 123
Flemish Cap 47.00N 45.00W 16
Flensburg 54.48N 9.26E 123
Floating platforms 106
Floods 56, 60
Florida current 44
Florida, Straits of 24.00N 80.00W 150
Flossie, typhoon 54
Flotta 58.49N 3.07W 123
Flotta 106, 135
Flounder 88
Flying fish 75
Flyndre oilfield 106
FOC (flag of convenience) 140, 141
FOC registers 140, 141
Fod, G. of 123
Foerstner 37
Fog (maps) 53, 154, 155, 156, 160
  collisions in 166–167
Folkestone 51.05N 1.12E 123
Follonica 42.55N 10.45E 122
Food & Agricultural Organisation *see FAO*
Food chains 68, 70, 78–79
Foraminifera 69, 71, 115
Forcados 5.20N 5.25E 133
Forcados 108, 135
Forces, naval *see Naval: forces*
Forecasting weather 160, 161
Forestville 48.46N 69.02W 126
Forsmark 60.25N 18.13E 123
Fortaleza 3.41S 38.33W 127
Fort-de-France 14.38N 61.04W 127
Forth ports, *see Burntisland, Grangemouth, Granton, Hound Point, Kirkaldy, Leith, Methil*
Forth, shipping forecast area 161
Forties, oilfield 102, 106
Forties, shipping forecast area 161
Fortune Bank 7.13S 57.00E 19
Fos 43.25N 4.53E 122, 123, 177
Fosbucraa Port 27.10N 13.11W 133, 135
Foulness Pt. 156
Four North Fracture Zone 4.00N 35.00W 18
Foveaux Strait 46.40S 168.00E 150, 151
Fowey 50.21N 4.38W 123
Fox Bay 184
Foxe Basin 66.00N 78.00W 16, 24
Foxe Channel 64.00N 80.00W 24
Foynes 52.36N 9.06W 123
Fracture zones 26, 27, (map) 32–33
Fram, ship 199
Fram Bank 67.18S 70.00E 25
France
  Anglo–French Continental Shelf case 1977–78 222
  aquaculture production 82, (map) 83
  coast of 156, 216
  fishing catch total 91, 93
  fishing fleet 86
  merchant fleet 138
  naval submarine strength 181, 182
  naval surface fleet 178, 182
  oyster & mussel industries 82
  pollution 177
  seaborne trade 144
  shellfish market 82
  tidal power schemes (map) 120
  tuna fishing 101
Franklin, Benjamin 198
Franklin class submarine 181
Fraserburgh 57.42N 2.00W 123
Fray Bentos 33.06S 58.18W 127
Fredericia 55.34N 9.44E 123
Frederikshåb 62.05N 49.30W 126
Frederikshavn 57.27N 10.33E 123, 182
Frederikssund 55.50N 12.04E 123
Frederiksted 17.43N 64.53W 127
Frederiksværk 55.59N 12.02E 123
Fredrikstad 59.12N 11.00E 123
Freeport, Bahamas 26.31N 78.46W 126, 134
Freeport, Bermuda 32.19N 64.51W 126
Free ports (free trade zones) 129
Freeport, USA 28.57N 95.21W 126, 134
Freetown 8.30N 13.14W 133
Freezing processes 119
Freight rates 143
  in relation to commodity prices 144
Fremantle 32.03S 115.45E 132, 135
French–American Mid Ocean Undersea Study (FAMOUS) 203
French Polynesia: fisheries 99
Fresh water 119
Freu de Menorca 40.00N 3.40E 151
Frigate Bird 76, 77
Frigates 178, 179
Frigg, & NE & E., oilfields 106
Frobisher Bay 63.44N 68.32W 120, 126
Frontera 18.32N 92.39W 126
Fronts 56
Fuego 37
Fuel consumption: ships 138
Fügley Bank 71.00N 20.00E 24
Fuik Bay 12.03N 68.50W 127
Fukuoka 96
Fukuyama 34.26N 133.27E 130
Fulmar oilfield 106
Funabashi, port 131
Funafuti 8.25S 179.10E 132
Funchal 32.38N 16.54W 133
Fundy, Bay of
  tidal power potential (map) 120
  tidal range 60, 120
Fungicides 172
Fushiki 36.49N 137.03E 130

G

Gabès 33.53N 10.06E 133
Gabon
  aquaculture production 82
  offshore oilfields (map) 108, 109
Gabon Coastal, oil basin 102, 103, 108, 109
Gaeta 41.12N 13.35E 122, 182
Galapagos Fracture Zone 1.00S 134.00W 23
Galapagos fur seal 210
Galapagos Is 114, 157
Galapagos Ridge 114
Galapagos Rift Zone 73
Galapagos Rise 12.00S 95.00W 23
Galathea expedition 198, (map) 202
Galaţi 45.25N 28.05E 122
Galeota Point 10.08N 61.00W 127
Gales 48, 57, 60, (map) 160–161
Galicia Bank 42.50N 11.50W 17
Galicia Bank 37
Galle 6.01N 80.13E 130
Gallego Rise 4.00S 120.00W 21, 23
Gallieni Fracture Zone 37.00S 52.15E 19
Gallipoli, Italy 40.03N 17.58E 122
Gallipoli, Turkey see Gelibolu
Galloper, light buoy 156
Galveston 29.20N 94.45W 126, 134
Galway 53.18N 9.05W 125
Gama, Vasco da 192
Gamba 2.42S 9.59E 133
Gambia Abyssal Plain 12.00N 28.00W 18
Gandia 38.58N 0.10W 122
Ganges Delta 54
Gannet 76, 77
Gardar Ridge 57.00N 27.00W 16
Garrett Fracture Zone 13.20S 112.00W 23
Garston 53.21N 2.54W 123
Gas carriers 138, 142, 148
Gascoyne Plain 16.00S 110.00E 19
Gascoyne Seamount 36.30S 156.30E 22, 36
Gas fields, offshore 106, 108, 109
Gas: liquid, trade 137
Gas, natural: trade 137
Gaspé 48.49N 64.29W 126
Gas tankers 137, 141
Gatun Locks 152
Gaul, factory trawler 164
Gauss, ship 199
Gavle 60.41N 17.10E 123
Gdańsk 54.21N 18.39E 123, 135
Gdynia 54.32N 18.34E 123, 135
GEBCO (General Bathymetric Chart of the Oceans) 203
Geelong 38.09S 144.22E 132, 135
Geese Bank 71.30N 46.30E 24
Gela 37.03N 14.16E 122
Gela desalination plant 118
Gelibolu 40.24N 26.40E 122
Gelibolu (Gallipoli) 155
Gelidonya, Cape 194
Gemlik 40.26N 29.09E 122
General Bathymetric Chart of the Oceans (GEBCO) 203
General Belgrano, cruiser 184
General Belgrano Bank 73.00S 50.00W 25
General cargo liners 138, 139
General Fisheries Council for the Mediterranean (GFCM) 211
Geneva Convention on the Continental Shelf 187, 222
Genoa: pollution 177
Genova (Genoa) 44.24N 8.54E 122, 135
Gent 51.02N 3.44E 123
Geodesy 204
Geodetic satellites 204
Geoid 204
Geomagnetic field 30
George Bligh Bank 58.55N 13.45W 17
George V Land 63
Georges Bank 41.15N 67.30W 16
Georges Bank/Gulf of Maine dispute 186
Georges Leygues, corvette 179
Georgetown, Canada 46.11N 62.31W 126
Georgetown, Cayman Is 19.17N 81.23W 126
Georgetown, Guyana 6.49N 58.10W 127
Georgetown, USA 33.21N 79.17W 126
Georgia Basin 51.00S 37.00W 18
Geo-synchronous orbit 204
Geothermal heat 39
Geraldton 28.46S 114.36E 132, 135
German Bight, shipping forecast area 161
GFCM (General Fisheries Council for the Mediterranean) 211
Ghana
  aquaculture production 82
  fishing catch 95
  fishing fleet 86
  offshore oil & gas 104
Ghazaouet 35.06N 1.52W 133
Giant tube worm 73
Gibraltar 36.07N 5.21W 122
Gibraltar, Rock of 157
Gibraltar, Straits of 157, 182, 219
Gibraltar, Straits of 36.00N 5.30W 150, 151
Gijón 43.34N 5.41W 122
Gilbert Is 36
Gilbert Seamount 36, 37
Gilbert Seamounts 2.00N 173.00E 22
Gill nets & netting 80, 84, 101
Gino, tanker 171
Gippsland oil basin 103
Giresun 40.56N 38.24E 122
Gisborne 38.40S 178.01E 132
Giulia–Ferdinandeo 37
Gizo 8.05S 156.52E 132
Glacial deposits 42
Glaciers 62, 64
Gladstone 23.50S 151.15E 132, 135
Glamorgan, destroyer 184
Glasgow 55.51N 4.16W 123
Glasson Dock (Lancaster) 54.00N 2.50W 123
Glass sponges 72
Glebe Island 132
Glenn oilfield 106
Global positioning system (GPS) 158
Globigerina ooze 42
Globigerinoides 71
Glomar Challenger 40, 202
Glomar Explorer 40
GLORIA, sonar 203
Glossopteris 35
Gloucester 42.36N 70.39W 126
Glückstadt 53.47N 9.28E 123
Goban Spur 49.25N 12.00W 17
Goderich 43.44N 81.43W 126
Godthåb 64.11N 51.40W 126
Gofar Fracture Zone 4.15S 106.00W 23
Gölcük 183
Gold 112, 113, 119
Golden Drake, tanker 170
Golden Gate 129
Golfito 8.37N 83.10W 126
Golfo San Jorge 120
Golfo San José 120
Golf class submarine 181
Golovasi 36.52N 35.55E 122
Gondwanaland 34, 35
Gonostoma bathyphilum 75
Goodwin Sands 156
Goole 53.42N 0.52W 123
Goose Bay 53.20N 60.24W 126
Goose Green 184
Goote Bank 156
Gorda plate 32
Gorgonian coral 72
Gorm oilfield 106
Gorontalo 0.30N 123.03E 132
Göteborg 57.45N 12.00E 123, 135
Göteborg, port & region (maps) 125
Gotland Basin 59.00N 20.00E 17
Gough Fracture Zone 40.30S 20.00W 18
Gough I. 37
Gove 12.12S 136.40E 132, 135
GPS (satellite global positioning systems) 158
Graham Land 62
Grain, I. of 51.28N 0.41E 56, 123
Grain, world trade 134, (map) 136, 137
Grand Bank 47.08N 55.50W 126
Grand Banks of Newfoundland 45.00N 53.00W 16
Grand Banks of Newfoundland 64, 93, 160
Grand Erg Oriental, oil basin 102
Grand Haven 43.04N 86.14W 126
Grand Turk 21.30N 71.09W 126
Grand Zenith, tanker 171
Grangemouth 56.02N 3.41W 123
Granton 55.59N 3.13W 123
Granville 48.50N 1.36W 122
Gravel deposits 112–113
Gravelines 196
Gravesend Reach 124
Gravity 204
Grays Harbor 46.55N 124.08W 126
Great Barrier Reef 42, 212, 224
Great Bitter Lake 153
Great Britain *see UK and British Isles*
Great Circle Route 148
Great Eastern, passenger liner 200

Great frigate bird 77
Great Meteor Seamount 30.00N 28.30W 16, 18
Great Meteor Seamount 36
Great Quoin 154
Great Shearwater 77
Great skua 77
Great Yarmouth 52.34N 1.44E 123
Greece 108
  aquaculture production 83
  naval submarine strength 181, 183
  naval surface fleet 178, 183
  registration of vessels 141
Greece–Turkey dispute 187
Green Bay 44.31N 88.00W 126
Greenland 64, 65, 92, 101, 215
  coast 63
  fishing catch 93
  ice cap 62
Greenland Abyssal Plain 75.00N 3.00W 24
Greenland Docks 124
Greenland–Iceland Rise 67.00N 27.00W 16
Greenland Sea 62, 64
Greenland Sea 76.00N 10.00W 24
Greenock 55.57N 4.46W 123
Green turtle 210
Greenwich 60, 61, 124
Grená 56.24N 10.55E 123
Greymouth 42.26S 171.13E* 132
Grijalva Ridge 5.00S 85.00W 23
Grimsby 53.34N 0.04W 123, 135
Grimstad 58.21N 8.36E 123
Gronigen gas field 106
Groningen 53.13N 6.34E 123
Groundfish stocks 96
Growler class submarine 101
Guadelupe fur seal 210
Guadeloupe Pass 16.30N 62.00W 150
Guafo Fracture Zone 45.00S 83.40W 23
Guam 99, 183
Guangzhou (Canton) 23.06N 113.14E 130
Guánica 17.57N 66.54W 127
Guano 52
Guantánamo Bay 19.58N 75.09W 126, 182
Guatemala 54
  fisheries 99
Guatemala Basin 11.00N 95.00W 23
Guayabal 20.42N 77.36W 126
Guayacán 29.58S 71.22W 127, 134
Guayanilla 18.00N 66.46W 127
Guayaquil 2.12S 79.54W 127
Guaymas 27.55N 110.55W 126
Gudrun oilfield 106
Guiana Plateau 8.00N 55.00W 18
Guimaras 10.20N 122.35E 132
Guinea 136
Guinea Bissau 187
Guinea Basin 0.00 5.00W 18
Guinea, G. of 104, 109
Guinea, G. of 3.00N 0.00 18
Gulfhavn 55.12N 11.16E 123
Gulf menhaden 88
Gulf of Alaska Seamounts 36
Gulf of Suez, oil basin 103
Gulf of Thailand, oil basin 103
Gulfport 30.21N 89.05W 126
Gulf Stream 51, (maps) 52, 64
  velocity field (diag) 44
Gulf, The 27.00N 52.00E 19
Gulf, The (map) 133, 134, 137, 154, 187
  Landsat imagery 205
  offshore oilfields (map) 109
  pollution 173
Gull 76, 77
Gulper eel 75
Gunboat diplomacy 190, *see also Appendix VIII*
Gunnerus Bank 68.00S 33.00E 25
Gunnerus Ridge 67.00S 34.50E 19, 25
Gunness 53.37N 0.40W 123
Gurnard 84
Gutenburg discontinuity 38
Guyana–Venezuela boundary dispute 186
Guyots 28, 36, 37
Gypsum 118
Gythion 194

H

Habomai 189
Hachinohe 40.33N 141.30E 96, 130
Hadal zone 26
Haddock 81, 84, 88
Haderslev 55.15N 9.30E 123
Hadsund 56.43N 10.07E 123
Haehyöp, see glossary 150
Hafnarfjördhur 64.04N 21.58W 92, 122
Hagen, tanker 167
Haifa 32.48N 35.01E 133, 135
Haifa 146
Haifa Bay 177
Haina 18.25N 70.01W 127
Hainan Strait 20.30N 111.00E 151
Haines 59.12N 135.26W 126
Haiphong 181
Haiphong 20.51N 106.49E 130
Haiti: floods 55
Hakata 33.36N 130.24E 130
Hake 84, 88, 90, 94, 95
Hakodate 41.47N 140.42E 130
Halden 59.07N 11.24E 123
Haldia 22.02N 88.05E 130, 131, 135
Halibut 84, 88, 96
Halieis 194
Halifax 44.39N 63.34W 126
Halifax 134, 146, 182

Halley, Edmond 198
Hallstavik 60.03N 18.35E 123
Halmstad 56.40N 12.51E 123
Hälsingborg 56.02N 12.41E 123
Halten Bank 64.45N 8.45E 17
Hälül I. 25.42N 52.28E 133, 135
Hamburg 53.33N 9.58E 123, 135
Hamburg America Line 140
Hamilton Bank 57.00N 59.00W 16
Hamilton, Bermuda 32.18N 64.48W 126
Hamilton, Canada 43.14N 79.51W 126
Hamina 60.34N 27.11E 122
Hammerfest 70.40N 23.48E 122
Hampton Roads 134, 213
Hampton Roads 36.50N 76.25W 126
Hangö 59.49N 22.58E 122
Hanish Is 154
Hantsport 45.04N 64.10W 126
Hargshamn 60.10N 18.29E 123
Harlingen 53.11N 5.25E 123
Härnösand 62.38N 17.57E 122
Harpoons 84
Harriers, aircraft 184
Harstad 68.48N 16.30E 122
Hartlepool 135
Hartlepool 54.41N 1.11W 123
Harwich 51.57N 1.17E 123
Harwich 156
Hastings 156
Hatchetfish 69, 74
Hatizyo–Sima 36
Hatteras Abyssal Plain 31.00N 71.00W 18
Hatteras Abyssal Plain (map) 29
Hatteras Canyon 34.40N 74.00W 16
Hatton Bank 58.00N 19.00W 17
Hatton Bank 16/17
Hatton–Rockall Basin 57.30N 16.30W 16/17
Haugesund 59.25N 5.12E 123
Havre Aubert 47.14N 61.50W 126
Havre St Pierre 50.14N 63.35W 126
Hawaiian Is 36, 37, 59, 121, 183
Hawaiian monk seal 210
Hawaiian Patriot, ship 171
Hawaiian Ridge 30.00N 178.00E 22
Hawaiian Ridge 36, 37
Hawaiian Trough 21.00N 155.00W 22
Hawksbill turtle 210, 211
Haydarpasa 41.00N 29.04E 122
Hayes Fracture Zone 33.40N 38.30W 16
Hay Point 21.16S 149.19E 132, 135
Hazards at sea 158, 160–169, 194
  ice casualties 163
  rig mishaps 162
  ship losses (map) 164–165
Heard I. 37
Heather oilfield 106
Heavy metals 118, 173, 174, 177
Heavy minerals 112
Hebridean Shelf 59.00N 5.00W 17
Hebrides, shipping forecast area 161
Hecate Seamount 52.17N 30.58W 16
Hecate Strait 53.00N 131.00W 150
Hekla 37
Helgafell 37
Helicopter carrier 178
Helm orders 166
Helmdal oilfield 106
Helsingør 56.02N 12.36E 123
Helsinki 60.10N 24.57E 122
Henry VIII 197
Henson, Victor 198
Hercynian–Appalachian orogenic belt 35
Hereke 40.49N 29.36E 122
Hermes, carrier 184
Hero Fracture Zone 23
Heron Reef 212
Herring & herring fisheries 81, 84, 88, 92, 93, 96, 97, 215
Hess, Harry Hammond 39
Hess Rise 36.45N 177.15E 20
Hewett oilfield 106
Heysham 54.02N 2.52W 123
Hibernia, oilfield 107, 162
Hilo 19.44N 155.05W 126
Himeji 34.50N 134.36E 130
Hiroshima 96
Hiroshima 34.25N 132.25E 130
Hirtshals 57.35N 9.57E 123
Hispaniola 192
Hispaniola Trough 20.50N 71.00W 16
Histioteuthis (squid) 69
Hjort Trench 58.00S 157.30E 22
Hobart 42.53S 147.20E 132
Hobro 56.38N 9.48E 123
Ho Chi Minh *10.46N 106.42E* 130
Hodder's Volcano 37
Hod, oilfield 106
Höganäs 56.12N 12.33E 123
Hokkaido: herring fishery 96, 97
Holbæk 55.43N 11.43E 123
Holland America Line 140
Hollandia, wreck 194
Holmes, A. 35
Holmestrand 59.29N 10.19E 123
Holothurians 72
Holsteinsborg 66.56N 53.30W 126
Holyhead *53.18N 4.38W* 123
Homer 59.40N 151.37W 126
Home Reef 37
Honavar 14.16N 74.27E 130
Honduras 54, 141
  fisheries 99
  fishing fleet 86

Honfleur 49.25N 0.14E 122
Honguedo Passage 149
Hong Kong 22.16N 114.10E 130
Hong Kong 54, 96
  aquaculture production 83
  commodity port 135
  desalination plant 118
  registration of vessels 141
Honiara 9.30S 160.00E 132
Honolulu 59
Honolulu 21.19N 157.52W 126
Hooghly R. 131
Hooke, Robert 198
Hook of Holland 51.59N 4.07E 124, 125
Hopa 41.25N 41.24E 122
Hormuz, Strait of 154, 184, 185, 187, 219
Hormuz, Strait of 26.30N 57.00E 150, 151
Hörnefors 63.37N 19.54E 122
Horse mackerel 88
Horsens 55.51N 9.52E 123
Horseshoe Seamounts 36.30N 15.00W 17
Horta 38.32N 28.38W 133
Horta Barbosa, tanker 167
Horten 59.25N 10.30E 123
Hososhima 32.26N 131.42E 130
Hotel class submarine 181
Hot spots 32, 37, 51
Hound Point 56.00N 3.30W 123, 135
Houston 29.45N 95.25W 126, 134
Höyanger 61.10N 6.04E 122
Huacho 11.14S 77.35W 127
Hua-lien 23.59N 121.37E 130
Huangpu (Whampoa) 23.05N 113.36E 130
Huasco 28.28S 71.15W 127, 134
Hudiksvall 61.44N 17.09E 122
Hudson Bay 60.00N 85.00W 21
Hudson Bay 26, 193
Hudson Canyon 39.27N 72.12W 16
Hudson River 128
Hudson Strait 63.00N 70.00W 16, 150
Huelva *37.17N 6.57W* 122
Hughes, Howard 40
Hull *53.44N 0.22W* 123
Humber, shipping forecast area 161
Humidity 204
Humpback whale 100, 210, 211
Hungary: aquaculture production 83
Hunter-killer submarine 80
Huron *41.24N 82.35W* 126
Hurricanes 48, (maps & graphs) 54–57
Húsavik 66.04N 17.18W 122
Husnes 59.52N 5.46E 123
Husum 54.28N 9.02E 123
Hutton oilfield 106
Hyalonema (cup sponges) 73
Hydrocarbons 188, 206
  basins 102, 103
  offshore 104–105
  resources 185
Hydrodynamic forces 58
Hydrogen 119
Hydrographic charts, *see Charts* 158
Hydrosphere 26
Hydrostatic pressure, effects of 75
Hydrothermal activity 114, 202
Hyperbolic navigation 158

I

IALA (International Association of Lighthouse Authorities) 159
IATTC (Inter-American Tropical Tuna Commission) 211
Iberian Abyssal Plain 43.45N 13.30W 17
Ibicuy 33.45S 59.15W 127
Ibiza 39.00N 1.30E 122
IBSFC (International Baltic Sea Fishery Commission) 211
ICCAT (International Commission for the Conservation of Atlantic Tuna) 211
Ice
  bergs 62, 64–65, 119, 160, 163
  breakers 148, 149
  bridges 149
  cap 62–63
  casualties (map) 163
  drift 63
  extent (maps) 50, 65, 66, 67
  fields 64
  floes 63, 64
  islands 64, 65
  offshore rigs affected 106
  packs 64–65, 148
  patrols 163
  permanent 62, 63
  regions 47, 148
  sheet 65
  shelves 63, 64
  ships affected 64–65, 106, 160, 161
  tracking stations (map) 203
Iceland 81
  fishing 85, 92
  fishing catch total 90, 93
  fishing fleet 86
Iceland Basin 60.00N 25.00W 16
Iceland–Faeroe Rise 64.00N 11.00W 17
Icelandic Plateau 69.30N 12.00W 17, 24
Icing
  Baltic ports 149
  St Lawrence ports 149
  vessels 64–65, 106, 160, 161
ICSEAF (International Commission for SE Atlantic Fisheries) 211
Icy Strait 58.20N 136.00W 150
IDOE (International Decade of Ocean Exploration) 207

IHB (International Hydrographic Bureau) 203
IHO (International Hydrographic Organisation) 158, 203
IJmuiden 52.27N 4.34E 123
Ilha de Maraca 120
Ilhéus 14.48S 39.02W 127
Il'ichëvsk 46.20N 30.39E 122
Iligan 8.13N 124.14E 132
Ilmenite 112
Ilo 17.38S 71.21W 127
Iloilo 10.41N 122.35E 132
Imabari 34.05N 133.00E 130
Iman Hasan 30.00N 50.00E 133
Imbituba 28.17S 48.40W 127
IMCO (Inter-governmental Maritime Consultative Organisation) 168
Immingham 53.37N 0.12W 123
IMO (International Maritime Organisation) 169, 208
Inch'on 37.28N 126.37E 130
Incidents, naval (map) 190–191
Indefatigable, oilfield 106
Independence, carrier 179, 189
Independentza, ship 171
India 108 ,136
  aquaculture production 83
  fisheries 98
  fishing catch total 91
  hurricanes (maps) 54–55
  naval submarine strength 181
  naval surface fleet 178
  offshore oil & gas 104
  pollution, marine 173
  ports 130
  satellites 204
India–Burma boundary 187
Indian Ocean
  bases, air & naval 185
  cyclonic storms 56
  exploration of sea floor (map) 202
  fisheries 98, 99
  fishing catch total (by FAO area) 91
  fleets 185
  mid-ocean ridge 29
  monsoon winds 161
  morphology 28, 29
  rises 28
  routeway 184
  salinity profile 66, 67
  strategic value 184, 185
  topographic view 26, 27
  voyages & exploration 192–193, 198
  Zone of Peace 185, 187
Indian Ocean Fishery Commission (IOFC) 211
Indispensable Strait 10.00S 160.00E 150, 151
Indomptable, submarine 180
Indonesia 155
  aquaculture production 83
  conservation areas 210
  fisheries (map) 98–99
  fishing catch total 91
  fishing fleet 87
  naval submarine strength 181
  naval surface fleet 178
  offshore oil & gas 104, (map) 108–109
  offshore placers 113
  pollution 173
  tin resources potential (map) 113
Indo–Pacific Fishery Commission (IPFC) 211
Indus Cone 19.00N 66.30E 19
Industrial waste 174
Industries associated with ports 123
Inertial Navigation System *see SINS*
Infrared images: Gulf Stream 52
Inga 60.01N 24.04E 122
Inhambane 23.50S 35.23E 133
Inman Company 140
INPFC (International N. Pacific Fisheries Commission) 211
Insecticides 172
Inter-American Tropical Tuna Commission (IATTC) 101, 211
Inter-governmental Maritime Consultative Organisation (IMCO) 168
Internal waters: legal definition 220
International Association of Lighthouse Authorities (IALA) 159
International Baltic Sea Fishery Commission (IBSFC) 211
International Commission for SE Atlantic Fisheries (ICSEAF) 211
International Commission for the Conservation of Atlantic Tuna (ICCAT) 211
International Convention for the Prevention of Pollution from ships (MARPOL) 168, 171, 176, 224
International Convention for the Prevention of Pollution of the Sea by oil (OILPOL) 168, 224
International Convention for the Safety of Life at Sea (SOLAS) 158, 163, 168, 224
International Convention on Civil Liability for Oil Pollution Damage 224
International Convention on Standards of Training, Certification and Watchkeeping of Seafarers 168
International Court of Justice 186, 222, 223
International Decade of Ocean Exploration (IDOE) 207
International Energy Agency 121

International Geographic Congress 203
International Halibut Commission 96
International Hydrographic Bureau (IHB) 203
International Hydrographic Conference 203
International Hydrographic Organisation, Monaco (IHO) 158, 203
International Ice Patrol 163
International Journal of Nautical Archaeology 194
International Maritime Organisation (IMO) 169, 208
International Maritime Satellite 158
International North Pacific Fisheries Commission (INPFC) 211
International Oceanographic Commission (IOC) 203
International Ocean Research 206
International Oil Pollution Compensation Fund 224
International Pacific Halibut Commission (IPHC) 211
International Pacific Salmon Fisheries Commission (IPSFC) 211
International Programme of Ocean Drilling (IPOD) (map) 40–41
International regulations for preventing collisions 166
International trade, seaborne 136
International Union for Conservation of Nature (IUCN) 213
International Whaling Commission (IWC) 100, 211
Inter-oceanic canals 150
Interstitial water 26
Intertidal zone 26, 72, 73
Intertropical Convergence Zone (ITCZ) 45, 46, 47, 49, 56, 66
Intrepid, assault ship 184
Invergordon 57.42N 4.10W 123
Investigator, ship 199
Investigator Ridge 11.30S 98.10E 19
Invincible, carrier 184
IOC (International Oceanographic Commission) 203
Iodides, in seaweed 83
Iodine, in sea water 66, 118
IOFC (Indian Ocean Fishery Commission) 211
Ionian Sea 38.00N 18.00E 17
IPFC (Indo-Pacific Fishery Commission) 211
IPHC (International Pacific Halibut Commission) 211
Ipnops 73
IPOD (International Programme of Ocean Drilling) (map) 40–41
IPSFC (International Pacific Salmon Fisheries Commission) 211
Ipswich 52.02N 1.10E 123
Iquique 20.15S 70.08W 127
Iráklion 35.20N 25.09E 122
Iran
fisheries 98
naval submarine strength 181
naval surface fleet 178
offshore oil & gas 104, 109
territorial waters 154
Iraq
fisheries 98
fishing fleet 86
naval fleet 178
Ireland, Rep. of
aquaculture production 83
offshore oil & gas 104
wrecks 196
Irenes Serenade, tanker 171
Irish formula 222, 223
Irish Sea 60, 160, 187, 214
Irminger Basin 62.00N 38.00W 16
Iron 112, 113
Iron ore: inter area trade 134, (map) 137
Irrawaddy Delta 57
Isabela 6.42N 121.58E 132
Isabela de Sagua 22.55N 80.01W 126
Ishinomaki 96
İskenderun 36.37N 36.10E 122
Island arcs 27, 29, 32, 33, 36, 37, 114
Islands, artificial 106, 111, 125, 133, 134
Islands: *see also* Atolls 36, 37
Islas Orcadas Rise 51.00S 27.00W 18
Islas Orcadas Seamounts 66.00S 24.00W 18, 25
Isle of Grain see Grain, I. of
Ismâ'ilîya 152
Isobath, 500 fathom 34
Isogonic maps 30
Israel
aquaculture production 82
naval submarine strength 181
naval surface fleet 178
pollution 177
İstanbul 41.00N 28.59E 122
Istiophorus platypterus (sailfish) 75
Isumrud Strait 3.30S 145.00E 151
Itajaí 26.53S 48.37W 127
Italy 108, 136, 216
aquaculture production 83
fishing catch 95
naval submarine strength 181, 182
naval surface fleet 178, 182
pollution 177
Itaqui 2.35S 44.22W 127
ITCZ (Intertropical Convergence Zone) 45, 46, 47, 49, 56
IUCN (International Union for Conservation of Nature) 213
IUCN Marine Programme 213
Ivan Grozny 36
Ivory Coast
aquaculture production 82
fishing catch 95
fishing fleet 86
Iwakuni 34.11N 132.10E 130
IWC (International Whaling Commission) 211
Iwo Jima, carrier 189
Ixtoc 1 blow-out 162, 170
İzmail 45.20N 28.51E 122
İzmir 38.26N 27.09E 122
İzmit 40.45N 29.55E 122
Izu-Ogasawara Trench 31.00N 142.00E 22

J

Jabal Dhanna 24.11N 52.37E 133
Jack mackerel 88
Jacksonville 30.20N 81.40W 126, 134, 182
Jack-up rigs 104, 105
Jacques Cartier Passage 50.00N 64.00W 149, 151
Jakarta 6.06S 106.52E 132
Jakob Maersk, tanker 171
Jakobstad 63.41N 22.41E 122
Jamaica 136
aquaculture 82
Jamaica Chan 18.00N 75.00W 150
James, wreck 195
James Matthews, wreck 194
James Ross Strait 70.00N 96.00W 150
Jamestown 15.55S 5.43W 133
Jan Mayen Fracture Zone 71.12N 8.00W 17, 24
Jan Mayen Ridge 69.00N 8.00W 17
Japan 108, 136, 137, 146, 155
aquaculture production 83
bonito 101
continental shelf 97
fisheries (map) 96–97
fishing catch total 91
fishing fleet 87, 97
fishing industry 90, 95, (maps) 96–97, 99
fishing ports (map) 96, 97
island arc 32
Kaimei power project 121
naval submarine strength 181
naval surface fleet 178
offshore oil & gas 104
pollution 173
ports 96, 97, 130
salmon 101
seaborne trade 145
shipbuilding 142
shipping casualties 165
surges 60
territorial claims 188–189
tsunami devastation 59
typhoons (map) 55
whaling 100
Japan Basin 43.00N 136.00E 20
Japan Rise 38.00N 145.00E 20
Japan Sea 41.00N 135.00E 20
Japan, Sea of 64, 121, 182, 188–189
Japan/S. Korea Joint Fisheries Commission (JKFC) 211
Japan/Soviet NW Pacific Fisheries Commission (JSFC) 211
Japan Trench 37.00N 143.00E 20
Japanese Sea lion 211
Java
fishing grounds 99
offshore oilfields 108, 109
storm frequency 57
Java Ridge 10.30S 115.00E 22
Java Sea 5.00S 107.00E 19, 22
Java Trench 10.30S 110.00E 19, 22
Jazīreh-ye Hormoz 154
Jazīreh-ye Larak 154
Jazīreh-ye Qeshm 154
Jersey City 128
Jersey, weather station 161
Jezebel sonar buoys 184
Jiddah 21.28N 39.14E 133, 135
Jijel 36.50N 5.47E 133
JKFC (Japan/S Korea Joint Fisheries Commission) 211
Jobos 17.56N 66.13W 127
Johore 130
Johor Baharu 1.27N 103.45E 130
Jolo 6.03N 121.00E 132
Jönköping 57.46N 14.10E 123
Jose Pañganiban 14.18N 122.40E 132
Josephine, oilfield 106
JSFC (Japan/Soviet NW Pacific Fisheries Commission) 211
Juan de Fuca Ridge 114
Juan de Fuca, Straits of 186
Juan de Fuca, Straits of 48.20N 124.00W 150
Juan Fernandez fur seal 210
Júcaro 21.37N 78.51W 126
Julianehåb 60.43N 46.03W 126
Juneau 58.18N 134.20W 126
Jurisdictional zones, ocean 218, 220

K

Kagoshima 31.36N 130.30E 130
Kahului 20.53N 156.28W 126
Kaikyō, *see glossary*
Kaimei project 121
Kainan Maru Seamounts 65.00S 35.00E 19, 25
Kaiwi Channel 21.15N 158.30W 150
Kakinada 16.56N 82.15E 130
Kalámai 37.01N 22.07E 122
Kalianget 7.02S 113.55E 132
Kalimantan: fishing grounds 99
Kalix 65.48N 23.17E 122
Kalmar 56.40N 16.22E 123
Kalmarsund 57.00N 16.28E 151
Kaloí Liménes 34.55N 24.49E 122
Kalundborg 55.40N 11.05E 123
Kamaishi 39.16N 141.54E 130
Kamatsushima 34.01N 134.36E 130
Kamchatka Basin 57.00N 168.00E 20
Kamchatskiy Proliv 55.00N 165.00E 150, 151
Kampuchea: *see Cambodia*
Kamsar 10.39N 14.37W 133, 135
Kanda 33.50N 130.59E 130
Kandla 23.00N 70.13E 130
Kane Fracture Zone 23.30N 45.00W 16, 18
Kane Seamount 21.08N 28.02W 17
Kao-hsiung 22.37N 120.16E 130, 135
Kao-hsiung harbour 55
Kaolack 14.09N 16.06W 133
Kara, Bay of 68.00N 68.00E 24
Karachi 24.48N 66.58E 130
Kara Sea 77.00N 75.00E 24, 62
Kara Strait 219
Karimsky 36
Karlshamn 56.11N 14.52E 123
Karlskrona 56.10N 15.36E 123
Karlstad 59.23N 13.31E 123
Karpathos Sea 151
Karpathos Strait 35.40N 27.30E 151
Karskär 60.40N 17.15E 123
Karua 36
Karwar 14.48N 74.06E 130
Kashin class (USSR) destroyer 179, 189
Kaskö 62.23N 21.13E 122
Kasos Strait 35.20N 26.30E 151
Katákolon 37.39N 21.20E 122
Kattegat 57.00N 11.00E 151
Kauai Chan 22.00N 160.50W 150
Kaulakahi Chan 22.00N 160.00W 150
Kavála 40.55N 24.25E 122
Kavieng 2.34S 150.48E 132
Kawasaki 35.29N 139.45E 130
Kawasaki, port 131
Keflavík 64.00N 22.33W 92, 122
Kelvin, Lord 198
Kelvin Seamounts 36
Kemi 65.44N 24.33E 122
Kemp Land 63
Kenai 107
Kenitra 34.20N 6.35W 133
Kennedy, carrier 189
Kennemerland, wreck 194
Kenosha 42.36N 87.48W 126
Kenya: fisheries 98
Kerchenskiy Proliv 45.20N 37.00E 151
Kerguelen Plateau 55.00S 75.00E 19
Kérkira 39.37N 19.55E 122
Kermadec Is 36
Kermadec Trench 30.00S 177.00W 22
Ketchikan 55.25N 131.38W 126
Key West 24.34N 81.48W 126
Khalkís 38.27N 23.36E 122
Khambhat, G. of 120
Khārg Island 29.12N 50.20E 133, 135
Khawr Fakkān 25.21N 56.22E 133
Kherson 46.38N 32.37E 122
Kholmsk 47.03N 142.03E 130
Khor al Amaya 29.47N 48.48E 133, 135
Khorramshahr 30.26N 48.10E 133
Kick-em-Jenny 36
Kiel 54.19N 10.08E 123
Kiel 152
Kiel Canal 149, 153
Kiel Canal 54.20N 9.30E 151
Kieta 6.14S 155.38E 132
Kiev 179
Kiire 31.21N 130.33E 130
Kijang 0.53S 104.37E 132
Kilauea 36, 37
Kiliya 45.24N 29.17E 122
Killingholme 53.40N 0.14W 123
Killybegs 54.40N 8.27W 123
Kimberley 120
King's Lynn 52.45N 0.24E 123
King's Lynn 194
Kingston, Canada 44.12N 76.30W 126
Kingston, Jamaica 18.01N 76.48W 126
Kingstown 13.09N 61.14W 127
Kings Trough 43.48N 22.00W 16/17
Kinsale 51.42N 8.32W 123
Kinuula 34.53N 136.57E 130
Kiribati: fisheries 81, 99
Kiritimati 1.57N 157.29W 132
Kirkaldy 56.07N 3.09W 123
Kirkenes 69.36N 30.03E 122
Kirkwall 58.59N 2.57W 123
Kisarazu 35.21N 139.57E 130
Kislaya Guba 120
Kismaayu (Chisimaio) 0.22S 42.34E 133
Kita-Kyūshū 33.56N 130.45E 130
Kithera Strait 36.00N 23.00E 151
Kitimat 53.59N 128.46W 126
Kittiwake (map) 77
Klaipėda 55.43N 21.07E 122
Klakksvig 62.14N 6.35W 122
Klondyking 87
Kōbe 34.40N 135.12E 130
Kōbe 96, 135
København 55.42N 12.37E 123, 135, 182
Koçek 36.45N 28.32E 122
Kōchi 33.31N 133.34E 130
Køge 55.26N 12.12E 123
Kohler Seamount 53.00S 64.50E 19
Kokkola 63.51N 23.08E 122
Koko 6.00N 5.28E 133
Kolbeinsey Ridge 69.00N 17.30W 17, 24
Kolding 55.29N 9.29E 123
Kolobrzeg 54.11N 15.34E 123
Kompong Som 11.40N 103.32E 130
Koper 45.33N 13.43E 122
Kopervik 59.17N 5.20E 107, 123
Kophobelemnon stelliferum (sea-pen) 72
Köping 59.31N 16.00E 123
Korsør 55.19N 11.09E 123, 182
Kota Kinabalu 5.59N 116.04E 130
Kotka 60.28N 26.57E 122
Kotlin, SAM classe (USSR destroyer) 179
Kotzebue, Otto von 198
Kotzebue Sound 67.00N 163.00W 20
Kovachi 36
Kozhikode 11.15N 75.47E 130
Kpémé 6.17N 1.39E 133, 135
Kpémé, port 133
Kragerø 58.52N 9.25E 123
Krakatoa 36
Kralendijk 12.15N 68.20W 127
Kribi 2.56N 9.54E 133
Krill 68, 69, 78, 79, 88, 89, 185
fishing 78–79, 97
food chain link 79
meal 79
Southern Ocean (map) 78–79
Kristiansand 58.08N 8.02E 123
Kristiansund 63.06N 7.44E 122
Kristiansund 85
Kristinehamn 59.19N 14.07E 123
Kristinestad 62.16N 21.23E 122
Kronshtadt 182
Krung Thep (Bangkok) 13.44N 100.30E 130
Krusenstern, A. J. 198
Krylou Seamount 17.35N 30.07W 17
Kuching 1.34N 110.21E 130
Kudat 6.53N 116.51E 130
Kumkale 155
Kunak 4.41N 118.15E 130
Kunashir 189
Kunsan 35.59N 126.43E 130
Kurchatov Fracture Zone 41.00N 30.00W 16
Kure 34.14N 132.33E 130
Kuril Basin 47.00N 150.00E 20
Kurile Harbour seal 210, 211
Kuril Is 36, 188
Kuril-Kamchatka Trench 47.00N 155.00E 20
Kuro Shio, current 45, 51
Kushiro 42.59N 144.22E 96, 130
Kutch, G of 120
Kutei–N. Makassar, oil basin 103
Kuwait 144
fisheries 98
Kuwait–Iraq: ownership of islands 187
Kwa Ibo 4.33N 7.59E 108, 133
Kyndby 55.49N 11.53E 123
Kyoto 96
Kyrenia shipwreck 197
Kyusyu-Palau Ridge 20.00N 136.00E 22

L

Labrador Basin 53.00N 48.00W 16
Labrador current 44, 64
Labrador: offshore oilfields 107
Labrador Sea 60.00N 50.00W 16
Labrador Sea 64
Labuan 5.17N 115.15E 130
La Ceiba 15.46N 86.50W 126
Lachine rapids 153
La Coruña 43.23N 8.22W 122
Lae 6.44S 147.00E 132
La Estacada 10.43N 71.33W 127
Lafayette class submarine 181
Lagoon 43, 80–81, 212
beach 80
fisheries 80–81
ports 123
reef 80–81
slopes 80
Lagos 6.25N 3.25E 133
La Guaira 10.37N 66.56W 127
La Habana 23.09N 82.21W 126
Lahad Datu 5.02N 118.20E 130
La Have 44.17N 64.21W 126
La Hondura 28.27N 16.16W 133
Lake Charles 30.13N 93.15W 126
Lakehead Harbour 48.27N 89.14W 126, 134
La Libertad 2.12S 80.55W 127
Lambasa 16.26S 179.22E 132
Laminaria saccharina 119
Lamma Chan. 22.20N 114.10E 151
Lancaster (Glasson Dock) 54.00N 2.50W 123
Lancaster Sound 74.00N 85.00W 24
Land bridges, linking ocean routes 146
Landlocked seas 66
Landsat 204–205
Landskrona 55.52N 12.50E 123
Langesund 59.00N 9.45E 123
Lantern fish 69, 74
La Palma, I. 37
La Pampilla 11.55S 77.08W 127
La Paz, Mexico 54
La Pérouse Strait 45.40N 142.00E 151
Lapithos 194
La Plata 34.52S 57.55W 127, 134
Laptev Sea 75.00N 130.00E 24
Laptev walrus 211
Larache 35.13N 6.07W 133
La Rance 60
tidal power scheme 120
Large Strait 154
Larnaca 34.55N 33.39E 122
Larne 54.51N 5.47W 123

La Rochelle 46.10N 1.10W 122
La Rochelle: oyster & mussel production 83
La Romana 18.24N 68.57W 127
Larvik 59.04N 10.03E 123
La Salina 10.22N 71.28W 127
La Salineta 27.58N 15.22W 133
LASH barge handling facilities 131
LASH (lighter aboard ship) 134, 136, 139, 147
La Soufrière 36
Las Palmas 28.09N 15.25W 133
La Spezia 44.04N 9.50E 122, 182
Lastdrager, wreck 194
Latakia 189
Latakia (Lattaquie) 35.32N 35.47E 133, 135
Latin American Nuclear Free Zone 184, 186
La Trinidad Velencera, wreck 195
Lau Basin 20.00S 177.00W 22
Launceston 41.27S 147.07E 132
Laurasia 34, 35
Lau Ridge 21.00S 178.30W 22
Lautoka 17.36S 177.26E 132
Lavan I. 26.47N 53.20E 133, 135
Lavanters (winds) 157
Lavera-Caronte 43.23N 4.58E 122
Lavoisier, Antoine Laurent de 198
Lávrion 37.42N 24.04E 122
Law of the Sea 206
Law of the Sea, Convention 1982 218–224 *see also Appendix XI*
Law of the Sea, Geneva conventions 218
Lazarev Sea 67.00S 7.00E 18, 25, 62
Leach's Storm Petrel 76
Lead 118, 173, 174, 175
Leathery turtle 210, 211
Lebanon 118, 141, 177
Leer 53.13N 7.28E 123
Legaspi 13.09N 123.45E 132
Le Havre 49.29N 0.06E 122, 135
Leirvik 59.47N 5.32E 123
Leith 55.59N 3.10W 123
Leith Harbour 184
Leixões 41.09N 8.42W 122
Leman Bank 106
Lemvig 56.32N 8.20E 123
Leningrad 59.54N 30.15E 122
Lennox Island 187
Lenz, Emil von 198
Leopard seal 79
Lepanto, Battle of, site 194
Lepidion eques (deep sea cod) 72
Lerwick 60.10N 1.08W 122
Les Escoumins 48.21N 69.23W 126
Lesotho: aquaculture 82
Les Sables d'Olonne 46.30N 1.47W 122
Lesseps, Ferdinand de 152
Lesser frigate bird (map) 77
Levuka 17.41S 178.51E 132
Lewis, Outer Hebrides 121
Liancourt Rocks 189
Liberia 136
flag of convenience 140, 141
Libourne 44.55N 0.14W 122
Libreville 0.23N 9.26E 133
Libya
Continental Shelf Case 1982, (Tunisia/Libya) 222
naval surface fleet 178
naval submarine strength 181
Licata 37.05N 13.56E 122
Licenses, dredging 112, (map) 113
Licensing of vessels 85
Lidköping 58.30N 13.10E 123
Lift nets 80
Lift-on lift-off (LoLo) container vessels 134
Ligeti Ridge 63.00S 28.00W 18
Lighter-aboard ship (LASH) 134, 136, 139, 147
Lightfish 89
Lightning, expedition (map) 198–199
Lightning 57
Light organs (in sea creatures) 74
Lightships 158
Lillesand 58.15N 8.24E 123
Limassol 34.42N 33.03E 122
Limerick 52.40N 8.37W 123
Limetree Bay 17.40N 64.44W 127, 134
Limhamn 55.36N 12.56E 123
Limited Test Ban Treaty 1963 172
Limón 10.00N 83.01W 126
Lincoln Sea 84.00N 55.00W 24, 62
Liner vessels 136, 146
Ling 84
Liparididae (sea snails) 73
Liquefied natural gas *see LNG*
Liquefied petroleum gas *see LPG*
Liquid cargoes 137
Lisboa 38.42N 9.11W 122
Lisbon 143, 182
Lithosphere 26, 30, 32, 33, 39
Lithospheric plates 29, 32
Little Minch 57.30N 7.00W 151
Little Narrows 46.03N 60.57W 126
Littoral zone 26
Liverpool, Canada 44.03N 64.42W 126
Liverpool, England 53.24N 3.00W 123, 135
Livorno 177
Livorno 43.33N 10.18E 122
Liza, hurricane 54
Lloyds Register of Shipping Casualty Returns 162, 164
LNG (liquefied natural gas) 134
carriers 138
world trade, growth in 137
Loadline rules 160–161, 208
Load on Top (LOT) 171, 224
Loanda 108
Lobito 12.20S 13.32E 133
Lobitos 4.27S 81.18W 127
Lobster 84, 88
Loch Fyne 200
Lockheed 121
Lofoten fishery 93
Loggerhead turtle 210, 211
LoLo (lift-on lift-off) container vessels 134
Lombok Strait 155, 184, 185
Lombok Strait, see Selat Lombok
Lomé 6.09N 1.20E 133
Lomé, port 133
Lomond oilfield 106
Lomonosov Ridge 88.00N 140.00E 24
London 51.30N 0.05W 123
London
Docks 124
port, commodities 135
port, development (maps) 124
Londonderry 55.00N 7.20W 123
London Trinity House 166
Long Beach 33.45N 118.12W 126, 134, 182
Long I. 36
Long line fishing 84
Long Range Mts 149
Longview 46.08N 122.56W 126
Lorain 41.28N 82.12W 126
Loran (long range navigation) system 158
Lord Howe Rise 32.00S 162.00E 22
Lord Howe Seamount Chain 28.00S 161.00E 22
Lorient 47.45N 3.21W 122
Lorient 182, 217
Los Angeles 34.00N 118.16W 126, 134
Los Angeles oil basin 102, (map) 105
LOT (load on top) 171, 224
Louisburg 45.55N 59.58W 126
Louisiana 55, 105
Louisville Ridge 31.00S 172.30W 22
Lousy Bank 60.27N 12.30W 17
Lowestoft 52.29N 1.45E 123
LPG (liquefied petroleum gas) 134
carriers 137, 138
Luanda 8.45S 13.18E 133
Luba 3.38N 8.30E 133
Lübeck 53.52N 10.41E 123
Luciferins 74
Lucina Terminal 3.39S 10.46E 133
Lucinda 18.32S 146.20E 132
Lüda 38.55N 121.39E 130
Lüderitz 26.40S 15.10E 133
Luleå 65.35N 22.09E 122
Lures 74, 80
Luzon Straits 20.00N 121.00E 150, 151
LVZ (low-velocity zone) 38
Lyell oilfield 106
Lyme Bay 169
Lysekil 58.16N 11.26E 123
Lyttelton 43.37S 172.42E 132, 135

M

Maasbanker fisheries 95
Maasvlakte 125
Mabahiss, ship 199
Mabel oilfield 106
Macau 22.11N 113.33E 96, 130
Macclesfield Bank 189
Macdonald 36
Maceió 9.41S 35.43W 127
Machilipatnam 16.12N 81.09E 130
Mackay 21.10S 149.14E 132, 212
Mackenzie Bay 69.00N 137.00W 24
Mackenzie Delta 106
Mackerel 84, 88, 95, 96, 97, 215, 217
Macquarie I. 36
Macquire Ridge Complex 53.00S 160.00E 22
Madagascar
fisheries 98
hurricanes (map) 54
Madagascar Basin 27.00S 53.00E 19
Madagascar Ridge 30.00S 45.00E 19
Madang 5.12S 145.49E 132
Madeira 192
Madeira Abyssal Plain 32.00N 22.00W 16, 18
Madeira, Arquipelago da 33.00N 17.00W 17
Madeira Rise 33.30N 18.00W 17
Madeline, hurricane 54
Madingley Rise 4.15S 61.00E 19
Madras 13.06N 80.18E 130, 135
Magallanes, oil basin 102
Magellan 192
Magellan Seamounts 17.30N 152.00E 22
Magellan, Strait of 120, 146, 150, 187, 192, 193
Magnesium 66, 118, 119
Magnetic
anomalies (maps) 30–31
anomaly detectors 182
compass 31
field of the Earth (map) 30, 35, 40
poles (map) 30, 35
Magnetite 113
Magnus oilfield 106
Mahajanga 15.43S 46.20E 133
Mahé 185
Mahón 39.50N 4.15W 122
Maize, *see Grain, trade in*
Maizuru 35.28N 135.20E 130
Makarov Basin 87.00N 170.00E 24, 62
Makassar Str 2.00S 118.00E 151
Mako shark 75
Malabo 3.45N 8.45E 133
Malacca 192
Malacca, Strait of 155, 184, 185
Malacca, Strait of 2.00N 101.50E 150, 151
Málaga 36.45N 4.24W 122
Malawi: aquaculture production 82
Malaysia 155
aquaculture production 83
fishing catch, total 91
offshore oil & gas 104, (map) 108–109
Maldives 37
fisheries 98
Maldonado 34.55S 55.00W 127
Male 4.00N 73.28E 130
Malin Head lighthouse 161
Malin, shipping forecast area 161
Malm 64.04N 11.14E 122
Malmö 55.37N 13.00E 123
Malouines, Isles 184
Måløy 61.56N 5.07E 122
Malpe 13.21N 74.41E 130
Malta Channel 36.30N 15.00E 151
Malvinas Chasm 53.00S 50.00W 18
Malvinas, Islas (Falkland Is) 184
Manakau 120
Mánáreyar 37
Manaus 3.08S 59.59W 127
Manatee 210, 211
Manchester 53.29N 2.14W 123, 135
Mandal 58.01N 7.27E 123
Mangalore 12.52N 74.54E 130
Manganese 118
nodules (map) 110–111, 114, 116, 173
ore, inter area trade 137
zone in N. Pacific 221
Mangrove swamps 210
Manhattan, tanker 148
Manhattan 128
Manihiki Plateau 11.00S 164.00W 22
Manila 14.35N 120.58E 132, 135
Manila galleons 192
Manistee 44.15N 86.20W 126
Manitowoc 44.06N 87.40W 126
Manning Strait 7.30S 157.20E 150, 151
Manta 1.00S 80.47W 127
Mantle, composition of 39
Manus Trench 1.00S 150.00E 22
Manzanillo, Cuba 20.21N 77.07W 126
Manzanillo, Dom. Rep. 19.43N 71.43W 127
Manzanillo, Mexico 19.03N 104.20W 126
Mapmakers Seamounts 25.00N 165.00E 22
Mapping: ocean floor 203
Maputo 25.58S 32.34E 133, 135
Maracaibo 10.41N 71.38W 127
Maracaibo L. oil basin 102, 104, (map) 105
Maranhão 120
Mar del Plata 38.00S 57.30W 127
Marennes: oyster production 83
Margate 156
Marginal plateaus 29
Marguerite, wreck 195
Marianas 36
Marianas Trench 173, 198
Marianas Trench 15.00N 147.30E 22
Maria Theresa Reef 36
Mariculture 82
Marie Byrd Land 63
Marie Byrd Seamount 70.00S 117.00W 25
Marie Celeste Fracture Zone 17.30S 66.00E 19
Mariehamn 60.06N 19.56E 122
Mariel 23.01N 82.46W 126
Mariestad 58.43N 13.50E 123
Marín 42.24N 8.42W 122
Marina di Carrara 44.02N 10.03E 122
Marine *see also Ocean, Sea*
aggregates 110, 112–113
aquaculture 80, 82–83, 96, 97
archaeology 194–197
biogeographic areas 68
biological zones 68
conservation 208, 210–214, 211, *see also Appendix X*
deposits 112
environments 212
geology 203
metalliferous deposits 110, 114
mineral resources (map) 110–111, (maps) 116–117
parks 212
pollution 170–172, 174–177, 224
products 96
recreation 216–217
research 110, 208, 209, 210, *see also Appendix IX*
Mariner Shoal 154
Marion Dufresne Seamount 54.00S 51.00E 19
Maritime
boundaries 220
disputes & conflicts *see Territorial claims & disputes*
exclusion zones 184, 185
law: collisions 166
museums *see Appendix IX*
tension 188–189
transport 146, 147
Maritime Industrial Development Area (MIDAS) 123
Markets for shellfish 82
Marks, buoyage system 159
Marlin 75, 96
Marmagao 15.25N 73.47E 130, 135
Marmara, Sea of 154, 155
MARPOL (International Convention for Prevention of Pollution from ships) 168, 171, 176, 224
Marquesas Fracture Zone 9.15S 127.00W 23
Marsa el Hamra 30.59N 28.52E 133
Marsala 37.47N 12.25E 122
Marsden Squares 164
Marseille 43.19N 5.22E 122
Marseilles (map) 123, 135, 177
Marshall Is 36
Marshall Seamounts 11.50N 165.00E 22
Marsigli, Count Luigi 198
Marssuak Channel 60.00N 35.00W 16
Marstrand 57.54N 11.35E 123
Martaban, G. of 187
Martinique Pass 15.00N 61.30W 150
Martin Vaz Fracture Zone 20.00S 19.00W 18
Mary 194
Maryland 213
Mary Rose, wreck 196, 197
Masan 35.11N 128.34E 130
Masaya 36
Mascarene Basin 15.00S 56.00E 19
Mascarene Plain 19.00S 52.00E 19
Ma'shūr 30.28N 49.11E 133
Masinloc 15.32N 119.55E 132
Maslinica 43.24N 16.12E 122
Masnedsund 55.00N 11.50E 123
Massawa 15.38N 39.28E 133
Matadi 5.49S 13.28E 133
Matane 48.49N 67.31W 126
Matanzas, Cuba 23.04N 81.37W 126
Matanzas, Venezuela 8.17N 62.51W 127
Matarani 17.00S 72.10W 127
Mathematicians Seamounts 15.00N 111.00W 23
Matrah 23.37N 58.34E 133
Matsuyama 33.50N 132.41E 130
Maturín, oil basin 102
Maud Rise 65.00S 3.00E 18, 25
Mauna Loa 36
Maureen oilfield 106
Maurice Ewing Bank 51.00S 43.00W 18, 29
Mauritius: fisheries 98
Mauritius Trench 23.30S 55.30E 19
Maury Channel 56.33N 24.00W 16
Maury, Matthew Fontain 203
Maxwell Fracture Zone 47.00N 25.00W 16
Mayaguana Pass. 22.20N 73.30W 150
Mayagüez 18.12N 67.09W 127
Mayport 182
Mazatlán 23.11N 106.26W 126
MCBSF (Mixed Commission for Black Sea Fisheries) 211
M'Clintock Channel 73.00N 103.00W 24
M'Clure Strait 75.00N 120.00W 24, 150
MCM (Mine countermeasure vessel) 181
Median Line 186, 220
Median rift valley 29
Mediterranean Action Plan 176
Mediterranean crisis 1973 189
Mediterranean monk seal 211
Mediterranean Ridge 34.00N 23.00E 17
Mediterranean Sea 66, 108, 155, 176, 189, 194, 214, 216
cables, submarine (map) 200–201
circulation (map) 52
currents 45 (map) 52, 157
disputes 187, 189
fishing catch total 91
pollution: sources (map) 176–177
port development 123
salinity 52
shipping casualties 165
waterspouts 57
Medway ports 124, 134
Medway ports, see also Grain, I. of; Sheerness
Melaka 2.15N 102.15E 130
Melanesian Basin 0.05N 160.35E 22
Melbourne 37.50S 144.58E 132, 135
Meli, hurricane 55
Melilla 35.17N 2.57W 133
Meltwater 67
Melville Bugt 62
Melville Fracture Zone 30.30S 60.40E 19
Melville I. 63, 148
Menard Fracture Zone 50.00S 120.00W 23
Mendaña Fracture Zone 16.00S 91.00W 23
Mendeleyev Ridge 81.00S 180.00 24, 63
Mendocino Seascarp 40.00N 140.00W 21
Menhaden industry 84, 95, 212
Mentawei Ridge 1.00S 98.40E 19
Merchant fleets, national & beneficial ownership (map) 140–141
Merchant seamen & fishermen, *see Appendix VI*
Merchant shipping
casualties (map) 164–165
Dardanelles 155
density 157
fleet, world 140–141
freight costs 144
types 138–139, (graph)141
Mercury 173, 174, 175, 177
Meresteyn, wreck 194
Mersin 36.47N 34.37E 122
Mesopelagic species 74, 89
Mesopelagic Squid 69
Mesopelagic zone 68, 74
Messina 38.10N 15.33E 122, 183
Metalliferous deposits 110, (map) 114
Metamorphism in ocean crust 39
Meteor expedition 198, (map) 199
Meteorological satellites 161, 204
Meteorological telecommunication system 161
Meteor Rise 45.00S 5.00E 18
Methil 56.11N 3.01W 123
Methyl mercury 173
Metis Shoal 36
Metlakatla 55.08N 131.35W 126
Metula, tanker 171
Meuse, R. 125

Mexico 108, 136, 146, 221
  aquaculture production 82
  fisheries 99
  fishing catch total 90, 94
  hurricanes 54
  naval fleet 178
  offshore oil & gas 104
  phosphorites, offshore 115
Mexico, G. of 21, 102, 109
  fisheries 94, 95
  floods 60
  hurricanes (map) 54
  offshore oil production 104, (map) 105, 162
  pollution 172
  shipping casualties 165
  tourism 213
  waterspouts 57
Mezen' 65.53N 44.07E 120, 122
Miami 25.46N 80.10W 126
Michael Sars, ship 199
Michipicoten 47.58N 84.54W 126
Microalgal feeders 79
MIDAS (Maritime Industrial Development Area) 123
Mid-Atlantic Ridge 0.00 20.00W 18
Mid-Atlantic Ridge 28, (profiles) 29, 32–33, 223
Middelburg 51.32N 3.39E 123
Middelfart 55.30N 9.44E 123
Middlesbrough (Teesport) 54.35N 1.12W 123
Mid-Indian Ridge 10.00S 80.00E 19
Midland 44.45N 79.56W 126
Mid North Sea High, oil basin 102
Mid-ocean ridges *see Ocean: ridges*
Mid-Pacific Seamounts 20.00N 170.00E 22, 36
Midway Atoll 37
Midway Is 36
Migrations
  humpback whale 100
  salmon 101
  seabirds (maps) 76–77
  tuna 101
  vertical, ocean 68, 71, 74, 75
Milazzo 38.12N 15.13E 122
Milbruk 6.10N 124.16E 132
Milford Haven 51.42N 5.04W 123, 135
Military reconnaissance 204
Military waste 172
Milkfish 80, 82–83, 88
  distribution (map) 83
Millbank 47.04N 65.27W 126
Millwall 124
Milne Seamounts 45.00N 40.00W 16
Milwaukee 43.01N 87.53W 126, 134
Mnā' 'Abd Allāh 29.01N 48.12E 133
Mnā' al-Aḥmadī 29.04N 48.10E 133, 135
Mina al Bakr 29.40N 48.38E 133, 135
Mnā' al Fahal 23.40N 58.30E 133, 135
Minamata 173
Mnā' Qābūs 23.37N 58.38E 133
Mnā' Rashīd 25.16N 55.16E 133, 135
Mnā' Sa'ūd 28.45N 48.24E 133
Mnā' Sulmān 26.12N 50.37E 133
Mnā' Zāyid 24.33N 54.20E 133
Mindanao Trench, see Philippine Trench
Mindoro Str. 12.30N 120.30E 151
Mine countermeasure vessel (MCM) 181
Minerals 118–119
  aggregate & placer deposits (map) 112–113
  extraction plants (map) 118
  nodules, ocean floor (map) 116–117
  phosphorites 115
  seabed (map) 110–111
  sea water 118–119
Mines 158, 181, 209
Mining, offshore 113
Minitrack 204
Minke whale 100
Miraflores locks 152
Mirage aircraft 185
Missiles, submarine 178, 184, 185
  ownership, nations (table) 180
  ranges (maps) 180–181
Mississippi, R. 26
  ports 147
Misumi 32.37N 130.28E 130
Mitilíni 39.05N 26.34E 122
Mixed Commission for Black Sea Fisheries (MCBSF) 211
Mobile 30.40N 88.05W 126, 134
Moçambique 15.04S 40.44E 133
Moçâmedes 15.11S 12.08E 133
Mocha Fracture Zone 40.00S 77.45W 23
Mocimboa da Praia 11.20S 40.20E 133
Modern Greece, wreck 194
Moengo 5.38N 54.25W 127
Mogadishu, see Muqdisho
Mohammedia 33.45N 7.22W 133
Mohns Ridge 72.30N 5.00E 24
Mohorovičic discontinuity 38, 39
Mo i Rana 66.20N 14.05E 122
Mokp'o 34.49N 126.23E 130
Molde 62.45N 7.10E 122
Molfetta 41.13N 16.38E 122
Mollusca 119, 82
Molokai Fracture Zone 23.00N 148.00W 23
Moluccas 192
Molybdenum 118
Mombasa 4.04S 39.40E 133
Mombasa, port 133
Monaco Bank 37
Mona Pass. 18.00N 68.00W 150, 151
Monazite 113
Mongstad 60.49N 5.02E 122

Monitor, wreck 194
Monitoring systems 182–183
Monk seal 210
Monks Islands 186
Monopoli 40.57N 17.18E 122
Monroe 41.55N 83.20W 126
Monrovia 6.21N 10.48W 133
Monrovia, port 133, 135
Monsoonal year & how monsoons occur 49
Monsoons 48, 49, 53, 58
Monsoon winds 46, 161
Monsunen, ship 184
Montague 46.10N 62.38W 126
Montevideo 34.55S 56.13W 127
Mont-Louis 49.14N 65.44W 126
Montoir 47.20N 2.08W 122
Montreal 149, 153
Montreal 45.30N 73.36W 126, 134
Montreux Convention of 1936 155
Montrose 56.42N 2.26W 123
Montrose, oilfield 102, 106
Mont Saint-Michel 120
Moonless Seamounts 30.40N 140.00W 23
Moray Firth, oil basin 102
Morecambe oilfield 106
Morehead City 34.43N 76.42W 126, 134
Mornington Abyssal Plain 53.00S 88.00W 23
Morocco 115, 136, 157
  aquaculture 82
  fishing industry & catch 95
  naval fleet 178
  phosphorites, offshore 115
  sardine fisheries 95
Morondava 20.17S 44.16E 133
Moroni 11.41S 43.15E 133
Mosjøen 65.51N 13.13E 122
Moss 59.27N 10.40E 123
Mosselbaai 34.10S 22.10E 133
Mostaganem 35.56N 0.05E 133
Mostyn 53.18N 3.16W 123
Motala 58.32N 15.03E 123
Motril 36.43N 3.31W 122
Moulmein 16.29N 97.37E 130
Mount Temple, ship 163
Mourilyan Har. 17.36S 146.07E 132
Mozambique Basin 30.00S 40.00E 19
Mozambique Chan. 20.00S 43.00E 151
Mozambique: fisheries 98
Mozambique Plateau 32.00S 35.00E 19
Mozambique Scarp 33.00S 36.30E 19
Mtwara 10.16S 40.11E 133
Muara 4.53N 114.56E 130
Mubarek oilfield 154
Mubarek Terminal 25.49N 55.11E 133
Mubarras 24.29N 53.23E 133
Mucuio 14.50S 12.12E 133
Mudanya 40.20N 28.53E 122
Muertos Trough 16.50N 66.30W 18
Muhammad Bin Qasim 24.46N 67.20E 130
Mukho 37.32N 129.07E 130
Mulgrave 45.37N 61.23W 126
Mullet 88
Mullet eel 221
Muncar 99
Muqdisho (Mogadishu) 2.02N 45.20E 133, 183
Murchison oilfield 106
Murex regius 119
Murman Rise 71.00N 36.00E 17, 24
Murmansk 69.00N 33.03E 122
Murmansk 120, 148, 182, 187
Muroran 42.21N 140.57E 130
Murray Fracture Zone 34.00N 135.00W 23
Murray Ridge 21.45N 61.50E 19
Murray, Sir John 199
Mururoa Atoll 172
Muscat 183
Museums *see Appendix IX*
Muskegon 43.15N 86.17W 126
Mussau Trough 1.00N 148.30E 22
Mussels 82, 83, 84, 88
Mustard gas 172
Myctophum punctatum (lanternfish) 74
Myojin-sho 36
Mysticeti 78

N

Naantali 60.28N 22.01E 122
Nacala 14.33S 40.40E 133
Nadeshda, ship 198
Nærsnes 59.46N 10.31E 123
Næstved 55.14N 11.45E 123
NAFO (N W Atlantic Fishery Organisation) 211
Nagasaki 32.44N 129.52E 96, 130
Nagoya 35.05N 136.53E 130
Naha 26.10N 127.40E 130
Nakhodka 146
Nakhodka 42.47N 132.52E 130
Nakskov 54.50N 11.08E 123
Namibia
  fishing catch 95
  phosphorites offshore 115
  pilchard fishery, collapse of 95
Namibia Abyssal Plain 30.00S 7.00E 18
Namsos 64.28N 11.31E 122
Nanaimo 49.10N 123.57W 126
Nansei Syoto Trench 24.45N 128.00E 22
Nansen Basin 84.30N 75.00E 24, 62
Nansen, Fridtjof 199
Nansha Islands 189
Nantes 47.14N 1.32W 122, 135
Napier, tanker 171
Napier 39.29S 176.55E 132

Naples, Bay of 177, 196
Napoli 40.50N 14.15E 122
Narawa region 131
Narcondom 187
Nares Abyssal Plain 23.30N 63.00W 16, 18, 21
Nares Abyssal Plain (map) 29
Nares Strait 81.00N 67.00W 24, 150
Narvik 68.25N 17.25E 122
Nasipit 8.59N 125.20E 132
Nassau 25.05N 77.20W 126
Natal 5.45S 35.15W 127
Natal Valley 31.00S 33.15E 19
National expedition (map) 198–199
NATO (North Atlantic Treaty Organisation) 155, 178, 180, 182, 187, 208
  naval fleet 178–179, 182–183
Natural gas 104
Naturaliste Plateau 34.00S 110.00E 19
Natural prolongation 186
Natural seeps 171
Nautical charts *see Charts*
Nautilus, submarine 148
Naval
  aircraft 178, 183
  bases 182–185
  blockades 181, 190
  fleet deployment 182–185
  forces 178–179, 184, 185, 186
  incidents (map) 190–191, *see also Appendix VIII*
  operations, Northern Hemisphere 182–183
  power 178
  strategy 180
  submarines 180
  submarine strengths (world map) 180–181, 182–183
  surface fleet strengths (world map) 178–179
NAVAREA (radio-navigational warning areas) 158
Navigation 109, 204, 208
  aids (map) 158
  buoys & marks 159
  equipment 158
  lights 159
  lights, ships' 166
  satellites 204
  systems 158
Navlakhi 22.58N 70.27E 130
Návplion 37.35N 22.49E 122
Navy, Royal *see Appendix VIII*
Nawiliwili 21.57N 159.21W 126
Nazareth Bank 14.30S 60.45E 19
Nazca Plate 32, 33
Nazca Ridge 20.00S 81.00W 23
Naze, The 156
NEAFC (NE Atlantic Fisheries Commission) 211
Neap tide 61
Necker Ridge 22.00N 167.15W 22
Nelson 41.16S 173.16E 132
Nematocyst 119
Nemuro-kaikyō 44.00N 145.20E 150, 151
Nephrops 88
Nerve gas 172
Netherlands
  aquaculture production 82, 83
  fishing catch 93
  fishing fleet 86
  floods 60
  naval submarine strength 181, 182
  naval surface fleet 178, 182
  offshore oil & gas 104, 106
  sea area 215
  seaborne trade 144
Neva, ship 198
New Amsterdam 6.17N 57.28W 127
Newark 128
New Bedford 41.38N 70.55W 126
New Britain Trench 6.00S 153.00E 22
New Caledonian Basin 30.00S 165.00E 22
Newcastle, Australia 32.55S 151.48E 132, 135
Newcastle, Canada 47.00N 65.33W 126
Newcastle (Tynemouth) 55.01N 1.24W 123
New England 92, 100
New England Seamounts 38.00N 61.00W 16
New England Seamounts 52
Newfoundland 92, 107, 192
Newfoundland Grand Banks *see Grand Banks*
Newfoundland Seamounts 43.45N 45.00W 16
New Guinea 193
Newham 124
New Haven 41.18N 72.55W 126
New Jersey 179
New Jersey 179
New London 41.20N 72.05W 126, 182
Newlyn 50.05N 5.35W 123
New Orleans 134, 147
New Orleans 30.00N 90.02W 126
Newport News, *see Hampton Roads*
Newport, USA 41.30N 71.20W 126, 182
Newport, Wales 51.33N 2.59W 123
New Ross 52.23N 6.56W 123
Newton, Isaac 98
New Westminster 49.10N 122.58W 126
New York–New Jersey 40.43N 74.00W 126
New York, port & region 128, 134
New Zealand
  aquaculture products 83
  fisheries 98, 99

naval fleet 178
  offshore oil & gas 104, 108
  phosphorites, offshore 115
Niagara Falls 153
Nicaragua: fisheries 99
Nice 43.42N 7.17E 122
Niceto de Larrinaga, ship 166
Nicholas, wreck 194
Nickel 110, 111, 118
  nodules (maps) 116–117
  trade 137
Nieuport 196
Nieuwe Maas 124, 125
Nieuwe Waterway 124, 125
Nieuw Nickerie 5.50N 56.59W 127
Niger Cone 4.00N 4.00E 18
Niger delta 109
Nigeria 184
  fishing catch 95
  naval fleet 178
  offshore oil & gas 104, (map) 108–109
Niger oil basin 102
Niger, R. 26
Niigata 37.54N 139.04E 130
Niigata, oil basin 103
Nile 152
Nile Cone 33.00N 31.00E 17
Nile Delta 177
Nimbus 5 satellite image 65
Nimitz 179
Nimrod, aircraft 184
Ninety east Ridge 5.00S 90.00E 19
Ninian, oilfield 102, 106
Niowerkerk 36
Nishino-shima 36
Niterói 22.54S 43.07W 127
Nitrates 174
Nitrates in seawater 52
Nitrogen 176
Noctiluca miliaris (dinoflagellate) 70
Noddy, seabird 76
Nodules 115, (maps) 116–117, 173, 221
Nome 64.30N 165.30W 126
Nome: gold beach deposits (map) 113
Noordhinder lightvessel 156, 161
Noordwinning oilfield 106
Nordenham 53.29N 8.29E 123
Nord-Ostsee Kanal 151
Nordenham 53.29N 8.29E 123
Nord-Ostsee Kanal 151
Nordenham
Norrköping 58.36N 16.12E 123
Norrsundet 60.56N 17.09E 123
North Apoi Field 4.40N 5.30E 133
North Atlantic Drift 44, 52, 67
North Atlantic *see Atlantic Ocean*
North Atlantic Treaty Organisation, *see NATO*
North Australia Basin 14.30S 116.30E 22
North Banda Basin 3.30S 124.30E 22
North Blake Plateau: phosphorites 115
North Cape 182
North Channel 55.00N 5.30W 151
North East Atlantic Fisheries Commission (NEAFC) 211
Northeast Georgia Rise 52.30S 32.30W 18
North East Passage 150
Northeast Providence Chan. 25.30N 77.00W 150
North Ellesmere I. 64
Northern bottlenose whale 210, 211
North Falls 156
North Fiji Basin 16.00S 174.00E 22
North Fiji Plateau 15.00S 172.00E 22
North Foreland 156
North Gabbard, radio beacon 156
North Hinder, radio beacon 156
North Kanin Bank 71.00N 42.00E 24
North Korea
  fisheries 96
  fishing catch 91
  fishing fleet 87
  naval submarine strength 181
  naval surface fleet 179
North Pacific Fur Seal Commission (NPFSC) 211
North Pacific Ocean *see Pacific Oc.*
North Pole 62, 148
North Scotia Ridge 53.00S 46.00W 18
North Sea 55.00N 0.00 17
North Sea 89, 109, 136, 137, 156, 214, 215
  aggregates 112
  Baltic connections 149
  coal beneath sea bed 111
  collisions 167
  Continental Shelf case 1969 222
  dredging 112
  engineering technology 106–107
  fisheries 215
  herring 84
  management 215
  oilfields 102, 104, (map) 106, 215
  pollution control 215
  pollution (map) 174
  resources 215
  surges (map) 60–61
  tides (map) 60–61, 153
  waves (maps) 59
  wind speeds (maps) 47
Northumberland Strait 46.00N 64.00W 150
North West Atlantic Fishery Organisation (NAFO) 211
Northwest Atlantic mid-ocean Channel 54.00N 48.00W 16
North West Cape 150
Northwest Georgia Rise 52.50S 37.50W 18

Northwest Hawaiian Ridge 33.00N 175.18W 22
Northwest Pacific Basin 40.00N 155.00E 22
North West Passage 148, 150, 186, 193
Northwest Providence Chan. 26.20N 78.00W 150
Northwind Ridge 63
North Yemen *see Yemen Arab Republic*
Norton Sound 64.00N 163.00W 20
Norway 63, 92, 93, 182, 215
  aquaculture products 83
  buoys: studies 121
  fishing catch 91, 93
  fishing fleet 86
  fishing rights 186
  naval submarine strength 181, 182
  naval surface fleet 178, 182
  North: exploration 106
  offshore oil & gas 104, 106
  Svalbard dispute (map) 186–187
  waves: studies 121
  whaling from remote bases 100
Norway pout 88
Norwegian Basin 70.00N 9.00E 17, 24
Norwegian Sea 62, 64, 67, 101, 214
Norwegian Sea 28.00N 10.00E 17, 24
Notostomus (deep sea prawn) 69
Notothenia 78
Nouadhibou 20.54N 17.03W 133, 135
Nouakchott 18.08N 16.00W 133
Nouméa 22.16s 166.25E 132
Nova Canton Trough 4.00s 179.00W 22
Novara Knoll 43.00s 74.00E 19
Nova Scotia 92
Nova Trough 2.30s 169.00W 22
Novaya Zemlya 62
Novaya Zemlya Trough 73.30N 59.00E 24, 62
Novorossiysk 44.43N 37.47E 122
NPFSC (N Pacific Fur Seal Commission) 211
Nuclear
  dumping 206
  missiles, submarine 180–181
  powers 184
  submarines 148, 180, 183
  vessels 148
Nuclear Free Zone, Latin American 184, 186
Nuclear-Powered Strategic Submarine, ballistic missiles (SSBN) 178, 179, 180, 182, 183
Nuclear-Powered Strategic Submarine, guided (cruise) missiles (SSGN) 180
Nuclear-Powered Strategic Submarine (SSN) 180
Nueva Island 187
Nueva Palmira 33.52s 58.20W 127
Nuevitas 21.33N 77.19W 126
Nuku'alofa 21.08s 175.12W 132
Nutrients in sea water 70, 76, 115, 177
Nyamaragira 37
Nyborg 55.18N 10.47E 123
Nyiragongo 37
Nykøbing, Falster 54.47N 11.52E 123
Nykøbing, Jutland 56.48N 8.52E 123
Nyköping 58.45N 17.02E 123
Nynäshamn 58.54N 17.57E 123

O

Oakland 129, 134
Oakland 37.50N 122.15W 126
Ob, G. of 70.00N 73.00E 24
OBO (ore-bulk-ore) carrier 138
Ob seamount 37
Observer Transatlantic, racing events 217
Ocean *see also Sea and individual oceans*
  age 30, 33, 40
  areas *see Appendix II*
  basins (map) 26–27, 28, 32, (maps) 40–41
  circulations 44–45 (maps) 50–51, 52
  conservation 210–211, *see also Appendix X*
  cruises (maps) 216
  crust 38–39, 40–41, 43
  currents 44–45, (maps) 50–51, 56, 62, 63, 64
  development (maps) 40–41
  energy sources 120–121
  exploration & expeditions 192–193, 198–199, 202
  floor: magnetic anomalies 30–31
  floor: mapping 202–203
  physiographic provinces 26 (map) 28–29
  pollution 170–174
  racing (maps) 217
  ranching 82
  research 44, 202–203, 206, 209, *see also Appendix IX*
  ridges 27, (map, profiles) 28–29, 32–34, 38, 40, 72, 110, 114
  rises 27, (map) 28–29, 114
  routes, shipping 146
  sediments 42–43
  surface waters 26, 45
  surges, storm 54, 55, 56, 57, 60–61, 156
  temperatures (maps & profile) 50–51, (maps) 53
  trenches 26, 27, 29, 32, 72, 73
  weather ships 47, 161
  weather stations 58, 161

yachting 216–217
  zones, biological environment 26, 27, 68–75
Ocean Falls 52.21N 127.41W 126
Oceanographer Canyon 40.30N 68.10W 16
Oceanographer Fracture Zone 35.00N 35.00W 16
Oceanography 189, 200, 202
Ocean Ranger, ship 160, 162
Octopus 88
Odda 60.04N 6.33E 123
Odense 55.24N 10.23E 123
Odessa 46.29N 30.44E 122
Odin oilfield 106
Odontoceti 78
OECD 142
Offshore
  deposits 112, 113
  engineering yards 106
  exploration 106
  fisheries 96, 97
  mining 113
  oil production (maps) 102–105, 106–107, 171
  platforms and rigs 58, 59, 64, 104–107, 160, 162
  rig mishaps (map) 162–163
Offshore Pollution Liability Agreement (OPOL) 224
Ogdensburg 44.40N 75.30W 126
O'Gorman Fracture Zone 12.00N 105.00W 21, 23
Ohi container terminal 131
Ohio class submarine 181
Oil
  basins, potential 40, (map) 102–103
  blow-outs 162, 170, 171
  consumption *see Appendix V*
  crisis, 1973 142, 143
  pollution 162, 169, (map) 170–171, 177
  prices 142
  products, seaborne trade 144
  production *see Appendix V*
  resources 108
  rigs (*see also offshore platforms*) 104–107, 109, 162
  routes 185
  spillages 170–171, 175, 205, 206
  supplies: transport 154, 155
  tankers 131
  trade, inter area (map) 137
  trade, seaborne 144
  trade, world 140, 141
  trap 42
  waste disposal 224
Oilfields
  developments 106
  producing (maps) 102–106
OILPOL (International Convention for Prevention of Pollution of the sea by oil) 224
Okha 22.28N 69.05E 130
Okhotsk, Sea of 55.00N 150.00E 20
Okhotsk, Sea of 53, 64, 108, 120
Oki-Daito Ridge 23.50N 133.00E 22
Okinawa Trough 25.30N 125.00E 22
Okrika 4.25N 7.04E 133
Olbia 40.53N 9.37E 122
Old Bahama Channel *22.30N 78.30W* 150
Oldenburg 53.08N 8.13E 123
Olga, typhoon 54
Olive turtle 211
Olympia 47.03N 122.54W 126
Oman 98, 178, 187
Oman Basin 23.20N 63.00E 19
Oman, G. of 154
Omega System 158
Onahama 36.56N 140.55E 96, 130
Onega 63.55N 38.06E 122
Onehunga 37.07s 174.30E 132
Onion Patch/Bermuda, racing event 217
Onomichi 34.23N 133.10E 130
O-O (ore-oil) carrier 138
Oostende 51.14N 2.56E 123
Oostende 156
Oosterschelde 82
Oozes 42, 69, 72
Ophidioid species 73
Ophiolites 114
Ophiolite sequences 38, 39
Opisthoproctus soleatus 74
OPOL (Offshore Pollution Liability Agreement) 224
Optimum Routes in Atlantic 148
Opua 35.20s 174.08E 132
Oran 35.42N 0.39W 133
Orange 30.04N 93.43W 126
Orange Cone 31.00s 11.00E 18
Oranjestad 12.31N 70.01W 127
Orchid, typhoon 55
Ore-bulk-ore (OBO) carrier 138
Ore carriers 139
Orehoved 54.57N 11.51E 123
Orestville 48.46N 69.02W 126
Öresund Straits 55.40N 12.50E 150, 151
Organic matter 177
Organochlorines 118
Orkney Is 106
Orkney Deep 61.00s 40.00W 18
Orkney Is 106
Örnsköldsvik 63.17N 18.43E 122
Orozco Fracture Zone *15.30N 104.30W* 23
Orphan Knoll 50.23N 46.24W 16
Ortelius, Abraham 193
Ösaka 34.38N 135.25E 130
Osaka 96
Osaka Bay 130

Osborn Plateau 14.45s 87.00E 19
Oscillating water column (OWC) 121
Oshawa 43.52N 78.50W 126
Oskarshamn 57.16N 16.28E 123
Oslo 59.55N 10.45E 123
Oslo Convention 215
Osprey 175
Osprey Reef 212
Osumi-kaikyō 31.00N 131.00E 151
Oswego 43.29N 76.30W 126
Otago Harbour 45.46s 170.43E 132
Otaru 43.12N 141.01E 130
OTEC (Ocean Thermal Energy Conversion) projects 121
Otranto, Str. of 40.30N 19.00E 151
Ottawa 45.25N 75.45W 126
Otterbäcken 58.57N 14.03E 123
Otter trawls 84, 95
Oude Maas 125
Oulu 65.01N 25.28E 122
Overfishing 84, 92, 93, 100–101, 215
OWC (oscillating water column) 121
Owen Fracture Zone 12.00N 58.00E 19
Owen Sound 44.34N 80.56W 126
Ownership of islands *see Territorial claims & disputes*
Oxelösund 58.40N 17.08E 123
Oya Shio 53
Oysters 82, 83, 84, 88

P

Pacay 36
Pacific–Antarctic Ridge 62.00s 157.00W 22, 25
Pacific Basin, Central 5.00N 175.00W 22
Pacific Basin, Northwest 40.00N 155.00E 22
Pacific Basin, Southwestern 40.00s 150.00W 22
Pacific Ocean 20–23
  exploration of sea floor (map) 203
  features (topographic view) 26, 27
  fisheries (map) 96–99
  fishing catch total by FAO area 90
  fog 53
  islands 136
  manganese nodule zone (map) 221, (maps) 116–117
  mid-ocean ridge 29
  morphology 29
  salinity profile 67
  temperatures, surface 53
  tropical storms & cyclones 56
  tsunamis 59
  voyages & exploration 192–193, 198–199
  weather hazards 160
Pacific Rise, East *see East Pacific Rise*
Pacific salmon 101
Pacific 169
Pack ice 63, 64, 65, 160
Padstow 50.34N 4.56W 123
Paelopatides gigantea (sea cucumber) 73
Pago Pago 14.17s 170.41W 132
Pailolo Channel 21.00N 156.40W 150
Paita 5.05s 81.07W 127
Pakistan 185
  fisheries 98
  naval submarine strength 181
  naval surface fleet 178
Palaeomagnetic research 30
Palamós 41.50N 3.07E 122
Palau Trench 6.30N 134.30E 22
Palawan, N W, oil basin 103
Palawan Trough 7.00N 115.00E 22
Palembang 2.59s 104.48E 132
Palenque 18.14N 70.09W 127
Palermo 38.08N 13.22E 122
Palk Str. 10.00N 80.00E 151
Pallice, la 46.10N 1.14W 122
Palma de Mallorca 39.32N 2.38E 122
Palm Beach 26.41N 80.03W 126
Palúa 8.22N 62.41W 127, 134
Panama 141
  fisheries 99
  fishing fleet 86
Panama Basin 5.00N 83.30W 23
Panama Canal 139, 146, 152
Panama Canal 9.00N 80.00W 150
Panama Canal Zone 152
Panama City 30.10N 85.41W 126
Panama Fracture Zone 4.00N 82.45W 23
Panama, Isthmus of 192
Panamax ships 142, 152
Pan American Highway 129
Pandora, wreck 195
Pangaea 34, 40
Pangkalansusu 4.07N 98.13E 132
Panjang 5.28s 105.19E 132
Panthalassa 34
Papeete 17.33s 149.34W 132
Papeete, port (map) 132
Papenburg 53.05N 7.22E 123
Papua Abyssal Plain 13.00s 152.00E 22
Papua New Guinea
  aquaculture production 83
  fisheries 99
Papua Plateau 11.00s 148.15E 22
Par 50.21N 4.42W 123
Paracel Is 109, 189
Paradip 20.15N 86.40E 130, 135
Paralytic shellfish poisoning 119
Paramaribo 5.49N 55.09W 127
Paranaguá 25.31s 48.30W 127, 134
Paranam 5.38N 55.05W 127
Parcel tankers 137

Parece Vela Basin 15.00N 137.00E 22
Paris 48.52N 2.20E 122
Paris Convention 215
Pasajes 43.20N 1.56W 122
Pascagoula 30.21N 88.31W 126
Paspébiac 48.02N 65.15W 126
Passenger ferries 138, 146
Patagonian hake 94, 95
Pataholm 56.27N 16.27E 123
Patrol boats 178
Pátrai 38.15N 21.45E 122
Patten Escarpment *32.30N 120.00W* 23
Pauillac 45.13N 0.44W 122
Paulo Petri 194, 196
Pavlof 36
Payardi 9.25N 79.49W 126
Paysandu 32.18s 58.02W 127
PCB (polychlorinated biphenols) 172, 174, 175
PCSP (Permanent Commission of the Conference on the Use and Conservation of the Marine Resources of the S. Pacific) 211
Pebble I. 184
Pectens 88
Pedro Miguel locks 152
Pelabuhan Kelang *3.00N 101.24E* 130
Pelagic
  fish 84, 210
  fisheries, industrial 88
  notothenids 79
  sediments 42
  stocks (menhaden & sardine) (map) 94–95
  trawls 84
  whaling 100
  zone 26
Pelican 76
Pelotas 31.48s 52.20W 127
Pemba Channel 5.00s 39.30E 151
Pemba, *see Porto Amelia*
P'eng hu Shui-tao, see Pescadores Chan.
Penguin (map) 76, 79
Peninnis Head 168
Penlee Lifeboat 164
Penrhyn Basin 7.30s 156.15W 22
Pensacola *30.25N 87.14W* 126
Pentland Firth 58.40N 3.20W 151
Penzance 50.08N 5.35W 123
Perim I. 154, 187
Periplus of the Erythraean Sea, The 192
Permanent Commission of the Conference on the Use and Conservation of the Marine Resources of the S Pacific (PCSP) 211
Pernambuco Abyssal Plain 10.00s 27.00W 18
Pernis 125
Persian Gulf, oil basin 103
Persian Gulf *see Gulf, The*
Perth 55, 185
Perth Basin 28.30s 110.00E 22
Peru
  anchovy fishery collapse 98, 99
  fisheries 85 99
  fishing catch total 91
  fishing fleet 86
  guano 53
  naval submarine strength 181
  naval surface fleet 178
  offshore oil & gas 104
  phosphorites offshore 115
Peru Basin 15.00s 85.00W 23
Peru Chile Trench 20.00s 73.00W 23
Peru current 53
Pervyy Kuril'skiy Proliv 50.00N 155.40E 150, 151
Pesaro 43.55N 12.54E 122
Pescadores Channel 24.00N 118.30E 151
Peterhead 57.30N 1.46W 106, 123
Petersen Bank 65.45s 109.55E 25
Peter the Great Bay 189
Petropavlovsk 183
Petrel (maps) 76, 79, 210
Petroleum *see also Oil*
  coke: trade in 137
  crude, transport 136, 144
  products: transport 136, 144
Phaeophyta 119
Phalarope, seabird 76
Phaselis, ancient harbour 194
Pheronema (glass sponges) 72
Philadelphia, see Ameriport
Philip II 196
Philippine Basin 17.00N 132.00E 22
Philippines
  aquaculture production 83
  disputed areas 188
  fisheries 99
  fishing catch total 91
  fishing fleet 87
  hurricanes (map) 54–55
  naval fleet 178
  offshore oil & gas 104
  territorial claims 189
  tsunami damage 59
  tuna industry 101
Philippine Sea 15.00N 135.00E 20, 22
Philippine Trench 9.00N 127.00E 22
Phnom Penh 11.33N 104.56E 130
Phosphates 110, 111, 174
  fertilisers 115
  sea water 52
  world trade (map) 136, 137
Phosphorite nodules 115
Phosphorites 110, 111, 115
Phosphorus 115, 118, 176

Photosynthesis 70, 213
Phuket 7.58N 98.24E 130
Physalia physalis (Portuguese man of war) 71, 119
Physeter catodon (sperm whale) 79
Phytoplankton 52, 68, (map) 70–71, 72, 73
Pico Fracture Zone 38.00N 35.00W 16
Pico I. 37
Picton 41.17S 174.00E 132
Picton Island 187
Pictou 45.41N 62.43W 126
Pigments in ocean animals 74
Pilchard 88
  fishing 95
  stocks off southern Africa 89, 95
Pillars of Hercules 157
Pimental 6.50S 79.58W 127
Pinang 135, 155
Pinang 5.25N 100.21E 130
Pink salmon 101
Pinne 37
Piombino 42.55N 10.31E 122
Pioneer Ridge 38.45N 128.00W 21
Pipelines 104, 106, 109, 136, 137
Piper oilfield 102, 106
Piracy 194
Piraeus 177
Piraiévs 37.56N 23.37E 122
Pirie Pt 154
Piteå 65.19N 21.29E 122
Placer deposits 110, (map) 112–113
Placid oilfield 106
Plaice 82, 84, 175
Plankton 70, 79, 84, 115
Planktonic crustaceans 88
Plate tectonics (map) 32–34, 38–40, 110, 114, 203
Platinum 112, 113
Pleistocene glaciation 28
Ploče 43.02N 17.25E 122
Plutonium 174
Plymouth, England 50.22N 4.07W 123
Plymouth, frigate 184
Plymouth, Montserrat 16.42N 62.13W 127
Plymouth, shipping forecast area 161
Plymouth, USA 41.57N 70.36W 126
P. & O. Company 140
Po Hai Str. 38.30N 121.30E 151
P'ohang 36.02N 129.23E 130
Point Cloates 197
Pointe-à-Pierre 10.19N 61.28W 127
Pointe-à-Pitre 16.13N 61.32W 127
Pointe-au-Père 48.32N 68.28W 126
Pointe-des-Galets 20.55S 55.18E 133
Pointe Noire, Congo 4.47S 11.50E 133
Point Fortin 10.10N 61.42W 127
Point Lisas 10.22N 61.29W 127
Point Reyes 115
Point Tembladora 10.41N 61.36W 127
Point Ubu 20.50S 40.40W 127
Poisonous marine life 119
Poland
  aquaculture production 83
  fishing catch total 91, 93
  fishing fleet 86
  naval submarine strength 181
  naval surface fleet 178
Polar
  easterlies 45
  ice packs 148
  oceans (maps & views) 62–63
  submarine routes 149
Polaris missiles 180, 181, 204
'Polar wandering' 30, 35
Polders 60
Pole Abyssal Plain 89.00N 100.00E 24
Pole of rotation (diags) 33, 34
Pollack 84
Pollutants (map) 172–173, 175, 176–177, 206, 208, 209, 224
Pollution 170, 171, 174–177, 224
  Baltic (map) 175
  conventions 224
  dumping 224
  Mediterranean 52, (map) 176–177
  monitoring by satellite imagery 205
  North Sea (map) 174–175, 215
  oil 162, 169, (map) 170–171, 177
  radioactive 173, 177
  types (chemicals, heavy metals etc.) 172–173, 176–177
Polyamyy 182
Ponce 17.58N 66.39W 127
Pondicherry 11.59N 79.50E 130
Ponds: fish culture 82, 83
Ponta Delgada 37.44N 25.40W 133
Poole 50.43N 1.59W 123
Po, R. 177
Porbandar 21.38N 69.37E 130
Porcupine expedition (map) 198–199
Porcupine Abyssal Plain 49.00N 16.00W 17
Porcupine Bank 53.20N 13.30W 17
Porcupine Seabight 50.00N 13.00W 17
Pori 61.29N 21.48E 122
Porifera (sponges) 119
Porpita 71
Porpoise 88
Porsgrunn 59.08N 9.39E 123
Port Adelaide 34.51S 138.30E 132, 135
Port Alberni 49.14N 124.50W 126
Port Alfred 48.20N 70.53W 126, 134
Port Alice 50.22N 127.28W 126
Port Alma 23.35S 150.53E 132
Port Alucroix 17.42N 64.46W 127
Port Angeles 48.08N 123.25W 126
Port Arthur 29.52N 93.56W 126, 134
Port Augusta 32.30S 137.46E 132
Port-au-Prince 18.33N 72.21W 126
Port Blair 11.45N 92.45E 130
Port Canaveral 28.24N 80.36W 126
Port Cartier 50.02N 66.47W 126, 134
Port Dickson 2.31N 101.47E 130
Port Edgar 184
Port Elizabeth 33.58S 25.37E 133, 135
Port Esquivel 17.53N 77.08W 126, 134
Port Everglades 26.05N 80.04W 126
Port Gentil 0.43S 8.48E 133
Port Giles 35.02S 137.46E 132
Port Harcourt 4.43N 7.05E 108, 133
Port Hawkesbury 45.37N 61.21W 126
Port Hedland 20.24S 118.35E 132, 135
Port Holland 6.32N 121.52E 132
Port Hueneme 34.09N 119.12W 126
Port Isabel 26.04N 97.14W 126
Port Jackson 132
Port Kembla 34.28S 150.55E 132, 135
Port Kent 184
Portland, Australia 38.21S 141.37E 132
Portland, England 50.35N 2.25W 123, 182
Portland (Me) 43.39N 70.14W 126, 134
Portland (Oreg) 45.32N 122.40W 126, 134
Portland, shipping forecast area 161
Port La Nouvelle 43.01N 3.04E 122
Port Latta 40.51S 145.23E 132
Port Lavaca 28.35N 96.40W 126
Port Lincoln 34.43S 135.52E 132
Port Louis 184
Port Louis 20.09S 57.30E 133
Port Morant 17.53N 76.20W 126
Port Moresby 9.30S 147.12E 132
Porto 41.09N 8.40W 122
Pôrto Alegre 30.02S 51.10W 127, 134
Porto Amboim 10.46S 13.40E 133
Porto Amelia 12.55S 40.30E 133
Porto Empedocle 37.16N 13.32E 122
Portoferráio 42.50N 10.21E 122
Porto Foxi 39.05N 9.05E 122
Port of Spain 10.38N 61.32W 127
Porto Grande 16.53N 25.00W 133
Porto Marghera 123
Porto Novo 6.30N 2.40E 133
Pôrto Santana 0.03S 51.10W 127
Pôrto Santos 23.56S 46.19W 127
Porto Santo Stéfano 42.26N 11.07E 122
Porto Torres 40.49N 8.25E 122
Porto Vesme 39.11N 8.23E 122
Port Phillip 38.18S 144.38E 132
Port Pirie 33.11S 138.01E 132, 135
Port Polnocny 54.24N 18.40E 123
Port Purcell 17.00N 64.40W 127
Port Rhoades 18.27N 77.26W 126, 134
Port Royal 194, 196
Port Royal, Jamaica 17.55N 76.52W 126
Port Royal, USA 32.22N 80.41W 126
Ports 122–133, 146, 147
  artificial 133
  commodity 134–135
  container 125, 128, 129, 131, 132
  delta 123, 125
  development and distribution (maps) 122–133
  estuary 124, 146
  island 124, 125, 127, 132
  lagoon 123, 132
  location 124, 127, 130
  river 124, 125, 147
  types 134
Port Said 31.17N 32.18E 133
Port St Joe 29.49N 85.19W 126
Port St Louis 43.23N 4.49E 122
Port San Carlos 184
Port San Luis 35.09N 120.45W 126
Portsmouth 182, 197
Portsmouth, England 50.48N 1.01W 123
Portsmouth (NH) 43.04N 70.46W 126
Portsmouth (Va), see Hampton Roads
Port Stanley, see Stanley
Port Stanvac 35.06S 138.28E 132
Port Sudan 19.36N 37.14E 133
Port Sulphur 29.28N 89.41W 126
Port Talbot 51.34N 3.49W 123
Port Talbot & region (maps) 125
Port Taranaki 39.03S 174.02E 132
Portugal
  fishing catch total 93
  fishing fleet 86
  naval submarine strength 181, 182
  naval surface fleet 178, 182
  voyages & exploration from 192
Portuguese man of war 71, 119
Port Vendres 42.31N 3.07E 122
Port Walcott 20.37S 117.11E 132, 135
Poseidon C-3, missile 180, 181
Potassium 66, 118
Poti 42.09N 41.39E 122, 183
Potiguar, oil basin 102
Pots, lobster etc. 84
Powell Basin 62.15S 49.30W 18, 25, 62
Powell River 49.52N 124.33W 126
'Power-driven vessel', term 166
Power production, tidal 120, 121
Pozzuoli 40.49N 14.07E 122
Praia 14.54N 23.28W 133
Pratt Guyot 37
Prawn 69, 88, 98, 210
Precipitation 47, 66
Predators 78, 79
Prescott 44.45N 75.30W 126
Preston 53.45N 2.45W 123
Prevailing winds 46, 64
Pribilof Islands 96
Prices of commodities/liner freight rates, ratios 144
Primary (P) seismic waves 38, 39
Prince Edward Fracture Zone 46.00S 35.00E 19
Prince Edward I. 37
Prince Regent Inlet 73.00N 90.00W 24
Prince Rupert 54.19N 130.19W 126
Princess Elizabeth Land 63
Princess Elizabeth Trough 64.00S 80.00E 19
Prionace glauca (blue shark) 75
Products tankers 138
Progreso 21.17N 89.39W 126
Proliv Bussol' 46.40N 151.30E 150, 151
Proliv Dmitriya Lapteva 72.00N 145.00E 151
Proliv Friza 45.40N 148.00E 150, 151
Proliv Karskiye Vorota 70.30N 57.30E 151
Proliv Kruzenshterna 48.30N 153.30E 150, 151
Proliv Litke 59.00N 163.20E 151
Proliv Longa 70.00N 180.00W 151
Proliv Matochkin Shar 72.50N 55.00E 151
Proliv Nevel'skogo 52.00N 141.30E 150, 151
Proliv Vil'kitskogo 85.00N 120.30E 151
Proliv Yekateriny 44.20N 156.40E 150, 151
Protozoa 70
Providence 41.49N 71.24W 126
Provideniya 64.30N 173.11W 126
Pteropod ooze 42
Puerto Barrios 15.43N 88.37W 126
Puerto Bolívar 3.19S 79.59W 127
Puerto Cabello 10.30N 68.03W 127
Puerto Cabezas 14.01N 83.23W 126
Puerto Cabo Blanco 4.29S 81.19W 127
Puerto Cortés 15.51N 87.58W 126
Puerto de Hierro 10.38N 62.05W 127
Puerto La Cruz 10.14N 64.38W 127
Puerto las Mareas 17.56N 66.08W 127
Puerto Libre Duarte 19.30N 69.50W 127
Puerto Madryn 42.46S 65.02W 127
Puerto Manatí 21.24N 76.48W 126
Puerto Miranda 10.46N 71.33W 127
Puerto Montt 41.29S 72.58W 59, 127
Puerto Ordaz 8.15N 62.43W 127, 134
Puerto Padre 21.13N 76.35W 126
Puerto Plata 19.49N 70.41W 127
Puerto Quepos 9.25N 84.10W 126
Puerto Rico Trench 20.00N 66.00W 18
Puerto Santa Cruz 120
Puerto Somoza 12.10N 86.50W 126
Puerto Viejo de Azua 18.30N 70.40W 127
Puffer fish 119
Pugwash 45.52N 63.40W 126
Pula 44.53N 13.50E 122
Punta Arenas 53.10S 70.54W 127
Punta Cardón 11.38N 70.15W 127
Punta Colorada 41.50S 65.05W 127
Punta de Palmas del Sur 10.26N 71.38W 127
Punta Quilla 50.15S 68.55W 127
Puntarenas 9.59N 84.50W 126
Purse-seining 84, 90, 93, 94, 95, 96, 100
Pusan 35.06N 129.04E 130, 135
Pyrrophyta 119

Q

Qaḍimah 22.20N 39.07E 133
Qaṣr Aḥmad 32.20N 15.17E 133
Qaṣr al Burayqah 30.25N 19.34E 133, 135
Qatar
  desalination plants 118
  fisheries 98
  offshore oil & gas 104, 109
Qeshm 109, 154
Qingdao 36.05N 120.19E 130
Qinhuangdao 39.54N 119.38E 130
Quahogs 84, 88
Quan Phu Quoc Island 109
Québec 46.49N 71.12W 126
Quebec 149
Quebrada Fracture Zone 3.00S 105.00W 23
Queen Elizabeth I. 62–63
Queen Maud Gulf 67.50N 102.00W 24
Queen Maud Land 63
Queen Maud Mts 63
Queensland Plateau 15.00S 149.00E 22
Quelimane 17.53S 36.53E 133
Quemadas, Islas 36
Quequén 38.32S 58.40W 127
Quilon 8.53N 76.36E 130
Quintero 32.47S 71.31W 127
Quirós Fracture Zone 22.30S 95.00W 23
Quseir 26.06N 34.17E 133

R

Raahe 64.41N 24.29E 122
Rabaul 4.13S 152.14E 132
Racing, ocean 217
Racon, echo enhancer 158
Radar(Radio Detection & Ranging) 158
  failure to use properly 166–167
  pictures 160, 205
  screen 156
Radioactively generated heat 39
Radioactive pollution 172–173
Radio communication 200
Radio-isotope dating 37
Radiolaria 69, 70
Radiolarian ooze 42
Raffles, Sir Stanford 131
Rafts 80, 82
Rainfall, statistics (map) 47, 49
Ramallo 33.30S 60.00W 127
Ramark, echo enhancer 158
Ramsgate 51.19N 1.25E 123
Ramsgate 156
Randers 56.27N 10.03E 123
Rangoon 16.46N 96.10E 120, 130
Raoul I. 36
Rapid, wreck 197
Rapid Bay 35.32S 138.12E 132
Raša 45.03N 14.04E 122
Ra's al Ghār 27.30N 49.15E 133
Ra's al Ju'aymah 26.56N 49.40E 133, 135
Ra's al Khafjī 28.25N 48.35E 133
Ra's al Tu'aymah 26.56N 49.40E 133
Ra's al Unūf 30.26N 18.45E 133
Ras Bahregan 29.43N 50.10E 133
Râs Shukheir 28.08N 33.16E 133, 135
Ra's Tannūrah 26.38N 50.10E 133, 135
Rat-tail fish 68, 72, 73
Rat-trap fish 75
Rattray Head, ship 167
Rauma 61.07N 21.30E 122
Ravenna 44.25N 12.15E 122
Ray 73, 84, 88
Raysūt 16.56N 54.01E 133
Recife 8.04S 34.52W 127
Reclamation of land 125, 132, 210, 215
Recreation, marine 208, 209, 213, 216–217
  activities 217
  Brittany (map) 217
  California 217
  Caribbean 212–213
  Chesapeake Bay 213
  Cruises (map) 216
  fishing 95, 216
  racing events (map) 217
  sailing 217
Red fish 88
Redi 15.45N 73.39E 130
Red Sea 20.00N 39.00E 19
Red Sea 108, 110, 114, 152, 154
  floor spreading 35, 114
  Landsat image 205
  metalliferous deposits (map) 114
  navigation rights 187
  pollution 173
  salinity profile 66,67
  temperature profile 51
Red Sea Commission 114
Red seaweed 88
Red tide 70, 173
Reef 42, 132, 155, 210–212
  lagoon 80–81
Reefer ships 138, 152
Reggio di Calabria 38.06N 15.45E 122
Regional Fisheries Advisory Commission for the SW Atlantic (CARPAS) 211
Registration of vessels 140, 141
Regulus, missile 181
Rendsburg 54.17N 9.40E 123
Renee oilfield 106
Reni 45.26N 28.18E 122
Rennell, James 198
Repair facilities 143
Researcher Ridge 15.15N 50.30W 16/17
Researcher Seamount 27.56N 68.14W 16
Research, marine 202–203, 206–207, 209 *see also Appendix IX*
Research & survey fleets (maps) 206–207
Réunion 98, 185
Revillagigedo, Islas 221
Reykjanes Ridge 62.00N 27.00W 16, 31
Reykjanes Ridge 31
Reykjavík 64.09N 21.56W 92, 122
Rhine 124, 125, 147, 176
Rhine–Main–Danube canal system 147
Rhodes 196
Rhodophyta 119
Rhône, R. 177
Rhumb line track 148
Rias 127
Richard's Bay 28.47S 32.05E 133, 135
Richibucto 46.41N 64.52W 126
Richmond 129
Richmond (Va) 37.32N 77.26W 126
Richter scale 38
Ridges, ocean, *see Ocean: ridges*
Rift valley 29
Riga 56.57N 24.07E 122, 182
Rights
  access 186, 218
  fishing 186, 210, 219
  navigation 187
Rigs, oil *see also offshore platforms* 104–107, 109, 162
  blow-outs 170
  mishaps (map) 162–163
Riiser-Larsen Sea 67.00S 20.00E 19, 25
Rijeka 45.19N 14.26E 122
Rimouski 48.25N 68.34W 126
Rio Benito 1.35N 9.38E 133
Rio Colorado 120
Rio de Janeiro 22.54S 43.10W 127, 135
Rio de Janeiro, harbour 127
Rio de la Plata, ship 184
Río Gallegos 51.35S 69.15W 120, 127
Rio Grande 32.03S 52.05W 127, 134
Rio Grande Fracture Zone 30.00S 20.00W 18
Rio Grande Gap 30.30S 39.10W 18
Rio Grande Plateau 31.00S 35.00W 18
Rises, ocean, see Ocean: rises
Rishiri-suidō 45.00N 141.20E 151
Risör 58.43N 9.14E 123
Ritter I. 36
River ports 124, 125
River run off 171
Riviera Fracture Zone 18.40N 107.15W 23
Rivière de Loup 47.50N 69.34W 126
Roadtown, St Thomas 18.20N 64.55W 127
Roaring Forties 46
Roar oilfield 106
Roatán 16.23N 86.30W 126
Robbie Ridge 10.15S 175.00W 22
Roberts Bank 49.00N 123.05W 126

Robeson Chan. 82.20N 60.00W 150
Rochefort 45.56N 0.57W 122
Rochester, England 51.23N 0.32E 123, 156
Rochester, USA 43.12N 77.36W 126
Rockall 81, 186, 214
dispute over sea areas (map) 186, 187
Rockall Bank 57.30N 13.50W 17
Rockall Plateau 59.00N 14.00W 17
Rockall, shipping forecast area 161
Rockall Trough 57.00N 12.00W 17
Rockhampton 212
Rødby 54.39N 11.21E 123
Rødhos 36.26N 28.14E 122
Rodriguez Ridge 19.30S 62.00E 19
Roggeveen Basin 31.30S 95.30W 23
Roll-on roll-off *see RoRo*
Romanche Fracture Zone 0.00 17.00W 18
Romania 142, 147
aquaculture production 83
fishing fleet 86
naval fleet 178
Ronaldsway, weather station 161
Rønne 55.06N 14.42E 123
Ronneby 56.13N 15.15E 123
Ronne Entrance 72.50S 75.00W 25
Ronne Ice Shelf 63
Roo Rise 12.00S 111.00E 19
Roosevelt, carrier 189
Roosevelt Roads 182
RoRo (roll-on, roll-of)
cargo 129
container vessels 124, 125, 136, 139
ferries 139
terminals 134
Rosario 33.00S 60.40W 127, 134
Roscoff 48.43N 3.58W 122
Roseau 15.17N 61.24W 127
Rosemary Bank 59.15N 10.10W 17
Ross Ice Shelf (Ross Sea) 63
Ross, James Clark: expedition (map) 198–199
Rosslare 52.16N 6.23W 123
Ross Sea 76.00S 180.00 25
Röst Bank 68.00N 11.30E 24
Rostock 54.09N 12.06E 123
Rosyth 182
Rota 182
Rotterdam (map) 124–125, 147, 215
Rotterdam (Europoort) 51.55N 4.30E 123, 135
Rouen 49.26N 1.05E 122
Rough oilfield 106
Round Britain, racing event 217
Routes
Arctic trade (map) 148–149
exploration (map) 192–193, (map) 198–199, 202
shipping (map) 146–147
submarine (map) 148–149, 182
weather (maps) 148
Rovinj 45.05N 13.38E 122
Rowley Shelf 19.00S 118.00E 22
Royal Air Force 169
Royal Indian Marine Survey 199
Royal Society of London 198
Royal Sovereign light-tower 161
Royal Sovereign Shoals 156
Royal Trough 16.10N 49.00W 16
Royal Victoria Docks 124
Ruapehu 36
Rudkøbing 54.56N 10.43E 123
Rumford, Count 198
Ruth oilfield 106
Rutile 113
Rwanda: aquaculture production 82
Ryukyu Is 189

S

Saavedra 192
Sacramento 129
Sacramento 38.31N 121.28W 126
Sacramento, wreck 195
Sado-kaikyō 37.50N 137.30E 151
Safaga 26.43N 35.55E 133, 135
Safety, navigational 208
Safety of Life at Sea, International Convention for (SOLAS) 158, 163, 168, 224
Safety of ships 158
Safi 32.19N 9.12W 133, 135
Saglek Bank 59.00N 61.40W 16
Sagua de Tánamo 20.40N 75.17W 126
Sagunto 39.39N 0.13W 122
Saharian Seamounts 25.00N 20.00W 17
Sahul Shelf 12.30S 125.00E 22
Saida 33.34N 35.21E 133
Sailfish 75
Sailing 216
Sailing ships 192
Saimaa seal 211
St Brieuc: mussel production 83
St Fergus 106
St George 32.23N 64.42W 126
St George's 12.03N 61.45W 127
St George's Channel 5.00S 152.30E 150, 151
St Helena Fracture Zone 18.00S 19.00W 18
St Hélier 49.11N 2.06W 122
Saint John 45.16N 66.03W 126, 134
St Johns, Antigua 17.06N 61.51W 127
St John's, Canada 47.34N 52.41W 126
St Katherine Docks 124
St Kitts: hurricane damage 55
St Lawrence, Gulf of (view) 149
St Lawrence, Gulf of 47.50N 61.00W 16
St Lawrence ports: icing 149
St Lawrence R 26, 124, 149
St Lawrence Seaway 153
St Lawrence Seaway 45.00N 75.00W 150
St Lucia Channel 14.20N 61.00W 150
St Lucia: hurricane damage 55
St Malo 48.38N 2.02W 122
St Malo: mussel production 83
St Nazaire 47.17N 2.12W 122
St Paul Fracture Zone 0.40N 24.40W 18
St Paul I. 37
St Peter, tanker 171
St Peter Port 49.27N 2.33W 123
St Petersburg 27.46N 82.38W 126
St Pierre 46.47N 56.12W 126
St Pierre Bank 39.00S 78.00E 19
St Pierre et Miquelon 92
St Vincent Pass 13.30N 61.00W 150
Sakai 96
Sakai 34.35N 135.28E 130
Sakaide 34.20N 133.51E 130
Sakata 38.56N 139.49E 130
Sakhalin 96
Sakurajima 36
Salalah 185
Salaverry 8.14S 79.00W 127
Salcedo–Urdaneta 192
Saldanha 33.01S 17.57E 133, 135
Salerno 40.39N 14.46E 122
Salīf 15.18N 42.41E 133
Salina Cruz 16.10N 95.12W 126
Salinity 52, (maps) 66–68, 70, 114, 120
affecting ice formation 64
Atlantic 27
Salmon 82, 84, 88, 221
fisheries 96, 100, (maps) 101
fishing 97, (maps) 101
industry 101
ranching 97, 100
species, oceanic distribution & migrations 101
Salt 118–119 *see also Salinity*
pans 118
precipitation 66
production 118
trade 137
Salter Duck, wave energy device 121
Salterns 66
Salvador 12.58S 38.31W 127
Salvage 197
Salyut 204
Samalga Pass 53.40N 169.00W 150
Samarinda 0.30S 117.08E 132
Sambu 1.15N 103.52E 132, 155
SAM missile destroyers 189
Samoa, American: fisheries 99
Samoa Basin 16.00S 166.00W 22
Samos 196
Samsun 41.16N 36.21E 122
San Antonio 33.37S 71.37W 127, 129
San Antonio Este 40.50S 64.42W 127
San Bernardino Str 12.50N 124.30E 151
San Carlos 184
San Carlos Bay 184, 185
San Carlos da la Rápita 40.35N 0.36E 122
Sandakan 5.50N 118.07E 130
Sandbanks (map) 42
Sand deposits 112–113
Sand-eel 84, 88
Sandefjord 59.08N 10.14E 123
San Diego 32.45N 117.10W 126, 182
San Diego Co. (map): sports fishing 217
Sandnes 58.52N 5.43E 123
Sand waves 42
Sandwich Islands 184
San Feliú de Guixols 41.35N 3.02E 122
San Fernando 16.37N 120.19E 129, 132
San Francisco 37.48N 122.25W 126
San Francisco
fog 53
port & region (maps) 129
reclamation 129
salterns 66
San Jorge I. 37
San José 13.58N 90.50W 126, 129
San José del Cabo 23.03N 109.41W 126
San Juan del Sur 11.14N 85.52W 126
San Juán, Peru 15.22S 75.07W 127
San Juan, Puerto Rico 18.28N 66.07W 127, 134
San Juan Seamount 36
San Lorenzo, Argentina 32.45S 60.40W 127
San Lorenzo, Honduras 13.24N 87.27W 126
San Lorenzo, Venezuela 9.47N 71.05W 127
San Martin 13.48S 76.20W 127
San Martin Seamounts 58.00S 95.00W 23
San Miguel 36
San Nicolas, Argentina 33.26S 60.16W 127, 134
San Nicolás, Peru 15.10S 75.15W 127
San Pablo Bay 129
San Pedro, Argentina 33.42S 59.39W 127
San Pedro de Macoris 18.26N 69.19W 127
San Pedro, Ivory Coast 4.44N 6.37W 133
San Sebastián 53.15S 68.20W 127
Santa Barbara 37
Santa Barbara Channel 171
Santa Cruz de la Palma 28.40N 17.33W 133
Santa Cruz del Sur 20.42N 77.59W 126
Santa Cruz de Tenerife 28.28N 16.15W 133
Santa Fé, submarine 184
Santa Fé 31.39S 60.42W 127
Santa Maria 7.45N 122.07E 132
Santa Maria de la Rosa, wreck 196, 197
Santa Marta 11.15N 74.13W 127
Santa Monica Bay 115
Santan 0.02S 117.32E 132
Santander 43.28N 3.48W 122
Santarem 2.24S 54.42W 127
Santa Rosalia 27.21N 112.16W 126
Santiago de Cuba 19.58N 75.52W 126
Santo 15.32S 167.08E 132
Santo Antonio de Tanna, wreck 195
Santo Christo de Castello, wreck 194
Santo Domingo 18.28N 69.53W 127
Santorin (Thera) 37
Santos 23.56S 46.19W 127
Santos Plateau 25.00S 43.00W 18
São Francisco do Sul 26.15S 48.38W 127
São Sebastião 23.57S 45.24W 127, 135
São Tomé 0.15N 6.35E 37, 133
Sapele 5.55N 5.45E 133
Sapphire, wreck 195
Sarawak, oil basin 103
Sardine 84, 88, 95
Californian fishery collapse 98, 99
fisheries 96, 97
Morocco, industry 95
Sardinia Cup, racing event 217
Sargasso Sea 44, 68, 70
Sarikei 2.08N 111.31E 130
Sarnia 43.00N 82.25W 126
Saroniba, G. of 177
Sarpsborg 59.17N 11.07E 123
Sasebo 33.10N 129.45E 130
Satellite
navigation systems 158, 204
photos 56, 65
radar 204
technology 202
tracking: buoys 52
tracking: iceberg 65
tracking stations (map) 204
Satellites 204–205
active 204
communications 200, 204
geodetic 204
meteorological 161, 204
navigation 204
passive 204
radar 205
reconnaissance 205
SATO (South Atlantic Treaty Organisation), proposals 184
Sattahip 12.35N 100.51E 130
Sauda 59.39N 6.21E 123
Saudi Arabia
desalination plants 118
naval fleet 178
offshore oil & gas 104, 109
seaborne trade 144
Sault Ste. Marie 46.30N 84.20W 126
Saury 88
Savannah 32.04N 81.05W 126
Savannah, port 128, 134
Savona 44.18N 8.30E 122
Saya de Malha Bank 10.30S 61.30E 19
SBM (single buoy mooring) 134
Scallop 83, 88
Scanraff 58.00N 11.00E 123
Scavengers, deep sea 72, 73
Scheldt, R. 125
Scheveningen 52.06N 4.15E 123
Schizophyta 119
Scientific Committee on Oceanic Research (SCOR) 203
Scilly Isles 168
Scilly (St Mary's) weather station 161
SCNEA (Sealing Commission for the NE Atlantic) 211
SCNWA (Sealing Commission for the NW Atlantic) 211
Scoop nets 80
Scoresby Sund 62
Scoresby Sund 70.30N 24.00W 16, 24
Scoresby, William 198
Scorpio, tanker 171
Scorpion fish 73
SCOR (Scientific Committee on Oceanic Research) 203
Scotia Arc 78
Scotia Sea 55.00S 60.00W 18
Scotland 215
Scott I. 36
Scott Seamounts 68.00S 180.00W 25
Scrabster 58.37N 3.33W 123
Scram oilfield 106
Scripps Institution of Oceanography 115, 121
SCSK (Shellfish Commission for Skagerrak–Kattegat) 211
SCUBA (self contained underwater breathing apparatus) 194, 212, 216, 217
Sea *see also Ocean and individual seas*
areas, *see Appendix II*
boundaries 214
coastal zones 208, 216
conservation 208–216
description, in Beaufort scale 48
European 214
farming 82
ice 62–64
jurisdictional zones 218
limits 26
management 208–216 *see also Appendix X*
mapping & exploration 202–203
minerals 116–117, 118–119
pollution 170–177
recreational use 208, 212, (maps) 216–217
research 202–203, 209
shelf 42, 215
surface waters 52, 53
surges 60–61
temperatures 50–51, 53, 56, 121
thermal power 121
tides (maps) 60–61
use: management 208–216, *see also Appendix X*
water levels 27, 120, 196
waves (maps) 58–59
weather hazards 160, 161
Sea algae *see Seaweed*
SEABEEs 134, 139, 147
Seabirds 76–77, 210
Seaborne trade, world 136–137, 144
Sea bream 84
Sea cucumber 72, 73
Sea floor 72, 73
dating 30–31
exploration (map) 202–203
mapping 203
metalliferous deposits (maps) 114
minerals (map) 110–111, (maps) 116–117
morphology (map) 28–29
phosphorite (maps) 115
spreading 29, 31, (map) 32–33, 34, 51, 73
Seafood, major consumers (map) 85
Seaham 54.50N 1.19W 123
Sea hares 72
Seal 79, 175, 210
Sealing Commission for the NE Atlantic (SCNEA) 211
Sealing Commission for the NW Atlantic (SCNWA) 211
Sea lion 210, 211
Sea, Ministry for the (France) 208
Seamounts 26, 27, 28, 36, 37, 115
Sean oilfield 106
Sea otter 210
Sea pen 72
Sea power 178
Searsport 44.28N 68.56W 126
Seasat, satellite 204–205
Sea smoke, *see Fog*
Sea snail 73
Sea spider 88
Sea Star, tanker 167, 170
Seattle 47.36N 122.20W 126, 134
Seattle 96
Sea urchin 88
Seaward Beach 80
Sea water 118
density 52, (maps, graph) 66–67
desalination plants 118
elements 66, 118, (table) 119
minerals 66, 118–119
salinity (maps, profiles) 66–67, 118–119
volume, total 26
Seaways 154, 155, 156
Seaweed 82, 83, 88
cultivation 83
fertiliser 83
food 83
gathering 97
harvests (map) 82, 83
industry 83
Secondary (S) seismic waves (diags) 38, 39
SECOR (Sequential Observation of Range) 204
Sedimentary formations (map) 42–43
Sediment cores 40
Sediments 28, 29, (map) 42–43, 72, 110, 112, (map) 114, 115
Seguam Pass. 53.30N 172.30W 150
Seine Abyssal Plain 34.00N 12.15W 17
Seiners 86, 87
Seines 80, 84
Seismic
layers of ocean crust 39
surveys 42, 43
warning station 59
waves 28, 29, 38, 39
Sei whale 78
Selat Alas 8.30S 116.40E 151
Selat Bali 8.30S 114.30E 151
Selat Bangka 2.30S 105.30E 151
Selat Berhala 0.40S 104.00E 151
Selat Gaspar 3.00S 107.00E 151
Selat Karimata 2.00S 109.00E 151
Selat Lombok 9.00S 115.00E 151
Selat Manipa 3.20S 127.10E 151
Selat Ombai 8.30S 125.20E 151
Selat Roti 10.30S 123.30E 151
Selat Sape 8.30S 119.30E 151
Selat Serasan 2.20N 109.00E 151
Selat Sunda 6.30S 105.00E 151
Selat Timpaus 2.00S 124.10E 151
Semarang 7.01S 110.27E 132
Senegal: fishing catch 95
Senkaku Islands 189
Seoul (Sŏul) 120
Sepetiba 23.00S 44.02W 127, 135
Sept Iles 50.11N 66.23W 126, 134
Sergipe–Alagoas, oil basin 102
Sérifos 37.07N 24.32E 122
Sète 43.24N 3.42E 122
Sète Bank 37
Setúbal 38.29N 8.56W 122
Seven Stones Reef 168
Severnaya Zemlya 62
Severn Estuary
tidal power potential 120
tidal range 60, 120
Severomorsk 182
Sevilla 37.22N 6.00W 122
Sewage 82, 174, 176
Sewage sludge 174
Seward 60.06N 149.34W 126
Sewell, R. B. Seymour 199
Seychelles 37, 185
fisheries 98
Seychelles Bank 4.45S 55.30E 19
Seydhisfjödhur 65.15N 14.01W 92, 122
Sfax 34.44N 10.46E 133

Shad 88
Shanghai 31.14N 121.29E 120, 130
Shannon, shipping forecast area 161
Shantou 23.21N 116.40E 130
Sharjah 25.23N 55.26E 133
Sharjah: offshore oil & gas 104, 154
Shark 73, 74, 84, 88
Sharpness 51.43N 2.29W 123
Shatt el Arab 187
Shearwater 76, (map) 77, 210
Shediac 46.14N 64.33W 126
Sheerness 124, 156
Sheerness 51.27N 0.45E 123
Sheet Harbour 44.56N 62.30W 126
Sheffield, destroyer 184
Shelburne 43.45N 65.19W 126
Shelf seas: oil resources 109
Shelikhova Gulf 60.00N 158.00E 20
Shelikof Strait 57.30N 155.00W 150
Shellfish 82, 84, 87
Shellfish Commission for Skagerrak–
    Kattegat (SCSK) 211
Shell fisheries 88, 97
Shepody Bay 120
Sherbro 7.32N 12.30W 133
Shetland E./Shetland W., oil basins
    102
Shetland Is 81, 106
    fisheries (maps) 81
Shetland models (boats) 86
Shikotan 189
Shimizu 35.00N 138.30E 130
Shimonoseki 33.59N 130.58E 130
Shinagawa 131
Shiogama 38.19N 141.04E 130
Shipbuilding
    successful firms in 140
    world trends, orders, completions
        142, 143
Shipowners, major 140
Shippegan 47.45N 64.42W 126
Shipping
    casualties (map) 164–165
    density 157
    distances (map) 146–147, *see also
        Appendix VII*
    lanes 143, 215
    lines 137, 140
    merchant 138–139, 141, 144, 155, 157,
        164–165
    naval 178–179, 182–185
    ocean routes (map) 146–147
    oil spills (map) 170–171
    routes 146–147, *see also Appendix VII*
    weather forecast areas 161
Ship's Inertial Navigation System
    (SINS) 158
Shipwrecks *see Wrecks*
Shipyards 142
Shirshov Ridge 57.30N 171.00E 20
Shoals 155, 156, 157
Shona Ridge 51.00S 3.00E 18
Shoreham 50.50N 0.15W 123
Short-tailed shearwater (map) 77
Shrimp 69, 84, 88, 94–95, 212
Shrimp industry 94,95
Shrimp trawler 87
Shu'aybah 29.02N 48.08E 133
Shuwaykh 29.21N 47.56E 133, 135
Sib 183
Šibenik 43.44N 15.54E 122
Siberia 96
Siboga, ship 198
Sibu 2.18N 111.49E 130
Sibutu Pass 7.00N 119.20E 151
Sicilian Channel 37.30N 12.00E 151
Sicilian Depression, oil basin 102
Sicily 95
Sidi Kerir 30.50N 29.00E 133, 135
Sierra Leone Basin 5.00N 17.00W 18
Sierra Leone Fracture Zone 6.00N 31.00W 18
Sierra Leone Rise 5.30N 21.00W 18
Sierra Leone Seamounts 37
Siglufjördhur 66.10N 18.50W 92, 122
Sigsbee Deep 25.00N 92.00W 21
Sikeå 64.11N 20.59E 122
Sikoku Basin 30.00N 137.00E 22
Siliceous deposits 43
Siliceous ooze 72
Silloth 54.52N 3.24W 123
Simonstown 34.11S 18.26E 133
Simrishamn 55.35N 14.20E 123
Singapore 1.16N 103.50E 132, 135
Singapore 137, 143, 155, 183, 185
    aquaculture production 83
    bunkering 130–131
    containers 134
    fisheries 98
    naval fleet 178
    port (map) 131, 135
    registration of vessels 141
    shipbuilding & repair 130
Singapore, Strait of 155, 157
Singapore, Strait of 1.20N 103.40E 150, 151
Single buoy mooring, (SBM) 122–133,
    134
Sin-Iwo-sima 36
Sinking, see Collisions
SINS (Ship's Inertial Navigation
    System) 158
Sint Nicolaas 12.26N 69.55W 127
Siphonophores 71
Sipontum, ancient port 194
Siqueiros Fracture Zone 8.10N 104.00W 23
Siracusa 37.03N 15.18E 122
Sirenians 210
Sir Galahad, landing ship 184
Siros 37.25N 24.50E 122
Sirri 25.52N 54.28E 133
Sir Tristram, landing ship 184

Sitala, tanker 166
Sitito–Iozima Ridge 33.00N 140.00E 22
Sitrah 26.10N 50.40E 133
Six, James 198
Sjaelland Rundt, racing event 217
Skælskør 55.15N 11.17E 123
Skagen 153
Skagen 57.43N 10.35E 123
Skagerrak 50.00N 9.00E 151
Skandia 125
Skaramanger 38.20N 21.28E 122
Skate 84
Skaw 182
Skellefthamn 64.42N 21.14E 122
Skien 59.12N 9.38E 123
Skikda 36.53N 6.54E 133
Skimmer 76
Skipjack tuna 101
Skive 56.34N 9.03E 123
Skoghall 59.19N 13.27E 123
Skua 76, (map) 77
Skudeneshavn 59.08N 5.16E 123
Skulskär 60.39N 17.23E 123
Skyhawk, aircraft 185
Slant range 204
Sleipner oilfield 106
Sligo 54.16N 8.28W 123
Slite 57.41N 18.49E 123
Smalkalden 5.30N 55.10W 127
Small Strait 154
Smelt 88
Smith Rock 36
Smiths Bluff 30.00N 93.59W 126
Snoek 88
Snorkel diving 212, 216
Söderhamn 61.18N 17.05E 123
Söderköping 58.29N 16.25E 123
Södertälje 59.12N 17.38E 123
Sodium, in sea water 66, 119
Sofala 19.51S 34.50E 133
Sohm Abyssal Plain 36.00N 55.00W 29
Sola 58.55N 5.35E 123
Solar energy 120
Solar evaporation 118
SOLAS (Safety of Life at Sea)
    Convention 1974 158, 163, 168,
    224
Sole, fish 88
Solent 197
Sole, shipping forecast area 161
Solomon Is: fisheries 99
Solomon Rise 1.00N 157.00E 20, 22
Solomon Sea 10.00S 153.00E 20, 22
Sölvesborg 56.03N 14.35E 123
Solway Firth 120
Sonagraph 202
Somalia 141
    fisheries 98
Somalia–Kenya Boundary 187
Somalian plate 32
Somali Basin 0.00 52.00E 19
Somali current 51
Sonar 84, 182
Sonar scanners 40
Sønderborg 54.55N 9.47E 123
Sooty Shearwater 77
Sooty tern 77
Sorel 46.03N 73.06W 126, 134
Sorong 0.53S 131.14E 132
SOSUS (sound surveillance systems)
    182, 183
Soulanges 153
Söul (Seoul) 120
Soundings 84, 198, 202
Sound surveillance systems (SOSUS)
    182, 183
Souris 46.21N 62.14W 126
Sousse 35.50N 10.38E 133
South Africa 108, 184
    fisheries 95, 98
    fishing catch total 95
    fishing fleet 86
    fishing industry 95
    naval submarine strength 181
    naval surface fleet 178
    phosphates offshore 115
South American marine otter 210
South American river turtle 210
Southampton 50.54N 1.24W 123, 124,
    135
South Atlantic Treaty Organisation
    (SATO), proposals 184
South Australia Basin 37.30S 130.00E 22
South China Basin 15.00N 115.00E 22
South China Sea 12.00N 117.00E 20
South China Sea 26, 155, 161
Southeast Indian Ridge 50.00S 110.00E 19,
    22
Southend-on-Sea 124
South Equatorial Current 49
Southern Ocean 26, 51, 63, 64, (map)
    65, 78, 157
    whale & krill distribution (map) 78–
    79
    whaling: expansion 100
Southern Ocean Racing Conference
    217
Southern Right whale 78, 100
Southern skua 77
South Falls 156
South Fiji Basin 26.00S 175.00E 22
South Foreland 156
South Georgia 100, 184
South Indian Abyssal Plain 59.00S 125.00E 22
South Korea
    aquaculture production 83
    fisheries 96
    fishing catch total 91
    fishing fleet 87

naval fleet 178, 179
    shipbuilding 142
    tuna fishing 101
    typhoons 55
South Orkney Is 62
South Polar Expedition 1901, German
    198
South Pole 63
South Riding Point 26.36N 78.13W 126
*South Sandwich Fracture Zone 62.00S
    25.00W* 18,
South Sandwich Is 62
South Sandwich Trench 56.30S 25.00W 18
South Scotia Ridge 60.50S 51.00W 18
South Shetland Is 62
South Shetland Trench 25
South Tasman Rise 49.00S 148.00E 22
Southwark 124
Southwestern Pacific Basin 40.00S 150.00W
    22/23
Southwest Indian Ridge 43.00S 40.00E 18/
    19
South Yemen (People's Dem. Rep. of
    Yemen) 154
    fisheries 98
    naval fleet 178
Sovereignty claims *see Territorial claims &
    disputes*
Sovetskaya Gavan 146, 183
Soviet AGIs 182
Soviet Union, *see USSR*
Soyuz 204
Space technology 204
Spain 157
    aquaculture production 83
    fishing catch total 91, 93, 95
    fishing fleet 86
    naval submarine strength 181
    naval surface fleet 178
    offshore oil & gas 104, 108
    pollution 177
    tuna fishing 101
Spanish Armada and wrecks 196, 197
Spears 80
Sperm whale 78–79, 100
    whaling activity 1729–1919 (map)
    100
Spheroid 204
Spitsbergen *see Svalbard*
Split 43.30N 16.26E 122
Sponges 72,, 73
Sports fishing 216, 217
'SPOT' satellite 204, 205
Spratly Is 188–189
Springdale 49.30N 56.05W 126
Spring tide 61
Squid 69, 79, 88, 96, 97
Sri Lanka 185, 223
    aquaculture production 83
    fisheries 98
    hurricane damage 55
SSBN (Nuclear Powered Strategic
    Submarine, ballistic missiles) 178,
    179, 180, 182, 183
SSBN, Typhoon class of 180
SSB (Strategic Submarine, ballistic
    missiles) 180
SSGN (Nuclear Powered Strategic
    Submarine, guided (cruise)
    missiles) 180
SSG (Strategic Submarine, guided
    missiles) 180
SSN (Nuclear Powered Strategic
    Submarine) 180
SS (Strategic Submarine) 180
Stanley 51.42S 57.15W 127
Stanley 184
St Anna Trough 80.00N 70.00E 24
Staten Island 128
Statfjord oilfield 106
Statue of Liberty, oil tanker 167
Stavanger 58.58N 5.44E 123
Stavanger 106
Steam
    ships 166
    technology 140
    trawling 84
Steam Navigation Act, The 166
Steel industry 136
Steinkjer 64.00N 11.30E 122
Stenón Kásou (Kasos Str.) 151
Stenungsund 58.05N 11.49E 123
Stephenville 48.30N 58.33W 126
Stingray 119
Stockholm 59.20N 18.03E 123
Stockholm 194
Stockholm, liner 167
Stocks Seamount 37
Stockton 129
Stockton 37.57N 121.19W 126
Store Bælt 55.30N 11.00E 151
Storegg Bank 67.00S 70.00E 25
Storm 54, 56–57, 59, 160, 161, 162
    Beaufort scale description 48
    losses 162
    surge 61
    warning systems 54
Stornaway 58.12N 6.22W 123
Storguns 57.50N 18.43E 123
Straits (map)
    Bab el Mandeb 154
    Dardanelles 155
    Dover 156
    Gibraltar 157
    Hormuz 154
    Malacca 155
    Singapore 155
    world 150–151
Stralsund 54.18N 13.05E 123

Strandings 164
Stranraer 54.55N 5.02W 123
Strategic routes in Atlantic 148
Strategic Submarine, *see SS*
Strathcona Sound 73.04N 84.33W 126
Straumsvik 64.03N 22.04W 122
Stretto di Messina 38.00N 15.30E 151
Stretto, *see glossary*
Striped mullet 177
Stromboli 37
Stromness 58.57N 3.18W 123
Strömstad 58.56N 11.11E 123
Strontium 174, 118
Struer 56.29N 8.37E 123
Stubbeköbing 54.53N 12.03E 123
Suba-Nipa 7.18N 122.56E 132
Subduction zones 32, 33, 35, 39
Subic Bay 14.45N 120.15E 132
Sublittoral zone, *see Continental Shelf*
Submarine
    cables 200
    canyons 28
    defence 180
    geology 202
    nuclear warfare: development 180
    strategy 180
    telegraphy 198
    terraces 28
Submarines 178,179
    Argentine: range 184, 185
    detection (map) 182–183
    missiles: range (maps) 180–181
    nuclear powered 184
    routes 148
    Soviet Echo II class 184
    strengths of principal navies (map)
    180–181
    Trident 181
Submerged cities and harbours 196,
    197
Submersibles 105, 114, 202–203
Suction dredgers 112
Sudan: fisheries 98
Suess, E. 34
Suez 29.58N 32.33E 133, 135
Suez Canal 67, 136, 137, 140, 146, 152–
    155, 157, 187
Suez Canal 31.00N 32.20E 151
Suez, G. of, oil basin 103
Sugar, raw: trade 137
Sulina 45.10N 29.40E 122
Sullom Voe 106, 135, 215
Sullom Voe 60.26N 1.20W 122
Sulphate ions in sea water 66
Sulphide deposits 73, 114
Sulphur dioxide 172
Sulphur: trade 137
Sulu Basin 8.00N 121.30E 22
Sulu Sea 8.00N 120.00E 22, 188
Sumatra 155
    fishing grounds 99
    tin, offshore 113
Sumburgh, weather station 161
Summerland oilfield 105
Summerside 46.23N 63.49W 126
Sunda, oil basin 103
Sunda Str. 151, 193
Sunda Trench 1.00N 96.00E 19
Sunda Trough 8.50S 109.30E 19
Sunderland 54.55N 1.21W 123
Sundsvall 62.23N 17.19E 122
Sungaipaknan 1.20N 102.09E 132
Superetendard: range 184, 185
Superior 46.42N 92.09W 126, 134
Surabaya 7.13S 112.44E 132
Surface fleet strengths of principal
    navies 178
Surface waters 26, 45
Surfing 216, 217
Surfsites (map) 217
Surges, storm 54, 55, 56, 57, 60–61, 156
Surigao Str. 10.30N 125.30E 151
Surrey Commercial Docks 124
Surtsey 37
Surveillance aircraft 180
Survey and research fleets (maps) 206–
    207
Susaki 33.23N 133.18E 130
Suspension feeders 72, 73
Suva 18.08S 178.26E 132
Suva 54
Suwanose Zima 37
Svalbard 62, 100, 182, 186
    Norway-USSR dispute (map) 186–
    187
Svelgen 61.46N 5.18E 122
Svendborg 55.03N 10.38E 123
Svolvær 68.14N 14.34E 122
Swansea 51.37N 3.55W 123
Sweden 136
    aquaculture production 83
    fishing catch 93
    merchant fleet 138
    naval submarine strength 181
    naval surface fleet 178
    ports 125
Swell, ocean 58, 59, 64
Swimming 216, 217
Swinoujscie 53.55N 14.15E 123
Switzerland: aquaculture production 83
Swordfish 75, 84
Sydney, Australia 33.50S 151.17E 132, 135
Sydney, Canada 46.09N 60.12W 126
Sydney, port (map) 132
Sylvania Guyot 36
Synthetic aperture radar 204
Syria
    aquaculture production 83
    naval fleet 178
Szczecin 53.25N 14.32E 123, 135

T

Tabaco 13.21N 123.44E 132
Tabasco–Campeche, oil basin 102
Tacloban 11.15N 124.59E 132
Tacoma 47.14N 122.28W 126, 134
Taconite Harbour 47.32N 90.52W 126
Tadotsu, tanker 171
Tadoussac 48.08N 69.43W 126
Tahiti 60, 132
T'ai-chung 24.15N 120.48E 130
T'ai pei 25.00N 121.30E 130
Taiwan 82
   aquaculture production 83
   fisheries 96
   naval submarine strength 181
   naval surface fleet 178, 179
   shipbuilding 142
   tuna fishing 101
   typhoon destruction 55
Taiwan Haixia 25.00N 119.00E 151
Takamatsu 34.21N 134.03E 130
Takeshima rocks 189
Takoradi 4.53N 1.45W 133
Takoradi, port 133
Talara 4.35S 81.17W 127
Talara, oil basin 102
Talcahuano 36.42S 73.05W 127
Tallinn 59.27N 24.45E 122, 182
Taltal 25.24S 70.29W 127
Tampa 27.57N 82.38W 126, 134
Tampico 22.15N 97.51W 126
Tanaga Pass 52.20N 179.20W 150
Tandoc 14.06N 123.18E 132
Tanega-shima-kaikyō 30.00N 130.00E 151
Tanga 5.04S 39.08E 133
Tanger 35.47N 5.48W 133
Tanggu 39.02N 117.41E 130
Tanjungpandan 2.36S 107.38E 132
Tanjunguban 1.05N 104.12E 132
Tanker
   disasters 168 (map) 170–171
   fleets, world 140, 141
   operational discharges 171
   routes 184
Tanker Owner's Voluntary Agreement
   concerning Liability for Oil
   Pollution (TOVALOP), 1969 224
Tankers 136, 137, 138, 142, 143, 154, 157
Tank washing 143
Tanzania: fisheries 98
Taolanaro 25.02S 47.01E 133
Tarakan 3.25N 117.40E 132
Taranaki, oil basin 103
Taranto 40.29N 17.12E 122, 183
Tarawa 1.21N 172.55E 132
Tarawa Atoll (map) 81
Tar balls 170, 172
Tarragona 41.07N 1.14E 122
Tarrawa 179
Tartan oilfield 106
Tartūs 34.54N 35.51E 133, 135
Tartūs 189
Task Force, British 184, 185
Tasman Sea 42.00S 160.00E 22
Tasman Abyssal Plain 34.30S 153.15E 22
Tatarskiy Proliv 50.00N 141.00E 150, 151
Tau 59.04N 5.55E 123
Tauranga 37.39S 176.11E 132
Tawau 4.15N 117.53E 130
Teal Inlet 184
Teesport (Middlesbrough) 54.35N 1.12W 123, 135
Teesside 106
Tegal 6.51S 109.08E 132
Tehuantepec Fracture Zone 54.00S 100.00W 23
Tehuelche Fracture Zone 54.00S 48.00W 18
Teignmouth 50.32N 3.30W 123
Tekirdağ 40.59N 27.32E 122
Tela 15.47N 87.30W 126
Telegraphy, submarine 198
Telica 36
Telok Anson 4.02N 101.01E 130
Telukbayur 0.58S 100.28E 132
Tema 5.38N 0.01E 133
Tema, port 133
Temperatures of oceans (maps) 50–51, (maps) 53
Tēnēs 36.32N 1.19E 133
Terminals: types 134
Termisa 5.00S 37.10W 127
Terneuzen 51.20N 3.49E 123
Tern oilfield 106
Tern 76, 77, 210
Terra Adélie 63
Terrigenous sediments 42
Territorial claims & disputes
   Anglo–French–Irish 186
   Antarctica 185
   Asia, E 188
   Asia, NE 189
   Asia, SE 189
   Beagle Channel Is 187
   Falkland Is 184–185
   Indian Ocean 185
   Mediterranean 187, 189
   Rockall 186
   South Georgia 184
   Svalbard 186, 187
   world: naval incidents 190–191
   world: 'trouble spots' 186–187

Territorial sea claims 218, 219
Territorial sea: legal definition 220, 222
Territorial waters 154
Tethys Sea 34, 40
TEU's *see glossary*
Texaco Denmark, tanker 170
Texaco Oklahoma, tanker 170
Texas 55
Texas City 29.23N 94.55W 126, 134
Thailand 109
   aquaculture production 83
   fishing catch total 91
   fishing industry & fisheries 80, 98, 99
   naval fleet 178
Thailand, G. of 10.00N 102.00E 19
Thailand, G. of 180, 189
   oil basin 103
   pollution 173
Thames
   Barrier 124
   Estuary 124, 156
   River 12, 124
Thamshamn 63.19N 9.53E 122
Theddlethorpe 106
Thelma, oilfield 106
Thelma, typhoon 55
Thermal energy 32, 39, 121
Thermoclines 51
Thessaloníki 40.37N 22.57E 122
Theta Gap 43.30N 12.40W 17
Thevenard 32.09S 133.39E 132
Thistle, oilfield 102, 106
Thompson, William 198
Thomson, Benjamin 198
Thomson, Sir Charles Wyville 198
Thorium 113
Thornton Bank, light buoy 156
Thousand Islands 153
Three Kings Ridge 30.30S 172.30E 22
Thunderstorms 56–57, 160, 161
Thunnus thynnus (bluefin tuna) 75
Thursday Island 10.35S 142.13E 132
Tianjin 39.07N 117.11E 130
Tiao-Yu-Tai 189
Tidal energy 120
   range 120, 121
   schemes for harnessing 60, (maps) 120
Tides 58, (maps & graphs) 60–61
   causes & behaviour 60
   cycles 120
   ranges 60–61, 155, 156
   types 60–61
Tijel 36.50N 5.47E 133
Tiki Basin 14.00S 135.00W 23
Tiko 4.04N 9.24E 133
Tilbury 51.28N 0.23E 123
Tilbury Docks (map) 124, 156
Tillerman, tanker 167
Timaru 44.24S 171.15E 132
Timor Sea 15.00S 130.00E 22
Timor Trough 9.50S 126.00E 22
Tin 110, 112–113
Tinakula 36
Tiran, Str. of 28.00N 34.30E 151
Tiree, weather station 161
Titanic, loss of the 64, 163
Titanium 112, 113
Titanium dioxide 174
Tlatelolco, Treaty of 186
Toamasina 18.10S 49.25E 133
Tocopilla 22.05S 70.11W 127
Todorokite 116
Tokara–Iwo-jima 36
Tokara-kaikyō 29.30N 129.00E 151
Tokuyama 34.04N 131.46E 130
Tōkyō 35.40N 139.45E 130
Tokyo 130, 131, 159
   commodity port 135
   port and region (maps) 130
Tokyo Bay 130
Toledo, Philippines *10.23N 123.38E* 132
Toledo, USA 41.42N 83.35W 126, 134
Toliara 23.23S 43.38E 133
Tomakomai 42.38N 141.36E 130
Tonga 36
   fisheries 99
Tonga–Kermadec arc 32
Tonga Trench 20.00S 173.00W 22
Tongking, G. of 188
Tongue, radio beacon 156
Tonnages, definitions *see Appendix I*
Tonnay-Charente 45.57N 0.55W 122
Tønsberg 59.16N 10.25E 123
Toothed whale 78, 79
Tordesillas, Treaty of 192
Tori-sima 36
Tornio 65.45N 24.09E 122
Tor & NW & SE, oilfields 102, 106
Toronto 43.38N 79.23W 126
Torre Annunziata 40.45N 14.29E 122
Torres Str. *10.00S 142.30E* 151
Torrevieja 37.59N 0.40W 122
Torrey Canyon, tanker (map) 169, 170, 224
Torshamenen 125
Torshavn 62.00N 6.47W 122
Toulon 43.07N 5.55E 122, 182
Tourism 216
TOVALOP, 1969 (Tanker Owners' Voluntary Agreement concerning Liability for Oil Pollution) 224
Tower Hamlets 124
Tower of London 197
Towle, tanker 170
Towns: undersea ruins 196, 197
Townsville 19.17S 146.48E 132
Toxic marine organisms 119

Toyama 36.47N 137.13E 130
Trabzon 41.01N 39.46E 122
Trace elements, sea water 66
Tracking, by satellites 204
Tra Co 189
Tracy, hurricane 54
Trader, tanker 170
Trade, seaborne 136, 140, 141, 144, 145
Trade, seaborne: national interest 144
Trade winds 44–45, 46, 47, 48, 49, 51, 58
Trading routes 192–193
Trafalgar, shipping forecast area 161
Traffic separation
   schemes 156, 157, 166
   zones, sea 154
Tramandai 30.00S 50.05W 127
Tramp
   freight markets, world 136
   routes 138
   ships 136, 137, 138, 146
   time charter index 143
Transantarctic Mts 63
Transatlantic telephone cable, first 200
'Transit passage' 218
TRANSIT Satellite Navigation System 158
Transkei Basin 35.30S 29.00E 19
Trans Pacific, racing event 217
Trans-polar surface route 148
Trans-Siberian Railway 146
Trápani 38.02N 12.31E 122
Traps 80, 84
Trawlers 86
Trawl gears 208
Trawls 84, 198
Treasure I. 182
Treguier 48.47N 3.14W 122
Trelleborg 55.22N 13.09E 123
Trematomus 79
Trenches, *see Ocean: trenches*
Trenton, see Ameriport
Tréport, le 50.04N 1.22E 122
Trichechus inunginis (manatee) 210
Trichodesmium 119
Trident missiles 181
Trident submarines 181
Trieste 45.39N 13.48E 122
Trincomalee 8.34N 81.14E 130
Trinidade Line 37
Trinidad & Tobago: offshore oil & gas 104, (map)105
Tripod fish 73
Tripoli, Lebanon 34.28N 35.49E 133
Tripoli, Libya 32.54N 13.11E 133
Tristan da Cunha 37
Tristan da Cunha Fracture Zone 38.00S 28.00W 18
Trois-Rivières 46.22N 72.34W 126, 134
Trolling 101
Trolltunga iceberg 65
Tromsø 69.39N 18.58E 122
Trondheim 63.26N 10.24E 122
Troodos Massif 39, 114
Troon 55.32N 4.42W 123
Trophic levels 71
Tropical
   cyclones 47, (maps & graphs) 54–57, 58, 160
   cyclone storm tracks (map) 56
   depressions 56
   revolving storm (TRS) 54
   storms 56, 160, 161
Tropic bird 76
Tropic Seamount 23.50N 20.40W 17
Trouble spots, world 186
Trout 82, 88
TRS (tropical revolving storm) 54
Tsugaru-kaikyō 41.20N 140.00E 151
Tsukumi 33.05N 131.52E 130
Tsunamis 58, (map) 59, 160
Tsuruga 35.40N 136.03E 130
Tsushima Strait 151, 183
Tuamotu Fracture Zone 12.30S 127.00W

Tuapse 44.05N 39.04E 122
Tubarāo 20.17S 40.14W 127, 135
Tuborg Havn 55.44N 12.35E 123
Tubruq 32.06N 24.00E 133
Tugs 148, 169
Tuktoyaktuk 69.27N 132.59W 126
Tuluman 36
Tumaco 1.50N 78.50W 127
Tuna 74, 75, 84, 85, 87, 88, 95, (maps) 101, 210
   catch, by FAO area 101
   clippers 86
   exports 101
   fisheries 96–101
   species and distribution 101
   vessels 86, 87
Tunas de Zaza 21.36N 79.36W 126
Tunb Islands 154, 187
Tungsten 113
Tunis 36.49N 10.18E 133
Tunisia
   aquaculture production 82
   Continental Shelf case, 1982, Tunisia/Libya 222
   naval fleet 178
   offshore oil & gas 104
Turbidity currents 28, 29, 42, 43
Turbot 82
Turbulence 76
Turkey 155
   aquaculture production 83
   fishing fleet 86
   naval submarine strength 181, 183
   naval surface fleet 178, 183
Turkey–Greece dispute 187

Turkish Straits 155
Turks I. Pass. 21.30N 71.20W 150
Turku 60.27N 22.16E 122
Turtle 88, 210
Tuscarora, expedition (map) 198–199
Tuticorin 8.48N 78.11E 130
Tuxpan 20.59N 97.19W 126
Tvedestrand 58.37N 8.54E 123
Twilight Zone 74
Twillingate 49.41N 54.48W 126
Tynemouth 55.01N 1.24W 123
Tyne, shipping forecast area 161
Typhoon class of SSBN 180, 181
Typhoons 54
Tyra oilfield 106
Tyrrhenian Sea 42.00N 14.00E 17

U

UAE (United Arab Emirates): offshore oilfields 109, 154
Ube 33.57N 131.15E 130
Uddevalla 58.21N 11.56E 123
Uithuizen 106
Ujungpandang 5.08S 119.24E 132
UK/France continental shelf boundary 187
UK/Rep. of Ireland boundary 187
UK (United Kingdom of Gt Britain & N. Ireland) 136, 156 *see also British Isles*
   aquaculture production 83
   boundaries, maritime 186, 187
   fishery zone claims 186
   fishing catch total 91, 93
   fishing fleet 86
   fishing industry 215
   naval submarine strength 181, 182–185
   naval surface fleet 178, 182–185
   offshore oil & gas 104, (map) 106
   power demand 121
Ula oilfield 106
Ulawun 36
ULMS (undersea long range missile system) 180
Ulsan 35.31N 129.15E 130
Umeå 63.42N 20.21E 122
Umm Qaṣr 30.02N 47.57E 133
Umm Qasr 185
Umm Sa'id 24.54N 51.34E 133
UNCLOS III (third UN convention on the Law of the Sea) 218–224, *see also Appendix XI*
UNCTAD (United Nations Conference on Trade & Development) 141
Undersea long range missile system (ULMS) 180
UNEP Regional Seas Programme 213
UNEP (United Nations Environmental Programme) 176, 208, 224
UNESCO 203
Ungava Bay 120
Unimak Pass. 54.30N 165.00W 150
United Arab Emirates, *see UAE*
United Kingdom, *see UK*
United Nations Conference on the Human Environment 224
United Nations Convention on the Law of the Sea (UNCLOS III) 218–224, *see also Appendix XI*
United Nations Conference on Trade & Development (UNCTAD) 141
United Nations Environmental Programme (UNEP) 176, 208, 224
United Nations Security Council Resolution 502 184
United Nations (UN) 172
United States of America, *see USA*
Unitised cargo 139
Unitised vessels 142
Uno 34.30N 133.57E 130
Upwelling 45, 50, 51, (map) 53, 57, 71, 76, 78, 85, 95, 110, 114
Uracas 36
Urangan 25.17S 152.54E 132
Uranium 119
Urquiola, tanker 171
Uruguay, fleet 178, 184
USA (United States of America) 136, 163
   aquaculture production 82
   barge transport system 147
   fisheries 94–95, 96
   fishing catch total 90, 93, 94
   fishing fleet 86
   maritime power 220
   naval fleet 178–179, 182–183, 189
   naval fleet deployment (map) 182–183
   naval submarine strength 181
   offshore oil & gas 104, 106, 107
   offshore sand & gravel (maps) 112–113
   phosphorite production 115
   pollution 172–173
   seaborne trade 144
   shrimp industry 87, 95
   strategic interest in the Indian Oc. 185
   Weather Bureau 54
Useless Loop 26.05S 113.24E 132
Ushant 169
Ushuaia 54.45S 68.20W 127